CHRONO...

of the

20TH CENTURY

CHRONOLOGY

of the

20TH CENTURY

based on

Chronology of the Modern World

by Neville Williams
Late Secretary of the British Academy, London

Edited by
Philip Waller
Merton College, Oxford

Consultant Editor
John Rowett
Brasenose College, Oxford

Preface by
Robert Dallek
Professor of History,
University of California, Los Angeles

Helicon

Chronology of the Modern World
© by Neville Williams 1966, 1969, 1975

Chronology of the 20th Century
© The Estate of Neville Williams and Helicon Publishing Ltd 1995,
1996

Additional material © Helicon Publishing Ltd 1995

This revised, updated paperback edition 1996

Helicon Publishing Ltd
42 Hythe Bridge Street
Oxford, Great Britain, OX1 2EP

Text and page design: Curtis Garratt Ltd

Jacket design: Richard Boxall

Typeset by Mendip Communications Ltd
Frome, Somerset

Printed and bound in Great Britain by
The Bath Press Ltd, Bath

ISBN 1–85986–174–1

British Library Cataloguing in Publication Data

A catalogue record for this book is available from the British Library

Papers used by Helicon Publishing Ltd are natural recyclable products made
from wood grown in sustainable forests. The manufacturing processes of
both raw materials and paper conform to the environmental regulations of
the country of origin.

Cover illustrations (starting top left): Queen Victoria (Topham); Model T
Ford (Topham); Chaplin in *The Kid*; Chrysler Building (Topham); 1940s
Utility Fashions (Topham); John Wayne; Indira Gandhi (Topham); Shuttle
Atlantis, 18 Oct 1989, carrying a crew of five and the spacecraft 'Galileo' on
its way to Jupiter (NASA); Mikhail Gorbachev addressing the UN General
Assembly, 7 Dec 1988 (Associated Press/Topham); Middle East Peace
Accord: Rabin, Clinton, Arafat (Associated Press/Topham).

Contents

Contributors

Lewis Baston
Nuffield College, Oxford

Martin Cloonan
University of York

Julia Colman
Formerly of Colgate University,
New York, and the Courtauld Institute,
London

David Crook
Formerly Researcher for the
Spencer Foundation, Chicago; Institute
of Education, London

Martin Goodman
Novelist, travel-writer, and tutor in creative
writing

Clare Griffiths
Wadham College, Oxford

Trevor Griffiths
University of Edinburgh

Frank James
Centre for the Study of Science
and Technology, Royal Institution,
London

Robert Peberdy
Formerly of Merton College, Oxford,
and the University of Leicester

Ann Swailes
St Hugh's College, Oxford

Jason Tomes
Formerly of Merton and Nuffield Colleges,
Oxford

Editors

Editorial Director
Anne-Lucie Norton

Managing Editor
Sheila Dallas

Contributing Editor
Robert Peberdy

Text Editor
Jane Anson

Indexer
Hilary Bird

Production
Tony Ballsdon

Note on the revised and updated edition

This updated and corrected edition includes the year 1995, with appropriate
amendments to the index. The editors and publisher welcome necessary corrections
and those readers who supplied them will recognize their inclusion here.

Preface

The Dutch historian Peter Geyl had it right: History is argument without end. But it is also a chronicle of events; a story of what and how things happened.

Nowadays, millions of young people in America and Great Britain, despite more and more years of education, seem to know less about the past than did earlier generations. Why bother with all those miserable dates and events when time can be passed more pleasurably in front of a television set being entertained? Students in America can rattle off current statistics about their favourite sport or identify the characters in some weekly TV drama, but they are hard pressed to identify the decade in which World War I occurred or to state on whose side Russia fought in World War II. 'Which were the last two states added to the Union?' American high school graduates were asked in a recent survey. 'Mexico and Canada' a distressingly large number replied.

We need all possible help in getting students and citizens generally to develop a more accurate knowledge of the past. How can democracies survive unless electorates know something about political history, their own as well as that of competing systems?

This *Chronology of the 20th Century* will bring the fundamentals within easy reach of students, teachers, journalists, and anyone needing access to basic details about the modern era. The book will appeal to both browsers and researchers with a specific question. The former, scanning the chronological lists, will be able to refresh their memories about particular times and places, and recall more clearly the sequence of events. The latter, intent on pinning down a fact in a particular category, can consult the comprehensive list of topics – be it politics, government, law, and economy; society, education, and religion; science, technology, and discovery; humanities; art, sculpture, fine arts, and architecture; music; literature and drama; births and deaths; everyday life; sport and recreation; and media. Readers can also consult the extensive index, which is a superb feature of this supremely useful book.

Robert Dallek
University of California, Los Angeles
Harmsworth Professor of American History,
University of Oxford, 1994–95

Introduction

The *Chronology of the 20th Century* is a calendar of events and a record of activities in the modern age. Though annals and chronicles have been compiled since ancient times, the construction of any new chronology offers a challenge. What picture of the world can or should the compilers present? What materials are available from which they can work?

The eighteenth-century historian Edward Gibbon, musing about the reign of the Roman Emperor Antoninus Pius in the mid-2nd century AD, commented, in his lapidary way, that history is 'little more than the register of the crimes, follies, and misfortunes of mankind'. The compilers of annals would not normally presume to take issue with the great philosophical historian, yet they cannot fail to notice a steady stream of honest endeavour – even heroic achievement – running with the tide of human error, organized cruelty, and natural disasters. Gibbon also commented that Antoninus' reign was 'marked by the rare advantage of furnishing very few materials for history'. By 'materials' he meant those of the miserable sort, since he believed that the period from the death of Emperor Domitian (AD 96) to the accession of Commodus (AD 180) was one of unexampled happiness and prosperity. But the surviving inventory for an historical stock-taking of that epoch – either good or bad – was altogether sparse.

For the compilers of the *Chronology of the 20th Century* it is not so. Modern chroniclers will never be found raising a cry about the paucity of material. The modern condition is more one of information surfeit and fatigue. The profusion of information from around the world is teeming and accumulating incessantly; and it is not confined to our planet alone, but even pours in from space itself. Selection, therefore, is not just an option but a matter of necessity.

The leading ambition which has guided us in the selection for the *Chronology* is a simple one: to include as much as may generally be found useful by those who habitually – even casually – have recourse to check for the dates of events and things in their work or leisure. There is no sophisticated philosophy involved in this. In 1789 the English philosopher Jeremy Bentham was disposed to extol the merits of Utility for mankind when he declared that 'the greatest happiness of the greatest number is the foundation of morals and legislation'.

The contributors to the *Chronology of the 20th Century*, by contrast, think of their utilitarianism as striving after the most practical. The principal purpose is to achieve a summary statement of events and things, without weighing causes or consequences. This approach has led neither to the production of the uniform nor to the exclusion of the unusual. Indeed, an outstanding virtue of such an aggregated record is that, in an almost involuntary way, it inspires fresh patterns of thought. That is because of the unexpected concurrences which will be found in the following pages. The *Chronology* establishes surprising simultaneities, and also permits the diligent user to trace lines of connection and sequence.

There is, however, one perennial problem shared by every historian – the consciousness that the things which are now thought important sometimes diverge completely from the things which mattered to the millions of the past. There is nothing to be done about this except to seek to strike a reasonable balance. For example, we have included in 1912, under Literature, *The Way of an Eagle*, the first best-seller of the prolific E M Dell (pseudonym of Ethel M Savage). In this instance, the author's plain popularity justifies inclusion; but for others, whose works may have had a tiny readership, their inclusion derives from judgements passed by literary scholars that the authors will enjoy a lasting significance and even canonical status because of their creative imagination, innovative technique, or special style, subject, and characterization.

The foundations of the present work lie in *The Chronology of the Modern World*, whose first edition covering 1763–1965 was compiled by Neville Williams and published in 1966 (and issued in a revised paperback edition in 1975). Reviewers and readers accorded Williams' *Chronology* an enthusiastic reception. It quickly established itself as an indispensable work of reference, not only because of the aggregate amount of information it contained. Its usability was outstanding – distinguished by its thematic organization and detailed index. A second edition of that work, extending the coverage of years to 1992, was completed by the present Editor and published in 1994. This *Chronology of the 20th Century* is not just a chip off the old block with sundry years added. While retaining the virtues of the previous work, the whole has been revised and at the same time substantially re-cast for a new generation of users. Most notably, the content of each year has been expanded to include many more entries on the United States and other countries to give a truly international coverage. The thematic categorization has also been revised and enlarged, providing more information on social developments, education, science, popular music, sport, and films.

The daily run of political and international 'events' appears throughout on the left-hand page, year by year, in monthly sections, wherever possible under precise chronological dates. The corresponding right-hand pages for each year are devoted to activities and achievements arranged under classified headings or 'themes'. Both the monthly sections of the left-hand pages and the subject paragraphs of the right-hand pages bear individual letters, enabling speedy reference from the Index (A to M on the left, O to Y on the right: 'I' has been omitted to avoid possible confusion with 'J'; 'N' has been reserved for any material within a year for which precise dates were inappropriate or could not be found).

Information in the 'themes' strand is grouped under multiple headings (for example, 'Politics, Government, Law, and Economy') and appears in an order corresponding to the subsections of the heading. Titles of works not written in English are usually given in their commonly known form. Where a book first appeared in a foreign language and was later translated into English, the English title is entered in the original year of publication. Plays are normally entered under the year of composition, and works of popular music under the year in which they became popular. Deaths listed under 'Births and Deaths' provide the person's age at death.

One recurring problem in the compilation was deciding the category in which to place items. Some non-political events which had great popular impact and are remembered along with the flux of contemporary politics (for example, the murder of former Beatle John Lennon in New York in 1980) have been entered on the left-hand pages. Other items could have been placed under two or more 'themes': for example, major legal decisions that had far-reaching social consequences, or technological developments that expanded the audience for popular music. These items have generally been placed under the heading to which they are most relevant.

Finally, the Editor must close by sounding two notes about help. Though these are customary, it does not lessen their fervour. The first is to invite readers to inform the publishers of necessary corrections of misplaced or misdescribed material. The second is to acknowledge a great indebtedness already incurred, to those who assisted in the compilation of this volume. New material has been gathered by an admirable group of methodical and resourceful scholars, who are named in the list of contributors. It will not be thought invidious if I make special mention of Robert Peberdy, as captain of, and greatest individual contributor to, the team. His organizational mastery has been decisive. Driving forces conventionally conjure up images of almost monstrous energy. Robert is the friendly version, considerate and co-operative, yet possessed of the desired dynamism and genius for combining miscellaneous contributions. As Editor, I have been in the habit of pestering experts to resolve occasional puzzles where the records have been obscure or discrepant; among them, my colleague at Merton, Robert Gildea, who has readily responded to queries about modern French history. Lastly, I thank most warmly John Rowett, Fellow and Tutor in Modern History at Brasenose College, Oxford, whose consultation about modern American history has been invaluable. As is the nature of things, John has advised about many other aspects too. This collaboration has not just lightened the toil of producing the volume but has made the exercise a cheerful one.

Philip Waller
Merton College, Oxford

CHRONOLOGY
of the
20TH CENTURY

Boer War in South Africa ... Boxer Rising in China ...

A January

1 British government assumes direct control of the Royal Niger Company's lands, which are added to Britain's Niger Coast Protectorate to form Southern Nigeria; Frederick Lugard is appointed high commissioner.

10 following four months of Boer advances in the South African or Boer War, Field Marshal Frederick Lord Roberts ('Bobs') lands in South Africa as the new commander in chief of the British army, with Lord Kitchener as chief of staff.

10 tension in British–German relations through Britain's seizure of a German vessel on suspicion of carrying contraband but, on 16 Jan, Britain gives way.

10 Emperor Franz Joseph of Austria appoints a ministry of bureaucrats under Ernst von Körber to resolve the conflict between German and Czech parties in Austria.

24 Battle of Spion Kop in South African War, when a Boer army forces a British army under Redvers Buller to retreat with heavy losses.

B February

15 in South African War, British army under General French relieves Kimberley (under siege by Boers since 15 Oct 1899).

22 bitter parliamentary conflict in Italy following the declaration by the Court of Cassation that the constitutional decrees of June 1899 are invalid.

27 in Britain, at conference in London, the Independent Labour Party, Fabian Society, Social Democratic Federation, and trade unions found the Labour Representation Committee to work for independent representation of working people in parliament; Ramsay MacDonald is appointed secretary.

27 Boer commander Piet Cronje and army surrender to Lord Roberts at Paardeberg.

28 Redvers Buller relieves Ladysmith in Natal (under siege by Boers since 30 Oct 1899).

28 Count Muraviev, Russian foreign minister, suggests that France and Germany put joint pressure on Britain to end South African War, but Germany rejects this (3 March) while France takes advantage of Britain's plight to advance its interests in Morocco.

C March

5 Presidents Kruger and Steyn of the Transvaal and Orange Free State offer peace proposals to the British government (rejected after capture of Bloemfontein);

10 Britain signs treaty with Uganda for regulating the government with the advice of a British commissioner.

13 in South Africa, Lord Roberts captures Bloemfontein, the capital of the Orange Free State.

14 Currency Act in USA declares paper and other money redeemable in gold.

D April

Republican bloc formed in France to defend the Republic against anti-Dreyfusard opponents.

7 US President William McKinley appoints commission with Judge W H Taft as president to extend US civil power in the Philippines (commences work in Sept, with appropriations for the construction of roads and harbours).

14 President Loubet of France opens the Paris International Exhibition (to 13 Nov).

30 Hawaii is organized as a territory of the USA.

E May

1 the Foraker Act for establishing civil government in Puerto Rico takes effect.

11 disorder in many Spanish cities in protest at new taxes.

17 in South Africa, British forces relieve the besieged town of Mafeking.

19 the Tonga Islands become a British protectorate.

24 Lord Roberts announces the annexation of the Orange Free State as the Orange River Colony.

31 British troops occupy Johannesburg and the Rand in the Transvaal.

F June

5 British troops capture Pretoria, capital of the Transvaal.

8 Czech members of the Austrian Reichsrat disrupt the sitting for seven hours with cymbals, trumpets, and other devices.

12 second German Naval Act aims at a fleet of 38 battleships in 20 years.

13 (–14 Aug) in China, rising of Boxers (supporters of the Society of Harmonious Fists) against Europeans.

18 General Pelloux resigns as prime minister following the success of the Left in Italian elections.

20 assassination of the German ambassador in Beijing begins the siege of foreign legations in the city by Boxers.

21 in USA, National Republican Convention at Philadelphia renominates McKinley for

Freud's Interpretation of Dreams ... *Speech transmitted by wireless ...*

o Politics, Government, Law, and Economy

Galveston, Texas, USA, is devastated by storms; to speed reconstruction, the town is run by five commissioners from 1901; the structure is retained in a charter of 1903, inaugurating the 'city commission' form of municipal government.

Civil Law Code introduced in Germany; similar codes are later adopted elsewhere in Europe and Japan.

Coal famine in Europe (Feb), due to strength of demand from industry.

In Germany, construction of the Elbe–Lübeck Canal, providing navigation south of the Jutland peninsula.

p Society, Education, and Religion

Major famine in India (Jan–March).

France limits the working day for women and children to 11 hours.

In USA, Carry Nation starts her campaign for Prohibition by breaking up saloons.

French senate approves the admission of women to practise at the Bar (14 Nov).

In USA, Charles Clinton Spaulding is appointed head of the North Carolina Mutual Life Insurance Company, which he builds into the largest African-American business.

The American Federation of Labor (AFL) is formed by 216 US unions.

Germany introduces compensation for accidents or illness caused by work.

'Zoning' introduced into city-planning in German cities, whereby different areas of cities have different designated functions.

Sigmund Freud, *The Interpretation of Dreams.*

C H Spurgeon, *Autobiography* (posthumous).

Leslie Stephen, *The Utilitarians.*

Wilhelm Wundt, *Comparative Psychology.*

Sex-education classes introduced in German schools.

Foundation of Birmingham University, England.

John Dewey, *The School and Society.*

Union of Free and United Presbyterian Churches in Scotland (31 Oct).

q Science, Technology, and Discovery

Magnetic tape invented.

The acetylene lamp is perfected.

In USA, J M Browning invents the revolver.

In Germany, first trial flight of Zeppelin airship (2 July).

Friedrich Dorn in Germany discovers the gaseous, nonmetallic element radon.

Karl Landsteiner in Austria divides blood into three groups.

William Crookes, in Britain, separates uranium.

Max Planck in Germany elaborates Quantum Theory.

Lord Rayleigh, *Scientific Papers*, Vol. 2.

Rediscovery by Dutch geneticist Hugo de Vries and others of the Moravian monk Gregor Mendel's work on heredity (dating from the 1850s and 1860s).

r Humanities

British archaeologist Arthur Evans discovers an unknown Bronze Age civilization at Knossos on Crete; Evans names it 'Minoan' after the legendary king of Crete.

J B Bury, *History of Greece.*

Henri Pirenne, *History of Belgium* (–1932).

A F Pollard, *England under Protector Somerset.*

Completion of the multi-volume *British Dictionary of National Biography* (first volume published in 1882).

Publication of the first volume of the *Victoria History of the Counties of England*, an encyclopedic account of every county and place in England (–).

Henri Bergson, *On Laughter.*

Bertrand Russell, *A Critical Exposition of the Philosophy of Leibniz.*

s Art, Sculpture, Fine Arts, and Architecture

First exhibition in France of Picasso's works, organized by Ambrose Vollard.

The Wallace Collection, Manchester Square, London, opened.

Painting, etc:

Paul Cézanne, *Still Life With Onions.*

Henri Matisse, *Male Model.*

Claude Monet, *Water Lilies, Harmony in Rose.*

Edvard Munch, *Golgotha.*

Pablo Picasso, *Moulin de la Galette*, his first Paris painting.

Pierre-Auguste Renoir, *Nude in the Sun* (pastel).

Henri Toulouse-Lautrec, *La Modiste.*

Sculpture:

Paul Gauguin, *Nude Woman.*

Auguste Rodin's reputation is established by exhibition at La Place de l'Alma, Paris.

Architecture:

Hector Guimard, Metro stations, Paris–Art Nouveau.

presidency and nominates Theodore Roosevelt for vice-presidency.

30 in China an international expedition, including troops from the USA and Japan, takes Tianjin; US secretary of state, John Hay, restates the policy of 'open door' in China.

G **July**

Following an excellent wine vintage, in both quantity and quality, the French government reduces retail duties to enable wine-growers to sell stocks.

9 Queen Victoria gives royal assent to Australian Federation Bill, providing for the establishment of the Commonwealth of Australia (from 1 Jan 1901).

29 King Humbert I of Italy is assassinated by an anarchist at Monza near Milan; succeeded by Victor Emmanuel III.

H **August**

14 international military force relieves besieged foreign legations in Beijing.

14 in South Africa, the British armies commanded by Roberts and Redvers Buller join at Vlakfontein.

27 Boer army under command of Louis Botha is defeated at Bergendal.

J **September**

The Sultan of Turkey announces the construction of the Hejaz railway, from Damascus to the Holy Places in Arabia, to be built by popular subscription as a Pan-Islamic project (–1908).

1 Lord Roberts formally proclaims the annexation of the Transvaal.

11 President Kruger crosses from the Transvaal into Portuguese South-east Africa (19 Oct, leaves for Europe).

30 in Ireland, Arthur Griffith founds Cumann na nGaedhael ('The League of Gaels'), which adopts the policy of Sinn Féin ('We Ourselves').

K **October**

6 President Kruger of the Transvaal, in Europe, is denied an audience by Kaiser Wilhelm II of Germany.

16 in the 'Khaki' election in Britain, the Conservatives, organized by Joseph Chamberlain, remain in power, with a majority of 134 (Conservatives and Unionists, 334 seats; Liberal Unionists, 68; Liberals, 184; Irish Nationalists, 82; Labour, 2). Lord Salisbury reconstructs his ministry, appointing Lord Lansdowne foreign secretary.

16 Yangzi Agreement between Britain and Germany to restrain foreign aggression in China and maintain open door for trade.

17 Bernhard von Bülow succeeds Prince Hohenlohe as German chancellor.

L **November**

Following British conquests, Boers resort to guerrilla tactics, with raids on communications and British outposts; Kitchener orders the internment in concentration camps of women and children related to Boer combatants and extends the 'scorched earth' policy started by Roberts, destroying Boer farms. Rising of the Ashanti in W Africa is suppressed by British forces.

5 Cuban constitutional convention begins to sit at Havana (–21 Feb 1901).

6 in US presidential election William McKinley, Republican, defeats William Jennings Bryan, Democrat, on an anti-imperialist platform, with 292 electoral votes to Bryan's 155; popular vote: McKinley, 7,207,923; Bryan, 6,358,133.

9 Russia, having completed the occupation of Manchuria with 100,000 troops, agrees with the Chinese governor to restore civil administration, but this agreement is abrogated by both central governments.

M **December**

14 secret Franco–Italian agreement to maintain French influence in Morocco and Italian interests in Tripoli.

4

Charles Rennie Mackintosh designs the Glasgow School of Art, Scotland.

Edwin Lutyens, Deanery Gardens, Sonning, England.

T Music

Gustave Charpentier, *Louise* (opera).

Edward Elgar, *The Dream of Gerontius* (oratorio).

Ruggiero Leoncavallo, *Zazà* (opera).

Edward MacDowell, Piano Sonata No. 4 ('Keltic').

Gustav Mahler, Symphony No. 4.

Giacomo Puccini, *Tosca* (opera).

Jean Sibelius, *Finlandia*.

First National Brass Championship for brass bands held in London.

In USA, Eldridge Johnson's Consolidated Talking Machine Company of Camden, New Jersey, markets the first gramophone records under the title 'His Master's Voice'.

U Literature and Drama

Frank Baum, *The Wonderful Wizard of Oz*.

Colette and Henri Gauthier-Villars, *Claudine at School*, the first of five 'Claudine' novels (–1907).

Joseph Conrad, *Lord Jim*.

Theodore Dreiser, *Sister Carrie*.

Maxim Gorky, *Three People*.

Jack London, *The Son of Wolf*.

Charles Péguy launches *Les Cahiers de la Quinzaine* (–1914).

Arthur Quiller-Couch, *Oxford Book of English Verse*.

Edmond Rostand, *L'Aiglon*.

Leo Tolstoy, *The Living Corpse*.

H G Wells, *Love and Mr Lewisham*.

Drama:

David Belasco and J L Long, *Madame Butterfly*.

Anton Chekhov, *Uncle Vanya*.

Frank Harris, *Mr & Mrs Daventry* (attributed to Oscar Wilde).

Romain Rolland, *Danton*.

George Bernard Shaw publishes *Three Plays for Puritans* with prefaces.

August Strindberg, *To Damascus*, Pt 1.

'The Hall of Fame' established in USA.

V Births and Deaths

Jan 20 John Ruskin dies (81).

Feb 5 Adlai Stevenson born (–1965).

Feb 22 Luis Buñuel born (–1983).

Feb 29 George Seferis born (–1971).

March 2 Kurt Weill born (–1950).

March 23 Erich Fromm born (–1980).

June 25 Louis (Earl) Mountbatten born (–1979).

June 25 Dennis Gabor born (–1979).

Aug 19 Gilbert Ryle born (–1976).

Aug 25 Hans Krebs born (–1981).

Aug 25 Friedrich Nietzsche dies (56).

Sept 20 Willem Visser't Hooft born (–1992).

Oct 3 Thomas Wolfe born (–1938).

Nov 14 Aaron Copland born (–1990).

Nov 30 Oscar Wilde dies (44).

Dec 27 Marlene Dietrich born (–1992).

W Everyday Life

'Cakewalk' dance craze.

New British royal yacht, *Victoria and Albert*, keels over while leaving Pembroke Dock and is jammed in entrance (Jan 3).

In France, opening of the Métropolitain or 'Métro' underground in Paris (19 July).

US engine driver Casey Jones dies on the footplate, trying to slow his engine before it hits another engine at Vaughan, Mississippi (30 April).

In USA, the Eastman Kodak Company launches the Brownie Box Camera, selling for just $1.

At the 'Stonehenge' prehistoric monument in S England, an upright stone and lintel fall (31 Dec), the first since 1797.

X Sport and Recreation

The 2nd Olympic Games are held in Paris (20 May–28 Oct), in connection with the Paris International Exhibition. France wins 29 gold medals; USA, 20; Britain, 17; Belgium, 8; Switzerland, 6; Austria, 4; Germany, 3.

In USA, Dwight Filley Davis presents an international challenge cup for lawn tennis (the Davis Cup); the USA wins the trophy, beating Great Britain 3–0 in Boston, Massachusetts (8–10 Aug).

Byron Bancroft Johnson founds the American League of Professional Baseball Clubs, challenging the established National League.

In the English County Cricket Championship, the winning team, Yorkshire, is the first side to remain unbeaten throughout an entire season.

The Prince of Wales is the first horse-owner to win the English Triple Crown (2,000 Guineas, Derby, and St Leger) and the Grand National in the same year.

Y Media

Associated Press news agency in USA moves from Chicago to New York, in order to

Birth of Commonwealth of Australia ... McKinley assassinated ...

A January

In South Africa, Kitchener launches two major offensives against Boer forces (–Feb); to combat the guerrilla actions of Boers, Kitchener builds a chain of blockhouses and starts denuding the country of its farms.

1 Commonwealth of Australia comes into being with Edmund Barton, federalist and protectionist, as prime minister.

22 death of Queen Victoria (at Osborne House, Isle of Wight, S England), after a brief illness; those present at her death include the German Kaiser, Wilhelm II; the Prince of Wales accedes to the throne as Edward VII (proclaimed, 23).

B February

7 the Italian government led by Giuseppe Saracco is overthrown for its feeble response towards striking dockers in Genoa (14, Giuseppe Zanardelli forms ministry).

8 on receiving Russia's proposals for evacuation of Manchuria, China appeals to the major powers and is supported by Britain, Japan, and, with hesitancy, by Germany.

11 death of Milan, father of Alexander I of Serbia.

23 British–German agreement on boundary between German East Africa and Nyasaland (modern Tanzania and Malawi).

28 in South Africa, Boer leader Louis Botha meets Kitchener at Middelburg; peace negotiations founder (16 March) because the British government refuses to accept a proposed amnesty for Boers and rebels in the Cape and Natal.

27 Russian minister of education, M Bogoljepoff, is wounded by an ex-student of Moscow University seeking to avenge repression of student agitation.

C March

In Russia, students and workers riot in major cities; many provinces are placed under martial law.

2 in USA, Orville Platt's amendment on the proposed Cuban constitution (reserving rights in Cuba to USA) and J C Spooner's amendment calling for civil government in the Philippines are added to Army Appropriations bill.

4 inauguration of President McKinley's second term of office in Washington, DC.

5 five Irish MPs are removed by police from the British House of Commons after they refuse to withdraw (following their refusal to take part in a division).

15 in the German Reichstag, Prince von Bülow declares that the Yangzi agreement of 1900 with Britain did not apply to Manchuria, and as a result the London discussions on the possibility of an British–German–Japanese bloc against Russia end abruptly.

D April

2 following protests from Britain and Japan, China refuses to sign a convention with Russia giving it control of Manchuria.

18 in the British budget, Chancellor Hicks Beach for the first time anticipates higher revenue from direct than from indirect taxes.

E May

7 (–14) general strike in Barcelona, Spain.

20 end of US military rule in Cuba.

29 a confidential memorandum by British prime minister Salisbury upholds the policy of isolation, marking the end of discussions for a British–German alliance.

F June

Moroccan mission to Paris, London, and Berlin seeking a British–German pact on Morocco.

12 new constitution for Cuba is agreed, reserving rights to the USA that make the country virtually a US protectorate.

17 David Lloyd George moves adjournment debate in British House of Commons,

maintain restrictive practices under New York law.

Alfred Harmsworth publishes the *New York World* as a 'tabloid newspaper'.

In Britain, C Arthur Pearson publishes the *Express*; a novel feature is news on the front page.

Primitive colour and sound systems are dem-onstrated at the Paris International Exhibition.

Film:

Hamlet's Duel (starring Sara Bernhardt).

Radio:

R A Fessenden first transmits speech by wireless.

J P Morgan forms US Steel ... Booker T Washington dines at the White House ...

o **Politics, Government, Law, and Economy**

The final Pendleton Act creates US career civil service.

Platt Amendment to Act of Congress provides for USA to withdraw its troops from Cuba when that country has established a republican form of government and has entered into other stipulations; the US will retain supervision of Cuba's foreign policy and acquire sites on Cuba for naval stations (March).

In Britain, the House of Lords rules on the Taff Vale Case (22 July): a trade union can be liable for damages caused by its members during a strike (the Taff Vale Railway Company had sued the Amalgamated Society of Railway Servants; the Society is fined £23,000).

The US Supreme Court rules, in the Insular cases, that inhabitants of Puerto Rico and other US overseas territories are US nationals, not citizens (2 Dec); the Constitution applies only in territories incorporated by Congress.

Discovery of oil in Texas, USA (10 Jan).

In USA, J P Morgan buys Andrew Carnegie's steel companies for $250 million, forming the US Steel Corporation (Feb).

Mass production of cars begins in Detroit, USA, with the Oldsmobile.

In USA, Henry E Huntington incorporates the Pacific Railway Company and starts building a network of electric inter-urban lines around Los Angeles (by 1913, the system reaches 42 incorporated cities); the development sets off a building boom.

The Shah of Persia grants an oil concession over 1.2 million sq km (480,000 sq mi) to William Knox D'Arcy (transferred to the Anglo-Persian Oil Company in 1909).

p **Society, Education, and Religion**

In Russia, criminals are no longer exiled to Siberia (from 14 Jan).

In USA, President Roosevelt entertains the African-American teacher Booker T Washington to dinner at the White House (16 Oct), arousing protest in southern states; Roosevelt seeks Washington's advice on African-American and southern appointments.

In the House of Lords, London, Earl Russell is tried by his peers for bigamy (18 July); he pleads guilty but states that he believed his divorce and remarriage in Nevada, USA, were valid; he is sentenced to three months' imprisonment.

Tenement Law in New York improves the minimum standards to be adopted in the design and building of tenement blocks (standards copied by many others US towns and cities).

Robert Hunter, *Tenement Conditions in Chicago*.

Booker T Washington, *Up from Slavery*.

Agnes Ozman speaks in tongues at Topeka, Kansas, USA; this is generally considered to be the beginning of the modern Pentecostal movement.

In Athens, serious disturbances in protest at the proposed publication of the Gospels in modern Greek; the Metropolitan and the government both resign (Nov).

Charles Gore, *The Body of Christ*.

A von Harnack, *The Essence of Christianity*.

A F Loisy, *L'Evangile et l'Eglise*.

W Wrede, *Das Messiasgeheimnis in den Evangelien*.

q **Science, Technology, and Discovery**

Guglielmo Marconi receives radio signals transmitted across Atlantic from Poldhu, SW England, to Newfoundland.

First petrol-engined motor-bicycle in Britain.

Max Planck, *Laws of Radiation*.

W Normann discovers process for hardening liquid fats.

Adrenalin is first manufactured, by Jokichi Takamine.

denouncing the management of concentration camps in South Africa (motion defeated by 253 to 154, with almost 50 Liberal Imperialists abstaining).

G July

In the Netherlands, a Liberal government is replaced by a government of Calvinists and Catholics led by Dr Abraham Kuyper (–1905). Negotiations begin in London for a British–Japanese alliance.

1 in France, the anticlerical Association Law is promulgated for compulsory regulation of all religious congregations and associations and the dissolution of those not authorized by the State.

4 in Philippines, civil government replaces military rule, with W H Taft as governor-general; he proclaims an amnesty for rebels who take the oath of allegiance to the USA.

16 Liberal ministry formed in Denmark, ending a long period of Conservative government.

20 Morocco grants France control of frontier police.

H August

7 in South Africa, Kitchener issues proclamation: leaders of Boer forces who do not surrender by 15 Sept will be permanently banished from South Africa; the property of other combatants who do not surrender will bear the cost of maintaining the combatants' families.

17 as expression of imperialist sentiment the Royal Titles Act adds the words 'and of the British Dominions beyond the Seas' to Edward VII's style.

J September

Visit of Russian Emperor to France provokes anti-militarist demonstrations. In South Africa, Boer raiders invade Natal and Cape Colony.

6 in USA, the anarchist Leon Czolgosz shoots President McKinley at a reception at Buffalo, New York (McKinley dies on 14 Sept, when Vice-President Roosevelt is sworn in as president; aged 42, he is the youngest man to hold the presidency).

7 Peace of Beijing formally ends the Boxer Rising; China is to pay an indemnity to the great powers.

25 Ashanti Kingdom annexed to Gold Coast Colony (modern Ghana).

K October

16 British–Japanese negotiations reopened in London by Tadasu Hayashi, the Japanese minister to Britain.

25 British colonial secretary Joseph Chamberlain makes an anti-German speech at Edinburgh, leading (on 27 Dec) to breakdown in negotiations for British–German alliance.

29 execution in electric chair in New York of Leon Czolgosz for murder of President McKinley.

L November

9 the Sultan of Turkey accepts a French ultimatum to stop interference with various French interests in Turkey.

18 riot in Birmingham, England, when David Lloyd George attempts to give speech about South African War; he leaves the town hall disguised as a police sergeant.

18 second Hay–Pauncefote Convention between the USA and Britain provides for the USA to construct a canal across the Isthmus of Panama; the canal zone will be under US jurisdiction (ratified by US Senate 16 Dec).

25 Prince Hirobumi Ito of Japan, visiting St Petersburg, seeks Russian agreement to Japanese claims in Korea.

M December

7 Japan drops negotiations with Russia, deciding instead to conclude an alliance with Britain.

7 British–Italian agreement for settling Sudan frontier.

25 last notable Boer victory in South African War, at Tweefontein.

26 completion of Uganda railway from Mombasa to Lake Victoria.

31 presidential election held in Cuba; Tomás Estrada Palma is elected (inaugurated 20 May 1902).

Nobel prizes first awarded: the Physics prize to Wilhelm Röntgen, the Chemistry prize to J H van't Hoff, and the Medicine prize to Emil von Behring

R Humanities
Max Weber, *The Protestant Ethic and the Birth of Capitalism*.
C H Firth, *Oliver Cromwell and the Rule of the Puritans in England*.
Woodrow Wilson, *History of the American People*.
Arnold White, *Efficiency and Empire*.
James Bryce, *Studies in History and Jurisprudence*.
US tycoon Andrew Carnegie donates $5.2 million to found New York Public Library.
Foundation of British Academy for the Promotion of Historical, Philosophical and Philological Studies (charter granted Aug).
Publication of *Man*, a journal of social anthropology.
Edmund Husserl, *Logical Investigations*.
Josiah Royce, *The World and the Individual*.

S Art, Sculpture, Fine Arts, and Architecture
Painting, etc:
Paul Gauguin, *The Gold in Their Bodies*.
Edvard Munch, *Girls on the Bridge*.
Pablo Picasso, *Self Portrait*–marks beginning of Blue Period.
Pablo Picasso, *Child Holding a Dove*.

Architecture:
Charles Rennie Mackintosh, Ingram Street Tea Rooms, Glasgow, Scotland.

T Music
Eduardo di Capua, 'O Sole Mio!'
Antonin Dvořák, *Rusalka* (opera).
Edward Elgar, *Cockaigne* Overture, *Pomp and Circumstance* March No. 1.
George Enescu, *Romanian Rhapsodies*.
Ignacy Paderewski, *Manru* (opera).
John Philip Sousa, *The Invincible Eagle* (march).
Charles Villiers Stanford, *Much Ado About Nothing* (opera).
'Ragtime' popular in the USA, but the American Federation of Musicians condemns it and recommends that its members refrain from playing it.
Introduction of the 10-in (25.4-cm) shellac gramophone record with a spiral groove.

U Literature and Drama
Samuel Butler, *Erewhon Revisited*.
Hall Caine, *The Eternal City*.
Miles Franklin, *My Brilliant Career*.
Thomas Hardy, *Poems of the Past and Present*.
Henry James, *The Sacred Fount*.
Rudyard Kipling, *Kim*.
Selma Lagerlöf, *Jerusalem*.
Maurice Maeterlinck, *Life of the Bee*.
Thomas Mann, *Buddenbrooks*.
Frank Norris, *The Octopus*.
G W Russell, W B Yeats, and others, *Ideals in Ireland*.

Drama:
August Strindberg, *Dance of Death*.
Anton Chekhov, *Three Sisters*.

V Births and Deaths
Jan 16 Fulgencio Batista y Zaldívar born (–1973).
Jan 27 Giuseppe Verdi dies (88).
Feb 3 Rosamund Lehmann born (–1990).
Feb 20 Louis Isadore Kahn born (–1974).
Feb 27 Marino Marini born (–1980).
March 24 Charlotte M Yonge dies (78).
March 27 Eisaku Sato born (–1975).
April 22 William Stubbs dies (76).
April 29 Hirohito born (–1989).
May 23 Edward Rubbra born (–1986).
June 6 Achmed Sukharno born (–1970).
Aug 4 Louis Armstrong born (–1971).
Aug 8 E O Lawrence born (–1958).
Sept 21 Learie Constantine born (–1971).
Oct 23 George von Siemens dies (62).
Nov 3 André Malraux born (–1976).
Nov 18 G H Gallup born (–1984).
Dec 5 Walt Disney born (–1966).
Dec 16 Margaret Mead born (–1978).

W Everyday Life
Invention of instant coffee.
In USA, King C Gillette start of production of the Gillette safety razor in Boston.
A court in London awards £75 damages to a woman against the London and North Western Railway Company for the destruction of a Peruvian mummy sent on their railway.

X Sport and Recreation
In Britain, the Professional Golfers' Association is founded.
Tottenham Hotspur of the English Southern League is the first team from outside the Football League to win the Football Association Cup; in a replay of the Final, they beat Sheffield United 3–1.
Peter O'Connor of Ireland establishes a new world long-jump record (5 Aug): 7.6 m (24 ft 11 in); the record stands until 1921.
American jockey Lester Reiff (champion jockey in 1900) has his licence to ride in Britain withdrawn by the Jockey Club for 'throwing' a race.

Y Media
Publication in Britain of *The Tatler* magazine.

End of Boer War ... Germany, Austria, and Italy renew alliance ...

A January

7 following suppression of the Boxer rising, the Chinese imperial court returns to Beijing.

30 Britain qualifies its isolationist foreign policy by signing a treaty with Japan, to safeguard their common interests in China and Korea; in the event of Britain or Japan being at war with a foreign power in East Asia, the other shall maintain strict neutrality, but shall assist its ally if a second foreign power should join the first.

B February

Italian government prevents general strike through calling up all railway workers on the reserve.

6 French agreement with Ethiopia to finance Djibouti–Addis Ababa railway provokes protests from Britain and Italy.

C March

20 Franco–Russian declaration acknowledging the terms of the British–Japanese alliance, but reserving their rights to safeguard their interests.

D April

8 signing in Beijing of Russo–Chinese Manchurian Convention for the gradual evacuation of Manchuria by Russia and guaranteeing of certain Russian rights.

12 in South Africa, following successful actions against Boer forces in Feb and March, Boer leaders meet Kitchener in Pretoria to discuss peace proposals.

15 Britain adjusts the Sudanese frontier with Ethiopia.

15 murder of Sipyagin, Russian minister of interior, by an ex-student; succeeded by Viacheslav Plehve who suppresses peasants' revolt and despoils the Armenian Church.

E May

12 coal strike in Pennsylvania, USA, over demands for higher wages and improved conditions (–13 Oct).

14 following severe financial crisis in Portugal, law passed confirming agreement of bondholders to a substantial reduction in the value of their capital and interest.

16 in Madrid, Spain, enthronement of King Alfonso XIII on his sixteenth birthday, ending minority.

31 signing of Peace of Vereeniging ends Boer War, in which British casualties numbered 5,774 killed (and 16,000 deaths from disease) against 4,000 Boers killed in action;

Boers accept British sovereignty but are promised self-government in the Orange River Colony and Transvaal, and £3 million from Britain for restocking farms.

F June

3 in France René Waldeck-Rousseau resigns, despite his majority in the Chamber, through lack of sympathy with extremists, and is succeeded by Émile Combes who directs a vigorous anti-clerical policy.

28 renewal of Triple Alliance between Germany, Austria, and Italy for six years (originally agreed in 1882).

28 US Congress passes Isthmian Canal Act which authorizes the president to purchase the rights of the French Panama Company and to acquire from Colombia perpetual control of the canal zone.

30 (–11 Aug) Colonial Conference in London supports the principle of Imperial Preference (i.e. Britain and the colonies setting preferential tariffs for each other's goods).

G July

11 Lord Salisbury retires as British prime minister; succeeded by his nephew Arthur Balfour on the following day.

H August

9 coronation of King Edward VII and Queen Alexandra in Westminster Abbey, London.

J September

5 British–Chinese commercial treaty.

27 Crown Lands ordinance inaugurates white settlement of East African uplands.

K October

16 President Roosevelt ends US coal strike by threatening to work the mines with federal troops; mine owners agree to the appointment of a commission to investigate miners' claims.

L November

1 Franco–Italian Entente, in which Italy assures France of its neutrality if France is attacked.

8 Spain holds back from signing agreement on Morocco with France from fear of antagonizing England.

13 Persia concludes favourable tariff with Russia, discriminating against British goods.

*Mahler's 'Fifth' ... Teddy Bears become popular ... Publication
of the* Times Literary Supplement ...

o Politics, Government, Law, and Economy

J A Hobson, *Imperialism*.

V I Lenin, *What Is To Be Done?*.

C F G Masterman, *The Heart of Empire*.

Moisei Ostrogorski, *Democracy and the Organization of Political Parties*.

Oliver Wendell Holmes is appointed to the US Supreme Court (–1932).

In USA, *McClure's* magazine publishes articles exposing corruption in US cities and attacking large companies.

In USA, foundation of Pepsi Cola and Minnesota Mining and Manufacturing (3M).

Theodore Roosevelt intervenes to settle a strike in the US coal industry (16 Oct).

Foundation in USA of the Texas Oil Company (Texaco).

In USA, J P Morgan effects merger of Canadian Copper and Orford Copper to form International Nickel.

Family farms are encouraged in the USA by the National Reclamation Act.

Werner Sombart, *Modern Capitalism* (2nd edition, 1916).

p Society, Education, and Religion

Immigration Restriction Act in Australia.

Australia introduces universal suffrage in federal elections (with voting age of 21); women hold a preponderance of votes in Melbourne and Sydney constituencies.

Imperial decree in China abolishes binding of women's feet and lifts ban on marriages between Chinese and Manchus.

Foundation of the American Automobile Association (AAA) in Chicago, Illinois, USA (4 March).

Ebenezer Howard, *Garden Cities of Tomorrow* (revised edition of *Tomorrow: A Peaceful Path to Real Reform* 1898).

The will of Cecil Rhodes provides funds for the establishment of scholarships at Oxford University for citizens of the British colonies, USA, and Germany.

In China, imperial edicts encouraging the study of Western science result in the opening of colleges in 11 provinces.

Education Act for England and Wales provides for secondary education, places schools under Committees of local authorities and brings denominational schools into the State system.

Charles Booth, *Life and Labour of the People in London*, Third Series: *Religious Influences* (7 volumes).

Paul Hoensbroech, *The Papacy in its Social and Cultural Influence*.

William James, *The Varieties of Religious Experience*.

q Science, Technology, and Discovery

J M Bacon crosses the Irish Channel in a balloon (Nov).

In Denmark, V Poulsen develops the arc generator for wireless telegraphy.

Oliver Heaviside states his conception of a layer in the atmosphere which aids the conduction of wireless waves.

Ernest Rutherford and Frederick Soddy discover Thorium X and publish *The Cause and Nature of Radioactivity*.

Pierre and Marie Curie in France isolate radium salt.

The US surgeon Harvey Cushing begins work on the pituitary body.

William Bayliss and Ernest Starling in England discover hormones.

C Richet discovers cases of 'maphylaxis', abnormal sensitiveness to antidiphtheria serum.

In USA, foundation of the Carnegie Institution in Washington, DC, to promote research.

r Humanities

Cambridge Modern History (–1911).

A F Pollard, *Henry VIII*.

James Gairdner, *History of the English Church in the Sixteenth Century from Henry VIII to Mary*.

R B Merriman, *Life and Letters of Oliver Cromwell*.

Charles Oman, *A History of the Peninsular War, 1807–14* (–1930).

H J Mackinder, *Britain and the British Seas*.

Jules Gilliéron and Edmond Edmont, *L'Atlas linguistique de la France* (–1910).

Scottish Historical Review issued (–1928; publication restarted 1947).

Benedetto Croce, *Aesthetics as the Science of Expression and General Linguistics*.

s Art, Sculpture, Fine Arts, and Architecture

Painting, etc:

Giacomo Balla, *Bankruptcy*.

Paul Cézanne, *La Dame en Bleu* (–1906).

Paul Gauguin, *Contes Barbares, Horsemen on the Beach*.

Claude Monet, *Waterloo Bridge*.

Pablo Picasso, *Woman with a Scarf*.

Sculpture:

Auguste Rodin, *Romeo et Juliette*.

M December
  10 official opening of Aswan Dam, Egypt.
  18 in London the Committee of Imperial
      Defence holds first meeting.

19 Germany, Britain, and Italy blockade
      Venezuela in protest at Cipriano Castro's
      refusal to meet claims for injuries caused
      during revolution.

Architecture:

Cass Gilbert, New York Customs House (–1907).

Charles Rennie Mackintosh, Hill House, Helensburgh, Scotland (–1903).

T Music

Francesco Cilea, *Adriana Lecouvreur* (opera).

Claude Debussy, *Pelléas et Mélisande* (opera).

Edward Elgar, 'Land of Hope and Glory' (words by A C Benson; adapted from Elgar's *Pomp and Circumstance* March No. 1).

Edward German, *Merrie England* (operetta).

Paul Lincke, 'Glow-worm idyll'.

Gustav Mahler, Symphony No. 5.

Jules Massenet, *Le Jongleur de Notre Dame* (opera).

Sergei Rachmaninov, Piano Concerto No. 2.

Jean Sibelius, Symphony No. 2.

In Italy, tenor Enrico Caruso makes his first recording (18 March), in the Hotel di Milano, with recording engineer Fred Gaisberg.

Scott Joplin, 'The Entertainer' rag.

Publication of 'Bill Bailey, Won't You Please Come Home' by Hughie Cannon.

U Literature and Drama

Hilaire Belloc, *The Path to Rome*.

Joseph Conrad, 'The Heart of Darkness' (published in *Youth and Other Stories*).

Arthur Conan Doyle, *The Hound of the Baskervilles*.

André Gide, *L'Immoraliste/The Immoralist*.

Henry James, *The Wings of the Dove*.

Rudyard Kipling, *Just So Stories*.

Maxim Gorky, *Night's Lodging*.

John Masefield, *Salt Water Ballads*.

Émile Verhaeren, *Les Forces Tumultueuses*.

Drama:

Gabriele D'Annunzio, *Francesca da Rimini*.

J M Barrie, *The Admirable Crichton*.

Anton Chekhov, *Three Sisters*.

Maxim Gorky, *The Lower Depths*.

V Births and Deaths

Jan 30 Nikolaus Pevsner born (–1983).

Feb 4 Charles Lindbergh born (–1974).

Feb 11 Arne Jacobsen born (–1971).

Feb 27 John Steinbeck born (–1968).

March 26 Cecil Rhodes dies (41).

March 29 William Walton born (–1983).

May 21 Marcel Lajos Breuer born (–1981).

June 28 Richard Rodgers born (–1979).

July 28 Karl Popper born (–1994).

Aug 9 Solomon born (–1988).

Aug 24 Fernand Braudel born (–1985).

Sept 20 Stevie Smith born (–1971).

Sept 29 Émile Zola dies (62).

Oct 5 Ray Kroc born (–1984).

Dec 9 R A Butler born (–1982).

Dec 13 Talcott Parsons born (–1979).

Ruhollah Khomeini born (–1989).

W Everyday Life

Sudden collapse of campanile in St Mark's Square, Venice (14 July).

Teddy bears start to become popular after an incident in which US President Theodore Roosevelt refused to shoot a bear cub.

Advances in refrigeration enable fish and chips to become a popular delicacy in London.

Underground railway opened in Berlin.

X Sport and Recreation

The first Rose Ball game in American college football is held; Michigan beats Stanford 49–0 (1 Jan).

The first £500 transfer fee in English football: Alf Common moves from Sheffield United to Sunderland.

In Scotland, 25 spectators are killed when a stand collapses at Ibrox Park, Glasgow, during the Home International Championship game between Scotland and England (5 April).

Alex Herd's victory in the British Open gold championship popularizes use of the Haskell golf ball, developed by Dr Coburn Haskell, a dentist in Ohio, USA; the ball uses a core of elastic thread, rather than of gutta percha, enabling players to hit the ball longer distances.

Sceptre wins four of the five English horse-racing classics: the 1,000 and 2,000 Guineas; the Oaks and the St Leger.

Y Media

In Britain, the *Times Literary Supplement* is published.

Film:

In France, Charles Pathé opens a film studio at Vincennes, Paris.

Trip to the Moon (director, Georges Méliès).

*Congo atrocities revealed ... USA obtains the Panama Canal
Zone ...*

A **January**
1 the Emperor of India (King Edward VII of Britain) holds a coronation durbar at Delhi; most Indian rulers attend together with 40,000 troops and 173,000 visitors (celebrations continue until 8 Jan).
22 Hay–Herrán pact for US acquisition of the Panama Canal Zone, but Colombia delays ratification.

B **February**
Germany, Britain, and Italy lift blockade against Venezuela (imposed in Dec 1902) on the Hague Tribunal appointing a commission to investigate the powers' claims for damages. Russia and Austria call for programme of reforms for pacifying Macedonia. British colonial secretary, Joseph Chamberlain, visits South Africa and directs British policy towards conciliation with Boers. Publication in Britain of report by Consul Roger Casement alleging atrocious treatment of African and Indian labourers in the Belgian Congo by white traders; a British government commission confirms the findings.

C **March**
15 British forces complete conquest of northern Nigeria.
21 end of hearings on grievances of US coal miners (following strike in 1902); contract miners are awarded a pay increase of 10 per cent and a shorter working day, but owners refuse to recognize the United Mine Workers Union.

D **April**
Britain and France withhold support for Germany's construction of a railway to Baghdad. Dutch government ends railway and dock strikes by calling in troops.

E **May**
In Britain, E D Morel launches the *West African Mail* to campaign against atrocities in Belgian Congo.
1 (–4) Edward VII's visit to Paris begins improvement in Anglo–French relations.
15 Joseph Chamberlain announces his conversion to Imperial Preference, which divides the Conservatives.
15 to counter Russian designs, British foreign secretary Lord Lansdowne declares that Britain would resist the establishment by

any power of a fortified base on the Persian Gulf.

F **June**
10 murders of King Alexander I and Queen Draga of Serbia (15, the Serbian Assembly elects Peter Karageorgevitch king as Peter I, –1921) and restores the 1889 constitution.

G **July**
6 (–9) visit to London of President Émile Loubet and Théophile Delcassé begins conversations leading to *Entente Cordiale*.
20 following death of Pope Leo XIII, Giuseppe Sarto is elected Pope Pius X.
21 Irish Land Purchase Act, providing inducements for landlords to sell estates to the Irish Land Commission, which will collect annuities from tenants rather than rent.
25 in Britain, Arthur Henderson wins parliamentary by-election at Barnard Castle, NE England, for the Labour Party in three-cornered fight.

H **August**
At London Congress the Russian Social Democratic Party splits into Mensheviks ('minority'), led by G V Plecharoff, and Bolsheviks ('majority'), led by V I Lenin.
2 start of rising in Macedonia; suppressed by Turks by end of Sept, but at the cost of considerable protest in W Europe and elsewhere at Turkish behaviour.
12 Japanese diplomatic note to Russia concerning the latter's failure to evacuate Manchuria.
29 dismissal of Count Witte, Russian finance minister, is taken as a victory for the group favouring Russian expansion in Manchuria and Korea.

J **September**
16 Franz Joseph's aim to bring Hungarian regiments into a unified army system provokes Magyar opposition.
18 British colonial secretary, Joseph Chamberlain, resigns to test feeling in country on Imperial Preference; leading free-traders also resign and Arthur Balfour reconstructs his Conservative ministry with Austen Chamberlain as chancellor of exchequer.

K **October**
Anglo-Russian conversations break down through Russian unwillingness to sacrifice interests in Persia.

*Krupp Company founded in Germany ... Dissolution of French
religious orders ... Grand Central Station, New York*

o Politics, Government, Law, and Economy

In USA, the state of Wisconsin institutes primary elections to enable voters to choose election candidates.

US Department of Commerce and Labor established.

President Theodore Roosevelt establishes the USA's first national wildlife refuge, Pelican Island off the E coast of Florida (by 1929, 87 federal refuges are established).

Foundation of Union of Liberation in Russia, supported by members of the professions, aiming at a liberal constitution.

In USA, Elkins Act strengthens Interstate Commerce Act (1887) by outlawing rebates paid by railway companies to favoured customers and requiring use of published charges.

Poor Prisoners' Defence Act creates the first legal aid scheme in Britain.

Regulation of motor-cars in Britain, with 20 mph (32 km/hr) speed limit.

Following the incorporation of the Ford Motor Company, Detroit (Michigan, USA) becomes the 'motor capital' of the world.

Krupp metal-working industries founded in the Ruhr region of Germany.

In Germany several electrical firms found the Telefunken Company.

Milton Hershey starts building a chocolate factory and a company town in Pennsylvania, USA.

F W Taylor, *Shop Management*, which helps to establish 'scientific management' of workforces.

New Zealand tariff favours British goods.

P Society, Education, and Religion

Major famine in Russia.

In Britain, Mrs Emmeline Pankhurst founds the Women's Social and Political Union (WSPU), a nonparty organization to campaign for female suffrage.

Establishment in USA of the Women's Trade Union League (WTUL).

The Senate of Dublin University, Ireland, votes to open its degrees to women (June).

W E B Du Bois, *The Souls of Black Folk*.

Increased sickness benefits for German workers.

Helen Keller, *The Story of My Life*.

Foundation of Letchworth Garden City in S England, an attempt by Ebenezer Howard to realize his 'garden city' ideal of well-planned urban centres which would include agricultural activities.

An infants' welfare centre opened in Ghent, Belgium.

Royal Naval College, Dartmouth, SW England, established.

Dissolution of most French religious orders (18 March).

Royal Commission on Ecclesiastical Discipline in England.

In England, Randall Davidson becomes Archbishop of Canterbury.

Mass said for the first time in the still incomplete Roman Catholic Cathedral, Westminster, London.

Johannes Haller, *The Papacy and Church Reform*.

Carol Munth founds Roman Catholic periodical *Hochland*.

Q Science, Technology, and Discovery

President Roosevelt of the USA inaugurates Pacific communications cable by sending a message around the world (4 July).

Orville and Wilbur Wright in North Carolina, USA, make the first successful flight in an aeroplane with a petrol engine (17 Dec).

C T R Wilson develops the sensitive electroscope.

R A Zsigmondy invents the ultramicroscope.

Agnes Clerke, *Problems in Astrophysics*.

J J Thomson, *The Conduction of Electricity Through Gases*.

W Ramsay discovers the gases krypton and xenon in the atmosphere.

Electrocardiography invented in the Netherlands by Willem Einthoven.

R Humanities

Max Uhlc, *Puchacamac*.

C H Overton, *The Non-Jurors: Their Lives, Principles and Writings*.

H Maxwell (ed.), *The Creevey Papers*.

H A L Fisher, *Studies in Napoleonic Statesmanship*.

John Morley, *Life of Gladstone*.

W S Holdsworth, *History of English Law* (–1966).

J Redlich and F W Hirst, *Local Government in England*.

Vierteljahrschrift für Sozial-und Wirtschaftsgeschichte issued.

G A Grierson, *Linguistic Survey of India* (–1928).

E K Chambers, *The Medieval Stage*.

E T Cook and A D D Wedderburn (eds.), *The Works of John Ruskin* (39 volumes; –1912).

Opening of German Museum, Munich.

Gottlob Frege, *Basic Laws of Arithmetic*, Volume 2.

1 (–3) Austro–Russian agreement at Mürz-stag for reforms in Macedonia is approved by powers.

20 settlement of Alaskan frontier by three-power commission; British representative gives casting vote in favour of USA, embittering Canada.

L **November**

Commission in Transvaal favours use of immigrant Chinese labour for Rand mines, which is later sanctioned by British prime minister Balfour.

3 fearing that the USA would choose alternative canal route if Colombia delayed further, a group of Colombians proclaims the independence of Panama from Colombia.

17 by the treaty of Petropolis, Bolivia cedes territory to Brazil in return for a rail and water outlet to the east.

M **December**

18 USA–Panama treaty places Panama Canal Zone in US hands in perpetuity for annual rent.

G E Moore, *Principia Ethica*.

Charles Sanders Peirce, *Lectures on Pragmatism*.

s Art, Sculpture, Fine Arts, and Architecture

First Salon d'Automne, Paris, France–includes a Gauguin retrospective.

National Art Collections Fund formed to raise money to prevent works of art leaving Britain.

Painting, etc:

Pablo Picasso, *L'ascete*, *La Vie*.

Architecture:

Antonio Gaudí, begins work on upper transept of Sagrada Familia church, Barcelona (church still unfinished).

Josef Hoffmann, Convalescent Home, Purkersdorf, Austria.

Charles Reed and Allen Stem, Grand Central Station, New York, USA (–1913).

New York Chamber of Commerce and Stock Exchange built.

т Music

Eugen d'Albert, *Tiefland* (opera).

Umberto Giordano, *Siberia* (opera).

Edvard Grieg, *Moods*.

Erik Satie, *Trois Morceaux en Forme de Poire*.

Arnold Schoenberg, *Pelleas und Melisande*.

The Wizard of Oz (musical), words by Frank L Baum, music by A Baldwin Sloane and Paul Tietjens (first work staged at the Majestic Theatre, New York, 20 Jan).

Production of the world's first unbreakable shellac disc claimed.

u Literature and Drama

Andy Adams, *The Log of a Cowboy*.

Mary Austin, *The Land of Little Rain*.

Samuel Butler, *The Way of All Flesh* (posthumous).

George Gissing, *The Private Papers of Henry Rycroft*.

Hugo von Hofmannsthal, *Electra*.

Henry James, *The Ambassadors*.

Jack London, *The Call of the Wild*.

Thomas Mann, *Tonio Kröger*.

Drama:

Oscar Hammerstein builds Drury Lane Theatre, New York (later the Manhattan Opera House).

Arthur Schnitzler, *Reigen*.

George Bernard Shaw, *Man and Superman*.

v Births and Deaths

Jan 10 Barbara Hepworth born (–1975).

Jan 11 Alan Paton born (–1988).

May 2 Dr Benjamin Spock born (–).

May 3 'Bing' Crosby born (–1977).

May 12 Lennox Berkeley born (–1989).

June 19 Lou Gehrig born (–1941).

June 25 George Orwell (Eric Blair) born (–1950).

July 2 Alec Douglas-Home (Lord Home) born (–1995).

July 10 Kenneth Clark born (–1983).

July 17 James Whistler dies (70).

Aug 7 Louis Leakey born (–1972).

Aug 22 Lord Salisbury (Robert Cecil) dies (73).

Aug 24 Graham Sutherland born (–1980).

Sept 25 Marc Rothko born (–1970).

Oct 22 W E H Lecky dies (87).

Oct 28 Evelyn Waugh born (–1966).

Nov 1 Theodore Mommsen dies (87).

Dec 8 Herbert Spencer dies (83).

Dec 13 John Piper born (–1992).

Dec 13 Paul Gauguin dies (55).

Dec 13 Camille Pissarro dies (72).

w Everyday Life

In USA, William Harley and the three Davidson brothers produce their first Harley-Davidson motorcycle.

First motor taxis in London.

x Sport and Recreation

Bury win the Football Association Cup in England without conceding a goal.

The National Federation of Anglers is formed in Britain at a meeting in Birmingham (May).

Baseball's World Series, between the winners of the American League and the National League, is inaugurated; the first title is won by the Boston Red Sox, who beat the Pittsburgh Pirates 5–3.

The Tour de France, organized by Henri Desgrange, editor of the French cycling magazine *L'Auto*, is run for the first time. The first winner is Maurice Garin, an Italian chimney sweep.

The Marylebone Cricket Club (MCC) takes over responsibility for English teams touring abroad.

In Britain, the Jockey Club takes action against the doping of horses.

y Media

In Britain, Alfred Harmsworth founds the *Daily Mirror* (Nov), a women's paper sold for a penny (Jan 1904, renamed the *Daily Illustrated Mirror* and published as an illustrated tabloid sold for a halfpenny).

Film:

The Great Train Robbery (starring G M Anderson).

Russo–Japanese War ... Theodore Roosevelt elected US president ...

B **February**

8 (–9) start of Russo–Japanese War: Japanese fleet makes surprise attack on Russian squadron at Port Arthur (Russian treaty port in NE China), damaging two battleships and a cruiser, and then blockades the port.

C **March**

11 army bill is passed in Hungary, despite Magyar obstruction, through using guillotine.

14 judgment in US Northern Securities case declares attempted mergers of railway interests as violation of anti-Trust Act.

D **April**

In Australia, John Christian Watson is prime minister of Labour government (–Aug).

8 *Entente Cordiale* settles British–French differences in Morocco, Egypt, and Newfoundland fishery; Britain recognizes Suez Canal Convention and surrenders claim to Madagascar.

23 USA acquires property of French Panama Canal company.

24 (–27) visit of French president and foreign minister, Émile Loubet and Théophile Delcassé, to King Victor Emmanuel III of Italy annoys Papacy.

E **May**

1 Japanese army (which had landed in Korea in March), attacks and defeats Russian army at Xinyizhou.

17 French ambassador at Vatican is recalled to Paris.

23 introduction of new cheap steerage rates encourages migration from Europe to the USA.

26 Battle of Nanshan: Japanese cut off Russian garrison in Port Arthur from other Russian land forces in Manchuria.

F **June**

G **July**

Rafael Reyes becomes dictator in Colombia and attempts to reorganize finances.

28 assassination of Vyacheslav Plehve, Russian minister of interior.

28 Germany signs commercial treaties with Belgium, Switzerland, Sweden, and Austria-Hungary.

H **August**

11 alteration to the drink licensing laws in Britain generates controversy by establishing compensation for publicans losing their drink licences as a matter of public policy; this fails to appease the temperance lobby.

25 (–3 Sept) Japanese defeat Russians at Liaoyang, China.

J **September**

General strike in Italy, culminating in violent incidents in Milan.

7 as the culmination of a British expedition to Lhasa, Colonel Francis Younghusband forces treaty on Tibet whose stipulations include a provision whereby the Dalai Lama will not concede territory to a foreign power without British consent.

K **October**

In Italian elections the socialists, discredited by strike action, lose heavily.

3 Insurrection of Hereros and Hottentots in German South-West Africa (–1908).

3 Franco–Spanish treaty for preserving independence of Morocco, with secret clauses aiming at ultimate partition.

20 Bolivia and Chile settle differences by treaty.

21 Russian fleet, bound for the Far East, fires on British trawlers in Dogger Bank area of North Sea, sinking one vessel and provoking wave of indignation in Britain (23).

28 following Dogger Bank incident, Tsar Nicholas II of Russia agrees to refer question of compensation to Hague international commission.

L **November**

Zemstvo Congress at St Petersburg demands a republican constitution and civil liberties.

8 in US presidential election, President Theodore Roosevelt (Republican) defeats Alton B Parker (Democrat) with 336 electoral votes to 140; popular vote: Roosevelt, 7,623,486; Parker, 5,077,911.

23 German–Russian negotiations for an alliance break down through Russia's unwillingness to sign before consulting France.

M **December**

2 members of the British Parliament representing Ulster form an organization (known as the Ulster Unionist Council from March 1905).

10 nationalist, anti-Austrian ministry takes office in Serbia.

Discovery of the Oseberg Viking Ship ... Teabag invented ...

o Politics, Government, Law, and Economy

John Christian Watson, prime minister of Australia, is the world's first head of government to be a representative of labor.

L T Hobhouse, *Democracy and Reaction.*

First official speed limits in USA (10 mph in populated areas, 15 mph in villages, and 20 on open roads; 16, 24, and 32 km/hr).

In Britain, Henry Royce and Charles Rolls start manufacturing and selling cars under the name Rolls-Royce (4 May).

USA acquires the Panama Canal zone (4 May).

In USA, James Buchanan Duke forms his tobacco companies into the American Tobacco Company (19 Oct).

Canada passes a protectionist tariff.

p Society, Education, and Religion

Telephone network covers the USA.

In USA, foundation of the National Child Labor Committee to coordinate the campaign for restrictions on use of child labour.

Robert Hunter, *Poverty.*

In England, foundation of the Workers' Educational Association by Albert Mansbridge.

The German anti-Jesuit law of 1872 is revised to permit the return of individual members of the order (8 March).

Émile Combes introduces bill for separation of Church and State in France, ending the 1801 Concordat (promulgated Dec 1905).

q Science, Technology, and Discovery

An ultra-violet lamp is made.

In Germany, J P L T Elster devises the photo-electric cell.

In Britain, J Fleming patents the diode valve.

In Spain Santiago Ramón y Cajal demonstrates that the nervous system is composed essentially of neurons (i.e., nerve cells).

r Humanities

Discovery of a Viking ship burial at Oseberg, Norway.

William Petrie, *Methods and Aims in Archaeology.*

Henry Adams, *Mont St. Michel and Chartres.*

G M Trevelyan, *England under the Stuarts.*

W Cunningham, *Growth of English Industry and Commerce in Modern Times.*

Herbert Levi Osgood, *The American Colonies in the Seventeenth Century* (–1907).

Bernard Berenson, *Drawings of the Florentine Painters.*

Fire destroys the National Library in Turin, including several hundred manuscripts (26 Jan).

First meeting, in Oxford, of Classical Association of England and Wales (28 May).

Benedetto Croce founds *La Critica* to reinvigorate Italian thought and to unite it with European idealist philosophy.

s Art, Sculpture, Fine Arts, and Architecture

Entire room reserved for Cézanne's works at the Salon d'Automne, Paris, France Mr Freer of Detroit, USA, buys Whistler's Peacock Room and ships the painted panels to the USA.

Painting, etc:

Giacomo Balla, *A Worker's Day.*

Frank Brangwyn, murals at the Skinners' Hall, London.

Paul Cézanne, *Mont Sainte Victoire* (–1906).

Henri Matisse, *Luxe, Calme et Volupté* (–1905).

William Nicholson, sets for *Peter Pan.*

Pablo Picasso, *Woman Ironing.*

Odilon Redon, *Portrait of Gauguin.*

Henri Rousseau, *The Wedding.*

Architecture:

Charles Rennie Mackintosh, The Willow Tea Rooms, Glasgow, Scotland.

Louis Sullivan, Carson, Pirie, and Scott store, Chicago, USA – early major work of the Chicago School.

Otto Wagner, Post Office Savings Bank, Vienna, Austria (–1906).

Frank Lloyd Wright, Larkin Building, Buffalo, New York, USA.

t Music

Frederick Delius, *Koanga* (opera).

Vincent d'Indy, Symphony No. 2.

Leoš Janáček, *Jenůfa* (opera).

Gustav Mahler, *Kindertotenlieder*, Symphony No. 6 ('Tragic').

Giacomo Puccini, *Madama Butterfly* (opera).

Florent Schmitt, Psalm 47.

Richard Strauss, *Sinfonia Domestica.*

u Literature and Drama

G K Chesterton, *The Napoleon of Notting Hill.*

Joseph Conrad, *Nostromo.*

O Henry, *Cabbages and Kings.*

Hermann Hesse, *Peter Camenzind.*

W H Hudson, *Green Mansions.*

Henry James, *The Golden Bowl.*

M R James, *Ghost Stories of an Antiquary.*

Jack London, *Sea Wolf.*

Romain Rolland, *Jean-Christophe* (–1912).

Drama:

J M Barrie, *Peter Pan.*

Anton Chekhov, *The Cherry Orchard.*

Attempted revolution in Russia ... Norway becomes independent ...

A January

Louis Botha forms *Het Volk* organization to agitate for responsible government in Transvaal.

2 Russian commander of Port Arthur surrenders the port to the Japanese.

22 'Bloody Sunday' in St Petersburg, when a procession of workers and their families, led by a priest (Father Gapon) and carrying a petition to the tsar, is fired on by guards outside the Winter Palace; over 100 are killed and riots break out elsewhere in Russia.

B February

Insurrection in Welle District of Belgian Congo.

19 (–10 March) Battle of Mukden between Japanese and Russians; Japanese capture the city of Mukden (Shenyang), a key point for control of Manchuria.

C March

3 Tsar Nicholas II promises to undertake religious and other reforms and to call a consultative assembly.

21 British–Persian agreement to counter Russian designs in the Near East.

30 Greeks in Crete revolt against Turkish rule.

31 Emperor William II's visit to Tangier sets off the 'First Moroccan Crisis', being seen as a test of the British–French Convention of 1904 which arranged for French predominance over Morocco.

D April

25 Transvaal is granted a constitution which Louis Botha regards as inadequate.

Thomas Hardy, *The Dynasts*.
Luigi Pirandello, *Il fu Mattia Pascal/The Late Mattia Pascal*.
J M Synge, *Riders to the Sea*.
First J E Vedrenne–Harley Granville-Barker season at the Court Theatre, London.
The Abbey Theatre, Dublin, opened by Miss E F Horniman.

v Births and Deaths
Jan 9 George Balanchine born (–1983).
Jan 14 Cecil Beaton born (–1980).
Feb 21 Alexei Nikolaievich Kosygin born (–1980).
Feb 22 Leslie Stephen dies (72).
March 5 Karl Rahner born (–1984).
April 16 Samuel Smiles dies (92).
May 1 Antonín Dvořák dies (62).
June 2 Johnny Weissmuller born (–1984).
July 2 Anton Chekhov dies (44).
July 12 Pablo Neruda born (–1973).
July 14 S J P Kruger dies (79).
Aug 21 Count Basie born (–1984).
Aug 22 Deng Xiaoping born (–).
Aug 26 Christopher Isherwood born (–1986).
Oct 2 Graham Greene born (–1991).
Nov 14 Michael Ramsey born (–1988).
Nov 17 Isamu Noguchi born (–1988).

w Everyday Life
Opening of Broadway Subway, New York, with electric trains running from City Hall to 145th Street.

In USA, the St Louis exposition popularizes the hamburger (produced by local German immigrants) and the ice cream cone.
Thermos flasks gain sudden popularity in the USA.
Safety razor blades are patented by King C Gillette in the USA.
Invention of the teabag by Thomas Sullivan in the USA.

x Sport and Recreation
England's cricketers regain the Ashes, beating Australia 3–2 in the five-match series in Australia.
The 3rd Olympic Games are held in St Louis, Missouri, USA, to coincide with the World Fair in the city. The United States wins 80 gold medals; Germany and Cuba, 5 each; Canada, 4; Hungary, 2 (1 July–23 Nov).
Charles W Follis becomes the first African-American professional player in US football.
The Federation Internationale de Football Association (FIFA), a world governing body for football, is founded, without British support.
US golfer Walter J Travis wins the British Amateur Golf Championship.

y Media
In USA, William Randolph Hearst founds the *Boston American*.

Einstein's special theory of relativity ... Debussy's La Mer *...*

o Politics, Government, Law, and Economy
In India, the viceroy, Lord Curzon, divides Bengal into East and West, uniting East Bengal with Assam; the action provokes opposition (Bengal reunited 1911).
In USA, President Theodore Roosevelt creates a forest service within the Department of Agriculture to manage national forests.
V I Lenin, *Two Tactics*.
The US Supreme Court strikes down a state law regulating hours of labour in Lochner v. New York.
A V Dicey, *Lectures on the Relation between Law and Public Opinion in England during the 19th Century*.
New York State investigates insurance houses following charges of corrupt practices.
Bethlehem Steel founded in Bethlehem, Pennsylvania, USA, as a rival to J P Morgan's US Steel.

Austin Motor Company founded in Britain.
Completion of the Trans-Siberian Railway (started 1891).

p Society, Education, and Religion
Anti-Jewish pogroms in numerous Russian towns and cities.
Foundation of 'Niagara Movement' of radical US African-Americans led by W E B Du Bois to work for civil equality (13 July).
Start of construction of Gary, Indiana, the largest 'company town' built by a US manufacturer (the US Steel Corporation); it is designed to house 200,000 people.
Jesse C Nichols starts buying land S of Kansas City, USA, for his exclusive residential district (Country Club District); it leads to the building of similar districts in the USA

30 British–French military conversations.

E May

1 (–5) Maurice Rouvier, French prime minister, fails to settle Moroccan question with Germany.

8 Union of Unions in Russia, under Paul Miliukov, combines various liberal elements demanding parliamentary institutions.

17 Britain proposes international discussions on Morocco.

27 (–28) Battle of Tsushima: Japanese sink two-thirds of the Russian Baltic fleet in Tsushima Strait (between Korea and Japan).

F June

6 Théophile Delcassé, French foreign minister since 1898, resigns under pressure from Germany.

7 Norwegian Storting (parliament) decides on separation from Sweden (ratified by plebiscite, Aug).

28 mutiny by sailors on the Russian battleship *Potemkin*, anchored off Odessa; unrest spreads through the Russian navy.

G July

Chinese boycott US goods, in protest at US restrictions on immigration into and visits to USA by Chinese.

8 France, assured of British support against unreasonable demands by Germany, agrees to a conference on Morocco.

23 (–4) William II and Nicholas II sign treaty of Björkö, for mutual aid in Europe (Prince von Bülow objects to the limitation to Europe and threatens to resign).

H August

Outbreak of Maji Maji rising in German East Africa (–1907).

12 British–Japanese alliance is renewed for 10 years.

19 Tsar Nicholas II issues an Imperial Manifesto, proposing to create an Imperial Duma (parliament), elected on limited franchise, and with only deliberative powers.

J September

1 Provinces of Alberta and Saskatchewan formed in Canada.

5 Treaty of Portsmouth (New Hampshire, USA), mediated by US president Roosevelt, ending Russo–Japanese War: Russia to cede Port Arthur and the Guangdong Peninsula, evacuate Manchuria and half of Sakhalin Island, and to recognize Japan's interests in Korea (Japan's demand for indemnity is not granted).

24 Sweden acquiesces in Norway's independence.

28 France and Germany agree to call a conference on Morocco.

K October

20 (–30) general strike in Russia.

26 delegates of strike committees in St Petersburg form the first Soviet ('council').

26 by Treaty of Separation between Norway and Sweden, Oscar II abdicates Norwegian crown.

30 in Russia, Tsar Nicholas II issues the 'October Manifesto' capitulating to demands for the Duma to have legislative powers, a wider franchise for its election, and civil liberties.

L November

Report of commission of inquiry into atrocities in Congo Free State excuses Leopold II.

16 Count Sergei Witte appointed prime minister of Russia.

18 Prince Charles of Denmark is elected King Haakon VII of Norway (25, the King and Queen Maud make their formal entry into Christiana (now Oslo)).

18 Japanese force the emperor of Korea to sign a treaty giving Japan control of Korea's foreign policy (through resident-general).

23 British Liberal Party leader Sir Henry Campbell-Bannerman makes speech in Stirling, Scotland, advocating Home Rule for Ireland 'by instalments' (25, former Liberal leader Lord Rosebery attacks the proposal).

M December

4 British Conservative prime minister Arthur Balfour resigns.

5 Sir Henry Campbell-Bannerman forms Liberal ministry with Sir Edward Grey as foreign secretary, Herbert Asquith as chancellor of exchequer and R B Haldane as war secretary; King Edward issues a warrant giving official recognition to the office of prime minister and according the holder precedence after the Archbishop of York.

12 King Nicholas of Montenegro grants constitution.

21 Japan declares Korea a protectorate.

22 insurrection of Moscow workers (–1 Jan 1906). Revolution in Persia begins.

during the 1920s and 1930s; inhabitants of such districts are controlled by covenants, which forbid the sale of houses to African-Americans.

Industrial Workers of the World ('The Wobblies') hold a convention in Chicago, USA.

Foundation in US of the Order of Sons of Italy, a mutual aid society for Italian-Americans.

Lawyer Paul Percy Harris, in Chicago, USA, founds the Rotary Club, an association of businessmen and professionals who meet by rota in members' offices for fellowship and also to promote work in the community.

The Aliens Act is the first piece of British legislation to restrict immigration (asylum-seekers are permitted entry, but not 'undesirables' without financial support).

The Automobile Association is founded in London.

Sigmund Freud, *Three Essays on the Theory of Sexuality*.

Separation of Church and State in France (9 Dec): freedom of worship guaranteed, without state recognition of any particular church; church property is to be held by associations (opposed by Pope Pius X).

Baptist World Alliance founded in London.

Q Science, Technology, and Discovery

Ejnar Hertzsprung in Denmark identifies the luminosity sequence of stars.

In Switzerland, Albert Einstein publishes his special theory of relativity, his mathematical analysis of Brownian motion, and his theory of the photoelectric effect.

Otto Hahn in Germany discovers radiothorium.

E Starling in England introduces the term 'hormone'.

E Zirm in Austria performs the first cornea transplant.

German surgeon H F W Braun introduces novocaine into clinical use.

In USA, foundation of the Audubon Society.

R Humanities

H W C Davis, *England under the Normans and Angevins*.

Andrew Lang, *John Knox and the Reformation*.

Edward Channing, *A History of the United States* (6 volumes; –1925).

E G Craig, *The Art of the Theatre*.

Ernst Mach, *Knowledge and Error*.

Charles Maurras, *The Future of Intelligence*.

George Santayana, *The Life of Reason*.

S Art, Sculpture, Fine Arts, and Architecture

Louis Vauxcelles coins the name 'Les Fauves'

('Wild Beasts') for the group of French artists led by Henri Matisse.

Die Brücke ('The Bridge') group of artists is formed in Dresden by Ernst Kirchner and revives interest in the graphic arts; the group's style is expressionism (–1913).

Painting, etc:

Paul Cézanne, *Les Grandes Baigneuses*.

André Derain, *Fishing Port, Collioure*.

Henri Matisse, *Portrait of Madame Matisse (The Green Line)*, *Bonheur de Vivre* (–1906).

Pablo Picasso, *Acrobat and Young Harlequin*, *Boy With Pipe*.

Henri Rousseau, *The Hungry Lion*.

John Singer Sargeant, *The Marlborough Family*.

Sculpture:

Thomas Brock, memorial to Queen Victoria, outside Buckingham Palace, London (posts and pedestal by Aston Webb).

Aristide Maillol, *The Mediterranean*.

Architecture:

Ernest Flagg, Singer Building, New York (–1908).

Antonio Gaudí, Casa Milà and Casa Batlló, Barcelona (–1910).

Josef Hoffmann, Palais Stoclet, Brussels, Belgium (–1911); interior mosaics by Gustav Klimt.

Frank Lloyd Wright, Unity Temple, Oak Park, Chicago, USA (–1906).

T Music

Claude Debussy, *La Mer*.

Edward Elgar, *Introduction and Allegro for Strings*.

Franz Léhar, *The Merry Widow* (operetta).

Gustav Mahler, Symphony No. 7.

Richard Strauss, *Salome* (opera).

Foundation of Juilliard School of Music in New York (1 Oct).

First double-sided record issued.

Harry Lauder, 'I Love a Lassie'.

U Literature and Drama

Rubén Darío, *Cantos of Life and Hope*.

Thomas Dixon, *The Clansman*.

E M Forster, *Where Angels Fear to Tread*.

Baron Corvo (pseudonym of Frederick Rolfe), *Hadrian the Seventh*.

August Strindberg, *Historical Miniatures*.

H G Wells, *Kipps*.

Edith Wharton, *House of Mirth*.

Oscar Wilde, *De Profundis* (posthumous).

Drama:

David Belasco, *The Girl of the Golden West*.

Tristram Bernard, *Triplepatte*.

Harley Granville-Barker, *The Voysey Inheritance*.

*Victory of Liberals in British election ... San Francisco
earthquake ...*

A **January**
1 Helmuth von Moltke becomes chief of German general staff.
10 British–French military and naval conversations.
12 Liberal landslide in British general election (Liberals, 400 seats, with majority of 130 over all parties; Unionists, 157; Irish Nationalists, 83; Labour, 30); Sir Henry Campbell-Bannerman's cabinet embarks on sweeping social reforms.
16 (–8 April) in southern Spain, Algeciras conference of great powers to settle their dispute over position of Morocco; cooperation of Britain and France isolates Germany.
17 Clément Fallières elected President of France, through Georges Clemenceau's influence.

B **February**

C **March**
10 colliery disaster in France (worst to date): explosion at the Courrières mine near Lens kills about 1,800 miners.
16 nationalization of Japanese railways.

D **April**
4 elections held for first Duma in Russia.
5 Kaiser Wilhelm II of Germany dismisses Count Friedrich Holstein (key adviser in foreign ministry), ending fear of German war with France over Morocco.
8 'Act of Algeciras' signed, ending the Moroccan Crisis; it gives France and Spain chief control in Morocco (under a Swiss inspector and respecting the sultan's authority).
18 (–19) major earthquake in San Francisco, USA; the quake and subsequent fires devastate the city, leaving over 200,000 people homeless and over 1,000 dead.

Hugo von Hofmannsthal, *Das gerettete Venedig*.
Charles Klein, *The Lion and the Mouse*.
George Bernard Shaw, *Major Barbara*.
Frank Wedekind, *Pandora's Box*.
The Aldwych Theatre opened in London.

v Births and Deaths

Jan 2 Michael Tippett born (–).
Feb 6 Wladyslaw Gomulka born (–1982).
Feb 9 Adolf Menzel dies (89).
March 2 Marc Blitzstein born (–1964).
March 29 Edward Burra born (–1976).
April 2 Serge Lifar born (–1986).
May Bill Brandt born (–1983).
May 24 Mikhail Sholokov born (–1984).
June 20 Lillian Hellman born (–1984).
June 21 Jean-Paul Sartre born (–1980).
July 1 John Hay dies (67).
Sept 5 Arthur Koestler born (–1983).
Sept 18 Greta Garbo born (–1990).
Oct 6 Helen Wills born (–).
Oct 15 C P Snow born (–1980).
Oct 22 Karl Jansky born (–1950).
Dec 9 Dag Hammarskjöld born (–1961).
Dec 21 Anthony Powell born (–).
Dec 24 Howard Hughes born (–1976).

w Everyday Life

Regular motor omnibus service in London; Bakerloo and Piccadilly underground lines are opened.
Neon signs are first displayed.

x Sport and Recreation

Eighteen players are killed during the American Football season; President Roosevelt threatens to ban the sport unless action is taken to curb the violence.
May Sutton of the USA becomes the first overseas player to win a title at the lawn tennis competition at Wimbledon, London.
The International Bowling Board, the governing body of lawn bowls, is founded (11 July).
In the first £1,000 transfer fee in English football, Alf Common moves from Sunderland to Middlesbrough.
The New Zealand Rugby Union 'All Blacks' make their first tour of the British Isles; their only loss is to Wales, 3–0 (Dec).

y Media

Film:
Raffles, the Amateur Cracksman.

Start of Pentecostalism in USA ... Hittite capital excavated ...
Invention of the jukebox ...

o Politics, Government, Law, and Economy

In USA, a presidential commission confirms the existence of insanitary conditions in Chicago's meat-packing trade (first exposed in Upton Sinclair's 1906 novel *The Jungle*); Congress later passes the Meat Inspection Act and the Pure Food and Drugs Act (establishing the Food and Drugs Administration).
In USA, the Antiquities Act permits the president to reserve federal lands for the protection of objects of scientific, prehistoric, or historic interest.
US National Forests Commission established.
Aga Khan III founds All India Muslim League.
Hepburn Act empowers the US Interstate Commerce Commission to regulate railroad services.
In Britain, the Trade Disputes Act reverses the Taff Vale judgement of 1901; peaceful picketing is allowed and unions are immune from claims for damage caused by strikes.
Marine Insurance Act codifies English common law on the subject; other legislation reforms conditions in the Merchant Navy.
Patents Act gives greater protection for inventors in Britain.
Establishment in New York of the first municipal reference bureau in the USA, to study local financial operations.
Crisis in French wine industry caused by declining prices.

p Society, Education, and Religion

Lunacy Commissioners in England and Wales report that on 1 Jan 121,979 persons are certified as insane.
International prohibition on night-shift working for women.
Confederazione Generale de Lavoro founded in Italy.
Term 'suffragette' coined to describe women campaigning for the vote.

E **May**

5 Turkey yields to British pressure over Egypt's frontier with Palestine. Fall of Count Witte in Russia, who is succeeded by the Conservative Ivan Goremykin.

6 Tsar Nicholas II promulgates the Fundamental Law of the Russian Empire, reaffirming autocratic rule.

8 the US Congress permits Alaska to elect a delegate to the Congress (first delegate arrives 3 Dec).

9 Chinese government decides to take over administration of Imperial Customs Service (of which Robert Hart has been inspector-general since 1863).

10 first Duma meets in Russia, resulting in deadlock through the Cadets' Party's criticism of Fundamental Laws (see 21 July).

11 Isvolsky becomes Russian foreign secretary.

19 João Franco becomes prime minister of Spain with dictatorial powers.

30 Giovanni Giolitti forms ministry in Italy (–Dec 1909).

F **June**

Peter Stolypin becomes prime minister of Russia.

5 third German naval bill provides for increases in construction of battleships.

G **July**

Universal suffrage bill introduced in Hungary. Revolt by Liberals in Cuba protesting against fraud by President Tomás Palma's government; Palma requests intervention by USA, which sends mediators.

4 Britain, France, and Italy guarantee the independence of Ethiopia.

12 in France, the guilty verdict against Alfred Dreyfus for treason (of Sept 1899) is annulled (22 July, Dreyfus is formally reinstated in the French Army and awarded the Legion of Honour).

21 on dissolution of Duma the Cadets adjourn to Finland and issue the Viborg Manifesto, calling on Russians to refuse paying taxes.

H **August**

British–Chinese convention on Tibet.

15 Edward VII's discussions with Kaiser Wilhelm II at Cronberg.

16 violent earthquake in Chile destroys parts of Santiago, Valparaiso and 40 to 50 smaller towns.

J **September**

18 typhoon hits Hong Kong, killing about 10,000 people.

20 in China, imperial edict orders end of use of opium within 10 years.

29 following the resignation of President Palma of Cuba, the USA declares a provisional government until order is restored.

K **October**

23 women suffragists demonstrate in outer lobby of House of Commons; 10 are charged the following day and sent to prison.

L **November**

22 Peter Stolypin introduces agrarian reforms in Russia.

M **December**

6 Britain grants self-government to Transvaal and Orange River Colonies.

13 through revolt of Centre Party, the German Reichstag opposes expenses on colonial wars; von Bülow dissolves the Reichstag and in subsequent elections the Socialists suffer losses.

Hampstead Garden Suburb, London, started; founded by Henrietta Barnett.

American Jewish Committee founded by senior members of the US Jewish community to promote Jewish concerns and interests.

Vilfredo Pareto, *Manual of Political Economy*.

School care committees established in Britain.

President Roosevelt decrees that presidential and other documents should be issued in reformed spelling (24 Aug).

The English Hymnal (edited by Percy Dearmer and Ralph Vaughan Williams).

The Azusa Street revival begins in Los Angeles, USA, under the leadership of William Seymour, the starting point for the world-wide spread of Pentecostalism.

Albert Schweitzer, *The Quest of the Historical Jesus*.

Q Science, Technology, and Discovery

Automatic railway coupling first used.

Simplon Tunnel (for electric railway) between Switzerland and Italy (begun in 1898) is opened (length, 19.8 km/12.3 mi).

Launch in Britain of the battleship HMS *Dreadnought*, with entirely large-calibre armament.

P Lowell in America publishes *Mars and its Canals*.

J J Thomson in England undertakes work on gamma rays.

W Nernst formulates the third law of thermodynamics.

Arthur Harden and W J Young discover cases of catalysis among enzymes.

The term 'allergy' coined by Austrian pediatrician Clemens von Parquet.

R Humanities

Excavations by German and Turkish scholars at Boghazköy (–1908) reveal that the city was ancient Hattusas, capital of the Hittites.

Ernst W Förstemann, *Commentary on the Maya Manuscript in the Royal Public Library at Dresden*.

Charles Oman, *The Great Revolt of 1381*.

P S Allen, *Erasmi Epistolae* (–1958).

Lord Acton, *Lectures on Modern History* (posthumous).

Winston Churchill, *Lord Randolph Churchill*.

Sidney and Beatrice Webb, *English Local Government* (9 volumes; — 1929).

E Cadbury, M C Matheson, and G Shann, *Women's Work and Wages*.

Giovanni Papini, *The Twilight of the Philosophies*.

S Art, Sculpture, Fine Arts, and Architecture

Exhibition of Ancient Iberian Art, Louvre, Paris, France.

Painting, etc:
Paul Cézanne, *The Gardener Vallier*.
André Derain, *Port of London*.
Henri Matisse, *The Young Sailor II*.
Paula Modersohn-Becker, *Old Poorhouse Woman with Glass Bottle and Poppy*.
Pablo Picasso, *Composition: les paysans, Two Nudes*.
Georges Rouault, *At the Mirror*.

Sculpture:
Aristide Maillol, *Chained Action*.
Medardo Rosso, *Ecce Puer* (–1907).

T Music

Granville Bantock, *Omar Khayyám* (–1909).
Charles Ives, *Central Park in the Dark*.
Charles Martin Loeffler, *A Pagan Poem*.
Arnold Schoenberg, Chamber Symphony No.1.
Ethel Smyth, *The Wreckers* (opera).
Invention of Gabel's 'Automatic Entertainer', i.e., the jukebox.
In France, debut of singer Maurice Chevalier.

U Literature and Drama

Endre Ady, *Új Versek* (New Poems).
John Galsworthy, *The Man of Property*, the first volume in The Forsyte Saga (–1922).
Robert Musil, *Young Törless*.
Upton Sinclair, *The Jungle*.
Mark Twain, *What is Man?*.
Paul Valéry, *Monsieur Teste*.
Foundation of 'Everyman's Library', cheap editions of important literary works published in Britain by Edward Dent.

Drama:
Paul Claudel, *Partage de Midi*.
Harley Granville-Barker, *Waste*.
Maxim Gorky, *Enemies*.
William Vaughan Moody, *The Great Divide*.
Arthur Wing Pinero, *His House in Order*.
Winchell Smith, *Brewster's Millions*.

V Births and Deaths

Jan 15 Aristotle Onassis born (–1975).
March 9 David Smith born (–1965).
March 13 Oscar Nemon born (–1985).
March 25 A J P Taylor born (–1990).
April 9 Hugh Gaitskell born (–1963).
April 13 Samuel Beckett born (–1989).
April 28 Kurt Gödel born (–1978).
May 23 Henrik Ibsen dies (78).
June 29 Albert Sorel dies (64).
July 8 Philip Johnson born (–).
Aug 7 Marcello Caetano born (–1980).
Aug 28 John Betjeman born (–1984).

Japan controls Korean government ... New Zealand becomes a
dominion ...

A January

10 in Austria, passing of bill extending suffrage to all males aged 24 or over (first election held on 14 May).

14 earthquake in Jamaica; Kingston is badly damaged and 700–800 people killed.

B February

19 war breaks out between Honduras, Nicaragua, and El Salvador (–Dec).

C March

Romanian army puts down Moldavian revolt with brutality.

5 Second Duma meets in Russia (–16 June).

29 in USA, serious train accident near Colton, California; 26 killed, about 100 injured (caused by derailment).

D April

8 British–French convention confirms independence of Siam (now Thailand).

21 in Ireland, political clubs merge to form the Sinn Féin League.

30 King Edward VII of Britain visits Rome and the Vatican.

E May

1 May Day labour demonstrations in many European capitals, including a general strike in Warsaw.

2 Edward VII visits President Fallières in Paris.

14 opening of Imperial Conference, London.

14 Sweden adopts proportional representation for elections to both chambers and universal adult suffrage for Second Chamber.

16 Pact of Cartagena between Britain, France, and Spain to counter German designs on Balearic and Canary Islands.

23 legislative council is created in Portuguese colony of Mozambique.

F June

10 Franco–Japanese agreement to preserve 'open door' in China.

14 female suffrage adopted in Norway (on same terms as for municipal elections).

Sept 25 Dmitry Shostakovich born (–1975).
Oct 22 Paul Cézanne dies (67).
Nov 2 Luchino Visconti born (–1976).
Nov 18 Alec Issigonis born (–1988).
Dec 19 Leonid Brezhnev born (–1982).
Dec 19 F W Maitland dies (56).
Dec 30 Paul Cézanne dies (67).

w Everyday Life

W K Kellogg Toasted Corn Flake Company launch their new breakfast cereal.

Coca-Cola Co. puts caffeine into its drink to replace cocaine.

Bodleian Library, Oxford, England, repurchases (for £3,000) a copy of the First Folio of Shakespeare which it had sold in 1664.

International Motor Car Exhibition held at Olympia, London.

x Sport and Recreation

South Africa's cricketers win a Test Match for the first time (4 Jan); they beat England 4–1 in the five-match series.

The Interim Olympic Games are held in Athens (22 April–2 May); France wins 18 gold medals; USA, 12; Greece and Britain, 8 each; Italy, 7; Switzerland, 5; Germany and Norway, 4 each.

The Intercollegiate Athletic Association redrafts the rules of American Football, allowing the forward pass for the first time.

The first motor-racing Grand Prix race is held at Le Mans (won by the Hungarian driver François Szisz, driving a Renault).

In England, the Northern Rugby Football Union reduces the size of each team from 15 to 13 (12 June).

Sport becomes part of the school curriculum in Britain.

y Media

In Britain, foundation of new Liberal national newspaper the *Tribune*.

Publication in Britain of the magazine *John Bull*.

Film:

In USA, the Biograph 14th Street film studio opens in Manhattan, New York.

Radio:

First known radio broadcast in USA (24 Dec), by R A Fessenden who broadcasts music, a poem, and a talk which are heard by ships' radio operators.

Famine in Russia ... First electric washing machine ... Record billiard break ...

o Politics, Government, Law, and Economy

In USA, Des Moines, the capital of Iowa, adopts the 'city commission' form of government pioneered in Galveston, Texas (in 1900), whereby commissioners run the municipal government.

The city government of New Haven, Connecticut, is the first city authority in the USA to establish a planning department (followed by Chicago in 1909).

Foundation of the Russell Sage Foundation, the oldest surviving research institute in the USA.

Financial panic in the USA; the government calls on the power of J P Morgan to revive the system (Morgan profits from the stock-market crash).

First British census of production.

Henry Deterding founds the Royal Dutch Shell oil company.

p Society, Education, and Religion

Famine in Russia kills several million people.

Bubonic plague in India kills 1.3 million people.

First women councillors elected in England in local elections (1 Nov).

In USA, controversy over magnitude of immigration from southern Europe and immigrants' effects on jobs and wage rates.

In USA, Edward H Bennett launches the Chicago Plan, aiming to 'beautify' the city, especially through the development of the lake front.

Alfred Adler, *The Inferiority of Organs*.

In Britain, Robert Baden-Powell founds the Boy Scouts.

In Britain, the Senate of Cambridge University approves abolition of designating the best mathematician in finals 'Senior Wrangler' and listing candidates in order of merit.

Start of medical inspection of school children in Britain.

Pope Pius X condemns Modernism in encyclical *Pascendi gregis*.

Charles Gore, *The New Theology and the Old Religion*.

15 (–18 Oct) reassembly of peace conference of great powers at the Hague, originally called at US President Roosevelt's suggestion in 1904, but postponed owing to the Russo–Japanese War in Far East; attempt at stopping the arms race fails, but progress is made in direction of voluntary arbitration of disputes, despite German opposition.

16 reactionary party in Russia forces Tsar Nicholas II to dissolve the Second Duma; an electoral edict increases representation of propertied classes and reduces representation of national minorities.

26 in Britain the House of Commons passes Prime Minister Campbell-Bannerman's resolution that the power of the Lords to prevent passage of bills must be restricted.

G **July**
Triple alliance between Germany, Austria, and Italy is renewed for six years, despite the reserved attitude of Italy.

1 revised constitution for Orange River Colony promulgated in Bloemfontein.

19 Emperor of Korea abdicates.

25 Korea agrees convention giving Japan control over its government (through presence of Japanese vice-ministers in major departments).

28 in USA, fire destroys numerous buildings at the New York seaside resort of Coney Island.

30 Russo–Japanese agreement over China.

30 elections for first assembly in Philippines.

H **August**
3 Kaiser Wilhelm II and Tsar Nicholas II meet at Swinemünde to discuss Baghdad Railway.

4 French fleet bombards Casablanca following anti-foreign outbreaks.

31 British–Russian Convention on Persia, Afghanistan, and Tibet is signed, removing obstacles towards an alignment of Russia with Britain and France against the Central Powers (Germany, Austria-Hungary, Italy).

J **September**
5 King Edward VII of Britain meets Alexander Izvolsky, Russian foreign minister, at Marienbad, Germany.

21 risings in German South-West Africa suppressed.

26 following a royal proclamation, the Colony of New Zealand is known as the Dominion of New Zealand.

K **October**
10 demonstrations and strikes are held in Budapest, Hungary, at opening of parliament, in demand of adult suffrage.

L **November**
14 the Third Duma meets in Russia (–1912), elected on a restricted franchise; leads to the suppression of revolutionary outbreaks.

16 in USA, Oklahoma is admitted to the union as the 46th state.

M **December**
For second time, leading Bolshevik Lenin leaves Russia (–1917).

6 frontier between Uganda and East Africa is defined.

7 first congress of Egyptian nationalist movement under Mustafa Kamil.

8 on Oskar II's death, Gustavus V succeeds as King of Sweden (–1950).

11 fire destroys the parliament buildings at Wellington, New Zealand.

16 a US fleet of 16 battleships departs on a round-the-world tour, to demonstrate the USA's military might (returns 22 Feb 1909).

Q Science, Technology, and Discovery

Leo Baekeland in the USA invents Bakelite (the first synthetic plastic).

Richard Anschütz and Max Schuler perfect the gyrocompass.

Auguste Lumière's improved process for colour reproduction through autochrome plates.

Emil Fischer, *Researches on the Chemistry of Proteins*.

C Pirquet devises a method for diagnosing tuberculosis.

C Ross Harrison develops tissue culture techniques.

Ivan Pavlov in Russia publishes *Conditioned Reflexes*.

R Humanities

Maurice Bloomfield, *Vedic Concordance*.

Frank Hrozny publishes the key to the translation of Hittite documents in the *Proceedings of the German Oriental Society*.

William A Dunning, *Reconstruction, Political and Economic, 1865–1877*.

Henry Adams, *The Education of Henry Adams: a study of XXth Century Multiplicity* (privately printed).

A C Benson and Viscount Esher (eds.), *Letters of Queen Victoria* (continued under editorship of G E Buckle; –1932).

Cambridge History of English Literature (–1927).

Henri Bergson, *Creative Evolution*.

William James, *Pragmatism: A New Name for Old Ways of Thinking*.

S Art, Sculpture, Fine Arts, and Architecture

Cézanne Retrospective at the Salon d'Automne, Paris, France.

Alfred Stieglitz expands gallery '291' in New York, and shows works by Henri Matisse, Francis Picabia, Constantin Brancusi, and Pablo Picasso, and African-American art.

National League of Handicrafts Societies leads to extension of the 'arts and crafts' movement in the USA.

Painting, etc:

André Derain, *Blackfriars Bridge, The Bathers*.

Augustus John, *W B Yeats*.

Henri Matisse, *Blue Nude; Luxe, Calme et Volupté, Memory of Biskra*.

Edvard Munch, *Amor and Psyche*.

William Orpen, *Hon. Percy Wyndham*.

Pablo Picasso, *Les Demoiselles d'Avignon*.

Henri Rousseau, *The Snake Charmer*.

Sculpture:

Constantin Brancusi, *The Kiss*.

Pablo Picasso, *Figure*.

Architecture:

Charles Rennie Mackintosh, Library Wing of Glasgow School of Art, Glasgow, Scotland (–1909).

T Music

In London, strike of music-hall artists and musicians.

Frederick Delius, *A Village Romeo and Juliet* (opera).

Paul Dukas, *Ariadne and Bluebeard* (opera).

Leo Fall, *The Dollar Princess* (operetta).

Gustav Mahler, Symphony No. 8 ('Symphony of a Thousand').

Jean Sibelius, Symphony No. 3.

Josef Suk, *Asrael*.

Follies of 1907, a spectacular music and dancing show (first performed at the Jardin de Paris, New York, 8 July), produced by Florenz Ziegfeld, the first of the 'Ziegfeld Follies' (–1931 under Ziegfeld's direction; –1956 under other directors).

Cecil Sharp, *English Folk Song*.

John Bratton, 'The Teddy Bears' Picnic'.

U Literature and Drama

Joseph Conrad, *Secret Agent*.

E M Forster, *The Longest Journey*.

Stefan George, *The Seventh Ring*.

Maxim Gorky, *Mother*.

Edmund Gosse, *Father and Son*.

Rainer Maria Rilke, *Neue Gedichte* (New Poems; –1908).

Frank Wedekind, *Such is Life*.

Drama:

August Strindberg, *The Ghost Sonata, The Dream Play*.

J M Synge, *Playboy of the Western World*.

V Births and Deaths

Jan 11 Pierre Mendès-France born (–1982).

Feb 21 W H Auden born (–1973).

May 12 Katharine Hepburn born (–).

May 12 J K Huysmans dies (59).

May 14 Muhammad Ayub Khan born (–1974).

May 22 Laurence Olivier born (–1989).

May 26 John Wayne born (–1979).

June 1 Frank Whittle born (–).

June 20 Lillian Hellman born (–1984).

Sept 4 Edvard Grieg dies (64).

Sept 12 Louis Macneice born (–1964).

Nov 28 Alberto Moravia born (–1990).

Dec 15 Oscar Niemeyer born (–).

Dec 15 Richard Crossman born (–1974).

Dec 16 Francis Thompson dies (47).

Dec 17 William Thomson (Lord Kelvin) dies (84).

W Everyday Life

The Hurley Machine Co. of Chicago markets

Labour government in Australia ... Austria annexes Bosnia and Herzegovina ...

A January

6 in Morocco, following popular unrest, the brother of Sultan Abdul Aziz, Mulai Hafid, rebels and is proclaimed Sultan at Fez.

27 Count Alois Aehrenthal, Austrian foreign minister, announces that the Austrian government will build a railway towards Salonika, to extend facilities for trade and Austro-Hungarian influence.

B February

1 King Carlos I of Portugal and the Crown Prince are murdered in Lisbon; Prince Manuel becomes king as Manuel II (–1910).

C March

4 in the USA, at Collinwood near Cleveland, Ohio, a fire in a primary school kills 180 children and 9 teachers.

D April

6 British prime minister Sir Henry Campbell-Bannerman resigns because of illness (22, dies).

8 King Edward VII, holidaying at Biarritz in SW France, appoints H H Asquith as British prime minister (12, new ministry announced, with David Lloyd George as chancellor of the exchequer).

E May

In Australia the government is defeated in a confidence vote; a Labour government takes office under Andrew Fisher.

F June

9 King Edward VII of Britain visits Russia and meets Tsar Nicholas II at Reval; the tsar agrees to introduce extensive reforms in Macedonia (still nominally under Turkish rule).

14 fourth German navy bill authorizes expenditure on four further capital ships.

23 Shah Mohammed Ali overthrows Persian constitution of Dec 1906.

23 USA severs diplomatic relations with Venezuela on Cipriano Castro's refusal to compensate US citizens for injuries.

G July

Pan Slav Conference in Prague.

the first electric washing machine in the USA.

Persil detergent is invented in Germany.

In Ireland, state jewels of the Order of St Patrick are stolen from Dublin Castle (6 July).

The largest diamond yet found, the Cullinan Diamond, is presented by the Transvaal to King Edward VII of Britain (9 Nov).

Launch in Britain of the luxury liners SS *Lusitania* and *Mauritania*.

Problems arise over the costume to be worn by Lady Godiva in a pageant in Coventry, England (Godiva allegedly rode naked through Coventry in the 11th century).

x Sport and Recreation

In billiards, Tom Reece of Oldham compiles a record break of 499,135 points using the cradle cannon (later outlawed) in 85 hours 49 minutes, spread over five weeks (3 June–6 July).

Northamptonshire are dismissed for 12 by Gloucestershire in the County Championship match at Gloucester (11 June); it remains the lowest total in first-class cricket.

The Association Football Players' Union (later the Professional Footballers' Association) is founded at a meeting in Manchester, England.

Arnaud Massy of France is the first overseas player to win the British Open Golf Championship.

The world's first specialized motor racing circuit is opened in Britain at Brooklands, on Lord Northcliffe's estate.

y Media

In USA, William Randolph Hearst founds International News Service press agency to supply news to his newspaper group.

Film:

20,000 Leagues Under the Sea (director, Georges Méliès).

Radio:

De Forest Radio Telephone Co. in the USA makes the first regular studio radio broadcasts.

The Ford Model T automobile ... Foundation of the Harvard Business School ... Invention of the paper cup ...

o Politics, Government, Law, and Economy

In USA, Staunton, Virginia, devises the 'municipal manager' system of government: the mayor and council hire a general manager to control the town administration; the manager has freedom to appoint subordinates (the model is adopted by other cities).

In USA, foundation (on 26 July) of the Bureau of Investigation (renamed, 1 July 1935, Federal Bureau of Investigation, or FBI).

Port of London Authority established.

In USA, President Theodore Roosevelt convenes a conference at the White House on nature conservation.

Frederick Meinecke, *Cosmopolitanism and the National State*.

Graham Wallas, *Human Nature in Politics*.

Woodrow Wilson, *Constitutional Government in the United States*.

International Convention on Copyright held in Berlin.

The American Bar Association adopts an ethics code.

Muller v. Oregon upholds a state's right to regulate maximum hours of work for women on health grounds; this case is the origin of the 'Brandeis brief' type of legal argument.

Henry Ford of the Ford Motor Company, USA, announces the production of the Model T car, which will sell for only $850.

In Detroit, USA, William C Durant of Buick Motor Company forms the General Motors Company as the basis for building a conglomerate of car-building companies (14 Sept).

p Society, Education, and Religion

Royal College of Surgeons in Britain decides to allow women to obtain the licence in dental surgery (15 Oct).

Mrs Garrett Anderson is elected mayor of Aldeburgh in E England, the first woman mayor in Britain (9 Nov).

First observation of Mother's Day, at Philadelphia, Pennsylvania, USA.

Regulation of hours of factory work for women and young persons in Germany (9 Dec).

Australia introduces pensions for the old and invalids.

In Britain, the Children Act abolishes the death

6 Young Turks under Niazi Bey stage revolt at Resina in Macedonia; the government troops sent to quell them desert.

24 the Sultan of Turkey, Abdul Hamid II, restores the constitution of 1876.

H August

20 Leopold II hands over Congo to Belgium (confirmed by act of Belgian parliament, 18 Oct).

23 Baltic Convention between Germany, Sweden, Denmark, and Russia, and North Sea Convention between Britain, Germany, Denmark, France, and the Netherlands to maintain the *status quo* on the shores of the two seas.

23 Mulai Hafid, the new Sultan of Morocco, defeats Sultan Abdul Aziz at Marrakesh.

J September

In Ireland, the Sinn Féin League becomes known as simply Sinn Féin.

1 opening of Hejaz railway, linking Damascus and Medina.

13 German Social Democrat rally at Nuremberg.

16 Buchlau conference between Count Aehrenthal and Alexander Izvolski, at which Austria undertakes not to oppose opening of the Dardanelles to Russian warships and Russia agrees to Austria's proposed annexation of Bosnia and Herzegovina.

25 Casablanca incident, when German deserters from the French Foreign Legion are taken by force from a German consular official.

K October

The Australian parliament agrees to the establishment of a new federal capital at Canberra near Sydney.

5 King Ferdinand I of Bulgaria declares Bulgaria's independence and assumes the title of tsar.

6 Austria annexes Bosnia and Herzegovina by decree.

7 Crete proclaims union with Greece.

12 South Africa constitutional convention meets at Durban, later removes to Capetown (–Feb 1909), agreeing on a Union of South Africa.

12 in London, international conference on electric units and standards with representatives of 18 countries.

12 in Paris, meeting of International Road Congress, with representatives of 29 countries.

27 The *Daily Telegraph* publishes remarks by Kaiser Wilhelm II of Germany in which he states the German people are hostile to Britain while he is a friend; strong feelings are aroused in Germany, both against Britain and against the Kaiser for making policy pronouncements without consulting the chancellor.

L November

3 in US presidential election William Howard Taft, Republican, with 231 electoral votes, defeats William Jennings Bryan, Democrat, with 162 votes; popular vote: Taft, 7,678,908; Bryan, 6,409,104.

9 Alexander Izvolski, Russian foreign minister, visits London.

10 (–11) in Germany, the Reichstag debates the *Daily Telegraph* interview, further embittering British–German relations.

14 Liberal victory in Cuban elections leads to José Gómez's presidency (–1913).

15 death of Guangxu, emperor of China (on 15, death of Cixi, the dowager empress).

M December

2 revolt in Bohemia.

4 abortive London naval conference of the powers to regulate conditions of warfare.

17 first meeting of Ottoman Parliament with large Young Turk majority.

28 earthquake in South Calabria and Sicily kills an estimated 200,000 people.

penalty and restricts imprisonment for those aged under 17.

Foundation of the Graduate School of Business Administration at Harvard University, USA.

Establishment of a national Roman Catholic hierarchy in the USA.

Protestant churches in the USA form the Federal Council of Churches of Christ in America, which supports social-welfare legislation.

Q Science, Technology, and Discovery

J E Brandenberger in France patents cellophane.

Ernest Rutherford and H Geiger invent the Geiger counter.

Hermann Minkowski elaborates four-dimensional geometry, the mathematics of relativity.

In Germany, Fritz Haber invents his process for synthesizing ammonia.

Heike Kamerlingh-Onnes in the Netherlands liquefies helium.

R Humanities

Joseph Déchelette, *Manuel d'archéologie préhistorique, celtique et gallo-romaine* (–1934; completed by Albert Grenier).

F W Maitland, *The Constitutional History of England*.

A L Lowell, *The Government of England*.

Earl of Cromer, *Modern Egypt*.

Henri Poincaré, *Science and Method*.

Josiah Royce, *The Philosophy of Loyalty*.

Georges Sorel, *Reflections on Violence*.

S Art, Sculpture, Fine Arts, and Architecture

Dinner held in honour of Le Douanier (Henri) Rousseau in Picasso's studio, Paris.

Painting, etc:

Pierre Bonnard, *Nude against the Light*.

Georges Braque, Landscape series at L'Estaques (e.g., *Trees at L'Estaque*), the first fully cubist landscapes.

Marc Chagall, *Nu Rouge*.

Wassily Kandinsky, *Blue Mountain*.

Henri Matisse, *Harmony in Red/La Desserte*.

Maurice Utrillo, white period (–1914).

Maurice Vlaminck, *The Red Trees*.

Sculpture:

Jacob Epstein, controversial figures for the building of the British Medical Associaton, London.

Henri Matisse, *The Back I*.

Architecture:

Peter Behrens, A E G Turbine Factory, Berlin (first building of steel and glass).

Frank Lloyd Wright, Robie House, Chicago, USA, the climax of the 'Prairie House'.

T Music

European conductors Arturo Toscanini and Gustav Mahler make their debuts at the New York Metropolitan Opera.

Béla Bartók, String Quartet No. 1.

Claude Debussy, *Golliwogg's Cake Walk*.

Edward Elgar, Symphony No. 1.

Charles Ives, *The Unanswered Question*.

Alexander Skryabin, *Poem of Ecstasy*.

Oscar Straus, *The Chocolate Soldier* (operetta).

Anton Webern, *Passacaglia*.

Double-sided records become the norm.

U Literature and Drama

Arnold Bennett, *The Old Wives' Tale*.

G K Chesterton, *The Man Who Was Thursday*.

Colette, *La Retraite Sentimentale*.

W H Davies, *Autobiography of a Super Tramp*.

E M Forster, *A Room With a View*.

John Fox, *The Trail of the Lonesome Pine*.

Anatole France, *L'île des pingouins/Penguin Island*.

Kenneth Grahame, *The Wind in the Willows*.

Herman Hesse, *Gertrud*.

Rabindranath Tagore, *Gora*.

In Britain Ford Madox Ford founds *The English Review*.

Drama:

J M Barrie, *What Every Woman Knows*.

V Births and Deaths

Jan 9 Simone de Beauvoir born (–1986).

Jan 25 'Ouida' (Louise de la Ramée) dies (67).

Apr ?? Henry Campbell-Bannerman dies (72).

May 22 W G Hoskins born (–1992).

May 28 Ian Fleming born (–1964).

June 24 Stephen Grover Cleveland dies (71).

July 2 Thurgood Marshall born (–1993).

July 6 Joel Chandler Harris ('Uncle Remus') dies (60).

July 8 Nelson Rockefeller born (–1979).

Aug 5 Harold Holt born (–1967).

Aug 27 Lyndon Baines Johnson born (–1973).

Aug 27 Donald Bradman born (–).

Oct 9 Jacques Tati born (–1982).

Nov 13 C Vann Woodward born (–).

Dec 10 Olivier Messiaen born (–1992).

Dec 11 Elliott Carter born (–).

Dec 17 W F Libby born (–1980).

W Everyday Life

In USA, introduction of the electric iron and the paper cup.

In Bristol in SE England, Arthur Hyne is covicted of bigamy; he had married and deserted five wives since 1905 and was

Sultan of Turkey deposed ... 'People's Budget' in Britain ...

A January
1 dismissal of Yuan Shikai from government posts places Chinese administration in Manchu hands.

B February
9 Germany recognizes France's special interests in Morocco in return for economic concessions.

13 Kiamil Pasha, grand vizier of Turkey, forced to resign by the Turkish nationalists.

21 Ferdinand I of Bulgaria visits Russia to obtain financial aid towards indemnity required by Turks for Bulgaria's independence.

26 Turkey recognizes Austria's annexation of Bosnia-Herzegovina and is paid compensation.

C March
2 the powers intervene to prevent a Serbo–Austrian war.

4 W H Taft inaugurated as president of USA (–1913); violent snowstorms and winds cause the transfer of the ceremony from outside the Capitol to the Senate chamber; trains carrying 30,000 guests are held up in the snow.

12 British alarm at growth of German navy leads to passage of naval bill.

25 press censorship imposed in Egypt to control Nationalists.

31 Serbia yields to Austria in Bosnian dispute.

D April
Strike of Paris postal workers (–May).

9 great powers recognize Austria-Hungary's annexation of Bosnia-Herzegovina.

9 army counter-revolution in Istanbul, Turkey, against rule of Mohammedan Union.

13 Turkey recognizes Bulgarian independence.

19 army of liberation captures Constantinople from rebels.

27 Young Turks depose Sultan Abdul Hamid who is succeeded by his brother as Mohammed V (–1918).

thought to be Witzhoff, wanted in the USA for similar offences.

Near Quebec city, Canada, the Plains of Abraham (scene of General Wolfe's victory over the French in 1759) are dedicated as a national monument (24 July).

Monosodium glutamate is identified in Japan as a taste enhancer.

Road race from New York to Paris via Vladivostok (won in 169 days).

Two further subway lines opened in New York.

x Sport and Recreation

Australia regains the Ashes, beating England 4–1 in the five-match home Test series.

W G Grace plays his last first-class cricket match, for the Gentlemen of England v. Surrey, at the age of 59 (20–22 April).

The 4th Olympic Games are held in London (27 April–31 Oct). Britain wins 56 gold medals; USA, 23; Sweden, 8; France, 5; Germany, Hungary, and Canada, 3 each.

In Britain, Signorinetta wins the Derby horse race at odds of 100–1.

First Australian Rugby League tour of the British Isles, including three Test Matches (12 Dec–15 Feb 1909).

Jack Johnson becomes the first African-American to win the World Heavyweight Boxing Championship, beating Tommy Burns in 14 rounds of their fight in Sydney, Australia (26 Dec).

Y Media

British Liberal paper the *Tribune* ceases publication (7 Feb).

In Britain, Lord Northcliffe (Alfred Harmsworth) acquires control of *The Times*.

J L Garvin is appointed editor of British Sunday paper the *Observer* (–1942).

Mary Baker Eddy founds the *Christian Science Monitor* in Boston, USA.

Film:

Pathé ends practice of selling films outright and rents them instead.

In USA, filming of *The Count of Monte Cristo* is completed near Los Angeles, California; in the next few years more film-makers are attracted to the low costs and reliable climate of California.

Romeo and Juliet (starring Florence Lawrence).

Tosca (starring Sara Bernhardt).

Radio:

Lee De Forest makes experimental broadcasts, including some from the Eiffel Tower, Paris, France.

Girl guides founded in Britain ... Establishment of youth hostels in Germany ...

o Politics, Government, Law, and Economy

J A Hobson, *The Crisis of Liberalism*.

V I Lenin, *Materialism and Empiric Criticism*.

Mahatma Gandhi launches the Hind Swaraj or Indian Home Rule movement.

Foundation of security agencies MI5 and MI6 in Britain.

First Town Planning Act passed in Britain.

In Britain, the Osborne Judgement: the House of Lords rules on the Osborne case (21 Dec), making compulsory union political levies illegal (resulting from an action by Walter Osborne to restrain his union from making a political donation to the Labour Party; principle reversed by legislation in 1913).

In USA, a comprehensive federal Copyright Act replaces previous legislation.

Payne-Aldrich tariff act passed in the USA.

Anglo-Persian Oil Company formed, which takes over William Knox D'Arcy's oil concession in Persia.

p Society, Education, and Religion

Women are admitted to German universities.

Girl Guides founded in Britain.

Conference in New York (30 May–June 1) leads to formation of the National Association for the Advancement of Colored People (NAACP).

Foundation of the Japanese Association of America.

First kibbutz founded in Palestine, at Degania Aleph.

Trade Boards Act provides for the regulation of wages in the 'sweated trades' of British industry.

USA bans the import of opium (except for medical use).

Compulsory military service in Australia.

William Beveridge, *Unemployment*.

H Croly, *The Promise of American Life*.

William James, *A Pluralistic Universe*.

C F G Masterman, *The Condition of England*.

The Pittsburgh Survey, of Pittsburgh, Pennsylvania, USA (6 volumes; –1914)

29 British chancellor Lloyd George introduces his 'People's Budget'; to raise money for defence and social expenditure it proposes taxes on land values, profits on land sales, and a 'super-tax' on high incomes.

E May

The Greek army forms a Military League, to influence policy of government.

25 Indian Councils Act gives greater powers to legislative councils, most of whose members are to be directly elected, and ensures appointment of an Indian to the viceroy's executive council.

F June

17 meeting of Tsar Nicholas II of Russia and the German Kaiser, Wilhelm II.

G July

14 Bernhard von Bülow resigns as German chancellor; succeeded by Theobald von Bethmann Hollweg.

16 Mohammed Ali, Shah of Persia, deposed in favour of Sultan Ahmad Shah, aged 12.

24 on Georges Clemenceau's resignation, Aristide Briand forms ministry in France.

26 general strike in Barcelona with rioting throughout Catalonia (–26 Sept).

30 earthquakes in Mexico; damage includes destruction of Acapulco.

H August

General strike in Sweden.

K October

13 Francisco Ferrer Guardia, leader of militant anti-clericals in Spain, executed.

21 Liberal ministry in Spain.

24 Russia and Italy sign Racconigi agreement for preserving *status quo* in Balkans.

25 murder (in Harbin, Manchuria) of Prince Ito of Japan, the resident in Korea, by a Korean fanatic; Japan imposes a dictatorship in Korea.

L November

British–German conversations on control of Baghdad Railway (–Dec).

5 after six months of debate, the British House of Commons gives a final reading to Chancellor Lloyd George's 'People's Budget', which then goes to the House of Lords.

13 in USA, explosion and fire in coal mine at Cherry, Illinois, kill about 250 miners.

30 the British House of Lords rejects the 'People's Budget' by 350 votes to 75, thereby creating a major constitutional crisis in Britain.

M December

Civil War in Honduras (–1911).

2 British prime minister Asquith denounces House of Lords for breach of constitution over finance bill and obtains dissolution of parliament.

2 Giovanni Giolitti is overthrown in Italy and Baron Sonnino forms a government.

17 on Leopold II's death, Albert I succeeds as King of the Belgians (–1934).

19 Juan Gómez seizes power in Venezuela.

provides the most thorough survey of the social conditions of any industrial city.

Sigmund Freud lectures in USA on psychoanalysis.

Pope Pius X beatifies Joan of Arc (18 April).

Q Science, Technology, and Discovery

Louis Blériot crosses the English Channel by monoplane.

R E Peary reaches North Pole (6 April).

Karl Hofmann in Germany produces synthetic rubber from butadiene.

Paul Ehrlich in Germany prepares salvarsan as cure for syphilis.

W Johannsen in the Netherlands introduces the term 'gene'.

T H Morgan in the USA begins research in genetics.

DNA and RNA discovered by P T Levene.

R Humanities

Arthur Evans, *Scripta Minoa*, Vol. 1.

Opening of the Victoria and Albert Museum, South Kensington, London.

Henri Bergson, *Time and Freewill*, *Matter and Memory*.

Benedetto Croce, *Logic as the Science of Pure Concept*.

William James, *The Meaning of Truth*.

S Art, Sculpture, Fine Arts, and Architecture

The American Federation of Arts founded, a nonprofit visual arts museum, program, and service which organizes travelling exhibitions.

Filippo Tommaso Marinetti, Italian poet and publicist, 'First Futurist Manifesto', published in *Le Figaro*, Paris, France.

Painting, etc:

Lawrence Alma-Tadema, *A Favourite Custom*.

Giacomo Balla, *Street Lamp* (study of light).

Georges Braque, *Violin and Palette*.

Wassily Kandinsky, *Mountain*.

Emil Nolde, *The Last Supper*.

Pablo Picasso, Landscape series at Horta de Ebro, the first fully defined statements of Analytic Cubism.

Henri Rousseau, *Flowers in a Vase*.

Architecture:

Edward Lutyens, St Jude's Church, Hampstead, London (–1911).

Frank Lloyd Wright, Robie House, Chicago, USA.

T Music

Isaac Albeniz, *Iberia* (piano suite).

Gustav Mahler, Symphony No. 9, *Das Lied von der Erde*.

Lionel Monckton and Howard Talbot, *The Arcadians* (operetta).

Nikolai Rimsky-Korsakov, *The Golden Cockerel* (posthumous opera).

Arnold Schoenberg, *Erwartung*, Five Pieces for Orchestra.

Jean Sibelius, *Voces intimae* (string quartet).

Richard Strauss, *Elektra* (opera).

Ralph Vaughan Williams, *Fantasia on a Theme of Thomas Tallis*.

Russian impresario Sergei Diaghilev presents a season of Russian opera and ballet in Paris; from this the Ballets Russes develop.

Bennett Scott, 'Ship Ahoy!' (All the nice girls love a sailor), words by A J Mills.

U Literature and Drama

Guillaume Apollinaire, *L'Enchanteur pourrissant*.

André Gide, *La Porte Étroite/Straight is the Gate*.

Gertrude Stein, *Three Lives*.

Rabindranath Tagore, *Gitanjali*.

Robert Walser, *Jakob von Gunten*.

H G Wells, *Tono-Bungay*.

Drama:

John Galsworthy, *Strife*.

D H Lawrence, *A Collier's Friday Night* (first performed in 1965 at the Royal Court Theatre, London).

Maurice Maeterlinck, *The Blue Bird*.

J M Synge, *Deirdre of the Sorrows*.

V Births and Deaths

Jan 1 Barry Goldwater born (–).

Jan 14 Joseph Losey born (–1984).

Feb 9 Dean Rusk born (–1994).

March 24 J M Synge dies (37).

March 30 E H Gombrich born (–).

April 10 Algernon Swinburne dies (72).

May 18 George Meredith dies (81).

May 30 Benny Goodman born (–1986).

June 6 Isaiah Berlin born (–).

Sept 21 Kwame Nkrumah born (–1972).

Oct 9 Donald Coggan born (–).

Oct 28 Francis Bacon born (–1992).

W Everyday Life

Death in Farnane, County Limerick, Ireland, of Mrs Johanna Leonard, aged 118 (reported 7 Jan).

US businessman H G Selfridge opens the first department store in Britain (Selfridge's in London).

X Sport and Recreation

The Imperial Cricket Conference, comprising England, Australia, and South Africa, is founded at a meeting at Lord's, London (15 July).

*Japan annexes Korea ... Revolution in Portugal ... Royal
Canadian Navy is formed.*

A **January**

In Greece, the Military League forces parliament and the king to summon a National Assembly to undertake revision of the 1864 constitution (the Cretan Venizelos acts for the League in negotiations with political leaders).

15 in Britain, general election held on Chancellor Lloyd George's budget, the power of the Lords, and Irish Home Rule, resulting in reduced Liberal majority (Liberals, 275 seats; Labour, 40; Irish Nationalists, 82; Unionists, 273).

15 reorganization of French Congo as French Equatorial Africa.

B **February**

20 Boutros-Ghali, the first native prime minister of Egypt and a Christian Copt, is shot by nationalist student (21, dies).

21 Edward Carson, member of the British Parliament, becomes leader of the Ulster Unionists.

C **March**

Luigi Luzzatti succeeds Baron Sonnino as Italian prime minister.

19 in USA, 'Insurgent' Republicans in the House of Representatives reduce the Speaker's customary power to appoint members of committees and control business by rejecting a nominee to the 'Rules Committee'.

31 in Greece, the Military League proclaims its dissolution.

D **April**

Albanian revolt is suppressed by Turkish army.

27 Louis Botha and James Hertzog found South African Party.

27 in Britain, the finance bill implementing the 'People's Budget' of 1909 is passed again by the House of Commons (28, by the Lords, after three hours of debate; 29, receives royal assent).

E **May**

6 death of King Edward VII at Buckingham Palace, London, after brief illness; succeeded by George V (–1936).

10 British House of Commons resolves that the House of Lords should have no power to veto money bills, only limited powers to postpone other bills, and that the maximum lifetime of Parliament should be reduced from seven to five years.

11 at Whitehaven, NW England, an explosion cuts off 132 men working in a mine under the sea (the decision to erect a brick wall to cut off the fire is controversial, even though no one is likely to have survived).

14 British–Belgian agreement assigns west shore of Lake Albert to Belgian Congo.

24 L Starr Jameson founds Unionist party in South Africa on imperialist platform.

26 Pope Pius X issues encyclical *Editio saepe*, which angers German Protestants because of its derogatory comments about Luther and the Reformation.

27 Prussian diet rejects reform of suffrage.

F **June**

11 Pope Pius X, on representations by Prussia, expresses regret about anti-Lutheran comments in his recent encyclical and orders German bishops to stop circulation in Germany.

In the first competitive Rugby Union match played at the Twickenham ground in London, Harlequins beat Richmond 14–10 (2 Oct).

The Jugendherbergen, a national network of hostels providing overnight accommodation for students, is established in Germany.

Y Media

The British newspaper the *People* settles a libel action brought by the British chancellor, David Lloyd George; an article alleged that the chancellor had commited adultery and had paid £20,000 to keep the case out of court.

In Britain, publication of the *Daily Sketch* (a halfpenny tabloid).

Film:

In Britain, Cinematograph Licensing Act for controlling cinemas exhibiting films.

In USA, D W Griffith transforms child actress Gladys Smith into Mary Pickford.

Friends (starring Lionel Barrymore).

Norman Angell's Great Illusion ... *Publication of* The Fundamentals ... *Return of Halley's comet ...*

O Politics, Government, Law, and Economy

In USA, revolt against 'Czar' Joe Cannon strips the speakership of the House of Representatives of much of its power.

US steel magnate Andrew Carnegie founds the Carnegie Endowment for International Peace, to conduct research into international law, economics, and history in order to advance international understanding.

Germany's machine-tool industry overtakes Britain's.

In Germany, electrification of part of Magdeburg–Halle mainline railway.

Swiss railways are nationalized.

The Ford Motor Company of the USA establishes its first factory in Britain.

A Development Commission is established to advise the British Treasury on loans for rural development and agriculture.

Norman Angell, *The Great Illusion: A Study of the Relation of Military Power in Nations to their Economic and Social Advantage.*

P Society, Education, and Religion

Launch (on 1 May) of the National Association for the Advancement of Colored People (NAACP), an organization of African-American radicals and liberals; it publishes *Crisis*, edited by W E B Du Bois.

In South Africa, end of use of Chinese labour in Rand mines.

First Labour Exchanges for the unemployed opened in Britain (1 Feb).

In USA, foundation of Boy Scouts of America and Camp Fire Girls.

In USA, first celebration (on 19 June) of Father's Day, founded by Mrs Dodd at Spokane, Washington.

Publication of the *Times Educational Supplement.*

Roman Catholic Priests obliged to take an oath against Modernism.

In London, consecration of the Roman Catholic Cathedral at Westminster.

First of the twelve volumes of *The Fundamentals* published, with contributions from many conservative Evangelical scholars in Europe and the USA.

Albert Schweitzer, *The Quest of the Historical Jesus.*

E Underhill, *Mysticism.*

Q Science, Technology, and Discovery

Charles Parsons' speed-reducing gear extends use of geared turbines.

First roller bearings produced by the Swedish Ball Bearing Factory.

G Claude invents the flourescent tube.

In USA, 2.54-m/100-inch reflecting telescope at Mount Wilson, California, completed.

Marie Curie and A Debierne in France isolate radium.

Marie Curie, *Treatise on Radiography*, published in France.

R A Millikan in the USA determines, in his oil-drop experiment, the charge on an electron.

J Herrick in the USA discovers sickle-cell anaemia.

R Humanities

Albrecht Penck and Eduard Brückner produce the system of four Pleistocene glaciations, named after Swiss sites (Günz, Mindel, Riss, Wurm).

Swedish archaeologist Gerhard de Geer pub-

G **July**

1 Union of South Africa becomes a dominion.

4 Russo–Japanese agreement on Manchuria and Korea.

H **August**

Austro-Hungarian commercial treaty with Serbia.

21 first meeting of the Greek National Assembly (official opening by king on 14 Sept).

22 Japan formally annexes Korea.

28 Montenegro is proclaimed an independent kingdom under Nicholas I.

31 former US president Theodore Roosevelt, on a speaking tour, propounds his concept of 'The New Nationalism', advocating tariff revision and greater federal control of working conditions.

J **September**

7 International Court of arbitration at The Hague settles dispute between Britain and USA over Newfoundland fisheries (referred to the court in Oct 1906).

15 South African party wins first South African elections and Louis Botha becomes prime minister.

K **October**

4 King Manuel II of Portugal flees to England on outbreak of revolution in Lisbon and, 5, Portugal is proclaimed a republic under Theophilo Braga.

10 Aristide Briand calls out troops in French railway strike, a general strike is averted and, 18, the railway workers resume work.

18 Eleutherios Venizelos becomes prime minister of Greece and begins financial reforms (25, National Assembly is dissolved).

L **November**

4 (–5) Tsar Nicholas II with his new foreign minister, Sergei Sazonov, agrees with German Kaiser Wilhelm II at Potsdam to cease opposition to the Baghdad Railway on condition that Russia is given a free hand in North Persia; (Britain is dismayed by Russia's negotiations with Germany on the railway question without consultation).

10 in Britain, break-up of constitutional conference.

28 British Prime Minister Asquith again appeals to the electorate.

M **December**

In British general election Liberals win 272 seats; Labour, 42; Irish Nationalists, 84; Unionists, 272 (making a majority for a Parliament Bill and Home Rule 126, an increase of 4 since Jan).

11 in the elections for the National Assembly in Greece the supporters of Venizelos win 300 seats out of 364.

lishes his notable paper, 'A Geochronology of the last 12,000 years'.

Charles P Bowditch, *The Numeration, Calendar Systems and Astronomical Knowledge of the Mayas.*

W F Monypenny and G E Buckle, *Disraeli* (–1920).

John Dewey, *How We Think.*

B Russell and A N Whitehead, *Principia Mathematica.*

s Art, Sculpture, Fine Arts, and Architecture

Manet and the Post-Impressionists, exhibition of recent French painting at the Grafton Galleries, London, organized by Roger Fry.

Hermetic phase of Cubism begins (–1911).

Exhibition of Islamic Art, Munich, Germany.

Painting, etc:

Umberto Boccioni, *Riot in the Galleria.*

Georges Braque, *Violin and Pitcher.*

Robert Delaunay, *The Eiffel Tower* (–1911).

Erich Heckel, *Franzi with Doll.*

Wassily Kandinsky, first abstract painting (gouache).

Ernst Kirchner, *Nude Behind a Curtain, Franzi* (–1926).

Fernand Léger, *Nues dans le fôret.*

Kasimir Malevich, *The Woodcutter.*

Henri Matisse, *La Danse II.*

Pablo Picasso, Portraits of *Ambrose Vollard, Kahnweiler,* and *Ude.*

Henri Rousseau, *The Dream.*

Sculpture:

Henri Matisse, *Jeanette III.*

Architecture:

Max Berg, Jahrhunderthalle, Breslau (now Wroclaw, Poland), using reinforced concrete (–1913).

T Music

Alban Berg, String Quartet.

Samuel Coleridge-Taylor, *Petite Suite de Concert.*

Gabriel Fauré, *Le Chanson d'Eve* (song cycle).

Victor Herbert, *Naughty Marietta* (operetta).

Engelbert Humperdinck, *Königskinder* (opera).

Giacomo Puccini, *The Girl of the Golden West* (opera).

Alexander Skryabin, *Prometheus* (symphonic poem).

Igor Stravinsky, *The Firebird* (ballet).

Ralph Vaughan Williams, Symphony No. 1 ('A Sea Symphony').

Thomas Beecham's first opera season at Covent Garden, London.

Pianist Solomon makes London debut at age of eight.

British singer and actress Gracie Fields makes her first professional appearance at the New Hippodrome Theatre, Rochdale, NW England.

Opening in London of the Palladium Theatre (popularly known as the London Palladium).

US band conductor and composer John Philip Sousa and his band make a world tour (–1911).

u Literature and Drama

Arnold Bennett, *Clayhanger*, the first volume of the Clayhanger trilogy (–1916).

Paul Claudel, *Cinq grandes odes.*

E M Forster, *Howard's End.*

Henry Newbolt, *Songs of the Fleet.*

Charles Péguy, *Le Mystère de la charité de Jeanne d'Arc.*

Edward Robinson, *The Town Down the River,* including 'Miniver Cheevy'.

H G Wells, *The History of Mr Polly.*

Drama:

John Galsworthy, *Justice.*

Harley Granville-Barker, *The Madras House.*

J M Synge, *Deirdre of the Sorrows.*

Gerald du Maurier manages Wyndham's Theatre, London (–1925).

v Births and Deaths

Feb 9 J L Monod born (–1976).

March 9 Samuel Barber born (–1981).

March 23 Akira Kurosawa born (–).

April 21 Mark Twain dies (74).

May 12 Dorothy Hodgkin born (–1994).

June 23 Jean Anouilh born (–1987).

Aug 13 Florence Nightingale dies (90).

Aug 27 William James dies (68).

Aug 27 Mother Teresa born (–).

Oct 29 A J Ayer born (–1989).

Nov 10 Leo Tolstoy dies (82).

w Everyday Life

Return of Halley's comet – the Earth passes through the comet's tail on 19 May; in the USA comet parties are held and there is a brisk sale for 'Comet Pills', allegedly an antidote to the poisonous gases thought to be in the comet's tail.

In Britain, season tickets are first issued on railways; second class accommodation is withdrawn.

Manhattan Bridge, New York, opened.

Tango dance craze.

Bert Williams is the first African-American entertainer to receive equal billing with whites on Broadway when he joins Ziegfeld Follies.

Parliament Act in Britain ... Russian prime minister assassinated ...

A January

7 Carnegie Trust Co., New York, closed by state supervisor of banks.

17 attempted assassination of Aristide Briand in French Chamber of Deputies.

20 Ecuador refuses to submit its dispute with Peru to Hague Tribunal.

21 in USA, foundation of the National Progressive Republican League led by Robert La Follette.

25 in Mexican civil war, US cavalry sent to preserve neutrality of Rio Grande and guard US territory against Mexican insurgents.

B February

6 British Labour Party elects Ramsay MacDonald chairman.

10 Persia appoints W Morgan Shuster to reorganize finances.

21 US–Japanese commercial treaty signed at Washington.

22 Canadian Parliament resolves to preserve union within British Empire, with control of own fiscal policy.

23 French Chamber of Deputies votes for building two battleships.

24 in Germany the Reichstag passes army bill.

27 in France, resignation of Aristide Briand's ministry.

28 Australian Prime Minister Andrew Fisher plans to nationalize monopolies.

C March

18 Italian Prime Minister Luzzatti resigns.

25 fire at Triangle Shirtwaist Company in New York kills 146; one escape door was locked, to prevent workers from sneaking off.

D April

3 progress of Parliament Bill through British House of Commons is accelerated by use of 'Kangaroo' clause.

3 British–Japanese commercial treaty.

4 US Congress meets in extraordinary sessions to deal with Reciprocity agreement with Canada (ratified by Senate 22 July).

11 French socialist leader Jean Jaurès announces scheme for socialist organization of France.

13 US House of Representatives votes in favour of direct election of senators.

24 British House of Commons rejects amendment to Parliament Bill providing for referendum.

E May

4 British chancellor Lloyd George introduces National Health Insurance bill.

8 Lord Lansdowne introduces Conservative bill for reconstruction of House of Lords in House of Lords.

15 British House of Commons passes the Parliament Bill.

15 US Supreme Court orders dissolution of Standard Oil Co.

23 Russia warns Turkey to withdraw troops from Montenegro frontier.

23 British Prime Minister Asquith opens Imperial Conference, London.

25 Porfirio Diaz resigns presidency of Mexico following rural unrest.

26 German Reichstag grants the former French territory of Alsace-Lorraine its own legislature and large measure of autonomy.

x Sport and Recreation

US African-American boxer Jack Johnson retains the World Heavyweight title, beating the former white champion Jim Jeffries in 15 rounds in Reno, Nevada (4 July).

The first Rugby Union Five Nations Championship is held, following the admission of France (to join England, Wales, Scotland, and Ireland).

Tony Wilding of New Zealand wins his fourth successive Men's Singles title in the Wimbledon tennis tournament, London.

Roller skating becomes a popular pastime in the USA and Britain.

y Media

Film:

Bronco Billy's Redemption.

In Neighbouring Kingdoms (starring John Bunny).

The Ranch Life in the Great Southwest (starring Tom Mix).

Radio:

Radio kits go on sale in the USA.

Lee De Forest broadcasts a programme from the Metropolitan Opera House, New York, including the singer Enrico Caruso.

Amundsen reaches South Pole ... Cubist works of art exhibited ...
'Alexander's Ragtime Band' ...

o Politics, Government, Law, and Economy

In USA, foundation of the Cooperative League, a progressive research institute interested in public policy (renamed the Twentieth Century Fund in 1919).

Official Secrets Act passed in Britain; it becomes a criminal offence for government officials to disclose certain categories of information.

Copyright Act in Britain provides for copyright in a work to last for 50 years after the author's death; books no longer have to be registered at Stationers' Hall.

R Michels, *Political Parties*.

In USA, John D Rockefeller's Standard Oil of New Jersey is broken up into 34 firms by anti-trust action.

Amalgamation of London General Omnibus Co., Metropolitan and District Railway Co., and Underground Electric Railways of London (1 Nov).

Buenos Aires to Valparaiso Railway completed.

I Fisher, *The Purchasing Power of Money*.

J Schumpeter, *Theory of Economic Development*.

F W Taylor, *The Principles of Scientific Management*.

p Society, Education, and Religion

In USA, foundation in New York of the National League on Urban Conditions Among Negroes, to help African-Americans from the South find industrial jobs.

Dillingham Immigration bill makes literacy a condition of entrance to the US (later modified to meet Japanese representations).

In USA, California enfranchises women.

Booker T Washington, *My Larger Life*.

T A Welton, *England's Recent Progress*.

On Long Island, USA, completion of Forest Hills Garden, designed by Frederick Law Olmsted, Jr, an settlement influenced by the 'garden city' movement.

In Britain, first nursery school opened by Rachel and Margaret McMillan in Deptford, London.

Phelps-Stokes Fund for education established in USA.

Separation of Church and State in Portugal.

World Missionary Conference, Edinburgh.

Women representatives attend the Conference of the Wesleyan Methodist Church in England for the first time.

Great meeting is held in the Albert Hall, London, to celebrate the tercentenary of the Authorised Version of the Bible (29 March); speakers include the prime minister and the archbishop of Canterbury; President Taft of the USA sends a message.

q Science, Technology, and Discovery

Aeronautical map of France published.

Norwegian explorer Roald Amundsen reaches the South Pole (15 Dec).

In USA, development of the first effective starter-motor for cars by C F Kettering.

H Kamerlingh-Onnes in the Netherlands discovers superconductivity.

V Hess in Austria discovers cosmic radiation.

Albert Einstein in Germany calculates the deflection of light caused by the sun's gravitational field.

F **June**
8 Birkbeck Bank, London, crashes.
11 revised Greek constitution.
13 reversal for Christian socialists in Austrian election.
22 coronation of King George V in Westminster Abbey, London.
28 Joseph Caillaux forms ministry in France.
28 Japan signs commercial treaty with France.

G **July**
1 arrival of German gunboat *Panther* in Agadir, Morocco, allegedly to protect German interests threatened by French involvement in Morocco; an international crisis ensues.
6 British–US treaty providing for arbitration of disputes.
10 Russia notifies Germany of its support for France in Moroccan crisis.
13 renewal of British–Japanese alliance for four years.
24 while British House of Commons debates the Lords' amendments to the Parliament Bill, Prime Minister Asquith is shouted down by Opposition members and the Speaker adjourns the House.
26 US President Taft signs Reciprocity bill with Canada.

H **August**
1 London dockers strike and, 7, refuse to return until other transport workers' claims are satisfied.
10 the British House of Lords passes the Parliament Bill, deciding (by 131–114 votes) not to insist on their amendments; the House of Lords' power to veto bills is converted into the power to suspend money bills for one month and other bills for a maximum period of two years; the maximum length of a parliament is reduced from seven to five years (except in an emergency situation).
10 British House of Commons votes to pay Members £400 per year.
10 (–28) military patrol streets of Liverpool in NW England; the city is paralysed by a transport strike.
14 South Wales miners end strike after 10 months.
15 British railway workers, led by J H Thomas, hold first national railway strike (–19).
20 Portugal adopts a Liberal constitution.
21 Kaiser Wilhelm II speaks at Hamburg on Germany's 'place in the sun' which its navy will secure.
31 Franco–Russian military conversations.

J **September**
11 in USA, attempt to repeal Maine prohibition laws defeated.
14 assassination of Peter Stolypin, Russian prime minister (19, Vladimir Kokovtsoff appointed prime minister).
21 in Canadian general election the Liberals, standing for Reciprocity with the USA, are defeated (the Reciprocity Agreement is later annulled).
29 Italy declares war on Turkey and Italian fleet bombards Tripoli coast.
29 first election in Sweden under Proportional Representation.

K **October**
9 launch of the super-Dreadnought battleship HMS *King George V* at Portsmouth, S England.
10 Robert K Borden forms Conservative ministry in Canada.
11 revolution breaks out in Central China.
17 Turkey promises Bulgaria to withdraw its troops and demobilize.
23 British cabinet changes, with Winston Churchill at Admiralty and Reginald McKenna home secretary.
26 Chinese Republic proclaimed.

L **November**
4 convention ending the 'Agadir Crisis' by which Germany allows France a free hand in Morocco in return for territory in the Congo.
5 Italy annexes Tripoli and Cyrenaica.
6 Francisco Madero becomes president of Mexico.
8 A J Balfour resigns leadership of British Conservative and Unionist Party (13, succeeded by Andrew Bonar Law).
16 Yuan Shikai forms cabinet in China.
16 Russia sends troops to Kazvin, Persia (on receiving no reply to ultimatum of Nov 11 to Persia); 23, Persia concedes demands.
21 Suffragette riots in Whitehall, London.
25 Chinese revolutionaries bomb Nanjing.
26 Italy's decisive victory in Tripoli.

M **December**
7 Chinese edict abolishing pigtails and ordering reform of calendar.
11 settlement of British railway workers' dispute.
12 George V holds Delhi Durbar.
30 Sun Yat-sen elected president of United Provinces of China by a revolutionary assembly in Nanjing.

Ernest Rutherford proposes the concept of the nuclear atom.

P Bleuler in Switzerland introduces term 'schizophrenia'.

R Humanities

Grafton Elliot Smith, *The Ancient Egyptians*.

British Museum's expedition to excavate Carchemish (–1920), which yields material from the Neolithic to the Roman period.

Cambridge Medieval History (–1936).

H W and F G Fowler, *Concise Oxford Dictionary of Current English*.

Hans Vaihinger, *The Philosophy of 'As If'*.

Opening of the New York Public Library in Fifth Avenue (23 May).

S Art, Sculpture, Fine Arts, and Architecture

At the Salon des Indépendents, Paris, cubism becomes a public phenomenon but Picasso and Braque do not exhibit.

Wassily Kandinsky and Franz Marc found *Blaue Reiter* (Blue Rider) group of artists in Munich.

Painting, etc:

Umberto Boccioni, *The City Rises, State of Mind I – The Farewells; Those Who Go; Those Who Stay*.

Georges Braque, *The Portuguese* — first use of stencilled letters.

Carlo Carrà, *Funeral of the Anarchist Galli*.

Marc Chagall, *Hommage to Apollinaire* (–1913).

Natalia Goncharova, *The Washerwoman* (–1912).

Juan Gris, *Man in a Café*.

Wassily Kandinsky, *Improvisation 21a*.

Henri Matisse, *The Red Studio*.

Pablo Picasso, *The Accordionist*.

Luigi Russolo, *Music*.

Sculpture:

Jacob Epstein, Tomb of Oscar Wilde, Paris, France.

Amedeo Modigliani, *Head* (–1913).

Architecture:

Walter Gropius and Adolph Meyer, Fagus Factory, Alfeld, Germany.

T Music

Edward Elgar, Symphony No. 2.

Enrique Granados, *Goyescas* (piano suite).

Maurice Ravel, *L'Heure espagnole* (opera).

Arnold Schoenberg, *Gurrelieder*.

Jean Sibelius, Symphony No. 4.

Richard Strauss, *Der Rosenkavalier* (opera).

Igor Stravinsky, *Petrushka* (ballet).

Ermanno Wolf-Ferrari, *Susanna's Secret* (opera).

'Alexander's Ragtime Band', by Irving Berlin.

'I'm Henry the Eighth I am', by R P Weston.

U Literature and Drama

Max Beerbohm, *Zuleika Dobson*.

Rupert Brooke, *Poems*.

G K Chesterton, *The Innocence of Father Brown*.

Ivy Compton-Burnett, *Dolores*.

Joseph Conrad, *Under Western Eyes*.

Norman Douglas, *Siren Land*.

Theodore Dreiser, *Jennie Gerhardt*.

Hugo von Hofmannsthal, *Jedermann*.

D H Lawrence, *The White Peacock*.

Katherine Mansfield (pseudonym), *In a German Pension*.

John Masefield, *The Everlasting Mercy*.

Ezra Pound, *Canzoni*.

Saki, *The Chronicles of Clovis*.

Rainer Maria Rilke, *Duimo Elegies* (–1922).

Hugh Walpole, *Mr. Perrin and Mr. Traill*.

H G Wells, *The New Machiavelli*.

Edith Wharton, *Ethan Frome*.

Georgian Poetry (edited by Edward Marsh, –1922).

Drama:

Robert Hitchen and Mary Anderson, *The Garden of Allah*.

The company of the Abbey Theatre, Dublin, makes its first visit to the USA.

In NW England, Basil Dean opens Liverpool Repertory Theatre.

V Births and Deaths

Feb 2 Jussi Bjoerling born (–1960).

Feb 6 Ronald Reagan born (–).

May 18 Gustav Mahler dies (50).

May 27 Hubert Humphrey born (–1978).

May 29 W S Gilbert dies (75).

June 9 Carry Nation dies (64).

July 5 Georges Pompidou born (–1974).

July 21 Marshall McLuhan born (–1980).

Aug 16 E F Schumacher born (–1977).

Aug 29 John Charnley born (–1982).

W Everyday Life

In France and Algeria, clocks are put back by 9 minutes and 21 seconds at midnight on 10–11 Mar, making Greenwich time the standard.

Mona Lisa by Leonardo da Vinci is stolen from the Louvre, Paris (21 Aug).

X Sport and Recreation

The Gordon-Bennett International Aviation Cup is awarded for the first time.

Wales wins the first Rugby Union Five Nations Grand Slam.

The Indianapolis 500 car race is run for the first time; the winner is Ray Harroun, driving a Marmon Wasp (May).

Johnny McDermott becomes the youngest winner of a major golf championship when he wins the US Open at the age of 19.

Republic in China ... War in Balkans ... Woodrow Wilson elected
US president ...

A January

　　Elections to German Reichstag leave the Socialists the strongest party.

3　Ulster Unionists resolve to repudiate the authority of any Irish parliament set up under Home Rule Bill.

6　in USA, New Mexico is admitted to the union as the 47th state.

10　in France, Prime Minister Joseph Caillaux resigns (14, Raymond Poincaré forms cabinet).

18　British miners ballot in favour of strike action.

B February

6　in China, Nanjing assembly endorses Yuan Shikai's proposals for constitutional reform.

10　French senate ratifies Moroccan agreement (of Nov 1911).

12　Manchu dynasty abdicates in China and a provisional republic is established.

14　in USA, Arizona is admitted to the union as the 48th state.

15　an amendment moved by the Labour Party in the British House of Commons favouring a minimum wage is rejected.

26　British coal strike begins in Derbyshire (becoming general, 1 March).

C March

9　the powers ask Italy to state terms on which it would accept arbitration to end Turkish war.

14　US President Taft forbids shipments of arms to Mexico (where government faces rebellion).

19　British Prime Minister Asquith introduces minimum wage bill to settle coal strike.

19　Tom Mann, the British Syndicalist leader, is arrested for inciting soldiers to mutiny.

28　British House of Commons rejects women's franchise bill.

29　the German government defeat in Reichstag on Post Office estimates.

30　Sultan of Morocco signs treaty making Morocco a French protectorate.

D April

4　Chinese Republic proclaimed in Tibet.

9　Canadian–West Indies preferential agreement.

15　(–15) the British liner *Titanic*, carrying 2,224 people on its maiden trans-Atlantic voyage, hits an iceberg S of Newfoundland and sinks; 1,513 are lost for want of sufficient lifeboats.

18　Turkey closes Dardanelles to shipping (–1 May).

23　Welsh Church Disestablishment bill is introduced in British House of Commons.

27　British–Belgian loan to China is cancelled after representations by other powers.

E May

22　in Hungary, Count Tisza, leader of the National Party of Work, is elected president of the Chamber; socialists proclaim a strike in support of male suffrage; riots occur in Budapest.

22　the German Reichstag is adjourned following socialist attacks on German emperor.

23　London transport workers strike.

F June

2　Clericals win Belgian elections on schools issue.

22　Taft is nominated Republican presidential candidate at Chicago convention, where Theodore Roosevelt makes proposals for a new Progressive Republican Party.

Dorothea Lambert Chambers wins her fifth consecutive Ladies' Singles title at the Wimbledon tennis tournament, London.

Y Media

In Britain, founding of the *Daily Herald* as a daily Labour and TUC paper (published as weekly 1914–19, then again as daily; formally taken over by the Labour Party in 1922).

Film:

In USA, David Horsley establishes the first studio in Hollywood, Los Angeles. 15 companies do likewise within the year.

First Keystone comedy film, produced by Max Sennett.

Anna Karenina.

La Dame aux camélias (starring Sara Bernhardt).

Pinocchio.

London eugenics conference ... Discovery of Piltdown Man ...

o Politics, Government, Law, and Economy

US House of Representatives resolves that election expenses of presidential and vice-presidential candidates should be published (20 April).

US excise bill, taxing net income from business sources (19 March).

Former US President Theodore Roosevelt founds the Progressive ('Bull Moose') Party.

Royal Flying Corps established in Britain.

Hilaire Belloc, *The Servile State.*

A B Keith, *Responsible Government in the Dominions.*

Switzerland introduces a Civil Code (which later serves as the model for Turkey's law code).

'D Notice' committee founded in Britain to 'guide' the press on matters concerning national security.

In USA, an amendment to the 1909 Copyright Act grants copyright in photoplays and other motion pictures.

In USA, Underwood–Simmons Act lowers tariffs, especially on raw materials.

Consumer Price index established to provide a guide for setting cost of living adjustments for US wages.

Parcel post is inaugurated in the USA.

US Supreme Court orders dissolution of Union Pacific and Southern Pacific railways merger (2 Dec).

British General Post Office takes over the telephone system.

p Society, Education, and Religion

Massachusetts is the first US state to enact law regulating wages for women and children (to come into force on 1 July 1913).

In USA, the states of Arizona, Kansas, and Wisconsin adopt women's suffrage (5 Nov).

US Senate passes Reed Smoot's pension bill.

British National Health Insurance Act in force (15 July).

First International Eugenics Congress held at the University of London (24–30 July).

In Britain, appointment of Royal Commissions on Divorce and Vivisection; the former leads to the Act of 1923.

Publication (13 July) of report by Roger Casement on atrocities at Putumayo, Peru.

C J Jung, *The Psychology of the Unconscious.*

Alfred Adler, *The Neurotic Constitution.*

Teachers' Registration Council founded in England.

Maria Montessori, *The Montessori Method.*

Church of Scotland revises Prayer Book.

Emile Durkheim, *The Elementary Forms of Religious Life.*

B M Streeter and others, *Foundations: A Statement of Christian Belief in Terms of Modern Thought.*

Ernst Troeltsch, *Socialism and the Christian Church.*

q Science, Technology, and Discovery

British explorer Robert Falcon Scott reaches the South Pole (18 Jan).

First use of the parachute for jumping from a moving aircraft (by Albert Berry in USA, 1 March).

G H Curtiss constructs the first sea-plane.

Henry Dreailey invents a type of stainless steel.

Irving Langmuir in America discovers that filling light bulbs with inert gases prolongs their life.

In Germany Max von Laue demonstrates that crystals scatter X– rays, the start of X-ray crystallography.

Alfred Wegener in Germany suggests idea of continental drift (published in 1915).

25 George Lansbury protests in British House of Commons against forcible feeding of imprisoned suffragettes.

G July

2 in USA, the Democratic Party convention at Baltimore, Maryland, nominates Woodrow Wilson as its presidential candidate.

7 German chancellor, Theobald von Bethmann Hollweg, visits Russian government in St Petersburg.

9 in New Zealand, following the electoral victory of the new Reform Party over the Liberals, W F Massey forms a ministry on the resignation of Thomas Mackenzie's.

18 Tewfik Pasha becomes Grand Vizier of Persia, following fall of Said Pasha's ministry.

24 riots in London docks and at Tower Hill meeting addressed by dockers' leader Ben Tillett.

30 in Japan, death of the Emperor Meiji (Mutsuhito); succeeded by Yoshihito.

H August

2 US Senate resolves to extend Monroe doctrine to foreign corporations holding territory on American continent.

5 (–16) French Prime Minister and Foreign Secretary Raymond Poincaré visits Russia.

5 in USA, convention of the Progressive Republican Party at Chicago nominates former president Theodore Roosevelt as its presidential candidate.

7 Russo–Japanese agreement determining spheres of influence in Mongolia and Manchuria.

17 British note to restrain China from sending military expedition to Tibet.

17 Britain protests to USA that Panama Canal rates infringe Hay–Pauncefote treaty of Nov 1901.

19 Britain accepts Austrian Prime Minister and Foreign Minister Count Berchtold's project for Balkan conversations.

J September

6 British Trades Union Congress votes against syndicalism.

13 revolution in Santo Domingo (modern Dominican Republic).

18 in northern Ireland, Anti-Home Rule demonstrations begin at Enniskillen under Edward Carson.

23 Chinese government declines six-powers loan in favour of loan by Birch, Crisp and Company of London.

28 in Northern Ireland, thousands of Unionist opponents of Home Rule sign the Solemn League and Covenant pledging themselves to resist Home Rule.

29 British and French forces pacify riots on Island of Samos after Turks withdraw troops (4 Sept).

30 Bulgarian and Serbian armies mobilize for war against Turkey.

K October

6 great powers back French proposals for averting Balkan war.

8 Montenegro declares war on Turkey.

12 Turkey declines to undertake reforms in Macedonia on which the powers insist.

14 a fanatic wounds US presidential candidate Theodore Roosevelt in Milwaukee, Wisconsin.

17 Turkey declares war on Bulgaria and Serbia.

18 Italy and Turkey sign peace treaty at Lausanne by which Tripoli and Cyrenaica are granted autonomy under Italian suzerainty, and Italy restores Dodecanese Islands to Turkey.

L November

3 Turkey asks powers to intervene to end Balkan war.

5 in US presidential election, Woodrow Wilson, Democrat, wins with 435 electoral votes against Theodore Roosevelt, Progressive, with 88, and President W H Taft, Republican, with 8 votes; popular vote: Wilson, 6,293,454; Roosevelt, 4,119,538; Taft, 3,484,980.

11 British government is defeated in House of Commons on amendment to Home Rule Bill.

11 Chile resumes diplomatic relations with Peru (after 30 months).

21 Turkey declares that peace terms of Balkan allies are unacceptable.

26 British Labour MP George Lansbury, who had resigned to test feeling of electorate on women's suffrage, is defeated in by-election at Bow, London.

27 run on savings banks in central and east Europe.

M December

3 armistice between Turkey, Bulgaria, Serbia, and Montenegro (Greece abstains).

14 Louis Botha resigns as South African prime minister to form new cabinet (20), omitting James Hertzog.

19 in Japan, prime minister Matsukata resigns following resignation of the minister for war; Prince Katsura forms cabinet.

20 at London peace conference between Turkey and Balkan states, ambassadors of great powers accept principle of Albanian autonomy, providing Serbia has canal access to Adriatic.

L O Howard, *The House Fly, Disease Carrier*.
Albert Einstein formulates the law of photochemical equivalence.
Casimir Funck introduces word 'vitamine'.

R Humanities

Discovery at Piltdown in south-east England of 'Piltdown Man', a human skull with an ape-like jaw (exposed as a forgery in 1953).
E Maude Thompson, *Introduction to Latin and Greek Palaeography*.
R E Prothero, *English Farming, Past and Present*.
James Harvey Robinson, *The New History*.
Lytton Strachey, *Landmarks in French Literature*.
G E Moore, *Ethics*.
Bertrand Russell, *The Problems of Philosophy*.

S Art, Sculpture, Fine Arts, and Architecture

Wassily Kandinsky, *On the Spiritual in Art* — first publication by an artist of a theory justifying abstraction.
Albert Gleizes and Jean Metzinger publish *Du Cubisme*.

Painting, etc:
Giacomo Balla, *Dynamism of a Dog on a Leash*.
Umberto Boccioni, *Materia*.
Georges Braque, creates first papiers collées e.g., *Fruit Dish & Glass*.
Giorgio de Chirico, *Melancholy, Place d'Italie*.
Robert Delaunay, *Windows Open Simultaneously*.
Marcel Duchamp, *Nude Descending A Staircase, II*.
Juan Gris, *Homage to Picasso*.
Wassily Kandinsky, *Deluge I*.
Ernst Kirchner, *Striding into the Sea*.
Mikhail Larionov, *Paysage Rayonniste*.
Emil Nolde, *The Missionary*.
Pablo Picasso, *Still Life with Chair Caning* — first Collage.
Gino Severini, *Blue Dancer*.

Sculpture:
Constantin Brancusi, *Mlle Pogany*.
Umberto Boccioni, *Development of a Bottle in Space*.
George Frampton, *Peter Pan* (in Kensington Gardens, London).
Pablo Picasso, *Guitar*.

T Music

Arnold Berg, *Five Altenberg Songs*.
Frank Bridge, *The Sea*.
Henry Cowell, *Tides of Manaunaun*.

Frederick Delius, *On Hearing the First Cuckoo in Spring*.
Maurice Ravel, *Daphnis et Chloé* (ballet).
Arnold Schoenberg, *Pierrot Lunaire*.
Leopold Stokowski becomes chief conductor of the Philadelphia Orchestra (Pennsylvania, USA).
In USA, W C Handy publishes 'Memphis Blues' (written 1909).
In Britain, the revue *Hullo, Ragtime* (first performed at the London Hippodrome, 23 Dec) encourages the craze for ragtime songs.
Jack Judge and Harry Williams, 'It's a Long, Long way to Tipperary'.

U Literature and Drama

Max Beerbohm, *A Christmas Garland*.
E M Dell, *The Way of an Eagle*.
Gerhart Hauptmann, *Atlantis*.
James Weldon Johnson, *The Autobiography of an Ex-Colored Man*.
Compton Mackenzie, *Carnival*.
Edna St Vincent Millay, *Renascence and Other Poems*.
Saki, *The Unbearable Bassington*.
Rabindranath Tagore, *Gitanjali*.
Junichiro Tanizaki, *Akuma/The Demons*.
'New Poetry' movement in USA.
Harriet Monroe founds *Poetry*, the first US periodical devoted exclusively to verse.

Drama:
Arnold Bennett and Edward Knoblauch, *Milestones*.
Paul Claudel, *L'Annonce faite à Marie*.
Stanley Houghton, *Hindle Wakes*.
Max Reinhardt's German spectacle *Sumurun*.
W B Yeats, *The Hour Glass*.
Actors' Equity Association founded in America.

V Births and Deaths

Feb 6 Christopher Hill born (–).
Feb 10 Joseph Lister dies (85).
Mar Robert Falcon Scott dies (41).
March 23 Werner von Braun born (–1977).
March 26 Tennessee Williams born (–1983).
March 27 James Callaghan born (–).
May 14 August Strindberg dies (63).
May 28 Patrick White born (–1990).
July 31 Milton Friedman born (–).
Aug 20 William Booth dies (83).
Sept 1 Samuel Coleridge-Taylor dies (37).
Sept 5 John Cage born (–1992).

W Everyday Life

Inauguration of new campanile in St Mark's Square, Venice (25 April).
Adoption of 'SOS' as a universal distress signal.
First regular air service, between Berlin and Friedrichshaven, in rigid airships *Victoria*, *Luise*, and *Hansa*.

Second Balkan War ... King of Greece assassinated ...

A January

2 Turkish garrison on the island of Chios surrenders to Greeks; Greece assumes rule.

5 Gottlieb von Jagow becomes German foreign minister (–1916).

6 London peace conference between Turkey and Balkan states suspended.

16 Irish Home Rule bill passes British House of Commons (but on 30 Jan is rejected by Lords).

17 Raymond Poincaré elected President of France (–1920).

18 Graeco–Turkish naval battle off the island of Tenedos.

21 in France, Aristide Briand succeeds Poincaré as prime minister and forms cabinet.

23 Nazim Pasha is murdered in Turkish coup and Shevket Pasha forms ministry.

28 Suffragettes demonstrate in London following withdrawal of a franchise bill (on 27 Jan) to which an amendment for women's suffrage might have been added.

B February

3 Bulgarians renew Turkish War (–16 April).

5 Welsh Church Disestablishment bill passes British House of Commons but on 13 Feb is rejected by Lords.

8 rebellion of part of army in Mexico City.

13 Franco–US agreement to extend 1908 arbitration convention for five years.

18 in Mexico, the commander of the army, Victoriano Huerta, joins rebel soldiers, forces President Madero to resign, and declares himself president; civil war breaks out (President Wilson of USA refuses to recognize Huerta).

23 murder of Madero, the deposed president of Mexico.

C March

In USA, flooding of the Ohio River devastates parts of Ohio and Indiana.

3 on the eve of the inauguration of the US president, 5,000 women parade in Washington, demanding women's suffrage.

4 Woodrow Wilson is inaugurated as the 28th president of the USA.

11 British–German agreement on frontier between Nigeria and Cameroons.

14 Balkan allies accept mediation of great powers.

18 King George I of Greece is assassinated by a Greek in newly occupied Salonika.

18 in France, the senate rejects Briand's plan for proportion representation; Briand resigns as prime minister.

x Sport and Recreation

England regains the Ashes in Australia, winning the five-match cricket series 4–1 (13 Feb).

The 5th Olympic Games are held in Stockholm. Sweden wins 24 gold medals; USA, 23; Britain, 10; Finland, 9; France, 7; Germany, 5. Races are timed electronically for the first time (5 May–22 July).

In cricket, a Triangular Tournament of nine test matches, involving England, Australia, and South Africa, is held in England.

In football, a rule change restricts goalkeepers to handling the ball in the penalty area, rather than in their own half of the field.

y Media

Mrs Joseph Pulitzer founds the School of Journalism at Columbia University, New York (2 July).

In Italy, the Benito Mussolini edits the Milan socialist paper *Avanti* (–1914).

In Russia, foundation of the socialist paper *Pravda*.

In Britain, Geoffrey Dawson appointed editor of *The Times* (–1919, 1923–41).

Foundation in Britain of the *Daily Herald*, published by members of the Labour movement.

Film:

London has 400 cinemas (90 in 1909); in USA, 5 million people visit cinemas daily.

In USA, first Warner Brothers films; formation of the Fox and Universal companies.

Formation of the British Board of Film Censors.

L'Homme nu (director, St Raime).

Voice of a Million (director, D W Griffith).

Radio:

Due to congestion of airwaves, the US Congress passes the Radio Act requiring operators to obtain a licence from the Department of Commerce and Labor (13 Aug).

Federal reserve established in the USA ... Stravinsky's Rite of Spring ... *Last horse-drawn bus in Paris ...*

o Politics, Government, Law, and Economy

The 16th Amendment to the US constitution takes effect (on 25 Feb), empowering the Congress to collect income tax.

The 17th Amendment to the US constitution (ratified 31 May) transfers election of senators from state legislators to a popular vote.

Secretaryship of Labor established in the USA.

US Congress passes the Federal Reserve Bank Act (23 Dec), establishing a Federal Reserve Board with power over monetary policy and 12 district Federal Reserve banks.

Prince Bernhard von Bülow, *Imperial Germany*.

In Britain, in the case Scott v. Scott, the House of Lords confirms the principle that 'every court in the Land is open to every subject of the King'.

Judge Archibald of the US federal commercial court is found guilty of corruption.

The Underwood Tariff Bill makes the biggest change to US tariffs since the mid-19th century; tariffs are removed from or reduced on over 1,000 items.

In Canada, first train on Transcontinental Railway, carrying grain.

Diesel-electric railway inaugurated in Sweden.

The USA's manufacturing output exceeds that of France, Germany, and Britain combined.

p Society, Education, and Religion

Universal suffrage introduced in Norway (with voting age of 25).

Miss Emily Duncan appointed first woman magistrate in England (26 May).

In Britain, Emily Wilding Davison, a member of the Women's Social and Political Union, an organization of militant suffragettes, dies after throwing herself at the King's horse Anmer, during the Derby at Epsom (4 June).

In USA, Alice Paul founds the Congressional Committee of the National American Woman's Suffrage Association.

In USA, B'Nai B'rith founds the Anti-Defamation League to fight antisemitism.

Old age and sickness insurance introduced in USA, France, and the Netherlands.

Rockefeller Foundation established in USA, to promote human well-being worldwide.

US automobile manufacturer Henry Ford introduces the conveyor-belt assembly technique into his Detroit-based company.

C G Jung, *The Psychology of the Unconscious*.

26 Bulgarians take Adrianople from the Turks.

28 Belgian army bill introduces universal military service.

31 Turkey accepts recommendations of great powers for a peace.

D **April**

3 in Britain, Mrs Emmeline Pankhurst is imprisoned for inciting persons to place explosives outside Chancellor Lloyd George's house.

8 opening of first Parliament of Chinese Republic.

8 in USA, President Wilson resumes delivery in person of the 'State of the Union' address to Congress after a break of 112 years.

16 Turkey signs armistice with Bulgaria.

E **May**

6 King Nicholas of Montenegro yields the Turkish town of Scutari (held by Montenegro since 1912) to the powers until an Albanian government is created (in Dec).

6 British House of Commons rejects a women's franchise bill.

30 peace treaty between Turkey and Balkan states signed in London, ending the first Balkan War.

30 Canadian Senate rejects naval bill (providing for high expenditure on ships for the Imperial Navy).

F **June**

18 British House of Commons debates the Marconi Report which acquits Chancellor Lloyd George and other ministers of corruption in assigning the imperial wireless contract to the Marconi Company.

24 (–7) President Poincaré of France visits England.

26 Bulgaria signs defensive treaty with Austria-Hungary.

28 Romania warns Bulgaria that it will not remain neutral in a war.

30 Second Balkan War opens, with Bulgaria attacking Serbian and Greek positions.

30 Reichstag passes bill to fund large increase of the German army.

G **July**

1 (–9), Hague opium conference.

7 British House of Commons passes Irish Home Rule bill (but rejected on 15 July by Lords).

8 following procedures established by the Parliament Act of 1911, the British House of Commons for a second time considers the bill to disestablish the Church in Wales; the Commons again passes the bill but it is again rejected by the House of Lords (22 July).

10 Russia declares war on Bulgaria.

12 Turkey re-enters war (20 July, recaptures Adrianople from Bulgaria).

23 outbreak of rebellion in Yangzi Valley and southern China (–Sept).

28 ambassadors of powers regulate establishment of Albanian principality.

31 Balkan states sign armistice in Bucharest.

H **August**

7 French army bill, imposing three years' military service.

10 Balkan states sign peace treaty in Bucharest.

J **September**

3 Nanjing falls to forces of Chinese ruler Yuan Shikai.

16 Japan sends flotilla to Yangzi river, on China's failure to honour reparations agreement.

18 Bulgarian–Turkish treaty settles frontier in Thrace; Adrianople remains under Turkish rule.

24 in Northern Ireland, Unionists appoint their own provisional government, to take power when the Irish Home Rule bill takes effect.

K **October**

6 Yuan Shikai is elected president of the Chinese Republic.

17 Serbs invade Albania.

21 royalist rising in Portugal (suppressed by government).

28 Britain, France, and Germany withhold recognition of Victoriano Huerta's government in Mexico until the USA defines its policy.

28 German–Turkish military conversations.

L **November**

In China, President Yuan Shikai outlaws the Guomindang party. The German general Otto Liman von Sanders is appointed a high commander of the Turkish army in Istanbul, heading a German military mission appointed to improve the Turkish army.

1 naval convention of Triple Alliance (Germany, Austria-Hungary, Italy).

3 USA demands withdrawal of General Huerta from Mexico.

5 joint declaration by Russia and China recognizing the autonomy of Outer Mongolia under Chinese suzerainty.

Six hundred Russian monks are deported from Mt Athos, Greece, for alleged heresy (July).

James Moffatt, *New Translation of the New Testament*.

Q Science, Technology, and Discovery

Niels Bohr in Denmark proposes a theory of atomic structure.

British scientist Frederick Soddy coins the term 'isotope'.

J J Thomson, *Rays of Positive Electricity and Their Application to Chemical Analysis*.

Bela Schick discovers test for immunity from diphtheria.

Richard Willstätter discovers composition of chlorophyll.

In USA, E McCollum isolates vitamin A.

R Humanities

H J Spinden, *A Study of Maya Art*.

Charles A Beard, *An Economic Interpretation of the Constitution of the United States*.

Elie Halévy, *A History of the English People in the Nineteenth Century*, (–1946).

G P Gooch, *History and Historians of the Nineteenth Century*.

Dictionary of the Irish Language (–1976).

Edward J Dent, *Mozart's Operas: A Critical Study*.

Sigmund Freud, *Totem and Taboo*.

Edmund Husserl, *Ideas: General Introduction to Pure Phenomenology*.

Walter Lippman, *Preface to Politics*.

S Art, Sculpture, Fine Arts, and Architecture

International Exhibition of Modern Art (exhibition of post-impressionist and cubist art), known as the 'Armory Show', held in New York.

Painting, etc:

Giocomo Balla, *Abstract Speed*.

Georges Braque, *Checkerboard: 'Tivoli Cinema'*.

Giorgio de Chirico, *The Uncertainty of the Poet*.

Natalia Goncharova, *The Cyclist*.

Wassily Kandinsky, *Improvisation 31 — Sea Battle*.

Ludwig Kirchner, *Berlin Street Scene*.

Kasimir Malevich, *The Black Cross*.

Henri Matisse, *Portrait of Mme Matisse*.

Francis Picabia, *Udnie*.

Pablo Picasso, *Man with a Guitar*.

Harold Gilman, Walter Sickert, and Wyndham Lewis form the London Group of artists, an exhibiting association (first exhibition, March 1914).

Guillaume Apollinaire's appraisal, *The Cubist Painters*.

Sculpture:

Umberto Boccioni, *Anti-graceful*.

Marcel Duchamp, *Bicycle Wheel* — the first 'readymade'.

Jacob Epstein, *Rock Drill*.

Wilhelm Lehmbruck, *Ascending Youth*.

Henri Matisse, *The Back, II*.

Architecture:

Cass Gilbert, Woolworth Building, New York (highest skyscraper until 1930).

Edwin Lutyens, Viceroy's House, New Delhi, India.

T Music

George Butterworth, *A Shropshire Lad* (symphonic rhapsody).

Claude Debussy, *Jeux* (ballet).

Ivor Gurney, *Five Elizabethan Songs*.

Italo Montemezzi, *L'Amore dei Tre Re* (opera).

Sergei Rachmaninov, *The Bells*.

Igor Stravinsky, *The Rite of Spring* (ballet).

Anton Webern, *Six Bagatelles*.

Guitarist Andrés Segovia makes debut in Madrid (1924, in Paris; 1928, in USA).

'Colonel Bogey', march by Kenneth J Alford.

'Hold Your Hand Out, Naughty Boy', by C W Murphy.

U Literature and Drama

Alain-Fournier, *Le Grand Meaulnes/The Lost Domain*.

Willa Cather, *O Pioneers!*

D H Lawrence, *Sons and Lovers*.

Compton Mackenzie, *Sinister Street* (–1914).

Osip Mandelstam, *Kamen/Stones*.

Thomas Mann, *Death in Venice*.

Marcel Proust, *Du côté de chez Swann*, the first part of *À la recherche du temps perdu* (–1927).

Miguel de Unamuno, *The Tragic Sense of Life*.

Edith Wharton, *The Custom of the Country*.

In Britain, Robert Bridges appointed Poet Laureate (–1930).

Drama:

George Bernard Shaw, *Androcles and the Lion, Pygmalion*.

The Palace Theatre opened on Broadway, New York.

Barry Jackson and John Drinkwater open Birmingham Repertory Theatre, England.

Lady Gregory, *Our Irish Theatre*.

V Births and Deaths

Jan 9 Richard Nixon born (–1994).

Jan 10 Gustáv Husák born (–1991).

Jan 18 Danny Kaye born (–1987).

March 28 Lord Wolseley dies (80).

March 31 J P Morgan dies (75).

May 16 Woody Herman born (–1987).

July 14 Gerald Ford born (–).

6 Mahatma Gandhi, leader of Indian Passive Resistance movement, is arrested.

13 Greek–Turkish peace treaty; the Greeks obtain Crete and Aegean islands apart from Tenedos, Imbros and the Dodecanese.

17 first vessel passes through Panama Canal.

20 Zabern incident, in which a German officer in Alsace-Lorraine insults Alsatian recruits, embittering Franco–German relations.

M **December**

5 British proclamation forbids sending of arms to Ireland.

13 Britain and France oppose German–Turkish military convention.

14 Greece formally annexes Crete.

Dispute between Mexico and USA ... Outbreak of First World War ...

A **January**

1 Northern and Southern Nigeria are amalgamated as the British Colony and Protectorate of Nigeria.

8 Gaston Calmette, editor of *Figaro*, makes charges of financial malpractice against Joseph Caillaux, the French minister of finance.

8 in Turkey, the German general Otto Liman von Sanders is promoted to inspector-general of the Turkish army.

11 in China, Yuan Shikai governs without parliament.

27 President Oreste of Haiti abdicates during revolt; US marines land to preserve order (General Zamon elected President, 8 Feb).

B **February**

15 Franco–German agreement on Baghdad Railway.

C **March**

8 Monarchist party wins Spanish elections.

10 Suffragettes damage the *Rokeby Venus* by Velázquez, in National Gallery, London.

14 Turkish–Serbian peace treaty.

16 in France, Mme Caillaux assassinates Gaston Calmette, editor of *Figaro*, for his smear campaign against her husband, the French finance minister.

20 the Curragh incident or 'mutiny': General Hubert Gough and 58 other British cavalry officers stationed at Curragh near Dublin indicate that they would resign if the army were to be ordered to undertake active operations in Northern Ireland to enforce Home Rule.

30 British Prime Minister Asquith assumes the post of secretary of state for war, having obtained the resignation of J E B Seely from that office in the wake of the Curragh 'mutiny'.

D **April**

1 Civil government established in Panama Canal Zone.

10 US sailors buying gasoline in Tampico, Mexico, are arrested; after their release, President Huerta refuses a US request for Mexican guns to salute the US flag.

Aug 11 Angus Wilson born (–1991).
Aug 13 Makarios III born (–1977).
Aug 16 Menachem Begin born (–1992).
Sept 12 Jesse Owens born (–1980).
Oct 1 Rudolf Diesel dies (56).
Nov 22 Benjamin Britten born (–1976).
Nov 22 Albert Camus born (–1960).
Dec 18 Willy Brandt born (–1992).

w Everyday Life

Last horse-drawn omnibus in Paris (11 Jan).
Recovery of Leonardo da Vinci's *Mona Lisa* (Dec), missing since 1911; the thief, Vincenzo Perugia, claimed he was retaliating against France for taking Italian art works from Italy.
New York World prints the first modern cross-word puzzle.
Coco Chanel's boutique at Deauville, N France, leads a trend toward more casual fashions in women's dress.
'Camel' cigarettes are launched in the USA with a huge advertising campaign; within five years they become the best-selling brand.
Foxtrot popular.

x Sport and Recreation

Francis Ouimet, a shop-assistant from Boston, becomes the first amateur golfer to win the US Open Championship.
Ladies' and Mixed Doubles championships are held for the first time at the Wimbledon tennis tournament, London.
In cricket, S F Barnes of England takes a record 17 South African wickets in the second Test at Johannesburg (26–30 Dec).
The International Lawn Tennis Federation is established in Paris.

y Media

Foundation of *New Statesman* periodical in Britain.

Film:

Are You a Mason? (starring John Barrymore).
The Fugitive (starring William S Hart).
The Sea Wolf (director, Hobart Bosworth).
The Student of Prague (director, Stellan Rye).
Charlie Chaplin makes 35 movies for Mack Sennet.
Mack Sennet makes Roscoe 'Fatty' Arbuckle a Keystone Kop.

Opening of Panama Canal ... Death of Westinghouse ... Elastic bra invented ...

o Politics, Government, Law, and Economy

Defence of the Realm Act passed in Britain, conferring emergency powers on the government (Aug).
US Supreme Court sustains the regulation of railway rates by the Interstate Commerce Commission in the Shreveport case.
Edward S Corwin, *The Doctrine of Judicial Review*.
In USA, Clayton Anti-Trust Act strengthens law against monopolist company policies and excludes unions and agricultural cooperatives from anti-combination laws; it also strengthens trade unions by forbidding the issue of injunctions against unions without notice.
Federal Trade Commission Act in USA establishes the Federal Trade Commission to prevent unfair competition in commerce.
Harrison Narcotic Act restricts the availability of drugs such as heroin in the USA.
Currency and Bank Notes Act, repealing Bank Charter Act, 1844, empowers Bank of England to issue £1 and 10-shilling notes.
Opening of the Panama Canal (15 Aug); about 6,000 workers died during its construction.
After outbreak of war in Europe, London Stock Market is closed (31 July–4 Jan 1915), followed by other markets.
E Cannan, *Wealth*.

p Society, Education, and Religion

Following a petition from Miss Anna Jarvis, the US Congress and president resolve that government executive departments will recognize Mother's Day as an annual holiday.
US campaigner for birth control, Margaret Sanger, publishes *The Woman Rebel* for subscribers.
In USA, racial segregation is extended to federal government employment.
Germany enacts maternity benefits.
Development of Billerica, Boston, USA, a 'garden' suburb.
Education (Provision of Meals) Act in England places a duty on local education authorities to provide school dinners.
In Belgium, introduction of compulsory school attendance for 6–12 year-olds.
Inception of the Assemblies of God, now the

22 US forces bombard and seize the port of Veracruz, Mexico (to prevent Germans landing munitions for President Huerta's forces; withdrawn 23 Nov).

E May

6 in the British Parliament, the Women's Enfranchisement Bill, introduced in the House of Lords, is defeated.

10 in Britain, the Liberal Unionists unite with Conservatives.

19 British House of Commons passes Welsh Church Disestablishment Bill for third time.

20 Argentina, Brazil, and Chile arbitrate at Niagara Falls between US and Mexico.

22 Britain acquires control of oil properties in Persian Gulf from Anglo–Persian Oil Company.

25 British House of Commons passes the Irish Home Rule bill.

F June

11 Niagara Falls delegates approve new Mexican government (24, peace with USA signed).

13 in France, following a political crisis, René Viviani forms a ministry.

13 Greece annexes the Aegean Islands of Chios and Mytilene or Lesbos (formerly Turkish).

15 British–German agreement on Baghdad Railway and Mesopotamia.

28 Archduke Franz Ferdinand of Austria-Hungary and his wife are assassinated at Sarajevo in Bosnia by Gavrilo Princip, an 18-year-old Bosnian Serb student linked with the Serbian nationalist society the 'Black Hand'.

G July

5 Germany promises support to Austria-Hungary for any conflict with Serbia.

8 the British House of Lords considers an Amending Bill to allow for the temporary exclusion of parts of Northern Ireland from Home Rule; the Lords vote to exclude Northern Ireland permanently, thus creating deadlock over Home Rule.

10 in Ireland, Ulster's provisional government re-affirms Ulster's determination to resist Home Rule.

16 announcement that President Huerta of Mexico has gone into exile and replaced by Carbajal as provisional president (Aug, Carbajal flees).

20 (–29) President Raymond Poincaré visits Russia.

21 (–24) conference on Irish Home Rule held at Buckingham Palace, London, at which parties fail to agree.

23 Austro-Hungary, suspecting Serbian involvement in the assassination of Franz Ferdinand, issues ultimatum to Serbia.

24 Edward Grey proposes four-power mediation of Balkan crisis, but Serbia appeals to Russia.

25 Serbia mobilizes army; Germany encourages Austria-Hungary to declare war on Serbia.

26 Austrian-Hungary mobilizes army on Russian frontier.

26 clash in Dublin between troops and Irish nationalists involved in gun-running.

28 Austria-Hungary declares war on Serbia.

30 Russia mobilizes army.

30 Leading French socialist Jean Jaurès (aged 55) is murdered in Paris.

31 Germany orders Russia to stop mobilization of army; France, Austria-Hungary, and Germany mobilize armies; Britain requests Germany to respect neutrality of Belgium.

H August

1 Germany declares war on Russia.

1 German–Turkish treaty signed at Constantinople.

2 Germany occupies Luxembourg and sends ultimatum to Belgium to allow passage of troops.

2 Russians invade East Prussia.

2 Italy declares neutrality in the European conflict.

4 Germany declares war on France and invades Belgium and France.

4 Britain declares war on Germany and establishes naval blockade of North Sea, Channel and Mediterranean to stop access to Central Powers.

4 President Wilson of the USA declares US neutrality respecting the European war.

5 German Second Army reaches Liège, where it is resisted by Belgian defenders until 16 Aug.

6 Austria-Hungary declares war on Russia.

6 Serbia and Montenegro declare war on Germany.

8 British troops land in France.

8 Britain and France occupy the German protectorate of Togoland (modern Togo and the Volta region of Ghana).

10 France declares war on Austria.

10 The German cruisers *Breslau* and *Goeben* escape British ships in the Mediterranean and enter the Black Sea, where they are purchased by Turkey to replace ships seized by the British.

12 Britain declares war on Austria-Hungary.

14 Russia promises autonomy to Russian Poland in return for Polish aid.

15 Japanese ultimatum to Germany demanding evacuation of the German treaty port of Jiaozhou in China.

20 Constitutionalist army, led by General Carranza, occupies Mexico City.

largest Pentecostal denomination in the United States.

Following the death of Pope Pius X (20 Aug), Giacomo Della Chiesa is elected Pope (3 Sept) and takes the name Benedict XV.

Q Science, Technology, and Discovery

Ernest Shackleton leads Antarctic expedition (–1917).

Arthur Eddington, *Stellar Movement and the Structure of the Universe*.

J H Jeans, *Report on Radiation and the Quantum Theory*.

Work of the National Physical Laboratory in England is extended to include the testing and certification of radium preparations.

James Dewar in England elucidates the composition of air.

Bottomley discovers fertilization through peat.

Alexis Carrel achieves successful heart surgery on a dog.

R Humanities

Journal of Egyptian Archaeology issued.

Robert Koldewey, *The Excavations at Babylon*.

Thomas A Joyce, *Mexican Archaeology*.

Austin Dobson, *Eighteenth-Century Studies*.

Theodore Roosevelt, *History as Literature*.

Edward VII Gallery of British Museum, London, opened.

Separate publication of the *Times Literary Supplement* (from 19 March).

F H Bradley, *Essays on Truth and Reality*.

C D Broad, *Perception, Physics, and Reality*.

E F Carritt, *Theory of Beauty*.

José Ortega y Gasset, *Meditations on Quixote*.

S Art, Sculpture, Fine Arts, and Architecture

In Britain, Vorticist group is formed in London.

Painting, etc:

Ernst Barlach, *The Avenger*.

Georges Braque, *Glass, Bottle and Newspaper*.

Carlo Carrà, *Words-in-Freedom: Interventionist Demonstration* (futurist collage).

Giorgio de Chirico, *The Enigma of a Day*, *Portrait of Guillaume Apollinaire*.

Otto Dix, *Self-Portrait as Soldier* (–1915).

Wassily Kandinsky, *Fugue*.

Wyndham Lewis, *Workshop* (–1915).

Kasimir Malevich, *The Aviator*.

Sculpture:

Henry Bacon, the Lincoln Memorial, Washington, DC, USA.

Constantin Brancusi, *Little French Girl*.

Marcel Duchamp, *Bottle Rack*.

Raymond Duchamp-Villon, *Horse*.

Henri Gaudier-Brzeska, *Hieratic Head of Ezra Pound*.

Ernst Kirchner, *Nude Woman, Sitting with Her Legs Crossed*.

Pablo Picasso, *Glass of Absinthe, Still Life*.

Architecture:

Walter Gropius and Adolph Meyer, Model Factory and Office Building, Werkbund Exhibition, Cologne, Germany.

Le Corbusier, Dom-ino (–1915), mass housing.

T Music

Rutland Boughton, *The Immortal Hour* (opera).

Ernst von Dohnányi, *Variations on a Nursery Song*.

Gustav Holst, *The Planets* (–1916; first performed, 1918).

Charles Ives, *Three Places in New England*.

Henri Rabaud, *Marouf* (opera).

Richard Strauss, *Josephslegende* (ballet).

Ralph Vaughan Williams, Symphony No. 2 ('A London Symphony'), *The Lark Ascending*.

Riccardo Zandonai, *Francesca da Rimini* (opera).

W C Handy, 'St Louis Blues'.

'Keep the Home Fires Burning', by Ivor Novello.

Following fires in music halls and theatres, London County Council bans eating and drinking in such places; music halls lose much of their special character.

Foundation of the American Society of Composers, Authors and Publishers (New York, 13 Feb).

Foundation of the Performing Rights Society in Britain.

U Literature and Drama

Joseph Conrad, *Chance*.

Emily Dickinson, *The Single Hound* (posthumous poems).

Robert Frost, *North of Boston* (poems).

Hermann Hesse, *Rosshalde*.

James Joyce, *Dubliners*.

Sri Ramana Maharshi, *Five Hymns to Arunachala*.

George Moore, *Hail and Farewell*.

Henry Newbolt, *Drake's Drum and other Songs of the Sea*.

Natsume Soseki, *Kokoro*.

Gertrude Stein, *Tender Buttons*.

Rabindranath Tagore, *Balaka*.

Miguel de Unamuno, *Niebla*.

Publication in Chicago, USA, of *The Little Review* (–1929).

Drama:

Percy Mackaye, *The Scarecrow*.

20 Germans occupy Brussels.
21 the British government orders the raising of the first 'New Army' of volunteers.
22 (–23) Battles of Namur and Mons.
22 retired general Paul von Hindenburg is appointed commander of the German Eighth Army in East Prussia.
23 Russian victory at Frankenau, East Prussia.
23 Japan declares war on Germany.
24 British and Belgians retreat from Mons (–Sept 7).
26 French cabinet reconstructed; General Galliéni is appointed governor of Paris.
26 (–28) Germans defeat Russians at Battle of Tannenberg in East Prussia.
27 the German general Liman von Sanders is appointed commander in chief of the Turkish army.
28 British navy, commanded by David Beatty, raids Bight of Heligoland.
28 Austria-Hungary declares war on Belgium.
30 Germans take Amiens.

J **September**
1 in Russia, the name of St Petersburg is changed to Petrograd.
2 French government moved to Bordeaux.
3 Germans cross the River Marne.
5 Pact of London between France, Russia, and Britain, each agreeing not to make a separate peace.
5 (–10) Battle of the Marne; 10 (–13), Germans retreat, stabilizing their line along the River Aisne.
6 (–15) Battle of the Masurian Lakes, East Prussia; Germans drive back the Russians.
8 (–12) Battle of Lemburg: Russians capture Austria-Hungary's fourth largest city.
14 Allies reoccupy Reims.
14 Erich von Falkenhayn succeeds Helmuth von Moltke as German commander in chief.
15 (–18) Battle of the Aisne: Allies attack the German line; the first trenches are dug.
15 in the Pacific, Germans in German New Guinea capitulate to British.
15 in Britain, bill suspends operation of Home Rule and Welsh Church Disestablishment Acts for duration of the war.
15 US troops withdraw from Vera Cruz.
17 (–18 Oct) the 'race to the sea' as Allied and German forces try to outflank each other; this establishes the Western Front, stretching from the North Sea through Belgium and France to Switzerland.
18 Paul von Hindenburg appointed to command all German armies in the East.
27 Russians cross the Carpathians and invade Hungary.
27 Duala in German Cameroons surrenders to British and French.

28 (–27 Oct) First Battle of Warsaw: Germans and Austrians attack Russia troops south of Warsaw, but are driven back.

K **October**
1 Turkey closes the Dardanelles.
9 Antwerp surrenders to Germans.
12 (–11 Nov) on Western Front, First Battle of Ypres (Belgium), when Germans attempt to break the Allied line.
13 Boer rebellion against British in South Africa under Christian de Wet.
14 first Canadian troops land in England.
17 (–30) on Western Front, Battle of Yser in Belgium prevents Germans from reaching Channel ports.
17 first units of Australian Expeditionary Force leave for France.
29 Turkish warships bombard Odessa and Sebastopol.
31 in Mexico, a Congress deposes General Carranza and elects General Carlos Gutierrez as provisional president.

L **November**
1 Battle of Coronel (west of Chile): a German squadron under Maximilius von Spee defeats a British naval force.
2 Russia declares war on Turkey.
3 in USA, large Republican gains in congressional elections.
5 France and Britain declare war on Turkey.
5 Britain annexes Turkish Cyprus, which it has occupied since June 1878.
9 German ship *Emden* sunk off Cocos Islands.
18 on Eastern Front, Germans break Russian line at Kutno.
18 French government starts transfer back to Paris.
21 Indian troops occupy the Ottoman city of Basra.
23 the British navy bombards Zeebrugge.

M **December**
2 Austrians take Belgrade (reoccupied by Serbians, 14).
5 (–17) on Eastern Front, Austrians defeat Russians at battle of Limanova, but fail to break Russian lines before Krakow.
6 on Eastern Front, Germans take Lódź.
8 Battle of the Falkland Islands: British naval force under Admiral Frederick Sturdee destroys German squadron.
17 British protectorate proclaimed in Egypt (18, Khedive Abbas II is deposed and Prince Husein Kemel succeeds him).
21 first German air raid on Britain (when south-coast towns are bombed).
22 (–18 Jan 1915) Turkish army makes unsuccessful attacks on Russian forces in the Caucasus.
26 the German government assumes control of food supplies and allocations.

Lilian Baylis first produces Shakespeare at the Old Vic Theatre, London.

v Births and Deaths

March 12 George Westinghouse dies (67).
May 13 Joe Louis born (–1981).
May 19 Max Perutz born (–).
July 2 Joseph Chamberlain dies (78).
Sept 2 George Brown born (–1985).
Oct 25 John Berryman born (–1972).
Oct 27 Dylan Thomas born (–1953).
Oct 28 Jonas Edward Salk born (–1995).
Nov 14 Frederick, Earl Roberts dies (82).

w Everyday Life

In USA, the 'Copperfield Affair', when the Governor of Virginia sends his secretary to administer the boom town of Copperfield; she closes all saloons within 80 minutes of arrival.

Elastic brassiere invented in New York by Mary Phelps Jacob; it finds much more commercial favour than previous bra designs.

x Sport and Recreation

England wins a second successive Five Nations Rugby Union Grand Slam.

King George V becomes the first reigning British monarch to attend the Football Association Cup Final; he sees Burnley beat Liverpool 1–0 at Crystal Palace (25 April).

Harry Vardon wins a record sixth British Open Golf title at Prestwick (his record still stands).

y Media

In Italy, Benito Mussolini founds the newspaper *Il Popolo d'Italia*.

In USA, foundation of *New Republic* by H D Croly.

Film:

My Official Wife (starring Rudolph Valentino).
The Typhoon (starring Sessue Hayakawa).

Allies invade Turkey ... Sinking of the Lusitania *... Execution of Edith Cavell ...*

A January

3 on Western Front, Germans start use of gas-filled shells.

8 (–5 Feb) on Western Front, heavy fighting in Bassée Canal and Soissons area of France.

12 in USA, the House of Representatives defeats proposal for women's suffrage.

13 South African troops occupy Swakopmund in German South-West Africa.

18 Japan delivers a secret ultimatum to China, demanding mineral and railway rights in the Shandong peninsula and leases in Manchuria.

19 first German Zeppelin airship raid on Britain; East Anglian ports are bombed.

23 (–mid April) on Eastern Front, heavy fighting in the Carpathian Mountains between Russian and Austro-Hungarian forces.

24 in the North Sea, the Battle of Dogger Bank: the British Navy sinks the German cruiser *Blücher*.

28 in USA, President Wilson vetoes immigration bill.

30 first German submarine attack without warning off Le Havre, on the N coast of France.

B February

3 in the Turkish Empire, a British force starts to advance along the River Tigris in Mesopotamia.

4 Germany declares the establishment of a submarine blockade around Britain and Ireland (from 18), and declares that any foreign vessel found is a legitimate target.

4 in Egypt, Turks repulsed from Suez Canal.

4 British Foreign Office announces that any vessel carrying corn to Germany will be seized.

8 (–22) on Eastern Front, Winter Battle of Masuria, in which Germans and Austro-Hungarians force the Russians to retreat.

10 US announces that Germany will be held responsible for any violation of US ships or citizens.

16 (–26) on Western Front, French bombard German forces in Champagne, France.

17 on Eastern Front, in north-west Germany, Germans recapture Memel (modern Klaipeda in Lithuania) from the Russians.

19 British and French fleets bombard Turkish forts at the entrance to the Dardanelles.

C March

6 in Greece, King Constantine dismisses prime minister Eleutherios Venizelos; Demetrios Gournaris forms ministry (Venizelos in office again from Aug to Oct).

10 (–13) on Western Front, Battle of Neuve Chapelle: British and Indian forces capture the village of Neuve Chapelle in NE France.

18 cotton declared an article of contraband.

18 in Turkey, British and French ships attempt to push through the Dardanelles but are repulsed by Turkish gun batteries; three major Allied ships are sunk.

21 German Zeppelin airships make bombing raid on Paris.

22 on Eastern Front, Russians take Przemysl (in the Polish area of NE Austria-Hungary).

D April

8 start of first war-time deportation and massacre of Armenians in Turkey.

22 (–27 May) on Western Front, Second Battle of Ypres: a German offensive pushes the Front in SW Belgium forward by 5 km/3 mi.

22 on Western Front, at Langemark near Ypres, Germans use poison gas from cylinders for the first time.

25 in Turkey, Allied landings on the Gallipoli Peninsula (British and French at Cape Helles; Australians and New Zealanders or ANZACS at Anzac Cove).

26 secret Treaty of London between Britain, France, and Italy; Italy to join war and at its end to be awarded land and reparations from Germany and Austria-Hungary.

26 on Eastern Front, German offensive in Courland (modern Latvia) and, 27, in Lithuania.

E May

1 US vessel *Gulflight* sunk by German submarines without warning.

2 (–30 Sept) on Eastern Front, Austro-German offensive in Galicia (NE Austria-Hungary) breaks Russian lines.

4 Italy denounces its Triple Alliance with Germany and Austria-Hungary (which had been renewed in Dec 1912).

4 (–18 June) on Western Front, Second Battle of Artois: after diversionary British attacks, the French push forward in NE France but gain little.

7 Germans sink the British liner *Lusitania* off the S coast of Ireland; 1,198 perish, including 128 US citizens.

9 (–10) on Western Front, Battle of Aubers Ridge: unsuccessful British attack in NE France.

Einstein's general theory of relativity ... 'Pack Up Your Troubles'
... Death of W G Grace ...

o Politics, Government, Law, and Economy

In Germany, industrialist Walter Rathenau organizes the War Raw Materials Department (Kriegsrohstoffabteilung or KRA), which establishes corporations to oversee the supply of raw materials to industry and procure extra supplies where necessary.

In Britain, production of war material is improved by creation of the Ministry of Munitions.

Lynn Haines, *Your Congress.*

German government takes control of the coal industry (12 July).

Leipzig railway station, the largest in Europe, completed.

P Society, Education, and Religion

National Registration Act in Britain (16 July) requires registration of men eligible for military service (National Register compiled on 15 Aug).

In Britain, enemy aliens are interned (from 14 May).

Denmark introduces universal suffrage (with voting age of 29).

Women magistrates are first appointed in Australia.

Women's Institute (WI) founded in Britain.

In USA, the Congressional Committee splits from its parent body, the National American Woman's Suffrage Association.

In Georgia, USA, William J Simmons revives the anti-black Ku Klux Klan.

Robert La Follette's Seamen's Act to improve conditions in US merchant fleet.

In Salt Lake City, Utah, USA, Joe Hill, organizer for the International Workers of the World, is executed (19 Nov) for murder of a grocer; he is immortalized in song.

Patrick Geddes, *Cities in Evolution.*

B Hutchins [Elizabeth Leigh], *Women in Modern Industry.*

Q Science, Technology, and Discovery

Hugo Junkers makes first all-metal aeroplane.

British Royal Navy uses paravanes as protection of vessels against mines (Oct).

Albert Einstein in Germany publishes his general theory of relativity.

W H and W L Bragg in England show that the atomic structure of crystals can be analyzed from the diffraction patterns of X-rays.

E C Kendall isolates thyroxine from thyroid gland.

The dysentery bacillus is isolated.

Outbreaks of tetanus in the trenches are controlled through serum injections.

K Yamagiwa and K Ichikawa, in Japan, identify the first carcinogen.

A Thorburn, *British Birds* (–1916).

R Humanities

Announcement that excavations at Mohenjo-daro and Harappa in NW India have revealed prehistoric sites (later shown to be centres of the Indus Valley civilization).

Carl L Becker, *The Beginnings of the American People.*

Charles A Beard, *Economic Origins of Jeffersonian Democracy.*

Heinrich Wölfflin, *Principles of Art History.*

Bernard Bosanquet, *Three Lectures on Aesthetic.*

S Art, Sculpture, Fine Arts, and Architecture

US collectors purchase many works of art at Christie's, London, where sales are held to aid British Red Cross.

British publisher Hugh Lane bequeaths works to English and Irish National Galleries.

Painting, etc:

Marc Chagall, *The Birthday.*

Marcel Duchamp, *The Large Glass* or *The Bride Stripped Bare by her Bachelors, Even* (–1923).

Wyndham Lewis, *The Crowd.*

Kasimir Malevich, *Suprematist Composition: Red Square and Black Square.*

Francis Picabia, *Very Rare Picture on the Earth.*

Pablo Picasso, *Harlequin.*

Liubov Popova, *The Philosopher.*

Gino Severini, *Armoured Train.*

Sculpture:

Marcel Duchamp, *In Advance of the Broken Arm.*

Vladimir Tatlin, *Counter-Corner Relief.*

T Music

Alban Berg, *Three Pieces for Orchestra.*

Emmerich Kalman, *The Gypsy Princess* (operetta).

Albert Ketèlbey, *In a Monastery Garden.*

Max Reger, *Variations and Fugue on a Theme of Mozart.*

Jean Sibelius, Symphony No. 5 (first version).

Richard Strauss, *Eine Alpensinfonie* (tone poem).

Alexander Zemlinsky, String Quartet No. 2.

In Britain, Clara Butt sings in aid of the Red Cross.

12 Louis Botha of South Africa occupies Windhoek, capital of German South-West Africa.

14 insurrection in Portugal leads to arrest of the military ruler, General Pimenta de Castro.

15 (–25) on Western Front, Battle of Festubert: unsuccessful British and Canadian offensive in NE France.

15 in Britain, John Fisher, First Sea Lord, resigns, disapproving of the cabinet's Dardanelles policy.

22 worst train disaster in British history, when a troop train hits a local train near Gretna Green, SW Scotland, and a third train hits the wreckage; 157 are killed.

23 Italy declares war on Austria-Hungary and seizes several areas of land belonging to Austria-Hungary.

25 China accepts Japanese ultimatum (of 18 Jan).

26 British Prime Minister Asquith forms a coalition government, with A J Balfour as first lord of the admiralty and Reginald McKenna chancellor of the exchequer; Winston Churchill leaves the admiralty for the chancellorship of Duchy of Lancaster; a new Ministry of Munitions is created with Lloyd George as minister.

27 Turkish government decides to deport Turkey's population of 1.8 million Armenians to Syria and Mesopotamia; a third are deported, a third massacred, and a third evade the order.

29 Theophilo Braga elected President of Portugal.

F **June**

1 first attack of Zeppelin airships on London.

3 on Eastern Front, the Russian southern front collapses with German recapture of Przemysl.

9 US Secretary of State William Jennings Bryan resigns in protest at President Wilson's increasingly belligerent attitude towards Germany (23, Robert Lansing appointed secretary of state).

9 riots in Moscow.

23 German Social Democrats issue manifesto asking for a peace to be negotiated.

23 on Eastern Front, in NE Austria-Hungary, German and Austro-Hungarian forces take Lemberg (modern Lvov, Ukraine) from the Russians.

23 (–7 July) First Battle of the Isonzo: Italians try to force bridgeheads held by Austrians on River Isonzo beyond NE Italy.

G **July**

9 in South-West Africa, German forces surrender to Louis Botha.

18 (–30 Aug) Second Battle of the Isonzo.

27 revolution in Haiti, when President Vilbrun Sam is killed by a mob (28, US marines land to restore order).

H **August**

4 in New Zealand, formation of coalition National Ministry.

5 on Eastern Front, Germans enter Warsaw in Russian Poland.

6 in Turkey, Allied troops land at Suvla Bay, Gallipoli, in an attempt to open a third front; little land is held.

6 Bernadino Machado elected president of Portugal.

25 Italy declares war on Turkey.

26 on Eastern Front, Germans capture Brest-Litovsk in E Russian Poland.

30 following protests from the USA, Germany orders its submarines and ships to warn enemy passenger vessels before sinking them.

J **September**

6 on Eastern Front, Russians check Germans at Tarnopol.

6 Bulgaria signs military alliances with Germany and Turkey.

8 Tsar Nicholas II takes personal command of the Russian armies.

9 the USA asks Austria to recall its ambassador (who leaves New York, 5 Oct).

18 Germany undertakes to withdraw its submarines from the English Channel and western approaches to reduce the danger to US ships.

18 on Eastern Front, Germans capture Vilna (modern Vilnius, Lithuania).

23 Greek army is mobilized.

25 (–Oct 14) on Western Front, Third Battle of Artois: French forces attack the German line in NE France and in Champagne to the SE; the British attack the line at Loos (–4 Nov); only small gains are made.

25 US lends $500 million to Britain and France.

28 British forces, advancing along the River Tigris in Mesopotamia, capture Kut-al-Imara in Mesopotamia.

K **October**

5 Allies land troops at Salonika in neutral Greece to aid Serbia.

6 Bulgaria enters the war on the side of the Central Powers.

6 in Britain, announcement that Lord Derby has been given charge of recruitment for the army (campaign runs to 12 Dec).

7 (–20 Nov) Austria-Hungary renews the invasion of Serbia and captures Belgrade (9 Oct); Serbia's army retreats to the SW;

Remains of Claude Joseph Rouget de Lisle, composer of *La Marseillaise*, are brought to the Invalides, Paris (4 July).

'Pack Up Your Troubles in Your Old Kit Bag', words by George Asaff, music by Felix Powell.

u Literature and Drama

Rupert Brooke, *1914 and Other Poems*.
John Buchan, *The Thirty-Nine Steps*.
Willa Cather, *The Song of the Lark*.
Joseph Conrad, *Victory*.
Norman Douglas, *Old Calabria*.
Ford Madox Ford, *The Good Soldier*.
D H Lawrence, *The Rainbow*.
Somerset Maugham, *Of Human Bondage*.
F Neumann, *Mitteleuropa*.
Ezra Pound, *Cathay* (poems).
Dorothy Richardson, *Pointed Roofs* (first volume of *Pilgrimage*, –1938).
Isaac Rosenberg, *Youth*.
H G Wells, *Boon*.
Virginia Woolf, *The Voyage Out*.

v Births and Deaths

March 21 F W Taylor dies (59).
April 14 Alexander Skryabin dies (43).
May 6 Orson Welles born (–1985).
May 20 Moshe Dayan born (–1981).
June 10 Saul Bellow born (–).
Aug 29 Ingrid Bergman born (–1982).
Sept 26 Keir Hardie dies (59).
Oct 16 J L Sundquist born (–).
Oct 17 Arthur Miller born (–).
Oct 23 W G Grace dies (67).
Oct 24 Tito Gobbi born (–1984).
Nov 12 Roland Barthes born (–1980).
Nov 14 Booker T Washington dies (59).
Dec 12 Frank Sinatra born (–).

x Sport and Recreation

US boxer Jess Willard, known as the 'Great White Hope', wins the World Heavyweight title, knocking out Jack Johnson in the 26th round of their fight in Havana, Cuba (5 April).

Wexford beats Kerry in the All-Ireland Gaelic Football final, the first of four consecutive victories.

In England, Huddersfield Rugby League club wins all four trophies for which it is eligible to compete: the League Championship; the Yorkshire League; the Challenge Cup; and the Yorkshire Cup. It is the second club to achieve this run (following Hunslet in 1908).

Sheffield United beat Chelsea 3–0 in the 'Khaki' Football Association Cup Final at Old Trafford, Manchester; the competition is then suspended for the duration of the War.

y Media

In Britain, end of the Labour newspaper the *Citizen*.

Foundation in Britain of the popular Sunday paper the *Sunday Herald* (later renamed the *Sunday Graphic*).

Lord Beaverbrook buys the *Daily Express* in Britain.

The British paper the *Globe* is suppressed (6–20 Nov) for spreading false rumour about Lord Kitchener's resignation.

Film:

Birth of a Nation (director, D W Griffith).
Carmen (director, C B de Mille).
Fatty and Mabel's Simple Life (starring Fatty Arbuckle).
The Lamb (starring Douglas Fairbanks).
The Meal Ticket (starring Gloria Swanson).
Just Nuts (starring Harold Lloyd).
Les Vampires (director, Louis Feuillade) — 1916.
A Welsh Singer (starring Edith Evans).

Bulgarian troops contain Allied forces in Salonika.

9 conference of Latin American states recognizes Venustiano Carranza as chief of *de facto* government in Mexico (recognized by USA, 19).

12 Germans execute the British nurse Edith Cavell in Brussels for harbouring British and French prisoners and aiding escapes.

12 Allies declare they will assist Serbia under Bucharest treaty of 10 Aug 1913.

12 Greece refuses Serbian appeal for aid under Serbo–Greek treaty of 1913.

13 Théophile Delcassé, French foreign minister, resigns in protest at dispatch of troops to Salonika.

15 Britain declares war on Bulgaria.

19 Japan becomes signatory to the Treaty of London, undertaking not to make a separate peace.

20 J B Hertzog's Nationalist Party's successes in South African elections leave South African Party government in a minority in the House.

21 (–4 Nov) Third Battle of Isonzo: Italians make small gains of territory.

27 in Australia, Andrew Fisher resigns as prime minister, to become High Commissioner in London; succeeded by W M Hughes.

28 René Viviani resigns as prime minister of France (29, Aristide Briand forms ministry).

L November

5 Chinese princes vote for establishment of a monarchy, with Yuan Shikai as emperor.

6 Sophocles Skouloudis forms ministry in Greece favourable to Allies.

10 (–2 Dec) Fourth Battle of the Isonzo.

12 Britain annexes the Gilbert and Ellice Islands (modern Tuvalu and Kiribati), converting the protectorate into a colony.

13 following the failure of the Gallipoli campaign, Winston Churchill resigns from the British cabinet.

21 Italy agrees with the Allies not to make a separate peace.

22 (–4 Dec) Battle of Ctesiphon: Turks force the British invaders of Mesopotamia back to Kut-al-Imara.

M December

3 Joseph Joffre becomes French commander in chief.

8 Turks besiege the British forces at Kut-al-Imara in Mesopotamia.

18 (–19) Allied troops withdraw from Suvla and Anzac on the Gallipoli Peninsula.

19 Douglas Haig succeeds John French as British commander in chief in France and Flanders.

21 William Robertson becomes British chief of staff.

28 British cabinet agrees on principle of compulsory service.

Battle of Verdun ... Easter Rising in Ireland ... Battle of the Somme ...

A January

8 (–9) Allied forces withdrawn from Cape Helles on the Gallipoli Peninsula, Turkey.

8 (–17) Austro-Hungarian attack on Montenegro; the Serbian army flees to Corfu.

10 (–18 April) Russian offensive against Turkey south of the Caucasus.

16 supporters of Mexican rebel 'Pancho' Villa kill 16 US citizens near Chihuahua, N Mexico.

27 conference of British Labour Party votes against conscription.

29 last Zeppelin airship raid on Paris.

B February

2 Boris Stürmer becomes Russian prime minister.

14 Allies guarantee Belgium a place at the peace conference.

15 (–17 March) Fifth Battle of the Isonzo, between Italians and Austro-Hungarians.

16 Russians capture Erzurum in NE Turkey.

18 last German garrison in Cameroons surrenders.

21 (–18 Dec) on Western Front, Battle of Verdun: Germans try to capture the French city of Verdun, but meet determined resistance; the Germans and French suffer about 400,000 casualties each.

29 issue in Britain of first 'Black List' of firms in neutral countries with whom trade is forbidden.

C March

2 Russians capture Bitlis in SE Turkey (reconquered by Turks, 7 Aug).

9 Germany declares war on Portugal.

9 Mexican rebel 'Pancho' Villa and men make incursion into USA, sacking town of

Conscription in Britain ... First woman elected to US House of Representatives ... Tanks introduced to warfare ...

o Politics, Government, Law, and Economy

Cabinet Secretariat is formed in Britain, the first move towards the creation of a prime-ministerial department.

Conscription introduced in Britain, overseen by the new Ministry of National Service.

USA establishes shipping board.

In USA, foundation of the Institute for Government Research.

Act of Congress establishes the National Park Service to manage national parks in the USA.

L Curtis, *The Problem of the Commonwealth*.

G Lowes Dickinson, *The European Anarchy*.

Louis Brandeis appointed to the US Supreme Court, serving until 1939; he is the first Jewish Associate Justice.

Foundation of Boeing aircraft company (by timber merchant William E Boeing) in Seattle, USA.

Rural Credits Act in USA.

V I Lenin, *Imperialism: the Highest Stage of Capitalism*.

p Society, Education, and Religion

War Food Office established in Germany (1 June) to rationalize price controls; the disastrous harvest of 1916 leads to severe rationing and the 'turnip winter' of early 1917.

In Britain, the first Military Service Act (given royal assent on 27 Jan) introduces compulsory military service for single men; a second act (royal assent, 25 May) extends conscription to married men.

In Australia, a proposal to introduce conscrip-

Columbus, New Mexico (19 US citizens are killed).

13 Germany loosens rules governing sinking of ships: submarines can sink British vessels around Britain if they appear not to be passenger ships.

15 US punitive expedition, under command of General John J Pershing, is sent into Mexico to pursue Villa.

15 Alfred von Tirpitz, German secretary of state for the navy, resigns.

17 (–4 Apr) in Scotland, strike of workers in munitions factories along River Clyde.

20 Allies agree on partition of Turkey.

20 Allied air attack on German submarine base at Zeebrugge, Belgium.

22 in China, President Yuan Shikai dies.

24 German submarine sinks the passenger ship *Sussex* without warning; victims include US citizens.

27 French prime minister Aristide Briand opens Paris inter-allied war conference.

D April

18 Russians capture Trebizond in NE Turkey.

20 USA threatens to break off diplomatic relations with Germany.

21 a German submarine lands Roger Casement in Ireland, to try to postpone planned Irish rising (24, is arrested; executed on 3 Aug for high treason).

24 (–29) Easter Rising in Dublin by members of the Irish Republican Brotherhood supported by Sinn Féin (15 leaders are later executed).

29 the Turks recapture Kut-al-Imara from the British.

E May

8 ANZAC troops arrive in France.

15 (–26 June) Asiago offensive: Austro-Hungarians attack Italy, but make few gains.

31 (–1 June) in North Sea, Battle of Jutland: major clash of British and German surface fleets; British lost most ships, but the German fleet remained in harbour for the rest of the war.

F June

4 (–10 Aug) on Eastern Front, the Brusilov offensive: Russian armies commanded by Alexei Brusilov push back the Austro-Hungarian line south of the Pripet Marshes; German reinforcements blunt the attack.

5 death of the British minister for war, Lord Kitchener, when the HMS *Hampshire* is sunk off the Orkney Islands by a German mine while sailing to Russia.

6 (–24) Allies blockade Greece.

6 start of Arab revolt against Turks in Hejaz (now part of Saudi Arabia).

9 Grand Sheriff of Mecca, Hussein, revolts against Turkey; Britain recognizes him as King of the Hejaz.

10 in USA, Republican Convention nominates Charles E Hughes as presidential candidate.

13 Jan Smuts, commander in chief of Allied troops, captures Wilhelmsthal in German East Africa (now Tanzania).

14 Allied economic conference in Paris.

15 in USA, Democratic Convention at St Louis, Missouri, nominates President Wilson as presidential candidate.

17 in Italy, coalition government formed (including Catholics and Reformist Socialists) under Paolo Boselli.

18 on Eastern Front, Russians take Czernowitz (now Chernovtsy in Ukraine).

21 in Mexico, Battle of Carrizal between US and Mexican troops.

23 Greece accepts Allies' demands for demobilization.

23 Convention of Ulster Nationalists agrees to exclude Ulster under Government of Ireland Act.

26 in USA, former president Theodore Roosevelt declines nomination as Progressive Republican presidential candidate.

G July

1 (–19 Nov) on Western Front, Battle of the Somme: massive offensive by French and British troops, which gains 8 km/5 mi; the British army suffers 60,000 casualties (including 20,000 dead) on the first day; during the campaign British and French casualties exceed 620,000 and German casualties amount to about 450,000.

6 in Britain, Lloyd George becomes war secretary in succession to Lord Kitchener.

9 German submarine *Deutschland* reaches the USA, having passed through the Allied naval blockade.

25 Sergei Sazonov, Russian foreign minister, resigns.

26 US protests against British 'Black List' forbidding trading with certain US firms.

H August

4 (–9 Jan) Turks are driven out of Egypt.

4 Danish government agrees to sell the Virgin Islands in the West Indies to the USA; the treaty is opposed in Denmark and is put to a referendum (on 14 Dec; the sale is approved).

6 (–17) Sixth Battle of the Isonzo: Italians advance and take Gorizia from the Austro-Hungarians.

17 (–11 Sept) Bulgarians attack the Allied enclave around Salonika.

tion is rejected by a small majority in a referendum (28 Oct).

In Canada, women magistrates are first appointed.

In elections to the US Congress, Miss Jeanette Rankin is the first woman to be returned, as a member of the House of Representatives for Montana (7 Dec).

Mrs Margaret Sanger opens her first birth-control clinic, in New York (16 Oct).

Reform of family law in Turkey modifies marriage and divorce regulations; women are admitted to university.

The Keating-Owen Act in the USA (signed Sept 1) outlaws work in mines and night-time work by children under 16 and limits day-time work to 8 hours; it also bans interstate commerce in products made by children under 14.

Marcus Garvey travels from Jamaica to the USA to spread his message of celebration of black culture.

New York is the sixth US city to adopt a 'zoning' law; its action is followed by several hundred US cities and towns.

In USA, foundation of the American City Planning Institute.

Stamford–Binet intelligence test compiled; US psychologist Lewis M Terman invents the term 'IQ' for 'intelligence quotient'.

In Britain, report of the Royal Commission on Venereal Diseases finds that 10 per cent of the population in large cities is infected with syphilis, and that for gonorrhea the proportion is much larger.

Wifredo Pareto, *Treatise of General Sociology.*

First Australian correspondence schools founded.

Foundation of the School of Oriental and African Studies, London University.

In Britain, the Committee on the Neglect of Science, led by Ray Lankester, starts press campaign (2 Feb) demanding greater awareness of science in Britain's schools, universities, and civil service.

John Dewey, *Democracy and Education.*

Q Science, Technology, and Discovery

Development of the first effective military tanks (first used in battle at the Somme, France, on 15 Sept).

British scientist Herbert Jackson succeeds in making optical glasses of the same standard as those of the Zeiss works at Jena.

The British government establishes a Department of Scientific and Industrial Research.

A Board of Scientific Societies is sponsored by the Royal Society to promote co-operation in pure and applied science for the service of Britain.

A Michelson in the USA determines that the Earth has a molten core.

British chemist G N Lewis states a new valency theory, which is later stated independently by Kossel.

Treatment of war casualties stimulates development of plastic surgery.

F W Mott develops the theory of shell-shock.

R Humanities

Closure of many British museums and galleries to save manpower, but the press campaigns successfully for keeping the British Museum Reading Room and the Natural History Museum open.

Giovanni Gentile, *General Theory of the Spirit as Pure Act.*

S Art, Sculpture, Fine Arts, and Architecture

In Canada, foundation of the Canadian War Memorials Fund includes scheme organized by Lord Beaverbrook to create an artistic record of wartime activity.

First official war artists commissioned in Britain (scheme expanded in 1917, after Lord Beaverbrook becomes minister of information).

The term 'Dada' is coined in Zurich, possibly by Tristan Tzara; the Dada movement (producing iconoclastic 'anti-art' works) lasts until 1922.

Painting, etc:

Jean Arp, *Collage with Squares arranged according to the Laws of Chance* (–1917).

Georg Grosz, *Metropolis.*

Kasimir Malevich, *Suprematist Composition.*

Henri Matisse, *Piano Lesson.*

Claude Monet, *Water Lilies* (murals at the Musée d'orangerie, Paris). Giorgio Morandi, *Still Life.*

Christopher Nevinson, *Troops Resting.*

Pablo Picasso, designs curtain for *Parade*, a play by Jean Cocteau; the design signals a return to classicism.

Mario Sironi, *The Cyclist.*

Sculpture:

Henri Matisse, *The Back, III.*

Architecture:

Eugène Freyssinet, Airship Hangars at Orly, France (first giant structure in reinforced concrete).

T Music

Manuel de Falla, *Nights in the Gardens of Spain.*

Charles Ives, Symphony No. 4.

Carl Nielsen, Symphony No. 4 ('The Inextinguishable').

19 Royal Navy damages the German battle-ship *Westfalen* in North Sea.

19 Germans bombard the English coast.

27 Romania joins the Allies and declares war on Austria-Hungary; it starts an offensive in Transylvania (then in Hungary).

28 Italy declares war on Germany.

30 Paul von Hindenburg appointed German chief of general staff.

30 Turkey declares war on Russia.

J September

1 Bulgaria declares war on Romania.

4 British troops take Dar es Salaam, the capital of German East Africa (now Tanzania).

6 Central Powers establish a Supreme War Council.

12 (–11 Dec) British and Serbs attack from Salonika, but cannot help Romania.

14 (–18) Seventh Battle of the Isonzo: Italians make small gains.

15 on Western Front, British first use tanks, during the Somme offensive.

25 former Greek prime minister Venizelos leaves Greece for Crete (early Oct, goes to Salonika).

K October

4 (–Dec) in Romania, successful Austro-German counter-offensive.

9 (–12) Eighth Battle of the Isonzo: Italians make small gains.

11 Greece accepts Allies' ultimatum to hand over Greek fleet.

16 Allies occupy Athens.

19 Franco–British conference at Boulogne recognizes Venizelist government of Greece at Salonika.

21 Count Carl Stürgkh, Austrian prime minister, assassinated.

24 (–5 Nov) on Western Front, French offensive east of Verdun.

28 (–10 Feb 1917) Germans forcibly deport 60,000 Belgians to work in Germany.

31 (–4 Nov) Ninth Battle of the Isonzo; Italians gain very little.

L November

5 Central Powers proclaim Kingdom of Poland.

7 Woodrow Wilson, Democrat, is re-elected US president with 277 electoral votes against Charles E Hughes, Republican, with 254 votes; popular vote: Wilson, 9,129,606; Hughes, 8,538,221; A L Benson, 585,113.

13 Cardinal Mercier, Archbishop of Malines in Belgium, protests against deportation of Belgians to Germany for forced labour.

21 death of Emperor Francis Joseph of Austria; succeeded by his grand-nephew as Charles I (–1918).

21 Arthur Zimmermann becomes German foreign minister.

24 in USA, US–Mexican protocol signed at Atlantic City, New Jersey (but, 18 Dec, President Carranza refuses to ratify).

25 Germany's air forces are established as a separate military division.

29 the Sheriff of Mecca, Hussein, is proclaimed King of the Arabs.

29 British government takes over South Wales coalfield under Defence of the Realm Act because of strikes.

29 David Beatty appointed commander in chief of British fleet and John Jellicoe First Sea Lord.

M December

5 in Britain, Lloyd George resigns from Asquith's cabinet after Prime Minister Asquith had rejected his proposal for a war committee not chaired by the prime minister; Asquith resigns several hours later.

6 in Romania, Germans occupy Bucharest (–30 Nov 1918).

7 in Britain, David Lloyd George is appointed prime minister, forms a coalition government, and (on 10 Dec) forms war cabinet, including the Conservatives A J Balfour, Andrew Bonar Law, Lord Curzon, and Lord Milner, and the Labour leader Arthur Henderson.

12 Robert Nivelle is appointed commander in chief of French armies in N and NE France.

12 Aristide Briand forms French War Ministry.

12 US Senate passes Immigration bill, with literacy test clause amended to meet Japanese criticism.

12 Germany's peace note to Allies saying the Central Powers were prepared to negotiate (30, reply sent via US ambassador in Paris).

13 in France, General Joffre is appointed 'technical adviser' to the government without powers of command (26, resigns).

15 (–17) on Western Front, French offensive between Meuse and Woëvre Plain.

19 British government takes control of shipping and of mines.

20 President Wilson of USA issues 'peace note' to belligerents in European war.

31 in Petrograd, Russia, a group of nobles murder Rasputin, the debauched holy man who had considerable influence over Tsarina Alexandra.

31 Allied ultimatum to Greece for withdrawal of forces from Thessaly.

Hubert Parry, *Jerusalem*.

Richard Strauss, *Ariadne auf Naxos* (opera, second version).

Attempt made in Britain to ban German music, but campaign makes little headway.

Nat Ayer, 'If You Were the Only Girl in the World'.

Frederic Norton, *Chu Chin Chow* (first performed at His Majesty's Theatre, London, 31 Aug); it was seen by many British soldiers on leave, and had a record run of 2,238 performances (not exceeded until the 1950s).

Period of emergence of term 'jazz' for syncopated, improvisational, highly rhythmic music of black origin, originating in the southern USA.

u Literature and Drama

John Buchan, *Greenmantle*.

Gabriele D'Annunzio, *La Leda Senza Gigno* (–1918).

Ronald Firbank, *Caprice*.

Robert Frost, *Mountain Interval* (poems).

James Joyce, *Portrait of the Artist as a Young Man*.

Frank Kafka, *Metamorphosis*.

George Moore, *The Brook Kerith*.

Arthur Quiller-Couch, *The Art of Writing*.

George Bernard Shaw publishes 'Prefaces' to *Androcles and the Lion*, *Overruled*, and *Pygmalion*.

Mark Twain, *The Mysterious Stranger* (posthumous).

H G Wells, *Mr Britling Sees it Through*.

Drama:

Leonid Andreyev, *He Who Gets Slapped*.

Algernon Blackwood, *Starlight Express*.

Harold Brighouse, *Hobson's Choice*.

Eugene O'Neill, *Bound East*.

v Births and Deaths

Feb 28 Henry James dies (72).

March 11 Harold Wilson born (–1995).

April 22 Yehudi Menuhin born (–).

May 20 Owen Chadwick born (–).

June 5 Lord Kitchener dies (66).

June 8 Francis Crick born (–).

July 9 Edward Heath born (–).

Sept 29 J M Wallace-Hadrill born (–1985).

Oct 26 François Mitterrand born (–1996).

Nov 14 'Saki' (H H Munro) dies (45).

Nov 21 Franz Joseph dies (86).

w Everyday Life

National Savings movement launched in Britain to raise money for the war effort.

British Summer Time (daylight saving) introduced in Britain.

Liquid nail polish is introduced in the USA.

Introduction in USA of car windscreen wipers.

x Sport and Recreation

Foundation of Professional Golfers Association in USA (17 Jan).

The 6th Olympic Games, scheduled for Berlin, are cancelled due to the War.

y Media

Publication of British edition of the US magazine *Vogue*.

In France, publication of socialist newspaper *Le Populaire*.

Forward, British Labour newspaper, suppressed for inciting Clydeside workers to refuse making munitions.

Film:

Intolerance (director, D W Griffith).

Judex (director, Louis Feuillade).

Love and Journalism (director, Mauritz Stiller).

War Brides (starring Alla Nazimova)

Radio:

American Radio and Research Corporation makes regular broadcasts two or three times a week.

*Revolutions in Russia ... USA declares war on Germany ... Third
Battle of Ypres ...*

A January

1 Britain, France, and Italy recognize the Kingdom of Hejaz in Arabia.

1 Turkey denounces the treaties of Paris, 1856, and Berlin, 1878, which had defined Turkish territories.

16 Greece accepts Allied ultimatum of Dec 1916, demanding withdrawal of forces from Thessaly.

B February

'Turnip winter' in Central Europe, when food shortages cause high mortality.

1 Germany declares policy of unrestricted submarine warfare.

2 bread rationing introduced in Britain.

3 German submarine sinks the US liner *Housatonic* off the coast of Sicily; the USA breaks diplomatic relations with Germany.

12 US President Wilson refuses to reopen negotiations with Germany until it abandons unrestricted naval warfare.

17 in Australia, supporters of Prime Minister Hughes form a coalition government with the Liberals (known as the Commonwealth War Government).

24 British forces in Mesopotamia recapture Kut-al-Imara and then advance along the Tigris.

C March

1 publication in USA of the 'Zimmermann telegram', a message from German Foreign Minister Arthur Zimmermann to the German minister in Mexico City; if war broke out between Germany and the USA, the minister was to propose an alliance with Mexico and support Mexico's reacquisition of territory lost to the USA in 1848.

8 US President Woodrow Wilson, without authority of Congress, orders arming of US merchant ships.

8 US marines land at Santiago, Cuba, at request of civil government.

8 (–14) (old style, 23 Feb–1 March) the 'February Revolution' in Russia: striking workers are joined, on 10, by soldiers; on 14 the Duma establishes a provisional government, headed by Prince G E Lvov.

11 in Mesopotamia, British forces capture Baghdad.

15 in Russia, Tsar Nicholas II abdicates throne for himself and son; his brother Grand Duke Michael refuses the throne, ending the Romanov dynasty's rule.

16 on Western Front, German troops withdraw to the specially constructed 'Hindenburg Line' between Arras and Soissons.

17 (–18) on the Western Front, British capture Bapaume and Péronne.

19 French prime minister Briand resigns; Alexandre Ribot forms cabinet.

20 Imperial war cabinet, of government leaders from British overseas territories, first meets in London.

26 (–8 April) Archibald Murray defeats Turks in Gaza, Palestine.

30 Russian provisional government guarantees independence of Poland.

31 USA finally acquires the Virgin Islands in the West Indies from Denmark, to prevent German acquisition and to protect the Panama Canal.

D April

2 in USA, President Wilson calls special sessions of Congress for declaration of war; 6, USA declares war on Germany.

7 Cuba declares war on Germany.

7 Kaiser Wilhelm II promises universal suffrage in Prussia.

9 (–16) on Western Front, Battle of Arras: British 3rd Army advances 6.5 km/4 mi.

9 (–14), on Western Front, Battle of Vimy Ridge: Canadians take Vimy Ridge.

16 (–9 May) on Western Front, the Chemin des Dames or Nivelle offensive (or Second Battle of the Aisne), along the River Aisne: French forces make tiny advances.

16 food strikes in Berlin.

16 Bolshevik leader Lenin arrives in Petrograd, having travelled with German assistance from Switzerland via Germany, Sweden, and Finland.

17 on Western Front, first mutiny in French army (more serious mutiny on 29; mutinies continue until Aug).

18 (–19) Second Battle of Gaza in Palestine: Turks, with German support, repulse British.

20 USA and Turkey sever relations.

28 in France, Henri Pétain, the hero of Verdun, is promoted to chief of the general staff.

30 British Prime Minister Lloyd George orders the admiralty to experiment with convoys of British merchant shipping.

E May

5 British foreign secretary A J Balfour is first non-American to address the US House of Representatives; he eulogizes democratic institutions.

12 (–8 June) Tenth Battle of the Isonzo: Italians make some advances.

*Draft introduced in USA ... Debut of Bertie Wooster and Jeeves
... Death of 'Buffalo Bill' ...*

o Politics, Government, Law, and Economy

In USA, the Liberty Loan Act (passed 24 April) authorizes the issue of war bonds.

Other wartime legislation in the USA includes the Espionage Act (passed 15 June), under which people can be fined or imprisoned for hindering the war effort; the federal government also takes control of railways (Dec).

The US government establishes several agencies to regulate its war effort: the War Industries Board, under financier Bernard M Baruch, coordinates war production (July 1917; reorganized March 1918); the Food Administration, under Herbert Hoover as chief, boosts food production and exports to the Allies; the Fuel Administration increases coal and oil production.

The US Congress passes the Jones Act or Organic Act for Puerto Rico (2 March) whereby the island becomes a US territory and its inhabitants have the rights of US citizens.

In USA, income tax revenues pass the total of customs duties collected for the first time.

Establishment of British Ministry of Labour and of a Civil Aerial Transport Committee.

H Fernau, *The Coming Democracy*.

V I Lenin, *The State and Revolution*.

The US Supreme Court in effect overrules Lochner v. New York (1905) *sub silentio* and upholds a state law regulating hours on health grounds in Bunting v. Oregon.

Completion of trans-Australian railway (started 1912).

In Russia, the Bolshevik government allow workers' committees to supervise businesses and nationalizes banks (27 Dec).

P Society, Education, and Religion

The Selective Service Act in the USA (passed 18 May) requires every male between 21 and 30 to register for the draft on 5 June; local boards will select about half a million men for service.

Second referendum in Australia seeking support for conscription is defeated (20 Dec).

A new constitution in Mexico provides means for the expropriation of land, stated rights for workers, and limits the role of the Catholic Church.

In Russia, following their seizure of power, the Bolsheviks abolish large landed estates without compensation and confiscate possessions of the royal family, the church, and monasteries (8 Nov).

In USA, New York is the first eastern state to enfranchise women.

In USA, 48 people (39 black and 9 white) are killed in race riots in East St Louis, Illinois.

Marcus Garvey establishes the New York Division of the United Negro Improvement Association; it expands to become the largest mass movement in African-American history.

Publication in USA of the radical African-American paper *The Messenger* (–1928).

School Certificate and Higher School Certificate examinations introduced in England and Wales.

In USA, the Smith–Hughes Act establishes a Federal Board of Vocational Education.

Pope Benedict XV promulgates a new code of canon law (which had been largely completed by Pius X), the *Codex Iuris Canonici*; Benedict appoints a committee to interpret the code.

Pope Benedict XV issues a seven-point peace plan, but it is unacceptable to all participants in the war.

In Russia, the provisional government of Alexander Kerensky approves a new constitution for the Russian Orthodox Church (Aug).

Basil Tikhon is elected Patriarch of Moscow (Oct).

Maude Royden becomes Assistant Preacher at the City Temple, London, the first Englishwoman to have a permanent pulpit.

Rudolph Otto, *The Idea of the Holy*.

Q Science, Technology, and Discovery

In USA, Clarence Birdseye develops freezing as a method for preserving food.

Institute of Technical Optics founded in South Kensington, London.

Radioactive element proactinium is independently discovered by three research groups.

R Humanities

History issued (journal of Britain's Historical Association).

Frank Hrozny, *The Hittite Language*.

J L and B Hammond, *The Town Labourer, 1760–1832*.

Benedetto Croce, *History: Its Theory and Practice*.

S Art, Sculpture, Fine Arts, and Architecture

French official war artists are assigned to particular zones or projects.

Pablo Picasso's sets and costumes for Sergei Diaghilev's ballet *Parade* are described by

15 in France, Nivelle is dismissed as commander in chief and replaced by Henri Pétain; Ferdinand Foch replaces Pétain as chief of the general staff.

18 Prince Lvov reforms cabinet in Russia to include socialists; Alexander Kerensky becomes minister of war.

22 Count Tisza, Hungarian prime minister, resigns.

23 Duan Qirui, prime minister of China, is dismissed.

F **June**

2 Brazil revokes its neutrality and seizes German ships.

3 Albanian independence under Italian protection is proclaimed.

7 (–14) on Western Front, Battle of Messines Ridge: British clear ground in SE Belgium for major offensive.

10 (–26) Italians attack Austro-Hungarians in the Trentino.

10 Sinn Féin riots in Dublin.

12 following demand from Allies, King Constantine I of Greece abdicates in favour of second son, Alexander (–1920).

14 American Expeditionary Force, commanded by General John J Pershing, arrives in France.

14 US mission under E Root arrives in Petrograd, to encourage continued Russian participation in war.

15 British government grants amnesty to those imprisoned after Easter Rising in Dublin, 1916.

16 first all-Russian congress of Soviets ('councils') held in Petrograd.

18 (–13 July) on Eastern Front, Russian minister of war, Alexander Kerensky, launches the Kerensky offensive: a series of attacks against the Germans, which are quickly repulsed.

19 British royal family renounces German names and titles, having adopted name of Windsor.

24 Russian Black Sea fleet mutinies at Sebastopol.

26 Eleutherios Venizélos returns from Salonika to Athens as prime minister.

29 Edward Allenby takes over command of British forces in Palestine.

29 Greece declares war on the Central Powers.

G **July**

12 Duan Qirui resumes Chinese premiership.

14 Theobald von Bethmann-Hollweg resigns as German chancellor; succeeded by George Michaelis.

16 (–17) in Petrograd, mass demonstrations against the provisional government; Bolsheviks attempt to encourage an insurrection, but crowds melt away.

19 (–4 Aug) on Eastern Front, counter-offensive by Germans and Austro-Hungarians; the Russian line is pushed back.

19 Zeppelin airships attack English industrial areas.

19 Reichstag passes motion for peace.

20 Corfu Declaration by representatives seeking state for Serbs, Croats, and Slovenes.

21 in Russia, Alexander Kerensky replaces Prince Lvov as prime minister.

25 in Dublin, meeting of Irish Convention of different Irish interests to seek scheme for self-government (Convention is enfeebled by absence of Sinn Féin and Ulster Unionist intransigence).

31 (–10 Nov) on Western Front, Third Battle of Ypres (or Battle of Passchendaele): British forces in Belgium advance about 13 km/8 mi at cost of massive casualties.

H **August**

1 Richard von Kühlmann becomes German foreign minister.

3 mutiny of sailors at German naval base of Wilhelmshaven.

3 on Eastern Front, Russians retake Czernowitz (now Chernovtsy in Ukraine).

11 Labour Party leader Arthur Henderson resigns from the War Cabinet, following disagreement over policy towards Russia.

13 revolt in Spain for home rule for Catalonia.

14 China declares war on Germany and Austria.

14 Pope Benedict XV makes unsuccessful attempt to arrange peace in European war.

17 (–12 Sept) Eleventh Battle of the Isonzo: Italians make minor advances.

25 (–28) in attempt to increase support for the Russian provisional government, Alexander Kerensky holds a State Conference in Moscow.

J **September**

In China the Guomindang party under Sun Yat-sen organizes its own provisional government, based in Guangzhou.

1 (–5) on Eastern Front, German offensive leads to occupation of Riga on River Dvina (now in Latvia).

9 General Lavr Kornilov, dismissed as Russian commander in chief, sends cavalry force to Petrograd; submits to delegates from soviets and workers (Kornilov is later arrested).

9 (–16) serious unrest at British training camp at Etaples in NE France.

12 in France, Paul Painlevé forms cabinet.

14 in Russia, prime minister Kerensky declares a republic.

Guillaume Apollinaire as 'Surrealist' — first use of the term.

Piet Mondrian launches *de Stijl* magazine in Holland.

Following the Bolshevik Revolution in Russia, all art collections are nationalized, all art academies are closed, and modernist art is officially patronized by the new State.

Painting, etc:
Giorgio de Chirico, *Disquieting Muses*.
Georg Grosz, *Homage to Oskar Panizza* (–1918).
Pablo Picasso, *Portrait of Olga in an Armchair*.

Sculpture:
Marcel Duchamp, *Fountain* — submitted under a pseudonym, R Mutt, for an exhibition organized by the Society of Independent Artists — is a signed urinal.

т Music
Arnold Bax, *Tintagel*.
Gabriel Fauré, Violin Sonata No. 2.
Hans Pfitzner, *Palestrina* (opera).
Sergei Prokofiev, Symphony No. 1 ('Classical').
Giacomo Puccini, *La Rondine* (opera).
Ottorino Respighi, *The Fountains of Rome*.
Erik Satie, *Parade* (ballet).
Jascha Heifetz, the Russian-born violinist, makes his debut in the USA (at Carnegie Hall, New York), aged 16 (27 Oct).
Oh, Boy! (musical), lyrics by P G Wodehouse, music by Jerome Kern (first performed at the Princess Theatre, New York, 20 Feb).
'Over There' by George M Cohan.
In USA, the Original Dixieland Jazz Band, an all white group from New Orleans, takes jazz to New York for the first time and makes the first jazz record with the Victor Talking Machine Company (including 'Original Dixieland One-step').
In USA, closure of Storyville in New Orleans, the area of the city where prostitution was licensed and jazz flourished (some jazz musicians move to Chicago and other cities).

u Literature and Drama
Lawrence Binyon, 'For the Fallen' (poem).
Norman Douglas, *South Wind*.
Arthur Conan Doyle, *His Last Bow*.
T S Eliot, *Prufrock and Other Observations* (poems).
Knut Hamsun, *Growth of the Soil*.
Henry James, *The Middle Years* (posthumous).

Juan Ramón Jiménez, *Diary of a Newly Married Poet*.
Frank Swinnerton, *Nocturne*.
Paul Valéry, *La jeune parque*.
Alec Waugh, *The Loom of Youth*.
Mary Webb, *Gone to Earth*.
P G Wodehouse, *The Man with Two Left Feet* (collection of stories in which Jeeves and Wooster first appear).
In USA, Pulitzer Prizes are first awarded (for literature, journalism, and music).

Drama:
Guillaume Apollinaire, *Les Mamelles de Tirésias*.
J M Barrie, *Dear Brutus*.
Luigi Pirandello, *Liola*.

v Births and Deaths
Jan 10 William F Cody ('Buffalo Bill') dies (70).
March 1 Robert Lowell born (–1977).
March 8 Ferdinand, Count Zeppelin dies (79).
April 1 Scott Joplin dies (48).
May 20 Richard Cobb born (–).
May 29 John F Kennedy born (–1963).
Aug 9 Ruggiero Leoncavallo dies (59).
Aug 30 Denis Healey born (–).
Sept 26 Edgar Degas dies (83).
Oct 15 Arthur Schlesinger, Jr, born (–).
Oct 21 'Dizzy' Gillespie born (–1993).
Nov 17 Auguste Rodin dies (77).
Nov 19 Indira Gandhi born (–1984).
Dec 17 Elizabeth Garrett Anderson dies (81).

w Everyday Life
In Britain, two new public honours are founded, the Companion of Honour and Order of the British Empire.
Women's need to cut hair short for work in factories leads to a fashion for the 'bob'.

y Media
In Russia, following the Bolshevik Revolution, *Pravda* becomes the leading newspaper, as mouthpiece of the Bolshevik (Communist) Party; *Izvestiya* is also founded.

Film:
The Butcher Boy (starring Buster Keaton).
The Girl from Stormycroft (director, Victor Sjöstrom).
A Poor Little Rich Girl (starring Mary Pickford).
Thomas Graal's Best Film (director, Mauritz Stiller).

29 (–1 Oct) German aircraft attack London on successive nights.

к October

6 in Russia, the Petrograd Soviet elects Trotsky as chairman; he establishes a committee to plan an insurrection.

15 Germans renew offensive in East Africa at Battle of Mahiwa.

15 execution in St Lazare, France, of French dancer Mata Hari (Gertrud Margarete Zelle), who had been convicted of spying for the Germans.

22 in Russia, Congress of Soviets passes resolution calling for armistice.

24 (–10 Nov) on the Italian Front, the Battle of Caporetto: Austro-Hungarians and Germans break the Italian line; Italians regroup along the River Piave.

28 Vittorio Orlando becomes Italian prime minister.

L November

1 Count von Hertling appointed German chancellor.

2 British foreign secretary A J Balfour issues the 'Balfour declaration' on Palestine in a letter to Lord Rothschild: Britain favours the establishment of a national home for the Jewish people without prejudice to non-Jewish communities.

5 (–9) Allied conference at Rapallo, NW Italy, decides on Supreme Allied War Council (which first meets, 29, at Versailles).

6 on Western Front, in SW Belgium, Canadians and British capture Passchendaele Ridge.

7 (old style, 26 Oct) in Russia, the 'October Revolution': Lenin and Bolsheviks seize the Winter Palace in Petrograd, overthrowing the provisional government.

7 at meeting of All-Russian Congress of Soviets in Petrograd, most Menshevik and other socialist walk out, leaving the Bolsheviks in control; Lenin forms a Soviet of People's Commissars (composed of Bolsheviks) to be the new government.

7 in Middle East, British take Gaza.

8 Lenin becomes chief of commissars of people and Trotsky is appointed prime minister.

10 (–12) in Russia, Kerensky's counter-revolution fails.

16 on Paul Painlevé's fall as prime minister of France, Georges Clemenceau forms cabinet.

17 in Palestine, British take Jaffa from Turks.

20 (–7 Dec) on Western Front, Battle of Cambrai, the first major battle involving tanks: a British tank force breaks the German line at Cambrai in NE France (British forces are then repulsed by the Germans).

20 Ukrainian republic proclaimed.

26 Russian Soviet government offers armistice to Germany and Austria.

29 in Britain, publication in the *Daily Telegraph* of letter from Lord Lansdowne, a former foreign secretary, advocating a compromise peace with Germany; Prime Minister Lloyd George rejects the proposal, declaring there is 'no half-way house between defeat and victory'.

м December

1 German East Africa cleared of German troops.

5 German and Russian delegates sign armistice at Brest-Litovsk (in modern Belarus).

6 Finland declares independence from Russia as republic (recognized by Russia's Bolshevik government).

7 USA declares war on Austria-Hungary.

9 Romania signs armistice with Central Powers at Focsani.

9 British led by Edmund Allenby capture Jerusalem from the Turks.

10 Italians torpedo Austrian battleship *Wien* in Trieste.

12 worst train crash in history: a passenger train leaves the rails at Modane, France, killing 543.

17 Robert Borden becomes Canadian prime minister after Unionist election victory.

21 start of peace negotiations at Brest-Litovsk between German and Russian delegates.

26 Bolsheviks establish a government in Kharkov in the Ukraine to rival the established rada in Kiev.

28 Bessarabia proclaims its independence as the Moldavian republic (modern Moldova).

28 US government takes control of railways.

President Wilson's 14 Points ... Treaty of Brest-Litovsk ...
Armistice on the Western Front ...

A **January**

4 Joseph Caillaux, former prime minister of France, is arrested and imprisoned on suspicion of planning coup and seeking a premature peace (sentenced to imprisonment April 1920).

8 in message to US Congress, Woodrow Wilson propounds Fourteen Points for peace settlement (including principles of national self-determination, free trade, open diplomacy, and foundation of a league of nations).

16 strike begins in Vienna.

18 Russian Constituent Assembly opens in Petrograd but, 19, is dispersed by Bolsheviks.

20 Turkish ship *Breslau* sunk near Dardanelles after making sortie in Mediterranean (the sister ship *Goeben* is damaged).

26 in Finland, left wing of Social Democratic Party seizes control in Helsinki and proclaims the Finnish Workers' Socialist Republic (suppressed in March by Germans and Finns).

27 Russia denounces British–Russian treaty of 1907.

28 (–3 Feb) strike in Berlin.

28 Bolsheviks occupy Helsinki, Finland.

28 in Russia, Bolsheviks issue decree founding the Red Army.

31 Russia adopts the 'New Style' Gregorian calendar.

B **February**

8 Bolshevik invaders capture Kiev in the Ukraine, forcing Ukrainian leaders to flee to Germans for help.

20 (–23) inter-allied Labour and Socialist conference in London.

21 Australians occupy Jericho.

25 meat and butter rationed in London and Southern England.

C **March**

British force lands in Murmansk, Russia.

1 Germans occupy Kiev in the Ukraine and, on 2, Narva in Estonia.

3 peace treaty of Brest-Litovsk between Russia and the Central Powers (Germany and Austria-Hungary): Russia cedes Baltic Provinces and Russian Poland to Central Powers and recognizes independence of Finland and the Ukraine; Turkey to take former Russian districts of Kars, Ardahan, and Batum.

3 the Bolsheviks move the Russian capital from Petrograd to Moscow, so that it is farther from the Germans.

6 (–8) 7th Congress of the Bolshevik Party, which approves the signing of the treaty of Brest-Litovsk and changes the party's name to Russian Communist Party.

12 Turks occupy Baku in Azerbaijan (–14 May).

21 (–17 July) on Western Front, German Spring offensive: Germans make great advance towards Paris.

23 (–15 Aug) Germans use massive gun to shell Paris from 120 km/75 mi away.

23 Lithuania proclaims independence from Russia.

26 French prime minister Clemenceau and Milner for Britain make the Doullens agreement, giving Ferdinand Foch command over French and British armies.

D **April**

1 in Britain, foundation of the Royal Air Force as separate military force (replacing the Royal Flying Corps).

8 (–10) meeting in Rome of representatives of Czecho-Slovaks, Romanians, Yugoslavs, and Poles.

14 agreement with Allies for US troops to fight as single army under command of General Pershing and under supreme command of Foch.

14 on Russians' withdrawal, Germans occupy Helsingfors (modern Helsinki, Finland).

19 Alfred Milner becomes British war secretary.

21 German air ace Manfred von Richthofen ('the Red Baron') is shot down.

22 (–23) raid by British ships on Zeebrugge, Belgium, blocks entrance to Bruges Canal and German submarine base (10 May, the British cruiser *Vindictive* is sunk at the entrance to the Ostend submarine base).

E **May**

1 Germans occupy Sebastopol on the north side of the Black Sea.

6 Allied break-through in Albania.

7 Romania signs the Peace of Bucharest with Germany and Austria-Hungary; Romania is allowed to annexe Bessarabia (but Russia refuses to recognize the annexation).

7 in Britain, letter by Major-General Sir Frederick Maurice published in *The Times* alleges that ministers gave misleading statements about military manpower to the House of Commons (9, Prime Minister Lloyd George defends the government in debate).

Strachey's Eminent Victorians ... *Ponselle's debut at the 'Met'* ...
Tarzan of the Apes ...

o Politics, Government, Law, and Economy

Oswald Spengler, *The Decline of the West*, Volume 1 (Volume 2 published in 1922).

The 8th Congress of the Russian Communist Party (March) establishes the Political Bureau ('Politburo'), Organization Bureau, and Secretariat.

New constitution adopted in Russia (10 July), as basic document of the new Russian Soviet Federated Socialist Republic (RSFSR).

In Britain, the Labour Party adopts a constitution (drafted by Sidney Webb and Arthur Henderson), which includes 'clause IV' seeking 'Common Ownership of the Means of Production' (Feb).

Australia introduces the 'alternative vote' system in elections.

Overman Act empowers US president to reorganize executive departments (14 May).

In Hammer v. Dagenhart the US Supreme Court strikes down a federal statute against child labour on the grounds that Congress has power over interstate commerce, not manufacturing.

In Russia, the Bolshevik government decrees the nationalization of industry (June).

p Society, Education, and Religion

Food shortage in Britain leads to establishment of National Food Kitchens (March) and rationing (14 July); the prime minister appeals to women to help with the harvest (25 June).

'Spanish flu' epidemic (–Spring 1919) kills at least 20 million people in Europe, America, and India.

Women over 30 achieve the right to vote in Britain, as do all men aged over 21 previously barred by residence and property qualifications.

In USA, Michigan, South Dakota, and Oklahoma enfranchise women.

'Fisher' Education Act raises school leaving-age in Britain to 14 and advocates part-time Day Continuation classes for school leavers.

In Russia, the Bolshevik People's Commission for Education publishes a radical blueprint for free, compulsory, non-religious schooling.

Progressive Education Association founded in USA.

In USA, University of North Dakota founded.

University Edict authorises the establishment of private and municipal universities and colleges in Japan.

Separation of Church and State decreed in Russia (2 Feb); antireligious riots are widespread.

q Science, Technology, and Discovery

Asdic sonar apparatus invented.

Telescope at Mount Wilson, California, USA, is first used.

Arthur Eddington, *Gravitation and the Principle of Relativity*.

r Humanities

Carl L Becker, *The Eve of the Revolution*.

Ulrich B Phillips, *American Negro Slavery*.

Lytton Strachey, *Eminent Victorians*.

W R Inge, *The Philosophy of Plotinus*.

Moritz Schlick, *General Theory of Knowledge*.

s Art, Sculpture, Fine Arts, and Architecture

Amédée Ozenfant and Le Corbusier, *Après le Cubisme*, a manifesto on 'Purism'.

Dada art spreads to Berlin (–1923).

Painting, etc:

Raoul Hausmann, *Men are Angels and Live in Heaven*.

Paul Klee, *Gartenplan*.

Kasimir Malevich, *La Cavalerie Rouge au Galop* (–1930), *Suprematist Composition: White on White*.

Paul Nash, *We are making a New World*.

Alexander Rodchenko, *Black on Black*.

Architecture:

Willis Polk, Hallidie Building, San Francisco, USA — continuous curtain wall of glass and steel.

Erich Mendelsohn, Einstein Tower, Potsdam, Germany (–1920) — Expressionist architecture.

t Music

Béla Bartók, *Duke Bluebeard's Castle* (opera).

Percy Grainger, *Country Gardens*.

Charles Griffes, *The Pleasure Dome of Kubla Khan*.

Giacomo Puccini, *Il Trittico* (opera).

Franz Schreker, *Die Gezeichneten* (opera).

Anton Webern, *Four Songs with Orchestra*.

US soprano Rosa Ponselle makes her debut at the Metropolitan Opera, New York.

The Original Dixieland Jazz Band records 'Tiger Rag'.

18 British planes make bombing raids on Germany.

23 Georgia proclaims independence from Russia.

29 on Western Front, Germans capture Soissons and Reims.

F **June**

9 (–13) on Western Front, German offensive near Compiègne.

15 (–23) Battle of the Piave: Austro-Hungarians attack the Italian line but are repulsed.

17 food riots in Vienna.

21 British government announces abandonment of Home Rule and conscription for Ireland.

G **July**

6 Montagu–Chelmsford Report on Constitution of India published, advocating that Indian ministers be given charge of aspects of provincial government.

13 Turkish offensive in Palestine checked.

15 (–17) on Western Front, Second Battle of the Marne: Allies halt the German advance towards Paris.

16 in Russia, execution at Ekaterinburg (now Sverdlovsk) of ex-Tsar Nicholas II and family on orders of Ural Regional Council.

18 (–10 Nov) on Western Front, Allied counteroffensive against Germans (with strong forward movement from 8 Aug).

22 on Western Front, Allies cross the River Marne.

H **August**

British forces land at Archangel, Russia.

2 on Western Front, the French recapture Soissons.

2 Japanese advance into Siberia.

3 British force lands at Vladivostok, Russia.

8 on Western Front, 'the black day of the German army', when British forces break the German line.

15 USA and Russia sever diplomatic relations.

J **September**

1 on Western Front, British take Péronne.

4 on Western Front, Germans retreat to Siegfried Line.

10 in India, Muslim riots in Calcutta.

12 (–16) on Western Front, Battle of St Mihiel: the US 1st Army under Pershing captures the St Mihiel salient.

14 Austro-Hungarian peace offer (which Allies refuse, 20).

14 in USA, leading socialist Eugene V Debs is sentenced to 10 years' imprisonment for violating the Espionage Act (10 March 1919, Supreme Court upholds the conviction).

15 Allied break-through in Bulgaria.

22 collapse of Turkish resistance in Palestine.

29 Belgians capture Dixmude, Belgium.

29 the German quartermaster general, Ludendorff, and commander in chief, Hindenburg, advocate that Germany should become a constitutional monarchy and approach the Allies for an armistice.

30 Bulgaria signs armistice with Allies.

30 George, Count Hertling, German chancellor, resigns.

K **October**

1 British and Arab forces occupy Damascus.

1 on Western Front, French take St Quentin.

3 Prince Max of Baden appointed German chancellor.

3 (–4) German–Austrian note to USA, via Switzerland, suggesting armistice based on President Wilson's Fourteen Points.

6 French occupy Beirut.

9 on Western Front, British take Cambrai and Le Cateau.

12 Germany and Austria agree to Woodrow Wilson's terms and that their troops should retreat to their own territory before an armistice is signed.

13 Laon falls to French and, 17, Lille to British troops.

14 Turks pass message to President Wilson proposing an armistice.

19 Belgians recapture Zeebrugge and Bruges.

20 Germany suspends submarine warfare.

24 (–2 Nov) Battle of Vittorio Veneto: conflict on Italian front leads to collapse of Austro-Hungarian army.

26 Ludendorff resigns as quartermaster general of German army.

27 Austria-Hungary asks Italy for an armistice.

28 mutiny of German sailors at Kiel.

30 Allies sign armistice with Turkey on the warship *Agamemnon* at Mudros.

30 Czechoslovakia proclaimed as an independent republic in Prague.

31 Hungarian prime minister, Count Tisza, is assassinated.

L **November**

1 British and French forces occupy Constantinople.

2 riots in Vienna and Budapest.

3 Allies sign armistice with Austria-Hungary (to come into force on 4).

3 riots and risings in Germany.

4 Allied conference at Versailles agrees on peace terms for Germany.

5 US Congressional elections result in Republican majority of 43.

6 German armistice commission meets Allied delegation under Foch in railway

First visit by a US jazz band to Britain, The Jazz Boys.

Establishment around this time of 78 revolutions per minute as the standard playing speed for records.

u Literature and Drama

Alexander Blok, *The Twelve*.

Rupert Brooke, *Collected Poems* (posthumous).

Gerard Manley Hopkins, *Poems* (posthumous).

Laurence Housman, *The Sheepfold*.

W H Hudson, *Far Away and Long Ago*.

Wyndham Lewis, *Tarr*.

Siegfried Sassoon, *Counter Attack*.

Booth Tarkington, *The Magnificent Ambersons*.

Rebecca West, *The Return of the Soldier*.

Drama:

John Drinkwater, *Abraham Lincoln*.

James Joyce, *The Exiles*.

Luigi Pirandello, *Six Characters in Search of an Author*.

v Births and Deaths

Jan 15 Gamal Abdel Nasser born (–1970).

Jan 26 Nicolae Ceauşescu born (–1989).

March 6 John Redmond dies (61).

March 25 Claude Debussy dies (55).

April 25 Ella Fitzgerald born (–).

May 11 Richard Feynman born (–1988).

Aug 25 Leonard Bernstein born (–1990).

Sept 27 Martin Ryle born (–1984).

Nov 7 Billy Graham born (–).

Dec 2 Edmund Rostand dies (50).

Dec 11 Alexander Solzhenitsyn born (–).

Dec 23 Helmut Schmidt born (–).

Dec 25 Anwar Sadat born (–1981).

Nelson Mandela born (–).

w Everyday Life

In Britain, standard clothing for male civilians is made by Board of Control of Textile Industries.

USA introduces Daylight Saving.

Three-colour traffic lights installed in New York.

x Sport and Recreation

Lady Jane Douglas becomes the first woman to own a Derby winner, Gainsborough.

Volleyball is introduced to Europe by American troops.

y Media

In Britain, the *Daily Chronicle* is purchased by a syndicate fronted by Sir Henry Dalziel and organized by the prime minister, David Lloyd George.

Film:

The Eyes of the Mummy (director, Fritz Lang).

Tarzan of the Apes (the original version, starring Elmo Lincoln).

carriage in Compiègne, France; armistice negotiated (to be effective from 11).

6 Polish republic proclaimed in Kraków.

6 on Western Front, US troops occupy Sedan.

7 Republic proclaimed in Bavaria, Germany.

9 to forestall the proclamation of a communist republic in Germany, the Social Democrat Philipp Scheidemann proclaims a republic; Max Ebert replaces Prince Max as chancellor; Kaiser Wilhelm II flees to the Netherlands.

10 in Germany, Ebert's government receives the support of the armed forces and of the workers' and soldiers' councils of Berlin.

11 armistice between Allies and Germany in force (from 11 am).

11 provisional government in Estonia proclaims independence.

12 Emperor Charles I abdicates in Austria (and, 13, in Hungary).

12 Austria proclaims union with Germany (subsequently forbidden by the Paris Peace Conference in the Treaties of Versailles, St Germain, and Trianon).

13 Soviet government annuls treaty of Brest-Litovsk.

13 in Egypt, organization of the nationalist Wafd Party, initially to provide for a delegation of Egyptians to attend the Paris Peace Conference.

14 British Labour Party decides to secede from coalition government.

14 German troops in Northern Rhodesia surrender.

14 Tomás Masaryk elected President of Czechoslovakia.

18 German troops evacuate France.

18 in Russia, Admiral Alexandr Kolchak establishes an anti-Bolshevik dictatorial regime at Omsk.

18 Belgian troops enter Brussels and Antwerp.

18 National Council proclaims independence of Latvia.

19 in Berlin, Ebert (now Chairman of the Council of People's Commissars) persuades the Congress of Soldiers' and Workers' Councils to agree to elections for a national assembly (to be held on 19 Jan 1919).

20 Germans surrender submarines at Harwich, E England (21, surrender surface fleet at Firth of Forth, Scotland).

22 in Britain, Prime Minister Lloyd George and Conservative leader Bonar Law issue coalition election manifesto.

23 in Berlin, sailors occupy the chancellery and take Ebert prisoner (24, Ebert is rescued by soldiers from Potsdam).

26 National Assembly in Montenegro proclaims the deposition of King Nicholas and the union of Montenegro with Serbia.

27 Red Army takes Narva in Estonia and invades Estonia.

29 in Berlin, Independent Socialists resign from the government, leaving Ebert and his Majority Socialists free to suppress revolutionary forces.

M December

Allied forces under French command land at Odessa and other ports in the Ukraine.

1 start of Allied occupation of Germany.

1 Convention of Romanians in Transylvania proclaims union with Romania (2, provisional government established).

1 Iceland becomes a sovereign state.

4 National Council proclaims formation of Kingdom of Serbs, Croats, and Slovenes with Alexander I (son of King Peter of Serbia) as prince-regent (country renamed Yugoslavia in 1929).

5 Germans blockade Baltic.

6 in Germany, Allies occupy Cologne.

8 Bolshevik rule in Estonia.

14 in British general election, Coalition has majority of 249: Coalition Conservatives, 335, Coalition Liberals, 133, Coalition Labour, 10 (total Coalition, 478); Irish Unionists, 25; Irish Nationalists, 7; Conservatives, 23; Liberals, 28; Labour, 63; Sinn Féin, 73; others, 10.

14 Sidonio Paes, President of Portugal, assassinated.

14 Woodrow Wilson arrives in Paris for peace conference.

20 Berlin conference of workers' and soldiers' delegates demands nationalization of industries.

27 Poles occupy Posen (modern Poznań, Poland).

30 Members of the Spartacists in Germany found the German Communist Party.

*Unrest in Germany ... Paris Peace Conference ... US Senate
rejects Peace Treaty ...*

A **January**

3 Herbert Hoover of USA becomes director-general of Commission for Relief and Reconstruction of Europe.

4 Bolsheviks take Riga (in Latvia).

5 (–15) Communist (Spartacist) revolt in Berlin.

5 in Germany, formation of German Workers' Party in Munich (12 Sept, Adolf Hitler attends for first time).

7 British Labour Party decides to go into opposition.

10 British army takes over administration of Baghdad Railway.

10 (–4 Feb) Soviet Republic of Bremen, NW Germany.

15 volunteer soldiers suppress the Spartacist rising in Berlin; the Spartacist leaders, Karl Liebknecht and Rosa Luxemburg, are arrested and shot.

17 Ignacy Paderewski becomes prime minister of Poland (resigns 18 May).

18 opening of Paris Peace Conference under chairmanship of Georges Clemenceau.

19 in Germany, elections are held for the national assembly: Social Democrats (38 per cent) and Centre Party (19 per cent) win largest proportions of vote.

21 Sinn Féin MPs elected to the Westminster parliament meet in Dublin as a constituent assembly for Ireland (the Dáil Eireann); they proclaim an Irish Republic and elect a president (Éamon de Valera) and ministers; meanwhile the Irish Republican Army (IRA) attacks British authorities in Ireland.

22 Czechs occupy the Teschen area (now in SW Poland), to press claim to part of Silesia.

25 Paris Peace Conference adopts principle of founding League of Nations.

29 Czechoslovakians defeat Poles in Galicia.

B **February**

3 (–9) Anton Denikin's White Russian army routs Bolsheviks in the Caucasus.

3 President Woodrow Wilson of USA presides at first League of Nations meeting, Paris.

3 international socialist conference, Berne, Switzerland.

6 Bolsheviks capture Kiev, Ukraine.

6 in Germany, national assembly convenes at Weimar (11, elects Friedrich Ebert as president of Germany; 12, Philipp Scheidemann forms ministry of Social Democrats and Centre Party members).

14 Woodrow Wilson lays League of Nations Covenant before Paris Peace Conference (adopted 25 March).

14 Bolsheviks invade Estonia.

20 Emir of Afghanistan murdered.

21 in Germany, Kurt Eisner, Bavarian prime minister, is assassinated in Munich.

28 in USA, Senator H C Lodge begins campaign against League of Nations.

C **March**

10 in Egypt, nationalist riots in Cairo, after British authorities deport nationalist leader Saad Zaghlul.

16 Karl Renner, Socialist, appointed chancellor of Austria.

21 Edmund Allenby becomes British high commissioner in Egypt.

22 Soviet government formed in Budapest, Hungary.

23 in Italy, Benito Mussolini founds Fasci d'Italiani di Combattimento; i.e., the Italian Fascist movement.

D **April**

4 Philippines demand independence from USA.

4 Soviet Republic established in Bavaria (–1 May).

5 Éamon de Valera is elected president of the Sinn Féin Dáil executive (suppressed Sept).

7 Allies evacuate Odessa, Ukraine.

8 Red Army enters Crimea.

10 (–14) riots in Portugal.

13 in N India, the 'Amritsar Massacre': following riots in Amritsar, Gurkha troops in British army fire on a crowd, killing 379 and wounding over 1,200.

28 German delegates arrive at Paris Peace Conference.

30 Paris Peace Conference grants German concession in Shandong peninsula to Japan, whereupon China leaves the Conference.

E **May**

In Russia, the Red Army begins counteroffensive against 'White' forces.

1 great strike in Winnipeg, Canada (–15 June).

1 Bavarian government troops capture Munich from Communists.

3 start of war between British India and Afghanistan following Afghanistan's demand for complete independence (8 Aug, peace agreement at Rawalpindi concedes independence).

Communist Third International founded ... Race riots in Chicago
... Alcock and Brown fly across the Atlantic ...

o **Politics, Government, Law, and Economy**

The Treaty of Versailles (signed 28 June) requires Germany to pay reparations for damage caused during the war and establishes the League of Nations and the International Labour Organisation.

Germany establishes a Ministry of Economics.

Communist Third International founded to encourage world revolution; affiliation to this body marks the split between socialist and communist movements and Parties.

Henry Campbell Black, The Relation of the Executive Power to Legislation.

In US Supreme Court, Schenck v. US establishes the 'clear and present danger' test for the restriction of free speech.

Abrams v. US, in the US Supreme Court, upholds convictions for inciting resistance to the war effort under the Espionage Act.

J M Keynes, *The Economic Consequences of the Peace*.

British parliament passes Imperial Preference Provisions Act (22 Aug).

Britain sets up Coal Commission under Lord Sankey (2 Feb; reports 23 June).

Rapid growth in the economy and share values in Britain and several other countries.

Bankruptcy of Canadian Grand Trunk Pacific Railway (9 March); is nationalized in 1920.

Anglo-American Corporation of South Africa founded by Ernest Oppenheimer to exploit the Witwatersrand goldfield.

p **Society, Education, and Religion**

In USA, the States ratify the 18th Amendment to the Constitution (29 Jan), which outlaws the manufacture, transport, and sale of alcoholic drinks (to take effect on 16 Jan 1920).

A referendum in New Zealand rejects Prohibition of alcohol (11 April).

Norway introduces Prohibition of alcohol (6 Oct).

Women are allowed to work as government clerks in France.

Women over 20 are enfranchised by the 'Weimar' German constitution.

In Britain, Lady Nancy Astor is elected in a by-election (28 Nov) and becomes the first woman Member of Parliament to take her seat.

W E B Du Bois convenes the first Pan-African Congress.

Marcus Garvey founds the Black Star Line, a black shipping company (–1922).

Race riots in Chicago, USA, cause the deaths of 38 people.

Delegates from American Expeditionary Force, meeting in Paris (15 March), found the American Legion organization of veterans, to support veterans' welfare and the defence of the USA.

International Labour Conference, inaugurating the International Labour Organisation, is held in Washington, DC, USA (opens 29 Oct).

Housing Act allows local authorities to issue bonds; the start of large-scale public housing in Britain.

In France, the Astier Laws make part-time technical education compulsory for young workers.

'Burnham' standing committee on teachers' salaries established in England.

University Grants Committee established in Britain.

Enabling Act in England brings the Anglican Church Assembly into existence.

Karl Barth, *The Epistle to the Romans*.

Henri Bergson, *L'Energie spirituelle*.

Martin Dibelius, *From Tradition to Gospel*.

Dean W R Inge, *Outspoken Essays*.

q **Science, Technology, and Discovery**

British aviators J W Alcock and A W Brown make the first trans-Atlantic flight, in 16 hrs 27 mins (14–15 June).

Ross Smith flies from London to Australia in 135 hours (10 Dec).

E Shackleton, *South*, an account of his 1914–17 expedition.

First successful helicopter flight.

First motor scooter.

Observations by Arthur Eddington of the total eclipse of the sun (29 May) bear out Albert Einstein's theory of relativity.

J and V Bjerknes introduce the term 'front' in meteorology.

Ernest Rutherford's 'transmutation', producing a simpler atom from a complex one.

F W Aston in England builds mass-spectograph and establishes the phenomena of isotopy.

T H Morgan, *The Physical Basis of Heredity*.

r **Humanities**

J B Huizinga, *The Waning of the Middle Ages*.

H L Mencken, *The American Language*.

C B Fawcett, *Provinces of England*.

J L and B Hammond, *The Skilled Labourer, 1760–1832*.

Edward S Corwin, *John Marshall and the Constitution*.

Leonard Woolf, *Empire and Commerce in Africa: A Study in Economic Imperialism*.

4 outbreak of riots in Beijing and other Chinese cities on news that the Paris Peace Conference had confirmed Japanese holdings in China.

6 Paris Peace Conference disposes of Germany's colonies, assigning German East Africa as a League of Nations mandate to Britain, and German South-West Africa as a mandate to South Africa.

7 at Paris Peace Conference, Allies present terms to Germany without giving opportunity for negotiation: Germany to lose large areas of land; Rhineland to be demilitarized and part occupied for 5–15 years; Germany to pay reparations; limits placed on size of Germany's armed forces; Germany to accept the 'war guilt' clause acknowledging responsibility for World War I.

15 with Allied support and protection of Allied ships, a Greek force occupies Smyrna (modern Izmir in Turkey).

28 Armenia declares independence.

29 Germany's delegates make counter-proposals to Paris Peace Conference.

30 at Paris Peace Conference, Britain agrees on transfer of part of German South-West Africa to Belgium.

F June

3 British reinforcements reach Archangel, Russia.

6 Finland declares war on Bolshevik Russia.

9 in Russia, Red Army takes Ufa.

10 Austria protests against terms of Peace Conference.

19 in Turkey, Mustafa Kemal and other nationalist leaders sign the Amasia Protocol, declaring their determination to resist the Allies' plans for Turkey and the Sultan's cooperation with them.

20 fall of German chancellor, Scheidemann, for opposition to peace treaty (21, Gustave Bauer, Social Democrat, forms cabinet comprising Social Democrats, Centre, and Democrats).

21 Francesco Nitti becomes prime minister of Italy.

21 German sailors scuttle fleet at the British Scapa Flow naval base in the Orkney Islands.

22 German national assembly at Weimar authorizes signature of peace treaty.

28 German representatives sign the peace treaty in the Hall of Mirrors of the Palace of Versailles near Paris.

28 Britain and USA guarantee France in event of an unprovoked German attack (US later refuses to ratify).

G July

12 Britain and France authorize resumption of commercial relations with Germany.

12 Irish MP Edward Carson demands repeal of Home Rule and threatens to call out Ulster Volunteers.

19 peace celebrations in Britain.

23 congress of Turkish nationalists convened at Erzurum, under leadership of Mustafa Kemal, to resist Allied dismemberment of Turkey (second congress held 4 Sept).

27 (–31) race riots in Chicago, followed by race riots and lynchings throughout the USA.

H August

1 Hungarian Socialist regime under Béla Kun overthrown.

4 (–14 Nov) Romanians occupy Budapest, Hungary.

5 in Canada, Mackenzie King is elected leader of Liberal Party.

6 Archduke Joseph becomes 'state governor' of Hungary (23, resigns on Allies' demand).

9 British–Persian agreement at Tehran to preserve integrity of Persia.

11 in Germany, the national assembly promulgates the 'Weimar constitution'.

14 revised constitution for Bavaria, Germany.

22 in New Zealand, break-up of coalition government (Massey remains prime minister of Reform Party government).

23 US Senate committee rejects clause of Versailles Treaty giving German concession in Shandong peninsula, China, to Japan.

31 press censorship abolished in Ireland.

J September

1 the US Socialist Party, meeting in Chicago, splits; factions form a Communist Party and a Communist Labor Party.

2 Anton Denikin's White Russian army enters Kiev, Ukraine.

10 Allied peace treaty agreed with Austria at St Germain-en-Laye, near Paris.

12 Gabriele d'Annunzio leads unofficial Italian army to seize Fiume before it is incorporated in Yugoslavia.

15 China terminates war with Germany.

22 steel strike in USA (–Jan 1920).

25 in USA, President Wilson, on a speaking tour, breaks down in Denver (2 Oct, suffers stroke).

25 Paris Peace Conference grants Norway sovereignty over the island of Spitzbergen in the Arctic Ocean.

27 British troops are withdrawn from Archangel, Russia.

Karl Kautsky, *The Dictatorship of the Proletariat.*

M Schlick, *Space and Time in Contemporary Physics.*

A N Whitehead, *Enquiry Concerning the Principles of Natural Knowledge.*

s Art, Sculpture, Fine Arts, and Architecture

The Bauhaus (School of Design, Building, and Crafts) founded by Walter Gropius in Weimar (transferred to Dessau, 1925).

First international Dada fair held, Berlin, Germany.

Painting, etc:
Marcel Duchamp, *L H O O Q.*
Raoul Hausmann, *The Art Critic* (–1920).
Fernand Léger, *Men in the City.*
El Lissitzky, *Beat the Whites with the Red Wedge.*
Amedeo Modigliani, *The Blue Nude*, *Portrait of Jeanne Hébuterne.*
Alfred Munnings, *Zennor Hill.*
Pablo Picasso, *Pitcher and Compotier with Apples*, sets for *The Three-Cornered Hat.*
Kurt Schwitters, *Merzpicture 36 Cuba Button* (–1920).

Sculpture:
Ernst Barlach, *Veiled Beggar Woman.*
Wax and plaster figures of dancers and horses, created by Edgar Degas 1890–1912, are cast in bronze.

Architecture:
Vladimir Tatlin, Monument to the Third International — model for Tatlin's Tower, early avant garde example of momumental architecture.

T Music
Hugo Alfvén, Symphony No. 4.
Edward Elgar, Cello Concerto.
Manuel de Falla, *The Three-Cornered Hat* (ballet).
Fritz Kreisler, *Apple Blossoms* (operetta).
André Messager, *Monsieur Beaucaire* (operetta).
Richard Strauss, *Die Frau ohne Schatten* (opera).
In San Francisco, USA, Paul Whiteman forms his own jazz orchestra.
The Original Dixieland Jazz Band makes its debut in London (7 April).

U Literature and Drama
Sherwood Anderson, *Winesburg, Ohio.*
Vicente Blasco Ibáñez, *The Four Horsemen of the Apocalypse.*

James Branch Cabell, *Jurgen.*
André Gide, *La Symphonie pastorale* (Two Symphonies).
Thomas Hardy, *Collected Poems.*
Hermann Hesse, *Demian.*
Rudyard Kipling, *Verse: Inclusive Edition.*
Somerset Maugham, *The Moon and Sixpence.*
Ezra Pound, *Quia Pauper Amavi.*
John Reed, *Ten Days that Shook the World.*
Shimaxaki Toson, *Shinsei/A New Life.*
Arthur Waley, *170 Chinese Poems.*

Drama:
George Bernard Shaw, *Heartbreak House.*
In New York, foundation of The Theatre Guild, a theatre production company using subscriptions as the basis for mounting productions.

V Births and Deaths
Jan 6 Theodore Roosevelt dies (60).
Jan 14 Giulio Andreotti born (–).
Feb 17 Wilfrid Laurier dies (78).
May 16 Liberace born (–1987).
May 18 Margot Fonteyn born (–1991).
June 6 Peter, Lord Carrington born (–).
July 15 Iris Murdoch born (–).
July 20 Edmund Hillary born (–).
July 31 Primo Levi born (–1987).
Aug 11 Andrew Carnegie dies (83).
Aug 27 Louis Botha dies (57).
Aug 28 G N Hounsfield born (–).
Oct 18 Pierre Trudeau born (–).
Oct 22 Doris Lessing born (–).
Oct 26 Muhammad Reza Shah Pahlavi born (–1980).
Nov 23 P F Strawson born (–).
Sept 27 Adelina Patti dies (76).
Dec 3 Pierre-Auguste Renoir dies (78).

X Sport and Recreation
The American Professional Football Association, comprising 14 teams, is formed at Canton, Ohio, USA.
Suzanne Lenglen, minus corsets, dominates the Wimbledon Lawn Tennis tournament in London.
US boxer Jack Dempsey, 'the Manassa Mauler', wins the World Heavyweight title, beating Jess Willard in three rounds in Toledo, Ohio, USA (4 July).
A record 1,580 crown-green bowlers enter the Talbot Handicap, held at Blackpool, NW England.
In USA, the Chicago White Sox lose the Baseball World Series to the Cincinnati Reds; eight Sox players ('The Black Sox') are subsequently banned for life for conspiracy to 'throw' the match.
The Royal and Ancient Golf Club (at St Andrews, Scotland) assumes responsibility

27 the Allied powers decide to refer the Polish–Czech dispute over part of Silesia to a plebiscite.

K October

10 referendum in Luxembourg votes in favour of the monarchy and for economic union with France.

12 British troops are withdrawn from Murmansk, Russia.

13 in Russian civil war, Anton Denikin's White Russian army captures Orel, SW of Moscow, but is soon driven out by the Red Army.

13 dock strike in New York.

22 in Russian civil war, Bolshevik Red Army defeats White army under Nicolai Yudenich, a Russian counter-revolutionary, near Petrograd (Yudenich retreats to Estonia).

27 Lord Curzon succeeds A J Balfour as British foreign secretary.

27 (–8) US President Woodrow Wilson vetoes Volstead Prohibition Enforcement bill, but House and Senate overturn his veto.

28 dissolution of British war cabinet.

L November

7 Allied Supreme Council demands withdrawal of Romanian troops from Hungary.

11 two minutes' silence in memory of war victims first observed in Britain.

15 in Russia, the Bolshevik Red Army takes Omsk.

19 US Senate votes against ratification of the Treaty of Versailles, thereby leaving the USA outside the League of Nations.

21 Allied Supreme Council gives Poland mandate over Galicia for 25 years.

27 Peace of Neuilly between the Allies and Bulgaria.

28 Latvia declares war on Germany.

M December

5 Serbo–Croat–Slovene Kingdom (Yugoslavia) agrees to peace treaties with Austria and Bulgaria.

9 US delegates leave Paris Peace Conference.

13 in Russia, Soviets capture Kharkov from the White Army of Anton Denikin.

15 Fiume, Yugoslavia, declares independence.

16 German troops evacuate Latvia and Lithuania.

20 US House of Representatives moves to curtail immigration.

League of Nations inaugurated ... President of Mexico assassinated ... Bolsheviks victorious in Russian Civil War ...

A January

5 Poles and Letts capture Dvinsk (Daugavpils, now in Lithuania) from the Bolsheviks.

8 in Russia, the White army leader Alexander Kolchak is defeated at Krasnoyarsk (7 Feb, executed by Bolsheviks).

10 ratification of the Treaty of Versailles brings the League of Nations into existence, with 29 initial members (out of 32 Allied signatories to the Versailles Treaty; the exceptions are the USA, China, Ecuador, and Nicaragua).

10 Eupen and Malmédy united with Belgium (ratified by plebiscites later in the year).

16 first meeting of the League of Nations' Council in Paris.

16 in USA, Prohibition comes into force.

16 US Senate votes against joining the League of Nations.

17 Paul Deschanel is elected president of France (takes office on 18 Feb).

23 The Netherlands declines to surrender ex-Kaiser Wilhelm II as demanded by the Supreme Allied War Council.

28 the new Turkish parliament, containing a nationalist majority, issues the pact of Ankara affirming the integrity of Turkish territory, based on the resolutions of the nationalist congresses of 1919.

B February

2 in treaty signed at Tartu in Estonia, Russia recognizes independence of Estonia and renounces claims.

8 Bolsheviks capture Odessa in the Ukraine.

9 Allies formally cede Spitsbergen in the Arctic Ocean to Norway (takes formal possession on 14 Aug 1925).

10 plebiscite in Schleswig north zone favours unification with Denmark (14 March, voters in middle zone favour union with Germany).

for managing the British Open Championship.

The first commercial greyhound race track is opened in Emeryville, California, USA.

γ Media

The *New York Daily News* is published as a tabloid paper.

In Britain, Arthur Mee founds the *Children's Newspaper*.

London Mercury founded.

Film:

Hans Vogt experiments with sound film system.

Charlie Chaplin, Douglas Fairbanks, and D W Griffith found United Artists (17 April).

Film industry in Russia is nationalized.

The Cabinet of Dr Caligari (director, Robert Wiene).

J'Accuse (director, Abel Gance).

Leaves from Satan's Book (director, Carl Dreyer).

Madame Dubarry (director, Ernst Lubitsch).

The Spiders (director, Fritz Lang) — 1920.

Radio:

In USA, the General Electric Company creates the Radio Corporation of America (RCA), to take over the American Marconi Company.

Ponzi swindle in USA ... US women enfranchised ... First radio stations ...

○ Politics, Government, Law, and Economy

Following the establishment of the League of Nations, numerous countries become members (Argentina, 13 Jan; Switzerland, 13 Feb; Norway, 5 March; Denmark, 8 March; Netherlands, 10 March; Austria, 3 Dec; Bulgaria, Costa Rica, Finland, and Latvia, 16 Dec; Albania, 17 Dec).

The Hague is selected as seat of the International Court of Justice (25 June).

Royal Institute of International Affairs (Chatham House) founded in London.

Oswald Spengler, *Prussianism and Socialism*.

In Ireland, the British government reinforces with Royal Irish Constabulary with ex-soldiers, known as 'Black and Tans' from their temporary uniforms (withdrawn after truce of Dec 1921).

Oliver Wendell Holmes, *Collected Legal Papers*.

A deflationary Budget and a rise in Bank Rate halt the economic boom in Britain and prices and output fall steeply while unemployment rises over one million, where it remains for the entire interwar period; the US economy also suffers a sharp slump.

Agricultural Act establishes farm price supports in Britain.

National Economic Council established in Germany.

System of works councils established in Germany, giving workers a share in control of management.

Esch–Cummins Act in the USA returns railways to private ownership and management (1 March).

In USA, the 'Ponzi swindle' is exposed: Charles Ponzi defrauds over 20,000 investors of over $10 million with a scheme for using International Reply Coupons to make large profits; no money was in fact invested.

Forest coverage in the USA reaches its historic low point.

13 following dispute with President Wilson, Robert Lansing resigns as US secretary of state (25, Bainbridge Colby is appointed).

15 Allies take over Memel (modern Klaipeda) in Lithuania.

26 in accordance with the Treaty of Versailles, the League of Nations takes over the Saar area between France and Germany; France takes control of the Saar's coal deposits.

27 Allies announce that Turkey will retain Istanbul, but the Dardanelles will be under international control.

28 Hungarian and, 29, Czechoslovak constitutions are adopted.

c March

1 Nicholas Horthy elected regent of Hungary, pending a possible restoration of the monarchy.

10 Ulster Unionist Council votes to accept the Government of Ireland Bill, partitioning Ireland into two states, north and south, each with its own Home Rule parliament.

11 national congress in Syria proclaims Feisal (third son of King Hussein of the Hejaz) king of an independent Syria.

13 (–17) in Germany, the 'Kapp Putsch': the US-born German journalist Wolfgang Kapp and military supporters seize Berlin; the government flees but the conspirators cannot establish their authority in the face of a general strike.

16 Allied forces in Istanbul, Turkey, arrest nationalists and the Sultan closes the parliament; some nationalists escape to Ankara.

19 the US Senate rejects the Versailles Treaty (and attached reservations).

27 following the 'Kapp Putsch', Gustav Bauer resigns as German chancellor and is succeeded by Hermann Müller (also a Social Democrat).

28 Bolsheviks take Novorossiisk on Black Sea; collapse of Anton Denikin's White Russian army.

d April

In Mexico, revolt begins against President Carranza provoked by his intention to force through the election of his nominee for president.

6 (–17 May) while German troops are suppressing a rebellion in the Ruhr (a demilitarized area) French troops occupy Frankfurt, Darmstadt, and Hanau until German forces have withdrawn.

23 opening of new Turkish assembly at Ankara, which elects Mustafa Kemal as president of the assembly and a new government (the assembly proclaims a new

constitution, the Law of Fundamental Organization).

25 Supreme Allied Council disposes of territories formerly in the Ottoman (Turkish) Empire: it assigns mandates over Mesopotamia and Palestine to Britain and over Syria and the Lebanon to France.

25 Polish offensive in the Ukraine under Józef Piłsudski against Russia (–12 Oct).

30 conscription abolished in Britain.

E May

5 Treaty of Berlin between Germany and Latvia.

8 in the Ukraine, Poles and Ukrainians enter Kiev.

20 assassination of President Carranza of Mexico (in response the US government suspends diplomatic relations); Adolfo de la Huerta takes office as provisional president.

27 in USA, President Wilson vetoes the Knox peace resolution terminating state of war with Germany.

27 Leonid Krassin, Soviet trade delegate, arrives in London

F June

4 Treaty of Trianon between the Allies and Hungary: removes various territories from Hungary; imposes limits on Hungary's armed forces; requires Hungary to pay reparations.

6 in Germany, the first elections held after the signing of the Treaty of Versailles produce a swing away from the Social Democrats and Centre towards extremist parties.

12 in USA, Republican Convention at Chicago nominates Warren G Harding for presidency and Calvin Coolidge for vice-presidency.

21 in Germany, Konstantin Fehrenbach of the Centre Party becomes chancellor; his coalition government of Social Democrats and Centre Party members is joined by members of the People's Party.

21 Supreme Allied Council agrees that Germany shall make 42 annual reparations payments largely to France, Britain, Italy, and Belgium.

G July

1 Robert Borden, prime minister of Canada, resigns because of ill health (10, succeeded by Arthur Meighen).

5 in USA, Democratic convention in San Francisco, California, nominates James M Cox for presidency, F D Roosevelt for vice-presidency.

P Society, Education, and Religion

Widespread famine in China (7 Nov–21 Dec).

In Mexico, following the new constitution of 1917, some land is redistributed and the government supports organized labour; the government also launches a school-building programme and commissions work by revolutionary artists.

Ratification in USA (on 26 Aug) of the 19th Amendment to the Constitution, permitting women to vote.

Formation of the League of Women Voters in USA.

Canada introduces universal suffrage (with voting age of 21).

League of Women Voters founded in the USA.

Foundation in USA of the American Civil Liberties Union.

In USA, James Weldon Johnson is appointed the first African-American secretary of the National Association for the Advancement of Colored People.

Land boom in Florida, USA (during the early 1920s), resulting from the construction of roads enabling tourists to visit the state during winter elsewhere.

Ralph Borsodi establishes a subsistence homestead outside New York city, symbolizing the 'back to the land' movement.

Max Weber, *The Protestant Ethic and the Spirit of Capitalism*.

In England, the Convocation of Oxford University passes statute admitting women to degrees (11 May); the University admits its first women members (7 Oct); Cambridge University rejects a proposal to admit women to full membership (8 Dec).

In USA, University of Maryland founded.

Percy Nunn, *Education: Its Data and First Principles*.

Pope Benedict XV canonizes Joan of Arc (16 May).

In England, first Anglo-Catholic Congress held in the Albert Hall, London.

Jacques Maritain, *Art and Scholasticism*.

Q Science, Technology, and Discovery

US gunsmith J T Thompson invents the sub-machine gun.

Baade discovers the planet Hidalgo, which orbits farthest from the sun.

R Goddard in America publishes the mathematics of rocket propulsion.

A Michelson in America makes first measurement of the size of a star other than the sun.

R Humanities

H G Wells, *Outline of History*.

F J Turner, *The Frontier in American History*.

Carl L Becker, *The United States: An Experiment in Democracy*.

Canadian Historical Review published.

Roger Fry, *Vision and Design*.

Samuel Alexander, *Space, Time, and Deity*.

John Dewey, *Reconstruction in Philosophy*.

A N Whitehead, *The Concept of Nature*.

S Art, Sculpture, Fine Arts, and Architecture

In Russia, Stalin's disapproval of the avant-garde leads to the departure of some artists; Kasimir Malevich and Vladimir Tatlin remain.

Antoine Pevsner and Naum Gabo issue the *Realistic Manifesto*, containing the principles of European Constructivism.

Bernard Leach establishes Leach Pottery at St Ives, Cornwall, England.

Spectators at the Exhibition of Dadaist art in Cologne, Germany, are provided with an axe to smash paintings.

Painting, etc:

Max Beckman, *Carnival*.

Juan Gris, *Guitar, Book and Newspaper*.

Pablo Picasso, *Seated Woman*.

Kurt Schwitters, *Spring Picture*.

Mario Sironi, *The White Horse and the Pier*.

Sculpture:

Ernst Barlach, *The Refugee*.

T Music

Leoš Janáček, *The Adventures of Mister Brouček* (opera).

Albert Ketèlbey, *In a Persian Market*.

Erich Korngold, *Die tote Stadt* (opera).

Darius Milhaud, *Le Boeuf sur le toit* (ballet).

Maurice Ravel, *La Valse*.

French critic Henri Collet refers to the group of composers comprising Darius Milhaud, Francis Poulenc, Arthur Honegger, Louis Durey, Germaine Tailleferre, and Georges Auric as 'Les Six'.

Marie Rambert founds the Rambert School of Ballet in London, leading to the establishment of the Marie Rambert Dancers.

Mamie Smith is first African-American singer to make a record (10 Dec), with 'Crazy Blues' by Perry Bradford (over one million copies sold in six months).

First electro-acoustic recording made, in London.

HMV, in Britain, makes the record autochanger.

U Literature and Drama

Sherwood Anderson, *Poor White*.

Agatha Christie, *The Mysterious Affair at Styles* (introducing Hercule Poirot).

5 (–16) Spa Conference between Allies and Germany on reparations.

5 Schleswig is transferred from Germany to Denmark.

6 Britain evacuates Batumi in Georgia.

6 (–12 Oct) start of Russian war with Poland.

8 Britain annexes East African Protectorate as Kenya Colony (a crown colony).

11 plebiscite in East and West Prussia: 97 per cent vote to remain in Germany.

12 peace treaty between Russia and Lithuania: Russia recognizes Lithuania's independence.

21 Sinn Féin supporters and Unionists riot in Belfast.

21 in Syria, King Feisal recognizes French mandate.

24 treaty of St Germain (signed 19 Sept 1919), comes into force.

25 France occupies Damascus, Syria; King Feisal leaves the country.

25 Greeks under King Alexander occupy Adrianople.

27 in Polish–Russian War, Russians take Pinsk and cross into Poland.

28 Teschen agreement between Czechoslovakia and Poland signed in Paris.

H August

8 Russia rejects proposal for armistice with Poland.

9 British Labour organizations appoint Council of Action to arrange general strike if Britain declares war on Russia.

10 Treaty of Sèvres between the Allies and Turkey; the Treaty awards part of eastern Thrace, the district of Smyrna (modern Izmir) and other territory to Greece.

10 New States treaty between Allies, Romania, Czechoslovakia, and Poland; and frontier treaty with Romania, Czechoslovakia, and the Kingdom of the Serbs, Croats, and Slovenes (Yugoslavia).

10 treaty between Greece and Italy assigns Dodecanese Isles to Greece.

11 Riga treaty between Russia and Latvia: Russia recognizes Latvia's independence.

14 Yugoslav–Czechoslovak alliance, which is joined, 17, by Romania to form the 'Little Entente'.

14 (–16) in Polish–Russian War, Poles defeat Russians at Warsaw.

18 the Milner–Zaghlul agreement: following discussions between Lord Milner for Britain and the Egyptian nationalist leader Saad Zaghlul, Britain agrees in principle to recognize the independence of Egypt provided that the two countries make a close alliance.

19 in Polish–Russian War, Poles enter Brest-Litovsk.

J September

In Italy, the 'occupation of the factories' when half a million steel and engineering workers occupy their factories and try to run them themselves; Prime Minister Giolitti intervenes and forces management to make concessions.

5 Alvaro Obregón is elected president of Mexico (takes office on 1 Dec).

7 Franco–Belgian military convention.

10 Russian–British negotiations are suspended owing to alleged Russian attempt to subsidize the British newspaper the *Daily Herald*.

16 bomb explodes on Wall Street, New York, killing about 30 people and injuring about 200.

23 Alexandre Millerand elected president of France as successor to Paul Deschanel (had resigned because of ill health, 16).

K October

1 new Austrian constitution.

9 Poland annexes Vilna (Vilnius in modern Lithuania).

10 plebiscite in the former Habsburg duchy of Carinthia favours Austria.

12 Russian–Polish peace treaty signed at Tartu (in Estonia).

20 Treaty of Ankara between France and Turkey.

20 US–Chinese tariff treaty.

27 Poland signs treaty with Danzig (modern Gdansk).

27 League of Nations headquarters are moved to Geneva.

L November

2 in US presidential election, Warren G Harding, Republican, wins with 404 electoral votes against James M Cox, Democrat, with 127; popular vote: Harding, 16,152,200; Cox, 9,147,353; Eugene V Debs, Socialist (in prison), 919,799.

12 by treaty of Rapallo, Italy obtains Istria and cedes Dalmatia to the Kingdom of the Serbs, Croats, and Slovenes (Yugoslavia); Fiume is to be independent.

14 in Greece, general election results in a crushing defeat for the supporters of prime minister Venizélos.

14 in Russia, the Red Army takes Sebastopol in the Crimea.

15 Danzig (modern Gdańsk) is proclaimed a free city (in early Dec its constitutional assembly is proclaimed the city parliament).

16 end of Russian civil war, with victory to the Bolsheviks.

17 Dowager Queen Olga becomes Regent of Greece.

Colette, *Chéri.*
John Galsworthy, *In Chancery.*
Franz Kafka, *The Country Doctor.*
Sinclair Lewis, *Main Street.*
Katherine Mansfield (pseudonym), *Bliss.*
Wilfred Owen, *Collected Poems.*
Sigrid Undset, *Kristin Lavransdatter* (–1922).
Paul Valéry, *Le Cimetière marin.*
Edith Wharton, *The Age of Innocence.*

Drama:
An-ski, *The Dybbuk.*
Karel Čapek, *R U R.*
John Galsworthy, *The Skin Game.*
Eugene O'Neill, *Beyond the Horizon.*
E Temple Thurston, *The Wandering Jew.*

v Births and Deaths
Jan 2 Isaac Asimov born (–1992).
Jan 20 Federico Fellini born (–1993).
May 18 Karol Wojtyla (Pope John Paul II) born (–).
June 14 Max Weber dies (56).
Oct 10 Thelonius Monk born (–1982).

w Everyday Life
First 'Miss America' beauty competition held in Atlantic City, New Jersey (7 Sept); winner is Miss Margaret Gorman.

x Sport and Recreation
The 7th Olympic Games are held in Antwerp, Belgium. The USA wins 41 gold medals; Sweden, 19; Britain and Finland, 15 each; Belgium, 14; Norway and Italy, 13 (20 April–12 Sept).
In England, cricketer Percy Fender, batting for Surrey, scores a century in 35 minutes against Northamptonshire in the County Championship match at Northampton (26 Aug).
The Third Division South of the English

Football League is founded, with 22 teams.
Timing clocks are made compulsory in pigeon racing.
Duke Kahanamoku of Hawaii establishes the world's first surfing club at Waikiki.

y Media
In Germany, supporters of the Nazi Party purchase the *Völkischer Beobachter* to serve as Hitler's mouthpiece.
Press Association in Britain leases telegraph wires for news distribution.
Time and Tide news magazine published in Britain.

Film:
Anna Boleyn (director, Ernst Lubitsch).
Dr Jekyll and Mr Hyde (starring John Barrymore).
Erotikon (director, Mauritz Stiller).
The Golem (directors, Paul Wegener and Carl Boese).
The Mark of Zorro (starring Douglas Fairbanks).
Way Down East (starring Lilian Gish, director, D W Griffith).

Radio:
The Westinghouse Company in the USA establishes the KDKA station in East Pittsburgh, Pennsylvania (first broadcast on 2 Nov 1920, of presidential election returns).
Between 1920 and 1922 570 radio stations are licensed in the USA.
First radio broadcasts in Europe, from the Hague in the Netherlands.
In Britain, the Marconi company makes radio broadcasts from Chelmsford in Essex (from Feb).
A British newspaper sponsors a broadcast by opera singer Dame Nellie Melba.

19 convention between Nicaragua, Honduras, and Costa Rica.

M **December**

2 following Turkish attack on Armenia, the Treaty of Alexandropol is concluded; Armenia cedes territory to Turkey.

5 plebiscite in Greece (following death of King Alexander in October) favours return of former King Constantine (19, returns).

9 Michael Hainisch elected first president of Austria.

10 Woodrow Wilson and Léon Bourgeois awarded Nobel Peace Prize.

12 in Ireland, martial law imposed in Cork.

15 (–22) Brussels conference on Germany's reparations.

23 British Parliament passes the Government of Ireland Act: Southern Ireland (26 counties) and Northern Ireland (six counties) each to have own parliament.

23 Franco–British convention on boundaries of Syria and Palestine.

29 conference of French Socialist Party at Tours votes for adhesion to the Moscow International; the Party becomes the French Communist Party while a minority, led by Léon Blum, form a new French Socialist Party.

Greek–Turkish War ... French troops occupy Ruhr ... Treaty between Britain and Ireland ...

A **January**

Greek offensive into Anatolia (Turkey), starting Greek–Turkish War. General congress of the Italian Socialist Party at Livorno results in the formation of a separate Communist Party.

10 in Germany, war trials begin in Leipzig before German supreme court.

16 Aristide Briand forms ministry in France.

22 deportation from USA of Mantes, self-styled Russian ambassador.

24 (–29) Paris conference of wartime Allies fixes Germany's reparation payments.

B **February**

The Red Army invades Georgia.

4 Sir James Craig elected Ulster Unionist leader, in succession to Sir Edward Carson.

8 in South African elections, Jan C Smuts gains majority of 20.

9 in India, state opening of central parliament (established under Government of India Act of 1919).

12 in Britain, Winston Churchill is appointed colonial secretary.

18 recall of US representative from Reparations Commission.

21 London conference of Allies and representatives of the Turkish Sultan's government and the nationalist government at Ankara.

26 Russia signs treaties with Persia and, on 28, with Afghanistan.

27 in Italy, riots between Communists and Fascists in Florence.

C **March**

1 Turkish treaty with Afghanistan.

4 Warren G Harding inaugurated as 29th president of the USA.

5 USA warns Costa Rica and Panama to settle frontier dispute by arbitration.

7 in Hungary, ex-Emperor Charles attempts coup.

7 (–18) following mutiny of sailors at Kronstadt naval base near Petrograd, military forces attack the base.

8 French troops occupy Düsseldorf and other towns in Ruhr because of Germany's failure to make preliminary reparations payment.

11 following nationalist opposition to French possession of Cilicia in SE Turkey, France agrees to leave; nationalist fighting against French continues.

15 Rwanda, East Africa, ceded to Britain by Belgian convention.

16 British–Russian trade agreement; British trade mission visits Moscow.

17 in Britain, Andrew Bonar Law resigns leadership of Conservatives in Commons (21, Austen Chamberlain elected leader).

17 Polish Constitution established.

18 Treaty of Riga between Russia and Poland delineates the countries' common frontier.

20 plebiscite held in Upper Silesia, part of pre-War Germany; 63 per cent vote for incorporation with Germany.

23 Germany announces that it will be unable to pay £600 million due as reparations on 1 May.

24 British Reparation Recovery Act imposes 50 per cent duties on German goods (reduced, 20 May, to 26 per cent).

24 Communist riots in Hamburg, Germany.

*Lenin's New Economic Policy in Russia ... Salzburg Festival
founded in Austria ... Caruso dies ...*

o **Politics, Government, Law, and Economy**

States admitted to the League of Nations include Estonia, Latvia, and Lithuania (22 Sept).

British Commonwealth of Nations founded.

Establishment in USA of the Bureau of the Budget to coordinate federal government spending (since 1970, the Office of Management and Budget).

General Accounting Office established by US Congress.

In USA, Port Authority of New York and New Jersey established.

In Britain, Lord and Lady Lee of Fareham donate the 'Chequers' house and estate near London for use by the prime minister, with an endowment to maintain the estate and pay for the minister's weekend visits (Lloyd George holds house-warming on 8 Jan 1921).

President Harding appoints former president W H Taft as Chief Justice of US Supreme Court (30 June; serves until 1930).

Benjamin Cardozo, *The Nature of the Judicial Process.*

Roscoe Pound, *The Spirit of the Common Law.*

At the 10th Congress of the Russian Communist Party, Lenin introduces his New Economic Policy (NEP), which restores some private business and freedom of trade, and affirms peasant ownership of land (17 March).

Safeguarding of Industries Act in Britain permits use of selective tariffs to prevent dumping of foreign manufactures (1 July).

Ending of wartime government direction of food, coal, and railways in Britain; mines are returned to private owners which leads to industrial conflict.

Federal Highway Act gives grants of 50 per cent of costs from the federal government for road construction.

p **Society, Education, and Religion**

Sweden introduces universal suffrage (with voting age reduced from 24 to 23).

Miss Olive Clapham is the first woman to be admitted as a barrister in England.

In USA, Wisconsin passes Equal Rights Law.

Emergency Quota Immigration Act in USA (19 May).

Foundation of British Legion, to provide care for ex-servicemen and women (24 May).

R H Tawney, *The Acquisitive Society.*

School attendance is made compulsory in Finland.

British Institute of Adult Education founded.

Famine in Russia results in persecution of Orthodox Church after Patriarch Basil Tikhon refuses to allow the sale of consecrated objects to raise funds for famine relief; Tikhon is imprisoned and the Metropolitan of St Petersburg is executed.

Rudolph Bultmann, *The History of the Synoptic Tradition.*

Charles Gore, *Belief in God.*

q **Science, Technology, and Discovery**

Ernest Rutherford and James Chadwick disintegrate all elements, except carbon, oxygen, lithium and beryllium, as a

25 USA refuses Russia's request to resume trading.

28 British Independent Labour Party refuses to affiliate with Communists.

31 in Britain, coal mines are returned to private ownership; new employment terms are rejected by miners (1 April–1 July, miners locked out).

D **April**

In Greek–Turkish War, following a Turkish victory over the Greek invaders, the Greek army withdraws.

12 President Harding declares that the USA could play no part in League of Nations.

19 Government of Ireland Act in force.

23 Czechoslovak–Romanian alliance.

24 Germany unsuccessfully asks USA to mediate in reparations controversy.

24 war crimes court in Leipzig, German, acquits General Erich von Ludendorff of breaches of laws of war.

27 Reparations Commission fixes Germany's liability at 132,000 million gold marks (£6,650 million).

E **May**

2 French troops are mobilized for occupation of Ruhr.

4 in Germany, Konstantin Fehrenbach's government resigns in protest at the size of the reparations payment.

5 Allied Supreme Council warns Germany that failure to accept the reparations figure, by 12 May, will lead to occupation of Ruhr.

6 peace treaty signed between Germany and Russia.

10 in German cabinet crisis Karl Joseph Wirth, Catholic Centre Party, becomes chancellor (11, Reichstag votes to accept Allies' ultimatum on reparations).

14 in Italian elections, 35 Fascists are returned.

20 Germany and China resume diplomatic relations.

24 election held to parliament of Southern Ireland; because of the guerrilla war conditions, no contests are held; 124 Sinn Féin and 4 Unionists (representing Dublin University) are returned unopposed.

28 German chancellor Wirth appoints industrialist Walter Rathenau as minister for reconstruction (including responsibility for reparations).

28 following discussions between the British government and the Sultan of Egypt, and the formation of new Egyptian government, nationalists riot in Alexandria, Egypt.

F **June**

5 agreement on the control of Fiume between Italy, Serbia, and the Kingdom of the Serbs, Croats, and Slovenes (Yugoslavia).

7 USA refuses to recognise Mexican government until international obligations are honoured.

7 opening of new Parliament of Northern Ireland in Belfast, with Sir James Craig as first prime minister of Northern Ireland (–1940, from 1927 as Viscount Craigavon).

7 alliance made between Romania and the Kingdom of the Serbs, Croats, and Slovenes (Yugoslavia).

19 the powers agree to mediate between Turkey and Greece (but, 25, Greece refuses the offer).

22 Labour Conference of Great Britain rejects affiliation with Communists.

26 in Italy, fall of Prime Minister Giolitti; succeeded by Ivanoe Bonomi.

27 treaty between Afghanistan and Persia.

G **July**

In Greek–Turkish War, Greeks resume invasion of Anatolia and press towards Ankara. Communist Party founded in China.

8 Éamon de Valera, on behalf of the self-declared Irish Republic, agrees a truce with the British authorities (11, fighting ends).

23 convention for internationalization of Danube.

25 Belgium and Luxembourg sign 50-year economic pact.

28 following the resistance to the proposed plebiscite in S Silesia, the Allied powers divide the area between Poland and Czechoslovakia.

29 in India, the Congress Party decides to boycott Prince of Wales's visit.

H **August**

11 the USA invites powers to conference on Far East and the limitation of armaments.

12 following conflict between Poles and Germans in Silesia, the Allied Supreme Council refers question of the assignment of Upper Silesia to the League of Nations.

16 the Sinn Féin members elected to the southern Irish parliament in May meet in Dublin and constitute themselves as a second Dáil Eireann; they appoint representatives (led by Arthur Griffith and Michael Collins) to negotiate with Britain on Irish independence.

23 Irish Dáil rejects British peace offer.

23 in Iraq, Feisal (the former king of Syria) is crowned king.

24 USA signs peace treaties with Austria.

preliminary experiment to splitting the atom (–1924).

R Humanities

J Gunnar Andersson discovers a cave at Yangshao Tsun in Honan, China, which was occupied in the Neolithic (in 1923 his *An Early Chinese Culture* defines the Yangshao culture).

Arthur Evans, *The Palace of Minos at Knossos* (–1935).

O G S Crawford, *Man and his Past.*

James Truslow Adams, *The Founding of New England.*

Albert K Weinberg, *Manifest Destiny: A Study of National Expansionism in American History.*

Lytton Strachey, *Queen Victoria.*

Lady Gwendolen Cecil, *Life of Robert, Marquis of Salisbury* (–1932).

Institute of Historical Research, London, founded, with A F Pollard as director.

John M'Taggart, *The Nature of Existence.*

Bertrand Russell, *The Analysis of Mind.*

Max Scheler, *Formalism in Ethics and Material Value Ethics.*

S Art, Sculpture, Fine Arts, and Architecture

Painting, etc:

Georges Braque, *Still Life with Guitar.*

Max Ernst, *Celebes.*

Raoul Hausmann, *Dada-Cino.*

Paul Klee, *The Fish.*

Fernand Léger, *Le Grand Déjeuner.*

Henri Matisse, *The Moorish Screen, Odalisque with Red Culottes* – first Matisse bought by a French museum.

Joan Miró, *The Farm.*

Piet Mondrian, *Composition with Red, Yellow, Blue and Black.*

Amédée Ozenfant, *Still Life with a Glass of Red Wine* (Purism).

Pablo Picasso, *Large Bather.*

Sculpture:

Marcel Duchamp, *Why not sneeze, Rose Sélavy?*

Architecture:

Michael de Klerk, Eigen Haard flats, Amsterdam.

T Music

Arthur Honegger, *Le Roi David* (dramatic oratorio).

John Ireland, *Mai-Dun.*

Leoš Janáček, *Katya Kabanova* (opera).

Pietro Mascagni, *Il piccolo Marat* (opera).

Sergey Prokofiev, *The Love for Three Oranges* (opera).

Edgard Varèse, *Amériques.*

Peter Warlock, *The Curlew.*

In Austria, Salzburg Festival established.

Musicians' Union founded in Britain.

Jazz outlawed on Broadway, New York.

U Literature and Drama

Anna Akhmatova, *Anno Domini MCMXI* (poems).

Walter de la Mare, *Memoirs of a Midget.*

John Dos Passos, *Three Soldiers.*

John Galsworthy, *To Let.*

Aldous Huxley, *Crome Yellow.*

D H Lawrence, *Women in Love.*

Rose Macaulay, *Dangerous Ages.*

George Moore, *Héloïse and Abelard.*

Italo Svevo, *The Confessions of Zeno.*

Paul Valéry, *L'Âme de la danse.*

Drama:

Gabriel Marcel, *La Grâce.*

Somerset Maugham, *The Circle.*

Eugene O'Neill, *Anna Christie, The Emperor Jones.*

Jean Sarment, *Le Pêcheur d'ombres.*

Opening of Ambassador Theatre, New York.

V Births and Deaths

Jan 1 César born (–).

March 25 Mary Douglas born (–).

May 2 Satyajit Ray born (–1992).

May 3 Sugar Ray Robinson born (–1989).

May 12 Joseph Beuys born (–1986).

Aug 2 Enrico Caruso dies (48).

Aug 17 G R Elton born (–1994).

Oct 2 Robert Runcie born (–).

Nov 27 Alexander Dubček born (–1992).

Dec 16 Camille Saint-Säens dies (86).

W Everyday Life

Chanel No. 5 perfume launched (5 May).

Kotex markets its sanitary towel products.

Band Aid sticking plasters are introduced.

X Sport and Recreation

Australia regains the Ashes, winning all five cricket Tests at home against England.

'Babe' Ruth hits a record 59 home runs for the New York Yankees, beating his own record set the previous season.

In winning the English Football League, Burnley go a record 30 consecutive games unbeaten.

The 20-team Third Division North of the English Football League is inaugurated.

Batting against South Africa in the second cricket Test at Johannesburg, Jack Gregory

24 (–16 Sept), Battle of the Sakkaria: Turks (commanded by Mustafa Kemal) prevent Greek forces from reaching Ankara; the Greeks retreat.

25 USA signs peace treaties with Germany and, on 29, with Hungary.

26 assassination of former German finance minister Mathias Erzberger by nationalist gang.

29 (–16 Dec) state of emergency proclaimed in Germany in the face of economic crisis.

J September

15 Guatemala, Honduras, and El Salvador agree to form a Republic of Central America (with its capital at Tegucigalpa, Honduras).

30 British–Russian commercial agreement.

30 French troops evacuate Ruhr.

K October

6 Franco–German agreement for supply of reparations in kind.

12 the Council of the League of Nations awards two-thirds of Upper Silesia (including most of the coal mines and steelworks) to Poland (25 Oct–10 Nov, Poland and Germany reluctantly accept the division).

13 treaty signed in Kars, Turkey, between Russia, the Caucasian republics, and the Turkish government in Ankara.

18 central executive of Russian government grants independence to Crimea.

19 revolution in Lisbon: insurgents force the prime minister to resign and make the president appoint their nominees.

20 Franco–Turkish agreement signed at Ankara, recognizing the Ankara government.

27 Germany agrees to accept Allies' conditions on reparations.

29 ex-Emperor Charles is expelled from Hungary on failure of further attempted coup (goes to Madeira, where he dies on 1 April 1922).

L November

1 Otto Braun, Socialist, forms ministry in Prussia.

4 Takashi Hara, prime minister of Japan, is murdered at Tokyo railway station.

5 treaty between Russia and Mongolia.

12 powers recognize Albanian government.

12 (–6 Feb 1922) in USA, Washington Conference on disarmament.

12 rapid fall of the German Mark.

M December

6 the British government and representatives of the Dáil Eireann sign the British–Irish Treaty providing for an independent southern Ireland with dominion status.

6 in Canadian election, Liberals defeat Conservatives.

7 USA and Austria resume diplomatic relations.

13 USA, British Empire, France, and Japan sign Washington Treaty to respect each other's rights over insular possessions in the Pacific; by this treaty the USA is drawn into consultation with other powers in matters of common concern.

14 in plebiscite held in Ödenburg, 65 per cent vote for union with Hungary rather than with Czechoslovakia.

15 Germany applies for moratorium on reparations payments.

16 the British Parliament ratifies the British–Irish treaty (in Ireland, Éamon de Valera, a signatory to the Treaty, repudiates it).

21 Russia and Turkey form alliance.

21 in Australia, Prime Minister Hughes reconstructs his government.

27 commercial agreement between Italy and Russia.

29 USA, British Empire, France, Italy, and Japan sign Washington Treaty to limit naval armaments.

29 in Canada, following defeat of the Conservatives in the general election, Arthur Meighen resigns as prime minister; the Liberal leader W L Mackenzie King is appointed, and governs with support from the Progressives.

of Australia scores the fastest century in Test cricket history: in 70 minutes off 67 deliveries.

v **Media**

Foundation in Germany of the Deutsche Allgemeine Zeitung.

Film:

US film comedian, writer, and director Roscoe ('Fatty') Arbuckle is arrested after a death at a party; although acquitted of rape and murder, his career never recovers.

L'Atlantide (director, Jacques Feyder).
The Beggar Maid (starring Mary Astor).
Destiny (director, Fritz Lang).
The Haunted Castle (director, F W Murnau).
Innocent (starring Basil Rathbone).
The Kid (starring Charlie Chaplin).
The Mountain Cat (director, Ernst Lubitsch).
Nosferatu (director, F W Murnau).
The Rotters (starring Stanley Holloway).
Shattered (director, Lupu Pick).
The Sheik (starring Rudolph Valentino).

Radio:

First medium-wave wireless broadcast, in USA.

Civil war in Irish Free State ... Italian Fascists march on Rome ...

A January

7 in Ireland, the Dáil Eireann ratifies the British–Irish Treaty by 64 to 57 (Éamon de Valera resigns as president; 9, replaced by Arthur Griffith).

10 in South Africa, strike in Rand gold mines.

13 conference at Cannes, France, decides to postpone Germany's reparation payments.

15 Raymond Poincaré forms ministry in France (following Aristide Briand's resignation on 12).

15 Michael Collins becomes the first prime minister of the Irish Free State and forms a provisional government.

26 legislative council of British Southern Rhodesia (now Zimbabwe) accepts draft constitution conferring limited self-government.

31 Walther Rathenau is appointed German foreign minister.

B February

1 in USA, Washington conference approves treaties restricting submarine warfare and poison gas.

4 Japan agrees to restore Shandong peninsula to China, reserving some mines and commercial interests.

9 (–25) in Italy, resignation of Prime Minister Bonomi produces crisis; on 25, Luigi Facta agrees to form government.

11 nine-power Treaty of Washington for securing China's independence and maintaining the 'open door'.

11 USA–Japan naval agreement.

28 British government announces its desire to recognize Egypt as an independent state, reserving certain British interests.

C March

1 trade agreement between Sweden and Russia.

6 USA prohibits export of arms to China.

10 in South Africa, strikes and martial law in Johannesburg.

15 modified reparations agreement, for Germany to pay with raw materials, signed by France and Germany (31, approved by Reparations Commission).

15 the Sultan of Egypt assumes the title of king as Fuad I; Sudan comes under joint British–Egyptian sovereignty.

15 in Ireland, Eamon de Valera organizes a Republican Society, to fight the Pro-Treaty Party (Cumann na nGaedheal).

17 Baltic states and Poland sign agreement on neutrality.

18 in India, Mahatma Gandhi sentenced to six years' imprisonment for civil disobedience.

20 President Harding orders return of US troops from Rhineland, Germany.

24 Allied conference in Paris recommends that Greeks and Turks should seek Armistice; Turks will only make peace if Greece evacuates Anatolia.

D April

1 (–15 Aug) coal strike in USA.

7 Britain concedes to Standard Oil Co. rights in Palestine.

10 (–19 May) economic conference of European powers held at Genoa, Italy.

14 Irish rebels seize the Four Courts, Dublin, from the Free State government.

16 Rapallo Treaty between Germany and Russia: Germany recognizes Russia as 'a great power' and both sides waive reparations claims; the treaty leads to the resumption of diplomatic and trade relations, and to cooperation between the two countries' armies.

E May

10 Genoa convention between Russia and the Vatican.

15 Germany cedes Upper Silesia to Poland.

24 Italy signs commercial treaty with Russia.

26 Russian leader Lenin suffers first stroke (second occurs in Dec).

F June

5 US Congress presents the Medal of Congress to the people of Verdun, France, honouring their resistance in World War I.

10 bankers' committee of Reparations Commission declines to recommend international loan for Germany.

16 election in the Irish Free State gives majority to Pro-Treaty candidates (58, against 35 anti-Treaty Republicans); anti-Treaty Republicans continue to oppose the new government, with the IRA taking large areas under its control.

22 in London, murder by two Irishmen of Field Marshal Sir Henry Wilson, an advocate of British reconquest of Ireland; the British government demands the restoration of order in the Irish Free State.

24 German foreign minister Walther Rathenau (aged 54) is murdered by antisemitic nationalists.

26 emergency decree in Germany to protect the economy.

28 in Dublin, anti-Treaty Republicans seize the assistant chief of staff of the Irish army

*Insulin is isolated ... Discovery of Tutankhamun's tomb ...
Foundation of the BBC ...*

o Politics, Government, Law, and Economy
USA sets up the 'Prohibition Navy' to prevent widespread liquor smuggling.

In Britain the budget makes expenditure cuts of £64 million, mainly in military spending but also in the civil service, following recommendations made by the Committee on National Expenditure chaired by Sir Eric Geddes (the reductions are popularly known as the 'Geddes Axe').

Publication of the journal *Foreign Affairs* in the USA.

Foundation in USA of the Institute of Economics.

George Rothwell Brown, *The Leadership of Congress*.

New hierarchy of courts introduced in Russia (people's courts, regional or territorial courts, supreme court of each republic, supreme court of state).

Permanent Court of International Justice holds first session at The Hague (15 Feb).

In Germany the value of the mark falls from 162 to over 7,000 to the dollar.

Fordney–McCumber tariff passed in USA, raising tariffs to the highest level ever.

Austin Seven production begins, making it the first British mass-produced car.

P Society, Education, and Religion
In USA, Mrs Rebecca L Fulton, aged 87, becomes the first woman member of the Senate when she succeeds her dead husband as a member of the Senate for one hour (before the introduction of the newly elected replacement).

US women who marry aliens are entitled to independent citizenship (6 June).

The Mann Act in the USA makes it a federal offence to transport a woman across a state line for immoral purposes.

Lady Rhondda's case at first allows a woman peer to take her seat in the British House of Lords, but this is reversed.

Marie Stopes holds meetings in London to campaign for birth control.

Herbert Hoover, *American Individualism*.

In Kansas City, USA, Jesse C Nichols builds the Country Club Plaza shopping centre in his exclusive Country Club District.

In Britain the 'Geddes Axe' expenditure cuts include £6 million from education, curtailing the implementation of provisions of 1918 Education Act ('Fisher Act').

R H Tawney, *Secondary Education for All*.

Following the death of Pope Benedict XV (22 Jan), Ambrogio Ratti is elected Pope (6 Feb) and takes the name Pius XI.

Charles Gore, *Belief in Christ*.

Q Science, Technology, and Discovery
British horologist John Harwood invents self-winding wrist-watch.

Danish physicist Niels Bohr propounds the theory that electrons travel in concentric orbits round the atomic nucleus.

In Britain, P S M Blackett undertakes experiments on the transmutation of elements.

First ionamide dyes are prepared.

In Canada, Frederick Banting and C H Best isolate insulin and a diabetic patient in Toronto receives an insulin injection.

In Britain, Alexander Fleming discovers lysozyme.

R Humanities
Howard Carter, supported by Lord Carnarvon, discovers the tomb of Pharaoh Tutankhamun at Luxor (4 Nov), the only ancient Egyptian pharaoh's tomb discovered complete with grave goods.

The Cambridge History of India (–1937).

Surendranath Dasgupta, *History of Indian Philosophy* (–1955).

Carl L Becker, *The Declaration of Independence*.

C E Montague, *Disenchantment*.

John Dewey, *Human Nature and Conduct*.

Ludwig Wittgenstein, *Tractatus Logico-Philosophicus*.

S Art, Sculpture, Fine Arts, and Architecture
Colonial Exhibition, Marseille, France.

Painting, etc:
Giorgio de Chirico, *Roman Villa*.
Joan Miró, *The Farm*.
Gerald Murphy, *Villa America*.
Pablo Picasso, *Dancing Couple*.
Clive Bell publishes *Since Cézanne*.
David Low, *Lloyd George and Co.* (a book of political cartoons).

Sculpture:
Constantin Brancusi, *The Fish*.
Kasimir Malevich, *Suprematist Architecton No. 3*.

Architecture:
E Freyssinet, Bridge of St. Pierre-du-Vauvray.
Le Corbusier, Ville Contemporaine, total plan for city.

and hold him hostage in the Four Courts building; the Irish army besieges the building, destroying the Irish public records (30, rebel forces surrender).

28 British Labour Party continues to rebuff Communist Party's attempt to affiliate.

G **July**

2 (–5) in Irish Free State, heavy fighting in Dublin.

8 Chile and Peru agree to submit dispute over Tacna and Arica territories (on border) to arbitration.

20 Council of League of Nations approves mandates for the former German colonies Togoland (now Togo), the Cameroons, and Tanganyika (now Tanzania) and (on 24) for Palestine.

29 ultimatum of Allied Powers forbidding Greek occupation of Istanbul.

30 in Ireland, National Troops capture Tipperary from anti-Treaty rebels.

30 Greek high commissioner in Smyrna (modern Izmir, Turkey) proclaims the autonomy of Greek-inhabited territory in Anatolia.

31 general strike begins in Italy, protesting at weakness of state in face of Fascist agitation; Fascists use the strike as the opportunity to seize power in several cities (including Milan and Genoa).

H **August**

1 Balfour Note circulated to Allies, stating that Britain would only expect to recover from its European debtors the sum the USA expected it to pay (thus placing the odium of war debts on the USA).

1 Britain, France, and Italy warn Greece against attempted occupation of Palestine.

4 (–8) fighting between Fascists and Socialists in Italian cities.

12 sudden death of Arthur Griffith, president of the Dáil of the Irish Free State.

22 Michael Collins (aged 31), prime minister of the Irish provisional government, killed by Republican ambush in west Cork.

24 Arab Congress at Nablus rejects British mandate for Palestine.

26 Turks return to the offensive and defeat the Greeks at the Battle of Afyon.

31 alliance between Czechoslovakia and the Kingdom of the Serbs, Croats, and Slovenes is signed.

31 Reparations Commission adopts Belgian proposal for Germany's payments by instalments on Treasury bills.

J **September**

9 the Dáil of the Irish Free State meets under heavy guard; it elects William T Cosgrave as president (to replace Arthur Griffith).

9 in Greek–Turkish War, Turks take Smyrna (modern Izmir) from the Greeks; many Greek inhabitants are massacred.

10 commercial treaty between Britain and Russia, which (in Oct) Russia refuses to ratify.

11 British mandate proclaimed in Palestine while Arabs declare a day of mourning.

13 Franco–Polish 10-year military convention.

18 Hungary is admitted to the League of Nations, the first of the defeated Central Powers to be admitted.

23 with the Turkish army now approaching the Straits, the Allies invite the Ankara government to a peace conference.

27 King Constantine of Greece abdicates for second time (departs, 30); succeeded by crown prince George.

30 conscription introduced in Russia.

K **October**

1 a reaffirmation of the new Turkish constitution provides for the separation of the sultanate and the caliphate; the sultanate is abolished.

4 Austria receives international loan.

13 the Armistice of Mudanya, ending the Greek–Turkish War and settling relations between the Allies and the Ankara government; the Allies allow Turkish troops to enter Istanbul.

17 in Britain, unemployed workers leave Glasgow, Scotland, on hunger march to London.

19 in Britain, following the 'Chanak Crisis' of Sept–Oct (when Lloyd George reinforced British troops at Chanak on the Dardanelles and threatened Turkey), Conservatives withdraw from the coalition government; Lloyd George resigns as prime minister (23, Andrew Bonar Law forms Conservative ministry).

24 in Italy, opening of Fascist Congress in Naples, where Mussolini demands participation in the government.

24 in Ireland, the Dáil adopts a constitution for Irish Free State, which provides for a governor-general to represent the British crown.

24 Friedrich Ebert re-elected president of Germany.

27 Italian cabinet offers resignation (declined by king).

27 referendum in Southern Rhodesia (modern Zimbabwe) votes against joining Union of South Africa.

T Music

George Antheil, *Airplane Sonata*.
Arthur Bliss, *Colour Symphony*.
Carl Nielsen, Symphony No. 5.
Ralph Vaughan Williams, Symphony No. 3 ('A Pastoral Symphony').
William Walton, *Façade* ('entertainment' to poems by Edith Sitwell).
Young Viennese composers found the International Society for Contemporary Music, with British musicologist Edward Dent as chairman.
Formation of the white jazz group New Orleans Rhythm Kings in Chicago (–1924).
Joe 'King' Oliver leads his Creole Jazz Band at Lincoln Gardens, Chicago, USA.
Ben Pollack leads the band at the Venice Ballroom, Los Angeles, USA.

U Literature and Drama

John Buchan, *Huntingtower*.
Ivan Bunin, 'Gentleman from San Francisco'.
e e cummings, *The Enormous Room*.
T S Eliot, *The Waste Land*.
F Scott Fitzgerald, *The Jazz Age*, including 'The Diamond as Big as the Ritz'.
R M du Gard, *Les Thibault* (–1940).
Jaroslav Hašek, *The Good Soldier Schweik*.
James Joyce, *Ulysses* (published in Paris).
D H Lawrence, *Aaron's Rod*.
Sinclair Lewis, *Babbitt*.
Katharine Mansfield, *The Garden Party*.
Rainer Maria Rilke, *Sonette an Orpheus*.
Jules Romains, *Psyche* (The Body's Rapture; –1929).
Hugh Walpole, *The Cathedral*.
Virginia Woolf, *Jacob's Room*.
P. E. N. (writers' association), London, founded by Mrs Dawson Scott.
In Britain, quarterly literary review *Criterion*, edited by T S Eliot, first published.

Drama:

Bertolt Brecht, *Drums in the Night*.
Somerset Maugham, *East of Suez*.
A A Milne, *The Dover Road*.
Anne Nichols, *Abie's Irish Rose* – New York run of 2,327 performances.
Eugene O'Neill, *The Hairy Ape*.
Luigi Pirandello, *Henry IV*.
Tanizaki Jun-ichiro, *Because One Loves*.
John Willer, *The Cat and the Canary*.

V Births and Deaths

Feb 24 Richard Hamilton born (–).
March 12 Jack Kerouac born (–1969).
April 16 Kingsley Amis born (–1995).
April 22 Charlie Mingus born (–1979).
June 10 Judy Garland born (–1969).
Aug 1 Alexander Graham Bell dies (75).
Aug 14 Alfred Harmsworth (Lord Northcliffe) dies (57).
Sept 10 Bernard Bailyn born (–).
Oct 7 Marie Lloyd dies (76).
Nov 8 Christiaan Barnard born (–).
Nov 15 Marcel Proust dies (51).
Nov 26 Charles Schulz born (–).

W Everyday Life

US magazine *Vanity Fair* employs the term 'Flapper' to denote a young woman who abjures femininity, dresses in a provocative manner, and smokes.
The number of telephone subscribers in Britain exceeds one million.

X Sport and Recreation

The National Football League is founded in the USA.
In the first £5,000 transfer in British football, Syd Puddefoot moves from West Ham United to Falkirk.
The All England Lawn Tennis and Croquet Club moves to new premises, at Church Road, Wimbledon, London.
Walter Hagen is the first US golfer to win the British Open, at Royal St George's, Sandwich, S England.
First Walker Cup match between the amateur golfers of Britain and Ireland, and the USA, at Long Island, New York; the USA wins 8–4 (29 Aug).
In Britain, the Northern Rugby Football Union changes its name to the Rugby Football League.

Y Media

DeWitt Wallace and his wife Lila Acheson publish the first issue of the *Reader's Digest* magazine in Greenwich Village, New York (5 Feb).
Publication in USA of *Better Homes and Gardens*.
Publication of a British edition of the US magazine *Good Housekeeping*.

Film:

In Hollywood, USA, foundation of the organization Motion Pictures Producers and Distributors of America to regulate film content and defend the film industry.
Dr Mabuse, The Gambler (director, Fritz Lang).
La Femme de Nulle Part (director, Louis Delluc).
Foolish Wives (director, Erich von Stroheim).
Orphans of the Storm (director, D W Griffith, starring Lilian Gish).

28 in Italy, Fascists march on Rome; Prime Minister Facta proposes state of emergency, but King Victor Emanuel refuses to sign the decree (30, Mussolini goes to Rome at the king's invitation and, 31, forms government composed of Liberals and Nationalists as well as Fascists).

24 in Irish Free State, execution of leading Republican Erskine Childers for possession of a firearm.

25 Italian parliament grants Mussolini temporary emergency powers to force through reforms.

28 six Greek ex-ministers and generals executed for failure in Greek–Turkish War.

L November

1 Kemal Pasha proclaims Turkish republic and abolition of the Sultanate.

1 civil war renewed in China.

2 (–7) Berlin conference of monetary experts on German currency.

7 elections to US Congress reduced Republican majority.

17 Far Eastern Republic votes for union with Russia.

17 in British general election, Conservatives win 345 seats, Labour 142, Lloyd George Liberals 62, and Asquith Liberals 54.

17 the caliph (and former sultan) of Turkey, Muhammad VI, leaves in a British warship and is declared deposed; his successor, Prince Abd ul-Mejid, renounces the sultanate and holds only the caliphate.

22 Wilhelm Cuno succeeds Wirth as German chancellor.

M December

1 Jozef Pilsudski, President of Poland, resigns.

6 the Dáil of the Irish Free State and the British Parliament ratify the British–Irish Treaty; Tim Healy is appointed governor-general.

7 Northern Ireland Parliament votes against inclusion in Irish Free State.

15 Franco–Canadian trade agreement.

16 in Australian elections, Nationalists win 27 seats, Labour 29 and the Country Party 14.

17 last British troops leave the Irish Free State.

26 Reparations Commission, against British vote, declares Germany has made a voluntary default in payments.

30 establishment of the Union of Soviet Socialist Republics (USSR) through confederation of Russia, Belarus, the Ukraine, and the Transcaucasian Federation.

Inauguration of the USSR ... Dictatorship in Spain ... Collapse of German currency ...

A January

10 Memel, under Allied occupation, is seized by Lithuanian forces.

11 because of Germany's failure to meet reparations payments, French and Belgian troops occupy the Ruhr; Germans respond with passive resistance and sabotage; the occupiers make arrests and deportations, and cut off the Rhineland from the rest of Germany.

14 in Italy, Fascist squads are formed into a militia.

28 French troops encircle the Ruhr.

31 Britain accepts terms of a commission for funding its war debt to the USA.

B February

2 Central American Republics sign treaty of amity in Washington, DC, USA.

2 in Australia, Prime Minister Hughes is forced to resign; Stanley Bruce forms a coalition ministry from the Nationalist and Country Parties.

10 Turkey forges an alliance with Afghanistan.

16 conference of ambassadors assigns Memel to Lithuania, with safeguards for Poland.

24 US Labor Party convention repudiates Communism.

C March

3 US Senate rejects proposal to join International Court of Justice.

4 in USA, the 'Teapot Dome' scandal: Secretary of the Interior Albert B Fall resigns as a senate committee investigates alleged unlawful leasing of government oil reserves and other matters (1929, Fall is fined and sentenced to a year in prison).

14 Allies recognize Vilna (modern Vilnius) and East Galicia as Polish.

21 Secretary of state Charles Hughes declares that the USA will not recognize the USSR unless it acknowledges foreign debts and restores alien property.

Witchcraft Through the Ages (director, Benjamin Christiansen).

Radio:

In the USA, establishment of the WEAF station by the American Telephone and Telegraph Company to provide broadcast facilities on a rental basis.

In Britain the Marconi Company broadcasts on the station 2LO in London from 11 May.

Following a decision that radio broadcasting should come within control of the Post Office, the British Broadcasting Company is founded; its first broadcast, on station 2LO, is on 14 Nov (though the company is not licensed until 18 Jan 1923); John Reith is appointed general manager; the broadcasts include commercials.

Cotton Club opens in New York ... The first supermarket ... First English cup final at Wembley ...

o Politics, Government, Law, and Economy

Interpol police co-ordination body founded at a Vienna conference.

Hyperinflation in Germany causes a temporary reversion to barter exchange in some transactions.

In USSR, inauguration of national airline Aeroflot (15 July).

A Marshall, *Money, Credit and Commerce*.

p Society, Education, and Religion

Following the Treaty of Lausanne between Greece and Turkey, 1.5 million Greeks migrate from Anatolia (W Turkey) to Greece.

In Britain the Matrimonial Causes Act gives women equality in divorce suits (July 18).

The Trades Union Congress in Britain elects its first woman Chairman of the General Council, Miss Margaret Bondfield.

In Adkins v. Children's Hospital the US Supreme Court strikes down minimum wages for adult women as a breach of the liberty of contract.

US Steel introduces an eight-hour day for its workers.

The University of Chicago establishes the Social Science Research Committee to coordinate research into social conditions in USA.

Foundation of the Regional Planning Association of America (–1933).

Nursery Schools Association founded in Britain with Margaret McMillan as founding president.

Giovanni Gentile, *The Reform of Education*.

Jean Piaget, *Language and Thought of the Child*.

q Science, Technology, and Discovery

British metallurgist John B Tytus invents continuous hot-strip rolling of steel.

Frederick Lindemann investigates the size of meteors and the temperature of the upper atmosphere.

D **April**

11 in Britain, the Conservative government is defeated in the House of Commons (by 145 votes to 138) on motion on ex-servicemen.

19 formal promulgation of Egyptian constitution, establishing parliamentary government.

26 Mexico recognizes oil concessions granted before 1917.

30 Irish anti-Treaty Republicans suspend offensive operations after the government accepts Éamon de Valera's terms as proclaimed on 27 April.

E **May**

8 British note to USSR objecting to dissemination of anti-British propaganda.

10 Vaslav Vorovski, USSR delegate at Lausanne, murdered.

20 British prime minister Andrew Bonar Law resigns because of ill health; 22, Stanley Baldwin forms Conservative ministry, with Neville Chamberlain as chancellor of exchequer.

25 Britain, France, Italy, and Belgium agree to reimburse the USA for the cost of the US army of the Rhine.

25 with British support, Emir Abdullah ibn Hussein (second son of King Hussein of the Hejaz) is proclaimed ruler of Transjordan (modern Jordan).

29 Palestine constitution suspended by British order in council because of Arabs' refusal to co-operate.

F **June**

1 New York State Prohibition Enforcement Act repealed (thereby making federal agencies responsible for enforcement of Prohibition).

9 coup in Bulgaria leads to fall of prime minister Alexander Stambolisky (who is assassinated on 15).

10 Swiss-Liechtenstein customs union.

19 British prime minister Stanley Baldwin and US secretary of state Andrew Mellon sign British–US convention on war debt.

26 German–Estonian commercial treaty.

G **July**

2 (–20 Aug) London dock strike.

6 the USSR (and its new constitution) formally comes into existence.

24 Treaty of Lausanne between Greece, Turkey, and the Allies; Greece to give up Eastern Thrace; Turkey obtained the islands of Imbros and Tenedos.

H **August**

2 in USA, President Harding dies suddenly (aged 57); succeeded, 3rd, by Vice-President Calvin Coolidge.

6 in Germany, following the resignation of Wilhelm Cuno, Gustav Stresemann is appointed German chancellor and foreign minister and forms a grand coalition of parties.

10 (–13) strikes and riots in Germany.

15 Irish Free State troops arrest Éamon de Valera (imprisoned until July 1924).

27 in Irish elections, Cumann na nGaedheal wins 63 seats, the anti-Treaty Republicans 44.

31 following the murder of an Italian helping to fix the course of the Greek–Albanian frontier (27 Aug), Mussolini demands a payment from Greece and then bombards and occupies Corfu town.

31 (–17 Sept) coal strike in USA.

J **September**

1 severe earthquake in Japan destroys all of Yokohama and most of Tokyo; about half a million people are killed.

3 USA recognizes Mexican government.

3 Greece appeals to League of Nations over Italian occupation of Corfu town.

10 Irish Free State admitted to League of Nations.

14 Miguel Primo de Rivera assumes dictatorship in Spain (ruling under King Alfonso XIII).

15 Germany's bank rate raised to 90 per cent.

26 German chancellor Stresemann calls for end to passive resistance to French and Belgian occupation of Ruhr.

27 state of emergency declared in Germany, under article 48 of the constitution.

27 Italy ends occupation of Corfu town.

28 Ethiopia is admitted to League of Nations.

29 British mandate in Palestine begins.

K **October**

1 failure of Black Reichswehr coup in Germany.

1 Southern Rhodesia becomes a self-governing British colony.

11 value of German Mark drops to rate of 10,000 million to £.

13 Ankara becomes new capital of Turkey (succeeding Istanbul).

21 France recognizes separatist government established in the Rhineland Palatinate of Germany.

26 (–8 Nov) British Empire conference in London; recognizes the right of Dominions to make treaties with foreign powers.

L A Bauer analyzes the Earth's magnetic field.
E N da C Andrade, *The Structure of the Atom.*

R Humanities

The Faculty of Advocates in Edinburgh donates its library to form the nucleus of a National Library of Scotland.

J B Bury (ed.), *The Cambridge Ancient History*; the first volume published is Bury's *History of the Later Roman Empire.*

Salvador de Madariaga, *The Genius of Spain.*

James Truslow Adams, *Revolutionary New England 1691–1776.*

Charles H McIlwain, *The American Revolution: A Constitutional Interpretation.*

Winston Churchill, *The World Crisis, 1911–1914.*

E K Chambers, *The Elizabethan Stage.*

W P Ker, *The Art of Poetry.*

Ernst Cassirer, *The Philosophy of Symbolic Forms,* Vol. 1.

Karl Korsch, *Marxism and Philosophy.*

Georg Lukács, *History and Class Consciousness.*

S Art, Sculpture, Fine Arts, and Architecture

Exhibitions of African and Oceanic art held in Paris and Strasbourg, France.

Royal Fine Art Commission is formed in Britain to advise the government on the design and siting of buildings and memorials.

Painting, etc:

Max Beckmann, *Self-Portrait with Cigarette.*

Marc Chagall, *The Green Violinist* (–24).

Max Ernst, *Pietà, or Revolution by Night.*

Fernand Léger designs costumes and scenery for ballet *La Création du Monde.*

Joan Miró, *The Tilled Field.*

Pablo Picasso, *Harlequin and Mirror, The Pipes of Pan.*

Sculpture:

Constantin Brancusi, *Bird in Space.*

El Lissitzky, *Proun Room.*

Architecture:

Paul Behrens, Basset-Lowke House, Northampton, England (–1926).

Raymond Hood, Chicago Tribune Building (–1925).

T Music

Henry Cowell, *Aeolian Harp.*

Arthur Honegger, *Pacific 231.*

Zoltán Kodály, *Psalmus Hungaricus.*

Darius Milhaud, *La création du monde* (ballet).

Igor Stravinsky, *Les Noces* (ballet).

Edgard Varèse, *Hyperprism.*

Eugène Ysaÿe, Six Sonatas for Solo Violin.

Review *Runnin' Wild* includes 'Charleston, South Carolina' by James P Johnson.

Introduction of the Charleston dance to New York audiences in the Ziegfeld Follies at the Amsterdam Theatre.

In US, first recording of 'Hillbilly' music (including John Carson's 'The Old Hen Cackled and the Rooster's Going to Crow').

Paul Whiteman Orchestra, 'Three O'Clock in the Morning'.

Opening of the Cotton Club in Harlem, New York, providing black music and entertainment for a white audience.

U Literature and Drama

Arnold Bennett, *Riceyman Steps.*

Colette, *The Ripening Seed.*

John Drinkwater, *Collected Poems.*

Robert Frost, *New Hampshire* (poems).

Khalil Gibran, *The Prophet.*

D H Lawrence, *Kangaroo.*

John Masefield, *Collected Poems.*

François Mauriac, *Génitrix.*

Dorothy L Sayers, *Whose Body?*

Wallace Stevens, *Harmonium.*

P G Wodehouse, *Leave it to Psmith.*

Drama:

Karel Čapek, *The Insect Play.*

Caradoc Evans, *Taffy*, causes riots in London.

James Elroy Flecker, *Hassan.*

Sean O'Casey, *Shadow of a Gunman.*

Luigi Pirandello, *The Late Mattia Pascal.*

Elmer Rice, *The Adding Machine.*

George Bernard Shaw, *Back to Methuselah.*

V Births and Deaths

Jan 9 Katherine Mansfield dies (34).
Feb 1 Ernst Troeltsch dies (57).
Feb 12 Franco Zeffirelli born (–).
March 2 Basil Hume born (–).
March 26 Sarah Bernhardt dies (77).
May 28 György Ligeti born (–).
June 10 Robert Maxwell born (–1991).
Sept 1 Rocky Marciano born (–1969).
Aug 2 Warren G Harding dies (57).
Aug 29 Richard Attenborough born (–).
Oct 23 Roy Lichtenstein born (–).
Oct 30 Andrew Bonar Law dies (65).
Dec 2 Maria Callas born (–1977).
Dec 27 Gustav Eiffel dies (91).

W Everyday Life

The first recognizable supermarket is opened in San Francisco, USA.

29 amendment to Turkish constitution passed: Turkey to be a republic; Mustafa Kemal is elected president.

L **November**

8 (–9) the 'Munich Putsch': Adolf Hitler and National Socialists attempt a coup in Munich.

14 the Italian parliament passes an election law, whereby the party that wins the greatest number of votes receives two-thirds of the seats.

20 value of German Mark drops to rate of 4,200,000 million to the dollar; the government introduces a new currency, the Rentenmark.

23 German chancellor Stresemann fails to win vote of confidence for changes to his government and resigns (succeeded by Wilhelm Marx of the Centre Party).

29 Reparations Commission appoints two committees of experts under Charles Dawes and Reginald McKenna to investigate German economy.

30 in Germany, end of separatist riots in the Rhineland.

M **December**

In Mexico, Adolfo de la Huerta attempts rising against government (–April 1924).

1 Wilhelm Marx manages to form a new coalition government and becomes chancellor.

6 in British general election the Conservatives, standing on platform of using a protective tariff to relieve unemployment, lose heavily (Conservatives, 258 seats, Labour, 191, Liberals, 159).

8 US treaty of friendship and commerce with Germany.

18 Britain, France, and Spain sign convention on Tangier.

19 King George II leaves Greece at the request of the ruling revolutionary committee.

Death of Lenin ... Labour Government in Britain ... Murder of Matteotti ...

A **January**

Nationalists win elections in Egypt; Saad Zaghlul forms ministry.

11 Eleutherios Venizélos accepts premiership of Greek national assembly (–4 Feb).

21 death of Soviet leader Lenin (3 Feb, Alexei Rykoff becomes prime minister).

21 in China, Congress of the Guomindang, the Chinese nationalist party, in Guangzhou, which admits communists to the party and welcomes Soviet advisers.

22 following defeat of Conservatives in general election (Dec 1923), British prime minister Stanley Baldwin resigns.

23 Ramsay MacDonald forms first Labour government (without an overall majority) in Britain, with Philip Snowden as chancellor of the exchequer.

23 convention between the USA and Britain permitting US seizure and inspection of ships thought to be infringing Prohibition; British ships are permitted to enter and leave US ports carrying liquor.

24 non-Fascist trade unions abolished in Italy.

25 French–Czechoslovak alliance formed.

B **February**

1 Britain recognises the USSR.

16 British dock strike (–26).

18 Edwin Denby, US navy secretary, is forced to resign through connection with oil leases.

19 Shah Ahmad of Persia is deposed.

23 Britain reduces reparation recovery duties on German goods to 5 per cent.

C **March**

3 the Turkish national assembly expels the Ottoman dynasty, abolishes the caliphate and other religious institutions, and establishes a commissariat of public instruction.

3 Germany signs treaty of friendship with Turkey.

In USA Frank Mars invents the Milky Way sweet bar.

x Sport and Recreation

The Yankee Baseball Stadium, the 'house that Ruth built', is opened in New York.

In Britain, the Football Association Cup Final is held at Wembley Stadium, London, for the first time; a crowd estimated at 200,000 sees Bolton Wanderers beat West Ham United 2–0 (28 April).

In Britain, Steve Donoghue, riding Papyrus, wins his third consecutive Derby horse race.

The first Wightman Cup match between the women tennis players of Britain and the USA is won by the USA 7–0.

Sir Henry Segrave becomes the first British driver to win a motor-racing Grand Prix, the French at Tours.

The dimensions of squash courts are standardized by a subcommittee of the Tennis and Rackets Association.

y Media

In the USA, Henry A Luce and Briton Hadden found the weekly news magazine *Time*.

In Britain, following death of Lord Northcliffe, Colonel J J Astor (later Lord Astor) becomes main proprietor of *The Times*; he reappoints Geoffrey Dawson as editor.

Foundation in Britain of *Radio Times*.

Film:

In the USA, Harry, Albert, Sam, and Jack L Warner found the film company Warner Bros.

Heape and Grylls make a rapid filming machine.

The Ancient Law (director, E A Dupont).

Raskolnikov (director, Robert Wiener).

Safety Last (starring Harold Lloyd).

The Smiling Madame Beudet (director, Germaine Dulac, viewed as the first feminist film).

Warning Shadows (director, Arthur Robson).

The White Sister (starring Ronald Colman and Lilian Gish).

Radio:

In Britain, daily weather forecasts broadcast by the British Broadcasting Corporation; the BBC also broadcasts the first radio play.

Television:

In USA, Vladimir Zworykin develops the iconoscope, an image-scanner, which can then produce electronic signals for reconstitution on the screen of a cathode ray tube.

J Edgar Hoover appointed to FBI ... Woman cabinet minister in Denmark ... Constitution for Mt Athos ...

o Politics, Government, Law, and Economy

Hugh Gunn (ed.), *The British Empire: A Survey* (12 volumes).

In USA, foundation of the Robert Brookings Graduate School of Economics and Government.

In USA, J Edgar Hoover is appointed acting director of the Bureau of Investigation (later the Federal Bureau of Investigation).

The British House of Commons censures the attorney-general in the 'Campbell case' concerning the government's authority over prosecutions.

Benjamin Cardozo, *The Growth of the Law*.

World Power Conference held at Wembley, London, to discuss standardization in power supplies (June).

In USA, the Computing-Tabulating-Recording Company is renamed International Business Machines (IBM).

p Society, Education, and Religion

The Johnson–Reed Act in the USA reduces the maximum number of European immigrants permitted each year to 164,000 and bans Japanese (26 May).

Denmark is the first country to appoint a woman cabinet minister, Nina Bang, minister for education (–1928).

Native Americans are allowed to receive full United States citizenship.

Native American Learned Hand is appointed a judge of the US Court of Appeals (serving until 1956).

Foundation in USA of the National Negro Finance Corporation.

In USA, the trustees of Vassar College, Poughkeepsie, New York, agree to the creation of a School of Euthenics.

Australia makes voting in elections compulsory.

Oregon Case in the US Supreme Court rules

9 Italy annexes the independent city of Fiume but abandons claims to Yugoslavia's Dalmatian coast.

25 Greece is proclaimed a republic (confirmed by plebiscite on 13 April; Admiral Pavlos Koundouriotis becomes president).

D **April**

1 in Germany, following the failed 'Munich Putsch' Adolf Hitler is sentenced to 5 years' imprisonment (released 20 Dec; in prison he dictates his political manifesto, *Mein Kampf/'My Struggle'*).

6 in general election in Italy, Fascists win 65 per cent of the vote although, because of widespread intimidation, the election cannot be considered a free one.

9 Committees under Charles Dawes and Reginald McKenna make reports on reparations issue.

11 in Denmark, Social Democrats form government after winning 55 seats to the Liberals with 44, Radicals with 20, and Conservatives with 28.

14 British–Soviet conference in London.

18 the League of Nations reorganizes Hungary's finances.

20 new, more democratic constitution adopted in Turkey; tithes are abolished and military service shortened.

24 Irish boundary conference in London; the Northern Ireland Government refuses to appoint a representative, and the British government appoints a commissioner on Northern Ireland's behalf.

E **May**

4 in elections to the German parliament, the Reichstag, Nationalists (95 seats) and Communists (62 seats) strengthen their position against the Social Democrats (100) and Centre Party (65); for the first time, the National Socialists/Nazi Party enter the Reichstag with 32 seats.

11 in French elections the Left Cartel emerges as the largest bloc, with 287 out of 581 seats.

15 international conference on immigration held at Rome.

19 Pan-American treaty signed to prevent conflicts between states.

26 in Germany, the government of Wilhelm Marx resigns on breakdown of negotiations for coalition.

31 China recognizes the USSR.

F **June**

10 abduction of Giacomo Matteotti, an Italian Socialist deputy who had attacked Mussolini's government; during June, when it becomes clear that Matteotti has been

murdered, opposition deputies withdraw from the Chamber (the 'Aventine Secession'); Matteotti's corpse is found on 15 Aug.

10 in USA, Republican Convention at Cleveland, Ohio, nominates Calvin Coolidge for the presidency and Charles Dawes for the vice-presidency.

10 Alexandre Millerand, president of France, resigns (13, Gaston Doumergue is elected his successor; 15, Édouard Herriot becomes premier).

24 Democratic Convention in New York nominates J W Davis for presidency and William Jennings Bryan for vice-presidency.

25 Britain states that it will not abandon the Sudan, despite Egyptian demands for complete evacuation.

30 in South Africa, J B Hertzog, Nationalist Party leader, forms ministry with Labour support, following defeat of J C Smuts' South African Party in elections.

G **July**

3 British prime minister Ramsay MacDonald refuses to sign treaty of mutual assistance prepared by the League of Nations.

11 (–15) rioting between Hindus and Muslims in Delhi.

16 at London conference on reparations, attended by Gustav Stresemann and Édouard Herriot, the Dawes Report (or Dawes Plan), which removes reparations from the sphere of political controversy, is approved.

H **August**

6 Lausanne treaty for re-establishing world peace comes into force.

16 French delegates at London conference agree to evacuate the Ruhr within a year (18, French troops leave Offenburg region).

29 the German Reichstag approves the Dawes Plan (1 Sept, comes into force).

30 the German Reichsbank becomes independent of the government and introduces a new Mark.

J **September**

5 in Chile a military junta takes power.

17 Italy abrogates treaty of Rapallo (made on 12 Nov 1920).

20 Britain takes dispute over Mosul in Iraq (claimed by Turkey) to the League of Nations.

25 (–3 Oct) visit of Saad Zaghlul to Britain to discuss Egyptian demand for sovereignty

that states cannot compel children of school age to attend school.

Abbots and elders of the Orthodox monasteries on Mt Athos, Greece, draw up a constitution for the ecclesiastical government of the Holy Mountain.

Charles Gore, *The Holy Spirit and the Church*.

Q Science, Technology, and Discovery

British astrophysicist Arthur Eddington discovers that the luminosity of a star is approximately a function of its mass.

Louis de Broglie in France argues that particles can also behave as waves, laying the foundations for wave mechanics.

The first insecticide developed.

British physicist Edward Appleton discovers that radion emissions are reflected by an ionized layer of the atmosphere.

R Humanities

Ancient Monuments Society founded in England.

A V Kidder, *An Introduction to the Study of South-Western Archaeology*.

A Mawer and F M Stenton (eds.), *Introduction to the Survey of English Place-Names*, first volume of the county series published by the English Place-Name Society.

Eileen Power, *Medieval People*.

Charles M Andrews, *The Colonial Background of the American Revolution*.

Léon Brunschvicg, *The Genius of Pascal*.

R G Collingwood, *Speculum Mentis*.

Étienne Gilson, *The Philosophy of St Thomas Aquinas*.

S Art, Sculpture, Fine Arts, and Architecture

André Breton publishes *Surrealist Manifesto*.

Fernand Léger makes film *Ballet Mécanique*.

Painting, etc:

Stuart Davis, *Odol*.

Gwen John, *The Convalescent*.

Joan Miró, *Harlequin's Carnival*.

Gerald Murphy, *Razor*.

Mario Sironi, *The Pupil*.

Stanley Spencer, *The Resurrection, Cookham* (–1926).

Architecture:

J J P Oud, Housing Estate at Hoek van Holland, Holland.

Gerrit Rietveld, Schroeder House, Utrecht, Holland.

T Music

George Gershwin, *Rhapsody in Blue*.

Leoš Janáček, *The Cunning Little Vixen* (opera).

Emmerich Kálmán, *Countess Maritza* (operetta).

Francis Poulenc, *Les Biches* (ballet).

Ottorino Respighi, *The Pines of Rome*.

Sigmund Romberg, *The Student Prince* (operetta).

Richard Strauss, *Intermezzo* (opera).

In USA, Serge Koussevitsky conducts Boston Symphony Orchestra.

Foundation of the Curtis Institute, Philadelphia, Pennsylvania, USA.

Lady Be Good! (musical), lyrics by Ira Gershwin, music by George Gershwin.

U Literature and Drama

E M Forster, *A Passage to India*.

John Galsworthy, *The White Monkey*.

David Garnett, *A Man in the Zoo*.

Robinson Jeffars, *Tamar and Other Poems*.

Thomas Mann, *The Magic Mountain*.

Katherine Mansfield, *Journal*.

Herman Melville, *Billy Budd* (posthumous).

A A Milne, *When We Were Very Young* (poems).

Pablo Neruda, *Twenty Love Poems and a Song of Despair*.

St John Perse (pseudonym), *Anabase*.

Mary Webb, *Precious Bane*.

Drama:

Maxwell Anderson and Laurence Stallings, *What Price Glory?*

Noël Coward, *The Vortex*.

Henri-René Lenormand, *L'Homme et ses Fantômes*.

Eugene O'Neill, *All God's Chillun Got Wings*, *Desire under the Elms*.

George Bernard Shaw, *St Joan*.

V Births and Deaths

Jan 21 Vladimir Ilyich Lenin dies (53).

Feb 3 Woodrow Wilson dies (67).

March 8 Anthony Caro born (–).

April 28 Kenneth Kaunda born (–).

May 12 Tony Hancock born (–1968).

June 3 Franz Kafka dies (40).

June 12 George Bush born (–).

June 14 James Black born (–).

July 13 Alfred Marshall dies (81).

Aug 2 James Baldwin born (–1987).

Aug 3 Joseph Conrad dies (67).

Sept 18 F H Bradley dies (78).

Oct 1 James Earl ('Jimmy') Carter born (–).

Oct 13 Anatole France dies (79).

Nov 29 Giacomo Puccini dies (66).

W Everyday Life

In USA, Clarence Birdseye founds the General Sea Foods Co. to undertake preparation and sale of frozen fish.

X Sport and Recreation

1st Winter Olympic Games are held at Chamonix, France (25 Jan–4 Feb).

over Sudan; rejected by Prime Minister MacDonald.

27 following election, Plutarcho Calles is declared president of Mexico (takes office on 1 Dec).

29 Germany states terms on which it will join the League of Nations, including a permanent seat on the Council.

K October

2 League of Nations adopts Geneva Protocol for the peaceful settlement of international disputes.

3 in Arabia, King Hussein abdicates throne of Hejaz in favour of his son Ali.

9 in Britain, Parliament is dissolved following defeat of Labour on question of prosecution of the acting editor of *Workers' Weekly*, J R Campbell, for inciting soldiers to mutiny rather than be used to break strikes.

9 in Britain, Irish Free State bill receives royal assent (17, passes Dáil in Dublin).

10 international loan to Germany arranged in London.

25 the British Foreign Office publishes the 'Zinoviev Letter', a document inciting revolutionary activity in the army and Ireland, which was said to be by Grigori Zinoviev, chairman of the External Committee of the Comintern (the Soviet-controlled Communist International).

25 Tsao Kun, president of China, resigns.

28 France recognizes the USSR.

29 Conservatives win British general election with 415 seats against Labour, 151, and Liberals, 44.

L November

4 Calvin Coolidge, Republican, wins US presidential election with 382 electoral votes, over J W Davis, Democrat, 136, and Robert M LaFollette, Progressive, 13; popular vote: Coolidge, 15,725,016; Davis, 8,386,503; LaFollette, 4,822,856.

4 Ramsay MacDonald resigns as British prime minister; a week later Stanley Baldwin forms a Conservative government with Austen Chamberlain as foreign secretary and Winston S Churchill as chancellor of the exchequer.

19 murder in Cairo of Sir Lee Stack, the British governor of the Sudan (22, Britain puts demands to Egyptian government).

20 revolt of Kurds in Turkey, which is put down with ferocity.

21 British prime minister Baldwin informs the USSR that Britain will not proceed with treaties negotiated by the Labour government.

30 last French and Belgian troops are withdrawn from the Ruhr.

30 following the murder of Sir Lee Stack, the Egyptian prime minister accepts most of the British demands.

M December

2 British–German commercial treaty.

7 in German elections, Communists (with 45 seats) lose ground to Social Democrats (131 seats); Conservative Nationalists (103 seats) also improve their strength while the Nazi Party slumps to 14 seats; the Centre Party has 69 seats.

15 (–15 Jan 1925) cabinet crisis in Germany.

24 Albania is proclaimed a republic.

Hindenburg elected president of Germany ... Locarno treaties ...

A January

1 Christiania, the Norwegian capital, resumes name of Oslo (disused in 1624).

3 in Italy, Mussolini announces that he will take dictatorial powers.

6 Allies inform Germany they will not now evacuate Cologne area on 10 Jan.

11 on Charles Hughes's resignation, F B Kellogg is appointed US secretary of state.

15 Hans Luther, Independent, succeeds Wilhelm Marx of the Centre Party as German chancellor, with Gustav Stresemann as foreign minister.

16 in the USSR, Leon Trotsky is dismissed from chairmanship of Revolutionary Military Council.

20 USSR–Japanese convention signed, establishing diplomatic relations and the basis for future cooperation.

20 British–Chinese Treaty of Beijing.

29 David Lloyd George succeeds Lord Oxford (H H Asquith) as Liberal leader.

B February

10 US–Canadian fishing agreement.

28 President Friedrich Ebert of Germany dies.

Billy Meredith plays for Manchester City in the Football Association Cup semi-final against Newcastle United at the age of 49.

The 8th Olympic Games are held in Paris. The USA wins 45 gold medals; Finland, 14; France, 13; Britain and Italy, 9 each; Switzerland, 7; Norway, 5 (4 May–27 July). Paavo Nurmi of Finland wins a record 5 golds, for the 1,500-m, 5,000-m, 10,000-m (both individual and team), and the 3,000-m team event.

The victory of Jean Borotra (the 'Bounding Basque') is the first of six consecutive Men's Singles titles won by French players at the Wimbledon tennis tournament, London.

In USA, the Gila Wilderness Area is created within the Gila National Forest, New Mexico; this is the first unmodified area to be set aside for recreational use.

Y **Media**

William Randolph Hearst founds the *Daily Mirror* tabloid paper in New York followed by Bernarr Macfadden's tabloid *Daily Graphic*: in New York's 'war of the tabs', the two papers battle with the *Daily News* for readers.

F M Ford founds *Transatlantic Review*.

Film:

'Fonofilm' system of talking pictures is developed.

In USA, foundation of Columbia Pictures and consolidation of Metro-Goldwyn-Mayer (MGM).

Alice's Wonderland (first cartoon by Walt Disney).

The Extraordinary Adventures of Mr West in the Land of the Bolsheviks (director, Lev Kuleshov).

The Iron Horse (director, John Ford).

Mikaël (director, Carl Dreyer; with an appearance by Sigmund Freud).

Die Nibelungen (director, Fritz Lang).

Sherlock Junior (starring Buster Keaton).

Wanderer of the Wasteland (nature feature in colour).

Waxworks (director, Paul Leni).

Radio:

Columbia University, New York, introduces educational radio broadcasting.

Two million radio sets are in use in the USA.

Hitler's Mein Kampf *... First woman state governor in USA ... Feast of Christ the King ...*

o **Politics, Government, Law, and Economy**

In Italy, new laws provide for the reduction of the king's prerogative, the dismissal of civil servants who frustrate government policy, and for the appointment of a governor of Rome (with governors being appointed for other cities in 1926).

Dominions Office established by British government.

In USA, Colonel William ('Billy') Mitchell, proponent of air power, is found guilty for insubordination by court martial (Dec) after he had accused the US War and Navy Departments of incompetence.

Adolf Hitler, *Mein Kampf/My Struggle*, Vol. 1.

Lord Beaverbrook, *Politicians and the Press.*

The Supreme Court of Judicature (consolidation) Act defines the structure of the High Court and Court of Appeal in England.

The Law of Property Act, the Land Charges Act, and the Land Registration Act consolidate and reform property law in England.

Britain returns sterling to the gold standard at the prewar parity of $4.86, leading to increasing difficulties for British industry.

In Mexico, the government requires oil companies to replace ownership of oil fields with 50-year leases.

c March

5 Labour opposition in British House of Commons leaves the House on suspension of Clydesider Member David Kirkwood (the suspension was withdrawn a few days later on the motion of the prime minister, Baldwin).

9 President Coolidge of USA arbitrates in Chilean–Peruvian dispute.

12 Britain refuses to sign Geneva protocol (of Oct 1924) for the peaceful settlement of international disputes.

d April

3 Britain repeals Reparation Recovery Act and re-establishes sterling on a gold basis at its pre-1914 rate.

3 Holland and Belgium sign convention on the navigation of the River Scheldt.

4 Japan evacuates Sakhalin (occupied in 1905 and 1918).

10 Paul Painlevé becomes prime minister of France on Édouard Herriot's defeat.

25 Paul von Hindenburg, the former military leader, is elected president of Germany; he entered the contest only in the second ballot and wins 48.5 % of the popular vote against 45.2 % for Wilhelm Marx of the Centre Party.

e May

Shooting of Chinese students by foreign municipal police in Shanghai and other incidents in Guangzhou provokes Chinese boycott of British goods.

1 Cyprus is declared a British Crown Colony.

4 (–17 June) Geneva Conference on arms traffic and use of poison gas in war.

30 Joseph Coates, Reform Party, becomes prime minister of New Zealand, following death of W F Massey (10 May).

f June

8 Britain and France accept in principle Germany's proposals (of 9 Feb) for a security pact to guarantee Franco–German and Belgian–German boundaries.

26 in Greece, coup in Athens: General Theodoros Pangalos seizes power.

30 in Britain, owners of coal mines give a month's notice of wage cuts (opposed by miners).

g July

7 South African Senate rejects colour-bar bill.

13 in Germany, French troops begin evacuation of Rhineland.

16 first elected parliament of Iraq opens in Baghdad.

18 insurrection of the Druses in Syria (–June 1927).

18 Treaty of Nettuno between Italy and the Kingdom of the Serbs, Croats, and Slovenes to settle disputes about Dalmatia.

31 provisional settlement of British miners' dispute, when the government agrees to provide subsidies for nine months and appoint a Royal Commission to investigate the raising of productivity.

h August

15 Norway annexes Spitzbergen.

18 US agreement with Belgium on war debts.

26 Henri Pétain takes command of French troops in Morocco.

28 Britain resumes diplomatic relations with Mexico, after break of eight years.

29 in Germany, amnesty for Kapp and promonarchical conspirators who mounted the 'Kapp Putsch' of March 1920.

k October

Greek army invades Bulgaria in reprisal for a soldier's murder; Bulgaria appeals to the League of Nations.

5 (–16) Locarno Conference, discussing question of security pact, strikes a balance between French and German interests by drafting treaties (a) guaranteeing the French–German and Belgian–German frontiers; (b) between Germany and France, Belgium, Czechoslovakia, and Poland respectively; (c) a mutual guarantee between France, Czechoslovakia, and Poland. Britain is involved in the guarantee of Franco–Belgian–German frontiers but not in the arrangements in Eastern Europe.

12 Soviet–German commercial treaty.

12 risings in Syria (18–20, French fleet bombards Damascus).

19 Italy completes occupation of Italian Somaliland under terms of 1889 Protectorate.

26 Chinese customs conference at Beijing.

29 Conservatives win seats in Canadian elections but W L Mackenzie King maintains precarious Liberal government with support of Progressives.

31 Reza Khan deposes the shah of Persia (now Iran) and becomes Shah.

l November

12 US agreement with Italy on war debts.

22 Free State representative on Irish boundary commission resigns.

27 Aristide Briand forms ministry in France.

m December

1 Locarno treaties signed in London.

P Society, Education, and Religion

Mrs Ross of Wyoming becomes first woman state governor in USA (1 Jan), when she takes office to complete her late husband's term.

First woman mayor (Burgomaster) appointed in Belgium (July).

Foundation at Smith College, Northampton, Massachusetts, USA, of the Institute to Coordinate Women's Interests (–1931).

Japan introduces adult male suffrage (29 March).

The Polish parliament provides for the voluntary breakup of great estates (Dec 28).

Turkish government abolishes the Fez and requires men to wear hats.

Al 'Scarface' Capone takes control of organized crime in Chicago, USA.

Egypt introduces free compulsory elementary education.

Inauguration of the Hebrew University in Jerusalem by Earl Balfour (2 April).

In USA, Guggenheim Foundation established.

'Project method' of learning evaluated in W H Kilpatrick, *Foundations of Method.*

Harold Rugg and Ann Shumaker, *The Child-Centred School.*

Trial (July) of John T Scopes in Dayton, Tennessee, USA, for teaching evolutionary theory, in contravention of a recent state act; Scope was found guilty but the conviction was later overturned on a legal technicality; the trial seen widely as a humiliation for the Fundamentalist cause.

Concordat between Poland and the Vatican (signed 10 Feb) provides for Church-organized religious instruction and requires consultation between Church and State for only the highest Church appointments.

Pope Pius XI introduces the Feast of Christ the King, to be celebrated on the last Sunday of October.

United Church of Canada is founded.

Songs of Praise (edited by Percy Dearmer).

Q Science, Technology, and Discovery

Bell laboratories founded in USA.

US physicist R A Millikan discovers the presence of penetrating radiations in the upper atmosphere.

British pathologist J B Collip obtains extract of the parathyroid gland for treating tetanus.

Goldberger isolates vitamins B and B2.

A N Whitehead, *Science and the Modern World.*

R Humanities

V Gordon Childe, *The Dawn of European Civilization.*

Henri Pirenne, *Medieval Cities.*

Hilaire Belloc, *History of England.*

Julius Pratt, *Expansionists of 1812.*

E D Adams, *Great Britain and the American Civil War.*

Viscount Grey of Fallodon, *Twenty-Five Years, 1892–1916.*

A Richards, *Science and Poetry.*

Virginia Woolf, *The Common Reader.*

Marcel Mauss, *The Gift: Forms and Functions of Exchange in Archaic Societies.*

Harold Laski, *A Grammar of Politics.*

S Art, Sculpture, Fine Arts, and Architecture

Exposition Internationale des Arts Décoratifs et Industriels Modernes, Paris, France — term 'Art Deco' originates here.

First Surrealist exhibition, held at the Galerie Pierre, Paris, France.

Central Committee of the Communist Party of the USSR criticizes abstract art.

Painting, etc:

Otto Dix, *Three Prostitutes on the Street.*

André Masson, *Automatic Drawing.*

Henri Matisse, *Decorative Figure on an Ornamental Ground* (–1926).

Pablo Picasso, *Three Dancers.*

Chaim Soutine, *Carcass of Beef.*

Sculpture:

Jacob Epstein, *Rima.*

Alfred Gibert, The Shaftesbury Memorial ('Eros').

Kurt Schwitters, *Merzbau* (–1936).

Architecture:

Walter Gropius, Bauhaus, Dessau (–1926).

Le Corbusier, pavilion of the Esprit Nouveau, Paris Exhibition, France.

T Music

Alban Berg, *Wozzeck* (opera).

Ferruccio Busoni, *Doktor Faust* (posthumous opera).

Aaron Copland, Symphony No. 1.

George Gershwin, Piano Concerto.

Carl Nielsen, Symphony No. 6 ('Sinfonia Semplice').

Sergei Prokofiev, Symphony No. 2.

Maurice Ravel, *L'Enfant et les Sortilèges* (opera).

Dmitry Shostakovich, Symphony No. 1.

In USA, start of regular broadcasting of country music from Nashville, Tennessee, with the *National Barn Dance* country variety programme (28 Nov) and the *Grand Ole Opry* radio show (10 Dec).

In Chicago, USA, Louis Armstrong starts making his Hot Five recordings.

1 British troops evacuate Cologne, Germany.
3 existing boundary between Irish Free State and Northern Ireland is confirmed; the same agreement relieves the Free State of its share of British National Debt and transfers powers of the planned Council of Ireland relating to Northern Ireland to the Northern Ireland government.
5 (–20 Jan 1926) cabinet crisis in Germany.

6 Italy makes agreement with Egypt on Cyrenaica.
15 Greece agrees to penalties imposed by League of Nations over its dispute with Bulgaria.
16 League of Nations settles disputed possession of Mosul in favour of Iraq.
17 USSR signs defensive alliance with Turkey.

US black singer Paul Robeson gives his first recital of Negro spirituals.

US industrialist Henry Ford starts a drive against jazz by organizing a series of folk dances.

Introduction of electrical recording for records in place of acoustical methods.

u Literature and Drama

Sherwood Anderson, *Dark Laughter*.

Martin Boyd, *Love Gods*.

Mikhail Bulgakov, *The White Guard*.

Ivy Compton-Burnett, *Pastors and Masters*.

e e cummings, *XLI Poems*.

John Dos Passos, *Manhattan Transfer*.

Theodore Dreiser, *An American Tragedy*.

Lion Feuchtwanger, *Jew Süss* (written 1921).

F Scott Fitzgerald, *The Great Gatsby*.

Ford Madox Ford, *No More Parades*.

André Gide, *Les Faux-Monnayeurs* (The Counterfeiters).

Dubose Heyward, *Porgy*.

Aldous Huxley, *Those Barren Leaves*.

Franz Kafka, *The Trial* (posthumous).

Sinclair Lewis, *Arrowsmith*, for which he declined a Pulitzer Prize.

Eugenio Montale, *Ossi di seppia/Cuttle-bones*.

Gertrude Stein, *The Making of Americans* (written 1906–08).

Jules Supervielle, *Gravitations* (poems).

P G Wodehouse, *Carry on Jeeves*.

Virginia Woolf, *Mrs Dalloway*.

Drama:

Noël Coward, *Hay Fever*.

Frederick Lonsdale, *The Last of Mrs Cheyney*.

Sean O'Casey, *Juno and the Paycock*.

Arnold Ridley, *The Ghost Train*.

In USA, foundation of the Goodman Theater Center of the Art Institute of Chicago.

v Births and Deaths

Feb 20 Robert Altman born (–).

Feb 21 Sam Peckinpah born (–1984).

March 12 Sun Yat-sen dies (58).

March 20 Lord Curzon dies (66).

March 26 Pierre Boulez born (–).

April 14 John Singer Sergeant dies (69).

May 12 Alfred, Lord Milner dies (71).

May 14 Henry Rider Haggard dies (69).

June 27 Michael Dummett born (–).

July 26 Gottlob Frege dies (76).

Sept 7 Laura Ashley born (–1985).

Sept 8 Peter Sellers born (–1980).

Sept 16 Charles Haughey born (–).

Oct 3 Gore Vidal born (–).

Oct 13 Margaret Thatcher born (–).

Oct 22 Robert Rauschenberg born (–).

Oct 24 Luciano Berio born (–).

Nov 10 Richard Burton born (–1984).

Nov 20 Robert Kennedy born (–1968).

w Everyday Life

Clarence Birdseye in USA extends deep-freezing process to pre-cooked foods.

The first motel opens in California, USA.

Lux soap goes on sale.

The 'Charleston' takes New York dance halls by storm.

Hungarian designer Marcel Breuer designs the tubular steel chair.

x Sport and Recreation

In American Football, Red Grange signs for the Chicago Bears for $100,000.

Batting for Surrey against Somerset at Taunton, English cricketer J B Hobbs surpasses W G Grace's record of 126 centuries in first-class cricket (18 Aug).

In a change in football's offside law, the number of players required to be between an attacking player and the goal is reduced from three to two.

For the first time, motor-racing mechanics are accommodated in pits, rather than being required to travel with the driver.

The New Zealand Rugby Union 'All Blacks' are undefeated on their 30-match tour of Britain and France.

The Fastnet Race for yachts is inaugurated (from the Isle of Wight, off S England, round the Fastnet rock off SE Ireland, and back to Plymouth, SW England).

y Media

In Britain the Press Association acquires major control of the Reuters news agency.

Publication of *The New Yorker*, founded by Harold Ross.

Tass press agency founded in USSR (10 July).

Film:

The Battleship Potemkin (director, Sergei Eisenstein).

The Chronicles of the Grey House (director, Arthur von Gerlach).

The Death Ray (director, Lev Kuleshov).

The Gold Rush (starring Charlie Chaplin).

Gribiche (director, Jacques Feyder).

Joyless Street (starring Greta Garbo in her last European role).

The Pony Express (director, James Cruze).

Radio:

Foundation (April) of the European Broadcasting Union (or UIR) as a forum for handling broadcasting issues affecting Europe.

In Britain, the BBC's long-wave transmitter at Daventry in the E Midlands is brought into service; its broadcasts are heard throughout Britain and in Europe.

General Strike in Britain ... Germany joins the League ...
British legation in Beijing declares Britain's sympathy with
Chinese Nationalist movement (Guomindang).

A **January**

3 in Greece, Theodoros Pangalos assumes dictatorial powers (April, is elected president).

4 Moderate ministry takes office in Bulgaria, offering amnesty to all political prisoners except Communists.

8 in Mecca, following conquests in Arabia and the abdication of Hussein ibn Ali, king of Hejaz (on 5 Oct 1924), Ibn Saud is proclaimed king of Hejaz.

14 (–30) Denmark, Sweden, Norway, and Finland make a series of agreements for the peaceful settlement of disputes.

B **February**

Tension between Italy and Austria over Germanization of South Tyrol.

10 Germany applies for admission to League of Nations (17 March, Brazil and Spain block Germany's admission, protesting against the plan to give Germany a seat on the Council, which they thought they should have instead).

C **March**

11 Éamon de Valera resigns as leader of Sinn Féin.

26 Romania and Poland form alliance.

D **April**

7 first of several attempts to assassinate Benito Mussolini.

22 Persia, Turkey, and Afghanistan sign treaty for mutual security.

24 Berlin treaty of friendship and neutrality between Germany and USSR.

E **May**

1 (–Nov) coal strike in Britain.

2 US troops land to preserve order in Nicaraguan revolt.

3 (–12) in Britain, first (and only) General Strike.

8 following revolt by Druse in Syria, French fleet bombards Damascus.

10 Vincent Witos, leader of the Peasants' Party, forms ministry in Poland.

12 (–14) in Poland, Józef Pilsudski and army units march on Warsaw and seize power (14, President Wojciechowski and Prime Minister Witos resign; the speaker of parliament becomes acting president).

12 in Germany, resignation of Chancellor Hans Luther (17, Wilhelm Marx of the Centre Party is appointed).

16 in Irish Free State, Éamon de Valera founds Fianna Fáil ('Soldiers of Destiny'), thereby splitting the anti-treaty party.

18 (–26) preparatory Disarmament Conference meets, attended by USA, but not by USSR.

23 France proclaims the Lebanon a republic.

26 in Morocco, end of the Riff war, with the Berber leader Abd-el-Krim's surrender to France.

31 in Poland, the parliament elects Józef Pilsudski as president, but he refuses to take office (1 June, Ignace Moscicki is elected president).

31 General Manuel de Oliveira Gomes da Costa leads coup in Portugal which deposes the president (Bernardino Machado).

F **June**

5 British–Turkish agreement on Mosul, with most of the area assigned to Iraq in accordance with League of Nations' award of Dec 1925).

7 Liberal ministry replaces Socialist government in Sweden.

10 Spain announces withdrawal from the League of Nations, but later rescinds decision.

26 in USA, McNary-Haugen Bill for tariff on agricultural products is defeated in Senate.

28 W L Mackenzie King resigns as result of Canadian customs scandals; Arthur Meighen forms Liberal ministry.

G **July**

1 British–Portuguese agreement on boundary between South West Africa (modern Namibia) and Angola.

9 Gomes da Costa is overthrown in Portugal by General António Oscar de Fragoso Carmona.

15 in France, fall of Aristide Briand's ministry as a result of financial crisis.

23 (–1929) Raymond Poincaré becomes prime minister of French National Union Ministry.

26 Philippines legislature calls for plebiscite on independence, which is vetoed by the governor.

28 USA–Panama alliance to protect the Panama Canal in wartime.

28 Belgian financial crisis: franc is devalued and King Albert I is given dictatorial powers for six months.

30 a treaty between Albania, Greece, and the Kingdom of the Serbs, Croats, and Slo-

Anticlerical legislation in Mexico ... Goddard develops liquid-powered rocket ... Death of Houdini ...

o Politics, Government, Law, and Economy

New constitution for Lebanon (a French mandate), which seeks to balance different communities in government by providing for a Maronite president, a Sunni Muslim as prime minister, and a Shi'ite Muslim as speaker of the chamber.

US Congress passes the Air Commerce Act (20 May), which makes the licensing of pilots and aircraft the responsibility of the Commerce Department.

Leonard D White, *Introduction to the Study of Public Administration.*

British Parliament appoints the Simon Commission, to examine the working of the 1919 Government of India Act (8 Nov).

Beatrice Webb, *My Apprenticeship.*

New law code adopted in Turkey (17 Feb), based on Swiss code (rather than Islamic principles); polygamy is prohibited.

France returns to the gold standard.

In Italy, the Fascist government undertakes (in theory at least) a 'corporatist' reorganization of industry with the declaration of 13 state-controlled corporations and the establishment of the National Council of Corporations; workers are represented by Fascist labour syndicates; strikes and lock-outs are declared illegal.

Central Electricity Generating Board established in Britain to regularize electrical supply and create a National Grid.

ICI (Imperial Chemical Industries) formed in Britain as a merger of companies, with a near monopoly in the British chemical industry.

p Society, Education, and Religion

League of Nations sponsors international convention on slavery, which defines slavery (Sept).

Civil marriage is established in Turkey (1 Sept).

A New York State Housing Law permits tax exemptions for cooperative housing projects, in an attempt to encourage the provision of low-cost housing.

In USA, the Ford Motor Company introduces a 5-day working week and 8-hour day (5 Sept).

Foundation of the Council for the Preservation of Rural England.

In Italy, foundation of the *Ballilla*, a Fascist youth organization (3 April).

Adoption is made legal in Britain.

Hadow Report backs transfer of all 11-year-old children in England from primary to differentiated secondary schools.

Foundation of Reading University, S England.

University of London Act provides a new constitution for the University's constituent colleges.

Cyril Burt, *The Measurement of Mental Capacities.*

Kenneth Lindsay, *Social Progress and Educational Waste.*

Anticlerical legislation in Mexico (2 July), which results in the Church's refusal to hold services for three years.

Father Charles Coughlin, a Roman Catholic priest, makes his first radio broadcast in Detroit, USA.

Rudolph Bultmann, *Jesus.*

Essays Catholic and Critical.

q Science, Technology, and Discovery

Alan Cobham flies from Croydon in southern England to Cape Town in South Africa and back (March) to discover possibilities of long-distance air routes.

Flights over North Pole by Roald Amundsen and by Richard Byrd.

Robert H Goddard of Clark University, Massachusetts, USA, develops a rocket powered by petrol and liquid oxygen.

Scott Polar Research Institute, Cambridge, opened.

F Lindemann, *The Physical Significance of the Quantum Theory.*

German physicists Max Born and Werner Heisenberg formulate a mathematical theory to explain quantum theory.

Austrian physicist Erwin Schrödinger develops wave mechanics.

US biochemist J B Sumner succeeds in isolating an enzyme (an achievement validated in the 1930s by the work of J H Northrop).

T H Morgan, *The Theory of the Gene.*

Liver extract first used for treating pernicious anaemia.

r Humanities

M Rostovtzeff, *Social and Economic History of the Roman Empire.*

Speculum, a Journal of Medieval Studies issued.

G M Trevelyan, *History of England.*

R H Tawney, *Religion and the Rise of Capitalism.*

Charles A Beard, *The Supreme Court and the Constitution.*

James Truslow Adams, *New England in the Republic, 1776–1850.*

J H Clapham, *An Economic History of Modern Britain* (–1938).

venes recognizes Albania's frontiers (registered with the League of Nations).

31 Afghanistan signs non-aggression pact with USSR.

H August

10 following devaluation of the French franc, a sinking fund is established to redeem the national debt.

17 Greece signs treaty of friendship with the Kingdom of the Serbs, Croats, and Slovenes (Yugoslavia).

22 in Greece, Theodoros Pangalos is overthrown by General Georgios Kondylis (who recalls former president George Koundouriotis).

J September

2 Italy agrees a treaty with the Yemen (start of Italy's attempt to dominate the east coast of the Red Sea).

6 in China, the Guomindang nationalist forces led by Chiang Kai-shek reach Hankou at the confluence of the Han and the Yangzi rivers; Hankou becomes the Guomindang capital.

8 Germany is admitted to the League, and in consequence Spain leaves (11).

17 Italian–Romanian treaty of friendship.

18 Poland signs treaty of friendship with the Kingdom of the Serbs, Croats, and Slovenes (Yugoslavia).

23 Aristide Briand and Gustav Stresemann discuss the Rhineland and reparations at Thoiry.

25 campaign against the Mafia begins in Sicily.

25 in Canada, following the defeat of the Conservatives in the House of Commons and in a general election, W L Mackenzie King forms another Liberal ministry.

K October

Union of National Peasants' Party founded in Romania.

2 in Poland, Józef Pilsudski becomes prime minister.

15 Ignaz Seipel, Christian Socialist, forms ministry in Austria, replacing Rudolf Ramek.

19 (–18 Nov) Imperial Conference in London, which decides that Britain and the Dominions are autonomous communities, equal in status.

19 in USSR, expulsion of Leon Trotsky and Grigory Zinoviev from the Politburo of the Communist Party, following Joseph Stalin's victory.

L November

In Italy, the Socialist, Republican, and Communist Parties are dissolved and the abstaining anti-Fascist deputies are declared to have forfeited their parliamentary seats. Communist revolt in Java (–July 1927).

10 Vincent Massey becomes first Canadian minister to Washington.

11 in Hungary, the Upper House of parliament, representing the landed aristocracy, is re-established.

19 British miners call off strike (begun 1 May).

27 Treaty of Tirana between Italy and Albania, with Italy recognizing the status quo in Albania and promising assistance.

M December

15 in Denmark, following minor losses by Social Democrats and Radicals in general election, the Liberals form a government but the Social Democrats remain the largest single party.

17 (–Jan 1927) cabinet crisis in Germany.

G P Gooch and H W V Temperley (eds.), *British Documents on the Origins of the War, 1898–1914* (–1938).

Max Scheler, *Forms of Knowledge and Society.*

A N Whitehead, *Religion in the Making.*

s Art, Sculpture, Fine Arts, and Architecture

Painting, etc:

Otto Dix, *The Poet Ivan von Lucken.*

Arshile Gorky, *Artist and Mother* (–1936).

George Grosz, *Eclipse of the Sun, Pillars of Society.*

Joan Miró, *Person Throwing a Stone at a Bird.*

Georgia O'Keefe, *Black Iris.*

Man Ray, *Black and White — photograph.*

Stanley Spencer, Murals for Burghclere Chapel, Berkshire, England (–1932).

Sculpture:

Alberto Giacometti, *Spoon Woman.*

Pablo Picasso, *Guitar.*

Architecture:

Le Corbusier, *The Coming Architecture* published.

t Music

Béla Bartók, *The Miraculous Mandarin* (ballet).

Alban Berg, *Lyric Suite.*

John Alden Carpenter, *Skyscrapers.*

Paul Hindemith, *Cardillac* (opera).

Leoš Janáček, *The Makropoulos Case* (opera) and *Glagolitic Mass.*

Zoltán Kodály, *Háry János* (opera).

Giacomo Puccini, *Turandot* (posthumous opera).

Karol Szymanowski, *King Roger* (opera).

Ray Henderson, 'The Black Bottom'.

The Desert Song (musical), music by Sigmund Romberg, text by Otto Harbach and others (first performed at the New York Casino Theatre, 30 Nov).

In USA, Jelly Roll Morton forms his band the Red Hot Peppers to record for the Victor label.

First *Blackbirds* revue in London, at the London Pavilion (11 Sept).

Foundation of *Melody Maker* magazine in Britain, which eventually helps the spread of jazz in the country.

u Literature and Drama

Georges Bernanos, *Under the Sun of Satan.*

Hart Crane, *White Buildings.*

William Faulkner, *Soldiers' Pay.*

Edna Ferber, *Show Boat.*

André Gide, *Si le grain ne meurt/If it die.*

Ernest Hemingway, *The Sun Also Rises* (published as *Fiesta* in Britain).

Langston Hughes, *The Weary Blues.*

Franz Kafka, *The Castle* (posthumous).

Rudyard Kipling, *Debits and Credits.*

D H Lawrence, *The Plumed Serpent.*

T E Lawrence, *Seven Pillars of Wisdom.*

Hugh MacDiarmid, *A Drunk Man Looks at the Thistle.*

Somerset Maugham, *The Casuarina Tree.*

A A Milne, *Winnie the Pooh.*

Vladimir Nabokov, *Mary.*

Sylvia Townsend Warner, *Lolly Willowes.*

The magazine *Voorslug* founded in South Africa by Roy Campbell and William Plomer.

Drama:

Paul Green, *In Abraham's Bosom.*

Margaret Kennedy and Basil Dean, *The Constant Nymph.*

Sean O'Casey, *The Plough and the Stars.*

Eugene O'Neill, *The Great God Brown.*

Ben Travers, *Rookery Nook.*

The Yiddish Art Theatre opened in New York by Maurice Schwartz.

v Births and Deaths

Feb 2 Valéry Giscard d'Estaing born (–).

Feb 9 Garret Fitzgerald born (–).

Feb 16 John Schlesinger born (–).

March 6 Andrzej Wajda born (–).

April 8 Jürgen Moltmann born (–).

April 21 Queen Elizabeth II born (–).

May 15 Peter Shaffer born (–).

June 1 Marilyn Monroe born (–1962).

June 3 Allen Ginsburg born (–).

Aug 3 Anthony Sampson born (–).

Aug 23 Rudolph Valentino dies (31).

Sept 3 Alison Lurie born (–).

Oct 15 Michel Foucault born (–1984).

Dec 5 Claude Monet dies (66).

Dec 20 Geoffrey Howe born (–).

Dec 29 Rainer Maria Rilke dies (51).

w Everyday Life

Sale in New York of a Gutenberg Bible for $106,000.

In USA, Harry Scherman founds the first bookclub, the Book-of-the-Month Club.

The Shakespeare Memorial Theatre at Stratford-upon-Avon, England, is burnt down.

Half a million telephones are now installed in London.

Charles Atlas (real name Angelo Siciliano) opens a gymnasium in New York to promote his body-building techniques.

US escape artist Harry Houdini dies from peritonitis after being punched (31 Oct).

x Sport and Recreation

England's cricket team regains the Ashes,

*Guomindang advances in China ... Trotsky expelled from Soviet
Communist Party ...*

A January

29 German cabinet crisis is resolved with Wilhelm Marx becoming chancellor.

31 inter-Allied military control of Germany ends.

B February

3 (−13) revolt in Portugal against the military dictatorship of General Carmona.

18 USA establishes direct diplomatic relations with Canada (not via Britain).

19 in China the Guomindang nationalists extract from Britain a reduction of the concessions at Hankou and Kiukiang.

C March

24 the Guomindang nationalists take Nanjing on the lower Yangzi.

D April

5 treaty of friendship between Italy and Hungary.

12 following the arrival of Guomindang forces in Shanghai, E China, Chiang Kai-shek and conservatives start purging communists and other leftist elements from the Guomindang.

15 USSR and Switzerland resume diplomatic relations.

17 bank crisis in Japan forces resignation of Reijiro Wakatsuki's ministry.

21 Italian labour charter issued, embodying principles of Fascist corporatism.

E May

2 (−23) economic conference at Geneva, attended by 52 nations, including USSR.

4 Henry Stimpson, US secretary of state, brings together factions in Nicaragua; the USA is asked to supervise elections.

9 in Australia, the Parliament House, Canberra, is opened.

20 by Treaty of Jiddah, Britain recognizes rule of Ibn Saud in the Hejaz.

26 Britain annuls trade agreement with USSR and breaks off diplomatic relations after discovery of documents relating to Soviet intrigues against the British Empire.

27 in Czechoslovakia, Tomáš Masaryk is re-elected President of Czechoslovakia.

27 Japan intervenes on the Shandong Peninsula, China, to block the advance of Chi-

beating Australia 1–0 in the five-match series in England (18 Aug).

Gertrude Ederle of the USA becomes the first woman to swim the English Channel (Aug).

Gene Tunney out-points Jack Dempsey to win the World Heavyweight boxing title in Philadelphia, Pennsylvania, USA (23 Sept).

Victoria establishes a new record score for first-class cricket of 1,107 runs in the Sheffield Shield match against New South Wales in Melbourne, Australia (24–29 Dec).

The International Table Tennis Federation is formed and the first world championships are held in the Memorial Hall, Farringdon St, London.

Y Media

Film:

Ben Hur (starring Ramon Navarro).
Faust (director, F W Murnau).
Mantrap (starring Clara Bowe).

Metropolis (director, Fritz Lang).
Mother (director, Vsevolod Pudovkin).
A Page of Madness (director, Teinosuke Kinugasa).
Secrets of a Soul (director, G W Pabst).
Slipping Wives (starring Laurel and Hardy).

Radio:

Following concern about the control of radio in Britain, the BBC is incorporated by royal charter as the British Broadcasting Corporation (effective from 1 Jan 1927), run by a crown-appointed chairman and governors and financed by a licence fee.

Over 2 million people in Britain hold radio licences.

In the USA, the National Broadcasting Company (NBC) purchases the WEAF station as the basis for establishing a national network of stations; programmes are a mixture of sponsored programmes and public-service programmes.

Television:

John Logie Baird demonstrates television system in Soho, London (26 Jan).

Lindbergh flies across the Atlantic ... Benda's Treason of the Intellectuals *... Show Boat ...*

O Politics, Government, Law, and Economy

In USA, the Institute for Government Research, Institute of Economics, and Robert Brookings Graduate School of Economics and Government are merged to form the Brookings Institution.

W F Willoughby, *Principles of Public Administration.*

Massachusetts is the first US state to introduce a compulsory car insurance fund.

Adolf Hitler, *Mein Kampf*, Vol. 2.

Mustafa Kemal, *The New Turkey.*

Walter Lippmann, *Public Opinion.*

In Italy, a new criminal code is published (Aug), reintroducing the death penalty and abolishing trial by jury.

Benjamin Cardozo, *The Paradoxes of Legal Science.*

In USA, execution of anarchists Nicola Sacco and Bartolomeo Vanzetti (23 Aug) for murder during robbery in 1920 causes outcry because of slim evidence (posthumous pardons awarded by Governor Dukakis of Massachusetts in 1977).

British Trades Union Act (passed 28 July)

declares general strikes and lock-outs illegal.

Pan American and Eastern airlines founded in USA.

Discovery of the Kirkuk oil field in north-eastern Iraq.

Florida land boom collapses after excessive speculation and some outright fraud.

P Society, Education, and Religion

The US Supreme Court rules, in Nixon v. Herndon, that a 'white primary' election in Texas is unconstitutional.

Frederick Thrasher, *The Gang.*

The German government introduces a comprehensive scheme of unemployment legislation.

World Population conference organized by Margaret Sanger.

Wilhelm Reich, *The Function of the Orgasm.*

World Conference on Faith and Order held at Lausanne, Switzerland.

Emil Brunner, *The Mediator.*

Q Science, Technology, and Discovery

US aviator Charles A Lindbergh flies from

nese Nationalists (the Guomindang) on Beijing.

F **June**
Rupture of relations between Albania and the Kingdom of the Serbs, Croats, and Slovenes (Yugoslavia) following frontier incidents. End of Druse revolt in Syria.
3 in Greece, promulgation of a new constitution.
9 in Irish Free State, election produces a deadlock: Cumann na nGaedheal, 47 seats; Fianna Fáil, 44; Labour, 22; Farmers' Union, 11; National League, 8; Republicans, 5; others, 16.
20 (–4 Aug) Britain, USA, and Japan confer at Washington, DC, USA, on naval disarmament, but fail to reach agreement.

G **July**
Unrest in Samoa (modern Western Samoa), fomented by Europeans (–Aug).
10 assassination of Kevin O'Higgins (Nationalist minister) provokes denunciation of tactics of Irish Republicans; in response the Irish Dáil passes the Public Safety Act declaring revolutionary societies as treasonable and giving increased powers to the government.
15 (–16) Socialist riots and general strike in Vienna, following acquittal of Nationalists for political murders.
27 Belgium and Portugal make territorial adjustments in the Congo (modern Zaire).

H **August**
7 international Peace Bridge between USA and Canada opened.
12 in the Irish Free State, following the introduction of a bill requiring election candidates to swear willingness to enter the Dáil, Éamon de Valera and other anti-Treaty Republicans agree to take up their seats in the Dáil.
22 Allied military control of Hungary abolished.
23 following the death of Saad Zaghlul, Nahas Pasha becomes leader of the Wafd nationalist party in Egypt.

J **September**
2 in Turkish elections Mustafa Kemal is empowered to nominate all candidates, giving the People's Party a monopoly.

15 in second general election of the year in the Irish Free State, Cumann na nGaedheal with 62 seats fail to win a clear majority over Fianna Fáil (57 seats) and other parties (Labour, 13; Farmers' Union, 6; National League, 2; others, 13); in Oct William Cosgrave forms a new ministry with support from the Farmers' Union and independents.
16 President Hindenburg of Germany, dedicating the Tannenburg memorial, repudiates Germany's responsibility for the War (article 231 of the Versailles Treaty).
22 slavery abolished in Sierra Leone.

K **October**
1 USSR–Persian non-aggression pact.
17 first Labour government formed in Norway, following general election in which Labour won 59 seats, Conservatives 30, Liberals 30, and Farmers' Party 26.

L **November**
11 treaty of friendship between France and the Kingdom of the Serbs, Croats, and Slovenes (Yugoslavia).
14 Leon Trotsky and Grigory Zinoviev are expelled from the Soviet Communist Party (expulsion confirmed on 2 Dec by 15th Party Congress).
15 Canada is elected to a seat on the Council of the League of Nations.
22 in reply to the treaty between France and the Kingdom of the Serbs, Croats, and Slovenes (Yugoslavia), Albania signs defensive alliance with Italy.
22 Persia claims Bahrein Island in the Persian Gulf.
30 Maxim Litvinov, the USSR's commissar for foreign affairs, proposes immediate disarmament at Geneva, but this is rejected as a 'Communist trick'.

M **December**
13 dispute between Lithuania and Poland is referred to the League of Nations.
14 Britain recognizes Iraq's independence and promises to support its application for membership of the League of Nations in 1932.
14 China and the USSR break off diplomatic relations.
17 F B Kellogg, US secretary of state, suggests pact for renunciation of war.

New York to Paris in 37 hours (20–21 May).

Gino Watkins leads expedition to Edge Island, Spitzbergen.

German metallurgist Siegfried Junghans develops process for continuous casting of non-ferrous metal.

US scientist Albert W Hall improves fluorescent lamps.

German physicist Werner Heisenberg propounds the 'uncertainty principle' in quantum physics.

W Heitler and F London make discoveries on the wave mechanics of valency.

Iron lung invented in USA by Philip Drinker.

R **Humanities**

Bones found recently at Zhoukoudian, China, and known as Beijing Man are identified as those of the early hominid *Homo erectus.*

H Maspero, *China in Antiquity.*

British archaeologist Leonard Woolley makes rich discoveries at the site of ancient Ur (now in Iraq).

O G S Crawford founds the archaeological journal *Antiquity.*

Economic History Review issued.

Ernst H Kantorowicz, *Frederick the Second.*

Charles A and Mary R Beard, *Rise of American Civilization.*

E M Forster, *Aspects of the Novel.*

Harley Granville-Barker, *Prefaces to Shakespeare* (–1948).

J L Lowes, *The Road to Xanadu: A Study in the Ways of the Imagination.*

Vernon Parrington, *Main Currents in American Thought* (–1930).

Julien Benda, *The Treason of the Intellectuals.*

Martin Heidegger, *Being and Time.*

Gabriel Marcel, *Metaphysical Journal.*

Bertrand Russell, *The Analysis of Matter.*

S **Art, Sculpture, Fine Arts, and Architecture**

Painting, etc:
Giorgio de Chirico, *Furniture in a Valley.*
Edward Hopper, *Drug Store.*
Fernand Léger, *Woman Holding a Vase.*
L S Lowry, *Coming Out of School.*

Sculpture:
Jacob Epstein, *Madonna and Child, Paul Robeson.*
Eric Gill, *Mankind.*

Architecture:
Alvar Aalto, Library, Viipuri, Finland (–1935).

T **Music**

George Antheil's 'ballet mécanique', scored for propellers, anvils, motor horns, etc.

Reinhold Glière, *The Red Poppy* (ballet).

Ernst Křenek, *Jonny spielt auf* (opera).

Arnold Schoenberg, String Quartet No. 3.

Dmitry Shostakovich, Symphony No. 2 ('To October').

Igor Stravinsky, *Oedipus Rex* (opera).

Jaromír Weinberger, *Schwanda the Bagpiper* (opera).

Production of the stage version of *The Jazz Singer* (musical) at Warners' Theatre in New York (6 Oct).

Show Boat (musical), text by Oscar Hammerstein, music by Jerome Kern (first performed at the Ziegfeld Theatre, New York, 27 Dec).

Shuffle Along, a pioneering US African-American musical, by Eubie Blake and Noble Sissle.

Strike Up the Band (musical), text by George S Kaufman, music by George Gershwin (first performed in Long Branch, New Jersey, USA, 19 Aug; revived in New York, 1930).

In Britain the *Daily Mail* declares that 'Victims of the dancing craze multiply with frequency of adapted jazz "melodies"'.

U **Literature and Drama**

Isaak Babel, *Jewish Tales.*

Willa Cather, *Death Comes for the Archbishop.*

Robert Graves, *Poems, 1914–1926.*

Ernest Hemingway, *Men Without Women.*

Hermann Hesse, *Steppenwolf.*

Robinson Jeffers, *The Women at Point Sur* (poems).

Franz Kafka, *America.*

Sinclair Lewis, *Elmer Gantry.*

Henri Michaux, *Qui je fus.*

Marcel Proust, *Le Temps retrouvé* (posthumous).

Dorothy Richardson, *Oberland.*

Henry Williamson, *Tarka the Otter.*

Virginia Woolf, *To The Lighthouse.*

Drama:
Paul Claudel, *Protée.*
Somerset Maugham, *The Letter.*
Ben Travers, *Thark.*
Thornton Wilder, *The Bridge of San Luis Rey.*
Openings of the Royale and Alvin Theatres, New York.

V **Births and Deaths**

Feb 19 Georg Brandes dies (85).
May 6 Hudson Maxim dies (74).
June 1 J B Bury dies (76).
June 14 Jerome K Jerome dies (68).
Aug 23 Saad Zaghlul dies (66).

King Fuad suspends Egyptian constitution ... Kellogg–Briand
Pact ... Strikes in India.

A January

13 Allied military control of Bulgaria abolished.

14 first Conservative administration in Latvia.

19 press announcement in USSR that 30 'oppositionists', including Leon Trotsky, have gone into internal exile.

29 treaty between Germany and Lithuania provides for arbitration over Memel.

B February

20 Transjordan becomes self-governing under the British mandate.

C March

13 in USA, dam burst in Santa Clara River Valley, California, kills 450 people.

16 nationalist leader Nahas Pasha is appointed prime minister of Egypt (–25 June).

25 General António Carmona is elected president of Portugal (–1951).

28 military service in France reduced to a year.

D April

6 in arbitration of dispute between the USA and the Netherlands, Palmas Island, near the Philippines, is awarded to the Netherlands.

13 US secretary of state F B Kellogg submits his plan for renunciation of war to the Locarno powers.

21 Aristide Briand proposes a draft treaty for outlawing war.

22 in French elections, parties of the Right win 325 out of 610 seats.

27 Antonio de Oliveira Salazar becomes minister of finance in Portugal with wide powers.

29 British ultimatum forces Egypt to provide for freedom of public meetings.

Oct 8 César Milstein born (–).

w Everyday Life
Great gale sweeps across Britain, with wind
speed reaching 160 kph/102 mph (Feb 28).
Transatlantic telephone services begin.

x Sport and Recreation
Abraham M Saperstein founds the Harlem
Globetrotters, an African-American US
professional basketball team.

Cardiff City are the first non-English team to
win the Football Association Cup, beating
Arsenal 1–0.

First Ryder Cup match between the pro-
fessional golfers of the USA and Great
Britain and Ireland; held at Worcester,
Massachusetts, the US team wins 9–2 (3–4
June).

US tennis-player Helen Wills wins the first of
eight Ladies' Singles titles at the Wimbledon tournament in London; seeding is
introduced into the championships.

Sir Henry Segrave establishes a new world
land speed record of 326 kph/203.79 mph
at Daytona, Florida, USA.

British snooker player Joe Davis wins the
inaugural World Professional Snooker
Championship, holding the title until 1940
and winning again in 1946.

y Media
Film:
Fox Movietone News begins, using the sound-
on-record system.
Bed and Sofa (director, Abram Room).
Berlin, Symphony of a Great City (director,
Walter Ruttman).
The End of St Petersburg (director, Vsevolod
Pudovkin).
The Italian Straw Hat (director, René Clair).
The Kiss of Mary Pickford (director, Sergei
Komarov).
Napoleon (director, Abel Gance).
October (director, Sergei Eisenstein).
The Underworld (director, Josef von
Sternberg).
Zvenigora (director, Alexander Dovzhenko).

Radio:
Radio Act in the USA establishes a Federal
Radio Commission to license airwaves.
Foundation in USA of the Columbia Broadcasting Corporation (CBS).
First outside sports broadcast on the BBC, of
commentary on the Grand National horse
race.
First regular programme of recorded music
broadcast on the BBC, presented by Christopher Stone, who is considered to be the
world's first disc-jockey.

First Five-Year Plan in USSR ... Gershwin's American in Paris *...*
Mickey Mouse makes first appearance in film ...

o Politics, Government, Law, and Economy
League of Nations attempts to create a full
system of legal arbitration of international
relations questions in the General Act for
the Peaceful Settlement of International
Disputes.

A new law in Italy reorganizes the membership of parliament: the 13 state corporations are to submit candidates' names to
the Grand Council of Fascism, which then
finalizes the lists and submits them to the
electorate for ratification or rejection.

Benito Mussolini, *My Autobiography*.

In USSR, Stalin ends the New Economic
Policy and introduces state-directed economic planning and distribution, the development of industry, and collectivization of
agriculture in accordance with the first
Five-Year Plan (from 1 Oct).

'Bull market' on US stock exchange as people
and institutions borrow money to buy
shares.

Overproduction of coffee causes a price slump
and economic crisis in Brazil.

Italy adopts the gold standard.

Cable and Wireless corporation formed in
USA.

p Society, Education, and Religion
Voting age for Women in Britain reduced from
30 to 21 (5 July).

G B Shaw, *The Intelligent Woman's Guide to
Socialism and Capitalism*.

Oscar De Priest, a Republican from Chicago,
becomes the first African-American
elected to the US Congress since
Reconstruction.

Turkey adopts Latin alphabet (3 Nov).

Ankara, the new capital of Turkey, is
replanned with the assistance of German
engineer H Jansen.

In USA, start of development of Radburn,

E May

3 (–11) in China, clashes between Guomindang nationalists and Japanese troops at Ji'nan in NE China, after which Japan reoccupies part of the Shandong Peninsula.

12 Italian electoral law reduces electorate from 10 million to 3 million.

20 in German elections Social Democrats increase their number of seats from 131 to 153 and are the largest party but without an overall majority: Centre, 62; Communists, 54; German National People's Party, 73; German People's Party, 45; Nazis, 12.

F June

8 in China, the Guomindang nationalists capture Beijing (though the Guomindang and now Chinese capital remains at Nanjing).

9 France convenes constituent assembly in Syria; it has a Nationalist majority.

23 explanatory note on Kellogg–Briand pact is sent to the powers.

24 the French franc is again devalued.

27 in Poland, following elections, Kazimierz Bartel replaces Pilsudski as prime minister (though Pilsudski remains minister of defence).

28 Hermann Müller, Social Democrat, is appointed German chancellor (following resignation of Wilhelm Marx's ministry, 13).

G July

3 following his return to Greece in March, Eleutherios Venizélos is again appointed prime minister.

17 Alvaro Obregón, newly elected president of Mexico, is assassinated before taking office; the Congress appointed Emilio Portes Gil as successor.

19 King Fuad's coup in Egypt, where parliament is dissolved and the constitution is suspended; the king rules by decree.

19 China annuls the 'unequal treaties' with European powers.

25 Italy becomes a signatory to Tangier statute, giving Spain greater control there.

H August

2 Italy signs 20-year treaty of friendship with Ethiopia.

8 Croats withdraw from parliament of the Kingdom of the Serbs, Croats, and Slovenes, and establish a separatist assembly in Zagreb.

19 general election in Greece produces victory for the Liberal Party supporters of Venizélos.

27 the Kellogg–Briand Pact, outlawing war and providing for pacific settlement of disputes, is signed in Paris by 15 states, including USA.

28 all-party conference at Lucknow votes for dominion status for India (but, 30, radical members form the Independence of India League).

J September

1 Albania is proclaimed a kingdom and Zog (Ahmed Beg Zogu) is elected king.

10 in Argentina, Chamber of Deputies votes to revoke oil concessions (Senate adjourns before considering the matter).

11 Portuguese treaty with South Africa regulates problems of transport and labour recruitment.

23 Italy signs friendship treaty with Greece.

26 an act of the League of Nations Assembly, embodying Kellogg–Briand Pact, is signed by 23 nations.

K October

2 in Sweden, Arvid Lindman forms Conservative ministry; in the general election the Social Democrats won 40 seats, Prohibitionist Liberals 28, Liberals 4, Conservatives 73, Agrarian Party 27, and Communists 8.

4 (–16) plebiscite in Germany against building new battleships fails.

6 Chiang Kai-shek is elected President of China.

7 in US presidential election, Herbert Hoover, Republican, wins with 444 electoral votes against Alfred E Smith, Democrat, with 87; popular vote: Hoover, 21,391,381; Smith, 15,016,443; Norman Thomas (Socialist), 267,835.

L November

14 in elections in New Zealand, United (Liberal) Party under Joseph Ward wins 25 seats, Reform 25, and Labour 19.

M December

Arrest of a Slovak deputy in Czechoslovakia for irredentist agitation in favour of Hungary provokes ill feeling.

5 Wilhelm Miklas elected President of Austria, in succession to Michael Hainisch.

6 war between Bolivia and Paraguay.

12 Peasants' Party wins Romanian elections.

20 Britain recognizes the Guomindang government in Nanjing, China.

22 a Committee under US financier Owen D Young is appointed to examine reparations question.

New Jersey, as a 'garden city' for 25,000 people (the project is ruined by the crash of 1929; only 1,500 homes are built).

Margaret Mead, *Coming of Age in Samoa.*

Selig Perlman, *A Theory of the Labor Movement.*

Louis Wirth, *The Ghetto.*

In USSR, mass campaign against adult illiteracy and for compulsory primary schooling.

By amendment to Turkish constitution, Islam ceases to be the recognized state religion (9 April).

Ecumenical Missionary Conference, held in Jerusalem, stresses partnership in a common undertaking.

Revised Prayer Book of the Church of England rejected by Parliament (14 June).

Cosmo Lang becomes Archbishop of Canterbury (succeeding Randall Davidson who had served from 1903 to 28, the longest tenure of the office since William Warham, 1504–32).

Q Science, Technology, and Discovery

First east–west transatlantic flights by Köhl and by Fitzmaurice.

German physicists H Geiger and W Müller improve the 'Geiger counter'.

In Britain, Alexander Fleming discovers penicillin.

The constitution of thyroxine is discovered.

T H Morgan, *The Theory of Sex.*

R Humanities

Start of excavations at Anyang, China, which reveal Anyang to have been a capital of the Shang dynasty in the mid-2nd millennium BC.

O G S Crawford and Alexander Keiller, *Wessex from the Air* – a pioneer archaeological study based on aerial photographs.

Kenneth Clark, *The Gothic Revival.*

J G Randall and David Herbert Donald, *The Civil War and Reconstruction.*

Albert J Beveridge, *Abraham Lincoln, 1809–1858.*

Completion of *New English Dictionary* (begun 1884).

Dictionary of American Biography (–1944).

Rudolf Carnap, *The Logical Structure of the World.*

Max Scheler, *The Place of Man in the Universe.*

S Art, Sculpture, Fine Arts, and Architecture

The USSR sells art treasures to finance development (–1933).

Painting, etc:

Max Beckmann, *Black Lilies.*

Charles Demuth, *I saw the Figure 5 in Gold.*

Max Ernst, *The Virgin spanking the Infant Jesus before three witnesses.*

André Breton, *Paul Eluard and the Artist.*

Henri Matisse, *Seated Odalisque.*

Pablo Picasso, *Bathers* series.

Architecture:

Congrès Internationaux d'Architecture Moderne, founded in Switzerland.

T Music

Ernest Bloch, *America.*

George Gershwin, *An American in Paris.*

Ildebrando Pizzetti, *Fra Gherardo* (opera).

Maurice Ravel, *Boléro* (ballet).

Arnold Schoenberg, *Variations for Orchestra.*

Richard Strauss, *Die ägyptische Helena* (opera).

Anton Webern, Symphony.

Kurt Weill, *The Threepenny Opera* (musical).

Pianist Vladimir Horowitz makes his British and American debuts.

Al Jolson, 'Sonny Boy', 'There's A Rainbow Around My Shoulder'.

Paul Robeson sings 'Ol' Man River' in the British production of *Show Boat.*

Jimmie Rodgers, 'The Soldier's Sweetheart'.

In New York, *Blackbirds of 1928* revue.

Clarence 'Pine Top' Smith, 'Pine Top's boogie-woogie' (considered the earliest commercial use of the term 'boogie-woogie').

Earl Hines founds his first band in Chicago, USA.

HMV introduce first autochange gramophone.

U Literature and Drama

Stephen Vincent Benét, *John Brown's Body.*

Aldous Huxley, *Point Counter Point.*

Christopher Isherwood, *All the Conspirators.*

D H Lawrence, *Lady Chatterley's Lover* (privately printed in Florence).

Federico García Lorca, *Gipsy Ballads.*

Katherine Mansfield, *Letters.*

Somerset Maugham, *Ashenden.*

Eugene O'Neill, *Strange Interlude.*

Ezra Pound, *A Draft of the Cantos 17–27.*

Theodore Francis Powys, *Mr Weston's Good Wine.*

Siegfried Sassoon, *Memoirs of a Foxhunting Man.*

Upton Sinclair, *Boston.*

Stephen Spender, *Nine Experiments.*

Edgar Wallace, *The Squeaker.*

Evelyn Waugh, *Decline and Fall.*

Wen-I-tuo, *Dead Water* (poems).

Virginia Woolf, *Orlando.*

W B Yeats, *The Tower* (poems).

Drama:
Bertolt Brecht, *The Caucasian Chalk Circle.*
Jean Giraudoux, *Siegfried.*
Ben Hecht and Charles MacArthur, *The Front Page.*
Vladimir Mayakovsky, *Klop/The Bedbug.*
Eugene O'Neill, *Strange Interlude.*
John Van Druten, *Young Woodley.*
John Gielgud first plays in New York, in *The Patriot* by Alfred Neumann.

v Births and Deaths
Jan 1 Thomas Hardy dies (87).
Jan 29 Douglas, Earl Haig dies (66).
Feb 15 H H Asquith dies (75).
March 12 Edward Albee born (–).
March 19 Hans Küng born (–).
April 6 James Watson born (–).
April 10 Stanley John Weyman dies (72).
May 1 Ebenezer Howard dies (78).
June 14 Ernesto 'Che' Guevara born (–1967).
June 14 Emmeline Pankhurst dies (69).
July 26 Stanley Kubrick born (–).
Aug 12 Leoš Janáček dies (74).
Sept 23 Roald Amundsen dies (56).
Nov 12 Grace Kelly born (–1982).
Dec 7 Noam Chomsky born (–).

w Everyday Life
The British War Office abolishes the use of the lance as a weapon of war.
The first stabilized, marketable peanut butter is produced.
The airship *Graf Zeppelin* completes the transatlantic flight from Friedrichshafen in Germany to New Jersey, USA, in 4 days 15.5 hours.

x Sport and Recreation
In Britain, the Grand National horse race is won by Tipperary Tim at odds of 100–1; only two of the 42 starters complete the course (30 March).
The 9th Olympic Games are held in Amsterdam (17 May–12 Aug). The USA wins 22 gold medals; Germany, 10; Finland, 8; Sweden, Italy, and Switzerland, 7 each; France and Holland, 6 each. Women's track and field events are held for the first time. India wins the first of six consecutive hockey golds.
The West Indies play Test cricket for the first time, losing all three matches against England.
In the first £10,000 transfer in English football: David Jack moves from Bolton Wanderers to Arsenal.
The Squash Rackets Association is formed.

y Media
Foundation, in Atlanta, Georgia, USA, of the African-American daily paper *Atlanta World.*
In Britain, Viscount Burnham sells the *Telegraph* to members of the Berry family.
Life and Letters first issued.

Film:
George Eastman in USA produces the first colour moving pictures.
L'Argent (director, Marcel L'Herbier).
Un Chien Andalou (director, Luis Buñuel).
Crossways (director, Teinosuke Kinugasa).
The Fall of the House of Usher (director, Jean Epstein).
The House of Trubnaya Square (director, Boris Barnet).
The Little Matchgirl (director, Jean Renoir).
The Man with the Movie Camera (director, Dziga Vertov).
The Seashell and the Clergyman (director, Germaine Dziga, viewed as the first surrealist film).
The Singing Fool (starring Al Jolson).
Steamboat Willie (director, Walt Disney; featuring Mickey Mouse).
Storm Over Asia (director, Vsevolod Potemkin).

Television:
John Logie Baird makes transatlantic television transmission and demonstrates colour television in Britain.

St Valentine's Day Massacre ... Wall Street Crash ...

A January

5 King Alexander I suppresses the constitution of the Kingdom of the Serbs, Croats, and Slovenes (Yugoslavia), and establishes a dictatorship.

5 inter-American treaty of arbitration, analogous to the Kellogg–Briand Pact, is signed in Washington, DC, USA.

21 Croat party in the Kingdom of the Serbs, Croats, and Slovenes (Yugoslavia) is dissolved.

31 Leon Trotsky is expelled from the USSR.

B February

6 Germany accepts the Kellogg–Briand Pact.

9 Litvinov Protocol, or Eastern Pact, between USSR, Estonia, Latvia, Poland and Romania for renunciation of war.

14 in Chicago, USA, the 'St Valentine's Day Massacre: gangsters dressed as policemen, working for Al 'Scarface' Capone, gun down seven members of the gang led by George 'Bugsy' Moran.

27 Turkey signs the Litvinov Protocol.

C March

6 Bulgarian–Turkish treaty of friendship.

17 Spanish government closes Madrid University to stifle student agitation.

24 Fascists 'win' single-party elections in Italy.

27 pact of friendship between Greece and the Kingdom of the Serbs, Croats, and Slovenes (Yugoslavia).

28 new Constitution in Ecuador ends military regime.

D April

3 Persia signs Litvinov Protocol.

24 in Denmark, Social Democrats (with 61 seats) form ministry after general election: Liberals win 43 seats, Conservatives 24, Radicals 16.

30 Ernst Streeruwitz appointed chancellor of Austria.

E May

1 in Germany, start of three days of clashes between Communist demonstrators and police in Berlin, leaving 15 dead.

16 restoration of Greek Senate, abolished in 1862, in hope of stabilizing republican regime.

20 Japan evacuates the Shandong Peninsula, China.

22 Emir Amanullah flees from Afghanistan (Nadir Khan proclaimed King, 15 Oct).

26 in Belgian election, Catholic parties have 77 seats, Workers Party 70, Liberals 78, Flemish Nationalists 11.

30 in British general election, the first held under universal adult suffrage, Labour wins 287 seats, Conservatives 260, Liberals, 59, others, 9.

F June

3 settlement of Arica–Tacna dispute, originating in 1910, by which Chile is awarded Arica, Peru gains Tacna, and Bolivia acquires railway rights.

5 in Britain, Ramsay MacDonald forms Labour ministry, with Arthur Henderson as foreign secretary, Philip Snowden as chancellor of the exchequer, and J R Clynes as home secretary.

7 Young Committee reviewing German reparations payments recommends that Germany should pay annuities, secured on mortgage of German railways, to an international bank until 1988.

27 the German Reichstag repeals the Protection of the Republic Act.

27 in Turkey, President Kemal suppresses Communist propaganda.

G July

2 fall of Giichi Tanaka ministry in Japan.

24 Kellogg–Briand Pact comes into force.

25 Pope Pius XI, no longer 'a voluntary prisoner' following the Lateran Treaty (of 11 Feb), leaves the Vatican, the first Pope to do so since 1870.

27 in France, Raymond Poincaré resigns because of ill health and Aristide Briand becomes prime minister.

H August

Ibn Saud, king of Hejaz and sultan of Nejd, signs treaty of friendship with Turkey (and, on 24, with Persia). Arab attacks on Jews in Palestine, following disputes over Jewish use of the Wailing Wall, Jerusalem.

6 (–13) at Reparations Conference at the Hague, Germany accepts the Young Plan; the Allies agree to evacuate the Rhineland by June 1930.

11 Iraq and Iran sign treaty of friendship.

J September

5 Aristide Briand proposes a European federal union.

12 Count Grandi is appointed Italian foreign minister.

14 the USA joins the International Court.

16 peace is signed between Bolivia and Paraguay.

Vatican State becomes independent ... Annales *published ...*
Graves' Goodbye To All That *...*

o Politics, Government, Law, and Economy

In Mexico, formation of the National Revolutionary Party or PNR (renamed the Party of the Mexican Revolution in 1938, and the Institutional Revolutionary Party in 1946).

E Pendleton Herring, *Group Representation Before Congress.*

The Warsaw Convention establishes the rules for air carriage of goods across international boundaries.

In USA, former secretary of the interior Albert B Fall (resigned 1923) is fined $100,000 and sentenced to one year in prison for accepting a bribe (in 'Teapot Dome' scandal).

The Migratory Bird Conservation Act in the USA provides authority and funds for the establishment of refuges for migrating birds.

Start of the most acute crisis of the world capitalist economy.

Motor industry becomes the largest sector of the US economy.

Unilever is formed by the merger of British and Dutch firms.

New Tilbury Dock, London, opened.

p Society, Education, and Religion

In USSR, the wealthier farmers ('Kulaks') oppose the collectivization of agriculture; Stalin responds by ordering the 'liquidation' of the kulaks (by murder or deportation).

Female suffrage in Turkey (6 Dec).

Miss Margaret Bondfield becomes the first woman cabinet minister in Britain.

Indian Trade Disputes Act and Public Safety Act to reduce radical Labour unrest (12 April).

In South Africa, the term 'Apartheid' (separate development) is first used in an Afrikaner text.

In USA illegal drinking places or 'Speakeasies' flourish.

Seven are killed in the 'St Valentine's Day Massacre' (14 Feb) in an organized crime feud in Chicago, USA.

Robert and Helen Lynd, *Middletown* (based on Muncie, Indiana, USA).

Harvey Zorbaugh, *The Gold Coast and the Slum.*

A N Whitehead, *The Aims of Education and Other Essays.*

Lateran Treaties between the Pope and Italy establish the independent Vatican City State in Rome and entail Papal recognition of the state of Italy.

The Presbyterian Churches in Scotland unite to form the Church of Scotland.

q Science, Technology, and Discovery

US explorer Richard Byrd flies over the South Pole.

Graf Zeppelin airship flies round the world.

In USA, the Kodak company develop a 16-mm colour film.

Tootal's discover a crease-resisting cotton fabric.

US astronomer Edwin Hubble publishes Hubble's Law, concerning the speed at which galaxies are receding.

James Jeans, *The Universe Around Us.*

Albert Einstein, *Unitary Field Theory.*

G Gamow, R Atkinson, and F Houtermans suggest that thermonuclear processes are the source of solar energy.

Neurologists E A Adrian and Matthews, using an ultra-sensitive galvanometer, are able to follow a single impulse in a single nerve fibre.

r Humanities

C L Woolley, *Ur of the Chaldees.*

Charles A Lindbergh and Anne Lindbergh take aerial photographs of Pueblo sites in SW USA and Mayan sites in British Honduras (modern Belize).

A F Pollard, *Wolsey.*

Lewis Namier, *The Structure of Politics at the Accession of George III.*

Ulrich Bonnell Phillips, *Life and Labor in the Old South.*

Annales d'histoire économique et sociale issued, founded by Lucien Febvre and Marc Bloch.

Journal of Modern History issued.

Lord David Cecil, *The Stricken Deer.*

14th edition of *Encyclopaedia Britannica.*

R Carnap, Hans Hahn, Otto Neurath, et al., *Scientific Conception of the World: The Vienna Circle.*

Martin Heidegger, *What is Metaphysics?*

Edmund Husserl, *Formal and Transcendental Logic.*

A N Whitehead, *Process and Reality.*

s Art, Sculpture, Fine Arts, and Architecture

Opening of the Museum of Modern Art, New York, with exhibitions of works by Paul

19 in USA, share values on the Wall Street stock exchange reach their highest point in 'bull' market.

26 Johann Schober forms ministry in Austria supported by Christian Socialists and Nationalists.

K October

Cessation of US loans to Europe, following Wall Street Crash.

3 the name of the Kingdom of the Serbs, Croats, and Slovenes is changed to 'Yugoslavia'.

3 Britain resumes relations with the USSR.

3 Julius Curtius appointed German foreign minister on Gustav Stresemann's death.

12 Labour Party wins Australian elections (22, James H Scullin forms ministry).

21 in Egypt, a general election results in a victory for the Wafd nationalist party.

24 (–29) crashes in share values on Wall Street stock market, New York, starting with 'Black Thursday' and continuing (after closure of the market from noon on 24 until 28) on 'Black Monday' (28) and 'Black Tuesday' (29).

31 Egyptian constitution is restored.

L November

13 Basle Bank for International Settlements is founded to deal with Germany's reparation payments under the Young Plan.

30 second Rhineland Zone is evacuated.

M December

Round Table conference between viceroy and Indian party leaders on Dominion status. China announces that foreign concessions will end on 1 Jan 1930 (but implementation is postponed).

22 referendum in Germany upholds the adoption of the Young Plan.

22 Khabarovsk Protocol between USSR and China: China to deal with the activities of anti-Soviet 'White' Russian bands based in Manchuria, and a conference to be held to settle other issues.

Cézanne, Paul Gauguin, Georges Seurat, and Vincent van Gogh.

Second Surrealist Manifesto; the Surrealist group is joined by Salvador Dalí.

First issue of dissident surrealist review *Documents*, edited by Georges Bataille.

Painting, etc:

Max Ernst, *La Femme 100 Têtes* — picture book of collages.

Paul Klee, *Fool in a Trance* (in one continuous line).

René Magritte, *The Treachery of Images ('This is not a Pipe').*

Kasimir Malevich, *Les Sportifs.*

Piet Mondrian, *Composition with Yellow and Blue.*

Pablo Picasso, *Nude in an Armchair.*

Christian Schad, *Agosta the Pigeon Chested Man and Rasha the Black Dove.*

Sculpture:

Henry Moore, *Mask.*

Pablo Picasso, *Woman in a Garden.*

Architecture:

Alvar Aalto, Convalescent Home, Paimio, Finland (–1933).

Le Corbusier, Salvation Army Hostel, Paris, France; Villa Savoye, Poissy, France (–1931).

Ludwig Mies van der Rohe, Barcelona Pavilion, International Exhibition, Barcelona, Spain.

T **Music**

Arnold Bax, Symphony No. 3.

Béla Bártok, String Quartets Nos. 3 and 4.

Max Brand, *Machinist Hopkins.*

Noël Coward, *Bitter Sweet* (operetta).

Constant Lambert, *The Rio Grande.*

Franz Léhar, *The Land of Smiles* (operetta).

In Britain, first Malvern Festival.

Fifty Million Frenchmen (musical comedy), lyrics and music by Cole Porter (his first major success, first performed at the Lyric Theatre, New York, 27 Nov).

'Happy Days are Here Again'.

'Stardust' by Hoagy Carmichael.

African-American revue *Hot Chocolates* first staged at Connie's Inn, Harlem, New York (includes 'Ain't Misbehavin' and 'What Did I Do To Be So Black and Blue?' by 'Fats' Waller).

In USA, Bessie Smith records a two-reel film of 'St Louis Blues', which is suppressed for its 'bad taste'.

In Britain, Ray Noble leads the EMI house band, the New Mayfair Orchestra.

Laurens Hammond invents the Hammond Organ (patented 1929, sold from 1935).

U **Literature and Drama**

Conrad Aiken, *Selected Poems.*

Robert Bridges, *The Testament of Beauty.*

Jean Cocteau, *Les Enfants terribles.*

Ivy Compton-Burnett, *Brothers and Sisters.*

Alfred Döblin, *Berlin-Alexanderplatz.*

John Dos Passos, *Airways, Inc.*

William Faulkner, *The Sound and the Fury, Sartoris.*

Robert Graves, *Goodbye To All That.*

Henry Green, *Living.*

Ernest Hemingway, *A Farewell to Arms.*

Hugo von Hofmannsthal, *Poems.*

Richard Hughes, *A High Wind in Jamaica.*

Sinclair Lewis, *Dodsworth.*

Alberto Moravia, *The Time of Indifference.*

Axel Munthe, *The Story of San Michele.*

Robert Musil, *The Man Without Qualities* (–1943).

Vladimir Nabokov, *The Defence.*

S J Perelman, *Dawn Ginsbergh's Revenge.*

John Cowper Powys, *Wolf Solent.*

J B Priestley, *The Good Companions.*

Erich Remarque, *All Quiet on the Western Front.*

Henry Handel Richardson, *The Fortunes of Richard Mahoney.*

Antoine de St Exupéry, *Courrier Sud/Southern Mail.*

Edith Sitwell, *Gold Coast Customs.*

Thomas Wolfe, *Look Homeward, Angel.*

Virginia Woolf, *A Room of One's Own.*

Drama:

Jean Giraudoux, *Amphitryon 38.*

Patrick Hamilton, *Rope.*

Elmer Rice, *Street Scene.*

George Bernard Shaw, *The Apple Cart.*

R C Sherriff, *Journey's End.*

Preston Sturges, *Strictly Dishonourable.*

V **Births and Deaths**

Jan 3 Sergio Leone born (–1989).

Jan 12 A C MacIntyre born (–).

Jan 15 Martin Luther King born (–1968).

Feb 15 Graham Hill born (–1975).

March 20 Ferdinand Foch dies (78).

May 23 Roger Bannister born (–).

May 1 Audrey Hepburn born (–1994).

May 14 Michael D Coe born (–).

May 21 Lord Rosebery dies (82).

June 18 Jürgen Habermas born (–).

July 15 Hugo von Hofmannsthal dies (55).

Aug 5 Millicent Garrett Fawcett dies (82).

Aug 19 Sergei Diaghilev dies (57).

Sept 10 Arnold Palmer born (–).

Gandhi begins civil disobedience campaign in India ... End of
Allied occupation of the Rhineland ...

A January

1 in Egypt, following the victory of the Wafd nationalist party, Nahas Pasha forms a Wafd ministry.

23 in Germany, Wilhelm Frick is appointed minister for the interior and education in Thuringia, the first Nazi Party member to become a minister in a state government.

28 in Spain, the dictator Primo de Rivera resigns, following the army's withdrawal of support; General Dámaso Berenguer forms ministry.

B February

US President Hoover sends commission to Haiti, to prepare for end of US occupation; it persuades President Borno to resign.

6 treaty of friendship between Austria and Italy.

18 (–24 March) tariff conference in Geneva, organized by League of Nations; little achieved.

C March

In USA, publication of Reuben J Clark's Memorandum of 1928 on Monroe doctrine.

12 in India, Mahatma Gandhi opens civil disobedience campaign in India with his 'salt march' (a march from Ahmedabad to the coast, where on 6 April Gandhi seizes salt to protest at the levying of salt tax on

Sept 15 Murray Gell-Man born (–).
Sept 17 Stirling Moss born (–).
Oct 3 Gustav Stresemann dies (51).
Nov 24 Georges Clemenceau dies (88).
Dec 9 Robert (Bob) Hawke born (–).
Dec 12 John Osborne born (–1994).

w Everyday Life

British playwright Sir James Barrie donates the rights to *Peter Pan* to the Hospital for Sick Children, Great Ormond Street, London.

The USA now has 377 skyscrapers with more than 20 storeys.

x Sport and Recreation

The first public women's cricket match is played at Beckenham, between London and District, and the Rest of England.

In American Football, the Green Bay Packers win the National Football League without losing a game, the first of three consecutive titles.

The Tote, run by the Racecourse Betting Control Board, is introduced in Britain; part of the money raised is ploughed back into horse racing.

In USA, the yo-yo is registered as a trademark by Louis Marx.

Regulation L-20 in the USA, which permits the heads of national forests to set aside wilderness areas for recreational use; by 1939 some 72 areas have been designated.

y Media

The *Listener* issued in Britain, reprinting talks from BBC radio.

Business Week magazine issued in the USA.

Retirement of C P Scott, editor of the *Manchester Guardian* since 1872 (succeeded by his son E T Scott).

Film:

The US Academy of Motion Picture Arts and Sciences presents its first awards, the gold-plated statuettes known as 'Oscars' (for 1927–8).

Arsenal (director, Alexander Dovschenko).

Blackmail (the first British all-talkie; director, Alfred Hitchcock).

Fragment of an Empire (director, Friedrich Ermier).

Hallelujah — the first all-black feature film (director, King Vidor).

The Mysterious Dr Fu Manchu (director, Rowland V Lee).

Pandora's Box (dircctor, G W Pabst, starring Louise Brooks).

The Phantom of the Opera (starring Lon Chaney).

The Virginian (starring Gary Cooper).

Radio:

In USA, start of popular *Amos 'n' Andy* series on NBC.

Television:

Demonstration of colour television at Bell Laboratories in the USA.

Anglicans accept artificial contraception ... Discovery of Pluto ...
First soccer World Cup ...

o Politics, Government, Law, and Economy

Harold Laski, *Liberty and the Modern State.*

Leon Trotsky, *The Permanent Revolution, Autobiography.*

Albert Rosenberg, *Myths of the 20th Century.*

France begins construction of the Maginot Line defence system along the French–German border.

In USA, Charles E Hughes appointed Chief Justice of the Supreme Court (serving until 1941).

First publication of *Restatement of Contracts.*

Jerome Frank, *Law and the Modern Mind.*

Bank for International Settlements founded.

In USA, the Smoot–Hawley Act imposes high tariffs (confirmed by President Hoover on 17 June).

Dunning tariff in Canada imposes high duties, but gives Britain preferential treatment (2 May).

Farm collectivization programme in the USSR gathers speed.

In USSR, Turkestan–Siberian railway completed.

Three US airlines merge to form Transcontinental and Western Air (TWA); meanwhile, Pan-Am merges with a smaller company and becomes the country's largest airline company.

J M Keynes, *Treatise on Money.*

poor people).

12 customs agreement between China and Japan, whereby Japan recognizes China's autonomy in setting tariffs (ratified in May).

27 in Germany, resignation of Hermann Müller's government, because Social Democrats oppose planned cuts in unemployment benefit.

30 Heinrich Brüning, Centre Party, forms a coalition of the Right in Germany, replacing the Social Democrats, but without a majority in the Reichstag.

31 revolt in Ethiopia, led by the empress's brother.

D April

3 Ras Tafari, regent of Ethiopia, becomes emperor on the death of empress Zauditu; he assumes the name Haile Selassie, 'Might of the Trinity' (crowned 2 Nov).

22 USA, Britain, France, Italy, and Japan end London Conference (held since 21 Jan), with signing of a treaty on naval disarmament, regulating submarine warfare and limiting aircraft carriers.

30 Italy announces naval programme (to build 29 new vessels).

E May

Opposition party founded in Turkey, favouring greater ties with the West.

8 breakdown of talks in London between the British government and Egypt regarding government of the Sudan.

11 in Moscow, USSR, opening of conference of Chinese and Soviet representatives to deal with outstanding problems between the two countries.

17 Young Plan for reparations in force.

24 Benito Mussolini champions revision of Versailles Treaty.

28 George W Forbes becomes prime minister of United Party ministry in New Zealand following resignation of Joseph Ward on 15 May, due to ill health (dies 8 July).

F June

8 Crown Prince Charles is elected King of Romania.

21 in Egypt, following the resignation of the Wafd government (after King Fuad had blocked the government's attempt to limit his powers), Ismail Sidky Pasha is appointed prime minister.

24 in Britain, publication of the Simon Report on India; it recommends self-government at provincial level.

27 treaty of arbitration signed by Scandinavian powers.

30 20-year treaty between Britain and Iraq, regulating relations between the countries.

30 last Allied troops leave Rhineland.

G July

Rising of Kurds on Persian–Turkish frontier.

16 President Hindenburg authorizes German budget by decree under article 48 of the constitution following the failure of Reichstag to pass it.

21 Maxim Litvinov becomes the USSR's foreign minister.

28 Conservatives win the Canadian general election, with 137 seats (Labour wins 91; other parties win 17); on 6 Aug, W L Mackenzie King resigns as prime minister; succeeded by Conservative leader Richard B Bennett.

30 National Union Party (neo-Fascist) founded in Portugal.

H August

17 in Spain, Pact of San Sebastián made between republicans and supporters of Catalan autonomy: autonomy to be granted to Catalonia if a republic is achieved.

25 following the outbreak of centre-left mass protests in Poland, Jozef Pilsudski forms ministry (30, parliament is dissolved; Sept, 70 opposition members are arrested and imprisoned).

25 in Peru, following revolt by an army garrison, a military junta takes power and forces Augusto Leguía to resign presidency (27 Aug, Colonel Luis Sánchez Cerro, leader of the original revolt, becomes president after march on Lima).

J September

6 in Argentina, demonstrations by crowds in Buenos Aires and revolt by army force President Hipólito Irigoyen to resign; General José Uriburu is appointed president.

8 (–22) special sessions of Canadian parliament to enact emergency laws dealing with depression.

14 in German elections Social Democrats win 143 seats and Communists 77, but National Socialists (Nazis), denouncing Versailles Treaty, gain 107 seats (Centre Party, 68; National People's Party, 41; others, 137).

15 removal of press censorship in Spain brings independent demands for a republic.

K October

National assembly elected in Haiti, which elects Sténio Joseph Vincent as president.

1 Britain restores the naval base of Weihaiwei to China (leased by Britain in 1898).

1 (–14 Nov) Imperial Conference in London, in which Britain rejects Canadian

P Society, Education, and Religion

World population passes 2 billion.

US emigration exceeds immigration for the first time in the Republic's history because of the economic slump and immigration restrictions.

White women enfranchised in South Africa (19 May).

International Labour Conference held by League of Nations adopts the Forced Labour Convention, to promote the restriction and abolition of forced labour (June); a subsequent commission reports the existence of forced labour in Liberia.

Workman's Insurance Law in France (30 April).

H Llewellyn Smith (ed.), *The New Survey of London Life and Labour* (9 volumes; –1935).

In Britain, Pilgrim Trust founded.

Albert Einstein, *About Zionism*.

Sigmund Freud, *Civilisation and its Discontents*.

Charles Johnson, *The Negro in American Civilisation*.

Charles Gore, *The Philosophy of the Good Life*.

In USA, Cochran v. Board of Education case declares valid the principle of supplying free textbooks to schoolchildren.

Foundation of the Institute for Advanced Study at the University of Princeton, New Jersey, USA.

In England, the Archbishop of Canterbury, Cosmo Gordon Lang, attacks the persecution of religion in the USSR (12 Feb).

Archbishop Lang issues an encyclical letter which states Anglican acceptance of the conscientious use of artificial methods of contraception; it also condemns 'trial marriages' and affirms the value of family life (14 Aug).

Pope Pius XI condemns birth control as a grave and unnatural sin.

Q Science, Technology, and Discovery

British aviator Amy Johnson makes solo flight from Britain to Australia (5–24 April).

British Arctic Air Route expedition (–1931).

Picture telegraphy service between Britain and Germany opened (7 Jan).

The photoflash bulb is invented.

German chemist J W Reppe makes artificial fabrics from acetylene base.

Acrylic plastics are invented (Perspex in Britain, Lucite in USA).

In USA, C Tombaugh discovers the planet Pluto (18 March).

Dutch chemist P J W Debye investigates the structure of molecules with X-rays.

US biochemist J H Northrop makes pepsin and trypsin in crystallized form.

R Humanities

C L Woolley, *The Sumerians*.

M Granet, *Chinese Civilization*.

G G Coulton, *The Medieval Scene*.

G M Trevelyan, *England Under Queen Anne* (–1934).

Samuel Eliot Morison, *Builders of the Bay Colony*.

J L and B Hammond, *The Age of the Chartists*.

Samuel Eliot Morison and Henry Steele Commager, *The Growth of the American Republic*.

I'll Take My Stand: The South and the Agrarian Tradition, by Twelve Southerners.

Harry Elmer Barnes, *Education versus Enlightenment*.

James Weldon Johnson, *Black Manhattan*.

R W Chambers, *William Shakespeare*.

G Wilson Knight, *The Wheel of Fire*.

William Empson, *Seven Types of Ambiguity*.

Margaret Mead, *Growing Up in New Guinea*.

Arthur Lovejoy, *The Revolt Against Dualism*.

Moritz Schlick, *The Problem of Ethics*.

S Art, Sculpture, Fine Arts, and Architecture

Dutch painter Theo van Doesburg first uses term 'Concrete Art'.

Painting, etc:

Isaak Brodsky, *Lenin at Smolny*.

Marc Chagall, *Lovers in the Lilacs*.

Paul Klee, *Prophet*.

Fernand Léger, *La Joconde with Keys*.

Joan Miró, *Painting*.

Pablo Picasso, *Crucifixion*.

Grant Wood, *American Gothic*.

Sculpture:

Alberto Giacometti, *Suspended Ball*.

Julio González, *Maternity* (–1932).

Arturo Martini, *Expectation* (–1931).

Architecture:

William Van Alen, Chrysler Building, New York (art deco skyscraper, completed).

R Hood, Daily News Building, New York.

Howe and Lescaze, Philadelphia Savings Fund Building, Philadelphia, USA.

Le Corbusier, Cité Universitaire, Paris (–1932).

Pier Luigi Nervi, Stadium, Florence, Italy (–1932).

T Music

Eric Coates, *By the Sleepy Lagoon*.

Hanns Eisler, *Die Massnahme* (musical play).

proposal for preferential tariff to help Dominion wheat.

4 following Liberal revolt in Brazil, to prevent accession of president-elect Dr Júlio Prestes, martial law is declared in three provinces (23 Oct, military leaders for President Luis to resign; 4 Nov, Getúlio Vargas is installed as temporary president).

5 (–12) conference of Balkan powers in Athens, origin of Balkan Entente (leading to pact of Feb 1934).

5 British airship R101 crashes and explodes near Beauvais, NE France, killing 44 people.

14 attempted Fascist coup in Finland.

20 publication in Britain of the Passfield White Paper on Palestine, which stresses the need to tackle the problem of shortage of land for Arab farmers and resulting destitution; the proposed policy threatens the expansion of the Jewish homeland in Palestine and is denounced by Zionists.

21 explosion in coal mine at Aachen, Germany, kills 262 (25, another explosion in a Saar coal mine kills about 100).

23 King Fuad of Egypt announces changes to the constitution: the king is to nominate the majority of senate members, and the chamber is to be elected by an indirect system.

30 treaty between Turkey and Greece signed at Ankara; governs exchange of populations.

L November

11 repressive legislation in Finland against Communism.

12 (–19 Jan 1931) first Round Table Conference on India held in London (without Congress Party representatives).

14 attempted assassination of Prime Minister Hamaguchi of Japan, by youth belonging to the Patriots organization.

16 in general election in Poland, the non-party bloc of government supporters wins 44.7 per cent of votes (4 Dec, Pilsudski resigns as prime minister but remains minister of defence).

17 (–28) Geneva Economic Conference discusses the world depression.

M December

3 Otto Ender, Christian Socialist, forms ministry in Austria.

9 Preparatory Commission on Disarmament adopts draft convention for discussions at League of Nations Conference in Feb 1932, but Germany and the USSR disapprove of draft.

12 last Allied troops leave the Saar.

15 in Spain, abortive military rising against the government.

30 Scandinavian states, Holland, Belgium, and Luxembourg, sign the Oslo agreements (–1938), against raising tariffs without prior consultation.

Jacques Ibert, *Divertissement*.
Leoš Janáček, *From the House of the Dead* (posthumous opera).
Albert Roussel, Symphony No. 3.
Kaikhosru Sorabji, *Opus clavicembalisticum*.
Igor Stravinsky, *Symphony of Psalms*.
Kurt Weill, *The Rise and Fall of the City of Mahagonny* (opera).
Adrian Boult is appointed musical director of the British Broadcasting Corporation (–1942).
Ralph Benatzky and Robert Stolz, *White Horse Inn* (musical).
Girl Crazy (musical), lyrics by Ira Gershwin, music by George Gershwin (New York opening at Alvin Theatre, 14 Oct).
Marlene Dietrich, 'Falling in Love Again'.

u Literature and Drama
W H Auden, *Poems*.
Agatha Christie, *Murder at the Vicarage*.
Hart Crane, *The Bridge*.
E M Delafield, *Diary of a Provincial Lady*.
John Dos Passos, *42nd Parallel*.
T S Eliot, *Ash Wednesday* (poem).
William Faulkner, *As I Lay Dying*.
Jose Maria Ferreira de Castro, *The Jungle*.
Robert Frost, *Collected Poems*.
Dashiell Hammett, *The Maltese Falcon*.
Hermann Hesse, *Narziss and Goldmund*.
Wyndham Lewis, *The Apes of God*.
Somerset Maugham, *Cakes and Ale*.
Salvatore Quasimodo, *Acque e terre*.
Jean Rhys, *After Leaving Mr Mackenzie*.
George Seferis, *Strophe*.
Sigrid Undset, *Burning Bush*.
Evelyn Waugh, *Vile Bodies*.
Sinclair Lewis is the first US writer to win the Nobel Prize for Literature.
In Britain, John Masefield succeeds as poet laureate on death of Robert Bridges.

Drama:
James Bridie, *The Anatomist*.
Marc Connelly, *The Green Pastures*.
Noël Coward, *Private Lives*.
Moss Hart and George Kaufmann, *Once in a Lifetime*.
Somerset Maugham, *The Breadwinner*.
Vladimir Mayakovsky, *The Bathhouse*.

v Births and Deaths
Jan 23 Derek Walcott born (–).
March 2 D H Lawrence dies (45).
March 6 Alfred von Tirpitz dies (81).
March 8 William Howard Taft dies (72).
March 16 Primo de Rivera dies (60).
March 19 A J Balfour dies (82).

March 22 Stephen Sondheim born (–).
April 3 Helmut Kohl born (–).
May 15 Jasper Johns born (–).
July 7 Arthur Conan Doyle dies (71).
July 15 Jacques Derrida born (–).
Aug 15 Tom Mboya born (–1969).
Aug 16 Ted Hughes born (–).
Sept 30 F E Smith (Lord Birkenhead) dies (58).
Oct 10 Harold Pinter born (–).

w Everyday Life
In Turkey, following the replacement of Arabic script by the Latin alphabet, the government orders the post office to return all mail not bearing the politically correct new spellings of place-names.
Ready-sliced bread is introduced under the brand name 'Wonder Bread'.

x Sport and Recreation
Batting in the 4th Test against the West Indies, in Kingston, Jamaica, Andrew Sandham of England becomes the first player to score a triple century in a Test Match; in the same match, Wilfred Rhodes becomes the oldest Test player, at 52 years 165 days (3–12 April).
Max Schmeling of Germany wins the World Heavyweight boxing title at the Yankee Stadium, New York, when Jack Sharkey is disqualified for a low punch (12 June).
Australia regains the Ashes, beating England 2–1 in the five-match series in England; during the series, the Australian batsman Donald Bradman scores a record 974 runs with a Test average of 139.14.
The first football World Cup is held in Uruguay; 11 nations take part in the event, which is won by the host nation (beating Argentina 4–2 in the Final in Montevideo); British teams are unable to participate, having withdrawn from FIFA in 1928.
Bobby Jones of the USA wins four national golf championships in one year: the US and British Opens, and the US and British Amateur Championships.
The Youth Hostel Association is formed in England and Wales.

y Media
In Britain, amalgamation of the *Daily Chronicle* and *Daily News* to form the *Daily News and Chronicle*.
In USA, William Randolph Hearst owns 33 newspapers with total circulation of 11 million.

*Revolution in Spain ... Formation of National Government in
Britain ... Japanese occupation of Manchuria ...*

A January
12 Allied military control committee is
dissolved.
26 in India, Mahatma Gandhi is released for
discussions with government.
27 Pierre Laval becomes prime minister of
France.

B February
The British Labour government, at Liberal
behest, appoints the May Committee to
propose economies.
14 in Spain, resignation of General Berenguer's government; Admiral Juan Bautista
Aznar is appointed prime minister.
20 in Britain, Oswald Mosley and five other
members of the Labour Party decide to
resign.
28 Oswald Mosley inaugurates the New Party.

C March
5 by Delhi Pact between the viceroy of India
(Lord Irwin, who becomes Lord Halifax in
1934) and Gandhi, the civil disobedience
campaign organized by the Indian National
Congress is suspended; the Congress Party
promises to participate in the Round Table
Conference, and political prisoners are
released.
15 Peasants' Party founded in Poland.
21 Austria and Germany agree to create a
customs union; after France, Italy, and
Czechoslovakia protest, the issue is
referred to the League of Nations and the
International Court of Justice.

26 treaty of friendship between Iraq and
Transjordan.

D April
12 following municipal elections in Spain, in
which republicans did well, Niceto Alcalá
Zamora, leader of a revolutionary committee in Madrid, demands the abdication
of the king (14, King Alfonso XIII flees
Spanish revolution; Alcalá Zamora
becomes president of a provisional
government).
22 treaty of friendship between Egypt and
Iraq, the first pact between Egypt and
another Arab state.

E May
5 People's Convention meets in Nanjing,
China (12, adopts constitution which is due
to come into effect on 1 June).
8 Farmers' Party in power in Norway.
11 bankruptcy of Credit-Anstalt in Austria
begins financial collapse of Central
Europe.
13 Paul Doumer is elected French President
(–May 1932).
28 in China, rebel members of the Guomindang establish another government at
Guangzhou.

F June
15 USSR–Polish treaty of friendship and
commerce.

Film:
Wider screen introduced.
L'Age D'Or (director, Luis Buñuel).
All Quiet on the Western Front.
À propos de Nice (director, Jean Vigo).
The Big House (director, George Hill).
The Blue Angel (starring Marlene Dietrich).
Hell's Angels (director, Howard Hawks).
Journey's End (director, James Whale).
Murder (director, Alfred Hitchcock).
Sous les Toits de Paris (director, René Clair).
Trader Horn (director, W S Van Dyke).

Radio:
Permission is given for Radio Luxembourg to begin broadcasting (29 Dec).

In Britain, 3,092,000 people hold wireless licences.

Television:
In Britain, a television set is installed in the prime minister's official home, 10 Downing Street, London (March); factory-made television sets ('Baird televisors') go on sale (May).

In Britain, the BBC makes the first broadcast of synchronized sound and pictures and of the first televised play, Luigi Pirandello's *The Man with the Flower in his Mouth.*

The first-ever television interview is given from the Ideal Home Exhibition in Southampton, S England.

Al Capone sent to prison ... Opening of the Empire State Building ... Dracula on screen ...

○ **Politics, Government, Law, and Economy**

The British Parliament passes the Statute of Westminster, enacting resolutions from the imperial conferences of 1926–30 and defining Dominion status (Dec); Dominions have legislative autonomy.

In USA, the Massachusetts State legislature requests repeal of the Prohibition amendment (March 13).

Political and Economic Planning (PEP) founded in London.

Norman Angell and Harold Wright, *Can Governments Cure Unemployment?*

In USA, nine African-Americans (the 'Scottsboro Nine') are convicted of raping two white girls (25 March); eight are sentenced to death and one to life imprisonment (7 Nov 1932, the US Supreme Court orders a retrial).

In USA, Chicago gang-leader Al 'Scarface' Capone is sentenced to 11 years in prison for tax evasion (17 Oct).

In USA, a record wheat crop leads to a collapse in prices and agricultural discontent.

National Coffee Department is established in Brazil and begins official destruction of surplus stocks.

Britain goes off the Gold Standard (20 Sept).

In southern Africa, opening of Benguella–Katanga railway (1 July), which completes first trans-African railway.

P **Society, Education, and Religion**

In S China, Communists establish the Jiangxi

Soviet; many of its social policies will be applied to the entire country after the Communist takeover in 1949.

In Britain, a 'means test' is introduced, by which the long-term unemployed who have exhausted their unemployment insurance contributions are required to evidence what resources they possess before further relief from public funds is given; this test, variably assessed by local public assistance committees, adds a further source of grievance and suffering to the plight of the unemployed in the 1930s.

The US state of Nevada faces a dire fiscal crisis; it decides to raise revenues by legalizing gambling and allowing divorces after six weeks of residence; Nevada becomes a centre for marriage, divorce, and recreation.

Elijah Muhammad (né Poole) founds the Black Muslims in Detroit, USA.

R H Tawney, *Equality.*

In London, foundation of the Courtauld Institute for the study of the history of art (as an institute of London University).

In Britain, the Hadow Report (*Report of the Consultative Committee on the Primary School*) recommends that the curriculum should 'be thought of in terms of activity and experience rather than of knowledge to be acquired and facts stored'.

Susan Isaacs, *Social Development in Young Children.*

In Spain, following the departure of the king, many churches are burnt, clergy attacked,

16 Bank of England advances money to Austria, but France withholds support.

20 US president Herbert Hoover proposes one-year moratorium for payment of reparations and war debts.

21 in Austria, Karl Buresch, Christian Socialist, forms ministry.

24 USSR–Afghanistan treaty of neutrality.

28 in a general election in Spain, the left parties win large majority.

G **July**

In Britain, the report of the May Committee estimates that the budget deficit could reach £120 million; proposed economies include cut in unemployment benefits, which divides the Labour cabinet.

1 anti-Chinese riots in Korea.

9 in Germany, the Nazi leader Adolf Hitler and Alfred Hugenberg of the German National Party agree to cooperate.

10 Norway's annexation of East Greenland provokes Danish protest (referred to the League of Nations which adjudicates against Norway in April 1933).

13 bankruptcy of German Danatbank leads to closure of all German banks until 5 Aug.

26 Cárlos Ibañez, President of Chile, resigns (succeeded on 4 Oct by Juan Montero).

H **August**

1 Franco–US loan to Britain.

11 London Protocol on Hoover moratorium.

19 French loan to Hungary.

19 Layton–Wiggin report calls for six-month extension of foreign credit to Germany.

24 British Prime Minister Ramsay MacDonald resigns; 25, forms National Government with other parties to balance the budget; Labour Party subsequently expels MacDonald, Philip Snowden, and J H Thomas, who serve with him; Arthur Henderson becomes leader of Labour Party.

28 the International Court of Justice at the Hague rules that the proposed customs union between Germany and Austria contravenes the Geneva Protocols of 24 Oct 1922.

J **September**

The Guangzhou rebel government sends troops towards the capital at Nanjing.

7 (–1 Dec) second Round Table Conference on India held in London (including attendance of Gandhi), but the Conference fails to reach agreement on the representation of religious minorities.

10 government's economy measures provoke riots in London and Glasgow and, 15, naval mutiny at Invergordon over pay cuts.

12 Mexico is admitted to the League of Nations.

13 in Austria, coup by the Heimwehr under Fascist leader Dr Pfrimer fails.

18 United and Reform parties form coalition in New Zealand.

18 Japan begins siege of Mukden, using bomber seaplanes, and occupies other strategic points in Manchuria.

K **October**

16 US delegates attend the League of Nations Council to discuss Japanese aggression in Manchuria.

20 Protection of Republic law in Spain.

27 in British general election National Government wins 554 seats, Opposition 61 (government supporters comprise 473 Conservatives, 35 National Liberals, 33 Liberals, 13 National Labour; the opposition comprises 52 Labour, 4 Lloyd George Liberals and 5 others); Oswald Mosley's New Party fails to win a seat.

L **November**

5 Ramsay MacDonald forms second National Government, with Neville Chamberlain as chancellor of the exchequer, Sir John Simon as foreign secretary, and Stanley Baldwin (leader of the Conservative Party) as lord president of the council.

M **December**

9 republican constitution promulgated in Spain (10, Alcalá Zamora elected president and Manuel Azaña appointed prime minister).

11 Japan abandons the gold standard.

and the primate (Cardinal Pedro Segura) is expelled (May).

Pope Pius XI issues the Encyclical *Quadragesimo Anno*, confirming teaching on social questions.

G Aulen, *Christus Victor*.

Ernst Troeltsch, *The Social Teaching of the Christian Churches*.

Q Science, Technology, and Discovery

Spicer-Dufay process of natural colour photography.

French physicist Auguste Picard is first person to ascend into the stratosphere.

The British chemicals company Imperial Chemical Industries (ICI) produces petrol from coal.

Julius A Nieuwland invents 'Neoprene' synthetic rubber process.

Publication of 'Gödel's proof' (*On Formally Undecidable Propositions of Principia Mathematica and Related Systems*), Kurt Gödel's questioning of the possibility of establishing dependable axioms in mathematics.

British physicist John D Cockcroft develops high-voltage apparatus for atomic transmutations.

US physicist Ernest O Lawrence devises the cyclotron (an 'atom-smasher').

Arthur Eddington, *The World of Physics*.

Large scale celebrations to mark the centenary of Michael Faraday's discovery of electomagnetic induction.

Swiss biochemist O P Karrer isolates vitamin A.

R Humanities

N H Baynes, *Constantine the Great and the Christian Church*.

Herbert Butterfield, *The Whig Interpretation of History*.

A E Feavearyear, *The Pound Sterling: A History of English Money*.

Walter Prescott Webb, *The Great Plains*.

Edmund Wilson, *Axel's Castle*.

John Dewey, *Philosophy and Civilisation*.

Edmund Husserl, *Cartesian Meditations*.

S Art, Sculpture, Fine Arts, and Architecture

Opening of the Whitney Museum of American Art, New York (13 Nov).

International Colonial Exhibition, Paris, France.

Painting, etc:

Salvador Dalí, *The Persistence of Memory*.

Lucio Fontana, *Scratched Tablet*.

Edward Hopper, *Route 6, Eastham*.

Piet Mondrian, *Composition with Two Lines*.

Pablo Picasso, *Figures on the Seashore*.

Sculpture:

Henri Matisse, *The Back IV*.

Henry Moore, *Composition*.

Pablo Picasso, *Head of a Woman*.

Architecture:

Raymond Hood, McGraw Hill Building, New York.

Reinhard and Hofmeister, Rockefeller Center, New York (–1939).

Shreve, Lamb, and Harmon, Empire State Building, New York.

T Music

Béla Bartók, Piano Concerto No. 2.

Ferde Grofé, *Grand Canyon Suite*.

Alois Hába, *Matka* (opera).

Albert Roussel, *Bacchus et Ariane* (ballet).

Deems Taylor, *Peter Ibbetson* (opera).

Edgar Varèse, *Ionisation*.

William Walton, *Belshazzar's Feast* (oratorio).

In London, Lilian Baylis reopens Sadler's Wells Theatre, London, as a venue for opera and ballet.

Sergei Rachmaninov's music is banned in the USSR as 'decadent'.

Cavalcade (musical), by Noël Coward (first performed at the Drury Lane Theatre, 13 Oct).

Of Thee I Sing (musical), lyrics by Ira Gershwin, music by George Gershwin (New York opening at the Music Box Theatre, Dec 26).

In Britain, singer and comedian George Formby, Jr, presents his own variety show (followed by numerous films and hit records in the 1930s and 1940s).

In Britain, merger of His Master's Voice and Columbia creates Electrical and Musical Industries (EMI).

U Literature and Drama

Conrad Aiken, *Preludes for Mennon*.

Georges Bernanos, *La Grande Peur des bien-pensants*.

Pearl Buck, *The Good Earth*.

Theodore Dreiser, *Dawn*.

William Faulkner, *Sanctuary*.

James Hanley, *Boy*.

Anthony Powell, *Afternoon Men*.

Vita Sackville-West, *All Passion Spent*.

Antoine de St-Exupéry, *Vol de nuit/Night Flight*.

George Santayana, *The Genteel Tradition at Bay*.

Wallace Stevens, *Harmonium*.

Lytton Strachey, *Portraits in Miniature*.

Tristan Tzara, *L'Homme approximatif.*
Virginia Woolf, *The Wave*s Drama:
Rudolph Besier, *The Barretts of Wimpole Street.*
Noël Coward, *Cavalcade.*
Eugene O'Neill, *Mourning Becomes Electra.*
Lynn Riggs, *Green Grow the Lilacs* (adapted as musical *Oklahoma*, 1943).

v Births and Deaths
Jan 3 Joseph Joffre dies (78).
Feb 1 Boris Yeltsin born (–).
Feb 23 Nellie Melba dies (72).
March 2 Mikhail Gorbachev born (–).
March 5 P Atiyah born (–).
March 11 Rupert Murdoch born (–).
March 27 Arnold Bennett dies (64).
May 31 Clint Eastwood born (–).
Aug 17 E A Wrigley born (–).
Aug 31 Hall Caine dies (78).
Sept 24 J M G M Adams born (–1985).
Sept 29 William Orpen dies (52).
Oct 4 Richard Rorty born (–).
Oct 7 Desmond Tutu born (–).
Oct 18 Thomas Edison dies (84).

w Everyday Life
'The Star Spangled Banner' is designated the national anthem of the USA (3 March).
In New York, opening of the George Washington Bridge between Manhattan and New Jersey (25 Oct), the longest suspension bridge yet built.
In USA, electric shavers are first sold by Schick Dry Shaver Inc.
Chevrolet manufactures the first pick-up truck, creating a US icon.
Alka-Seltzer, a combination of indigestion and headache relief designed to cope with hangovers, is introduced to Prohibition-bound America.

Freon (a CFC) is introduced as an aerosol propellant.
A fire in the Vatican Library destroys about 15,000 books (22 Dec).

x Sport and Recreation
New Zealand's cricketers play their first Test Match in England.
An English Ice Hockey League is formed and is won by Oxford University.
France are banned from the amateur Rugby Union Five Nations Championship for professionalism.
The National Council of Ramblers' Federations (from 1935, the Ramblers' Association) is founded at a meeting in the English Peak District.
Opening of the Royal Zoological Society's Zoological Gardens at Whipsnade, England.

y Media
Film:
À Nous la Liberté (director, René Clair).
City Lights (starring Charlie Chaplin).
Congress Dances (director, Erik Charrell).
Dracula (starring Bela Lugosi).
Emil and the Detectives (director, Gerhard Lamprecht).
Frankenstein (starring Boris Karloff).
The Front Page (director, Lewis Milestone).
M (director, Fritz Lang).
Mädchen in Uniform (starring Dorothea Wieck).
Mata Hari (starring Greta Garbo).
The Million (director, René Clair).
The Public Enemy (starring James Cagney).
Sally in Our Alley (starring Gracie Fields).
Trader Horn.

Television:
First broadcasts in the USA.
In Britain, the BBC televises horses finishing the Derby horse race (3 June).

Outbreak of Chaco War ... Iraq becomes independent ...
F D Roosevelt elected US president ...

A January

4 Japanese troops occupying Manchuria reach Shanhaiguan at the E end of the Great Wall of China.

4 following Mahatma Gandhi's return to India, and the revival of civil disobedience, the Indian government is granted emergency powers for six months; the Indian National Congress is declared illegal and Gandhi is arrested.

7 US Secretary of State Henry L Stimson sends notes to China and Japan setting out what becomes known as the Stimson Doctrine: he opposes Japanese aggression in Manchuria and states that the USA will not recognize gains made by armed force.

7 Chancellor Heinrich Brüning declares that Germany cannot, and will not, resume reparations payments.

15 France completes pacification of French Morocco.

21 USSR and Finland sign three-year non-agression pact.

25 USSR–Polish nonaggression pact.

28 in China, Japanese capture Shanghai.

B February

2 (–July 1932) 60 states, including USA and USSR, attend Geneva Disarmament Conference, at which French proposal for an armed force under international control is opposed by Germany.

6 in Lithuania, fascist coup in Klaipeda (formerly Memel).

7 by Oslo convention, Scandinavian countries, Belgium, and Netherlands undertake economic co-operation.

8 Bulgaria renounces further reparations payments.

9 foundation in the Irish Free State of the Army Comrades Association (20 July 1933, renamed the National Guard; nicknamed the 'Blueshirts').

16 in the Irish Free State, Fianna Fáil, led by Éamon de Valera, win the general election (with 72 seats; Cumann na nGaedheal wins 57, others, 24).

16 French senate overthrows the Laval government; 23, André Tardieu forms ministry in France.

18 Japanese puppet republic of Manzhouguo proclaimed in Manchuria, with former Chinese emperor Pu Yi as chief executive (1 March, is proclaimed emperor).

29 (–3 March) in Finland, the government suppresses the Mantsälä Rising, a threatened revolt by members of the Fascist Lapua movement who had massed at Mantsälä.

C March

1 in Britain, the Import Duties Act comes into force, in effect ending 80 years of free trade.

3 Chinese drive back Japanese forces from Shanghai.

9 the Dáil of the Irish Free State elects Éamon de Valera as president of the executive council.

13 in German presidential election Paul von Hindenburg receives 18.6 million votes (49.6 per cent) against Adolf Hitler's, 11.3 million (30.1 per cent), and the Communist Ernst Thälmann's 4.9 million (13.2 per cent), but 0.4 per cent below the required absolute majority (new election held on 10 April).

D April

6 (–8) four-power conference held in London about navigation on the Danube; the conference fails because Germany and Italy decline to leave the problem to the Danubian states.

10 Paul von Hindenburg is re-elected German president (19.5 million votes; 53 per cent) against Hitler (13.4 million; 36.8 per cent), and Thälmann (3.7 million; 10.2 per cent).

24 in Germany, Nazi successes in elections in Prussia, Bavaria, Württemberg, and Hamburg; in Prussia the Nazi Party becomes the largest single party in the state parliament.

E May

6 President Paul Doumer of France assassinated by Russian *émigré* (dies on 7; succeeded on 10 by Albert Lebrun).

8 Left parties emerge from second round of French elections with gain of about 100 seats.

15 murder of Tsuyoshi Inukai, prime minister of Japan, by young naval and military officers (succeeded by Makoto Saito).

19 in the Irish Free State, the Dáil votes for abolition of oath of loyalty to British crown, but opposition in the senate prevents enactment.

20 Engelbert Dollfuss, Austrian chancellor, forms a coalition of Christian Socialists and Agrarians.

30 President Hindenburg of Germany withdraws support from Chancellor Heinrich Brüning, who resigns.

Suicide of fraudster Ivar Kreuger ... Karl Barth's
Church Dogmatics ... Tarzan the Ape Man ...

o Politics, Government, Law, and Economy

The Australian federal government is strengthened by passage of Financial Agreement Enforcement Act.

Chief Justice Benjamin Cardozo of the New York Court of Appeals, whose theory of judicial decision-making enabled judges to respond to pressures for both continuity and change in the law, is appointed a Justice of the Supreme Court (–1938).

In Britain, in the case Donoghue v. Stevenson, Lord Atkin creates the modern law of negligence.

New rules of procedure in the British High Court and Court of Appeal allow sworn affidavits for factual testimony, obviating the need for some witnesses to attend.

Creation in the USA of the Reconstruction Finance Corporation to provide finance to firms in difficulty (Jan); in July it is empowered to provide money to states for public works.

Reorganization of US federal reserve system (27 Feb).

Imperial Economic Conference in Ottawa attempts to expand trade within the British Empire but results in the Import Duties Act imposing full protectionism in Britain.

Exchange Equalisation Account starts dealing in foreign currency on behalf of Britain.

Interest rates in Britain fall to 2 per cent (30 June), starting seven years of cheap money.

In the Netherlands, the Zuider Zee drainage scheme is completed.

In Germany, the Cologne–Bonn autobahn is opened, one of the world's first motorways or express highways.

The Swedish 'match king', Ivar Kreuger, commits suicide in Paris, France (12 March); after his death it is discovered that his companies' assets were overstated and the declared profits largely fictitious; his national and international business empire collapses.

Greek businesmann Aristotle Onassis purchases six freight ships, the start of his shipping fortune.

A A Berle and G C Means, *The Modern Corporation and Private Property.*

p Society, Education, and Religion

Famine in USSR.

In India, Mahatma Gandhi leads a campaign of civil disobedience to protest against the treatment of the harijans (untouchables).

In USA, veterans of World War I petitioning the Hoover administration for payment of bonuses are dispersed by armed force (28 July).

Agrarian Law in Spain provides for the expropriation of landed estates (15 Sept); to be administered by an Institute of Agrarian Reform.

British Ministry of Health issues circular to local authorities urging vigorous policy of slum clearance (6 April).

By new language regulations in Belgium (18 July), French becomes official language of Walloon provinces, Flemish the language of Flanders.

Basic English founded as a prospective international language.

In USA, the Norris-La Guardia Act makes organization easier for trade unions: federal judges cannot issue injunctions in a strike except when unlawful acts involve substantial damage to an employer's property.

In USA, Mary Dewson organizes the Reporter Plan, for women to inform communities around the country about 'New Deal' legislation.

Catholic Eucharistic Congress held in Ireland for the first time (June), coinciding with celebrations of the 1,500th anniversary of the arrival of St Patrick.

Wesleyan Methodists, Primitive Methodists, and the United Methodist Church form the Methodist Church of Great Britain and Ireland.

Publication of the first volume of Karl Barth's *Church Dogmatics* (unfinished at author's death).

Henri Bergson, *The Two Sources of Morality and Religion.*

Martin Buber, *The Kingship of God.*

Reinhold Niebuhr, *Moral Man and Immoral Society.*

q Science, Technology, and Discovery

US aviator Amelia Earhart is the first woman to make a solo flight across the Atlantic (20–21 May).

US aviator Paul Codos flies from Paris to Hanoi, Indochina (now Vietnam) in 3 days 5 hrs 40 mins (Jan).

US physicist Karl Jansky pioneers radio astronomy through his detection of a constant source of 'static' coming from the direction of Sagittarius.

British physicist James Chadwick discovers the 'neutron'.

US chemist Harold C Urey and atomic physicist J Washburn discover that electrolysed water is denser than ordinary water,

F June

A bloodless revolution in Siam (now Thailand), led by lawyer Luang Pradit Phanomyong, establishes a constitutional monarchy (constitution promulgated in Dec).

2 in Germany, Franz von Papen (a repudiated Centre Party member) forms a nonparty 'cabinet of barons'.

4 second ministry of Édouard Herriot in France.

6 (–18) revolt in Chile in which the military make Carlos Dávila, a socialist, president.

13 British–French pact of friendship signed at Lausanne.

15 start of Chaco War between Bolivia and Paraguay (–June 1935), when Bolivians attack Paraguayan positions in the disputed border territory of Chaco Boreal.

16 (–9 July) at Lausanne reparations conference, Germany accepts proposal for a final conditional payment of 3,000 million Reichsmarks.

16 in Germany, ban on Nazi Storm Troopers (in operation since April) is lifted.

G July

2 in accepting the nomination of the Democratic Party for the US presidential election, F D Roosevelt first uses the term 'New Deal' (coined by adviser Raymond Moley).

5 in Portugal, President Carmona appoints Oliveira Salazar as prime minister.

9 (–2 Oct) in Brazil, unsuccessful revolt in São Paulo against government.

15 by Geneva protocol Austria is granted loan on condition it renounces *Anschluss* (union with Germany) until 1952.

18 Turkey is admitted to the League of Nations.

20 following a growth in lawlessness in Prussia, German Chancellor Franz von Papen removes the state's Social Democrat prime minister (Otto Braun) and the minister of the interior (Severing).

21 (–20 Aug) Imperial Conference at Ottawa, Canada, favours extension of imperial preference.

31 in Reichstag elections Nazis win 230 seats, Social Democrats 133, Centre 75, Communists 89, National People's Party 37 (others, 44), producing stalemate, since neither Nazis nor Social Democrats would enter a coalition.

H August

10 in Spain, revolt of General José Sanjurjo in Seville is suppressed.

13 Adolf Hitler refuses President Hindenburg's request to serve as vice-chancellor under Franz von Papen.

J September

In Chile, the military oust President Dávila.

1 a band of Peruvians enters Leticia on the Amazon in Colombia, seeking to recover the port; Peru backs the claim.

14 Germany withdraws temporarily from the Geneva Disarmament Conference (until Dec), demanding the principle of being allowed aramaments equal to those of other powers.

14 Belgian government is granted wide powers to deal with financial crisis.

25 in Spain, Catalonia is granted autonomy, with its own flag, language, and parliament.

28 in Britain, Sir Herbert Samuel and other Liberal free-traders resign from cabinet over policy of imperial preference; Sir John Simon becomes leader of the Liberals supporting the National Government.

30 following a financial crisis and the resignation of Count Károlyi, Julius Gömbös forms ministry in Hungary.

K October

1 Oswald Mosley launches the British Union of Fascists (renamed the British Union of Fascists and National Socialists in summer 1936).

2 Lytton Report to League of Nations on Manchuria recognizes Japan's special interests and recommends an autonomous state under Chinese sovereignty but Japanese control.

3 British mandate over Iraq terminated; Iraq becomes independent and joins the League of Nations.

31 in Greece, following an inconclusive general election, Eleutherios Venizelos resigns as prime minister; succeeded, on 4 Nov, by Panyoti Tsaldaris, a moderate Royalist.

L November

6 German elections produce further deadlock, with some Communist gains from Nazis (Nazis, 192 seats; Social Democrats, 121; Centre, 70; Communists, 100; National People's Party, 52; others, 45).

8 F D Roosevelt wins US presidential election in Democrat landslide with 472 electoral votes over Herbert Hoover, Republican, with 59; popular vote: Roosevelt, 22,821,857; Hoover, 15,761,841; Norman Thomas (Socialist), 881,951.

leading to the discovery of deuterium ('heavy hydrogen').

German chemist Gerhard Domagk discovers that the Prontosil Red dye can control streptococcal infections in mice (published in 1935).

Vitamin C isolated by C G King and W A Waugh.

In Germany the biochemist Hans Krebs describes the citric acid cycle in cells, which converts sugars, fats and proteins into carbon dioxide, water, and energy.

R Humanities

F M Stenton, *The First Century of English Feudalism, 1066–1166.*

Cyril Fox, *The Personality of Britain.*

Pieter Geyl, *The Revolt of the Netherlands.*

Carl L Becker, *The Heavenly City of the Eighteenth-Century Philosophers.*

Allan Nevins, *Grover Cleveland: A Study in Courage.*

Andrew C McLaughlin, *The Foundations of American Constitutionalism.*

J L Garvin, *The Life of Joseph Chamberlain* (Volumes 1–3, –1934; Volumes 4–6, by Julian Amery, 1951–69).

Paul Harvey, *The Oxford Companion to English Literature.*

F R Leavis, *New Bearings in English Poetry.*

Q D Leavis, *Fiction and the Reading Public.*

In USA, opening of the Folger Library, Washington, DC.

Karl Jaspers, *Philosophy.*

Jacques Maritain, *The Degrees of Knowledge.*

G H Mead, *The Philosophy of the Present.*

Edvard Westermarck, *Ethical Relativity.*

S Art, Sculpture, Fine Arts, and Architecture

Painting, etc:

Thomas Hart Benton, *Arts of the West.*

Kazimir Malevich, *The Red House.*

Henri Matisse, *Dance* (–1933).

Pablo Picasso, *Girl Before a Mirror.*

Alberto Savinio, *Annunciation.*

Ben Shahn, *The Jury Box.*

Man Ray, *Observatory Time – The Lovers* (–1934).

Sculpture:

Alexander Calder invents 'mobiles' (sculptures moved first by engines or hand, later by air currents) soon followed by 'stabiles' which did not move.

Jean Arp, *Constellation.*

Alexander Calder, *Mobile* (–34).

Alberto Giacometti, *The Palace at 4 am, Woman with her Throat Cut.*

Eric Gill, *Prospero and Ariel* (for Broadcasting House, London; –1937).

Henry Moore, *Composition* — first sculpture with a hole through it.

Pablo Picasso, *Reclining Nude.*

Architecture:

'The International Style: Architecture since 1920', exhibition at the Museum of Modern Art, New York — identifies the International Style as universal (Philip Johnson and H R Hitchcock coin the term 'International Style').

Liverpool Metropolitan Cathedral begun on Edwin Lutyens' plans (later abandoned, but Lutyens' crypt was incorporated in the final building).

Sir Giles Scott, Battersea Power Station, London (–1934).

T Music

Mario Castelnuovo-Tedescu, Violin Concerto No. 2.

George Gershwin, *Cuban Overture.*

Gian Francesco Malipiero, *Pantea.*

Nikolai Miaskovsky, Symphony No. 12.

Maurice Ravel, Piano Concerto in G.

Carl Ruggles, *Sun-treader.*

Thomas Beecham founds London Philharmonic Orchestra.

Gay Divorce (musical), music and lyrics by Cole Porter (first performed at the Ethel Barrymore Theatre, New York, 29 Nov).

Tommy Dorsey, 'I'm Getting Sentimental Over You'.

'Brother, Can You Spare a Dime?' by Jay Gourlay.

Debut in Britain of Louis Armstrong, including concert at the London Palladium.

U Literature and Drama

W H Auden, *The Orators.*

Louis-Ferdinand Céline, *Voyage au bout de la Nuit/Journey to the End of the Night.*

John Dos Passos, *1919.*

Hans Fallada, *Little Man, What Now?.*

James T Farrell, *Young Lonigan.*

William Faulkner, *Light in August.*

Lewis Grassic Gibbon, *Sunset Song.*

Stella Gibbons, *Cold Comfort Farm.*

Ernest Hemingway, *Death in the Afternoon.*

Aldous Huxley, *Brave New World.*

Rosamund Lehmann, *Invitation to the Waltz.*

François Mauriac, *Le Noeud de Vipères.*

Henri Michaux, *Un Barbare en Asie.*

Charles Morgan, *The Fountain.*

Boris Pasternak, *Second Birth* (poems).

Jules Romains, *Les hommes de bonne volonté* (–1947).

Damon Runyon, *Guys and Dolls.*

14 in Yugoslavia, Croats and Serbian democrats opposed to the royal dictatorship demand a new constitution.

17 Franz von Papen resigns as German chancellor, to allow a new coalition to be formed following the elections.

19 (–24) at President Hindenburg's invitation, Adolf Hitler attempts to form a coalition commanding a majority in the German parliament, but fails.

19 (–24 Dec), third India Round Table Conference in London (concerned with reports on franchise, finance, and the states).

29 French–USSR nonaggression pact.

29 Persia annuls Anglo–Persian Oil Co. agreement of 1901.

M December

In Chile, Arturo Alessandri is elected president.

4 Kurt von Schleicher forms ministry in Germany, attempting to conciliate the Centre and the Left.

9 Japanese invade Jehol (Chengde).

11 Britain, France, Germany, and Italy make the 'No Force Declaration', renouncing the use of force for settling differences; with signing of Geneva Protocol on Germany's equality of rights with other nations, Germany returns to the Geneva Disarmament Conference.

16 National Union in Lithuania adopts Fascist programme.

18 in France, Édouard Herriot resigns, after defeat in Chamber of proposal to pay debt to USA, and Joseph Paul-Boncour forms cabinet.

27 South Africa leaves gold standard.

28 US Congressional resolution against cancellation of Germany's war debt.

George Bernard Shaw, *The Adventures of the Black Girl in Her Search for God.*

James Thurber, 'The Secret Life of Walter Mitty'.

Drama:

Bertolt Brecht, *The Mother.*

J B Priestley, *Dangerous Corner.*

Shakespeare Memorial Theatre, Stratford-on-Avon, England, opened.

v Births and Deaths

Jan 7 André Maginot dies (54).

Jan 17 Charles Gore dies (78).

Jan 21 Giles Lytton Strachey dies (51).

Feb 6 François Truffaut born (–1984).

Feb 10 Edgar Wallace dies (57).

Feb 18 Miloš Forman born (–).

March 7 Aristide Briand dies (69).

March 14 George Eastman dies (77).

March 18 John Updike born (–).

May 24 Arnold Wesker born (–).

June 11 Athol Fugard born (–).

July 6 Kenneth Grahame dies (73).

July 22 R A Fessenden dies (65).

Aug 17 V S Naipaul born (–).

Oct 27 Sylvia Plath born (–1963).

Oct 30 Louis Malle born (–).

Nov 29 Jacques Chirac born (–).

w Everyday Life

The baby son of aviator Charles Lindbergh and Anne Lindbergh is kidnapped (1 March; body is found on 12 May); Bruno Hauptmann is executed for the murder on 3 April 1936.

Zippo lighters are first manufactured in Pennsylvania, USA.

Opening of Lambeth Bridge, London, and Sydney Harbour Bridge.

In USA, Route 66 from Chicago to Los Angeles is completed.

x Sport and Recreation

A mass trespass on Kinder Scout in the English Peak District is organized by the British Workers' Sports Federation, an offshoot of the Communist Party of Great Britain; the protest is held to demand free access to moorland (24 April).

In USA, Jack Sharkey out-points Max Schmeling over 15 rounds of their fight at Long Island to win the World Heavyweight boxing title (21 June).

The X Olympic Games are held in Los Angeles, USA (30 July–14 Aug); the USA wins 41 gold medals; Italy, 12; France, 10; Sweden, 9; Japan, 7; Hungary, 6; Finland, 5. National flags are used in medal ceremonies for the first time.

India's cricketers play their first Test Match.

The first Curtis Cup match between the women golfers of the USA and those of Great Britain and Ireland is held at Wentworth, Surrey, England; the USA team wins the match 5–3.

y Media

In Britain, foundation of the Communist paper the *Daily Worker.*

In USA, publication of *Family Circle*, an early 'store magazine' given away in Piggly Wiggly supermarkets (–1946; then sold as a monthly).

Film:

Publication of *Cinema Quarterly.*

127 sound films made (compared with eight in 1929).

The Blue Light (director, Leni Riefenstahl).

Boudu Saved from Drowning (director, Jean Renoir).

Cavalcade (director, Frank Lloyd).

Doctor Jekyll and Mr Hyde (director, Rouben Mamoulian).

A Farewell to Arms (starring Gary Cooper).

Grand Hotel (director, Edmund Golding).

I am a Fugitive from a Chain Gang (director, Mervy LeRoy) .

I Was Born, But (director, Yasujiro Ozu).

La Maternelle (starring Jean Benoit-Lévy).

Scarface (director, Howard Hawks).

Shanghai Express (starring Marlene Dietrich).

Tarzan the Ape Man (starring Johnny Weissmüller; the first Tarzan film).

Trouble in Paradise (director, Ernst Lubitsch).

Radio:

Agreements signed at the Madrid convention of the International Telecommunications Union are the first provisions for the international regulation of radio communications, including radio.

King George V of Britain makes the first Christmas broadcast by the British head of state.

*Adolf Hitler becomes German chancellor ... Batista takes power
in Cuba ...*

A January

2 in Spain, rising of anarchists and syndicalists in Barcelona.

13 US Congress votes for independence for the Philippines, after a period of transition; President Hoover immediately vetoes the bill; Congress overturns the veto on 17 Jan, but in Oct the Philippines legislature rejects the arrangements.

16 Eleuthérios Venizélos again appointed Prime Minister of Greece (–10 March).

24 in the Irish Free State, Éamon de Valera's Fianna Fáil party gains a majority of one in general election (Fianna Fáil, 77; Cumann na nGaedheal, 48; others, 28).

25 in Norway, a Liberal ministry replaces the Agrarian Party government.

28 in Germany, Kurt von Schleicher's ministry falls, following failure to conciliate the Centre and Left.

30 Adolf Hitler is appointed chancellor of Germany; his cabinet includes only two Nazis, Hermann Goering (minister without portfolio) and Wilhelm Frick (minister of the interior); Franz von Papen is vice-chancellor, Constantin von Neurath, foreign minister.

31 Edouard Daladier becomes prime minister of France.

B February

9 in Britain, the Oxford Union debating society carries the motion 'that this House will in no circumstances fight for its King and its Country'.

14 the governor of Michigan, USA, closes banks in his state for eight days (to prevent the bankruptcy of the two largest); similar proclamations are made in other states.

15 gunman Giuseppe Zingara attempts to assassinate US president-elect F D Roosevelt (the Mayor of Chicago is hit; he dies from wounds on 6 March).

16 fearing German threats, the 'Little Entente' (Czechoslovakia, Romania, and Yugoslavia) is reorganized, with a permanent council.

23 (–12 March), the Japanese army advances south-west from Manchuria into Jehol (Chengde), NE of the Great Wall, and later advances southwards.

24 the Lytton Report (stating that the sovereignty of Manchuria belongs to China) is adopted by the League of Nations, despite its rejection by Japan (the power occupying Manchuria).

27 fire destroys the Reichstag (parliament) in Berlin; though it was started by a Dutch worker, Marinus van der Lubbe, the Nazis denounce the fire as a Communist plot and use it as the pretext for suspending civil liberties and freedom of the press.

C March

4 inauguration of F D Roosevelt as 32nd president of the USA; he declares that 'the only thing we have to fear is fear itself'; in the evening he addresses the Nation on radio; Cordell Hull is appointed secretary of state.

5 general election in Germany, in which the Nazis win 288 seats; Social Democrats, 120; Communists, 81; Centre, 74; National People's Party, 52; others, 32.

5 in the USA, President Roosevelt summons Congress to Washington on 9 March, for a special session, and declares a banking holiday from 6 to 9 March.

7 Engelbert Dollfuss, chancellor of Austria, suspends the Austrian Parliament.

9 (–16 June) special session of the US Congress, to deal with economic and social problems; it immediately grants President Roosevelt control over gold and silver bullion and foreign exchange; during the 'Hundred Days' the Congress passes 15 major bills.

12 President Roosevelt's first 'fireside chat' by radio to the US people; he announces that it is safe to bank savings.

16 at the League of Nations Disarmament Conference in Geneva, Britain's plan for a reduction in the size of armies fails, because Germany insists that Storm Troopers should not be included in the total.

19 Benito Mussolini, prime minister of Italy, proposes a pact with Britain, France, and Germany (signed 15 July).

23 in Germany, the Enabling Act gives Adolf Hitler dictatorial powers until April 1937.

26 new constitution in Portugal.

27 Japan announces that it will leave the League of Nations (effective from 1935).

30 in South Africa, J B M Hertzog forms a National Coalition government, with J C Smuts as deputy prime minister.

D April

1 start of official persecution of the Jews in Germany, with a national boycott of Jewish shops, businesses, and professionals.

8 Western Australia, irritated by federal taxation, votes to secede from the Commonwealth of Australia.

10 British Labour Party moves censure vote on government in British House of Com-

'New Deal' legislation ... 'Bodyline' crisis on cricket tour ... King Kong ...

o Politics, Government, Law, and Economy

Norman Angell, *The Great Illusion Now.*

Leon Trotsky, *History of the Russian Revolution.*

After the Nazis come to power in Germany, the Nazi SA take control of police forces; they are then taken under Himmler's control; Hermann Goering forms the Geheime Staatspolizei or Gestapo (secret police).

Twentieth Amendment to the US Constitution advances the inauguration date of new presidents to 20 Jan, with senators and representatives taking office on 3 Jan (ratified on 5 Oct).

Children and Young Persons Act in Britain raises the age of criminal responsibility from 7 to 8 and the range of juvenile courts to 17.

Against Norway's claim, the International Court at The Hague rules that Greenland is a Danish possession (5 April).

In the USA, economic legislation under F D Roosevelt's 'New Deal' includes the Agricultural Adjustment Act (12 May), which attempts to raise prices by providing grants to farmers for reducing areas under cultivation and livestock numbers; the Federal Securities Act (27 May), which compels disclosure of information about security issues; the National Industrial Recovery Act (16 June), which encourages joint economic planning by government and business through the National Recovery Administration and appropriates $3.3 billion for public works projects; and the Glass Steagall Banking Act, which creates the Federal Bank Deposit Insurance Corporation to guarantee deposits under $5,000 (effective from Jan 1934). The Tennessee Valley Authority is formed to build dams and hydroelectric plants.

USSR launches second Five-Year Plan (22 Jan), envisaging growth of heavy industry but also production of more consumer goods (Plan redrafted and adopted by 27th Party Congress in Feb 1934).

Foundation of airline Air France.

The London Passenger Transport Board takes control of all public transport in London except main-line railways.

J M Keynes, *The Means to Prosperity.*

p Society, Education, and Religion

Germany opens concentration camps for enemies of the Nazi regime; the first camp is at Dachau, near Munich (opened 20 March).

Germany inaugurates a four-year plan (the Schacht Plan) for abolishing unemployment by expanding public works.

In USA, social legislation under the 'New Deal' extends government involvement in social provision. The Federal Emergency Relief Act (12 May) provides money to states for unemployment relief projects and establishes the Public Works Administration, which constructs roads and buildings and runs numerous other projects.

In USA, President Roosevelt appoints John Collier, secretary of the Indian Defence Association, his Commissioner for Indian Affairs.

Frances Perkins is the first woman cabinet member in the USA, as secretary of labor.

The 21st Amendment to the US Constitution repeals Prohibition (ratified 5 Dec).

C G Jung, *Modern Man in Search of a Soul.*

George Orwell, *Down and Out in Paris and London.*

H G Wells, *The Shape of Things to Come.*

I L Kandel, *Comparative Education.*

Associations Law in Spain nationalizes church property and closes church schools (17 May).

The Vatican and the German government initial a new concordat, defining the position of the Catholic Church in Germany (9 July).

The Lutheran Churches in Germany are formed into the German Evangelical Church League (July); the national synod elects the pro-Nazi Ludwig Müller as Reich Bishop (27 Sept). Opponents rally around Martin Niemöller and form the anti-Nazi Confessional Church.

In USA, first publication of the *Catholic Worker* as the organ of the Catholic Worker Movement.

E W Barnes, *Scientific Theory and Religion.*

W R Inge, *God and the Astronomers.*

Nathan Söderblom, *The Living God* (Gifford Lectures).

q Science, Technology, and Discovery

The Marconiphone Company makes the first all-metal wireless valve.

E Armstrong in the US patents Frequency Modulation (FM) in radio.

Wiley Post flies round the world in 7 days, 18 hours, 49 minutes.

US scientists C D Anderson and Robert Millikin, while analysing cosmic rays, discover positive electrons ('positrons').

In Germany, Ernst Ruska builds the first electron microscope that is more powerful

mons, for driving thousands of unemployed to seek means-tested assistance (a government amendment detailing proposed changes to assistance arrangements is carried by 384 votes to 46).

19 President Roosevelt makes a proclamation removing the US dollar from the Gold Standard.

25 Canada abandons the gold standard.

27 trade agreement between Britain and Germany.

27 Anglo–Persian oil dispute is settled with new agreement.

E **May**

2 in Germany, trades unions are suppressed.

3 oath of allegiance to the British Crown is removed from the Irish Constitution; appeals to the Privy Council are made illegal.

10 in the Chaco War, Paraguay makes a formal declaration of war on Bolivia.

17 in elections in South Africa, the National Coalition wins 138 seats, the Opposition, 12.

26 Australia claims a third of Antarctica.

28 Nazis win elections in the free city of Danzig (now Gdansk in Poland); a new government is formed on 2 June.

31 armistice between China and Japan; Japanese forces in China to withdraw to the north of the Great Wall (completed by 7 Aug).

F **June**

6 Rome Pact initialled, binding France, Britain, Germany, and Italy to support the Covenant of the League of Nations, the Locarno Treaties, and the Kellogg–Briand Pact.

12 (–27 July) 64 countries attend the World Monetary and Economic Conference in London but fail to reach agreement on how to achieve currency stabilization.

15 Britain makes token final payment to the USA for debts from First World War.

19 in Austria, Chancellor Dollfuss dissolves the Nazi Party, but Nazi agitation continues.

20 coup by army in Siam (now Thailand).

G **July**

3 USSR and countries in its ambit sign the London Convention defining aggression.

14 in Germany, suppression of political parties other than the Nazi Party.

H **August**

5 Poland makes agreement with the free city of Danzig (modern Gdansk in Poland).

12 the Cuban army, led by Fulgencio Batista and supported by the USA, overthrows President Machedo.

22 in the Irish Free State, the 'Blueshirts' are outlawed.

25 Canada, USA, USSR, Australia, and Argentina sign the Wheat Agreement to raise and stabilize prices.

J **September**

2 in the Irish Free State, the opposition parties of the National Guard, the Centre, and Cumann na nGaedhael form Fine Gael, under Owen O'Duffy (from 22, led by William Cosgrave).

14 Greece and Turkey agree 10-year nonaggression pact.

11 Latin American countries sign the Rio de Janeiro nonaggression pact.

K **October**

Increasing unrest in Palestine.

14 Germany withdraws from the League of Nations and its Disarmament Conference.

16 in Norway, the Labour Party wins the general election (Labour 69 seats; Conservatives, 30; Liberals, 24; Farmers' Party, 23; others, 4).

23 Albert Sarraut becomes prime minister of France.

L **November**

12 in German election, 92 per cent of voters vote for the Nazi Party list of candidates (96 per cent of electorate vote).

16 British Liberal Party leaves National Government and joins Opposition.

16 President Getúlio Vargas of Brazil acquires dictatorial powers.

17 the USA recognizes the USSR and resumes trade.

19 in Spain, the Spanish Confederation of Autonomous Right Wing Groups (CEDA) wins the largest number of seats (115) in the general election, followed by the Radicals (with 102); the Centre parties win 167, the Left, 99; members of CEDA enter the Radical government led by Alejandro Lerroux.

22 Camille Chautemps becomes prime minister of France.

M **December**

Jews in Palestine protest at immigration restrictions.

5 ratification of the 21st amendment to the US Constitutiton, repealing prohibition.

9 (–19) radical rising in Spain.

15 an African-American released by a court in Tennessee, USA, is lynched by a white mob.

than a light microscope (magnification × 12,000).

In Austria, R Kuhn, A von Szent-Györgyi and J Wagner-Jauregg discover Vitamin B2 (riboflavin).

E Graham makes the first successful removal of a human lung.

Arthur Stanley Eddington, *The Expanding Universe*.

J B S Haldane, *The Causes of Evolution*.

R Humanities

The discovery of the Steinheim skull leads to the rejection of the theory that Neanderthal Man was in the line of descent of *Homo sapiens*.

Arthur Bryant, *Samuel Pepys* (–1942).

Winston Churchill, *Marlborough: His Life and Times* (–1938).

Arthur M Schlesinger, *The Rise of the City, 1878–1898*.

Completion of publication of the late Ludwig Pastor's *History of the Popes from the Close of the Middle Ages* (16 volumes).

The Warburg Institute is transferred from Hamburg to London (and incorporated in London University in 1944).

F N Robinson (ed.), *The Complete Works of Geoffrey Chaucer*.

Shorter Oxford English Dictionary.

E Starkie, *Baudelaire*.

T S Eliot, *The Use of Poetry and the Use of Criticism*.

Alfred Tarski, *The Concept of Truth in the Languages of Deductive Sciences*.

A N Whitehead, *Adventures of Ideas*.

S Art, Sculpture, Fine Arts, and Architecture

Following the accession of the Nazis in Germany, Kandinsky, Klee, and other artists leave the country.

Closure of the Bauhaus design school in Germany.

First issue of *Minotaure*, a mainstream surrealist review (editors, André Breton, Marcel Duchamp, Paul Éluard).

Painting, etc:

British critic Herbert Read publishes *Art Now*.

Max Beckmann, *Departure*.

Paul Klee, *Von der Liste Grestrichen*.

Sculpture:

Jean Arp, *Human Concretion*.

Architecture:

Arne Jacobsen, Bellavista Housing Estate near Copenhagen, Denmark.

T Music

Kurt Atterberg, *A Varmland Rhapsody*.

Béla Bartók, Piano Concerto No. 2.

Louis Gruenberg, *The Emperor Jones* (opera).

Roy Harris, Symphony No. 1.

Olivier Messiaen, *The Ascension*.

Richard Strauss, *Arabella* (opera).

Kurt Weill, *The Seven Deadly Sins* (cantata).

George Balanchine and Lincoln Kirstein found the School of American Ballet.

Debut in Britain of Duke Ellington's orchestra from the USA.

U Literature and Drama

Sherwood Anderson, *Death in the Woods*.

Erskine Caldwell, *God's Little Acre*.

John Drinkwater, *Summer Harvest*.

Georges Duhamel, *Chronique de Pasquier/ The Pasquier Chronicles* (–1945).

Lewis Grassic Gibbon, *Cloud Howe*.

Walter Greenwood, *Love on the Dole*.

André Malraux, *La condition humaine/Man's Estate*.

Thomas Mann, *The Tales of Jacob* (first volume of 'Joseph and his Brothers') (–1943).

John Cowper Powys, *Weymouth Sands*.

Raymond Queneau, *The Bark Tree*.

George Santayana, *The Last Puritan*.

Dorothy L Sayers, *Murder Must Advertise*.

Gertrude Stein, *The Autobiography of Alice B Toklas*.

Helen Waddell, *Peter Abelard*.

Nathanael West, *Miss Lonelyhearts*.

Antonia White, *Frost in May*.

Drama:

Federico García Lorca, *Blood Wedding*.

Eugene O'Neill, *Ah, Wilderness!*.

V Births and Deaths

Jan 1 Joe Orton born (–1967).

Jan 2 Keith Thomas born (–).

Jan 5 Calvin Coolidge dies (60).

Jan 21 George Augustus Moore dies (80).

Jan 31 John Galsworthy dies (66).

March 19 Philip Roth born (–).

April 22 Frederick Henry Royce dies (60).

July 23 Richard Rogers born (–).

Aug 18 Roman Polanski born (–).

Sept 7 Edward Grey (Lord Grey) dies (81).

Dec 4 Stefan George dies (65).

Dec 6 Henryk Górecki born (–).

Dec 23 Akihito born (–).

W Everyday Life

Ritz crackers introduced to the US consumer.

The British Imperial Chemical Industries (ICI) makes the first commercially produced synthetic detergent.

In London, Lyons opens its 'Corner House' fast food restaurant with seats for 2,000 (23 Oct).

18 Newfoundland Constitution suspended because of mismanagement of economic affairs.

21 Newfoundland loses status as British dominion; reverts to Crown Colony.

29 in Romania, the fascist Iron Guard murders the Liberal prime minister Ion Duca; succeeded by George Tartarescu.

Death of Stavisky in France ... 'Night of the Long Knives' in Germany ... Murder of Austrian chancellor ...

A January

8 in France, death of Alexander Stavisky (by suicide or murder), who had been accused of issuing fraudulent bonds (with official backing).

14 in Spain, elections in Catalonia are won by Left, while elsewhere the Right predominates.

26 Germany signs 10-year nonaggression pact with Poland.

30 Édouard Daladier forms ministry in France.

B February

1 (–16) in Austria, political parties are forcibly dissolved except for Chancellor Engelbert Dollfuss's Fatherland Front; a general strike called on 12 Feb fails to stop the dissolution.

6 (–7) riots in Paris protesting at the corruption implied by the Stavisky affair; 8, Paul Doumergue forms National Union ministry of all parties, except Royalists, Socialists, and Communists, to avert civil chaos.

9 pact signed between Greece, Turkey, Romania, and Yugoslavia, forming the 'Balkan Entente' as a counterpart to the Little Entente, to prevent Balkans from encroachment by the great powers.

12 (–13) general strike in France, in protest at danger posed by rise of Fascism.

15 Civil Works Emergency Relief act in USA.

16 British–Russian trade pact.

17 death of King Albert I of Belgium in climbing accident; succeeded by Leopold II.

21 (–16 March) French troops combat Berbers in SW Morocco.

21 in Nicaragua, murder of former guerrilla leader César Sandino by National Guard under command of Anastasio Somoza.

x Sport and Recreation

England regains the Ashes on the 'Bodyline' tour of Australia: diplomatic relations between the two countries are threatened when protests are made over the English tactics of bowling short on the line of the batsman's body.

Peggy Scriven is the first Briton to win a Singles title at the French Tennis Championships.

In USA, Primo Carnera of Italy knocks out Jack Sharkey in the sixth round of their fight at Long Island to win the World Heavyweight boxing title (29 June).

Fred Perry becomes the first British tennis player to win the US Championship since 1903 (10 Sept).

The British jockey Gordon Richards beats Fred Archer's record of riding 246 winners in one season (8 Nov).

The National Playing Fields Association is established in Britain.

y Media

Foundation of union for journalists in the USA, the American Newspaper Guild.

In Germany, Hitler persuades President Hindenburg to use article 48 of the constitution (the president's emergency powers) to suspend or close down several hundred newspapers.

Australian Women's Weekly published.

Newsweek magazine published in Britain.

In Britain, Arthur Christiansen edits the *Daily Express* (–1957).

In India, Mahatma Gandhi founds the weekly publication *Harijan*.

Film:

A Voz do Carnival (starring Carmen Miranda).

Dinner at Eight (starring Jean Harlow).

Duck Soup (starring The Marx Brothers).

Ecstasy (starring a nude Hedy Lamarr).

Footlight Parade (starring James Cagney).

42nd Street introduces the choreography of Busby Berkeley.

The Invisible Man (starring Claude Rains).

King Kong (directors, Merian C Cooper and Ernest Shoedsack).

Little Women (director, George Cukor).

The Private Lives of Henry VIII (director, Alexander Korda; starring Charles Laughton).

14 Juli (director, René Clair).

Queen Christina (starring Greta Garbo).

She Done Him Wrong (starring Mae West).

The Testament of Dr Mabuse (director, Fritz Lang).

Viktor und Viktoria (director, Reinhold Schünzel).

Zéro de Conduite (director, Jean Vigo).

British Film Institute founded.

Odeon Cinema circuit founded in Britain.

Synod of Barmen opposes Nazism ... Coward's 'Mad Dogs and Englishmen' ... Deaths of Elgar, Holst, and Delius ...

o Politics, Government, Law, and Economy

John Wheeler-Bennett, *The Disarmament Deadlock*.

Incitement to Disaffection Act (the 'Sedition Bill') passed in Britain, providing for summary treatment of anyone who undermines allegiance of armed forces.

Road Traffic Act introduces driving tests in Britain (26 March).

B Graham, *Security Analysis*.

Special commissioners (all Nazis) are placed in charge of state governments in Germany; state parliaments are abolished.

In Germany, SS leader Himmler takes control of the secret police; on 20 July, the SS is made an independent organization inside the Nazi Party.

Law Revision Committee established in Britain.

British Council founded, to promote British culture overseas.

In Britain, Hendon Police College founded to provide training for police.

Federal Farm Mortgage Corporation set up in USA, to take over farm mortgages and stem foreclosures (31 Jan).

The Gold Reserve Act in the USA allows the president to devalue the dollar by 60 per cent.

In USA, formation of the Securities and Exchange Commission, to police acts of Congress that regulate the securities market and thereby prevent recurrence of the abuses of the 1920s and the 1929 Crash (6 June).

Five-Year Plan launched in Turkey, to expand textile, metal, paper, chemical, and other industries (Jan).

Opening of oil pipeline from Mosul, Iraq, to Tripoli, Lebanon (14 July).

c **March**

The French high commissioner in Syria dismisses the cabinet and prorogues parliament for seven months.

8 for first time the Labour Party wins a clear majority on the London County Council over Municipal Reform and Liberal Parties.

16 (–17) Rome protocols signed between Italy, Austria, and Hungary to a form Danubian bloc against Little Entente (Czechoslovakia, Romania, and Yugoslavia).

24 in USA, the Tydings–McDuffie act declares independence of the Philippines from 1945.

d **April**

In Spain, Socialists lead strike in Barcelona.

7 in India, Mahatma Gandhi suspends civil disobedience campaign.

7 extension of 1932 USSR–Finnish nonaggression pact for 10 years.

e **May**

14 Unemployment Bill given third reading in British House of Commons, intending to take the question of unemployment relief 'out of politics' by transferring responsibility for setting benefit rates to a new statutory body, the Unemployed Assistance Board.

15 Karlis Ulmanis becomes dictator in Latvia.

24 Colombia and Peru agree to continue discussions over disputed port of Leticia.

26 in Portugal, Prime Minister Salazar calls a meeting of the National Congress and announces that elections will be held.

f **June**

5 J C Smuts' South African Party unites with J B M Hertzog's followers in Nationalist Party to form United South African Nationalists, while other Nationalists reform under D F Malan.

8 Oswald Mosley addresses mass meeting of British Union of Fascists at Olympia, London.

9 USSR renews relations with Czechoslovakia and, on 10, with Romania.

11 Geneva Disarmament Conference ends in failure.

12 political parties banned in Bulgaria.

12 US Congress grants President Roosevelt powers to conclude agreements for reducing tariffs.

12 Cape Parliament retains right to secede from Commonwealth in South African Status bill.

14 (–15) meeting in Venice, Italy, between Hitler and Mussolini, which fails to improve relations because of divergent interests in the Danube Valley.

19 US Silver Purchase Act authorizes the purchase of silver to provide partial backing for the dollar.

20 Britain and Italy exchange notes defining the frontier between Sudan and Libya.

23 following six-week war, Saudi Arabia and the Yemen sign peace agreement.

29 (–30) in Germany, 'Night of the Long Knives': a Nazi purge to break the power of the SA or Storm Troopers; those murdered include Ernst Roehm, head of the SA, General Kurt von Schleicher, over 70 leading Nazis, and many others (executions continue until 2 July).

g **July**

1 Germany suspends all cash transfers on debts abroad.

2 Lazaro Cárdenas elected president of Mexico.

7 Keisuke Okada forms ministry in Japan.

12 Belgium prohibits uniformed political parties.

16 new constitution promulgated in Brazil; it enlarges the powers of the chamber and reduces those of the president (17, chamber elects Getúlio Vargas president).

19 in Britain, the acting prime minister, Stanley Baldwin, announces increase in size of the Royal Air Force.

25 Engelbert Dollfuss, chancellor of Austria, is murdered in attempted Nazi coup.

30 Kurt Schuschnigg is appointed Austrian chancellor.

h **August**

1 Australia's prohibitive duty on imported cottons provokes boycott of Australian produce in Lancashire, NW England.

2 in Germany, death of President Paul von Hindenburg (aged 87); soon afterwards the presidency is merged with the chancellorship and all members of the armed forces take an oath of loyalty to Adolf Hitler as Führer ('Leader').

6 US marines withdraw from Haiti, after 19 years of military occupation.

19 German plebiscite on vesting of sole executive power in Adolf Hitler as Führer; 89.9 per cent of voters approve the change.

j **September**

9 Fascist and anti-Fascist demonstrations in Hyde Park, London.

12 Baltic states sign treaty of collaboration.

15 in general election in Australia, the United Australia Party wins the largest number of seats with 32 (Labour, 18; Country Party, 15; New South Wales Labour, 9); on 17,

British Iron and Steel Federation formed to set prices and plan the industry.

Bank Secrecy Act passed in Switzerland.

In USA, textile strike in the S and strikes in mining areas.

P Society, Education, and Religion

The Nazi government develops a plan for labour regulation and reducing German reliance on foreign trade; unemployment in Germany falls rapidly.

Enfranchisement of women in Turkey (14 Dec).

In Turkey, family names are made obligatory from 1 Jan 1935 and titles are abolished; Mustafa Kemal adopts the name Kemal Atatürk, 'Chief Turk' (26 Nov).

James Weldon Johnson, *Negro Americans, What Now?*

In USA, Indian Reorganization Act recognizes tribal authority.

Lewis Mumford, *Technics and Civilization*.

Wilhelm Reich, *The Mass Psychology of Fascism*.

Bertrand Russell, *Freedom and Civilisation*.

Gordonstoun School at Elgin, Scotland, founded by Kurt Hahn.

German Protestant leaders meet at the Synod of Barmen to organize resistance to Nazism (May); they produce the Barmen Declaration, which affirms basic Christian doctrines and condemns attempts to accommodate Christianity to Nazism (more synods are held until 1937).

In USA, the Fraternal Council of Negro Churches is established, with the intention of campaigning for social change.

The Evangelical Synod of North America and the Reformed Church of the United States unitc to form thc Evangclical and Reformed Church (26 June).

In USA the 'radio priest' Father Charles E Coughlin founds the National Union for Social Justice and attracts 5 million members.

Karl Barth, *Nein! Antwort an Emil Brunner*.

William Temple, *Nature, Man and God*.

Q Science, Technology, and Discovery

The cat's eye reflector invented.

Chilling process for meat cargoes discovered.

Soviet balloon *Osoaviakhim* ascends 20.8 km/13 mi into the stratosphere (30 Jan).

US explorer and biologist William Beebe descends in a bathysphere to a record 922.9 m/3,028 ft in the Atlantic off Bermuda (16 Aug).

French physicists Frédéric Joliot and Irène Curie-Joliot discover induced radioactivity.

US physicist Ernest O Lawrence constructs the 'cyclotron', for accelerating particles.

Italian physicist Enrico Fermi suggests that neutrons and protons are the same fundamental particles in two different quantum states.

Alexander Fleming and G F Petrie, *Recent Advances in Vaccine and Serum Therapy*.

Tadeusz Reichstein, in Switzerland, makes pure Vitamin C.

R Humanities

Abbé Breuil, *L'Evolution de l'Art Pariétal dans les Cavernes et Abris Ornées de France*.

Arnold Toynbee, *A Study of History* (–1961).

Oxford History of England, edited by G N Clark (–1965).

J E Neale, *Queen Elizabeth*.

Earl Jefferson Hamilton, *American Treasure and the Price Revolution in Spain, 1501–1650*.

Charles McLean Andrews, *The Colonial Period in American History* (–1938).

A J A Symons, *The Quest for Corvo*.

Harold Nicolson, *Curzon, the Last Phase*.

G M Young (ed.), *Early Victorian England*.

Ruth Benedict, *Patterns of Culture*.

Maurice Blondel, *Thought*.

R Carnap, *The Logical Syntax of Language*.

D T Suzuki, *An Introduction to Zen Buddhism*.

S Art, Sculpture, Fine Arts, and Architecture

Following the first Congress of Soviet Writers, Socialist Realism becomes the official style of art in the Soviet State.

Painting, etc:

Salvador Dalí, *Mae West* (–1936).

René Magritte, *The Human Condition*.

Sculpture:

Max Beckmann, *The Man in Darkness*.

Lucio Fontana, *Abstract Sculpture*.

Alberto Giacometti, *The Invisible Object*.

Pablo Picasso, *Woman with Leaves*.

Architecture:

Maxwell Fry and Walter Gropius, Impington Villa College, near Cambridge, England (–1937).

Tecton Group, Penguin Pool, London Zoo (–1938).

T Music

Jacques Ibert, Flute Concerto.

Sergei Rachmaninov, *Rhapsody on a Theme of Paganini*.

Franz Schmidt, Symphony No. 4.

Dmitry Shostakovich, *The Lady Macbeth of Mtsensk* (opera).

Virgil Thomson, *Four Saints in Three Acts* (opera).

US violinist Yehudi Menuhin makes his first world tour.

Joseph Lyons forms a United Australia Party ministry.

18 the USSR is admitted to the League of Nations.

ᴋ October

2 Royal Indian Navy founded.

4 Alejandro Lerroux forms ministry of Right in Spain, provoking, on 5, strike called by the Left.

9 King Alexander of Yugoslavia is assassinated in Marseilles, France, by Croat; succeeded by his young son Peter II.

21 in China, start of the 'Long March' of Chinese Communists led by Mao Zedong (–20 Oct 1935); under attack from the Guomindang army, an estimated 100,000 people leave the Jiangxi Soviet in S China and march 9,600 km/6,000 mi to Yan'an in the northern province of Shaanxi.

23 (–19 Dec) discussions in London on naval disarmament, involving delegates from Japan, USA, and Britain; no conclusions are achieved.

24 Gandhi withdraws from Indian National Congress, disillusioned with its tactical use of disobedience; he invests his efforts in the All-India Village Industries Association.

30 dissolution of Greek–Turkish Commission (established in 1923).

ʟ November

Moroccan nationalist movement founded.

3 the French high commissioner in Syria suspends parliament indefinitely.

7 in Australia, Joseph Lyons, United Australia Party, forms coalition ministry with the Country Party.

9 in France, following the resignation of Paul Doumergue (because of opposition to his plans for constitutional reform) Pierre Flandin forms a coalition ministry.

20 Depressed Areas Act in Britain provides funds and two commissioners for promotion of economic development and social improvement.

30 in Egypt, following riots by supporters of the Wafd Party, King Fuad suspends the constitution.

ᴍ December

Daniel Salamanca, president of Bolivia, overthrown by military coup, following Paraguayan victories in the Chaco War.

1 in USSR, assassination of Sergei Kirov, the fourth highest communist leader, probably with Stalin's connivance; the assassin, 13 accomplices, and 103 others are summarily executed.

5 clashes between Italian and Ethiopian troops on Somaliland frontier.

16 general elections held in Portugal; no opposition parties are allowed to put forward candidates.

19 Japan denounces Washington treaties of 1922 and 1930.

21 British–Irish coal and cattle pact.

John Christie founds opera festival at his country house of Glyndebourne, S England.

Anything Goes (musical), text by Guy Bolton and P G Wodehouse, music by Cole Porter (first performed at the Alvin Theatre, New York, 21 Nov).

Blue Mountain Melody (musical) by Charles Zwar staged at the Theatre Royal in Sydney, Australia.

Noël Coward, 'Mad Dogs and Englishmen'.

First 'Oscars' awarded for best film song ('The Continental' from *The Gay Divorcée*) and best film score (*One Night of Love*).

Belgian jazz guitarist Django Reinhardt and French violinist Stéphane Grappelli form the Quintette du Hot Club de France in Paris.

In USA, pianist 'Fats' Waller emerges as leading jazz performer and composer.

u Literature and Drama

Louis Aragon, *Hourra l'Oural* (poem).
Paul Brunton, *A Search in Secret India*.
James Cain, *The Postman Always Rings Twice*.
Eleanor Dark, *Prelude to Christopher*.
F Scott Fitzgerald, *Tender is the Night*.
Lewis Grassic Gibbon, *Grey Granite*.
Robert Graves, *I, Claudius*.
Henry Miller, *Tropic of Cancer*.
Henry de Montherlant, *The Bachelors*.
Edwin Muir, *Variations on a Time Theme*.
Vladimir Nabokov, *Despair*.
William Saroyan, *The Daring Young Man on the Flying Trapeze*.
Dorothy L Sayers, *The Nine Tailors*.
Mikhail Sholokhov, *Quiet Flows the Don*.
Ben Traven, *The Treasure of the Sierra Madre*.
Evelyn Waugh, *A Handful of Dust*.
H G Wells, *Experiment in Autobiography*.
William Carlos Williams, *Collected Poems, 1922–1931*.
In USSR, first Congress of Soviet Writers held, under Maxim Gorky.

Drama:

Jean Cocteau, *La Machine infernale*.
Lillian Hellman, *The Children's Hour*.
Federico García Lorca, *Yerma*.
Sean O'Casey, *Within the Gates*.
J B Priestley, *Eden End*.
Robert Sherwood, *The Petrified Forest*.

v Births and Deaths

Feb 21 César Sandino dies (40).
Feb 23 Edward Elgar dies (76).
May 9 Alan Bennett born (–).
May 25 Gustav Holst dies (59).
June 10 Frederick Delius dies (71).
July 4 Marie Curie dies (66).
July 13 Wole Soyinka born (–).
Aug 2 Paul von Hindenburg dies (87).
Sept 9 Roger Fry dies (67).
Sept 20 Sophia Loren born (–).
Oct 15 Raymond Poincaré dies (74).
Nov 23 Arthur Wing Pinero dies (79).
Nov 24 Alfred Schnittke born (–).

w Everyday Life

In Louisiana, USA, police kill the murderers Bonnie and Clyde (Bonnie Parker and Clyde Barrow; 23 May); in Chicago, FBI agents kill the notorious bank-robber John Dillinger.

In USA, the Prison Bureau acquires the island of Alcatraz in San Francisco Bay as site for a new federal prison.

Regular air-mail service from London to Australia is inaugurated (8 Dec).

In London, 60 official pedestrian crossing places established on roads (June).

Opening of Mersey Tunnel in Liverpool, NW England (18 July).

Luxury liner SS *Queen Mary* is launched in Scotland (26 Sept).

The Southern Railway in England launches the first train ferry.

x Sport and Recreation

The US Masters, the fourth of golf's major championships, is held for the first time in Augusta, Georgia; the winner is Horton Smith of the USA.

In USA, Max Baer of the USA knocks out Primo Carnera in the 11th round of their World Heavyweight title fight at Long Island (14 June).

The second football World Cup is held in Italy; Italy wins the trophy, beating Czechoslovakia 2–1 in the final in Rome.

Australia regains the Ashes, beating England 2–1 in the five-match series in England (22 Aug).

In American Football, Beattie Feathers of the Chicago Bears becomes the first player to 'rush' 1,000 yards.

y Media

Film:

L'Atalante (director, Jean Vigo).
The Black Cat (starring Boris Karloff).
Cleopatra (director, Cecil B de Mille).
The Count of Monte Cristo (starring Robert Donat).
Forgotten Men.

Government of India Act ... Anti-Jewish Nuremberg laws in
Germany ... Italy invades Ethiopia ...

A January

Constitutional Convention held in the Philippines (23 March, US President Roosevelt confirms that the proposed constitution conforms with the Tydings–McDuffie Act of 1934).

4 British cotton-spinners vote in favour of reducing their industry's productive capacity.

7 French–Italian Agreement of Marseilles, settling disputes between the two countries (including problems in Africa).

9 Britain signs trade pact with India.

13 plebiscite in the Saarland: 90.8 per cent of voters favour incorporation in Germany.

15 (–17) in the USSR, Grigory Zinoviev, Lev Kamenev, and 17 other former leading Communists are tried and imprisoned for 'moral responsibility' for Kirov's murder in 1934; thousands more around the country are arrested.

17 former British prime minister David Lloyd George makes speech at Bangor, NW Wales, advocating a statutory council to prepare plans for economic development; the proposal is dubbed his 'New Deal'.

28 Labour leader George Lansbury leads attack in British House of Commons on proposed reduction in some unemployment payments.

B February

1 (–3) British–German conference in London to discuss Germany's rearmament.

22 Italian troops depart for East Africa.

C March

1 (–11) rising in Greece; Eleuthérios Venizélos in Crete accepts leadership of the rebels, but after suppression of the uprising flees to France.

1 restoration of Saarland to Germany.

16 Germany repudiates disarmament clauses of the Versailles Treaty and introduces conscription.

20 in Norway, following defeat of the government in parliament, Labour forms a ministry with Johan Nygaardsvold as prime minister.

23 USSR sells its interest in the Chinese Eastern Railway (in Manchuria) to Japan.

25 in Belgium, Paul van Zeeland forms ministry of National Unity and devalues the Belgian franc.

D April

11 (–14) prime ministers of Italy, France, and Britain, confer at Stresa in NW Italy where they issue protest at German rearmament and agree to act together against Germany.

23 adoption of new constitution in Poland; President Moscicki signs it to the accompaniment of a 101-gun salute.

E May

2 French–USSR treaty of mutual assistance for five years.

16 USSR–Czechoslovakia pact of mutual assistance.

19 in Czechoslovakia, the Sudeten German (Nazi) Party wins 44 out of 300 seats, making it the second largest party in parliament.

The Last Millionaire (director, René Clair).
Lives of a Bengal Lancer (starring Gary Cooper).
The Lost Son (director, Luis Trenker).
The Scarlet Empress (director, Joseph von Sternberg).
The Scarlet Pimpernel (producer, Alexander Korda).
The Thin Man (director, W S Van Dyke).

Triumph of the Will (director, Leni Riefenstahl).

Radio:
In USA, creation of the Federal Communications Commission (FCC) to regulate broadcasting (as successor of the Federal Radio Commission), telephone services, and telegraph services.

'New Deal' in Canada ... Gershwin's Porgy and Bess *... Launch of 'Monopoly' ...*

o **Politics, Government, Law, and Economy**

In Britain, publisher Victor Gollancz founds the Left Book Club (first publication May 1936).

Foundation in Britain of the Peace Pledge Union (after a mass meeting in the Albert Hall, London, on 14 July), to oppose rearmament and resort to war.

In Schechter Poultry Corporation v. US, the Supreme Court strikes down the National Industrial Recovery Act (27 May), because of improper delegation of legislative powers to the executive and for exceeding the reach of the commerce clause of the Constitution.

In USA, the National Labor Relations Act (or Wagner Act) outlaws unfair practices by employers and creates a new National Labor Relations Board to manage union elections and bargain for workers; the Act establishes the right to join a trade union and to engage in collective bargaining.

George Gallup founds the American Institute of Public Opinion (known as the Gallup Poll) to conduct political and market research by scientific methods.

Persia changes name, becoming Iran.

The US Supreme Court reverses the convictions of the 'Scottsboro Nine', a group of African-Americans convicted in 1931 and again in 1932 of raping two white girls (1 April).

Oil pipelines from Kirkuk in Iraq to Haifa and Tripolis opened (Jan).

Large windstorm brings further devastation to the 'dust bowl' area of the mid-west USA, causing large-scale migration to other states.

A hydrogenerator plant, for extracting petrol from coal, is opened at Billingham, NE England (June).

p **Society, Education, and Religion**

In Canada, Prime Minister Richard Bennett announces a 'New Deal' for Canada (Jan); subsequent legislation provides for unemployment and social insurance, maximum hours and minimum wages in industry, farm credit supported by the federal government, and an agricultural marketing board.

In USA, in a second round of New Deal legislation, President Roosevelt establishes the Resettlement Administration (1 May), to help owners and tenants move to better land; the Works Progress Administration (WPA) to provide public works programmes; the Rural Electrification Administration (REA) to provide loans to companies for the construction of electricity supply networks in rural areas. The Social Security Act (signed, 14 Aug) provides pensions to the over-65s, help for the disabled and blind, and unemployment assistance (from 1942), paid for by contributions rather than from tax revenues.

In USA, eight unions seeking the establishment of industry-based unions, break away from the American Federation of Labor and found the Committee for Industrial Organization (CIO).

In USA, the National Association for the Advancement of Colored People appoints leading African-American lawyer Charles Hamilton Houston as full-time special counsel; he handles important civil-rights cases and initiates a campaign against segregation in colleges.

French trade unions recognize the right of women to hold employment.

Irish Free State makes the import and sale of contraceptives illegal (28 Feb).

Sidney and Beatrice Webb, *Soviet Communism: A New Civilisation?*

27 in Britain, Stanley Baldwin announces large expansion of Royal Air Force, including introduction of new heavy bomber.

31 ministry of Pierre Flandin, who had demanded extensive powers, is overthrown in France.

F June

3 Croats boycott the Yugoslav Parliament.

4 Pierre Laval forms ministry in France.

7 in Britain, Stanley Baldwin, Conservative, succeeds J Ramsay MacDonald as prime minister and forms a new National Government with MacDonald as lord president of the council, Sir John Simon as home secretary, and Sir Samuel Hoare as foreign secretary.

9 general election held in Greece; the Populists (Monarchists) win 243 seats (though the Liberal Party boycotts the election).

12 formal truce in Chaco War between Paraguay and Bolivia (treaty agreed in July 1938).

18 British–German Naval Agreement: Germany undertakes that its navy will not exceed a third of the tonnage of Britain's Royal Navy.

23 Britain's minister for League of Nations affairs, Anthony Eden, responds to Italian threats in East Africa by offering the Italian prime minister, Benito Mussolini, land in Somaliland if he will abandon designs on Ethiopia; Mussolini rejects the offer.

27 the League of Nations Union in Britain announces the results of its 'peace ballot': 11.6 million have registered support for the League's aims.

G July

Anti-Roman Catholic riots in Belfast, Northern Ireland.

1 (–2) in Britain, conference of the Council of Action for Peace and Reconstruction founded by former prime minister David Lloyd George; the Council will support parliamentary candidates who support its aims.

4 Austria, encouraged by Mussolini, abolishes anti-Hapsburg laws and restores some imperial property.

13 USSR–USA trade pact.

25 (–20 Aug) meeting of the Third International (Soviet-controlled international Communist organization) declares that Communists in democratic countries should support their governments against Fascist states.

27 French government is granted emergency financial powers.

H August

2 Government of India Act reforms governmental system, separates Burma (now Myanmar) and Aden from India, grants provincial governments greater self-government, and creates a central legislature at Delhi (to come into force on 1 April 1937).

J September

10 assassination in Baton Rouge, Louisiana, USA, of Senator Huey Long, the domineering former governor of Louisiana.

10 assembly of white settlers in Kenya denounces government policy and advocates closer union with Uganda and Tanganyika.

15 in Germany, at the Nuremberg Nazi Party rally, Hitler announces the anti-Jewish 'Nuremberg Laws': legislation will define Jews, ban them from professions, and forbid marriage and sexual intercourse with non-Jews; the Swastika will become Germany's official flag.

K October

2 Italy invades Ethiopia.

7 following Italy's invasion of Ethiopia, the League of Nations Council declares and denounces Italy as aggressor.

7 (–17) Kurt Schuschnigg's 'bloodless' coup in Vienna in collaboration with Prince Starhemberg against Emil Fey, minister of interior, and his Nazi allies.

8 in Britain, George Lansbury resigns as leader of the Labour Party, because he cannot support the Party's decision to support the use of force against Italy; Clement Attlee is chosen as acting leader for the remainder of the parliamentary session.

14 general election in Canada: the Liberal Party wins an overwhelming victory with 173 seats to the Conservatives' 40 seats (and 32 seats to other parties); 23, W L Mackenzie King is appointed prime minister.

19 the League of Nations imposes sanctions against Italy.

L November

3 plebiscite in Greece supports restoration of King George II, with 97 per cent voting in favour.

3 French Socialist groups merge as Socialist and Republican Union, under Léon Blum; this soon forms close relations with Radical Socialists and Communists to found a Popular Front.

In Britain, speed limit of 48 kph/30 mph is enforced in built-up areas (from 12 March).

Green Belt scheme in operation around London to prevent excessive development.

Foundation in Akron, Ohio, USA, of Alcoholics Anonymous, a group for dealing with drinking problems by mutual support.

Riots in New York after police are accused of brutal treatment of an African-American arrested for shoplifting (19–21 March).

F H Hinsley appointed as Cardinal Archbishop of Westminster, London.

Karl Barth, *Credo*.

S Bulgakov, *The Orthodox Church*.

Q Science, Technology, and Discovery

British driver Malcolm Campbell at Daytona Beach, Florida, USA, drives *Bluebird* at 445.4 kph/276.8 mph.

SS *Normandie* crosses Atlantic in 107 hours 33 mins.

The 35-mm 'Kodachrome' film devised.

American seismologist Charles Richter introduces Richter scale for measuring power of earthquakes.

British physicist Robert Watson-Watt builds first practical radar equipment for detecting aircraft.

US chemist W H Carothers discovers the fibre-forming potential of polyamides, which leads to the development of synthetic fibres.

US biochemist E C Kendall isolates the steroid hormone Cortisone from the adrenal cortex.

R Humanities

R Syme, *The Roman Revolution*.

R H Hodgkin, *History of the Anglo-Saxons*.

A Herrmann, *Historical and Commercial Atlas of China*.

Andrew C McLaughlin, *The Constitutional History of the United States*.

W E B Du Bois, *Black Reconstruction in America*.

George Dangerfield, *The Strange Death of Liberal England*.

Carl L Becker, *Every Man His Own Historian*.

H A L Fisher, *A History of Europe*.

Ruth Benedict, *Zuni Mythology*.

T E Lawrence, under pseudonym of T E Shaw, publishes translation of *The Odyssey of Homer*.

Donald Tovey, *Essays in Musical Analysis*, 6 volumes (–1939).

Brockhaus Encyclopaedia completed.

Sidney Hook, *From Hegel to Marx*.

Karl Jaspers, *Reason and Existence*.

Karl Popper, *The Logic of Scientific Discovery*.

S Art, Sculpture, Fine Arts, and Architecture

Exhibition 'Chinese Art' at Burlington House, London — the first of its kind in Europe.

In USA, the Federal Art Project employs tens of thousands of artists for public works of art including Arshile Gorky, Jackson Pollock, and Ben Shahn; artists are paid from the federal payroll.

Painting, etc:

Fernand Léger, *Adam and Eve*.

Ben Nicholson, *White Relief*.

Pablo Picasso, *Minotaurmachy* etchings.

Sculpture:

Barbara Hepworth, *Three Forms*.

Henry Moore, *Family*.

Architecture:

Edward Mendelssohn and Sergei Chermayeff, The De la Warr Pavilion, Bexhill, Sussex, England.

T Music

Alban Berg, Violin Concerto.

Henry Cowell, *Mosaic Quartet*.

George Gershwin, *Porgy and Bess* (opera).

Ivor Novello, *Glamorous Night* (operetta).

Sergey Prokofiev, Violin Concerto No. 2.

Richard Strauss, *Die Schweigsame Frau* (opera).

Karol Szymanowski, *Harnasie* (ballet).

In USA, publication of the tune 'Good Morning to All' as 'Happy Birthday to You' (words by Patty Smith Hill, music by Mildred J Hill).

In USA, start (on 20 April) of world's first ratings show, *Your Lucky Strike Hit Parade*, featuring the 15 most popular songs of the week (–1959).

In USA, manufacture of first Gibson electro-acoustic guitar.

Count Basie's band achieves fame through performances at the Famous Door Club, New York.

US jazz musician Artie Shaw founds his first band.

In Britain, first recordings by dance band of Victor Silvester.

The British Ministry of Labour effectively bans US jazz musicians by stipulating that they can only play in Britain if there are reciprocal arrangements with the American Federation of Musicians. As a result, few foreign jazz musicians play in Britain for 17 years.

4 German–Polish economic agreement.

5 Milan Hodza, Agrarian Party, forms ministry in Czechoslovakia.

7 USSR–Turkish treaties extended for 10 years.

14 in British general election Government parties win 429 seats, Opposition, 184 (Conservatives, 388, National Liberal, 33, National Labour, 8; Liberal, 21, Labour, 154, Independent Labour Party, 4, Communist, 1, others 4); Ramsay MacDonald is defeated by Emmanuel Shinwell at Seaham Harbour.

15 Commonwealth of Philippines is inaugurated as largely self-governing with Manuel Quezon as president (elected 17 Sept); Douglas MacArthur from the US Army is appointed to reorganize defence forces.

15 Canada–USA reciprocal trade agreement.

20 British miners ballot to press for wage increase.

26 in Britain, Clement Attlee defeats Herbert Morrison and Arthur Greenwood in election for Labour Party leader.

27 general election in New Zealand results in Labour victory (Labour, 53 seats; National Party, 17; others, 6); on 29, Michael Savage forms first Labour government in New Zealand.

M December

1 Chiang Kai-shek elected president of Chinese (Guomindang) executive.

9 Hoare–Laval Pact, whereby the British foreign minister (Samuel Hoare) and the French prime minister (Pierre Laval) propose to cede the most fertile part of Ethiopia to Italy; in both countries public outcry denounces the plan and the British prime minister disowns it.

12 in Egypt, Wafd nationalists demand restoration of the Egyptian Constitution of 1923.

13 Eduard Beneš succeeds Tomáš Masaryk as president of Czechoslovakia.

18 following criticism of the Hoare–Laval pact, Samuel Hoare resigns as British foreign secretary (23, succeeded by Anthony Eden).

German radio bans jazz of African-American or Jewish origin (Oct).

u Literature and Drama

E F Benson, *Mapp and Lucia*.
Elias Canetti, *Die Blendung/Auto-Da-Fé*.
Ivy Compton-Burnett, *A House and its Head*.
Cyril Connolly, *The Rock Pool*.
Cecil Day Lewis, *A Time to Dance*.
Walter de la Mare, *Poems, 1919–34*.
T S Eliot, *Four Quartets* (poems; –1942).
Christopher Isherwood, *Mr Norris Changes Trains*.
André Malraux, *Le temps du mépris*.
Herbert Read, *The Green Child*.
John Steinbeck, *Tortilla Flat*.
Wallace Stevens, *Ideas of Order*.

Drama:

W H Auden and Christopher Isherwood, *The Dog Beneath the Skin*.
T S Eliot, *Murder in the Cathedral*.
Clifford Odets, *Waiting for Lefty*.
Robert Sherwood, *The Petrified Forest*.
Emlyn Williams, *Night Must Fall*.
New York Drama Critics' Circle Founded.

v Births and Deaths

Jan 8 Elvis Presley born (–1977).
March 6 Oliver Wendell Holmes dies (93).
May 12 Józef Pilsudski dies (67).
May 19 T E Lawrence ('Lawrence of Arabia') dies (46).
June 1 Norman Foster born (–).
June 13 Christo born (–).
June 21 Françoise Sagan born (–).
July 17 G W Russell (A) dies (68).
Sept 16 Carl André born (–).
Oct 20 Arthur Henderson dies (72).
Oct 22 Edward Carson dies (81).
Oct 24 Henri Pirenne dies (72).
Nov 5 Lester Piggott born (–).
Nov 13 George Carey born (–).
Nov 20 John (Earl) Jellicoe dies (75).
Dec 1 Woody Allen born (–).
Dec 24 Alban Berg dies (50).

w Everyday Life

Launch of 'Monopoly' board game, invented by Charles B Darrow of Philadelphia, USA.
Pan-American Airways ('Pan-Am') start trans-Pacific service from California.
Lower Zambesi railway bridge, the longest in world, opened to traffic (14 Jan).
In Britain, introduction of streamlined steam locomotive 'Silver Jubilee' on line between London and Newcastle (followed in 1937 by 'Coronation', running to Edinburgh, and 'Coronation Scot', running to Glasgow).

x Sport and Recreation

The draft system is introduced into American Football, whereby the team in last place in the National Football League is allowed first choice of players graduating from college.
Arsenal wins the English Football League Championship for the third successive season.
James Braddock out-points Max Baer over 15 rounds to win the World Heavyweight boxing title (23 June).
Barham is the first horse to win the English Triple Crown since Rock Sand in 1903.
In cricket, Clarrie Grimmett of Australia becomes the first bowler to take 200 Test wickets.
In England, Ted Drake scores a record 7 goals for Arsenal in the soccer League match against Aston Villa (14 Dec).
Wilderness Society founded in USA, to promote walking and preservation of natural areas.

y Media

Film:

In the USA, the Fox Company merges with Twentieth Century to form the film company Twentieth Century Fox.
Anna Karenina (starring Greta Garbo).
Becky Sharp (director, Rouben Mamoulian).
The Bride of Frankenstein (starring Boris Karloff).
Cyrano de Bergerac.
David Copperfield (director, David O Selznick).
Hopalong Cassidy (first of a series of 66 films starring William Boyd).
Lives of a Bengal Lancer.
Les Misérables (starring Fredric Marsh).
Mutiny on the Bounty (starring Charles Laughton and Clark Gable).
A Night at the Opera (starring The Marx Brothers).
The 39 Steps (director, Alfred Hitchcock).
Toni (director, Jean Renoir).
Top Hat (starring Fred Astaire and Ginger Rogers).

Television:

In Germany, the Reichspost starts regular low-definition television broadcasting (22 March).
Experimental low-definition television broadcasts begin in France.

German troops enter the Rhineland ... Popular Front in France
... Start of Spanish Civil War ...

A January

6 (–25 March) resumption of London Naval Conference; Japan withdraws on 15 Jan, because other countries refuse to accept its demand for a common upper limit on naval strength.

20 in Britain, death of King George V (succeeded by Edward VIII).

23 in France, resignation of Prime Minister Pierre Laval following attacks on the Hoare–Laval Pact of Dec 1935; Albert Sarraut forms ministry.

B February

16 in Spanish elections the Popular Front coalition of Left parties wins 256 seats against 165 for the Right and 52 for the Centre parties; Manuel Azaña becomes prime minister and re-establishes the constitution of 1931; across Spain, land is seized and churches attacked.

17 British–Irish trade pact ends tariff war.

26 military rebellion in Japan: junior officers murder three government ministers; Prime Minister Keisuke Okada resigns and is succeeded by Koki Hirota.

C March

Britain's first civil defence anti-gas school is opened; a new cabinet post is created, that of minister for the co-ordination of defence, with Sir Thomas Inskip as the first minister.

3 British defence budget leaps from £122 million to £158 million, to increase Fleet Air Arm, add 250 aircraft for home defence, and to provide four new infantry battalions.

7 German troops occupy the demilitarized zone of the Rhineland, thereby violating the Treaty of Versailles.

23 Italy, Austria, and Hungary sign Rome Pact: none to discuss matters relating to the Danube without first consulting the other two countries.

25 Britain, USA, and France sign the London Naval Treaty, which defines categories of ship, permitted tonnages and gun sizes, and requires advance notification of building programmes.

29 99 per cent of electorate vote for official Nazi candidates in German elections.

31 Lord Eustace Percy, minister without portfolio, resigns from the British cabinet, allegedly because of unhappiness about foreign policy.

D April

1 Austria reintroduces conscription, thereby repudiating obligations under the Treaty of St Germain of 1919 (first troops called up in Oct).

7 Cape parliament passes the Native Representation Bill, permitting natives to elect three Europeans to represent them in the parliament of South Africa, and establishing a native representative council with only advisory powers.

8 USSR–Mongolia treaty of mutual assistance.

10 the Spanish parliament dismisses President Zamora.

13 following the inconclusive general election of 26 Jan, a period of uncertainty, and the death of Prime Minister Demerdjis, General John Metaxas becomes Greek prime minister.

15 (–Nov) serious Arab unrest in Palestine; Jews are murdered and Jewish property attacked.

28 death of King Fuad of Egypt; succeeded by 16-year-old son Farouk.

E May

2 general election in Egypt results in victory for the Wafd nationalists; Nahas Pasha forms a Wafd Party ministry.

3 in France, left-wing parties supporting the Popular Front win 376 seats in general election (Socialists, 147; Radicals, 106; Communists, 72; others, 51); other parties, 232.

5 Italians occupy the Ethiopian capital, Addis Ababa, ending the Ethiopian war (9, Ethiopia is formally annexed by Italy).

10 Manuel Azaña elected president of Spain.

21 in Austria, Chancellor Kurt Schuschnigg is given power over the Fatherland Front, the only permitted political party.

22 in Britain, J H Thomas, colonial secretary, resigns over his leakage of budget information.

24 in Belgian general election, Rexists (Fascist) win seats for the first time (21 out of 202).

28 Senate of Irish Free State is abolished (its final act is to commit a casket presented by the late Mrs A S Green to the Royal Irish Academy).

F June

4 Léon Blum, Socialist, forms Popular Front ministry in France.

First Butlin Holiday Camp in Britain ... Messiaen's Poèmes pour Mi
... Death of Venizélos ...

o Politics, Government, Law, and Economy

Leon Trotsky, *The Revolution Betrayed.*

In USA, the Gallup poll successfully predicts the re-election of President Roosevelt, while the larger but less scientific effort of the *Literary Digest* forecasts his defeat (from which the magazine did not recover).

George Gallup founds the British Institute of Public Opinion.

Public Order Act in Britain bans political uniforms and gives the police more powers in response to Fascist disturbances in London.

New constitution in USSR, with a supreme council and a two-chamber parliament (5 Dec).

Reserve Bank of New Zealand is nationalized.

In US v. Butler, the US Supreme Court declares the Agricultural Adjustment Act of 1933 unconstitutional (6 Jan) because it misused the taxing power; the Court, however, rules that the minimum-wage law in Washington state is constitutional.

In US v. Curtiss-Wright Export Corporation, the US Supreme Court, upholding an arms embargo, states that the federal government's powers of external sovereignty do not depend on affirmative statements in the constitution.

In the British mandate of Palestine, a criminal-law code based on English law replaces the Ottoman code.

Opening of the Hoover Dam on the Colorado River (on the border of Arizona and Nevada), to provide hydroelectricity; the lake behind the dam, Lake Mead, is the largest artificial lake in the USA.

In Germany Adolf Hitler announces a second Four-Year Plan to make the country self-sufficient in raw materials.

France abandons the gold standard.

In Germany, Hitler opens the first Volkswagen factory (26 Feb), for the production of mass-market cars.

Rapid expansion of aircraft construction in Britain.

J M Keynes, *General Theory of Employment, Interest and Money.*

p Society, Education, and Religion

The American Federation of Labor grants a charter to the Brotherhood of Sleeping Car Porters (an African-American union); the Pullman Company recognizes the union in 1937.

In USA, Mary McLeod Bethune is appointed director of the Division of Negro Affairs of the National Youth Administration (serving until 1944).

40-hour week in France (12 June).

Decree in USSR revokes 1920 legalization of abortion; divorce procedures are tightened.

In Britain, Billy Butlin opens a holiday camp at Skegness, Lincolnshire; it proves a success and Butlin opens more camps.

Dale Carnegie, *How to Win Friends and Influence People.*

The new constitution of the USSR enacts freedom of non-religious propaganda, but only allows freedom of worship, not propaganda to the Orthodox Church.

Michael Ramsey, *The Gospel and the Catholic Church.*

q Science, Technology, and Discovery

The *Wupperthal*, first diesel-electric vessel, launched.

British aviator Amy Johnson flies from England to Cape Town in 3 days 6 hrs 25 mins (4–7 May).

Solar eclipse observed (19 June) by expeditions in Kamishari, North Japan, and Omsk, Siberia.

In USA, foundation of National Wildlife Federation, concerned with the preservation of animal species.

r Humanities

Grahame Clark, *The Mesolithic Settlement of Northern Europe.*

V Gordon Childe, *Man Makes Himself.*

A J Carlyle completes *History of Medieval Political Theory in the West.*

Arthur O Lovejoy, *The Great Chain of Being.*

Samuel Eliot Morison, *The Puritan Pronaos.*

Samuel Flagg Bemis, *A Diplomatic History of the United States.*

G M Young, *Victorian England, Portrait of an Age.*

R C K Ensor, *England, 1870–1914.*

A B Keith, *A Constitutional History of India, 1600–1935.*

Eilert Ekwall, *The Concise Oxford Dictionary of English Place-names.*

C S Lewis, *The Allegory of Love.*

T E Tallmadge, *The Story of Architecture in America.*

Nikolaus Pevsner, *Pioneers of the Modern Movement.*

Werner Sombart, *Sociology.*

A J Ayer, *Language, Truth, and Logic.*

Rudolf Carnap, *Testability and Meaning.*

Edmund Husserl, *The Crisis of European Sciences and Transcendental Phenomenology.*

9 Count Galeazzo Ciano (Prime Minister Mussolini's son-in-law) is appointed Italian foreign minister.

17 Canadian supreme court nullifies most of 'New Deal' legislation of R B Bennett's government in 1935.

18 in Irish Free State, the Irish Republican Army (IRA) is declared illegal.

23 in the British House of Commons, opposition leader Clement Attlee moves a vote of censure on Stanley Baldwin's government for pursuing a weak and dangerous foreign policy (defeated by 384 votes to 170).

24 Paul van Zeeland, prime minister of Belgium, proposes radical programme of social reform, providing a minimum wage, 40-hour week in some industries, paid holidays, an increased school-leaving age, and sickness and unemployment insurance.

30 suppression of French Fascist Party.

G **July**

11 Austrian–German convention acknowledges Austria's independence.

15 League of Nations raises sanctions against Italy.

17 munitions industry in France is nationalized.

17 army mutiny in Spanish Morocco, led by Francisco Franco, to uphold religion and traditional values; other mutinies occur throughout Spain, thereby starting the Spanish Civil War;

20 by Montreux Convention Turkey recovers sovereignty over Dardanelles and Bosphorus.

21 revised means-test regulations introduced in Britain.

24 Committee of National Defence established by Spanish nationalists at Burgos in N Spain.

H **August**

2 France suggests to Britain a policy of nonintervention in Spain.

4 in Spanish Civil War, Franco's nationalist army captures Badajoz in the SW, enabling forces in N and S to combine.

4 martial law is proclaimed in Greece, in order to preempt a general strike.

11 in China, Guomindang leader Chiang Kai-shek enters Guangzhou for the first time since 1926, thereby strengthening the Guomindang's hold on S China.

24 Germany adopts two-year compulsory military service.

26 treaty ends British protectorate over Egypt, except for the Canal Zone, and forms British–Egyptian alliance for 20 years.

J **September**

Japan makes secret demands to China about employment of Japanese in Chinese government and presenting united front against Communists; rejected by the Chinese government.

9 (–17) conference in London on Spanish Civil War; 27 countries join a Nonintervention Committee charged with preventing the supply of war material and intervention of foreign forces in the War.

9 France signs treaties of friendship with Syria, where mandate is to end in 1939, and, on 19, with the Lebanon.

10 the German propaganda minister, Joseph Goebbels, accuses Czechoslovakia of harbouring USSR aircraft.

27 France, Switzerland, and the Netherlands abandon gold standard.

K **October**

1 USSR accedes to London Naval Treaty of 25 March.

1 Spanish nationalists appoint General Francisco Franco chief of state.

2 France devalues the franc.

5 (–11 Nov) in Britain, the Jarrow march, when 200 men march from Jarrow in NE England to London to protest against high unemployment.

5 Italy devalues the lira.

6 conference of British Labour Party rejects application of Communist Party for affiliation.

10 in Austria, Chancellor Kurt Schuschnigg dissolves the Heimwehr (Fascist militia), incorporating it in the Fatherland Front.

12 in Britain, the leader of the British Union of Fascists, Oswald Mosley, leads an anti-Jewish march along the Mile End Road, a Jewish part of London.

14 alarmed at the German occupation of Rhineland, Belgium renounces its military alliance with France and resumes liberty of action.

22 martial law proclaimed in Belgium, to combat the Rexists.

28 in the Republican area of Spain, unions collectivize agriculture and industry and ban Christian worship.

L **November**

1 following the visit of Italian Foreign Minister Ciano to Berlin, the Italian prime minister Benito Mussolini proclaims the Rome–Berlin axis.

3 in US presidential election F D Roosevelt, Democrat, is re-elected, with 523 electoral votes over Alfred M Landon, Republican, with 8, and carries every state except Maine and Vermont; popular vote: Roose-

s Art, Sculpture, Fine Arts, and Architecture

Coup d'état by General Franco in Spain results in severe cultural repression in early years of his dictatorship.

In USA, 'Cubism and Abstract Art' and 'Fantastic Art, Dada, and Surrealism' exhibitions are held at the Museum of Modern Art, New York.

Painting, etc:
Arshile Gorky, *Organization*.
Wassily Kandinsky, *Dominant Curve*.
Laura Knight, *Ballet*.
Piet Mondrian, *Composition in Red and Blue*.
Mario Sironi, *Corporate Italy*.

Sculpture:
Max Beckman, *Adam and Eve*.
Salvador Dalí, *Lobster Telephone*.
Julio González, *Montserrat (–1937)*.
Meret Oppenheim, *Object* (Fur Breakfast).

Architecture:
Alvar Aalto, Factory and Workers' Housing, Sumila, Finland (–1939).
Walter Gropius and E M Fry, Film Studios, Denham, Bucks.
Frank Lloyd Wright, Kaufman House, 'Falling Water', Bear Run, Pennsylvania (–1937), and Johnson Wax Factory (with umbrella columns), Racine, Wisconsin, USA.
Tecton, Highpoint Flats I, London.

T Music

George Enescu, *Oedipe* (opera).
Berthold Goldschmidt, *Ciaconna Sinfonica*.
Olivier Messiaen, *Poèmes pour Mi.*
Sergei Prokofiev, *Peter and the Wolf.*
Arnold Schoenberg, Violin Concerto, String Quartet No. 4.
Edgard Varèse, *Density 21.5.*
On Your Toes (musical), lyrics by Lorenz Hart, music by Richard Rodgers.
'Pennies From Heaven', by Arthur Johnston.
In USA, start of the 'swing' era of jazz, with band leader and broadcaster Benny Goodman labelled 'The King of Swing'.
US clarinettist Woody Herman takes over Isham Jones's band, which is renamed 'The Band That Plays the Blues'.

u Literature and Drama

W H Auden, *Look Stranger*.
Djuna Barnes, *Nightwood*.
Georges Bernanos, *Journal of a Country Priest*.
James Cain, *Double Indemnity*.
John Dos Passos, *The Big Money* (completing the trilogy *USA*).
William Faulkner, *Absalom, Absalom!*.
Miles Franklin, *All that Swagger*.
Robert Frost, *A Further Range* (poems).

Aldous Huxley, *Eyeless in Gaza*.
Margaret Mitchell, *Gone With The Wind*.
Henry de Montherlant, *Les jeunes filles* (–1939).
George Orwell, *Keep the Aspidistra Flying*.
Dylan Thomas, *Twenty-five Poems*.
W B Yeats (ed.), *The Oxford Book of Modern Verse, 1892–1935*.
In Britain, John and Rosamund Lehmann found *New Writing*.
British publisher Allen Lane founds Penguin Books in London, starting the paperback revolution.

Drama:
Federico García Lorca, *The House of Bernarda Alba*.
Terence Rattigan, *French Without Tears*.
Armand Salacrou, *Un Homme comme les autres*.
Robert Sherwood, *Idiot's Delight*.
Publication of Konstantin Stanislavsky's *An Actor Prepares*.

v Births and Deaths

Jan 18 Rudyard Kipling dies (70).
Jan 19 Zia ur-Rahman born (–1981).
March 4 Jim Clark born (–1968).
March 11 David (Earl) Beatty dies (65).
March 18 Eleuthérios Venizélos dies (71).
March 18 F W de Klerk born (–).
April 30 A E Housman dies (77).
May 8 Oswald Spengler dies (55).
May 12 Frank Stella born (–).
June 14 G K Chesterton dies (62).
June 18 Maxim Gorky dies (68).
July 19 Herbert Boyer born (–).
July 28 Gary Sobers born (–).
Aug 1 Louis Blériot dies (64).
Oct 5 Václav Havel born (–).
Dec 10 Luigi Pirandello dies (69).

w Everyday Life

In London, the Crystal Palace, at Sydenham, is destroyed by fire (30 Nov).

x Sport and Recreation

Joe Louis, the 'Brown Bomber', loses to Max Schmeling in the 12th round of their non-title fight at the Yankee Stadium, New York (19 June).
In cricket, a record 588 runs are scored on the second day of the Second Test between England and India at Old Trafford, Manchester (27 July).
The 11th Olympic Games are held in Berlin (1–16 Aug). Germany wins 33 gold medals; USA, 24; Hungary, 10; Italy, 8; Finland and France, 7 each; Sweden and

velt, 27,751,597; Landon, 16,679,583; William Lemke (National Union for Social Justice), 882,479.

6 in Spanish Civil War, siege of Madrid begins (–28 March 1939); the republican defenders are joined by supporters from abroad belonging to the International Brigade; the Spanish government moves to Valencia.

14 Germany denounces clauses of Versailles Treaty about internationalization of its waterways.

16 in Britain, King Edward VIII gives official notification that he plans to marry Mrs Wallis Simpson, a divorced US citizen; Prime Minister Baldwin warns that the marriage would offend public opinion and damage the prestige of the throne.

18 Germany and Italy recognize Franco's government in Spain.

23 Expropriation law in Mexico empowers government to seize private property.

25 Germany and Japan sign Anti-Comintern Pact; the countries agree to work together against international communism; Germany also recognizes Japan's regime in Manchuria.

M December

1 (–16) Pan-American peace conference in Buenos Aires, Argentina.

3 in Britain, the press, after a period of self-restraint, breaks the news of King Edward's intention to marry Mrs Wallis Simpson.

5 new constitution in USSR, with a supreme council and a two-chamber parliament.

11 in Britain, King Edward VIII abdicates (12, proclamation of Duke of York's accession as George VI; Edward is created Duke of Windsor).

12 in the Irish Free State the Constitution (Amendment) Act removes the king from membership of the Irish parliament and deprives the governor-general of most of his functions; the Executive Authority (External Relations) Act gives effect to King Edward's abdication.

12 President Chiang Kai-shek of China is held under arrest in NW China for several days by Marshal Chang Hsüeh-liang, who wanted stronger opposition to the Japanese (Chiang is released after intervention by a British adviser).

Explosion of airship Hindenburg *... Japan invades China ... Irish Free State becomes Eire ...*

A January

1 in Britain, the Public Order Act comes into force; it proscribes political uniforms and permits the police to ban processions when there is danger of disorder.

2 British–Italian agreement affirming free passage on Mediterranean.

6 in USA, President Roosevelt renews the Neutrality Act forbidding shipments of arms to Spain.

7 Poland signs agreement with the free city of Danzig (now Gdansk in Poland).

9 after living in Turkey and Paris, the former leading Soviet Communist Leon Trotsky arrives in Mexico.

14 in Britain, Communists, the Independent Labour Party, and the Socialist League form the Unity Campaign, opposing rearmament and aiming to transform the Labour movement (27, the Socialist League is expelled from the Labour Party).

15 Austria declares amnesty for Nazis.

23 (–30) in USSR, trial and conviction of Karl Radek and 16 other Communist leaders, accused of conspiring with Trotsky, Germany, and Japan; Radek and three others are imprisoned, and the rest shot dead.

24 Bulgaria and Yugoslavia sign treaty of perpetual peace.

B February

The All-India Congress Party is the most successful party in Indian elections.

8 in Spanish Civil War, nationalists take Malaga in S with Italian aid.

14 in Austria, Chancellor Kurt Schuschnigg reserves the initiative to organize any restoration of the Hapsburg monarchy.

20 Paraguay withdraws from the League of Nations.

27 French defence plan creates ministry of defence, extends Maginot Line, and nationalizes the Schneider–Creusot arms factory.

C March

1 Adam Koc forms Camp of National Unity in Poland; a Workers' and Peasants' Camp is formed in opposition to him.

Holland, 6 each; Japan, 5; the US African-American athlete Jesse Owens wins 4 golds, in the 100 m, the 200 m, the Long Jump, and the 4x100 m relay.

At the World Table Tennis Championships in Prague, the match between Michael Haguaneur of France and Dvoboj Marin of Romania lasts over 7 hours.

Y Media

In USA, publication of the profusely illustrated *Life* magazine by Henry Luce, publisher of *Time*.

Film:

As You Like It (director, Paul Czinner).
César (director, Marcel Pagnol).
The Charge of the Light Brigade (starring Errol Flynn).

A Day in the Country (director, Jean Renoir).
Flash Gordon (starring Buster Crabbe).
The Great Ziegfeld (director, Robert Leonard).
Mr Deeds Goes to Town (director, Frank Capra).
Modern Times (starring Charlie Chaplin).
These Three (director, William Wyler).
Things to Come (producer, Alexander Korda).

Television:

In Britain, an English Football League match, Arsenal v. Everton, is televised for the first time (29 Aug).

The BBC starts the world's first high-definition television service from its transmitter at Crystal Palace, London (2 Nov–1939).

German television broadcasts from the Berlin Olympic Games, including Jesse Owens' victory in the 200-m race.

Pope's anti-Nazi encyclical ... Shostakovich's Symphony No. 5 ...
Renoir's La Grande Illusion *...*

O Politics, Government, Law, and Economy

British Institute of Public Opinion founded to spread Gallup's methods to Britain.

Stephen Spender and others, *The Mind in Chains: Socialism and the Cultural Revolution*.

W K Hancock, *Survey of British Commonwealth Affairs* (–1942).

In USA, the state of Nebraska replaces a bicameral legislature with a single chamber, as a cost-cutting measure.

W E Binkley, *The Powers of the President: Problems of American Democracy*.

In Britain, the Ministers of the Crown Act revises the salaries paid to ministers and institutes a salary for the leader of the opposition; the Act places the terms 'cabinet', 'cabinet minister', and 'prime minister' on the British statute book for the first time.

In USA, the Supreme Court Retirement Act (passed 1 March) allows the Court's judges to retire at 70 with full pay; President Roosevelt also proposes that if judges

over 70 refuse to retire, the president can appoint extra judges, but opposition in Congress forces him to withdraw the proposal (July).

The US Supreme Court reverses stance on New Deal legislation; in National Labor Relations Board v. Jones and Laughlin Steel Corporation and West Coast Hotel Co. v. Parrish cases it allows union organization and minimum wages as part of the 'constitutional revolution' of 1937.

Hugo Black of Alabama, an outspoken liberal, is appointed to the US Supreme Court (serving until 1971).

T Arnold, *The Folklore of Capitalism*.

P Society, Education, and Religion

Major floods in mid-West USA, caused by Ohio, Mississippi, and Allegheny rivers; a million people are left homeless (Jan–Feb).

In USA, the National Housing Act (Wagner-Steagall Act) creates the United States Housing Authority, to make housing for people on low incomes more affordable

2 in Mexico, nationalization of oil and establishment of the National Petroleum Corporation to administer oil-producing lands.

16 Benito Mussolini visits Libya (an Italian colony).

18 in Spanish Civil War, defeat of Italian legionaries at Brihuega checks nationalists' threat to Madrid.

18 Committee of All-India Congress Party votes to accept invitations to form provincial governments provided that governors undertake not to use special powers.

25 Italy and Yugoslavia sign Belgrade Pact of assistance for five years.

D April

1 Indian Constitution in force; because provincial governors refuse to give formal undertakings not to use special powers, the All-India Congress Party refuses to form governments.

1 in Spanish Civil War, nationalists launch a major offensive in the N.

2 South Africa prohibits political activity by foreigners in South-West Africa (a League Mandate under South African control).

19 the two main right-wing Spanish parties, the Falange and the Traditionalists, merge to form the Falange Española Tradicionalista.

22 Austrian chancellor Kurt Schuschnigg meets Italian prime minister Benito Mussolini in Venice.

24 Britain and France release Belgium from obligations under the Locarno Treaty of 1925.

27 in Spanish Civil War, aircraft from the German Condor Legion bomb Guernica, the ancient Basque capital in N Spain.

E May

3 (–10) rising of Anarchists and Syndicalists in Barcelona, SE Spain.

6 the giant German airship *Hindenburg* explodes as it attempts to moor at Lakehurst Naval Station, New Jersey, USA; 36 are killed.

8 Montreux convention abolishes Egyptian capitulations (i.e., right of foreign powers to protect non-Muslim inhabitants as if under separate jurisdictions).

10 (–23) bus strike in London.

12 coronation of King George VI at Westminster Abbey, London, followed by Imperial Conference (14–15 June).

15 Muslim rising in Albania; suppressed within a few days.

26 Egypt joins the League of Nations.

28 on Stanley Baldwin's retirement Neville Chamberlain forms a National Government, with Sir John Simon as chancellor of the exchequer and Anthony Eden as foreign secretary.

F June

In USSR, several high-ranking generals are tried, convicted, and shot for collaboration with Germany; there follows a purge of the armed forces.

1 in Japan, following several short-lived ministries, Prince Fumimaro Konoe becomes prime minister of a national union ministry, with Koki Hirota as foreign minister.

3 in France, the Duke of Windsor (the former King Edward VIII of Britain) marries Mrs Wallis Simpson.

14 in Irish Free State, the Dáil approves de Valera's Constitution for Ireland, which changes the name of the Irish Free State, abolishes the governor-general, and provides for a new form of senate, and a president (to be introduced on 29 Dec).

19 in Spanish Civil War, nationalists capture Bilbao, the Basque capital in the NE.

21 on French Senate refusing Léon Blum's demands for emergency fiscal powers, he resigns and Camille Chautemps forms Radical–Socialist ministry.

23 Germany and Italy withdraw from Nonintervention Committee (barring involvement in Spain).

G July

1 Irish elections result in stalemate but Éamon de Valera is again prime minister (Fianna Fáil win 69 seats, Fine Gael, 48; others, 21); a referendum approves the new constitution, with 56.5 per cent of voters in favour.

7 in China, incident at Marco Polo Bridge, SE of Beijing, is followed by Japanese invasion of NE China.

7 Royal Commission on Palestine recommends end of mandate and partition of country into British area, Jewish State, and Arab area joined with Transjordan.

8 Afghanistan, Iran, Iraq, and Turkey sign nonaggression pact.

17 naval agreements between Britain and Germany and Britain and USSR.

28 in Japanese–Chinese War, Japanese seize Beijing and, on 29, Tianjin in NE China.

H August

6 trade pact between USA and USSR.

8 in Japanese–Chinese War, Japanese launch an amphibious assault on Shanghai, on E coast of China (–11 Nov).

11 Bakr Sidqi, dictator of Iraq, is assassinated.

14 W L Mackenzie King, prime minister of Canada, announces establishment of com-

(signed 15 Sept); it creates the US Housing Authority, which takes over PWA projects and can make 60-year loans to local agencies for slum clearance and the building of new accommodation.

In USA, first state contraception clinic is opened in North Carolina, as birth control also wins endorsement from the American Medical Association.

Grand Mufti of Islam permits Muslims to use contraceptives where both parties agree.

Appointment of William H Hastie as first African-American Federal judge in the USA.

In USA, the Marijuana Tax Act, passed under the influence of Bureau of Narcotics' director Harry Anslinger, makes possession of cannabis a federal offence; a moral panic about 'Reefer Madness' follows.

Matrimonial Causes Act, introduced by A P Herbert, equalizes position of women in divorce proceedings in England and Wales (23 May).

A wave of strikes takes place in the US car industry (from 30 Dec 1936), in which workers occupy their factories; the dispute ends with an agreement made on 30 March in which General Motors recognizes the United Automobile Workers.

In USA, the Committee on Industrial Organization is expelled from the American Federation of Labor; it establishes itself on a formal basis as the Congress of Industrial Organizations.

Romansch recognized as fourth national language in Switzerland.

Karen Horney, *The Neurotic Personality of Our Times*.

Arthur Koestler, *Spanish Testament*.

Walter Lippmann, *The Good Society*.

G A N Lowndes, *The Silent Social Revolution*.

George Orwell, *The Road to Wigan Pier*.

Talcott Parsons, *The Structure of Social Action*.

Seebohm Rowntree, *The Human Needs of Labour*.

In Germany, the ministry of education decrees that all educational institutions should 'educate German youth for membership of the racial community and full commitment to the Führer'.

In England, Lord Nuffield donates £1 million plus a site for the foundation of Nuffield College, Oxford, for the study of social, economic, and political problems.

Pope Pius XI orders the encyclical *Mit brennender Sorge*, branding Nazism as fundamentally anti-Christian, to be read from all Catholic pulpits in Germany.

In Germany, the leading anti-Nazi pastor and preacher Martin Niemöller is arrested (1 July; tried Feb 1938, when acquitted and rearrested; then sent to a concentration camp).

Pope Pius XI issues the encyclical *Divini Redemptoris*, on Atheistic Communism.

International conference on 'Church, Community and State' held in Oxford, England (12–26 July).

The Holy Synod of the Ecumenical Patriarch grants autocephalic status to the Albanian Orthodox Church.

Q Science, Technology, and Discovery

British engineer Frank Whittle builds first prototype jet engine.

Xerography pioneered in USA by C F Carlson.

USSR establishes observation station on an ice floe near the North Pole.

Zinc protamine insulin is successfully used in cases of diabetes.

Crystalline Vitamin A and Vitamin K concentrate are obtained.

In USA, J Aneurin synthesizes Vitamin B.

R Humanities

Skull of *Pithecanthropus*, an early hominid, found in Java.

Henri Pirenne, *Mohammed and Charlemagne*.

James G Randall, *The Civil War and Reconstruction*.

In Britain, National Maritime Museum, Greenwich, opened.

Yvor Winters, *Primitivism and Decadence*.

Charles Hartshorne, *Beyond Humanism*.

Wyndham Lewis, *Blasting and Bombardiering*.

Charles W Morris, *Logical Positivism, Pragmatism, and Scientific Empiricism*.

S Art, Sculpture, Fine Arts, and Architecture

International Exhibition held in Paris, France, for which Fernand Léger and his students paint mural *Le Transport des Forces*; Pablo Picasso paints *Guernica*; Léger designs sets for the play *Naissance d'une Cité*; Vera Mukhina produces *Worker and Collective Farm Girl*, a monumental Socialist Realist sculpture atop the Soviet Pavilion.

Paul Mellon endows National Gallery of Art, Washington, DC, USA.

In Germany, Nazi exhibition of 'Degenerate Art' held in Munich.

Painting, etc:

In London, William Coldstream and Lawrence Gowing found the Euston Road Group of artists, advocating a return to a realistic conception of painting.

mission to re-examine the structure of the confederation.

25 in Spanish Civil War, nationalists capture Santander in N.

J September

3 in Britain, the National Council of Labour declares that another war in Europe is not inevitable and supports Britain's role in the League of Nations.

10 (–14) at Nyon Conference, convoked by Britain, nine nations adopt system of patrols in Mediterranean to deal with submarine piracy arising from Spanish Civil War.

25 (–28) Italian prime minister Benito Mussolini visits Berlin, to confer with Hitler.

26 in Palestine, Arabs murder the British district commissioner for Galilee.

K October

1 in Spain, General Francisco Franco assumes the leadership of the nationalists and outlines the main policies to be followed by a nationalist government.

13 Germany guarantees the inviolability of Belgium.

16 Fascist groups in Hungary form National Socialist Party.

17 riots in Sudeten (German) area of Czechoslovakia.

21 in Spanish Civil War, nationalists take Gijón, capturing the last major town in the N.

23 Labour defeated in Australian elections by United Australia and Country parties (United Australia Party wins 29 seats; Country Party, 16; Labour Party, 29).

24 Paul van Zeeland, prime minister of Belgium, resigns on charges of corruption over National Bank; succeeded by Paul Janson, Liberal.

28 the Spanish government moves from Valencia to Barcelona.

L November

3 (–24) Brussels conference of powers discusses Japanese–Chinese War.

5 Air Raid Precautions bill introduced in British House of Commons.

6 Italy joins German–Japanese Anti-Comintern Pact.

10 the president of Brazil, Getúlio Vargas, declares the 1934 constitution cancelled and his tenure of office extended by six years.

11 in Japanese–Chinese War, Japanese troops finally capture Shanghai.

15 extraordinary session of the US Congress opens to promote legislative programme.

17 (–21) British cabinet minister Lord Halifax visits Adolf Hitler, to attempt peaceful settlement of Sudeten problem.

18 discovery of Fascist plot in Paris.

24 Walter Funk replaces Dr Schacht as German minister of economics.

28 General Franco begins naval blockade of Spanish coast.

29 Sudeten Germans leave Czech parliament following ban on political meetings.

M December

The British Labour leader, Clement Attlee, visits Spain to encourage Republican leaders.

4 in Spanish Civil War, republicans launch offensive in Aragon (–Jan 1938).

11 Italy withdraws from the League of Nations.

5 (–13) in Japanese–Chinese War, Japanese troops take Nanjing, NW of Shanghai; their victory is followed by the 'rape of Nanjing', when around a quarter of a million Chinese are killed.

14 political parties banned in Brazil.

16 French–Syrian convention.

24 in Japanese–Chinese War, Japanese capture Hangzhou, SW of Shanghai.

28 Octavian Goga, anti-Semite, forms ministry in Romania, on fall of Nicholas Titulescu.

29 new Irish Constitution comes into force; Irish Free State becomes Eire.

30 in Egypt, the Liberal Constitution Party forms ministry.

Salvador Dalí, *Sleep*.

Max Ernst, *The Angel of the Hearth*.

Pablo Picasso, *On The Beach*.

Sculpture:

Jean Fautrier, *Head*.

Barbara Hepworth, *Conicoid: Sphere and Hollow*.

Käthe Kollwitz, *Pietà* (–1938).

т Music

Alban Berg, *Lulu* (posthumous opera, unfinished).

Ernest Bloch, *Voice in the Wilderness*.

Benjamin Britten, *Variations on a Theme by Frank Bridge*.

Carl Orff, *Carmina Burana*.

Dmitry Shostakovich, Symphony No. 5.

Pianist Artur Rubinstein tours USA to great acclaim.

In USA, foundation of the NBC Symphony Orchestra, with Arturo Toscanini as conductor (–1954).

The Cradle Will Rock, controversial left-wing musical drama by Marc Blitzstein (first performed at the Venice Theatre, New York, on 16 June after protests had forced cancellation of original planned performance elsewhere).

Me and My Girl (musical), text by L Arthur Rose and Douglas Furber, music by Noel Gay (first performed at the Victoria Palace, London, 16 Dec); includes the song-and-dance routine 'The Lambeth Walk'.

Bing Crosby, 'Sweet Leilani', the first of Crosby's 22 million-selling records.

Death of US jazz singer Bessie Smith from loss of blood after she is turned away from a whites-only hospital in Coahome, Mississippi (26 Sept).

US folk singer Woody Guthrie stars in the radio show *Here Come Woody and Lefty Lou* on KFVD in Los Angeles.

u Literature and Drama

Karen Blixen, *Out of Africa*.

A J Cronin, *The Citadel*.

Oliver St John Gogarty, *As I Was Going Down Sackville Street*.

Ernest Hemingway, *To Have and Have Not*.

Sadiq Hidayat, *The Blind Owl*.

Christopher Isherwood, *Sally Bowles*.

David Jones, *In Parenthesis*.

Yasunari Kawabata, *The Snow Country*.

Rudyard Kipling, *Something of Myself*.

André Malraux, *L'Espoir/Days of Hope*.

Jean-Paul Sartre, *Nausée/Nausea*.

Stevie Smith, *A Good Time was Had By All*.

John Steinbeck, *Of Mice and Men*.

Wallace Stevens, *The Man with the Blue Guitar* (poems).

Rex Warner, *The Wild Goose Chase*.

Viginia Woolf, *The Years*.

Charles Williams, *Descent into Hell*.

Drama:

W H Audèn and Christopher Isherwood, *The Ascent of F6*.

Bertolt Brecht, *A Penny for the Poor*.

Jean Giraudoux, *Elektra*.

Laurence Housman, *Victoria Regina*.

J B Priestley, *Time and the Conways*.

The Mercury Theatre founded by Orson Welles and John Houseman.

v Births and Deaths

Jan 30 Vanessa Redgrave born (–).

Jan 31 Philip Glass born (–).

March 16 Austen Chamberlain dies (73).

April 22 Jack Nicholson born (–).

May 23 John D Rockefeller dies (97).

June 19 J M Barrie dies (77).

June 24 Anita Desai born (–).

July 2 Amelia Earhart dies (38).

July 3 Tom Stoppard born (–).

July 9 David Hockney born (–).

July 11 George Gershwin dies (38).

July 20 Guglielmo Marconi dies (63).

Aug 11 Edith Wharton dies (75).

Aug 18 Robert Redford born (–).

Sept 14 Tomáš Masaryk dies (87).

Oct 19 Ernest (Lord) Rutherford dies (66).

Nov 9 Ramsay MacDonald dies (71).

Dec 20 Erich Ludendorff dies (72).

Dec 21 Frank Billings Kellogg dies (80).

Dec 28 Maurice Ravel dies (62).

w Everyday Life

Opening of the Golden Gate Bridge, San Francisco, USA; the longest suspension bridge to date at 1,965 m/6,450 ft.

US spinach growers erect a statue to Popeye in honour of his achievements in boosting the image of their product.

The 'Nylon' synthetic fibre is patented by the US chemicals company Du Pont.

x Sport and Recreation

In USA, Joe Louis wins the World Heavyweight boxing title by knocking out James Braddock in the eighth round of their fight in Chicago (22 June).

A US Lacrosse team tours England for the first time.

At the Wimbledon tennis tournament in London, Donald Budge of the USA becomes the first player to win three titles

*Austria united with Germany ... Chamberlain capitulates to
Hitler at Munich ... Kristallnacht in Germany ...*

A January

4 Britain postpones scheme for partition of Palestine and appoints commission under John Woodhead to study boundaries; the commission is boycotted by Arabs (reports 9 Nov).

9 in Spanish Civil War, republicans take Teruel, in E Spain, from the nationalists.

10 in Japanese–Chinese War, Japanese enter the port of Qingdao in NE China.

14 Socialists leave French cabinet, which Camille Chautemps reorganizes as a Radical ministry.

B February

4 in Germany, the commander in chief of the army, Field Marshal Werner von Blomberg, resigns; Hitler formally declares himself commander with Wilhelm Keitel as chief of staff; Hitler appoints Joachim von Ribbentrop foreign minister.

12 Austrian Chancellor Kurt Schuschnigg visits Adolf Hitler at Berchtesgaden and is ordered to appoint the Nazi sympathizer Arthur Seyss-Inquart to his government and to release imprisoned Austrian Nazis (16, Austrian government announces amnesty for Nazis).

18 French Chamber cancels Labour code.

20 British Foreign Minister Anthony Eden resigns in protest at Prime Minister Neville Chamberlain's priorities in foreign affairs; Chamberlain had declined President Roosevelt's suggestion of a conference on international relations and was determined to obtain an agreement with Italy; Eden is succeeded on 25 by Lord Halifax.

21 in British House of Commons, Winston Churchill leads an outcry against Chamberlain and, on 22, 25 members of the administration vote against the government in censure motion.

22 in Spanish Civil War, the nationalists recapture Teruel in E Spain and drive towards the Mediterranean.

C March

1 (–24) in Japanese–Chinese War, Japanese advance southwards from Ji'nan in N China, but are blocked by a large Chinese army at Tai'erzhuang and forced to withdraw.

2 (–14) in USSR, trial of the former leading Communist Nikolai Bukharin and other political leaders (Bukharin is convicted and shot on 14 March).

9 Austrian Chancellor Kurt Schuschnigg announces plebiscite on 12 on whether Austria should remain independent.

12 German troops enter Austria, which, on 13 is declared part of the German Reich.

13 Léon Blum forms Popular Front ministry in France (–10 April).

19 Lithuania capitulates to Poland's demands to reopen the frontier.

19 following the failure of US and British oil companies in Mexico to comply with a pay-and-conditions award of Dec 1937, the government declares the expropriation of the companies' Mexican assets.

at the tournament: the Men's Singles, the Men's Doubles, and the Mixed Doubles.

Y Media

In Britain, the *Morning Post* is absorbed into the *Daily Telegraph*, to form the *Daily Telegraph and Morning Post*.

Film:

The 'Prix Louis Delluc' founded, for the best French film of the year.

The Awful Truth (starring Irene Dunne and Cary Grant).

Camille (starring Greta Garbo).

Captains Courageous (starring Spencer Tracy).

The Edge of the World (director, Michael Powell).

Fire Over England (director, William K Howard).

The Good Earth (director, Sidney Franklin).

La Grande Illusion (director, Jean Renoir).

Lost Horizon (director, Frank Capra).

Pepe Le Moko (director, Julien Duvivier).

The Prisoner of Zenda (producer, David O Selznick).

Snow White and the Seven Dwarfs (producer, Walt Disney).

The Stage Door (starring Katharine Hepburn and Ginger Rogers).

They Won't Forget (director, Mervyn LeRoy; starring Allyn Joslin, Claude Rains, and Lana Turner).

Television:

In USA, NBC makes regular experimental broadcasts.

Coelacanth discovered ... Disney's Snow White and the Seven Dwarfs *... Martians invade USA ...*

O Politics, Government, Law, and Economy

In USA, establishment of the House Un-American Activities Committee (its revival after the war marked the start of the anti-Communist witch hunts).

David Lloyd George, *The Truth About the Peace Treaties*.

Civil Aeronautics Bureau established in USA.

In USA, Supreme Court ruling in Erie Railroad Co. v. Tompkins declares that there is no federal common law, only state.

In the USA, the second Agricultural Adjustment Act replaces the Act of 1933, which was struck down by the Supreme Court in 1936.

Temporary National Economic Commission investigates the power of monopolies in USA.

P Society, Education, and Religion

In USA, the Emergency Relief Appropriations Act allocates $3.75 billion for the creation of public works programs.

The Fair Labor Standards Act in the USA sets a minimum wage (40 cents an hour) and a maximum number of hours per week for workers in companies involved in interstate commerce, and prohibits the hiring of children under 16.

In Norway, women are permitted to hold all government posts.

Medical tests are required for marriage licences in New York state, USA.

State Medical Service established in New Zealand.

In Britain, publication of report of the Amulree Committee recommending the extension to most workers of a week's paid annual holiday, on grounds of social justice and industrial welfare and efficiency.

In USA, President Roosevelt's Advisory Committee on Education recommends that the federal government should be given powers to relieve the unsatisfactory state of education.

Spens Report in England supports the division of secondary education into grammar, technical, and modern streams.

H Kraemer, *The Christian Message in a non-Christian World*.

Q Science, Technology, and Discovery

Howard Hughes in monoplane *New York World Fair* flies round world in 3 days 19 hrs 17 mins (10–14 July).

Polyamide plastic 'Perlon' (similar to American nylon) is discovered in Germany.

Werner von Braun is appointed technical director at the German rocket research centre at Peenemünde.

The Soviet physicist Pyotr Kapitza publishes studies on Helium II, about the state of Helium at $-456°F$.

British biochemist William Ewins and H Phillips synthesize sulphapyridine ('M and B 693').

28 Japanese install puppet government of Chinese Republic at Nanjing.

D April

1 in Japanese–Chinese War, one Japanese force again advances southwards from Ji'nan while another advances northwards from Nanjing; they meet at Xuzhou on 20 May.

3 in Spanish Civil War, nationalists capture Lérida, W of Barcelona.

10 Édouard Daladier, radical socialist, forms ministry in France, supported by Léon Blum.

15 in Spanish Civil War, nationalists take Vinaroz on the Mediterranean coast, dividing the republicans in Catalonia from those in SE Spain.

16 by British–Italian pact, Britain recognizes Italian sovereignty over Ethiopia and Italy undertakes to withdraw troops from Spain (in force 16 Nov).

17 in Romania, almost 200 members of the Fascist Iron Guard are arrested following the discovery of a plot (27 May, Iron Guard leader Corneliu Codreanu is sentenced to 10 years in prison; others sentenced on 28 June).

24 Konrad Henlein, the leader of the Sudeten Germans in Czechoslovakia (acting on order from Adolf Hitler), demands autonomy for the Sudetenland.

25 British three-year agreement with Eire settles outstanding disputes.

27 Greek–Turkish treaty of friendship.

E May

3 (–9) Adolf Hitler visits Benito Mussolini in Rome.

4 Douglas Hyde, a Protestant, is elected first president of Eire by popular vote under the 1937 constitution (holding the powers of the former governor-general but not representing the British monarch); he is installed on 25 June.

12 Germany recognizes the Japanese puppet state in Manchuria, Manzhouguo.

13 Paul Spaak, socialist, forms coalition in Belgium.

18 United Party under J B M Hertzog confirmed in power in South African elections.

F June

1 (–July 1) in Japanese-Chinese War, Japanese advance west from Xuzhou; they take Kaifeng on 6 June, but as they approach Zhengzhou the Chinese break dykes on the Huang (Yellow) River, halting the advance.

17 in general election in Eire, Fianna Fáil wins 77 seats, the Opposition, 61 (Fine Gael, 45; others, 16).

G July

11 (–Aug 11) Soviet troops clash with Japanese on border of Manzhouguo.

19 (–21) King George VI of Britain visits Paris.

21 peace treaty agreed between Paraguay and Bolivia, ending the dispute over Chaco Boreal; Paraguay gains about 70 per cent of the claimed territory.

30 US car magnate Henry Ford receives the Grand Cross of the German Eagle (19 Oct, US aviator Charles Lindbergh receives a lower German order).

31 Bulgaria signs nonaggression pact with Greece and other powers of the Balkan Entente (Turkey, Romania, Yugoslavia).

H August

1 in Japanese–Chinese War, Japanese advance south-west from Xuzhou.

3 Lord Runciman from Britain arrives in Prague to mediate between the Czech government and the Sudeten Germans.

12 Germany mobilizes armed forces.

21 (–23) the Little Entente (Czechoslovakia, Romania, and Yugoslavia) recognizes the right of Hungary to rearm.

J September

7 Sudeten Germans in Czechoslovakia break off relations with the Czech government after clashes between rival parties; France calls up reservists.

15 British Prime Minister Neville Chamberlain visits Adolf Hitler at Berchtesgaden; Hitler states his determination to annex the Sudetenland in Czechoslovakia on the principle of self-determination.

16 in Britain, Lord Runciman's main recommendations about Czechoslovakia are reported to the cabinet; Runciman advocates transfer of the Sudetenland to Germany without a plebiscite (report published on 28).

18 British and French make proposals for Czechs to accept Germany's terms over the Sudetenland; rejected by Czechs on 20, accepted on 21.

22 (–24) British Prime Minister Chamberlain visits Adolf Hitler at Bad Godesberg; Hitler now proposes that Germany should make an immediate military occupation of the Sudetenland; on returning to London, Chamberlain seeks British, French, and Czech acquiescence for Hitler's plan.

22 in Czechoslovakia, Milan Hodza's cabinet resigns.

The Swiss biochemist O Paul Karrer synthesizes Vitamin E.

A coelacanth (an ancient fish assumed to be extinct) is discovered in Indian Ocean (Dec).

Lancelot Hogben, *Science for the Citizen*.

R Humanities

Curtis Nettes, *The Roots of American Civilization*.

Carl Bridenbaugh, *Cities in the Wildnerness*.

E L Woodward, *The Age of Reform, 1815–1870* ('Oxford History of England' series).

Christopher Caudwell, *Studies in a Dying Culture*.

L Mumford, *The Culture of Cities*.

J B Huizinga, *Homo Ludens*.

Frank Luther Mott, *A History of American Magazines* (–1968).

Raymond Aron, *Introduction to the Philosophy of History*.

John Dewey, *Logic: The Theory of Inquiry*.

Hans Reichenbach, *Experience and Prediction*.

Edmund Wilson, *The Triple Thinkers*.

S Art, Sculpture, Fine Arts, and Architecture

Musée de l'Homme opens, Paris, France.

Painting, etc:

Max Beckmann, *Birds' Hell*.

Paul Delvaux, *The Call of the Night*.

Augustus John, *Dylan Thomas*.

Paul Klee, *Dark Message*.

Joan Miró, *Head of a Woman*.

Jackson Pollock, *Man with a Knife* (–1941).

Sculpture:

Eric Gill, relief for the League of Nations Building, Geneva, Switzerland.

Architecture:

Frank Lloyd Wright, Taliesin West, Phoenix, Arizona, USA.

T Music

Samuel Barber, *Adagio for Strings* (adapted from String Quartet).

Arthur Benjamin, *Jamaican Rumba*.

Aaron Copland, *Billy the Kid* (ballet).

Howard Hanson, Symphony No. 3.

Paul Hindemith, *Mathis der Maler* (opera).

Walter Piston, *The Incredible Flutist* (ballet).

Sergei Prokofiev, *Romeo and Juliet* (ballet).

Richard Strauss, *Friedenstag*, *Daphne* (operas).

Anton Webern, String Quartet.

Irving Berlin, 'God Bless America'.

Artie Shaw, 'Begin the Beguine'.

Benny Goodman Band gives sensational jazz concert at Carnegie Hall, New York (Jan).

In the USA, Glenn Miller forms his second band (–1942), which achieves success with 'Moonlight Serenade' and other hits.

U Literature and Drama

W H Auden (ed.), *The Oxford Book of Light Verse*.

Samuel Beckett, *Murphy*.

Elizabeth Bowen, *The Death of the Heart*.

Cyril Connolly, *Enemies of Promise*.

e e cummings, *Collected Poems*.

Cecil Day Lewis, *Overtures to Death*.

Lawrence Durrell, *The Black Book* (published in Paris).

Daniel Fagunwa, *The Forest of a Thousand Demons*.

William Faulkner, *The Unvanquished*.

Robert Graves, *Collected Poems 1914–1938*.

Graham Greene, *Brighton Rock*.

Richard Hughes, *In Hazard*.

Christopher Isherwood, *Goodbye to Berlin*.

Somerset Maugham, *The Summing-Up*.

Daphne du Maurier, *Rebecca*.

Vladimir Nabokov, *Invitation to a Beheading*.

George Orwell, *Homage to Catalonia*.

Laura Riding, *Collected Poems*.

Rex Stout, *Too many Cooks*.

Evelyn Waugh, *Scoop*.

Drama:

Jean Anouilh, *Le voyageur sans bagage/ Traveller without Luggage*.

Philip Barry, *Here Come the Clowns*.

Jean Cocteau, *Les Parents terribles*.

Patrick Hamilton, *Gaslight*.

Thornton Wilder, *Our Town*.

Emlyn Williams, *The Corn is Green*.

Antonin Artaud in *Le Théâtre et son Double* proposes 'the theatre of cruelty'.

V Births and Deaths

Jan 5 King Juan Carlos born (–).

Feb 16 John Corigliano born (–).

March 1 Gabriele D'Annunzio dies (75).

March 7 David Baltimore born (–).

April 19 Henry Newbolt dies (75).

April 27 Edmund Husserl dies (79).

June 26 James Johnson dies (67).

July 9 Benjamin Cardozo dies (68).

Aug 9 Rod Laver born (–).

Sept 15 Thomas Wolfe dies (37).

Nov 10 Kemal Atatürk dies (57).

W Everyday Life

Trolleybuses begin to replace trams in London (6 March).

Luxury liner SS *Queen Elizabeth* launched in Scotland.

Introduction of fibreglass and teflon.

The Hungarians J Ladisla and Georg Biro patent their ballpoint pen; a few more refinements are needed for success.

26 partial mobilization of French armed forces; 27, the British Royal Navy is mobilized.

27 the League of Nations pronounces Japan to be the aggressor in China.

29 (–30) the Munich conference, when British Prime Minister Neville Chamberlain, French Prime Minister Édouard Daladier, Adolf Hitler, and Benito Mussolini agree to Germany's military occupation of the Sudetenland, while the remaining frontiers of Czechoslovakia are guaranteed; Germany becomes the dominant power in Europe and both the Little Entente and the French system of alliances in Eastern Europe are shattered; on his return to London, Chamberlain declares that he has brought back 'peace with honour. I believe it is peace in our time.'

κ October

1 Czechs accept Polish ultimatum for the cession of Teschen in north-central Czechoslovakia.

1 (–10) Germany occupies the Sudetenland in Czechoslovakia.

1 in Britain, Alfred Duff Cooper resigns as first lord of the admiralty in protest at the Munich agreement.

1 the League of Nations separates its Covenant from the Versailles Peace Treaty (in which it was originally contained).

2 Japan withdraws from the League of Nations.

4 end of the Popular Front in France when Socialists and Communists abstain from vote of confidence.

5 Eduard Beneš, president of Czechoslovakia, resigns.

6 Czechoslovakia grants autonomy to Slovakia and, on 8, Ruthenia.

6 the Grand Fascist Council in Italy passes antisemitic legislation; Jews are to be excluded from public activities (such as journalism) and are to cede property to the state (confirmed, 10 Nov; Pope Pius XI condemns the legislation).

10 in Japanese–Chinese War, Japanese capture Hankou, which had been the seat of Chiang Kai-shek's government (moved to Chongqing).

25 in Japanese–Chinese War, Japanese take Guangzhou (and the port of Fuzhou on 23 Nov).

25 Libya is declared to be part of Italy.

29 Belgium withdraws from the Nonintervention Committee (barring involvement in Spain).

L November

2 Hungary annexes Southern Slovakia.

8 mid-term elections in the USA result in Democrats having 69 seats in he Senate and 261 in the House of Representatives, while Republicans have 23 in the Senate and 168 in the House.

9 (–10) Kristallnacht ('Crystal night'), when Jewish houses, synagogues, and schools in Germany are burnt down and shops looted; attacks continue until 14.

10 death of Kemal Atatürk; on 11, Ismet İnönü is elected president of Turkey.

26 USSR–Polish declaration of friendship renews nonaggression pact.

30 speeches in Italian Chamber claim Nice and Corsica for Italy.

30 in Romania, Corneliu Codreanu and other members of the Fascist Iron Guard are shot while attempting to escape from prison.

30 Emil Hacha elected president of Czechoslovakia.

M December

1 Britain establishes national register for war service.

6 French–German pact on inviolability of existing frontiers.

14 Italian Chamber of Deputies is replaced by Chamber of Fasces and Corporations.

17 Italy denounces 1935 agreement with France.

23 in Spanish Civil War, the nationalists begin offensive in Catalonia, with the aim of capturing Barcelona.

26 Pan-American Conference makes Declaration of Peru against all foreign intervention.

28 Iraq severs relations with France.

x Sport and Recreation

US boxer Henry 'Homicide Hank' Armstrong becomes the first boxer to hold three world professional titles simultaneously: at featherweight; welterweight, and lightweight.

In soccer, Raith Rovers win the Scottish Second Division, scoring a record 142 goals in 34 matches.

Great Britain and Ireland win the Walker Cup for the first time, beating the USA 7½–4½ at St Andrews (3–4 June).

The third football World Cup is held in France; Italy retains the trophy, beating Hungary 4–2 in the final in Paris.

England scores 903–7 declared in the final Test against Australia at The Oval, winning the match by an innings and 579 runs; during England's innings, Len Hutton establishes a new record individual Test score of 364 (20–24 Aug).

US player Donald Budge is the first male tennis player to win the Grand Slam of all four major tournaments (Wimbledon, US, French, and Australian championships).

y Media

In Britain, Edward Hulton founds the illustrated news magazine *Picture Post*.

Following the union of Germany and Austria, many old Austrian newspapers are suppressed.

Film:

The Adventures of Robin Hood (starring Errol Flynn).

Alexander Nevsky (director, Sergei Eisenstein).

Angels with Dirty Faces (starring James Cagney).

Break the News (director, René Clair).

The Childhood of Maxim Gorky (director, Mark Donskoy).

Dance from the Volcano.

Dawn Patrol (director, Edmund Goulding).

The Lady Vanishes (director, Alfred Hitchcock).

Olympiad (director, Leni Riefenstahl).

Pygmalion (starring Leslie Howard and Wendy Hiller).

Le Quai des Brumes (Port of Shadows) (director, Marcel Carné).

Snow White and the Seven Dwarfs (director, Walt Disney).

Radio:

In USA, great fright and hysteria caused by broadcast on CBS radio of a play about an invasion of Martians, by Orson Welles and his Mercury Theatre (30 Oct).

In Britain, the BBC starts foreign-language broadcasting.

Television:

Experimental transmissions begin in the USSR (July).

In Britain, the BBC broadcasts Neville Chamberlain's return from Munich, waving Hitler's guarantee of peace (30 Sept).

Dismemberment of Czechoslovakia ... Nationalists victorious in Spanish Civil War ... Nazi–Soviet Pact ... Britain and France at war with Germany ...

A January

1 (–6) Édouard Daladier, the French prime minister, visits Algiers, Tunisia, and Corsica to affirm the integrity of the French Empire and counter Benito Mussolini's demands for extra Italian colonies in North Africa and elsewhere.

4 in USA, President Roosevelt asks Congress for $552 million for defence.

10 British Prime Minister Neville Chamberlain and Foreign Secretary Lord Halifax visit Rome for conversations with Benito Mussolini.

21 Adolf Hitler dismisses Dr Schacht, president of the Reichsbank, replacing him by Walter Funk, minister of economics.

26 in Spanish Civil War, the nationalists take Barcelona.

B February

10 in Japanese–Chinese War, Japanese troops occupy the Chinese island of Hainan in the South China Sea and other Chinese ports.

27 Britain and France recognize General Franco's government in Spain (USA grants recognition on 1 April).

C March

6 the Czech government dismisses the autonomous government of Ruthenia, and, on 9–10, the Slovak government.

14 responding to an ultimatum from Hitler, the former prime minister of Slovakia, Josef Tiso, proclaims the region's independence from Czechoslovakia.

15 German troops occupy Bohemia and Moravia in Czechoslovakia; Hitler makes a triumphal entry into Prague in the evening; the regions become a protectorate ruled by Constantin von Neurath.

16 Slovakia is placed under German 'protection', while Hungary annexes Ruthenia (formerly part of Czechoslovakia).

17 Édouard Daladier is granted wide powers by the French parliament to accelerate rearmament.

20 the US government recalls its ambassador from Berlin in protest at the dismemberment of Czechoslovakia.

21 Germany demands of Poland that Germany should acquire the Free City of Danzig (modern Gdansk) and routes through the 'Polish Corridor' (which provides Poland with access to the Baltic); Poland rejects the demands.

23 Germany annexes Memel (modern Klaipeda) from Lithuania and forces Lithuania to sign a treaty.

28 in Spanish Civil War, Madrid surrenders to nationalists; remaining republican areas and places surrender the next day, ending the War.

28 Adolf Hitler denounces Germany's nonaggression pact with Poland (of Jan 1934).

31 Britain and France pledge to support Poland in any attack on Polish independence (pact of mutual assistance agreed on 6 April).

D April

7 Italy invades Albania.

7 Spain joins Germany, Italy, and Japan in the Anti-Comintern Pact.

7 in Australia, death of Prime Minister J A Lyons of the United Australia Party; succeeded on 24 by Robert Menzies.

11 Hungary withdraws from the League of Nations.

13 Britain and France guarantee the independence of Romania and Greece.

15 US President Roosevelt asks Adolf Hitler and Benito Mussolini for assurances that they will not attack 31 named states.

18 USSR proposes a triple alliance with Britain and France.

27 introduction in Britain of conscription for men aged 20–21.

28 Adolf Hitler denounces 1935 British–German naval agreement and repeats demands on Poland.

E May

3 in USSR, Vyacheslav Molotov is appointed commissar of foreign affairs in place of Maxim Litvinov.

8 Spain leaves the League of Nations.

12 Britain and Turkey form pact of mutual assistance.

17 Sweden, Norway, and Finland reject Germany's offer of nonaggression pacts, but Denmark, Estonia, and Latvia accept.

22 Adolf Hitler and Benito Mussolini sign 10-year political and military alliance (the 'Pact of Steel').

23 the British Parliament approves a plan for an independent Palestine by 1949, which is later denounced by Jews and by Arabs in Palestine.

F June

8 (–11) King George VI of Britain visits the USA at end of tour of Canada.

Bloch's Feudal Society ... *Thurber's* Walter Mitty ... *Retirement of Lou Gehrig* ... Gone With the Wind ...

o Politics, Government, Law, and Economy

E H Carr, *The Twenty Years' Crisis.*

Michael Oakeshott, *The Social and Political Doctrines of Contemporary Europe.*

In USA, Executive Office of the President is founded to assist the president in controlling the executive.

New ministries of Supply (11 July) and Information (5 Sept) are established in Britain.

Hatch Act in USA restricts political activities by civil servants.

In USA, in Mulmfard v. Smith, the Supreme Court sustains the Agricultural Adjustment Act of 1938.

Felix Frankfurter appointed to the US Supreme Court (serving until 1962).

Opening of Trans-Iranian Railway, Caspian Sea to Persian Gulf (Jan).

British Overseas Airways Corporation (BOAC) established.

Hewlett-Packard company founded in California, USA.

p Society, Education, and Religion

German Jewish refugees on the SS *St Louis* are turned back by US authorities at Havana; European countries eventually take them, but many are captured by the Nazis in 1940; Britain also restricts Jewish immigration to Palestine.

British government distributes air-raid shelters in areas likely to be bombed in wartime (from Feb).

Evacuation of children from major British cities begins (31 Aug).

Miss Dorothy Garrod is the first woman to be elected a professor in Cambridge University, England (8 May, elected to the Disney Professorship in Archaeology).

In Gaines v. Canada, the US Supreme Court rules that 'separate but equal' must mean that the facilities are of equal standard for black and white.

E Franklin Frazier, *The Negro Family in the United States.*

Amendments are made to the US Social Security Act: a Federal Security Agency is created, with six boards under its jurisdiction; more workers become eligible for pensions and sickness insurance; the first payment of benefits is advanced from 1942 to 1940 and certain family members become entitled to benefits.

In USA, Food Stamps programme starts in Rochester, New York state, run by the US Department of Agriculture.

'The World of Tomorrow', the New York World Fair (April 30–1940).

James Agee and Walker Evans, *Let Us Now Praise Famous Men.*

S Chakotin, *The Rape of the Masses.*

Karen Horney, *New Ways in Psycho-Analysis.*

Paul S Taylor and Dorothea Lange, *An American Exodus: A Record of the Human Erosion.*

These Are Our Lives (autobiographies produced under the auspices of the Works Progress Administration in the USA).

In USA, education, formerly a bureau in the Department of the Interior, becomes the responsibility of the Federal Security Agency.

Following the death of Pope Pius XI (10 Feb), Eugenio Pacelli is elected and takes the name Pius XII (2 March); at Christmas he proposes a five-point peace plan, but neither side will accept it.

Frank Buchman's revivalist Oxford Group operates under the name 'Moral Rearmament'.

T S Eliot, *The Idea of a Christian Society.*

Karl Rahner, *Spirit in the World.*

q Science, Technology, and Discovery

John Cobb at Bonneville Salt Flats, Utah, USA, drives (23 Aug) at 590 kph/368.85 mph.

Malcolm Campbell's water speed record of 226.7 kph/141.7 mph.

Streamlined diesel train achieves 212.8 kph/133.6 mph between Hamburg and Berlin, Germany.

The first Messerschmitt military jet plane, the Me 109, sets a world speed record of 774 kph/481 mph.

Flight of one of the first effective helicopters, the VS-300 designed by US engineer Igor Sikorsky's (14 Sept).

The British Imperial Chemical Industries (ICI) begins the commercial production of polythene.

In USA, a letter from the physicist Albert Einstein, outlining the possibility of creating atomic power, causes President Roosevelt to establish the Advisory Committee on Uranium; it aims to accelerate research into nuclear reactions at US universities.

German physicists Otto Hahn and F Strassman discover nuclear fission by bombarding uranium with neutrons.

French physicist Frédéric Joliot demonstrates the possibility of splitting the atom of uranium isotope 235.

14 Japanese blockade of British concession at Tianjin.

G July

9 Winston Churchill urges Britain to make military alliance with USSR.

16 USA denounces its 1911 trade pact with Japan.

H August

5 British military mission leaves for Moscow (arriving there, 11).

18 commercial agreement between the USSR and Germany.

23 Nazi–Soviet Pact; the parties agree not to fight each other; secret protocols provide for the partition of Poland and for the USSR to operate freely in the Baltic States, Finland, and Bessarabia.

23 British Prime Minister Neville Chamberlain warns Adolf Hitler that Britain will stand by Poland and pleads for settlement of German claims on Danzig.

24 British Parliament passes the Emergency Powers Bill in a day, enabling the government to maintain public safety and prosecute war by order in council.

25 British–Polish treaty of mutual assistance signed in London.

26 (–31) attempts by Daladier and Chamberlain to negotiate with Hitler fail.

30 in France, start of evacuation of children from Paris (31, evacuation of women and children from London begins).

31 USSR Supreme Soviet ratifies the Nazi–Soviet Pact.

J September

1 Germany invades Poland and annexes Danzig; Italy declares neutrality.

2 British National Service bill, calling up men aged 18–41, in force.

3 Britain and France declare war on Germany, following Germany's failure to reply to ultimata on Poland; Australia and New Zealand also declare war.

3 British ministerial changes: Chamberlain forms a war cabinet, with Winston Churchill as first lord of the admiralty.

3 Germans sink *Athenia* off Ireland.

4 French–Polish agreement.

4 in South Africa, a motion proposing neutrality in the European war is defeated; Prime Minister J B M Hertzog resigns and, on 5, J C Smuts of the United Party forms a coalition government.

7 Germans overrun Pomerania and Silesia and, by 10, control western Poland.

13 in France, Édouard Daladier reforms ministry, becoming foreign secretary himself.

14 in Japanese–Chinese War, Japanese troops advance S towards Changsha but are repulsed; it turns out to be the end of Japanese expansion in central China until 1944.

17 Germans reach Brest-Litovsk.

17 USSR invades Poland from east.

17 President Ignace Moscicki and the government of Poland enter Romania where they are interned.

19 British warship HMS *Courageous* sunk by a German submarine.

19 British Royal Air Force begins 'leaflet' raids on Germany.

21 Armand Calinescu, prime minister of Romania, is assassinated by the Fascist Iron Guard.

27 in Britain, an emergency Budget raises standard rate of income tax from 5s.6d. to 7s.6d. (from 25.5 to 37.5 new pence) in the pound.

27 in Poland, Warsaw surrenders after three-day German bombardment.

28 Polish army surrenders; Germany and the USSR conclude a treaty partitioning Poland.

28 USSR pact with Estonia.

30 in Romania, President Ignace Moscicki of Poland resigns in favour of Wladyslaw Raczkiewicz, speaker of the senate, now in France; General Wladyslaw Sikorski forms a Polish government-in-exile in Paris.

K October

3 USA declares neutrality in European war.

5 USSR pact with Latvia.

6 Adolf Hitler's peace-feelers are summarily rejected by Britain and France.

8 Germany incorporates western Poland into the Reich.

10 USSR cedes Vilna (modern Vilnius), hitherto in Poland, to Lithuania.

10 deportation of Polish Jews to Lublin reserve begins.

12 'discussions' start between the USSR and Finland; the USSR demands a mutual assistance pact, but Finland refuses.

14 British warship HMS *Royal Oak* sunk in Scapa Flow by Germans.

L November

4 US President Roosevelt signs bill enabling Britain and France to purchase arms in USA on 'cash and carry' basis, amending the Neutrality Act of May 1937.

15 in Japanese–Chinese War, Japanese invade S China and capture Nanning, cutting the railway between Hanoi (Vietnam) and Changsha.

American chemist Linus Pauling develops theory of the chemical bond.

Swiss chemist Paul Müller invents the insecticide DDT.

R Humanities

Discovery of remains of a 7th-century ship burial at Sutton Hoo, Suffolk, E England.

Marc Bloch, *Feudal Society* (–1940).

Mediaeval Studies issued (by Pontifical Institute of Medieval Studies, Toronto).

Perry Miller, *The New England Mind*.

Robert R Palmer, *Catholics and Unbelievers in Eighteenth-Century France*.

Completion of Carl Sandburg's six-volume *Abraham Lincoln* (1926–39).

Robert Graves and Alan Hodge, *The Long Weekend*.

Charles Beard with Mary Beard, *America in Midpassage*.

C S Lewis and E M W Tillyard, *The Personal Heresy*.

Isaiah Berlin, *Karl Marx*.

Brand Blanshard, *The Nature of Thought*.

John Dewey, *Freedom and Culture*.

Edmund Husserl, *Experience and Judgment* (posthumous).

S Art, Sculpture, Fine Arts, and Architecture

Solomon R Guggenheim Foundation Museum of Non-Objective Painting opens in New York.

Painting, etc:

Paul Klee, *La Belle Jardinière*.

Pablo Picasso, *Bust of a Woman with Striped Hat*.

Ben Shahn, *Hard Ball*.

'Grandma Moses' (Anna M Robertson) becomes famous overnight in 'Unknown American Painters' Exhibition.

T Music

Béla Bartók, String Quartet No. 6.

Roy Harris, Symphony No. 3.

Zoltán Kodály, *Peacock Variations*.

Arnold Schoenberg, Chamber Symphony No. 2.

Heitor Villa-Lobos, Bachiana Brasiliera No.5.

William Walton, Violin Concerto.

In Britain, Myra Hess organizes lunch-time concerts at the National Gallery in London, which popularize pianoforte and chamber music and help to sustain morale.

In USA, the African-American singer Marian Anderson sings at the White House (invited by President Roosevelt) after the Daughters of the American Revolution had refused a concert booking for her at their Constitution Hall in Washington, DC.

Americans buy 45 million 'popular' music records and 5 million 'classical' records.

US jazz trombonist Jack Teagarden founds the first of several bands.

U Literature and Drama

Joyce Cary, *Mister Johnson*.

Raymond Chandler, *The Big Sleep*.

T S Eliot, *Old Possum's Book of Practical Cats* (poems).

Patrick Hamilton, *Hangover Square*.

James Joyce, *Finnegans Wake* (written from 1922).

Ernst Jünger, *On the Marble Cliffs*.

Richard Llewellyn, *How Green Was My Valley*.

Thomas Mann, *Lotte in Weimar*.

Henry Miller, *Tropic of Capricorn*.

Dorothy Parker, *Here Lies*.

John Steinbeck, *The Grapes of Wrath*.

Jan Struther, *Mrs Miniver*.

James Thurber, *The Secret Life of Walter Mitty*.

J R R Tolkien, *The Hobbit*.

Drama:

Philip Barry, *The Philadelphia Story*.

T S Eliot, *The Family Reunion*.

Lillian Hellman, *The Little Foxes*.

V Births and Deaths

Jan 28 W B Yeats dies (73).

March 20 Brian Mulroney born (–).

April 7 Francis Ford Coppola born (–).

April 12 Alan Ayckbourn born (–).

June 26 Ford Madox Ford dies (66).

July 8 Havelock Ellis dies (80).

Sept 17 E M Dell dies (58).

Sept 23 Sigmund Freud dies (83).

Dec 23 Anthony Fokker dies (49).

W Everyday Life

Pan-American Airways begin regular commercial flights between USA and Europe (20 May).

Cup sizing is introduced for brassieres.

X Sport and Recreation

A crowd of 118,570 attends the Glasgow 'Derby' between Rangers and Celtic at Ibrox Park, the first six-figure gate in British League football (2 Jan).

The 5th cricket Test between South Africa and England at Durban, South Africa, is abandoned as a draw after 10 days; England (at 654 for 5, needing 696 to win) have to leave to catch their boat home. The game is the last 'timeless Test' (3–14 March).

In baseball, Lou Gehrig retires after making 2,130 consecutive appearances for the New York Yankees (2 May).

18 magnetic mines, laid by German submarines, sink 60,000 tons of shipping on English east coast in a week.

30 USSR invades Finland, with main offensive to north of Lake Ladoga.

M **December**

13 Battle of the River Plate, between British and German warships, ends on 17 with scuttling of *Graf Spee* off Montevideo.

14 USSR is expelled from League of Nations.

Germany invades Denmark and Norway ... Germany conquers the Low Countries and France ... The Battle of Britain ...

A **January**

21 British first lord of the admiralty, Winston Churchill, advises neutral states in Europe to side with Britain before they suffer German aggression.

B **February**

1 in Russo–Finnish War, USSR launches attacks on Karelian Isthmus and near Lake Kuhmo.

11 USSR attack on Mannerheim Line, the line of forts along Finland's SE border between Lake Ladoga and the Baltic.

C **March**

3 USSR troops capture Vyborg in Finland.

12 end of Russo–Finnish War: Finland signs peace treaty with USSR, ceding the Karelian Isthmus and shores of Lake Ladoga.

20 in France, Édouard Daladier resigns as prime minister; succeeded by Paul Reynaud.

28 Britain and France agree not to conclude a separate peace with Germany.

D **April**

3 changes made to government in Britain, with Lord Woolton appointed minister for food and Lord Beaverbrook minister for aircraft production.

9 German troops invade Denmark and Norway; in Norway the major ports and cities are occupied.

10 (–11) in Norway, First Battle of Narvik, when a British fleet attacks German destroyers at Narvik; further attack made in Second Battle on 13.

14 British forces land at Namsos, Norway, and, on 17, at Andalsnes (French and Polish forces arrive in Norway on 19 April).

15 British cryptanalysts make their first decipherment of a key used for encoding messages on the German 'Enigma' machine (for radio transmission); thereafter the Allies decipher a large proportion of German communications.

In London, Bobby Riggs of the USA wins all three Wimbledon titles on his first and only appearance in the championships.

In Italy, Enzo Ferrari founds his car company, the Auto Avio Construzione.

ᵧ Media

After the German annexation of Czechoslovakia and the invasion of Poland, the press is closed down in both countries.

Film:

The Adventures of Sherlock Holmes (starring Basil Rathbone).

Derrière la Façade (directors, Yves Mirade and Georges Lacombe).

Gone With the Wind (producer, David O Selznick, starring Vivien Leigh and Clark Gable).

Goodbye Mr Chips (starring Robert Donat).

The Hunchback of Notre Dame (starring Charles Laughton).

Daybreak (director, Marcel Carné).

Ninotchka (director, Ernst Lubitsch, starring Greta Garbo).

The Rules of the Game (director, Jean Renoir).

Stagecoach (director, John Ford, starring John Wayne).

The Stars Look Down (director, Carol Reed).

The Wizard of Oz (starring Judy Garland).

Wuthering Heights (starring Laurence Olivier and Merle Oberon).

Radio:

Many countries (mainly in Europe) start foreign-language broadcasts, including Vatican Radio.

BBC broadcasts *ITMA (It's That Man Again)*, with Tommy Handley.

Germany begins overseas broadcasts in English (April). After the outbreak of war, a posh voice on the service is nicknamed 'Lord Haw-Haw' by British journalist Jonah Barrington. Towards the end of the war, William Joyce uses the character of Haw-Haw in propaganda broadcasts from Germany; in 1945 he is captured and convicted in Britain of treason; hanged on 3 Jan 1946.

Television:

In USA, NBC starts the first regular television service, with President Roosevelt opening the New York World Fair (30 April).

In Britain, the BBC's television service is terminated in the middle of a Mickey Mouse film (1 Sept).

Howard Florey develops penicillin for medical use ... Rodrigo's guitar concerto ... Chaplin's 'Great Dictator' ...

○ Politics, Government, Law, and Economy

In Japan, political parties dissolve themselves and are replaced by the Imperial Rule Association (July).

In attempt to seek Indian support for Britain's war effort, the viceroy, Lord Linlithgow, announces that the aim of British policy in India is to provide Dominion status under a constitution framed by Indians (Jan, Aug).

George Gallup, *The Pulse of Democracy: The Public Opinion and How It Works*.

Harold J Laski, *The American Presidency: An Interpretation*.

United States Air Defense Command created (26 Feb) to provide coordinated air defence for the USA.

In USA, President Roosevelt establishes the National Defense Advisory Commission and, with Canadian prime minister W L Mackenzie King, creates the Permanent Joint Board of Defense to protect North America against attack.

In USA, Office of Strategic Services, the precursor of the Central Intelligence Agency, is established.

In Britain, the Local Defence Volunteers are reformed as the 'Home Guard' (July).

Export Control Act passed to conserve US resources as war advances in Asia and Europe.

In USA, establishment of the Fish and Wildlife Service.

Order Number 1305 proclaimed in Britain, that provides for compulsory arbitration in industrial disputes (repealed 1951).

Agreement between Germany and Romania, whereby Romania supplies oil to Germany (22 May).

Rationing of basic foods begins in Britain (bacon, butter, and sugar rationed from 8 Jan).

Ploughing-up scheme is introduced in Britain to boost agricultural production.

Publication (Jan) in Britain of the *Report on the Distribution of the Industrial Population* (the Barlow Report); it urges the establishment of a National Industries

30 British forces are evacuated from Andalsnes, Norway (and on 1 May); troops are evacuated from Namsos on 2–3 May.

E May

4 (–31 May) Germany troops in Norway advance northwards along the Arctic Highway to Rosvik; they advance to Narvik from 9–13 June.

7 in Britain, Prime Minister Neville Chamberlain is attacked for the failure of British troops in Norway; 10, resigns, when Winston Churchill forms a coalition government, including Labour Party members Clement Attlee as lord privy seal, A V Alexander as first lord of the admiralty, and Ernest Bevin as minister of labour; Chamberlain is lord president and Halifax foreign secretary.

10 (–14) Germany invades the Netherlands, Belgium, and Luxembourg.

10 Local Defence Volunteers (later 'Home Guard') formed in Britain.

13 Winston Churchill makes his 'blood and toil' speech in the British House of Commons, rallying confidence in his leadership.

14 Dutch army surrenders; (–23) Germans pierce French defences near Sedan and head NW for the English Channel, dividing Allied (British and French) forces into two groups.

22 British government granted wide emergency powers.

23 Adolf Hitler orders the German armies in Belgium and France to halt their advance; the advance resumes on 25.

26 (–2 June) over 300,000 British and French soldiers trapped in NE France are evacuated from Dunkirk.

28 Belgian army surrenders; King Leopold III is taken prisoner.

30 former British Labour member of Parliament Stafford Cripps is appointed British ambassador to the USSR, initially to organize trade relationships.

31 in Britain, the leader of the British Union of Fascists, Oswald Mosley, is interned (–Nov 1943); internees in Britain include 763 other members of the Union.

F June

5 (–27) German armoured forces conquer N and SW France.

9 cease-fire in Norway at midnight; King Haakon VII flees to Britain.

10 in France, German forces cross the River Seine at Rouen; the government leaves Paris (arrives in Bordeaux, 14 June).

10 Italy declares war on France and Britain.

13 Winston Churchill visits the French prime minister, Paul Reynaud, at Tours, to plead for French resistance to the Germans and for France to appeal to the USA for support.

14 Germans enter Paris.

15 France appeals to the USA for help against the German invasion; the USA rejects the plea.

15 (–17) USSR occupies the Baltic States (Estonia, Latvia, Lithuania).

16 Winston Churchill offers France union with Britain, as a means to continue the war after the defeat of France; the French government rejects the idea and Reynaud resigns as prime minister (succeeded by Marshal Henri Pétain).

17 in France, Pétain announces that France is negotiating an armistice with Germany; General Charles de Gaulle flees from Paris to Britain.

22 France concludes armistice with Germany, dividing the country into two zones: a German-occupied zone in the N and SW and a so-called autonomous 'Vichy' French State with responsibility for French overseas territories (French government established in Vichy on 1 July).

24 armistice between Vichy France and Italy, including the withdrawal of French colonies from the war.

25 Japanese forces land at Haiphong in French Indochina, to cut the Haiphong–Kunming railway and therefore stop supplies reaching the Chinese government by that route.

26 USSR demands Bessarabia and Bukovina from Romania; Romania requests German support for rejection of the demand, but Hitler refuses; 27, Romania cedes the territories which are occupied on 28 by Soviet troops.

28 Britain recognizes General de Gaulle as leader of the Free French.

30 Germany occupies the Channel Islands.

G July

3 British Royal Navy sinks the French fleet at Mers el-Kebir, near Oran, Algeria.

5 the government of Vichy France breaks relations with Britain.

9 Romania places itself under German protection.

10 start of Battle of Britain: German planes attack shipping convoys in British waters and English ports (–18 Aug).

11 Marshal Pétain becomes president of the French State (Vichy France); 12, Pierre Laval appointed vice-president.

18 at Japan's request, Britain closes the 'Burma Road', the main supply route for China running from Lashio in Burma (Myanmar) to Kunming.

Board to encourage the dispersal of industry throughout Britain.

P Society, Education, and Religion

The Germans transport Polish Jews to the 'General Government' area of German-occupied Poland.

In USA, Alien Registration Act (or Smith Act) requires the registration of aliens and gives the federal government powers to suppress political associations.

Government edict in Japan (Sept) orders the establishment of community councils and neighbourhood associations to motivate people in support of the war effort.

British women to receive old-age pension at 60 (21 Feb).

Free milk provided in Britain for mothers and children (July).

The George Cross is instituted in Britain (24 Sept), intended primarily to acknowledge civilian acts of the greatest heroism and courage in circumstances of extreme danger.

Trade unions and employers' organizations are abolished in Vichy France, which also strips Jews of citizenship and bans them from public service.

Ruth Benedict, *Race: Science and Politics*.

Mirra Komarovsky, *The Unemployed Man and His Family*.

Karl Mannheim, *Man and Society*.

In USA, the Office of Education is authorized to provide 'short intensive courses of college grade, designed to meet the shortage of engineers in activities essential to national defence', marking the start of the Engineering Defence Training programme.

Selective Training and Service Act in USA (signed 16 Sept); it provides for men aged 21–35 to be called up for one year of military training.

Fred Clarke, *Education and Social Change*.

Portugal makes new concordat with the Vatican.

Inauguration in the United Kingdom of the National Free Church Council.

Installation of the 14th Dalai Lama, Bstan' dzin-rgy a-mtsho (Ten zin Gyat so), as spiritual leader of Tibetan Buddhists (22 Feb).

C G Jung, *Psychology and Religion*.

Q Science, Technology, and Discovery

M Minnaert, G Mulders, and J Houtgast, *Photometric Atlas of the Solar System*.

Albert Einstein states in his paper to the American Scientific Congress at Washington, DC, that there is as yet no theory which can provide a logical basis for physics.

Rockefeller grant for University of California, USA, to build a giant cyclotron, under E O Lawrence's direction, for producing mesotrons from atomic nuclei.

Edwin McMillan and F Abelson discover neptunium (element 93).

Invention in Britain of the cavity magnetron, a valve that makes radar more sensitive.

First electron microscope demonstrated at RCA laboratories.

Howard Florey, in Oxford, England, develops penicillin for medical use.

R Humanities

Schoolboys discover the Palaeolithic painted and engraved cave at Lascaux, France (12 Sept).

V Gordon Childe, *Prehistoric Communities of the British Isles*.

Dom David Knowles, *The Monastic Order in England, 943–1216*.

George Ostrogorsky, *History of the Byzantine State*.

A J Marder, *The Anatomy of British Sea Power*.

D W Brogan, *The Development of Modern France, 1870–1939*.

Allan Nevins, *John D Rockefeller: The Heroic Age of American Business*.

F W Bateson (ed.), *Cambridge Bibliography of English Literature*.

George Orwell, *Inside the Whale*.

A J Ayer, *The Foundation of Empirical Knowledge*.

Gaston Bachelard, *The Philosophy of No*.

Bertrand Russell, *An Inquiry into Meaning and Truth*.

S Art, Sculpture, Fine Arts, and Architecture

Following the Nazi occupation of France, many artists flee Paris, but Picasso remains, protected by his prestige; he is forbidden to exhibit or sell.

In Britain, official war artists are appointed: Edward Ardizzone, Muirhead Bone, Henry Lamb, John Nash, Paul Nash, Eric Ravilious, Stanley Spencer.

Painting, etc:

Augustus John Exhibition held at the Tate Gallery, London.

Max Ernst, *Europe after the Rain, II*.

Jean Fautrier, *Eyes*.

Wassily Kandinsky, *Sky Blue*.

Paul Klee, *Death and Fire*.

Willem de Kooning, *Seated Woman*.

Joan Miró, *Constellation* series.

John Piper, *St Mary le Port, Bristol*.

Stanley Spencer, *Shipbuilding on the Clyde* series (–1947).

21 Britain recognizes the Czechoslovak National Committee in London as a provisional government.

22 in Japan, Prince Fumimaro Konoe (out of office since 1939) is reappointed prime minister; he declares that Japan's aim is to establish a 'New Order in greater East Asia'.

22 French-administered New Hebrides (now Vanuatu) join the Free French; by 24 Sept numerous French territories apart from those in North Africa do likewise.

23 purchase tax imposed in Britain.

H August

4 Italians advance from Ethiopia into British Somaliland.

5 Britain signs agreements with Polish Government in London and, on 7 with Free French under Charles de Gaulle.

8 Indian Congress Party rejects the viceroy's invitation to serve on a War Advisory Council.

15 in Battle of Britain, the Royal Air Force shoots down 180 German planes.

20 in Battle of Britain, the German emphasis shifts to attacking British airports and aircraft factories.

23 all-night German bombing raid on London begins the period of intense bombing known as the 'Blitz'.

J September

3 USA sells 50 destroyers to Britain in return for 99-year rent-free leases of bases in Newfoundland and the Caribbean.

4 in Romania, Ion Antonescu assumes dictatorial powers (as 'Conducator'); 6, King Carol II abdicates in favour of his son Michael and flees to Switzerland with his mistress.

15 (–16) Italian forces in Libya advance into Egypt, to Sidi Barrani.

22 Japanese troops occupy the area around Hanoi in French Indochina (now Vietnam).

27 British and Free French forces attempt to occupy Dakar, the capital of Senegal (a French territory that had remained loyal to Vichy France), but are repulsed.

27 Tripartite Pact, between Germany, Italy, and Japan, pledging military and economic cooperation.

30 during September Britain loses 160,000 tonnes of shipping to enemy action.

K October

3 Neville Chamberlain retires from the British government (dies, 9 Nov), and is succeeded by Sir John Anderson; Sir Kingsley Wood and Ernest Bevin enter the cabinet as, respectively, chancellor of the exchequer and minister of labour.

4 Adolf Hitler meets Benito Mussolini in Brenner Pass for discussions.

7 by agreement, German troops enter Romania and take control of oilfields.

12 Adolf Hitler postpones 'Operation Sea Lion', the planned invasion of Britain; in the Battle of Britain, the range of targets is extended, with large-scale bombing of London (especially 13–21) and other cities.

18 Britain reopens the Burma Road, enabling supplies again to reach China.

28 Italy demands cession of strategic points in Greece but Greece rejects demands; an Italian invasion follows.

L November

3 British forces occupy Suda Bay, Crete.

5 in USA, F D Roosevelt, Democrat, is re-elected President for an unprecedented third term, with 449 electoral votes, against Wendell L Wilkie, Republican, with 82; popular vote: Roosevelt, 27,244,160; Wilkie, 22,305,198.

11 (–12) British attack and cripple Italian fleet at Taranto, SE Italy.

12 (–14) Soviet foreign minister Vyacheslav Molotov visits Berlin, for discussions with Adolf Hitler and Joachim von Ribbentrop, the foreign secretary; the Germans are evasive about the USSR's place in their plans and Molotov doubts their ability to conquer Britain.

14 (–15) Germans bomb Coventry in central England, killing 568 people, destroying the city centre and cathedral, and severely damaging industrial production (16, Britain retaliates with a raid on Hamburg).

20 agreement between USA and Britain for partial standardization of weapons and pooling of technical knowledge.

20 Hungary and, on 23, Romania, endorse German–Italian–Japanese Tripartite Pact of 27 Sept.

20 in the month's air raids, 4,558 persons killed in Britain.

M December

9 (–9 Feb) in North Africa, Operation Compass: Eighth Army under Archibald Wavell advances from Egypt into Libya (crossing the border on 15).

22 Lord Halifax, the British foreign secretary, is appointed British Ambassador to USA; 23, Anthony Eden appointed British foreign secretary.

Sculpture:
Joseph Cornell, *Soap Bubble Set.*

Architecture:
Frank Lloyd Wright, Chapel of Florida Southern College, Florida, USA.

т Music
Benjamin Britten, *Sinfonia da Requiem.*
Aram Khachaturian, Violin Concerto.
Elisabeth Lutyens, *Three Pieces.*
Frank Martin, *Le vin herbé* (oratorio).
Sergei Prokofiev, Piano Sonata No. 6.
Joaquin Rodrigo, *Concierto de Aranjuez* (for guitar and orchestra).
Randall Thompson, *Alleluia.*
Anton Webern, *Variations for Orchestra.*
Foundation of the Stan Kenton band (–1947).
In USA, formation of The Almanac Singers by Pete Seeger, Lee Hayes, and Millard Lampell, joined in 1941 by Woody Guthrie (–1942).
Introduction of the world's first record chart in US magazine Billboard (20 July).
In Britain, the BBC launches the radio series *Sincerely Yours,* starring Vera Lynn, who popularizes 'We'll Meet Again' and 'White Cliffs Of Dover'.

u Literature and Drama
Dino Buzzati, *Tartar Steppe.*
Raymond Chandler, *Farewell My Lovely.*
Graham Greene, *The Power and the Glory.*
Ernest Hemingway, *For Whom the Bell Tolls.*
Arthur Koestler, *Darkness at Noon.*
Carson McCullers, *The Heart is a Lonely Hunter.*
Michael Sadleir, *Fanny by Gaslight.*
Upton Sinclair, *Between Two Worlds.*
C P Snow, *Strangers and Brothers.*
Howard Spring, *Fame is the Spur.*
Dylan Thomas, *Portrait of the Artist as a Young Dog.*
Edmund Wilson, *To the Finland Station.*

Drama:
Ernest Hemingway, *The Fifth Column.*
Eugene O'Neill, *Long Day's Journey into Night* (first produced in 1956).

v Births and Deaths
Jan 21 Jack Nicklaus born (–).
Feb 1 John Buchan dies (63).
March 16 Bernardo Bertolucci born (–).
April 18 H A L Fisher dies (75).
May 7 George Lansbury dies (81).
Aug 21 Leon Trotsky dies (61).
Aug 30 J J Thompson dies (83).
Oct 9 John Lennon born (–1980).

Oct 14 Cliff Richard born (–).
Oct 23 Pele born (–).
Nov 9 Neville Chamberlain dies (71).
Nov 17 Eric Gill dies (58).
Nov 26 Harold Harmsworth (Lord Rothermere) dies (72).
Dec 21 F Scott Fitzgerald dies (44).

w Everyday Life
Nylon stockings are marketed in the USA, proving an instant success.
In USA, Colonel Sanders concocts his special recipe for Kentucky Fried Chicken.
Willys Corporation in the USA produces the jeep.
British writer Agatha Christie's novel *Ten Little Niggers* is released in the USA as *Ten Little Indians.*

x Sport and Recreation
In USA, the Chicago Bears beat the Washington Redskins 73–0 in the National Football League Championship game.
The 12th Olympic Games, due to be held in Tokyo, Japan, are cancelled because of the War.

y Media

Film:
US actress Hattie McDaniel is the first African-American woman to win an Oscar (best supporting actress in *Gone With the Wind*).
The Bank Dick (starring W C Fields).
A Day in the New World.
Fantasia (producer, Walt Disney).
The Grapes of Wrath (director, John Ford).
The Great Dictator (starring Charlie Chaplin).
Pinocchio (producer, Walt Disney).
Rebecca (director, Alfred Hitchcock).
The Road to Singapore (the first 'road' film starring Bing Crosby, Bob Hope, and Dorothy Lamour).
The Thief of Baghdad (producer, Alexander Korda).
The Westerner (director, William Wyler).
A Wild Hare (in which Bugs Bunny makes his debut).

Television:
In USA, CBS demonstrates its colour-television system, developed by engineer Peter Goldmark, making the world's first broadcast in colour.
Germany continues broadcasts (–23 Nov 1943) and takes over the Eiffel Tower transmitter in Paris after the invasion of France (–1944).

*Germany invades the USSR ... Japan bombs US fleet at Pearl
Harbour ... USA enters the war ...*

A **January**

3 in N Africa, Italians surrender Bardia in NE Libya to the British (advancing from Egypt).

6 in USA, President Roosevelt sends Lend-Lease Bill to Congress; it provides for the president to sell, lend, or lease material to countries whose defence is important to the USA.

30 South Africans drive Italians from Kenya, E Africa.

30 pro-British rising in Ethiopia.

B **February**

6 in N Africa, British forces advancing across Libya occupy Benghazi; 9, reach El Agheila.

12 German General Erwin Rommel arrives in Tripoli, Libya, to take control of German reinforcements and stiffen Italian resistance to the British.

19 in E Africa, British troops invade Italian Somaliland from Kenya.

27 Britain signs pact of friendship with Hungary.

C **March**

1 Prime minister of Bulgaria signs the Tripartite Pact (of 27 Sept 1940), allying Bulgaria with the Axis powers (5, in protest Britain orders departure of its minister in Sofia).

7 British troops invade Italian-controlled Ethiopia.

11 in USA, the Lend-Lease Bill is signed after two months' controversy.

19 Germany resumes air raids on London.

24 in N Africa, German and Italian forces commanded by General Rommel take El Algheila in Libya from the British; Rommel launches his first offensive.

24 USSR undertakes to support Turkey if it becomes the victim of aggression.

25 Yugoslavia joins the Tripartite Pact (Germany, Italy, Japan, and others).

27 Prince Paul, Regent of Yugoslavia, is deposed in *coup d'état* organized by airforce officers who were exploiting the unpopularity of adherence to the Tripartite Pact; succeeded by Peter II (a minor who is declared to be of age).

27 British forces in the Italian E African territory of Eritrea capture Keren (after a long battle, from 5 Feb).

28 in the Mediterranean, Battle of Cape Matapan: a small British fleet sinks six or seven Italian ships off Cape Matapan (also known as Cape Taínaron, S Greece).

D **April**

2 in Iraq, army officers dismiss the prime minister and appoint Rashid Ali, a former prime minister; the regent is later declared deposed; Britain sends troops to Iraq under the terms of the 1930 treaty.

5 USSR offers goodwill to Yugoslavia in the event of a German invasion.

5 British forces in Italian-controlled Ethiopia take Addis Ababa and, on 6, Massawa in Eritrea.

6 German ultimatum to Greece and Yugoslavia; Germany, Italy, and Bulgaria invade Yugoslavia; Germany invades Greece (Britain sends 60,000 troops to Greece).

7 British Budget raises standard rate of income tax to 10 shillings in the pound.

10 Croatia in Yugoslavia declares independence.

11 German bombers attack aircraft factories around Coventry in Midland England.

13 Joseph Stalin for the USSR signs neutrality pact with Japan.

17 Yugoslavia signs surrender to German invaders.

20 in N Africa, Axis forces under Erwin Rommel attack Tobruk in NE Libya.

21 Greek army surrenders to Germans (22–2 May, British forces evacuate Greece); 27, Athens surrenders.

25 in N Africa, the German-led offensive against the British across Libya reaches Egypt.

E **May**

1 Iraq, siding with Germany, demands withdrawal of British forces; on 2, fighting breaks out.

6 Joseph Stalin, the secretary of the Soviet communist party, assumes the post of prime minister.

10 Rudolf Hess, the deputy leader of the German Nazi party, flies to Scotland, where he seeks to arrange peace but is treated as a prisoner.

10 heaviest German bombing raid on London; the chamber of the House of Commons is destroyed.

12 Adolf Hitler and Admiral François Darlan, vice-president of Vichy France, meet for discussions; Darlan makes concessions (approved by the Vichy government on 14).

18 Bulgaria seizes the Greek and Yugoslav sections of Macedonia.

20 Germans invade Crete.

*Start of the 'Manhattan Project' in USA ... 'Big Boy' goes into
service ... Orson Welles' Citizen Kane ...*

o Politics, Government, Law, and Economy

In USA, Office of Price Administration established (April) to control war-related inflation; price controls are tightened in succeeding years.

In USSR, State Committee of Defence established under Joseph Stalin, as supreme wartime organ of government.

In USA, Harlan Stone is appointed Chief Justice of the Supreme Court (serving until 1946).

In USA, in US v. Darby Lumber Co., the Supreme Court unanimously overrules Hammer v. Dagenhart (1918), which had declared federal regulation of transportation of products of child labour unconstitutional.

In Britain the White Paper *The Sources of War Finance* marks the introduction of national income-based budgetary policy.

The Essential Work Order (March) and registration of the work force in Britain enables the minster of labour (Ernest Bevin) to direct labour to where it is needed in the war economy.

In USSR, 1,360 heavy industrial plants in western areas are dismantled and moved eastwards (many E of the Urals), to enable the continuation of industrial production after the German invasion.

Rice-rationing introduced in Japan (April).

P Society, Education, and Religion

In the wake of the German invasion of the USSR, German 'Action Groups' (Einsatzgruppen) slaughter 400,000–500,000 Jews.

The Germans transport Jews from Germany to the 'General Government' area of occupied Poland, where they are placed in ghettos or (from Dec) killed.

In Vichy France, Jews are rounded up and turned over to the Germans (May–June).

In USA, President Roosevelt establishes the Fair Employment Practices Commission (25 June), to investigate alleged discrimination on basis of colour, race, national origin, or creed (the action is to avoid a mass march on Washington by African-Americans complaining about discrimination by companies working on government contracts).

British government announces intention to call up women aged 20–30 for war service (Dec).

Unemployment is virtually eliminated in Britain.

National Fire Service established in Britain (18 Aug).

Heavy penalties for British black-marketeers (17 Dec).

B S Rowntree, *Poverty and Progress: A Second Social Survey of York.*

Rudolf Bultmann, *New Testament and Mythology.*

Etienne Gilson, *God and Philosophy.*

Nathaniel Micklem, *The Theology of Politics.*

Reinhold Niebuhr, *The Nature and Destiny of Man* (–1943). Karl Rahner, *Hearers of the Word.*

Q Science, Technology, and Discovery

Creation of the Office of Scientific Research and Development in USA.

In Britain, J R Whinfield and J T Dickson develop the synthetic polyester fibre 'Terylene' ('Dacron' in the USA).

A Ferry Command aircraft crosses the Atlantic from the west in 8 hrs 23 mins.

J D Bernal investigates the physics of air raids.

In USA, the 'Manhattan Project' of atomic research (to develop an atomic bomb) starts in Chicago and Los Angeles under the direction of G B Pegram and H C Urey (Dec).

In USA, G T Seaborg and E M McMillan isolate plutonium.

R Humanities

Cambridge Economic History of Europe (–).

Cecil Roth, *History of the Jews in England.*

Eileen Power, *The Wool Trade in English Medieval History.*

A L Rowse, *Tudor Cornwall.*

Robert R Palmer, *Twelve Who Ruled.*

A J P Taylor, *The Habsburg Monarchy, 1815–1918.*

James Burnham, *The Managerial Revolution.*

Oscar Handlin, *Boston's Immigrants: A Study in Acculturation.*

The Oxford Dictionary of Quotations.

Erich Fromm, *Escape from Freedom.*

Herbert Marcuse, *Reason and Revolution.*

S Art, Sculpture, Fine Arts, and Architecture

In Paris, France, Picasso writes play *Le Desir Attrapé par la Queue*, referring to the privations of the Occupation, especially food.

Henry Moore makes crayon drawings of refugees in air-raid shelters during the London Blitz.

In USA, National Gallery opens in Washington, DC (buildings funded by the late Andrew W Mellon and the collection based around Mellon's collection).

24 Naval battle: the German battleship *Bismarck* sinks the British battle-cruiser HMS *Hood* off Greenland.

24 (–30) collapse of anti-British government in Iraq; Rashid Ali and others flee abroad (1 June, deposed regent returns to Baghdad).

27 the German battleship *Bismarck*, which had been attacking commercial shipping around Britain, is sunk by the British Royal Navy west of Brest, but its companion ship *Prinz Eugen* escapes.

29 British evacuate Iráklion, the largest city on Crete, and on 31 make a final withdrawal of troops to Egypt, leaving Crete under German occupation.

F **June**

8 (–14 July) British and Free French Forces invade Syria to prevent establishment of Axis bases.

12 first conference of Allies held in London; countries pledge mutual assistance.

22 Operation Barbarossa: Germany invades the USSR, with three army groups aiming to capture, respectively, Leningrad, Moscow, and the Ukraine (Romanian troops support the invasion).

25 following Germany's invasion of the USSR, Finland declares that it is at war with the USSR; Finns invade eastern Karelia (which is re-conquered by the end of Aug).

27 Hungary declares war on the USSR.

27 in the USSR, Germans from the north and centre army groups converge to the east of Minsk, trapping about 300,000 Soviet troops.

G **July**

6 USSR troops abandon occupied Poland and Baltic states, retiring to 'Stalin Line' on former frontier with Poland.

7 US troops relieve British in occupation of Iceland.

12 in USSR, British–Soviet agreement of mutual assistance signed in Moscow.

16 in USSR, Germans pierce the Stalin Line and take Smolensk.

23 following Japan's demand for bases in Indochina, Britain and USA freeze Japanese assets.

24 Japanese troops begin occupation of C and S Indochina.

25 in USSR, Germans take Tallinn (formerly the capital of Estonia).

27 in USSR, Germans enter the Ukraine.

29 Romania reoccupies Bessarabia and Bukhovina, which it had ceded to the USSR in June 1940.

H **August**

11 Winston Churchill and F D Roosevelt, meeting on a ship off Newfoundland (now part of Canada), sign the Atlantic Charter (published on 14); it condemns territorial changes and affirms human rights.

12 British–Soviet trade agreement.

25 (–17 Sept) USSR and Britain invade Iran following the Shah's refusal to reduce numbers of resident Germans (16 Sept, Reza Khan Pahlavi abdicates in favour of his son Muhammad Reza Shah Pahlavi).

J **September**

Campaign in Britain for opening of a Second Front against Germany.

8 in USSR, German forces reach Leningrad (now St Petersburg) but fail to capture the city; they start a siege (–27 Jan 1944).

19 in USSR, Germans capture Kiev, capital of the Ukraine.

24 Allied conference in London endorses Atlantic Charter.

29 (–10 Oct) Lord Beaverbrook for Britain and Averell Harriman for the USA visit Moscow to arrange provision of war supplies to the USSR.

K **October**

1 in USSR, Germans advance from Smolensk towards Moscow.

3 in USSR, Germans take Orel, S of Moscow.

13 British Royal Air Force bombs the German city of Nuremberg.

15 as Germans are 100 km/60 mi from Moscow, the order is given for the Soviet government to be transferred to Kuybyshev on the River Volga, but Joseph Stalin stays in Moscow.

16 in USSR, the port of Odessa falls and, on 27, Perekop on the Sea of Azov.

16 in Japan, Prince Fumimaro Konoe resigns as prime minister; succeeded by Hideki Tojo.

22 Britain resumes diplomatic relations with Mexico (broken since May 1938).

24 in USSR, Germans take Kharkov, the second largest city of the Ukraine.

25 failure of first German offensive against Moscow.

L **November**

3 in USSR, Germans take Kursk.

13 British aircraft carrier *Ark Royal* is torpedoed by a German submarine near Gibraltar; it sinks the following day.

13 US Congress votes to amend the Neutrality Act, allowing US merchant ships to be armed and to enter war zones.

Painting, etc:

Francis Gruber, *Hommage to Jacques Callot*, a symbol of French resistance to Nazi occupation.

Renato Guttuso, *Crucifixion*.

Pablo Picasso, *Boy with a Crayfish*.

T Music

Richard Addinsell, *Warsaw Concerto*.

Henry Cowell, *Tales of Our Countryside*.

Luigi Dallapiccola, *Canti di Prigioniera*.

Olivier Messiaen, *Quartet for the End of Time*.

Harry Partch, *San Francisco Newsboy Cries*.

William Schuman, Symphony No. 3.

Noël Coward, 'London Pride'.

In USA, Lionel Hampton founds the Hampton Big Band.

U Literature and Drama

James Agee and Walker Evans, *Let Us Now Praise Famous Men*.

Louis Aragon, *Le Crève-Coeur*.

Joyce Cary, *Herself Surprised*.

Ivy Compton-Burnett, *Parents and Children*.

Ilya Ehrenburg, *The Fall of Paris*.

F Scott Fitzgerald, *The Last Tycoon* (posthumous).

John Masefield, *The Nine Days Wonder*.

Vladimir Nabokov, *The Real Life of Sebastian Knight*.

Edna St Vincent Millay, *Collected Sonnets*.

Stephen Spender, *Ruins and Visions*.

Franz Werfel, *The Song of Bernadette*.

Drama:

Bertolt Brecht, *Mother Courage and her Children*.

Noël Coward, *Blithe Spirit*.

Lillian Hellman, *Watch on the Rhine*.

Richard Wright, *Native Son*.

In USA, Piscator's Studio Theatre, New York, founded to present social drama.

V Births and Deaths

Jan 5 Henri Bergson dies (81).

Jan 8 Robert Baden-Powell dies (83).

Jan 8 Amy Johnson dies (38).

Jan 13 James Joyce dies (58).

March 8 Sherwood Anderson dies (65).

March 28 Virginia Woolf dies (59).

May 7 J G Frazer dies (87).

May 18 Werner Sombart dies (78).

May 24 Bob Dylan born (–).

June 2 Lou Gehrig dies (37).

June 4 Kaiser Wilhelm II dies (82).

June 29 Ignacy Paderewski dies (80).

July 11 Arthur Evans dies (90).

Aug 7 Rabindranath Tagore dies (80).

Oct 5 Louis Brandeis dies (84).

W Everyday Life

In USA, completion of the Mount Rushmore Memorial (to presidents Washington, Jefferson, Roosevelt, and Lincoln).

'Cheerios' breakfast cereal is launched in USA.

In USA, the Muzak Company, providing piped music to public places, is acquired and expanded by William Benton.

'Big Boy', thought to be the biggest steam locomotive ever built, goes into service for the Union Pacific railroad company in the USA.

There are now 38.8 million private cars in the USA, 2.2 million in Britain.

In Britain, closure of Sanger's Circus (founded 1820).

'Utility' (standardized) clothing and furniture introduced in Britain, where clothes are rationed (from 1 June).

Double Summer Time introduced in Britain.

Germany adopts Roman type instead of Gothic (31 May).

X Sport and Recreation

In USA, Jackie Robinson is the first African-American player in Major League baseball.

Y Media

In USA, Marshall Field founds the *Chicago Sun* (tabloid from 1947).

In Britain, retirement of Geoffrey Dawson as editor of *The Times*; replaced by R M Barrington Ward.

The British Communist paper, the *Daily Worker*, is suppressed (Jan–Sept 1942).

Film:

The Big Store (last film starring the Marx Brothers).

Citizen Kane (director and star, Orson Welles).

Dumbo (producer, Walt Disney).

The First of the Few (starring Leslie Howard).

49th Parallel (directors, Michael Powell and Emeric Pressburger).

Friedmann Bach.

High Sierra (starring Humphrey Bogart).

How Green Was My Valley (director, John Ford).

Kipps (director, Carol Reed).

The Maltese Falcon (director, John Huston).

Nous les Gosses.

Radio:

Brains Trust broadcast by BBC.

The BBC broadcasts the serial *The Man Born to be King* by Dorothy L Sayers (at monthly intervals from Dec to Oct 1942).

Television:

In USA, the Federal Communications Commission endorses recommendation of the

16 in USSR, second German offensive against Moscow.

18 in N Africa, British forces in Egypt launch Operation Crusader; they relieve Tobruk in Libya (7 Dec) and advance across Libya (–1942).

27 in USSR, Marshal Semyon Timoshenko launches Soviet counterattacks against the Germans, forcing them to evacuate Rostov-on-Don on 28, the first German loss of territory in the East.

M **December**

5 (–5 Jan 1942) in USSR, Soviet forces launch counteroffensive N and S of Moscow to relieve pressure on the capital.

5 Britain declares war on Finland, Hungary, and Romania on their refusing to withdraw from the war against the USSR.

5 British Foreign Secretary Anthony Eden visits Moscow to discuss the military situation with Stalin and foreign secretary Vyacheslav Molotov (returns 27 Dec).

7 Japanese make surprise air attack on the US naval base at Pearl Harbor, Hawaii; eight battleships and over 300 aircraft are destroyed or damaged.

8 USA and Britain declare war on Japan.

8 Japanese forces attack Wake Island and Guam (and, on 10, Makin), US possessions in the Pacific Ocean; they then occupy the islands.

8 Japanese forces capture Victoria Point airfield in S Burma (Myanmar) and advance into Malaya; British forces retreat to Singapore.

9 National Service Bill in Britain lowers age of call-up to 18½ and renders single women aged 20–30 liable to military service.

9 in NW USSR, Soviet forces recapture Tikhvin, easing the pressure on Leningrad.

10 Japanese forces start a series of landings on Luzon, Philippines (others on 12 and 22).

10 Japanese aircraft sink the British ships *Prince of Wales* and *Repulse*, weakening the defence of Malaya.

11 Germany and Italy declare war on the USA.

16 in USSR, German forces on Moscow front begin retreat.

19 commander of German chiefs of staff, General Walther von Brauchitsch, resigns; Adolf Hitler takes personal control.

19 British withdraw from island of Penang off the W coast of Malaya.

19 following bombardment (from 8 Dec), Japanese forces land on Victoria, Hong Kong.

22 (–14 Jan) Arcadia Conference in Washington, DC, USA: President Roosevelt and Winston Churchill establish a joint chiefs of staff committee to plan war strategy; they also agree on invasion of NW Africa.

24 in N Africa, British reoccupy Benghazi and regain control of Cyrenaica, Libya.

25 British Chinese territory of Hong Kong surrenders to Japanese.

26 USA and Britain agree alliance with China.

26 in USSR, Germans withdraw from Kaluga, SW of Moscow.

*Fall of Singapore ... Germans fight to take Stalingrad in USSR ...
Battle of El Alamein ...*

A **January**

2 in Washington, DC, USA, the USA, Britain, USSR, China, and 22 other Allies (calling themselves the United Nations) pledge not to make separate peace treaties with the enemy.

5 (–31 March) in USSR, Soviet Winter offensive: the Red Army launches an offensive on all fronts, and makes progress in the north and centre.

6 in N Africa, British advancing westwards through Libya reach Mersa Brega, near El Agheila.

11 Japanese advancing through Malaya take Kuala Lumpur.

20 in Germany, the Wannsee Conference: Nazi leaders and senior officials meet in a Berlin suburb to discuss 'the Final Solution of the Jewish Question'; that is, the destruction of European jewry.

20 Japanese cross Thailand and invade Burma (now Myanmar), capturing Rangoon (now Yangon) on 8 March.

21 (6 Feb) in N Africa, Rommel launches new offensive against the British forces in Libya; the British retreat eastwards to NE Libya (to a line between Gazala and Bir Hacheim).

23 in Pacific, a Japanese force captures Rabaul in New Britain.

National Television System Committee to make 525 lines the standard for US television broadcasting (from 1 July); on that date the Columbia Broadcasting System (CBS) begins regular television broadcasting (in competition with NBC).

Germans establish 'death camps' for mass murder of Jews ...
First electronic computer ... Sinatra's New York debut ...

o Politics, Government, Law, and Economy

E H Carr, *Conditions of Peace.*

Ministry of Production formed to coordinate the British war economy. Ministry of Fuel and Power created in Britain.

Office of War Production established in USA (Jan).

In USA, Office of War Information created to manage government's information activities (13 June).

In the USA, a new act of Congress (Oct) empowers the Office of Price Administration to impose a freeze on prices, wages, and rents (from 3 Oct).

In Britain, Duncan v. Cammell Laird establishes that a minister can withhold documents and items on grounds of national interest.

The Welsh Courts Act allows the use of Welsh in court proceedings in Wales.

The USA expands industrial production for the war effort; among items produced is the 'Liberty Ship', a freighter of simple design.

In USA, civilian automobile production is halted for the duration of the war to allow for war production; petrol (gasoline) is also rationed (from Sept).

Campaigns started in Britain ('Dig for Victory') and USA ('Victory Gardens'), encouraging cultivation of gardens and public space to increase food production.

B February

1 British forces in Malaya withdraw to Singapore, the key British naval base for all of SE Asia.

1 in Norway, the Fascist leader Vidkun Quisling is appointed prime minister.

1 (–4 March) US carrier aircraft attack Japanese bases on the Marshall, Gilbert, Wake, and Marcus islands.

7 Japanese land on Singapore island.

15 Singapore, and over 70,000 British and Commonwealth soldiers and airmen, surrenders to the Japanese; described by Winston Churchill as 'the worst disaster and largest capitulation in British history'.

16 (–20) in Pacific, Japanese troops land at several places in the Dutch East Indies (16, seize Palembang; 18, occupy Bali; 19, land on Timor).

19 in Pacific, Japanese planes bomb Darwin in N Australia.

19 (–22) in Britain, Winston Churchill reconstructs his ministry, with Clement Attlee as deputy prime minister and Sir Stafford Cripps entering the war cabinet as lord privy seal; Lords Beaverbrook and Greenwood resign from the government, and the chancellor of the exchequer, Kingsley Wood, leaves the war cabinet.

28 in Pacific, Japanese land on Java.

C March

23 Japanese forces occupy N Sumatra and the Nicobar and Andaman Islands in the Indian Ocean.

28 British commandos raid St Nazaire in NW France, seeking to destroy the dry dock.

28 British air force bombs the port of Lübeck in N Germany, destroying most of the medieval city.

30 (–30 April) Japanese forces advance through Burma (Myanmar).

D April

Continuous intensive Axis air raids made on Malta to hamper British attempts to disrupt the supply of materiel to the Axis forces in N Africa.

5 Japanese bomb Colombo in Ceylon (now Sri Lanka) and Trincomalee on 9 April.

8 (–15) General George Marshall and Harry Hopkins of USA visit London to discuss attacking Germany in order to relieve pressure on the USSR; on 14, the combined commanders group concludes that a second front cannot be opened in Europe in 1942.

9 in Philippines, US and Filipino forces holding out against the Japanese on the Bataan Peninsula surrender (15–29, survivors are taken on a forced march, the 'Bataan death march', during which about 10,000 are killed or die).

18 (–29 July) in USSR, the German Spring Offensive: the Germans press into E Ukraine, aiming to capture the oil fields in the Caucasus.

18 the Doolittle Raid: 16 US bombers from a carrier make a bombing raid on Tokyo and other Japanese cities, some then flying on to China.

18 in the (Vichy) French State, Pierre Laval becomes president and minister for foreign affairs and the interior.

23 (–30) German bombers make raids on Exeter, Bath, and other historic places in Britain, the so-called 'Baedeker' raids named after the German guidebooks.

E May

1 in Burma (Myanmar), Japanese take Mandalay, while British withdraw along the Chindwin Valley to India.

4 (–8) in Pacific, indecisive Battle of the Coral Sea between USA and Japanese naval forces E of Papua New Guinea.

5 British troops invade the (Vichy) French territory of Madagascar.

6 in the Philippines, the US and Filipino force on the island of Corregidor surrenders to the Japanese.

24 the Nazi 'Protector' of Bohemia and Moravia, Reinhard Heydrich, is shot in Prague by nationalists; dies on 26.

26 Vyacheslav Molotov in London signs British–Soviet treaty for closer cooperation in prosecution of the war.

26 British–USSR 20-year alliance signed in London.

27 (–5 Sept) in N Africa, Rommel's forces outflank the British forces; the British retreat eastwards into Egypt.

30 (–31) first British 'thousand bomber' raid on Germany, against Cologne.

F June

4 (–5) in Pacific, Battle of Midway, when US carrier planes sink four Japanese carriers.

5 Japanese seize Attu and, on 7, Kiska, two islands in the US Aleutian chain.

10 in Czechoslovakia, Nazis destroy the village of Lidice in revenge for the death of Reinhard Heydrich; males over 16 are shot, all others deported.

17 (–21) Washington Conference, between President Roosevelt and Winston Church, to discuss war production and military strategy.

21 in N Africa, the Axis forces under Rommel retake Tobruk in NE Libya from the British.

28 in N Africa, British retreat eastwards to El Alamein in N Egypt.

Sugar rationing introduced in the USA (14 May).

Coal Commission takes over colliery leases in Britain under 1938 Act (1 July).

In USA, the Alaska Highway is opened (Oct).

Foundation in USA of the Committee for Economic Development.

J A Schumpeter, *Capitalism, Socialism and Democracy.*

P Society, Education, and Religion

Following the Wannsee Conference in Berlin (Jan), the Germans expand the killing of Jews, using gas; mobile gas vans kill many Jews, but facilities for large-scale murder are established at six 'death camps' (Chelmo; Bergen-Belsen, March; Sobibor, April; Auschwitz, June; Treblinka, July; Majdanek, autumn); Jews are transported by train from occupied Europe (France, Belgium, Netherlands, etc) to the death camps; Auschwitz sends up to 10,000 Jews to the gas chambers every day. 30,000 Jews are arrested by police in Paris (16 July) and sent to German concentration camps.

In USA, Executive Order 9066 (signed by President Roosevelt on 21 March) establishes the War Relocation Authority to move Japanese-Americans away from the Pacific Coast; some 110,000 are interned in WRA camps (most of the 150,000 Japanese in Hawaii are not interned).

President Roosevelt creates the National Wage Labor Board to adjudicate in wage disputes in the USA (Jan).

Office of Civilian Defense is created in USA to organize the civilian contribution to defence.

In USA, the Works Progress Administration, a 'New Deal' public works and relief agency, is wound up (4 Dec).

During the war, US women are recruited on a large scale for the war effort; between 1942 and 1945 the number of working women increases by 50 per cent.

Oklahoma is the last state in the USA to remove bar on women holding the senior offices of state (governor, lieutenant governor, and attorney general).

In Japan, community councils and neighbourhood associations are ordered to take over the organization of food and clothing rations (Oct).

William Beveridge, *Social Security and Allied Services* (the 'Beveridge Plan', published in Dec).

King George VI of Britain awards the George Cross to the people of Malta for their endurance of German bombardment (15 April).

Foundation in Oxford, England (31 July), of the Oxford Committee for Famine Relief (later 'Oxfam').

Women's Auxiliary Army Corps founded in USA (14 May).

Uthwatt Report rejects land nationalization in Britain in favour of controlled land use, development, and town planning.

C S Lewis, *The Screwtape Letters.*

In England, William Temple is appointed as Archbishop of Canterbury and publishes *Christianity and the Social Order.*

Inauguration of the British Council of Churches with service in St Paul's Cathedral, London (preacher, Archbishop Temple).

Q Science, Technology, and Discovery

First launch of the V2 rocket in Germany.

Flight of the first jet fighter, the German Messerschmidt Me 262 (July).

In USA, magnetic tape is invented.

Enrico Fermi at Chicago, USA, initiates a controlled chain-reaction in the first nuclear reactor (2 Dec).

Pure uranium produced in USA for use in atomic bomb.

American scientists develop ENIAC, the first electronic computer.

In Canada, H R Griffith and E Johnson use curare as a muscle relaxant during surgery.

R Humanities

Discovery, near the Mildenhall airbase in E England, of the Mildenhall Treasure, a collection of silver tableware and other objects (now in the British Museum, London).

V Gordon Childe, *What Happened in History.*

G M Trevelyan, *English Social History.*

M L Campbell, *The English Yeoman under Elizabeth and the Early Stuarts.*

Avery Craven, *The Coming of the Civil War.*

Paul Henry Lang, *Music in Western Civilisation.*

R G Collingwood, *The New Leviathan.*

Susanne Langer, *Philosophy in a New Key.*

Hans Reichenbach, *Philosophy Foundations of Quantum Mechanics.*

S Art, Sculpture, Fine Arts, and Architecture

'Artists Aid Russia' Exhibition at Hertford House, London.

Painting, etc:

Piet Mondrian, *Broadway Boogie-Woogie* (–1943).

Pablo Picasso, *Woman with a Hat in the Shape of a Fish.*

Yves Tanguy, *Infinite Divisibility.*

Sculpture:

Jean Fautrier, *Great Tragic Head.*

G July

Georgi Zhukov replaces Timoshenko as commander of the Soviet southern armies.

1 (–3) debate in British House of Commons on motion of no confidence 'in the central direction of the war'; defeated by 25–476.

7 in Pacific, Japanese troops spreading through the Solomon Islands land on the island of Guadalcanal.

21 (–22 Jan 1943) in Pacific, Japanese troops land on New Guinea and move towards the capital of Papua, Port Moresby.

26 British air force raids Hamburg.

27 in London, 60,000 people demonstrate in Trafalgar Square demanding the opening of a Second Front in Europe, to take pressure off the German–Soviet Front.

28 in USSR, Germans take Rostov and over-run the northern Caucasus.

H August

7 in Pacific, US troops capture an airfield (named Henderson Airfield) on the island of Guadalcanal and hold it against a series of Japanese counterattacks (–7 Feb 1943); the US success at Guadalcanal turns the Japanese tide.

8 in India, the Congress Party passes a motion calling upon the British to 'quit India' immediately; civil disorder follows in the autumn.

12 (–15) in USSR, Averell Harriman for the USA and Winston Churchill for Britain confer with Joseph Stalin in Moscow.

19 Canadian and British force raid Dieppe in NE France; casualties include 3,500 Canadians.

19 General Bernard Montgomery is appointed commander of Britain's 8th Army, in N Africa.

J September

13 (–2 Feb 1943) in USSR, Battle of Stalingrad: Germans try to capture the city of Stalingrad (now Volgograd) on the River Volga against determined Soviet resistance.

K October

US National Labour Service Act.

23 (–4 Nov) in N Africa, (second) Battle of El Alamein: British forces in Egypt under General Bernard Montgomery attack the Axis forces under Rommel.

L November

4 in N Africa, Axis forces under Rommel retreat westwards, pursued by the British.

7 (–8) in N Africa, Operation Torch: Allied troops under command of US General Dwight D Eisenhower land in Morocco and Algeria.

11 Adolf Hitler orders the German occupation of Vichy France.

11 General Dwight Eisenhower recognizes Admiral François Darlan as French chief of state in N Africa, arousing British indignation.

13 British forces in NE Libya retake Tobruk.

18 in USSR, the German drive into the Caucasus reaches its furthest extent; Soviet resistance forces the Germans to withdraw, isolating the army attacking Stalingrad.

19 in USSR, Soviet counteroffensive at Stalingrad surrounds besieging German army.

22 in Britain, Sir Stafford Cripps leaves the war cabinet and is replaced by Herbert Morrison (Labour, home secretary).

M December

12 (–23) in USSR, German troops under General Erich von Manstein attempt to relieve the trapped German army at Stalingrad.

16 (–20) in USSR, Soviet troops rout Italians on the River Don.

19 British and Indian troops begin advance in Burma (Myanmar).

21 in N Africa, British reoccupy Benghazi in Libya.

24 Admiral François Darlan, chief of state in French N Africa, is assassinated in Algiers.

31 British Royal Navy beats off massive German air attack on convoy to Russia.

Architecture:

Oscar Niemeyer, Casino, club, and Church of St Francis, Pampulha, Belo Horizonte, Brazil (–1943).

Frank Lloyd Wright, design for the new Guggenheim Museum, New York.

T Music

John Cage, *The Wonderful Widow of Eighteen Springs*.

Alfredo Casella, *Paganiniana*.

Aaron Copland, *Lincoln Portrait*, *Rodeo* (ballet).

Aram Khachaturian, *Gayaneh* (ballet).

Sergei Prokofiev writes score for Sergei Eisenstein's film *Ivan the Terrible* (–1945).

Arnold Schoenberg, *Piano Concerto*.

Dmitry Shostakovich, Symphony No. 7 ('Leningrad').

Richard Strauss, *Capriccio* (opera).

'White Christmas' by Irving Berlin, sung by Bing Crosby, features in the film *Holiday Inn* (and in 1954 in the film *White Christmas*).

Frank Sinatra makes a sensational first stage appearance in New York.

Dooley Wilson sings 'As Times Goes By' in the film *Casablanca*.

The RCA Company presents the Glenn Miller orchestra with a gold record to mark sales of 1.2 million records of 'Chattanooga choo choo' (Feb), probably the first presentation of a 'gold disc' for sales of one million.

Glenn Miller disbands his own band to direct the American Air Force Band.

U Literature and Drama

Albert Camus, *The Outsider*.

T S Eliot, *Little Gidding*.

Camilo José Cela, *Pascal Duarte's Family*.

Patrick Kavanagh, *The Great Hunger*.

John Steinbeck, *The Moon is Down*.

Wallace Stevens, *Notes Towards a Supreme Fiction* (poems).

Eudora Welty, *The Robber Bridegroom*.

Drama:

Maxwell Anderson, *The Eve of St Mark*.

Jean Anouilh, *Antigone*.

Rose Franken, *Claudia*.

Sean O'Casey, *Red Roses For Me*.

Terence Rattigan, *Flare Path*.

Thornton Wilder, *The Skin of our Teeth*.

V Births and Deaths

Jan 8 Stephen Hawking born (–).

Jan 17 Muhammad Ali born (–).

Jan 22 Walter Sickert dies (81).

Jan 31 Derek Jarman born (–1994).

March 12 William Bragg dies (79).

March 28 Neil Kinnock born (–).

Sept 5 Werner Herzog born (–).

Nov 5 George M Cohan dies (64).

Nov 17 Martin Scorsese born (–).

Nov 21 J B M Hertzog dies (76).

Nov 27 Jimi Hendrix born (–1970).

Moamer al Khaddafi born (–).

W Everyday Life

In Britain, the government orders the baking of white bread to stop (order made 11 March, order in force 6 April).

British Budget doubles entertainment tax (14 April).

X Sport and Recreation

Cornelius Warmerdam of the USA establishes a new record for the pole vault of 4.75 m/15 ft 7 in; it remains the highest vault using a bamboo pole (23 May).

Y Media

In Britain, J L Garvin resigns as editor of the *Observer* (28 Feb; editor since 1928).

In New York, the *Evening Post* becomes the tabloid *New York Post*.

Press censorship is introduced in the USA and some publications suppressed.

The US Army sponsors *Yank* magazine (published from 17 June).

Stars and Stripes, a daily paper for US troops in Europe, is published from the office of *The Times* in London (from 2 Nov).

John H Johnson publishes the monthly *Negro Digest* in Chicago, USA.

Film:

Casablanca (starring Ingrid Bergman and Humphrey Bogart).

The Cat People (director, Jacques Tourneur).

Holiday Inn (starring Bing Crosby).

The Magnificent Ambersons (director, Orson Welles).

Mrs Miniver (director, William Wyler; starring Greer Garson).

Ossessione (director, Luchino Visconti).

The Ox-Bow Incident (director, William Wellman).

Woman of the Year (starring Spencer Tracy and Katharine Hepburn).

Radio:

ITMA (*It's That Man Again*), starring Tommy Handley, is broadcast by BBC on 21 April as the first royal command performance of a radio programme.

Germans army surrenders at Stalingrad ... Allies invade Italy ...
Fall of Mussolini ...

A January

2 in USSR, German withdrawal from Caucasus begins.

11 Britain makes treaty with China renouncing British extra-territorial rights in China.

12 (–23) Casablanca Conference: F D Roosevelt and Winston Churchill confer on grand strategy; they agree that Germany and Japan must surrender unconditionally.

18 (–16 June) Japan deploys submarines off the E coast of Australia.

18 German air attack on London renewed.

23 in N Africa, the British, advancing westwards across Libya, enter Tripoli in NW Libya.

24 in USSR, Soviet forces drive the Germans from Voronezh, on the River Don S of Moscow.

31 in USSR, the German commander at Stalingrad, Friedrich von Paulus, and his army surrender to the Red Army.

B February

8 in USSR, Soviet army retakes Kursk from the Germans.

9 in Pacific, organized Japanese resistance to US forces on Guadalcanal comes to an end.

10 in N Africa, the British army advancing westwards through Libya reaches the Tunisian frontier.

10 in Britain, support in Ashford by-election for the Commonwealth Party (a Christian Socialist body founded in July 1942 by the former Liberal Sir Richard Acland MP) indicates dissatisfaction with government's social policy, but Winston Churchill's broadcast on 22 March, advocating four-year plan for post-war reconstruction, retrieves government's popularity.

14 in USSR, Soviet army recaptures Rostov and, on 16, Kharkov.

14 (–24 April) British and Gurkha troops under the command of Orde Wingate, known as the 'Chindits', leave Imphal in India on sabotage mission in Burma behind Japanese lines.

21 King George VI of Britain announces the presentation of a sword of honour to Stalingrad (handed by Winston Churchill to Joseph Stalin at Tehran Conference in Nov).

21 Allied armies in N Africa are placed under US General Dwight Eisenhower's supreme command.

25 following a decision made at the Casablanca Conference in Jan, British and American bombers begin round-the-clock bombing of Germany.

C March

7 (–11) in N Africa, the British repulse heavy Axis counterattacks in Tunisia.

12 Allied conference agrees two-pronged strategy for reconquest of Japanese-occupied territories in the Pacific and SE Asia: a sweep across the C Pacific and campaigns in the SW Pacific Area.

15 in USSR, Germans force Soviet forces to evacuate Kharkov.

20 (–28) in N Africa, British forces advancing westwards attack and break, on 28, the Axis 'Mareth Line' in Tunisia.

D April

British and US bombers make heavy air raids on the Ruhr industrial region in Germany.

6 in N Africa, Axis forces under Rommel retreat north from Gabes Gap in Tunisia, enabling US and British armies to link up on 8.

7 in Britain, the Commonwealth Party wins its first contested seat in the Eddisbury by-election (in Cheshire, NW England).

8 General Rommel leaves N Africa and is replaced by General Hans-Jürgen von Arnim.

12 discovery of the 'Katyn massacre': Germans find the grave of 4,500 Polish officers at Katyn near Smolensk in the USSR; they announce the discovery on 13, claiming the Poles were murdered by the Soviets; Soviet authorities deny this.

19 (–16 May) in Poland, uprising in the Warsaw ghetto.

25 USSR breaks off diplomatic relations with General Wladyslaw Sikorski's London Polish government, claiming that he had falsely blamed the USSR for the Katyn massacre.

E May

1 US coal-miners' strike (settled 3 Nov).

7 in N Africa, Allies take Tunis and Bizerta, while Germans retire to Cap Bon Peninsula.

11 (–29) US force retakes Attu in the Aleutian Islands, N Pacific; on 29 the Japanese evacuate Kiska.

11 (–25) Washington Conference: F D Roosevelt and Winston Churchill meet in the US capital and agree on the next Allies' next steps: invasion of Sicily, invasion of Italy, invasion of N Europe.

13 German Army in Tunisia surrenders.

16 Operation Chastise: British bombers, led by Wing-Commander Guy Gibson, attack

*Danish Jews evacuated to Sweden ... Stenton's Anglo-Saxon
England ... Bernstein's debut with the New York Philharmonic ...*

o **Politics, Government, Law, and Economy**

Harold Laski, *Reflections on the Revolution of Our Times.*

Walter Lippmann, *US Foreign Policy: Shield of the Republic.*

Indian nationalist Subhas Chandra Bose, working with the Japanese, establishes a provisional government of free India and (in July) an Indian National Army (of Indian defectors) which serves with the Japanese against British and Indian troops in Burma.

After the surrender of Italy (Sept), leaders of the former Italian Popular Party found Christian Democracy.

Office of War Mobilization created in USA (May), to coordinate government agencies involved in supplying the war effort by establishing priorities, allocating basic materials, and setting production targets.

The Smith–Connally Act in the USA (June) authorizes the president to seize any plant where a strike threatens to interfere with war-related production.

Ministry of Munitions created in Japan (Nov).

Foundation of the American Enterprise Association (renamed the American Enterprise Institution for Public Policy Research in 1960).

US Congress approves the 'Pay-As-You-Go' scheme whereby employers will deduct income tax from salaries and wages (9 June).

During the war, the US government raises tax rates for both individuals and corporations; income-tax payers increase from 5 per cent of the adult population in 1939 to 74 per cent in 1945.

In USA, in West Virginia Board of Education v. Barnette, the Supreme Court rules that compulsory saluting of the flag is unconstitutional (14 June), reversing the decision in Minersville School District v. Gobitis (1940).

Unemployment in the USA is virtually eliminated and production of war materials reaches staggering levels.

In USA, 'Big inch' oil pipeline from Texas to eastern seaboard is opened.

Compulsory arbitration introduced in British coal industry (1 May).

Introduction in Britain of system of balloting National Service boys to provide extra manpower in coal mines (Dec); in 1944–45, 21,000 ballottees (popularly known as 'Bevin boys', after Ernest Bevin, minister of labour) work in the pits.

Meat rationing introduced in the USA.

P **Society, Education, and Religion**

Severe famine in Bengal.

Worst rice crop for 50 years in Japan leads to privation.

Most Jews in Denmark (about 7,200) are evacuated to Sweden, to save them from deportation to the German death camps (Oct).

United Nations Relief and Rehabilitation Administration (UNRRA) founded in Washington, DC, USA, to provide relief in war-torn countries (relief programmes in Europe continue until 30 June 1947).

Civil conscription of women in Germany (27 Jan).

In Britain, part-time work is made compulsory for women aged 18–45 (3 May).

Women are admitted to membership of the Amalgamated Engineering Union in Britain.

Riots in Detroit, USA, caused by racial tensions (June); the war production boom has resulted in many southerners, whites and African-Americans, migrating north and west to work in industry.

In USA, James Farmer and five other pacifists form the Congress of Racial Equality (CORE) in Chicago, to challenge discrimination against African-Americans using nonviolent direct action.

British–US Conference in Bermuda on European refugee problem (April); results only in the transfer of 21,000 refugees (including 5,000 Jews) from Spain to N Africa.

Albert Hoffman, a Swiss research chemist, discovers the hallucinogenic properties of the drug LSD.

Karl Mannheim, *Diagnosis of Our Time.*

Formation of the Nuffield Foundation in Britain, which the car manufacturer William Morris (Viscount Nuffield) endows with £10 million for medical and social projects.

Barlow Report recommends that British universities should double their output of scientists.

In Britain, Winston Churchill (with support from President Roosevelt) appoints committee to study ways of extending the use of Basic English (devised by C K Ogden, supported by George Bernard Shaw).

In USSR, Stalin meets three patriarchs of the Russian Orthodox Church (4 Sept); it leads

three dams in the Ruhr region of Germany using the spinning or 'bouncing' bombs designed by Barnes Wallis; two dams are breached.

22 in USSR, Joseph Stalin dissolves the Third Communist International or Comintern (formed in 1919).

27 in France, creation of National Resistance Council of political parties, unions, and others under Jean Moulin (21 June, Moulin is betrayed to the Germans and dies on 8 July after torture).

F June

3 French Committee of National Liberation is formed, led by General Charles de Gaulle and General Henri Giraud.

11 the island of Pantelleria, in the Mediterranean between Tunisia and Sicily, surrenders to the Allies after bombardment.

11 agreement on post-war relief signed at end of Hot Springs Conference of 44 countries, held in USA.

G July

US Congress passes anti-strike act over President Roosevelt's veto.

1 (–25 Nov) in SW Pacific, Operation Cartwheel Phase One: US troops recapture important islands in the Solomon Islands.

4 (–20) in USSR, German forces attack the Kursk Salient, a protruding part of the Soviet Front; the attack inaugurates the largest tank battle in history.

4 head of the Polish government-in-exile, General Wladyslaw Sikorski, is killed in air crash at Gibraltar during tour of inspection of Polish troops in Mediterranean.

10 (–17 Aug) in Italy, Operation Husky: US and British troops land in Sicily.

12 (–15) in USSR, N of the Kursk Salient, Soviet forces attack the Orel area of the Front, to increase pressure on the Germans attacking Kursk.

19 first Allied air raid on Rome.

20 Adolf Hitler calls off the German attack on the Kursk Salient in the USSR; the Soviet army breaks out of the salient and pushes back the Germans who, from this point, are incapable of mounting any further offensives on the Eastern Front.

22 in Italy, US troops occupy Sicily's main city, Palermo.

25 in Italy, King Victor Emmanuel III dismisses Benito Mussolini as prime minister and asks Marshal Badoglio to form a government.

H August

1 Burma is declared independent under Japanese 'protection'.

4 in USSR, Soviet army captures Orel.

5 capture of Catania gives Allies command of Sicilian Straits.

12 (–15) Winston Churchill stays with President Roosevelt at his home in Hyde Park, New York State, USA; the leaders agree that their countries will pool atomic research and together develop the atomic bomb in the USA.

14 (–24) Quadrant Conference of Allied leaders in Quebec, Canada; President Roosevelt and Winston Churchill accept plan to defeat Germany before Japan, and to aim for invasions of France in May 1944.

17 in Italy, US troops occupy Messina in Sicily, at the crossing point to the mainland.

22 in USSR, German forces withdraw from Kharkov, S of Kursk.

24 US and Britain grant limited recognition to the French Committee of National Liberation, based in Algiers.

25 in SW Pacific, US troops complete reconquest of New Georgia in the Solomon Islands.

J September

3 Italy surrenders unconditionally (surrender announced by General Dwight Eisenhower on 8).

3 (–20) in Italy, Operation Baytown: British forces advance across the SW Italian mainland, reaching Auletta on 19 and Potenza on 20.

4 (–23 March 1944) in SW Pacific, Operation Cartwheel Phase Two: US and Australia forces invade NE New Guinea.

9 (–19) in Italy, Operation Avalanche: US and British forces land in the Gulf of Salerno; the Germans withdraw to the Gustav Line across the peninsula N of Naples.

9 (–30 Nov) in Italy, Operation Slapstick: British forces land at Taranto on the 'heel' of Italy and advance along the coast towards the German Gustav Line.

10 Germans occupy Rome.

11 (–5 Oct) Free French and French resistance forces liberate Corsica.

12 in Italy, Operation Oak: a small German force frees former prime minister Benito Mussolini from prison in the Abruzzi mountains.

15 Benito Mussolini proclaims the new Italian Social Republic, which is established with its capital at Salò on Lake Garda.

17 British drop Fitzroy Maclean by parachute into Yugoslavia on mission to Tito's headquarters, to coordinate Allied help to Yugoslav partisans.

to a Church–State compact whereby the holy synod is re-established, and churches and seminaries are re-opened; the Archbishop of Moscow is elected Orthodox Patriarch of All Russia.

Papal Encyclical *Divino Afflante Spiritu* sets out the official Roman Catholic approach to biblical scholarship.

Archbishop Suhard of Paris founds worker-priest movement.

Bertrand Griffin is appointed Archbishop of Westminster, London, as successor to Cardinal Arthur Hinsley.

Dom Gregory Dix, *The Shape of the Liturgy*.

Jacques Maritain, *Christianity and Democracy*.

Q Science, Technology, and Discovery
Fully-laden glider is towed across Atlantic from Montreal in 28 hrs.

In Britain, penicillin is successfully applied to treat chronic diseases.

R Humanities
Mortimer Wheeler is appointed Director-General of Antiquities in India; his work in the sub-continent (–1947) includes major excavations at Mohenjo-daro and Harappa, leading centres of the Indus Valley civilization.

F M Stenton, *Anglo–Saxon England* ('Oxford History of England' series).

Medievalia et Humanistica issued.

E M W Tillyard, *The Elizabethan World Picture*.

J M Thompson, *The French Revolution*.

Samuel Flagg Bemis, *The Latin American Policy of the United States*.

Erwin Panofsky, *The Life and Art of Albrecht Dürer*.

Nikolaus Pevsner, *An Outline of European Architecture*.

Eugène Vinaver (ed.), *The Works of Sir Thomas Malory*.

In Britain, the Pilgrim Trust purchases Sir Isaac Newton's library.

Albert Camus, *The Myth of Sisyphus*.

Jean-Paul Sartre, *Being and Nothingness*.

S Art, Sculpture, Fine Arts, and Architecture

Painting, etc:
Jean Dubuffet, *Metro*.
Arshile Gorky, *Waterfall*.
Paul Nash, *Vernal Equinox*.
Jackson Pollock, *Mural*.

Sculpture:
Henry Moore, *Madonna and Child*, Northampton, England.
Pablo Picasso, *Le Crane, Bull's Head*.

T Music
Béla Bartók, *Concerto for Orchestra*.
Benjamin Britten, *Serenade for Tenor, Horn, and Strings*.
Aaron Copland, *Fanfare for the Common Man*.
Morton Gould, *Cowboy Rhapsody*.
Ralph Vaughan Williams, Symphony No. 5.
Leonard Bernstein makes public debut as conductor of the New York Philharmonic Orchestra (14 Nov), deputizing at short notice for Bruno Walter.
New York City Opera founded.
Carmen Jones (musical, adapted from Bizet's *Carmen*), with new libretto by Oscar Hammerstein (first performed at the Broadway Theatre, New York, 2 Dec, featuring African-American cast).
Oklahoma (musical), music by Richard Rodgers and Oscar Hammerstein (first performed at the St James Theatre, New York, 31 March).
In Britain, revue *Sweet and Low*, starring Hermione Gingold (at the Ambassadors Theatre, London, from 10 June).
US jazz pianist Art Tatum founds his famous trio with Slam Stewart and Tiny Grimes (–1956).
US blues singer Muddy Waters starts singing career in Chicago (after being discovered by folk singer Alan Lomax on a plantation in 1941).

U Literature and Drama
Jane Bowles, *Two Serious Ladies*.
Henry Green, *Caught*.
Hermann Hesse, *The Glass Bead Game*.
Henri Michaux, *Exorcismes*.
Ricardo Molinari, *Mundos de la Madrugada* (poems).
Romain Rolland, *Péguy*.
Antoine de Saint-Exupéry, *The Little Prince*.
Denton Welch, *Maiden Voyage*.
New Writing and Daylight, edited by John Lehmann.

Drama:
Bertolt Brecht, *The Good Woman of Sezuan, The Life of Galileo*.
Jean-Paul Sartre, *Les mouches/The Flies*.

V Births and Deaths
Jan 9 R G Collingwood dies (54).
Feb 11 Mary Quant born (–).
March 13 J P Morgan dies (75).
March 28 Sergei Rachmaninov dies (69).
March 29 John Major born (–).
April 30 Beatrice Webb dies (85).
July 4 Wladyslaw Sikorski dies (62).
July 10 Arthur Ashe born (–1993).
Sept 29 Lech Walesa born (–).

20 in Britain, sudden death of Sir Kingsley Wood, the chancellor of the exchequer (succeeded on 24 by Sir John Anderson).

24 in USSR, the Soviet army, moving westwards, crosses the River Dnieper N of Kiev.

25 in USSR, the Soviet army retakes Smolensk.

κ **October**

1 in Italy, British forces advancing from the Gulf of Salerno occupy Naples.

12 Portugal grants Britain facilities in the Azores.

13 the government of Italy, based in Brindisi, declares war on Germany.

14 Japan proclaims the independence of the Philippine Islands.

18 (–30) Moscow Conference of Allied foreign ministers; it decides to establish the European Advisory Council to provide a forum for US, British, and Soviet consultation on the future of Europe.

19 German forces in Italy pull back from the Volturno river.

L **November**

1 in SW Pacific, US force lands on Bougainville in the Solomon Islands (fighting continues until April 1944).

6 in USSR, the Soviet army recaptures Kiev from the Germans.

11 Lord Woolton appointed first British minister for reconstruction, with seat in the war cabinet.

19 release on health grounds of Oswald Mosley, imprisoned since 1940 under Defence Regulations, divides British Labour Party.

23 (–27 and 2–7 Dec) Cairo Conference: F D Roosevelt, Winston Churchill, and Chiang Kai-shek agree measures for defeating Japan.

23 in Pacific, US troops occupy Makin in the Gilbert Islands.

28 (–1 Dec) Tehran Conference: F D Roosevelt and Winston Churchill outline to Joseph Stalin the plan for an invasion of France in 1944.

29 in Yugoslavia, congress of the Anti-Fascist National Liberation Committee held in the Bosnian town of Jajce; its resolves to create a Federal Republic of Yugoslavia with Tito (Josip Broz) as Marshal.

M **December**

12 USSR–Czechoslovak treaty for post-war co-operation.

24 in USSR, the Soviet army, having retaken two-thirds of the territory conquered by the Germans, launch an offensive in the Ukraine (–May 1944).

26 British ships sink the German battle-cruiser *Scharnhorst* in Arctic waters.

Allied armies land in Normandy ... Bomb explodes in Hitler's HQ ... Battle of Leyte Gulf ... Battle of the Bulge ...

A **January**

7 in Britain, the Commonwealth Party wins another parliamentary seat in by-election at Skipton in NE England.

14 in USSR, the Soviet army launches an offensive in the NW, near Leningrad.

17 in Italy, British and US forces attempt to break the Germans' Gustav Line at Monte Cassino.

20 British air force drops 2,300 tons of bombs on Berlin (provoking, on 9 Feb, protests in the House of Lords about the bombing of German cities).

22 in Italy, US and British troops land at Anzio, SE of Rome, in an attempt to outflank the Germans' Gustav Line; the Germans besiege them until late May.

24 General Dwight Eisenhower of the USA is appointed supreme commander of Allied forces in Europe.

27 in USSR, the Soviet army clears German troops from the Leningrad–Moscow railway line, ending the siege of Leningrad.

29 (–25 July) in Pacific, US forces launch a series of offensives, to retake various Pacific islands.

B **February**

In Britain, miners' strike in S Wales (–March 19).

1 (–7) in Pacific, US forces retake Kwajalein atoll from the Japanese in heavy fighting.

15 (–17) in Italy, US and British troops make a second attack on the Germans' Gustav Line at Monte Cassino; the monastery is bombed.

17 (–21) in Pacific, US forces take Eniwetok island from the Japanese.

19 (–26) heaviest German air raids on London since May 1941.

Nov 22 Billie Jean King born (–).

w Everyday Life
Zoot suits become high fashion in USA.

x Sport and Recreation
In England, a match is played at Headingley, Leeds, under Rugby Union rules between Northern Command Rugby League and Northern Command Rugby Union; the Rugby League players win 18–11 (23 Jan).

y Media
In Germany, the *Frankfurter Zeitung* (founded 1855) is ordered to cease publication.

Film:
The Adventures of Baron Münchhausen (director, Josef von Baky).

For Whom the Bell Tolls (director, Sam Wood; starring Gary Cooper and Ingrid Bergman).
The Gentle Sex (directors, Leslie Howard and Maurice Elvey).
I Walked with a Zombie (director, Jacques Tourneur).
Jane Eyre (director, Orson Welles).
Lassie Come Home (starring the male dog Pal in Lassie's screen debut).
The Life and Death of Colonel Blimp (producers, Michael Powell and Emeric Pressburger).
Stage-Door Canteen (starring 48 musicians, entertainers, and others).
Stalingrad: One Day of War.

Radio:
In USA, Edward Noble founds the American Broadcasting Co. (ABC).

The 'GI Bill of Rights' ... Francis Bacon's Three Studies ... *Death of Glenn Miller ...*

o Politics, Government, Law, and Economy
Conference of major powers held at Dumbarton Oaks mansion, Washington, DC, USA, establishes general structure for new international organization, the United Nations (Aug–Oct).

Pay-As-You-Earn system for payment of income tax is introduced in Britain (in force from 10 Feb).

The US Supreme Court, in Smith v. Allwright, rules that whites-only primary elections are unconstitutional, but does not question the fundamental doctrine of 'separate but equal' established in Plessy v. Ferguson 1896.

In England, Alfred Thompson Denning (later Lord Denning) is appointed to the High Court.

Roscoe Pound, *The Task of Law.*

United Nations Monetary and Financial Conference at Bretton Woods, New Hampshire, USA (July), establishes a new world economic order based on fixed exchange rates but not a return to the gold standard; the International Monetary Fund (IMF) and the World Bank are founded to provide liquidity and loans to keep international financial transactions viable.

In Britain, the largest merger yet seen in the history of building societies when the Abbey Road Building Society and the National Building Society merge to form the Abbey National.

J von Neumann and O Morgenstern, *Theory of Games and Economic Behavior.*

The Polish Committee for National Liberation decrees (on 6 Sept) the expropriation of farms with more than 50 ha/123.5 acres of arable or over 100 ha/247 acres; some

20 saboteurs blow up a ferry on Lake Tinnsjo, Norway, carrying Germany's supply of 'heavy water' (used in atomic research).

28 British begin operations in Upper Burma (Myanmar).

c March

6 US bombers begin daylight attacks on Berlin.

10 in Greece, formation of the Greek Provisional National Liberation Committee, comprising resistance groups.

15 in Italy, US and British launch a third attack on Monte Cassino.

17 at the S end of the Soviet Front, the Soviet army crosses the River Dniester.

19 following Germans' discovery of Hungarian negotiations with the Allies, German troops occupy Hungary.

29 (–22 June) in NE India, Battle of Imphal: Japanese troops besiege the city of Imphal in Assam.

d April

During April, Allies drop 81,400 tonnes of bombs on Germany and occupied Europe.

2 at the S end of the Soviet Front, the Soviet army enters Romania.

11 (–18) in USSR, liberation of Crimea (except for Sevastopol).

18 in Britain, the Labour Member of Parliament Aneurin Bevan agitates for annulment of powers conferred on the minister of labour for dealing with strikes.

22 in SW Pacific, US troops land at Aitape and Hollandia, New Guinea; it takes until 5 Aug to defeat the Japanese occupiers.

e May

1 (–16) conference of British Dominion premiers held in London.

1 Spain makes agreement with Britain to reduce Spain's exports of the ore wolfram to Germany.

11 (–18) in Italy, Allied forces make a fourth attack on the Gustav Line at Monte Cassino and break through; Poles storm the monastery on 18; the German defeat enables troops at Anzio to break out.

11 in USSR, Germans withdraw from Sebastopol.

21 plebiscite in Iceland confirms parliament's vote to cancel Act of Union with Denmark (republic inaugurated 17 June).

f June

3 the French Committee of National Liberation (in Algiers) renames itself the Provisional Government of the French Republic.

4 in Italy, Allied forces enter Rome.

6 'D-Day', the start of Operation Overlord: Allied forces surprise the Germans with landings on five beaches in Normandy, NW France; the beachheads are joined on 12.

10 USSR starts offensive against Finland.

10 in W France, massacre at Oradour-sur-Glane: German SS detachment burns 642 villagers alive in their parish church in revenge for a French Resistance raid elsewhere.

13 (–30) in NW France, US troops take the Cotentin Peninsula, capturing Cherbourg on 27.

13 first German V1 flying-bombs launched from mainland Europe against Britain (fired intermittently until end of March 1945).

15 (–13 July) in Pacific, US forces capture Saipan island in the Marianas.

22 in USSR, the Soviet army launches Operation Bagration, an offensive in the central part of the Front (–23 Aug).

26 in USSR, the Soviet army enters Vitebsk, W of Moscow.

g July

3 in USSR, the Soviet army takes Minsk, capturing over 150,000 Germans.

4 the Soviet army crosses the 1939 Polish–USSR border.

9 in NW France, Allies capture Caen.

18 in Japan, following the loss of Saipan, General Tojo is forced to resign as prime minister; succeeded by Kuniaki Koiso.

20 in E Prussia, Germany, attempt to assassinate Adolf Hitler: a bomb explodes near Hitler in his eastern headquarters at Rastenburg, but fails to kill him; the man who placed the bomb, Count Claus von Stauffenberg, is shot the same evening and in the following months 5,000 people are executed for complicity.

22 the Soviet army reaches Lublin in Poland, where the Polish Committee for National Liberation is established and declares itself the executive authority in Poland; Joseph Stalin recognizes the Committee.

28 in Poland, the Soviet army takes Brest-Litovsk.

h August

1 (–2 Oct) the Warsaw Rising: Poles in Warsaw rebel against the German occupiers, but the Soviet army does nothing to help and forbids supplies from the West.

14 in S France, start of Operation Dragoon: Allies land on the coast between Toulon

expropriated land is passed to smallholders and agricultural workers, while some estates are turned into state farms; forests are nationalized.

P **Society, Education, and Religion**

Following the German occupation of Hungary, Hungarian Jews are rounded up and sent to extermination camps; about 400,000 are gassed.

In USA, the Servicemen's Readjustment Act, popularly known as the 'GI Bill of Rights', gives assistance to members of the armed services returning to civilian life through education grants and low-cost housing loans (signed 22 June).

In France, the Provisional Government enfranchises women and allows them to sit in parliament.

The statutes of the Royal Society in London are amended to permit the admission of women as fellows.

In USA, the War Department revokes the order of 1942 excluding Japanese-Americans from the Pacific Coast (17 Dec); the following day the Supreme Court, in Korematsu v. US, upholds the evacuation but rules, Ex parte Endo, that the federal government had no right to detain 'concededly loyal' citizens.

Adam Clayton Powell, Jr, is elected as New York's first African-American congressman.

In USSR, Stalin takes revenge on ethnic groups that collaborated with the German invaders, involving mass deportations and removal of local autonomy; the Volga Autonomous German Republic is abolished.

William Beveridge, *Full Employment in a Free Society.*

Friedrich von Hayek, *The Road to Serfdom.*

E Huxley and M Perham, *Race Relations.*

Lewis Mumford, *The Condition of Man.*

Gunnar Myrdal, *An American Dilemma: The Negro Problem and Modern Democracy.*

In England and Wales, the 'Butler' Education Act (named after R A Butler, president of the Board of Education) raises the Board's status to that of ministry; it divides education into primary, secondary, and further stages (following the Norwood Report of 1943); introduces the 'eleven plus' exam; provides for the raising of the school-leaving age to 15 (and 16 as soon as possible); makes religious education and worship compulsory in schools; reduces the number of local education authorities from 315 to 146 and makes them responsible for education of the handicapped and regular medical inspection of children.

McNair Report recommends longer training for teachers in England and Wales, a wider field of recruitment, and salary increases.

Fleming Report on independent schools in Britain advocates closer links between such schools and the state education sector.

Brother Roger Schutz founds ecumenical monastic community at Taize, near Cluny, France.

C G Jung, *Psychology and Religion.*

Vladimir Lossky, *The Mystical Theology of the Eastern Church.*

William Temple, *The Church Looks Forward.*

Q **Science, Technology, and Discovery**

First non-stop flight London–Canada (8 Sept).

Second uranium pile built at Clinton, Tennessee, USA, for manufacturing plutonium for an atomic bomb.

New cyclotron of Department of Terrestrial Magnetism, Carnegie Institution, Washington, USA, completed.

Quinine is synthesized in USA by R B Woodward and W von E Doering.

In USA, Selman A Waksman publishes description of the antibiotic streptomycin, which is used as a treatment for tuberculosis.

In USA, Alfred Blalock successfully operates on 'blue babies'.

Kidney machine invented by W J Kolff in occupied Netherlands

R **Humanities**

Discovery in a peat bog near Viborg, Denmark, of the well-preserved body of man who died by hanging in the 1st century BC (the so-called Tollund man).

J H Clapham, *The Bank of England: A History.*

B H Sumner, *Survey of Russian History.*

Eric Eustace Williams, *Capitalism and Slavery.*

Morris R Cohen, *Preface to Logic.*

Charles Stevenson, *Ethics and Language.*

S **Art, Sculpture, Fine Arts, and Architecture**

In Paris, following Liberation, the Salon d'Automne is named Salon de la Libération, with a special gallery for Picasso's works (first official recognition accorded to him by the French).

Painting, etc:

Francis Bacon, *Three Studies for Figures at the Base of a Crucifixion.*

Jean Bazaine, *Mass of the Armed Man/La Messe de l'homme armé).*

Jean Dubuffet, *Vue de Paris — Le Petit Commerce.*

Francis Gruber, *Job.*

and Cannes and push 32 km/20 mi inland on the first day.

16 in NW France, British troops capture Falaise; to the south is a large German force, in the 'Falaise Gap', threatened by the advance of British troops from the N and US troops from the S.

19 in Italy, British troops take Florence.

20 in NW France, US troops cross the River Seine at Mantes.

21 in NW France, Allied troops seal the 'Falaise Gap': some 50,000 Germans have been captured, but about 20,000 have escaped.

23 in Romania, a coup led by King Michael overthrows the pro-German government of Ion Antonescu and seeks an armistice with the Allies.

24 in France, a French armoured unit enters Paris; Charles de Gaulle arrives on 25, and on 26 organizes a procession along the Champs Elysées (on 28, the Provisional Government is transferred from Algiers to Paris).

31 Soviet army enters Bucharest, capital of Romania.

J September

1 in Yugoslavia, the British air force and Yugoslav partisans launch Operation Ratweek, attacks on roads and railways intended to prevent Germans withdrawing from Yugoslavia.

3 in Belgium, British troops enter Brussels.

4 Allies capture Antwerp in Belgium and destroy flying-bomb sites in Pas de Calais, France.

4 cease-fire between Finns and Soviet forces on Finnish front.

5 USSR declares war on Bulgaria; Bulgaria declares war on Germany and requests armistice with USSR.

8 Germans fire first V2 rockets at Britain.

10 (–17) Octagon Conference: F D Roosevelt and Winston Churchill meet in Quebec, Canada; they approve plans for the Allied advance into Germany, for the establishment of zones of occupation after Germany's defeat, and for the de-industrialization of Germany as proposed by the 'Morgenthau Plan'.

10 in France, the Provisional Government abolishes the Vichy legislature.

10 US troops enter the Duchy of Luxembourg.

11 US troops cross from Luxembourg into Germany near Trier.

12 Romania signs armistice with USSR, USA, and Britain.

17 (–28) in the Netherlands, Operation Market Garden: US airborne troops land at Eindhoven and Nijmegen, to seize bridges over

the Rivers Maas and Waal, and British troops at Arnhem on the Rhine, in an attempt to open a route to the Ruhr; German opposition makes the Arnhem operation a disaster.

19 Finns signs armistice with the USSR.

24 in France, decree integrates the Resistance into the French army.

25 in Germany, Adolf Hitler calls up all remaining males between 16 and 60 for service .in the Volksturm, a home defence force.

28 in N France, Canadians liberate Calais.

29 Soviet army invades Yugoslavia.

K October

2 in Poland, end of the Warsaw Rising: the insurgent Poles surrender to the Germans; many are deported and the city is destroyed; the German victory has eliminated many Poles loyal to the London Polish government, thereby strengthening Stalin's hand in Poland.

4 British troops land in Greece.

6 Soviet army enters Hungary.

8 in Egypt, King Farouk dismisses the Wafd government led by Nahas Pasha.

9 (–18) Moscow Conference: Winston Churchill and Averell Harriman for the USA visit Joseph Stalin in Moscow to discuss military plans.

14 in Greece, British troops liberate Athens from the Germans.

14 in Germany, Field Marshal Erwin Rommel commits suicide, under threat of trial for participation in the bomb plot of 20 July.

17 (–25) in Pacific, Battle of Leyte Gulf in the Philippines: the greatest naval battle in history, in which US ships destroy the Japanese fleet (Japanese losses include four carriers, three battleships, ten cruisers, and nine destroyers); on 25, the Japanese use 'Kamikazes' (bomb-carrying aircraft flown against the enemy by suicide pilots).

17 in Hungary, German troops occupy Buda and arrest Admiral Horthy.

18 Soviet army enters Czechoslovakia.

20 (–31 Dec) US troops retake the island of Leyte in the Philippines.

20 in Yugoslavia, Russians and Yugoslavs enter Belgrade.

22 USA, USSR, and Britain recognize General Charles de Gaulle's Provisional Government of France.

25 General Douglas MacArthur returns to the Philippines.

28 new government in Bulgaria signs armistice with Allies.

30 Soviet army attacks Budapest, Hungary, but the Germans hold the city until Feb 1945.

Willem de Kooning, *Pink Lady*.
Clifford Still, *No. 1*.

Sculpture:
Barbara Hepworth, *Wood and Strings*.
Pablo Picasso, *L'Homme à l'agneau*.

T Music

Leonard Bernstein, *Jeremiah Symphony*.
Aaron Copland, *Appalachian Spring* (ballet).
Roy Harris, *Gettysburg Address Symphony*.
Sergei Prokofiev, Symphony No. 5.
Richard Strauss, *Die Liebe der Danae* (opera).
Michael Tippett, *A Child of Our Time*.
Viktor Ullman, *Der Kaiser von Atlantis* (opera).
In London, Sir Henry Wood conducts his last Promenade Concert.
On the Town (musical), text by Betty Comden and Adolph Green, music by Leonard Bernstein (first performed at the Adelphi Theatre, New York, 28 Dec).
In Britain, revue *Sweeter and Lower*, with music by Charles Zwar and Geoffrey Wright, starring Hermione Gingold (at Ambassadors Theatre, London, from 17 Feb).
First jazz concert to be given at the New York Metropolitan Opera House (17 Jan).
In Britain, Ted Heath founds the Ted Heath Band (first tour of USA, 1956).
Dizzy Gillespie, 'Groovin' High'.
Death of band leader Glenn Miller in air crash (16 Dec).
US jazz promoter Norman Granz stages a jazz concert at the Philharmonic Hall, Los Angeles, the first in the series 'Jazz At The Philharmonic' (which continues in various cities until 1967).
In USA, Capitol Records starts recording in Nashville, Tennessee (studios built, 1950).

U Literature and Drama

H E Bates, *Fair Stood the Wind for France*.
Jorge Luis Borges, *Fictions*.
Joyce Cary, *The Horse's Mouth*.
Alex Comfort, *The Power House*.
Ivy Compton-Burnett, *Elders and Betters*.
Cyril Connolly, *The Unquiet Grave*.
T S Eliot, *Four Quartets* (poems).
Aldous Huxley, *Time Must Have a Stop*.
Rosamund Lehmann, *The Ballad and the Source*.
Somerset Maugham, *The Razor's Edge*.
Alberto Moravia, *Agustino*.
Karl Shapiro, *V-Letter and Other Poems*.
Christina Stead, *For Love Alone*.

Drama:
Terence Rattigan, *Love in Idleness*, *The Winslow Boy*.

Jean-Paul Sartre, *In Camera*.
Tennessee Williams, *The Glass Menagerie*.

V Births and Deaths

Jan 1 Edwin Lutyens dies (75).
Jan 18 Paul Keating born (–).
Jan 23 Edvard Munch dies (80).
Jan 28 John Tavener born (–).
March 28 Stephen Leacock dies (74).
May 9 Ethel Smyth dies (86).
May 12 Arthur Quiller-Couch ('Q') dies (80).
June 16 Marc Bloch dies (57).
Aug 19 Henry Wood dies (75).
Sept 13 Heath Robinson dies (72).
Oct 26 William Temple dies (63).
Nov 7 Geoffrey Dawson dies (70).
Nov 22 Arthur Stanley Eddington dies (61).
Dec 13 Wassily Kandinsky dies (77).

W Everyday Life

In USSR, the 'Internationale' is replaced as the national anthem by a patriotic song.

X Sport and Recreation

The 13th Olympic Games, scheduled for London, are cancelled due to the War.

Y Media

Only four prewar national French newspapers are allowed to resume publication, because they refused to collaborate during the war.
In France, the news agency Agence France-Presse is established, taking over assets of the older Havas agency.
The Times newspaper of Britain publishes an 'Air Edition' on India paper (from 1 Aug).
Al-Akhbar newspaper published in Cairo, Egypt.
Publication in USA of *Seventeen*, a magazine aimed at teenage girls.

Film:
Arsenic and Old Lace (director, Frank Capra).
Double Indemnity (director, Billy Wilder).
Henry V (director and star, Laurence Olivier).
Ivan the Terrible, Part 1; Part 2, 1946 (director, Sergei Eisenstein).
Lifeboat (director, Alfred Hitchcock).
The Miracle of Morgan's Creek (director, Preston Sturges).
This Happy Breed (director, David Lean).
To Have and Have Not (director, Howard Hawks).
The Way Ahead (director, Carol Reed).
The White Cliffs of Dover (director, Clarence Brown).

L **November**

3 the Allies reopen the port of Antwerp, Belgium, to shipping.

7 F D Roosevelt, Democrat, wins US Presidential election, for a fourth term, with 432 electoral votes over Thomas E Dewey, Republican, with 99; popular vote: Roosevelt, 25,602,504; Dewey, 21,969,170; Dewey fails to carry his own state of New York.

11 end of liberation of Greece from the Germans, but the resistance organization, the National People's Liberation Army (known as ELAS and part of the Communist-controlled National Liberation Front or EAM), refuses to demobilize; ELAS rebels seize part of Athens and Piraeus.

12 British bombers sink the Germany's last battleship, the *Tirpitz*, in Tromsö Fjord, Norway, enabling Britain's large ships to be released for service in the Pacific War.

24 in France, Allies capture Strasbourg.

24 in Pacific, B-29 bombers from Saipan make the first US bombing raid on Tokyo since the Doolittle raid of April 1942; bombing raids on Japan continue into 1945.

27 following Cordell Hull's resignation as US secretary of state (because of ill health), Edward Stettinius is appointed.

M **December**

3 police action against National Liberation Front demonstrations in Athens raises criticisms of British policy in Greece; to restore confidence Winston Churchill visits Athens (24).

5 in Italy, Allies take Ravenna.

16 in the Ardennes (Luxembourg and Belgium), the German army launches an offensive, aiming to reach the Meuse at Namur (the 'Battle of the Bulge', –28 Jan 1945).

18 North Burma (Myanmar) is cleared of Japanese.

22 in Hungary, a Provisional Government, based at Debrecen, is formed under Soviet supervision; the prime minister is General Béla Miklós.

Death of President Roosevelt ... Germany surrenders ... USA drops atomic bombs on Japan ... Japan surrenders ...

A **January**

1 (–3) in Pacific, US forces capture the island of Mindoro in the Philippines.

1 British army opens new offensive in Burma (Myanmar).

1 in Poland, the Lublin Committee proclaims itself Poland's Provisional Government (5, recognized by USSR, thereby excluding the London-based Polish government).

6 (–8) in Pacific, US fleet fights its way into Lingayen Gulf, at the NW end of Luzon in the Philippines.

8 general election in Egypt, boycotted by the Wafd nationalists, results in majority for Ahmed Pasha, the prime minister.

11 Communists agree to truce in Greek civil war.

12 in Poland, the Soviet army launches an offensive from the River Vistula, aiming to reach the River Oder and press towards Berlin (–early Feb).

14 in the 'Battle of the Bulge' in Belgium, US forces reach Bastogne, rescuing US soldiers who had been trapped there by the German offensive.

17 in Poland, the Soviet army takes Warsaw; on 19, captures Kraków; on 23, Tilsit (now Sovetsk in Russia).

18 German forces in Budapest surrender to the Soviet army.

20 provisional Hungarian government at Debrecen under General Miklós concludes armistice with Allies.

22 near Oppeln in Germany (now Opole in Poland), first crossing of the River Oder by Soviet troops.

27 Soviet forces liberate the Auschwitz death camp in Poland.

B **February**

3 in Philippines, US troops besiege Manila; falls on 3 March.

4 (–11) F D Roosevelt, Winston Churchill, and Joseph Stalin confer at Yalta (in Russia in the Crimea) to plan for Germany's unconditional surrender (and division of the country into four zones of occupation, with four zones in Berlin), to settle the Polish question, and to make arrangements for the first United Nations conference at San Francisco, USA; Stalin agrees that the

Foundation of Arab League ... Germans and Magyars expelled from Czechoslovakia ... A J P Taylor's Course of German History ...

O Politics, Government, Law, and Economy

League of Arab States ('Arab League') founded by a treaty signed at Cairo (22 March).

D W Brogan, *The Free State*.

The USSR establishes five Länder (states) in its zone of Germany (July).

Christian Democrat parties are founded in the zones of occupied Germany.

In Bulgaria, members of the wartime administration are tried; 2,680 are sentenced to death, 6,870 to imprisonment; leading government members are all executed.

The International Military Tribunal, sitting at Nuremberg, to judge crimes against peace, war crimes, and crimes against humanity, rules that an individual's obedience to orders is an insufficient defence for having committed such acts.

In USA, strikes from Nov (–March 1946) hamper production.

French government nationalizes the Bank of France and other private banks, Air France, and the Renault car company.

In the Soviet zone of Germany, all banks are closed on 26 July and inhabitants are ordered to hand over gold and silver currency, foreign bank notes, and valuables; the Soviet authorities remove factories and railway lines to the USSR as reparations.

In Czechoslovakia, decrees nationalize key industries and banking (24 Oct), implementing part of the Košice Programme.

In Poland, a Central Planning Office is established (10 Nov; becomes the State Planning Commission in 1949).

By the Washington Loan Agreements, the USA makes loan to Britain of $3.75 billion (6 Dec).

End of rationing of petrol and fuel oil in USA (15 Aug).

P Society, Education, and Religion

In Australia, the Re-establishment and Employment Act (June) provides for the demobilization of armed forces and war workers; training in 400 trades is provided by the Commonwealth Reconstruction Training scheme.

In Czechoslovakia, as part of the Košice

USSR will enter the war against Japan after the defeat of Germany and receive an occupation zone in Korea (Korea will be divided into two, along the 38th parallel).

4 in Pacific, US bombers make an 'experimental' low-level attack on Kobe, Japan, using incendiary bombs; their success leads to similar attacks on other Japanese cities on an increasingly large scale.

8 opening of the Allies' Rhineland campaign (–21 March) with 'Operation Veritable': Canadians begin a drive S from Nijmegen in the Netherlands to capture land between the Rivers Rhine and Maas and so clear German troops from the W bank of the Upper Rhine.

13 (–15) Allies bomb Dresden in eastern Germany, to prevent the transfer of German troops to the Soviet Front; at least 60,000 are killed and the city's historic centre is destroyed.

19 (–24 March) in Pacific, US marines capture the Japanese island of Iwo Jima after fierce fighting which results in 27,499 US casualties.

24 Ahmed Pasha, prime minister of Egypt, is assassinated after announcing Egypt's declaration of war against Germany.

c March

2 at Soviet insistence, Petru Groza is appointed prime minister of Romania and forms a pro-Soviet government.

7 in Germany, US troops find the Ludendorff railway bridge at Remagen, S of Bonn, intact and capture it; by evening 100 US troops have crossed the Rhine (the Allies build six bridges across the Rhine in the next fortnight; the Remagen bridge collapses on 17 March).

20 in Burma (Myanmar), British and Indian troops enter Mandalay.

22 US troops in Germany cross the River Rhine at Nierstein and Oppenheim, 32 km/20 mi W of Frankfurt, and secure bridgeheads.

23 British and Canadian troops in Germany cross the River Rhine at Rees and Wesel (near the German–Netherlands border).

25 in Germany, US troops break out of their Rhine bridgeheads to the S of the Ruhr industrial region (28, British forces in the northern part of the Rhineland also break out of their bridgeheads).

29 Soviet army crosses into Austria.

30 Soviet army captures Danzig (now Gdansk in Poland).

d April

1 (–22 June) in Pacific, US forces capture Okinawa, the largest of the Japanese Ryu-

kyu islands (total US casualties are about 49,000, the heaviest US toll for an action in the Pacific war; the Japanese lose about 110,000).

2 (–end April) in Italy, Allied offensive across northern Italy (under command of General Alexander).

3 President Eduard Beneš of Czechoslovakia, after returning to the country from London via Moscow and now based at Košice, appoints a Provisional Government with Socialist Zdenek Fierlinger as prime minister, Jan Masaryk as foreign minister, and Communist Václav Nosek as interior minister; the 'Košice Programme' envisages a socialist and national state.

5 USSR denounces neutrality pact with Japan of 13 April 1941.

10 in northern Germany, US troops take Hanover, but Germans resist attack on Bremen.

11 in Germany, US troops reach the River Elbe, near Wittenberge, 120 km/75 mi NW of Berlin.

12 in USA, President Roosevelt dies (aged 63) and is succeeded by Vice-President Harry S Truman.

13 Soviet army takes Vienna and establishes a Provisional Government of Social Democrats, Social Christians, and Communists with Karl Renner as prime minister.

16 in Germany, Soviet army launches offensive from its bridgehead on the River Oder, aiming to capture Berlin.

25 US and Soviet troops meet at Leckwitz, near Stehla, and at Torgau on the River Elbe.

25 (–26 June) founding conference of the United Nations held in San Francisco, California, USA; at the conclusion, 51 countries sign the UN Charter.

28 in Italy, Benito Mussolini, his mistress Clara Petacci, and members of his entourage are shot by partisans (the bodies of Mussolini and Petacci are displayed in Milan the following day).

29 surrender of German army on Italian front.

29 in Germany, Adolf Hitler marries his mistress, Eva Braun, in their Berlin bunker.

30 in Germany, Adolf Hitler shoots himself in his bunker in Berlin; Eva Braun takes poison (1 May, Admiral Doenitz announces Hitler's death and declares himself Hitler's successor).

e May

2 Berlin surrenders to Soviet army.

2 in Germany, British forces reach Lübeck, to the SE of the Jutland peninsula, aiming to prevent Soviet occupation of Denmark.

4 in Burma (Myanmar), Rangoon (Yangon) is captured from the Japanese.

Programme, a decree (18 June) orders the expulsion of all Germans and Magyars who had not been anti-Fascists (most leave by the end of 1946).

In Hungary, large estates are expropriated (most of the land is converted into state farms).

In the Soviet zone of Germany, the Communist secretary for agriculture, Erwin Hörnle, organizes the break-up of large estates and their transfer to smallholders (Sept–Dec).

Introduction of Family Allowance in Britain, a state payment to mothers.

First woman Metropolitan Police Magistrate appointed in Britain, Miss Sybil Campbell (4 April).

Founding of the Medal of Freedom in USA, to reward outstanding civilian endeavour.

Karl Popper, *The Open Society and Its Enemies.*

World Trade Union Conference held in London (opens 6 Feb), organized by British Trades Union Congress and attended by representatives from Allied and neutral countries.

Publication in Britain of the *Greater London Plan, 1944* (the Abercrombie Report, named after its author Sir Leslie Abercrombie); it envisages post-war London as a set of concentric circles with different economic activities and population densities.

Foundation of the United Nations Educational, Scientific, and Cultural Organization (UNESCO).

In Britain, abolition of fees in state-maintained secondary schools.

Percy Report advocates an increase in the provision of higher technological education in Britain.

In Germany, the leading anti-Nazi Pastor Dietrich Bonhoeffer (in prison since 5 April 1943) is hanged (9 April).

In England, following the death of Archbishop Temple in Oct 1944, Geoffrey Fisher is appointed Archbishop of Canterbury (enthroned on 19 April).

Collection of Coptic Gnostic manuscripts discovered at Nag Hammadi, Egypt.

Occupation authority in Japan order the disestablishment of State Shinto (state rites conducted by the emperor); replaced by Shrine Shinto (private practices of the imperial family); on 31 Dec, Emperor Hirohito broadcasts repudiation of divinity on radio.

Martin Buber, *For the Sake of Heaven.*

C J Webb, *Religious Experience.*

Q Science, Technology, and Discovery

First atomic explosion (16 July), in the New Mexico desert, USA, reveals the discovery of releasing and controlling atomic energy.

Britain establishes Atomic Research Centre at Harwell, Berkshire.

British scientist Henry Dale pleads for the abolition of secrecy in science.

Hungarian scientist Lajos Jánossy investigates cosmic radiation.

Z Bay of Hungary reflects radar signals from the Moon.

Synthesis of Vitamin A.

R Humanities

E W Tristram, *English Medieval Wall-Painting.*

A J P Taylor, *The Course of German History: A Survey of the Development of Germany since 1815.*

Arthur M Schlesinger, Jr, *The Age of Jackson.*

James G Randall, *Lincoln the President* (4 volumes; –1955).

Ruth Benedict, *The Chrysanthemum and the Sword.*

Maurice Merleau-Ponty, *Phenomenology of Perception.*

S Art, Sculpture, Fine Arts, and Architecture

Painting, etc:

Balthus, *Les Beaux Jours.*

Willem de Kooning, *Pink Angels.*

Jean Dubuffet, *Wall with Inscriptions.*

Jean Fautrier exhibits *Otages/Hostages,* paintings done during the Occupation of Paris.

Pablo Picasso, *The Charnel House.*

Graham Sutherland, *Thorn Trees.*

Boris Taslitsky, *The Small Camp at Buchenwald.*

Wols, *Drunken Boat.*

Sculpture:

Alexander Calder, *Red Pyramid* (mobile).

Henry Moore, *Family Group.*

Architecture:

Charles Eames, Eames House, Santa Monica, California, USA (–1949), a prefabricated building based on doors and windows ordered from a mail-order catalogue.

Ludwig Mies van der Rohe, Farnsworth House, Illinois, USA (–1950).

T Music

Béla Bartók, Piano Concerto No. 3.

Benjamin Britten, *Peter Grimes* (opera).

Paul Creston, Symphony No. 2.

Bohuslav Martinu, Piano Concerto No. 3.

Richard Strauss, *Metamorphosen.*

Arts Council of Great Britain established, to encourage performance in the arts (royal charter, 1946).

7 near Reims in France, in the presence of General Dwight Eisenhower and other Allied officers, General Alfred Jodl signs surrender of Germany (effective from 8 May); the German state will cease to exist and be replaced by the Allies' zones of occupation.

8 'VE' (Victory in Europe) Day in Western Europe and the USA; in Germany, near Berlin, Wilhelm von Keitel and other German military leaders sign surrender document in presence of Marshal Georgi Zhukov of the USSR and other Allied commanders.

9 'VE' Day in USSR.

9 in Czechoslovakia, Germans in Prague surrender to Soviet forces.

25 in Britain, the Coalition government is replaced by a 'Caretaker' Conservative ministry with Winston Churchill remaining prime minister.

F **June**

5 Allied Control Commission proclaims its control of Germany and authority over the definition of Germany's territories and borders.

9 USSR forms the Soviet Military Administration in the eastern part of Germany.

10 José Bustamente becomes president of Peru.

11 Liberals under W L Mackenzie King win Canadian general election (with 125 seats; Conservatives win 67; the Cooperative Commonwealth Federation, 28; other parties, 25).

26 in Eire, Sean O'Kelly becomes president on retirement of Douglas Hyde.

28 after round-table conference in Moscow (from 17 June), a National Unity Government is formed for Poland, comprising 16 ministers from the old Provisional Government and five new ministers; Edward Osobka-Morawski is prime minister.

G **July**

1 Edward Stettinius resigns as US secretary of state (and is appointed US ambassador to the United Nations); succeeded by James F Byrnes.

3 US, British, and French occupy zones in Berlin (in addition to the Soviet zone).

5 in Pacific, General MacArthur announces liberation of the Philippines from the Japanese.

5 the USA and Britain recognize the new government in Poland, withdrawing recognition from the London government-in-exile.

5 death of John Curtin, prime minister of Australia (succeeded on 12 by Joseph Chifley).

17 (–2 Aug) in Germany, Potsdam Conference is held, attended by Joseph Stalin, Harry Truman, Winston Churchill, and Clement Attlee, to organize the occupation of Germany; German land east of the Oder–Neisse is left under Polish jurisdiction; Austria is to be divided into occupation zones.

26 Labour landslide in British general election with 393 seats, against Conservatives with 199, Liberals with 12, and National Liberals with 11; other parties, 25. (On 27, Clement Attlee forms ministry with Ernest Bevin as foreign secretary and Hugh Dalton as chancellor of the exchequer).

H **August**

Following the defeat of Japan, conflict breaks out in China between the Nationalist government (Guomindang) and Communists; the USA attempts to mediate.

6 in Pacific, US plane drops atomic bomb on the Japanese city of Hiroshima.

8 USSR declares war on Japan and invades Manchuria.

9 in Pacific, US plane drops atomic bomb on the Japanese city of Nagasaki.

12 Soviet forces occupy N Korea, Sakhalin, and the Kurile Islands; in Korea they organize the Executive Committee of the Korean People.

13 World Zionist Congress demands admission of 1 million Jews to Palestine.

14 announcement made that the Japanese emperor will formally proclaim Japan's acceptance of the Allies' terms for ending the war; ie, surrender (his recorded message is broadcast on radio at midday on 15).

14 USSR treaty with Nationalist China for recognizing the independence of Outer Mongolia.

15 in France, General Henri Pétain sentenced to death for collaboration with the Germans (commuted to life imprisonment).

16 USSR and Poland sign treaty demarcating new Soviet–Polish frontier.

17 Indonesian leaders proclaim Indonesia's independence, but this is rejected by the Netherlands.

19 the Vietminh enter Hanoi in Vietnam and force Emperor Bao Dai to abdicate.

24 President Harry Truman of USA orders cessation of lend–lease which has cost the USA $48.5 billion.

27 US forces land on the Japanese mainland.

J **September**

2 Japan signs capitulation on board USS *Missouri*; Korea is placed under US and Soviet occupation until a democratic government is established; Outer Mongolia

Carousel (musical), by Richard Rodgers and Oscar Hammerstein (first performed at the Majestic Theatre, New York, 19 April).

Perry Como, 'Till the End of Time'.

In USA, Bluegrass music, based on hillbilly music, becomes popular through performances by Bill Monroe's Bluegrass Boys.

First album sales chart issued in the USA.

u Literature and Drama

Ivo Andric, *The Bridge on the Drina.*

W H Auden, *For the Time Being* (poems).

Stig Dagerman, *The Serpent.*

Robert Frost, *Masque of Reason* (poems).

Henry Green, *Loving.*

John Hersey, *A Bell for Adano.*

Chester Himes, *If He Hollers Let Him Go.*

Pierre Jean Jouve, *La Vierge de Paris.*

Carlo Levi, *Christ Stopped at Eboli.*

George Orwell *Animal Farm.*

Jean-Paul Sartre, *The Age of Reason.*

John Steinbeck, *Cannery Row.*

Evelyn Waugh, *Brideshead Revisited.*

Denton Welch, *In Youth is Pleasure.*

Richard Wright, *Black Boy.*

In France, the Prix Goncourt is awarded to a woman for the first time: to Else Triolet for *Le premier accroc coûte 200 francs.*

v Births and Deaths

Jan 26 Jacqueline du Pré born (–1987).

Feb 1 J B Huizinga dies (72).

March 26 David Lloyd George dies (81).

April 12 F D Roosevelt dies (63).

April 22 Käthe Kollwitz dies (77).

April 28 Benito Mussolini dies (61).

April 30 Adolf Hitler dies (56).

July 19 Heinrich Wölfflin dies (81).

July 20 Paul Valéry dies (74).

Sept 15 Anton Webern dies (61).

Sept 26 Béla Bartók dies (64).

Oct 15 Pierre Laval dies (62).

Dec 4 T H Morgan dies (79).

Dec 21 George S Patton dies (60).

Dec 28 Theodore Dreiser dies (74).

w Everyday Life

Ballpoint pens, based on the Biro design, cause mystification but are a commercial craze when sold in New York.

'Bebop' sweeps the USA.

x Sport and Recreation

Matt Busby is appointed manager of Manchester United soccer club in NW England.

The Moscow Dynamo football team remains unbeaten on a tour of Britain.

y Media

In Germany, the occupying powers publish several newspapers, including *Die Neue Zeitung* in Munich, the *Tägliche Rundschau* in Berlin, and *Die Welt* in Hamburg; these titles continue after the end of the occupation.

In USA, John H Johnson publishes the illustrated monthly magazine *Ebony*, aimed at African-Americans.

Film:

Brief Encounter (director, David Lean; script, Noel Coward).

Les Enfants du Paradis (director, Marcel Carné).

The Lost Week-end (director, Billy Wilder).

Mildred Pearce (starring Joan Crawford).

Rome, Open City (director, Roberto Rossellini).

The Southerner (director, Jean Renoir).

Radio:

In Britain the BBC extends its range of programmes with the establishment of the Home Service and the Light Programme.

Television:

Start of regular television broadcasting in the USA (following delay caused by the War).

is recognized as under Soviet control, while China regains sovereignty over Inner Mongolia and Manchuria, Formosa (modern Taiwan), and Hainan; General MacArthur of USA assumes supreme power in Japan, under directions from the US government.

2 Ho Chi Minh proclaims independent Democratic Republic of Vietnam (the French refuse to recognize the Republic).

6 in S Korea, Communist-influenced Korean nationalists proclaim the Korean People's Republic (8, US troops land in S Korea where they establish a military administration, refusing to recognize the Republic).

10 Vidkun Quisling sentenced to death in Norway for collaboration (executed 24 Oct).

12 the USSR creates a central administration for its zone of Germany, under the chairmanship of Marshal Georgi Zhukov.

20 (–23) All-India Congress Committee under Gandhi and Pandit Nehru rejects British proposals for self-government and calls on Britain to 'quit India'.

23 Egypt demands revision of the 1936 British–Egyptian treaty, the end of military occupation, and the return of the Sudan.

27 in India, the Congress Party and the Muslim League win most seats in elections for Central Legislative Assembly.

к October

7 in Portugal, Prime Minister Salazar permits formation of opposition parties (but, on 14, reimposes press censorship).

9 in France, Pierre Laval sentenced to death for collaboration with Germans (shot on 15 Oct).

11 in China, breakdown of negotiations between Chiang Kai-shek and Communist leader Mao Zedong leads to fighting between Nationalists and Communists in N China for control of Manchuria.

15 Labour and Dominion parties in South Africa withdraw from coalition, leaving J C Smuts prime minister of a United Party government.

20 Egypt, Iraq, Syria, and Lebanon warn USA that creation of a Jewish state in Palestine would lead to war; foundation of Arab League.

21 elections in France show swing to left;

Communists win 148 seats; Socialists, 134; Radical Socialists, 35 (the Popular Republican Movement wins 141 seats; Conservatives, 62; others, 2); simultaneous referendum votes to consider the new Assembly a Constituent body, thereby ending the Third Republic (founded 1875).

24 the United Nations comes into formal existence with ratification of its Charter by 29 nations.

25 Liberals in Brazil secure resignation of Getúlio Vargas and the election of José Linhares as President.

30 Danish elections leave Social Democrats the strongest single party, but Erik Eriksen forms coalition of Liberals and Conservatives.

L November

4 general election held in Hungary, with Communists winning only 17 % of votes; the election is won by the Smallholders with 60 % (Zoltan Tildy of the Smallholders Party, forms coalition).

10 Communist-dominated government of Albania, under Enver Hoxha, recognized by Western powers.

11 Marshal Tito's National Front wins elections to Yugoslav Constituent Assembly.

13 in France, Charles de Gaulle is elected president of Provisional Government.

18 Communist rising in Azerbaijan province, Iran; troops sent to quell it are stopped by USSR forces at Kazvin.

18 in Portugal, Prime Minister Salazar's National Union Party wins general election (boycotted by opposition).

18 Communist-dominated Fatherland Front wins Bulgarian elections.

20 in Nuremberg, Germany, opening of trial of 24 leading Nazis before Allied International Military Tribunal (–31 Aug 1946).

20 Allied Control Commission in Europe approves plan to transfer 6.6 million Germans from Austria, Hungary, and Poland to Germany pending a peace settlement.

25 People's Party wins Austrian elections.

29 Federal People's Republic of Yugoslavia proclaimed.

м December

2 Enrico Dutra elected president of Brazil.

28 Karl Renner elected President of Austria.

*Perón elected president of Argentina ... War trials in Nuremberg
and Tokyo ...*

A January

7 Western powers recognize Austrian Republic with 1937 frontiers.

10 truce in Chinese Civil War (–14 April).

10 first session of United Nations General Assembly opens in London, with Paul Spaak of Belgium as president.

11 constituent assembly in Albania proclaims a People's Republic.

20 in France, Charles de Gaulle resigns presidency of Provisional Government because of continued Communist opposition (succeeded, on 22, by the Socialist Félix Gouin).

31 new constitution in Yugoslavia creates six constituent republics (Serbia, Montenegro, Croatia, Slovenia, Bosnia-Herzegovina, Macedonia), but these are subordinated to the central authority, on the model of the USSR.

B February

British government decides to send mission to India, to discuss the country's future constitution with political leaders. In S Korea, the US military government establishes the Representative Democratic Council, chaired by Syngman Rhee; in N Korea, the Executive Committee is replaced by the Provisional People's Committee for North Korea; Kim Il Sung becomes head of the N Korean government.

1 Trygve Lie, Norwegian Socialist, is elected secretary general of the UN (serving until 1953).

1 Hungarian Republic proclaimed, with Zoltan Tildy, leader of Smallholders' Party, as president.

17 Christian Socialists win Belgian elections, but the position of the monarchy hampers the formation of a coalition.

24 Juan Perón elected president of Argentina.

25 following mediation of US Secretary of State George Marshall, Nationalists and Communists in China agree to merge their armies; but the parties fail to keep the agreement, leading to civil war (–1949).

C March

4 USA, Britain, and France appeal to the Spanish to depose General Franco.

5 Winston Churchill, former British prime minister, delivers speech at Fulton, Missouri, USA, in which he declares that Stalin has lowered an 'iron curtain ... from Stettin in the Baltic to Trieste in the Adriatic', and warns that the USSR is aiming for 'the infinite expansion of [its] power and doctrines'; his speech signals for many the formal start of the Cold War.

6 France recognizes Vietnam as a Democratic Republic within the Indochinese Federation.

10 Britain and France begin evacuating Lebanon.

22 Britain recognizes independence of Transjordan (proclaimed 25 May), with Abdullah Ibn Hussein as king.

26 Allied Control Commission limits level of German production.

29 new constitution in Gold Coast, which becomes first British African colony with a majority of Africans in the legislature.

D April

5 USSR agrees to withdraw troops from Iran on promise of reforms in Azerbaijan.

10 Japanese election favours moderate parties.

18 League of Nations assembly dissolves itself.

19 USA recognizes Yugoslavia Republic.

22 in Soviet zone of Germany, the Social Democrats merge with the Communists to form the Socialist Unity Party of Germany (SED).

27 in Tokyo, Japan, opening of the main war crimes trial of the International Military Tribunal for the Far East (–12 Nov 1948); charges are brought against Hideki Tojo, the former prime minister, and 27 associates (one defendant is declared unfit to stand trial; two die during the trial).

29 British–US committee advises against partition of Palestine.

E May

Civil war breaks out in Greece, between monarchists backed by Britain and Communists supported by Albania, Bulgaria, and Yugoslavia.

5 referendum in France rejects draft constitution.

9 King Victor Emmanuel III of Italy abdicates and Umberto II proclaims himself king.

17 Ion Antonescu, wartime prime minister of Romania, is sentenced to death.

17 US government takes control of railways, dislocated by strikes, and, on 20, coal mines.

20 British House of Commons passes bill for nationalization of coal mines.

26 general election in Czechoslovakia, in which the Communists win the largest

1946

Dr Spock's Baby and Child Care ... *First US saint ... Bikinis
modelled in Paris ... Alistair Cooke's first* Letter from America ...

o **Politics, Government, Law, and Economy**

George B Galloway, *Congress at the Crossroads.*

Frederick Meinecke, *The German Catastrophe.*

Christian Social Union (CSU) founded in Bavaria, Germany.

Douglas MacArthur purges extreme nationalists in Japan.

In USSR, Council of Ministers, with Joseph Stalin as chairman, replaces Council of People's Commissars (19 March).

The USA organizes state elections (June) in its zone in Germany; state governments are then formed; the USSR organizes elections to state councils in its zone in Oct.

Britain co-ordinates armed services under a single defence committee (30 Dec).

The International Court of Justice is established at The Hague, Netherlands, as successor to the Permanent Court of International Justice and as the judicial body of the United Nations.

Verdicts of the International Military Tribunal at Nuremberg, Germany, establish that individuals can be guilty of war crimes and punished for crimes against international law.

In Britain, the Privy Council rules that a Canadian Bill to stop appeals from Canadian courts to the Council is valid.

Trades Disputes Act, 1927, which had outlawed general and sympathetic strikes and imposed 'contracting in' for the political levy, is repealed in Britain (13 Feb).

In USA, Fred Vinson is appointed Chief Justice of the Supreme Court (serving until 1953).

USSR adopts fourth Five-Year Plan (15 March); its main aim is to restore industry in the area devastated during the Second World War (about 7,000 large enterprises are constructed or reconstructed).

Widespread dismissals of staff in Soviet industry for incompetence (28 June).

In France, the Monnet Plan suggests a technocratic restructuring of industry and agriculture.

Hyperinflation in Hungary is history's most extreme, resulting in the printing of a 100-trillion-pengo note.

British government nationalizes the Bank of England (1 March; Bank incorporated in 1694).

Nationalization of transport bill published in London (28 Nov).

Heavy industry is nationalized in Austria.

In Poland, industrial enterprises employing more than 50 workers per shift plus all former German businesses are nationalized (3 Jan).

First completely automated production lines are introduced at Ford Motors, USA.

In USA, major strikes take place in the steel, automobile, coal, electrical equipment, and meat industries; 116 million working days are lost.

World wheat shortage leads to bread rationing in Britain (21 July).

Foundation of the Kuwait Oil Company; Kuwait becomes the largest oil-producing country in the Middle East.

Opening of London airport at Heathrow (March 31).

p **Society, Education, and Religion**

United Nations establishes the International Refugee Organization (IRO) to take over the refugee work of the United Nations Relief and Rehabilitation Administration (–1952).

Start of the 'post-war baby boom', with 3.4 million births in the USA and continuing high birth rates into the 1950s.

Royal Commission favours equal pay for women in Britain (6 Nov).

In France, women are granted a statutory right to equal pay.

Italian women enfranchised.

US Supreme Court, in Morgan v. Virginia, rules that the segregation of African-Americans on interstate buses is unconstitutional (3 June).

Indian Claims Commission established in USA (13 Aug), to receive and deal with compensation claims from Native Americans (for loss of land, etc).

Bombay, India, removes discrimination against the harijans ('untouchables').

British National Insurance Act consolidates social services (27 July).

Foundation of the National Health Service in Britain (from 6 Nov).

Canada introduces family allowance.

Benjamin Spock, *Common Sense Book of Baby and Child Care.*

Cultural Relaxation Centre (COC) in the Netherlands is the first cultural facility established for homosexuals.

In Britain, the report of the Reith Committee leads to the founding of New Towns as growth points in Britain.

In France, official support is given to child-centred teaching methods in experimental 'classes nouvelles'.

number of votes (about 38 per cent); Communist Klement Gottwald becomes prime minister.

30 in Netherlands, the Catholic People's Party wins general election; J Beel forms new coalition.

F **June**

2 in election for French Constituent Assembly, the Popular Republican Movement wins the largest number of seats with 160 (Communists win 146; Socialists, 115; Radical Socialists, 39; Conservatives, 62).

2 Britain and USA restore military bases in Azores to Portugal.

2 in Italy, referendum produces majority in favour of a republic.

3 South African parliament passes Asiatic Land Tenure and Indian Representation Bill.

3 King Umberto II leaves Italy; Alcide de Gasperi, the prime minister, becomes provisional head of state.

19 Georges Bidault elected president of French Provisional Government.

27 foreign ministers of USA, Britain, France, and USSR transfer Dodecanese Islands from Italy to Greece and areas of Northern Italy to France.

28 Enrico de Nicola elected president of Italy.

30 referendum in Poland favours a single-house assembly and wide nationalization.

G **July**

French hold conference at Fontainebleau, France, on future of Indochina; Ho Chi Minh, leader of the Vietminh, walks out.

4 independent Philippine Republic inaugurated (replacing the Commonwealth of the Philippines).

7 election of Miguel Alemán, a civilian, as president of Mexico, leads to closer ties with USA.

14 anti-Jewish pogrom in Kielce, Poland.

15 in USA, President Truman signs bill of credit for $3.75 billion for Britain.

15 Canadian commission reports on Soviet espionage.

22 in Palestine, Zionist terrorists blow up part of the King David Hotel in Jerusalem containing British government and military offices, killing 91.

29 (–15 Oct) Peace Conference of 21 nations that had opposed the Axis meets in Paris to draft peace treaties.

H **August**

20 Allied Control Commission dissolves the German army.

25 'closed shop' dispute in British transport industry begins.

J **September**

London conference on Palestine meets (–Dec), but is boycotted by Zionists.

1 plebiscite in Greece favours the monarchy (on 28, King George II returns to Athens).

2 in India, provisional government formed by Congress Party takes office; Jawaharlal Nehru is vice-president to the viceroy, Lord Wavell.

6 J F Byrnes, US secretary of state, makes speech in Stuttgart, Germany, bidding for German co-operation.

8 referendum in Bulgaria supports establishment of a republic (King Simon II and Queen Mother leave country on 16 Sept).

18 Archbishop Stephinac of Croatia imprisoned in Yugoslavia.

30 in Nuremberg, Germany, the judges of the International Military Tribunal deliver their judgment; on 1 Oct they announce verdicts and sentences: Joachim von Ribbentrop, Hermann Goering, and ten other leading Nazis (including Martin Bormann, tried in absentia) are sentenced to death; Rudolf Hess, Walter Funk, and Erich Raeder are sentenced to life imprisonment; four others receive long sentences, but Dr Hjalmar Schacht, Franz von Papen, and Hans Fritzsche are acquitted.

K **October**

Spain signs commercial agreement with Argentina following President Juan Perón's visit to General Franco. In S Korea, the Representative Democratic Council is replaced by an Interim Legislative Assembly.

5 Tage Erlander, Social Democrat, becomes prime minister of Sweden on Per Hansson's death.

13 in France, Constituent Assembly adopts revised constitution (with many deputies abstaining from vote).

13 Siam accepts verdict of UN for returning territory to Indochina.

15 in Nuremberg, Germany, former leading Nazi Hermann Goering, in prison awaiting execution, commits suicide (by swallowing cyanide).

16 in the early hours of the morning, 10 of the defendants at the Nuremberg war trial are hanged in the prison gym by US hangman John C Woods.

23 General Assembly of UN meets in New York.

27 general election in Bulgaria, after which a Fatherland Front government is formed

In Australia, establishment of the federal government's Commonwealth Office of Education to manage the education systems of the six states.

In USA, foundation of the Fulbright Scholarships, to enable US citizens to study abroad, and people from abroad to study in the USA.

Pope Pius XII creates 32 cardinals.

Mother Frances Xavier Cabrini (1850–1917) is the first US citizen to be canonized.

Committee of provisional World Council of Churches drafts plans for a reconstructed world international assembly.

International Christian Conference at Cambridge, England, aims at closer relations between Protestant and Orthodox Churches.

Q Science, Technology, and Discovery

US scientists win all of the Nobel science prizes.

Fairey Aviation Co. construct a pilotless radio-controlled rocket missile.

The magnetic north pole observed by aircraft to be 400 km/250 mi north of the charted position.

The Williamson diamond mine, Tanganyika, is found to be the world's largest.

USSR's first nuclear reactor is started up.

Development, separately, of nuclear magnetic resonance by E W Purcell in USA and F Bloch in Switzerland.

British scientists Edward Appleton and Donald Hay discover that sun-spots emit radio waves.

Electronic computer is built at Pennsylvania University, USA.

Discovery of carbon-13, an isotope for curing metabolic diseases.

R Humanities

E V Rieu's translation of Homer's *Odyssey*.

John Summerson, *Georgian London*.

G D H Cole and R Postgate, *The Common People, 1746–1938*.

Joseph Dorfman and Bray Hammond, *The Economic Mind in American Civilization* (5 volumes, –1959).

Charles A Beard, *American Foreign Policy in the Making, 1932–40*.

John Rewald, *The History of Impressionism*.

Alfred Einstein, *Mozart: His Character, His Work*.

George F Black, *The Surnames of Scotland: Their Origin, Meaning and History*.

In Britain, King George VI opens the New Bodleian Library in Oxford (24 Oct).

Ernst Cassirer, *The Myth of the State*.

R G Collingwood, *The Idea of History*.

Bertrand Russell, *History of Western Philosophy*.

Jean-Paul Sartre, *Existentialism and Humanism*.

S Art, Sculpture, Fine Arts, and Architecture

Art et Resistance exhibition in Paris, France.

Pablo Picasso founds the pottery at Vallauris, S France.

Painting, etc:

Barnett Newmann, *Pagan Void*.

Mark Rothko, *Sacrifice*.

Sculpture:

Barbara Hepworth, *Pelagos*.

Architecture:

Richard Neutra, Deset House, Colorado, USA.

T Music

Samuel Barber, *Serpent of the Heart* (Medea) (ballet).

Lennox Berkeley, *Five Songs*.

Aaron Copland, Symphony No. 3.

Gian Carlo Menotti, *The Medium* (opera).

Sergei Prokofiev, *War and Peace* (opera, first version).

Arnold Schoenberg, String Trio.

Kurt Weill, *Street Scene* (musical).

Musical *Annie Get Your Gun* produced in New York at the Imperial Theatre (16 May).

Edith Piaf, 'La vie en rose'.

U Literature and Drama

Miguel Asturias, *El Presidente*.

Herman Broch, *The Death of Vergil*.

Theodore Dreiser, *The Bulwark*.

Jean Genet, *Our Lady of the Flowers*.

André Gide, *Journal, 1939–42*.

John Hersey, *Hiroshima*.

Nikos Kazantzakis, *Zorba the Greek*.

Philip Larkin, *Jill*.

Robert Lowell, *Lord Weary's Castle* (poems).

Jacques Prévert, *Paroles* (poems).

Dylan Thomas, *Deaths and Entrances* (poems).

Robert Penn Warren, *All the King's Men*.

Eudora Welty, *Delta Wedding*.

Richard Wilbur, *The Beautiful Changes* (poems).

Paramahansa Yogananda, *Autobiography of a Yogi*.

Drama:

Jean Cocteau, *The Eagle Has Two Heads*.

headed by Communist Georgi Dimitrov (who returns from Moscow on 21 Nov).

L November

4 Chinese–US treaty of friendship and commerce.

4 Republicans (246 seats) win US Congressional elections (with Democrats holding 188 seats).

9 in USA, President Truman removes controls, excepting those on certain food stocks and rent.

10 in elections to the French National Assembly, Communists win the largest number of seats, with 166 (the Popular Republic Movement wins 158; Socialists, 90; Radical Socialists, 55; Conservatives, 70; Gaullists, 5); the result is political deadlock.

19 elections held in Romania; in the government formed afterwards, Communists hold key positions.

23 French troops bombard Haiphong in NE Vietnam, killing around 20,000; this incident marks the beginning of the French Indochina War (–1954).

27 Labour Party retains power in New Zealand elections, winning 42 seats, against 38 for the National Party.

M December

2 J F Byrnes, US secretary of state, and Ernest Bevin, British foreign secretary, agree to economic union of US and British occupation zones in Germany (in force from 1 Jan 1947).

5 New York City is chosen as site for the permanent headquarters of the UN.

9 Indian constituent assembly meets to discuss independence, but is boycotted by the Muslim League.

11 the UN bars Spain from its activities (on 14, rejects South African proposal for incorporation of South-West Africa in South Africa).

16 Léon Blum forms Socialist government in France.

20 in Vietnam, French troops occupy Ho Chi Minh's residence in Hanoi (Ho flees, calling for resistance to the French).

30 Atomic Energy Commission of UN approves US plan for control.

Eduardo de Filippo, *Filumena Maturano*.
Eugene O'Neill, *The Iceman Cometh*.
Jean-Paul Sartre, *Morts sans sépulture*.

v Births and Deaths

Jan 29 Harry L Hopkins dies (56).
April 17 George Köhler born (–).
April 21 John Maynard Keynes dies (60).
May 31 Rainer Werner Fassbinder born (–1982).
June 8 Gerhart Hauptmann dies (83).
June 10 Jack Johnson dies (68).
June 14 John Logie Baird dies (57).
July 29 Gertrude Stein dies (72).
Aug 13 H G Wells dies (70).
Aug 19 William J Clinton born (–).
Aug 31 Harley Granville-Barker dies (69).
Dec 10 Damon Runyon dies (62).

w Everyday Life

Vespa scooters are brought onto the Italian market, to the gratitude of subsequent generations of young Italian men.
The first bikinis cause a sensation when modelled in Paris (5 July).
'Tide' becomes the first commercially available washing powder.
The first drive-in bank is opened.

x Sport and Recreation

The All-America Football Conference is established as a challenge to the National Football League; rivalry persists, until the Conference folds in 1949.
In England, 33 spectators are killed when a wall collapses during the Football Association Cup tie between Bolton Wanderers and Stoke City at Burnden Park (9 March).
Sugar Ray Robinson out-points Tommy Bell to win the World Welterweight boxing title at Madison Square Garden, New York (20 Dec).
Walter Winterbottom becomes the first England football manager.

The first US Women's Open Golf Championship is staged.
In lawn tennis, the USA beats Britain 7–0 in the Wightman Cup match, without losing a set.

y Media

The press agency Allgemeiner Deutscher Nachrichtendienst is founded in Soviet zone of Germany.
In Britain, new governing body established to maintain the independence of the *Observer*.

Film:
La Belle et la Bête (director, Jean Cocteau).
The Best Years of Our Lives (director, William Wyler).
The Big Sleep (director, Howard Hawks).
Great Expectations (director, David Lean).
It's a Wonderful Life (director, Frank Capra; starring James Stewart).
The Killers (starring Burt Lancaster in his screen debut).
Notorious (director, Alfred Hitchcock).
Paisa (director, Roberto Rossellini).
Les Portes de la Nuit (director, Marcel Carné).
The Postman Always Rings Twice (director, Tay Garnet).
Shoeshine (director, Vittorio de Sica).
Stairway to Heaven (producers, Michael Powell and Emeric Pressburger).

Radio:
In Britain, first broadcast by BBC of Alistair Cooke's 'Letter from America' (–).
The BBC founds the Third Programme (29 Sept).
Foundation of Asociación Interamericana de Radiodifusión (AIR).

Television:
Revival in Britain of regular television broadcasts by the BBC, with fewer than 12,000 viewers (7 June).

*Announcement of the 'Truman Doctrine' ... 'Marshall Aid'
provided for Europe ... India and Pakistan become independent ...*

A **January**
1 Britain grants Nigeria modified self-government.
7 George Marshall succeeds J F Byrnes as US secretary of state.
16 Vincent Auriol elected president of France.
21 J C Smuts, prime minister of South Africa, refuses to place South-West Africa under United Nations trusteeship.
21 P Ramadier forms coalition in France, on Léon Blum's resignation.
26 Egypt breaks off diplomatic relations with Britain, for revising 1936 treaty, and for stating that it will prepare the Sudan for self-government; it refers the question to the UN.
27 Regional Advisory Commission for the Pacific established.
29 USA abandons efforts at mediation in China.

B **February**
Fuel crisis in Britain (–April).
1 in Italy, Alcide de Gasperi forms new ministry of Christian Democrats, Communists, and Left Socialists.
7 British proposal for dividing Palestine into Arab and Jewish zones with administration as a trusteeship is rejected by Arabs and Jews.
10 by peace treaties, signed in Paris, (i) Italy loses Adriatic Islands and part of Venezia Giulia to Yugoslavia, the Dodecanese Islands to Greece and small frontier regions to France, renounces sovereignty over its North African colonies, agrees to the establishment of Trieste as a free territory, pays reparations, and reduces its forces to 300,000 men; (ii) Romania loses Bessarabia and North Bukovina to the USSR, but regains Transylvania; (iii) Bulgaria retains South Dobrudja; (iv) Hungary is reassigned 1938 frontiers; and (v) Finland cedes Petsamo to the USSR.
20 British government announces its intention to transfer power in India to Indians by not later than June 1948.
21 British government informs the USA that it cannot afford to keep troops in Greece and will withdraw them by the end of March.

C **March**
1 Allied Control Commission in Germany decrees that the Prussian state, a 'promoter of militarism and reaction in Germany', has ceased to exist.
3 in USSR, Nikolai Bulganin replaces Joseph Stalin as defence minister.

4 British–French treaty of alliance.
10 (–24 April) Moscow Conference of foreign ministers, which fails through division between the West and the USSR over problem of Germany.
12 in USA, President Harry Truman, in speech to Congress announces plan to give aid to Greece and Turkey and thereby outlines the 'Truman Doctrine': he pledges that the USA will support 'free peoples who are resisting attempted subjugation by armed minorities or by outside pressures'.
19 in Belgium, Paul Spaak forms coalition of Catholics and Socialists.
19 Chinese Nationalists capture Communist capital of Yan'an.
23 Lord Wavell resigns as viceroy of India; succeeded by Lord Mountbatten (who consults local leaders and announces that Muslim-dominated areas must become a separate independent state).
29 nationalist revolt against France in Madagascar (–July).

D **April**
2 Security Council of the UN appoints the USA as Trustee for Pacific islands formerly under Japanese mandate.
2 Britain refers the Palestine question to the UN.
14 in France, Charles de Gaulle organizes the Rassemblement du Peuple Français or RPF ('Gaullists'), to rally non-Communists to unity and reform.
16 ex-President Joseph Tiso of Slovakia executed.

E **May**
Serious strikes in France.
29 Ferenc Nagy, prime minister of Hungary, resigns while on holiday in Switzerland (after he has been charged with complicity in a plot to overthrow the Hungarian regime; he finds asylum in the USA); succeeded by Lajos Dinnyés, also of the Smallholders' Party.
31 in Italy, Alcide de Gasperi forms government of Christian Socialists and Independents (following resignation, on 13, after friction with the Left).

F **June**
2 German Economic Council is established.
5 in speech at Harvard University, USA, Secretary of State George Marshall calls for a European Recovery Program funded by the USA (Marshall Aid).

New constitution in Japan ... Discovery of the Dead Sea Scrolls
... First US presidential address on television ...

o Politics, Government, Law, and Economy

R McCallum and A Readman, *The British General Election of 1945*, the first work of psephological analysis.

In Germany, Britain and France organize elections (April and May respectively) in their occupation zones; state governments are formed.

New constitution introduced in Japan (3 May), with approval of the Diet, the emperor, and the people by means of a referendum (in which women vote for the first time); the emperor's powers are limited and the country renounces the use of war.

Pakistan and the Yemen are admitted to the United Nations (30 Sept).

Presidential Succession Act establishes the order of succession to the US presidency between elections: the vice-president, followed by the speaker of the House of Representatives.

In USA, the National Security Act (signed 26 July) merges the War and Navy Departments into a single War Department under a cabinet secretary; military activity will be coordinated by the Joint Chiefs of Staff; a National Security Council will advise the president on military affairs, and the new Central Intelligence Agency (CIA) is created to collect intelligence.

The US government introduces security and loyalty checks on its employees (March), following several leaks of government papers.

The US Army Air Force is established as a separate US Air Force (USAF).

Commonwealth Relations Office and Colonial Development Corporation established in Britain.

Leo Amery, *Thoughts on the Constitution*.

Oliver Franks, *Central Planning and Control in War and Peace*.

US Congress passes Taft–Hartley act over President Truman's veto, prohibiting use of union funds for political purposes, outlawing the 'closed shop' and strengthening the government's hands in strikes and lockouts (23 June).

In Britain, the Crown Proceedings Act enables citizens, in most circumstances, to institute civil proceedings against the government on the same basis as actions against private individuals.

In Christie v. Leachinsky the British House of Lords establishes that suspects have a right to be told of their arrest and have the reasons for it explained.

In Britain, in the 'High Trees' case, Judge Denning introduces the principle of promissory estoppel into English contract law, whereby someone whose offer to forego something has been accepted and relied upon cannot then enforce the original rights.

General Agreement on Tariffs and Trade (GATT) founded to negotiate lower tariffs worldwide to prevent repetition of the events of the 1930s.

Economic crises in Britain caused by the harsh winter and the resumption of convertibility of the pound.

In Britain, the coal industry is nationalized (from 1 Jan); acts of parliament (Aug) nationalize railways and road transport (from 1948).

In Hungary, launch of Three-Year Plan (Aug) under which banking, industry, mining, and most trade are nationalized.

Yugoslavia launches Five-Year Plan, aiming to collectivize half of the country's agricultural land and develop industry.

In Australia, banks are nationalized (27 Nov).

p Society, Education, and Religion

Indian constituent assembly outlaws 'untouchability' (29 May).

Partition of India into India and Muslim Pakistan leads to massacres and killings, especially in divided Bengal and Punjab; within a year of independence over 6 million people move state.

Ferdinand Lundberg and Marynia Farnham, *Modern Woman: The Lost Sex*.

Commission on Civil Rights appointed in USA.

In USA, construction of Levittown on Long Island, New York, starts the trend to mass suburbanization.

G D H Cole, *The Intelligent Man's guide to the Post War World*.

John Gunther, *Inside USA*.

Town and Country Planning Act in Britain imposes planning control throughout the country; each major local authority is also required to prepare and maintain a development plan.

Australia, New Zealand, the USA, Britain, and France found the South Pacific Commission, to coordinate social and economic development in South Pacific.

Fundamental Law on Education reshapes the Japanese school system along American lines.

School-leaving age in Britain raised to 15.

17 Constituent Assembly in Burma (now Myanmar) resolves for independence.

G July

6 Spanish bill of succession, for restoring monarchy on General Franco's death or resignation.

12 (–15) 16 West European nations meet in Paris to discuss proposed 'Marshall Plan' for economic recovery.

20 in Indonesia, Dutch troops launch 'police action' against independence movement and succeed in establishing rule over Dutch estates.

28 in Romania, dissolution of the National Peasant Party (the most popular political party).

H August

1 Security Council of the UN calls for cease-fire in Indonesia (leads to truce on 17 Jan 1948).

15 Independence of India proclaimed, partitioning India; Nehru becomes prime minister of India, Muhammad Ali Jinnah (leader of the Muslim League) becomes viceroy of Pakistan with Liaquat Ali Khan prime minister; British authority in remaining states ends.

31 Communist successes in Hungarian elections.

J September

2 American republics sign treaty of mutual assistance at Rio de Janeiro, Brazil.

14 Poland denounces 1925 concordat with Catholic Church.

26 Don Stephen Senanayake becomes prime minister of Ceylon (now Sri Lanka).

K October

In India the state of Kashmir (with 75 per cent of its population Muslim, but a Hindu ruler) is invaded by Pathan tribesmen; Indian troops assist the ruler, who agrees to accede to India (fighting continues until Jan 1949).

5 Warsaw Communist conference establishes the Cominform (Communist Information Bureau) to co-ordinate activities of European Communist Parties.

19 (–26) Charles de Gaulle's RPF party becomes strongest group in French municipal elections, winning 38.7 per cent of the vote.

21 General Assembly of UN calls on Greece and Balkan powers to settle disputes by peaceful means.

29 Belgium, Netherlands, and Luxembourg ratify customs union (Benelux) (effective from 1 Nov).

L November

13 Social Democrats form minority cabinet in Denmark.

14 the General Assembly of the UN adopts resolution requiring elections to be held throughout Korea under a UN Temporary Commission on Korea.

19 in France, P Ramadier resigns as prime minister; on 23, Robert Schuman of the Popular Republican Movement forms ministry supported by Socialists.

20 in Britain, Princess Elizabeth marries Philip Mountbatten (created Duke of Edinburgh).

22 Iran assembly nullifies oil agreement with USSR.

25 (–16 Dec) London Conference of powers on Germany fails through USSR's demands for reparations.

29 UN adopts plan for partition of Palestine, with Jerusalem under UN Trusteeship; fighting breaks out between Jews and Arabs in Palestine.

M December

14 Rómulo Gallegos, Democratic Action, elected president of Venezuela.

16 USSR devalues currency.

19 Romanian–Yugoslav treaty of friendship.

22 new constitution in Italy centralizes government and provides for popularly elected senate.

27 Greek government dissolves the Communist Party and the Communist-controlled National Liberation Front (EAM).

30 Kashmir conflict referred to the UN.

30 under Communist pressure, King Michael of Romania abdicates.

Cambridge University, England, votes to admit women to membership and degrees (6 Dec).

The Church of South India is inaugurated by union of Anglicans, Methodists, and the South Indian United Church.

Michael Polanyi, *Science, Faith and Society*.

Q Science, Technology, and Discovery

British government sets up Advisory Committee on Scientific Policy.

First supersonic air flight by US plane.

Captain Odom flies round world in 73 hr 5 min (Aug).

John Cobb's ground world speed record (16 Sept) of 634.39 kph/394.196 mph.

Printed circuit board developed in Britain by J A Sargrove.

Britain's first atomic pile at Harwell comes into operation (Aug).

British scientist P M S Blackett advances theory that all massive rotating bodies are magnetic.

L Essen determines the speed of radio waves in a vacuum.

Dennis Gabor invents holography, the production of three-dimensional images.

C F Powell and G P S Occhialini in Britain discover the pi-meson (or pion) atomic particle.

R Humanities

In Palestine, discovery of main series of Dead Sea Scrolls at Qumran on the shores of the Dead Sea.

John Harvey, *Gothic England*.

F M Powicke, *King Henry III and the Lord Edward*.

Oscar and Mary Handlin, *Commonwealth*.

John Hope Franklin, *From Slavery to Freedom*.

Allan Nevins, *Ordeal of the Union*.

Documents on British Foreign Policy, 1919–39 (–).

H R Trevor-Roper, *The Last Days of Hitler*.

H W Garrod, *Scholarship; Its Meaning and Value*.

Theodor Adorno and Max Horkheimer, *Dialectic of Enlightenment*.

Rudolf Carnap, *Meaning and Necessity*.

Pierre Lecomte du Noüy, *Human Destiny*.

C I Lewis, *An Analysis of Knowledge and Valuation*.

Hans Reichenbach, *Elements of Symbolic Logic*.

S Art, Sculpture, Fine Arts, and Architecture

Existentialism becomes popular in Paris, France; artists such as Alberto Giacometti and Wols closely reflect Jean-Paul Sartre's existentialist aesthetic in their work.

The cleaning of Rembrandt's *Woman Bathing* and other pictures in the National Gallery provokes controversy on the principles of cleaning canvases.

Painting, etc:

Jean Dubuffet, *Will to Power*.

Arshile Gorky, *Agony*.

Jean Helion, *À Rebours*.

Jackson Pollock, *Full Fathom Five*.

Diego Rivera, *Alameda Park* (–1948).

Sculpture:

Alberto Giacometti, *Tête d'Homme sur Tige*, *The Nose*.

Marino Marini, *Horseman*.

David Smith, *The Royal Bird*.

Architecture:

Alvar Aalto, Hall of Residence, Massachusetts Institute of Technology, Boston, USA (–1949).

Wallace K Harrison and others, United Nations Headquarters, New York (–1950).

Le Corbusier, Unité d'habitation, Marseilles, France (–1952).

Ludwig Mies van der Rohe, Promontory Apartments, Chicago, USA.

Frank Lloyd Wright, Unitarian Church, Madison, Wisconsin, USA.

T Music

Milton Babbitt, *Three Compositions for Piano*.

Benjamin Britten, *Albert Herring* (opera).

Gottfried von Einem, *Dantons Tod* (opera).

Roger Sessions, Symphony No. 2.

Elie Siegmeister, Symphony No. 1.

Virgil Thomson, *The Mother of Us All* (opera).

In Scotland, foundation of the Edinburgh Festival of Music and Drama.

Brigadoon (musical) by Alan Jay Lerner and Frederick Loewe (first performed at the Ziegfeld Theatre, New York, 13 March).

Finian's Rainbow (musical), text by E Y Harburg and Fred Sady, music by Burton Lane (first performed at the 46th Street Theatre, New York, 10 Jan).

Classic period of innovative playing by US jazz saxophonist Charlie 'Yardbird' or 'Bird' Parker.

Capitol Records use tape for recordings.

U Literature and Drama

Italo Calvino, *The Path to the Nest of Spiders*.

Albert Camus, *The Plague*.

Osamu Dazai, *The Setting Sun*.

Anne Frank, *The Diary of Anne Frank*.

Jean Genet, *Querelle de Brest*.

L P Hartley, *Eustace and Hilda*.

Malcolm Lowry, *Under the Volcano*.
Compton Mackenzie, *Whisky Galore*.
Alberto Moravia, *The Woman of Rome*.
St John Perse, *Vents*.

Drama:

Maxwell Anderson, *Joan of Lorraine*.
Arthur Miller, *All My Sons*.
John Van Druten, *The Voice of the Turtle*.
Tennessee Williams, *A Streetcar Named Desire*.
The Actors' Studio founded in New York, by Elia Kazan, to propagate the 'Method' principles of experimental, introspective acting.
The American Theatre Wing establishes the Tony Awards to honour outstanding Broadway productions and those involved in them.

v Births and Deaths

April 7 Henry Ford dies (82).
April 24 Willa Cather dies (73).
May 8 H G Selfridge dies (90).
June 19 Salman Rushdie born (–).
Aug 21 Ettore Bugatti dies (65).
Oct 4 Max Planck dies (89).
Oct 31 Sidney Webb dies (88).
Nov 30 David Mamet born (–).
Dec 14 Stanley Baldwin dies (80).
Dec 30 A N Whitehead dies (86).

w Everyday Life

The first microwave ovens go on sale, but the public are slow to buy them.
Motorcycle riots in California, USA.
The first recorded sighting of an unidentified flying objects (UFO) occurs in the sky over Kansas, USA.

x Sport and Recreation

France is readmitted to Rugby Union's Five Nations Championship.
In USA, Jackie Robinson signs for the Brooklyn Dodgers, becoming the first African-American player in major-league baseball since Moses Fleetwood Walker in 1884.

In football, Britain beats the Rest of Europe 6–1 in a match at Hampden Park to mark the British Associations' readmission to FIFA (10 May).
In the course of the English first-class cricket season, Denis Compton and Bill Edrich of Middlesex score 7,355 runs, including 30 centuries.
In the first £20,000 transfer in British football, Tommy Lawton moves from Chelsea to Notts County of the English Third Division North.

y Media

Fuel crisis in Britain forces reduction in size of newspapers and curtailment of magazine publication (17 Feb–3 March, with further reductions on 21 July).
Publication in Germany of the news magazine *Der Spiegel*.

Film:

Black Narcissus (producers, Michael Powell and Emeric Pressburger).
Brighton Rock (director, John Boulting).
The Fugitive (director, John Ford).
It Always Rains on Sunday (director, Robert Hamer).
Monsieur Verdoux (director and star, Charlie Chaplin).
Odd Man Out (director, Carol Reed).
Quai des Orfèvres (director, Henri Clouzot).
Le Silence est d'or (director, René Clair).
La Terra Trema (director, Luchino Visconti).

Radio:

US State Department begins 'Voice of America' station, a Russian-language service broadcasting to the USSR.
In Britain, Prime Minister Clement Attlee makes the first 'Party Political Broadcast' on the BBC (18 March), under a scheme to give major parties equal access to radio (Anthony Eden replies for the Conservatives).

Television:

In USA, President Truman makes the first presidential address to the nation on television (5 Oct).

1948

Gandhi assassinated ... Foundation of Israel ... National Party
wins election in South Africa ... Blockade of West Berlin ...

A **January**

4 Union of Burma (now Myanmar) proclaimed as an independent republic.

7 the USA and Britain expand the German council running the bizone and add a Länderrat containing two representatives from each state.

17 Netherlands and Republic of Indonesia sign truce.

20 in Delhi, India, Mahatma Gandhi is assassinated by an extremist Hindu, Nathuram Godse.

B **February**

1 Federation of Malaya proclaimed (Chinese in Malaya form Malayan Communist Party, which launches guerrilla attacks; state of emergency declared on 16 June).

4 Ceylon (now Sri Lanka) becomes a self-governing dominion.

20 in Czechoslovakia, 11 anti-Communist government ministers resign in protest at increasing Communist strength in police force; popular protests against the government are crushed.

25 President Beneš of Czechoslovakia accepts an all-Communist cabinet, though Jan Masaryk remains foreign minister.

C **March**

2 the Communist government of Czechoslovakia subordinates Slovakia to rule from Prague.

10 in Prague, Jan Masaryk is found dead.

16 United Nations Palestine commission reports that it cannot implement partition into Arab and Jewish areas because of local opposition.

17 France, Belgium, Netherlands, Luxembourg, and Britain sign Brussels Treaty, for 50-year alliance against armed attack in Europe and providing for economic, social, and military cooperation.

20 in response to developments in the US and British bizone in Germany, Soviet delegates walk out of Allied Control Commission for Germany.

29 Chiang Kai-shek, re-elected president of China by Nanjing Assembly, is granted dictatorial powers.

31 US Congress passes Marshall Aid Act, contributing $5.3 billion for European recovery.

D **April**

1 USSR begins to interfere with traffic between Berlin and West Germany.

6 Central Legislature of British East Africa holds first sessions at Nairobi.

6 USSR agrees treaty of mutual assistance with Finland, aimed at Germany.

13 Romanian Constitution is remodelled on Soviet lines.

16 meeting in Paris, France, of countries participating in the European Recovery Programme; sets up the Organization for European Economic Co-operation (OEEC).

18 Christian Democrats win absolute majority in Italian elections (winning 305 out of 574 seats).

E **May**

7 Hague Congress of movement for European unity under Winston Churchill.

9 in Czechoslovakia, Constituent Assembly accepts new constitution for a 'People's Democracy', but President Beneš refuses to sign it.

10 elections are held in S Korea, supervised by the UN Temporary Commission (the USSR had denied the Commission entry to N Korea).

11 Luigi Einaudi elected president of Italy.

14 as British mandate in Palestine ends, the Jewish National Council and General Zionist Council in Tel Aviv proclaim the establishment of a Jewish state, Israel, and assume the role of Provisional Government; David Ben-Gurion becomes prime minister (16 May, Chaim Weizmann is elected president); the USA recognizes the new state (as does the USSR on 17).

15 Egypt, Transjordan, Iraq, and Syria invade Israel and occupy areas in the S and E; the Arab Legion of Transjordan captures the old city of Jerusalem.

26 in South African election, J C Smuts's coalition of United and Labour Parties is defeated by the Nationalists and the Afrikaner Party, who advocate 'apartheid'; on 3 June, D F Malan becomes prime minister and forms government of Afrikaners.

31 National Assembly meets in S Korea and elects Syngman Rhee chairman (adopts constitution in July, elects Rhee as president on 20 July).

F **June**

7 USA, Britain, France, and Benelux countries agree a programme for the development of the US, British, and French occupation zones of Germany, to include a constituent assembly and federal government.

*End of racial segregation in US armed forces ... Invention of
transistor ... Richard Strauss's* Four Last Songs *...*

o Politics, Government, Law, and Economy

Foundation of the Organization of American States (OAS) at the 9th Pan-American Conference, at Bogotá, Colombia (charter signed 30 April).

In USA, incorporation of the RAND Corporation (policy research institute) in Santa Monica, California.

Electoral reform in Britain abolishes plural voting, including the business vote and university seats.

The Military and Political Consequences of Atomic Energy by P M S Blackett argues that an independent nuclear deterrent is beyond Britain's means; Blackett is excluded from government advisory circles for over a decade.

The US Supreme Court, in Shelley v. Kramer, invalidates restrictive covenants that prevent inhabitants of exclusive districts from selling their houses to African-Americans.

In USA, in Sipeul v. Board of Regents, the US Supreme Court rules that black applicants must be admitted to whites-only law schools unless equivalent black law tuition is provided (12 Jan).

Institute of Advanced Legal Studies founded in London.

In Hungary, the government announces its intention to bring about the collectivization of agriculture (richer small landowners are then persecuted).

In Romania, completion of nationalization of finance, industry, and commerce.

Indian government passes resolution on industrial policy (April): state to develop key sectors of industry where neglected by private enterprise.

In Britain, railways (from 1 Jan), the electricity industry (from 1 April), and gas are nationalized.

End of bread-rationing in Britain.

p Society, Education, and Religion

The General Assembly of the United Nations adopts the Universal Declaration of Human Rights.

Belgian women enfranchised.

Women are permitted to hold all judicial offices in France.

In USA, Margaret Chase Smith is the first elected woman senator (2 Nov).

US armed services are desegregated by order of President Truman (July 30).

Departure of the *Empire Windrush* from Kingston, Jamaica, with 492 passengers, all intending to start a new life in Britain, marks the start of immigration to Britain from the West Indies (8 June).

British Citizenship Act confers status of British subjects on all Commonwealth citizens (30 July).

A C Kinsey (and others), *Sexual Behaviour in the Human Male.*

World Health Organization (WHO) founded, as United Nations agency, in Geneva, Switzerland.

Foundation of the British National Health Service (effective from 5 July).

US Selective Service Act requires men aged 19–25 to register for military duty and provides for 19-year-olds to be called up (19 June).

Conscription in Britain for men aged 18 to 26 (12 Dec).

John Jewkes, *Ordeal by Planning.*

Law passed 'to make culture, training and education democratic' (Czechoslovakia).

Foundation of Nottingham University, England.

Representatives of 147 churches from 44 countries meet in Amsterdam, Netherlands (22 Aug–4 Sept), to inaugurate the World Council of Churches (WCC).

Formation of the Evangelical Church in Germany by Lutheran, Reformed, and United Churches.

In USA, in McCollum v. Board of Education, the US Supreme Court rules that time provided at the start of the school day for prayer is unconstitutional (8 March).

In Hungary, the Protestant Christian Churches and the Jewish community accept composition payments for their educational establishments and recognize the authority of the state; the Catholic Church, under Cardinal József Mindszenty, refuses to accept a similar arrangement and its schools are forcibly nationalized (26 Dec, Mindszenty is arrested and on 8 Feb 1949 sentenced to life imprisonment).

World Jewish Congress held at Montreux, Switzerland.

G K A Bell, *Christian Unity.*

Rudolph Bultmann, *Kerygma and Myth* (–1955), *Theology of the New Testament* (–1953).

W R Inge, *Mysticism in Religion.*

Thomas Merton, *The Seven Storey Mountain* (published in Britain, 1948, as *Elected Silence*).

P Tillich, *The Shaking of the Foundations.*

7 President Beneš of Czechoslovakia resigns; succeeded, on 14, by Klement Gottwald, who ratifies the new constitution.

11 in Israel, United Nations mediator Count Bernadotte obtains a cease-fire for four weeks.

14 in Hungary, under pressure, the Social Democrats merge with the Communists to form the Hungarian Workers' Party.

20 reform of currency in US, British, and French zones of Germany is implemented.

28 Yugoslavia is expelled from Cominform for hostility to USSR.

G July

Amnesty proclaimed in Philippines, but the rebels refuse to comply.

8 in Netherlands, William Drees, Labour, forms coalition.

10 in N Korea, the Provisional People's Committee adopts a draft constitution.

18 after renewed fighting between Arabs and Jews in Israel, a second truce is agreed, but fighting continues and the Jews extend their territory.

24 USSR stops road and rail traffic between Berlin and the West forcing Western powers to organize massive airlift (–30 Sept 1949).

29 Marshal Tito denies Cominform charges and is given vote of confidence by Yugoslav Communist Party, which is later purged of Cominform supporters.

30 (–18 Aug) conference of 10 nations meets in Belgrade to consider the future of the River Danube.

30 in Hungary, Zoltan Tildy resigns as president after his son-in-law is arrested (succeeded from 2 Aug by Árpád Szakasits).

H August

10 Gaston Eyskens, Christian Socialist, forms coalition in Belgium with Liberal support.

15 Republic of Korea proclaimed in Seoul; end of US military administration in S Korea.

25 USSR breaks off diplomatic relations with USA, alleging that the USA had kidnapped two Soviet teachers in the USA (the USA claims that the teachers had chosen to stay).

J September

3 Wladyslaw Gomulka, leader of Communist Polish Workers' Party, is forced to resign; replaced by Boleslaw Bierut.

4 Queen Wilhelmina abdicates in Netherlands for health reasons; succeeded, on 6, by Queen Juliana.

9 in N Korea, the Supreme People's Assembly proclaims the Democratic People's Republic of Korea, with its capital at Pyongyang, claiming authority over the entire country; the prime minister is Kim Il Sung.

10 Henri Queuille, Radical, forms ministry in France, with Robert Schuman foreign minister.

17 Count Folke Bernadotte, United Nations mediator in Israel, is assassinated by Jewish terrorists (succeeded by deputy, Ralph Bunche).

17 Hyderabad surrenders to Indian forces and agrees to join Indian Union.

18 Indonesian Communists set up a soviet government in Java, but are forced to withdraw.

24 first conference in London of representatives from Britain's African colonies.

K October

7 Democratic–Liberal government formed in Japan by Shigeru Yoshida.

25 USSR vetoes proposal of non-permanent members of United Nations Security Council for ending Berlin blockade.

29 military junta ends José Bustamente's government in Peru.

L November

In Chinese Civil War, Communists (commanded by Lin Baio) complete the conquest of Manchuria from the Nationalists; massive forces (Communists commanded by Zhu De) then fight for Xuzhou, which is captured in early Jan 1949.

2 in US presidential election, Harry Truman, Democrat, wins 304 electoral votes against Thomas E Dewey, Republican, 189, confounding public opinion polls; popular vote: Truman, 24,105,695; Dewey, 21,969,170; J Strom Thurmond, State-Rights Democrat, 1,169,021; Henry A Wallace, Progressive, 1,156,103. In Congressional elections, Democrats gain majority in both Houses.

7 in France, Charles de Gaulle's RPF gains large number of seats in elections for the Council of the Republic.

12 in Tokyo, Japan, end of the main war crimes trial: Hideki Tojo and six others are sentenced to death by hanging; 16 receive life imprisonment; 2 are given lesser sentences (executions carried out on 23 Dec).

15 resignation and retirement of W L Mackenzie King, prime minister of Canada; succeeded by Louis St Laurent.

27 in Britain, Prime Minister Clement Attlee appoints Lynskey tribunal to investigate charges of corruption at the Board of Trade

Q Science, Technology, and Discovery

Wilfred Thesiger crosses Arabian desert and penetrates Oman Steppes.

Radar is installed at Liverpool Docks, NW England, to supervise shipping approaches in fog, etc.

French scientist Auguste Piccard constructs bathyscaphe for deep descent into oceans.

H Bondi and T Gold, *The Steady State Theory of the Expanding Universe*.

Transistor invented in USA by J Bardeen, W H Brattain, and W Shockley at the Bell Telephone Laboratories.

Lajos Jánossy, *Cosmic Rays and Nuclear Physics*.

Soviet biologist T D Lysenko denounces non-Michurin geneticists in USSR, which leads to purges of scientific committees.

In USA, A E Mirsky discovers RNA (ribonucleic acid) in chromosomes.

Arthur Keith, *A New Theory of Human Evolution*.

Preparation of new antibiotics, aureomycin and chloromycetin.

R Humanities

W W Taylor, *A Study of Archaeology*.

Thor Heyerdahl, *The Kon-Tiki Expedition*.

C P Groves, *The Planting of Christianity in Africa* (–1958).

Sylvia L Thrupp, *The Merchant Class of Medieval London*.

T S Ashton, *The Industrial Revolution, 1760–1830*.

Leon Radzinowicz, *A History of English Criminal Law and its Administration, from 1750* (–1986; last volume with Roger Hood).

Daniel Boorstin, *The Lost World of Thomas Jefferson*.

Richard Hofstadter, *The American Political Tradition and the Men Who Made It*.

Winston S Churchill, *The Gathering Storm* (first volume of *The Second World War*).

L B Namier, *Diplomatic Prelude, 1938–9*.

J W Carter and Graham Pollard, *Thomas J Wise in the Original Cloth*, which exposes Wise's literary forgeries.

F R Leavis, *The Great Tradition*.

T S Eliot, *Notes Towards the Definition of Culture*.

Antonio Gramsci, *Prison Notebooks*.

R M Hare, *The Language of Morals*.

Bertrand Russell, *Human Knowledge: Its Scope and Limits*.

S Art, Sculpture, Fine Arts, and Architecture

The influx of US funds into Europe through the Marshall Plan causes US influence to penetrate European artistic culture.

Painting, etc:

Bill Brandt, *Camera in London* (photographs).

Bernard Buffet, *Absinthe Drinker*.

Willem de Kooning, *Mailbox*.

André Fougeron, *Les Parisiennes aux Marché*.

Barnett Newman, *Onement I*.

Jackson Pollock, *Composition No. 1* (action painting).

Nicolas de Staël, *Marathon*.

Sculpture:

Max Ernst, *Capricorn*.

Henry Moore, *Family Group* for Stevenage New Town, England.

Architecture:

Luigi Figini and Gino Pollini, Olivetti Building, Ivrea, Italy (–1950).

Buckminster Fuller, first sizeable geodesic dome constructed at Black Mountain College, Carolina, USA.

Pier Luigi Nervi, Exhibition Hall, Turin (single-roof structure, in undulating pre-fabrication).

Eero Saarinen, General Motors Technical Center, Warren, Michigan, USA (–1956).

T Music

Havergal Brian, *Gothic Symphony*.

Dmitri Kabalevsky, Violin Concerto in C.

Olivier Messiaen, *Turangalîla Symphony*.

Wallingford Riegger, Symphony No. 3.

Richard Strauss, *Four Last Songs*.

Virgil Thomson, *Louisiana Story* (suite).

Benjamin Britten founds Aldeburgh Festival (in E England).

Sir Malcolm Sargent becomes chief conductor of the Promenade Concerts, London.

Kiss Me, Kate (musical), text by Bella and Samuel Spewack, music by Cole Porter (first performed at the New Century Theatre, New York, 1948).

Ella Fitzgerald, 'My Happiness'.

Duke Ellington is given permission to play in Britain–the first US jazz act to appear in Britain since the Second World War.

Humphrey Lyttelton forms jazz band.

Columbia Record Company releases the first long-playing record (LP); by 1950 the playing speed of 33.3 revolutions per minute is established.

U Literature and Drama

Harold Acton, *Memoirs of An Aesthete*.

W H Auden, *The Age of Anxiety: A Baroque Eclogue* (poems).

Truman Capote, *Other voices, Other Rooms*.

Graham Greene, *The Heart of the Matter*.

Norman Mailer, *The Naked and the Dead*.

Thomas Merton, *Seven Storey Mountain*.

(report published on 25 Jan 1949 finds most charges are baseless).

M **December**

1 Arab Congress at Jericho proclaims Abdullah ibn Hussein of Transjordan as king of Palestine.

5 Ernst Reuter, Social Democrat, elected mayor of Berlin.

9 (–10) UN General Assembly adopts convention on prevention and punishment of genocide and the declaration of human rights.

12 UN General Assembly recognizes the government in Seoul, South Korea, as the lawful government of Korea and recommends that occupying powers should withdraw.

15 in Poland, the Polish Workers' Party and Polish Socialist Party merge to form the Polish United Workers' Party, led by Boleslaw Bierut.

18 following breakdown of negotiations, Dutch renew their offensive in Indonesia and capture Ahmed Sukarno's government.

25 the USSR claims to have withdrawn its forces from North Korea.

27 refusal of Catholics in Hungary to make concessions to government leads to arrest of Cardinal Mindszenty.

28 USA, Britain, France, and Benelux countries establish an International Ruhr Authority.

28 Nokrashy Pasha, prime minister of Egypt, is assassinated.

Alan Paton, *Cry, the Beloved Country.*
Ezra Pound, *The Pisan Cantos.*
Georges Simenon, *Pedigree.*
Gore Vidal, *The City and the Pillar.*
Patrick White, *The Aunt's Story.*
Thornton Wilder, *The Ides of March.*

Drama:
Albert Camus, *State of Siege.*
Christopher Fry, *The Lady's Not for Burning.*
Jean Genet, *The Maids.*
Moss Hart, *Light Up the Sky.*
Terence Rattigan, *The Browning Version.*

v Births and Deaths
Jan 8 Kurt Schwitters dies (60).
Jan 30 Mahatma Gandhi dies (79).
Jan 30 Orville Wright dies (76).
March 8 Jonathan Sacks born (–).
March 22 Andrew Lloyd Webber born (–).
July 23 D W Griffith dies (73).
Aug 16 (George Herman) 'Babe' Ruth dies (53).
Sept 3 Eduard Beneš dies (65).
Sept 11 Muhammad Ali Jinnah dies (71).
Nov 14 Prince Charles born (–).

w Everyday Life
'Scrabble' word game launched in USA.
Long-distance travel is made more comfortable by the invention of both car air-conditioning and Dramamine (an antihistimine used to counter travel sickness).
In USA, Richard and Maurice McDonald open a drive-in hamburger cafe.
In Britain, launch of the Morris Minor car (designed by Alec Issigonis); 1,293,331 vehicles are sold by the time of its withdrawal in 1971.

x Sport and Recreation
The International Rugby League Board, comprising Australia, Britain, France, and New Zealand, is established at a meeting in Bordeaux, France (25 Jan).
Ireland wins the Rugby Union Five Nations Grand Slam for the first time.
The 14th Olympic Games are held in London (29 July–14 Aug). The USA wins 38 gold medals; Sweden, 16; France and Hungary, 10 each; Italy and Finland, 8 each; Turkey and Czechoslovakia, 6 each; Switzerland, Denmark, and Holland, 5 each. Mrs Fanny Blankers-Koen of the Netherlands wins 4 golds, for the 100-m, the 200-m, the 80-m hurdles, and the 4 × 100-m relay.
Donald Bradman plays his last Test innings for Australia against England at The Oval, England; dismissed for 0, he retires with a Test average of 99.94 (14 Aug).

y Media
In USA, Marshall Field combines the *Chicago Sun* and *Times* to form the *Sun-Times.*
In Britain, death of R M Barrington Ward, editor of *The Times* since 1941; succeeded by W F Casey.

Film:
Abbot and Costello Meet Frankenstein.
Bicycle Thieves (director, Vittorio de Sica).
Bitter Rice (director, Giuseppe de Santi).
Drunken Angel (director, Akira Kurosawa).
The Fallen Idol (director, Carol Reed; starring Ralph Richardson).
Fort Apache (director, John Ford; starring Henry Fonda).
Hamlet (director and star, Laurence Olivier).
Key Largo (director, John Huston; starring Humphrey Bogart).
The Lady from Shanghai (director, Orson Welles).
The Naked City (director, Jules Dassin).
Red River (director, Howard Hawks; starring John Wayne).
The State of the Union (director, Frank Capra; starring Spencer Tracy and Katherine Hepburn).
The Winslow Boy (director, Anthony Asquith; starring Robert Donat).

Radio:
International Conference for redistribution of wavelengths (15 Sept).
BBC broadcasts *Any Questions?* (–).

Television:
New programmes in the USA include *Candid Camera* and *Hopalong Cassidy* (first Western series).
CBS broadcasts *The Toast of the Town*, which becomes *The Ed Sullivan Show* (–1971).

*Foundation of NATO ... Eire becomes a Republic ... Communists
win Chinese Civil War ... Indonesia becomes independent ...*

A **January**
7 Dean Acheson succeeds George Marshall as US secretary of state.
10 in China, Communist army under Zhu De captures Xuzhou, exposing the Nationalists' capital at Nanjing.
15 in Chinese Civil War, the Communists capture Tianjin in NE China.
18 Council for Mutual Economic Assistance formed in Moscow to further economic co-operation between the USSR and its satellites (25, Poland joins the Council).
20 in USA, President Harry Truman, in inaugural address, states Four-Point programme, including economic aid for underdeveloped countries.
20 United Nations Security Council calls for end of hostilities in Burma (now Myanmar).
21 Chiang Kai-shek resigns presidency of China, following successive reversals for Nationalist Armies.

B **February**
1 clothes rationing ends in Britain.
8 Eire declares that it cannot participate in proposed North Atlantic Treaty Organization while Ireland remains divided.
24 Israel and Egypt agree armistice (followed by armistices between Israel and Lebanon in March, with Transjordan on 3 April, with Syria on 20 July).

C **March**
4 in USSR, Andrei Vyshinsky replaces Vyacheslav Molotov as foreign minister.
13 Belgium, Netherlands, and Luxembourg agree to implement full economic union as soon as possible; on 26, France and Italy sign similar agreement.
31 Newfoundland joins Dominion of Canada as tenth province.

D **April**
4 foundation of the North Atlantic Treaty Organization ('NATO'): the North Atlantic Treaty is signed in Washington, DC, USA, by foreign ministers of USA, Canada, Britain, France, Luxembourg, Belgium, Netherlands, Italy, Portugal, Denmark, Iceland, and Norway, providing for mutual assistance against aggression.
10 USA, Britain, and France promulgate new occupation statute for their zones in Germany; the French zone is to be merged with the 'bizone' and a new West German state created with full self-government except for reserved matters (constitution or Basic Law of new state adopted by German

parliamentary council on 8 May and approved by Western military governors).
18 Republic of Ireland is formally proclaimed in Dublin; Ireland leaves the Commonwealth.
19 US Foreign Assistance bill authorizes $5.43 billion for European Recovery Programme.
24 in Chinese Civil War, Communists capture Nanjing, the Nationalist capital.

E **May**
5 Statute of Council of Europe is signed in London by Belgium, Denmark, France, Britain, Ireland, Italy, Luxembourg, Netherlands, Norway, and Sweden (and subsequently by Greece, Iceland, and Turkey); members commit themselves to support freedom and the rule of law; Strasbourg is chosen as seat of the Council; the Council's institutions include a Consultative Assembly, a Committee of Ministers, and the European Court of Human Rights.
11 Israel is admitted to the United Nations.
11 Siam changes name to Thailand.
12 Berlin blockade is officially lifted.
12 to aid Japan's recovery, the Far Eastern Commission terminates Japan's reparation payments.
14 United Nations General Assembly invites India, Pakistan, and South Africa to discuss alleged discrimination against Indian races in South Africa.
23 Federal Republic of Germany (West Germany) comes into being, with capital at Bonn (West Berlin is excluded from the new state but associated with it).
23 Communist armies in China, commanded by Zhu De, resume offensive, to drive Nationalist armies off the mainland.
30 in Germany, a People's Congress in the Soviet zone adopts a new constitution (providing for a People's Chamber and a Chamber of States).

F **June**
2 British parliament passes the Ireland Bill, which recognizes independence of the Republic of Ireland, but declares special relationship of Irish citizens to the United Kingdom and reaffirms the position of Northern Ireland within the United Kingdom unless its parliament decides otherwise.
2 Transjordan is renamed the Hashemite Kingdom of Jordan.

President Truman announces 'Fair Deal' ... South Pacific *in New York ... Orwell's* Nineteen Eighty-four *...*

o Politics, Government, Law, and Economy

James MacGregor Burns, *Congress on Trial: The Legislative Process and the Administrative State.*

V O Key, *Southern Politics.*

In the new state of Israel, a single-chamber parliament, the Knesset, is established, which (in place of a constitution) passes an interim organic law defining legislative, executive, and judicial powers; religious tribunals are to operate alongside the civil courts.

New constitution in Hungary, which establishes a Soviet-type state (Aug).

Constituent Assembly in India adopts new constitution (Nov; to come into force on 26 Jan 1950).

The US War Department is retitled Department of Defense (10 Aug).

The British Commonwealth is henceforth referred to as the Commonwealth.

UN International Court of Justice delivers first decision, holding Albania responsible for incidents in Corfu Channel in 1946 and awarding damages to Britain (9 April).

A comprehensive Legal Aid system is enacted in Britain (to come into force in 1950).

British Parliament Act reduces power of Lords to delay passage of legislation to two parliamentary sessions and a year and one month from the second reading of a bill in the House of Commons (16 Dec).

In USA, 11 Communists are convicted under the Smith Act of 1940, for advocating forcible overthrow of the government (the Supreme Court upholds the conviction in 1951 in Dennis v. US).

Alger Hiss, a former senior officer of the US State Department and suspected of espionage for the USSR, is tried for perjury (July); the jury fails to reach a verdict and a retrial is ordered (verdict announced 1950).

Council for Mutual Economic Assistance (Comecon) formed by the Soviet bloc.

Czechoslovakia launches a Five-Year Plan (from 1 Jan).

Romania starts collectivization of agriculture.

In USA, General Motors, Standard Oil, and other companies are found guilty of conspiracy to tear up municipal electric tram services, but are charged only nominal fines.

Devaluation of the pound from $4.03 to $2.80 coincides with devaluations in Germany, Belgium, and Italy.

British export drive successful, with a doubling of exports over those of 1946 and continuing growth.

In Britain, Iron and Steel Act passed to nationalize that industry, but its operation is suspended until the 1950 election.

Saudi Arabia grants a 60-year concession to Getty Oil of the USA, controlled by J P Getty (the deal makes Getty a billionaire).

p Society, Education, and Religion

In USA, President Truman (in his inaugural address on 20 Jan) announces his 'Fair Deal': a plan to extend social legislation; social security is to be expanded; the minimum wage to be raised; and the federal public housing program vastly enlarged; the Housing Act is passed (15 July), providing federal funds for slum clearance and construction of low-cost housing.

In USA, the minimum wage is raised from 40 cents to 75 cents an hour.

In South Africa, social legislation begins the implementation of 'apartheid'; the South African Citizenship Act suspends automatic granting of citizenship to Commonwealth immigrants after five years; the Prohibition of Mixed Marriages Act outlaws marriage between Europeans and non-Europeans; an amendment to the Immorality Act of 1927 bans sexual intercourse between Europeans and Coloureds; the Population Registration Act starts the process of defining people as White, Coloured, or African.

Simone de Beauvoir, *The Second Sex.*

R Lewis and Angus Maude, *The English Middle Classes.*

Margaret Mead, *Male and Female.*

Basic Law of the German Federal Republic (West Germany) restores control of education to the Länder (states).

Following the Communists' victory in the Chinese Civil War, the Common Programme establishes the right of all citizens to education and the responsibility of the state to provide it.

In England and Wales, the Teachers' Registration Council is abolished, having failed to register more than half of the profession since its inception in 1912.

University College of North Staffordshire is granted a charter to award its own degrees (becomes Keele University in 1962).

The Bible in Basic English.

Rudolph Bultmann, *Primitive Christianity in its Contemporary Setting.*

Eric Mascall, *Existence and Analogy.*

14 Vietnam State is established by French, with capital at Saigon, but conflict with Vietminh continues.

16 Communist purge in Hungary.

27 Liberals, led by Louis St Laurent, win majority in Canadian general election; Liberals win 193 seats; Conservatives, 41; others, 28.

27 start of coal strike in Australia (ends 15 Aug, after emergency legislation authorizes troops to work mines).

27 (–28 June) British dock strike (ends after the government implements the 1920 Emergency Powers Act for the first time).

29 USA completes withdrawal of occupying forces from South Korea.

G **July**

Former emperor of Vietnam Bao Dai returns to Vietnam at invitation of French and becomes prime minister.

16 Chinese Nationalists organize Supreme Council under Chiang Kai-shek, which begins to remove forces to the island of Formosa (now Taiwan; evacuation completed, 8 Dec).

18 fresh agreement between Iran and Anglo-Iranian Oil Company (but is later rejected by Iran assembly).

29 United Nations Atomic Energy Commission suspends meetings until a broader basis for agreement among powers is reached.

H **August**

5 US aid to Nationalist China ceases.

10 Christian Socialists and Liberals form coalition ministry in Belgium.

14 first general election held in West Germany; Christian Democrats win 139 seats; Social Democrats, 131; Free Democrats, 52; others, 80.

J **September**

2 United Nations Commission warns of danger of civil war in Korea.

12 Theodor Heuss, Free Democrat, is elected president of West Germany and Konrad Adenauer, Christian Democrat, chancellor; Adenauer forms government of Christian Democrats, Free Democrats, and the German Party.

18 Britain devalues the pound (from exchange rate of $4.03 to $2.80); most European states subsequently devalue their currencies.

21 in West Germany, Allied High Commission replaces Allied Military government.

27 USSR denounces treaty with Yugoslavia.

30 Berlin Airlift ends, after 277,264 flights.

K **October**

1 in China, Communist leader Mao Zedong proclaims the establishment of the People's Republic, with its government based in Beijing (Zhou Enlai is prime minister and foreign minister).

1 Bulgaria and, on 21, Romania denounce treaties of friendship with Yugoslavia.

6 in USA, President Truman signs Mutual Defense Assistance Act for provision of military aid to NATO countries.

7 Democratic Republic established in East Germany (on 11, Wilhelm Pieck is elected president and Otto Grotewohl as prime minister).

9 Socialist vote falls in Austrian elections.

14 leaders of the Communist Party of America are convicted of conspiracy.

15 in Chinese Civil War, Communists capture Guangzhou.

16 defeat of rebels ends Greek Civil War (since May 1946).

28 Georges Bidault forms coalition in France, following Henri Queuille's resignation over financial crisis.

L **November**

11 (–13) Polish United Workers' Party is purged of members with Titoist leanings.

21 United Nations General Assembly votes for ultimate independence of Italy's former colonies.

24 Allied High Commission makes further economic concessions to West Germany on its accession to the International Ruhr Authority.

26 India adopts constitution as a federal republic, remaining within the Commonwealth (to come into force on 26 Jan 1950).

M **December**

5 United Nations General Assembly requires member states to submit information on armaments and armed forces.

8 Nationalists driven by Communists from the Chinese mainland declare Taipei on the island of Formosa (now Taiwan) to be the capital of the Republic of China.

8 United Nations calls on Powers to recognize political independence of China.

14 Israeli government moves capital from Tel Aviv to Jerusalem, disregarding United Nations resolution for internationalization of Jerusalem.

15 West Germany becomes full member of Marshall Plan for European recovery.

17 Robert Menzies, Liberal, forms new coalition in Australia.

27 Netherlands transfers sovereignty to United States of Indonesia (comprising all the former Dutch East Indies except western New Guinea).

30 France transfers sovereignty to Vietnam.

Q Science, Technology, and Discovery

Opening of Mount Palomar observatory.

USA tests first multistage rocket.

First atomic bomb tests in USSR.

US physicist Richard Feynman publishes his re-casting of the theory of quantum electrodynamics.

US physician Philip Hench discovers Cortisone (compound E) as cure for rheumatism.

US biologist Selman A Waksman isolates antibiotic neomycin.

Dorothy Hodgkin in Britain works out chemical structure of penicillin.

R Humanities

Start of excavations by S I Rudenko of 5th-century-BC Scythian tombs at Pazyryk, Siberia, USSR.

Alberto Ruz begins the excavation of the Temple of Inscriptions at the Maya city of Palenque; the discovery of a pyramid, skeletons, and funerary goods demonstrates that Maya pyramids were funerary buildings.

J E Neale, *The Elizabethan House of Commons*.

Fernand Braudel, *The Mediterranean and the Mediterranean World in the Age of Philip II*.

Samuel F Bemis, *John Quincy Adams and the Foundations of American Policy*.

W K Hancock and M M Gowing, *British War Economy*.

Marc Bloch, *The Historian's Craft*.

Kenneth Clark, *Landscape into Art*.

Axel Hägerström, *Philosophy and Religion*.

Arthur Koestler, *Insight and Outlook*.

Gilbert Ryle, *The Concept of Mind*.

S Art, Sculpture, Fine Arts, and Architecture

'L'Art Brut Préféré aux Arts Culturels', exhibition curated by Jean Dubuffet, Paris, France; includes, among others, art collected from mental hospitals and raises question of who or what defines art.

Life magazine features Jackson Pollock: 'Jackson Pollock: Is he the greatest living painter in the US?'.

Painting, etc:

Josef Albers begins the *Homage to the Square* series, continuing until his death in 1976.

Karel Appel, *Questioning Children*.

Constant, *Après nous la liberté*.

Willem de Kooning, *Asheville*.

Henri Matisse, *The Tree of Life*, maquette for stained glass for Chapel of the Rosary of the Dominican Nuns, Vence, France.

Robert Motherwell begins series *Elegy to the Spanish Republic*.

Graham Sutherland, *Somerset Maugham*.

Wols, *Bird*.

Sculpture:

Jacob Epstein, *Lazarus*.

Lucio Fontana, *Ambiente Spaziale a Luce Nera*.

Pablo Picasso, *Pregnant Woman*.

Architecture:

Philip Johnson, Johnson 'Glass' house, New Canaan, Connecticut, USA.

Frank Lloyd Wright, Laboratory tower for S C Johnson & Son, Wisconsin, USA.

T Music

Leonard Bernstein, *The Age of Anxiety*.

Marc Blitzstein, *Regina* (opera).

Benjamin Britten, *Spring Symphony*.

Gerald Finzi, *Clarinet Concerto*.

Goffredo Petrassi, *Il Cordovano* (opera).

Gentlemen Prefer Blondes (musical), lyrics by Leo Robin, music by Jule Styne (first performed at the Ziegfeld Theatre, New York, on 8 Dec).

South Pacific (musical), lyrics by Oscar Hammerstein, music by Richard Rodgers (first performed at the Majestic Theatre, New York, 7 April).

Foundation of US folk group The Weavers (disbanded for political reasons in 1952; reformed in 1955).

Sidney Bechet, 'Les oignons'.

Billboard introduces the term 'Rhythm and blues' as description for the current range of African-American music.

In USA, start of *Billboard* Country and Western chart.

RCA release the first single record at the playing speed of 45 revolutions per minute.

U Literature and Drama

H E Bates, *The Jacaranda Tree*.

Enid Blyton's first *Noddy* books published.

Elizabeth Bowen, *The Heat of the Day*.

Paul Bowles, *The Sheltering Sky*.

James Broughton, *The Playground* (poems).

Paul Eluard, *Une Leçon de morale* (poems).

Jean Genet, *The Thief's Journal*.

Paul Goodman, *The Grand Piano*.

Fitzroy Maclean, *Eastern Approaches*.

Louis MacNeice, *Collected Poems 1925–1948*.

Nancy Mitford, *Love in a Cold Climate*.

Charles Morgan, *The River Line* (dramatised 1952).

George Orwell, *Nineteen Eighty-four*.

Cesare Pavese, *The House on the Hill*.

*The Schuman Plan ... Outbreak of Korean War ... NATO agrees
creation of integrated defence force ...*

A **January**

3 in Egypt, general election results in an
overwhelming majority for the Wafd Party,
ending five years of government by minority administrations.

5 Alexander Diomedes, prime minister of
Greece, resigns; his successor (from 7),
John Theotokis, Populist, heads a caretaker
government.

6 Britain recognizes Communist China.

6 Franco–German parliamentary conference
opens in Basle, Switzerland, to discuss the
two countries' economic and political
relations within the framework of a united
Europe.

9 in USA, Senator Joseph McCarthy alleges
that 205 Communists are working in the
State Department (22, Senate Foreign
Relations Committee is given job of investigating charges).

12 in Egypt, Mustafa an-Nahas Pasha forms
Wafd government which includes all ministers dismissed in 1944.

12 state of emergency in Gold Coast (now part
of Ghana), caused by strikes.

Frank Sargeson, *I Saw in My Dreams*.

Drama:
T S Eliot, *The Cocktail Party*.
Arthur Miller, *Death of a Salesman*.
Sean O'Casey, *Cock-a Doodle Dandy*.
In the USA, inauguration of the Shakespeare Festival in Balboa Park, San Diego.
Berliner Ensemble founded by Bertolt Brecht, at the Theater am Schiffbauerdamm in East Berlin.

v Births and Deaths
May 6 Maurice Maeterlinck dies (86).
Sept 6 Richard Strauss dies (85).
Sept 23 Bruce Springsteen born (–).
Oct 30 Edward R Stettinius dies (49).

w Everyday Life
'Silly Putty' is invented when a chemical process goes wrong.

x Sport and Recreation
After 25 successful title defences, Joe Louis retires as World Heavyweight boxing champion (1 March); Ezzard Charles outpoints Jersey Joe Walcott over 15 rounds to win the National Boxing Association version of the vacant title (22 June).
In Britain, the Badminton Olympic Three-Day Event (horse-riding) is held for the first time on the Duke of Beaufort's estate.
Seventeen members of the Torino side, Italian football champions for 5 successive years, are killed in a plane crash at Superga.
Photo-finish cameras are introduced to decide the results of English classic horse-races in close finishes.

The National Parks and Access to Countryside Act is passed, creating National Parks and long-distance footpaths in England and Wales.

y Media
In Germany, foundation in Hamburg of the press agency Deutsche Presse-Agentur.
Publication of *Paris-match*, an illustrated French news magazine.

Film:
All The King's Men (director, Robert Rossen; starring Broderick Crawford).
The Blue Lamp (starring Jack Warner as a police constable who is killed in a shooting; he is revived by the BBC in 1955 for *Dixon of Dock Green*).
Les Enfants terribles (director, Jean Melville).
The Heiress (director, William Wyler; starring Olivia de Havilland).
Kind Hearts and Coronets (director, Robert Hamer; starring Alec Guinness).
She Wore a Yellow Ribbon (director, John Ford; starring John Wayne).
The Third Man (director, Carol Reed; starring Orson Welles).
White Heat (director, Raoul Walsh; starring James Cagney).

Television:
RCA in the USA produces a colour television system.
New programmes in the USA include *The Lone Ranger*.
The radio series *Amos 'n' Andy* becomes a television series with African-American actors.

E H Gombrich's Story of Art *... Maria Callas sings at La Scala*
... First Formula One racing championship ...

o Politics, Government, Law, and Economy
R H S Crossman (ed.), *The God That Failed: Six Studies in Communism* (contributors are: Louis Fischer, André Gide, Arthur Koestler, Ignazio Silone, Stephen Spender, and Richard Wright).
Denmark annuls 1918 Act of Union with Iceland (a republic since 1944).
In Indonesia, a centralized state organization replaces the Dutch federal system (17 Aug).
In West Germany, Christian Democratic parties unite (Oct) as the Christian Democratic Union (CDU).
Stephen K Bailey, *Congress Makes a Law*.
In USA, Congress passes the Internal Security (or McCarran) Bill (Sept), requiring registration of Communist organizations and forbidding the employment of Communists in defence companies (vetoed by President Truman, but passed over his veto in 1951).
International Law Commission, established by the United Nations in Nov 1947, submits its formulation of the 'Nuremberg principles' to the General Assembly (concern-

13 UN Security Council rejects motion of USSR (proposed on 10) that the representatives of Nationalist China (Formosa, now Taiwan) should be removed; Soviet delegates then boycott UN (–1 Aug).

26 inauguration of the Republic of India, with Rajendra Prasad (a supporter of the late Mahatma Gandhi) as president.

27 bilateral agreements for aid in defence signed in Washington, DC, USA, between USA and (separately) Britain, France, Belgium, Netherlands, Luxembourg, Norway, Denmark, and Italy.

27 in Italy, following resignation of Democratic Socialist minister in Nov 1949 and withdrawal of Liberal support, Alcide de Gasperi forms new coalition of Christian Democrats, Democratic Socialists, and Republicans.

29 in South Africa, first series of riots in Johannesburg provoked by government racial policy.

30 Britain, Norway, Denmark, and Sweden sign agreement for economic co-operation.

31 in USA, President Truman instructs Atomic Energy Commission to proceed with development of the hydrogen bomb (a far more powerful kind of atomic weapon).

B February

1 Vlko Chervenkov becomes prime minister of Bulgaria on Vasil Kolarov's death.

13 conference opens in Bangkok, Thailand, of heads of US missions in 14 Asian countries to discuss US support for moves for independence.

14 in Moscow, USSR, the USSR and Communist China sign a 30-year Treaty of Friendship, Alliance, and Mutual Assistance (in the event of attack) and other agreements.

20 USA severs diplomatic relations with Bulgaria, after Bulgaria refuses to withdraw charge that Donald Heath, a US minister, had been involved with Traicho Kostov (a former senior Communist who was executed in 1949).

23 general election in Britain results in a reduced Labour majority (315 seats; Conservatives, 298; Liberals, 9; others 3).

28 British Prime Minister Clement Attlee reconstructs his ministry, though most changes are below cabinet rank; Hugh Gaitskell is appointed minister for economic affairs.

C March

1 Chiang Kai-shek resumes presidency of Nationalist China (Formosa, now Taiwan).

3 French government signs agreements with the government of the Saar, confirming the Saar's autonomy in legislative, administrative, and juridical matters, but reserving control over foreign policy and security; the Saar remains in economic union with France.

8 Marshal Klement Voroshilov announces that USSR possesses the atomic bomb.

12 in Belgium, a referendum supports (by a small majority) the return of King Leopold III (on 18, government resigns because of disagreement on the question of his return).

16 Dean Acheson, US secretary of state, makes speech suggesting ways in which the USSR could end the Cold War.

21 Konrad Adenauer, chancellor of West Germany, advocates economic union between his country and France.

D April

1 Somalia, which had been occupied by British troops 1941–49, becomes a UN Trust Territory under Italian administration (the greater part of modern Somalia, known as British Somaliland, continues as a British Protectorate, 1887–1960).

8 India and Pakistan sign Delhi Pact, each committing itself to upholding the rights of its minority populations.

11 following the shooting down of a US aircraft on 8, USSR complains to USA that a US Flying Fortress bomber had entered Soviet air space in Latvia (18, USA implies that USSR had shot down a private plane bound for Sweden).

13 members of the Arab League sign a security pact, whereby they will coordinate their defence arrangements.

19 (–1 May) dock strike in London.

27 Communist Party is outlawed in Australia.

27 Britain recognizes Israel.

E May

9 announcement in Paris of the Schuman Plan, for placing the French and German coal industries and iron and steel production under a single authority which could then be joined by other countries.

11 foreign ministers of Britain, France, and USA confer in London on the future of Germany.

22 Chinese Communist government offers Tibet regional autonomy if it will adopt Communist system.

30 Albania and Yugoslavia sever relations.

F June

5 in USA, President Truman signs bill providing US foreign aid of $3,121 million (including funds for the 'Marshall Aid' programme).

ing war crimes, crimes against peace, and crimes against humanity).

The Council of Europe produces the European Convention on Human Rights, providing for a European Court of Human Rights and a Commission to enforce the Convention.

Capital punishment reintroduced in USSR (12 Jan).

In USA, Alger Hiss is found guilty of perjury in concealing membership of Communist Party (25 Jan).

In Britain, the atomic scientist Klaus Fuchs is sentenced to 14 years' imprisonment for betraying atomic secrets to Soviet agents (1 March); his evidence in confession to MI5 is used to incriminate his contact in the USA, Harry Gold, and Julius and Ethel Rosenberg.

Legal Aid comes into force in Britain (2 Oct).

The Korean War leads to tax rises and a burst of inflation in western countries.

President Truman bans US trade with the People's Republic of China (8 Dec).

Colombo Conference of Commonwealth foreign ministers held to prepare plans for co-operating in the economic development of Asiatic states (9 Jan).

European Payments Union (EPU) established (from 30 June, with retrospective agreement signed on 19 Sept); to manage and settle trade deficits and surpluses between 15 countries plus the sterling area (–30 June 1952).

Hungary launches Five-Year Plan, to develop heavy industry.

In USA, the Celler-Kefauver Act makes horizontal mergers between firms in the same industry illegal.

In USA, the 'Treaty of Detroit', a five-year agreement between General Motors and the United Auto Workers (signed 23 May), delivers high wages and industrial peace.

The London Stock Exchange starts compensation fund to guarantee investors against the default of member firms.

Rationing ends in West Germany, apart from sugar (1 March).

Wealthy US industrialist Howard Hughes becomes a recluse.

P **Society, Education, and Religion**

In South Africa, an amendment to the 1949 Immorality Act prohibits sexual intercourse between Europeans and Coloureds; the Population Registration Act provides for the eventual registration of the entire population as either White, Coloured, or African; and the Group Areas Act establishes machinery for demarcating areas in which members of each racial group are permitted to live; the Suppression of Communism Act gives the minister of justice considerable power to deal with any organization opposing government policy.

Polygamy, infanticide, and child marriage are banned in the People's Republic of China (1 May).

In USA, cartoonist 'Herblock' (Herbert Lawrence Block) coins term 'McCarthyism'.

The Kefauver Committee investigates the extent of organized crime in the USA.

Congress for Cultural Freedom meets in West Berlin.

David Riesman, Reuel Denney, and Nathan Glazer, *The Lonely Crowd*.

L Ron Hubbard, *Dianetics: The Modern Science of Mental Health*.

Holy Year of the Roman Catholic Church.

Pope Pius XII issues encyclical *Humani Generis*, against Existentialism and 'erroneous' scientific theories.

In *Munificentissimus Deus*, Pope Pius XII promulgates the dogma of the bodily Assumption of the Virgin Mary (1 Nov).

In Yugoslavia, the Macedonian Orthodox Church is separated from the Serbian patriarchate.

In Hungary, following government decree (7 Sept), most religious orders are closed, their buildings closed, and their members evicted.

In USA, National Council of Churches of Christ is established.

R A Knox, *Enthusiasm*.

Q **Science, Technology, and Discovery**

Jet-propelled, pilotless aircraft constructed in Australia.

US Atomic Energy Commission separates plutonium from pitchblende concentrates.

Existence of 'V'-particles is confirmed in Pasadena, California, USA, and on the Pic du Midi d'Ossau.

G T Seaborg of California University, USA, discovers element 98 (californium).

New calculations for the speed of light obtained through use of radio waves at National Physical Laboratory, Teddington, Britain, and at Stanford University, USA.

R **Humanities**

Thor Heyerdahl, *The Kon-Tiki Expedition*.

E V Rieu's translation of Homer's *The Iliad*.

Brian Hope-Taylor excavates remains of a large Anglo-Saxon hall at Yeavering, Northumberland, NE England.

Bernard Lewis, *The Arabs in History*.

S T Bindoff, *Tudor England*.

A L Rowse, *The England of Elizabeth*.

F A Pottle (ed.), *Boswell's London Journal, 1762–3*.

6 Trygve Lie, appointed to a fresh term of office as secretary general of UN, announces 20-year peace programme, envisaging more regular meetings of foreign ministers, creation of a permanent UN military force, admission of new members to UN, and greater aid for poorer countries.

15 West Germany admitted to Council of Europe.

24 Georges Bidault, French prime minister, resigns after his government is defeated in a vote on a technical issue.

25 North Korean forces invade South Korea with several armies advancing southwards; UN Security Council passes resolution demanding withdrawal of North Korean forces (26 in US).

27 President Truman of USA orders US air and naval forces in E Asia to resist N Korean aggression and sends reinforcements; order ratified by UN Security Council which passes resolution calling on UN members to help South Korea repel the invasion by the North.

28 North Koreans capture Seoul in South Korea; most of the South Korean army is destroyed.

G **July**

1 in Korea, first UN troops arrive at Pusan at SE end of the peninsula (16 UN members send contingents to Korea, though most troops are from the USA).

7 UN Security Council instructs the USA to appoint a supreme commander of UN forces in Korea (8, USA appoints Douglas MacArthur).

11 René Pleven forms French government in which Guy Mollet and other Socialists serve.

19 in USA, President Truman sends message to Congress urging vast military budget.

20 in USA, the Senate accepts committee report denying Senator Joseph McCarthy's charges (of 9 Feb) of Communist infiltration of the State Department.

22 King Leopold III returns to Belgium after six years' exile (23, Socialist demonstrations in Brussels protesting against his return).

H **August**

1 King Leopold III abdicates in favour of his son Prince Baudouin.

1 Jacob Malik of USSR chairs meeting of UN Security Council, ending the Soviet boycott.

11 at the meeting in Strasbourg, France, of the Consultative Assembly of the Council of Europe, Winston Churchill of Britain sup-

ports a motion calling for creation of a European army; the motion is passed by 89 votes to 5.

15 in Belgium, Paul van Zeeland forms Christian Socialist ministry.

J **September**

1 North Koreans attack across the Naktong River at the SE end of the Korean peninsula.

4 new constitution adopted in Syria, curtailing the powers of the president.

19 emergency session of British Parliament for passing defence measures for Korean War.

12 Louis A Johnson resigns as US secretary of defence; succeeded by George Marshall.

15 in South Korea, US forces (for UN) make surprise amphibious landing at Inchon, W of Seoul; North Koreans panic and retreat.

15 national service in Britain is extended to two years.

26 in Korea, UN forces recapture Seoul, the capital of South Korea.

28 Indonesia is admitted to the UN.

29 in Korea, General MacArthur is authorized to organize advance of UN forces into North Korea.

K **October**

1 in Korea, South Korean and UN troops, moving north, cross the 38th parallel (the border line between North and South).

4 Turkey agrees to co-operate with NATO defence plans for the Mediterranean.

7 Dean Acheson, US secretary of state, proposes plan for strengthening UN's powers to resist aggression: if the Security Council is unable to adopt course of action against act of aggression, the General Assembly should recommend a course of action to members (adopted on 19).

15 East German elections result in 99.7 per cent of voters supporting the National Front (dominated by the Communists).

19 in Britain, Stafford Cripps resigns as the chancellor of the exchequer because of ill health; succeeded by Hugh Gaitskell.

20 in Korea, UN troops capture Pyongyang, the capital of North Korea.

21 Chinese forces occupy Tibet, with Tibetan army accepting defeat.

21 representatives of the Soviet bloc (chaired by Vyacheslav Molotov, the Soviet foreign minister) meet in Prague, Czechoslovakia, to discuss the future of Germany.

24 in Paris, France, Prime Minister René Pleven announces to the National Assembly a plan for creation of a European Military Community, including a European Army (the Pleven Plan).

Harold A Innis, *Empire and Communication*.
Henry Nash Smith, *Virgin Land: The American West as Symbol and Myth*.
Allan Nevins, *The Emergence of Lincoln*.
Cecil Woodham-Smith, *Florence Nightingale*.
Henry Steele Commager, *The American Mind: An Interpretation of American Thought and Character since the 1880s*.
E H Carr, *History of Soviet Russia* (14 volumes, nos. 9 and 10 with R W Davies; –1978).
R M Titmuss, *Problems of Social Policy*.
Journal of Ecclesiastical History issued (–).
E H Gombrich, *The Story of Art*.
Geiriadur Prifysgol Cymru/A Dictionary of the Welsh Language, (–).
Nicholas Berdyaev, *Dream and Reality*.
Rudolf Carnap, *Logical Foundations of Probability*.
Stephen Toulmin, *An Examination of the Place of Reason in Ethics*.

s Art, Sculpture, Fine Arts, and Architecture

Influence of Paris as the world's art centre begins to decline, threatened by rise of New York and challenged by other European capitals.
Parisian art critic Michel Tapié coins term 'Art Informel' to denote the European expressionist style running parallel with Abstract Expressionism in the USA.

Painting, etc:
Jean Dubuffet, *Corps de Dames* series (–1951).
Asger Jorn, *Buttadeo*.
Franz Kline, *Chief*.
Barnett Newman, *Vir Heroicus Sublimis* (–1951).
Serge Poliakoff, patchwork-type paintings reach maturity.
Jackson Pollock, *Autumn Rhythm*.
Robert Rauschenberg, *White Painting* – first monochrome by US artist.
Mark Rothko, *Number One*.
Clyfford Still, *1950-A, No. 2*.
Emilio Vedova, *Concentration Camp*.

Sculpture:
Alberto Giacometti, *Falling Man*.
Pablo Picasso, *The She-Goat*.
Germaine Richier, crucifixion for the church at Assy, France (outcry forces its removal).
David Smith, *Tanktotem* series.

Architecture:
Gordon Bunshaft, Lever Building, New York (–1952).
Le Corbusier, Chapel of Nôtre-Dame-du-Haut at Ronchamp, France (–1954).

Ludwig Mies van der Rohe, Farnsworth House, Plano, Illinois, USA.
Mario Pani and Enrique del Moral, University City, Mexico.
Powell and Moya, Pimlico Housing Estate, Westminster, London.

T Music

Lennox Berkeley, *Sinfonietta*.
Carlos Chavez, Violin Concerto.
Luigi Dallapiccola, *Il Prigioniero* (opera).
David Diamond, Piano Concerto.
Quincey Porter, String Quartet No. 8.
Maria Callas makes debut at La Scala Opera, Milan, Italy.
Call Me Madam (musical), by Irving Berlin (first performed at the Imperial Theatre, New York, 12 Oct).
Guys and Dolls (musical), by Frank Loesser and Abe Burrows (first performed at the 46th Street Theatre, New York, 24 Nov).
Fats Domino, 'The Fat Man'.

U Literature and Drama

W H Auden, *Collected Shorter Poems*.
Sri Aurobindo, *Savitri*, the longest verse epic in English.
Ray Bradbury, *The Martian Chronicles*.
Marguerite Duras, *The Sea Wall*.
William Goyen, *The House of Breath*.
Julien Green, *Moira*.
G I Gurdjieff, *Beelzebub's Tales to his Grandson*.
Ernest Hemingway, *Across the River and Into the Trees*.
Doris Lessing, *The Grass is Singing*.
Pablo Neruda, *General Song*.
P D Ouspensky, *In Search of the Miraculous*.
Cesare Pavese, *The Moon and Sixpence*.
Ezra Pound, *Seventy Cantos*.
Carl Sandburg, *Collected Poems*.
I B Singer, *The Family Moskat*.
C P Snow, *The Masters*.
Richard Wilhelm (translator), *The I Ching*.
Angus Wilson, *Such Darling Dodos*.

Drama:
Jean Anouilh, *La Répétition ou l'amour puni*.
Stig Dagerman, *The Man Condemned to Die*.
Christopher Fry, *Venus Observed*.
William Inge, *Come Back Little Sheba*.
Eugène Ionesco, *The Bald Prima Donna*.
John Van Druten, *Bell, Book and Candle*.

V Births and Deaths

Jan 9 Alec Jeffreys born (–).
Jan 21 George Orwell (Eric Blair) dies (46).
Feb 14 Karl Jansky dies (44).
Feb 26 Sir Harry Lauder dies (79).

28 in Denmark, following a general election and the resignation of Hans Hedtoft, the Liberal Agrarian leader Erik Eriksen forms a coalition ministry of his own party and Conservatives.

30 nationalist rising in Puerto Rico.

N November

1 in USA, two Puerto Ricans attempt to assassinate President Truman.

3 French forces withdraw from frontier of N Indochina.

4 UN General Assembly revokes 1946 resolutions on Spain (which had barred Spain from membership of the UN and had recommended members not to maintain diplomatic relationships with Spain).

5 Douglas MacArthur, UN commander in Korea, reports the massing of Chinese troops in North Korea.

7 in US elections, Republicans gain 30 seats in House of Representatives.
Tibet appeals to UN against Chinese aggression.

18 meeting of Consultative Assembly of the Council of Europe, which hears speech by Robert Schuman, French foreign minister, supporting the Pleven Plan for establishment of a European Defence Community and European Army.

24 in Korea, UN troops launch offensive into NE Korea.

26 Chinese troops enter Korean War, forcing UN forces to retreat southwards.

27 delegates of Communist government in China attend UN as observers.

28 Poland and East Germany proclaim the Oder–Neisse line as the frontier between the two countries.

M December

13 Marshall Aid to Britain ceases.

13 South Africa refuses to place South-West Africa (a mandate from the former League of Nations) under UN trusteeship.

16 state of emergency proclaimed in USA following reversals of UN forces in Korea.

19 conference of North Atlantic Conference (established under the North Atlantic Treaty of April 1949) agrees to create an integrated defence force, under the supreme command of General Dwight Eisenhower.

27 China refuses UN appeal for a cease-fire in Korea.

27 USA and Spain resume diplomatic relations.

28 in Korea, Chinese forces moving southwards cross the 38th parallel into South Korea.

March 12 Heinrich Mann dies (78).
March 19 Edgar Rice Burroughs dies (74).
March 30 Léon Blum dies (77).
April 3 Kurt Weill dies (50).
April 8 Vaslav Nijinsky dies (60).
July 22 W L Mackenzie King dies (75).
Sept 11 J C Smuts dies (80).
Oct 23 Al Jolson dies (64).
Nov 2 George Bernard Shaw dies (94).

w Everyday Life

In USA, Charlie Brown appears in Charles Schulz's first syndicated cartoon.

Smokey the Bear survives a forest fire in USA to become an emblem of National Park fire safety.

Diners' Club cards issued in New York, the first modern charge card.

In USA, a special tax and colouring restrictions on margarine are lifted at federal level.

In Britain, the first £100,000 winner of the football pools is declared.

Opening of J Sainsbury's first self-service shop in Croydon, S London (31 July).

The stone of Scone (the Scottish coronation stone) is stolen from the throne in Westminster Abbey, London (25 Dec; recovered in Scotland on 11 April 1951).

x Sport and Recreation

Argentina wins the first world basketball championship, held in Buenos Aires, Argentina.

The West Indies win a Test Match in England for the first time, winning the second Test at Lord's by 326 runs; 18 England wickets fall to the spinners Sonny Ramadhin and Alf Valentine (24–29 June).

The fourth football World Cup is held in Brazil, when Uruguay beats Brazil 2–1 in the final, witnessed by 199,854 spectators (July 16); British sides compete for the first time, England losing 1–0 to the USA (June 29).

The first Formula One World Motor Racing Championship is won by the Italian Giuseppe Farina, driving an Alfa Romeo.

y Media

Film:

All About Eve (director, Joseph L Mankiewicz, starring Bette Davis).
Annie Get Your Gun (lyrics and music by Irving Berlin).
The Asphalt Jungle (director, John Huston).
La Beauté du diable (director, René Clair).
Diary of a Country Priest (director, Robert Bresson).
Les Enfants terribles (director, Jean Cocteau).
Orphée (director, Jean Cocteau).
Rashomon (director, Akira Kurosawa).
Rio Grande (director, John Ford).
Summer Interlude (director, Ingmar Bergman).
Sunset Boulevard (director, Billy Wilder; starring Gloria Swanson and William Holder).
The Wooden Horse (director, Jack Lee).
The Young and the Damned (director, Luis Buñuel).

Radio:

Formation of a new European Broadcasting Union, representing mainly countries in Western Europe.

In Britain, start of *The Archers* (May) in the Midland region of the BBC; broadcast nationally from 1 Jan 1951 (–).

Television:

Start of regular colour broadcasts in USA.

New programmes in USA include *Your Show of Shows* with Ed Caesar, and *What's My Line?*

In Britain, the BBC broadcasts *Watch with Mother* (–1980), featuring Andy Pandy.

The BBC introduces the current affairs discussion programme *In the News* (–13 April 1956); regular participants in the early years include Robert Boothby, W J Brown, Michael Foot, and A J P Taylor.

The BBC programme *Television Crosses the Channel*, celebrating the centenary of the laying of the submarine cable between Britain and France, is the first programme broadcast across the English Channel, from Calais, France (27 Aug).

President Truman dismisses General MacArthur ... Libya becomes independent ... Conservatives win general election in Britain ...

A **January**

1 in Korea, North Korean and Chinese forces break United Nations lines on 38th parallel and, on 4 take Seoul, the capital of South Korea.

17 in Britain, Aneurin Bevan is appointed minister of labour.

26 in Korea, UN forces launch counteroffensive against Chinese and North Koreans.

B **February**

8 President Truman orders army to control US railways during strike.

13 British Commonwealth Consultative Committee meets at Colombo to discuss development plan for S and SE Asia.

15 conference opens in Paris to discuss formation of the European Defence Community and Army (following the Pleven Plan of 1950).

19 in Iran, Dr Muhammad Mossadeq, chairman of the oil commission of the Iranian Majlis (parliament), proposes that the oil industry in Iran should be nationalized.

28 René Pleven's coalition in France falls on issue of electoral reform.

C **March**

2 purge of Czechoslovak Communist Party.

4 International Socialist Conference meeting in London adopts name 'Socialist International'.

5 (–21 June) deputy foreign ministers of Britain, France, USA, and USSR meet in Paris to prepare agenda for future conference, but problem of disarmament hampers progress.

7 General Ali Razmara, prime minister of Iran, is assassinated by a militant nationalist.

9 in Britain, Ernest Bevin resigns as foreign secretary because of ill health; succeeded by Herbert Morrison.

10 Henri Queuille forms ministry in France, ending political deadlock.

20 in Iran, oil nationalization bill becomes law, leading to dispute with Britain: under the 1933 Oil Convention, the concession to the Anglo-Iranian Oil Company should not be altered unilaterally and disputes should be referred to arbitration.

29 USA completes draft peace treaty with Japan which is circulated to the powers.

29 Chinese government rejects Douglas MacArthur's offer of truce discussions but, on 31, India, and, on 2 April, Britain again urge truce in Korean War.

31 in Korea, UN forces have moved northwards again to the 38th Parallel; General MacArthur advocates extending the war into China, using atomic bombs.

D **April**

11 President Truman of USA relieves General MacArthur of command in Korea, because of his public advocacy of war with China; succeeded by Matthew Ridgway; UN forces how fight to hold their line on the 38th Parallel (on 19, MacArthur argues against the US administration's policies in address to joint session of Congress).

22 in Britain, Aneurin Bevan (minister for labour) and Harold Wilson (president of the board of trade) resign from Labour cabinet in protest at imposition of health service charges to meet increasing defence spending.

22 (–25) in Korea, Battle of Imjin River: defensive action by UN troops against Chinese and North Koreans.

28 in Iran, after a fortnight's rioting in Abadan, the shah appoints Dr Muhammad Mossadeq prime minister.

E **May**

7 (–25 June) in USA, George Marshall and other witnesses testify before the Foreign Relations Committee and Armed Services Committee of the Senate on Douglas MacArthur's removal as UN commander in Korea.

17 in Korea, Chinese launch offensive along most of the front in central Korea, forcing back the United Nations forces.

25 in Britain, diplomats Guy Burgess and Donald Maclean are warned by art historian and Soviet spy Anthony Blunt that they are under suspicion for espionage; they leave Britain (their presence in Moscow, USSR, is revealed on 11 Feb 1956).

26 Britain submits dispute with Iran over nationalization of oil to the International Court of Justice (26 June, oil tankers leave Abadan).

F **June**

3 Indian Socialist Party organizes mammoth demonstration in Delhi in protest at the government's food and housing policies.

13 following a general election in the Republic of Ireland (on 30 May), the prime minister, Dr John Costello, is not re-elected by the Dáil; Éamon de Valera returns to power as head of a coalition government.

British Witchcraft Act repealed ... Atomic energy generates
electric power ... Rauschenberg's Black Painting ...

o Politics, Government, Law, and Economy

Hannah Arendt, *The Origins of Totalitarianism*.

In Britain, Lord Radcliffe gives the Reith Lectures (on radio) on 'Power and the State'.

Communist-sponsored World Peace Council meets in East Berlin (opens 21 Feb).

The 21st Amendment to the US constitution restricts presidents to a maximum of two elected terms (a vice-president who has succeeded a president during a term of office may in addition serve a maximum of two years of the former president's term).

In Dennis v. US, the US Supreme Court upholds Smith Act prosecutions against American communists by a weakened version of the 'clear and present danger' test.

In USA, Julius Rosenberg, an electrical engineer, and his wife Ethel are tried under the Espionage Act of 1917 and found guilty of passing information on atomic weapons to the USSR (6–29 March); they are sentenced to death (the first US civilians to be sentenced for death for espionage).

Fifth Five-Year Plan due in USSR (–1955), but plans are not announced until 1952.

Major oil refinery opened at Fawley, Hampshire, S England.

Shah of Iran makes order for his land to be sold to peasants (28 Jan).

p Society, Education, and Religion

Severe drought in Australia (–1953).

In South Africa, the Native Representative Council (established in 1936 to advise the government) is abolished; the Separate Representation of Voters Bill, to remove Coloured voters from the Common Roll in the Cape, is passed by both houses of Parliament, but then challenged in court (1952); the Bantu Authorities Act provides for African chiefs and officials, appointed and paid by the government, to maintain law and order in tribal areas; the Prevention of Illegal Squatting Act empowers the minister of native affairs to compel Africans to leave public or private land and authorizes local authorities to establish resettlement camps.

United Nations High Commission for Refugees established.

Servicemen's Indemnity Act in USA (signed 25 April) provides for $10,000 to be paid to survivors of combatants killed in Korea and in future conflicts.

Festival of Britain held in London (3 May–30 Sept).

B S Rowntree and G R Lavers, *Poverty and the Welfare State, English Life and Leisure*.

Fraudulent Medium Act in Britain repeals provisions of the Witchcraft Act of 1735.

In Britain, Royal Commission on Betting, Lotteries, and Gaming (established in 1949) issues report (17 April); finds that in the main regular gambling is not a direct cause of social problems; recommends allowing off-course betting shops for horse races.

Talcott Parsons, *The Social System*.

In England and Wales, the General Certificate of Education 'Ordinary' and 'Advanced' examinations (popularly known as O and A levels) replace the 'School Certificate'.

In Australia, start of 'Schools of the Air', broadcasting radio 'lessons' to students in rural communities, via the Flying Doctor Service network.

World Muslim Conference held in Karachi with delegates from 30 countries.

In Northern Ireland, Rev Ian Paisley and followers found the Free Presbyterian Church of Ulster (11 March).

Dietrich Bonhoeffer, *Letters and Papers from Prison*.

Paul Tillich, *Systematic Theology* (3 volumes; –1963).

q Science, Technology, and Discovery

John Brown and Co. make a peat-fired gas turbine on Clydebank, Scotland.

The 'flying spot' microscope is devised.

Electric power is satisfactorily produced from atomic energy at Arcon, Idaho, USA (Dec).

Second British plutonium pile, at Sellafield, Cumberland, in operation.

Dutch–Norwegian joint atomic energy research establishment opened at Hjeller, near Oslo, Norway.

Krilium, a synthetic chemical, is developed from acrylonitrile for use in fertilizers.

r Humanities

Louis Leakey, *Olduvai Gorge* (–1965).

Henri Frankfort, *The Birth of Civilization in the Near East*.

Stephen Runciman, *History of the Crusades* (–1958).

Dumas Malone, *Jefferson and the Rights of Man*.

George R Taylor, *The Transportation Revolution, 1815–1860*.

C Vann Woodward, *Reunion and Reaction*.

17 in elections for French National Assembly Gaullists win 107 seats; Communists, 97; Socialists, 94; Conservatives, 87; Popular Republicans, 82; Radical Socialists, 77.

23 (–29) in Korea, further attempts to negotiate armistice end in failure.

G July

3 India complains to UN Security Council against Pakistan for violating cease-fire agreement in Kashmir.

5 in dispute between Iran and Britain over oil nationalization, the International Court issues interim order, which is rejected by Iran (15, President Truman sends Averell Harriman to Iran to urge a compromise settlement).

10 in Korea, armistice negotiations open between the commanders of the opposing sides.

20 King Abdullah of Jordan assassinated in Jerusalem (succeeded by his son Talal, who is proclaimed king on 6 Sept).

H August

5 Matthew Ridgway, supreme commander of Allied forces in Korea, breaks off armistice talks, charging Communist North Koreans with violation of demilitarization rules; further negotiations fail.

5 'World Youth Festival', a mammoth Communist youth rally, opens in East Berlin.

7 US Congress rejects Soviet proposal for agreement on arms and atomic weapons, advising it to honour existing obligations first.

11 French ministerial crisis (since elections on 17 June) ends with René Pleven forming a coalition of the Centre.

30 USA–Philippines mutual defence pact.

J September

1 in San Francisco, California, USA, the USA, Australia, and New Zealand sign the Pacific Security Agreement providing for mutual assistance if any signatory power is attacked.

8 peace treaty with Japan signed at San Francisco by representatives of 49 powers, though USSR and satellites boycott final session of peace conference.

10 foreign ministers of USA, Britain, and France discuss plans to combat Soviet aggression and to use West German troops in NATO army.

13 UN Conciliatory Commission discusses Palestine problem with Israeli and Arab delegates, but by 21 Nov the talks fail.

K October

5 US House of Representatives approves $56.9 billion armed forces appropriation bill.

6 Henry Gurney, British high commissioner in Malaya, is assassinated by Communist.

9 David Ben-Gurion ends eight months' ministerial crisis in Israel by forming coalition government.

12 Britain's dispute with Iran is placed before the UN Security Council.

16 Liaquat Ali Khan, prime minister of Pakistan, is assassinated by Afghan fanatic (civil disorder follows).

25 negotiations for armistice in Korea are renewed at Panmunjom.

25 in British general election Conservatives win 321 seats (net gain 23) over Labour with 295 (net loss 20) and Liberals with 6 (net loss 3), United Ireland, 3.

27 in Britain, Winston Churchill forms ministry, with Anthony Eden as foreign secretary and R A ('Rab') Butler as chancellor of exchequer.

27 Egypt abrogates 1936 treaty of alliance with Britain and 1899 agreement over Sudan.

L November

Coup in Thailand by senior military officers, while king is in Switzerland, restores constitution of 1932 (Dec), but is modified in March 1952 (Pibul remains prime minister).

8 Dean Acheson presents disarmament proposals to UN General Assembly, which are countered by the USSR with a rival plan.

10 France, Britain, USA, and Turkey announce security programme for Near East.

11 Juan Perón is re-elected president of Argentina.

14 USA alleges that North Koreans have murdered 5,970 UN prisoners and about 250,000 Korean civilians.

16 Egypt offers to let future of Sudan be decided by plebiscite under UN supervision.

29 in Syria, army mounts coup, instigated by the chief of staff, Colonel Chichekli.

M December

6 East and West Germany agree to send representatives to UN to discuss holding of free elections in Germany, but USSR opposes the project.

13 French National Assembly ratifies the Schuman Plan (placing French and German coal, iron, and steel industries under

C Vann Woodward, *Origins of the New South, 1877–1913.*

Oscar Handlin, *The Uprooted.*

J A Schumpeter, *Imperialism and Social Classes.*

History Today issued (–).

Nelson Goodman, *The Structure of Appearance.*

Michael Polanyi, *The Logic of Liberty.*

Hans Reichenbach, *The Rise of Scientific Philosophy.*

David Riesman, *The Lonely Crowd.*

s Art, Sculpture, Fine Arts, and Architecture

Exhibition 'L'Ecole de Paris 1900–1950' is held at the Royal Academy, London, presenting progressive French painting.

'Véhémences Confrontées' exhibition, Paris, France, the first confrontation in an exhibition space of art by US and French artists.

Painting, etc:

Peter Lanyon, *Porthleven.*

Henri Matisse, *Blue Nude I.*

Jackson Pollock, *Echo no. 25.*

Robert Rauschenberg, *Black Painting* (–1952).

Mark Rothko, develops mature colourfield works, continuing throughout decade.

Sculpture:

Kenneth Armitage, *People in a Wind.*

Lucio Fontana, *Neon Structure*, Triennale, Milan, Italy.

Henry Moore, *Reclining Figure.*

Pablo Picasso, *Baboon and Young.*

Germaine Richier, *Berger des Landes.*

David Smith, *Hudson River Landscape.*

Architecture:

Alvar Aalto, Village Hall, Saynatsalo, Finland.

Gerald Barry's plan for centenary of the 1851 'Great Exhibition', on the South Bank, London, with Hugh Casson director of architecture; Robert Matthew, Royal Festival Hall; Ralph Tubbs, Dome of Discovery.

Louis Kahn, D Orr, Yale University Art Gallery, with a space-frame ceiling (–1953).

Le Corbusier, Law Courts and Secretariat, Chandigarh, India.

Ludwig Mies van der Rohe, Lake Shore Drive, Chicago, USA.

Basil Spence's design for Coventry Cathedral, England, wins award open to Commonwealth architects.

t Music

Benjamin Britten, *Billy Budd* (opera).

Julian Carrillo, *Horizontes.*

Elliott Carter, String Quartet No. 1.

Norman Dello Joio, *The Triumph of St Joan Symphony.*

Gian Carlo Menotti, *Amahl and the Night Visitors* (opera).

Dmitry Shostakovich, *Twenty-Four Preludes and Fugues.*

Igor Stravinsky, *The Rake's Progress* (opera).

The King and I (musical), text by Oscar Hammerstein, music by Richard Rodgers (first performed at the St James Theatre, New York, (29 May).

Paint Your Wagon (musical), text by Alan Jay Lerner, music by Frederick Loewe (first performed at the Shubert Theatre, New York, 12 Nov).

'Charmaine', arranged by Mantovani and played by the Mantovani Orchestra.

Johnnie Ray, 'Cry'.

Foundation of the Dave Brubeck jazz quartet (–1967).

In the USA, Fender produce the first electric bass guitar.

First 33.3 rpm long-playing records go on sale in West Germany (31 Aug).

u Literature and Drama

Isaac Asimov, *Foundation.*

Ray Bradbury, *The Illustrated Man.*

Albert Camus, *The Rebel.*

Camilo José Cela, *The Hive.*

Arthur C Clarke, *The Sands of Mars.*

Keith Douglas, *Collected Poems* (posthumous).

Janet Frame, *Lagoon and Other Stories.*

Robert Frost, *Complete Poems.*

James Jones, *From Here to Eternity.*

Yasunari Kawabata, *Thousand Cranes.*

Carson McCullers, *The Ballad of the Sad Cafe.*

Nicholas Monsarrat, *The Cruel Sea.*

Marianne Moore, *Collected Poems.*

Shohei Ooka, *Fires on the Plain.*

Anthony Powell, *A Question of Upbringing,* the first of 12 volumes in the sequence *A Dance to the Music of Time* (–1975).

J D Salinger, *The Catcher in the Rye.*

Herman Wouk, *The Caine Mutiny.*

John Wyndham, *The Day of the Triffids.*

Marguerite Yourcenar, *Memoirs of Hadrian.*

Drama:

Jean Anouilh, *Colombe.*

Donald Bevan and Edmund Trzcinski, *Stalag 17.*

N C Hunter, *Waters of the Moon.*

Jean-Paul Sartre, *Le Diable et le Bon Dieu.*

Peter Ustinov, *The Love of Four Colonels.*

John Van Druten, *I am a Camera.*

John Whitney, *Saint's Day.*

Tennessee Williams, *The Rose Tattoo.*

v Births and Deaths

Jan 10 Sinclair Lewis dies (65).

common authority to which other European nations might accede) by 377 to 233 votes.

19 Marshal Andrei Vyshinsky, Soviet foreign minister, demands UN to require USA to revoke its Mutual Security Act.

20 Greece is elected to the UN Security Council after 19 ballots, in preference to Belarus, which had been nominated by Russia (USSR).

24 Libya (an Italian colony from 1911 to 1942, and under British military administration since then) becomes an independent federation under King Idris I, previously emir of Cyrenaica. This is in conformity with a resolution of the UN General Assembly (21 November 1949), and makes Libya the first independent state to be created by the UN.

27 Korean armistice talks fail on exchange of prisoners and building of airfields in North Korea.

30 public announcement made in Paris at meeting of foreign, finance, and defence ministers of France, Italy, Luxembourg, Belgium, Netherlands, and West Germany that the proposed European defence force is to be called the European Defence Community; and that they envisage that one day the Community will be replaced by a federal body.

31 Mutual Security Agency replaces Economic Co-operation Administration of Marshall Plan.

Jan 27 Carl Mannerheim dies (83).
Jan 30 Ferdinand Porsche dies (75).
Feb 19 André Gide dies (81).
March 6 Ivor Novello dies (58).
April 14 Ernest Bevin dies (70).
April 18 Dom Antonio Carmona dies (81).
April 23 Charles Dawes dies (85).
April 29 Ludwig Wittgenstein dies (62).
July 13 Arnold Schoenberg dies (76).
July 23 Henri Philippe Pétain dies (95).
Aug 14 William Randolph Hearst dies (88).
Oct 6 W K Kellogg dies (91).
Oct 16 Liaquat Ali Khan dies (56).
Dec 31 Maxim Litvinov dies (75).

w Everyday Life

'Crazy Horse Saloon' opens in Paris, the first such establishment in post-war Europe.

Transcontinental dial telephone service inaugurated in USA (10 Oct).

x Sport and Recreation

The International Amateur Athletic Federation establishes a series of area championships: the Asian Games, first held in New Delhi, India; the Pan-American Games, first held in Buenos Aires, Argentina; and the Mediterranean Games, first held in Alexandria, Egypt.

The University Boat Race in England is cancelled after Oxford sinks (24 May); Cambridge win by 12 lengths when the race is re-run (26).

Randolph Turpin of Britain out-points Sugar Ray Robinson to win the World Middleweight title at Earl's Court, London (10 July); Robinson regains the title from Turpin 64 days later, at the New York Polo Grounds (12 Sept).

Jersey Joe Walcott knocks out Ezzard Charles in the seventh round of their World Heavyweight title fight in Pittsburgh, Pennsylvania, USA (18 July).

Len Hutton is dismissed 'obstructing the field' in the final Test against South Africa at The Oval, London (18 Aug).

In American Football, Norm van Brocklin passes a record 506.5 m/554 yd for the Los Angeles Rams against the New York Yankees (28 Sept).

In Scotland, the Braemar caber, 5.8 m/19 ft in length and weighing over 54.5 kg/120 lb is tossed for the first time by George Clark.

y Media

Press Association in Britain uses teletypsetting machines for distributing news.

Film:

British Board of Film Censors introduces 'X' category (from 1 Jan), for films totally unsuitable for anyone under 16.

Fred Waller in USA invents Cinerama.

The African Queen (director, John Huston; starring Humphrey Bogart and Katherine Hepburn).

An American in Paris (director, Vincente Minelli; starring Gene Kelly and Leslie Caron).

Bedtime for Bonzo (starring Ronald Reagan).

The Day the Earth Stood Still (director, Robert Wise).

The Man in the White Suit (director, Alexander Mackendrick; starring Alec Guinness and Joan Greenwood).

Miracle in Milan (director, Vittorio de Sica).

Othello (director, Orson Welles).

An Outcast of the Islands (director, Carol Reed; starring Trevor Howard).

A Place in the Sun (director, George Stevens).

Le Plaisir (director, Max Ophül).

Rashomon (director, Akira Kurosawa).

The Red Badge of Courage (director, John Huston; starring Audie Murphy).

Strangers on a Train (director, Alfred Hitchcock).

A Streetcar Named Desire (director, Elia Kazan; starring Vivien Leigh and Marlon Brando).

Radio:

In Britain, the BBC broadcasts *Crazy People* (from May), starring Michael Bentine, Spike Milligan, Harry Secombe, and Peter Sellers; renamed *The Goon Show* in June 1952 (–Jan 1960).

Television:

In USA, the first programme of *See It Now* (18 Nov), with Ed Murrow (CBS), features a split screen showing Brooklyn Bridge in New York and the Golden Gate Bridge at San Francisco, demonstrating that broadcasting is now nationwide.

New programmes in USA include: *Dragnet* (NBC), a police drama series; *I Love Lucy*, starring Lucille Ball and husband Desi Arnaz; *The Roy Rogers Show*; and the 'soap operas' *Love of Life* and *Search for Tomorrow*.

In Britain, *The Final Test* by Terence Rattigan is the first play to be broadcast on television (BBC).

The BBC broadcasts *What's My Line?*, derived from the US show of the same title.

*Accession of Queen Elizabeth II ... Hussein becomes King of
Jordan ... Mau Mau violence in Kenya ... Dwight Eisenhower
elected president of USA ...*

A **January**

7 in France, René Pleven's ministry falls after plans to reorganize nationalized industries and social services are defeated (22, Edgar Faure, Radical, forms coalition).

14 Tunisia (a French protectorate) unsuccessfully appeals to the United Nations Security Council to be permitted to state its case for autonomy.

15 USA, Britain, and France submit draft treaty on Austria to the USSR, proposing that Austria should become an independent, democratic state with the frontiers of 1 Jan 1938 (USSR rejects treaty in Aug).

15 General Sir Gerald Templer becomes high commissioner in Malaya (–1954); turns tide against Communist guerrillas.

18 (–27) anti-British riots in Egypt, which end with King Farouk's dismissal of Mustafa an-Nahas Pasha and the appointment of Ali Maher Pasha as prime minister (–1 March).

24 Vincent Massey is first Canadian to be appointed governor general of Canada (–Sept 1959).

26 representatives of France, Italy, Luxembourg, Belgium, Netherlands, and West Germany, meeting in Paris, agree the outlines of the army to be established under the European Defence Community.

B **February**

6 death of George VI; accession of Queen Elizabeth II (while on visit to Kenya; proclaimed on 8).

20 (–25) NATO Council, meeting in Lisbon, Portugal, approves establishment of the proposed European Defence Community; members agree to provide 50 divisions for NATO service by Dec.

26 Winston Churchill, the British prime minister, announces that Britain has produced its own atomic bomb.

29 in France, Edgar Faure's ministry falls, on failing to obtain the National Assembly's assent to tax increases; Antoine Pinay, Conservative, forms cabinet with some Gaullist support.

C **March**

1 in India's first national elections Pandit Nehru's Congress Party wins 364 of 489 seats in the National Assembly.

1 in Egypt, Ali Maher Pasha resigns as prime minister following differences in the cabinet; succeeded by Ahmed Nagib al Hilaly.

10 USSR note proposes four-power conference on unification and rearmament of Germany (to which the Western Powers reply, on 23, that free elections would be a prerequisite, that Germany should not be empowered to rearm, and that its boundaries, as settled by the Potsdam Conference, 1945, would be subject to revision).

10 in Cuba, Fulgencio Batistá (in exile since 1944) overthrows the government.

20 South Africa Supreme Court holds the apartheid legislation of D F Malan's government as unconstitutional.

21 the prime minister of Ceylon (now Sri Lanka), Don Stephen Senanayake, is thrown from horse (22, dies; succeeded on 26 by son Dudley Senanayake).

29 in USA, President Truman announces he will not be a candidate in the presidential election.

30 anti-French riots in Tangier, French Morocco.

D **April**

8 in USA, President Truman orders seizure of the steel industry in response to strike (strike continues until 2 May; the seizure continues until after the Supreme Court decision of 2 June).

10 USSR proposes that all-German elections be held under a four-power commission, instead of under UN supervision, and rejects the West's views on Germany's frontiers.

15 Britain declares it will sign a mutual defence treaty with the proposed European Defence Community.

22 in South Africa, Prime Minister D F Malan introduces bill to make Parliament a high court, in order to prevent the Supreme Court from invalidating apartheid race legislation.

28 Dwight Eisenhower is relieved of his post as Supreme Allied Commander in Europe at his own request and is succeeded by Matthew Ridgway (who is succeeded in Far East by Mark Clark).

E **May**

20 rioting of Communist prisoners of war at Koje Island prison camp, South Korea.

27 (–31) foreign ministers of France, Italy, Luxembourg, Belgium, Netherlands, and West Germany treaty signed in Paris establishing European Defence Community, with reciprocal NATO–EDC guarantees.

*John Cage's 4'33" ... Rocky Marciano wins World Heavyweight
title ... Flowerpot Men on British TV ...*

o Politics, Government, Law, and Economy

Samuel Lubell, *The Future of American Politics.*

Following peace treaty of Sept 1951, Japan regains sovereignty and independence (28 April).

New constitution promulgated in Poland, based on the Soviet constitution of 1947; the Sejm is the highest state authority, though the 15-member council of state has considerable powers (its chairman is nominal head of state).

Revised constitution in Romania (24 Sept); disfranchises all except members of the Workers' Party and their associates.

Puerto Rico granted status of a 'Commonwealth' associated with the USA.

In West Germany, the Länder (states) of Baden, Württemberg-Baden, and Württemberg-Hohenzollern are merged to form Baden-Württemberg.

In Youngstown v. Sawyer, the US Supreme Court rules (2 June) that President Truman went beyond his constitutional powers in ordering the seizure of the steel industry (only the third time the court has restricted the president's power).

The Court of Justice of the European Coal and Steel Community becomes operational (5 July).

In Britain, the Bentley case: Derek Bentley is convicted of murdering a policeman and sentenced to death (11 Dec), even though the fatal shots were fired by accomplice Christopher Craig who, at age 16, is too young to suffer capital punishment (Bentley is hanged on 28 Jan 1953); the case remains controversial because of Bentley's ambiguous instruction to Craig, 'Let him have it Chris', which could refer to either the gun itself or to firing the gun.

In USSR, 19th Congress of Communist Party adopts directives for the Fifth Five-Year Plan (6 Oct); the plan envisages an increase in industrial production by 1955 of 70 per cent over 1950 production and large increases in agricultural output.

In USA, foundation of the Resources for the Future research institute.

In France, hydro-electric power station and dam opened at Donzère-Mondragon in the Rhône Valley (25 Oct).

In Britain, Morris Motors and the Austin Motor Company merge to form the British Motor Corporation.

In East Germany, start of production of the Trabant motor car.

p Society, Education, and Religion

In USA, the Veterans' Readjustment Assistance Act (known, like its post-World War II predecessor, as the 'GI Bill of Rights') provides educational grants, housing assistance, and loan guarantees for service personnel returning from the Korean War.

No lynchings reported in USA for first time since records began in 1881.

Immigration and Naturalization Act passed in USA over President Truman's veto (27 June); it limits total immigration and establishes quotas based on national origin.

In South Africa, the Natives (Abolition of Passes and Coordination of Documents) Act replaces 'passes' with new 'reference books' containing details of birth, employment, taxation, and movement; black male adults are required to carry them at all times.

In South Africa, an amendment to the Native Laws Amendment Act stipulates that no African can remain in an urban area for longer than 72 hours unless they have lived there for 15 years or worked for the same employer for 10 years.

West Germany agrees to pay Israel £293 million as compensation for war-time atrocities.

A winter smog in London, consisting of high concentrations of sulphur dioxide and other pollutants, leads to over 2,000 deaths.

In England, University College, Southampton, is incorporated as a university by royal charter.

G H Bantock, *Freedom and Authority in Education.*

Reinhold Niebuhr, *Christ and Culture.*

Paul Tillich, *Courage To Be.*

q Science, Technology, and Discovery

British driver John Cobb is killed establishing a water speed record of 332.9 kph/206.89 mph at Loch Ness, Scotland (5 Oct).

The British jet-powered passenger aircraft the Comet makes its first scheduled commercial flight, from London to Johannesburg (4 May; made maiden flight on 27 July 1949).

Britain's first atomic bomb tests, in Monte Bello Islands, NW Australia (3 Oct).

USA explodes the first hydrogen bomb, at Eniwetok island in the Pacific (6 Nov).

Rapid extension of use of radio-isotopes in scientific research, medicine and industry.

G D Searle laboratories in the USA make a contraceptive tablet of phosphorated hesperidin.

28 Communist demonstrations in Paris, France.

F **June**

1 in Ceylon (now Sri Lanka), United National Party under Dudley Senanayake wins election.

18 British scheme for Central African Federation published.

20 in USA, President Truman signs Foreign Aid Bill.

23 US Air Force bombs hydro-electric plants in North Korea.

G **July**

6 Adolfo Ruíz Cortines elected president of Mexico.

22 in Iran, following riots in Tehran, Dr Muhammad Mossadeq is reappointed prime minister with emergency powers for six months.

22 The International Court at the Hague rules it has no jurisdiction in case between Iran and Anglo-Iranian Oil Co. (arising from Iran's nationalization of oil in March 1951).

23 General Muhammad Neguib seizes power in Egypt (7 Sept, forms government).

24 India makes agreement with head of the government of Kashmir.

25 European Coal and Steel Community in force.

26 in Egypt, King Farouk abdicates in favour of infant son, Fuad.

26 in Argentina, death from cancer of Eva ('Evita') Perón, wife of President Juan Perón; her death begins the gradual erosion of his appeal.

H **August**

4 (–25 Sept) conference in Honolulu of Pacific Council (Australia, New Zealand, and USA; held under Pacific Security Treaty of Sept 1951).

5 Japan resumes diplomatic relations with Nationalist China (Formosa, now Taiwan).

11 in Jordan, parliament declares the termination of the reign of King Talal, because of his chronic schizophrenia; his son Hussein, educated in England at Harrow and Sandhurst, is proclaimed king (Hussein, a minor, will reach majority age on 2 May 1953).

14 in Hungary, Mátyás Rákosi, secretary of the Hungarian Workers' Party, is also appointed prime minister.

17 large Chinese mission, led by Zhou Enlai, visits USSR for discussions (–22 Sept).

23 Arab League Security Pact of 1950 comes into force following ratification by member states.

J **September**

1 William Drees, Labour, reforms coalition in Netherlands after general election.

4 General Carlos Ibáñez elected president of Chile.

11 UN settlement for Eritrea, federation with Ethiopia, is ratified by Emperor Haile Selassie of Ethiopia; Eritrea has autonomy in domestic affairs.

18 Finland completes reparation payments to USSR.

30 Council of Europe adopts Eden Plan, for making the Council a framework into which the Coal and Steel Community and Defence Community can be fitted.

K **October**

2 Chinese government holds 'Asia and Pacific Peace Conference' in Beijing, with delegates from 37 countries.

3 USSR demands that USA recall George Kennan, its ambassador in Moscow, for his comments made in Germany about the 'icy cold' isolation of Western diplomats in Moscow (USA repudiates Soviet complaints, but Kennan does not resume post).

4 China and Mongolia sign ten-year agreement.

5 opening of 19th Congress of the USSR Communist Party, the first Congress since 1939.

13 Egypt reaches agreement with Sudan over waters of Nile.

17 Council of Socialist International meets in Milan.

20 state of emergency proclaimed in Kenya because of Mau Mau (nationalist) disturbances; about 200 leading members of the Kenya African Union are arrested.

22 Iran breaks diplomatic relations with Britain over oil dispute.

L **November**

In Czechoslovakia, trials and convictions of Rudolf Slansky, former secretary of Czech Communist Party, Vladimir Clementis, former foreign minister, and 11 others (all Jews) for 'Titoism' (all but three are hanged on 2 Dec). Bill introduced in British Parliament to denationalize iron and steel.

4 Republican landslide in US presidential election with Dwight D Eisenhower winning 442 electoral votes over Adlai Stevenson, Democrat, with 89; popular vote: Eisenhower, 33,936,252; Stevenson, 27,314,992.

10 the secretary of the UN, Trygve Lie, makes surprise announcement of his resignation (hoping, in view of Soviet opposition to his

In USA, at the Pennsylvania Hospital, Philadelphia, an artificial heart keeps a patient alive for 80 minutes (8 March).

K Hamburger in Denmark performs the first successful sex-change operation.

R Humanities

Archaeologists use radioactive carbon (C14) tests for dating finds.

Grahame Clark, *Prehistoric Europe: The Economic Basis*.

Kathleen Kenyon begins her excavation at Jericho, Jordan.

J M Wallace-Hadrill, *The Barbarian West, 400–1000*.

Lucy Sutherland, *The East India Company in Eighteenth-Century Politics*.

Edgar Johnson, *Charles Dickens*.

Noel Annan, *Leslie Stephen*.

Walter P Webb, *The Great Frontier*.

Eric F Goldman, *Rendezvous with Destiny*.

Luigi Albertini, *The Origins of the War of 1914* (–1957).

Harold Nicolson, *King George V, His Life and Reign*.

Alan Bullock, *Hitler: A Study in Tyranny*.

Past and Present issued (–).

T S R Boase (ed.), *Oxford History of English Art* series (–1940).

Hugh S Morrison, *Early American Architecture from the First Colonial Settlements to the National Period*.

Paul Hindemith, *A Composer's World*.

F R Leavis, *The Common Pursuit*.

Middle English Dictionary (–).

Werner Heisenberg, *Philosophic Problems of Nuclear Science*.

John Wisdom, *Other Minds*.

S Art, Sculpture, Fine Arts, and Architecture

British government broadly accepts proposals of the Waverley Committee for restricting the export of works of art from Britain.

Painting, etc:

Balthus, *Le Passage du Commerce Saint André* (–1954).

Edward Burra, *John Deth*.

Alberto Burri, *Sack*.

Sam Francis, *St Honoré*.

Helen Frankenthaler, *Mountains and Sea*.

Willem de Kooning, *Woman with Lipstick*.

Henri Matisse, *The Swimming Pool*.

Sculpture:

Henry Moore, *King and Queen*.

Architecture:

Alvar Aalto, Church at Imatra, Finland (–1958).

Luigi Figini and Gino Pollini, Church of Madonna dei Poveri, Milan, Italy (– 1956).

I M Pei, Mile High Center, Colorado, USA (–1956).

Skidmore, Owings, and Merrill, Lever House, New York; Manufacturers Trust Bank, New York (–1954).

T Music

Earle Brown, *Folio*.

John Cage, *4′33″*.

Lukas Foss, *A Parable of Death*.

Hans Werner Henze, *Boulevard Solitude* (opera).

Otto Luening, *Fantasy in Space*.

Michael Tippett, *The Midsummer Marriage* (opera).

Ralph Vaughan Williams, *Sinfonia Antarctica* (Symphony No. 7), *Romance* (for harmonica, written for Larry Adler).

White US disc jockey Alan Freed plays African-American music on his programme 'Moondog's Rock 'n' Roll Party' (popularizing the term Rock 'n' Roll).

New Musical Express publishes Britain's first pop singles chart (14 Nov).

In Britain the BBC launches its first televised pop show, *Hit Parade*.

Gibson in the USA produce the Les Paul solid electric guitar.

U Literature and Drama

Paul Bowles, *Let It Come Down*.

Ralph Ellison, *The Invisible Man*.

Ernest Hemingway, *The Old Man and the Sea*.

Doris Lessing, *Martha Quest*.

Norman Lewis, *Golden Earth*.

Mary McCarthy, *The Groves of Academe*.

Flannery O'Connor, *Wise Blood*.

Frank O'Hara, *A City Winter*.

John Steinbeck, *East of Eden*.

Dylan Thomas, *Collected Poems*.

Laurens van der Post, *Venture to the Interior*.

Evelyn Waugh, *Men at Arms*.

Angus Wilson, *Hemlock and After*.

Drama:

George Axelrod, *The Seven Year Itch*.

Marcel Aymé, *La Tête des Autres*.

Truman Capote, *The Grass Harp*.

Agatha Christie, *The Mousetrap*.

Clifford Odets, *Winter Journey*.

Terence Rattigan, *Deep Blue Sea*.

V Births and Deaths

Feb 6 King George VI of Britain dies (56).

March 4 C S Sherrington dies (94).

April 21 Stafford Cripps dies (62).

reappointment, that it will enable the five permanent powers to cooperate).

16 Field Marshal Alexandros Papagos forms ministry in Greece following success of Greek Rally in elections.

20 in Poland, following the first general election held under the new constitution (26 Oct), Boleslaw Bierut (Communist) is elected prime minister by the Sejm.

27 (–11 Dec) Commonwealth Economic Conference held in London.

M December

2 Dwight Eisenhower, president-elect of USA, visits Korea.

3 UN General Assembly adopts Indian proposal for armistice in Korean War.

4 Winston Churchill, prime minister of Britain, announces that Britain will curtail defence expenditure.

7 riots in French Morocco.

8 following Chaim Weizmann's death (on 9 Nov), Itzhak Ben-Zvi becomes president of Israel.

10 Egypt abolishes 1923 Constitution.

12 Communist world conference held in Vienna.

15 China rejects Indian plan for armistice in Korea.

23 Antoine Pinay, French prime minister, resigns following growth of dissension within his government and opposition to his fiscal policies (by the end of the year the 1953 budget had not been voted on).

May 6 Maria Montessori dies (81).
July 26 Eva Perón dies (30).
Aug 20 Kurt Schumacher dies (56).
Sept 26 George Santayana dies (88).
Oct 28 W M Hughes dies (88).
Nov 9 Chaim Weizmann dies (77).
Nov 20 Benedetto Croce dies (86).

w Everyday Life

Wayfarer sunglasses, based on a military model, become commercially available.

The last London tram runs (6 July), from Woolwich to New Cross; on the final stage of the journey the tram, being driven by the deputy-director of the transport authority, breaks down and has to be rescued by a 'retired' tram.

'Smog' hits London (Dec).

In Britain, the Hypnotism Act authorizes local authorities to regulate or prohibit public hypnotism displays, and forbids public hypnotism of anyone under 21.

Holiday Inn founded in Memphis, Tennessee, USA.

x Sport and Recreation

India wins a cricket Test for the first time, beating England by an innings and 8 runs in Madras, India (10 Feb).

Newcastle United, in beating Arsenal 1–0, becomes the first English soccer team since Blackburn Rovers in 1891 to win two successive Football Association Cup finals (3 May).

The 15th Olympic Games are held in Helsinki (19 July–3 Aug). The U. S. A. wins 40 gold medals; USSR, 22; Hungary, 16; Sweden, 12; Italy, 8; Czechoslovakia, 7; France, Finland, and Australia, 6 each. In the course of one week, the Czech athlete, Emil Zatopek wins the 5,000 m, the 10,000 m, and the marathon (20–27 July).

Rocky Marciano defeats Jersey Joe Walcott (both of USA), to win the World Heavyweight Boxing title (23 Sept).

Alberto Ascari of Italy, driving a Ferrari, wins six of this year's seven Grand Prix.

Professionals boycott the World Snooker Championship; only two players are left to compete for the title.

y Media

Associated Press news agency in USA inaugurates first overseas teleprinter link.

In Britain, retirement of W F Casey, editor of *The Times*; succeeded by Sir William Haley.

Film:

Charlie Chaplin leaves USA after he is alleged to have connections with subversive causes; 17 April 1953, announces that he will never return to the USA after he is informed that his re-entry would be challenged (settles at Vevey, Switzerland).

The Bad and the Beautiful (director, Vincente Minelli; starring Kirk Douglas).

Breaking the Sound Barrier (director, David Lean).

B'wana Devil (first three-dimensional film).

Casque D'Or (director, Jacques Becker).

El (director, Luis Buñuel).

Forbidden Games (director, René Clement).

The Greatest Show on Earth (director, Cecil B de Mille).

High Noon (director, Fred Zinnemann; starring Gary Cooper and Grace Kelly).

Ikiru (director, Akira Kurosawa).

Limelight (director and star, Charlie Chaplin; with Claire Bloom).

Moulin Rouge (director, John Huston; starring Jose Ferrer).

Peter Pan (producer, Walt Disney).

The Quiet Man (director, John Ford; starring John Wayne and Maureen O'Hara).

Singin' in the Rain (director and star, Gene Kelly).

Summer With Monika (director, Ingmar Bergman).

This is Cinerama (opens on Broadway, New York, in Sept).

Radio:

Sony of Japan markets the first pocket-sized transistor radio.

Television:

The Liberace Show is a nationwide success on US television.

Other new US programmes include *This Is Your Life* (NBC, derived from radio), and *Inspector Mark Saber — Homicide Squad* (–1954).

During the US presidential election, Dwight Eisenhower's team produces a series of one-minute commercials in support of their candidate.

In Britain, the BBC transmits the first thriller serial, *The Broken Horseshoe* by Francis Durbridge.

The BBC's *Watch With Mother* programmes introduce Bill and Ben, *The Flowerpot Men*.

The BBC broadcasts *Paris Panorama* from France to Britain, the first transmission between countries with different television systems.

The BBC makes experimental broadcasts to six schools in Middlesex, S England.

Death of Stalin ... Rising in East Berlin ... Armistice signed in Korea ... Khrushchev appointed secretary of USSR Communist Party ...

A January

1 conference held in London of representatives of British government and those of Northern Rhodesia, Southern Rhodesia, and Nyasaland (respectively modern Zambia, Zimbabwe, and Malawi), regarding proposed creation of federation of those countries to handle external affairs, defence, and currency (scheme to establish Central African Federation published on 5 Feb; created by Federation (Constitution) Order in Council on 1 Aug).

1 the Maldive Islands become independent under British protection (the new president, Amin Didi, plays centre forward in a ceremonial football match).

5 British Prime Minister Winston Churchill visits US president-elect Dwight Eisenhower.

6 Asian Socialist conference held at Rangoon, Burma (now Yangon in Myanmar).

8 riots in Karachi, Pakistan (followed by others elsewhere in the country, reflecting difficult economic conditions and dissatisfaction with the government).

8 in France, René Mayer, Radical, forms government.

10 first meeting of the Assembly of the European Coal and Steel Community.

12 Yugoslav National Assembly adopts new constitution (on 14, Marshal Tito is elected first president of Yugoslav Republic).

14 Consultative Assembly of Council of Europe meets in Strasbourg to draft constitution for European Political Community (adopted 10 Feb).

16 in Egypt, General Neguib dissolves political parties.

20 Dwight Eisenhower is inaugurated as 34th president of the USA.

21 electoral reform bill (providing bonus seats in the Chamber for any party or alliance that wins over 50 per cent of votes) passes Italian Chamber, with Communists abstaining (passes Senate on 29 March).

B February

10 in Egypt, General Neguib is voted dictatorial powers for three years.

12 announcement of British–Egyptian agreement on Sudan, providing transitional period of self-government for Sudan, followed by self-determination.

12 USSR severs relations with Israel.

16 in South Africa, passing of the Public Safety Act, which gives the governor general (or in some cases the minister of justice) the power to declare a state of emergency and issue regulations overriding acts of parliament.

22 People's Party and Socialists win seats in Austrian elections.

24 Rome Conference of foreign ministers of the European Defence Community countries.

28 treaty of friendship between Greece, Turkey, and Yugoslavia.

C March

5 Joseph Stalin dies (6, Georgi Malenkov, designated by Stalin, succeeds as chairman of council of ministers).

16 President Tito of Yugoslavia makes state visit to Britain.

19 West German Bundestag approves Bonn agreement and Paris agreement establishing a European Defence Community.

31 Dag Hammarskjöld of Sweden is elected secretary general of the United Nations by the Security Council in succession to Trygve Lie (7 April, ratified by General Assembly).

D April

2 in Austria, Julius Raab, People's Party, succeeds Dr Figl as chancellor and forms coalition government of People's Party and Socialists similar to the previous one.

6 German Chancellor Konrad Adenauer visits New York (and, on 14 May, London).

8 in Kenya, following a massacre at Lari in the Rift Valley, Jomo Kenyatta and five other Kikuyu convicted of organizing Mau Mau terrorism.

11 UN force and Communists arrange for exchange of prisoners in Korea.

11 Vietnamese insurgents renew offensive on Laos.

13 opening of conference in London to consider establishment of British West Indies Federation.

15 National Party under D F Malan secures clear majority in South African elections.

17 the governor general of Pakistan dismisses the government of Khwaja Nazimuddin and appoints Muhammad Ali as prime minister.

21 Social Democrats gain clear majority in Danish general election.

30 in British Guiana (now Guyana), the first general election to be held under a new constitution is won by the left-wing

First US woman ambassador ... Separate Amenities Act in South Africa ... Wittgenstein's Philosophical Investigations ... Songs by Tom Lehrer ...

o Politics, Government, Law, and Economy

R Kirk, *The Conservative Mind.*

Daniel Boorstin, *The Genius of American Politics.*

Denmark adopts new constitution (30 March); the Upper House is abolished and the voting age reduced to 23.

In USA, creation of the Department of Health, Education, and Welfare.

Earl Warren appointed Chief Justice of US Supreme Court, serving until 1969; contrary to expectations the 'Warren Court' proves the high point of judicial activism.

In USA, Julius and Ethel Rosenberg, sentenced as atomic spies in 1951, are executed (19 June).

In Britain, the trial and conviction of the 'Rillington Place murderer' John Christie (for the murder of four women, including his wife) casts doubt on the conviction and execution of Timothy Evans in 1950 (Christie was a prosecution witness at the trial of Evans for the murder of his wife and daughter; Christie now claims to have killed Evans' presumed victims); Christie is executed on 15 July.

In Britain, the Royal Commission on Capital Punishment issues report (23 Sept); it concludes that it is impossible to differentiate murder into degrees of culpability and recommends that juries should decide whether a murderer should suffer death or life imprisonment.

First Five-Year Plan in China, aiming to achieve rapid industrialization (with assistance from the USSR) and to amalgamate mutual-aid teams into collective farms.

In USA, the Office of Price Stabilization lifts controls on wages and salaries.

In countries of the European Coal and Steel Community (France, Italy, Luxembourg, Belgium, Netherlands, West Germany), common market for coal and iron ore comes into operation on 10 Feb, for scrap on 15 March, and for steel on 1 May.

Economic Commission for Europe publishes report, *Economic Survey of Europe since the War.*

In Britain, steel is denationalized (March), followed by road transport (May).

London Stock Exchange opens public galleries.

The Tidelands Oil Act in the USA transfers deposits off the Gulf of Mexico and along the Pacific Coast to state ownership.

Walt W Rostow, *The Process of Economic Growth.*

p Society, Education, and Religion

Widespread floods in the Netherlands and E England, killing, respectively, at least 1,000 and 280 people (3 Feb).

Clare Boothe Luce is the first woman to serve as an ambassador of the USA (in Italy; –1956).

In Britain, Florence Horsbrugh is appointed minister of education, the first Conservative woman cabinet member (3 Sept).

Mirra Komarovsky, *Women in the Modern World.*

In South Africa, the Reservation of Separate Amenities Act forces different races to use separate facilities in many areas of life; the Native Labour (Settlement of Disputes) Act in South Africa outlaws strikes by Africans and denies legal recognition to black trade unions.

In Britain, over 300,000 new homes are built.

F Osborne, *The Limits of Our Earth.*

In USA, publication of Arthur Bestor's anti-progressive *Educational Wastelands*, amid fears of university and school teachers' links with communism.

In South Africa, the Bantu Education Act authorizes the government to take over the education of Africans (mainly from missionary societies); expenditure is related to African taxes plus a government contribution; the government determines curricula.

The Communist regime places severe pressure on the Catholic Church in Poland; by decree (9 Feb) the state claims the right to make and terminate all Church appointments; a supplementary order gives local authorities the power to extract an oath of loyalty to the state from clergy.

In USA, Demos Shakarian founds the Full Gospel Businessmen's Fellowship International, a body which will play a significant part in spreading charismatic experience within the mainstream Protestant denominations in the USA.

Reinhold Niebuhr, *Christian Realism and Political Problems.*

q Science, Technology, and Discovery

Edmund Hillary and Norkey Tenzing from John Hunt's expedition climb Mt Everest (summit reached 29 May).

Austro–German expedition climbs Nanga Parbat in Himalayas (summit reached 4 July).

British Comet jet airliner crashes near Calcutta, India (2 May), killing all 43 on board; further crashes occur in 1954.

People's Progressive Party led by Cheddi Jagan.

E May

12 General Aldred Gruenther of USA is appointed supreme Allied commander in Europe.

20 France signs agreement with the Saar.

21 in France, René Mayer resigns as prime minister following defeat on vote of confidence; his resignation is followed by the longest interregnum of the fourth republic (–26 June).

25 President Eisenhower of USA states principles on which UN peace proposals for Korea were based.

F June

2 in Britain, coronation of Queen Elizabeth II at Westminster Abbey, London.

3 in London, opening of Conference of Commonwealth prime ministers.

7 in Italian elections, Christian Democrats and their allies win seats from Socialists and Communists.

8 Kenya African Union is proscribed.

17 in East Berlin, strike of 16 June turns into rising against East Germany's Communist government; in the afternoon the Soviet commandant of Berlin proclaims a state of emergency, establishes summary courts, and employs Soviet military forces to put down the rising.

18 Republic proclaimed in Egypt, with General Neguib as president and prime minister, and Colonel Abdel Nasser as deputy prime minister and minister of the interior.

18 South Korea releases 26,000 non-Communist North Korean prisoners.

26 Joseph Laniel, Independent (Right), forms ministry in France.

G July

2 in Republic of Ireland, following loss of a Fianna Fáil seat in by-election, Éamon de Valera calls and wins (73–71) a vote of confidence in his government.

4 International Confederation of Free Trade Unions meets in Stockholm, Sweden.

5 in Hungary, Mátyás Rákosi is removed as prime minister and replaced by Imre Nagy, leading to more relaxed regime.

9 in USSR, Lavrenti Beria, minister of internal affairs, is arrested, dismissed from the Communist Party, and accused of attempting to seize power (he is shot as a traitor on 23 Dec).

10 (–14) US, British, and French foreign ministers meet in Washington, DC, USA, discussing the situation of Germany among other matters.

12 following election, Brigadier Chichekli becomes president of Syria.

14 in Malta, Dr Giorgio Olivier's coalition is defeated on vote of confidence.

15 Kenya Supreme Court quashes Jomo Kenyatta's conviction (upheld, 22 Sept, by East African Court of Appeal).

15 Britain proposes four-power conference on Germany (involving also USA, USSR, and France).

20 USSR and Israel resume diplomatic relations.

26 in Cuba, Fidel Castro leads attempt to overthrow the Batista government (Castro is imprisoned; released under amnesty in 1955 and goes to Mexico).

27 Korean armistice is signed at Panmunjom.

28 in Italy, the new coalition government of Alcide de Gasperi is defeated in the Chamber; Giuseppe Pella forms government of Christian Democrats with two non-party experts (approved by parliament on 24 Aug).

30 Britain signs alliance with Libya.

H August

6 following announcement of change in retirement age for public workers, widespread strikes begin in France (–late Aug).

8 USA–South Korea mutual defence treaty agreed.

10 in Canada, Liberals retain power following general election; Liberals win 171 seats; Progressive Conservatives, 51; others, 43.

13 Shah of Iran appoints General Zahedi prime minister (19, army takes control of capital; 20, Dr Muhammad Mossadeq, the former prime minister, is arrested and later sentenced to three years' solitary confinement; Mossadeq's foreign minister, Hussein Fatemi, is executed for treason).

15 Giuseppe Pella forms Christian Democrat ministry in Italy.

20 France deposes sultan of Morocco.

23 USSR cancels East German reparations.

24 Kenya government calls on Mau Mau to surrender.

30 Hungary and Yugoslavia resume relations.

J September

6 Christian Democratic Union wins West German general election, winning 243 seats; Social Democrats win 151; Free Democrats, 48; others, 45.

12 in USSR, Nikita Khrushchev is appointed first secretary of central committee of Communist Party.

26 Cardinal Stefan Wyszynski, primate of Poland, is arrested.

Astronomers in Australia, South Africa, and USA discover a new scale of space outside the solar system.

Cosmic ray observatory is established on Mt Wrangell, Alaska, USA.

In England, the Royal Observatory is moved from Greenwich to Herstmonceux, Sussex (–1956).

International laboratory for nuclear research opened at Meyrin, near Geneva, Switzerland.

In Britain, pioneer US atomic scientist Robert Oppenheimer gives the Reith Lectures (on radio) on *Science and the Common Understanding* (published as book in 1954).

In USA, C H Townes develops the MASER (Microwaves Amplified by the Stimulated Emission of Radiation), a means of amplifying microwave radiation.

Myxomatosis spreads from continental Europe to Britain, killing millions of rabbits.

J Gibbon in USA performs the first successful open-heart operation.

In USA, at the University of Iowa Medical School, a woman is impregnated with a frozen sperm.

Francis Crick and James Watson announce discovery the double helix structure of DNA, the basic material of heredity (25 April).

R Humanities

W Le Gros Clark and others prove that the skull of 'Piltdown Man', found in S England in 1912, is a fraud (21 Sept).

Discovery of an ancient Egyptian boat alongside the pyramid of Cheops at Giza, Egypt.

British architect and archaeologist Michael Ventris publishes his decipherment of the Minoan writing called 'Linear B'.

René Joffroy discovers the rich grave of a princess's burial at Vix, France, dating from 525–500 BC.

R W Southern, *The Making of the Middle Ages*.

F M Powicke, *The Thirteenth Century* ('Oxford History of England' series).

G R Elton, *The Tudor Revolution in Government*.

Edmund S Morgan and Helen M Morgan, *The Stamp Act Crisis*.

Perry Miller, *The New England Mind from Colony to Province*.

Norman Gash, *Politics in the Age of Peel*.

J Fairbank, *Trade and Diplomacy on the China Coast*.

Philip Mason, *The Men Who Ruled India* (–1954).

John Wheeler-Bennett, *Nemesis of Power; the German Army in Politics*.

Agricultural History Review issued (–).

Margaret Mead (ed.), *Cultural Patterns and Technical Change*.

Nikolaus Pevsner (ed.), 'Pelican History of Art' series (–).

Anthony Blunt, *Art and Architecture in France 1500–1700* ('Pelican History of Art' series).

Rupert Gunnis, *Dictionary of British Sculptors, 1660–1851*.

Ralph Kirkpatrick, *Domenico Scarlatti*.

Aaron Copland, *Music and Imagination*.

Leon Edel, *Henry James* (5 volumes; –1970).

Karl Jaspers, *Tragedy is Not Enough*.

Willard V Quine, *From a Logical Point of View*.

Ludwig Wittgenstein, *Philosophical Investigations* (posthumous).

S Art, Sculpture, Fine Arts, and Architecture

'Mexican Art' exhibition (from Pre-Columbian art to the mid-20th century), Royal Academy, London.

Painting, etc:

André Fougeron, *La Civilisation Transatlantique*.

Ellsworth Kelly, *Black, Two Whites*.

Henri Matisse, *The Snail*.

Jackson Pollock, *Blue Poles* (Number 11).

Robert Rauschenberg, *Untitled* (Red Painting).

Larry Rivers, *Washington crossing the Delaware*.

Nicolas de Staël, *Agricento*.

Mark Tobey, *Edge of August*.

Sculpture:

Institute of Contemporary Art, London, holds competition for sculpture of *The Unknown Political Prisoner*; won by Reg Butler.

Architecture:

Pier Luigi Nervi and others, UNESCO Conference Hall, Paris (–1957).

Eero Saarinen, Kresge Auditorium, Massachusetts Institute of Technology, Boston, USA (–1955); Yale University Hockey Rink, New Haven, Connecticut, USA (–1959).

Skidmore, Owings, and Merrill, Connecticut General Life Insurance, Hartford, Connecticut, USA (–1957).

T Music

Tadeusz Baird, Concerto for Orchestra.

Paul Ben Haim, *The Sweet Psalmist of Israel*.

Boris Blacher, *Abstrakte Oper No. 1* (opera).

Benjamin Britten, *Gloriana* (opera).

Frederick Delius, *Irmelin* (Thomas Beecham conducts first production of opera completed in 1892).

Gottfried von Einem, *The Trial* (opera).

27 Japan establishes a national defence force.

30 following general election in Denmark (on 22 Sept, the first under the new constitution), in which the Social Democrats won the largest number of seats, their leader, Hans Hedtoft, forms a minority government.

к October

6 fearing the establishment of communism in British Guiana (now Guyana), by the People's Progressive Party, Britain sends troops; on 9, the constitution is suspended and the governor rules under a state of emergency; party-leaders are arrested.

8 USA and Britain decide to hand over administration of Zone A of Trieste to Italy.

9 Arab Liberation movement wins Syrian elections.

12 Labour majority in Norwegian elections.

12 the prime minister of Ceylon (now Sri Lanka), Dudley Senanayake, retires; Sir John Kotalawala forms ministry.

20 Konrad Adenauer forms new government in West Germany.

23 federal constitution of Central African Federation (North and South Rhodesias and Nyasaland, now Zambia, Zimbabwe, and Malawi) comes in force.

26 USA publishes report on Communist outrages in Korea.

30 general strike in Austria, as protest against occupation.

ʟ November

2 Constituent Assembly in Pakistan decides to declare the country a republic as the 'Islamic Republic of Pakistan'.

8 all seats in Portuguese elections won by Prime Minister Salazar's National Unity Party.

17 non-party government in Finland under the governor of the Bank of Finland.

23 Queen Elizabeth and Prince Philip of Britain depart from London for tour of the Commonwealth (−15 May 1954).

29 in Vietnam, French airborne troops capture the village of Dien Bien Phu in the N, to establish French command of an important position between Hanoi and Laos.

30 British government announces that it has withdrawn recognition from the kabaka of Buganda, in Uganda; the governor of Uganda orders Kabaka Mutesa II to be deported.

м December
In Britain, national strike of engineers and shipyard workers, affecting over 1 million workers.

4 (−8) President Eisenhower of USA, British Prime Minister Winston Churchill, and Joseph Laniel, the French prime minister, and their foreign ministers meet in Bermuda to discuss matters of common concern.

5 Britain and Iran resume diplomatic relations.

7 in Israel, David Ben-Gurion resigns as prime minister after prolonged tension in coalition (succeeded on 9 by Moshe Sharett).

8 in 'Atoms for Peace' speech, President Eisenhower proposes to UN General Assembly the establishment of an International Atomic Energy Agency to monitor the spread of atomic technology used for peaceful purposes.

18 Godfrey Huggins, Federal Party, forms ministry in Central African Federation.

20 Fatherland Front is the sole party in Bulgarian elections.

21 in Iran, Dr Muhammad Mossadeq, former prime minister, is sentenced to three years' confinement.

23 René Coty elected president of France.

Dmitry Shostakovich, Symphony No. 10.

Michael Tippett, *Fantasia Concertante on a Theme by Corelli.*

The Boy Friend (musical), by Sandy Wilson (first performed at the Players' Theatre, London, 14 April).

Kismet (musical), text by Charles Lederer and Luther Davis, using music by Alexander Borodin (first performed at the Ziegfeld Theatre, New York, 3 Dec).

Wonderful Town (musical), lyrics by Betty Comden and Adolph Green, music by Leonard Bernstein (first performed at the Winter Garden Theatre, New York, 25 Feb).

Tom Lehrer, *Songs By Tom Lehrer.*

Marty Robbins, 'Singin' the Blues'.

u Literature and Drama

James Baldwin, *Go Tell It On The Mountain.*

Saul Bellow, *The Adventures of Augie March.*

Ray Bradbury, *Fahrenheit 451.*

William Burroughs, *Junkie.*

Raymond Chandler, *The Long Goodbye.*

Cecil Day Lewis, *An Italian Visit.*

William Faulkner, *Requiem for a Nun.*

Ian Fleming, *Casino Royale* (the first 'James Bond' thriller).

E M Forster, *The Hill of Devi.*

L P Hartley, *The Go-Between.*

Rosamund Lehmann, *The Echoing Grove.*

Czeslaw Milosz, *The Captive Mind.*

Theodore Roethke, *The Waking* (poems).

John Wain, *Hurry on Down.*

Richard Wright, *The Outsider.*

Drama:

Arthur Adamov, *Professor Taranne.*

Robert Anderson, *Tea and Sympathy.*

T S Eliot, *The Confidential Clerk.*

Graham Greene, *The Living Room.*

Arthur Miller, *The Crucible.*

In Canada, first summer festival at Stratford, Ontario.

v Births and Deaths

Feb 20 Francesco Nitti dies (84).

March 5 Joseph Stalin dies (73).

March 5 Sergei Prokofiev dies (61).

March 24 Queen Mary of Britain dies (85).

June 16 Margaret Bondfield dies (80).

July 16 Hilaire Belloc dies (82).

July 31 Robert Taft dies (63).

Oct 30 Arnold Bax dies (69).

Nov 9 Ibn Saud dies (about 73).

Nov 9 Dylan Thomas dies (39).

Nov 27 Eugene O'Neill dies (65).

Dec 19 R A Millikan dies (85).

w Everyday Life

In Britain, launch of the Ford Popular, the world's cheapest four-cylinder motor car.

In USA, the wedding of Mr John Fitzgerald Kennedy and Miss Jacqueline Lee Bouvier (12 Sept), in Newport, Rhode Island.

x Sport and Recreation

English soccer player Stanley Matthews, at 38, wins first medal at Football Association Cup Final (when his team Blackpool beat Bolton Wanderers 4–3, 2 May).

In Britain, Sir Gordon Richards, riding Pinza, wins his first Derby horse race at the age of 49 (6 June).

US golfer Ben Hogan wins the US Masters, the US Open, and the British Open; he is unable to compete in the year's fourth 'major', the US PGA, because the date clashes with that of the British Open.

In cricket, England regains the Ashes after 20 years, beating Australia 1–0 in the five-match series in England (19 Aug).

In tennis, US player Maureen 'Little Mo' Connolly becomes the first woman to win the Grand Slam (US, French, Australian Opens and Wimbledon, London).

In soccer, England lose at Wembley, London, for the first time to an overseas team, beaten 6–3 by Hungary (25 Nov).

y Media

In Britain, foundation of the Press Council, a voluntary organization representing owners, editors, and journalists.

The *Indian Express* is published, and achieves the highest circulation among English-language newspapers in India.

In USA, publication of 'girlie' magazine *Playboy* (Dec), founded by Hugh Hefner.

TV Guide published in USA (from 3 April).

Film:

The Big Heat (director, Fritz Lang; starring Glenn Ford).

The Cruel Sea (director, Charles Frend; starring Jack Hawkins).

Four Chimneys (director, Heinosuke Gosho).

From Here to Eternity (director, Fred Zinnemann; starring Burt Lancaster and Frank Sinatra).

Gentlemen Prefer Blondes (director, Howard Hawks; starring Jane Russell and Marilyn Monroe).

Monsieur Hulot's Holiday (director and star, Jacques Tati).

The Robe (first film in 'Cinemascope').

Roman Holiday (director, William Wyler; starring Gregory Peck and Audrey Hepburn).

Shane (director, George Stevens; starring Alan Ladd).

Stalag 17 (director, Billy Wilder).

Fall of Dien Bien Phu in Vietnam to Vietminh ... French
parliament rejects European Defence Community ... Nasser head
of state in Egypt ...

A January

5 in Italy, resignation of Giuseppe Pella as prime minister (18, Amintore Fanfani forms ministry of Christian Democrats).

8 (–15) Commonwealth finance ministers meet at Sydney, Australia, under Australian Prime Minister Robert Menzies, to consolidate economic progress of the sterling area and Commonwealth.

17 expulsion from Yugoslav Communist Party of Chairman Milovan Djilas, who had pleaded for greater freedom of expression.

23 in USA, publication of report of Randall Commission on Foreign Economic Policy, recommending that the president should be given greater flexibility to reduce tariffs.

24 Moshe Sharett forms new coalition in Israel.

25 (–18 Feb) foreign ministers of USA, USSR, Britain, and France meet in Berlin to reduce world tension, but USSR rejects the West's proposal for the reunification of Germany through free elections (conference ends with proposal for a further conference in Apr at Geneva with Chinese and Korean representatives).

30 in Italy, Amintore Fanfani resigns as prime minister after losing vote of confidence.

B February

10 Mario Scelba forms coalition of Christian Democrats, Social Democrats, and Liberals in Italy, with parliamentary support from Republicans.

23 the British colonial secretary, Oliver Lyttelton, announces the intention to turn the protectorate of Uganda into a self-governing state; this would involve not recognizing the authority of the kabaka of Buganda; in Uganda, supporters of the kabaka bring a legal action claiming that withdrawal of recognition of Nov 1953 was illegal.

25 in Egypt, Colonel Gamal Abdel Nasser usurps power as prime minister (but, on 27, General Muhammad Neguib is again in control).

25 President Chichekli of Syria flees, following army revolt (on 1 March, Sabri el Assali forms government).

C March

1 USA announces that it has tested a hydrogen bomb in the Marshall Islands, over 500 times more powerful than the bomb dropped on Hiroshima in 1945; the bomb's shock wave and fall-out cause great concern in the USA and elsewhere.

1 opening of meeting of Organization of American States in Caracas, Venezuela; delegates support US motion denouncing international communism as a threat to 'the sovereignty and political independence' of the Americas.

4 following the death of President Amin Didi in Jan, the sultanate is restored in the Maldive Islands, with Amir Mohammed Didi as sultan.

8 USA and Japan make mutual defence agreement.

Tokyo Story (director, Yasujiro Ozu).
Ugetsu Monogatavi (director, Kenji Mizoguchi).
I Vitelloni (director, Federico Fellini).
Where Chimneys are Seen (director, Heinosuke Gosho).

Radio:
In Britain the British Broadcasting Corporation's charter is renewed in modified form.

Television:
Programmes first recorded on tape.
The inauguration of the US president, Dwight Eisenhower, is broadcast throughout the country for the first time (20 Jan).

The Coronation of Queen Elizabeth II is televised (2 June), stimulating purchase of television sets in Britain.
In USA, Ed Murrow, on *The Case Against Milo Radulovich, A0589839*, attacks McCarthyism.
Experimental colour broadcasts in USA (Dec).
First television broadcasts in the Philippines (22 Oct).
In Britain, new BBC programmes include *Panorama* on current affairs (–), the variety programme *The Good Old Days* (–1983), and *The Quatermass Experiment*, the first of Nigel Kneale's Quatermass serials; the glove puppet Sooty makes his first appearance with Harry Corbett.

Racial segregation in US schools ruled unconstitutional ...
Karajan appointed to Berlin Philharmonic ... Amis's Lucky Jim
... First four-minute mile ...

o **Politics, Government, Law, and Economy**
New constitution in Nigeria (British protectorate) establishes Federation of Nigeria, comprising Northern, Eastern, and Western regions, the Southern Cameroons (UN Trust territory) and Federal Territory of Lagos.
In Britain, publication (June) of report of the Public Inquiry into the controversial 'Crichel Down' affair (in 1937 the Air Ministry had taken 725 acres of land in Dorset for a bombing range; after the war the land was let by the Agricultural Land Commission to a new tenant); the report criticizes civil servants for their insensitivity in ignoring requests of original owners and tenants to reacquire the land.
In Britain, the Landlord and Tenant Act provides security of tenure for tenants not covered by the Rent Act.
In England, the High Court of Chivalry sits for the first time since 1731 (21 Dec) in Manchester Corporation v. Manchester Palace of Varieties Ltd; it rules that the Palace cannot use Manchester Corporation's arms and issues injunction.
International convention on the prevention of oil pollution at sea.
In USA, Ray Kroc buys the McDonalds company (which produces hamburgers using the assembly-line principle) and presides over its massive growth worldwide (first new restaurant opened on 15 April 1955 at Des Plaines, Illinois).
In USA, President Eisenhower signs St Lawrence Seaway bill (13 May), for the con-

struction of a deep-draught route from Montreal in Canada to Lake Erie (opened 1959).
In Britain, rationing ends (3 July).
In USA, Vice-President Richard Nixon announces plan for construction of network of interstate and intercity highways (12 July).
In USA, General Motors produces its 50 millionth car (23 Nov), a gold-painted Chevrolet sport coupe.
The Anglo-Iranian Oil Company is renamed the British Petroleum Company (Dec).
J A Schumpeter, *History of Economic Analysis* (posthumous).

P **Society, Education, and Religion**
In USA, in Brown v. Topeka Board of Education, the Supreme Court rules (May 17) that racial segregation in schools is unconstitutional, thereby repudiating the doctrine of 'separate but equal'; extension of the ruling in later cases deems segregation of other public facilities unconstitutional.
Women enfranchised in national elections in Mexico.
Divorce legalized in Argentina (14 Dec).
Natives Resettlement Act in South Africa gives the state government power to remove black settlements (the black township of Sophiatown, near the centre of Johannesburg, is cleared).
Richard Wright, *Black Power*.
Two-thirds of Chinese prisoners released in Korea by UN forces are unwilling to return to China.
In Britain, the Beaver Committee on air pollution (appointed July 1953) issues report

9 Centre and Right gain in Finnish election.

13 in Vietnam, Vietminh begin siege of French forces at Dien Bien Phu (–7 May).

23 Israel withdraws from UN Mixed Armistice Commission, complaining of its ineffectiveness.

31 USSR offers to join NATO.

D **April**

5 in USA, President Eisenhower makes broadcast about the H-bomb and the Communist threat.

12 in British Guiana (now Guyana), Dr Cheddi Jagan, former prime minister and leader of the People's Progressive Party, is sentenced to six months in prison for violating order restricting his movements.

12 in Belgian elections Christian Socialists lose absolute majority to Socialists and Liberals (22, Achille van Acker, Socialist, forms coalition).

13 Vladimir Petrov of the Soviet embassy in Canberra is granted asylum in Australia.

16 President Eisenhower pledges US support to the six countries forming the European Defence Community (France, Italy, Luxembourg, Belgium, Netherlands, West Germany).

18 General Nasser becomes prime minister and military governor of Egypt.

21 US Air Force flies a French battalion to Indochina to defend Dien Bien Phu in N Vietnam.

21 the shah of Iran reappoints General Zahedi prime minister.

22 in USA, Senate Sub-Committee on Investigations of Government Operations holds televised hearings at which Senator Joseph McCarthy continues making allegations about Communist infiltration of the army and other government institutions (17 June).

26 (–21 July) at Geneva conference on Korea and Indochina, UN powers insist on free elections in Korea.

28 prime ministers of India, Pakistan, Burma (now Myanmar), Indonesia, and Ceylon confer at Colombo, Ceylon (now Sri Lanka).

28 India signs commercial and cultural agreement with China.

29 first election in Honduras.

E **May**

7 in N Vietnam, Vietminh siege of French forces at Dien Bien Phu ends with surrender of French.

18 European Convention on Human Rights in force.

18 general election in Ireland; Fianna Fáil win 65 seats; Fine Gael, 50; Labour, 19.

29 Thailand complains to UN Security Council that Communists in Indochina threaten its security.

29 in Australian general election, Robert Menzies' coalition of Liberal and Country parties is re-elected with a slightly reduced majority (Liberals win 47 seats; Country Party, 17; Labor, 57).

31 state of emergency declared in Buganda, Uganda (British territory).

31 President Tito of Yugoslavia visits Greece.

F **June**

2 in Republic of Ireland, following the election in May, John Costello (Fine Gael) replaces Éamon de Valera as prime minister and forms coalition government.

12 French government defeated in National Assembly after the defeat of the French army by the Vietnamese at Dien Bien Phu.

15 in Gold Coast (now Ghana), Convention People's Party wins elections (21, Dr Kwame Nkrumah forms government).

18 Pierre Mendès-France, Radical, becomes prime minister of France.

29 following the meeting of President Eisenhower and Winston Churchill in Washington, DC, USA, the Potomac Charter, or six-point affirmation of Western policy, is issued.

G **July**

2 French evacuate southern part of Red River delta, Indochina.

17 Theodor Heuss is elected president of West Germany.

17 Finnish–USSR trade pact.

20 armistice for Indochina signed in Geneva by which France evacuates N Vietnam; the Communists evacuate S Vietnam, Cambodia, and Laos; and France undertakes to respect the independence of Cambodia, Laos, and Vietnam; Ho Chi Minh forms government in N Vietnam.

23 Indochina settlement is approved by French National Assembly.

30 US Senate censures Senator Joseph McCarthy for behaviour unbecoming to a senator and establishes a committee to investigate him.

H **August**

5 announcement of agreement between Iran and consortium of eight foreign companies for the production and export of oil (signed by shah on 29 Oct).

19 fearing vote against the European Defence Community treaty of May 1952 in the French government submits a revised treaty to its co-signatories, but the draft is rejected (22).

(25 Nov); recommends 'Clean Air Scheme' of 10–15-year programme of subsidies and legislation to reduce smoke emissions in densely populated areas.

Filter-tip cigarettes grow in popularity as further evidence of the health risks of smoking is published.

In England, University College, Hull (founded 1929), is incorporated as a university by royal charter (the University's librarian from March 1955 to December 1985 is the poet Philip Larkin).

Canonization of Pope Pius X, Pope 1903–14 (declared saint on 29 May).

The Second Assembly of the World Council of Churches is held at Evanston, Illinois, USA (28–30 Aug).

US evangelist Billy Graham holds massive meetings in London, Berlin, and New York.

C E Raven, *Natural Religion and Christian Theology.*

Paul Tillich, *Love, Power and Justice.*

Q Science, Technology, and Discovery

British Comet jet airliners crash near Elba (10 Jan, killing 35) and N of Messina (9 April, killing 21); the jets are grounded and metal fatigue in a section of the cabin roof is thought to be the cause of the crashes (announced 19 Oct).

In USA, Boeing 707, four-engine jet passenger aircraft, makes maiden flight, from Seattle (15 July).

Italian expedition under Ardito Desio climbs Mt Godwin Austen (K2) in the Himalayas (reaches summit 21 July).

Launch in USA of the first nuclear-powered submarine, the *Nautilus* (21 Jan).

First 'flying bedstead' aircraft, with vertical take-off.

Composite photograph of the night sky completed by Lisk Observatory, California, USA.

Central Observatory of Soviet Academy of Sciences, near Leningrad, opened (21 May).

Bell Telephone Laboratories develop solar battery capable of converting the sun's radiation into electricity.

Atomic-powered railway locomotive designed at Utah University, USA.

National Cancer Institute in the USA suggests link between smoking and lung cancer.

John Charnley starts research that leads to effective hip replacement operations (from 1961).

Polio vaccine prepared by US physician Jonas E Salk is released for general use.

R Humanities

Joseph Needham, *Science and Civilisation in China* (7 volumes and 25 parts; –).

Mortimer Wheeler, *The Indus Civilization.*

W G Grimes discovers remains of a Roman Temple of Mithras in the City of London.

Charles Singer et al. (eds.), *The History of Technology* (5 volumes; — 1958).

M W Beresford, *The Lost Villages of England.*

Benjamin P Thomas, *Abraham Lincoln.*

Asa Briggs, *Victorian People.*

A J P Taylor, *The Struggle for Mastery in Europe, 1848–1918.*

Brinley Thomas, *Migration and Economic Growth: A Study of Great Britain and the Atlantic Economy.*

Henry Pelling, *The Origins of the Labour Party, 1880–1900.*

Isaac Deutscher, *A Study of Trotsky* (–1963).

David M Potter, *People of Plenty: Economic Abundance and the American Character.*

John Harvey, *English Medieval Architecture: A Biographical Dictionary down to 1550.*

Howard Colvin, *A Biographical Dictionary of English Architects, 1660–1840.*

New Oxford History of Music (–1990).

Thurston Dart, *The Interpretation of Music.*

Isaiah Berlin, *Historical Inevitability.*

Max Black, *Problems of Analysis.*

Arthur Koestler, *The Invisible Writing.*

Gilbert Ryle, *Dilemmas.*

S Art, Sculpture, Fine Arts, and Architecture

Death of Henri Matisse (3 Nov).

Painting, etc:

Robert Rauschenberg, *Pink Door.*

Ad Reinhardt, *Abstract Painting, Black.*

Mark Rothko, *Untitled* (Yellow, Orange, Red on Orange).

Graham Sutherland, *Winston Churchill* (later destroyed by Mrs Churchill, who disliked it).

Sculpture:

Kenneth Armitage, *Seated Group Listening to Music.*

Barbara Hepworth, *Two figures, Menhirs.*

Henry Moore, *Internal and External Forms.*

T Music

Benjamin Britten, *The Turn of the Screw* (opera).

Aram Khachaturian, *Spartacus* (ballet).

Rolf Liebermann, *Penelope* (opera).

Witold Lutoslawski, Concerto for Orchestra.

Vincent Persichetti, Symphony No. 4.

Sergei Prokofiev, *The Fiery Angel* (completed

23 Greece, Yugoslavia, and Turkey sign treaty of mutual assistance.

30 French parliament votes against ratification of the 1952 treaty establishing the European Defence Community, which is destroyed by the decision.

J September

8 South-East Asian Defence treaty (for mutual defence) and Pacific Charter signed in Manila, Philippines by USA, Australia, New Zealand, Pakistan, Thailand, Philippines, Britain, and France (the Defence treaty establishes SEATO, the South-East Asia Treaty Organization, based in Bangkok, Thailand).

15 (–28) in Beijing, first meeting of the All-China People's Congress, which, on 20, adopts new constitution for China; on 27, it elects Mao Zedong chairman, Zhu De vice-chairman, and Zhou Enlai prime minister.

27 US Senate Select Committee reports that Joseph McCarthy acted improperly in making government employees hand over documents.

K October

3 nine-power conference in London on European unity agrees that West Germany should enter NATO.

5 USA, Britain, Italy, and Yugoslavia agree that the Free Territory of Trieste should be divided into Italian and Yugoslav zones.

8 Communist forces occupy Hanoi, N Vietnam.

11 the People's Republic of China complains to the UN about US aggression towards 'China's territory of Formosa' (now Taiwan).

18 in Britain, Winston Churchill reconstructs cabinet, with Harold Macmillan as minister of defence.

19 Colonel Nasser of Egypt signs British–Egyptian agreement; it terminates the treaty of 1936; states timetable for withdrawal of British troops from canal zone; and reserves right of Britain to intervene if the canal is threatened (in force from 6 Dec).

23 USA, Britain, France, and USSR agree to end occupation of Germany; nine-power agreement on Western European Union signed, permitting Italy and Germany to accede to the Brussels treaty of 1948.

24 state of emergency declared in Pakistan; the governor general declares that the Constituent Assembly has lost the people's confidence.

26 France and West Germany sign economic and cultural agreement.

30 (–1 Nov) insurrection in Algeria, with over 60 attacks on French police and troops; the rebels call themselves the Front for National Liberation (FLN) and call for the establishment of an independent Algeria.

L November

4 in Uganda, judgment of high court supports legality of Uganda government in withdrawing recognition of the kabaka of Buganda.

5 Burma (now Myanmar) signs peace treaty with Japan.

13 success of Social Credit Party in New Zealand elections reduces National government's majority.

14 in Egypt, President Neguib is deposed (18, General Nasser becomes head of state).

29 Moscow Conference of representatives of Soviet satellite states opens; attended by observers from Communist China.

M December

France sends 20,000 troops to Algeria.

1 USA signs pact of mutual security with Nationalist China (Formosa, now Taiwan).

2 US Senate censures Joseph McCarthy.

2 J G Strijdom, Nationalist, forms ministry in South Africa on D F Malan's retirement.

14 riots in Athens, Greece, by supporters of union (Enosis) of Cyprus with Greece; during 1954, EOKA (National Organization of Cypriot Fighters) under George Grivas emerges as pro-Enosis terrorist organization.

17 President Tito of Yugoslavia visits Delhi, India.

20 USSR threatens to annul alliance treaty of May 1942 with Britain if Paris agreement of 23 Oct on Germany is ratified.

1923, revised 1927, and now given first performance on Paris radio).

Arnold Schoenberg, *Moses and Aron* (posthumous opera).

Edgard Varèse, *Déserts*.

William Walton, *Troilus and Cressida* (opera).

In Germany, Herbert von Karajan of Austria succeeds Wilhelm Furtwängler as conductor of the Berlin Philharmonic Orchestra.

Joyce Grenfell Requests the Pleasure, revue starring Joyce Grenfell.

The Pajama Game (musical), lyrics and music by Richard Adler and Jerry Ross (first performed at the St James Theatre, New York, 13 May).

Salad Days (musical), by Julian Slade (first performed at the Vaudeville Theatre, London, 5 Aug).

Eddie Calvert, 'Oh, my Papa'.

Doris Day, 'Secret Love'.

Bill Haley and the Comets, 'Rock Around the Clock'.

Elvis Presley, 'That's All Right' (by Arthur 'Big Boy' Crudup).

In USA, first jazz festival at Newport, Rhode Island (18 July).

Fender in USA produce the twin reverb amplifier.

u Literature and Drama

Kingsley Amis, *Lucky Jim*.

John Betjeman, *A Few Late Chrysanthemums* (poems).

Peter De Vries, *The Tunnel of Love*.

William Golding, *Lord of the Flies*.

Thomas Mann, *The Confessions of Felix Krull, Confidence Man*.

John Masters, *Bhowani Junction*.

Françoise Sagan, *Bonjour Tristesse*.

J R R Tolkien, *The Lord of the Rings*, Vols. 1 and 2 (Vol. 3, 1955)

Drama:

Enid Bagnold, *The Chalk Garden*.

Jane Bowles, *In the Summer House*.

Truman Capote and Harold Arlen, *House of Flowers*.

Paddy Chayefsky, *The Bachelor Party* (for TV).

Christopher Fry, *The Dark is Light Enough*.

Charles Morgan, *The Burning Glass*.

Dylan Thomas's dramatic poem (a 'play for voices', written for radio) *Under Milk Wood*; broadcast on BBC Third Programme, 25 Jan.

Tennessee Williams, *Cat on a Hot Tin Roof*.

New York Shakespeare Festival founded by Joseph Papp.

v Births and Deaths

Jan 11 John Simon dies (80).

April 10 Auguste Lumière dies (91).

May 19 Charles Ives dies (79).

Aug 19 Alcide de Gasperi dies (73).

Aug 24 Getúlio Vargas dies (71).

Aug 25 Elvis Costello born (–).

May 19 Charles Ives dies (79).

Sept 8 André Derain dies (74).

Oct 7 Seebohm Rowntree dies (83).

Nov 3 Henri Matisse dies (84).

Nov 30 Wilhelm Furtwängler dies (68).

w Everyday Life

Northland shopping mall, north of Detroit, USA, opens; it will lead the way to new patterns of suburban living.

The cha cha cha is introduced to the USA.

US actress Marilyn Monroe makes second marriage, to baseball star Joe DiMaggio (14 Jan); sues for divorce on 5 Oct.

Flashing directional indicator lights are compulsory on cars in Britain (from 1 Jan).

Formation of the Federation of British Sun Clubs (nudist clubs).

x Sport and Recreation

Roger Bannister is the first man to run a mile in under 4 minutes, at the Iffley Road Sports Ground, Oxford, England (6 May).

Miss D Leather of Birmingham University, England, is the first woman to run a mile in under 5 minutes (30 May).

Soviet rowing crews enter the Henley Royal Regatta, England, for the first time, winning the Grand Challenge Cup (for eights), the Stewards' Cup (for coxswainless fours), and the Silver Goblets (for coxswainless pairs).

The fifth football World Cup is held in Switzerland; West Germany beats Hungary 3–2 in the final in Berne.

Pakistan win a Test on their first cricket tour of England, winning the final match at The Oval by 24 runs (17 Aug).

The Union des Associations Européennes de Football (UEFA) is formed, with a view to establishing regular European cup competitions.

y Media

Publication of the French women's magazine *Marie-Claire*.

Film:

Bad Day at Black Rock (director, John Sturges; starring Spencer Tracey).

The Belles of St Trinians (starring Alistair Sim).

The Caine Mutiny (starring Humphrey Bogart).

Carmen Jones (director, Otto Preminger).

Les Diaboliques (director, Henri Clouzot).

The Divided Heart (director, Charles Crichton).

Winston Churchill retires as British prime minister ... Bandung
Conference ... West Germany enters NATO ...

A **January**

10 following introduction of new constitution in 1954, the Federal House of Representatives of Nigeria first meets.

18 the governor of Kenya (British colony) proclaims amnesty: no prosecutions to be brought against Mau Mau rebels who surrender (about 1,000 surrender by end of amnesty on 10 July).

21 in Norway, following the retirement the Labour Prime Minister Oscar Torp, Einar Gerhardsen, resumes the premiership.

24 because of increased tension between the People's Republic of China and Formosa (now Taiwan), President Eisenhower of the USA asks Congress for authority to protect Formosa (granted within four days).

25 USSR decrees end of state of war with Germany.

25 Jacques Soustelle, Left Republican, appointed governor general of Algeria, with task of restoring order.

B **February**

5 in France, Pierre Mendès-France resigns as prime minister after defeat of his government in a vote of confidence on its North Africa policy.

8 Georgi Malenkov, prime minister of USSR, resigns following opposition to his policy of reducing arms production; succeeded by Nikolai Bulganin.

23 foreign ministers of SEATO countries (established in Sept 1954) confer at Bangkok, Thailand.

23 Edgar Fauré, Radical, forms ministry in France.

24 Turkey and Iraq sign treaty of alliance, the Baghdad Pact, which provides for mutual support against Communist militants.

24 in Cuba, Fulgencio Batista is elected president (without opposition) for four years.

East of Eden (director, Elia Kazan; starring Raymond Massey and, in his first role, James Dean).

Executive Suite (director, Robert Wise; starring Fredric March and Barbara Stanwyck).

A Generation (director, Andrzej Wajda).

Genevieve (director, Henry Cornelius; starring Kenneth More).

On the Waterfront (director, Elia Kazan; starring Marlon Brando, Rod Steiger, and Lee J Cobb).

Rear Window (director, Alfred Hitchcock; starring James Stewart and Grace Kelly).

Seven Brides for Seven Brothers (director, Stanley Donen; starring Howard Keel).

The Seven Samurai (director, Akira Kurosawa).

A Star is Born (director, George Cukor; starring Judy Garland and James Mason).

La Strada (director, Federico Fellini; starring Giulietta Masina).

Voyage in Italy.

White Christmas (director, Michael Curtiz; starring Bing Crosby and Danny Kaye).

The Wild One (starring Marlon Brando).

Radio:

BBC broadcasts *Hancock's Half Hour*, with Tony Hancock and Sid James (Nov–Dec 1959).

Television:

First regular broadcasts in colour in USA (from 1 Jan).

'Miss America' beauty competition (held in Atlantic City, New Jersey) is televised throughout the USA (11 Sept).

Meeting of US cabinet televised for first time (25 Oct).

New programmes in USA include *Disneyland* (ABC); the current affairs programme *Face the Nation*; *The Secret Storm* (–1974); *Tonight Show* (NBC) with Steve Allen; *Twelve Angry Men*, a Studio 1 drama by Reginald Rose.

The Eurovision network is formed, linking companies in eight countries (first broadcast on 6 June features Pope Pius XII).

In Britain, Richard Baker presents the first *BBC Television News* (5 July).

Other new BBC programmes include *The Grove Family*, Britain's first television 'soap opera'; *1984*; the zoological programme *Zoo-Quest*, with David Attenborough (–1961).

In Britain, the Television Act establishes the Independent Television Authority to manage the introduction of commercial television (from 1955).

Montgomery bus boycott ... Larkins' Less Deceived *... Opening of 'Disneyland' ... Death of Grace Archer ...*

o **Politics, Government, Law, and Economy**

In USA, William F Buckley founds *National Review*, a review of politics and current affairs.

Louis Hartz, *The Liberal Tradition in America*.

Walter Lippmann, *The Public Philosophy*.

Albania, Austria, Bulgaria, Cambodia, Ceylon (now Sri Lanka), Finland, Hungary, Republic of Ireland, Italy, Jordan, Laos, Libya, Nepal, Portugal, Romania, and Spain are admitted to United Nations (14 Dec).

In USA, the Yarmolinsky Report, financed by the Ford Foundation, reveals absurd aspects of US security precautions.

In Britain, Ruth Ellis is hanged (13 July) for murdering her lover; she is the last woman to be hanged in Britain.

New York Housing Authority is ruled to have exceeded its powers by requiring loyalty oaths from tenants.

Universal Copyright Convention comes into force.

Commonwealth Law conference held at Westminster.

Five-Year Plan launched in Pakistan, to increase agricultural output and expand power generation and industry.

In USA, creation of Chase Manhattan Bank by merger.

In West Germany, the airline Lufthansa is revived.

p **Society, Education, and Religion**

In USA, after the Interstate Commerce Commission orders the end of segregation in transport (Nov 25), Rosa Parks, an African-American, in Montgomery, Alabama, is arrested for sitting at the front of a bus (in the section reserved for whites); 50,000 African-Americans, led by Dr Martin

c **March**

2 Egypt and Syria establish defensive alliance.

3 Greece, Yugoslavia, and Turkey set up a consultative parliamentary council (of 20 deputies from each country).

7 general election in Malta won by the Labour Party, led by Dom Mintoff, which fought on platform of seeking integration with Britain.

11 Italy, West Germany (on 18), and France (on 27) ratify Paris agreement of Oct 1954 for establishing Western European Union.

24 new constitution in force in Tanganyika (now Tanzania).

27 state of emergency declared in Pakistan.

31 purge of Chinese Communist Party.

d **April**

1 US Senate ratifies Paris agreement of Oct 1954 for establishing Western European Union.

4 Britain signs treaty with Iraq, and Parliament decides to adhere to the Baghdad Pact (of 24 Feb).

5 in Britain, Winston Churchill resigns as prime minister because of age and ill health (succeeded on 6 by Anthony Eden who, on 7, re-forms Conservative ministry, with Harold Macmillan as foreign secretary and R A Butler chancellor of the exchequer).

14 Chinese prime minister and foreign minister Zhou Enlai visits Rangoon, Burma (now Yangon in Myanmar).

15 USSR–Austrian economic agreement.

17 Vietnam appeals to United Nations over alleged breach of Geneva agreement by the Vietminh (nationalists).

18 (–24) Bandung or Afro-Asian Conference, held in Bandung, Indonesia, at invitation of President Sukharno; ministers of 29 non-aligned states meet to form 'non-aligned bloc' of countries opposed to the 'imperialism' and 'colonialism' of the superpowers.

18 in Hungary, Imre Nagy is forced to resign as prime minister; Ándras Hegedüs becomes nominal prime minister, but Mátyás Rákosi returns to post of secretary of Hungarian Workers' Party.

20 in USA, President Eisenhower asks Congress for $3,530 million for foreign aid appropriations.

29 Giovanni Gronchi, Christian Democrat, is elected president of Italy.

e **May**

5 end of occupation régime in West Germany.

6 Britain submits dispute with Argentina and Chile over ownership of Falkland Islands to International Court; but those countries refuse to present counter-claims.

7 USSR annuls treaties with Britain and France in retaliation for the ratification of the Paris agreement on European Union.

9 West Germany is admitted a member of NATO.

14 Warsaw Treaty (of Friendship, Co-operation, and Mutual Assistance) signed by USSR, Albania, Bulgaria, Czechoslovakia, East Germany, Hungary, Poland, and Romania, establishing the 'Warsaw Pact'; provides for unified military command (with headquarters in Moscow) and stationing of Soviet military units in member countries.

15 USA, USSR, Britain, and France sign Vienna treaty restoring Austria's independence.

24 (–4 July) dock strike in Britain.

26 in British general election Conservatives win 345 seats over Labour with 277, Liberals with 6, and United Ireland with 2.

26 Nikolai Bulganin and Nikita Khrushchev of USSR visit Yugoslavia (2 June, sign treaty of friendship).

29 (–14 June) railway strike in Britain.

f **June**

6 Western Powers propose summit conference at Geneva to ease tension (18 July, USSR agrees to meeting).

11 in USA, President Eisenhower proposes financial and technical aid to non-Communist countries for development of civil atomic energy.

15 USA and Britain sign atomic energy agreement, providing for exchange of information.

22 resignation of Mario Scelba's coalition in Italy; Antonio Segni, also Christian Democrat, forms coalition.

30 military aid agreement between USA and West Germany.

g **July**

4 Britain undertakes to return naval base at Simonstown, South Africa, to that country's government (by 31 March 1957) while retaining right to use the base.

5 Assembly of Western European Union holds first meeting at Strasbourg, France.

18 (–23) summit conference of USA, USSR, Britain, and France at Geneva, Switzerland; no agreements are reached; the USSR states that it will only agree to German reunification within the framework of a collective security system for Europe (on 24, Harold Macmillan, at press conference on return from summit, declares: 'There ain't gonna be no war').

Luther King, mount a boycott of local buses (1 Dec–Nov 1956), demanding an end to segregation.

Emmett Till, a 14-year-old African-American, is lynched in Mississippi, USA.

President Eisenhower increases the US minimum wage from 75 cents to $1 per hour.

In USA, merger of the American Federation of Labor and the Congress of Industrial Organizations agreed (5 Dec), forming the AFL-CIO.

In Britain, Political and Economic Planning (PEP) issues report *World Population and Resources*, urging research into the control of human fertility.

Clean Air Act passed in Britain in response to the 1952 smog.

Amphetamine abuse surges in Japan.

In USA, the Progressive Education Association is disbanded.

In England, University College, Exeter (founded 1922), is incorporated as a university by royal charter.

In USA, L Ron Hubbard formally establishes the Church of Scientology, having found no professional support for his eccentric views on mental health.

W Herberg, *Protestant-Catholic-Jew*.

Q Science, Technology, and Discovery

British aviator Walter Gibb, in a Canberra jet, flies at new record altitude of 20,000 m/65,876 ft.

First flight in USSR of A N Tupolev's Tu-104 jet passenger aircraft.

First vertical take-off plane built in Britain, the PD11.

USA and USSR announce they will attempt launching of Earth satellites in International Geophysical Year (1957–58).

First use of atomically generated power in USA, at Schenectady (18 July).

During the Geneva conference on Peaceful Uses of Atomic Energy (8–20 Aug), British publisher Robert Maxwell rents villa for the entertainment of delegates; many agree to publish revised versions of their conference papers in the series 'Economics of Nuclear Power', to be issued by Maxwell's Company Pergamon Press in competition with the official publication of conference proceedings; the deals turn Pergamon (founded 1951) into a major publisher of scientific journals.

Audouin Dolfus ascends 7.2 km/4½ mi above the Earth to make photoelectric observations of Mars.

In USA, B F Burk discovers that Jupiter emits radio waves (announced in May).

In USA, Radio-physicists of Massachusetts Institute of Technology develop use of Ultra High-Frequency waves.

In Britain, chemist Dorothy Hodgkin discovers composition of Vitamin B12.

British biochemist Frederick Sanger completes elucidation of the structure of the insulin molecule (to date, the largest protein molecule whose chemical structure has been determined).

R Humanities

Robert Graves, *The Greek Myths*.

Dorothy Whitelock, *English Historical Documents, c.* 500–1042, first volume of David Douglas (ed.), 'English Historical Documents' (–).

Stephen Runciman, *The Eastern Schism*.

Walter Ullmann, *The Growth of Papal Government in the Middle Ages*.

W G Hoskins, *The Making of the English Landscape*.

G R Elton, *England under the Tudors*.

J E Neale, *Elizabeth I and her Parliaments* (Volume 2, 1957).

Bernard Bailyn, *The New England Merchant in the Seventeenth Century*.

Philip D Curtin, *Two Jamaicas*.

E P Thompson, *William Morris: Romantic to Revolutionary*.

C Vann Woodward, *The Strange Career of Jim Crow*.

John Higham, *Strangers in the Land: Patterns of American Nativism, 1860–1925*.

J B Frantz and J E Choate, *The American Cowboy: The Myth and Reality*.

A J P Taylor, *Bismarck: The Man and the Statesman*.

Richard Hofstadter, *The Age of Reform*.

C L Mowat, *Britain Between the Wars, 1918–1940*.

J K Galbraith, *The Great Crash*.

John Pope-Hennessy, *Italian Gothic Sculpture*.

J A Westrup, *An Introduction to Musical History*.

E S de Beer (ed.), *The Diary of John Evelyn*.

Bibliography of American Literature (–).

Etienne Gilson, *History of Christian Philosophy in the Middle Ages*.

Claude Lévi-Strauss, *A World on the Wane* (in USA, published as *Tristes Tropiques*).

Herbert Marcuse, *Eros and Civilization*.

Pierre Teilhard de Chardin, *The Phenomenon of Man*.

S Art, Sculpture, Fine Arts, and Architecture

Painting, etc:

Pietro Annigoni, *HM Queen Elizabeth II*.

Karel Appel, *Amorous Dance*.

Alberto Burri, *Wood Combustion*.

Willem de Kooning, *Composition*.

Jasper Johns, first *Flag*, *Target*, and *Number* paintings.

20 headquarters of the International Armistice Commission in Saigon, Vietnam, are sacked.

21 Greece proposes that the Cyprus question be put before UN General Assembly.

24 Nikolai Bulganin and Nikita Khrushchev of USSR visit East Germany.

30 conscription introduced in China.

31 devaluation of the Pakistan rupee.

H August

1 Communist Youth Congress held in Warsaw, Poland.

8 (–20) International Conference on the Peaceful Uses of Atomic Energy held in Geneva, Switzerland; attended by 1,428 delegates from 73 countries and eight agencies, and by 1,350 academic and commercial observers.

8 barter agreement between Egypt, USSR, and Romania (Egypt to exchange cotton and cotton yarns for oil and paraffin).

11 Muslim-dominated right-wing ministry takes office in Indonesia.

13 five armed members of the Irish Republican Army are arrested while trying to steal arms from a British army training centre at Arborfield, Berkshire, S England.

15 Buganda transitional agreement signed in Kampala, Uganda, which will permit the return of the Kabaka.

15 Indians attempt to enter the Portuguese colony of Goa, India.

20 anti-French riots in Morocco, on anniversary of sultan's deposition in 1953.

20 outbreak of FLN attacks on French in Algeria, including massacre near Philippeville.

30 (–7 Sept) conference in London of foreign ministers of Greece, Turkey, and Britain to discuss Cyprus and E Mediterranean; Britain's proposals for government of Cyprus are rejected.

J September

6 anti-Greek riots in Istanbul and Izmir, Turkey.

13 announcement made at end of meeting of meeting of West German Chancellor Konrad Adenauer with Soviet leaders in Moscow that diplomatic relations will be restored (23, German Bundestag approves; Soviet ambassador appointed 8 Jan 1956).

16 rising in Córdoba under General Eduardo Lonardi spreads throughout Argentina.

19 Juan Perón resigns as president of Argentina, going into exile (23, General Lonardi assumes presidency).

24 in USA, President Eisenhower suffers a heart attack.

25 British government appoints John Harding governor of Cyprus.

30 France withdraws from UN General Assembly after the Assembly votes (28–27) to debate the Algerian situation (item deleted from agenda on 25 Nov, after which the French delegation returns).

K October

12 goodwill visits of British Royal Navy to Leningrad, USSR (now St Petersburg, Russia) and of Soviet Navy to Portsmouth, Britain.

17 in Morocco, a Council of the Throne is instituted to enable Franco-Moroccan negotiations to be resumed (resigns on 2 Nov).

17 the Kabaka returns to Buganda, Uganda.

23 referendum in South Vietnam advocates deposition of Emperor Bao Dai (26, republic is proclaimed under Ngo Dinh Diem).

23 plebiscite in Saar, on plan to place the Saar under control of the Western European Union; rejected by 423,434 votes to 201,973; after election in Dec, France agrees that the Saar can return to Germany.

26 in Britain, R A Butler introduces autumn Budget, consisting of credit squeeze to deal with Britain's unfavourable balance of payments.

27 (–16 Nov) Geneva conference of US, USSR, British, and French foreign ministers on security and position of Germany.

L November

1 John Foster Dulles, US secretary of state, visits General Franco in Spain and, on 6, President Tito in Yugoslavia.

2 in Israel, David Ben-Gurion, the former prime minister, now back from retirement, forms coalition ministry.

3 Iran joins the (Iraq–Turkey) Baghdad Pact.

6 the deposed Sultan of Morocco agrees conditions with France for his return; constitutional government to be established and terms for self-government to be negotiated with France.

9 South Africa withdraws from UN General Assembly, because UN decides to continue consideration of Cruz Report of 1952 on 'apartheid'.

16 the deposed Sultan of Morocco returns (first all-Moroccan government formed on 7 Dec).

26 John Harding, governor of Cyprus, proclaims state of emergency in the island.

M December

9 Adnan Menderes forms ministry in Turkey.

Robert Rauschenberg, *Bed*.
Cy Twombly, *Free Wheeler (New York City)*

Sculpture:
Robert Rauschenberg, *Monogram* (–1959).

Architecture:
Frederick Gibberd, buildings for London Heathrow Airport.
Le Corbusier, La Torette, Eveaux-sur-l'Arbresle, Lyons, France.
Ludwig Mies van der Rohe and Phillip Johnson, Seagram Building, New York (–1958).
Pier Luigi Nervi and Gio Ponti, Pirelli Skyscraper, Milan, Italy (–1958).
Eero Saarinen, General Motors Technical Center, Michigan, USA.

T **Music**
Easley Blackwood, Symphony No. 1.
Pierre Boulez, *Le Marteau sans Maître*.
Carlisle Floyd, *Susannah* (opera).
Alan Hovhaness, *Mysterious Mountain*.
Bohuslav Martinů, *Fantaisies Symphoniques*.
Iannis Xenakis, *Metastaseis*.
Marian Anderson is the first African-American singer to perform at the Metropolitan Opera House in New York (7 Jan).
Damn Yankees (musical), music and lyrics by Richard Adler and Jerry Ross (first performed at 46th Street Theatre, New York, 5 May).
Chuck Berry, 'Maybelline', 'Roll Over Beethoven'.
'Tennessee' Ernie Ford, 'Sixteen Tons' (written by Merle Travis in 1947), 'Give Me Your Word'.
Slim Whitman, 'Rosemarie'.
Foundation in Britain of Ivor Novello awards for achievement in popular and light music.
RCA build the first moog synthesiser.
In USA, jazz saxophonist and composer Charlie 'Yardbird' or 'Bird' Parker dies at age of 34, killed by heroin and alcohol.

U **Literature and Drama**
James Baldwin, *Notes of a Native Son*.
Edward Blishen, *Roaring Boys*.
Heinrich Böll, *The Bread of Our Early Years*.
Paul Bowles, *The Spider's House*.
Ivy Compton-Burnett, *Mother and Son*.
J P Donleavy, *The Ginger Man*.
Graham Greene, *The Quiet American*.
Robin Jenkins, *The Cone Gatherers*.
Philip Larkin, *The Less Deceived* (poems).
Vladimir Nabokov, *Lolita*.
Patrick White, *The Tree of Life*.

Drama:
Samuel Beckett, *Waiting for Godot*.
Ugo Betti, *The Queen and the Rebels*.
William Inge, *Bus Stop*.

Raymond Evenor Lawler, *The Summer of the Seventeenth Doll*.
Arthur Miller, *A View from the Bridge*.
Sean O'Casey, *The Bishop's Bonfire*.
Thornton Wilder, *The Matchmaker*.
In London, playwright Ronald Duncan founds the English Stage Company, to perform the work of young and experimental playwrights and foreign contemporary drama.

V **Births and Deaths**
March 11 Alexander Fleming dies (73).
April 18 Albert Einstein dies (76).
Aug 12 Thomas Mann dies (80).
Oct 28 Bill Gates born (–).
Nov 5 Maurice Utrillo dies (71).
Nov 27 Arthur Honegger dies (63).

W **Everyday Life**
'Disneyland' theme park opens in Anaheim, California, USA (18 July).
'Flying saucers' attract attention.
Tight jeans are fashionable in N America and western Europe.
In Britain, Princess Margaret decides not to marry Peter Townsend, a divorcee (30 Oct).

X **Sport and Recreation**
In the second Test in Auckland, New Zealand are dismissed by England for 26, the lowest total in Test cricket history (29 March).
Eighty-three spectators and one driver are killed in an accident during the Le Mans 24-hour race (11 June).
Charles Dumas of the USA is the first man to clear 2.1 m/7 ft in the High Jump (29 June).
Louison Bobet of France becomes the first cyclist to win three consecutive Tours de France.
In football, the European Cup is inaugurated; Scottish clubs participate in the competition, but not English clubs.
In Britain, Donald Campbell becomes the first man to exceed 321 km/200 mph on water (16 Nov).

Y **Media**
The British government bans the import of 'horror comics' after a moral panic.

Film:
US heartthrob cinema actor James Dean dies in car crash, near Los Angeles, at age of 24 (30 Sept).
The Blackboard Jungle (director, Richard Brooks; starring Glenn Ford).
The Dam Busters (director, Michael Anderson; starring Michael Redgrave and Richard Todd).
The Ladykillers (the last of the Ealing Comedies).

13 in Britain, following retirement of Clement Attlee as leader of the Labour Party, Hugh Gaitskell is elected leader by Labour MPs and peers with 157 votes, against 70 for Aneurin Bevan and 40 for Herbert Morrison.

19 Sudan's parliament passes resolution calling on Egypt and Britain to recognize Sudan as an independent state (recognition granted on 1 Jan 1956; Sudan joins Arab League on 19 Jan).

20 in Britain, Anthony Eden reshuffles cabinet, with Harold Macmillan as chancellor of the exchequer, Selwyn Lloyd foreign secretary, and R A Butler as leader of the House of Commons.

Khrushchev denounces Stalin ... Suez crisis ... Soviet invasion of Hungary ...

A January

2 Communists and 'Poujadists' (Union for the Defence of Traders and Artisans, called after their leader Pierre Poujade) gain seats in French elections (Communists win 147 compared with 97 in 1951; Poujadists, contesting their first election, win 51).

5 in Cairo, Egypt, meeting between Marshal Tito of Yugoslavia and Colonel Nasser of Egypt.

18 (–8 Feb) conference held in London to discuss future of Malayan federation; recommends that Britain should grant independence by Aug 1957.

23 Nikolai Bulganin, prime minister of USSR, proposes 20-year pact of friendship between USA and USSR.

B February

1 South Africa requests USSR to close its consulates.

1 in USA, President Eisenhower and Anthony Eden, prime minister of Britain, issue Declaration of Washington, reaffirming joint policy in Middle East.

1 following general election of 2 Jan, Guy Mollet, Socialist, forms ministry in France; he announces plan to bring peace to Algeria, but unrest continues there.

4 USSR protests to USA about its launching of balloons with photographic equipment over Soviet territory.

7 (–23) conference held in London to advance plans for establishing British Caribbean Federation (from 1958; Act to establish Federation given royal assent on 2 Aug).

11 (–12) referendum in Malta (a British colony) favours integration with Britain (but only 45 per cent of electorate vote).

12 USSR states that the dispatch of US or British troops to the Middle East would violate the United Nations Charter.

25 in USSR, at closed session of the 20th Conference of the Communist Party, general secretary Nikita Khrushchev denounces policies of Stalin (speech made public on 18 March).

29 Pakistan parliament passes bill containing constitution for independent Islamic Republic of Pakistan (2 March, decides to stay in Commonwealth; 23 March becomes independent, with Iskander Mirza, the governor general, as provisional president).

Lola Montes (director, Max Ophüls).

The Night of the Hunter (director, Charles Laughton; starring Robert Mitchum).

Pather Panchali (director, Satyajit Ray).

Rebel Without A Cause (director, Nicholas Ray; starring James Dean).

Rififi (director, Jules Dassin).

The Seven Year Itch (director, Billy Wilder; starring Marilyn Monroe).

Radio:

Sony of Japan launch the first mass-produced transistor radio.

Television:

Eisenhower is the first US president to hold a televised news conference (19 Jan).

New programmes in USA include: *Alfred Hitchcock Presents* (–1962); *Cheyenne*, starring Clint Walker (–1962); *Douglas Fairbanks Presents* (–1959); *Dragnet*, about Los Angeles detectives; *The Phil Silvers Show*, which introduces Sergeant Bilko; and *The $64,000 Question* (CBS).

In USA, the series *Sam and Friends* features The Muppets.

In Britain, commercial television is introduced (22 Sept), supervised by the Independent Television Authority (ITA); the BBC spoils ITA's first evening by killing Grace Archer, a leading character in the popular radio series *The Archers*, in a fire.

The first programmes on commercial television include: *The Benny Hill Show* (–1989); *Double Your Money*, a quiz game with Hughie Green; *Free Speech*, featuring the original team of the BBC's *In The News*, who had been dropped by the BBC; *Robin Hood*; *Sunday Night at the Palladium*.

New BBC programmes include: *Crackerjack* for children, presented by Eamonn Andrews (–1984); *Dixon of Dock Green*, starring Jack Warner (–1976).

The BBC makes experimental colour broadcasts (from 10 Oct).

The police series *Dragnet* is the first US drama series to be broadcast in Britain.

W H Whyte's Organization Man ... *Development of FORTRAN ...
Elvis Presley's 'Love Me Tender' ... John Osborne's* Look Back
in Anger ...

○ **Politics, Government, Law, and Economy**

Anthony Crosland, *The Future of Socialism*.

C Wright Mills, *The Power Elite*.

Clinton Rossiter, *Conservatism in America*, *The American Presidency*.

William S White, *Citadel: The Story of the US Senate*.

India and Indonesia sign mutual aid treaty (28 Feb).

National People's Army formed in East Germany (28 Jan).

West Germany amends constitution to permit introduction of conscription (8 March).

In Griffin v. Illinois the US Supreme Court makes the first broad statement that economic inequality should not be a barrier to equality before the law.

Restrictive Practices Act sets up Restrictive Practices Court in Britain (9 July), to deal with unfair trading.

In Britain, Sydney Silverman's bill for abolition of death penalty passes Commons (28 June) but is defeated in the House of Lords (10 July).

Norman St John-Stevas, *Obscenity and the Law*.

In USSR, Sixth Five-Year Plan is adopted at Party Congress (Feb), aiming to achieve further increases in industrial and agricultural production; but the plan is abandoned a year later and not replaced.

In USA, the Defense Interstate Highway Act grants $33.5bn over 14 years to develop the interstate road system.

Container port opened at Elizabeth, New Jersey, USA, transforming the nature of docks.

British bank rate raised to 5.5 per cent, highest rate since 1932, to curb inflation (16 Feb).

Life insurance is nationalized in India (30 May).

Tube Investments Ltd brings into operation the first multi-purpose industrial high-energy plant in Europe.

Bread subsidy ends in Britain after 15 years (29 Sept).

P **Society, Education, and Religion**

The bus boycott campaign of 1955 in Montgomery, Alabama, USA, ends when the Supreme Court rules that the segregation of bus passengers is unconstitutional (13 Nov).

c March

2 France recognizes independence of Morocco (Spain grants recognition on 7 April).

2 King Hussein of Jordan dismisses General J B ('Pasha') Glubb from command of Arab Legion.

5 Britain begins jamming of radio broadcasts from Radio Athens to Cyprus, which were encouraging terrorist activities (jamming continues until Dec).

9 British authorities deport Archbishop Makarios and three others from Cyprus to the Seychelles, suspecting them of involvement with EOKA terrorists.

12 Greek government asks for Cyprus question to be put before UN General Assembly; UN agrees, but accepts British counter-proposal as well.

20 France recognizes independence of Tunisia; the Bey of Tunis is head of state with Habib ben Ali Bourguiba as prime minister.

d April

10 general election in Ceylon (now Sri Lanka) is won by the Sri Lanka Freedom Party; Solomon Bandaranaike replaces Sir John Kotalawala as prime minister.

17 USSR abolishes the Cominform (Communist Information Bureau, established in 1947), in move to help rapprochement with Yugoslavia and the West.

18 (–27) visit of Soviet leaders Nikolai Bulganin and Nikita Khrushchev to Britain.

21 military alliance signed by Egypt, Saudi Arabia, and Yemen at Jiddah, Saudi Arabia.

22 China appoints Dalai Lama chairman of committee to prepare Tibet for regional autonomy within Chinese People's Republic.

29 Dag Hammarskjöld, UN secretary general, obtains agreement of Israel and Jordan to respect cease-fire undertakings (similar agreement obtained on 1 May from Lebanon and on 2 May from Syria).

29 British admiralty announces disappearance of Lionel Crabb, a navy frogman who was diving near the cruiser of the Soviet leaders in Portsmouth Harbour (Crabb's headless body is found in sea, 26 June 1957).

e May

1 in Argentina, Peronist constitution is revoked and replaced by liberal constitution of 1853.

9 plebiscite in British Togoland votes for integration with Gold Coast.

14 USSR complains that US planes have violated its air space.

27 India claims suzerainty over Chitral, a princely state which has been under Pakistani administration since 1947.

28 France formally cedes former French settlements in India to Republic of India.

f June

1 in USSR, Vyacheslav Molotov is dismissed as foreign minister; succeeded by Dmitri Shepilov.

2 President Tito of Yugoslavia visits Moscow, USSR, marking improvement in relations.

4 Egypt declares that it will not extend the Suez Canal Company's concession after expiry in 1968.

5 in Luxembourg, Chancellor Konrad Adenauer of Germany and Prime Minister Mollet of France agree future of the Saar; Saar to have political union with West Germany from 1 Jan 1957 and economic union over longer period (formal agreement signed on 27 Oct).

13 last British troops leave Suez Canal base, in accordance with British–Egyptian treaty of Oct 1954.

22 in Austria, following general election on 13 May, Julius Raab forms new coalition of People's Party and Socialists.

24 Colonel Nasser (unopposed) is elected president of Egypt by popular vote, which also approves new constitution.

28 labour riots at Poznań, Poland, put down with heavy loss of life.

30 Leeward Islands federation dissolved to enable islands to enter Caribbean federation.

g July

11 in USSR, the separate Finno-Karelian Republic is abolished and incorporated as the Karelian Autonomous Republic within the Russian Federation.

17 Kwame Nkrumah, People's Party, increases majority in Gold Coast elections.

19 (–20) USA and Britain inform Egypt that they cannot at present participate in financing proposed Aswan High Dam on the River Nile.

26 in Egypt, President Nasser announces nationalization of the Suez Canal (owned partly by France and Britain), under decree outlawing the company (–31, Britain, France, and USA retaliate with financial measures).

h August

2 Britain rejects request of Federation of Rhodesia and Nyasaland for status as separate state within Commonwealth.

D S Saund is first US Congressman of Asian descent (elected 6 Nov).

In Ceylon (now Sri Lanka), following the election victory of the Sri Lanka Freedom Party, Sinhalese replaces English as the official language (7 July).

In South Africa, publication of the report of the Tomlinson Commission on the potential for economic and social development of African areas; it states that the European population is unwilling to sacrifice its ethnic identity and recommends that African reserves should be grouped into seven areas and developed in order to stem the flow of Africans from the countryside to the towns.

Legislation passed in South Africa (following appointment of new judges to the appeal court and enlargement of the senate) abolishing the Coloured vote; the Industrial Conciliation Act permits the government to reserve jobs for whites in certain industries.

M E Tower is first woman to be ordained a presbyterian minister in the USA.

Report of the Guillebaud Committee on the British National Health Service (published 25 Jan) approves the Service's general structure and state and argues that fundamental reforms are unnecessary.

Gunnar Myrdal, *Development and Underdevelopment*.

F Pollock and A Weber, *Revolution of the Robots*.

W H Whyte, *The Organization Man*.

In Japan, nationwide system of testing pupils is introduced.

James B Conant, *The American High School Today*.

In Britain, Colleges of Advanced Technology, along the lines recommended in the 1945 Percy Report, are established, but a White Paper on technical education unfavourably compares British efforts to increase scientific and technical manpower with progress in the USA, USSR, and Western Europe.

The German Evangelical Churches begin revision of the Lutheran text of the New Testament.

Buddhist Council held in Rangoon, Burma (now Yangon in Myanmar) in ending in May; the sixth such council since 483 BC.

'In God We Trust' adopted as US national motto by act of Congress.

Rudolf Bultmann, *Essays Philosophical and Theological*.

Trevor Huddleston, CR, *Naught for your Comfort*.

Q Science, Technology, and Discovery

British aviator Peter Twiss captures air-speed record with flight at 1,821 kph/1,132 mph in a Fairey Delta research aircraft (10 March).

Scientists from seven countries encamp in Antarctica in preparation for International Geophysical Year.

In Britain, Queen Elizabeth II opens Calder Hall in NW England, the world's first large-scale nuclear power station (17 Oct); by year end it supplies 65,000 KW.

In USA, Bell Telephone Company develops 'visual telephone', transmitting pictures simultaneously with sound.

Development in USA of FORTRAN, the first computer-programming language.

US physicist Erwin Wilhelm Müller develops the field ion microscope, enabling individual atoms to be seen.

Mullard image-dissector camera, capable of taking very rapid photographs.

H P Wilkins and P Moore, *The Moon*.

Edward Appleton's Reith Lectures, *Science and the Nation*.

'Dido' reactor at Harwell, Britain, opened (21 Nov).

Detection of the 'neutrino' (a particle of no electric charge) at Los Alamos Laboratory, USA.

Discovery of the anti-neutron at California University, USA.

P Berg in USA discovers transfer-RNA.

G E Palade in USA discovers ribosomes.

R Humanities

Edmund S Morgan, *The Puritan Family*.

Harold Acton, *The Bourbons of Naples*.

Winston Churchill, *History of the English-Speaking Peoples* (–1958).

Kenneth M Stampp, *The Peculiar Institution*.

Margery Perham, *Lugard: The Years of Adventure (1858–98)*.

Lord Beaverbrook, *Men and Power, 1917*.

James Macgregor Burns, *Roosevelt: The Lion and the Fox*.

Nikolaus Pevsner, *The Englishness of English Art*.

A J Ayer, *The Problem of Knowledge*.

Alfred Tarski, *Logic, Semantics, and Metamathematics*.

Eric Voegelin, *Order and History*.

S Art, Sculpture, Fine Arts, and Architecture

'This is Tomorrow', exhibition at the Whitechapel Gallery, London, which launches Pop Art, an art that draws on consumer culture.

Painting, etc:

Raymond Hains, *Paix en Algerie*.

Richard Hamilton, *What is it that makes today's homes so different, so appealing?*

Hans Hartung, *10*.

3 Gold Coast League Assembly adopts Kwame Nkrumah's resolution demanding independence (granted by Britain, 18 Sept).

4 Indonesia repudiates debts to Netherlands.

16 (–23) international conference on Suez Canal held in London by British and French governments, attended by representatives of 22 countries (but not Egypt); 18 countries support the Dulles Plan for an international Suez Canal Board associated with the UN to manage the Canal.

22 John Harding, British governor of Cyprus, offers surrender terms to EOKA guerrillas, which they reject.

J September

9 President Nasser of Egypt rejects Dulles Plan for international control of the Suez Canal.

19 second London conference on Suez held in London, attended by delegates of 18 countries supporting the Dulles Plan (21, establishes Canal Users' Association, which first meets in London on 18 Oct).

23 Britain and France refer Suez dispute to UN Security Council.

30 (–1 Oct) secret meeting in Montparnasse, Paris, of French and Israeli delegations (the Israelis led by Foreign Secretary Golda Meir), to discuss possible coordination of military action against Egypt (known sometimes as the Conference of St Germain, after the district where the Israelis stayed).

K October

8 Israel withdraws from Israeli–Jordan Mixed Armistice Commission.

12 Britain informs Israel it will assist Jordan, if attacked (under 1948 treaty).

13 UN Security Council adopts first part of British–French resolution on Suez Canal, but USSR vetoes second part requiring Egypt to comply with set of principles.

16 British Prime Minister Anthony Eden and Foreign Secretary Selwyn Lloyd visit Paris to discuss participation in action against Egypt with French Minister Guy Mollet and Foreign Minister Christian Pineau.

21 (–22) secret meeting at Sèvres, Paris, of Israelis (including Prime Minister David Ben-Gurion), French (including Prime Minister Guy Mollet) and British Foreign Secretary Selwyn Lloyd to discuss coordinated action against Egypt.

21 in Poland, former leader Wladyslaw Gomulka returns to power when he is elected first secretary of the Communist Party.

23 demonstrations in Hungary, starting with university students in Budapest, call for democratic government, return of Imre Nagy to power, withdrawal of Soviet troops, and release of Cardinal Mindszenty; the prime minister, Ernö Gerö (appointed 18 July) calls in Soviet troops.

24 Imre Nagy is appointed prime minister of Hungary and promises reforms.

25 Egypt, Jordan, and Syria establish joint command of their armed forces.

28 Cardinal Wyszynski, primate of Poland, is released from prison.

29 Israeli troops invade Sinai Peninsula of Egypt.

29 János Kádár becomes leader of Central Committee of Hungarian Workers' Party.

30 Britain and France present ultimatum to Egypt and Israel, calling for cease-fire and withdrawal of forces 16 km/10 mi from Suez Canal; Israel accepts but not Egypt.

30 in Hungary, Cardinal Mindszenty is released after eight years' captivity; Soviet reinforcements invade Hungary.

31 British and French planes bomb Egyptian airfields; public outcry in Britain over the Suez War.

31 Roy Welensky succeeds Lord Malvern as prime minister of Federation of Rhodesia and Nyasaland.

31 USA suspends aid to Israel.

L November

1 in Hungary, Prime Minister Imre Nagy forms new government, including non-Communists.

1 Jordan prohibits use of British air bases in Jordan for operations against Egypt.

1 (–2) emergency session of UN General Assembly to consider the Suez crisis; John Foster Dulles, US secretary of state, attacks the British–French–Israeli action; the Assembly votes for a cease-fire.

2 Hungarian government renounces Warsaw Treaty (of 1955) and appeals to UN and Western powers for assistance against Soviet invasion.

2 USSR vetoes Western powers' request for UN Security Council to consider critical state in Hungary.

3 Britain and France accept Middle East cease-fire if UN force will keep the peace.

4 UN General Assembly adopts Canadian resolution to send international force to Middle East, with Britain and France abstaining.

4 Soviet forces attack Budapest; Imre Nagy takes refuge in Yugoslav Embassy; defection of János Kádár who forms a 'revolutionary peasant-worker' government.

5 in Egypt, British paratroops land at Port Said, at the N end of the Suez Canal.

Yves Klein, first blue monochrome (he patents the colour in 1960 as YKB (Yves Klein Blue).

Kenneth Noland paints his first characteristic circle painting.

Antoni Tàpies, *Earth + Paint*.

Victor Vasarely, *Tlinco*.

Sculpture:

Alberto Giacometti, *Femmes de Venise* series.

Architecture:

Lucio Costa wins competition for plans of Brasilia, new capital of Brazil.

William Holford's plan for redevelopment of area around St Paul's Cathedral, London, published.

Eero Saarinen's design for the United States Embassy, London, wins open competition (–1960).

Eero Saarinen, TWA Terminal at J F Kennedy Airport, New York (–1962).

T **Music**

Henk Badings, *Kain* (ballet).

Benjamin Britten, *The Prince of the Pagodas* (ballet; first performed 1957).

Hans Werner Henze, *König Hirsch* (opera).

Frederick Loewe, *My Fair Lady* (musical).

Olivier Messiaen, *Oiseaux Exotiques*.

Douglas Moore, *The Ballad of Baby Doe* (opera).

Karlheinz Stockhausen, *Gesang der Jünglinge*.

Maria Callas makes debut at the New York Metropolitan Opera, singing role of Norma.

Candide (musical), by Leonard Bernstein (first performed at the Martin Beck Theatre, 1 Dec).

My Fair Lady (musical), text by Alan Jay Lerner, music by Frederick Loewe (first performed at the Mark Hellinger Theatre, New York, 15 March).

Revue *At the Drop of a Hat*, starring Michael Flanders and Donald Swann, opens at the New Lindsey Theatre, London (31 Dec).

Pat Boone, 'I'll be home'.

The Coasters, 'Down In Mexico'.

Doris Day, 'Que será, será' (by Jay Livingston).

Fats Domino, 'Blueberry Hill'

Elvis Presley, 'Heartbreak Hotel', 'Don't Be Cruel', 'Love Me Tender'.

In the USA, Asa Cater, secretary of the North Alabama White Citizens Council, declares that 'Rock "n" Roll is a means of pulling the white man down to the level of the Negro' (May).

In Britain, Member of Parliament Robert Boothby calls for banning of the film *Rock Around the Clock*, following disturbances around the country.

In Britain, the popularity of Lonnie Donegan's 'Rock Island Line' (recorded 1954) triggers the skiffle craze (small-scale, jazz-type music).

The BBC starts the Eurovision Song Contest (–).

U **Literature and Drama**

James Baldwin, *Giovanni's Room*.

John Berryman, *Homage to Mistress Bradstreet* (poems).

Anthony Burgess, *The Malayan Trilogy* (–1959).

Albert Camus, *The Fall*.

Gerald Durrell, *My Family and Other Animals*.

Allen Ginsberg, *Howl and Other Poems*.

Laurie Lee, *Cider with Rosie*.

Rose Macaulay, *The Towers of Trebizond*.

Compton Mackenzie, *Thin Ice*.

Naguib Mahfouz, *The Cairo Trilogy* (–1957).

V S Pritchett, *Collected Stories*.

Kathleen Raine, *Collected Poems*.

Simone Weil, *Notebooks*.

Patrick White, *The Tree of Man*.

Angus Wilson, *Anglo-Saxon Attitudes*.

W H Auden is elected Professor of Poetry at the University of Oxford, England (9 Feb).

Drama:

Jean Anouilh, *Poor Bitos*, *The Waltz of the Toreadors*.

Friedrich Dürrenmatt, *The Visit*.

Jean Genet, *The Balcony*.

John Osborne, *Look Back in Anger* (opens 8 May; the first major success of the English Stage Company, at the Royal Court Theatre, London).

Bertolt Brecht's Berliner Ensemble visits Britain for first London production of *The Threepenny Opera*.

Michael Croft founds the National Youth Theatre in Britain (27 Aug).

V **Births and Deaths**

Jan 23 Alexander Korda dies (62).

Jan 29 H L Mencken dies (75).

Jan 31 A A Milne dies (74).

Feb 10 Hugh Trenchard dies (83).

March 12 Boleslaw Bierut dies (63).

April 15 Emil Nolde dies (88).

May 20 Max Beerbohm dies (83).

Aug 14 Bertolt Brecht dies (58).

Aug 25 Alfred Kinsey dies (62).

Sept 22 Frederick Soddy dies (79).

Sept 28 William E Boeing dies (74).

Oct 7 Clarence Birdseye dies (69).

Oct 18 Martina Navratilova born (–).

Oct 31 Marshal Pietro Badoglio dies (86).

6 in US presidential election, Dwight D Eisenhower, Republican, is re-elected with 457 electoral votes over Adlai Stevenson, Democrat, with 73; popular vote: Eisenhower, 35,575,420; Stevenson, 26,033,066; Republicans fare badly in state elections.

7 Britain and France accept cease-fire in Egypt, but Britain declares it will evacuate troops only on arrival of UN force.

8 UN General Assembly demands withdrawal of Soviet troops from Hungary.

9 Constituent Assembly of South Vietnam is inaugurated.

12 János Kádár refuses entry to Hungary for UN observers but accepts UN relief.

15 UN emergency force arrives in Egypt.

17 Constituent Assembly in Jammu and Kashmir, India, adopts new constitution (to be in force from 26 Jan 1957) and reaffirms accession to Republic of India.

20 Lauris Norstad succeeds Alfred Gruenther as Supreme Allied Commander in Europe.

21 UN General Assembly censures USSR over Hungary.

23 (–14 Dec) Anthony Eden, British prime minister, leaves London for recuperation in Jamaica (R A Butler, home secretary, deputizes).

M December

2 Fidel Castro and followers land in Cuba; after an initial setback they begin a campaign of guerrilla war, aiming to overthrow Batista's government.

5 in South Africa, 150 Europeans, Asians, and Natives are in arrested in dawn raids and charged with treason (preliminary hearing held 19–9 Jan, though defendants are released on bail for Christmas).

5 British and French forces begin withdrawal from Egypt (completed, 22 Dec).

6 in Britain, the government wins a vote of confidence over the Suez action (with 15 Conservative abstentions).

8 in Hungary, call for general strike leads to proclamation of martial law and mass arrests.

17 petrol rationing introduced in Britain.

18 Japan is admitted to UN.

19 Lord Radcliffe's proposals for Cyprus constitution published, involving proportional representation of Greek and Turkish communities (proposals rejected by Greece because they do not provide for self-determination).

27 UN-sponsored fleet begins clearance of Suez Canal.

w Everyday Life

In Britain, six members of the Surrey Walking Club, wearing 11th-century dress and arms, march 32 km/20 mi to prove that in 1066 King Harold and his army could have marched 320 km/200 mi from Yorkshire to the Battle of Hastings in 10 days; on arrival the Surrey walkers do not feel ready for a fight (March).

In Britain, Harold Macmillan, chancellor of the exchequer, introduces premium savings bonds in budget (17 April; go on sale on 1 Nov).

US film star Grace Kelly marries Prince Rainier of Monaco (19 April).

Abolition of third-class coaches on British trains (3 June).

Marilyn Monroe marries US writer Arthur Miller (29 June); they divorce in 1961.

Transatlantic telephone service inaugurated (25 Sept).

x Sport and Recreation

The first floodlit English Football League match, between Portsmouth and Newcastle United, is disrupted when the lights fuse (22 Feb).

In the Grand National horse race at Aintree in Britain, Devon Loch, owned by Queen Elizabeth the Queen Mother, collapses when only 45 m/50 yd from winning the race (24 March).

Rocky Marciano retires as undefeated World Heavyweight champion (21 April); Floyd Patterson beats Archie Moore in five rounds in Chicago, USA, to win the vacant title (30 Nov).

In cricket, Jim Laker takes a record 19 wickets in the fourth Test for England against Australia at Old Trafford, Manchester, NW England (27–31 July).

During the fifth game in Baseball's World Series, Don Larsen of the New York Yankees pitches the first perfect game in the Series' history (8 Oct).

The 16th Olympic Games, held in Melbourne, Australia (22 Nov–8 Dec), are affected by political boycotts: Egypt, Lebanon, Netherlands, Spain, and Switzerland refuse to take part following the French–British–Israeli action in Egypt, and the Soviet invasion of Hungary. China also withdraws in protest at the participation of Formosa (Taiwan). The USSR wins 37 gold medals; the USA, 32; Australia, 13; Hungary, 9; Italy and Sweden, 8 each; Britain, 6; West Germany, 5.

The director of the US National Parks, Conrad L Wirth, announces 'Mission 66', a plan to improve visitor facilities and undertake considerable restoration in the parks.

y Media

Foundation, in USA, of the African-American daily paper *Chicago Daily Defender*.

Lock-out in British printing industry forces many periodicals to be printed abroad (15 Feb–23 March).

Film:

Anastasia (starring Ingrid Bergman).

Aparajito (director, Satyajit Ray).

Baby Doll (director, Elia Kazan; script by Tennessee Williams; starring Karl Malden and Carroll Baker).

Carousel (music and lyrics by Richard Rodgers and Oscar Hammerstein).

Early Spring (director, Yasujiro Ozu).

Giant (director, George Stevens; starring Rock Hudson, Elizabeth Taylor, and James Dean).

The King and I (starring Yul Brynner and Deborah Kerr).

Lust for Life (starring Kirk Douglas).

Nuit et Brouillard (director, Alain Resnais).

Reach for the Sky (director, Lewis Gilbert; starring Kenneth More).

Richard III (director and star, Laurence Olivier).

The Seventh Seal (director, Ingmar Bergman).

A Town Like Alice (director, Jack Lee).

Television:

In USA, Elvis Presley appears on *The Ed Sullivan Show*, attracting 82 per cent of the potential audience.

New programmes in USA include: *Gunsmoke* (CBS), starring James Arness as Marshall Matt Luhan; *Highway Patrol*, starring Broderick Crawford; *Tic Tac Dough* (NBC), a panel game (–1959).

Armchair Theatre, broadcast by ABC in the USA, is an influential series showing television drama from Britain (–1969).

New programmes in Britain include: *The Billy Cotton Band Show*; *Opportunity Knocks*, a talent show, transferred from radio and presented by Hughie Green; *Zoo-Time*, presented from London Zoo by Desmond Morris.

The BBC's *Watch With Mother* series introduces *The Woodentops*.

Hancock's Half Hour, with Tony Hancock and Sid James, appears on television as well as radio (–1961).

*Macmillan appointed British prime minister ... King of Jordan
survives coup ... Launch of Sputnik ...*

A **January**

5 in USA, President Eisenhower announces the 'Eisenhower Doctrine': the USA will protect political independence of states of Middle East, fearing that the USSR is behind Arab nationalist movements (Senate approves doctrine on 7 March).

7 Zhou Enlai, prime minister of Chinese People's Republic, visits Moscow, USSR.

8 (–26 Feb) conspiracy trials in Syria resulting in life sentences on ex-president Chichekli and others.

9 Anthony Eden resigns as prime minister of Britain.

10 United Nations General Assembly establishes Special Committee on the Problems of Hungary (denied entry to Hungary, but studies documents and takes evidence from over 100 refugees; report published 20 June).

10 in Britain, Queen Elizabeth, after consulting former prime minister Winston Churchill and senior Conservative peer the Marquess of Salisbury, appoints Harold Macmillan prime minister; on 13, he forms ministry with R A Butler as home secretary, Selwyn Lloyd foreign secretary, and Peter Thorneycroft chancellor of the exchequer.

22 Israeli forces complete withdrawal from Sinai Peninsula of Egypt but remain in 'Gaza Strip' (Egyptian territory to SW of Israel).

30 UN General Assembly calls on South Africa to reconsider its apartheid policies.

B **February**

15 in USSR, Andrei Gromyko replaces Dmitri Shepilov as foreign minister.

5 general election held in Ireland (following withdrawal of Clann na Poblachta from the Fine Gael-led coalition on 28 Jan); Fianna Fáil, with 78 seats, wins majority over all other parties (69 seats, of which 40 are won by Fine Gael); on 20 March, Éamon de Valera becomes prime minister again, at age of 75.

6 Israeli troops hand over Gaza Strip to UN force.

6 the Gold Coast (comprising the former colonies of the Gold Coast, Ashanti, the Northern Territories, and Trans-Volta–Togoland) becomes an independent state, within the Commonwealth, as Ghana (8, is admitted to UN); Kwame Nkrumah is prime minister.

11 (–11 April) Singapore Constitutional Conference held in London; agrees on internal self-government during 1958.

C **March**

13 agreement between Britain and Jordan, ending 1948 treaty; British forces to be withdrawn by 15 Sept and Jordan to purchase British military installations.

14 EOKA guerrillas in Cyprus offer to suspend terrorist activities on release of Archbishop Makarios.

14 following unrest in Indonesia, President Sukharno declares a state of siege and takes power into his own hands.

20 Britain accepts NATO offer to mediate in Cyprus, but rejected by Greece.

21 Dag Hammarskjöld, UN secretary general, visits President Nasser of Egypt to discuss solution of Suez Canal problem; President Nasser insists that Egypt is to receive tolls for use of the canal.

21 (–24) Bermuda Conference, of President Eisenhower of USA and Harold Macmillan prime minister of Britain; re-establishes the 'special relationship' which had been strained by Suez Crisis; USA undertakes to make certain guided missiles available to Britain, with warheads remaining under US control.

25 Belgium, France, West Germany, Italy, Luxembourg, and Netherlands (the 'Six') sign the Treaty of Rome establishing the European Economic Community (EEC) or 'Common Market' and a second Rome treaty establishing the European Atomic Energy Authority or 'Euratom' (to take effect from 1 Jan 1958).

28 Britain releases Archbishop Makarios from imprisonment in the Seychelles; he is free to travel, except to Cyprus; General George Grivas, leader of the EOKA guerrillas, is offered safe conduct to Greece.

29 ships of small draught begin using Suez Canal (open to ships of maximum draught on 9 April).

D **April**

9 King Hussein of Jordan dismisses Prime Minister Nabulsi after he declares intention of establishing a republic in Jordan; on 13, King Hussein foils a coup planned by General Abu Nuwar.

17 in India, Jawaharlal Nehru forms new Congress government, with Krishna Menon as minister of defence.

18 representatives of Burma (now Myanmar), Ceylon (Sri Lanka), India, Indonesia, Iraq,

Integration crisis in Little Rock, USA ... West Side Story ...
Patrick Moore presents The Sky at Night ...

o Politics, Government, Law, and Economy

Milovan Djilas, *The New Class.*

A Downs, *An Economic Theory of Democracy.*

V P Menon, *The Transfer of Power in India.*

In Britain, Ralph Harris and Arthur Seldon found the Institute of Economic Affairs (IEA), a 'think tank'.

International Atomic Energy Agency comes into being (29 July).

Under the Treaty of Rome (25 March, in force from 1 Jan 1958), the European Steel and Coal Community Court becomes the European Court of Justice (also covering the European Economic Community and Euratom).

Homicide Act creates a category of non-capital murder in Britain.

In Britain, the Rent Act removes controls on rents (royal assent, 6 June).

Trans-Iranian pipeline, Abadan–Tehran, completed (31 Jan).

In USA, Armand Hammer leaves retirement to take charge of Occidental Petroleum.

In USA, the Ford Edsel proves a failure with the motoring public despite heavy market research and advertising spending.

Vance Packard, *The Hidden Persuaders.*

In Britain, publication of *Which?* magazine by the Consumers' Association.

p Society, Education, and Religion

In USA, Governor Orval Faubus of Arkansas attempts to prevent the admission of African-American pupils to a school in Little Rock (5 Sept); President Eisenhower sends federal troops to enforce integration and protect the children.

Passage in USA of the Civil Rights Act (the first since Reconstruction in the 19th century); establishes the Civil Rights Commission to investigate the denial of voting rights to African-Americans and empowers it to sue where necessary.

In South Africa, 'God Save the Queen' is dropped leaving 'Die Stem van Suid Afrika' as the only national anthem (May 2); the Union Jack ceases to have any standing as a flag of the Union.

The State-Aided Institutions Act in South Africa permits the government to enforce racial segregation in places controlled by public authorities (such as libraries, concert halls, and sports venues); the Native Laws Amendment Bill permits the government to prohibit classes, entertainment, and church services attended by Africans in White areas.

Publication in Britain of *Declaration* by several 'Angry Young Men', setting forth their beliefs.

In Britain, the Wolfenden Report (by the Home Office Committee on Homosexual Offences and Prostitution, established in 1954) recommends the decriminalization of private homosexual acts between consenting adult males and measures to prevent street prostitution (4 Sept; recommendations rejected by government, 4 Dec).

Richard Hoggart, *The Uses of Literacy.*

W Sargent, *The Battle for the Mind.*

Michael Young and P Willmott, *Family and Kinship in East London.*

In USA, President Eisenhower calls for a nationwide system of testing for high school students; in the wake of the Soviet *Sputnik* launches, incentives are offered to students to pursue scientific and professional studies.

In England, University College, Leicester (founded 1918), is incorporated as a university by royal charter.

In USA, foundation of the Southern Christian Leadership Conference led by Martin Luther King, Jr.

First conference of European Rabbis under Israel Brodie.

Paul Tillich, *Dynamics of Faith.*

q Science, Technology, and Discovery

Canadian ship HMCS *Labrador* discovers new north-west passage (through to Baffin Bay), enabling ships supplying radar stations in the unfrozen Beaufort Sea to leave later for their home ports (before they would be prevented from returning by ice).

Soviet non-magnetic ship *Star* sets sail on expedition to take magnetic recordings.

US expedition is flown in to South Pole.

International Geophysical Year begins (1 July), with scientists concentrating on Antarctic exploration, oceanographic and meteorological research, and the launching of satellites into space (–31 Dec 1958).

USSR launches the artificial satellite *Sputnik 1* (4 Oct) to study the cosmosphere; weighing 83.4 kg/184 lb, it circles the Earth in 95 minutes.

Sputnik 2 is placed in orbit a month later (3 Nov) carrying the dog Laika, to study living conditions in space.

Manchester University's radio telescope, at Jodrell Bank, NW England, under Bernard Lovell, tracks *Sputnik 1.*

Syria, and Japan attend first meeting in New Delhi, India, of Asian Legal Consultative Committee.

20 USA resumes aid to Israel (suspended Oct 1956).

20 Japan makes protest to USSR over nuclear tests.

23 Albert Schweitzer sends letter to Norwegian Nobel Committee urging mobilization of world opinion against nuclear tests.

24 Ibrahim Hashem forms conservative, pro-Western ministry in Jordan, following demonstrations.

25 King Hussein proclaims martial law in Jordan; USA dispatches 6th Fleet to E Mediterranean (29, provokes protest from USSR).

28 King Hussein of Jordan visits King Saud of Saudi Arabia; 29, the monarchs state that the crisis in Jordan is an internal affair; Saudi Arabia pays first instalment of subsidy to Jordan.

E **May**

6 in Italy, government of Antonio Segni resigns on withdrawal of Social Democrats' support (19, Adone Zoli, Christian Democrat, forms ministry).

10 USSR appeals to USA and Britain to cease nuclear tests.

15 Britain explodes its first thermonuclear bomb in megaton range in Central Pacific.

21 Guy Mollet, Socialist, resigns as prime minister of France, following defeat of government in Assembly.

23 (–26 June) Nigerian Constitutional Conference held in London, to determine division of power between regions and the state; the Conference recommends that Western and Eastern Regions should have immediate self-government, and Northern Region in 1959.

30 Britain relaxes restrictions on trade with Communist China.

F **June**

5 Britain and US atomic authorities agree on exchange of information.

6 in Britain, royal assent is given to the Rent Act, removing many rent controls; in protest against the Act, Labour MPs boycott the procession to the House of Lords for announcement of the assent.

10 Progressive Conservatives win Canadian elections, with 112 seats; Liberals win 105, Cooperative Commonwealth Federation wins 25; others, 23 seats (17, Louis St Laurent, Liberal, resigns; 21, John Diefenbaker forms Conservative ministry, ending 22 years of Liberal rule).

12 Maurice Bourgès-Manoury, Radical, forms ministry in France.

20 publication of report of UN Special Committee on the Problems of Hungary; finds that the Hungarian revolt of 1956 was a spontaneous resulting from grievances against the USSR and conditions in Hungary, and that the Kádár regime had been imposed by the USSR (report discussed by UN Assembly on 10 Sept).

G **July**

4 in USSR, Vyacheslav Molotov, Dmitri Shepilov, and Georgi Malenkov are expelled from the presidium of the Central Committee of Communist Party.

15 General Franco announces that the Spanish monarchy will be restored on his death or retirement.

19 (–14 Aug) the Imam of Oman revolts against the Sultan of Oman, who requests British aid.

25 Constituent Assembly in Tunisia abolishes the monarchy (the former Bey is assigned a residence in a suburb of Tunis); Habib Bourguiba becomes president.

29 USA, Britain, France, and West Germany issue declaration on principles for German reunification and call for free elections.

H **August**

7 announcement of purge of top-ranking officers in Syrian army, with pro-Communist Afif Bizri appointed commander in chief; Turkey fears that the USSR is advancing its influence in Syria.

12 following Britain's decision to restore self-government in Guiana (now Guyana), an election is held for 14 seats on a new Legislative Council; Cheddi Jagan's People's Progressive Party wins 9 seats; on 15, Jagan forms government.

30 All-African Federal Executive Council formed in Nigeria, with Alhaji Abubakar Tafawa Balewa as prime minister.

31 independence of Malayan Federation in force.

J **September**

4 Egypt and Syria agree to create an economic union.

10 special session of UN General Assembly to consider report of the UN's Committee on Hungary; adopts report and passes resolution condemning the USSR for depriving the Hungarian people of their liberty.

11 USSR complains to Turkey about concentrations of Turkish troops on Syrian borders.

In Britain, a serious accident occurs at the Windscale reactor of the Atomic Energy Authority's plant at Windscale, NW England (10 Oct); some radiation escapes into the atmosphere.

Artificial rain in New South Wales, Australia, increases rainfall by 25 per cent and in Queensland saves crops.

At Stockholm, Sweden, the element nobelium (no. 102) is discovered.

British Medical Research Council publishes report arguing that there is a strong relationship between smoking and lung cancer (26 June).

Giberellin, a growth-producing hormone, is isolated.

DNA synthesized by Arthur Kornberg in USA.

A B Sabin in USA produces an oral polio vaccine.

R **Humanities**

Kathleen Kenyon, *Digging up Jericho.*

H W Parke and D Wormell, *The Delphic Oracle.*

R H C Davis, *A History of Medieval Europe.*

W G Hoskins, *The Midland Peasant.*

New Cambridge Modern History (–1979).

Herbert Butterfield, *George III and the Historians.*

A J P Taylor, *The Trouble Makers: Dissent over Foreign Policy, 1792–1939.*

Marvin Meyers, *The Jacksonian Persuasion: Politics and Belief.*

Arthur M Schlesinger, Jr, *The Crisis of the Old Order, 1919–33.*

Samuel P Hays, *The Response to Industrialism: 1885–1914.*

Kenneth Clark, *The Nude.*

Alec Harman and Wilfrid Mellers, *Man and his Music* (4 volumes; –1959).

F H Cross, *The Oxford Dictionary of the Christian Church.*

J A Passmore, *A Hundred Years of Philosophy.*

Noam Chomsky, *Syntactic Structures.*

Fred Hoyle, *Man and Materialism.*

Ernest Nagel, *Logic Without Metaphysics.*

S **Art, Sculpture, Fine Arts, and Architecture**

The Institute of Contemporary Art, London, exhibits and sells paintings by apes at London Zoo; the works resemble tachisme; sales are stopped by the Zoo's secretary, Sir Solly Zuckerman (whereupon the value of works already sold increases).

Painting, etc:

Francis Bacon, *Screaming Nurse.*

Richard Hamilton, *Hommage à Chrysler Corp.*

Franz Kline, *August Day.*

Sidney Nolan, *Gallipoli* series (–1958).

Mark Rothko, *Browns.*

Sculpture:

H G Adam, *Beacon of the Dead* (monument for the Auschwitz death camp; — 1958).

Alexander Calder, *Mobile*, at J F Kennedy Airport New York.

Jacob Epstein, *Christ in Majesty* (for Llandaff Cathedral, S Wales).

Alberto Giacometti, *Buste aux grands yeux.*

Henry Moore, *Reclining Figure*, at UNESCO building, Paris, France.

Architecture:

Walter Gropius, United States Embassy, Athens, Greece (–1961).

Le Corbusier, Tokyo Museum (–1960).

Oscar Niemeyer is named chief architect of Brasilia, Brazil.

Jorn Utzon wins competition for design of the Opera House, Sydney, Australia.

T **Music**

Paul Hindemith, *Die Harmonie der Welt* (opera).

Francis Poulenc, *Les Dialogues des Carmélites* (opera).

Gardner Read, *String Quartet.*

Edmund Rubbra, Symphony No. 5.

Igor Stravinsky, *Agon* (ballet).

In Britain, Sadlers Wells Ballet is chartered as the Royal Ballet (16 Jan).

West Side Story (musical), lyrics by Stephen Sondheim, music by Leonard Bernstein (first performed at the Winter Garden Theatre, New York, 26 Sept).

Harry Belafonte, 'Mary's Boy Child'.

Pat Boone, 'Love Letters in the Sand'.

Everly Brothers, 'All I Have To Do Is Dream', 'Wake Up Little Susie'.

Lonnie Donegan, 'Cumberland Gap'.

Buddy Holly, 'Peggy Sue', 'Rave On'.

Elvis Presley, 'All Shook Up' (his first 'number one' in Britain), 'Jailhouse Rock'.

Tommy Steele, 'Singing the Blues'.

U **Literature and Drama**

James Agee, *A Death in the Family.*

Sibylle Bedford, *A Legacy.*

John Braine, *Room at the Top.*

John Cheever, *The Wapshot Chronicle.*

Lawrence Durrell, *Justine* (the first volume in 'The Alexandrian Quartet', –1960).

Max Frisch, *Homo Faber.*

Ted Hughes, *The Hawk in the Rain* (poems).

Jack Kerouac, *On the Road.*

Mary McCarthy, *Memories of a Catholic Girlhood.*

Bernard Malamud, *The Assistant.*

V S Naipaul, *The Mystic Masseur.*

Studs Terkel, *Giants of Jazz.*

Alan Watts, *The Way of Zen.*

Rebecca West, *The Fountain Overflows.*

15 sweeping victory for Konrad Adenauer's Christian Democratic Union in West German elections.

16 (–17) military coup in Thailand; Prime Minister Pibul Songgram flees and is replaced by Pote Sarasin, secretary general of SEATO (interim constitution promulgated on 28 Jan 1958).

20 Sir Sidney Holland retires as prime minister of New Zealand; succeeded by Keith Holyoake.

21 death of King Haakon VII of Norway; succeeded by Olaf V.

26 Dag Hammarskjöld of Sweden, is re-elected secretary general of the UN for further term of five years.

K October

2 Poland, with support of Czechoslovakia and East Germany, outlines Rapacki Plan, for a denuclearized zone in Central Europe, to UN General Assembly.

4 USSR launches *Sputnik 1*, the world's first artificial satellite.

4 in Yugoslavia, Milovan Djilas, former vice-president, is sentenced to further term of imprisonment for spreading hostile propaganda.

12 Nikita Khrushchev, secretary general of Soviet Communist Party, sends letters to Labour and Socialist Parties in Britain and Europe urging them to prevent aggression by USA and Turkey in Middle East.

16 following incidents on frontier with Turkey, Syria declares state of emergency.

16 John Foster Dulles, US secretary of state, warns USSR against attacking Turkey.

19 West Germany severs relations with Yugoslavia, on the latter's recognition of East Germany.

26 in USSR, Marshal Georgi Zhukov, minister of defence, is relieved of his duties.

29 Fulgencio Batistá suspends Cuban constitution.

30 Felix Gaillard, Radical Socialist, forms ministry in France.

L November

4 Sir John Harding retires as British governor of Cyprus (succeeded on 3 Dec by Sir Hugh Foot, who announces desire to make fresh start on solving the Cyprus problem).

11 full internal self-government in force in Jamaica.

14 Britain and USA send token consignments of arms to Tunisia (to forestall supply of arms from Soviet bloc), provoking, on 15, French delegation to leave NATO Conference (France fears Tunisian support for Algerian nationalists).

26 International Court of Justice declares itself competent to adjudicate in India–Portuguese dispute over Portuguese enclaves in India.

30 in Indonesia, attempt made on life of President Sukharno during time of crisis in relations with the Netherlands (Dutch nationals leave Indonesia and Dutch consulates to close from 9 Dec).

30 general election in New Zealand is won by the Labour Party with a majority of one seat; Labour Leader Walter Nash becomes prime minister.

M December

8 merger of four small left-wing parties in France, forming the Union de la Gauche Socialiste ('Union of the Socialist Left').

15 at UN General Assembly, Greek resolution that Cyprus is entitled to self-determination fails to gain two-thirds majority required for adoption.

20 European Nuclear Energy Agency formed, to operate within the Organization for European Economic Co-operation.

30 in Malta, fearing that Britain may not maintain investment in the island, the Legislative Assembly passes an emergency resolution, that Malta has no obligations to Britain unless employment is found for discharged dockyard workers.

Patrick White, *Voss*.

In USA, Kerouac's novel *On the Road*, describing a journey across the USA by drop-outs, inspires the 'Beatniks', who scorn materialism and seek ways of avoiding the 'rat race'.

Drama:

Samuel Beckett, *Endgame*.

Robert Bolt, *The Flowering Cherry*.

John Osborne, *The Entertainer*.

Gore Vidal, *Visit to a Small Planet*.

In Britain, entertainment duty is abolished on theatre and reduced on films.

v Births and Deaths

Jan 14 Humphrey Bogart dies (57).

Jan 16 Arturo Toscanini dies (89).

Feb 9 Nicholas Horthy dies (88).

March 20 C K Ogden dies (67).

May 2 Joseph McCarthy dies (47).

July 3 Frederick Lindemann (Lord Cherwell) dies (71).

July 11 Aga Khan III dies (79).

Aug 7 Oliver Hardy dies (65).

Sept 20 Jean Sibelius dies (91).

Oct 19 V Gordon Childe dies (65).

Nov 30 Beniamino Gigli dies (67).

w Everyday Life

Detector vans introduced by British Post Office to look for television licence-dodgers (9 Jan).

ERNIE ('Electronic Random Number Indicator Equipment') draws first premium bond prizes in Britain (1 June).

The Mousetrap by Agatha Christie becomes Britain's longest-running play, with its 1,998th performance (13 Sept), in London (–).

British Post Office announces plan to introduce post codes (12 Nov).

Regular London–Moscow air service opens (19 Dec).

Prince Philip, the Duke of Edinburgh, grows beard during the last stage of his world tour (15 Oct 1956–16 Feb); the beard is much appreciated in St Helena, where inhabitants grow beards in his honour.

Five-day working week introduced for civil servants in Britain.

x Sport and Recreation

The Whitbread Gold Cup is the first horse race in Britain to be sponsored.

In football, Juventus of Italy pay a British transfer record of £70,000 for John Charles of Leeds United (19 April).

Althea Gibson of the USA becomes the first African-American player to win a Singles title at the Wimbledon championship, London.

In yachting, the Admiral's Cup, created by the Admiral of the Royal Ocean Racing Club, Sir Miles Wyatt, is held for the first time (in the English Channel).

Great Britain and Ireland's golfers win the Ryder Cup 7½–4½ at Lindrick, Yorkshire, their first win in the series for 23 years (5 Oct).

y Media

Closure of the British illustrated news magazine *Picture Post*.

Film:

Bonjour Tristesse (director, Otto Preminger).

The Bridge on the River Kwai (director, David Lean; starring Alec Guinness).

The Cranes are Flying (director, Mikhail Kalatozov).

Gunfight at the OK Corral (director, John Sturges; starring Burt Lancaster and Kirk Douglas).

Kanal (director, Andrzej Wajda).

A King in New York (director, Charlie Chaplin).

Paths of Glory (director, Stanley Kubrick; starring Kirk Douglas).

Porte des Lilas.

The Prince and the Showgirl (director, Laurence Olivier; starring Marilyn Monroe).

Quiet Flows the Don.

Throne of Blood (director, Akira Kurosawa).

Twelve Angry Men (director, Sidney Lumet; script by Reginald Rose; starring Henry Fonda).

Wild Strawberries (director, Ingmar Bergman).

Radio:

The BBC in Britain broadcasts the new channel 'Network Three', providing for various minority interests (from Sept).

Television:

In USA, about 100,000 people now own colour television sets.

New programmes in USA include: *The Army Game* (–1961); *Maverick*, starring James Garner (–1962); *Perry Mason*, starring Raymond Burr; *Wagon Train* (–1965).

Hawkeye and the Last of the Mohicans is produced in Canada.

NHK in Japan broadcasts *The True Face of Japan* (–1964).

Queen Elizabeth II of Britain gives her first Christmas talk on television.

New programmes in Britain include: *Emergency — Ward 10* (ITV), a 'soap opera' set in a hospital; *The Sky at Night* (BBC), presented by Patrick Moore (–).

On ITV in Britain, historian A J P Taylor delivers three unscripted, live lectures on the Russian Revolution (Aug), the first of many such lecture series.

The BBC starts its service to schools (24 Sept).

*European Economic Community in force ... Execution of Imre
Nagy ... Charles de Gaulle elected president of France ...*

A January

1 European Economic Community (EEC) and European Atomic Energy Commission (Euratom) in force.

1 some West German armed forces (including two armoured divisions) are placed under NATO command.

3 West Indies Federation in force.

6 in Britain, the chancellor of the exchequer, Peter Thorneycroft, and treasury ministers Enoch Powell and Nigel Birch resign from the government because of cabinet's refusal to prune expenditure estimates; Derick Heathcoat Amory appointed chancellor (on 7, Prime Minister Macmillan dismisses the resignations as 'little local difficulties').

20 USSR threatens Greece with economic sanctions if it agrees to installation of NATO missile bases on its territory.

B February

1 presidents of Egypt and Syria sign documents creating union as the United Arab Republic, intended as the first step in creation of a larger Arab State (21, plebiscite approves President Nasser of Egypt as head of state).

3 treaty signed at The Hague, Netherlands, by Belgium, Luxembourg, and Netherlands, establishing 'Benelux' Economic Union (for 50 years).

5 North Korea proposes withdrawal of all foreign troops from North and South Korea (7, China agrees to remove its troops from North Korea, but UN refuses to withdraw troops unless free elections are held throughout Korea; withdrawal of Chinese troops completed 28 Oct).

8 French forces bomb Tunisian town of Sakiet Sidi Youssef as reprisal for alleged Tunisian complicity in Algerian attack on French patrol in Algeria near the frontier on 11 Jan; Tunisia confines French troops in the country to barracks.

11 Tunisia informs France that French warships will no longer be allowed to use the port at Bizerta.

14 Rapacki Plan, proposed by Polish foreign minister Adam Rapacki, for denuclearized zone in Central Europe, delivered to foreign envoys in Warsaw (rejected by USA on 3 May, by Britain on 18 May).

14 kingdoms of Iraq and Jordan unite in Arab Federation, with King Faisal II of Iraq as head of state.

17 following the ousting of Garfield Todd, prime minister of Southern Rhodesia (now Zimbabwe), as leader of the United Federal Party (8 Feb), Sir Edgar Whitehead forms ministry.

17 France and Tunisia accept mediation of USA and Britain.

20 in Accra, Ghana, President Kwame Nkrumah inaugurates the Foundation for Mutual Assistance in Africa South of the Sahara, supported by eight governments.

27 (–8 March) general election held in Sudan; the Umma Party wins the largest number of seats but lacks a majority.

C March

5 Syria accuses King Saud of Saudi Arabia of organizing plot to overthrow Syrian régime and destroy union with Egypt.

27 in USSR, Nikita Khrushchev ousts and replaces Nikolai Bulganin as prime minister (chairman of Council of Ministers; 6 Sept, Bulganin is dismissed from Communist Party Presidium; becomes Chairman of Soviet State Bank).

31 in general election in Canada, the Progressive Conservatives win a much larger majority (Conservatives win 208 seats; Liberals, 49; Cooperative Commonwealth Federation, 8); John Diefenbaker remains prime minister.

31 USSR suspends testing of nuclear weapons (–30 Sept).

D April

8 President Eisenhower of USA proposes mutual inspection as a means of enforcing atomic test ban.

15 (–22) in Accra, Ghana, President Kwame Nkrumah hosts conference of independent African states (attended by delegates from eight countries).

16 sweeping victory for Nationalists in South African elections.

16 French Assembly defeat's government's proposals for restoring relations with Tunisia; Felix Gaillard's government resigns.

21 Dom Mintoff's Labour government in Malta finds Britain's terms for Malta's integration with Britain unacceptable and resigns; failing to find an alternative government, the British governor, Sir Robert Laycock, assumes control (following demonstrations in Valetta, the governor declares a state of public emergency on 30 April).

23 in Southern Rhodesia (now Zimbabwe), Garfield Todd and six others leave the United Federal Party and found a new United Rhodesia Party.

*Polygamy abolished in Tunisia ... Invention of hovercraft
announced ... Pasternak's* Dr Zhivago *... Munich air crash ...*

o Politics, Government, Law, and Economy

Foundation in Britain of the Campaign for Nuclear Disarmament, at public meeting in London on 17 Feb; speakers include philosopher Bertrand Russell, author J B Priestley, politician Michael Foot, historian A J P Taylor, and the chairman Canon John Collins (holds first 'Aldermaston March', from London to nuclear research centre at Aldermaston, on 7 April).

J D Stewart, *British Pressure Groups.*

In Britain, the Life Peerages Act dilutes the hereditary content of the House of Lords (first life peerages created 24 July).

USA and Canada establish North American Air Defense Command (12 May).

Public Records Act provides for most British government documents to be available for inspection after 50 years.

The Criminal Law Revision Committee is established to provide recommendations on the updating of English criminal law.

First Offenders Act states that no adult is to be imprisoned by a British magistrates' court if there is a more appropriate outcome.

Potter Stewart is appointed to the US Supreme Court, serving until 1981.

Conference on the Law of the Sea held in Geneva, Switzerland.

China launches the 'Great Leap Forward', aiming to increase industrial output at great speed (especially the production of steel, in 'backyard furnaces'); agricultural communes become universal.

The 'Delaney clause' in the USA forbids use of food additives shown to be carcinogenic.

Recession in the USA marks a temporary halt to the growth of prosperity; unemployment peaks at 5 million in March.

British Budget makes 'dividend stripping' (a tax avoidance measure) illegal (15 April).

One thousand electronic computers are in use in the USA, 160 in Britain.

First section of motorway is opened in Britain (5 Dec), the Preston bypass in NW England (closed because of frost damage, 29 Jan 1959).

p Society, Education, and Religion

In USA, new crisis at Little Rock, Arkansas, over racial integration of education: 21 June, District Court permits two-year suspension of integration, which is overturned by the Supreme Court on 12 Sept; Governor Faubus then orders the town's High Schools to close from 15 Sept.

Moroccan women are permitted to choose their own husbands and polygamy is restricted.

Polygamy abolished in Tunisia (1 Jan) and women are permitted to vote in municipal elections for the first time (5 May).

Women take seats in the British House of Lords (21 Oct).

Serious race riots in Notting Hill Gate, London (8–9 Sept).

In Britain, Queen Elizabeth II abolishes custom of presenting débutantes at court (last presentation, 26 July).

J K Galbraith, *The Affluent Society.*

Herman Lantz, *People of Coaltown.*

Claude Lévi-Strauss, *Structural Anthropology.*

C N Parkinson, *Parkinson's Law.*

In USA, the National Defense Education Act authorizes federal assistance for education of $4 billion over four years; spending priorities include higher education, student loans, and the teaching of science, mathematics, and modern languages.

Education Pact reforms Belgian education.

Following the death of Pius XII (9 Oct), Cardinal Angelo Roncalli is elected Pope at the age of 81 (25 Oct) and takes the name John XXIII.

In USA, the Church of the Brethren, at its 250th meeting at Des Moines, Iowa, approves ordination of women.

Evangelical Church of the Palatinate, West Germany, decides to admit women to ordination.

Legislation to admit women to Swedish Lutheran pastorate is passed by convocation and parliament.

Formation in USA of the United Presbyterian Church (May), the country's fourth largest denomination with 3 million members.

US Congregationalists and Evangelicals form United Church of Christ (June) with 2 million members.

Supreme Religious Centre for World Jewry is dedicated in Jerusalem (8 May).

q Science, Technology, and Discovery

British Section of Commonwealth Transantarctic Expedition, under Vivian Fuchs, makes first complete crossing of Antarctica ('the last great journey in the world'); leaves Shackleton Base in Nov 1957, reaches South Pole on 20 Jan, and reaches Scott Base on 2 March.

In USA, successful flight of the Rotocycle (Hiller XROE-1), a one-man helicopter.

International Geophysical Year ends (31 Dec).

E **May**

2 following attacks by Yemeni tribesmen, state of emergency declared by Governor Sir William Luce in Britain's Aden colony.

3 President Eisenhower of USA proposes that 12 countries involved in exploration of Antarctica should freeze claims and refrain from militarizing the continent (subsequently accepted by countries concerned).

8 John Foster Dulles, US secretary of state, declares in Berlin House of Representatives that an attack on Berlin would be regarded as an attack on the Western Allies.

13 in Algeria, French settlers in Algiers protest at idea that the French government might negotiate with nationalist rebels, sparking political crisis in France.

14 in France, Pierre Pflimlin, Popular Republican, forms ministry (–28).

15 in France, General Charles de Gaulle states readiness to assume the powers of the republic; on 19, praises achievements of the French army in Algeria.

16 because of opposition of French settlers in Algeria to any concessions to Algerian nationalists, the French government is granted emergency powers for three months.

25 general election in Italy; Christian Democrats win the largest number of seats but lack an absolute majority.

27 following floods, labour unrest, and ethnic conflict a state of emergency declared in Ceylon (now Sri Lanka).

F **June**

1 in France, following the resignation of Pierre Pflimlin on 28 May, Charles de Gaulle forms government (on 2, de Gaulle is granted emergency powers for six months; on 3, is granted authorization to draw up new constitution and submit it to a popular referendum).

1 Iceland extends limit reserved for its own fishing vessels to 19 km/12 mi.

16 USA and Britain both sign agreements with Japan for ten-year cooperation on atomic energy.

17 execution in Hungary of Imre Nagy, former prime minister, after secret trial.

18 President Eisenhower admits imprudence of Sherman Adams, assistant to the president, after hearings of Senate Committee on bribery charges involving Bernard Goldfine (Adams resigns on 22 Sept).

19 Britain announces new plan for Cyprus, involving representatives of the Greek and Turkish governments in the island's administration (rejected by Archbishop

Makarios and the Greek government; plan is implemented on 1 Oct, with participation by Turkey).

20 Indonesia bans operations of Royal Dutch Shell Oil group.

25 Amintore Fanfani, Christian Democrat, forms Italian coalition in succession to Adone Zoli (resigned 19 June).

G **July**

1 (–21 Aug) eight-power conference of experts at Geneva on detection of nuclear explosions.

1 Sudan diverts Nile waters as first stage of Managil project.

3 USA and Britain make agreement for co-operation in development of atomic weapons.

14 in Baghdad, Iraq, Brigadier Abdul Karim Kassem mounts coup: King Faisal II, his heir, and prime minister Nuri-es-Said are murdered; and King Hussein of Jordan assumes power as head of Arab Federation.

15 following coup in Iraq, USA dispatches forces to Lebanon at request of President Camille Chamoun.

15 South Africa resumes full membership of United Nations.

17 following coup in Iraq, British paratroops land in Jordan at request of King Hussein (remain until 2 Nov).

19 United Arab Republic (Egypt and Syria) and Iraq sign treaty of mutual defence (on 20, the UAR severs relations with Jordan).

19 Nikita Khrushchev of USSR proposes summit on 22 to discuss situation in Middle East (USA, Britain, and France suggest that the UN Security Council should consider the situation).

26 in Britain, Prince Charles (aged 9) is created prince of Wales.

31 (3 Aug) Nikita Khrushchev, prime minister of USSR, visits Beijing; he and Mao Zedong issue statement calling for end of nuclear tests, closure of overseas bases, and summit conference.

H **August**

1 King Hussein dissolves the Federation of Jordan with Iraq.

5 Nikita Khrushchev withdraws previous support for UN Security Council meeting on Middle East (given on 28 July) and proposes meeting of UN General Assembly, which is accepted by USA and Britain.

14 Britain, France, and other NATO countries announce relaxation of prohibitions on trade with Soviet bloc and Communist China; but USA maintains embargo on

Volcanic eruption on the moon observed by Soviet scientist (3 Nov).

US nuclear submarine *Nautilus* passes under ice cap at North Pole, demonstrating the practicability of shortening sea routes.

USSR launches nuclear-powered ice-breaker *Lenin*.

Discovery of submarine current in equatorial Pacific.

Creation in USA of the National Aeronautics and Space Administration or NASA (29 July).

The USA places five artificial satellites in orbit round the Earth; the first, *Explorer 1* (launched 31 Jan), studies cosmic rays; *Vanguard 1* (17 March) tests solar cells; *Explorer 3* (26 March) studies cosmic rays and meteors; *Explorer 4* studies intense radiation above 960 km/600 mi; *Atlas* (18 Dec) is an experimental radio relay station (it records and re-transmits to Earth a Christmas message from President Eisenhower). The USA also fires *Pioneer* rockets towards the Moon.

USSR places *Sputnik 3* in orbit (15 May) for aerodynamic studies, and also fires a rocket carrying two dogs to a height of 450 km/279 mi (27 Aug) and brings it safely back to Earth.

In Britain, announcement of the development of the hovercraft by Christopher Cockerell (23 May; first craft tested, June 1959).

R Humanities

Glyn Daniel, *The Megalith Builders of Western Europe*.

G R Willey and Philip Phillips, *Method and Theory in American Archaeology*.

Ronald Syme, *Tacitus*.

A L F Rivet, *Town and Country in Roman Britain*.

Stephen Runciman, *Sicilian Vespers*.

R H Tawney, *Lionel Cranfield*.

Thomas W Copeland (ed.), *The Correspondence of Edmund Burke* (–1978).

Daniel J Boorstin, *The Americans: The Colonial Experience*.

David Landes, *Bankers and Pashas*.

John Wheeler-Bennett, *King George VI, His Life and Reign*.

John Pope-Hennessy, *Italian Renaissance Sculpture*.

P H Reaney, *A Dictionary of British Surnames*.

The Yale Edition of the Works of Samuel Johnson.

Hannah Arendt, *The Human Condition*.

Werner Heisenberg, *Physics and Philosophy*.

Ludwig Wittgenstein, *The Blue Book* and *The Brown Book* (posthumous).

s Art, Sculpture, Fine Arts, and Architecture

Garçon au gilet rouge by Paul Cézanne sells for £220,000 at auction in London, double the highest price yet paid for a single picture at auction.

Exhibition of works by Jackson Pollock held at the Whitechapel Gallery, London.

In Britain, foundation of the Victorian Society to safeguard Victorian and Edwardian buildings threatened by demolition.

The Gulbenkian Fund's Committee reviews the needs of the arts in Britain.

Lord Bridges, in Oxford, England, gives the Romanes Lecture on 'The State of the Arts'; he calls for greater co-operation between central and local bodies in the arts, and for greater involvement by universities.

Painting, etc:

Ben (Ben Vaultier), first paintings of hand written-words on plain background.

Lucio Fontana, *Concetto Spaziale, Attese* (first slashed canvas).

Lucian Freud, *Woman Smiling* (–1960).

Raymond Hains, *Alleg*.

Morris Louis, first of *Veil* paintings, using one of first acrylic paints, 'Magna'.

Piero Manzoni, *Achrome*.

Mark Rothko, commissioned to paint Seagram murals (eventually donated to Tate Gallery, London, by the artist in 1964).

Leon Polk Smith, *Amitou*.

Sculpture:

César, *Compression*.

Jasper Johns, *Light Bulb*.

David Smith, *8 planes and 7 bars*.

Architecture:

Louis Kahn, Richards Medical Research Building, Philadelphia, USA (–1960).

Ludwig Mies van der Rohe and Philip Johnson, Seagram Building, New York.

Pier Luigi Nervi and Gio Ponti, Palazzo dello Sport, Rome (–1960); Pirelli Building, Milan.

Pier Luigi Nervi and Jean Prouvé, Exhibition Hall Rond-Point de la Défense, Paris, France.

Oscar Niemeyer, President's Palace, Brasilia.

Eero Saarinen, Dulles Airport, Washington DC, USA (–1963); Yale Hockey Rink, New Haven, USA.

Bernard Zehrfuss, Pier Luigi Nervi, and Marcek Breuer, UNESCO Building, Paris.

T Music

Samuel Barber, *Vanessa* (opera).

Luciano Berio, *Ommagio à Joyce*.

Benjamin Britten, *Noye's Fludde*.

Jean Françaix, *Divertimento*.

Cemal Rey, *The Conqueror*.

trade with China, North Korea, and North Vietnam.

23 People's Republic of China begins bombarding Quemoy, an island near the Chinese mainland ruled from Formosa (now Taiwan).

24 death of J G Strijdom, prime minister of South Africa; succeeded on 3 Sept by Hendrik Verwoerd.

J **September**

1 Icelandic patrols board British fishing vessels within 19-km/12-mi limit.

7 Nikita Khrushchev states that any US attack on China will be regarded as an attack on USSR.

14 (–15) Konrad Adenauer, chancellor of West Germany, visits Prime Minister de Gaulle at his home at Colombey-les-deux-Eglises, N France, to discuss Franco–German relations.

15 (–26) Commonwealth Trade and Economic Conference, Montreal.

18 President Eisenhower signs four-year extension of Reciprocal Trade Agreements Act, enabling him to adjust tariffs in accordance with political situations.

19 UN rejects Indian proposal to consider admission to UN of People's Republic of China.

19 in Cairo, Egypt, Algerian rebel leader Ferhat Abbas proclaims establishment of Provisional Government of the Republic of Algeria.

28 referendum held in France, Algeria, and territories overseas approves constitution for Fifth French Republic (promulgated on 5 Oct followed by electoral law on 13); gives president greater powers and strengthens position of the government in the Assembly.

30 USSR resumes nuclear tests.

K **October**

7 following unrest throughout Pakistan, President Iskander Mirza proclaims martial law and suspends the constitution.

20 military coup in Thailand.

23 Charles de Gaulle, prime minister of France, says he is willing to discuss a ceasefire with nationalist rebels in Algeria (no reply from Algerian Provisional Government; unrest continues).

23 USSR makes loan to United Arab Republic for building Aswan Dam on River Nile.

24 President Mirza of Pakistan forms a presidential cabinet, with General Ayub Khan as prime minister (President Mirza resigns on 27, when Ayub Khan assumes presidency and abolishes post of prime minister).

L **November**

4 in USA, Democratic victory in mid-term Congressional elections, leaving Democrats with 62 seats in Senate (Republicans, 34) and 281 seats in House of Representatives (Republicans, 153).

10 (–18 Dec) Ten-power Conference on Measures against Surprise Attack held in Geneva, Switzerland; representatives from the West and the Soviet bloc attend but fail to reach any agreement.

12 in Central African Federation, United Federal Party of Prime Minister Roy Welensky wins general election.

12 East Germany sends notes to 60 countries, requesting recognition.

17 in Sudan, the army assumes power with General Ibrahim Aboud as head of state, prime minister, and commander of armed forces.

23 Ghana and Guinea announce they will form nucleus of a union of West African states.

27 the USSR demands that troops be withdrawn from Berlin and the city established as a 'free city' (14 Dec, rejected by meeting of US, British, and French foreign ministers, and on 16 Dec by NATO council).

30 in France, Neo-Gaullist Union for a New Republic (UNR) wins largest number of seats in general election (198 out of 465).

M **December**

3 Indonesia nationalizes Dutch businesses.

8 (–13) All-Africa People's Conference held in Accra, Ghana, with representatives from most countries; establishes permanent secretariat and resolves to work for freedom of Africa.

11 in Netherlands, following differences between coalition members on a tax issue, William Drees, Labour, resigns as prime minister; succeeded on 20 Dec by J M Beel, Catholic People's Party.

12 in Algeria, civilian government is partly restored, with General Raoul Salan becoming inspector general of national defence.

21 Charles de Gaulle elected president of French Republic by electoral college, with 78.5 per cent of votes (Communist candidate wins 13.1 per cent, the candidate of the Union of Democrat Forces, 8.4 per cent).

27 Britain announces convertibility of sterling for non-resident holders.

27 France devalues the Franc and makes it convertible to non-resident holders.

30 French West African states (Chad, Congo, Gabon, Mali, Mauritania, and Senegal) decide to form a federation within the French Community.

Edgard Varèse, *Poème électronique*.
La Monte Young, *String Trio*.
Max Bygraves, 'You Need Hands'.
Perry Como, 'Magic Moments' (written 1957 by Burt Bacharach).
Connie Francis, 'Stupid Cupid', 'Who's Sorry Now'.
Jim Reeves, 'Anna Marie'.
Phil Spector, 'To Know Him Is To Love Him'.
Formation of British folk group The Spinners.
Start of the US National Academy of Recording Arts and Sciences 'Grammy' awards.
In USA, first stereophonic ('stereo') records sold.

u Literature and Drama
Chinua Achebe, *Things Fall Apart*.
H E Bates, *The Darling Buds of May*.
Brendan Behan, *Borstal Boy*.
Albert Camus, *Exile and the Kingdom*.
Truman Capote, *Breakfast at Tiffany's*.
Evan Connell, *Mrs Bridge*.
Yasar Kemal, *Mehmed, My Hawk*.
Jack Kerouac, *Dharma Bums*.
Giuseppe di Lampedusa, *The Leopard*.
Iris Murdoch, *The Bell*.
Eric Newby, *A Short Walk in the Hindu Kush*.
Boris Pasternak, *Dr Zhivago*.
Barbara Pym, *A Glass of Blessings*.
Theodore Roethke, *Words for the Wind* (poems).
Alan Sillitoe, *Saturday Night and Sunday Morning*.
Leon Uris, *Exodus*.
Laurens Van der Post, *The Lost World of the Kalahari*.
T H White, *The Sword in the Stone*.
The 'Beatnik' movement, originating among young poets of California, spreads to Britain; devotees are unkempt, penurious, and take drugs.

Drama:
Fernando Arrabel, *The Two Executioners*.
Samuel Beckett, *Krapp's Last Tape*.
T S Eliot, *The Elder Statesman*.
Max Frisch, *Biedermann und die Brandstifter/ The Firereaisers*.
Jean Genet, *The Blacks*.
Graham Greene, *The Potting Shed*.
Archibald Macleish, *J B*.
Harold Pinter, *The Birthday Party*.

v Births and Deaths
March 14 Christabel Pankhurst dies (77).
March 29 Sir William Burrell dies (96).
April 18 Maurice Gamelin dies (85).
May 29 Juan Ramón Jiménez dies (76).
June 17 Imre Nagy dies (62).
Aug 16 Madonna born (–).
Aug 24 J G Strijdom dies (65).
Aug 26 Ralph Vaughan Williams dies (85).

Aug 28 F O Lawrence dies (57).
Aug 29 Michael Jackson born (–).
Oct 2 Marie Stopes dies (78).
Oct 9 Pope Pius XII dies (82).
Oct 24 G E Moore dies (84).
Dec 15 Wolfgang Pauli dies (59).

w Everyday Life
Radar used in Britain to check for speeding drivers (from 20 Jan).
US singer Elvis Presley reports for two years' military service (24 March).
Parking meters introduced in Mayfair, London (10 July).
First scheduled transatlantic jet services, by British Overseas Airways Corporation flying the Comet IV between London and New York (from 4 Oct), followed by Pan-Am flying the Boeing 707 between Paris and New York (26 Oct).
The hula hoop is developed by the Wham O Manufacturing Co., of San Gabriel, California, USA.
Bank of America (California) issues the first recognisable multi-purpose credit card; American Express charge card also launched.

x Sport and Recreation
Eight members of the Manchester United football side from England are killed in an air crash at Munich, Germany, while returning from a European Cup tie in Belgrade (6 Feb).
Batting for the West Indies against Pakistan in Kingston, Jamaica, Gary Sobers establishes a new record individual Test innings score of 365 not out (26 Feb–4 March).
The sixth football World Cup tournament is held in Sweden. All four British teams qualify for the finals for the first time. Brazil wins, beating the host nation 5–2 in the final in Stockholm.
Great Britain wins the Wightman Cup for tennis for the first time since 1930.
Water-skiing becomes popular.

y Media
In USA, Associated Press and International News Service merge to form United Press International.

Film:
Ashes and Diamonds (director, Andrzej Wajda).
Ballad of Narayama (director, Keisuke Kinoshita).
Gigi (director, Vincente Minnelli; starring Audrey Hepburn).
The Hidden Fortress (director, Akira Kurosawa).
Mon Oncle (director and star, Jacques Tati).
The Rickshaw Man (director, Hiroshi Inagaki).

Agreement for independence of Cyprus ... de Valera becomes president of Ireland ... Makarios elected president of Cyprus ...

A January

1 in Cuba, the guerrilla campaign of the 26 July Movement forces President Fulgencio Batistá to resign and flee to Dominica; military junta appoints Carlos Piedra as provisional president.

2 in Cuba, the 26 July Movement ignores the military junta and proclaims Dr Manuel Urratía provisional president; announces cabinet on 3, with Fidel Castro as prime minister (takes oath on 16 Feb).

3 in USA, Alaska is admitted to the union as the 49th state.

4 disturbances at Léopoldville, Belgian Congo (now Zaire), which force Belgium, on 13, to grant reforms.

8 in France, General de Gaulle is proclaimed president of Fifth Republic; he appoints Michel Debré as prime minister.

10 USSR proposes conference to draw up German peace treaty (West replies on 16 Feb by suggesting four-power foreign ministers' conference, which meets in Geneva, Switzerland, on 11 May).

19 in South Africa, re-opening of treason trial of those arrested in Dec 1956.

26 Amintore Fanfani resigns as prime minister of Italy, because of dissensions among Christian Democrats (6 Feb, Antonio Segni, Christian Democrat, forms ministry supported by Liberals and Monarchists).

B February

9 USA supplies arms to Indonesia.

11 Laos announces that it will recognize UN as sole arbiter of disputes, provoking denunciation by North Vietnam.

19 agreement signed in London by prime ministers of Greece, Turkey, and Britain for independence of Cyprus; Cyprus to be republic with presidential regime; president to be Greek, vice-president Turkish; the two communities are to be allowed considerable autonomy. Britain will retain two military bases on the island, and Enosis (union with Greece), for which EOKA has been fighting, is ruled out.

20 disturbances in the British territory of Nyasaland (now Malawi) where, 3 March, state of emergency is declared and Hastings Banda and other leaders of Nyasaland African Congress are arrested.

21 (–3 March) Harold Macmillan, prime minister of Britain, and Selwyn Lloyd, foreign secretary, visit USSR (Macmillan wears plus-fours when visiting a collective farm and his Old Etonian tie at the ballet).

26 (–20 May) Sir Edgar Whitehead, prime minister of southern Rhodesia, declares state of emergency and bans four African National Congress parties, fearing spread of trouble from Nyasaland (now Malawi).

28 Egypt and Britain settle claims arising from Suez crisis of 1956.

c March

1 Archbishop Makarios III returns to Cyprus from exile.

1 (–9) unsuccessful army revolt in Mosul, Iraq.

3 in Kenya, the 'Hola incident': incident at Hola Camp causes death of 11 Mau Mau prisoners; news of the deaths, on 7, is followed by protests in Kenya and Britain.

Room at the Top (director, Jack Clayton; starring Lawrence Harvey and Simone Signoret).

South Pacific (music and lyrics by Richard Rodgers and Oscar Hammerstein).

Touch of Evil (director, Orson Welles).

Les Tricheurs (director, Marcel Carné).

Vertigo (director, Alfred Hitchcock; starring James Stewart and Kim Novak).

The Wind Cannot Read (starring Dirk Bogarde).

Television:

New programmes in USA include: *Bronco*, starring Ty Hardin (–1962); *Sea Hunt*, starring Lloyd Bridges; *77 Sunset Strip* (–1964).

East German television produces the fairy tale *The Singing Ringing Tree*.

New programmes in Britain include: *The Black and White Minstrel Show* (BBC; –1978); *Blue Peter*, for children (–); *Grandstand*, showing live broadcasts of sport (BBC) (–); *Monitor* (BBC), an arts programme (–1965); *Oh Boy!* (popular music show).

Scottish television broadcasts *The Wonderful World*, presented by John Grierson.

Antarctic Treaty ... Stockhausen's Gruppen *... Launch of the Mini Minor ... Quiz show scandal in USA ...*

o **Politics, Government, Law, and Economy**

S M Lipset, *Political Man*.

C Wright Mills, *The Causes of World War III*.

Antarctic Treaty signed, freezing territorial claims and aiming to prevent development (valid June 1961–Dec 1989).

Cabinet government introduced to Trinidad and Tobago (20 July).

First meeting of European Court of Human Rights at Strasbourg (23–28 Feb).

Intergovernmental Maritime Consultative Organization (since 1982 called the IMO) starts overseeing the law of the sea.

The Obscene Publications Act codifies the British law on the subject and offers protection to literature and other documents of merit; Vladimir Nabokov's *Lolita* (1955) is published in Britain.

The US Post Office Court rules that *Lady Chatterley's Lover* by D H Lawrence (privately published in Florence in 1928) is not objectionable (21 July); a complete edition is published.

The Landrum–Griffin Act in the USA regulates the internal affairs of trade unions.

In Cuba, courts martial are established to try members of the previous Batista regime; some 450–550 people are convicted and shot.

Queen Elizabeth opens St Lawrence Seaway, linking the Atlantic with Chicago and other ports in the Great Lakes of USA (6 June).

Britain announces removal of controls on imports of many consumer goods from dollar area, with increased import quotas on other goods (28 May).

Opening in Britain of the first section of the M1 (London–Leeds motorway) (1 Nov).

De Beers of Johannesburg manufacture a synthetic diamond (17 Nov).

A Martial Law Regulation in Pakistan implements land reform in West Pakistan: the maximum holding is fixed at 500 acres, the minimum at 50 acres, and subsistence holdings at 12.5 acres (smaller areas cannot be sold or fragmented); dispossessed landlords are to be compensated.

In Cuba, the Agrarian Reform Act (passed in June) transfers land from large landowners to those who work it, provides land for the unemployed, and reduces the power of US-owned sugar mills (the maximum personal holding is 1,000 acres, with 3,300 acres for sugar, rice, and cattle farms).

Following the uprising in Tibet and the flight of the Dalai Lama (March), the Chinese announce programme of land expropriation and redistribution (3 July).

Vance Packard, *The Waste makers*.

p **Society, Education, and Religion**

Disastrous crop failures in China.

Swiss referendum rejects female suffrage in federal elections (1 Feb).

United Nations General Assembly passes a resolution condemning racism.

In South Africa, the government establishes a Coloured Affairs Department and a Union Council on Coloured Affairs (comprising 15 nominated and 12 elected members); the Promotion of Bantu Self-Government Act provides for the establishment of eight African 'homelands', of which Africans will become citizens (thereby losing right of representation in Parliament).

In South Africa, the Extension of University Education Act (11 June) ends racially

9 (–23) British Prime Minister Macmillan and foreign secretary Selwyn Lloyd visit President de Gaulle (France), Chancellor Adenauer (Germany), Prime Minister Diefenbaker (Canada), and President Eisenhower (USA) to report on visit to USSR.

12 in Northern Rhodesia, the Zambia African National Congress is banned for intimidating Africans planning to vote in election on 20.

17 USSR and Australia resume diplomatic relations (severed in April 1954).

17 Colonel Grivas, leader of EOKA guerrillas in Cyprus, returns to Athens from Cyprus under safe conduct granted by governor.

17 Tibetan rising against Chinese garrison; the Dalai Lama is smuggled out of Lhasa (31, arrives in India after journey of 480 km/300 mi; 9 Sept, appeals for UN intervention).

20 United Federal Party wins Northern Rhodesian elections.

24 Iraq withdraws from Baghdad Pact (and the 1956 British–Iraqi agreement lapses).

27 US aircraft first 'buzzed' in Berlin air corridor (connecting West Germany and West Berlin) by Soviet jet fighters.

D **April**

4 (–30 May) Ivory Coast signs series of agreements with Niger, Upper Volta (now Burkina Faso), and Dahomey (now Benin) to form Sahel–Benin Union.

15 in USA, President Eisenhower announces resignation of John Foster Dulles, the secretary of state (effective on 16; Christian A Herter appointed on 18 as successor; Dulles dies of cancer on 24).

17 Malaya and Indonesia sign treaty of friendship.

26 detachment of Cubans invades Panama (arrested and flown to Havana, Cuba, where imprisoned).

27 Liu Shaoqi elected chairman of Chinese Republic in succession to Mao Zedong, who remains head of Communist Party.

E **May**

2 Afro-Asian Organization for Economic Co-operation, at meeting in Cairo, Egypt, announces exclusion of USSR from the Organization.

4 USSR sends note to Japan urging removal of US bases in Japan; offers to guarantee permanent neutrality for Japan.

7 agreement between Britain and USA enabling Britain to purchase components of atomic weapons other than warheads from USA.

11 (–5 Aug) conference of foreign ministers held in Geneva, Switzerland, to discuss Berlin and a German peace treaty.

19 in Netherlands, following indecisive outcome of general election of 12 March, J E de Quay forms four-party coalition ministry; the Labour Party goes into opposition for the first time since 1945.

22 Canada and USA make agreement for co-operation in use of atomic energy for mutual defence.

25 (–4 June) Nikita Khrushchev of USSR visits Albania.

30 Iraq terminates US military assistance agreements because they now conflict with its policy of neutrality.

F **June**

3 Singapore becomes self-governing.

4 Cuban government expropriates US-owned sugar mills and plantations.

5 (–10) Atlantic Congress, London, sponsored by NATO Parliamentarians' Conference and attended by representatives of 15 NATO countries.

14 USA agrees to provide Greece with nuclear information and supply ballistic rockets.

17 Éamon de Valera resigns as prime minister of Ireland to become third president (in succession to Sean O'Kelly) on 23, Sean Lemass becomes prime minister.

25 USSR proposes denuclearized zone in Balkans and Adriatic (rejected by West, 11–13 July).

G **July**

1 Heinrich Lübke is elected president of West Germany in succession to Dr Heuss (Konrad Adenauer's opposition prevented Dr Ludwig Erhard standing as Christian Democrat candidate).

4 Jamaica is granted internal self-government within the West Indies Federation.

5 Ghana boycotts South African goods.

5 completion of incorporation of the Saar in the West German economic system.

5 President Sukarno dissolves Indonesian constituent assembly (sitting since 1956) and issues decree restoring the constitution of 1945, with its greater presidential powers.

17 Nikita Khrushchev of USSR reaffirms guarantee of Oder–Neisse frontier (between East Germany and Poland) and calls for European denuclearized zone.

17 in Cuba, Manuel Urratía is replaced as president by Osvaldo Dórticos (–1976).

19 the presidents of Ghana, Guinea, and Liberia propose holding conference of independent African states in 1960, to form a 'Community of African States'.

integrated education at Cape Town and Witwatersrand Universities and creates separate institutions of higher education for Coloureds, Indians, and Africans.

In Britain, novelist and educationalist C P Snow delivers the Richmond Lecture *The Two Cultures and the Sciences.*

In Britain, the Crowther Report recommends that compulsory full-time education should continue to 16 and part-time education to 18.

In France, President de Gaulle's educational reforms permit public funds to be allocated to Catholic schools.

Segregation is enforced in higher education in South Africa.

World Refugee Year begins (1 June).

At press conference (20 June), the Dalai Lama claims that the Chinese have destroyed 1,000 monasteries in Tibet since 1956, attempting to eradicate Buddhism.

Pope John XXIII announces the calling of the first Vatican Council since 1870.

The Vatican orders the French worker-priest movement, founded in 1943, to be discontinued.

President Celal Bayar of Turkey is the first Muslim ruler to visit the Pope (June).

Start of restoration of the Dome of the Rock, Jerusalem, with gifts from Muslim governments.

Karl Barth, *Dogmatics in Outline.*

Pierre Teilhard de Chardin, *The Phenomenon of Man.*

Q Science, Technology, and Discovery

Launching in USA of first atomic-powered passenger-cargo ship, *Savannah* (21 July).

British hovercraft crosses the Channel in two hours (25 July).

Discovery of the Arctic submarine plateau.

The USA places 11 artificial satellites in orbit around the Earth; *Explorer 6* (launched 7 Aug) investigates the Van Allen radiation belt around the Earth (discovered in 1958 by *Explorer 1*); the Moon probe *Pioneer 4* (launched 3 March) passes within 59,000 km/37,000 mi of the Moon.

The USA also launches two monkeys in a rocket to a height of 480 km/300 mi and recovers them alive (28 May).

The USSR places *Lunik 3* in orbit round the Earth (launched 4 Oct); it also launches three Moon probes. *Lunik 1* passes within 6,400 km/4,000 mi of the Moon; *Lunik 2* (launched 12 Sept) hits the Moon; *Lunik 3* (launched 4 Oct) passes behind the Moon and goes into orbit around the Earth, having taken photographs of the Moon's surface (including the hidden side).

Alvarez discovers the neutral *xi*-particle.

R Humanities

Mary Leakey discovers a human skull thought to be 1.75 million years old at Olduvai Gorge, Tanganyika (now Tanzania); Louis B Leakey finds the skull of 'the Nutcracker Man', 600,000 years old.

Remains of Nonsuch Palace are excavated successfully during Britain's driest summer for 200 years.

R V Lennard, *Rural England, 1086–1135.*

W G Hoskins, *Local History in England.*

Garrett Mattingly, *The Defeat of the Spanish Armada.*

Stanley M Elkins, *Slavery: A Problem in American Institutional and Intellectual Life.*

Samuel Flagg Bemis, *A Short History of American Foreign Policy and Diplomacy.*

Asa Briggs, *The Age of Improvement.*

H J Hanham, *Elections and Party Management.*

Allan Nevins, *The War for the Union.*

Eric Stokes, *The English Utilitarians and India.*

Keith Sinclair, *A History of New Zealand.*

Deryck Cooke, *The Language of Music.*

Iona and Peter Opie, *The Lore and Language of Schoolchildren.*

Ernst Bloch, *The Principle of Hope.*

Ernest Gellner, *Words and Things.*

S Art, Sculpture, Fine Arts, and Architecture

'New American Painting' exhibition at the Tate Gallery, London.

International exhibition of Surrealism, Paris, France; includes works by contemporary American artists (Jasper Johns and Robert Rauschenberg).

Pablo Picasso, *La Belle Hollandaise*, sells for £55,000, the highest price paid for a work by living artist.

Painting, etc:

Francis Bacon, *Sleeping Figure.*

Peter Blake, *Girly Door.*

Jean Dubuffet, *Corps d'Hommes* series.

Jasper Johns, *False Start.*

Robert Rauschenberg, *Canyon.*

Frank Stella, *Die Fahne Hoch!*

Cy Twombly, *Settebello.*

Sculpture:

John Chamberlain, *Zaar.*

David Smith, *Cubi* series (–1960).

Architecture:

Louis Kahn, Salk Institute Laboratories, La Jolla, California, USA (–1965).

Skidmore, Owings, and Merrill, Banque Lambert, Brussels, Belgium.

Frank Lloyd Wright, Beth Sholom Synagogue, Elkin Park, Pennsylvania, USA.

28 Indian police party seized by Communist Chinese in Jammu and Kashmir area.

H August

7 Chinese forces make incursion into NE India.

16 United Arab Republic (Egypt and Syria) restores diplomatic relations with Jordan (severed 20 July 1958).

21 following withdrawal of Iraq from Baghdad Pact (24 March), the Pact changes name to Central Treaty Organization, known as CENTO (moves headquarters to Ankara, Turkey).

21 in USA, Hawaii is admitted to the union as the 50th state.

J September

4 emergency in Laos, following alleged aggression by North Vietnamese.

7 USA, USSR, Britain, and France issue statements announcing proposal to establish 10-power disarmament committee.

16 President de Gaulle makes broadcast on Algeria: he proposes a referendum offering Algerians a choice between secession or continued association with France, to be held within four years of the effective end of the rebellion.

18 Nikita Khrushchev addresses UN General Assembly on disarmament.

22 UN votes against admission of People's Republic of China.

25 Nikita Khrushchev visits Beijing, China.

25 Solomon Bandaranaike, prime minister of Ceylon (Sri Lanka), is assassinated by a Buddhist monk; succeeded by Wijayananda Dahanayake.

K October

8 in British general election, Conservatives under Harold Macmillan win 365 seats; Labour, 258; Liberals, 6; other, 1.

20 Inter-American Nuclear Energy Commission holds first meeting in Washington, DC, USA.

21 UN General Assembly adopts motion calling for the restoration of religious and civil liberties in Tibet (denounced by Chinese government on 23).

26 Basic Democracies Order promulgated in Pakistan, providing for a four-tier hierarchy of councils, part elected, part nominated; Rawalpindi is chosen as provisional capital.

L November

8 United Arab Republic (Egypt and Syria) and Sudan sign agreement on sharing the Nile waters after construction of Aswan High Dam.

8 President Bourguiba's Neo-Destour Party win all seats in Tunisian assembly.

10 UN General Assembly condemns apartheid in South Africa and racial discrimination in any part of the world.

10 announcement of ending of emergency in Kenya after ten years (proclamation signed by governor on 12 Jan 1960).

13 at conference in Johannesburg, South Africa, the South African Progressive Party is founded.

20 (–29) conference at Stockholm, Sweden, at which the finance ministers of Austria, Denmark, Great Britain, Norway, Portugal, Sweden, and Switzerland (the 'Seven') initial convention establishing the European Free Trade Association or EFTA.

M December

3 (–23) President Eisenhower of USA makes tour of European capitals.

6 UN General Assembly resolves that Togoland trusteeship territory (now Togo) should achieve independence in April 1960.

9 Britain and United Arab Republic (Egypt and Syria) resume diplomatic relations (severed in Nov 1956).

10 USA begins withdrawal of troops from Iceland.

13 UN decides not to intervene in question of Algeria.

14 in Cyprus, Archbishop Makarios III is elected president.

19 Western powers at Paris meeting invite Nikita Khrushchev of USSR to attend summit conference in April 1960.

25 USSR agrees to give financial and technical aid to Syria.

т Music

Karl-Birger Blomdahl, *Aniara* (opera).

Elliott Carter, Second String Quartet.

Nam Paik, *Hommage à Cage*.

Francis Poulenc, *La voix humaine* (opera).

Alan Rawsthorne, Symphony No. 2 ('Pastoral').

Karlheinz Stockhausen, *Gruppen*.

Australian soprano Joan Sutherland sings role of Lucia di Lammermoor at Covent Garden, London, to great acclaim.

Gypsy (musical), lyrics by Stephen Sondheim, music by Jule Styne (first performed at the Broadway Theatre, New York, 21 May).

The Sound of Music (musical), lyrics by Oscar Hammerstein, music by Richard Rodgers (first performed at the Lunt-Fontanne Theatre, New York, 16 Nov).

Shirley Bassey, 'As I Love You'.

Russ Conway, 'China Tea'.

The Drifters, 'There Goes my Baby'.

Cliff Richard, 'Livin' Doll', 'Travellin' Light'.

Buddy Holly dies in plane crash (3 Feb).

In Detroit, USA, Berry Gordy founds Motown Records (a major black-owned record company) and launches the Tamla record label.

US jazz pianist and composer Thelonius Monk forms his own big band.

British jazz musician Ronnie Scott opens his jazz club at Gerrard Street, London.

u Literature and Drama

Saul Bellow, *Henderson the Rain King*.

James Blish, *A Case of Conscience*.

Heinrich Böll, *Billiards at Half-Past Nine*.

William Burroughs, *The Naked Lunch*.

William Faulkner, *The Mansion*.

Günther Grass, *The Tin Drum*.

Robert Lowell, *Life Studies*.

Colin MacInnes, *Absolute Beginners*.

Norman Mailer, *Advertisement for Myself*.

Anaïs Nin, *Cities of the Interior*.

James Purdy, *Malcolm*.

Alan Sillitoe, *The Loneliness of the Long Distance Runner*.

Muriel Spark, *Memento Mori*.

Philip Whalen, *Self-Portrait from Another Direction* (poems).

Drama:

Edward Albee, *The Zoo Story*.

John Arden, *Sergeant Musgrave's Dance*.

Brendan Behan, *The Hostage*.

Shelagh Delaney, *A Taste of Honey*.

Jack Gelber, *The Connection*.

Harold Pinter, *The Caretaker*.

Arnold Wesker, *Roots*.

Tennessee Williams, *Sweet Bird of Youth*.

Jerzy Grotowski creates the Theatre Laboratory in Opole, Poland.

In the City of London, Bernard Miles opens the Mermaid Theatre, at Puddle Dock near Blackfriars Bridge (28 May 1959), the first new theatre in the City for 300 years.

v Births and Deaths

Jan 14 G D H Cole dies (69).

Jan 21 Cecil B de Mille dies (77).

Feb 7 D F Malan dies (84).

March 26 Raymond Chandler dies (70).

April 9 Frank Lloyd Wright dies (89).

July 6 George Grosz dies (65).

July 15 Ernest Bloch dies (78).

May 24 John Foster Dulles dies (71).

Aug 19 Jacob Epstein dies (78).

Sept 26 Solomon Bandaranaike dies (60).

Oct 9 Henry Tizard dies (74).

Oct 16 George Marshall dies (78).

Dec 23 Lord Halifax dies (78).

w Everyday Life

In Britain, launch of the Mini Minor, designer Alec Issigonis (the one millionth vehicle is produced in 1965).

First drive-in bank in Britain, in Liverpool.

In USA, invention of pantyhose (known as tights in Britain).

British Post Office introduces post codes and automatic sorting machines (28 July).

During visit of President Eisenhower to Britain, Prime Minister Harold Macmillan escorts him from Heathrow Airport to central London via several Conservative marginal constituencies; the two leaders appear on television in discussion at 10 Downing Street (31 Aug).

Nikita Khrushchev of USSR, on visit to the USA, is refused entry to the Disneyland amusement park for security reasons (20 Sept).

x Sport and Recreation

Batting for Karachi against Bahawalpur in Karachi, Pakistan, Hanif Mohammad establishes a new record individual score for first-class cricket of 499; he is run out attempting his 500th run (8–12 Jan).

Australia regains the Ashes, beating England 4–0 in the five-match series in Australia (4 Feb).

US golfer Jack Nicklaus wins the US Amateur Golf Championship at Broadmoor, Colorado, USA, at the age of 19.

In soccer, Billy Wright of Wolves and England becomes the first player to win 100 international caps (4 April).

Ingemar Johansson of Sweden beats Floyd Patterson in three rounds in New York to win the World Heavyweight Boxing title;

*Harold Macmillan's 'Wind of Change' speech ... Sharpeville
massacre in South Africa ... Kennedy elected president of the
USA ...*

A **January**

1 French Cameroon becomes the independent Republic of Cameroon.

6 (–5 Feb) Harold Macmillan, prime minister of Britain, visits Ghana, Nigeria, Rhodesia (now Zimbabwe), and South Africa; on 3 Feb, speaking in Cape Town to South Africa's Parliament, he declares: 'The wind of change is blowing through this continent .... and our national policies must take account of it.'

8 in Northern Rhodesia (now Zambia), Kenneth Kaunda (imprisoned in 1959) is released from prison (soon afterwards he becomes president of the United National Independence Party, which seeks independence by Oct).

12 in Kenya, state of emergency declared in 1952 is terminated.

12 in Indonesia, President Sukarno forms National Front.

16 (–18) London conference on independence terms for Cyprus; ends without agreement.

in the third round, Patterson is floored seven times (26 June).

Bill Shankly is appointed manager of English Second Division soccer side Liverpool (1 Dec); in his first match in charge, Liverpool lose 4–0.

γ **Media**

In Cuba, many newspapers close and others are later suppressed, following the accession of Fidel Castro.

Six-week printing strike in Britain (June–July) which affects all publications except London newspapers.

Film:

Publication (posthumous) of *Notes of a Film Director* by Soviet director Sergei Eisenstein (1898–1948).

Anatomy of a Murder (director, Otto Preminger).

Ben Hur (director, William Wyler; starring Charlton Heston).

Black Orpheus (director, Marcel Camus).

Boris Godunov (director, V Stroyerai).

Compulsion (director, Richard Fleischer).

The Four Hundred Blows (director, François Truffaut).

Good Morning (director, Yasujiro Ozu).

The Gordeyev Family (director, Mark Donskoy).

Hiroshima, mon Amour (director, Alain Resnais).

Look Back in Anger (director, Tony Richardson; starring Richard Burton and Mary Ure).

Our Man in Havana (director, Carol Reed).

Peeping Tom (director, Michael Powell).

Pickpocket (director, Carl Bresson).

Rio Bravo (director, Howard Hawks; starring John Wayne).

Some Like it Hot (director, Billy Wilder; starring Marilyn Monroe, Jack Lemmon, and Tony Curtis).

Le Testament d'Orphée (director, Jean Cocteau).

The World of Apu (director, Satyajit Ray).

Television:

Sony of Japan produces a transistorized television receiver.

Television introduced to India, with station and sets in community centres in Delhi.

First television service started in Africa, at Ibadan, Nigeria (31 Oct).

In USA, the 'Quiz Show Scandal' when participants in the quiz show *Twenty-One* confess that they had been supplied with answers before the show.

New programmes in USA include: *Bonanza*, starring Lorne Green (–1973); *For Whom the Bell Tolls*, a *Playhouse 90* production starring Jason Robards; *Rawhide* (–1966); *The Untouchables*.

In Britain, first coverage of general election (Oct).

New programmes in Britain include: *Face to Face* (BBC), interviews by John Freeman; *Juke Box Jury* (BBC; –1967); *No Hiding Place* (ITV; –1967); *Para Handy – Master Mariner* (BBC), a Scottish comedy series (–1960); *Whicker's World* (BBC), presented by Alan Whicker.

South Africa rejects introduction of television (28 Oct).

'Lady Chatterley' case in Britain ... Development of the laser ...
End of National Service in Britain ... Beatles play in Hamburg ...

ο **Politics, Government, Law, and Economy**

Donald R Matthews, *US Senators and their World*.

Elmer Eric Schattschneider, *The Semi-Sovereign People*.

In USA, evolution of the Hoover Library into the Hoover Institution on War, Revolution, and Peace.

The first Polaris-armed nuclear-powered submarine, the USA's *George Washington*, becomes operational (15 Nov).

In South Africa, the Promotion of Bantu Self-Government Act comes into force (30 June).

Capital of Brazil moved to Brasilia.

In Britain, Viscount Stansgate dies (17 Nov); his son, A N Wedgwood Benn, a member of the House of Commons, succeeds as the 2nd Viscount, but returns his Letter Patent to Queen Elizabeth II (23), in a bid to renounce his title and remain in the Commons; on 29 he submits a petition to the House of Commons.

Canada passes a Bill of Rights.

In Britain, in the celebrated 'Lady Chatterley'

18 (–21 Feb) Kenya constitutional conference, London, at first boycotted by African elected members, who take their places on 25; the conference agrees new constitution.

19 US–Japanese Treaty of Mutual Co-operation and Security signed in Washington, DC, USA.

20 (–20 Feb) conference in Brussels, Belgium, agrees on programme for achieving independence for Belgian Congo (now Zaire) on 30 June.

24 (–1 Feb) in Algeria, French settlers riot in Algiers, sparked by President de Gaulle's offer of self-determination for Algeria and his dismissal of General Jacques Massu as commander of the Central Algiers Region.

B **February**

5 Anastas Mikoyan, deputy prime minister of USSR, opens Soviet exhibition in Havana, Cuba.

10 (–5 March) Nikita Khrushchev of USSR visits India, Burma (now Myanmar), and Indonesia.

14 Muhammad Ayub Khan elected president of Pakistan.

17 USA and Britain agree to build early-warning station for detection of ballistic missiles at Fylingdales, NE England.

19 in Britain, Queen Elizabeth II gives birth to Prince Andrew (first birth to a reigning sovereign since 1857).

24 in Italy, Antonio Segni, Christian Democrat, resigns as prime minister after Liberals withdraw their support; after protracted deadlock, Amintore Fanfani, Christian Democrat, succeeds in forming ministry, 22 July.

29 earthquake hits Agadir in Morocco, the worst earthquake recorded in Africa; 12,000 are killed.

C **March**

5 President Sukarno suspends Indonesian parliament; on 27, announces formation of 'Mutual Co-operation' legislature, to comprise members nominated by himself (meets on 25 June).

15 ten-power disarmament committee meets in Geneva (–27 June, when Soviet and East European delegates walk out).

15 presidential election held in South Korea, which is won by 85-year-old Syngman Rhee by fraudulent methods; demonstrations spread throughout the country; on 27 April, the four-times president resigns following loss of support from army and USA.

19 general election in Ceylon (now Sri Lanka), in which the two main parties win a

similar number of seats; on 21, Dudley Senanayake, United National Party, forms ministry but it is defeated on confidence vote on 22 April, when new elections are called.

21 in South Africa, the 'Sharpeville massacre': at Sharpeville township near Vereeniging (S of Johannesburg) members of the Pan-Africanist Congress demonstrate against pass laws; the police panic and shoot into the crowd, killing 69 Africans and wounding 186.

30 following demonstrations, strikes, and marches by Africans, the South African government proclaims a state of emergency (–31 Aug) and passes the Unlawful Organizations Act; on April 8, the African National Congress and Pan-African Congress are banned (Nelson Mandela and others form Umkonto we Sizwe, 'Spear of the Nation', as the guerrilla wing of the ANC).

D **April**

1 In Nyasaland (now Zimbabwe), nationalist leader Dr Hastings Banda is released from prison (15 June, state of emergency lifted).

9 in South Africa, Hendrik Verwoerd, prime minister, is shot and wounded by David Pratt, a wealthy European farmer and businessman who had been refused a visa to visit his second wife in the Netherlands.

27 (–4 May) constitutional conference in London on future of Sierra Leone proposes independence in April 1961.

27 the French-governed part of Togoland becomes the independent Republic of Togo, Africa's smallest independent country.

28 (–25 May) in Turkey, students demonstrate in Ankara and Istanbul.

E **May**

1 In USSR, Soviet military forces shoot down a US high-altitude U-2 spy aircraft over the Ural Mountains, flown by Gary Powers (19 Aug, Powers is sentenced to 10 years' imprisonment for espionage).

3 European Free Trade Association (EFTA) comes into force, with 20 per cent tariff cuts between members from July.

7 Leonid Brezhnev replaces Marshal Klement Voroshilov as president of the USSR.

16 (–19) summit meeting in Paris, France, of Nikita Khrushchev (USSR), Harold Macmillan (Britain), President Eisenhower (USA), and Charles de Gaulle (France); Khrushchev uses the U-2 incident to break up the summit, when President Eisenhower refuses to give a public apology for the

case, the jury rules that *Lady Chatterley's Lover* by D H Lawrence is not obscene (2 Nov); Penguin Books stand by with 200,000 copies for sale (during the trial, the prosecuting lawyer asks if it is a book one would allow one's 'wife or servants' to read).

International Development Association, a lending agency under the World Bank, begins operations.

In Britain, foundation of the National Economic Development Council (known as 'Neddy'), with representatives from government, management, and unions (Trades Union Congress makes decision to join on 14 Feb 1962).

Seven Latin American countries establish the Latin American Free Trade Association (18 Feb).

In Britain, the Guillebaud Committee's report on railwaymen's pay embodies principle of fair comparison with other employment (published 3 March).

Collectivization of East Germany's agriculture completed (14 April).

Kariba Dam, Rhodesia (now Zimbabwe), opened (17 May).

Britain, France, Netherlands, and USA sign agreement to provide a Caribbean organization for economic and social co-operation (21 June); it replaces the Caribbean Commissions founded in 1949.

Meeting in Baghdad, Iraq (Sept) of representatives of Iran, Iraq, Kuwait, Saudi Arabia, and Venezuela votes to establish the Organization of Petroleum-Exporting Countries (OPEC), a permanent organization to represent their oil interests (OPEC formed in 1961).

India and Pakistan treaty on Indus waters development (19 Sept).

In Cuba, land expropriation continues; in July the government seizes the Shell and Esso oil refineries; in July the USA suspends purchases of sugar.

Walt W Rostow, *The Stages of Economic Growth: A Non-Communist Manifesto*.

P Society, Education, and Religion

'The Pill' (oral contraceptive tablet for women) is introduced in the USA for general use as a contraceptive (approved by Food and Drug Administration 9 May).

In USA, sit-ins begin (2 Feb) in Greensboro, North Carolina, to protest against segregated lunch counters; Martin Luther King is arrested in Georgia; the Student Nonviolent Co-ordinating Committee (SNCC) is founded to organize civil rights campaigning.

Civil Rights bill for safeguarding African-

Americans' voting rights passes US Senate (10 April).

UN Food and Agriculture Organization launches Freedom from Hunger Campaign (1 July).

West Germany agrees to compensate French victims of Nazi persecution (15 July).

Neo-Nazi groups are banned in West Germany after antisemitic incidents.

California passes New York as the US state with the largest population.

Robert Blood and Donald Wolfe, *Husbands and Wives: The Dynamics of Married Living*.

R D Laing, *The Divided Self*.

The education of women is permitted in Saudi Arabia.

In Britain, Masters of Arts of the University of Oxford elect Prime Minister Harold Macmillan as chancellor (5 March; installed on 1 May).

Beloe Report in Britain advocates a secondary-school examination for average and below-average children.

Education Act increased the central government's control of education (Czechoslovakia).

Jerome S Bruner, *The Process of Education*.

A S Neill, *Summerhill*.

Three women are admitted to the pastorate of the Swedish Lutheran Church.

Kneel-in campaign by African-Americans in segregated churches in US Southern States.

Bishop Ambrose Reeves of Johannesburg is expelled from South Africa for his protest against the Sharpeville Massacre.

Dr Geoffrey Fisher, archbishop of Canterbury, visits Jerusalem, Istanbul, and Rome.

A church in Herne Bay, Kent, SE England, is dedicated for use jointly by Anglicans and Methodists.

A M Ramsey, *From Gore to Temple*.

Q Science, Technology, and Discovery

US bathyscaphe *Trieste*, designed by Belgian marine biologist Professor Auguste Piccard, dives to the bottom of Challenger Deep, of the Pacific island of Guam, about 10,600 m/35,800 ft.

US nuclear-powered submarine Triton makes an underwater circumnavigation of the globe, taking 84 days (Feb–May).

Twenty artificial satellites are in orbit.

US Air Force recovers *Discoverer* satellite from Pacific, and USSR recovers dogs that made 17 orbits of the Earth.

USA launches *Tiros 1*, a weather satellite (2 April), and a radio-reflector satellite (12 Aug).

US physicist T H Maiman develops the prototype laser (Light Amplification by Stimu-

incident and to pledge that there would be no further intrusions into Soviet air space.

23 Israel announces arrest (after abduction in Argentina) of Adolf Eichmann, who had been responsible for organizing the Germans' mass extermination of Jews in World War II.

27 in Turkey, following a period of unrest (including a battle with inkpots and furniture in the National Assembly), the military overthrows President Adnan Menderes; General Cemal Gürsel assumes presidency.

27 USA ends aid to Cuba.

F **June**

14 President de Gaulle renews offer to Algerian provisional government to negotiate cease-fire; the Front for National Liberation (FLN) agrees, but rejects subsequent French conditions.

15 Japanese students riot in protest against Mutual Co-operation and Security Treaty with USA; planned visit by President Eisenhower is postponed (19, Japanese Diet ratifies treaty).

24 Greece, Yugoslavia, and Turkey dissolve Balkan alliance of Aug 1954.

26 Madagascar proclaimed independent as the Malagasy Republic (remains within the French Community; 20 Sept, admitted to UN).

26 British Somaliland becomes independent and, on 27, joins Somalia.

30 Belgian Congo becomes independent as the Congo Republic (now Zaire), with Joseph Kasavubu as president and Patrice Lumumba prime minister.

G **July**

1 Soviet military shoot down US aircraft over the Barents Sea, N of the Russian mainland.

1 Britain and Cyprus settle final terms for independence of Cyprus, including conditions for British bases (on 10, announcement that power will be transferred on 16 Aug).

5 (–6) in Congo Republic (now Zaire), the army mutinies; Europeans flee from Léopoldville (now Kinshasa) area to Brazzaville (French Congo).

8 Belgium sends troops to Congo Republic; Patrice Lumumba appeals to the UN for military assistance.

11 in Congo Republic, Moïse Tshombe, prime minister of Katanga province, proclaims independence.

11 (–12), France agrees to independence from Aug of the Republics of Dahomey (now Benin), Niger, Upper Volta (now Burkina

Faso), Ivory Coast, Chad, Central Africa (now the Central African Republic), and Congo.

14 government of the Congo Republic (now Zaire) severs relations with Belgium.

15 UN emergency force arrives in Congo Republic.

18 following the cancellation of President Eisenhower's visit to Japan, Nobusuke Kishi resigns as prime minister; succeeded by Hayato Ikeda.

19 USSR protests at US proposal to equip West German army with Polaris missile.

20 Poland asks NATO powers to acknowledge Oder–Neisse line, the border of Poland with East Germany (12 Aug, Britain states that Germany's frontiers depend on achieving a peace treaty).

20 end of general election in Ceylon (now Sri Lanka), which is won by the Sri Lanka Freedom Party; on 21, Mrs Sirimavo Bandaranaike, widow of the prime minister assassinated in the previous September, is appointed prime minister (the first woman prime minister of the Commonwealth).

25 (–4 Aug) constitutional conference held in London on future of Nyasaland (now Malawi); reaches agreement on new constitution (to be implemented after review of the Central African Federation).

27 in Britain, Derick Heathcoat Amory retires as chancellor of the exchequer; replaced by Selwyn Lloyd, who is replaced as foreign secretary by the Earl of Home.

31 official end of the 'Malayan Emergency' (operations against Communist insurgents in Malaya, from 1948 onwards).

H **August**

8 UN demands evacuation of Belgian troops from Congo Republic (last leave, 2 Sept).

8 (–9) coup in Laos, by parachute battalion; leads to appointment of General Souvanna Phoumi on 17 Aug.

12 government of Ceylon (now Sri Lanka) takes over press.

12 in Congo Republic, Dag Hammarskjöld, UN secretary general, and UN troops enter Katanga province.

15 President Sukarno of Indonesia announces nominated membership of new People's Consultative Congress, intended as the highest authority in the state (first meets on 10 Nov).

16 Cyprus becomes an independent republic with Archbishop Makarios as president and Turkish Cypriot Dr Fazil Kütchük as vice-president.

25 manifesto of the Soviet Communist Party condemns dogmatism of Chinese leader Mao Zedong.

lated Emission of Radiation), a device producing an intense beam of parallel light.

Surgeons at Birmingham, England, develop a pacemaker for the heart.

German chemist K H Hofman synthesizes pituitary hormone.

British chemist G N Robinson discovers methicillin, an antibiotic drug.

British biophysicist J C Kendrew elucidates three-dimensional structure of the protein myoglobin.

Chlorophyll is synthesized simultaneously by Martin Strell of Munich, Germany, and R B Woodward of Harvard University, USA.

R **Humanities**

In Egypt, archaeologists begin saving treasures in Aswan High Dam region of Nubia before flooding begins.

Excavations at Stonehenge, S England, by officials of Ministry of Works.

Further Biblical texts are discovered in Dead Sea region.

B H Slicher von Bath, *Agrarian History of Western Europe, 500–1850.*

Gideon Sjoberg, *The Preindustrial City, Past and Present.*

Philippe Ariès, *Centuries of Childhood: A Social History of Family Life.*

Henry Steele Commager, *The Era of Reform.*

L M Thompson, *The Unification of South Africa, 1902–1910.*

William L Shirer, *The Rise and Fall of the Third Reich.*

Welsh History Review issued (–).

E H Gombrich, *Art and Illusion.*

Friedrich von Hayek, *The Constitution of Liberty.*

Hans-Georg Gadamer, *Truth and Method.*

W V Quine, *Word and Object.*

S **Art, Sculpture, Fine Arts, and Architecture**

First manifesto of Nouveau Réalisme, Paris.

Painting, etc:

Jim Dine, *Car Crash*, a Happening.

David Hockney, *Adhesiveness.*

Jasper Johns, *Painting with 2 Balls.*

Yves Klein, first *Anthropométries*, a Happening in which women's bodies are used as paintbrushes.

Mark Rothko, *Black on Dark Sienna on Purple.*

Frank Stella, *Six Mile Bottom.*

Cy Twombly, *School of Fontainebleau.*

Andy Warhol, *Superman.*

Sculpture:

Musée Léger opened at Biot, France, with the 'Children's Garden' in the forecourt.

Arman, *Portrait Robot d'Iris Clert.*

Jasper Johns, *Painted Bronze* (Ale Cans).

Edward Kienholz, *And Sugerplums Danced in Their Heads.*

Piero Manzoni, *Artist's Shit.*

Niki de Saint-Phalle, *Two Guns and One Knife.*

George Segal, first sculptures cast using live models encased in plaster.

Jean Tinguely, *Striptease Machine.*

Architecture:

Brasilia, the new capital of Brazil, is officially opened.

Frank Lloyd Wright, Guggenheim Museum, New York, completed.

T **Music**

Jean Barraqué, *au delà du hazard.*

Luciano Berio, *Circles.*

Benjamin Britten, *A Midsummer Night's Dream* (opera).

Olivier Messiaen, *Chronochromie.*

Krzysztof Penderecki, *Threnody for the Victims of Hiroshima.*

William Walton, Symphony No. 2.

Camelot (musical), by Alan Jay Lerner (first performed at the Majestic Theatre, New York, 3 Dec).

Oliver! (musical), text and music by Lionel Bart (first performed at the Wimbledon Theatre, London, 10 June).

Ray Charles, 'Georgia On My Mind'.

Eddie Cochran, 'Three Steps to Heaven'.

Lonnie Donegan, 'My Old Man's a Dustman'.

Everly Brothers, 'Cathy's Clown'.

Johnny Mathis, 'The Shadow of Your Smile'.

Edith Piaf, 'Non, je ne regrette rien'.

Jim Reeves, 'He'll Have to Go'.

First public performance by John Lennon, Paul McCartney, George Harrison, and Pete Best as The Beatles (in Hamburg, West Germany).

U **Literature and Drama**

John Barth, *The Sot-Weed Factor.*

John Betjeman, *Summoned by Bells.*

Lawrence Durrell, *Clea.*

Gunner Ekelöf, *A Moelna Elegy.*

George Friel, *The Bank of Time.*

Randall Jarrell, *The Woman at the Washington Zoo* (poems).

John Knowles, *A Separate Peace.*

Alain Robbe-Grillet, *Dans la labyrinthe.*

I B Singer, *The Magician of Lublin.*

Gary Snyder, *Myths and Texts.*

John Updike, *Rabbit Run.*

Drama:

Edward Albee, *The Sandbox.*

Robert Bolt, *A Man For All Seasons.*

Eugène Ionesco, *The Rhinoceros.*

Harold Pinter *The Caretaker.*

Murray Schisgal, *The Typists.*

Arnold Wesker, *I'm Talking About Jerusalem.*

29 assassination of Hazza el-Majali, prime minister of Jordan (by bombs thought to have been placed by Syrian intelligence agents).

30 East Germany imposes partial blockade of West Berlin (further restrictions on entry, 8 Sept).

J September

2 USSR provides aircraft for Patrice Lumumba in the Congo Republic.

2 Cuba recognizes Communist China and denounces 1952 military aid treaty with USA.

5 President Kasavubu of Congo Republic (now Zaire) dismisses Prime Minister Patrice Lumumba; Joseph Ileo forms ministry.

10 Prince Boun Oum of S Laos declares martial law throughout Laos.

23 Nikita Khrushchev of USSR addresses UN General Assembly on colonial peoples and disarmament, attacking the Western World and especially the USA. (On 29, during Harold Macmillan's speech, Khrushchev bangs on desk with shoe; Macmillan responds: 'Mr President, perhaps we could have a translation, I could not quite follow.')

28 NATO introduces unified system of air defence command.

K October

1 Nigerian Federation becomes independent, with Nnamdi Azikiwe as governor general.

5 in, Britain, the Labour Party Conference votes in favour of unilateral nuclear disarmament against the policy of the Leader, Hugh Gaitskell.

6 referendum in South African favours establishment of republic (52.14 per cent of votes in favour, 47.42 against).

11 publication in Britain of the Monckton Report on the Constitution of Rhodesia and Nyasaland (Central African Federation); recommends continuation of the Federation for economic reasons, but advocates a devolution of many powers to the territories, a broader franchise, greater participation of Africans in the Assembly, and removal of discriminatory legislation.

15 in Turkey, 800 members of former President Menderes' régime are put on trial, charged with corruption.

19 US imposes embargo on shipments to Cuba.

L November

1 In Britain, Prime Minister Harold Macmillan announces plan to provide facilities for US Polaris-armed submarines at Holy Loch in Scotland.

8 in US presidential election, John F Kennedy, Democrat, wins 303 electoral votes over Richard Nixon, Republican, with 219; popular vote: Kennedy, 34,227,096; Nixon, 34,108,546; 502,773 for minor candidates. Democrats lose 21 seats in House of Representatives.

25 after four months of unrest, parliament of South Rhodesia (now Zimbabwe) passes the Law and Order Maintenance Act, despite protests from churches, the bar, and the press; the Act gives the police extra powers and provides heavy penalties for many offences (1 Nov, the Chief Justice of the Central African Federation resigns in protest).

26 general election in New Zealand is won by the National Party with 46 seats over Labour with 34; Keith Holyoake is appointed prime minister and his government sworn in on 12 Dec.

28 Mauritania proclaims independence from France as Islamic Republic.

M December

Announcement in North Vietnam of the formation of the National Front for the Liberation of South Vietnam and its military arm, the National Liberation Army, known as the Vietcong ('Vietnamese Communists'); it aims to replace President Diem's government and unite Vietnam.

2 Britain refuses request of Buganda (in Uganda) for independence.

5 opening in London of constitutional conference to review future of Central African Federation (adjourned on 17; territorial conference on Southern Rhodesia met between same dates; Northern Rhodesia conference met and adjourned, 19–20 Dec).

9 General Souvanna Phouma and ministers flee from Laos to Cambodia, following rebellion of General Phoumi and Prince Boun Oum; on 13 Dec, the prince is approved as new prime minister by the Assembly and the king.

14 convention of Organization for Economic Co-operation and Development (OECD) signed in Paris, France, by USA, Canada, and 18 member countries of the Organization for European Economic Co-operation (OEEC), replacing the OEEC and providing an Atlantic economic community.

21 King Saud takes over Saudi Arabian government on resignation of prime minister, Emir Faisal.

31 Cuba requests UN Security Council to consider its complaint about US aggression.

Beyond the Fringe, satirical revue starring Alan Bennett, Peter Cook, Jonathan Miller, and Dudley Moore (first presented at the 'fringe' of the Edinburgh Festival and in London from 10 May 1961, in New York from 27 Oct 1962).

In Britain, inauguration of the Royal Shakespeare Company; in addition to its theatre at Stratford-Upon-Avon, it acquires the Aldwych Theatre, London.

v Births and Deaths

Jan 4 Albert Camus dies (46).
May 30 Boris Pasternak dies (69).
May 31 Walter Funk dies (69).
July 6 Aneurin Bevin dies (62).
July 16 Albert Kesselring dies (74).
Aug 19 Lewis Namier dies (72).
Aug 23 Oscar Hammerstein dies (65).
Sept 9 Jussi Bjoerling dies (49).
Sept 27 Sylvia Pankhurst dies (78).
Nov 5 Mack Sennett dies (80).

w Everyday Life

Häagen-Dazs ice cream is devised in the Bronx, New York.

Pentel felt-tip pens are sold in Japan.

The Twist is the dance craze of the year.

Go-karting becomes popular.

In Britain, Queen Elizabeth II announces that all her descendants, except those enjoying the style of Royal Highness, will bear the name Mountbatten-Windsor (8 Feb).

In Britain, Princess Margaret marries Antony Armstrong-Jones (6 May).

King Baudouin of Belgium marries Doña Fabiola of Spain (14 Dec).

x Sport and Recreation

In football, Real Madrid win the European Cup for the fifth successive season, beating Eintracht Frankfurt 7–3 at Hampden Park, Glasgow (18 May).

In beating Ingemar Johansson in five rounds of their fight in New York, Floyd Patterson becomes the first boxer to regain the World Heavyweight title (20 June).

Armin Hary of West Germany becomes the first man to run 100 m in 10 seconds (21 June).

Eighty-four nations compete in the 17th Olympic Games, held in Rome (25 Aug–11 Sept). The USSR wins 43 gold medals; the USA, 34; Italy, 13; West Germany, 10; Australia, 8; Turkey, 7, Hungary, 6. Cassius Clay of the USA wins the light-heavyweight boxing gold.

In USA, the American Football League (AFL) is formed to challenge the National Football League (NFL).

The first cricket Test between Australia and the West Indies in Brisbane, Australia, ends with scores level. It is the first Test Match to end in a tie (9–14 Dec).

Francis Chichester of Britain wins the first solo Transatlantic race from Plymouth, SW England, to Newport, Rhode Island, USA, in his yacht *Gypsy Moth III*.

y Media

In Britain, the *Manchester Guardian* is renamed the *Guardian*.

The British newspaper the *Sunday Graphic* is closed down.

Film:

À Bout de Souffle (director, Jean-Luc Godard; starring Jean-Paul Belmondo).

The Apartment (starring Jack Lemmon and Walter Matthau).

L'Avventura (director, Michelangelo Antonioni).

La Dolce Vita (director, Federico Fellini).

The Entertainer (director, Tony Richardson; starring Laurence Olivier).

Exodus (director, Otto Preminger).

I'm Alright Jack (director, John Boulting; starring Ian Carmichael and Peter Sellers).

The Magnificent Seven (director, John Sturges; starring Yul Brynner and Steve McQueen).

Never on Sunday (starring Melina Mercouri).

Psycho (director, Alfred Hitchcock).

Rocco and his Brothers (director, Luchino Visconti).

Saturday Night and Sunday Morning (director, Karel Reisz; starring Albert Finney).

Shadows (the cinema of improvisation).

Sons and Lovers (director, Ken Russell).

Spartacus (director, Stanley Kubrick; starring Kirk Douglas).

Television:

In USA, presidential candidates John F Kennedy and Richard Nixon debate on television, establishing a precedent for several subsequent elections (26 Sept); viewers consider the outcome to be a draw.

New programmes in Britain include: *Coronation Street* (Granada), which becomes Britain's most successful 'soap opera'; *Danger Man*, starring Patrick McGoohan; *The Flying Doctor*; *How Green Was My Valley*; *Maigret* (–1963); *Soldier Soldier*, by John Arden; *A Walk in the Desert*, by John Whiting, the first in the BBC series *The Sunday-Night Play*.

Tales of the Riverbank is produced in Canada.

Army revolt in Algeria ... South Africa becomes republic ...
Building of the Berlin Wall ... Death of Dag Hammarskjöld in the
Congo ...

A January

3 USA severs diplomatic relations with Cuba.

6 Dag Hammarskjöld, United Nations secretary general, visits South Africa to discuss apartheid.

6 referendum held in Algeria (–8), France (on 8), and other French territories (also on 8) on President de Gaulle's policy for Algeria; 75 per cent of voters in France support the policy, and 69 per cent in Algeria (though the FLN boycott the referendum); policy is for Algeria to vote on self-determination and France to ratify the outcome.

7 Casablanca Conference of heads of state in Africa; adopts African Charter, which provides for the establishment of four permanent committees to coordinate policies.

17 in Congo Republic (now Zaire), Patrice Lumumba, the former prime minister, is killed near Elisabethville (now Lubumbashi) by agents of President Tshombe's government in Katanga province.

20 John F Kennedy is inaugurated as 35th president of the USA (the first Roman Catholic and the youngest person to be elected).

26 Britain and United Arab Republic (Egypt and Syria) resume full relations.

28 Rwanda provisional government proclaims republic, and is placed under UN trusteeship.

31 (–17 Feb) the constitutional conference on Northern Rhodesia (now Zambia) reconvenes in London, but two African parties boycott the talks; no agreement is reached.

B February

4 (–5) Nationalist disturbances in Luanda, in the Portuguese territory of Angola (15 March, outbreak of revolt in northern provinces, with attacks on Portuguese settlers).

9 in Congo Republic (now Zaire), President Kasavubu issues decree establishing a government with Joseph Ileo as prime minister.

10 USA relinquishes rights in many defence bases in West Indies (acquired under 1941 agreement with Britain).

11 plebiscite held in British-administered Cameroon, supervised by UN; the north votes to join Nigeria, the south to join the Republic of Cameroon.

21 UN Security Council adopts resolution authorizing UN forces to use force to prevent the outbreak of civil war in the Congo Republic (now Zaire); calls for Congo parliament to convene and foreign advisers to leave the country.

22 Nikita Khrushchev of USSR wages campaign against Dag Hammarskjöld, UN secretary general, and calls on commission of African states to supervise restoration of an independent Congo.

27 Britain and Iceland settle fisheries dispute: after three years, British ships will not fish within 19.2 km/12 mi of Iceland's coast.

C March

8 (–17) meeting of Commonwealth prime ministers in London; Hendrik Verwoerd announces that South Africa will leave the Commonwealth on 31 May.

8 (–12) conference of political leaders from Congo Republic (now Zaire) in Tananarive (now Antananarivo) in Madagascar; agrees on formation of confederation of 18 states.

9 Dalai Lama appeals to UN to restore independence of Tibet.

26 in Belgian elections, Christian Socialists lose overall majority and form coalition government with Socialists; Théodore Lefèvre succeeds Gaston Eyskens (both Christian Socialists) as prime minister.

26 President Kennedy of USA meets Harold Macmillan, prime minister of Britain, at Key West, Florida, USA, to discuss the situation in Laos.

29 28 people (including Nelson Mandela) tried for treason in South Africa are all acquitted.

D April

7 UN General Assembly condemns South African policies in South West Africa (a UN Mandate, now Namibia).

11 Nigeria imposes boycott on trade with South Africa.

12 USSR puts first person in space, Yuri Gagarin, who orbits the Earth and returns after flight lasting 108 minutes (5 May, US astronaut Alan Shepard makes 15-minute suborbital flight).

13 UN General Assembly condemns apartheid in South Africa.

17 1,500 Cuban exiles, trained by US military instructors, invade Cuba; an expected sympathetic rising fails to occur and the invaders are killed or captured.

18 following elections in Kenya, the Kenya African Democratic Union agrees to join the government provided that a house is

Trial of Adolf Eichmann in Israel ... Hart's Concept of Law ...
Michael Ramsey becomes Archbishop of Canterbury ... Christo's
first project for a wrapped building ...

o Politics, Government, Law, and Economy

US Supreme Court rules (5 June) that Communist Party should register as a foreign-dominated organization (Party refuses, 17 Nov).

R Dahl, *Who Governs?*.

V O Key, *Public Opinion and American Democracy*.

Theodore White, *The Making of the President, 1960*.

In Israel, Adolf Eichmann is tried and found guilty of crimes against the Jewish people during the Holocaust (executed 31 May 1962).

Hannah Arendt, *Eichmann in Jerusalem*.

In USA, the retiring president, Dwight Eisenhower, warns Americans of the danger of allowing too much influence to what he calls the 'military–industrial complex' (17 Jan).

First successful hijacking of airliner (lands in Havana, Cuba, 27 Dec).

The 23rd Amendment to the US Constitution gives residents of the District of Columbia (i.e., the capital, controlled by Congress) a vote in presidential elections.

In Britain, a ring of five people led by Gordon Lonsdale (and known as the 'Portland Spies', because they passed on information from the Underwater Warfare Establishment at Portland in S England) are convicted of spying (March).

In Britain, the KGB spy and former diplomat George Blake pleads guilty to espionage and is sentenced to 42 years in prison (3 May).

In British House of Commons, 67 Conservative backbench members support an amendment to Criminal Justice Bill to bring back the birch (11 April).

In Britain, the Committee of Privileges of the House of Commons reports that the 2nd Viscount Stansgate, Mr A N Wedgwood Benn, ceased to be a member of the House on succeeding to his peerage; a by-election is held (4 May) in Benn's constituency (Bristol SE), which returns Benn, but he is refused admission to the Commons (8 May).

H L A Hart, *The Concept of Law*.

Latin American Free Trade Area and Alliance for Progress in force (from 2 June); aims to cement free trade, growth, and US economic interests in the western hemisphere.

Organization for Economic Co-operation and Development (OECD) founded (from 30 Sept), as successor to the Organization for European Economic Co-operation (OEEC); the OECD includes the USA and Canada among its founder members.

Eight-year development plan launched in Indonesia, to achieve 'Indonesian socialism'.

South Africa introduces new decimal coinage, the Rand (in force from 14 Feb).

The national electrical grids of France and Britain are connected by cable.

Britain imports methane from the Sahara to supplement coal-gas.

P Society, Education, and Religion

In USA, the Campaign for Racial Equality (CORE) organizes the Freedom Rides; a group of people travel around the South to check that bus services have introduced desegregation; the riders face violent opposition.

Oral contraceptive pill licensed for use in Britain (on sale from 30 Jan).

New Zealand introduces compulsory selective national service (14 Sept).

President Nasser confiscates property of wealthy Egyptians (21 Oct).

John F Kennedy establishes Peace Corps of Young Americans for overseas service (1 March).

Frantz Fanon, *The Wretched of the Earth*.

Michel Foucault, *Madness and Civilisation*.

M Harrington, *The Other America*.

Jane Jacobs, *The Death and Life of Great American Cities*.

Michael Young, *The Rise of the Meritocracy*.

In England, foundation of the University of Sussex, at Falmer near Brighton (buildings designed by Basil Spence).

Michael Ramsey appointed 100th Archbishop of Canterbury (19 Jan) following announcement of retirement of Archbishop Fisher (Ramsey enthroned 27 June 1961).

Papal Encyclicals issued on Catholic Social Doctrine (*Mater at Magistra*) and on Christian reconciliation under Roman Primacy (*Aeterna Dei*).

The first Pan-Orthodox Conference meets at Rhodes.

Delhi meeting of World Council of Churches is joined by members of Russian Orthodox Church and of Pentecostal Churches of Chile, and is attended by Roman Catholic observers.

The International Missionary Council is integrated with the World Council of Churches.

built for Jomo Kenyatta in Kiambu district (Kenyatta is released by governor, 14 Aug).

21 in Algeria, revolt by army rebels under General Maurice Challe, members of the OAS (Secret Army Organization); President de Gaulle declares a state of emergency in France on 23; the coup collapses on 26; rebel leaders are tried on 11 July, and eight are sentenced to death (including General Raoul Salan, who was tried in absentia).

24 at Coquilhatville conference of Congolese delegates, President Tshombe of Katanga province denounces President Kasavubu's agreement with UN and is arrested after walking out of conference.

27 British territory of Sierra Leone becomes independent within the Commonwealth.

E May

1 UN Trust Territory of Tanganyika (now Tanzania) achieves internal self-government with Julius Nyerere as prime minister.

1 Kwame Nkrumah takes control of Convention People's Party in Ghana.

2 warring factions in Laos agree to ceasefire; on 8 an International Control Commission arrives in the country.

9 Ali Amini, new prime minister of Iran, dissolves parliament and bans political meetings.

16 (–July 1962) 14-nation conference on Laos convened in Geneva, Switzerland (soon becomes bogged down).

24 Cyprus becomes 16th member of Council of Europe.

27 Tunku Abdul Rahman, prime minister of Malaya, proposes formation of a Greater Malaysian Federation.

29 Western European Union agrees that West Germany will be allowed to build destroyers equipped to fire nuclear weapons.

31 South Africa becomes an independent republic outside the Commonwealth, with C R Swart as president.

31 Ghana refuses to recognize South Africa.

F June

4 Nikita Khrushchev of USSR proposes to President Kennedy of USA a German peace conference to conclude a treaty and establish Berlin as a free city; also proposes that disarmament discussions should proceed simultaneously with talks about ban on nuclear tests (rejected by West, 17 July).

9 UN calls on Portugal to cease repressive measures in Angola.

13 Austria refuses application of Archduke Otto von Habsburg to return as a private individual.

19 by arrangement, Kuwait abrogates its agreement with Britain of 1899 (Britain declares itself ready to assist Kuwait if necessary).

19 US and USSR representatives begin disarmament talks in Washington, DC, USA.

22 President Tshombe of Katanga province in the Congo (now Zaire) is freed.

25 General Abdul Karim Kassem, prime minister of Iraq, declares Kuwait an integral part of Iraq and calls upon Kuwait to surrender to Iraq.

30 following Iraq's threat to Kuwait, Britain sends troops (withdrawn by 13 Aug, when Arab troops under Saudi command are in position).

G July

10 (–25) Kwame Nkrumah, president of Ghana, visits USSR.

20 Kuwait is admitted to Arab League, but membership of UN is vetoed by USSR (30 Nov).

22 UN orders ceasefire in Tunisia, after clashes between French and Tunisians.

25 emergency Budget in Britain: Chancellor Selwyn Lloyd introduces wages pause; bank rate is raised from 5 to 7 per cent.

26 parliament of Congo Republic meets at Léopoldville (now Kinshasa); confirms President Kasavubu's choice of prime minister, Cyrille Adoula.

26 referendum in South Rhodesia (now Zimbabwe) approves new constitution (approved in Britain by order in council on 6 Dec).

H August

10 Britain applies for membership of the European Economic Community.

13 East Germany seals off border between East and West Berlin, closing the Brandenburg Gate.

15 general election held in Nyasaland (now Malawi), under constitution agreed in 1960; Dr Hastings Banda's Malawi Congress Party (MCP) is victorious (new ministers, including Dr Banda, are sworn in on 12 Sept); the MCP demands an end to the Central African Federation.

17 (–18) East German building workers construct the Berlin Wall, a near-impregnable physical barrier sealing off West Berlin and preventing the escape of East Germans to the West.

19 President Kennedy of USA sends Vice-President Lyndon Johnson to Berlin to

Closure of Synagogues in Moscow.

In USA, the Evangelical and Reformed Church unites with the Congregational Christian Churches to form the United Church of Christ (July).

The New English Bible, New Testament (complete Bible published in 1970).

N Zernov, *Eastern Christendom*.

Q Science, Technology, and Discovery

The Atlas computer, the world's largest, is installed at Harwell, Britain, to aid atomic research and weather forecasting.

British astronomer Martin Ryle concludes from radio-astronomical observations that the universe changes with time; his burial of 'the steady state' theory is challenged by Fred Hoyle.

British chemist Francis Crick and South African chemist Sydney Brenner claim to determine the structure of deoxyribonucleic acid (DNA), thus breaking the genetic code.

Conference held in Tanganyika (now Tanzania) for preserving African wildlife (Sept).

World Wildlife Fund (now Worldwide Fund for Nature) established to promote conservation.

R Humanities

Graham Clarke, *World Prehistory*.

Colin McEvedy, *The Penguin Atlas of Medieval History*.

V H Galbraith, *The Making of Domesday Book*.

Lewis Mumford, *The City in History*.

J H Hexter, *Reappraisals in History*.

T G P Spear, *India: A Modern History*.

William A Williams, *The Contours of American History*.

Lee Benson, *The Concept of Jacksonian Democracy: New York as a Test Case*.

A J Marder, *From the Dreadnought to Scapa Flow* (–1970).

Fritz Fischer, *Germany's Aims in the First World War*.

A J P Taylor, *The Origins of the Second World War*.

Lord Hankey, *The Supreme Command*.

Michel Foucault, *History of Madness*.

Martin Heidegger, *Nietzsche*.

Ernest Nagel, *The Structure of Science*.

S Art, Sculpture, Fine Arts, and Architecture

Aristotle Contemplating the Bust of Homer by Rembrandt is bought by the Metropolitan Museum, New York, for $2,300,000 at auction, the highest price paid for a work of art at auction.

Exhibition 'Le Nouveau Réalisme à Paris et à New York' held in Paris, France.

Painting, etc:

Jean Dubuffet, 'Hourloupe' series.

David Hockney, *Typhoo Tea*.

Jasper Johns, *Map*.

Ellsworth Kelly, *Orange White*.

Roy Lichtenstein, *Popeye*.

Niki de Saint-Phalle, first *Tir* paintings; she shoots at canvas containing bags filled with paint and food; e.g., *Tir de Bob Rauschenberg*, *Tir de Jasper Johns*.

Tom Wesselman, *Great American Nude No. 1*.

Sculpture:

Anthony Caro, *Sculpture Three*.

Christo, first project for a wrapped building.

Jasper Johns, *The Critic Sees*.

Edward Kienholz, *Roxy's*.

Claes Oldenburg, *Lunch-Box*, *The Store*.

Larry Rivers and Jean Tinguely, *Turning Friendship of America and France*.

George Segal, *Gas Station*.

Architecture:

Philip Johnson, Amon Carter Museum, Fort Worth, Texas, USA.

In London, Hardwick's neo-classical arch at Euston Station is demolished, despite protests.

T Music

Luciano Berio, *Visage*.

Elliott Carter, Double Concerto for Harpsichord and Piano.

Hans Werner Henze, *Elegy for Young Lovers* (opera).

György Ligeti, *Atmosphères*.

Bohuslav Martinů, *The Greek Passion* (opera).

Luigi Nono, *Intolleranza 1960* (opera).

Robert Ward, *The Crucible* (opera).

British cellist Jacqueline du Pré makes her debut as a soloist in London, aged 16.

Soviet ballet star Rudolf Nureyev defects to the West while at Le Bourget airport, Paris (16 June).

Billy Fury, 'Halfway to Paradise'.

Bert Kaempfert, 'Wooden Heart'.

'Moon River' by Henry Mancini.

Elvis Presley, 'Are You Lonesome Tonight?'

Neil Sedaka, 'Happy Birthday, Sweet Sixteen'.

Helen Shapiro, 'Walking Back to Happiness'.

Debut of The Beatles at the Cavern Club, Liverpool, NW England (21 March).

Debut of Bob Dylan at the Gaslight Cafe in Greenwich Village, New York (6 Sept).

In Britain, formation of The Rolling Stones.

In USA, first elections to the Country Music Hall of Fame in Nashville, Tennessee.

assure Berliners that the USA guarantees their freedom.

21 election in British Guiana (now Guyana); Cheddi Jagan's People's Progressive Party retains power.

27 Ben Khedda replaces Ferhat Abbas as head of the Algerian Provisional Government.

J September

1 UN breaks off relations with government of Katanga in Congo (now Zaire); attempts of UN to arrest members of the government lead to heavy fighting in Elisabethville (now Lubumbashi) and Jadotville (now Likasi).

1 (–6), non-aligned powers meet in Belgrade, Yugoslavia, under Jawaharlal Nehru of India and Kwame Nkrumah of Ghana.

17 Christian Democratic Union and allies lose overall majority in West German elections.

17 (–18) Dag Hammarskjöld, UN secretary general (aged 56), is killed in air crash in Congo Republic while travelling to see President Tshombe of Katanga province (U Thant of Burma is acting secretary general from 3 Nov).

18 (–9 Oct) Uganda constitutional conference held in London; ends with agreement for internal self-government in Oct 1962.

19 referendum in Jamaica votes for secession from West Indies Federation.

28 in Ghana, President Kwame Nkrumah imprisons leading members of the opposition, claiming a plot to assassinate him.

28 army coup in Damascus, Syria; 29, Syria secedes from United Arab Republic and forms Syrian Arab Republic.

K October

4 At Conference in Blackpool, British Labour Party reverses vote of previous year's Conference and switches back from policy of unilateral to bilateral disarmament.

10 volcanic eruption in Tristan da Cunha; inhabitants are evacuated (return in 1963 and 1967).

27 Mauritania and Mongolia admitted to UN.

29 Constantine Karamanlis forms new ministry in Greece after victory of National Radical Union in elections.

L November

2 David Ben-Gurion forms new coalition in Israel after long negotiations.

8 start of negotiations for Britain's entry into the European Economic Community; Britain's chief negotiator is Edward Heath.

19 in South Rhodesia (now Zimbabwe), Garfield Todd holds inaugural meeting of Rhodesian New African Party.

21 British government fails to stop Electricity Council granting substantial wage increase, which defies wages pause.

24 President de Gaulle of France visits Harold Macmillan, the British prime minister.

24 UN General Assembly resolves to treat Africa as a denuclearized zone.

24 (–29) Reginald Maudling, British colonial secretary, visits Kenya to take soundings about the country's future; announces constitutional conference in Feb 1962.

M December

4 In general election in Barbados, the Labour Party led by Grantley Adams, prime minister of West Indies Federation, loses to the Democratic Labour Party of Errol Barrow, further weakening the Federation.

4 People's National Movement led by Eric Williams returns to power in Trinidad.

5 in the Congo Republic (now Zaire), following numerous attacks on UN personnel in Katanga province, Katangan forces attack UN positions (fighting continues until cease-fire on 18).

6 order in council made in Britain for Southern Rhodesian Constitution; to come into effect after holding of new elections.

9 in Southern Rhodesia (now Zimbabwe), the National Democratic Party is banned; within a week, its leader, Joshua Nkomo, founds the Zimbabwe African People's Union (ZAPU).

9 Tanzania becomes an independent state within the Commonwealth.

9 USSR breaks off relations with Albania.

15 UN General Assembly rejects Soviet proposal to admit People's Republic of China.

16 USA agrees to make loan to Ghana for Volta River project (for generation of hydro-electric power).

18 Indian forces invade the Portuguese territory of Goa, on India's E coast (Goa surrenders on 19).

21 President Tshombe of Katanga province in Congo Republic (now Zaire) agrees to end the province's secession.

21 (–22) President Kennedy of USA and Harold Macmillan of Britain meet in Bermuda to discuss relations with the USSR and nuclear weapons.

31 Lebanese army prevents *coup* of Syrian Popular Party in Beirut.

u Literature and Drama

M Anantanarayanan, *The Silver Pilgrimage*.
Robert Heinlein, *Stranger in a Strange Land*.
Joseph Heller, *Catch 22*.
Richard Hughes, *The Fox in the Attic*.
LeRoi Jones, *Preface to a Twenty Volume Suicide Note* (poems).
Iris Murdoch, *A Severed Head*.
V S Naipaul, *A House for Mr Biswas*.
R K Narayan, *The Maneater of Malgudi*.
Ogden Nash, *Collected Verse*.
J D Salinger, *Franny and Zooey*.
Muriel Spark, *The Prime of Miss Jean Brodie*.
Irving Stone, *The Agony and the Ecstasy*.
Philip Toynbee, *Pantaloon, or The Valediction*.
Patrick White, *Riders in the Chariot*.

Drama:

Edward Albee, *The American Dream*.
Jean Anouilh, *Becket*.
John Osborne, *Luther*.
Arnold Wesker, *The Kitchen*.
John Whiting, *The Devils*.

v Births and Deaths

Jan 17 Patrice Lumumba dies (35).
March 8 Thomas Beecham dies (81).
June 6 Carl Gustav Jung dies (85).
July 1 Lady Diana Spencer born (–).
July 2 Ernest Hemingway dies (61).
July 22 Lee De Forest dies (87).
Sept 18 Dag Hammarskjöld dies (56).
Sept 24 Sumner Welles dies (68).
Nov 2 James Thurber dies (66).

w Everyday Life

Last journey of *Orient Express*, Paris–Bucharest, after 78 years (28 May).
Twist dance craze in USA, generated by Chubby Checker's song 'The Twist'.

x Sport and Recreation

France wins the Rugby Union Five Nations Championship outright for the first time.
In soccer, Tottenham Hotspur is the first side to win both the English League and the Football Association Cup double since Aston Villa in 1897.
In baseball, Roger Maris of the New York Yankees hits a record 61 home runs in the season.
The maximum wage of £20 a week for English football league players is abolished;

Johnny Haynes of Fulham becomes the first English player to earn £100 a week.
Azam Khan of Pakistan wins his fourth consecutive British Open Squash title.
Antonio Abertondo of Argentina becomes the first swimmer to achieve a double crossing of the English Channel (Sept).

y Media

In USSR, foundation of the news agency Novosti, which distributes material to foreign publications as well as Soviet ones.
Royal Commission on British Press appointed (9 Feb).

Film:

Accatone (director, Pier Paolo Pasolini).
L'Année dernière à Marienbad (director, Alain Resnais).
Breakfast at Tiffany's (starring Audrey Hepburn).
El Cid (director, Anthony Mann; starring Charlton Heston).
Jules et Jim (director, François Truffaut; starring Jeanne Moreau).
The Misfits (script by Arthur Miller; director, John Huston; starring Clark Gable and Marilyn Monroe).
La Notte (director, Michelangelo Antonioni).
One Hundred and One Dalmatians (producer, Walt Disney).
A Taste of Honey (director, Tony Richardson).
Victim (starring Dirk Bogarde).
West Side Story (directors, Robert Wise and Jerome Robbins).
Whistle down the Wind (director, Bryan Forbes; starring Hayley Mills and Bernard Lee).
Yojimbo (director, Akira Kurosawa).

Radio:

In Britain, end of *Children's Hour*, broadcast since 1922 (April).

Television:

In USA, broadcast of *The Defenders* (CBS).
The Old Man and the Hawk, by Junichi Ushiyama, is broadcast by NTV in Japan.
In Britain, new programmes include: *The Avengers*, starring Patrick MacNee and Diana Rigg (–1969); *Chicago–Portrait of a City* (joint BBC and ABC production); *Comedy Playhouse*, the BBC's showcase for comic writing (– 1974); *Compact* (BBC), a 'soap opera'; *The Morecambe and Wise Show*; *Songs of Praise* (–); *Survival* (Anglia TV); and *Where the Difference Begins*, the first of a trilogy of plays by David Mercer.

*Independence of Algeria ... Cuba missile crisis ... Independence
of Tanzania ...*

A January

1 Western Samoa becomes first sovereign independent Polynesian State.

3 President Sukarno of Indonesia proclaims West New Guinea an independent province.

6 princes of Laos invited to Geneva, Switzerland, for joint negotiations.

9 trade pact between Cuba and USSR.

22 Julius Nyerere resigns in Tanganyika (now Tanzania), to devote himself to the Tanganyika African National Union; Rashidj Kawawa forms ministry.

25 African heads of state of Monrovia group (Liberia, Togo, Nigeria, and Cameroon) issue Lagos Charter for pan-African co-operation.

29 collapse of three-power conference (USA, USSR, Britain), on Discontinuance of Nuclear Weapon Tests, which had met 353 times at Geneva, Switzerland, since 31 Oct 1958.

B February

8 US military council established in South Vietnam.

10 Nikita Khrushchev of USSR proposes that an 18-nation disarmament committee should meet at summit level.

14 constitutional conference on Kenya opens in London; agreement is reached for establishment of two-chamber parliament and regional assemblies on 21 March.

16 anti-government riots in Georgetown, British Guiana (now Guyana), in protest at austerity measures in budget (announced 31 Jan).

17 (–19) general election in Malta, during which the Catholic Church attacks the Labour Party; election won by Dr Borg Olivier's Nationalist Party with 25 seats, with 16 to Labour, and 9 for other parties (3, Dr Borg Olivier, Nationalist, forms ministry in Malta).

C March

1 Uganda attains full internal self-government, with Benedicto Kiwanuka as prime minister.

2 Britain applies to join European Coal and Steel Community (and on 5, to join Euratom).

2 military coup in Burma (now Myanmar), when Ne Win overthrows U Nu.

14 17 foreign ministers attend disarmament conference in Geneva, Switzerland, but France refuses to participate.

14 in Britain, Eric Lubbock, Liberal, wins Orpington by-election with 7,855 majority, overturning a Conservative majority (in 1959) of 14,760.

18 following secret discussions (completed at Évian-les-Bains, France), the French government and the Provisional Government of Algeria make the 'Évian agreements'; a Provisional Muslim-French government is to be installed in Algeria and a referendum held on self-determination.

19 West Germany agrees to contribute to costs of the British Army of the Rhine (BAOR).

23 Scandinavian States of Nordic Council sign Helsinki Convention on Nordic Co-operation.

31 end of pay pause in Britain.

D April

11 Alexander Bustamante, Labour, forms ministry in Jamaica.

14 in France, Michel Debré, Radical, resigns as prime minister; succeeded, on 15, by Georges Pompidou, Gaullist.

18 following Jamaica's vote to leave the West Indies Federation (Sept 1961), Britain's Parliament passes the West Indies Act, dissolving the Federation.

20 rebel French leader in Algeria, Raoul Salan (who was tried in absentia in 1961) is captured in Algiers.

22 renewed fighting in Laos.

27 in the Central African Federation, the United Federal Party is returned in elections, which are boycotted by the European Opposition and all the African political parties.

E May

6 Antonio Segni elected president of Italy on 9th ballot.

7 negotiations held in Laos between leaders of the three warring parties; reach agreement on 12; Provisional Government of National Unity is established on 23.

24 Conference of Barbados, Windward, and Leeward Islands in London ends with proposal of the 'Little Eight' to form a new West Indies federation.

18 Progressive Conservatives lose overall majority in Canadian elections, but John Diefenbaker remains as prime minister; Conservatives win 116 seats, Liberals, 100, others, 49.

F June

22 Philippines claim part of British North Borneo.

Sampson's Anatomy of Britain ... *Establishment of the EEC's
Common Agricultural Policy ... Hitchcock's* The Birds ...

o Politics, Government, Law, and Economy

In USA, foundation of the Center for Strategic and International Studies (originally affiliated with Georgetown University).

In USA, the *Port Huron Declaration* of the Students for a Democratic Society sets the political agenda of the 'New Left'.

New constitution in Pakistan, establishing presidential government; the president is chief executive and appoints government ministers (constitution inducted and new National Assembly meets on 8 June).

Agreement between USA and USSR on co-operation for peaceful uses of outer space (5 Dec).

J P Mackintosh, *The British Cabinet.*

In Britain, a committee on reform of the House of Lords recommends that an heir should be able to disclaim his peerage (17 Dec).

In USA, the Supreme Court rules in Engel v. Vitale that prayers in public schools are unconstitutional (25 June).

In USA, the Supreme Court rules, in Baker v. Carr, that malapportionment is contrary to equal protection under the law and therefore unconstitutional; voting districts must be equalized.

In Britain, the Restrictive Practices Court rules that the Net Book Agreement (by which publishers set the retail price of books) is not against the public interest (Oct 30).

In Britain, six members of the Committee of 100 of the Campaign for Nuclear Disarmament (CND) are found guilty of a breach of the Official Secrets Act in conspiring to enter an air force base; sentenced to imprisonment (12 Feb).

South African General Law Amendment bill imposes death penalty for sabotage (12 May).

Milovan Djilas, former vice-president of Yugoslavia, is given further sentence for publishing *Conversations with Stalin* (14 May).

In Britain, W John Vassall, a clerk in the admiralty formerly stationed in Moscow, USSR, is sentenced to 18 years' imprisonment for spying (22 Oct).

In Britain, Lord Denning is appointed Master of the Rolls.

Second stage of integration of the European Economic Community, following agreement on the establishment of the Common Agricultural Policy (agreement reached 14 Jan, but backdated to 1 Jan).

British Budget introduces levy on speculative gains (9 April).

The US Congress passes President Kennedy's Trade Expansion Act (11 Oct), providing for the reduction or elimination of certain categories of tariffs.

In USA, the company Electronic Data Systems is founded by H Ross Perot.

Wal-Mart store opened in Rogers, Arkansas, USA; the chain expands rapidly.

Milton Friedman, *Capitalism and Freedom.*

p Society, Education, and Religion

In USA, the Committee on Equal Employment Opportunity is created, chaired by Vice-President Lyndon Johnson.

In USA, James Meredith gains admission to the University of Mississippi under federal guard against racist violence.

In Britain, the Commonwealth Immigrants Act, aiming to reduce immigration from the 'New Commonwealth', comes into force.

Hugh Hefner, *The Playboy Philosophy.*

Anthony Sampson, *The Anatomy of Britain.*

In Cambridge, England, the literary critic F R Leavis gives the Richmond Lecture in which he attacks C P Snow's argument about the emergence of 'two cultures', one humanist, the other scientific (expounded by Snow in his Rede Lecture of 1959).

In Austria, the School Organization Act introduces wide-ranging reforms in curricula and administration.

New technical schools introduced in Japan.

In Sweden, the Education Act creates mandatory nine-year comprehensive schools with a common curriculum in the lower and middle grades.

In England and Wales, the Ministry of Education set up a Curriculum Study Group.

University College of North Staffordshire in England becomes Keele University.

The Universities' Central Council on Admissions (UCCA) is established to provide a clearing house for university applicants in Britain.

United World College of the Atlantic is founded in Wales by Kurt Hahn.

Pope John XXIII insists on retention of Latin as the language of the Roman Catholic Church.

Second Vatican Council opens in Rome, with observer delegates from other Christian Churches; Pope John XXIII orders the controversial document on Sources of Revelation to be revised.

In USA, African-Americans are refused admission to the Mormon Priesthood.

26 Portuguese in Mozambique require Indian nationals to leave within three months of release from internment camps.

G **July**

1 Robert Soblen, sentenced to life imprisonment in USA for spying, arrives in London, following deportation from Jordan (British home secretary refuses to grant asylum and Soblen commits suicide, 11 Sept).

1 independence of Rwanda Republic and of Kingdom of Burundi.

3 France proclaims independence of Algeria, following referendum (on 1) of 91 per cent in favour; the Provisional Government in exile returns.

12 in Britain, the 'Night of Long Knives': Prime Minister Harold Macmillan dismisses seven of his cabinet, including Chancellor Selwyn Lloyd, in an attempt to retrieve Conservative fortunes; Reginald Maudling becomes chancellor of the exchequer.

20 conference in Geneva, Switzerland (sitting since May 1961), guarantees the neutrality of Laos (conference ends on 23; Laos reverts to civil war by early 1964).

31 Britain and Malayan governments sign agreement to establish a wider Malaysian Federation, by 31 Aug (including the Federation of Malaya, Singapore, Sarawak, and North Borneo).

H **August**

In South Africa, the leader of Umkonto we Sizwe, Nelson Mandela, is arrested when returning to Johannesburg from Natal (tried in Nov and convicted of inciting workers to strike and leaving the country without valid documents; sentenced to five years' imprisonment).

6 Jamaica becomes independent within the Commonwealth.

7 United Arab Republic (Egypt) sign agreement for compensating British subjects whose property was seized after the Suez crisis of 1956.

15 following mediation by the UN, the Netherlands and Indonesia settle their dispute over West New Guinea (UN to administer the territory from 1 Oct to 1 May 1963, followed by Indonesia, which is to make arrangements for self-determination by the inhabitants).

16 agreement signed in London for Aden to enter the Federation of South Arabia.

16 Algeria is admitted to the Arab League.

20 following breakdown of talks for financial aid (which had started on 27 June), Malta requests independence within the Commonwealth.

31 Trinidad and Tobago (previously members of the West Indies Federation) become an independent nation within the Commonwealth.

J **September**

1 Singapore, and on 12, North Borneo, vote to join Malaysian Federation.

2 USSR agrees to send arms to Cuba.

3 in Congo, the government of Katanga province accepts plan of U Thant, United Nations acting secretary general, for reunification of Congo.

7 Laos establishes diplomatic relations with the People's Republic of China and North Vietnam.

8 Chinese troops cross McMahon line on India's NE frontier.

9 (–13) France resumes relations with Syria, Jordan, and Saudi Arabia.

20 government of Southern Rhodesia (now Zimbabwe) declares Zimbabwe African People's Union an unlawful body.

25 Fidel Castro states that the USSR intends to establish a base for its fishing fleet in Cuba.

26 Ahmed Ben Bella elected prime minister of Algeria.

27 in North Yemen, Imam Mohammed is overthrown by a military coup led by Colonel Abdullah al-Sallal.

K **October**

1 UN takes over administration of West New Guinea from British.

5 French National Assembly censures proposed referendum to sanction future president's election by popular mandate; Georges Pompidou, prime minister, resigns, but President de Gaulle asks him to continue in office.

9 Uganda becomes independent within the Commonwealth, with Milton Obete as prime minister (elected in April).

10 *Der Spiegel* publishes article on NATO exercise criticizing weakness of West German army (the offices of the paper are occupied by the police, 16).

11 Hugh Foot resigns as a British representative at the UN in protest at his government's defence of the actions of Southern Rhodesia's government.

16 ceasefire in Congo Republic.

20 China launches offensive on Indian border positions (21 Nov).

22 start of the 'Cuba missile crisis': in USA, President Kennedy announces in broadcast that the USSR has installed a missile base in Cuba; he declares a naval blockade to prevent the delivery of missiles and calls on Nikita Khrushchev of the USSR to eliminate the threat to world peace.

1,100 Mormon missionaries campaign in England.

In England, 8,800 members of the Exclusive Brethren are expelled because of their unwillingness to accept decree forbidding contact with non-members.

Q Science, Technology, and Discovery

Twenty years after the beginning of the nuclear age, the USA has 200 atomic reactors in operation, Great Britain and the USSR, 39 each.

US spacemen John Glenn (20 Feb) and Malcolm Scott Carpenter (May) are put in Earth orbit.

The Satellite *Telstar* is launched from Cape Canaveral, USA (10 July), circles the earth every 157.8 minutes, enabling live television pictures transmitted from Andover, Maine, to be received at Goonhilly Down, Cornwall, SW England, and in Brittany, France (11 July).

USA also launches the rocket *Mariner*, to explore Venus, and the British satellite *Aerial*, to study cosmic radiation.

European Space Research Organization established at Paris (14 June).

Soviet scientist K Chudinov claims to have revived fossil algae some 250 million years old.

The German drug thalidomide, used as a sedative by pregnant women, is established as the cause of an increase in babies born with congenital malformations; the drug is banned in many countries.

Report of Royal College of Physicians on Smoking and Health.

R Humanities

Michael D Coe, *Mexico*.

Winchester Excavations Committee organizes major programme of archaeological and documentary research into the history of the city of Winchester in S England (findings published in the series Winchester Studies).

J Gernet, *Daily Life in China on the Eve of the Mongol Invasion*.

Helen M Cam, *Law-finders and Law-makers in Medieval England*.

A R Bridbury, *Economic Growth: England in the Later Middle Ages*.

Jasper Ridley, *Thomas Cranmer*.

B R Mitchell and Phyllis Deane, *Abstract of British Historical Statistics*.

H J Habakkuk, *American and British Technology in the Nineteenth Century*.

A H Hourani, *Arabic Thought in the Liberal Age, 1798–1939*.

Alfred D Chandler, Jr, *Strategy and Structure:*

Chapters in the History of the American Industrial Enterprise.

George Woodcock, *Anarchism: A History of Libertarian Ideas and Movements*.

F W Deakin, *The Brutal Friendship*.

J L Austin, *Sense and Sensibilia* (posthumous).

Thomas S Kuhn, *The Structure of Scientific Revolutions*.

Claude Lévi-Strauss, *The Savage Mind*.

S Art, Sculpture, Fine Arts, and Architecture

The Second Vatican Council (–1965) includes an appeal to contemporary artists to continue the tradition of Christian art; the Vatican Collection of Contemporary Art is the result (opened 1973).

Painting, etc:

Peter Blake, *Toy Shop*.

Christo, *Wrapped Portrait of Brigitte Bardot*.

Jasper Johns, *Diver, Fools House*.

Michelangelo Pistoletto, *Man Seen from the Back*.

Robert Rauschenberg, *Glider*.

Ad Reinhardt, *Abstract Painting No. 5*.

Gunther Uecker, *Breathing Volume*.

Andy Warhol, *Campbell's Soup Cans*, *210 Coca-Cola Bottles*, first of the *Marilyn Monroe* series.

Sculpture:

Phillip King, *Rosebud*.

Eduardo Paolozzi, *Four Towers*.

Martial Raysse, *Raysse Beach*.

David Smith, *Voltri IV*.

Architecture:

Coventry Cathedral is consecrated; architect, Basil Spence; engraved windows, John Hutton; sculpture, Jacob Epstein; baptistery window, John Piper; ten nave windows, Lawrence Lee; tapestry, Graham Sutherland.

Pan-American Airways Building, New York, provides world's largest office accommodation.

Louis Kahn, Unitarian Church, Rochester, New York, USA.

T Music

Grazyna Bacewicz, *Concerto for Orchestra*.

Pierre Boulez, *Pli selon pli*.

Benjamin Britten, *War Requiem*.

John Cage, *O'OO"*.

György Ligeti, *Poème Symphonique pour 100 Metronomes*.

Dmitry Shostakovich, Symphony No. 13 ('Babi-Yar').

Michael Tippett, *King Priam* (opera).

Jacqueline Du Pré plays Elgar's cello concerto at the Festival Hall, London.

26 Nikita Khrushchev sends letter to President Kennedy of the USA; on 27, publishes message saying that he is prepared to remove weapons 'regarded as offensive' if the USA removes its missiles from Turkey; Kennedy rejects the condition and states that work on the missile bases in Cuba must stop.

28 Nikita Khrushchev of USSR announces that he has ordered the withdrawal of the 'offensive weapons' from Cuba.

28 referendum in France favours election of president by universal suffrage.

30 UN General Assembly rejects Soviet proposal to admit the People's Republic of China.

31 following Chinese attack's on India's frontier, Krishna Menon, Indian defence minister, resigns.

31 UN General Assembly requests Britain to suspend enforcement of new constitution in Southern Rhodesia (now Zimbabwe), but constitution comes into effect on 1 Nov.

L **November**

2 President Kennedy announces that USSR has been dismantling bases in Cuba.

2 Julius Nyerere elected president of Tanganyika (now Tanzania).

2 British businessman Greville Wynne is arrested on espionage charge in Budapest and is later extradited to USSR.

5 Franz Joseph Strauss, West German defence minister, is relieved of his duties over the *Spiegel* affair because it is alleged that he was involved in police action against the magazine (on 19, five Free Democrat ministers resign in protest at government involvement).

5 US Congressional elections leave Democrats in control of both houses.

5 Saudi Arabia breaks off diplomatic relations with United Arab Republic (Egypt), following a period of unrest partly caused by the defection of several Saudi princes to Egypt.

8 in Britain, Thomas Galbraith, former civil lord of the admiralty and now undersecretary of state for Scotland, resigns over the Vassall affair (the spy John Vassall had worked in his office at the admiralty).

9 constitutional conference in London on British Guiana (now Guyana) breaks down.

14 in Britain, Harold Macmillan appoints Radcliffe tribunal to appraise the security services.

20 USSR agrees to withdraw Ilyushin bombers from Cuba and USA announces end of blockade.

21 China agrees to cease-fire on Sino–Indian border and forces subsequently withdraw.

27 Britain signs agreement to provide India with arms to resist Chinese aggression.

29 British–French agreement signed to develop the *Concorde* supersonic airliner.

30 U Thant of Burma (now Myanmar) is elected UN secretary general.

M **December**

4 Western European Union Assembly in Paris calls for single NATO nuclear force.

9 Tanganyika (now Tanzania) becomes a republic within the Commonwealth, with Julius Nyerere as president.

11 formation in West German of coalition government of Christian Democrats, Christian Socialists, and Free Democrats.

14 in elections in Southern Rhodesia (now Zimbabwe), Winston Field's right-wing Rhodesian Front defeats Edgar Whitehead's United Federal Party.

14 first African-dominated government formed in Northern Rhodesia (now Zambia), under Kenneth Kaunda.

19 conference at Nassau, Bahamas, of President Kennedy of USA and Harold Macmillan of Britain; USA agrees to supply Britain with Polaris missiles instead of Skybolt (as Kennedy arrives the local band plays 'Oh, Don't Deceive Me').

19 Britain acknowledges the right of Nyasaland (now Malawi) to secede from the Central African Federation.

27 India and Pakistan reopen talks on Kashmir.

28 UN troops engaged in heavy fighting in Katanga province, Congo Republic; on 29, they occupy Elisabethville (now Lubumbashi).

A Funny Thing Happened on the Way to the Forum (musical), music and lyrics by Stephen Sondheim (first performed at the Alvin Theatre, New York, 8 May).

Herb Alpert, 'The Lonely Bull'.

The Beach Boys, 'Surfin' Safari'.

Tony Bennett, 'I Left My Heart in San Francisco'.

Acker Bilk 'Stranger on the Shore'.

Nat 'King' Cole, 'Ramblin' Rose'.

Bob Dylan, 'Blowin' in The Wind'.

The Four Seasons, 'Sherry'.

Frank Ifield, 'I Remember You'.

Elvis Presley, 'Return to Sender'.

Neil Sedaka, 'Breaking Up Is Hard To Do'.

The Shadows, 'Wonderful Land'.

The Tornadoes, 'Telstar'.

The Beatles sign a management contract with Brian Epstein (24 Jan) and a recording contract with the Parlophone record label (9 May).

u Literature and Drama

James Baldwin, *Another Country*.

Giorgio Bassani, *The Garden of the Finzi-Continis*.

Robert Bly, *Silence in the Snowy Fields*.

Jorge Luis Borges, *Labyrinths*.

Ray Bradbury, *Something Wicked This Way Comes*.

William Faulkner, *The Reivers* (posthumous).

Ken Keasey, *One Flew Over the Cuckoo's Nest*.

Doris Lessing, *The Golden Notebook*.

Alison Lurie, *Love and Friendship*.

Vladimir Nabokov, *Pale Fire*.

Katherine Anne Porter, *Ship of Fools*.

Jean Renoir, *Renoir, My Father*.

Clancy Sigal, *Going Away*.

Alexander Solzhenitsyn, *One day in the Life of Ivan Denisovich*.

Drama:

Edward Albee, *Who's Afraid of Virginia Woolf?*

Friedrich Dürrenmatt, *The Physicists*.

Arnold Wesker, *Chips with Everything*.

v Births and Deaths

Jan 16 R H Tawney dies (81).

July 6 William Faulkner dies (64).

July 20 G M Trevelyan dies (86).

Aug 5 Marilyn Monroe dies (36).

Sept 3 e e cummings dies (67).

Nov 7 Eleanor Roosevelt dies (78).

Nov 18 Niels Bohr dies (77).

Nov 28 Queen Wilhelmina of the Netherlands dies (82).

Dec 7 Kirsten Flagstad dies (67).

w Everyday Life

Ring-pull drink cans are devised.

British weather reports give temperatures in centigrade as well as Fahrenheit (from 15 Jan).

x Sport and Recreation

The seventh football World Cup is held in Chile. Brazil retains the trophy, beating Czechoslovakia 3–1 in the final in Santiago.

In cricket, in England, the Gentlemen v. Players match is played for the last time, as the MCC votes to abolish the distinction between amateurs and professionals (18–20 July).

Sonny Liston beats Floyd Patterson in the first round of their World Heavyweight title fight in Chicago (25 Sept).

Off-course betting shops, legalized under the Betting and Gaming Act of 1960, are established across Britain.

Rod Laver of Australia is the first man to win tennis Grand Slam since 1938.

Graham Hill, driving a BRM, wins the world Grand Prix championship. He is only the second Briton to do so.

y Media

The British newspaper the *Sunday Times* introduces a separate colour magazine (4 Feb).

Publication in Britain of satirical magazine *Private Eye* (Feb; saved from financial difficulties by comedian Peter Cook in April).

The weekly sociology magazine *New Society* is published in Britain.

In Spain, press censorship is lifted in theory, though not entirely in practice.

In South Africa, the press establishes the Press Board of Reference to deal with complaints of misreporting; it enables the press to escape direct state control.

Weekly news magazine *Panorama* is published in Italy.

Film:

Advise and Consent (director, Otto Preminger; starring Don Murray and Charles Laughton).

The Birds (director, Alfred Hitchcock).

Divorce, Italian Style (starring Marcello Mastroianni).

Doctor No (the first James Bond movie, starring Sean Connery as Bond).

Exterminating Angel (director, Luis Buñuel).

How the West Was Won (director, John Ford).

A Kind of Loving (director, John Schlesinger, starring Alan Bates).

Lawrence of Arabia (director, David Lean).

Lolita (director, Stanley Kubrick).

Profumo affair in Britain ... Mass demonstration in Washington
for civil rights ... Assassination of President Kennedy ...

A January

2 General Lemnitzer succeeds General Norstad as Supreme Allied Commander Europe.

3 in Congo Republic, United Nations force captures Jadotville in Katanga province.

14 President de Gaulle of France states objections to Britain's entry into the European Economic Community (EEC) and rejects US offer of Polaris missiles.

15 President Tshombe of Katanga province, Congo Republic (now Zaire), accepts UN plan for secession of Katanga.

18 Hugh Gaitskell, leader of British Labour Party, dies suddenly from a viral infection.

22 President de Gaulle and Konrad Adenauer sign Franco–German treaty of co-operation.

23 'Kim' Philby, a former British diplomat and MI5 officer, now working in Beirut, Lebanon, disappears.

24 Italy accepts US plan for multilateral nuclear force.

29 Britain is refused entry into the EEC.

B February

1 Nyasaland (now Malawi) becomes self-governing with Hastings Banda as prime minister.

5 in Canada, John Diefenbaker's government is defeated in Parliament; Diefenbaker obtains a dissolution (election held on 8 April).

8 rebels in Baghdad, Iraq, assassinate prime minister Abdel Karim Kassem; succeeded by Abdul Salam Arif.

9 USSR releases Archbishop of Lvov (former head of the Ukrainian Catholic Church) after 18 years' imprisonment (he had been imprisoned when Ukrainian Catholics were forcibly united with the Russian Orthodox).

14 Harold Wilson is elected leader of British Labour Party, defeating deputy leader George Brown by 144 votes to 103 (James Callaghan was eliminated in an earlier round).

19 USSR agrees to withdraw troops from Cuba.

20 USA recommends that surface ships should be used to carry Polaris missiles in NATO force.

C March

17 Typhoid epidemic breaks out in Zermatt, Switzerland.

22 in British House of Commons, John Profumo, secretary of state for war, denies rumours that he had shared the favour of Miss Christine Keeler, a model, with Captain Ivanov, an attaché at the Soviet embassy in London.

25 in Northern Ireland, Terence O'Neill succeeds Lord Brookeborough (Basil Brooke) as prime minister (Brooke had held the post since 1943).

D April

6 Britain and USA sign Polaris missile agreement.

8 general election in Canada, won by the Liberals with 129 seats; Progressive Conservatives win 95 seats; others, 41 seats.

9 the USA makes Winston Churchill, former British prime minister, an honorary citizen.

The Loneliness of the Long Distance Runner (director, Tony Richardson).

Mama Roma (director, Pier Paolo Pasolini).

The Manchurian Candidate (director, John Frankenheimer).

Phaedra (director, Jules Dassin).

Ride the High Country (director, Sam Peckinpah).

A Taste of Honey (director, Tony Richardson).

To Kill a Mockingbird (starring Gregory Peck).

The Trial (director, Orson Welles).

Winter Night (director, Ingmar Bergman).

Television:

During the Cuba missile crisis, President Kennedy of the USA delivers his ultimatum to the USSR in a television address.

In USA, Johnny Carson takes over *The Tonight Show*.

In Japan, TBS broadcasts *Young Man* and *Bilbilly Sings*, two dramas by Katsumi Oyama.

New programmes in Britain include: *Animal Magic* (BBC), presented by Johnny Morris (–1984); *Dr Finlay's Casebook* (–1971); *Oliver Twist* (BBC); *The Saint*, starring Roger Moore (–1969); *Steptoe and Son* (BBC; –1965); *That Was The Week That Was* ('TW3'), presented by David Frost; *Z Cars* (BBC; –1978).

'Hot line' from Washington to Moscow is operational ...
Publication of Honest to God *... Cleopatra with Elizabeth Taylor*
and Richard Burton ...

o Politics, Government, Law, and Economy

Hannah Arendt, *On Revolution*.

Charles L Capp, *The Congressman: His Work as He Sees It*.

Rowland Egger and Joseph P Harris, *The President and Congress*.

Robert L Peabody and Nelson W Polsby (eds.), *New Perspectives on the House of Representatives*.

In USA, foundation of the Institute for Policy Studies.

Organization of African Unity (OAU) founded by conference of African leaders in Addis Ababa, Ethiopia (May); it aims to maintain solidarity between African leaders and remove colonialism from the Continent.

In USA, New Hampshire is the first state to introduce a state lottery, as a device to raise revenue without having to raise personal or sales taxes.

'Hot line' direct link between the White House, Washington, DC, USA, and the Kremlin in Moscow, USSR, becomes operational (30 Aug); it is intended to provide faster communications at times of international crisis.

In Britain, Prime Minister Harold Macmillan appoints Lord Hailsham, the minister for science and leader of the House of Lords, as special adviser to the cabinet on dealing with unemployment in NE England and stimulating industrial growth there (9 Jan).

The Peerage Act in Britain allows members of the House of Lords to disclaim their titles (and thus be eligible for membership of the House of Commons; existing peers can disclaim within six months, new peers within one month of succession to title); the 2nd Viscount Stansgate, formerly Mr A N Wedgwood Benn, renounces his peerage (31 July; in Aug 1972, changes name to Tony Benn).

London Government Act reshapes local government in London, creating a Greater London Council (GLC) and 32 London Boroughs covering most of the metropolitan area (first elections for the GLC are held on 9 April 1964).

Pope John XXIII appoints a Commission to revise Canon Law.

In USA, in Gideon v. Wainwright, the Supreme Court requires the state to appoint counsel if a defendant cannot afford a lawyer privately (18 March).

In USA, closure of the prison on Alcatraz Island, San Francisco (opened 1909).

In Britain, minimum prison age is raised to 17 by Criminal Justice Act (1 Aug).

Natural gas deposits in Groningen, Netherlands, are developed.

In Britain, the Beeching Report (published 27 March) recommends the closure of a quarter of all passenger rail lines and over 2,100 stations.

Milton Friedman and A Schartz, *A Monetary History of the USA, 1867-1960*.

p Society, Education, and Religion

In the USA, turbulence continues in the South, with resistance to integration in the Ala-

12 Indonesian forces make armed attack on Malaysia.

15 in Britain, disorder breaks out during last
• stages of the Aldermaston March (a protest march from London to the nuclear research centre at Aldermaston, organized by the Campaign for Nuclear Disarmament).

17 United Arab Republic (Egypt), Syria, and Iraq agree to federate.

17 in Canada, Prime Minister John Diefenbaker resigns following defeat of the Progressive Conservatives in the general election; on 22, Lester B Pearson, Liberal, forms ministry.

20 in Britain, the National Incomes Commission or 'Nicky' (announced in July 1962 and intended to judge wage claims in the light of public interest) issues its first report; it rejects an agreement for a 40-hour week in the Scottish building industry.

22 (–8 July) general strike in British Guiana (Guyana), with rioting and terrorism.

25 in Britain, publication of report of Radcliffe tribunal on Vassall spy case; it clears admiralty ministers for not spotting the spy John Vassall.

28 Fidel Castro, prime minister of Cuba, visits USSR.

E May

9 State of emergency declared in British Guiana (now Guyana) by governor at Prime Minister Cheddi Jagan's request.

11 in Moscow, USSR, end of trial of Oleg Penkovsky, a Soviet intelligence officer who spied for the West, and Greville Wynne, a British businessman and Penkovsky's go-between; Penkovsky is sentenced to death, Wynne to eight years' imprisonment.

16 Chief Enahoro of Nigeria is deported from Britain (7 Sept, he is sentenced in Lagos; the attorney general, John Hobson, is later charged unsuccessfully before his Inn for his share in the deportation).

16 Indian–Pakistani talks on Kashmir break down.

16 Geneva Conference on General Agreement on Tariffs and Trade (GATT) begins 'Kennedy round' of negotiations for tariff cuts.

F June

5 In Britain, John Profumo resigns from the government, admitting that he misled the House of Commons on 22 March (on 9, the *News of the World* publishes Christine Keeler's account).

11 Constantine Karamanlis, Greek prime minister, resigns in protest against King Paul's state visit to Britain.

19 in USA, President Kennedy gives address to Congress on civil rights.

20 agreement between USA and USSR to establish a telegraph and radio 'hot line' from the White House, Washington, DC, to the Kremlin, Moscow.

21 France withdraws naval Atlantic forces from NATO.

25 in Congo Republic, President Tshombe is forced to resign as prime minister of Katanga province.

26 during tour of West Germany (23–27), President Kennedy visits West Berlin; he tells a crowd of 150,000 Berliners: 'All free men ... are citizens of Berlin. And therefore, as a free man, I take pride in the words, "Ich bin ein Berliner".'

G July

1 In Britain, it is revealed that 'Kim' Philby was the 'third man' involved in espionage for the USSR with Guy Burgess and Donald Maclean.

11 in South Africa, the Security Police raid the headquarters of Umkonta we Sizwe in the Johannesburg suburb of Rivonia; Walter Sisulu and others are captured, together with weapons and incriminating documents.

20 end of USSR–Chinese ideological talks in Moscow.

21 British Prime Minister Harold Macmillan appoints Lord Denning to inquire into security aspects of the Profumo affair.

26 in Yugoslavia, earthquake hits Skopje (now capital of Macedonia).

30 Soviet newspaper *Izvestia* announces that British double-agent 'Kim' Philby, who disappeared from Beirut in Jan, has been granted asylum in USSR.

H August

1 Britain agrees to grant independence to Malta in 1964.

5 USA, USSR, and Britain sign nuclear test ban treaty (subsequently signed by 96 states, but not France, before coming into force, 1 Oct).

8 in Britain, the 'Great Train Robbery', the work of a 15-man gang, who fake a red light to stop the London–Glasgow mail train (near Cheddington in Buckinghamshire) and steal £2½ million in bank notes.

21 in South Vietnam, Buddhists are arrested and martial law imposed.

28 in USA, 200,000 African-Americans take part in a peaceful demonstration for civil rights in Washington, DC; they are addressed by the Reverend Martin Luther King, who proclaims: 'I have a dream that one day this nation will rise up and live out the true meaning of its creed: "We hold these truths to be self-evident, that all men are created equal".'

bama education system, the bombing of an African-American church in Birmingham, Alabama (15 Sept), and other terrorist incidents.

The Publications Control Board is established in South Africa, with powers to prohibit the import of offensive or blasphemous works and films.

Equal pay law for men and women passed in the USA.

In Britain, the Labour Member of Parliament Ben Parkin raises the problem of 'slum landlords' in the House of Commons (July) by exploiting the fact that Miss Mandy Rice-Davies (involved in the Profumo affair) had once cohabited with the notorious landlord Peter Rachman; an independent inquiry is established to investigate housing in London (22 July).

In USA, Timothy Leary is dismissed from his lectureship in psychology at Harvard University after running a popular series of experiments into the effects of psychedelic drugs such as psilocybin.

British Consumer Council appointed under Lady Elliot (26 March).

In Britain, publication of the Buchanan Report, *Traffic in Towns*.

James Baldwin, *The Fire Next Time*.

Betty Friedan, *The Feminine Mystique*.

Carl Gustav Jung, *Memories, Dreams, Reflections*.

Martin Luther King, *Letter from Birmingham Jail*.

In Britain, the Newsom Report, about the education of less academic children, argues that schools must relate 'more directly to adult life, and especially by taking a proper account of vocational interests'.

The Robbins Report marks the beginning of a 10-year period of expansion in higher education; the Universities of East Anglia (at Norwich), Newcastle-upon-Tyne (formerly part of the University of Durham), and York are founded.

E H Erikson, *Childhood and Society*.

Robin Pedley, *The Comprehensive School*.

Pope John XXIII issues encyclical *Pacem in Terris*, which deals with the peaceful settlement of disputes and with relations with non-Catholics and with Communists.

Following the death of Pope John XXIII (3 June), Cardinal Giovanni Battista Montini is elected Pope (21 June) and takes the name Paul VI.

Vatican Council approves the use of vernacular liturgies.

Mary Lusk appeals to be ordained in the Church of Scotland.

Publication (in March) of *Honest to God* by John Robinson, Bishop of Woolwich in London, arouses widespread controversy; a newspaper article about the book is headed 'Our Image of God Must Go' and helps to sell almost a million copies within three years; Archbishop Michael Ramsey responds with *Images Old and New*.

Alec Vidler and others, *Objections to Christian Belief*.

Towards a Quaker View of Sex.

Q Science, Technology, and Discovery

Committee of the Royal Society in Britain reports emigration of British scientists (21 Feb).

Friction welding is invented.

USSR puts Valentina Tereshkova into orbit (16 June) for three-day flight in space to study the problem of weightlessness in a woman; another astronaut launched the same day makes 49 orbits.

US astronaut Gordon Cooper, launched in an Atlas rocket, makes 22 orbits (15 May).

USA orbits a belt of copper needles as test for secure system of global radio communications.

Space research provides much data on conditions on Mars and Venus.

Discovery of anti-xi-zeno, a fundamental atomic particle of contra-terrene matter.

US physicist Murray Gell-Man and George Zweig independently suggest the existence of the quark, a subatomic particle.

Vaccine for measles is perfected.

British neurologist Alan Hodgkin and Australian neurologist John Eccles make discoveries in the transmission of nerve impulses.

Queen Elizabeth Hospital, Hong Kong, the largest in the Commonwealth, completed.

Rachel Carson, in her book *The Silent Spring*, draws attention to the dangers of chemical pesticides.

R Humanities

Alvar Ellegård, *A Statistical Method for Determining Authorship*.

A computer is used to investigate the authorship of St Paul's Epistles.

J H Elliott, *Imperial Spain*.

W G Hoskins, *Provincial England*.

F M L Thompson, *English Landed Society in the Nineteenth Century*.

Edward Crankshaw, *The Fall of the House of Hapsburg*.

Asa Briggs, *Victorian Cities*.

John Higham, *Strangers in the Land: Patterns of American Nativism 1860– 1925*.

William E Leuchtenburg, *Franklin D Roosevelt and the New Deal*.

Jürgen Habermas, *Theory and Practice*.

R M Hare, *Freedom and Reason*.

J September

4 Riots over school desegregation in Birmingham, Alabama, USA (on 15, bomb kills African-Americans in Birmingham).

8 new constitution in Algeria establishes presidential government; Ahmed ben Bella is president.

16 Malaya, North Borneo, Sarawak, and Singapore form Federation of Malaysia which, on 17, breaks off relations with Indonesia, following Sukarno's increased hostility.

18 UN Special Committee on apartheid in South Africa calls for prohibition of arms and petroleum traffic with South Africa.

19 British–French report favours Channel Tunnel project.

21 Vilian Siroký, prime minister of Czechoslovakia, is dismissed.

26 in Britain, publication of Lord Denning's report on the Profumo affair; he says that there was no breach of security, and reports that government ministers were not involved in promiscuous behaviour.

K October

In South Africa, opening of the 'Rivonia trial' of the leaders of Umkonto we Sizwe, including Nelson Mandela and Walter Sisulu, charged with sabotage and conspiracy to overthrow the government (–June 1964).

1 Nigeria becomes a republic within the Commonwealth, with Nnamdi Azikiwe as president.

1 Britain agrees to join discussions about a NATO mixed-crewed nuclear fleet.

3 army coup in Honduras.

4 release of Archbishop Beran of Prague after 14 years' imprisonment.

4 devastating hurricane in Caribbean.

7 UN Trusteeship Committee calls on Britain not to transfer armed forces of Rhodesian Federation to Southern Rhodesia.

9 Milton Obote declares Uganda a republic; the kabaka of Buganda, Mutesa II, is elected president.

11 the UN General Assembly condemns repression in South Africa by 106 votes to 1.

15 Ludwig Erhard becomes chancellor of West Germany on Konrad Adenauer's resignation.

18 in Britain, Harold Macmillan resigns as prime minister for reasons of health, and on 19, is succeeded by the Scottish peer the 14th Earl of Home (who later disclaims peerage, is made a Knight of the Thistle, and becomes Sir Alec Douglas-Home; on 8 Nov he is elected a member of the House of Commons, for Kinross).

20 Iain Macleod and Enoch Powell refuse to serve in Sir Alec Douglas-Home's new Conservative ministry.

22 (–31) reopening in London of constitutional conference on British Guiana (suspended in 1962); ends without agreement.

25 Vatican Council approves principle of a fixed Easter.

26 Nikita Khrushchev states that the USSR would not race the USA to place a person on the Moon.

31 Britain suspends aid to Indonesia.

L November

1 Army *coup* in South Vietnam; President Ngo Dinh Diem is assassinated and succeeded by General Duong Van Minh.

22 in USA, President Kennedy is assassinated in Dallas, Texas; Vice-President Lyndon Baines Johnson is sworn in as president.

24 Lee Harvey Oswald, arrested in Dallas, USA, for the murder of President Kennedy, is shot by Jack Ruby.

30 general election in Australia, in which the Liberal and Country Party coalition increases its majority; Liberal Party wins 52 seats, Country Party, 20 seats, and the Labor Party, 50 seats.

M December

3 In Britain, Lord Mancroft resigns from board of Norwich Union Insurance Society through Arab pressure (influential Arabs disapproved of his ties with Israel).

4 UN Security Council votes for partial embargo on sale and shipment of arms to South Africa.

10 Zanzibar becomes independent within the Commonwealth (now part of Tanzania).

11 in Ghana, President Kwame Nkrumah dismisses the chief justice following acquittals in treason trials.

12 Kenya becomes independent within the Commonwealth.

18 in USSR, African students riot in Red Square, Moscow, after the death of a Ghanaian.

22 clashes in Cyprus between Greeks and Turks lead to a major breakdown in relations between the two communities; on 30, following visit by Duncan Sandys, the British Commonwealth secretary, a neutral zone is agreed upon.

22 Greek liner *Lakonia* catches fire and sinks in North Atlantic with loss of 150 lives.

25 state of emergency declared in Somalia frontier region of Kenya.

31 dissolution of Central African Federation of Rhodesia and Nyasaland (now Zambia, Zimbabwe, and Malawi).

s Art, Sculpture, Fine Arts, and Architecture

Georges Braque dies (31 Aug).

Painting, etc:

Peter Blake, *The Lettermen.*

Richard Hamilton, *Towards a Definite Statement on the Coming Trends and Accessories in Menswear.*

Roy Lichtenstein, *I Know... Brad, Whaam!*

Sigmar Polke, *The Sausage Eater.*

Bridget Riley, *Fall.*

Mimmo Rotella, *The Assault.*

Niki de Saint-Phalle, *La Femme eclatée ou l'Acouchement du Taureau.*

Andy Warhol, *Ambulance Disaster*, *Electric Chair* series, *Race Riot* series.

Sculpture:

Marcel Duchamp, *Box in a Valise, Series E.*

David Smith, *Cubi I.*

Architecture:

G Bunshaft, Beinecke Library (a windowless building), Yale University, New Haven, USA.

Louis Kahn, Indian Institute of Management, Ahmedabad, India.

Le Corbusier, Carpenter Center for the Visual Arts, Harvard University, Cambridge, USA.

Ludwig Mies van der Rohe, Lafayette Towers, Detroit, Michigan, USA.

T Music

Leonard Bernstein, *Kaddish.*

Wolfgang Fortner, *Pfingstgeschichte nach Lukas.*

Karl Hartmann, Symphony No. 8.

Dmitry Shostakovich, String Quartet No. 9.

Michael Tippett, Concerto for Orchestra.

Italian tenor Luciano Pavarotti makes debut at Covent Garden, London, singing in *La Bohème.*

Half a Sixpence (musical), lyrics and music by David Heneker (first performed at the Cambridge Theatre, London, 21 March).

Oh, What a Lovely War! (musical), using songs of World War I (director, Joan Littlewood; first performed at the Theatre Royal, Stratford, London).

Revue *At the Drop of Another Hat*, starring Michael Flanders and Donald Swann, opens at the Haymarket Theatre, London (2 Oct).

Gerry and the Pacemakers, 'You'll Never Walk Alone'.

The Beatles, 'Please Please Me' (album of same title recorded in 12 hours at EMI's Abbey Road studios, London), 'She Loves You', 'I Want to Hold Your Hand'.

Gene Pitney, '24 Hours from Tulsa'.

Cliff Richard, 'Bachelor Boy', 'Summer Holiday'.

The Searchers, 'Sweets For My Sweet'.

u Literature and Drama

James Baldwin, *The Fire Next Time.*

Charles Bukowski, *It Catches My Heart in its Hands.*

G I Gurdjieff, *Meetings With Remarkable Men* (posthumous).

Wilson Harris, *The Secret Ladder* (completes 'The Guyana Quartet').

Mary McCarthy, *The Group.*

Joyce Carol Oates, *By the North Gate.*

Sylvia Plath, *The Bell Jar* (poems).

Maurice Sendak, *Where the Wild Things Are.*

Muriel Spark, *The Girls of Slender Means.*

John Updike, *The Centaur.*

The New York Review of Books is founded.

New York court allows publication of John Cleland's *Fanny Hill* (written 1748–9), but in England magistrates' courts oppose publication.

Drama:

John Arden, *The Workhouse Donkey.*

Rolf Hochhuth, *The Representative.*

Eugène Ionesco, *Exit the King.*

Henry de Montherlant, *Le Chaos et la Nuit.*

Neil Simon, *Barefoot in the Park.*

In Minneapolis, USA, opening of the Guthrie Theatre (7 May), a specially designed theatre planned by Tyrone Guthrie for presenting the classical repertory free from commercial pressures.

In Britain, first performance of the new National Theatre, London (22 Oct); the architect Denys Lasdun is commissioned to design a permanent home for the company.

v Births and Deaths

Jan 18 Hugh Gaitskell dies (56).

Jan 29 Robert Frost dies (88).

Jan 30 Francis Poulenc dies (64).

Feb 11 Sylvia Plath dies (30).

March 16 William Beveridge dies (84).

Aug 22 William Morris (Lord Nuffield) dies (85).

Aug 27 W E B Du Bois dies (95).

Aug 31 Georges Braque dies (81).

Oct 11 Jean Cocteau dies (74).

Nov 22 John F Kennedy dies (46).

Nov 22 Aldous Huxley dies (69).

Dec 30 Paul Hindemith dies (68).

w Everyday Life

Weight Watchers is founded in New York.

US Post Office introduces ZIP (Zone Improvement Plan) codes (1 July).

*Conflict in Cyprus ... Independence of Zambia ... Lyndon Johnson
wins US presidential election ...*

A January

7 As part of trade drive with Europe, Cuba orders 400 British buses.

8 in USA, President Johnson, in his State of the Union message to Congress, proposes reduction in defence spending.

9 anti-US riots in Panama which, on 10, breaks off diplomatic relations with USA.

12 rebellion in Zanzibar (now part of Tanzania), which is declared a republic; the sultanate is abolished and the sultan banished.

15 constitutional conference on Cyprus opens in London, but fails to reach agreement.

20 (–24) in Tanzania, mutiny of Tanganyika Rifles, followed by troop mutinies in Uganda and Kenya; quelled by British military forces.

21 (–17 Sept) sixth session of 17-nation disarmament conference held in Geneva, Switzerland.

22 Kenneth Kaunda, president of the United National Independence Party, becomes first prime minister of Northern Rhodesia (now Zambia).

24 (–31) referendum in Ghana, which supports giving the president the power to remove judges from the supreme and high court and establishing the Convention People's Party as the sole party (results announced 3 Feb).

27 France establishes diplomatic relations with the People's Republic of China.

28 riots in Salisbury (now Harare), Southern Rhodesia (now Zimbabwe).

Construction of the Victoria Underground line, London, begun.

Britain endures coldest Jan and Feb since 1740.

x Sport and Recreation

Alf Ramsey is appointed England's football manager (1 May).

Tottenham Hotspur becomes the first British side to win a European football trophy, winning the European Cup Winners' Cup Final against Atletico Madrid in Rotterdam (15 May).

Cricket's first limited-overs competition, sponsored by Gillette, is held in England. In the final at Lord's, Sussex beat Worcestershire by 14 runs (7 Sept).

Mr Justice Wilberforce judges that the 'retain and transfer' system in English football, whereby clubs can refuse to transfer a player, constitutes an unreasonable restraint of trade.

Arnold Palmer is the first golfer to win over $100,000 in a single season on the US circuit.

The first world netball championships are held in England, with 11 nations competing; Australia are the winners.

y Media

Daily Mirror in New York ceases publication.

In Britain, new constitution for Press Council (18 June; 11 Dec, Lord Devlin becomes chairman).

Film:

Billy Liar (director, John Schlesinger).

The Cardinal (director, Otto Preminger).

Cleopatra (director, Joseph L Mankiewicz; starring Elizabeth Taylor and Richard Burton; costing a record £12 million).

From Russia with Love (starring Sean Connery).

The Great Escape (director, John Sturges).

Irma La Douce (director, Billy Wilder).

The Leopard (director, Luchino Visconti).

Le Mépris (director, Jean-Luc Godard).

Muriel (director, Alain Resnais).

Tom Jones (director, Tony Richardson).

The Running Man (director, Carol Reed).

The Silence (director, Ingmar Bergman).

This Sporting Life (director, Lindsay Anderson).

Radio:

The Italian island of Capri bans transistor radios.

Television:

'Admags', programmes built around commercials, are banned in Britain.

In Britain, the BBC ends the controversial satire programme *That Was The Week That Was* (27 Dec).

New programmes in Britain include: *Doctor Who* (BBC), with William Hartnell as the first of many actors to play the lead role; *Ready Steady Go* (BBC; –1966); *World in Action* (Granada; –).

Fogel's Railroads and Economic Growth ... Fiddler on the Roof
... *Death of Roscoe Pound* ... Mary Poppins ...

o Politics, Government, Law, and Economy

Randolph Churchill, *The Fight for the Leadership of the Conservative Party*.

François Mauriac, *De Gaulle*.

In USA, the Warren Report into the assassination of President John F Kennedy (Nov 1963) concludes that Lee Harvey Oswald acted alone; its findings were later challenged by a House committee investigation in 1978.

In USA, the Free Speech Movement in Berkeley marks the start of a period of campus protest.

The new Labour government in Britain establishes a ministry of technology. In Britain, the Plowden Committee recommends union between Foreign Office and Com-

monwealth Relations Office overseas staff (27 Feb).

In USA, the 24th Amendment to the Constitution bans the use of poll taxes as a condition of voter rights in federal elections.

In USA, in Reynolds v. Simms, the Supreme Court rules that the Constitution's rules about equal protection imply an equal population rule for the apportionment of legislative districts.

United Nations establishes the Conference on Trade and Development (UNCTAD), to promote trade and negotiate trade agreements between countries.

In USA, the Teamsters' Union succeeds in obtaining a uniform contract for all truckers.

30 coup d'état in South Vietnam: General Duong Van Minh is replaced by General Nguyen Khanh (Minh remains the nominal head of state).

B February

11 fighting between Greeks and Turks at Limassol, Cyprus.

21 attempted assassination of Ismet Inönü, Turkish prime minister (and former president).

23 Britain recognizes President Abdul Amari Karume's régime in Zanzibar (now part of Tanzania).

C March

6 Death of King Paul I of Greece; succeeded by Constantine II.

9 fighting in Ktima, Cyprus.

11 South Africa withdraws from the International Labour Organization.

25 Sakari Tuomioja of Finland is appointed mediator in Cyprus dispute.

25 violence spreads in British Guiana (now Guyana) after eight-week strike of sugar-workers (strike ends, 26 July).

27 UN peace force under General Gyani, India, takes over from British troops in Cyprus.

31 military coup in Brazil deposes President João Belchio Goulart; on 2 April the presidency is declared vacant and is assumed by Marshal Humberto Castello Branco on 11.

D April

2 Yemen alleges British air attack on 28 March.

4 Archbishop Makarios abrogates 1960 treaty between Greece, Turkey, and Cyprus; heavy fighting occurs in the NW of the island.

13 Winston Field resigns as prime minister of Southern Rhodesia (now Zimbabwe) over question of unilateral declaration of independence if Britain insists on enfranchisement of African majority; Ian Smith forms ministry.

16 in Britain, 12 of those responsible for the 'Great Train Robbery' receive sentences totalling 307 years (12 Aug, Charles Wilson is helped to escape from Winson Green Prison).

16 in Southern Rhodesia (now Zimbabwe), Joshua Nkomo, leader of the Zimbabwe African People's Union, is placed under restriction.

22 Greville Wynne, British businessman sentenced in Moscow, USSR, in 1963, for spying, is exchanged at Berlin border for Gordon Lonsdale, the KGB agent sentenced in London for espionage, 1961.

27 Tanganyika and Zanzibar are united, with Julius Nyerere as president (29 Oct, the state is named the United Republic of Tanzania).

E May

In Jordan, the Palestine Liberation Organization (PLO) is founded in attempt to reconcile Palestinian factions.

14 Nikita Khrushchev of the USSR opens the Aswan Dam in the United Arab Republic (Egypt).

19 USA complains to the government of the USSR about microphones found in its Moscow embassy.

22 because of considerable unrest, a state of emergency is declared in British Guiana (now Guyana); British troops are flown in.

24 135 spectators at Peru versus Argentina football match in Lima, Peru, die in riot and over 500 are injured, after the referee disallowed an equalizing Peruvian 'goal'.

27 death (aged 74) of Jawaharlal Nehru, prime minister of India since independence in 1947; succeeded on 2 June by Lal Bahadur Shastri.

F June

11 Greece rejects direct talks with Turkey over Cyprus.

11 in South Africa, at the end of the 'Rivonia trial', Nelson Mandela is sentenced to life imprisonment for sabotage and conspiracy to overthrow the government; eight defendants receive lesser sentences, and one is discharged.

12 USSR and East Germany sign 20-year treaty of friendship.

19 in Congo Republic (now Zaire), rebels take Albertville (now Kalemi) in the north.

20 summit held in Tokyo, Japan, between President Macapagal of the Philippines, President Sukarno of Indonesia, and Tunku Abdul Rahman of Malaysia, to discuss friction between Indonesia and Malaysia; talks break down on 21.

30 end of UN military operations in the Congo Republic (now Zaire).

G July

6 Nyasaland Protectorate, renamed Malawi, becomes independent within the Commonwealth (becomes republic in 1966).

6 in Mexico, the candidate of the Institutional Revolutionary Party, Gustavo Ordaz, is elected president in succession to López Mateos (takes office on 1 Dec).

Abolition of Resale Price Maintenance (by Resale Prices Act) on most goods in Britain facilitates the rise of cost-cutting supermarkets (in force from 16 July).

British government grants licences to drill for oil and gas in the North Sea.

P Society, Education, and Religion

In USA, the Civil Rights Act 1964 prohibits racial discrimination in employment, unions, public accommodation, and restaurants (signed 3 July).

US Baptist minister and civil rights leader Martin Luther King is awarded the Nobel Peace Prize.

The Economic Opportunity Act in the USA (Aug) provides help for the unemployed, increases educational opportunities for poor children, and establishes VISTA, the domestic peace corps Volunteers in Service to America.

Food Stamp Act in the USA vastly expands the programme of providing food aid.

Murder of Kitty Genovese in New York and the callous reaction of local residents to her cries leads to introspection on the loss of community in US cities.

In South Africa, the Bantu Laws Amendment Act (passed 6 May) attempts to control the settlement of Africans in peripheral areas of towns and cities.

Outbreaks of anti-Muslim violence in India (22 March).

Industrial tribunals are established in Britain.

E Berne, *Games People Play*.

Hans Eysenck, *Crime and Personality*.

Marshall McLuhan, *Understanding Media*.

In USA, the Civil Rights Act is followed by a comprehensive survey of educational opportunities for the disadvantaged.

In Canada, the federal government introduces loans for university students.

In Australia, the report of the Martin Committee on technical education marked the beginning of a period of federal-funded college and university expansion.

Creation of the Department of Education and Science for England and Wales, which assumes the responsibilities of the previous Ministry of Education and also for universities.

Schools Council for Curriculum and Examinations established in Britain.

In Britain, the Council for National Academic Awards is established to award degrees in non-university institutions, including polytechnics and colleges of technology.

Foundation of the Universities of Essex (at Colchester) and Lancaster in England and Strathclyde in Scotland.

J W D Douglas, *The Home and the School*.

John Holt, *How Children Fail*.

Pope Paul VI makes pilgrimage to the Holy Land (4–6 Jan).

The Vatican signs an accord with Hungary (15 Sept).

Roman Catholic hierarchy in England and Wales rules against the use of the contraceptive pill (7 May), but authorizes joint prayers with other churches (6 Dec).

Arthur Koestler, *The Act of Creation*.

Q Science, Technology, and Discovery

US divers live on *Sealab* for nine days, at depth of 58.5 m/192 ft, off Bermuda coast, to study effects of depth on the mind and body.

Britain's advanced military fighter aircraft, the TSR-2, makes its maiden flight (28 Sept).

Britain's *Blue Streak* rocket is launched.

Ranger 7, launched from Cape Kennedy, succeeds in obtaining close-up photographs of the Moon's surface before crashing (31 July).

US *Mariner 4* and Soviet *Zond 2* are launched with equipment for photographing Mars.

USA develops uncrewed satellites 'Syncom' for relaying pictures of Olympic Games from Tokyo, and 'Nimbus'.

In USA, scientists at the Brookhaven National Laboratory, Upton, Long Island, discover the fundamental particle omega-minus through using the 'Nimrod' cyclotron.

Fred Hoyle and J V Narlikar of Cambridge University, England, propound new theory of gravitation, which solves the problem of inertia.

British chemist Dorothy Hodgkin wins the Nobel Prize for Chemistry for her work on X-ray crystallography (she is the third woman to win the prize).

The living brain of a rhesus monkey is isolated from its body by neurosurgeons at Cleveland General Hospital.

Successful experiments are made in finger-tip colour reading.

US surgeon general's report *Smoking and Health* confirm the links between cigarette smoking and lung cancer and heart disease.

R Humanities

A H M Jones, *The Later Roman Empire, 284–602: A Social, Economic and Administrative Survey*.

A G Dickens, *The English Reformation*.

Philip D Curtin, *The Image of Africa*.

W L Burn, *The Age of Equipoise*.

Robert Fogel, *Railroads and American Growth*.

H A Clegg, A Fox, and A F Thompson, *A History of British Trade Unions since 1889*, Volume 1.

10 Moïse Tshombe succeeds Cyrille Adoula as prime minister of the Congo Republic (now Zaire).

15 Anastas Mikoyan succeeds Leonid Brezhnev as president of the USSR.

18 race riots in Harlem, New York, the beginning of the 'ghetto revolts'.

22 (–30) constitutional conference in London on future of Gambia; agrees to independence in Feb 1965.

26 USSR calls for new 14-power meeting on Laos.

26 in British Guiana (now Guyana), strike of sugar-workers is called off.

27 (–30) disturbances in Northern Rhodesia (now Zambia), involving Lumpa Church, led by Alice Lenshina (death toll rises to 491).

27 in Britain, Winston Churchill (prime minister 1940–5, 1951-5) makes his last appearance in the House of Commons.

H August

2 The US destroyer *Maddox* is attacked off North Vietnam, in the Tonkin Gulf, by North Vietnamese torpedo boats; US aircraft bomb naval bases in North Vietnam in reprisal (on 4, the *Maddox* and the destroyer *C Turner Joy* are attacked).

5 in Congo Republic (now Zaire), rebels capture Stanleyville (now Kisangani); on 7, declare foundation of a People's Republic of the Congo.

7 in South Vietnam, General Nguyen Khanh proclaims a state of emergency and ousts President Duong Van Minh.

8 Turkish planes attack Cyprus; on 9, UN orders ceasefire.

11 Alice Lenshina surrenders in Northern Rhodesia (now Zambia), but further incidents occur.

13 General Grivas assumes command of Greek Cypriot forces.

17 Greece withdraws units from NATO.

24 white mercenaries arrive in Congo Republic (now Zaire) to fight rebels.

25 following protests in South Vietnam, President Nguyen Khanh resigns (on 27, General Duong Van Minh becomes chairman of Provisional Leadership Council).

26 in Rhodesia (now Zimbabwe), the nationalist movements People's Caretaker Council and the Zimbabwe African National Union (ZANU) are banned.

J September

2 Indonesian army lands at Labis in Malaysia; on 4, Commonwealth troops move in.

21 Malta becomes an independent state within the Commonwealth.

24 Berlin Passes agreement is signed between authorities of West Berlin and East Germany, whereby the Berlin Wall will be open for a fortnight four times a year, so that West Berliners can visit relatives in the East.

K October

5 (–11) conference in Cairo, United Arab Republic (Egypt), of 58 non-aligned states, but Moïse Tshombe, Congo Republic (now Zaire), is not permitted to attend.

14 Martin Luther King, US African-American leader, is awarded the Nobel Peace Prize.

15 in British general election Labour win 317 seats, Conservatives, 304, with Liberals, 9; (Labour receives 44.1 per cent of votes cast, Conservatives, 43.4, and Liberals, 11.2; overall national swing to Labour 3.2 per cent).

15 Nikita Khrushchev is replaced as first secretary of Soviet Communist Party by Leonid Brezhnev and as prime minister by Alexei Kosygin.

16 China explodes an atomic bomb.

16 in Britain, Alec Douglas-Home resigns as prime minister and Harold Wilson forms Labour ministry, with Patrick Gordon Walker, defeated at Smethwick, as foreign secretary, George Brown secretary of state for economic affairs, James Callaghan chancellor of the exchequer, and Lord Gardiner as lord chancellor.

20 civilian ministry established in South Vietnam, under Tran Van Huong.

24 Northern Rhodesia, renamed Zambia, becomes an independent republic within the Commonwealth, with Kenneth Kaunda as president (Southern Rhodesia is now known as just Rhodesia).

27 Harold Wilson states that a unilateral declaration of independence by Rhodesia (now Zimbabwe) would be an open act of defiance.

29 Indonesian landings on west coast of Malaysia, but Commonwealth troops capture the invaders.

L November

2 In Saudi Arabia, King Saud is deposed and replaced by his brother Faisal.

3 in US elections President Lyndon Baines Johnson, Democrat, with 486 electoral votes, has sweeping victory over Barry Goldwater, Republican, with 52; popular vote: Johnson, 43,126,506; Goldwater, 27,176,799; the Democrat gains in the House of Representatives leave them with 295 seats against the Republicans with 140.

5 in referendum in Rhodesia (now Zimbabwe), 90 per cent (of a 61 per cent poll) of white voters favour independence.

R Koebner and H D Schmidt, *Imperialism*.
Roy Jenkins, *Asquith*.
Alexander Werth, *Russia at War*.
W L Morton and D G Creighton (eds.), *The Canadian Centenary Series* (17 volumes; –1972).
Wilfrid Mellers, *Music in a New Found Land*.
Roman Ingarden, *The Controversy over the Existence of the World*.
Claude Lévi-Strauss, *Introduction to the Science of Mythology* (– 1971).
Herbert Marcuse, *One-dimensional Man*.

s Art, Sculpture, Fine Arts, and Architecture

Merger of art auction companies Sotheby of London and Parke-Burnet of New York.
US artist Robert Rauschenberg wins the Grand Prix at the Venice Biennale, seen as the defeat of the School of Paris and marking US domination.
New York art critic Clement Greenberg coins the term 'Post-Painterly Abstraction', referring to art after the gestural work of the New York school, with colour used for its optical effect alone.

Painting, etc:
'OP' art — geometric designs which give illusion of movement.
Jasper Johns, *Watchman*.
Robert Rauschenberg, *Retroactive II*.
Martial Raysse, *America America*.
Gerhard Richter, *Christa and Wolfi*.
Andy Warhol, *Most Wanted Men* series.

Sculpture:
Dan Flavin, *Monument 7 for V Tatlin* (–1965).
Claes Oldenberg, *Giant Soft Toothpaste*.
George Segal, *Woman Standing in a Bathtub*.
Andy Warhol, *Boxes*.

Architecture:
Arne Jacobsen, St Catherine's College, Oxford, England.

t Music

Milton Babbitt, *Philomel*.
Gottfried von Einem, *Die Zerissene* (opera).
Alberto Ginastera, *Don Rodrigo* (opera).
Vagn Holmboe, *Requiem for Nietzsche*.
Gustav Mahler, Symphony No. 10 (posthumous completion by Deryck Cooke).
Olivier Messiaen, *Colours of the Celestial City*.
Fiddler on the Roof (musical), lyrics by Sheldon Harnick, music by Jerry Bock (first performed at the Imperial Theater, New York, 22 Sept).
Hello, Dolly! (musical), lyrics and music by Jerry Herman (first performed in successful version at the St James Theatre, New York, 16 Jan).

The Animals, 'The House of the Rising Sun'.
Louis Armstrong, 'Hello Dolly'.
The Beatles, 'A Hard Day's Night' (single, album, and film).
Cilla Black, 'Anyone Who Had a Heart', 'You're My World'.
John Coltrane, 'A Love Supreme'.
Val Doonican, 'Walk Tall'.
Herman's Hermits, 'I'm Into Something Good'.
Roy Orbison, 'Oh, Pretty Woman', 'It's Over'.
The Rolling Stones, 'Rolling Stones No. 1'.
The Supremes, 'Baby Love'.
The Beatles and The Rolling Stones make their first visits to the USA.
First offshore 'pirate' radio station broadcasting to Britain, Radio Caroline (transmission starts 29 March).

u Literature and Drama

Chinua Achebe, *Arrow of God*.
Saul Bellow, *Herzog*.
John Berryman, *77 Dream Boys* (poems).
Richard Brautigan, *A Confederate General from Big Sur*.
Carlos Fuentes, *The Death of Artemio Cruz*.
William Golding, *The Spire*.
Ernest Hemingway, *A Moveable Feast* (posthumous).
Christopher Isherwood, *A Single Man*.
Philip Larkin, *The Whitsun Weddings* (poems).
Robert Lowell, *For the Union Dead*.
V S Naipaul, *An Area of Darkness*.
Frank O'Connor, *Fish for Fridays and Other Stories*.
Kathleen Raine, *The Hollow Hill* (poems).
Jean-Paul Sartre, *Les Mots*.
Hubert Selby, *Last Exit to Brooklyn*.
Frank Tuohy, *The Ice Saints*.
Gore Vidal, *Julian*.

Drama:
Ama Ata Aidoo, *Dilemma of a Ghost*.
John Arden, *The Workhouse Donkey*.
Enid Bagnold, *The Chinese Prime Minister*.
James Baldwin, *The Amen Corner*.
Arthur Miller, *After the Fall*.
John Osborne, *Inadmissible Evidence*.
Harold Pinter, *The Homecoming*.
Jack Richardson, *Gallow Humour*.
Peter Shaffer, *The Royal Hunt of the Sun*.
Peter Weiss, *Marat/Sade*.
Lanford Wilson, *Balm in Gilead*.
In London, closure of Joan Littlewood's Theatre Workshop, Stratford East, and the Windmill Theatre (non-stop vaudeville).

v Births and Deaths

Jan 22 Marc Blitzstein dies (58).
April 5 Douglas MacArthur dies (84).
May 27 Jawaharlal Nehru dies (74).
June 9 Max Aitken (Lord Beaverbrook) dies (85).

5 Zhou Enlai, prime minister of People's Republic of China, visits Moscow for summit talks of Communist states.

7 Ian Smith rejects proposed visit of Commonwealth secretary to Rhodesia (now Zimbabwe).

8 ceasefire in force in the Yemen.

8 Eisaku Sato becomes prime minister of Japan.

10 Kenya becomes a single-party state, after members of parliament belonging to the Kenya African Democratic Union join the Kenya African National Union.

12 high court in Rhodesia (now Zimbabwe) rules that Joshua Nkomo's detention is illegal; he and other African leaders are released on 16, and taken to restrictive areas.

16 in South Africa, start of trial in Johannesburg, under Suppression of Communism Act, of 14 whites, including Abraham Fischer, who had led defence in Rivonia trial.

17 Britain states its intention of banning exports of arms to South Africa.

24 in Congo Republic (now Zaire), Belgian paratroopers, the Congolese army, and white mercenaries capture Stanleyville (now Kisangani) from rebels and rescue 1,500 hostages (and, 26, rescue hostages from Paulis), although 30 hostages are killed by Christophe Gbenye's rebel forces.

26 Britain borrows $3,000 million from foreign bankers to save pound.

M December

2 Juan Perón, former president of Argentina, is detained in Brazil on his way to Argentina; is compelled to return to Spain.

6 Antonio Segni, president of Italy, resigns for health reasons; succeeded on 28 by Giuseppe Saragat.

12 Kenya becomes a republic within the Commonwealth with Jomo Kenyatta as president; ministers include Tom Mboya.

14 in British Guiana (now Guyana), following an election in which Cheddi Jagan's People's Progressive Party lost its majority, the governor dismisses Jagan as prime minister and appoints Forbes Burnham of People's National Congress.

16 the British government, Trades Union Congress, and employers sign a statement on productivity, prices, and incomes, intended as the first stage in development of an incomes policy.

17 announcement of free prescriptions in British Health Service from Feb 1965.

18 UN extends mandate for force in Cyprus to March 1965.

23 cyclone in Ceylon and southern India.

July 1 Roscoe Pound dies (93).
Aug 12 Ian Fleming dies (56).
Sept 3 Louis MacNeice dies (63).
Sept 18 Sean O'Casey dies (84).
Sept 20 Herbert Hoover dies (90).
Oct 15 Cole Porter dies (73).
Dec 9 Edith Sitwell dies (77).

w Everyday Life

The peak of 'Beatlemania' is reached, with the Beatles' appearance on *The Ed Sullivan Show* in the USA.

US postal service introduces Zip Codes.

Opening of two notable suspension bridges, the Forth Bridge in Scotland (4 Sept), and the Verrazano Narrows Bridge (the world's longest) at the entry to New York harbour.

British government changes August Bank Holiday to last Monday in month from 1965 (4 March).

Marriage of actors Elizabeth Taylor and Richard Burton (15 March), in Montreal, Canada.

In Britain, outbreaks during the Easter week-end of Mods *v*. Rockers disturbances in Clacton, Margate, and other south-coast resorts (30 March).

x Sport and Recreation

Cassius Clay beats Sonny Liston after six rounds of their fight in Miami, USA, to win the World Heavyweight title (25 Feb); Clay then announces his conversion to Islam, changing his name to Muhammad Ali.

In cricket, Fred Trueman of England becomes the first bowler to take 300 Test wickets (15 Aug).

The 18th Olympic Games are held in Tokyo (10–24 Oct). The USA wins 36 gold medals; the USSR, 30; Japan, 16; Italy and Hungary, 10; West Germany and Poland, 7; Australia, 6; Czechoslovakia, 5.

US boxer Sugar Ray Robinson retires from professional boxing with 174 victories in 201 bouts.

In British soccer, three Sheffield Wednesday players are accused of conspiring to 'fix' the result of a match against Ipswich Town; all three are subsequently jailed.

John Surtees is the first driver to win world championships on two and four wheels.

John White, Tottenham Hotspurs' international soccer star, is killed by a bolt of lightning on a golf course at Enfield, England (21 July).

y Media

In Britain, the Trades Union Congress sells its shares in the *Daily Herald*, which appears for the last time on 14 Sept; it reappears on 15 as the *Sun*.

Publication of the 'supermarket magazine' *Family Circle* in USA and Britain.

Petticoat published for girls of 14–19 in Britain.

Film:

Doctor Strangelove (director, Stanley Kubrick; starring Peter Sellers).

Eight and a Half (director, Federico Fellini).

A Fistful of Dollars (director, Sergio Leone; starring Clint Eastwood).

Goldfinger (director, Guy Hamilton; starring Sean Connery and Honor Blackman).

The Gospel According to St Matthew (director, Pier Paolo Pasolini).

Hamlet (director, Grigori Kozintsev).

A Hard Day's Night (starring The Beatles).

King and Country (director, Joseph Losey; starring Dirk Bogarde and Tom Courtenay).

Lord of the Flies (director, Peter Brooks).

Mary Poppins (starring Julie Andrews).

Muriel (director, Alain Resnais).

The Passenger (director, Andrzej Munk).

The Pumpkin Eater (director, Jack Clayton; starring Anne Bancroft, Peter Finch, and James Mason).

Red Desert (director, Michelangelo Antonioni).

Silken Skin (director, François Truffaut).

Woman of the Dunes (director, Hiroshi Teshigahara).

Zorba the Greek (starring Anthony Quinn).

Zulu (director, Cy Endfield).

Television:

Peyton Place (Twentieth Century Fox) is broadcast in the USA.

New programmes in Britain include: *Crossroads* (–1988), a 'soap opera' based in the Midlands; *Great Temples of the World*, presented by Sir Kenneth Clark; *Horizon* (BBC), a science magazine programme; *Ready Steady, Go!* (ITV); *Top of the Pops* (BBC); *The Wednesday Play* (BBC).

*Death of Winston Churchill ... Race riots in Watts District of Los
Angeles ... Rhodesia declares independence ...*

A January

2 In Pakistan, President Ayub Khan gains clear victory over Miss Fátima Jinnah in presidential elections.

2 Indonesia withdraws from the United Nations (the first member to do so); and on 8, more Indonesian landings in Malaysia.

14 the prime ministers of Northern Ireland and of the Republic of Ireland meet for the first time on Irish soil since partition in 1921.

20 in USA, inauguration of Lyndon Baines Johnson as president for new term.

21 Patrick Gordon Walker, foreign secretary, who lost his seat in the general election of Oct 1964, is defeated in by-election at Leyton; he resigns and is succeeded on 22 by Michael Stewart.

24 death of Winston Churchill, former prime minister of Britain; state funeral is held on 30, with service in St Paul's Cathedral, London, and burial at Bladon in Oxfordshire, near his birthplace of Blenheim Palace, Woodstock.

B February

7 US aircraft bomb North Vietnam, following attacks on US areas in South Vietnam; attack leads to regular US bombing of North Vietnam.

11 in Britain, following proposals from the government for a new pay structure, the British Medical Association advises family doctors to resign from the health service (doctors vote in favour of government's proposals for new pay structure, 5 Nov).

18 Gambia becomes independent within the Commonwealth.

21 in USA, Malcolm X, Muslim African-American leader, is shot dead in Manhattan, New York.

23 remains of Roger Casement (executed in 1916) are exhumed from Pentonville Prison, London, and sent to the Republic of Ireland for reinterment (given state funeral in Dublin on 30).

24 British government rejects Robbins Committee's recommendations for creating more new universities.

25 Regional Economic Planning Councils are set up in Britain.

C March

3 Bechuanaland (now Botswana), a British territory, becomes self-governing with Seretse Khama as prime minister.

7 in USA, violence at Selma, Alabama (9, whites kill a white civil rights worker).

8 3,500 US marines land in South Vietnam.

17 in Britain, Aubrey Jones is appointed first chairman of National Board for Prices and Incomes.

21 in USA, Martin Luther King heads procession of 4,000 civil rights demonstrators from Selma to Montgomery, Alabama, to deliver petition on grievances of African-Americans.

25 in USA, Ku Klux Klan shoot Viola Liuzzo, a white civil rights worker, in Selma, Alabama.

25 Dudley Senanayake forms ministry in Ceylon (now Sri Lanka) following defeat of Mrs Sirimavo Bandaranaike in elections.

28 serious earthquake in Chile, killing about 400 people.

D April

4 North Vietnamese Mig aircraft shoot down US jets.

7 President Johnson of USA proposes aid for vast development programme in SE Asia, which the governments of North Vietnam and the People's Republic of China reject.

8 members of the European Coal and Steel Community, the Economic Community, and Euratom sign treaty providing for the merging of the Communities' superior institutions into a single Commission and Council of Ministers.

9 clashes between Indian and Pakistani forces on Kutch–Sind border (between India and W Pakistan).

11 in USA, tornadoes devastate the mid-West.

17 student demonstrations in Washington, DC, USA, against US bombing of North Vietnam.

21 114-nation Disarmament Commission resumes talks in New York after five-year interval.

23 large-scale US raid over North Vietnam.

29 Australia decides to send troops to South Vietnam.

E May

7 In general election in Rhodesia (now Zimbabwe), Ian Smith's Rhodesian Front Party wins sweeping victory.

11 cyclone in East Pakistan (now Bangladesh).

12 West Germany establishes diplomatic relations with Israel; Arab states break off relations with West Germany.

18 in Britain, the first reference on a wage increase is made to the Prices and Incomes Board (for the printing industry).

President Johnson envisages the 'Great Society' ... First space walks ... Dr Zhivago ...

o Politics, Government, Law, and Economy

Political violence in Indonesia culminates in the massacre of the Communist Party by the new military regime.

M Olson, *The Logic of Collective Action*.

US poet Allen Ginsburg coins term 'Flower Power' at an anti-war rally.

Amalgamation of the British Foreign and Commonwealth Services as the Diplomatic Service (1 Jan).

In USA, in Griswold v. Connecticut (a case concerning birth control), the Supreme Court rules that there is a constitutional right to privacy expressed in the Bill of Rights.

Murder (Abolition of Death Penalty) Act suspends the application of the death penalty in Britain until 1970 (in force 9 Nov).

Britain accepts the jurisdiction of the European Court of Human Rights.

In Rice v. Connolly the British Court of Appeal holds that citizens cannot be compelled to assist police investigations by detention.

The English and Scottish Law Commissions are established in Britain, to undertake continuous reviews of the law in their jurisdictions and recommend reforms.

West Germany extends time limit for trials of former Nazis from May 1965 to Dec 1969 (25 March).

In West Germany, after a 20-month trial of former officials of the Nazi death camp at Auschwitz, a court sitting in Frankfurt sentences six men to life imprisonment (19 Aug).

The British government announces the *National Plan* with an ambitious target for growth (not achieved, because of currency crisis and austerity package in 1966).

British Petroleum Company strikes oil in the North Sea (21 Sept), but rig collapses (27 Dec).

In Britain, Jimmy Goldsmith founds Cavenham Foods.

Queen's Awards for Industry established in Britain.

Confederation of British Industry founded as a merger of three employer organizations.

Donovan Commission on Trade Unions and Employer Associations appointed.

Ralph Nader, *Unsafe at any Speed*.

p Society, Education, and Religion

In USA, in his State of the Union address (4 Jan), President Johnson proclaims the building of the 'Great Society', to comprise extensive federal programmes to support education (Head Start), medicine for the poor and elderly (Medicaid and Medicare), urban development schemes (Model Cities), and welfare benefits (AFDC).

Medical Care for the Aged Bill is signed by President Johnson on 30 July (at the Harry S Truman Library, Independence, Missouri).

In USA, Lorna Elizabeth Lockwood is the first woman to be appointed chief justice of a state supreme court (Arizona; named on 8 Jan).

In England, Judge Elizabeth Lane is the first woman to be appointed a High Court Judge.

In USA, the Voting Rights Act enforces the right of African-Americans to register and vote.

US abolishes the national quota system for immigration.

In Britain, White Paper on Commonwealth immigration proposes annual limit of 8,500 on work permits (2 Aug).

Race Discrimination Act bans discrimination in public places in Britain.

Hindi becomes an official language of India.

Dr Timothy Leary, *The Psychedelic Reader*.

In USA, enabling legislation is passed for the Head Start programme, designed to give disadvantaged children supplementary educational, nutritional, and health care before they enrol in school; the Elementary and Secondary Education Act targets federal spending on schools to poor areas and funds educational research; the Higher Education Act provides federal assistance to universities and colleges and provides undergraduate scholarships.

First 'teach-in' against the Vietnam War held at University of Michigan, USA.

In West Germany, foundation of the Education Council to provide advice.

In Britain, the Labour government publishes Circular 10/65, requesting all local authorities to submit plans for secondary school reorganization along comprehensive lines.

The Certificate of Secondary Education is introduced in England and Wales for children of average and lower ability, along the lines recommended by the Beloe Report in 1962.

Universities of Kent (at Canterbury) and Warwick are found in England and the University of Ulster (at Coleraine) in Northern Ireland.

E G West, *Education and the State*.

F **June**

2 In Congo Republic (now Zaire), European hostages are reported killed by Congolese rebels.

8 US forces in South Vietnam are authorized to engage in offensive operations against the Vietcong.

17 at Commonwealth prime ministers' conference, London, a Commonwealth secretariat is established.

19 Ahmed ben Bella, president of Algeria, is deposed; his former defence minister, Colonel Houari Boumédienne, heads revolutionary council.

24 South Vietnam breaks off relations with France.

30 India–Pakistan ceasefire signed.

G **July**

2 France announces boycott of all European Economic Community meetings apart from those concerned with day-to-day management of existing problems.

8 British Labour member of Parliament Harold Davies arrives in Hanoi, North Vietnam, as emissary of British Prime Minister Harold Wilson; no Vietnamese ministers meet the emissary.

15 King Constantine of Greece dismisses prime minister George Papandreou (after weeks of unrest Stephen C Stefanopoulos becomes prime minister, Sept 17).

22 in Britain, Alec Douglas-Home resigns as leader of the Conservative Party; on 27, Edward Heath is elected leader under new voting procedure (Heath wins 150 votes, Reginald Maudling, 133, Enoch Powell, 15; although Heath fails to win the majority plus 15 per cent required for victory, Maudling concedes defeat).

H **August**

3 In London, preparatory talks for a constitutional conference on Aden and the South Arabian federation; talks break down on 7.

8 Singapore secedes from Malaysia; Yusof Bin Ishaq becomes president (with Lee Kuan Yew remaining prime minister).

11 (–16) race riots in the Watts District of Los Angeles, California, USA, which break out after an African-American is arrested for drunken driving.

24 United Arab Republic (Egypt) and Yemen sign cease-fire agreement.

J **September**

1 Pakistani troops cross Kashmir cease-fire line.

1 terrorists in Aden shoot the speaker of the legislative council (26, Britain suspends the Constitution).

3 civil war breaks out in Dominica.

6 India invades West Pakistan and bombs Lahore.

7 (–24) constitutional conference in London on future of Mauritius; ends with promise of independence in 1966.

8 Rhodesia (now Zimbabwe) appoints an 'accredited representative' in Lisbon, Portugal.

22 ceasefire in war between India and Pakistan, which is subsequently violated by both sides.

29 USSR admits to supplying arms to North Vietnam.

K **October**

1 Six generals attempt coup against President Achmed Sukarno in Indonesia.

4 (–11) Ian Smith, prime minister of Rhodesia (now Zimbabwe), attends talks in London on Rhodesia.

13 in Congo Republic (now Zaire), President Kasavubu dismisses Moïse Tshombe, the prime minister.

17 demonstrations in USA and London against the war in Vietnam.

19 in USA, the Un-American Activities Committee of the House of Representatives begins public hearing on Ku Klux Klan.

25 (–30) Harold Wilson, prime minister of Britain, visits Salisbury, Rhodesia (now Harare, Zimbabwe), for talks with Ian Smith and African leaders.

25 kidnapping in Paris, France, of Mehdi Ben Barka, exiled Left Moroccan leader.

26 in Britain, at meeting in Aberdeen, the Archbishop of Canterbury, Michael Ramsey, states that if the British government had to use force in Rhodesia this would have the support of Christians (remarks cause storm in the Press; on 29 and 30, respectively, vandals spray paint in Canterbury Cathedral and York Minster).

L **November**

8 In Canadian elections, Lester B Pearson's Liberals are the largest party but fail to win an overall majority (Liberals win 131 seats; Progressive Conservatives, 97; others, 37).

11 Ian Smith, prime minister of Rhodesia (now Zimbabwe) makes Unilateral Declaration of Independence; Britain declares the régime illegal and introduces exchange and trade restrictions.

19 constitutional congress on future of British Guiana (now Guyana) ends with agreement for independence in May 1966.

25 in Congo Republic (now Zaire), General Sese Seko Mobutu deposes President Kasavubu.

Pope Paul VI visits New York to address the United Nations General Assembly; before the Vatican Council closes, promulgates a document exonerating the Jews of responsibility for the death of Christ.

The Vatican allows the resumption of worker-priests in France (suspended 1959).

The Orthodox Church annuls its excommunication of the Church of Rome in 1054.

In Britain, Westminster Abbey, founded by King Edward the Confessor, begins its 900th anniversary celebrations (commemorating the consecration of the Abbey, on 28 Dec 1065).

H E Cox, *The Secular City*.

Q Science, Technology, and Discovery

Soviet Antonov AN-22 heavy transport aircraft makes flight with 720 passengers.

Soviet cosmonaut Alexei Leonov leaves spacecraft *Voskhod 2* and floats in space for 20 minutes (18 March).

US space-ship *Gemini 3* is manoeuvred by pilots Virgil Grissom and John Young during orbit (23 March).

Edward White walks for 20 minutes in space from US *Gemini 4* (3 June), and *Gemini 5* makes 120 orbits (21–29 Aug).

Gemini 7 (launched 4 Dec), meets *Gemini 6* in orbit and returns (on 18 Dec) after flight of record length.

US satellite *Mariner 4* transmits close-up photographs of Mars (15 July).

First French satellite is launched (26 Nov).

R Humanities

Grahame Clark and Stuart Piggott, *Prehistoric Societies*.

Arnold J Toynbee, *Hannibal's Legacy*.

E R Dodds, *Pagan and Christian in an Age of Anxiety*.

W H C Frend, *Martyrdom and Persecution in the Early Church*.

Identification of a coffin found in Stepney, E London as containing the remains of Anne Mowbray, Duchess of York (died 1481).

The Complete Works of Sir Thomas More (–).

Martin Walzer, *The Revolution of the Saints*.

Christopher Hill, *Intellectual Origins of the English Revolution*.

Peter Laslett, *The World We Have Lost*.

Lawrence Stone, *The Crisis of the Aristocracy*.

A J P Taylor, *English History, 1914–1965* ('Oxford History of England' series).

Arthur Schlesinger, Jr, *Thousand Days*.

The Letters of Charles Dickens (Pilgrim Edition), (–).

Louis Althusser, *For Marx*.

Monroe Beardsley, *Philosophical Thinking*.

S Art, Sculpture, Fine Arts, and Architecture

Painting, etc:

Francis Bacon, *Study from Portrait of Pope Innocent X*.

Joseph Beuys, *How to Explain Pictures to a Dead Hare*.

Peter Blake, *Roxy, Roxy*.

Roy Lichtenstein, *Red and Yellow Brushstrokes*.

Kenneth Noland, *Transwest*.

A R Penck, *Method of Coping*.

Michelangelo Pistoletto, *Vietnam*.

Mark Rothko, the Rothko Chapel paintings, Houston, Texas, USA (–1966).

Sculpture:

Edward Kienholz, *The Beanery*.

Architecture:

Frederick Kiesler, Shrine of the Book, Jerusalem.

Viljo Revell, City Hall, Toronto, Canada.

Eero Saarinen, Gateway Arch, St Louis, Missouri, USA.

Lord Snowdon, new Aviary, London Zoo.

Kenzo Tange, Roman Catholic Basilica of St Mary, Tokyo, Japan.

T Music

Leonard Bernstein, *Chichester Psalms*.

Pierre Boulez, *Éclat*.

Sylvano Bussotti, *La Passion selon Sade*.

Krzysztof Penderecki, *St Luke Passion*.

Terry Riley, *In C*.

Bernd Zimmermann, *Die Soldaten* (opera).

In Britain, inauguration of National Youth Championship for brass bands.

The Beach Boys, 'California Girls'.

The Beatles, 'Help' (single, album, and film), 'Ticket to Ride', 'Day Tripper'.

The Byrds, 'Mr Tambourine Man'.

Petula Clark, 'Downtown'.

The Hollies, 'I'm Alive'.

Tom Jones, 'It's Not Unusual'.

The Rolling Stones, 'Satisfaction'.

The Seekers, 'I'll Never Find Another You'.

The Temptations, 'My Girl'.

In Chicago, USA, formation of the Association for the Advancement of Creative Musicians, a collective to encourage self-employment by black jazz musicians.

Philips Records launches the 'musicassette', i.e., 'cassette' tape recording, at the Berlin Radio Show.

U Literature and Drama

Basil Bunting, *Loquitur*.

Margaret Drabble, *The Millstone*.

Günter Grass, *Dog Years*.

Jerzy Kosinski, *The Painted Bird*.

Cormac McCarthy, *The Orchard Keeper*.

M December

5 In France, first round of presidential election; Charles de Gaulle wins largest percentage of vote but fails to obtain clear majority.

8 new Rent Act in force in Britain, gives greater security to tenants.

9 Nikolai Podgorny replaces Anastas Mikoyan as president of the USSR.

17 Britain imposes oil embargo on Rhodesia (now Zimbabwe); 19, begins airlift of oil to Zambia.

18 nine African states break off diplomatic relations with Britain for not using force against Rhodesia.

19 Charles de Gaulle defeats François Mitterrand in second round of presidential election.

29 President Ho Chi Minh of North Vietnam rejects unconditional peace talks offered by USA.

29 independence for Bechuanaland (now Botswana) announced for Sept 1966.

31 the executives of the European Economic Community, the European Coal and Steel Community, and Euratom are merged into one executive authority.

Norman Mailer, *An American Dream*.
Peter Matthiessen, *At Play in the Fields of the Lord*.

Drama:
Frank Marcus, *The Killing of Sister George*.
John Osborne, *A Patriot for Me*.
Neil Simon, *The Odd Couple*.
Michel Tremblay, *Les Belles Soeurs*.
The Vivian Beaumont Theatre opened at the Lincoln Center for Performing Arts, New York.

v Births and Deaths
Jan 4 T S Eliot dies (76).
Jan 24 Winston Churchill dies (90).
Feb 15 Nat 'King' Cole dies (45).
Feb 23 Stan Laurel dies (74).
March 6 Herbert Morrison dies (77).
March 17 King Farouk dies (45).
May 21 Geoffrey de Havilland dies (82).
May 23 David Smith dies (59).
June 13 Martin Buber dies (86).
June 20 Bernard Baruch dies (94).
July 14 Adlai Stevenson dies (65).
Aug 27 Le Corbusier dies (77).
Sept 4 Albert Schweitzer dies (90).
Nov 16 William T Cosgrave dies (85).

w Everyday Life
Miniskirts, first designed in France, rapidly become fashionable across the western world.
Britain decides to adopt metric measurements.
In Britain, opening in London of the Post Office Tower (now the Telecom Tower), the tallest building in Britain (7 Oct).

x Sport and Recreation
In Britain, Stanley Matthews, the first professional footballer to be knighted (1 Jan), plays his last football league match, for Stoke City against Fulham, five days after his 50th birthday (6 Feb).
British driver Jim Clark, driving a Lotus, becomes the first European for 45 years to win the Indianapolis 500 races in the USA (May).
Substitutes are allowed in British soccer league matches for the first time (21 Aug).
In golf, the Walker Cup match between Great Britain and Ireland, and the USA in Baltimore, USA, ends in a tie, 12–12 (3–4 Sept).
Mme Vaucher, the first woman to climb the Matterhorn, climbs the mountain's north wall on the centenary of the first ascent.

Australia wins the first women's world Softball championships, held in Melbourne, Australia.

y Media
Film:
Alphaville (director, Jean-Luc Godard).
The Battle of Algiers (director, Gillo Pontecorvo).
The Cincinnati Kid (director, Norman Jewison; starring Steve McQueen and Edward G Robinson).
The Collector (starring Samantha Eggar).
Darling (director, John Schlesinger; starring Julie Christie).
Doctor Who and the Daleks (director Gordon Fleming; starring Peter Cushing and Roy Castle).
Doctor Zhivago (director, David Lean).
The Knack (starring Rita Tushingham).
Repulsion (director, Roman Polanski).
The Shakespeare Wallah (director, James Ivory).
Simon of the Desert (director, Luis Buñuel).
The Sound of Music (starring Julie Andrews).

Television:
The funeral of Winston Churchill in Britain (24 Jan) is watched by an estimated 350,000,000 people worldwide.
Early Bird, US commercial communications satellite, is first used by television (2 May).
In USA, the programme *Actions of a Vietnamese Marine Battalion* (NTV) shows startling scenes from the Vietnam War.
In Britain, cigarette advertising is banned from commercial television (from 1 Aug).
New programmes in Britain include: *The Magic Roundabout*, showing the original French film with a new English narration by Eric Thompson (BBC; –1975); *Man Alive* (BBC; –1982); *Not Only–But Also ...* (BBC) a comedy series starring Peter Cook and Dudley Moore; *The Power Game*, starring Patrick Wymark; *Tomorrow's World* (BBC), a technology and science magazine programme.
The BBC programme *The War Game*, about the possible effects of a nuclear attack on Britain, is considered too disturbing to be shown.
The Tea Party, by dramatist Harold Pinter, is one of Britain's contributions to the European Broadcasting Union's joint drama commissions.
In Britain, Mrs Mary Whitehouse founds the National Viewers' and Listeners' Association to campaign against offensive and immoral broadcasting.

*France withdraws from NATO command structure ... Cultural
Revolution in China ...*

A January

1 Pope Paul VI appeals for peace in Vietnam.

1 Colonel Jean-Bedel Bokassa seizes power in the Central African Republic.

1 (–13), transport strike in New York.

8 major US offensive against the 'Iron Triangle', stronghold of the Vietcong.

10 Tashkent peace agreement between India and Pakistan.

11 death of Lal Bahandra Shastri, Prime Minister of India; succeeded by Indira Gandhi (19).

13 Robert Weaver appointed secretary of housing and urban development, the first African-American in US cabinet.

16 General Ironsi takes power in Nigeria after military coup.

20 Robert Menzies retires as prime minister of Australia; succeeded by Harold Holt (25).

27 (–25 Aug) 18-nation disarmament conference in Geneva.

30 France ends boycott of EEC meetings.

31 US resumes bombing of North Vietnam after 37-day pause.

31 Britain bans trade with Rhodesia.

B February

1 China protests to Britain about US warships in Hong Kong.

1 British government tightens credit squeeze.

7 (–8) President Johnson meets South Vietnamese leaders in Honolulu.

18 Dean Rusk states that USA has exhausted every procedure for bringing peace to Vietnam.

19 British Navy Minister Christopher Mayhew resigns in protest at proposed reduction in commitments east of Suez (in White Paper published on 22).

21 President de Gaulle of France calls for dismantling of NATO.

23 military junta seizes power in Syria.

24 British government publishes Prices and Incomes Bill.

24 overthrow of President Nkrumah of Ghana by military coup while away on tour of Asia.

C March

1 Rebellion in Eastern Assam, India.

2 Britain protests to Portugal about oil supplies reaching Rhodesia via Mozambique.

5 Organization of African Unity urges Britain to use force against Rhodesia (now Zimbabwe).

6 (–12) food riots in West Bengal, India, spreading to Calcutta and Delhi.

8 Australia triples its forces in Vietnam to 4,500 troops.

10 France requests removal of NATO bases from French territory.

11 after anti-Communist demonstrations, President Sukarno of Indonesia transfers all political powers to General Raden Suharto.

11 Canadian government orders inquiry into involvement of former cabinet ministers with East German spy Gerda Munsinger.

30 National Party wins sweeping victory in South African general election.

31 in British general election Labour win 363 seats, Conservatives, 253, with Liberals, 12 (Labour receives 47.9 per cent of votes cast, Conservatives, 41.9 per cent, and Liberals, 8.5 per cent).

D April

2 Unrest breaks out in Saigon, as protesters demand end of military rule in South Vietnam (14, government promises elections within 3–5 months).

6 (–8) increased ferry tolls spark riots in Hong Kong.

9 Spain eases press censorship.

9 UN authorizes Britain to prevent oil shipments to Rhodesia by force.

14 in USA, Sandoz Pharmaceuticals Inc. withdraws drug LSD after widespread misuse.

15 wave of anti-Chinese violence begins in Indonesia.

16 General Abdul Rahman Arif succeeds his brother as President of Iraq.

16 Rhodesia (now Zimbabwe) demands departure of British diplomats from Salisbury (now Harare) (28, withdrawal suspended).

18 People's Party forms a government in Austria.

27 (–20 May) clashes between police and students at Spanish universities.

28 in USA, President Johnson asks Congress for new civil-rights legislation to end discrimination in housing and jury service.

E May

3 British Budget introduces selective employment tax and corporation tax at 40 per cent.

3 USA admits shelling Cambodia.

4 British Government accepts Kindersley Report's recommendation for £1,000 p.a. increase in doctors' pay.

Trial in London of the 'Moors murderers' ... Opening of the new
'Met' in New York ... Death of Walt Disney ...

o Politics, Government, Law, and Economy

Henry Steele Commager, *Freedom and Order: A Commentary on the American Political Scene.*

W Fulbright, *The Arrogance of Power.*

Department of Housing and Urban Development established in USA, with Robert C Weaver as head of department and the first African-American in the US cabinet (appointed 17 Jan).

The opening of Britain's Parliament is televised for the first time (1 April).

In Miranda v. Arizona, the US Supreme Court rules that evidence obtained by confession is only valid when the police can show that the suspect's right to silence was observed and the suspect was aware of the rights given in the constitution (13 June).

In Harper v. Virginia Board of Elections, the US Supreme Court rules that poll taxes as a requirement to vote are unconstitutional (25 March).

South Africa extends its apartheid laws to South West Africa (now Namibia).

In Britain, the Lord Chancellor announces that the House of Lords would not consider itself absolutely bound by its own precedents (26 July).

In Britain, the Court of Appeal and the Court of Criminal Appeal are merged.

In London, trial of the 'Moors murderers' (4 April–6 May): Ian Brady and Myra Hindley are both convicted of the murder of a child and a youth, and Brady for the murder of another child, and receive life imprisonment. One child was buried on Saddleworth Moor in the Pennines; Brady and Hindley are thought to be responsible for the deaths of two other missing children.

In Britain, Queen Elizabeth II grants a posthumous pardon to Timothy Evans, who was hanged for murder in 1950 and is now thought to have been 'probably innocent' (18 Oct).

Members of the European Free Trade Association (EFTA) abolish tariffs on industrial goods, creating a customs union (31 Dec).

Australia adopts decimal currency (14 Feb).

In USA, the Fair Packaging and Labeling Act (signed 3 Nov) regulates package sizes and money-off claims, and requires net weight to be stated on packaging.

In Britain, peak of manufacturing employment.

The British steel industry is nationalized; the Industrial Reorganization Corporation is founded to aid mergers.

In Britain, businessman Freddie Laker forms Laker Airways to provide cheap flights to the USA (–1982).

p Society, Education, and Religion

In USA, author Betty Friedan founds the National Organization of Women (NOW).

In USA, Stokely Carmichael of Student Non-violent Coordinating Committee (SNCC) calls for 'Black Power'.

Foundation in USA of the militant African-American paramilitary organization the Black Panthers.

British government introduces Supplementary Benefit for the sick, disabled, unemployed, and widows.

In USA, the Child Nutrition Act (signed 11 Oct) grants federal funds to provide food for impoverished school children.

In USA, the Demonstration Cities and Metropolitan Redevelopment Act (signed 3 Nov), known as the Model Cities Act will provide $1 billion for the rebuilding of 60–70 inner cities.

Demolition of New York's Pennsylvania Station causes a public reaction in favour of conserving urban landmarks.

W Masters and V Johnson, *Human Sexual Response.*

H Thompson, *Hell's Angels.*

In China, as part of the Cultural Revolution, all universities are closed for re-educational purposes and school lessons become geared towards increasing productive labour in factories and in the countryside.

In Finland, five universities are founded.

In Britain, foundation of the Universities of Aston (in Birmingham), Bath, and Surrey (at Guildford), Brunel University (Uxbridge), City University (London), Heriot-Watt University (Edinburgh), and Loughborough University of Technology; 30 polytechnics are created.

In England, establishment of Wolfson College, Oxford; foundation of Clare Hall and Fitzwilliam College, Cambridge.

In Britain, the US evangelist Billy Graham mounts the Greater London Crusade.

Archbishop Michael Ramsey of the Church of England pays an official visit to Pope Paul VI (23 March), the first by the English primate since the mid-16th century.

Red Guards in Beijing, People's Republic of China, close churches and fly red flags on the Roman Catholic Cathedral.

Office of Inquisitor abolished at the Vatican.

Index of books prohibited to Roman Catholics is abolished.

7 Nicolae Ceauşescu declares that Romania recognizes no supreme authority within international Communist movement.

9 (–20) talks between British and Rhodesian officials in London (second round in Salisbury, 2 June–5 July).

16 (–1 July) British seamen's strike (23, state of emergency proclaimed to allow government control of ports).

18 Spain and Britain begin discussions on future of Gibraltar (talks end without agreement, 14 July).

23 South Vietnamese troops crush Buddhist rebellion in Da Nang after a week of fighting.

24 Ugandan army drives out the kabaka of Buganda (kingdom dissolved, 10 June).

26 British Guiana becomes independent as Guyana.

28 violent protests against creation of unitary state in Nigeria.

F June

2 Éamon de Valera re-elected president of Ireland.

3 purge of 'rightists' in Chinese leadership begins.

7 demonstrators in East Pakistan demand greater autonomy.

20 (–30) President de Gaulle visits USSR.

22 South Vietnamese army moves into Quang Tri, last stronghold of Buddhist opposition.

26 major civil-rights rally in Jackson, Mississippi, USA.

29 USA bombs Hanoi and Haiphong. Britain dissociates itself from bombing of populated areas.

G July

1 France withdraws its forces from NATO command structure.

1 British Steel Renationalisation Bill published.

3 Frank Cousins, the first minister of technology, resigns over prices and incomes policy; succeeded by A N Wedgwood Benn.

6 North Vietnamese parade 50 captured US airmen through streets of Hanoi.

11 USSR announces further aid to North Vietnam.

12 (–23) in USA, race riots in Chicago, Cleveland, and Brooklyn.

14 British bank rate rises from 6 to 7 per cent.

14 Israeli jets raid Syria in retaliation for border incursions.

20 British government announces six-month wage and price standstill, dividend curbs, and credit and exchange controls.

24 EEC reaches agreement on Common Agricultural Policy.

25 Chinese newspapers carry front-page pho-

tos of Mao Zedong during 14-km (9-mi) 65-minute swim down the Yangzi on (16).

29 General Yakubu Gowon succeeds General Ironsi as ruler of Nigeria after army mutiny.

31 British Colonial Office dissolved; remaining responsibilities assumed by Commonwealth Office.

H August

10 George Brown replaces Michael Stewart as British foreign secretary.

11 three-year-old undeclared war between Indonesia and Malaysia ends with agreement to decide status of Sarawak and Sabah by referendum.

13 Central Committee of Chinese Communist Party, in first plenary session since 1962, endorses the 'Great Proletarian Cultural Revolution', the movement to 'purify' Chinese Communism through young Red Guards violently removing members of the intelligentsia.

15 Israeli and Syrian forces clash around Sea of Galilee.

16 (–19) disorderly hearings of US Un-American Activities Committee on bill to penalize US citizens aiding Vietcong.

18 Red Guards make their first appearance in Beijing. Four days of anti-Western demonstrations follow.

19 earthquake in eastern Turkey kills 2,000.

J September

6 H F Verwoerd, prime minister of South Africa, is stabbed to death in Parliament in Cape Town. succeeded by B J Vorster (13).

6 (–14) Commonwealth conference in London commits Britain to seeking UN mandatory sanctions against Rhodesia (now Zimbabwe).

9 Rhodesian High Court rules that Ian Smith's regime is unlawful but the only effective administration.

16 China accuses USA of bombing Chinese territory near North Vietnamese frontier.

19 US Civil Rights Bill to end housing discrimination defeated by Senate filibuster.

23 US discloses that its planes are defoliating jungle areas in central Vietnam to deny cover to enemy.

27 in USA, race riots in San Francisco after shooting of African-American boy.

30 Bechuanaland becomes independent as Botswana, with Sir Seretse Khama as President.

30 Albert Speer and Baldur von Schirach released from Spandau Prison, Berlin, after serving 20 years for war crimes.

Publication of The Jerusalem Bible.

T J J Altizer, *The Gospel of Christian Atheism.*

Q Science, Technology, and Discovery

Soviet spacecraft *Luna 9* makes the first soft landing on the Moon (3 Feb), followed by US *Surveyor 1* (2 June).

Soviet probe *Venera 3* crashes on Venus (1 March), the first human-made object to land on another planet.

US *Gemini 8* achieves the first link-up of a crewed space craft with another object, an *Agena* rocket (16 March).

Soviet *Luna 11* goes into orbit around the Moon (Aug).

US *Lunar Orbiter 1* enters Moon orbit (10 Aug) and transmits pictures of the dark side.

Gemini 12, the last of the *Gemini* two-person space missions (launched 11 Nov).

Soviet *Luna 13* lands on the Moon (24 Dec) and sends back data about the soil.

In USA, astronomers at the Naval Research Laboratory discover powerful X-rays emitted from within the constellation Cygnus.

Molecular biologists discover that DNA is not confined to chromosomes but is also contained within cells in the mitochondria.

A French medical group defines death as brain inactivity rather than heart stoppage.

US scientists Harry M Meyer and Paul D Parman develop a live virus vaccine for rubella (German measles), which reduces the incidence of the disease.

Konrad Lorenz, *On Aggression.*

David Lack, *Population Studies of Birds.*

R Humanities

K V Flannery and associates begin detailed survey of the Valley of Oaxaca, Mexico.

Michael Coe and associates from Yale University, USA, begin detailed study of Olmec culture, Mexico.

E Le Roy Ladurie, The Peasants of Languedoc.

E A Wrigley, *An introduction to English Historical Demography.*

Robert Blake, *Disraeli.*

J R Vincent, *The Formation of the Liberal Party, 1857–1868.*

Owen Chadwick, *The Victorian Church*, Volume 1 (Volume 2, 1970).

J W Burrow, *Evolution and Society.*

Raymond Carr, *Spain, 1808–1939.*

Douglass C North, *Growth and Welfare in the American Past: A New Economic History.*

Dictionary of Canadian Biography (–).

Foundation in USA of the National Endowment for the Humanities.

Barrington Moore, *Social Origins of Dictatorship and Democracy.*

Theodor Adorno, *Negative Dialectics.*

Jacques Lacan, *Ecrits.*

S Art, Sculpture, Fine Arts, and Architecture

Severe floods in Florence leave the Renaissance centre under 2 m/6 ft of water (4 Nov).

Multi-part homage to Picasso in Paris, France, with exhibitions at the Bibliothèque Nationale, Grand Palais, and Petit Palais.

Painting, etc:

Term 'Arte Povera' coined by Germano Celant, Italy.

Allan Kaprow, *Gas — Collective Happening.*

Joseph Kosuth, *Titled (Art as an Idea).*

Malcolm Morley, *SS 'Amsterdam' in Front of Rotterdam.*

Sculpture:

Carl André, *Equivalent 8.*

Architecture:

John Andrews and Page and Steele, Scarborough College, University of Toronto, Canada.

Marcel Breuer and Hamilton Smith, new building for the Whitney Museum, New York.

Gio Ponti, Secretariat Buildings, Islamabad, Pakistan.

T Music

Samuel Barber, *Antony and Cleopatra* (opera).

Cathy Berberian, *Stripsody.*

Hans Werner Henze, *The Bassarids* (opera).

György Ligeti, *Aventures et Nouvelles Aventures.*

Arvo Pärt, Symphony No. 2.

Steve Reich, *Come Out.*

Eduard Tubin, Symphony No. 8.

Opening of new Metropolitan Opera House in New York.

Cabaret (musical) by John Kander and Fred Ebb (first performed at the Broadhurst Theater, New York, 20 Nov).

The Beach Boys, 'Good Vibrations'.

The Beatles, 'Paperback Writer', 'Eleanor Rigby', 'Yellow Submarine'.

The Byrds, 'Fifth Dimension'.

Cream, 'Fresh Cream'.

Neil Diamond, 'Cherry, Cherry', 'I Got the Feeling'.

Bob Dylan, 'Blonde on Blonde'.

The Four Tops, 'Reach Out, I'll Be There'.

Tom Jones, 'Green, Green Grass of Home'.

The Seekers, 'Georgy Girl'.

Simon and Garfunkel, 'Sounds of Silence'.

Frank Sinatra, 'Strangers in the Night'.

In Liverpool, NW England, closure of the Cavern Club, 'the home of the Beatles' (28 Feb).

κ October

1 Chinese defence minister, Lin Biao, accuses USSR of plotting with USA over Vietnam.

4 Basutoland becomes independent as Lesotho under King Moshoeshoe II.

5 Prices and Incomes Act gives British government powers to freeze wages and prices.

5 Spain closes frontier with Gibraltar to all traffic except pedestrians (refuses to accept Gibraltar passports from 12 Nov).

7 USSR expels all Chinese students.

14 heaviest US air raids on North Vietnam to date.

17 US President Lyndon Johnson begins 17-day tour of Far East and Pacific.

21 slag heap at Aberfan, Glamorgan, S Wales, slips and engulfs school, killing 116 children and 28 adults.

22 George Blake, serving 42 years for espionage, escapes from Wormwood Scrubs, London.

24 (–25) Manila Conference of Vietnam war allies: South Vietnam, USA, Australia, New Zealand, Philippines, South Korea, Thailand.

27 China announces successful test-firing of a guided nuclear missile.

27 UN Assembly ends South Africa's mandate over South-West Africa. South Africa refuses to accept the decision.

28 President de Gaulle of France calls for US withdrawal from Vietnam.

28 Britain and France agree plans for Channel Tunnel.

ʟ November

2 Enver Hoxha allies Albania with China and denounces USSR.

4 extensive flooding in central and northern Italy.

7 riots in Delhi over cow slaughter laws.

8 in US mid-term elections, Democrats retain control of Congress with reduced majorities.

10 Harold Wilson declares Britain's determination to become a member of the EEC.

13 Israeli forces attack Hebron area of Jordan (25, UN censures Israel).

22 Spanish Cortes passes new constitution proposed by General Franco (95 per cent approval in referendum, 14 Dec).

23 Red Guards demand dismissal of Chinese head of state, Liu Shaoqi, and party secretary, Deng Xiaoping.

30 Barbados becomes independent within Commonwealth.

30 Britain abolishes 10 per cent surcharge on imports.

ᴍ December

1 Kurt Kiesinger becomes chancellor of West Germany, following resignation of Ludwig Erhard.

2 UN unanimously elects U Thant of Burma for second term as secretary general.

2 (–4) Harold Wilson and Ian Smith meet aboard HMS *Tiger* and prepare plan for settlement of Rhodesian dispute (5, Rhodesia rejects the plan).

7 Arab Defence Council in Cairo co-ordinates military response to any Israeli attack.

8 Syria seizes Iraq Petroleum Company pipeline.

13 US raid on Hanoi suburbs kills over 100 civilians.

16 UN Security Council approves selective mandatory sanctions against Rhodesia (now Zimbabwe).

20 Britain rules out legal independence for Rhodesia except under black majority rule.

22 Ian Smith declares Rhodesia a republic.

24 Cardinal Spellman, Archbishop of New York, in sermon at US base near Saigon, says Vietnam is a war for civilization and anything less than victory is inconceivable.

30 Britain invites USA, South Vietnam, and North Vietnam to meet on British territory to arrange ceasefire.

31 Yugoslavia releases Communist dissident, Milovan Djilas, from prison.

John Lennon speculates that The Beatles are more popular than Jesus Christ (4 March); in response, Beatles records are burnt in the US 'Bible belt'. The Beatles give their last concert, at Candlestick Park, San Francisco, USA (29 Aug).

Avant-garde rock band the Velvet Underground does multi-media shows with Pop artist Andy Warhol.

u Literature and Drama
Truman Capote, *In Cold Blood*.
John Fowles, *The Magus*.
Graham Greene, *The Comedians*.
P J Kavanagh, *The Perfect Stranger*.
Bernard Malamud, *The Fixer*.
Yukio Mishima, *The Sailor who fell from Grace with the Sea*.
Vladimir Nabokov, *Despair*.
Anaïs Nin, *Diary* (Volume 1).
Sylvia Plath, *Ariel* (poems).
Thomas Pynchon, *The Crying of Lot 49*.
Jean Rhys, *The Wide Sargasso Sea*.
Susan Sontag, *Against Interpretation*.
Martin Walser, *The Unicorn*.
Patrick White, *The Solid Mandala*.

Drama:
Edward Albee, *A Delicate Balance*.
Edward Bond, *Saved*.
Emilio Carballido, *I, Too, Speak of the Rose*.
Aimé Césaire, *A Season in the Congo*.
Jorge Díaz, *The Toothbrush*.
Joe Orton, *Loot*.

v Births and Deaths
Feb 1 Buster Keaton dies (70).
April 10 Evelyn Waugh dies (62).
Sept 21 Paul Reynaud dies (87).
Dec 15 Walt Disney dies (65).
Dec 30 Christian Herter dies (71)

w Everyday Life
In Britain, the soccer world cup (the Jules Rimet Trophy) is stolen while on show at a stamp exhibition in London (found a week later, on 27 March, wrapped in newspaper).

x Sport and Recreation
Arkle, ridden by Pat Taaffe, wins the Cheltenham Gold Cup in Britain for the third successive year (17 March).

Following a court case, the British Jockey Club allows women to hold licences for training race horses.

Alan Ball is the first British soccer player to be transferred for £100,000 (from Blackpool to Everton).

In American professional football, a merger is agreed between the American Football League and the National Football League (8 June).

Host nation England wins soccer's World Cup, beating West Germany in the final 4–2 after extra time (30 July).

In lawn tennis, Australia wins the Davis Cup for the third successive year, beating India in the final.

Australian Jack Brabham wins the World Formula One motor racing championship in a car manufactured by his own company (4 Sept).

The first world Orienteering Championships are held.

y Media
The Times of London appears in new format with news on front page (3 May); Lord Thomson buys *The Times* from Gavin Astor (30 Sept).

The *Daily Worker* in Britain changes its name to *Morning Star* (May).

Three New York newspapers merge to form the *World Journal Tribune* (Sept).

Film:
Alfie (director, Lewis Gilbert; starring Michael Caine).
Andrei Rublev (director, Andrei Tarkovsky).
Georgy Girl (director, Silvio Narizzano; starring James Mason and Lynn Redgrave).
A Man and a Woman (director, Claude Lelouch).
A Man for All Seasons (script by Robert Bolt; director, Fred Zinnemann; starring Paul Scofield).
Two or Three Things I Know about Her (director, Jean-Luc Godard).

Television:
New programmes in USA include: *Batman*; *The Monkees*; *Star Trek*.
New programmes in Britain include: *Cathy Come Home* (BBC), *Softly Softly* (BBC; –1970), *Thunderbirds*, *Till Death Us Do Part* (BBC), written by Johnny Speight and starring Warren Mitchell.
Laurence Olivier's production of Shakespeare's *Othello* is broadcast in Britain.

*Greek military coup ... Six-Day War ... France vetoes British
entry into EEC ...*

A January

6 US and South Vietnamese forces launch major offensive in Mekong Delta.

10 President Johnson's State of Union address proposes 6 per cent war tax surcharge (increased to 10 per cent, 3 Aug).

10 US Supreme Court upholds right of travel to Communist countries regardless of State Department prohibitions.

15 (–24) Harold Wilson and George Brown tour EEC capitals to argue for British membership.

18 Jeremy Thorpe succeeds Jo Grimond as leader of the British Liberal Party.

26 (–12 Feb) Red Guards besiege Soviet embassy in Béijing, alleging mistreatment of Chinese students in Moscow.

28 USSR sends note to Potsdam signatories accusing West Germany of neo-Nazism and militarism.

30 France abolishes exchange controls and frees the gold market.

B February

2 President Johnson offers to halt US bombing of North Vietnam, if North Vietnamese cease infiltration of South Vietnam (Ho Chi Minh rejects proposals, 5 Mar).

2 General Somoza, Jr, becomes president of Nicaragua.

6 (–13) Soviet Prime Minister Kosygin visits Britain and discusses Vietnam with Harold Wilson.

10 curfew imposed in Aden after nationalist riots.

11 Chinese army takes over Public Security Ministry and places Beijing under military rule.

14 21 nations sign treaty in Mexico City prohibiting nuclear weapons from Latin America.

15 (–21) ruling Congress Party sustains heavy losses in Indian general election.

21 18-nation disarmament conference reopens in Geneva, Switzerland.

22 US and South Vietnamese forces begin Operation Junction City.

26 Chinese Premier Zhou Enlai calls for return to order and discipline.

28 (–12 Mar) British–Maltese conference in London on rundown of British forces in Malta.

C March

2 Accidental US bombing of Lang Vei kills 80 South Vietnamese civilians.

6 Svetlana Alliluyeva, Stalin's daughter, requests asylum at US embassy in Delhi.

12 French general election reduces Gaullist-led coalition government's majority in National Assembly to one.

13 (–21) student 'sit-in' at London School of Economics in protest over disciplinary action.

18 Liberian tanker *Torrey Canyon* runs aground off Land's End, England. Oil extends over 260 sq km (100 sq mi).

19 French Somaliland rejects independence in referendum.

28 U Thant discloses his Vietnam peace plan, accepted by USA, but rejected by North Vietnam.

29 US Court of Appeals in New Orleans orders complete desegregation of schools in Alabama, Florida, Georgia, Louisiana, Texas, and Mississippi.

31 supreme headquarters of NATO moves from France to Casteau in Belgium.

D April

1 in Britain, Sir Edward Compton takes office as first Parliamentary Commissioner for Administration (Ombudsman).

1 President Thieu of South Vietnam promulgates new constitution.

2 (–7) UN diplomatic mission to Aden. General strike and terrorist campaign by Arab nationalists.

7 border clashes between Syria and Israel around Lake Tiberias.

8 fighting resumes between Greek and Turkish Cypriots near Limassol.

13 heavy Labour losses in British county council elections. In Greater London, Conservatives have 82 seats, Labour 18.

21 military coup in Athens establishes the regime of the 'Greek Colonels'.

27 (–29 Oct) 'Expo 67' exhibition in Montreal marks centenary of Canadian confederation.

E May

2 (–10) Bertrand Russell International War Crimes Tribunal in Stockholm finds US guilty of aggression in Vietnam.

4 British bank rate down to 5.5 per cent (lowest since 1964).

6 outbreak of rioting in Hong Kong.

10 Greek military junta takes control of Greek Orthodox Church.

11 Britain, Denmark, and Ireland formally apply to join EEC.

11 in Britain, Conservatives make net gain of 535 seats in borough elections.

Foundation of ASEAN ... Race riots in USA ... First heart transplant ... The Beatles' Sergeant Pepper album ...

o Politics, Government, Law, and Economy

W N Chambers and W D Burnham, *The American Party Systems.*

Treaty banning nuclear weapons from outer space signed by 60 countries, including USA and USSR (27 Jan).

The 25th Amendment to the US Constitution clarifies the succession in the event of the death or disablement of the president.

In USA, establishment of secretaryship of transportation.

Thurgood Marshall is the first African-American to be appointed to the US Supreme Court, serving until 1991.

In USA, the 'Boston strangler', Albert de Salvo, is sentenced to life imprisonment for sex offences and robbery.

Criminal Justice Act introduces majority verdicts, suspended sentences, and parole in England and Wales.

The Leasehold Reform Act enables tenants of houses in Britain held on long leases at low rent to acquire freehold or extended lease.

Indonesia, Malaysia, Singapore, Thailand, and the Philippines form the Association of South-East Asian Nations (ASEAN), to promote regional growth and western security interests in SE Asia; they establish a secretariat in Jakarta, Indonesia.

End of the 'Kennedy Round' of negotiations of the General Agreement on Trade and Tariffs (GATT).

Under legislation against horizontal mergers, the US Justice Department prevents a merger between soap-manufacturer Proctor and Gamble and liquid-bleach manufacturer Clorox.

First landing of North Sea gas in Britain (7 March).

p Society, Education, and Religion

In USA, extremely destructive race riots take place in Detroit, Michigan, Newark, New Jersey, and about 70 other cities (July); they accelerate the trend of the 'white flight' to the suburbs.

In South Africa, instructions issued to magistrates (Dec) accelerate provision of towns and resettlement villages for Africans.

Colorado is the first state in the USA to permit abortion.

Birth control techniques are legalized in France.

In Britain, the Sexual Offences Act decriminalizes homosexual acts between consenting males over 21 (27 July).

Latey Committee report recommends lowering the age of majority in Britain from 21 to 18 (20 July).

In Tanzania, President Julius Nyerere makes the Arusha Declaration, outlining a version of 'African socialism'; his programme for the development of his country includes nationalization of major enterprises and the creation of ujamaa ('familyhood') villages, rural centres where basic services and education are provided.

Air Quality Act and National Environment Policy Act passed in USA.

Denmark and the Netherlands stop prosecuting cases of possession of the drug marijuana for personal use.

Martin Luther King, *Where do we go from here?*

In USA, a report of the Commission on Civil Rights concludes that racial integration in schools needs to be accelerated in order to reverse the underachievement of African-American children.

In Britain, the Plowden Report, *Children and their Primary Schools* (published 10 Jan), generally favours child-centred learning in the classroom and also backs the establishment of 'Educational Priority Areas' to combat inequality.

Foundation of the Universities of Dundee and Stirling in Scotland and Salford in England.

Order of Deacons is revived in the Roman Catholic Church.

Roman Catholics are forbidden to attend prayers for unity in All Saints' Anglican Church, Rome.

Occupation of Old City of Jerusalem by Jews for the first time since CE 135.

Consecration of the Roman Catholic Cathedral of Christ the King in Liverpool, England.

q Science, Technology, and Discovery

In Britain, Donald Campbell is killed on Coniston Water while trying to break the world water-speed record in his jet-powered *Bluebird* (4 Jan).

S Manabe and R T Wetherald warn that the increase in carbon dioxide in the atmosphere, produced by human activities, is causing a 'greenhouse effect', which will raise atmospheric temperatures and cause a rise in sea levels.

People's Republic of China explodes its first hydrogen bomb (announced on 17 June).

Invention of Dolby noise-reduction system for use in tape recording.

Introduction of direct dialling from New York to Paris, France, and London (1 March).

12 British government chooses Stansted for third London airport (local protestors win fresh inquiry, Feb 1968).

16 President de Gaulle, in press conference, virtually vetoes British entry into EEC.

18 100,000 Chinese demonstrate in Beijing against British possession of Hong Kong.

19 UN withdraws peace-keeping force from Israeli–Egyptian border at request of UAR (Egypt).

20 Arab League Council declares that an attack on one Arab State would be an attack on all.

22 President Nasser of UAR closes Gulf of Aqaba to Israeli shipping. Israel and UAR call up reserves.

23 USA tells UAR to respect freedom of international waterways. USSR warns Israel against aggression.

28 secession of Biafra under Colonel Chukwuemeka Odumegwu-Ojukwu provokes civil war in Nigeria.

F **June**

5 War breaks out between Israel and Arab States (UAR, Syria, Jordan, Lebanon and Iraq); Arab states declare oil embargo on Britain and USA; Israel destroys over 300 enemy aircraft.

6 President Nasser closes Suez Canal and alleges that US and British forces are aiding Israel.

7 Duchess of Windsor (wife of former King Edward VIII) makes first official appearance in Britain at unveiling of plaque to Queen Mary.

8 Israel wins control of Sinai Peninsula, Gaza strip and Old Jerusalem. UAR and allies agree to ceasefire.

9 Israel attacks Syria after breach of ceasefire.

10 end of Six-Day War. USSR breaks off diplomatic relations with Israel.

17 China announces explosion of its first hydrogen bomb.

20 Arab mutineers in Aden kill 22 British soldiers.

21 Soviet President Nikolai Podgorny visits Cairo to discuss re-armament of UAR.

23 (–25) summit talks between President Johnson and Soviet Premier Kosygin at Glassboro, New Jersey.

30 46 nations sign Final Acts of 'Kennedy Round' of General Agreement on Tariffs and Trade.

G **July**

1 Commissions of EEC, European Coal and Steel Community and Euratom merge into a Commission of the European Communities (EC).

2 fighting begins in Eastern Congo between army and white mercenaries (mercenaries flee to Rwanda, 4 Nov).

14 UN orders Israel to desist from unifying Jerusalem.

16 Hong Kong government arrests 600 Communists (20, government assumes emergency powers).

18 British Defence White Paper announces drastic reduction in commitments in Far East.

24 President de Gaulle of France angers Canadian government by shouting 'Vive le Quebec libre!' during visit to Montreal.

25 Margaret Herbison, British minister for social security, resigns over spending curbs.

27 in USA, outbreak of race riots in Detroit. President Johnson appoints commission to investigate causes.

H **August**

15 in USA, Martin Luther King urges African-Americans to launch a campaign of massive civil disobedience.

22 Red Guards set fire to British embassy in Beijing.

24 USA and USSR present draft nuclear non-proliferation treaty to Geneva disarmament conference.

25 British troops start their withdrawal from Aden.

28 British Prime Minister Harold Wilson takes direct command of Department of Economic Affairs.

28 Belgium suspends all aid to Congo.

J **September**

1 Arab summit conference lifts boycott on oil to Britain and USA imposed during Six-Day War.

5 Britain appeals for negotiations with nationalist forces in Aden.

10 referendum in Gibraltar: 12,138 vote for retaining links with Britain, 44 for union with Spain.

12 (–15) Indian and Chinese troops clash on Tibet–Sikkim frontier.

18 end of casual dock labour in British ports; several unofficial strikes follow.

20 in Scotland, Queen Elizabeth launches Cunard liner *Queen Elizabeth II*.

25 nationalists call for cease-fire in Aden and Federation of South Arabia.

K **October**

9 Revolutionary guerrilla Che Guevara is executed in Bolivia.

13 Communists plant over 100 bombs in Hong Kong.

US scientist Gene Amdahl proposes the use of parallel processors in computers to produce faster processing speeds.

Three US astronauts die in a fire during a training exercise on the *Apollo* spacecraft (27 Jan).

Soviet cosmonaut dies during the descent of his *Soyuz 1* spacecraft (24 April).

Soviet *Venera 4* lands on Venus, the first soft landing on another planet (18 Oct).

Jocelyn Bell and Anthony Hewish discover the first pulsar (July; announced in 1968); later shown to be a collapsed neutron star emitting bursts of radio energy.

Installation of a tank containing 455,000 litres (100,000 gallons) of cleaning fluid in a former gold mine in South Dakota, USA, to detect neutrinos from the Sun.

Sheldon Lee Glashow, Abdus Salam, and Steven Weinberg separately develop the electroweak unification theory, explaining 'electromagnetic' interactions and the 'weak' nuclear force.

US scientist Charles T Caskey and associates demonstrate that identical forms of messenger RNA produce the same amino acids in a variety of living beings, showing that the genetic code is common to all life forms.

Dr Christiaan Barnard performs the first heart transplant operation, in South Africa (3 Dec); the patient, Louis Washkansky, survives for 18 days.

Rene Favaloro in Cleveland, USA, develops the coronary bypass operation.

Introduction of mammography (an X-ray technique) for the detection of breast cancer.

Desmond Morris, *The Naked Ape*.

'Crown' ethers discovered by C J Pedersen.

R Humanities

Start of excavation of Mycenaean palace (and frescoes) at Akrotiri on the Aegean island of Thera.

Henry Chadwick, *The Early Church*.

Peter Brown, *Augustine of Hippo*.

Sheppard Frere, *Britannia*.

R H C Davis, *King Stephen*.

Maurice Beresford, *New Towns of the Middle Ages*.

The Agrarian History of England and Wales (–).

H R Trevor-Roper, *Religion, the Reformation and Social Change*.

Patrick Collinson *The Elizabethan Puritan Movement*.

J H Plumb, *The Growth of Political Stability in England*.

Bernard Bailyn, *The Ideological Origins of the American Revolution*.

Christopher Hill, *Reformation to Industrial Revolution*.

Ray Allen Billington, *Westward Expansion*.

Maurice Cowling, *1867: Disraeli, Gladstone and Revolution*.

Paul Smith, *Disraelian Conservatism and Social Reform*.

Robert H Wiebe, *The Search for Order, 1877-1920*.

Paul Conkin, *The New Deal*.

G R Elton, *The Practice of History*.

Jacques Derrida, *Of Grammatology*.

In Canada, the National Library, Ottawa, Ontario, is established.

S Art, Sculpture, Fine Arts, and Architecture

Alfred Barr retires as Director of Collections, Museum of Modern Art, New York.

Tate Gallery purchases Roy Lichtenstein's *Whaam* of 1963.

Painting, etc:

David Hockney, *A Neat Lawn*.

Andy Warhol, *Marilyn Monroe*.

Sculpture:

Anthony Caro, *Prairie*.

Richard Long, *A Line Made by Walking* (sculpture).

Robert Morris, *Untitled (Felt sculpture, soft)*.

George Segal, *Execution* (sculpture).

Architecture:

Paul Koralek, Trinity College Library, Dublin.

Le Corbusier, Centre Le Corbusier Heidi-Weber, Zurich.

Frederick Gibberd, Cathedral Church of Christ the King, Liverpool, NW England.

T Music

Richard Rodney Bennett, *A Penny for a Song* (opera).

Morton Feldman, *In Search of an Orchestration*.

Alexander Goehr, *Arden Must Die* (opera).

Witold Lutoslawski, Symphony No. 2.

Elizabeth Maconchy, String Quartet No. 8.

Karlheinz Stockhausen, *Hymnen*.

Toru Takemitsu, *November Steps*.

Hair (musical), lyrics by Gerome Ragni, music by Galt MacDermot (first performed at the Public Theatre, East Greenwich Village, New York, 29 Oct).

The Beatles, *Sergeant Pepper's Lonely Hearts Club Band*.

The Bee Gees, 'Massachusetts'.

Glenn Campbell, 'Gentle On My Mind', 'By the Time I Get to Phoenix'.

The Doors, *The Doors*.

The Jimi Hendrix Experience, *Are You Experienced?*, *Axis: Bold As Love*.

Engelbert Humperdinck, 'The Last Waltz'.

Jefferson Airplane, 'Somebody to Love', 'White Rabbit'.

19 Arab nationalists kill British administrator in Aden.

21 UAR (Egypt) navy sinks Israeli destroyer off Sinai (24, Israeli artillery destroys Suez oil refineries).

21 demonstrations against Vietnam War in Washington, London, and other capitals.

25 in Britain, foot-and-mouth epidemic begins in Shropshire (ends March 1968).

26 Shah Mohammad Reza Pahlavi formally crowns himself at ceremony in Tehran, Iran.

27 UN Trusteeship Committee condemns British failure to overthrow Smith regime in Rhodesia (now Zimbabwe).

28 Kenya and Somalia end four-year border conflict.

L **November**

2 (–7) rival nationalist groups fight in streets of Aden.

3 Greek military government abolishes trial by jury for all common and political crimes.

7 USSR celebrates 50th anniversary of Bolshevik Revolution.

8 British Commonwealth secretary, George Thomson, holds talks with Ian Smith in Salisbury (now Harare, Zimbabwe).

9 British bank rate rises to 6.5 per cent (18, rises to 8 per cent).

14 Britain borrows £90 million from Bank of International Settlements.

18 devaluation of sterling from $2.80 to $2.40.

21 (–29) negotiations in Geneva between Britain and nationalists on transfer of power in South Arabia.

25 Cyprus asks UN Security Council to prevent Turkish invasion (Turkey, Greece, and Cyprus agree peace formula, 3 Dec).

26 proclamation of People's Republic of South Yemen (29, last British troops leave Aden).

29 in Britain, Roy Jenkins replaces James Callaghan as chancellor of the exchequer.

30 Britain accepts $1.4 billion loan from International Monetary Fund.

M **December**

6 Demonstrations in New York as part of 'Stop the Draft Week'.

7 Nicolae Ceauşescu becomes Romanian head of state as well as Party general secretary.

13 King Constantine of Greece attempts to oust military junta (14, goes into exile).

16 UN General Assembly demands South African withdrawal from South-West Africa.

17 Harold Holt, prime minister of Australia, drowns near Portsea, Victoria.

19 at EC Council, France vetoes negotiations for British entry; Britain states application will not be withdrawn.

The Monkees, 'I'm A Believer', 'Last Train to Clarksville', 'Daydream Believer'.

Procul Harum, 'A Whiter Shade of Pale'.

Sandie Shaw, 'Puppet on a String' (Britain's winning entry for Eurovision Song Contest).

Velvet Underground, *The Velvet Underground and Nico.*

Publication, in San Francisco, of US pop music magazine *Rolling Stone.*

In Britain, the Beatles' manager, Brian Epstein, is found dead, killed by an overdose of sleeping pills (27 Aug).

In Britain, start of the BBC's national pop station, Radio One (30 Sept).

Successful development of the Moog Synthesizer by US engineer Robert A Moog (popularized in 1968 by Walter Carlos's album *Switched On Bach*).

u Literature and Drama

Paul Bailey, *At the Jerusalem.*

John Barth, *Giles Goat-boy.*

Paul Bowles, *Up Above the World.*

Mikhail Bulgakov, *The Master and Margarita.*

J P Donleavy, *The Saddest Summer of Samuel F.*

Gabriel García Márquez, *One Hundred Years of Solitude.*

Robert Lowell, *Near the Ocean* (poems).

Najob Mahfouz, *Miramar.*

Flann O'Brien, *The Third Policeman.*

Michel Tournier, *Friday.*

Thornton Wilder, *The Eighth Day.*

Drama:

Griselda Gambaro, *Los Siameses.*

Peter Nichols, *A Day in the Death of Joe Egg.*

Harold Pinter, *The Homecoming.*

George Ryga, *The Ecstasy of Rita Joe.*

Tom Stoppard, *Rosencrantz and Guildenstern are Dead.*

Derek Walcott, *Dream on Monkey Mountain.*

Martin Walser, *Home Front.*

Charles Wood, *Dingo.*

v Births and Deaths

Feb 28 Henry R Luce dies (68).

April 19 Konrad Adenauer dies (91).

May 12 John Masefield dies (88).

June 7 Dorothy Parker dies (73).

Aug 9 Joe Orton dies (34).

Aug 31 Ilya Ehrenburg dies (75).

Sept 18 John Cockcroft dies (70).

Oct 7 Norman Angell dies (92).

Oct 8 Clement Attlee dies (84).

Oct 9 Che Guevara dies (39).

Dec 17 Harold Holt dies (59).

Dec 29 Paul Whiteman dies (77).

Dec 30 Vincent Massey dies (80).

w Everyday Life

The summer of 1967 is designated the 'Summer of Love'.

Hippie era–the Grey Line Bus Co. offers a 'Hippie Hop' tour of San Francisco, USA.

Sweden changes to driving on the right (3 Sept).

British Road Safety Act introduces breath tests (from 10 Oct).

Opening of first Laura Ashley shop in London.

British model Twiggy popularises a waif-like look.

x Sport and Recreation

In American football, the first Superbowl match is held (between the winners of the National Football League and the American Football League); the Green Bay Packers beat the Kansas City Chiefs 35–10 in Los Angeles (15 Jan).

Queen's Park Rangers becomes the first English Third Division side to win a Wembley soccer cup final, beating West Bromwich Albion 3–2 in the League Cup (14 March).

Foinavon, ridden by John Buckingham, wins the Grand National at odds of 100–1 (8 April).

The World Boxing Association strips Muhammad Ali (formerly Cassius Clay) of his World Heavyweight title for refusing the US Army draft (28 April).

Glasgow Celtic is first Scottish team to win soccer's European Cup, beating Inter Milan 2–1 in Lisbon (25 May).

The British Lawn Tennis Association abolishes the distinction between amateurs and professionals (5 Oct) — as does the International Lawn Tennis Federation in 1968.

After 226 days (starting 27 Aug 1966), Francis Chichester, in his yacht *Gipsy Moth IV*, completes the first solo round-the-world voyage (12 Dec).

y Media

In Britain, closure of the co-operative movement's paper the *Sunday Citizen* and of the *Boy's Own Paper* (founded 1879).

New York's *World Journal Tribune* ceases publication.

Film:

Accident (script by Harold Pinter; director, Joseph Losey; starring Dirk Bogarde).

Bonnie and Clyde (director, Arthur Penn; starring Warren Beatty and Faye Dunaway).

Assassination of Martin Luther King ... 'May Events' in Paris ...
Soviet invasion of Czechoslovakia ...

A January

4 Number of US troops in Vietnam reaches 486,000.

5 Alexander Dubček becomes first secretary of Czechoslovak Communist Party.

8 battle between Israeli and Jordanian forces south of Sea of Galilee.

10 John Grey Gorton becomes 20th prime minister of Australia.

12 Soviet dissidents Yuri Galanskov and Alexander Ginsburg are sentenced in Moscow to hard labour.

16 British government proposes complete military withdrawal from east of Suez (except Hong Kong) by 1971.

21 31 North Koreans raid Seoul in attempt to assassinate President Pak of South Korea.

23 North Korea seizes US intelligence ship *Pueblo* (crew released, 23 Dec).

30 Vietcong launch Tet offensive against South Vietnamese cities.

30 students in Warsaw demonstrate against political censorship.

31 UN trust territory of Nauru becomes independent (population 6,000).

B February

7 Flemish campaign against French-speakers at University of Louvain brings down Belgian government.

8 in USA, three African-American students killed in Orangeburg, South Carolina, after attempt to desegregate bowling alley.

9 in South Africa Transvaal Supreme Court imprisons 30 men accused of terrorism in South-West Africa.

21 bomb explodes at Soviet Embassy, Washington.

25 President Makarios of Cyprus re-elected by huge majority.

26 (–5 March) meeting in Budapest, Hungary, to plan World Communist Summit.

27 Arab Emirates of Persian Gulf announce intention to federate when British troops leave in 1971.

C March

1 Speculative flight from US dollar into gold starts to destabilize international monetary system (London Gold Market closed, 15–1 April).

1 emergency legislation restricts immigration of Kenyan Asians into Britain.

2 Queen Elizabeth reprieves three Africans sentenced to death in Rhodesia (6, they are hanged in Salisbury, now Harare, Zimbabwe).

11 major US and South Vietnamese offensive in Saigon area.

12 in New Hampshire primary election in USA, Senator Eugene McCarthy, fighting on a policy of making peace in Vietnam, almost defeats president Johnson.

15 in Britain, George Brown resigns as foreign secretary; replaced by Michael Stewart.

16 US Senator Robert Kennedy announces candidacy for Democratic presidential nomination.

The Dirty Dozen (director, Robert Aldrich).

Far from the Madding Crowd (director, John Schlesinger).

Point Blank (director, John Boorman; starring Lee Marvin).

The Producers (director, Mel Brooks).

Radio:

In Britain, the BBC replaces its Light, Home, and Third Services with four numbered stations.

In Britain, the BBC starts local radio.

Television:

The Public Broadcasting Act (signed 22 June) establishes a corporation to spend funds (federal and private) on non-commercial radio and television broadcasting.

New programmes in USA include: *Ironside* (NBC); *Morley Safer's Vietnam* (CBS); *Rowan and Martin's Laugh-In* (NBC; –1973). *The Testimony of Hideo Den from Hanoi* is the first Japanese report from inside North Vietnam.

New programmes in Britain include: *The Forsyte Saga* (BBC); *Callan*, with Edward Woodward; *The World About Us* (BBC; –1986), presented by David Attenborough.

BBC2 makes Europe's first broadcasts in colour (official start of colour service, 2 Dec).

The European team knock-out game, *Jeux Sans Frontières*, is first broadcast.

Discovery of oil in Alaska ... Pope issues Humanae Vitae *...*
Richard Hamilton's Swinging London *... Stanley Kubrick's*
2001 *...*

o Politics, Government, Law, and Economy

J-J Servan-Schreiber, *The American Challenge*.

In USA, foundation of the Urban Institute research organization.

In South Africa, the Union Council for Coloured Affairs is wound up and replaced by the Coloured Persons' Representative Council.

White Paper on British House of Lords proposes abolition of the hereditary element (1 Nov).

British Commonwealth merges with the Foreign Office, to form the Foreign and Commonwealth Office (16 Oct).

Fulton Report criticizes the British civil service for class stratification, amateurism, and insularity (published 26 June).

In USA, in Witherspoon v. Illinois, the Supreme Court rules that the rules used by states for jury selection in capital cases are unconstitutional.

British law case Conway v. Rimmer gives courts power to inspect government documents privately to see if suppression for security reasons would prejudice the administration of justice.

The Theft Act in Britain redefines theft as the illegitimate assumption of rights of ownership rather than taking and carrying away.

Following international gold crisis, central banks agree a two-tier system for gold: official dealings at $35 per ounce, commercial dealings at free price (17 March).

Consumer Credit Protection Act regulates the fast growing credit sector of the US financial system.

Large quantities of oil are discovered in Alaska under land fronting the Arctic Ocean.

In Britain, the Royal Commission on Trade Unions and Employers' Associations urges end to national wage agreements and formation of labour tribunals (13 June).

Formation in Britain of the British Leyland motor company, formed by a government-aided merger of firms.

The first decimal coins are introduced in Britain.

British Post Office introduces second class postage (16 Sept).

The Integrated Electronics (Intel) company is founded in California, USA.

p Society, Education, and Religion

Kerner Report on 1967 riots in the USA, prepared by the National Advisory Committee on Civil Disorders (published 29 Feb), warns that the USA is becoming 'two societies, one black, one white, separate and unequal'; it urges re-organization of welfare services and bans on discriminatory practices.

In USA, President Johnson announces an 'affirmative action' program whereby all government contractors must give preferential treatment to African-Americans and other minorities.

Open Housing Law in USA prohibits racial

18 heavy fighting in northern Rhodesia (now Zimbabwe) between government forces and African nationalists.

22 President Novotný of Czechoslovakia resigns (30, succeeded by General Ludvik Svoboda).

31 President Johnson announces decision not to seek re-election and restricts US bombing of North Vietnam.

D April

3 USA and North Vietnam agree to establish direct contact as first step towards negotiated peace.

4 assassination of Martin Luther King in Memphis, Tennessee; for a week there are riots and looting in major US cities in protest.

8 new Czechoslovak government takes office under Oldřich Černik.

9 East Germany adopts new constitution.

9 British Race Relations Bill published.

11 riots in west Berlin follow attempted assassination of student leader Rudi Dutschke.

19 Josef Smrkovský, chairman of Czechoslovak National Assembly, promises freedom of press, assembly, and religion.

20 Enoch Powell attacks coloured immigration to Britain: 'like the Roman, I seem to see the River Tiber foaming with much blood' (21, dismissed from Shadow Cabinet).

21 Pierre Trudeau succeeds Lester Pearson as prime minister of Canada.

21 US Vice-President Hubert Humphrey announces candidacy for Democratic presidential nomination.

23 (– 30) in USA, student takeover of Columbia University, New York, protesting at proposed building of a university gym in adjacent African-American area and at the university's affiliation to the Institute for Defense Analysis; police storm occupied buildings.

30 in USA, Nelson Rockefeller announces candidacy for Republican presidential nomination.

E May

2 Violent clashes between students and police begin in Latin Quarter of Paris.

3 (– June 23) in USA, Poor People's March from Memphis, Tennessee, to Washington, DC, led by Ralph Abernathy, Jr, in place of the late Martin Luther King.

5 Spain further restricts access to and from Gibraltar.

9 Conservatives take control of 27 out of 32 London boroughs in local elections.

10 'Night of the Barricades' in Paris (11, French government makes concessions to student demands).

13 US and North Vietnamese negotiators begin peace talks in Paris.

14 Czechoslovak government announces wide range of liberalizing reforms.

17 students and strikers occupy factories and hold protest marches in French cities.

17 Soviet Prime Minister Andrei Kosygin and Defence Minister Marshal Andrei Grechko visit Prague, Czechoslovakia.

24 rioters set fire to Paris Bourse; President de Gaulle asks for vote of confidence in referendum.

26 French government raises minimum wage by 33.3 per cent.

30 President de Gaulle postpones referendum and calls general election, as riots continue.

31 Nigerian–Biafran peace talks in Kampala, Uganda, break down.

F June

5 in USA, Senator Robert Kennedy is shot in Los Angeles after winning California primary election (6, dies).

10 General William Westmoreland hands over US command in Vietnam to General Creighton Abrams.

11 East Germany announces that West Berliners will require visas to cross its territory.

12 French government bans demonstrations and dissolves 11 student organizations.

18 British House of Lords rejects Rhodesian Sanctions Order (20, Harold Wilson promises radical reform of Upper House).

19 India accuses Pakistan and the People's Republic of China of aiding rebels in Nagaland and Mizo.

20 total US combat deaths in Vietnam exceed 25,000.

24 (–25 July) negotiations between Greek and Turkish Cypriots in Nicosia (second round, 29 Aug–9 Dec).

26 Earl Warren announces resignation as Chief Justice of US Supreme Court.

27 Czechoslovak National Assembly passes laws abolishing censorship and rehabilitating political prisoners.

30 Gaullists win landslide victory in second round of French general election.

G July

1 61 nations, including Britain, USA, and USSR sign Treaty on Non-Proliferation of Nuclear Weapons.

2 Britain offers famine relief to Nigeria and Biafra (4, Biafra refuses it while Britain sells arms to Nigeria).

9 Couve de Murville succeeds Georges Pompidou as French prime minister.

discrimination in the sale or letting of housing (signed April 10).

Shirley Chisholm is the first African-American woman to be elected to the US Congress (5 Nov).

Immigration and Nationality Act in force in USA (from 1 July), replacing preference system based on country of origin with system based on certain categories (such as possession of special skills).

In USA, Hispanic César Chávez of the United Farm Workers' Union leads a boycott of grapes in protest against the treatment of Hispanic workers.

The Race Relations Act outlaws racial discrimination in Britain.

The Miss America contest in the USA is disrupted by feminists protesting at its portrayal of women.

Abortion is made lawful in Britain, when pregnancy endangers the physical or mental health of a woman or child (27 April).

Prescription charges are re-imposed in Britain with some exceptions (announced 16 Jan).

E Cleaver, *Soul on Ice*.

R Ehrlich, *The Population Bomb*.

V Solanas, *The SCUM Manifesto*.

Violent university campus demonstrations in the USA, France, and England, prompting regulatory legislation in France.

In Italy, state nursery schools are established.

The Gittins Report on primary education in Wales advocates school reorganization and the establishment of bilingual schools.

The Newsom Committee calls for the integration of British independent schools with state schools (22 July).

Publication of the Papal Encyclical *Humanae Vitae* (29 July), prohibiting use of artificial contraception by Roman Catholics.

All laws dealing with Church–State relations in Albania are abrogated, implying that religious bodies have been eliminated and that Albania has therefore become the world's first complete atheist state.

The South African Council of Churches declares the doctrine of racial separation to be 'truly hostile' to Christianity.

Fourth Assembly of the World Council of Churches meets in Uppsala, Sweden.

Tenth Lambeth Conference of Anglican bishops meets at Westminster, London.

Church of Scotland votes (22 May) to ordain women as ministers.

Q Science, Technology, and Discovery

First demonstration flight of Soviet Tupolev Tu-144, the world's first supersonic airliner (31 Dec).

The first 'supertanker' for carrying oil goes into service.

Regular hovercraft services begin across the English Channel.

Completion of tidal power station on the River Rance, France.

Soviet spacecraft *Zond 5* (launched 14 Sept) flies around the Moon and returns to Earth.

First crewed US Apollo space mission, *Apollo 7*, tests *Apollo* spacecraft (11–22 Oct); *Apollo 8* makes the first crewed mission to the Moon; it completes 10 orbits and returns to Earth (21–27 Dec).

Mark Ptashne and Walter Gilbert separately identify the first repressor genes.

New fertility drugs cause a British woman to give birth to sextuplets.

Oral contraceptives are shown to cause blood clots in some women.

M Arnstein develops a vaccine against meningitis.

Dr Christiaan Barnard performs his second heart transplant operation; the patient lives for 74 days.

Epidural anaesthetic technique devised, to ease childbirth (announced 11 Sept).

J D Watson, *The Double Helix*, about Crick and Watson's discovery of DNA.

First experimental fusion reactors (Tokomaks) built.

Survey ship *Glomar Challenger* starts drilling cores in the sea bed as part of the Deep Sea Drilling Project.

Elso S Barghorn and associates report the discovery of remains of amino acids in rocks 3 billion years old.

R Humanities

David Clarke, *Analytical Archaeology*.

The Cambridge History of Iran (–1991).

J J Scarisbrick, *Henry VIII*.

Carl Bridenbaugh, *Vexed and Troubled Englishmen*.

Bernard Bailyn, *The Origin of American Politics*.

Winthrop Jordan, *White Over Black: American Attitudes Toward the Negro, 1550-1812*.

Henry Steele Commager and E Giordanetti, *Was America A Mistake?*

David M Potter, *The South and Sectional Conflict*.

M R D Foot and H C G Matthew (eds.), *The Gladstone Diaries* (–1994).

Bernard Semmel, *Imperialism and Social Reform: English Social–Imperial Thought, 1895–1914*.

Gordon Haight, *George Eliot*.

Max Black, *The Labyrinth of Language*.

Michel Foucault, *The Archaeology of Knowledge*.

Jürgen Habermas, *Knowledge and Human Interests*.

9 Czechoslovakia rejects Soviet demand for meeting of Communist Party leaders.

14 USSR halts withdrawal of troops from Czechoslovakia after Warsaw Pact exercises.

15 Malaysia rejects Philippine claim to Sabah in North Borneo.

16 Soviet, East German, Hungarian, Polish, and Bulgarian leaders declare Czechoslovak reforms unacceptable.

24 conference of Spanish bishops proclaims workers' right to strike and form independent trade unions.

27 Alexander Dubček states that Czechoslovakia will continue on its chosen road and not retreat one step.

29 (–1 Aug), Czechoslovak and Soviet leaders hold talks at Cierna-nad-Tisou.

H August

4 Israeli aircraft bomb Palestinian guerrilla bases in Jordan.

5 Spain declares state of emergency in Guipuzcoa after Basque separatists murder police chief.

8 Richard Nixon secures Republican nomination for US presidency and chooses Spiro Agnew as running-mate for vice-presidency.

15 Nigeria forbids International Red Cross to fly relief supplies to starving Biafrans from neutralized airstrip.

20 Soviet and allied forces invade Czechoslovakia and arrest reform leaders.

21 Congress of Czechoslovak Communist Party, meeting in secret, rejects collaboration and re-elects Dubček as first secretary.

23 President Ludvik Svoboda of Czechoslovakia flies to Moscow for talks (25, secures release of Dubček).

24 Yugoslavia and Romania jointly condemn invasion of Czechoslovakia.

25 France explodes hydrogen bomb in South Pacific, thus becoming fifth thermonuclear Power.

28 in USA, Democratic Party convention in Chicago nominates Hubert Humphrey as presidential candidate. Violent demonstrations against the Vietnam War take place around the convention hall.

28 Czechoslovak National Assembly declares Soviet occupation illegal.

31 earthquakes in Iran kill 12,000.

J September

2 USSR tells West Germany to stop exerting itself in Eastern Europe and hints at possible invasion (17, USA, Britain, and France warn USSR against attacking West Germany).

5 British TUC massively rejects statutory incomes policy and approves voluntary wage restraint only by narrow margin.

6 Swaziland becomes independent under King Sobhuza II.

12 Albania formally quits Warsaw Pact.

15 Organization of African Unity appeals to Biafra to abandon independence struggle.

18 President Marcos proclaims Philippine sovereignty over most of Sabah (19, Malaysia withdraws diplomats from Manila).

26 Antonio Salazar resigns as prime minister of Portugal after 36 years; succeeded by Marcello Caetano.

27 USSR postpones World Communist Summit planned for Nov.

K October

4 Czechoslovak leaders visiting Moscow, USSR, agree to dismantle remnants of reform.

5 (–6) crowds in Londonderry, Northern Ireland, clash with police during civil rights march.

9 (–13) Harold Wilson of Britain and Ian Smith of Rhodesia (now Zimbabwe) hold talks about Rhodesia problem aboard HMS *Fearless* at Gibraltar.

12 Equatorial Guinea wins independence from Spain.

16 USSR and Czechoslovakia sign treaty on eventual withdrawal of Warsaw Pact forces.

21 anti-US demonstrations in Tokyo, Japan.

27 Big protest march in London against Vietnam War.

27 during a presentation ceremony at the Mexico City Olympic Games, winning US athletes Tommy Smith and John Carlos raise gloved fists in a 'black power' salute during the playing of the US anthem.

28 West German government initiates security review after spate of suicides of top secret service and military officials with access to secret information.

31 President Johnson halts bombing of North Vietnam and announces agreement on Vietnamese delegations for peace talks.

31 Chinese Communist Party expels President Liu Shaoqi.

L November

5 in US elections Richard Nixon, Republican, with 302 electoral votes, wins narrow victory over Hubert Humphrey, Democrat, with 191, and George Wallace, Independent, with 45; popular vote: Nixon, 31,770,237; Humphrey, 31,270,533; Wallace, 9,906,141. Democrats keep control of Congress.

s Art, Sculpture, Fine Arts, and Architecture

Henry Moore exhibition held in the Tate Gallery, London, and worldwide.

'Art of the Real' exhibition at the Museum of Modern Art, New York.

Supports/Surfaces movement, France.

Painting, etc:

Richard Hamilton, *Swinging London.*

Sculpture:

Anselmo, *Structure Which Eats Salad.*

Barry Flanagan, *Heap 3.*

César, *Compressions.*

Sol Lewitt, *Untitled Cube (6).*

Architecture:

Hubert Bennett and architects of Greater London Council, Hayward Gallery, London.

Ludwig Mies van der Rohe, National Gallery, West Berlin.

Skidmore, Owings, and Merrill, John Hancock Building, Chicago, USA.

James Stirling, History Faculty Building, Cambridge University, Cambridge, England.

t Music

Luciano Berio, *Sinfonia.*

Harrison Birtwistle, *Punch and Judy* (opera).

Pierre Boulez, *Domaines.*

Luigi Dallapiccola, *Ulisse* (opera).

Edison Denisov, *Ode in Memory of Ché Guevara.*

Allan Pettersson, Symphony No. 7.

John Tavener, *The Whale.*

Claudio Abbado becomes principal conductor at La Scala, Milan.

Joseph and the Amazing Technicolour Dreamcoat (musical), first performed at Colet Court School, London (1 March; first commercial theatre performance of longer version, 16 Oct 1972).

Foundation of World Championship for brass bands.

The Band, *Music from Big Pink.*

James Brown, 'Say It Loud, I'm Black and I'm Proud'.

Leonard Cohen, *The Songs of Leonard Cohen.*

Marvin Gaye, 'I Heard It Through the Grapevine'.

Joni Mitchell, *Songs To A Seagull.*

Van Morrison, *Astral Weeks.*

The Rolling Stones, *Beggar's Banquet.*

Simon and Garfunkel, 'Mrs Robinson'.

Dusty Springfield, 'Son of a Preacher Man'.

In Britain, second Isle of Wight pop festival, starring Bob Dylan (29–31 Aug).

Eric Clapton organizes first (short-lived) 'supergroup', Blind Faith.

Introduction of quadraphonic sound reproduction system.

u Literature and Drama

Richard Brautigan, *Trout Fishing in America.*

Philip K Dick, *Do Androids Dream of Electric Sheep.*

Lawrence Durrell, *Tunc.*

Allen Ginsberg, *Airplane Dreams* (poems).

Ursula Le Guin, *A Wizard of Earthsea.*

Norman Mailer, *The Armies of the Night.*

Amos Oz, *My Michael.*

Alexander Solzhenitsyn, *Cancer Ward.*

John Updike, *Couples.*

Gore Vidal, *Myra Breckinridge.*

Marguerite Yourcenar, *The Abyss.*

Yasunari Kawabata awarded Japan's first Nobel Prize for Literature.

Drama:

Peter Barnes, *The Ruling Class.*

Alan Bennett, *Forty Years On.*

Peter Handke, *Kaspar.*

Israel Horovitz, *The Indian Wants the Bronx.*

Thomas Kilroy, *The Death and Resurrection of Mr Roche.*

Arthur Miller, *The Price.*

Howard Sackler, *The Great White Hope.*

Peter Terson, *Zigger Zagger.*

Michael Tremblay, *The Sisters-in-Law.*

The Theatres Act in Britain abolishes theatre censorship, previously exercised by the Lord Chamberlain (end of censorship, 26 Sept).

In USSR, the Moscow Arts Theatre Company moves to a new theatre on the same site.

v Births and Deaths

Feb 21 Howard Florey dies (69).

April 4 Martin Luther King dies (39).

April 7 Jim Clark dies (32).

June 1 Helen Keller dies (87).

June 6 Robert Kennedy dies (42).

June 25 Tony Hancock dies (44).

Oct 2 Marcel Duchamp dies (81).

Nov 26 Upton Sinclair dies (90).

Nov 28 Enid Blyton dies (71).

Dec 10 Karl Barth dies (82).

Dec 20 John Steinbeck dies (66).

Dec 30 Trygve Lie dies (72).

w Everyday Life

Introduction in New York of '911' emergency telephone system (for police, fire, ambulance), the first such system to be established in the USA.

Jacuzzi Brothers, makers of farm pumps in California, USA, introduce the Jacuzzi Whirlpool Bath.

Adoption in Britain of British Standard Time,

5 South Vietnam objects to composition of planned Paris peace talks (26, agrees to attend).

15 new Greek constitution comes into force with articles on personal freedom suspended.

16 in Northern Ireland, 5,000 civil-rights marchers defy ban on demonstrations in Londonderry.

17 Anglo-Rhodesian talks in Salisbury end in deadlock.

20 European exchange markets close after heavy speculation against French franc (23, President de Gaulle refuses to devalue).

22 Northern Ireland government proposes reforms in housing and local franchise.

29 Arab guerrillas attack potash plant on Dead Sea (1 Dec, Israeli jets blow up two bridges in Jordan).

30 violence erupts between Catholic and Protestant demonstrators in Armagh, Northern Ireland.

M **December**

2 Iraqi artillery in Jordan shells Israeli villages (4, Israel bombs Iraqi bases).

6 rumours of coalition government and Queen's abdication cause panic selling on London stock market.

9 USSR objects to cruise of two US destroyers in Black Sea.

13 President Costa e Silva of Brazil assumes emergency powers to prevent left-wing coup.

16 Spain annuls 1492 decree expelling Jews.

18 UN General Assembly declares colonial rule in Gibraltar incompatible with UN Charter.

23 USA proposes to close, re-locate, or share control of 50 military bases in Japan.

26 two Arabs attack Israeli airliner in Athens (28, Israel bombs Beirut airport, wrecking 13 aircraft).

Nixon becomes US president ... Resignation of de Gaulle ...
Disturbances in Northern Ireland ...

A **January**

1 Czechoslovakia becomes a two-state federation.

3 Roman Catholic and Protestant demonstrators clash in Londonderry, Northern Ireland (11, in Newry).

6 France bans sale of military supplies to Israel.

10 Sweden becomes first Western government to recognize North Vietnam.

16 Czech student, Jan Palach, publicly burns himself to death in Prague in protest at Soviet occupation.

17 British government issues *In Place of Strife: A Policy for Industrial Relations*.

18 South Vietnamese and National Liberation Front join expanded peace talks in Paris.

20 Richard Nixon takes oath as 37th US president.

24 General Franco imposes martial law in Spain.

24 (–19 Feb) London School of Economics closed after student disorders.

27 Iraq executes 14 men accused of spying for Israel.

B **February**

1 Yugoslavia and Romania jointly refute Brezhnev doctrine on supremacy of international Communist interests.

one hour ahead of Greenwich Mean Time (18 Feb).

'I'm Backing Britain' campaign launched (1 Jan), when five typists in Surbiton, London, give half an hour free to their employer to counter gloom about the British economy.

x Sport and Recreation

Former world champion racing driver Jim Clark killed in accident at Hockenheim circuit, West Germany (7 April).

Manchester United becomes the first English soccer team to win the European Cup, beating Benfica of Portugal 4–1 in the final in London (29 May).

In London, at the first 'open' Wimbledon tennis championship, the Singles titles are won by Rod Laver of Australia and Billie Jean King of the USA.

The 19th Olympic Games are held in Mexico City (12–27 Oct). The USA wins 45 gold medals; USSR, 29; Japan, 11; East Germany, 9; France and Czechoslovakia, 7 each; West Germany, Britain, and Poland, 5 each; Romania, 4; Bob Beamon of the USA establishes a new Long Jump world record of 8.89 m/29 ft 2.5 in.

In Britain, Gary Sobers, batting for Nottinghamshire against Glamorgan at Swansea, hits six sixes in one over off Malcolm Nash (31 Aug).

The South African prime minister, B J Vorster, cancels the tour of South Africa by the MCC team from Britain after the MCC includes the Cape Coloured player Basil D'Oliveira in the MCC team (24 Sept).

y Media

Sir William ('Pissing Billy') Carr sells a 51 per cent stake in the British paper the *News of the World* to Rupert Murdoch of Australia, having rejected an offer from British businessman Robert Maxwell.

Film:

Bullitt (director, John Boorman).

Butch Cassidy and the Sundance Kid (director, George Roy Hill; starring Paul Newman and Robert Redford).

The Good, The Bad and the Ugly (director, Sergio Leone).

The Graduate (director, Mike Nichols).

In the Heat of the Night (director, Norman Jewison; starring Sidney Poitier and Rod Steiger).

If.. (director, Lindsay Anderson).

The Lion in Winter (starring Katharine Hepburn and Peter O'Toole).

Night of the Living Dead (director, George Romero).

Planet of the Apes (director, Franklin Schaffer; starring Charlton Heston).

Romeo and Juliet (director, Franco Zeffirelli).

2001, A Space Odyssey (director, Stanley Kubrick).

Television:

In USA, broadcaster Walter Cronkite delivers a personal and influential denunciation of the Vietnam War (6 March).

Hawaii Five-O is broadcast in the USA.

New programmes in Britain include: *Dad's Army*; *The Stanley Baxter Show* (both BBC).

Warren Burger appointed Chief Justice of US Supreme Court ...
First humans on the Moon ... Human egg cell fertilized in vitro ...

o Politics, Government, Law, and Economy

Isaiah Berlin, *Four Essays on Liberty*.

David Butler and D Stokes, *Political Change in Britain*.

Roger H Davidson, *The Role of the Congressman*.

J McGinniss, *The Selling of the President 1968*.

Julius Nyerere, *Freedom and Socialism*.

K Phillips, *The Emerging Republican Majority*.

Elmer Eric Schattschneider, *Two Hundred Million Americans in Search of a Government*.

In USA, Ron Ziegler, White House press secretary, coins the term 'photo-opportunity'.

'Weathermen' War Council in Flint announces the start of terrorist operations in the USA.

Ninth Chinese Communist Party Congress ends the Cultural Revolution and reestablishes authority structures.

In Britain, the Redcliffe-Maud Report (report of the Royal Commission on Local Government) recommends a radical simplification of the structure (published 11 June).

Warren Burger appointed Chief Justice of the US Supreme Court serving until 1986.

3 Palestine Liberation Organisation elects Yassir Arafat as chairman.

7 Anguilla votes to break all ties with Britain.

12 Ndabaningi Sithole, leader of Zimbabwe African National Union, convicted of incitement to murder Ian Smith.

18 Palestinian terrorists attack El Al airliner at Zurich airport.

22 France disputes British account of talks with President de Gaulle on future of the EC.

23 (–2 Mar) President Nixon of USA tours Western European capitals.

24 Northern Ireland general election reveals Unionists' divisions over reform.

c March

1 In Laos, the Pathet Lao opposition rejects government's offer of talks to end civil war.

1 Soviet–Chinese border conflict at Ussuri River.

3 British House of Commons approves *In Place of Strife* White Paper despite 49 Labour Noes and 40 Labour abstentions.

5 London gangsters Ronald and Reginald Kray sentenced to life imprisonment.

10 in USA, James Earl Ray convicted of murdering Martin Luther King (Apr 1968).

12 in Anguilla, British emissary forced to leave at gun-point (19, 250 British troops land and re-establish control).

25 military government takes over in Pakistan amid escalating violence; President Ayub Khan is replaced by General Yahya Khan.

27 Harold Wilson arrives in Nigeria for talks with General Gowon.

27 in Britain, Conservatives take Walthamstow, East from Labour in by-election.

28 anti-Soviet demonstrations in Prague.

d April

4 (–1 July) UN representatives of US, USSR, Britain, and France hold talks on Middle East in New York.

8 Arab guerrillas attack Eilat; Israeli jets retaliate with attack on Aqaba, Jordan.

10 King Hussein of Jordan proposes six-point Middle East peace plan (16, rejected by Palestinian organizations).

15 British Budget increases corporation tax, selective employment tax, and petrol duty.

15 North Korea shoots down US naval intelligence plane.

17 Gustav Husak succeeds Alexander Dubček as first secretary of Czechoslovak Communist Party.

17 British government drops Bill to reform House of Lords.

17 in Northern Ireland, 21-year-old civil rights activist Bernadette Devlin wins Mid-Ulster by-election.

20 British troops guard public utilities in Northern Ireland after post offices bombed.

22 Nigerian forces capture Umuahia, the administrative capital of Biafra.

23 Northern Ireland government concedes universal adult suffrage in local elections.

27 referendum in France narrowly rejects constitutional reforms.

28 resignation of President de Gaulle; Alain Poher becomes interim President.

e May

1 James Chichester-Clark succeeds Terence O'Neill as prime minister of Northern Ireland (6, grants amnesty to arrested rioters).

9 wave of currency speculation peaks with West German refusal to revalue mark.

10 local elections leave Labour in control of only 28 out of 342 borough councils in England and Wales.

11 Vietcong launch rocket and ground attacks throughout South Vietnam.

14 President Nixon suggests mutual withdrawal of US, Allied, and North Vietnamese troops from South Vietnam.

15 violence in Kuala Lumpur, Malaya, between Malays and Chinese.

20 government of Laos offers to halt US bombing of Pathet Lao opposition if North Vietnamese withdraw from Laos.

30 Gibraltar's constitution comes into effect (30 July, general election).

30 West Germany ends policy of automatically severing relations with governments which recognize East Germany.

f June

2 Australian aircraft carrier *Melbourne* collides with USS *Frank E Evans* during manoeuvres in China Sea.

5 (–17) delegates from 75 countries attend World Communist Conference in Moscow.

8 President Nixon announces withdrawal of 25,000 US troops from Vietnam (further 35,000, 16 Sept).

8 Spain completely closes land frontier with Gibraltar (27, suspends ferry service from Algeciras).

9 in Britain, Enoch Powell calls for repatriation of black immigrants.

15 Georges Pompidou becomes president of France (20, appoints Jacques Chaban-Delmas as prime minister).

18 British government abandons Trade Union Reform Bill in return for TUC pledge to deal with unofficial strikes.

(President Johnson first nominated Assistant Justice Abe Fortas as Chief Justice but the nomination was withdrawn because of the latter's association with a fraudulent stock operator. Fortas subsequently resigned from the Court.)

President Nixon is forced to withdraw two nominations to the US Supreme Court, Clement Haynsworth and George Carswell (the latter in 1970) after revelations of racism and incompetence.

In USA, the National Environmental Policy Act requires an environmental impact statement for each government decision.

In Los Angeles, USA, cult gang directed by Charles Manson invades the home of actress Sharon Tate, killing her and her unborn child, three guests, and a passer-by (10 Aug).

Capital punishment is permanently abolished in Britain and is replaced by a mandatory life sentence for murder.

Representation of the People Act 1969 reduces voting age in Britain from 21 to 18 (12 May).

Charter of the International Monetary Fund (IMF) is amended to allowing to issue Special Drawing Rights to increase world liquidity.

Japan's Gross National Product exceeds that of West Germany for the first time (March).

Dow Jones share index in USA crosses the 1,000 mark for the first time.

Internet established by the US Department of Defense.

'Hot Autumn' of strikes in Italy.

P **Society, Education, and Religion**

In USA, leading members of the Black Panther group are killed in a sudden police raid in Chicago.

In USA, President Nixon appoints Louis R Bruce, a Mohawk-Sioux, as commissioner for Native American affairs (19,400 hectares of tribal land are later returned to the Taos Pueblo Native Americans).

In Britain, the Divorce Reform Act (passed 17 Oct), known as the 'Casanova's Charter', permits divorce by consent of both parties after two years' separation and at the wish of one party after five years.

Strike by women workers at the Ford plant in Dagenham, east London, against pay discrimination.

In USA, the report of the Commission on Obscenity and Pornography recommends an end to censorship.

Official Languages Act makes Canada officially bilingual.

Riots follow a police raid at the Stonewall Tavern in New York, leading to the 'gay rights' movement.

C Booker, *The Neophiliacs*.

Vine Deloria, Jr, *Custer Died For Your Sins*.

Theodore Roszak, *The Making of a Counterculture*.

In Britain, publication of the first two anti-egalitarian *Black Papers* on education, edited by Professor C B Cox of Manchester University.

A scheme for Anglican–Methodist union in England fails to reach the necessary 75 per cent majority in the Convocations of Canterbury and York of the Church of England.

Catherine McConnochie is ordained as the first woman minister in the Church of Scotland.

Publication of the papal decree *Paschalis Mysterii* (9 May), revising calendar of saints' days.

Q **Science, Technology, and Discovery**

USA in effect bans use of DDT pesticide.

Thirty-nine nations meet in Rome to discuss pollution.

Creation of 'bubble memory' device, which enables computers to retain information after electrical power is switched off.

In USA, maiden flight of the Boeing 747 'jumbo jet' airliner (9 Feb) and in France of prototype 001 of the French–British supersonic airliner *Concorde* (2 March).

Two Soviet spacecraft (*Soyuz 4* and *5*) are locked together for four hours to form the first experimental space station (16 Jan).

US *Apollo 9* mission (3–13 March) tests Apollo Moon vehicles in Earth orbit, followed by *Apollo 10* mission in which the lunar module descends to within 15,250 m/50,000 ft of the Moon's surface (22 May).

US *Apollo 11* space mission (16–24 July) leads to the first crewed landing on the Moon and first walk on the Moon (20 July).

Foundation of Fermi National Accelerator Laboratory ('Fermilab') near Chicago.

Astronomers identify a visible star with a pulsar known from radio surveys.

In USA, Jonathan Beckwith and associates at the Harvard Medical School isolate a single gene for the first time.

R G Edwards of the Cambridge Physiological Laboratory, Cambridge, England, makes the first in vitro fertilization of human egg cells (15 Feb).

Development and implant of the first effective artificial human heart, used as a temporary device for patients requiring transplants.

British scientist Dorothy Hodgkin announces the structure of insulin (Aug).

Publication of *The Red Book* by James Fisher,

20 Rhodesia (now Zimbabwe) votes to become a republic (24, Britain cuts last official links).

25 in USA, the Senate passes resolution calling on president not to commit troops to foreign countries without Congressional approval.

26 (–24 Aug) strike at Port Talbot steel works, S Wales.

30 Nigerian government takes control of all relief operations in Nigeria–Biafra war.

G **July**

1 Formal investiture of Prince Charles as prince of Wales at Caernarvon Castle.

4 General Franco offers Spanish citizenship to all Gibraltarians.

13 border incidents follow defeat of Honduras by El Salvador in qualifying round of World Cup.

14 El Salvador invades Honduras (30, agrees to withdraw).

19 in USA, car driven by Senator Edward Kennedy plunges into river at Chappaquiddick Island; his passenger, Mary Jo Kopechne, drowns.

19 Indira Gandhi issues ordinance for nationalization of 14 major Indian banks.

20 Neil Armstrong becomes first human to walk on the Moon.

22 General Franco names Prince Juan Carlos as his eventual successor.

23 (–3 Aug) President Nixon of USA visits southern Asia, Romania, and Britain.

24 USSR exchanges British spy Gerald Brooke, arrested 1965, for 'Portland spies', Peter and Helen Kroger.

24 heaviest fighting between UAR (Egypt) and Israel since Six-Day War.

27 North Vietnam denies military intervention in Laos.

H **August**

8 France devalues the franc by 12 per cent.

11 in Zambia President Kenneth Kaunda announces nationalization of copper mines.

12 arson and street-fighting in Belfast and Londonderry, Northern Ireland (14, British troops intervene to separate rioters).

13 USSR forces cross Chinese border in Xinjiang.

15 Republic of Ireland mobilizes reserves and moves troops near Northern Ireland frontier.

17 Unionists in Northern Ireland rule out coalition government at Stormont.

19 British army assumes full responsibility for security in Northern Ireland.

21 50,000 protesters in Prague, Czechoslovakia, mark anniversary of Soviet invasion.

25 Arab League meets in Cairo, UAR, to plan 'holy war' against Israel.

28 prime minister of Ireland, John Lynch, proposes federation of the Republic and Northern Ireland.

29 British and Northern Ireland governments agree on civil-rights reforms.

31 military junta takes power in Brazil following illness of President Costa e Silva.

J **September**

1 Colonel Moamer al Khaddhafi deposes King Idris of Libya.

3 death of President Ho Chi Minh of North Vietnam (23, succeeded by Ton Dac Thang).

7 Laos, with US aid, begins offensive against North Vietnamese on Plain of Jars.

9 Israel attacks UAR military bases south of Suez.

10 British troops start to dismantle barricades in Belfast and Londonderry.

11 Soviet Prime Minister Kosygin makes surprise visit to Beijing.

17 week of violence between Hindus and Muslims breaks out in Gujarat.

22 World Islamic Conference opens at Rabat to consider consequences of arson attack on Al Aqsa mosque, Jerusalem, on 21 Aug.

27 purge of reformers in Czechoslovak government.

27 President Thieu of South Vietnam says US withdrawal will take 'years and years' as his country has 'no ambition' to take over the fighting.

28 in West German elections Christian Democrats wins 46 per cent of votes, Social Democrats 43 per cent.

K **October**

3 Greek government restores press freedom, abolishes arbitrary arrest and limits military powers.

4 President Ferdinand Marcos recalls Philippine troops from Vietnam.

5 British government abolishes Department of Economic Affairs and creates Ministry of Local Government and Regional Planning.

10 Lord Hunt's committee recommends disarming Royal Ulster Constabulary and disbanding part-time police, the 'B' specials (11, intense rioting in Belfast).

10 Czechoslovakia imposes drastic restrictions on foreign travel.

15 millions demonstrate across USA in peaceful 'moratorium' against Vietnam War.

21 Social Democrat Willy Brandt becomes Chancellor of West Germany.

listing animals and plants in imminent danger of extinction.

'Cryptates' discovered, making salts soluble in organic solvents such as chloroform.

R Humanities

Kenneth Clark, *Civilisation*.

David Landes, *The Unbound Prometheus: Technological Change and Industrial Development in Western Europe from 1750 to the Present*.

Gordon S Wood, *The Creation of the American Republic, 1776-1787*.

M Wilson and L Thompson (eds.), *The Oxford History of South Africa*, Volume 1 (Volume 2, 1971).

C A Macartney, *The Habsburg Empire, 1790–1918*.

E R J Owen, *Cotton and the Egyptian Economy, 1820–1914: A Study in Trade and Development*.

Harold Perkin, *The Origin of Modern English Society*.

David Dilks, *Curzon in India* (–1970).

Z S Steiner, *The Foreign Office and Foreign Policy, 1898–1914*.

K D Bracher, *The German Dictatorship*.

Angus Calder, *The People's War*.

Kathleen Coburn (ed.), *The Collected Works of Samuel Coleridge Taylor* (–).

Isaiah Berlin, *Four Essays on Liberty*.

Herbert Marcuse, *An Essay on Liberation*.

J R Searle, *Speech Acts*.

S Art, Sculpture, Fine Arts, and Architecture

'When Attitude Becomes Form' exhibition, Institute of Contemporary Art, London.

Retrospective exhibitions of works of Roy Lichtenstein and David Smith at the Guggenheim Museum, New York.

Painting, etc:

Georg Baselitz, *The Wood on its Head*.

Sculpture:

Dan Flavin, *Monument for V Tatlin*.

Michael Heizer, *Double Negative*.

Donald Judd, *Untitled* (minimal sculpture, vertically arranged metal and glass boxes).

Niki de Saint Phalle, *Black Nana*.

Architecture:

Denys Lasdun and Partners, First Phase of University of East Anglia, Norwich, England.

Wurster, Bernardi and Emmons, Skidmore, Owings and Merrill, and Pietro Belluschi as consultants, Bank of America World Headquarters, San Francisco, USA.

T Music

Peter Maxwell Davies, *Eight Songs for a Mad King*.

Henryk Górecki, *Old Polish Music*.

Olivier Messiaen, *The Transfiguration of Our Lord Jesus Christ*.

Krzysztof Penderecki, *The Devils of Loudon* (opera).

Henri Pousseur, *Votre Faust* (opera).

Dmitry Shostakovich, Symphony No. 14.

Captain Beefheart and the Magic Band, *Trout Mask Replica*.

Johnny Cash, 'A Boy Named Sue'.

Jimmy Cliff, 'Wonderful World, Beautiful People', one of the first reggae hits.

Leonard Cohen, *Songs From A Room*.

Cream, *Goodbye*.

Led Zeppelin, *Led Zeppelin I*.

The MC5, *Kick Out the Jams*.

Joni Mitchell, 'Clouds'.

The Stooges, *The Stooges*.

The Who, *Tommy*.

Frank Zappa, *Hot Rats*.

In the USA, half a million people attend the three-day Woodstock Music and Arts Fair (21–24 Aug).

In Britain, BBC television launches *The Old Grey Whistle Test*, featuring British and US pop stars (1977, renamed *Whistle Test*).

U Literature and Drama

First Booker Prize for fiction awarded in Britain.

Robert Coover, *Pricksongs and Descants*.

Michael Crichton, *The Andromeda Strain*.

John Fowles, *The French Lieutenant's Woman*.

Thomas McGuane, *The Sporting Club*.

Vladimir Nabokov, *Ada*.

Mario Puzo, *The Godfather*.

Philip Roth, *Portnoy's Complaint*.

Wilfred Thesiger, *Arabian Sands*.

William Trevor, *Mrs Eckdorf in O'Neill's Hotel*.

Kurt Vonnegut, *Slaughterhouse Five*.

Robert Penn Warren, *Audubon: A Vision*.

Drama:

Woody Allen, *Play it Again, Sam*.

Mart Crowley, *The Boys in the Band*.

Athol Fugard, *Boesman and Lena*.

Arthur Kopit, *Indians*.

Joe Orton, *What the Butler Saw*.

Neil Simon, *Last of the Red Hot Lovers*.

V Births and Deaths

Feb 3 Boris Karloff dies (81).

Feb 16 Kingsley Martin dies (71).

Feb 25 Karl Jaspers dies (86).

March 28 Dwight D Eisenhower dies (78).

26 Portuguese government holds every seat in first significantly contested elections since 1926 (8 Nov, opposition parties dissolved).

28 USA submits new Middle East peace plan (rejected by Israel, 22 Dec).

29 new cabinet of young 'technocrats' takes office in Spain.

29 US Supreme Court demands immediate integration of 30 schools in Mississippi.

30 Libya requests early closure of British bases.

L **November**

1 Congress Party of India formally splits into two factions.

3 President Nixon promises complete withdrawal of US ground forces from Vietnam on secret timetable (50,000 more troops withdrawn, 15 Dec).

8 navy of UAR (Egypt) shells Israeli positions in Sinai (11, air battle over Suez Canal).

11 UN General Assembly rejects admission of Communist China for 20th time.

17 US–Soviet talks on strategic arms limitation (SALT) open in Helsinki.

19 details emerge of shooting of over 100 Vietnamese civilians by US troops at My Lai on 16 Mar 1968.

19 Ghana expels 500,000 alien immigrants.

21 USA agrees to return Okinawa to Japan in 1972 and remove all nuclear weapons.

24 USA and USSR ratify nuclear non-proliferation treaty.

25 President Nixon orders destruction of US germ warfare stocks.

29 National Party wins fourth successive victory in New Zealand general election.

M **December**

2 EC summit agrees to prepare for negotiations on British entry.

8 Soviet Foreign Minister Gromyko begins talks with West German ambassador in Moscow on mutual renunciation of force.

9 USA calls on Israel to withdraw from occupied territories in return for binding peace agreement.

12 Greece withdraws from Council of Europe to pre-empt expulsion for abrogating democratic freedoms.

15 Alexander Dubček becomes Czechoslovak ambassador to Turkey.

18 East Germany proposes diplomatic relations with West Germany as between foreign states.

19 USA partially lifts embargo on trade with Communist China.

25 Israel launches heavy attack on UAR positions around Suez.

27 UAR, Libya, and Sudan form alliance.

June 22 Judy Garland dies (47).
July 5 Walter Gropius dies (86).
July 5 Tom Mboya dies (38).
Aug 17 Ludwig Mies van der Rohe dies (86).
Aug 31 Rocky Marciano dies (45).
Sept 3 Ho Chi Minh dies (79).
Oct 21 Jack Kerouac dies (47).

w Everyday Life

Beatle John Lennon and his new wife Yoko Ono make their honeymoon, at the Hilton Hotel, Amsterdam, Netherlands, a 'bed-in' for peace (March).

The mini dress is followed by the ankle-length 'maxi'.

In Britain, the Duke of Edinburgh, talking about the Royal Family's financial difficulties, says that he may have to give up polo (9 Nov).

'Sex Fair' held in Copenhagen, Denmark (1–6 Nov).

x Sport and Recreation

Robin Knox-Johnston wins the first single-handed round-the-world yacht race (22 April).

British driver Graham Hill wins the Monaco Grand Prix for a record fifth time (18 May).

In London, at the Wimbledon tennis tournament (4 July), Ann Jones wins the Women's Singles title, beating Billie Jean King of the USA in the Final; she is the first British winner of the title since 1961.

Tony Jacklin wins the British open golf championship (12 July), the first Briton to win since Max Faulkner in 1951.

Rod Laver of Australia achieves his second Grand Slam (8 Sept), winning all four major tennis championships (the Australian Open, the French Open, Wimbledon, and the US Open) in the same calendar year.

The New York Mets become the first 'expansion' side, added to the major leagues in the 1960s, to win baseball's World Series.

US professional football is reorganized into two 'conferences', the National Football Conference (NFC) and the American Football Conference (AFC), each with 13 teams.

y Media

Australian Rupert Murdoch buys the British paper the *Sun*, which is relaunched as a tabloid.

In Britain, the *Daily Telegraph* prints news on the front page.

Film:

Easy Rider (director, Dennis Hopper).

In the Heat of the Night (director, Norman Jewison; starring Rod Steiger and Sidney Poitier).

Midnight Cowboy (director, John Schlesinger).

Oh! What a Lovely War (director, Richard Attenborough).

The Prime of Miss Jean Brodie (starring Maggie Smith).

Satyricon (director, Federico Fellini).

The Wild Bunch (director, Sam Peckinpah).

Women in Love (director, Ken Russell).

Z (director, Constantin Costa-Gavras).

Television:

New programmes in USA include: *The Bill Cosby Show*; *Sesame Street*, first shown on almost 200 non-commercial stations.

There are now 81 million television sets in the USA.

The concert *Stones in the Park* is broadcast from New York.

New programmes in Britain include: *Civilisation*, presented by Kenneth Clark (BBC); *Monty Python's Flying Circus* (BBC); *On The Buses* (LWT); *Pot Black* (BBC), which starts a craze for snooker.

West German Ostpolitik ... US offensive in Cambodia ...
Palestinian Terrorism ...

A January

1 Britain abolishes limit of £50 for use during foreign travel.

1 Mao Zedong accuses USSR of 'Fascist dictatorship' and 'moribund neo-colonialism'.

5 in Britain, teachers' pay talks break down (selective strikes until 3 Mar).

7 British government revises rules for pay increases; practical end of statutory incomes policy.

11 Biafran leader, General Ojukwu, flies into exile (15, Nigeria accepts unconditional surrender of Biafra).

19 British anti-apartheid campaigners raid cricket grounds due to be visited by South African team.

20 abortive coup in Iraq (40 executed in following days).

30 severe fighting between Israel and Syria on Golan Heights.

B February

4 British government proposes making introduction of comprehensive schools compulsory.

6 UAR frogmen sink Israeli supply ship at Eilat. Israeli jets sink UAR minesweepers in Gulf of Suez.

10 publication of White Paper *Britain and the European Communities — An Economic Assessment.*

10 Jordan places tighter controls on Palestinian guerrilla movement.

12 Israeli air raid on factories near Cairo kills 70 civilians.

12 North Vietnamese offensive in north-east Laos.

18 President Nixon presents document to Congress entitled *US Foreign Policy for the 1970s: A New Strategy for Peace.*

21 Swiss airliner crashes near Baden, killing 47 passengers. Palestinian terrorists claim responsibility.

23 Guyana becomes a republic within the Commonwealth.

C March

1 Socialists win unexpected victory in Austrian general election.

2 Rhodesia (now Zimbabwe) formally declares itself a republic (Clifford Dupont becomes president, 14 Apr).

5 British bank rate falls from 8 to 7.5 per cent (to 7 per cent, 14 Apr).

8 group of Greek Cypriots attempt to assassinate President Makarios.

10 Knesset defines what constitutes a Jew under Israeli law.

11 Iraq recognizes Kurdish autonomy, thus ending nine-year war.

12 (–3 May) Queen Elizabeth tours New Zealand and Australia as part of Cook bi-centenary celebrations.

18 overthrow of Prince Norodom Sihanouk of Cambodia.

19 first-ever meeting of East and West German heads of government takes place at Erfurt (21 May, Willi Stoph and Willy Brandt meet again at Kassel).

23 USA refuses to supply 25 Phantom fighter-bombers to Israel (sale of 18 agreed, 9 Sept).

29 attack on a police station in Londonderry (1 Apr, riots in Belfast).

30 Japanese students hijack a Boeing 727 and fly to North Korea.

31 Guatemalan guerrillas kidnap West German Ambassador, Count von Spreti (one of many political kidnappings in Latin America in 1970).

D April

1 France proposes international conference on Vietnam, Laos, and Cambodia.

1 Vietcong launch major assaults throughout South Vietnam after six-month lull.

3 500 British troops fly to Northern Ireland to reinforce 6,000 already there.

7 US Senator Edward Kennedy is spared legal action in respect of Chappaquiddick car crash of July 1969.

8 Israeli bombs fall on primary school in Nile delta, killing 30 children.

10 Greek government relaxes martial law (14, release of 332 political prisoners).

19 Pathet Lao advances on Phnom Penh (20, Cambodian government appeals for US assistance).

20 President Nixon announces withdrawal of a further 150,000 US troops from Vietnam.

22 USSR celebrates centenary of Lenin's birth.

24 Gambia becomes a republic within the Commonwealth.

30 US and South Vietnamese forces attack Communist sanctuaries in Cambodia.

E May

2 USA bombs North Vietnam for first time since Nov 1968.

4 US National Guardsmen shoot dead four anti-war demonstrators at Kent State University, Ohio.

Studs Terkel's Hard Times ... *End of The Beatles ... Death of Alexander Kerensky ... Frankie Howerd's* Up Pompeii ...

o Politics, Government, Law, and Economy

W D Burnham, *Critical Elections and the Mainsprings of American Politics.*

Peter Jenkins, *The Battle of Downing Street.*

George E Reedy, *The Twilight of the Presidency.*

R M Scammon and B J Wattenberg, *The Real Majority.*

In USA, foundation of the Joint Center for Political and Economic Studies, a research unit interested in issues relating to African-Americans.

Environmental Protection Agency established in USA.

Occupational Health and Safety Administration formed in USA to regulate working conditions (29 Dec).

In England and Wales, the Administration of Justice Act constitutes a commercial court as part of the Queen's Bench division of the High Court; it also leads to the creation of the Family Division and abolishes imprisonment for debt.

The British Petroleum company makes major oil discovery in the North Sea (19 Oct).

p Society, Education, and Religion

In USA, President Nixon announces that Native Americans will be given greater autonomy without being cut off from federal attention and financial support.

In South Africa, the Bantu Homelands Citizen Act attaches citizenship for Africans to one of the Bantu homelands.

Parliament in South Africa empowers the minister of Bantu administration to prohibit the employment of Africans in any area of work (3 April, notice given of banning of employment of Africans as shop assistants, receptionists, telephone operators, etc, but plans revised after protests).

Cosmas Desmond, *The Discarded People* (banned in South Africa in 1971).

In USA, James Hodgson, the secretary of labor, announces that federal contracts will contain a clause requiring contracted companies to employ a certain quota of women.

US attorney-general, John Mitchell, initiates suits under the Civil Rights Act requiring large corporations to end discrimination against the employment of women.

The Equal Pay Act in Britain makes discrimination in wages and conditions of employment on the basis of sex illegal from 1975.

Family Law Reform Act reduces the age of majority in England and Wales from 21 to 18 (from 1 Jan); separate acts reduce the age in Scotland and Northern Ireland.

Divorce becomes legal in certain cases in Italy (1 Dec).

Clean Air Amendment Act passed in USA.

'Earth Day' is celebrated in the USA.

Cynthia Fuch Epstein, *Women's Place.*

Germaine Greer, *The Female Eunuch.*

Kate Millett, *Sexual Politics.*

Richard Titmuss, *The Gift Relationship.*

In USA, the first desegregated classes are held in over 200 school districts in the South (31 Aug).

In West Germany, a constitutional amendment gives the federal government greater involvement in education.

In Japan, the ministry of education starts providing financial assistance to private colleges and universities, in order to raise standards.

In Britain, the new Conservative secretary of state for education, Margaret Thatcher, issues Circular 10/70, seeking to reverse Labour's policy of making education authorities introduce comprehensive schools.

In Britain, inauguration of the Open University (Jan), an institution of higher education catering mainly for adults studying part-time, making extensive use of broadcasting media.

Caroline Benn and Brian Simon, *Half Way There.*

Paulo Freire, *Pedagogy of the Oppressed.*

The World Council of Churches holds its first consultation on 'Dialogue with Men of Living Faiths'.

Publication of the complete New English Bible (in Britain, a million copies are sold within a week).

The British Methodist Church votes to allow women to become ministers (June).

The General Synod of the Church of England is inaugurated.

q Science, Technology, and Discovery

The Boeing 747 'jumbo jet' airliner begins scheduled flights (21 Jan).

British–French supersonic airliner Concorde exceeds twice the speed of sound (4 Nov).

In USA, the IBM company develops the 'floppy disc' for storing computer data.

Carbon dioxide lasers first used for industrial cutting and welding.

Japan (11 Feb) and the People's Republic of China (24 April) place artificial satellites in Earth orbit.

6 Irish Finance Minister, Charles Haughey, dismissed for alleged association with IRA gun-running (23 Oct, acquitted by High Court).

9 demonstrations in Washington, DC, against US intervention in Cambodia.

15 International Olympic Committee expels South Africa.

21 heavy floods cause extensive damage and loss of life in Romania.

22 British Cricket Council cancels tour by South Africans at government request.

22 Palestinian terrorists ambush Israeli school bus and kill 12 people.

23 Portuguese forces attack African guerrilla headquarters in Angola.

25 (–27) New York Stock Exchange extremely volatile.

27 opposition wins general election in Ceylon (31, Mrs Bandaranaike becomes prime minister).

31 earthquake in northern Peru kills over 50,000.

F **June**

5 France ends 15-month boycott of Western European Union.

7 fighting breaks out between Jordanian army and Palestinian guerrillas (10, King Hussein and Yassir Arafat agree cease-fire).

15 12 Russians, mainly Jews, attempt hijack at Leningrad airport.

18 in British general election, Conservatives win 330 seats, Labour, 287, and Liberals, 6 (Conservatives win 46.4 per cent of votes cast, Labour, 43, and Liberals, 7.4).

19 Harold Wilson resigns as British prime minister and Edward Heath forms Conservative ministry, with Sir Alec Douglas-Home as foreign secretary, Iain Macleod as chancellor of the exchequer and Reginald Maudling as home secretary.

25 USA proposes 'Rogers Plan' for ceasefire and UN mediation in Middle East (accepted by UAR, 23 July and by Israel, 4 Aug).

26 violence in Belfast as Bernadette Devlin MP starts prison sentence for incitement to riot.

26 Czechoslovak Communist Party expels Alexander Dubček.

28 US ground troops withdraw from Cambodia.

30 Britain, Denmark, Norway, and Ireland open negotiations in Luxembourg for EC membership.

G **July**

3 Security forces begin search for arms in Falls Road area of Belfast, Northern Ireland.

6 Irish Foreign Minister, Dr Hillery, makes secret visit to Northern Ireland and criticizes behaviour of British troops.

10 US Roman Catholic missionary, Bishop James Walsh, released after 12 years in Shanghai prison.

12 China agrees loan to Tanzania and Zambia to build 'TanZam' railway.

16 (–29) British national dock strike over pay; government declares State of Emergency.

20 Britain expresses readiness to supply arms to South Africa for maritime defence.

20 death of British chancellor Iain Macleod (25, Anthony Barber becomes chancellor).

22 Tanzania, Uganda, and Zambia threaten to leave Commonwealth if Britain sells arms to South Africa.

23 Northern Ireland government bans all marches for six months.

23 tear-gas bombs thrown from gallery force evacuation of British House of Commons.

H **August**

7 Start of 90-day truce between Israel, UAR, and Jordan (5 Nov, renewed for 90 days).

12 West Germany and USSR sign treaty in Moscow renouncing use of force.

13 IRA bomb store found in Tooting, London.

25 UN mediator, Gunnar Jarring, meets representatives of Israel, UAR, and Jordan in New York.

J **September**

3 Panama rejects US draft treaties on status of Canal Zone.

5 Marxist candidate, Salvador Allende, wins Chilean presidential election (24 Oct, Chilean Congress ratifies his election).

6 Palestinian terrorists hijack four aircraft, one to Cairo, UAR, two to Dawson's Field, Jordan, and one to Heathrow, London, where hijacker Leila Khaled is arrested.

7 Indian presidential decree abolishes titles and privileges of Ruling Princes (15 Dec, deemed unconstitutional).

9 Palestinians hijack BOAC airliner to Dawson's Field, Jordan.

19 hijackers blow up three aircraft at Dawson's Field (30, remaining hostages go free, after Britain, West Germany, and Switzerland release Palestinian prisoners).

16 King Hussein orders Jordanian army to disband Palestinian militia (17, house-to-house fighting begins in Amman).

19 Syrian tanks invade Jordan in support of Palestinians.

27 King Hussein, Yassir Arafat and other Arab leaders sign agreement in Cairo to end civil war in Jordan.

US *Apollo 13* (launched 11 April) aborts planned Moon landing because of explosion in the Command module (13 April).

Soviet uncrewed *Luna 16* lands on the Moon, collects soil and returns to Earth (Sept); *Luna 17* lands on the Moon (17 Nov) and deploys the *Lunokhod 1* Moon vehicle.

Scientists at the University of Wisconsin, USA, assemble a gene from its chemical components.

Howard Temin and David Baltimore separately discover that RNA (ribonucleic acid) can be converted into DNA by the reverse transcriptase enzyme.

First successful nerve transplant achieved in West Germany.

P R and A H Ehrlich, *Population, Resources, and Experimental Issues in Human Ecology*.

R Humanities

The Cambridge History of Islam.
Roland Bainton, *Erasmus of Christendom.*
Christopher Hill, *God's Englishman: Oliver Cromwell and the English Revolution.*
R C Latham and W Matthews (eds.), *The Diary of Samuel Pepys* (–1983).
Richard Cobb, *The Police and the People.*
Eric Foner, *Free Soil, Free Labor, Free Men: The Ideology of the Republican Party before the Civil War.*
Paul Kleppner, *The Cross of Culture: A Social Analysis of Mid-Western Politics, 1850–1900.*
Studs Terkel, *Hard Times: An Oral History of the Great Depression.*
John Summerson, *Victorian Architecture.*
C C Gillispie (ed.), *Dictionary of Scientific Biography.*
T S Kuhn, *The Structure of Scientific Revolution.*
Willard Quine, *Philosophy of Logic.*

S Art, Sculpture, Fine Arts, and Architecture

Record price paid for a *Campbell's Soup Tin* by Andy Warhol — £25,000.

Painting:

David Hockney, *Mr and Mrs Ossie Clark and Percy.*
On Kawara, *I Am Still Alive.*
Denis Oppenheim, *Reading Position for a Second Degree Burn.*

Sculpture:

John De Andrea, *Standing Man.*
Sol Lewitt, *Five Modular Units.*
Mario Merz, *Igloo Fibonacci.*

Robert Smithson, *Spiral Jetty.*

Architecture:

Belluschi and Nervi, Roman Catholic Cathedral, San Francisco, USA.
Kisho Kurokawa, Takara Beautillon, Expo '70, Osaka, Japan.
Yamasaki, World Trade Center, first tower topped out, New York.

T Music

Luciano Berio, *Opera.*
George Crumb, *Black Angels.*
Henri Dutilleux, *Tout un monde lointain...*
Witold Lutoslawski, *Cello Concerto.*
Donald Martino, *Pianississimo.*
Krzysztof Penderecki, *Utrenia.*
William Still, *Western Hemisphere.*
Michael Tippett, *The Knot Garden* (opera).
The Beatles, 'Let It Be' (single and album).
The Carpenters, 'We've Only Just Begun' (by Burt Bacharach).
Creedence Clearwater Revival, *Cosmo's Factory.*
The Grateful Dead, *Workingman's Dead, American Beauty.*
Sacha Distel, 'Raindrops Keep Falling on my Head'.
George Harrison, 'My Sweet Lord'.
Jackson Five, 'I'll Be There'.
Elton John, *Elton John, Tumbleweed Connection.*
Led Zeppelin, *Led Zeppelin II, III.*
Joni Mitchell, *Ladies of the Canyon.*
Simon and Garfunkel, 'Bridge Over Troubled Water' (single and album).
The Beatles officially split up, all four of them releasing solo albums.
Death from drug overdose of superstar guitarist Jimi Hendrix (18 Sept).

U Literature and Drama

Maya Angelou, *I Know Why the Caged Bird Sings.*
Richard Bach, *Jonathan Livingston Seagull.*
Elizabeth Bowen, *Eva Trout.*
Ted Hughes, *Crow* (poems).
W S Merwin, *The Carrier of Ladders* (poems).
Iris Murdoch, *Bruno's Dream.*
Michel Tournier, *The Erl King.*
John Updike, *Bech: A Book.*
Eudora Welty, *Losing Battles.*
Patrick White, *The Vivisector.*
Japanese author Yukio Mishima commits ritual suicide after failed coup (25 Nov).

Drama:

Antonio Buero Vallejo, *The Sleep of Reason.*
Dario Fo, *Accidental Death of an Anarchist.*
Athol Fugard, *Boesman and Lena.*

28 President Nasser of Egypt dies (29, succeeded by Anwar Sadat).

K October

5 Quebec separatists kidnap Jasper Cross, British Trade Commissioner in Canada (3 Dec, released).

7 President Nixon proposes five-point peace plan for Indochina (14, North Vietnam rejects plan).

9 Cambodia declares itself the Khmer Republic.

10 Fiji becomes independent within the Commonwealth.

11 Quebec separatists kidnap Pierre Laporte, minister of labour (17, body found).

13 China establishes diplomatic relations with Canada (6 Nov, with Italy).

15 British governmental re-organization creates Department of Trade and Industry and Department of the Environment.

27 in Britain, Anthony Barber introduces mini-Budget: 6d. cut in standard rate of income tax, lower corporation tax, higher charges for some welfare services.

28 British government announces retention of 4,500 troops in Far East.

L November

1 The *Sunday Times* alleges that Jack the Ripper was Albert Victor, Duke of Clarence.

2 abolition of British Prices and Incomes Board.

3 in US Congressional elections, Republicans gain one Senator, but lose 10 Representatives.

8 UAR, Libya, and Sudan agree to federate (27, joined by Syria).

9 preliminary British–Rhodesian talks begin in Pretoria to seek basis for settlement.

11 British government lends £48 million to Rolls Royce Ltd, to offset losses.

12 cyclone and tidal wave kill 150,000 in East Pakistan.

20 UN General Assembly votes to admit Communist China, but majority is less than required two-thirds.

22 Portuguese mercenaries attempt to invade Guinea.

M December

2 Portugal grants a measure of autonomy to Angola and Mozambique.

3 British government publishes Industrial Relations Bill to make collective agreements enforceable at law.

3 (–28) trial of Basque separatists at Burgos prompts strikes and demonstrations.

7 West Germany and Poland sign treaty recognising Oder–Neisse Line as frontier.

7 Awami League of Bengali nationalists wins first free elections in Pakistan since 1948.

7 nationwide power-cut in Britain due to industrial action (14, work-to-rule ends).

13 Polish government sharply increases food, fuel and clothing prices (14, strikes, riots and arson begin in Gdansk, spreading to other Baltic ports).

20 Edward Gierek replaces Wladyslaw Gomulka as first secretary of Polish Communist Party.

30 Vietnam peace talks in Paris end second full year with all sides agreeing there had been no progress.

War in Pakistan ... Industrial Relations Act in Britian ... United Nations admits China ...

A January

2 Stampede at Ibrox Park football stadium, Glasgow, Scotland, crushes 66 people to death (the ensuing Wheatley Report recommends that stadia with capacities of 10,000 or more be licensed by the local authority).

3 Mujibur Rahman, leader of Awami League, pledges to seek full autonomy for East Pakistan in proposed new constitution.

4 Lord Robens resigns as Chairman of British National Coal Board in protest at plans to sell parts of nationalized industries.

5 Israel, Egypt, and Jordan resume indirect peace talks with UN mediator.

8 left-wing Tupamaros guerrillas kidnap Geoffrey Jackson, British ambassador to Uruguay (9 Sept, released).

12 'Angry Brigade' anarchists bomb home of British employment secretary, Robert Carr.

12 Selwyn Lloyd succeeds Horace King as speaker of British House of Commons.

Christopher Hampton, *The Philanthropist*.
David Mercer, *After Hegarty*.
Peter Nichols, *The National Health*.
David Storey, *The Contractor* and *Home*.

v Births and Deaths

Feb 2 Bertrand Russell dies (98).
Feb 25 Marc Rothko dies (66).
April 1 Semyon Timoshenko dies (75).
June 4 Hjalmar Schacht dies (93).
June 7 Edward Morgan Forster dies (90).
June 11 Alexander Kerensky dies (89).
June 21 Achmed Sukarno dies (69).
June 22 Erich Remarque dies (72).
July 27 Antonio Salazar dies (81).
Sept 1 François Mauriac dies (84).
Sept 18 Jimi Hendrix dies (27).
Sept 28 John Dos Passos dies (74).
Sept 28 Gamal Abdel Nasser dies (52).
Oct 10 Edouard Daladier dies (86).
Nov 9 Charles de Gaulle dies (79).

w Everyday Life

x Sport and Recreation

Joe Frazier becomes boxing's undisputed World Heavyweight champion, beating Jimmy Ellis in four rounds in New York (16 Feb).

In USA, Diane Crump is the first woman jockey in the Kentucky Derby (2 May); she finishes 12th on Fathom.

Brazil is victorious in the soccer World Cup, held in Mexico, for the third time (beating Italy by 4–1 in the final); it wins the Rimet Trophy outright (21 June).

Tony Jacklin wins the US Open at Hazeltine Golf Club, Minnesota (21 June); he is the first Briton to win since Ted Ray in 1920.

Nijinsky, ridden by Lester Piggott, wins the Derby in the fastest time since 1936 (4 June). In the same season Nijinsky also wins the 2,000 Guineas, the King George VI and Queen Elizabeth Diamond Stakes, and the St Leger, completing the first Triple Crown of major British races since 1935.

Margaret Court of Australia becomes only the second woman, after Maureen Connolly in 1953, to win the Grand Slam of all four major tennis tournaments (13 Sept).

y Media

National newspaper strike in Britain (10–15 June).

Film:
The Conformist (director, Bernardo Bertolucci).
Five Easy Pieces (director, Bob Rafelson; starring Jack Nicholson).
Kes (director, Ken Loach).
Love Story (director, Arthur Hiller; starring Ali MacGraw and Ryan O'Neal).
M*A*S*H (director, Robert Altman; starring Donald Sutherland and Elliott Gould).
The Passenger (director, Andrzej Munk).
Performance (director, Nicholas Roeg).

Television:
New programmes in USA include: *The Mary Tyler Moore Show*.
New programmes in Britain include: *Play for Today* (BBC), which includes John Osborne's *The Right Prospectus*; *The Six Wives of Henry VIII* (BBC); *Up Pompeii* (BBC), starring Frankie Howerd.

End of agreed exchange rates ... Religion and the Decline of Magic ... Jesus Christ Superstar ...

o Politics, Government, Law, and Economy

Formation of the South Pacific Forum on initiative of New Zealand; provides for occasional meetings of heads of state of S Pacific countries.

Sixty-three nations, including the USA, USSR, and Britain, sign treaty banning atomic weapons from the sea-bed (11 Feb).

Greenpeace international environmental campaign organization founded.

The 26th Amendment to the US Constitution extends full voting rights to 18 year-olds (30 June).

In USA, Federal Election Campaign Act requires disclosure of large campaign contributions from 1972.

In South Africa, administration of Bantu areas is vested in 16 Administration Boards (later 12), reporting directly to the government in Pretoria, thereby removing responsibility of town councils for their areas (in force from July 1973).

The Bantu Homelands Constitution Act enables the state president to proclaim

15 President Sadat of UAR (Egypt) and USSR President Podgorny inaugurate the Aswan High Dam.

20 (–8 Mar) nation-wide strike by British postal workers.

25 in Uganda, General Idi Amin deposes President Obote and seizes power.

31 telephone service between East and West Berlin re-established after 19 years.

B **February**

1 (–31 Mar) strike halts Ford car production in Britain.

4 Egypt extends ceasefire and offers to re-open Suez Canal if Israel withdraws from Sinai.

5 Robert Curtis is first British soldier to be killed on duty in Northern Ireland.

8 South Vietnam invades Laos to close Ho Chi Minh Trail to North Vietnamese (24 Mar, withdraws).

14 international oil companies accept higher prices demanded by Gulf States.

14 USSR announces ninth Five-Year Plan, with high priority for consumer goods.

15 Britain introduces decimal currency.

15 Israel affirms Jewish settlement policy in occupied territories.

20 Spanish bishops call for separation of Church and State.

20 emergency warning of nuclear attack broadcast by mistake in USA.

23 in Britain, nationalization of aero-engine and marine divisions of Rolls Royce Ltd.

24 British government publishes Immigration Bill to restrict rights of abode of Commonwealth citizens.

C **March**

1 Postponement of Pakistani Constituent Assembly provokes general strike in East Pakistan.

7 expiry of Middle East ceasefire, but accompanied by decision to withhold fire along Suez Canal.

10 USSR Jews, demanding emigration permits, occupy offices of Supreme Soviet.

10 three off-duty British soldiers murdered in public house near Belfast, Northern Ireland.

10 Indira Gandhi's Congress Party wins landslide victory in Indian general election.

10 William MacMahon succeeds John Gorton as prime minister of Australia.

12 in Northern Ireland, demonstrators in Belfast demand internment of IRA leaders (18, Britain sends 1,300 more troops).

23 Brian Faulkner becomes prime minister of Northern Ireland.

26 Awami League declares independence of East Pakistan as Bangladesh; troops from West Pakistan fight separatists.

26 renewal of conflict between Jordanian army and Palestinians.

30 British Budget halves selective employment tax, increases child allowances and old age pensions, and reforms taxation of high incomes, reducing top rate to 75 per cent.

31 US Lieutenant William Calley sentenced to life imprisonment for My Lai massacre of Mar 1968 (20 Aug, sentence reduced to 20 years).

D **April**

1 British bank rate falls from 7 to 6 per cent (2 Sept, falls to 5 per cent).

2 Pakistan protests at Indian support for East Pakistani separatism.

5 (–23) violent left-wing rebellion in Ceylon.

7 President Nixon announces withdrawal of 100,000 more troops from Vietnam.

10 US table tennis team arrives in China (14, US relaxes restrictions on Chinese trade and travel).

13 riots in East Belfast, Northern Ireland, after IRA gunmen fire on Orange parade.

15 Britain restores telephone link with China (cut in 1949).

17 Egypt, Syria, and Libya sign Benghazi Agreement to establish Federation of Arab Republics.

19 Sierra Leone becomes a republic within the Commonwealth.

19 British unemployment, at 3.4 per cent, reaches highest level since 1940.

21 death of President François Duvalier of Haiti (known as 'Papa Doc'); succeeded by his teenage son, Jean-Claude Duvalier.

25 200,000 demonstrate in Washington, DC, against Vietnam War (12,000 protestors arrested during following week).

26 British government decides to build third London airport at Foulness.

29 US combat deaths in Vietnam exceed 45,000.

E **May**

3 Erich Honecker succeeds Walter Ulbricht as first secretary of Socialist Unity Party of East Germany.

5 European currency markets close after flight from US dollar into marks (9, West Germany and Holland float their currencies).

6 Greece and Albania re-establish diplomatic relations.

11 120 Labour MPs declare opposition to British entry into EC.

13 in British borough elections, Conservatives lose 1,943 seats.

14 plot to overthrow President Sadat of Egypt foiled.

self-government for any of the eight African Territorial Authorities (KwaZulu proclaimed self-governing on 30 March 1972, Bophutatswana in May 1972, Ciskei on 28 July 1972, followed by five others).

In USA, Charles Manson and three women are sentenced to death (in practice, life imprisonment) for the murder of actress Sharon Tate and others in 1969 (29 March).

In Britain, the Assizes and Quarter Sessions are replaced by the Crown Court.

The British Industrial Relations Act establishes a completely new system of labour law, with a National Industrial Relations Court and legally binding contracts.

John Rawls, *A Theory of Justice*.

In USA, President Nixon introduces a 'New Economic Policy', in which the Bretton Woods system (founded in 1944) of agreed exchange rates is effectively ended despite an attempt to patch matters up at the Smithsonian conference; domestically wages and prices are subjected to direct controls.

In USA, Amtrak (the National Railroad Passenger Corporation) takes over the running of passenger trains (from 1 May).

General Motors in the USA starts the largest recall of cars in history, to install restraint mounts in 6.7 million vehicles.

Consolidation of British income tax and surtax into one graduated income tax (from 1973).

P **Society, Education, and Religion**

In Swann v. Charlotte-Mecklenburgh Board of Education, the US Supreme Court rules that busing should be used to ensure racial balance in school district systems (29 Apr).

Immigration Act places Commonwealth citizens on the same footing as foreigners while in Britain.

Referendum in Switzerland approves the introduction of female suffrage (7 Feb).

Divorce Reform Act in Britain permits the dissolution of marriage by consent after two-year separation (Jan).

Canadian Medicare system established.

Provisional returns from the 1971 British census show considerable decrease in populations of London and other big cities (Aug).

F Fox Piven and R Cloward, *Regulating the Poor*.

B F Skinner, *Beyond Freedom and Dignity*.

In the People's Republic of China, universities are re-opened.

In Britain, the Department of Education allocates £132 million to remove 6,000 slum primary schools (25 June).

Ivan Illich, *Deschooling Society*.

President Tito of Yugoslavia is first Communist head of state to be received officially by the Pope.

Joyce Bennett and Jane Hwang Hsien Yuen are ordained priests by the Anglican Bishop of Hong Kong.

General Synod of the Church of England allows baptized members of other Christian denominations to receive communion in Anglican churches.

Hans Küng, *Infallible? An Enquiry*.

Q **Science, Technology, and Discovery**

Introduction of quadraphonic sound reproduction system.

Japan launches world's largest supertanker, the *Nisseki Maru* (372,000 tonnes).

Canada inaugurates world's first nuclear power station with cooling by ordinary water.

Intel in the USA introduces the microprocessor, a minute device on a single 'chip' for processing information within a computer.

Swiss scientist Niklaus Wirth develops the computer language Pascal.

US *Apollo 14* mission (31 Jan–9 Feb) collects 44.5 kg/98 lb of Moon rock; astronauts on the *Apollo 15* mission (lands 30 July) drive around the Moon on the lunar rover.

USSR launches *Salyut 1* space station (19 April) which is visited by a three-person crew in June (7–29); the cosmonauts die during their descent to Earth when a faulty valve causes their capsule to lose pressure.

US space probe *Mariner 9* becomes first human-made object to orbit another planet (Mars); it transmits (from 12 Nov) 7,329 photographs of the planet.

Soviet craft *Mars 2* goes into orbit around Mars (27 Nov); a capsule from *Mars 3* lands on the planet, but its transmitters go dead after 20 seconds.

Surgeons develop the fibre-optic endoscope for looking inside the human body.

In USA, Choh Hao Li and associates at the University of California Medical Centre announce the synthesis of a human growth hormone, somatotropin (6 Jan).

Jacques Monod, *Chance and Necessity*.

R **Humanities**

C W Ferguson of the University of Arizona, USA, establishes a tree-ring chronology dating back to *c.* 6000BC.

Cambridge Ancient History, Volumes 1, 2, 3rd edition (–1977).

Peter Brown, *The World of Late Antiquity*.

Norman Davis, *Paston Letters and Papers of the 15th Century*, Part 1 (Part 2, 1976).

Keith Thomas, *Religion and the Decline of Magic*.

20 (–21) Edward Heath and President Pompidou, meeting in Paris, reach general agreement on terms for British membership of EC.

27 Egypt signs 15-year treaty of friendship with USSR.

28 Chile and USSR sign agreement on economic co-operation.

31 India requests international aid for millions of refugees from war in East Pakistan.

F **June**

7 Deals between Britain and EC on Commonwealth sugar and status of sterling (23, final agreement on British entry).

10 USA ends embargo on trade with China.

13 the *New York Times* begins publication of secret Pentagon Papers detailing US government deception in handling of Vietnam War (30, US Supreme Court upholds right to publish).

21 International Court of Justice rules South 'African administration of South-West Africa illegal.

22 Dom Mintoff, prime minister of Malta, demands resignation of governor general and re-negotiation of British–Maltese defence agreement.

25 British education secretary, Margaret Thatcher, announces end of free milk for primary school children.

30 Yugoslav Federal Assembly passes 23 amendments to 1963 constitution, devolving power to constituent republics.

G **July**

3 Indonesian government wins clear victory in first general election for 16 years.

7 White Paper, entitled *The United Kingdom and the European Communities*, outlines terms for British entry.

9 in Northern Ireland, troops shoot dead two rioters in Londonderry (15, nationalist SDLP withdraws from Stormont Parliament after inquiry is refused).

15 President Nixon of USA announces he will visit China in 1972.

18 Iraq closes border with Jordan in protest at suppression of Palestinian guerrilla movement (23, Syria closes border).

19 British government cuts purchase tax, raises capital allowances, and abolishes hire purchase restrictions.

25 East Caribbean states sign Declaration of Grenada on political union.

28 National Executive of British Labour Party votes to oppose EC membership on current terms.

H **August**

9 Northern Ireland government introduces internment and forbids processions.

9 (–11) in Northern Ireland, over 22 people die in fighting between troops and IRA in Belfast, Newry, and Londonderry; Ireland opens refugee camps for Catholics.

14 Bahrain declares independence from Britain (Qatar becomes independent 14 Sept).

15 after the USA reports its first trade deficit since 1894, President Nixon suspends conversion of dollars into gold and imposes 90-day price freeze and 10 per cent import surcharge.

16 (–23) closure of European currency markets, after which sterling finds its own level (28, Japan floats the yen).

18 Australia and New Zealand announce withdrawal of forces from Vietnam.

20 Britain's first auction of North Sea oil and gas concessions.

31 British Government orders inquiry into alleged ill-treatment of internees in Northern Ireland.

J **September**

2 United Arab Republic (UAR) reverts to historical name of Egypt.

3 USA, Britain, France, and USSR sign Berlin Agreement on communications between West Berlin and West Germany.

9 (–13) riots in Attica prison, New York, leave 42 dead.

24 Britain requests departure of 105 Soviet officials for alleged espionage (8 Oct, USSR expels or bars 18 Britons).

27 (–28) Edward Heath, John Lynch, and Brian Faulkner meet at Chequers to discuss Northern Ireland; they agree only to condemn violence.

27 Cardinal Mindszenty leaves Hungary after 15 years as refugee in US embassy.

K **October**

1 Joseph Luns succeeds Manlio Brosio as secretary general of NATO.

4 in Britain, Labour Party conference passes anti-EC resolution.

5 Emperor Hirohito of Japan visits Britain for first time since World War II.

7 Britain sends 1,500 more soldiers to Northern Ireland.

12 Iran celebrates 2,500th anniversary of Persian monarchy.

13 in Britain, Conservative Party conference votes 8 to 1 in favour of EC entry.

20 West German Chancellor Willy Brandt awarded Nobel Peace Prize.

25 UN General Assembly votes to admit Communist China and expel Taiwan (15 Nov, China takes its seat).

Geoffrey Best, *Mid-Victorian Britain, 1851–1870.*
Brian Harrison, *Drink and the Victorians.*
Mark Girouard, *The Victorian Country House.*
P F Clarke, *Lancashire and the New Liberalism.*
F S L Lyons, *Ireland since the Famine.*
Winifred Gerin, *Emily Brontë.*
Valerie Eliot (ed.), *The Waste Land: A Facsimile and Transcript of the Original Drafts.*
Charles Rosen, *The Classical Style.*
Alisdair MacIntyre, *Against the Self-Images of the Age.*
Jean Piaget, *Structuralism.*

s Art, Sculpture, Fine Arts, and Architecture

Conceptual art dominates Paris Biennale, Prospect 71, Düsseldorf, West Germany, and 6th Guggenheim International, New York.
Tate Gallery, London, acquires by gift from A McAlpine 59 works by Turnbull, Tucker, King, and Scott.
'Art in Revolution' exhibition at Hayward Gallery, London.

Painting, etc:
David Hockney, *Rubber Ring Floating in a Swimming Pool.*
Anselm Kiefer, *Mann im Wald.*

Sculpture:
Louise Bourgeois, *Trani Episode.*
Gilbert and George, *Underneath the Arches.*

Architecture:
Marcel Breuer and Hamilton Smith, Cleveland Museum of Art, Cleveland, Ohio, USA.
Pier Luigi Nervi, Audience Hall, The Vatican.
Destruction of Pruitt Igoe public housing blocks in St Louis, Missouri, USA (architect Minoru Yamasaki), heralds end of modern architecture.

t Music

Benjamin Britten, *Owen Wingrave* (opera).
Gottfried von Einem, *Der Besuch der alten Dame* (opera).
Mauricio Kagel, *Staatstheater* (opera).
Dmitry Shostakovich, Symphony No. 15.
Karlheinz Stockhausen, *Trans.*
Follies (musical), lyrics and music by Stephen Sondheim (first performed at the Winter Gardens, New York, 4 April).
Godspell (rock musical), lyrics and music by Stephen Schwartz.
Jesus Christ Superstar (rock musical), lyrics by Tim Rice, music by Andrew Lloyd Webber (first performed at the Mark Hellinger Theatre, New York, 12 Oct).

David Bowie, 'The Man Who Sold the World'.
Marvin Gaye, 'What's Going On?' Janis Joplin, *Pearl.*
Carole King, *Tapestry.*
Led Zeppelin, *Led Zeppelin IV.*
Jerry Reed, 'When You're Hot, You're Hot'.
The Rolling Stones, 'Brown Sugar', *Sticky Fingers.*
Rod Stewart, 'Maggie May', *Every Picture Tells a Story.*
T Rex, 'Hot Love', *Electric Warrior* — glitter rock starts in Britain.

u Literature and Drama

Albert Camus, *A Happy Death.*
E L Doctorow, *The Book of Daniel.*
Jane Gardam, *A Long Way from Verona.*
Geoffrey Hill, *Mercian Hymns.*
Jerzy Kosinski, *Being There.*
Herman Raucher, *The Summer of '42.*
Iain Crichton Smith, *Love Poems and Elegies.*
Alexander Solzhenitsyn, *August 1914.*

Drama:
Edward Bond, *Lear.*
John Guare, *The House of Blue Leaves.*
Wole Soyinka, *Madmen and Specialists.*
David Williamson, *The Removalists.*

v Births and Deaths

Jan 10 Coco Chanel dies (87).
March 7 Stevie Smith dies (68).
March 8 Harold Lloyd dies (77).
March 24 Arne Jacobsen dies (69).
April 6 Igor Stravinsky dies (88).
June 4 György S von Lukács dies (86).
June 16 John Reith dies (81).
July 1 W L Bragg dies (81).
July 1 Learie Constantine dies (69).
July 6 Louis Armstrong dies (69).
July 23 W V S Tubman dies (75).
Sept 11 Nikita Khrushchev dies (77).
Sept 20 George Seferis dies (71).
Oct 12 Dean Acheson dies (78).
Nov 11 A P Herbert dies (81).
Nov 17 Gladys Cooper dies (82).

w Everyday Life

In Orlando, Florida, USA, opening of Disney World (1 Oct).
The dismantled London Bridge is reopened in Lake Havasu City, Arizona, USA (10 Oct).
'Hot Pants' worn by young women in West (including Princess Anne of Britain).

x Sport and Recreation

First limited-overs one-day cricket international; Australia beats England in Melbourne (5 Jan).
In Test cricket, England regain the Ashes after 12 years from Australia (17 Feb).
Joe Frazier beats Muhammad Ali over 15

27 President Mobutu changes name of Congo to Zaire.

28 House of Commons votes 356 to 244 in favour of EC entry. 69 Labour MPs vote with Government, 39 Conservative MPs vote with Opposition.

31 Britain reverts to Greenwich Mean Time after three years of British Standard Time.

L November

3 Britain annexes Rockall in north Atlantic.

10 (–4 Dec) Fidel Castro, prime minister of Cuba, visits Chile.

12 President Nixon proclaims end of US offensive role in Vietnam War and withdraws 45,000 more troops.

15 British Foreign Secretary Sir Alec Douglas-Home opens talks with Ian Smith in Salisbury (now Harare, Zimbabwe; 24, agreement on new Rhodesian constitution).

16 Compton Report rejects allegations of brutality in internment camps in Northern Ireland.

17 military coup in Thailand.

22 Pakistan accuses India of invading East Pakistan.

25 Harold Wilson, leader of opposition in British House of Commons, proposes unification of Ireland in 15 years.

28 Palestinian terrorists murder Wasfi Tell, prime minister of Jordan (1 Dec, King Hussein rules out further talks with Palestinian guerrillas).

30 Iran occupies Tunbs Islands in Persian Gulf one day before British protectorate expires. Iraq severs diplomatic relations with Iran and Britain, alleging collusion.

M December

1 Abu Dhabi, Sharjah, Dubai, Umm al Qaiwain, Ajman, and Fujairah form United Arab Emirates.

1 President Tito purges Croat leadership of nationalists.

2 in Britain, report of Select Committee on Civil List proposes doubling Queen Elizabeth's income.

3 Pakistan bombs Indian air-fields.

4 in Northern Ireland, explosion in Belfast public house kills 15 (subsequent reprisals bring annual death-toll to 173, including 43 troops).

6 India recognizes independence of Bangladesh; war breaks out along border between India and West Pakistan.

16 East Pakistan forces surrender to India; India orders ceasefire on West Pakistan front.

16 Zimbabwe leaders form African National Council with aim of rejecting Anglo–Rhodesian settlement.

17 end of Indo–Pakistan War; East Pakistan becomes independent as Bangladesh.

18 USA devalues dollar by 7.9 per cent; realignment of other major currencies.

20 Zulfikar Ali Bhutto replaces Yahya Khan as president of Pakistan.

22 Mujibur Rahman is released from prison in West Pakistan to become president of Bangladesh.

24 Maltese ultimatum to Britain: pay £18 million for use of naval bases or withdraw by end of year (31 Dec, Malta extends deadline).

31 Kurt Waldheim takes office as UN secretary general.

President Nixon visits China ... Direct rule in Northern Ireland ...
East–West détente ...

A January

9 British national coal strike begins (9 Feb, state of emergency proclaimed).

10 President Mujibur Rahman of Bangladesh arrives in Dacca (12, resigns presidency in order to become prime minister).

11 (–12 Mar) Lord Pearce heads British Commission to Rhodesia to assess opinion on proposed new constitutional arrangements (agreed on 24 Nov 1971, report issued on 23 May).

14 talks between British Defence Secretary, Lord Carrington, and Maltese Premier,

Dom Mintoff, in Rome (16, withdrawal of British forces from Malta suspended).

14 death of King Frederik IX of Denmark; succeeded by Margarethe II.

20 number of unemployed in Britain exceeds 1 million.

22 Britain, Denmark, Ireland, and Norway sign Treaty of Accession to EC in Brussels.

25 in USA, President Nixon reveals that Henry Kissinger, his national security adviser, has been conducting secret peace negotiations with North Vietnam since 1969.

30 'Bloody Sunday' in Northern Ireland:

rounds at Madison Square Garden, New York, and retains the World Heavyweight title (8 March).

Britain and Ireland's amateur golfers win the Walker Cup match against the USA (27 May) — Britain and Ireland's first Walker victory since 1938.

The British Lions win a rugby Test series in New Zealand for the first time.

ʏ Media

In Britain, the *Daily Sketch* is merged into the *Daily Mail* (May), which is then relaunched as a tabloid.

Film:

Carnal Knowledge (director, Mike Nichols).

A Clockwork Orange (director, Stanley Kubrick).

Death in Venice (director, Luchino Visconti).

Dirty Harry (director, Don Siegel; starring Clint Eastwood).

Fiddler on the Roof (director, Norman Jewison; starring Topol).

The French Connection (director, William Friedkin; starring Gene Hackman and Fernando Rey).

The Garden of the Finzi-Continis (director, Vittorio de Sica).

Get Carter (director, Mike Hodges; starring Michael Caine).

The Godfather (director, Francis Ford Coppola; starring Marlon Brando and Al Pacino).

The Go-Between (director, Joseph Losey).

Klute (director, Alan J Pakula; starring Jane Fonda and Donald Sutherland).

The Last Picture Show (director, Peter Bogdanovich).

Play Misty for Me (director and star, Clint Eastwood).

Straw Dogs (director, Sam Peckinpah).

Sunday Bloody Sunday (director, John Schlesinger).

Two-Lane Blacktop (director, Monte Hellman).

Television:

New programmes in Britain include: *Edna the Inebriate Woman* (BBC), starring Patricia Hayes; *Elizabeth R* (BBC), starring Glenda Jackson; *The Old Grey Whistle Test* (BBC); *The Onedin Line* (BBC; — 1980); *The Two Ronnies* (BBC; –1986), with Ronnie Barker and Ronnie Corbett; *Upstairs Downstairs* (LWT; –1975).

Launch of Britain's 'University of the Air', the Open University, using television and radio broadcasts among its teaching media.

Tutankhamun exhibition at the British Museum ... Tate Gallery buys André's 'bricks' ... First computer game ... Alistair Cooke's America ...

o Politics, Government, Law, and Economy

In USA, foundation of the Center for National Policy, Washington, DC, and of the Institute for Contemporary Studies in San Francisco.

In USA, the Democratic Party introduces new nomination and delegate seating procedures.

In South Africa, the government abolishes Coloured representation on municipal councils in the Cape and substitutes nominated consultative committees.

Local Government Act provides for the first full-scale re-organization of local government in Britain since 1889 (to be effective from 1974); the scheme adopted does not follow the recommendations of the Redcliffe-Maud Report of 1969.

In USA, in Furman v. Georgia, the Supreme Court rules that the death penalty is unconstitutional (29 June).

In Kleindienst v. Mandel, the US Supreme

British troops shoot dead 13 civilians when violence erupts at anti-internment march in Bogside, Londonderry.

30 Pakistan leaves the Commonwealth in anticipation of British recognition of Bangladesh (Feb 4).

B February

2 demonstrators burn down British embassy in Dublin, Republic of Ireland.

7 Sir Keith Holyoake retires as prime minister of New Zealand; succeeded by John Marshall.

11 Greece demands that Cyprus surrender secret armaments and accept coalition government (Mar 14, Cyprus yields arms to UN peacekeepers but refuses ministerial changes).

11 British House of Commons approves second reading of European Communities Bill by 309 votes to 301.

18 Wilberforce Commission recommends pay increases for British miners of up to £6 per week (equivalent to 22 per cent; 28, coal strike ends after further government concessions).

21 (–27) President Nixon visits China.

22 IRA bomb kills seven people at Aldershot, S England.

27 Israel attacks south Lebanon in reprisal for Palestinian raids.

28 Japan acknowledges China's territorial rights over Taiwan.

C March

2 British Prime Minister Edward Heath forbids use of 'intensive' interrogation techniques in Northern Ireland, following Parker Report on security forces.

4 in Northern Ireland, bomb explosion in restaurant in Belfast kills two and injures 136.

13 Britain resumes ambassadorial relations with China and closes its consulate in Taiwan.

15 King Hussein of Jordan proposes creation of autonomous Palestinian state on West Bank (6 April, Egypt breaks off relations in protest).

19 India and Bangladesh sign mutual defence pact.

22 British government establishes Industrial Development Executive, to direct government money into industrial investment (Christopher Chataway appointed minister for industrial development).

26 Britain and NATO agree to pay Malta £14 million per year for use of military bases.

29 North Vietnamese launch major offensive in Quang Tri province.

30 Britain assumes direct rule over Northern

Ireland, with William Whitelaw as secretary of state.

D April

4 USSR refuses visa to Swedish Academy official due to deliver Nobel Prize for Literature to Alexander Solzhenitsyn.

6 President Allende of Chile vetoes constitutional amendment that would have made expropriation of property subject to congressional approval.

7 release of 73 internees in Northern Ireland.

9 USSR and Iraq sign 15-year treaty of friendship and co-operation.

10 Britain, USA, and USSR sign multilateral convention prohibiting the stock-piling of biological weapons.

10 Roy Jenkins resigns as deputy leader of British Labour Party after Shadow Cabinet calls for referendum on EC membership.

19 Widgery Report on 'Bloody Sunday' shootings in Londonderry, Northern Ireland, concludes that IRA fired first.

19 North Vietnamese aircraft attack US 7th Fleet in Gulf of Tonkin.

23 in French referendum, 67.7 per cent vote in favour of enlargement of EC.

27 British government lifts ban on marches in Northern Ireland and declares amnesty for 283 convicted of participating in illegal marches.

27 US Senator Edmund Muskie withdraws from contest for Democratic presidential nomination.

E May

1 Quang Tri city falls to North Vietnamese (recaptured by South Vietnamese, 15 Sept).

8 President Nixon orders blockade and mining of North Vietnamese ports.

10 referendum in Republic of Ireland records 83 per cent support for EC membership.

14 Ulster Defence Association sets up first Protestant 'no go' areas in Belfast.

14 (–20) demonstrations in Kaunas demand freedom for Lithuania.

15 candidate for Democratic presidential nomination, George Wallace, shot and paralyzed in Maryland.

17 West German Bundestag ratifies 1970 treaties with USSR and Poland with Christian Democrats abstaining.

22 (–29) Richard Nixon becomes first US president to visit USSR (26, signs treaty limiting anti-ballistic missile sites).

22 Ceylon ceases to be a British dominion and becomes a republic within the Commonwealth as Sri Lanka.

23 Britain abandons Rhodesian settlement proposals after Pearce Commission reports that black opinion is unfavourable.

Court rules (29 June) that freedom of expression implies the right to receive information as well.

European Communities Act gives European institutions power to override British law.

The property qualification for service on English juries is abolished on the recommendation of the Morris Committee.

'Diplock Courts' without juries are introduced for some trials in Northern Ireland.

Community service, deferred sentences, and criminal bankruptcy orders are introduced in Britain as alternatives to imprisonment.

USSR starts making large-scale purchases of surplus US grain.

Legislation passed in USA for federal government to share its tax revenues with states.

Sterling is floated on world currency markets, only to start sinking.

The Bank of England replaces fixed bank rate with fluctuating minimum lending rate (MLR) tied to discount rate of Treasury bills (13 Oct).

The British government sells off the Thomas Cook travel agency (26 May).

P Society, Education, and Religion

In USA, the National Black Political Assembly in Gary, Indiana, fails to reach agreement on founding a black political force; African-American advancement is increasingly through the Democratic Party.

Andrew Young is the first African-American to be elected from the South to the US Congress since Reconstruction in the mid-19th century (9 Nov).

Native Americans march on Washington, DC, and occupy the Bureau of Indian Affairs.

The US Congress passes the Equal Rights Amendment, but it fails to achieve ratification by the states.

Juanita Kreps is the first woman governor of the New York stock exchange (20 Jan).

In USA, Consumer Products Safety Act is passed.

In USA, Federal Water Pollution Control Act Amendments (known as the Clean Water Act), Coastal Zone Management Act, and Noise Control Act.

In West Germany, financial support and additional holidays are granted to part-time adult learners following vocational courses.

In Pakistan, a new education policy launched, including the development of a People's Open University (based on the British

model) and the nationalization of most private elementary schools (Pakistan).

In Britain, the White Paper, *Education: A Framework for Expansion* (published 6 Dec), proposes the provision of nursery education for 90 per cent of four-year-old children within 10 years.

James Report on teacher training published in Britain.

C Jencks and others, *Inequality: A Reassessment of the Effect of Family and Schooling in America.*

Dimitrios, Metropolitan of Imroz and Tenedos, is elected as Ecumenical Patriarch of Constantinople.

The first meeting held in London of the Standing Conference of Jews, Christians and Muslims.

Formation of United Reformed Church by union of Congregational Church in England and Wales and Presbyterian Church in England.

John V Taylor, *The Go-Between God.*

Q Science, Technology, and Discovery

First home video-cassette recorders introduced.

US craft *Pioneer 10* is launched (2 March), destined to travel beyond the solar system (which it leaves on 13 June 1983).

Soviet craft *Venus 8* (launched 27 March) makes a soft landing on Venus (22 July).

US *Apollo 16* Moon mission (16–27 April), followed by *Apollo 17* (7–19 Dec), the final *Apollo* crewed mission to the Moon.

Launch of *Landsat 1* (23 July), the first of a series of satellites for surveying Earth's resources from space.

US scientist Murray Gell-Mann presents the theory of quantum chromodynamics (QCD), which envisages that quarks interact according to their 'colour'; strongly interacting particles consist of quarks, which are bound together by gluons.

CAT (computerized axial tomography) scanning introduced to provide cross-sectional X-rays of human brain.

R Humanities

'Treasures of Tutankhamun' exhibition at the British Museum, London, to celebrate the 50th anniversary of the discovery of Tutankhamun's tomb.

Discovery of tomb of Han dynasty prince south of Beijing, China, including jade suits.

Mark Elvin, *The Pattern of the Chinese Past.*

Jean Gernet, *A History of Chinese Civilization.*

Michael Baxandall, *Painting and Experience in Fifteenth-Century Italy.*

30 three pro-Palestinian Japanese terrorists kill 26 Israelis at Lod airport, Israel.

F **June**

1 (–15) West German police round up Baader–Meinhof urban guerrilla group.

10 in Northern Ireland, battle between troops, Catholics, and Protestants in Belfast leaves six dead.

15 Soviet President Podgorny begins four-day visit to North Vietnam.

17 US police arrest five intruders planting electronic 'bugs' at the Democratic Party headquarters in the Watergate apartment complex, Washington, DC.

18 BEA Trident airliner crashes at Staines, west of London, killing 118.

23 British government temporarily floats the pound to halt drain on reserves.

26 (–9 July) IRA ceasefire in Northern Ireland.

27 French Socialist and Communist Parties agree on a common programme.

G **July**

2 India and Pakistan agree to renounce force in settlement of disputes.

5 Pierre Messmer succeeds Jacques Chaban-Delmas as prime minister of France.

5 Kakuei Tanaka succeeds Eisaku Sato as prime minister of Japan.

7 William Whitelaw holds secret talks with IRA in London.

8 President Nixon announces that USSR will purchase $750 million worth of US grain over three years.

12 in USA, Democratic Party convention in Miami nominates George McGovern as presidential candidate (14, approves Thomas Eagleton for Vice-Presidency).

17 (–11 Aug) trials of Czechoslovak dissidents in Prague and Brno.

18 Reginald Maudling resigns as British home secretary as consequence of connections with John Poulson, an architect facing bankruptcy and a police investigation for suspected corruption; succeeded by Robert Carr.

18 President Sadat of Egypt expels 20,000 Soviet advisers after accusing USSR of failing to supply promised armaments.

21 in Northern Ireland, 22 bombs explode in Belfast shopping centres and bus stations, killing 13 and injuring 130.

21 five dockers go to prison for contempt of court after refusing to stop 'blacking' container depots at Hackney, London (26, released).

28 (–16 Aug) in Britain, nationwide dock strike, after union rejects Jones–Aldington proposals to ease unemployment resulting from 'containerization'.

31 in Northern Ireland, army destroys Catholic and Protestant barricades to end 'no go' areas in Belfast and Londonderry.

H **August**

1 in Britain, TUC and CBI agree to set up independent conciliation service.

1 Egypt and Sudan announce plans for full union by Sept 1973.

4 President Amin asserts that Ugandan Asians are frustrating the involvement of Africans in Uganda's business and commercial life; he gives them 90 days to leave the country.

5 Sargent Shriver becomes Democratic candidate for US vice-presidency after revelation of psychiatric treatment prompts withdrawal of Thomas Eagleton.

12 heavy US air-raids on North Vietnam accompany departure of US combat infantry from South Vietnam.

12 Chinese Communist Party accuses USSR of complicity in plot to assassinate Mao Zedong.

16 British government offers £50,000 reward for information on murders without motive in Northern Ireland.

16 Moroccan fighter pilots attempt to shoot down airliner carrying King Hassan (17, Moroccan defence minister commits suicide).

22 in USA, Republican Party convention in Miami nominates President Nixon for a second term (23, re-nominates Vice-President Agnew).

25 China vetoes admission of Bangladesh to UN.

J **September**

1 Iceland unilaterally extends its fishing limit from 12 to 50 miles (5, Icelandic gunboat cuts fishing gear of British trawler).

4 (–9) in Britain, TUC conference at Blackpool suspends 32 unions for registering under Industrial Relations Act.

5 Arab terrorists murder 11 members of Israeli Olympic team at Munich. West German police kill five terrorists in gun battle.

7 South Korea withdraws its 37,000 troops remaining in Vietnam.

11 US Democratic Party accuses Republican campaign finance chairman, Maurice Stans, of political espionage.

17 Ugandan exiles attempt to invade Uganda from Tanzania.

18 first plane-load of expelled Ugandan Asians arrives in Britain (22, President Amin orders 8,000 Asians to leave within 48 hours).

21 William Whitelaw ends internment without trial in Northern Ireland.

Henry Mayr-Harting *The Coming of Christianity to Anglo-Saxon England*.

G R Elton, *Policy and Police: The Enforcement of the Reformation in the Age of Thomas Cromwell*.

Christopher Hill, *The World Turned Upside Down: Radical Ideas during the English Revolution*.

J D Chambers, *Population, Economy, and Society in Pre-Industrial England*.

Joyce M Bellamy and John Saville (eds.), *Dictionary of Labour Biography*, Volume 1.

José Harris, *Unemployment and Politics: A Study in English Social Policy, 1886–1914*.

C H Feinstein, *National Income, Expenditure, and Output of the United Kingdom, 1855–1965*.

Karl Popper, *Objective Knowledge*.

Stephen Toulmin, *Human Understanding*.

s Art, Sculpture, Fine Arts, and Architecture

'Inquiry into Reality: Images of Today', 5th Documenta, Kassel, West Germany.

Sculpture:

Michelangelo's *Pietà* in St Peter's Basilica, Vatican, is attacked with a hammer by lunatic.

Tate Gallery, London, makes controversial purchase of Carl André's 'bricks' (*Equivalent 8*, 1966).

Stuart Brisley, *And for Today — Nothing*.

Christo, *Valley Curtain, Colorado*.

Bruce Nauman, *Run From Fear/Fun From Rear*.

Nam June Paik, *Paik-Abe Video Synthesizer*.

Richard Serra, *Shift*.

Architecture:

Alvar Aalto, North Jutland Museum at Aalborg, Denmark.

Louis Kahn, Kimbell Art Museum, Fort Worth, Texas, USA.

Kisho Kurokawa, Nagakin Capsule Tower, Tokyo, Japan.

James Stirling, Florey Building, The Queen's College, Oxford, England.

T Music

Harrison Birtwistle, *The Triumph of Time*.

Sylvano Bussotti, *Lorenzaccio* (opera).

Peter Maxwell Davies, *Taverner* (opera).

Jacob Druckman, *Windows*.

Andrzej Panufnik, Violin Concerto.

George Rochberg, String Quartet No. 3.

Michael Tippett, Symphony No. 3.

Grease (musical), lyrics and music by Jim Jacobs and Warren Casey (first performed at the Eden Theatre, New York, 14 Feb).

Chuck Berry, 'My ding-a-ling'.

David Bowie, *The Rise and Fall of Ziggy Stardust*.

Alice Cooper, 'School's Out'.

Roberta Flack, 'The First Time I Ever Saw Your Face'.

Gladys Knight and the Pips, 'Help Me Make It Through the Night'.

Don Maclean, 'American Pie' (single and album).

Johnny Nash, 'I Can See Clearly Now'.

Harry Nilsson, 'Without You'.

Donny Osmond, 'Puppy Love'.

Helen Reddy, 'I Am Woman'.

The Rolling Stones, *Exile on Main Street*.

Roxy Music, *Roxy Music*.

The Wailers, *Catch a Fire*.

Stevie Wonder, *Innervisions*.

Era of 'Teenybop', with prominence of singers appealing to teenagers (The Bay City Rollers, The Jackson Five, The Osmonds, and David Cassidy).

u Literature and Drama

Anthony Burgess, *A Clockwork Orange*.

Margaret Drabble, *The Needle's Eye*.

Frederick Forsyth, *The Day of the Jackal*.

Tove Jansson, *The Summer Book*.

V S Naipaul, *In a Free State*.

Andrew Tuttle (ed.), *The Journal of Andrew Bihaley*.

Eudora Welty, *The Optimist's Daughter*.

Sir John Betjeman is appointed Britain's Poet Laureate.

In Britain, John Berger's *G* wins the Booker Prize for fiction; the author gives half the proceeds to the Black Panthers (African-American urban guerrilla group) in protest at the source of the money.

Drama:

Samuel Beckett, *Not I*.

David French, *Leaving Home*.

Athol Fugard, *Sizwe Banzi is Dead*.

Dorothy Hewett, *The Chapel Perilous*.

Jack Hibberd, *A Stretch of the Imagination*.

Franz Kroetz, *Farmyard*.

David Rabe, *The Basic Training of Pavlo Hummel*.

Sam Shepard, *The Tooth of Crime*.

Tom Stoppard, *Jumpers*.

Ted Whitehead, *Alpha Beta*.

v Births and Deaths

Jan 1 Maurice Chevalier dies (83).

Jan 7 John Berryman dies (57).

April 16 Yasunari Kawabata dies (72).

April 27 Kwame Nkrumah dies (62).

May 2 J Edgar Hoover dies (77).

May 4 E C Kendall dies (86).

24 53.5 per cent vote against EC membership in Norwegian referendum.

25 three-day conference on future of Northern Ireland opens at Darlington, NE England.

26 British government proposes wage and price restraint to TUC and CBI (tripartite talks continue until 2 Nov).

27 (–13 Oct) border fighting between North and South Yemen.

29 Japan and China agree to end the legal state of war existing since 1937.

κ October

1 Danish referendum approves EC entry.

3 US and USSR sign final SALT accords limiting submarine-carried and land-based missiles (SALT II talks begin in Geneva, 21 Nov).

3 pro-EC Labour MP for Lincoln, Dick Taverne, at odds with his constituency party over British membership of EC, announces his intention to stand down and fight by-election as independent 'Democratic Labour' candidate.

7 Britain names Christopher Soames and George Thomson as its first EC Commissioners.

17 Queen Elizabeth II begins a State visit to Yugoslavia, the first by a British monarch to a Communist country.

21 EC summit in Paris approves principle of economic and monetary union by 1980.

26 North Vietnam publishes ceasefire agreement with USA; Henry Kissinger says peace is at hand in Indochina.

26 in Britain, Liberals win Rochdale from Labour in by-election, with Cyril Smith as new MP (7 Dec, win Sutton and Cheam from Conservatives).

29 Palestinian hijackers of Lufthansa flight secure release of Arab terrorists held in West Germany since 5 Sept.

29 (–2 Nov) British Foreign Secretary Sir Alec Douglas-Home visits China.

30 Pierre Trudeau's Liberal Party wins narrow victory in Canadian general election.

30 British Green Paper promises greater political power for Catholics in Northern Ireland.

λ November

1 President Thieu of South Vietnam rejects US ceasefire plan.

5 in Britain, Peter Walker becomes secretary of state for trade and industry. James Prior becomes leader of the Commons.

6 British government imposes 90-day freeze on price, pay, rent, and dividend increases as Phase One of anti-inflation programme.

7 in US elections Richard Nixon, Republican, with 520 electoral votes, wins landslide victory over George McGovern, Democrat, with 17; popular vote: Nixon, 47,168,963. McGovern, 29,169,615. Republicans lose 2 Senators and gain 12 Representatives. Democrats keep control of both Houses.

8 deadline for Asians to leave Uganda (25,000 go to Britain by end of year).

9 Bank of England demands special deposits from clearing banks in attempt to control money supply.

19 West German general election returns Social Democrats with increased majority.

21 eight-hour battle between Israel and Syria on Golan Heights.

22 rebel British Conservative MPs defeat government on new immigration rules favouring EC citizens over white Commonwealth.

22 preparatory talks for European Security Conference begin in Helsinki.

24 Finland is first western nation formally to recognize East Germany.

25 Norman Kirk becomes prime minister of New Zealand after Labour Party wins sweeping electoral victory.

28 British–Icelandic talks on fisheries dispute break down.

μ December

2 Australian Labour Party wins general election (5, Gough Whitlam becomes prime minister).

6 in Britain, four 'Angry Brigade' anarchists jailed for conspiracy to cause explosions after record 111-day trial.

11 British Trade and Industry Secretary Peter Walker announces £175 million subsidy for National Coal Board and writes off £475 million deficit.

11 India and Pakistan agree on truce line in Jammu and Kashmir.

13 British Conservative Party nominates its 18 members of EC Parliament. Labour refuses to send any representatives.

18 (–30) heavy US bombing of North Vietnam.

20 Diplock Commission recommends wider powers of arrest in Northern Ireland and suspension of trial by jury in certain cases.

21 West and East Germany sign Basic Treaty to establish 'neighbourly relations on the basis of equality'.

23 earthquake devastates Managua, capital of Nicaragua.

27 Britain ignores Maltese ultimatum demanding 10 per cent increase in rent for military bases.

31 Northern Ireland Office reports total of 467 killings in 1972.

May 22 Cecil Day-Lewis dies (68).
May 28 Duke of Windsor dies (77).
July 31 Paul Spaak dies (72).
Sept 21 Henry de Montherlant dies (76).
Oct 1 Louis Leakey dies (69).
Oct 26 Igor Sikorsky dies (83).
Nov 1 Ezra Pound dies (87).
Nov 30 Compton Mackenzie dies (89).
Dec 23 A N Tupolev dies (84).
Dec 26 Harry S Truman dies (88).
Dec 27 Lester Pearson dies (75).

w Everyday Life

In USA, the Dallas Cowboys become the first football team to introduce professional cheerleaders.

'Pong' is the first known computer game.

x Sport and Recreation

Eddie Merckx of Belgium wins his fourth consecutive Tour de France cycling race.

Bob Massie of Australia takes 16 England wickets in the second cricket Test at Lord's (22–26 June) — a record for an Australian bowler.

The 20th Olympic Games are held in Munich, West Germany (26 Aug–11 Sept). USSR wins 50 gold medals; USA, 33; East Germany, 20; West Germany and Japan, 13 each; Australia, 8; Poland, 7; Hungary and Bulgaria, 6 each; Italy, 5; Sweden and Britain, 4 each; Mark Spitz of the USA wins 7 gold medals in swimming, all in world record times.

Bobby Fischer of the USA beats Boris Spassky of the USSR in World Chess Championship in Reykjavik, Iceland (1 Sept).

The British Jockey Club allows women jockeys to compete in horse-racing.

y Media

In Australia (June), Rupert Murdoch purchases the *Sydney Daily Telegraph* and *Sunday Telegraph*.

In USA, closure of *Life* magazine (last issue 29 Dec).

In USA, publication of the feminist women's magazine *Ms.*

Film:

The Bitter Tears of Petra Von Kant (director, Rainer Werner Fassbinder).

Cabaret (director, Bob Fosse; starring Liza Minnelli).

The Concert for Bangladesh.

The Decameron (director, Pier Paolo Pasolini).

The Discreet Charm of the Bourgeoisie (director, Luis Buñuel).

The Getaway (director, Sam Peckinpah; starring Steve McQueen and Ali MacGraw).

Last Tango in Paris (director, Bernardo Bertolucci).

Play It Again, Sam (director and star, Woody Allen).

Radio:

In Britain, broadcast of the last *Goon Show*.

Television:

New programmes in USA include: *M*A*S*H* (–1983); *The Waltons*.

Broadcast in Japan of the samurai series *Underground Executioner*.

In the Philippines, President Ferdinand Marcos closes down all channels apart from the state one.

New programmes in Britain include: *America* (BBC), a history of the USA presented by Alistair Cooke; *Colditz*; *The Lotus Eaters* (BBC); *Mastermind* (BBC), a general and specialist knowledge competition, with Magnus Magnusson; *Van der Valk*, starring Barry Foster.

In Britain, the BBC launches CEEFAX, a television information system.

US withdrawal from Vietnam ... Yom Kippur War ...
Energy crisis ...

A **January**
1 Britain, Ireland, and Denmark become members of the EC.
4 Australia abandons colour bar in admission of new settlers.
6 Portuguese revolutionaries explode 12 bombs in Lisbon in protest at colonial wars.
8 in USA, trial opens in Washington, DC, of seven men accused of bugging Democratic Party headquarters in the Watergate apartment complex.
9 Rhodesia (now Zimbabwe) closes its border with Zambia after terrorist attacks.
15 USA suspends all military action against North Vietnam.
17 in Britain, Edward Heath announces creation of Pay Board and Prices Commission.
17 President Marcos of Philippines proclaims new constitution under which he will rule indefinitely.
20 inauguration of Richard Nixon for second term as US president.
27 USA, North and South Vietnam, and Vietcong sign ceasefire agreement in Paris.

B **February**
7 Protest strikes, arson, and gun battles in Northern Ireland, following first detention of Protestant terrorist suspects.
8 Archbishop Makarios returned unopposed as president of Cyprus.
12 North Vietnam and Vietcong release first US prisoners of war.
13 USA devalues dollar by 10 per cent by raising gold price to $42.22 per ounce.
14 (–23 Mar) strike by British gas workers cuts off supplies in some areas.
19 French right-wing extremists steal body of Marshal Pétain from tomb on Île d'Yeu.
21 104 die when Libyan airliner crashes in Sinai after interception by Israeli jets.
21 government of Laos and Pathet Lao sign ceasefire agreement in Vientiane.
22 China and USA agree to establish high-level liaison offices in Washington and Beijing.
27 (–8 May) 200 Ogdala Sioux occupy hamlet of Wounded Knee, South Dakota, and hold residents hostage in protest at treatment of US Indians.
27 first-ever full strike by British civil servants.

C **March**
1 In Republic of Ireland, Fine Gael coalition wins general election (14, Liam Cosgrave becomes prime minister).

1 Dick Taverne, independent Democratic Labour candidate, defeats official Labour candidate in Lincoln by-election, achieving majority of over 13,000 votes.
1 (–14 Apr) hospital ancillary workers strike for higher pay.
2 (–19) closure of European exchange markets in face of new currency crisis.
2 Palestinian terrorists murder US ambassador to Sudan after invading reception at Saudi Arabian Embassy in Khartoum.
6 neutral British Budget introduces VAT at 10 per cent (supplanting other excise duties and the Selective Employment Tax) and increases pensions.
8 IRA car bombs at Great Scotland Yard and Old Bailey, London, kill 1 and injure 238.
8 in Northern Ireland referendum, 591,820 (59 per cent turn-out) vote to remain in United Kingdom, 6,463 to join Ireland.
10 following period of political tension, Sir Richard Sharples, governor of Bermuda, is assassinated in Hamilton.
11 Perónist candidate, Hector Campora, wins Argentinian general election (13 July, resigns to make way for General Perón).
16 finance ministers from 14 countries, meeting in Paris, agree to establish floating exchange rate system.
20 White Paper on Northern Ireland proposes new assembly, power-sharing executive, and talks on an all-Ireland council.
29 last US troops leave Vietnam and last US prisoners of war are released.

D **April**
1 Phase Two of British government's anti-inflation programme limits pay rises to £1 per week plus 4 per cent.
4 British government provides £15 million subsidy to prevent mortgage rate exceeding 9.5 per cent for next three months.
9 Palestinian terrorists attack home of Israeli ambassador to Cyprus (10th, Israeli commandos raid Beirut and kill three Palestinian guerrilla leaders).
12 Labour wins control of Greater London Council and six new metropolitan councils.
16 British Embassy opens in East Germany.
17 in USA, President Nixon drops ban on White House staff appearing before Senate Committee on Watergate affair (hearings begin, 17 May).
23 Henry Kissinger, head of US National Security Council, in major speech in New York calls for new 'Atlantic Charter' governing relations between America, Europe and Japan.

Roe v. Wade in USA ... Calf produced from frozen embryo ...
Women's cricket world cup ...

o Politics, Government, Law, and Economy

Noam Chomsky, *For Reasons of State.*

Arthur M Schlesinger, Jr, *The Imperial Presidency.*

James L Sundquist, *Dynamics of the Party System: Alignment and Realignment of Political Parties in the United States.*

James Q Wilson, *Political Organizations.*

In USA, foundation of the Heritage Foundation.

The US Congress passes the War Powers Act over President Nixon's veto (7 Nov), restricting the ability of the president to maintain troops overseas without Congressional approval.

Kilbrandon Commission on the Constitution recommends devolved parliaments for Scotland and Wales (31 Oct).

Queen Elizabeth, on Australian tour, assents to change of title there to Queen of Australia (19 Oct).

The US Supreme Court introduces the test of 'redeeming social value' for obscenity cases.

The British lord chief justice rules that physical obstruction on picket lines is unlawful (10 April).

World economies undergo a simultaneous boom with commodity prices increasing drastically; the rise in the price and restriction of supply in oil after war breaks out in the Middle East cause disruption to western economies.

Multi-fibre Agreement on textile prices.

European Trade Union Confederation, with 29 million members, is formed in the 14 countries belonging to the European Community and the European Free Trade Association (Feb).

Opening of the first market for share options, in Chicago, USA.

Federal Express in USA begins parcel delivery services.

E F Schumacher, *Small is Beautiful: A Study of Economics as if People Mattered.*

P Society, Education, and Religion

In USA, the Supreme Court, in Roe v. Wade, legalizes abortion (in the first six months of pregnancy) in all states (22 Jan).

The US state of Oregon decriminalizes the possession of small amounts of cannabis.

Daniel Bell, *The Coming of Post-Industrial Society.*

In USA, Thomas Bradley is elected first African-American mayor of Los Angeles (29 May).

Erich Fromm, *The Anatomy of Human Destructiveness.*

N Poulantzas, *Political Power and Social Classes.*

Sheila Rowbotham, *Women's Consciousness in a Man's World.*

In USA, the Carnegie Commission devises a classification to facilitate the comparison and analysis of diverse institutions of higher education.

The Ministry of Education in France is reorganized.

The creation of a Department of Education in Australia subjects state policies to closer federal control.

In Japan, foundation of Tsukuba University.

In Britain, the school leaving age is raised to 16.

Mother Teresa of Calcutta receives the first Templeton Prize for Progress in Religion.

The Pope condemns 'Christian fratricide' in Northern Ireland.

Golda Meir becomes the first prime minister of Israel to visit the Vatican (15 Jan).

Cypriot Orthodox bishops announce the deposition of Archbishop Makarios (8 Mar).

Geza Vermes, *Jesus the Jew.*

Q Science, Technology, and Discovery

Bar codes first used in supermarkets.

Opening of pipeline for transmission of natural gas from Ukraine to West Germany.

Start of construction of Thames Flood Barrier, London.

USA launches the first *Skylab* space station (14 May), which is visited by a three-person crew (25 May–22 June); the third mission to *Skylab* (launched 16 Nov) lasts a record 84 days and gathers data relevant to long space flights.

US probe *Pioneer 10* passes within 130,000 km/81,000 mi of Jupiter and transmits pictures and data.

Researchers at the European Centre for Particle Research (CERN, France/Switzerland) find some confirmation for the electroweak force when they discover neutral currents in neutrino reactions.

The US biochemist Herbert Boyer develops the technique of recombinant DNA, whereby different strands of DNA can be joined together and then be inserted into living organisms.

The first calf is produced from a frozen embryo.

In Britain, Paul Lauterbur obtains the first NMR (nuclear magnetic resonance) image.

In USA, Endangered Species Act passed.

27 Andrei Gromyko and Yuri Andropov enter Soviet Politburo in first major reshuffle since 1964.

30 in USA, President Nixon accepts responsibility for bugging of Watergate building but denies any personal involvement.

E May

1 in Britain, TUC calls one-day protest strike against pay policies.

7 British government introduces butter subsidies after outcry at EC sales of surplus butter to USSR.

11 US court dismisses all charges against the *New York Times* in Pentagon Papers trial because of 'Government misconduct'.

11 Joop den Uyl becomes Dutch prime minister after record 164-day ministerial crisis.

18 (–21) Soviet leader, Leonid Brezhnev, visits West Germany.

22 in Britain, Anthony Lambton, under-Secretary for defence, resigns after revelations about cannabis and call-girls (24, Lord Jellicoe, lord privy seal, also resigns).

22 Britain and USA veto UN resolution to extend Rhodesian sanctions to South Africa and Portuguese colonies for breaking embargo.

23 Greek government foils naval mutiny.

26 Icelandic gunboat shells British trawler Everton.

30 Erskine Childers succeeds Éamon de Valera as president of Eire.

31 US Senate votes to cut off funds for bombing of Cambodia and Laos (15 Aug, bombing ends).

F June

1 British Honduras changes name to Belize.

7 Labour Party announces plans to nationalize Britain's top 25 companies. Harold Wilson publicly repudiates the policy.

7 Icelandic coastguard vessel rams British warship in escalation of 'Cod War'.

9 General Franco confers Spanish premiership on Admiral Carrero Blanco.

15 second ceasefire begins in Vietnam.

20 in Argentina, 35 die in riots at Buenos Aires airport as Juan Perón returns from 18-year exile.

24 Leonid Brezhnev, during visit to USA, declares that the Cold War is over.

25 in USA, former White House counsel, John Dean, informs Senate Committee of President Nixon's complicity in Watergate cover-up.

26 newly formed 'Ulster Freedom Fighters' murder Senator Paddy Wilson of SDLP in Belfast, Northern Ireland.

28 election by proportional representation of new Northern Ireland Assembly leaves official Unionists dependent on SDLP and Alliance support.

G July

3 European Security Conference opens in Helsinki with 35 foreign ministers in attendance.

5 terrorists kidnap 273 people from mission school in Rhodesia (now Zimbabwe) (17, only eight remain missing).

10 in Britain, *The Times* alleges that Portuguese troops massacred 400 people in Mozambique in 1972.

10 the Bahamas become independent within the Commonwealth.

16 parents of British children disabled by thalidomide drug accept £25 million compensation from Distillers Company.

16 in USA, Alexander Butterfield tells Senate Committee that President Nixon secretly tape-records all conversations in his office.

17 bloodless coup deposes King Mohammed Zahir Shah of Afghanistan.

19 British government announces weekly cash payments to mothers of £2 per child.

21 France resumes nuclear tests at Mururoa Atoll despite protests from Australia and New Zealand.

26 in Cyprus, EOKA terrorists blow up Limassol police station in continuing campaign for Enosis (union with Greece).

31 militant Protestants, led by Revd Ian Paisley, disrupt first sitting of Northern Ireland Assembly.

H August

3 (–7) Race riots at University of Rhodesia (now Zimbabwe).

5 Arab terrorist attack at Athens airport kills four people.

6 (–8) accidental US bombing of friendly Laotian villages causes hundreds of casualties.

10 Israeli fighters force down Iraqi airliner, but wanted Palestinian guerrilla is not on board.

14 new Pakistani constitution takes effect, with Zulfikar Ali Bhutto as president.

19 formal abolition of Greek monarchy; George Papadopoulos becomes president.

24 Scotland Yard blames IRA for week of letter-bomb incidents in Britain.

29 Presidents Sadat and Khaddafi proclaim unification of Egypt and Libya, including plan for a joint Constituent Assembly (3 Oct, first meeting held).

R Humanities

The Cambridge History of China (–).

M I Finley, *The Ancient Economy*.

G R Elton, *Reform and Renewal: Thomas Cromwell and the Common Weal*.

Francis Godwin James, *Ireland in the Empire 1688–1770*.

L A Marchand (ed.), *Byron's Letters and Journals* (–1982).

Theodore Zeldin, *France, 1848–1948*, Volume 1 (Volume 2, 1977).

H J Dyos and M Wolff (eds.), *The Victorian City: Images and Realities*.

Sam B Warner, Jr, *The Urban Wilderness: A History of the American City*.

David M Potter, *History and American Society*.

Allardyce Nicoll, *English Drama 1900–1930: The Beginnings of the Modern Period* (a companion to Nicoll's six-volume *History of the English Drama, 1660–1900*).

Clifford Geertz, *Interpretation of Cultures*.

Michael Dummett, *Frege: Philosophy of Language*.

Saul Kripke, *Naming and Necessity*.

S Art, Sculpture, Fine Arts, and Architecture

Auctioneers Christie's offer shares to the public.

Pablo Picasso dies.

Painting, etc:

Richard Estes, *Paris Street Scene*.

Sculpture:

Barry Flanagan, *3rd February 1973* (sculpture).

Robert Smithson, *Amarillo Ramp* (sculpture).

Architecture:

Patrick Hodgkinson, Brunswick Centre, London.

John Portman and Associates, Hyatt-Regency Hotel, San Francisco, USA.

Jorn Utzon, Hall, Todd and Littlemore, Sydney Opera House, Sydney, Australia.

Minoru Yamasaki and Associates, World Trade Centre, New York.

T Music

Malcolm Arnold, Symphony No. 7.

Benjamin Britten, *Death in Venice* (opera).

Aaron Copland, *Night Thoughts*.

György Ligeti, *Clocks and Clouds*.

Bruno Maderna, *Satyricon* (opera).

A Little Night Music (musical), lyrics and music by Stephen Sondheim.

David Bowie, *Aladdin Sane*.

Roberta Flack, 'Killing Me Softly With His Song'.

Gary Glitter, 'I'm the Leader of the Gang'.

Elton John, 'Goodbye Yellow Brick Road' (single and album), *Don't Shoot Me, I'm Only the Piano Player*.

Led Zeppelin, *Houses of the Holy*.

The New York Dolls, *New York Dolls*.

Mike Oldfield, *Tubular Bells*.

Pink Floyd, *The Dark Side of the Moon*.

Lou Reed, *Berlin*.

The Rolling Stones, 'Angie', *Goat's Head Soup*.

Slade, 'Cum On Feel The Noize', 'Skweeze Me Pleeze Me'.

Stevie Wonder, 'I Believe'.

U Literature and Drama

Richard Adams, *Watership Down*.

Graham Greene, *The Honorary Consul*.

Richard Hughes, *The Wooden Shepherdess*.

Iris Murdoch, *The Black Prince*.

Thomas Pynchon, *Gravity's Rainbow*.

Tom Sharpe, *Riotous Assembly*.

Derek Walcott, *Another Life* (poems).

Patrick White, *The Eye of the Storm*.

Drama:

Alan Ayckbourn, *The Norman Conquests*.

Edward Bond, *Bingo*.

Hugh Leonard, *Da*.

John McGrath, *The Cheviot, The Stag, and the Black, Black Oil*.

Peter Shaffer, *Equus*.

V Births and Deaths

Jan 22 Lyndon Baines Johnson dies (64).

Feb 22 Elizabeth Bowen dies (73).

March 26 Noël Coward dies (73).

April 8 Pablo Picasso dies (91).

April 28 Jacques Maritain dies (90).

May 26 Jacques Lipchitz dies (81).

July 6 Otto Klemperer dies (88).

July 8 Wilfred Rhodes dies (95).

Aug 1 Walter Ulbricht dies (80).

Aug 6 Fulgencio Batistá y Zaldivar dies (72).

Aug 31 John Ford dies (78).

Sept 2 J R R Tolkien dies (81).

Sept 23 Pablo Neruda dies (69).

Sept 28 W H Auden dies (66).

Oct 21 Alan Cobham dies (79).

Oct 22 Pablo Casals dies (96).

Dec 1 David Ben-Gurion dies (87).

Dec 5 Robert Watson-Watt dies (81).

Dec 25 Ismet Inönü dies (84).

W Everyday Life

Skateboarding, a land recreation for surfers, becomes widely popular in USA following the development of the urethane wheel.

X Sport and Recreation

George Foreman defeats Joe Frazier to win world Heavyweight boxing title in Kingston, Jamaica (22 Jan).

In soccer, Sunderland becomes the first

30 Kenya bans hunting of elephants and trade in ivory.

J **September**

3 Henry Kissinger becomes US secretary of state.

3 in Britain, TUC expels 20 unions for registering under Industrial Relations Act.

5 (–8) Jordanian terrorists hold 13 hostages in Saudi Arabian Embassy in Paris.

7 Iceland threatens to break off diplomatic relations with Britain over fishing dispute.

11 (–12) military junta, headed by General Augustó Pinochet, seizes power in Chile; over 2,500 die in fighting; President Allende reportedly commits suicide.

13 major air battle between Israel and Syria.

14 British mortgage rate reaches unprecedented 11 per cent.

15 death of King Gustaf VI Adolf of Sweden; succeeded by King Carl XVI Gustaf.

17 Edward Heath meets Prime Minister Cosgrave of Ireland at military airfield near Dublin; first official visit to Ireland by a British prime minister.

18 UN admits East and West Germany.

23 Juan Perón and wife Isabel are elected president and vice-president of Argentina (inaugurated 12 Oct).

29 Austria closes transit camp for emigrating Soviet Jews on demand of Arab kidnappers.

K **October**

6 Full-scale war in Middle East, as Egypt and Syria attack Israel while Jews are observing Yom Kippur.

10 USSR starts airlift of military supplies to Arab states. Iraq joins war against Israel (as do Saudi Arabia and Jordan on 13).

10 US Vice-President Spiro Agnew resigns after pleading guilty to tax evasion charges.

11 counter-attacking Israelis break through on Golan Heights and invade Syria.

12 US Court of Appeals orders President Nixon to hand over Watergate tapes.

15 Britain and Iceland end 'Cod War' with agreement on fishing rights.

16 Israelis cross Suez Canal and invade Egypt (19, President Nixon asks Congress to approve $2,000 million worth of military aid for Israel).

17 11 Arab states agree to cut oil production by 5 per cent each month until US changes its Middle Eastern policy.

20 President Nixon dismisses special prosecutor in Watergate case; US attorney-general, Elliot Richardson, resigns in protest.

21 Henry Kissinger and Leonid Brezhnev, meeting in Moscow, agree plan to stop war

in Middle East (22, Egypt and Israel accept UN ceasefire, but fighting continues).

23 US House of Representatives orders judiciary committee to assess evidence for impeachment of President Nixon.

24 Syria accepts ceasefire and fighting halts on both fronts.

25 USA puts its forces on precautionary alert in response to fears of Soviet intervention in Middle East.

28 UN reports that drought has caused up to 100,000 deaths in Ethiopia.

L **November**

1 Phase Three of British government's anti-inflation programme limits pay rises to 7 per cent or £2.25 per week.

5 (–9) Henry Kissinger tours Arab capitals on peace mission.

7 US Congress overturns presidential veto on Bill limiting Executive powers to wage war without congressional approval.

8 in by-elections, Scottish Nationalists (SNP) win Govan from Labour, Liberals win Berwick-on-Tweed from Conservatives.

11 Israel and Egypt accept US plan for ceasefire observance and prisoner exchange.

12 British coal-miners begin over-time ban in protest at pay offer.

13 energy crisis prompts British government to declare state of emergency (19, 10 per cent cut in fuel and petrol supplies).

13 in Britain, minimum lending rate rises to 13 per cent after record balance of payments deficit.

21 in Britain, National Union of Mineworkers (NUM) rejects any pay deal under Phase Three.

21 Northern Ireland parties agree on formation of new power-sharing Executive.

25 General Phaidon Gizikis ousts President Papadopoulos of Greece.

29 distribution of petrol rationing coupons begins in Britain; 6 Dec, speed limit of 80 kph/50 mph and widespread extinguishing of street-lights.

M **December**

2 in Britain, William Whitelaw becomes secretary of state for employment. Francis Pym succeeds him as Northern Ireland secretary.

6 Gerald Ford takes oath as 40th vice-president of USA.

6 in Britain, Financial Times Share Index records most drastic fall since first compiled in 1935.

9 talks at Sunningdale, England, between Irish and British governments reach agreement on formation of a Council of Ireland

second-division side to win the English Football Association Cup Final since 1931, beating Leeds United 1–0 (5 May).

Members of the Association of Tennis Professionals boycott the tennis tournament at Wimbledon, London, because Nikki Pilic of Yugoslavia had allegedly refused to play in the Davis Cup.

The first women's cricket World Cup (final 28 July).

Y Media

Film:

The Canterbury Tales (director, Pier Paolo Pasolini).

Day for Night (director, François Truffaut).

Don't Look Now (director, Nicholas Roeg).

Enter the Dragon (director, Robert Clouse; starring Bruce Lee).

The Exorcist (director, William Friedkin).

Fear Eats the Soul (director, Rainer Werner Fassbinder).

The Last Detail (director, Jack Nicholson).

The Long Goodbye (director, Robert Altman).

Mean Streets (director, Martin Scorsese).

O Lucky Man (director, Lindsay Anderson).

Pat Garrett and Billy the Kid (director, Sam Peckinpah).

A Touch of Class (starring Glenda Jackson and George Segal).

Radio:

In Britain, launch (8 Oct) of the first legal commercial radio station, the London Broadcasting Company (LBC), specializing in new and current affairs, followed by Capital Radio (9 Oct), specializing in entertainment and music.

Television:

New programmes in USA include: *An American Family*, following the Louds family of California; *Kojak*.

New programmes in Britain include: *Are You Being Served?* (BBC; –1983); *The Ascent of Man* (BBC), presented by Jacob Bronowski; *Last of the Summer Wine* (BBC); *That's Life* (BBC; –1994), with Esther Rantzen.

with representatives from both governments. It is also agreed that the status of
Northern Ireland will not be changed without majority support in the province.

11 West Germany and Czechoslovakia agree
to invalidate Munich Agreement of 1938
and establish diplomatic relations.

12 in Britain, train-drivers' overtime ban
starts to disrupt British Rail.

13 Edward Heath, British prime minister,
orders industry to work three-day week
from 31 Dec to save energy.

17 Arab terrorists kill 32 in attack on Rome
airport.

17 Anthony Barber's emergency Budget cuts
spending by £1,200 million and restores
hire purchase controls.

18 IRA launches Christmas bombing campaign in London.

20 assassination of Spanish prime minister,
Carrero Blanco, in Madrid (29, succeeded
by Carlos Arias Navarro).

21 (–22) Middle East peace conference in
Geneva sets up working party to discuss
disengagement of troops on Egyptian front.

23 Shah of Iran announces that Gulf states will
increase oil price from $5.10 to $11.65 a
barrel from 1 Jan.

Revolution in Portugal ... Resignation of President Nixon ...
Partition of Cyprus ...

A **January**

1 Brian Faulkner takes office as chief executive of Northern Ireland (7, resigns leadership of Unionist Party).

2 introduction of entrance charges at British
national museums and galleries (30 Mar,
abolished).

8 in Britain, establishment of Department of
Energy under Lord Carrington.

14 in Britain, talks between Edward Heath and
TUC on miners' dispute break down (28,
Heath accuses Mick McGahey of NUM of
aiming to bring down government).

15 riots in Jakarta, Indonesia, against visit by
Japanese Premier.

18 Israel and Egypt agree on disengagement
of forces along Suez Canal.

25 Britain offers industrial goods worth £110
million to Iran in exchange for 5 million
extra tons of oil.

30 President Nixon makes slip of tongue in
State of Union address, mentioning need
'to replace discredited president — er,
present — system...'.

B **February**

4 in Britain, IRA bomb kills 12 people
(servicemen and their families) on bus
from Manchester to Catterick.

7 British Prime Minister Edward Heath
announces general election to be held on 28
Feb, on the issue 'Who Governs Britain?'.

7 Grenada becomes independent within the
Commonwealth.

10 British mineworkers begins all-out strike in
support of pay claim of 30–40 per cent.

11 John Poulson, a British architect who
undertook numerous contracts for local

authorities and other public bodies, is
sentenced to five years' imprisonment for
corruption (15 Mar, sentenced to another
seven years on further charges).

13 USSR deports dissident author Alexander
Solzhenitsyn.

17 British opposition leader Harold Wilson
announces 'social contract' between
Labour Party and TUC, whereby a Labour
government will sponsor social legislation
in return for wage restraint.

22 Pakistan recognizes Bangladesh at start of
Islamic summit conference at Lahore,
Pakistan.

23 Enoch Powell urges anti-EC Conservatives
to vote Labour in British election.

26 Confederation of British Industry calls for
repeal of Industrial Relations Act.

27 new constitution strips Swedish monarchy
of all remaining powers.

28 British general election produces no overall majority, as Labour win 301 seats,
Conservatives, 297, Liberals, 14, Scottish
Nationalists, 7, Plaid Cymru, 2 (Conservatives win 37.9 per cent of votes cast,
Labour, 37.1 per cent, and Liberals, 19.3
per cent).

C **March**

3 347 die when Turkish airliner crashes near
Paris.

4 Edward Heath resigns as British prime
minister after Liberals refuse to enter
coalition.

4 EC proposes economic co-operation with
20 Arab countries.

5 in Britain, Harold Wilson forms minority
Labour government, with James Callaghan
as foreign secretary, Denis Healey as chan-

Freedom of Information Act in USA ... Discovery of the Chinese emperor's 'terracotta army' ... Death of Duke Ellington ...

o Politics, Government, Law, and Economy

D Mayhew, *Congress: the Electoral Connection.*

Robert Nozick, *Anarchy, State and Utopia.*

Bob Woodward and Carl Bernstein, *All the President's Men.*

In US v. Richard M Nixon, the US Supreme Court rules that executive privilege does not cover evidence of criminal conduct, forcing Nixon to surrender subpoenaed Watergate tapes; the judgement confirms that the Supreme Court and not the president is the final arbiter of the Constitution.

In USA, Congress passes several bills designed to deal with abuses that came to light during the Watergate scandal; the Federal Election Campaign Amendments Act limits the scale of individual and corporate campaign contributions and provides for the Treasury to match funds if they have been raised in at least 20 states; the Budget and Impoundment Control Act which establishes the Congressional Budget Office to provide independent advice on government finance.

In USA, Congress passes the Freedom of Information Act over President Ford's veto (21 Nov); it prohibits government from denying access to documents without good cause and requires federal agencies to supply documents without delay.

The US Congress grants 'home rule' to the District of Columbia (the capital territory), which now has its own council, mayor, and Congressional observer delegates.

New National Health Service management (from 1 April) and local government systems in operation in England and Wales.

Rehabilitation of Offenders Act in England and Wales allows old convictions to become 'spent' and makes it an offence to refer to convictions after a certain lapse of time.

Rent Act in Britain extends indefinite security of tenure to tenants in furnished accommodation without a resident landlord.

'Lucky' Lord Lucan disappears from London (12 Nov) after the murder of his children's nanny (tried in absentia and convicted of murder on 19 June 1975).

In USA, Karen Silkwood dies in mysterious circumstances (13 Nov) after expressing concern at safety in Kerr McGee nuclear plants in Oklahoma.

The United Nations calls for a New International Economic Order, in which the development of the Third World is a priority.

Inflation becomes a serious problem in many countries; in USA President Ford launches the 'Whip Inflation Now' economic programme (8 Oct).

British Airways formed from a merger of British Overseas Airways Corporations (BOAC) and British European Airways (BEA).

p Society, Education, and Religion

World population passes 4 billion.

In USA, white pupils in Boston, Massachusetts, riot over use of busing to enforce desegregation of schooling (Sept–Dec).

cellor of the exchequer, Roy Jenkins as home secretary, and Michael Foot as secretary for employment.

9 British industry returns to five-day working week.

11 state of emergency ends in Britain after miners' union accepts £103 million pay deal.

14 heavy fighting between Kurdish rebels and Iraqi forces on Iraqi-Turkish border.

19 food riots in Bihar, India.

20 British Princess Anne escapes kidnap attempt in the Mall, London.

26 British Budget increases income tax by 3p, raises pensions and allocates £500 million for food subsidies.

D **April**

1 re-organisation of local government in England and Wales re-draws county boundaries.

2 Alain Poher becomes interim president of France on death of Georges Pompidou.

3 President Nixon agrees to pay $432,787 in unpaid income tax.

11 Palestinian terrorists kill 18 Israelis, mostly women and children, at Kiryat Shemona.

11 (–13) strike by 6 million Japanese workers.

17 number of killings in Northern Ireland since 1969 reaches 1,000.

19 Israeli–Syrian air battle over Golan Heights.

25 General Antonio de Spinola effects military coup in Portugal (26, junta vows to dismantle authoritarian state and end wars in Angola, Mozambique and Guinea).

30 President Nixon releases 1,308-page edited transcript of Watergate tapes to Judiciary Committee of House of Representatives.

E **May**

1 release of political prisoners and end of censorship in Portugal.

5 Harold Wilson condemns NIRC sequestration of AUEW funds (8, anonymous industrialists pay outstanding AUEW fines to end protest strike).

8 Willy Brandt resigns as West German chancellor after aide, Gunther Guillaume, admits to spying.

8 (–28) national rail strike in India.

15 20 children die when Israeli troops storm school occupied by Palestinian terrorists at Ma'alot (16, Israel bombs Palestinian refugee camps in Lebanon).

17 three bomb explosions in Dublin, Ireland, kill 32 people.

18 atomic bomb test makes India the world's sixth nuclear power.

19 Valéry Giscard d'Estaing wins second round of French presidential election with 50.8 per cent of votes to François Mitterrand's 49.2.

19 Protestant general strike begins in Northern Ireland against Sunningdale agreement and power-sharing (22, Executive postpones Council of Ireland till after 1977).

24 (–4 Apr) Edward Heath British opposition leader visits China (two giant pandas presented by China arrive at London Zoo, 14 Sept).

27 Jacques Chirac becomes prime minister of France.

28 Northern Ireland Executive collapses when all Unionist members resign (29, Britain re-imposes direct rule and general strike ends).

31 Henry Kissinger secures agreement between Syria and Israel to disengage forces on Golan Heights.

F **June**

1 in Britain, 29 die when Nypro chemical plant at Flixborough blows up.

3 IRA hunger-striker, Michael Gaughan, dies in Parkhurst prison, S England.

4 James Callaghan presents British conditions for re-negotiation of EC entry.

4 Itzhak Rabin succeeds Golda Meir as prime minister of Israel.

12 (–19) President Nixon tours the Middle East (27–3 July, in USSR).

15 student dies in fighting between left-wing and right-wing demonstrators in Red Lion Square, Holborn, London.

17 IRA explodes bomb outside Westminster Hall, London, injuring 11 people (17 July, bomb at Tower of London kills 1 and injures 37).

20 British House of Commons rejects plans for greater state control over industry (one of over 20 government defeats between Mar and Oct).

28 Ethiopian armed forces take control of government buildings and broadcasting.

28 President Makarios asks Greek officers to leave Cypriot National Guard.

G **July**

1 Isabel Perón becomes president of Argentina on the death of her husband.

2 start of sporadic industrial action against pay beds in British NHS hospitals.

14 left-wing government takes office in Portugal under Colonel Vasco Goncalves.

15 Cypriot National Guard, with Greek support, overthrows President Makarios and installs former EOKA terrorist Nicos Sampson in his place.

20 Turkey invades Cyprus, claiming right of intervention under 1960 treaty (22, ceasefire).

In USA, Hispanics are elected as governors of New Mexico and Arizona.

In USA, in the state of Connecticut, Ella Grasso is the first woman to be elected a state governor in her own right (5 Nov).

In Italy a referendum upholds the liberalization of the laws relating to divorce.

In Britain, inauguration of National Health Service family planning service (28 March).

In USA, an amendment to the Social Security Act provides for payment of a cost-of-living allowance (3 Jan).

In USA, Safe Drinking Water Act.

Kenya abolishes tuition fees for basic education.

The new British secretary of state for education, Reg Prentice, proposes abolition of the 11-plus examination and the establishment of a fully comprehensive school system (11 March).

In Britain, five men's colleges at Oxford University admit women (Oct).

Pope Paul VI inaugurates a Holy Year.

Roman Catholics are permitted to become Freemasons in countries where this does not involve anti-clericalism.

In USA, four bishops of the Episcopalian Church ordain 11 women to the priesthood, defying Church law (29 July).

Brother Roger Schutz of Taizé is awarded the Templeton Prize for Progress in Religion.

Donald Coggan, Archbishop of York, is appointed Archbishop of Canterbury to succeed Michael Ramsey (Coggan's appointment announced May 14; enthroned 24 Jan 1975).

Maurice Wiles, *The Remaking of Christian Doctrine*.

Q Science, Technology, and Discovery

US firm Hewlett Packard introduces the first programmable pocket calculator.

M Molina and F S Rowland warn that chlorofluorocarbons (used in fridges and as propellants in sprays) may be damaging the atmosphere's ozone layer (which filters out ultraviolet radiation from the Sun).

US probe *Mariner 10* (launched 3 Nov 1973) photographs the upper atmosphere of Venus (Feb) and then takes photographs of Mercury (March and Sept).

US probe *Pioneer 11* reaches Jupiter (Dec).

US astronomer Charles T Kowal announces discovery and naming of Leda, the 13th moon of Jupiter (Sept).

US physicists Burton Richter and Samuel Chao Chung Ting announce (16 Nov) they have separately discovered a new subatomic particle, later called the J/psi particle.

H M Georgi and S L Glashow propose the first Grand Unified Theory about the origins of the Universe.

R Humanities

Discovery of the 'terracotta army' — over 6,000 life-size model soldiers — guarding the tomb of China's first Emperor, Qin Shihuangdi, near Xi'an in central China.

Colin Renfrew, *Before Civilization: The Radiocarbon Revolution and Prehistoric Europe*.

Robert Fogel and Stanley Engerman, *Time on the Cross: The Economics of American Negro Slavery*.

Forrest McDonald, *The Presidency of George Washington*.

Bernard Bailyn, *The Ordeal of Thomas Hutchinson*.

Ross McKibbin, *The Evolution of the Labour Party, 1910–24*.

Jennifer Sherwood and Nikolaus Pevsner, *Oxfordshire*, the final volume in Pevsner's 'Buildings of England' series.

Encyclopaedia Britannica, 15th edition, in three sections: Propaedia, Micropaedia, Macropaedia.

George Watson (ed.), *New Cambridge Bibliography of English Literature*.

Times Literary Supplement abandons anonymity of authors of reviews and articles.

J L Mackie, *The Cement of the Universe*.

P F Strawson, *Freedom and Resentment*.

S Art, Sculpture, Fine Arts, and Architecture

Venice Biennale cancelled.

First major exhibition of photography by Arts Council in London, looks at work of American Diane Arbus.

Art Gallery of Ontario, Toronto, Canada, opens extended Building including Henry Moore Sculpture Centre.

Painting, etc:

Anselm Kiefer, *Resumptio*.

Sculpture:

Joseph Beuys, *I Like America and America Likes Me*.

Richard Long, *A Line in Ireland*.

Architecture:

John Andrews and Webb Zerata, Canadian National Tower, Toronto, is topped out, world's tallest freestanding structure.

Arata Isozaki, Gunma Prefectural Museum of Fine Arts, Japan.

Kenzo Tange, two new wings for Minneapolis Institute of Art, Minneapolis, USA.

T Music

Gordon Crosse, *The Story of Vasco* (opera).

23 Greek military government resigns (24, Constantine Karamanlis returns from exile to form civilian administration).

23 in Northern Ireland, nationalization of Harland and Wolff shipyard in Belfast to save 12,000 jobs.

24 US Supreme Court orders President Nixon to surrender all Watergate tapes to special prosecutor.

25 (–30) foreign ministers of Britain, Turkey, and Greece discuss future of Cyprus in Geneva.

27 US House Judiciary Committee votes for first article of impeachment charges against President Nixon.

31 in Britain, repeal of Industrial Relations Act and abolition of NIRC.

H August

1 Restoration of 1952 constitution in Greece.

5 in USA, President Nixon admits complicity in the Watergate cover-up.

9 President Nixon resigns; Vice-President Gerald Ford becomes 38th US President.

12 Turkey issues 24-hour ultimatum demanding creation of autonomous Turkish cantons in Cyprus (14, Turkish forces in Cyprus resume offensive).

14 Greece withdraws from NATO in protest at its failure to oppose Turks in Cyprus.

16 in Cyprus, second ceasefire leaves 40 per cent of land under Turkish control.

31 death of Norman Kirk, prime minister of New Zealand (6 Sept, succeeded by Wallace Rowling).

J September

4 USA and East Germany establish diplomatic relations.

5 in Britain, senior Conservative Sir Keith Joseph makes speech at Preston questioning the basis of post-war British economic policy and arguing for monetarism.

8 in USA, President Ford issues pardon, for any offences former President Richard Nixon might have committed in office.

12 military coup deposes Emperor Haile Selassie of Ethiopia.

20 nationalist government takes office in Mozambique under Jacques Chissano.

30 General Francisco Costa Gomes succeeds General Spinola as Portuguese president.

K October

5 IRA bombs kill 5 and injure 65 in two public houses in Guildford, Surrey, England.

10 British general election gives Labour an overall majority of 3, with 319 seats to Conservatives, 277, Liberals, 13, Scottish Nationalists, 11, Plaid Cymru 3 (Labour take 39.2 per cent of votes, Conservatives, 35.8 per cent, and Liberals, 18.3 per cent).

15 violent protests in Boston, USA, against integration of schools by 'busing'.

18 US Senator Henry Jackson announces informal deal linking US trade concessions to freedom of emigration from USSR.

28 20 Arab nations recognise the Palestine Liberation Organization (PLO) as sole legitimate representative of Palestinian people.

28 (–30) Chancellor Schmidt of West Germany holds talks with Leonid Brezhnev in Moscow, USSR.

31 Britain, France, and USA veto motion to expel South Africa from UN.

L November

6 Democrats gain 4 Senators and 43 Representatives in US mid-term elections.

13 PLO leader, Yassir Arafat, addresses UN General Assembly.

20 British Labour MP John Stonehouse disappears in Miami (24 Dec, arrested with false passport in Australia).

21 IRA bombs two public houses in Birmingham, killing 21 people and injuring 120.

23 (–25) President Ford and Leonid Brezhnev discuss arms control at Vladivostok, USSR.

26 Kakuei Tanaka resigns as Japanese prime minister amid allegations of corruption (9 Dec, succeeded by Takeo Miki).

28 following spate of IRA outrages in Britain, the Prevention of Terrorism Bill is passed through Parliament in 24 hours. Police are given power to hold terrorist suspects for five days without charge and suspects can be banned from the British mainland or deported to Northern Ireland.

M December

2 Israel announces that it possesses means to manufacture nuclear weapons.

7 President Makarios returns to Cyprus after five months in exile.

8 in Greece 62 per cent vote in referendum against restoration of monarchy.

9 (–10) EC summit in Paris reaches agreement on revised British contribution to budget.

11 Ian Smith calls constitutional conference to end guerrilla war in Rhodesia (now Zimbabwe).

25 cyclone devastates Darwin, Australia.

31 during 1974 British retail prices have risen by 19 per cent, wage rates by 29 per cent, while total industrial production fell by 3 per cent (each sum a post-war record).

Hans Werner Henze, *Tristan*.
Olivier Messiaen, *Des canyons aux étoiles*.
Karlheinz Stockhausen, *Inori*.
David Bowie, *Diamond Dogs*.
Can, *Soon Over Babaluma*.
Eric Clapton, *461 Ocean Boulevard*.
Carl Douglas, 'Kung Fu Fighting'.
Kraftwerk, *Autobahn*.
Mud, 'Tiger Feet'.
Status Quo, 'Down, Down'.
Steely Dan, *Pretzel Logic*.
Ray Stevens, 'The Streak'.
Barbara Streisand, 'The Way We Were' (single and album).
Swedish pop group Abba win the Eurovision Song Contest with 'Waterloo' and shoot to international stardom.
Bob Dylan and The Band undertake a classic US tour, giving 39 shows.
The film *The Sting* revives ragtime.

u Literature and Drama
Beryl Bainbridge, *The Bottle Factory Outing*.
Erica Jong, *Fear of Flying*.
Philip Larkin, *High Windows* (poems).
John Le Carré, *Tinker, Tailor, Soldier, Spy*.
Alison Lurie, *The War Between the Tates*.
Elsa Morante, *History*.
Alexander Solzhenitsyn is expelled from the USSR after publication of *The Gulag Archipelago, 1918–56*.

Drama:
Thomas Berhard, *The Force of Habit*.
Howard Brenton, *The Churchill Play*.
Alexander Buzo, *Norm and Ahmed*.
Dario Fo, *Can't Pay? Won't Pay!*
John Romeril, *The Floating World*.
Ntozake Shange, *For Coloured Girls who have Considered Suicide when the Rainbow is enuf*.
Tom Stoppard, *Travesties*.

v Births and Deaths
March 17 Louis Isadore Kahn dies (73).
April 2 Georges Pompidou dies (62).
April 5 Richard Crossman dies (66).
April 20 Mohammed Ayub Khan dies (66).
May 24 Duke Ellington dies (75).
June 18 Georgi K Zhukov dies (77).
July 1 Juan Perón dies (78).
July 10 Earl Warren dies (83).
July 13 P M S Blackett dies (76).
July 29 Erich Kästner dies (75).
Aug 26 Charles Lindbergh dies (72).
Dec 14 Walter Lippmann dies (85).
Dec 14 Kurt Hahn dies (88).

w Everyday Life
In USA and Britain, 'streaking' (running nude in public places) enjoys a burst of popularity at sports fixtures.
First observance of New Year's Day as a public holiday in England and Wales.

x Sport and Recreation
Sir Alf Ramsey is sacked as manager of the English soccer team (1 May).
Host nation West Germany wins the World Cup, defeating Holland by 2–1 in the Final in Munich, West Germany (7 July).
Gary Sobers retires from Test cricket, holding the record for the number of runs: 8,032, from 93 Tests.
In rugby football, the British Lions win their first Test series in South Africa.
Muhammad Ali beats George Foreman to regain the World Heavy-weight boxing title in Kinshasa, Zaire (29 Oct).

y Media
World-wide shortage of newsprint.

Film:
Aguirre, Wrath of God (director, Werner Herzog).
Amarcord (director, Federico Fellini).
Celine and Julie Go Boating (director, Jacques Rivette).
Chinatown (director, Roman Polanski).
The Conversation (director, Francis Ford Coppola; starring Gene Hackman).
Godfather II (director, Francis Ford Coppola; starring Al Pacino and Robert de Niro).
Lacombe Lucien (director, Louis Malle).
Papillon (starring Dustin Hoffman and Steve McQueen).
700 million video-cassettes are rented in the USA.

Radio:
In USA, *The Prairie Home Companion* with Garrison Keillor.

Television:
In France, ORTF is abolished and replaced by three 'commercial' stations, but the state is the only shareholder.
New programmes in Britain include: *Arena* (BBC), an arts programme; *The Family*, the BBC's 'fly on the wall' documentary about living with the Wilkins family; *Happy Days*; *Porridge* (BBC), a comedy series set in a prison, starring Ronnie Barker; *Rising Damp* (Yorkshire TV).

Communist victory in Vietnam ... Emergency in India ... First British North Sea oil ...

A January

1 In USA, aides of former President Nixon H R Haldeman, John D Ehrlichman, and John N Mitchell are found guilty of Watergate offences (21 Feb, sentenced to 2½–8 years in prison).

2 British hospital consultants start work-to-rule over new contracts.

4 Phuoc Binh province of South Vietnam falls to North Vietnamese.

6 Financial Times Share Index falls to 145.5 (having been at 339 on 28 Feb. 1974), the lowest level since 1954 (by 31 Dec London shares gain over 150 per cent).

15 Portugal agrees to grant independence to Angola.

15 British government proposes to nationalize the aircraft construction industry.

15 President Ford reports that the State of the Union is 'not good'.

20 British government abandons the Channel Tunnel project.

23 government decides to hold a referendum on the revised terms for British membership of the EC.

31 Industry Bill published in Britain, establishing a National Enterprise Board to facilitate state intervention in industry.

B February

4 In Britain, in the first ballot of the Conservative leadership election Margaret Thatcher wins 130 votes, Edward Heath 119, and Hugh Fraser 16. Heath resigns.

6 500 Spanish civil servants sign a pro-democracy manifesto.

8 IRA declares a ceasefire in Northern Ireland.

11 Margaret Thatcher elected leader of the British Conservative Party, with 146 votes (William Whitelaw wins 79 votes, with 49 for three other challengers).

13 Northern Cyprus declares separate existence as the Turkish Federated State of Cyprus.

24 Bangladesh becomes a one-party state.

27 Peter Lorenz, Chairman of West Berlin Christian Democratic Union, is kidnapped by terrorists (5 Mar, released after his captors' demands are met: five terrorists are released from jail in West Germany and flown out of the country).

28 43 die in crash of London Underground train at Moorgate station.

28 Lomé Convention signed, giving 46 developing countries preferential access to EC markets.

C March

2 Iran becomes a one-party state.

18 British government decides to recommend a 'Yes' vote in the EC referendum.

19 troops sent to Glasgow, Scotland, to clear rubbish heaps after a nine-week strike.

25 King Faisal of Saudi Arabia assassinated, succeeded by King Khalid.

27 in Britain, collective cabinet responsibility suspended for the first time for the duration of the EC referendum campaign.

30 North Vietnamese forces capture the central city of Da Nang.

D April

5 Chiang Kai-shek dies (6, succeeded by Yen Chia-kan as president of Taiwan).

9 British House of Commons vote confirms EC membership, by 396 to 170.

13 civil war starts in Lebanon when violent clashes between Palestinians and Christian Falangists outside a Beirut church leave 30 dead.

15 British Chancellor Denis Healey's 'rough and tough' Budget raises income tax by 2p and cuts spending by £900 million.

17 in Cambodia Khmer Rouge revolutionaries capture Phnom Penh; there is considerable brutality as people flee the city.

24 British government decides to take a majority shareholding in British Leyland motors.

25 the first free elections in Portugal since the 1920s produce no overall majority, the Socialists under Mario Soares emerge as the largest party.

25 South African government decides to abolish many measures of 'petty apartheid'.

29 last US personnel flee Saigon, South Vietnam, by helicopter from the US Embassy compound.

30 publication of bill to establish British National Oil Corporation.

30 President Minh of South Vietnam surrenders Saigon to Communist forces.

E May

1 British government takes 50 per cent stake in Ferranti Electronics.

1 Ulster Unionists win majority in elections for Northern Ireland Constitutional Convention.

5 Barbara Castle announces the British government's intention to abolish pay beds in NHS hospitals.

9 British Environment Secretary Anthony Crosland tells local authority leaders that

*Financial crisis of New York City ... Personal computers on sale
in USA ... Death of P G Wodehouse ... Arthur Ashe wins
Wimbledon ...*

o Politics, Government, Law, and Economy

Richard Crossman, *Diaries of a Cabinet Minister.*

T White, *Breach of Faith.*

New members of the US Congress overturn the seniority system and disperse the power of committee chairmen to subcommittees and members.

In USA, abolition of the Internal Security Committee of the House of Representatives, formerly known as the Un-American Activities Committee.

Ecology Party founded in Britain (known since 1985 as the Green Party).

In USA, the Supreme Court rules that defendants in criminal cases can conduct their own defence rather than accept the services of a court-appointed lawyer (30 June).

New York City suffers shortage of funds; bailed out by New York state and federal government aid (bill for federal loan signed on 9 Dec, two days before the city would have defaulted on debts).

The Lomé convention allows access to European markets for 58 Third World nations.

The International Monetary Fund (IMF) abandons the remaining role of gold in world monetary affairs (31 Aug).

Britain establishes the National Enterprise Board to co-ordinate government industrial holdings.

British government nationalizes the British Leyland motor company (11 Aug).

In USA, foundation of the Worldwatch Institute, a research institute dealing with the interdependence of the world economy and the environment.

Microsoft founded by Bill Gates, aged 19, and a friend.

P Society, Education, and Religion

Indian Self-determination Act passed in USA.

The United Nations declares 1975 International Women's Year.

Sex Discrimination Act in Britain outlaws discrimination in employment or education on grounds of sex or marital status and establishes the Equal Opportunities Commission.

Birth control becomes a priority in India; abortion is legalized and the government launches campaigns advocating vasectomy.

The British Appeal Court rules that Sikhs living in Britain can have only one wife (9 May).

Adopted children in Britain over 18 are granted right to information about their natural parents.

In USA, the Age Discrimination in Employment Act (passed 28 Nov) strengthens the law against age discrimination in the work place.

The Supreme Court of Alaska, USA, rules that personal possession and cultivation of marijuana is protected by the state constitution (27 May).

Michel Foucault, *Discipline and Punish.*

In USA, the Education for All Handicapped Children Act requires public schools to provide appropriate education for every school-age handicapped child, irrespective of disability (signed 29 Nov).

In Denmark, the New School Act legislates for primary and secondary comprehensive 'folk' schools.

In New Zealand, legislation facilitates the integration of private schools into the state system.

Parental complaints about 'progressive' teaching at the William Tyndale Primary School, London, forces an official inquiry.

Rhodes Boyson, *Crisis in Education.*

In England, the new Archbishop of Canterbury, Donald Coggan issues a 'call to the nation' for moral and spiritual renewal.

o Science, Technology, and Discovery

The first 'personal computer' is marketed in the USA.

Liquid crystals first used for display purposes in electronic devices.

US–German space probe *Helios 1* passes the Sun at a distance of 46.2 million km/28.7 million mi (15 Mar).

US *Apollo 18* and Soviet *Soyuz 19* spacecraft dock in Earth orbit (17–19 July).

Soviet craft *Venera 9* and *10* (22 and 25 Oct) land on Venus and transmit the first pictures from the surface.

Foundation of European Space Agency (1 Aug).

US astronomer Charles T Kowal discovers the 14th moon of Jupiter.

Astronomers at Leiden University estimate that the 'radio galaxy' spans a distance of 18 million light years.

Discovery of tau lepton or tauon atomic particle (Aug).

In USA, production of 'U' sub-atomic par-

407

'the party's over' for further expansion of local welfare services.

12 Cambodian navy seizes the USS *Mayaguez* (15, recaptured by US forces).

F June

4 First live broadcast of British parliament.

5 consultative referendum approves Britain's membership of EC; turn-out is 64.5 per cent, of whom 67.2 per cent vote in favour.

5 Suez Canal reopened.

9 (–15 Aug) in Britain, trial in Lancaster of the 'Birmingham Six' charged with the 1974 pub bombings in Birmingham; all are found guilty and sentenced to life imprisonment. They are released after successful appeal in March 1991.

10 in USA, report of Rockefeller Commission into CIA activities reports illegal domestic operations and extensive mail-opening programme.

10 Municipal Assistance Corporation formed to help New York City escape bankruptcy.

11 Uganda-based British lecturer Denis Hills, who had referred to President Amin in an unpublished text as a 'village tyrant', is sentenced to death (10 July, released following interventions by several parties and visit by British Foreign Secretary James Callaghan).

12 Indira Gandhi found guilty of electoral corruption but remains Indian prime minister pending appeals.

18 first North Sea Oil pumped ashore in Britain.

25 Mozambique becomes independent with Samora Machel as president.

26 Indira Gandhi declares a state of emergency in India; censorship is imposed and opposition leaders, including Morarji Desai, are imprisoned.

G July

2 Australian Deputy Prime Minister James Cairns dismissed because of his involvement in a loans scandal.

5 Cape Verde Islands gain independence.

6 Comoro Islands declare independence.

11 in Britain, White Paper *The Attack on Inflation* is published, proposing an incomes policy for 1975–76 which would allow only a flat-rate £6 per week increase.

12 São Tomé e Principe gains independence.

24 Reg Prentice, British Education Secretary, is refused renomination by his local Labour Party in Newham North-East constituency.

29 coup in Nigeria replaces General Gowon with Brigadier Murtala Mohammed.

29 Organization of American States lifts ban on relations with Cuba.

H August

1 Helsinki Conference on Security and Co-operation in Europe issues 'Final Act', signed by 30 states: states are to respect each other's equality and individuality, avoid use of force in disputes, and respect human rights.

12 British inflation peaks at 26.9 per cent.

15 President Mujibur Rahman of Bangladesh is murdered; his successor is Khandakar Mushtaq Ahmed.

19 in Britain supporters of imprisoned robber George Davis damage pitch of Headingley cricket ground in protest at Davis's imprisonment and prevent play in Test Match.

23 Greek colonels found guilty of treason and sentenced to death (25, sentence commuted).

J September

3 TUC supports the British government's incomes policy.

4 in USA, introduction of school busing for desegregation in Louisville, Kentucky, is followed by riots.

5 in USA, Lynette 'Squeaky' Fromme, a follower of murderer Charles Manson, attempts to assassinate President Ford (26 Nov, found guilty of attempted assassination).

16 Papua New Guinea becomes independent from Australia.

17 New York City narrowly averts bankruptcy through last-minute loan of $150 million from the teachers' union.

18 kidnapped US heiress Patricia Hearst arrested for armed robbery.

22 in USA, Sara Jane Moore attempts to assassinate President Ford.

22 15 die in bombings in nine Northern Ireland towns.

23 Israel and Egypt reach agreement on Israeli withdrawal from the Sinai peninsula.

29 British Labour Party conference supports the new incomes policy.

K October

1 The British Lord Chief Justice rules that the first volume of *The Crossman Diaries* can be published.

8 fighting resumes in Lebanon.

10 part of Israeli-occupied Sinai returned to Egypt.

15 the Liberal and National opposition decides to use its Senate majority to block the Australian government's supply of finance.

15 start of the 'Cod War', when Iceland increases its territorial waters from 80 to 320 km (50 to 200 mi) and confronts German trawlers with gunboats.

21 British unemployment breaches 1 million for first time since 1940s.

ticles at the accelerator at Stanford University, California.

C Milstein and G Köhler produce the first monoclonal antibodies (identical microorganisms), in Cambridge, England.

Derek Brownhall produces the first clone of a rabbit in Oxford, England.

J Hughes discovers endorphins (morphine-like chemicals) in the brain.

Swiss scientists publish details of the first chemically directed synthesis of insulin.

The EMI company introduces the CAT body-scanner.

R Humanities

Discovery of 'Lucy', the remains of a hominid about 3 million years old, at Hadar in Ethiopia.

20,000 clay tablets with cuneiform texts found at Tell Mardikh (ancient Ebla) in Syria.

The Cambridge History of Africa (–1986).

John Matthews, *Western Aristocracies and Imperial Court, AD 364–425*.

C N L Brooke and Gillian Keir, *London 800–1216: The Shaping of a City*.

R H Hilton, *The English Peasantry in the Later Middle Ages*.

US Department of Commerce and the Bureau of the Census, *Historical Statistics of the United States: Colonial Times to 1970*.

Carl Bridenbaugh, *The Spirit of '76: The Growth of American Patriotism Before Independence, 1607–1776*.

E P Thompson, *Whigs and Hunters*.

Edmund S Morgan, *American Slavery, American Freedom*.

Willard B Gatewood, Jr, *Black Americans and the White Man's Burden, 1898– 1903*.

Paul Fussell, *The Great War and Modern Memory*.

A J P Taylor, *The Second World War: An Illustrated History*.

Paul Addison, *The Road to 1945*.

Paul Feyerabend, *Against Method*.

Michel Foucault, *Discipline and Punish*.

H-G Gadamer, *Truth and Method*.

S Art, Sculpture, Fine Arts, and Architecture

'British Photography 1840–1950' exhibition at Hayward Gallery, London.

500th anniversary of Michelangelo's birth.

Painting, etc:

Rebecca Horn, *Unicorn*.

Sculpture:

John De Andrea, *Woman in Bed*.

Architecture:

Foster Associates, Willis, Faber, Dumas Building, Ipswich, England.

I M Pei, John Hancock Tower, Boston, Massachusetts, USA.

Kevin Roche, John Dinkeloo and Associates, Lehman Pavilion, Museum of Modern Art, New York.

T Music

Pierre Boulez, *Rituel in memoriam Bruno Maderna*.

Elliott Carter, *A Mirror on Which to Dwell*.

Joonas Kokkonen, *The Last Temptation* (opera).

György Ligeti, *San Francisco Polyphony*.

Witold Lutoslawski, *Les Espaces du sommeil*.

Luigi Nono, *Al gran sole carico d'amore* (opera).

Aulis Sallinen: *The Horseman* (opera).

James Levine becomes musical director of the Metropolitan Opera, New York.

A Chorus Line (musical), lyrics by Edward Kleban, music by Marvin Hamlisch (first performed at the Public Theatre, New York, 15 April).

The Bay City Rollers, 'Bye Bye Baby'.

Bee Gees, 'Jive Talkin''.

The Carpenters, 'Only Yesterday'.

Bob Dylan, *Blood on the Tracks*.

Elton John, *Captain Fantastic and the Brown Dirt Cowboy, Rock of the Westies*.

Led Zeppelin, *Physical Graffiti*.

Queen, 'Bohemian Rhapsody' (single and the first major rock video).

Patti Smith, *Horses*.

Bruce Springsteen, 'Born to Run' (single and album).

Rod Stewart, 'Sailing'.

U Literature and Drama

John Ashbery, *Self-Portrait in a Convex Mirror* (poems).

Saul Bellow, *Humboldt's Gift*.

Jorge Luis Borges, *The Book of Sand*.

Joyce Carol Oates, *Assassins*.

Ruth Prawer Jhabvala, *Heat and Dust*.

Primo Levi, *The Periodic Table*.

Paul Theroux, *The Great Railway Bazaar*.

Michel Tournier, *Gemini*.

In Britain, P G Wodehouse is knighted, just before his death.

Drama:

Michael Cook, *Jacob's Wake*.

Athol Fugard, *Statements*.

Trevor Griffiths, *Comedians*.

Terence McNally, *The Ritz*.

David Mamet, *American Buffalo*.

Harold Pinter, *No Man's Land*.

James Reeney, *Handcuffs* — completes 'The Donnelly Trilogy'.

Tadeusz Rozewicz, *Mariage Blanc*.

21 New York financial crisis leads to large cuts and a loss of power by elected officials.

22 in Britain, the 'Guildford Four' are sentenced to life imprisonment after being found guilty of planting IRA bombs in pubs in Guildford and Woolwich (released 17 Oct 1989).

24 one-day general strike of women in Iceland.

24 Young Liberal leader Peter Hain accused of robbing a London bank.

26 Transkei becomes the first nominally independent South African black 'homeland'.

27 British House of Commons votes to abolish grants to 'direct grant' schools.

29 House of Lords passes the Community Land Bill, putting development land under control of local authorities.

L **November**

1 (–29 Dec) British doctor Sheila Cassidy is imprisoned and tortured in Chile (30 Dec, British ambassador in Santiago recalled in protest).

3 in Britain, Queen Elizabeth makes formal opening of North Sea Oil pumps.

3 Bangladesh government imposes martial law.

6 (–9) unarmed Moroccan invasion of Spanish Sahara.

7 electoral corruption verdict on Indira Gandhi quashed by the Supreme Court (after India's parliament, the Lok Sabha, retrospectively legalized her actions).

10 Angola becomes independent with Agostinho Neto as president, but civil war breaks out between the government party, the Popular Movement for the Liberation of Angola (MPLA), and UNITA.

11 Sir John Kerr, the governor general of Australia, dismisses Prime Minister Whitlam and appoints the opposition leader, Malcolm Fraser.

12 the British House of Lords passes laws on industry, planning, and sex discrimination but rejects trade union law reform because it would allow journalists to establish closed shops, which is seen as a threat to freedom of the press.

14 Spain agrees with Morocco and Mauritania to pull out of the Sahara by Feb 1976 and organize consultations about the area's future.

15 Scottish Development Agency established.

20 in Spain, General Franco dies (22, the monarchy is restored and Juan Carlos becomes king of Spain).

20 interim US Senate report reveals that the CIA had plotted to kill foreign leaders, including Castro and Lumumba.

25 Surinam (former Dutch Guyana) becomes independent.

25 British government sends three frigates to protect trawlers in Icelandic fishing grounds.

26 attempted coup by left-wing Portuguese soldiers defeated.

27 British White Paper *Our Changing Democracy* proposes devolution for Scotland and Wales.

27 IRA murders British publisher and right-wing activist Ross McWhirter.

28 Fretilin liberation movement declares Portuguese (East) Timor independent.

29 New Zealand National Party defeats the Labour government. Robert Muldoon becomes prime minister.

M **December**

2 (–14) train hijacked in the Netherlands by South Moluccan terrorists.

3 Communist forces take control of Laos; the king abdicates.

5 last 46 Northern Ireland internees released.

6 (–12) IRA gang is besieged at Balcombe Street in London and eventually surrenders.

7 Indonesian forces invade East Timor and commit numerous atrocities.

11 first shots fired in the Cod War around Iceland.

13 general election in Australia gives large majority to the newly installed Fraser government.

16 the British government bails out the Chrysler UK car company with £162.5 million in assistance.

21 terrorists capture some OPEC oil ministers at their conference in Vienna, Austria.

23 Richard Welch, head of CIA operations in Greece, is shot dead in Athens following his exposure by newspaper as a spy.

27 Indian general election postponed, for a year, until 1977.

30 former dictator of Greece, Colonel Papadopoulos, is imprisoned for a further 25 years for shootings at Athens Polytechnic in Nov 1973.

Wole Soyinka, *Death and the King's Horseman*.

Peter Hall becomes Director of Britain's National Theatre.

v Births and Deaths

Jan 28 Antonin Novotný dies (70).
Feb 14 P G Wodehouse dies (93).
Feb 14 Julian Huxley dies (87).
Feb 24 Nikolai Bulganin dies (79).
March 15 Aristotle Onassis dies (69).
March 27 Arthur Bliss dies (83).
April 5 Chiang Kai-shek (87).
April 16 Sarvepalli Radhakrishnan dies (86).
May 20 Barbara Hepworth dies (72).
June 3 Eisaku Sato dies (74).
Aug 9 Dmitri Shostakovich dies (68).
Aug 27 Haile Selassie dies (83).
Aug 29 Éamon de Valera dies (92).
Sept 4 Ivan Maisky dies (91).
Oct 22 Arnold Toynbee dies (86).
Nov 29 Graham Hill dies (46).

w Everyday Life

Over a million 'Pet Rocks' are sold in the USA.

The first 'drive-thru' McDonald's hamburger store is opened.

x Sport and Recreation

Junko Tabei of Japan is the first woman to climb Mt Everest.

In cricket, Australia regains the Ashes from England (9 Jan).

Anatoly Karpov of the USSR becomes world chess champion when Bobby Fischer fails to meet the deadline for their match in Manila, Philippines (3 April).

Stable boys in England strike in pursuit of a pay rise; they picket the Ascot racecourse on Gold Cup day (19 June).

Arthur Ashe of the USA becomes the first African-American Men's singles champion at the Wimbledon tennis tournament, London (July 5).

Muhammad Ali beats Joe Frazier on points in Manila, Philippines, to retain the world Heavyweight boxing title (30 Sept).

y Media

The *Scottish Daily News* is launched by a workers' co-operative (5 May), but later fails (Oct), following an attempt by British businessman Robert Maxwell to save the paper.

Film:

Dog Day Afternoon (director, Sidney Lumet).
Every Man for Himself and God Against All (director, Werner Herzog).
Jaws (director, Steven Spielberg).
Nashville (director, Robert Altman).
One Flew Over the Cuckoo's Nest (director, Milos Forman).
The Passenger (director, Michelangelo Antonioni).
The Rocky Horror Picture Show (director, Jim Sharman).

Television:

New programmes in USA include: *Saturday Night Live* (NBC); *Starsky and Hutch*; *Wheel of Fortune* (NBC).

New programmes in Britain include: *Fawlty Towers* (BBC), starring John Cleese; *The Naked Civil Servant* (Thames TV), with John Hurt as Quentin Crisp; *Rumpole of the Bailey*; *The Sweeney*; *The World at War*.

Death of Chairman Mao ... Jimmy Carter elected US president ...
IMF crisis in Britain ...

A January

1 Venezuelan government nationalizes its oil industry.

4 (–5) 15 die in sectarian murders in South Armagh, Northern Ireland (6, the elite SAS (Special Air Service) is sent in to control the situation).

7 government of Aldo Moro in Italy resigns after the Socialist Party withdraws support.

8 Zhou Enlai, prime minister of China, dies (9 Feb, replaced by Hua Guofeng).

13 Argentina suspends diplomatic ties with Britain over Falkland Islands.

18 British Labour MPs Jim Sillars and John Robertson launch the Scottish Labour Party (SLP) to campaign for greater devolution for Scotland.

21 inaugural Concorde flights from London to Bahrain and from Paris to Rio de Janeiro, Brazil.

23 following an anti-Communist speech delivered by Margaret Thatcher, a report in the USSR newspaper *Red Star* brands her the 'Iron Lady'.

28 Spanish prime minister proposes lifting ban on political parties (enacted 14 July).

29 in Britain, a male model, Norman Scott, alleges in court that he was the homosexual lover of Liberal Party leader Jeremy Thorpe in the 1960s; a Department of Trade report criticises Thorpe's judgement in becoming involved with a crashed 'secondary bank'.

31 population of the world reaches 4 billion.

B February

4 Lockheed bribery scandal exposed, with serious consequences for politicians and officials in Japan, Italy, and the Netherlands.

11 in Italy Aldo Moro forms a minority Christian Democrat government.

13 the head of state of Nigeria, General Murtala Mohammad, is killed during an unsuccessful coup and succeeded by General Olusegun Obasanjo.

17 MPLA forces secure control over most Angolan territory. 19 Iceland breaks off diplomatic relations with Britain over the 'Cod War'.

24 Governor Jimmy Carter emerges as the surprise winner of the New Hampshire Democratic primary.

24 (–5 Mar) 25th Congress of the Communist Party of the Soviet Union (27, Italian Communist leader Enrico Berlinguer announces to the conference that a communist Italy would stay in NATO and remain pluralist).

27 Polisario Front declares the independence of Western Sahara, but an assembly of tribal chiefs votes for union with Morocco.

C March

5 The pound falls below $2 for the first time ever.

9 in Britain, Harold Wilson alleges that there had been 'South African participation' in allegations made against Jeremy Thorpe.

9 British House of Lords passes the Trade Union and Labour Relations Bill.

12 Lebanese army leaders set up an interim military council until political control of country is restored.

15 the French franc is forced out of the European currency 'snake'.

16 in Britain, Harold Wilson announces that he is to resign as prime minister.

20 US heiress Patricia Hearst found guilty of armed robbery with the 'Symbionese Liberation Army'.

24 military coup deposes President Isabel Perón of Argentina; all political parties and unions are 'suspended'.

25 in Britain, Michael Foot wins the first ballot for the Labour Party leadership with 90 votes. James Callaghan wins 84, Roy Jenkins 56, Tony Benn 37, Denis Healey 30, Anthony Crosland 17. A second ballot follows (30) with three contestants only, giving Callaghan 141, Foot 133, and Healey 38.

D April

2 A new Portuguese constitution with a commitment to socialism is promulgated.

3 in Britain, James Callaghan wins final ballot of Labour leadership election with 176 votes to 137 for Foot (5, Callaghan becomes prime minister).

4 government of Thailand defeated in general election (18, new coalition formed).

4 Prince Sihanouk retires as head of state of Cambodia, replaced by Khieu Samphan of the Khmer Rouge.

5 rioting in China over the removal by 'ultra-leftists' of wreaths laid in memory of Zhou Enlai.

7 British Labour government loses its overall majority with the defection of John Stonehouse to the 'English National Party'.

9 in Britain, Peter Hain, leader of the Young Liberals, is acquitted of bank robbery — evidence emerges that South Africans had tried to frame him.

Concorde in service ... J M Roberts' History of the World ...
Górecki's Third Symphony ... The Muppet Show ...

o Politics, Government, Law, and Economy

Valéry Giscard d'Estaing, *La Démocratie Française*.

Bob Woodward and Carl Bernstein, *The Final Days*.

In South Africa, the Republic of Transkei becomes nominally independent (Oct).

In Britain, publication of the reports of the Layfield Commission into local government finance (19 May) and of the Salmon Commission on Standards in Public Life (15 July).

In USA, in Buckley v. Valeo, the Supreme Court rejects placing limits on spending for political campaigns (31 Jan).

The US Supreme Court rules in Gregg v. Georgia that capital punishment is not unconstitutional (2 July).

Death penalty abolished in Canada (14 July).

In Virginia State Board of Pharmacy v. Virginia Consumer Council the US Supreme Court rules (24 May) that commercial speech is protected by the 1st Amendment to the Constitution.

Police Complaints Board is established in Britain.

The Organization of Petroleum Exporting Countries (OPEC) establishes its Special Fund for international development to recycle cash surpluses generated by the oil shock.

Apple Computers founded in USA by Steven Jobs and Stephen Wozniak.

p Society, Education, and Religion

Race Relations Act in Britain makes inciting racial hatred an offence and establishes the Commission for Racial Equality.

California allows the terminally ill to authorize the removal of life-support equipment (introduced on 1 Jan 1977).

West Germany legalizes abortion.

Shere Hite, *The Hite Report: A Nationwide Study on Female Sexuality.*

In USA, the Supreme Court rules that states have the right to enforce laws banning homosexual acts (29 March).

Foundation in USA of the Ethics and Public Policy Center and the Rockford Institute (dealing with family and religious issues).

In Britain, a speech by Prime Minister James Callaghan at Ruskin College, Oxford, criticizes educational standards and launches a 'Great Debate' on the curriculum and teaching methods.

The Education Act in England and Wales requires local education authorities who have not introduced comprehensive education to plan for comprehensivization.

Episcopalian Church in USA approves ordination of women to the priesthood (16 Sept).

Cardinal Suenens of Belgium is awarded the Templeton Prize for Progress in Religion.

The Roman Catholic Bishop of Umtali, Rhodesia (now Zimbabwe), is sentenced to 10 years' imprisonment for anti-government activities.

Basil Hume is appointed Roman Catholic Archbishop of Westminster, London.

Christian Believing, a report by the Doctrine Commission of the Church of England.

q Science, Technology, and Discovery

The Monotype company in Britain introduces laser typesetting.

British–French supersonic airliner Concorde begins regular passenger service across the Atlantic.

The German company Keuffel und Esser makes its last slide-rule.

A massive release of poisonous dioxin gas from a pesticide plant near Seveso in Italy kills domestic and farm animals in the surrounding region (26 July).

US spacecraft *Viking 1* and *Viking 2* soft-land on Mars (20 July, 3 Sept) and transmit detailed pictures of the surface and scientific data.

In USA, astronomers at Harvard College Laboratory discover bursts of X-rays coming from a star cluster 30,000 light years from Earth.

Japanese molecular biologist Susumu Tonegawa demonstrates that antibodies are produced by large numbers of genes working in combination.

R B Woodward and A Eschenmoser synthesize Vitamin B12.

In San Francisco, USA, foundation of Genentech, the world's first genetic engineering company.

In USA, a mystery disease afflicts people who attended the meeting of the American Legion in Philadelphia; 29 die within a month and the disease becomes known as Legionnaire's disease.

r Humanities

J M Roberts, *The Hutchinson History of the World.*

G Westermann, *Grosser Atlas zur Weltgeschichte.*

W G Hoskins, *The Age of Plunder: King Henry's England, 1500–1547.*

14 Western Sahara is divided between Morocco and Mauritania.

16 India and Pakistan normalise diplomatic relations, for the first time since the war of 1971.

26 (–5 Aug) In Britain, trial of John Stonehouse, resulting in seven years' imprisonment for fraud, theft, and forgery.

30 new Moro government in Italy collapses and an election is called.

E **May**

5 British government announces its pay policy for 1976–77, recommending 4.5 per cent for wage rises.

9 German terrorist leader Ulrike Meinhof commits suicide in prison.

11 in Britain, a supporters' campaign achieves the release of George Davis, imprisoned for armed robbery; he is released under royal prerogative because of faulty identification evidence.

12 in Britain, Jeremy Thorpe resigns as Liberal leader and is replaced by Jo Grimond as interim leader.

12 Icelandic gunboat attacks British trawler.

27 in Britain, Harold Wilson's resignation Honours List causes controversy.

27 Michael Heseltine, an opposition front bench spokesman, causes the suspension of the British House of Commons by whirling the mace around his head.

31 Syrian soldiers and tanks enter Lebanon.

F **June**

1 Cod War ends with agreement between Iceland and Britain about fishing.

8 (–12) Polish leader Edward Gierek visits Bonn and decides to normalize relations between Poland and West Germany.

10 Arab countries meeting in Cairo call for Syrian withdrawal from Lebanon.

16 (–25) South African police kill 76 students in Soweto and other townships during protests and riots about teaching in Afrikaans (6 July, Afrikaans education plan dropped).

16 British TUC approves the new incomes policy.

16 US ambassador to Lebanon kidnapped and murdered.

20 Italian general election produces a major advance for the Communist Party.

21 Arab Protection Force troops under the aegis of the Arab League arrive in Lebanon to take control from the Syrians.

24 Polish government announces big price rises, causing rioting in factory areas (9 Sept, price rises suspended).

25 Idi Amin is declared Uganda's president for life.

27 Palestinian terrorists hijack an Air France plane and force it to fly to Entebbe, Uganda (July, Israeli paratroopers rescue the 110 hijack victims at Entebbe).

29 Seychelles gains independence.

G **July**

1 Adolfo Suárez becomes prime minister of Spain.

2 North and South Vietnam are formally unified.

4 in USA bicentenary of Declaration of Independence is marked by nationwide celebrations.

7 in Britain, David Steel wins the Liberal leadership election, defeating John Pardoe.

14 Jimmy Carter is nominated as presidential candidate at the Democratic convention in New York.

14 Drought Bill published in Britain to deal with water shortages, with fines for excessive use of water.

18 cash worth a record £6 million is stolen when thieves tunnel from sewers into the vaults of a bank in Nice, France.

21 IRA assassinates Christopher Ewart-Biggs, British ambassador in Dublin, Ireland.

26 Scottish Labour Party breaks away from Labour Party.

27 former Japanese Prime Minister Kakuei Tanaka is charged with accepting bribes from US company Lockheed.

28 earthquake in Dangshan, China, kills 650,000.

28 Britain breaks off relations with Uganda over the disappearance of a former Entebbe hostage.

29 formation of new Italian government, led by Giulio Andreotti and dependent on Communist acquiescence.

30 amnesty for political prisoners in Spain.

H **August**

1 Trinidad and Tobago becomes independent.

2 British House of Lords rules that Tameside council, near Manchester, can defy a government directive to introduce comprehensive schools.

4 (–13 Sept) further rioting in Soweto and Port Elizabeth, South Africa.

19 in USA, Gerald Ford narrowly wins renomination against a challenge from Ronald Reagan at the Republican convention in Kansas City.

24 in Britain, Denis Howell appointed Minister for Drought.

25 Jacques Chirac, prime minister of France, resigns suddenly.

27 Howell claims success when rain falls in eastern England.

Peter Clark and Paul Slack, *English Towns in Transition, 1500–1700*.

T W Moody, F X Martin, F J Byrne (eds.), *Early Modern Ireland, 1534–1691*, the first volume in 'A New History of Ireland' (–).

E S de Beer (ed.), *The Correspondence of John Locke* (–1989).

The Statistical History of the United States.

Herbert George Gutman, *The Black Family in Slavery and Freedom, 1750– 1925*.

Ernest May, *The Making of the Monroe Doctrine*.

Louis Althusser, *Essays in Self-Criticism*.

Noam Chomsky, *Reflections on Language*.

Imre Lakatos, *Proofs and Refutations*.

s Art, Sculpture, Fine Arts, and Architecture

Venice Biennale rehabilitated.

'Sand Circles', exhibition at Hayward Gallery, London.

Painting, etc:

Claude Viallat, *Window in Tahiti, Homage to Matisse*.

Sculpture:

Daniel Buren, *On Two Levels With Two Colours*.

César, *Le Pouce*.

Christo, *Running Fence*.

Architecture:

Tadao Ando, Row House Sumiyoshi, Osaka, Japan.

Arata Isozaki, Kaijima House, Kichijoji, Musashino City, Japan.

Denys Lasdun, National Theatre, South Bank Centre, London.

Roche and Dinkeloo, One UN Plaza, New York.

T Music

Louis Andriessen, *De Staat* (opera).

Dominick Argento, *The Voyage of Edgar Allan Poe* (opera).

Malcolm Arnold, *Philharmonic Concerto*.

Benjamin Britten, String Quartet No. 3.

David Del Tredici, *Final Alice*.

Philip Glass, *Einstein on the Beach* (opera).

Henryk Górecki, Symphony No. 3 ('Symphony of Sorrowful Songs').

Abba, 'Dancing Queen'.

The Eagles, 'Hotel California'.

Four Seasons, 'December 1963 (Oh What a Night)'.

Peter Frampton, *Frampton Comes Alive*.

Elton John and Kiki Dee, 'Don't Go Breaking My Heart'.

Led Zeppelin, *Presence*.

The Ramones, *The Ramones*.

Rolling Stones, *Black and Blue*.

Rod Stewart, 'Tonight's the Night'.

Tom Waits, *Small Change*.

Pop group Abba become Sweden's biggest export earner after Volvo.

u Literature and Drama

Lisa Alther, *Kinflicks*.

Forrest Carter, *The Education of Little Tree*.

Raymond Carver, *Will You Please be Quiet, Please*.

Alex Haley, *Roots*.

Maxine Hong Kingston, *The Woman Warrior*.

Ryu Murakami, *Almost Transparent Blue*.

David Storey, *Saville*.

Patrick White, *A Fringe of Leaves*.

The Diaries of Evelyn Waugh (edited by Michael Davie).

Drama:

David Edgar, *Destiny*.

Barry Humphries, *Housewife — Superstar!*

Alexander Vampilov, *Duck Hunting*.

Britain's National Theatre opens in its new building on the South Bank, London.

v Births and Deaths

Jan 5 John A Costello dies (84).

Jan 8 Zhou Enlai dies (77).

Jan 12 Agatha Christie dies (85).

Jan 23 Paul Robeson dies (77).

Feb 23 L S Lowry dies (88).

March 17 Luchino Visconti dies (69).

March 24 Bernard L Montgomery dies (88).

April 1 Max Ernst dies (84).

April 5 Howard Hughes dies (70).

April 24 Henrik Dam dies (81).

May 11 Alvar Aalto dies (78).

May 26 Martin Heidegger dies (86).

May 31 J L Monod dies (66).

June 6 J Paul Getty dies (83).

July 6 Zhu De dies (90).

Aug ? Fritz Lang dies (85).

Sept 9 Mao Zedong dies (83).

Oct 6 Gilbert Ryle dies (76).

Oct 22 Edward Burra dies (71).

Nov 11 Alexander Calder dies (78).

Nov 19 Man Ray dies (86).

Nov 19 Basil Spence dies (69).

Nov 23 André Malraux dies (75).

Dec 4 Benjamin Britten dies (63).

w Everyday Life

Drought in Britain necessitates water standpipes in the streets of many cities.

x Sport and Recreation

Liverpool wins the English Football League Championship for record ninth time (4 May).

The 21st Olympic Games are held in Montreal, Canada (opened 31 July), boycotted by 20 African nations, Iraq, and Guyana following New Zealand's rugby tour of South

28 peace marches held all over Ireland — 25,000 march in Belfast.

30 (–2 Sept) violence mars the Notting Hill Carnival in London.

J September

9 Mao Zedong, chairman of the Chinese Communist Party, dies.

19 Swedish general election ends 40 years of government by Social Democrats (7 Oct, Thorbjörn Fälldin becomes Conservative prime minister).

19 Ian Smith accepts the principle of majority rule in Rhodesia (now Zimbabwe).

28 British Chancellor of the Exchequer Denis Healey, at Heathrow Airport en route to a conference, turns back to deal with a steep fall in the value of the pound.

29 British government approaches the International Monetary Fund for a $3.9 billion standby loan.

K October

3 Helmut Schmidt's Social Democrat-led coalition returns to power in West Germany with reduced majority.

4 US Agriculture Secretary Earl Butz resigns after making racist comments.

6 military coup in Thailand.

6 US President Ford declares 'there is no Soviet domination of Eastern Europe'.

7 in China, Hua Guofeng succeeds Mao Zedong as chairman; the 'Gang of Four', including Mao's widow, are arrested and denounced for plotting to take power.

11 more colour than black and white TV licences in Britain.

17 Riyadh summit of Arab countries produces ceasefire plan for Lebanon (21, implemented).

28 (–12 Dec) conference on Rhodesia in Geneva, at which the parties led by Joshua Nkomo and Robert Mugabe form the Patriotic Front (26 Nov, tenuous agreement on an independence plan).

29 Chairman Hua repudiates congratulations from Soviet bloc countries.

L November

2 In US presidential election Jimmy Carter, Democrat, defeats Republican President Gerald Ford, with 297 electoral college votes to 241. Popular vote: Carter, 40,828,587; Ford, 39,147,613. Congress retains large Democratic majorities in both Houses of Congress.

11 political parties are legalized in Egypt.

15 Parti Québecois wins large victory in Quebec provincial elections and new prime minister, René Levesque, promises a vote on independence by 1980.

15 Syrian troops take control of Beirut.

26 Catholicism ceases to be the state religion of Italy.

30 British government publishes bill for devolution in Scotland and Wales.

M December

4 Swiss voters reject proposal to cut the working week to 40 hours.

5 Japan's ruling Liberal Democratic Party suffers losses in general election.

5 Jacques Chirac re-founds the Gaullist party as the RPR (Rassemblement pour la République).

5 Jean-Bedel Bokassa proclaims the Central African Republic an Empire.

15 mini-Budget in Britain cuts £2.5 billion from public spending in accordance with terms for the IMF loan.

15 referendum in Spain approves transition to democracy.

20 Rabin coalition in Israel breaks up and calls an election.

20 in USA, death of Richard Daley, mayor of Chicago since 1955.

21 Reg Prentice, minister for overseas development, resigns out of dissatisfaction with British government policy.

24 Takeo Fukuda replaces Takeo Miki as prime minister of Japan.

Africa; Taiwan withdraws after the Canadian government refuses to recognize it as the Republic of China. The USSR wins 49 gold medals; East Germany, 40; USA, 34; West Germany, 10; Japan, 9; Poland, 7; Bulgaria and Cuba, 6 each; Romania, Hungary, Finland, and Sweden, 4 each. Nadia Comaneci of Romania achieves 7 'perfect' scores of 10 in the gymnastics events.

In tennis, Sue Barker is first Briton to win the Women's Singles final in the French Open Championships since 1966.

First women's cricket match is played at Lord's, London (4 Aug).

West Indies cricketer Viv Richards scores a record 1,710 Test runs in a calendar year.

Ɣ Media

Death of Lord Thomson, owner of *The Times* of London and many other newspapers (4 Aug).

US Supreme Court rules in Nebraska Press Association v. Stuart (30 June) against 'gag' orders whereby courts restrict press coverage of criminal trials.

Film:

Assault on Precinct 13 (director, John Carpenter).

Kings of the Road (director, Wim Wenders).

The Man Who Fell to Earth (director, Nicholas Roeg).

Marathon Man (director, John Schlesinger; starring Laurence Olivier and Dustin Hoffman).

Network (director, Sidney Lumet).

The Outlaw Josey Wales (starring Clint Eastwood).

Rocky (director, John G Avildsen; starring Sylvester Stallone).

Sebastiane (director, Derek Jarman).

Television:

In USA, Barbara Walters leaves NBC's *Today* to present ABC's evening news for $1 million per year.

Broadcast in USA of *The Muppet Show*.

New programmes in Britain include: *Bar Mitzvah Boy* (BBC), by Jack Rosenthal; *Bill Brand* series (Thames TV), by Trevor Griffiths; *I, Claudius*; *Nuts in May* (BBC), devised by Mike Leigh.

Indira Gandhi and Zulfikar Ali Bhutto lose power ... Death of
Steven Biko ... Coronation of Bokassa ...

A January

1 US Episcopal Church ordains its first women priests.

3 IMF lends Britain $3.9 billion.

6 Roy Jenkins takes office as president of the EC Commission.

7 advocates of human rights in Czechoslovakia publish 'Charter 77' manifesto, pressing for implementation of rights guarantees given at Helsinki conference in 1975.

17 Gary Gilmore is first person to be executed in USA since 1967.

18 in India, Indira Gandhi calls an election and releases opposition leaders from prison.

20 inauguration of Jimmy Carter as the 39th president of the USA.

21 Carter pardons people who evaded the draft for the Vietnam War.

24 Ian Smith's government rejects British proposals on Rhodesia (now Zimbabwe).

B February

1 Khmer Rouge incursion into Thailand kills 30.

3 Colonel Mengistu Haile Maram becomes leader of Ethiopia after killing eight fellow members of the ruling military council.

9 in Britain, Balcombe Street IRA gang sent to prison for at least 30 years.

16 Archbishop Janani Luwum, a Ugandan human-rights advocate who had denounced abuse of power by security forces, is killed by Amin's forces.

17 bill to nationalize British aircraft manufacture and shipbuilding is declared a 'hybrid bill' because it includes provision to nationalize some ship-repairing companies (2 Mar, discriminatory provisions concerning ship-repair companies are dropped).

19 Anthony Crosland, British foreign secretary, dies in office (21, Dr David Owen appointed).

22 in Britain, guillotine motion on the Devolution Bill fails after 22 Labour Noes and 21 abstentions and the Bill is dropped.

C March

2 Euro-communist leaders in France, Italy and Spain meet in Madrid.

4 earthquake in Romania kills 1,500 and wrecks much of Bucharest.

7 Zulfikar Ali Bhutto claims massive victory in Pakistan's general election.

9 (–11) Hanafi Muslim gunmen seize three buildings in Washington, DC, USA.

11 (–23) widespread violent protests in Pakistan allege that Bhutto's election victory is fraudulent.

12 political parties in Chile banned and censorship tightened.

15 British government nationalizes aircraft and shipbuilding industries.

16 Lebanese Muslim leader Kamal Jumblatt assassinated; violence follows.

20 Congress Party defeated in Indian election and Indira Gandhi loses her seat (24, Morarji Desai becomes prime minister of a Janata Party government).

20 large gains for the Left in French local elections, but conservative Jacques Chirac becomes the first elected mayor of Paris since the 1870s.

23 British Prime Minister James Callaghan and Liberal leader David Steel agree a pact between Labour and Liberals (the 'Lib–Lab Pact') to avoid defeat in a confidence motion.

27 world's worst air disaster in Tenerife kills 582 when two 747 'jumbo jets' collide.

29 British Budget cuts income tax by 2p in return for another year of pay restraint.

D April

7 Baader–Meinhof terrorists assassinate Siegfried Buback, the chief prosecutor of West Germany.

7 in Israel, Itzhak Rabin withdraws as prime ministerial candidate after being investigated for banking violations.

9 Spanish Communist Party is legalized.

20 US President Jimmy Carter proposes a radical energy conservation plan.

21 Zia ur-Rahman inaugurated as president of Bangladesh.

24 in West Germany, Andreas Baader and two other terrorists are imprisoned.

28 in British by-elections, Conservatives gain Ashfield on a 20 per cent swing but fail in more marginal Grimsby.

E May

2 (–13) unsuccessful Protestant general strike in Northern Ireland.

5 in Britain, huge Conservative gains in county elections and a strong National Front vote in Greater London.

11 Peter Jay (son-in-law of Prime Minister Callaghan) appointed British ambassador to USA.

13 in Britain, six members of the Metropolitan Police Obscene Publications Squad are jailed for 3–12 years on corruption charges.

Dworkin's Taking Rights Seriously ... *Latin abolished in Italian middle schools ... First AIDS deaths in New York ... Star Wars ...*

o Politics, Government, Law, and Economy

Roger H Davidson and Walter J Oleszek, *Congress against Itself.*

C Lindblom, *Politics and Markets.*

In South Africa, following riots, Urban Bantu Councils are replaced by Community Councils.

In USA, Richard Nixon, the former US president, gives a series of lengthy interviews to David Frost and discusses Watergate (May), his first major appearance in public since his resignation.

Foundation of the Cato Institute in USA.

Adam Smith Institute founded in London to research and promote free market policies.

Department of Energy established in the USA, intended to develop a plan for energy conservation and development after the 'oil shock'.

Sixth European Community Directive on Value Added Tax (VAT) unifies the organization of VAT throughout the Community (apart from the rates charged).

Gary Gilmore is executed in Utah (17 Jan), the first execution in the USA since 1967.

The US Supreme Court rules (19 April) that spanking school children is not unconstitutional (under the 8th Amendment).

The Unfair Contract Terms Act restricts the legitimacy of exclusion clauses in England and Wales.

Criminal Law Act in Britain allows British magistrates to try more cases.

The number of jury challenges allowed to a defendant in England and Wales is reduced from seven to three.

Conspiracy law overhauled in England and Wales.

Ronald Dworkin, *Taking Rights Seriously.*

The per capita Gross National Product of West Germany exceeds that of the USA for the first time.

The European Community (EC) and the European Free Trade Association (EFTA) agree to free trade in industrial goods (from 1 July).

Minimum wage in US raised to $2.65 an hour (bill signed 1 Nov).

Inauguration of 1,300-km/800-mi trans-Alaska oil pipeline (20 June).

Aerospace and shipbuilding industries are nationalized in Britain.

Publication of Bullock Report on industrial democracy (26 Jan), recommending that British companies with over 2,000 employees should be run by boards comprising equal numbers of employee representatives, ownership representatives, and co-opted directors.

p Society, Education, and Religion

In USA, the 'Hyde Amendment' limits federal funds for abortion (9 Dec).

In USA, First National Women's Conference held in Houston, Texas (18–21 Nov).

Foundation in Britain of the women's publishing house Virago.

Joseph Lason, Roman Catholic bishop of Biloxi, is the first African-American bishop in the USA since the 19th century (installed 6 June).

In Britain, the anti-obscenity campaigner Mary Whitehouse secures the conviction of the British homosexual newspaper *Gay News* for blasphemy.

In USA, Clean Air Act Amendment.

In Italy, Latin is abolished as a compulsory subject in middle schools.

In China, competitive higher education entrance examinations are reinstated.

In Britain, the Department of Education announces plans for the national testing of children in mathematics, reading, and writing (26 Oct).

Foundation of Robinson College, Cambridge, England.

Copies of the Torah (10,000) are shipped from the USA to the Moscow Synagogue, USSR, for the first time since 1917.

In USA, following the decision of the Episcopalian Church to ordain women (1976), a breakaway group founds the Anglican Church in North America, claiming to be true heirs to the Anglican tradition (16 Sept).

The Anglican–Roman Catholic Commission advises that the Anglican Communion should recognize the primacy of the Pope.

John Hick (ed.), *The Myth of God Incarnate.*

q Science, Technology, and Discovery

Bell Telephone Company in the USA transmits television signals over distance of 2.4 km/1.5 mi using fibre optics.

Introduction of the Apple II, the first mass-produced personal computer.

In USA, the human-powered aircraft *Gossamer Condor* makes its first flight.

Dutch scientists discover that the wastes from incinerators are contaminated by dioxins — chemicals thought to cause cancer.

Launches of the US spacecraft *Voyager 1* (5 Sept) and *2* (20 Aug), intended to explore Jupiter and the outer planets of the solar system.

17 Likud bloc wins Israeli elections for the first time (21 June, Menachem Begin becomes prime minister).

23 (–11 June) in the Netherlands, South Moluccan terrorists hijack a train.

25 Labour gains in the Netherlands general election.

30 USA and Cuba agree to exchange diplomats with effect from 1 Sept.

F **June**

4 Fourth constitution of the USSR published, making explicit the leading role of the Communist Party (adopted 7 Oct).

5 (–11) Jubilee week in Britain celebrates 25 years of reign of Queen Elizabeth II.

5 Albert René takes power in coup in the Seychelles.

8 Uganda excluded from Commonwealth conference for human rights abuses.

15 Adolfo Suárez and the Democratic Centre Party win small majority in Spain's first elections since 1936.

16 in USSR, Leonid Brezhnev combines post of head of state with that of Communist Party secretary.

16 Fianna Fáil wins large victory over the governing coalition in Republic of Ireland.

19 The *Daily Mail* publishes a forged document alleging that a minister had nodded through bribe payments by British Leyland.

27 Djibouti gains independence from France.

30 South-East Asia Treaty Organization (founded 1954) is dissolved.

G **July**

5 General Zia ul-Haq takes power in coup in Pakistan.

12 Sir John Kerr to resign as Australian governor general from Dec 1977.

13 electricity blackout in New York leads to chaos and looting.

14 three British MPs criticized by report on the Poulson scandal (22, John Cordle resigns from the Commons).

15 in Britain, a mini-Budget declares 10 per cent pay policy but rescinds half of March's tax cut.

21 (–25) border war between Libya and Egypt.

21 Junius Jayawardene defeats the Bandaranaike government in Sri Lankan elections.

22 'Gang of Four' expelled from the Chinese Communist Party and Deng Xiaoping reinstated as deputy premier.

23 Somali forces invade Ogaden area of Ethiopia.

30 allegations surface that the British security services plotted against Harold Wilson (31 Aug, call for an inquiry rejected).

31 Tamil separatist MPs in Sri Lanka start drafting a new constitution.

H **August**

1 a total ban on alcohol by 1981 is proposed in India.

4 in USA, President Carter creates a Department of Energy.

13 a National Front march in Lewisham, south London, sparks violent scenes.

16 Elvis Presley dies at home in Memphis.

18 11th Chinese Communist Party Congress indicates a swing away from hard-line Maoism towards giving priority to economic improvement.

26 French becomes the only official language of Quebec, Canada.

31 in Rhodesia (now Zimbabwe) Ian Smith's Rhodesian Front wins all 50 white seats in the 66-seat Parliament.

J **September**

1 Cyrus Vance and David Owen propose peace plan for Rhodesia, recommending a large role for Nkomo and Mugabe's Patriotic Front.

5 West German business leader Hans-Martin Schleyer kidnapped (19 Oct, found dead in France).

7 USA and Panama sign the Panama Canal Treaty which returns the canal zone to Panama.

10 (–20) national strike of bakery workers in Britain.

12 South African black leader Steve Biko is killed in police custody.

21 in USA, Bert Lance resigns as Carter's budget director after allegations are made about dubious bank loans.

21 alliance between Socialists and Communists in France breaks up.

26 first Laker 'Skytrain' flight from London to New York, for $102 a ticket.

28 in Britain, Liberal Assembly votes to support the Lib–Lab Pact.

K **October**

1 General Zia cancels the elections due in Pakistan on 18.

8 British MP Reg Prentice defects from Labour to Conservative.

18 German commandos storm a hijacked plane in Mogadishu, Somalia.

18 in West Germany, Andreas Baader and two other terrorists kill themselves in prison.

20 military coup in Thailand.

27 in Britain Jeremy Thorpe, former leader of the Liberal Party, denies involvement in alleged plot to harm Norman Scott.

Several groups of astronomers discover rings around Uranus (March).

Leon Lederman discovers the upsilon sub-atomic particle.

In Cambridge, England, L F Sanger describes the full sequence of bases in a viral DNA.

Tomas G M Hökfelt discovers that most neurons contain not one but several neurotransmitters.

Production of images of human tissues using NMR (nuclear magnetic resonance) scanning.

In New York two homosexual men are diagnosed as having the rare cancer Karposi's sarcoma; they are thought to have been the first victims of AIDS (Acquired Immune Deficiency Syndrome) in New York.

A baby mammoth, 40,000 years old, is found frozen in ice in the USSR.

R **Humanities**

Fergus Millar, *The Emperor in the Roman World, 31 BC–AD 337.*

H C Darby, *Domesday England.*

Lawrence Stone, *The Family, Sex and Marriage, 1500–1800.*

Philippe Ariès, *The Hour of Our Death.*

Simon Schama, *Patriots and Liberators.*

Mark Girouard, *Sweetness and Light: The 'Queen Anne' Movement, 1860–1900.*

Alfred D Chandler, Jr, *The Visible Hand: The Managerial Revolution in American Business.*

David Marquand, *Ramsay MacDonald.*

José Harris, *William Beveridge: A Biography.*

J K Galbraith, *The Age of Anxiety.*

H Orton, S Sanderson, J Widdowson (eds.), *The Linguistic Atlas of England.*

Thomas Kuhn, *The Essential Tension.*

S **Art, Sculpture, Fine Arts, and Architecture**

In Italy, extra Venice Biennale held, devoted to art of dissent and dissidents, especially in Eastern Europe and USSR.

Exhibition of unofficial Soviet art at Institute of Contemporary Art, London.

Duchamp exhibition, Pompidou Centre, Paris.

Sculpture:

Walter De Maria, *Lightening Field.*

Richard Long, *Throwing a Stone Around MacGillycuddy 's Rocks.*

Architecture:

Louis Kahn; Pellechia and Myers, Yale Centre for British Art, New Haven, Connecticut, USA.

Renzo Piano, Richard Rogers, and Gio Franco Franchini, Centre National d'Art et de Culture Georges Pompidou ('Pompidou Centre'), Paris.

T **Music**

William Alwyn, *Miss Julie* (opera).

Elliott Carter, *A Symphony for Three Orchestras.*

Leon Kirchner, *Lily* (opera).

Thea Musgrave, *Mary Queen of Scots* (opera).

Alfred Schnittke, *Requiem.*

Michael Tippett, *The Ice Break* (opera).

In Paris, France, opening of the Institut de recherche et de co-ordination acoustique–musique (IRCAM), a complex of laboratories and electronic studios (in the Pompidou Centre) for experimenting with modern compositional methods; the director is composer and conductor Pierre Boulez.

Annie (musical), by Martin Charnin and Charles Strouse (first performance in New York at the Alvin Theatre, 21 Apr).

Abba, *Arrival*, 'Knowing Me Knowing You'.

The Clash, *The Clash.*

Elvis Costello, *My Aim is True.*

Fleetwood Mac, *Rumours.*

Iggy Pop, *Lust for Life.*

The Sex Pistols, 'God Save the Queen'.

Barbara Streisand, 'Evergreen'.

Television, *Marquee Moon.*

Wings, 'Mull of Kintyre'.

Death of Elvis Presley from drug overdose at his home, Graceland in Memphis, Tennessee, USA (16 Aug).

'Punk' rock music prominent.

U **Literature and Drama**

Bruce Chatwin, *In Patagonia.*

John Cheever, *Falconer.*

Joan Didion, *A Book of Common Prayer.*

Patrick Leigh Fermor, *A Time of Gifts.*

Olivia Manning, *The Fortunes of War* (–1980).

Leonardo Sciascia, *Candido.*

Paul Scott, *Staying On.*

Mario Vargas Llosa, *Aunt Julia and the Scriptwriter.*

Drama:

Steven Berkoff, *East.*

John Murrell, *Waiting for the Parade.*

Peter Nichols, *Privates on Parade.*

Kid Stakas, *The Doll Trilogy.*

The Lindsay Kemp Company, *Flowers and Salome.*

Pieter-Dirk Uys, *Paradise is Closing Down.*

V **Births and Deaths**

Jan 14 Anthony Eden dies (79).

Feb 4 Ludwig Erhard dies (80).

27 (–11 Nov) unofficial action by British power station workers causes sporadic blackouts.

L **November**

1 USA quits the International Labour Organization, but Carter raises the minimum wage.

4 UN imposes strict arms embargo on South Africa.

8 Ed Koch wins mayoral election in New York City.

9 President Sadat of Egypt makes peace overtures to Israel, alienating other Arab states and his own foreign minister but winning acceptance from Israeli Prime Minister Begin.

11 Anti-Nazi League set up to combat the apparent growth of the National Front in Britain.

14 British firemen go on strike (–12 Jan 1978).

17 in Britain, publication of Third Report of Royal Commission on the Distribution of Income and Wealth.

19 (–21) Egyptian President Sadat visits Israel and addresses the Knesset.

24 Ian Smith proposes a new Rhodesian constitution with equal votes for blacks and whites.

30 ruling National Party wins record majority in South African elections.

M **December**

2 (–4) Tripoli conference of Arab states condemns Egypt.

4 Bophuthatswana, a black homeland in South Africa, becomes nominally independent.

4 coronation of Emperor Bokassa of Central Africa.

5 strike of US coal miners begins (8, violent incidents in Ohio and Utah).

10 Fraser government wins another large majority in Australian federal elections.

16 opening of London Underground extension to Heathrow Airport, making Heathrow the first airport in the world to be connected to a city rail system.

24 (–25) Israeli Prime Minister Begin visits Egypt.

31 violent deaths in Northern Ireland fall sharply in 1977, with 111 killed compared with 297 in 1976.

Year of three Popes ... Camp David agreement ... Murder of former Italian prime minister ...

A **January**

3 Indian Congress Party splits (from 25 Feb the rump led by Indira Gandhi is called the Congress (I) Party).

6 picket killed in violent incidents during US coal mines dispute.

12 Andreotti government collapses in Italy.

16 (–18) talks in Jerusalem between Egypt and Israel.

18 European Court of Human Rights clears British government of torture but finds it guilty of inhuman and degrading treatment of prisoners in Northern Ireland.

23 (–7 Feb) general strike in Nicaragua.

23 Sweden bans aerosol sprays because of damage to environment, the first country to do so.

24 the Superior Court in Quebec rejects important parts of the language law enforcing use of French.

25 amendment passed to Scottish and Welsh devolution bill requiring approval of 40 per

April 11 Jacques Prévert dies (77).
June 16 Werner von Braun dies (65).
July 2 Vladimir Nabokov dies (78).
Aug 3 Makarios III dies (63).
Aug 16 Elvis Presley dies (42).
Aug 23 Naum Gabo dies (87).
Sept 4 E F Schumacher dies (66).
Sept 12 Robert Lowell dies (60).
Sept 16 Maria Callas dies (53).
Oct 14 Bing Crosby dies (73).
Nov 18 Kurt von Schuschnigg dies (79).
Dec 25 Charlie Chaplin dies (88).

w Everyday Life

In Britain, British Gas completes conversion of 40 million appliances from coal gas to North Sea gas.

Skateboarding popular in Britain; Prime Minister James Callaghan is seen riding a board and some local authorities build skateboard parks (soon disused when the craze wanes).

x Sport and Recreation

In cricket, Australia beats England by 45 runs in the Centenary Test Match at Melbourne, Australia, exactly the same result as in the first match (12–17 March).

In Britain Red Rum, ridden by Tommy Stack, wins its third Grand National horse race (2 April).

Virginia Wade is first British woman since 1969 to win a Singles title at the Wimbledon tennis tournament, London (1 July).

In cricket, England regains the Ashes (15 Aug).

After failing to win the rights to televise Test cricket in Australia, Kerry Packer, owner of Channel Nine Television, signs up 66 leading players to participate in his own series of matches; all are barred from Test cricket.

y Media

In Britain, circulation of the *Sun* overtakes that of the *Daily Mirror*.

In Britain, Max Aitken sells the *Express* group of newspapers to the business conglomerate Trafalgar House (30 June).

Australian newspaper-owner Rupert Murdoch acquires the *New York Post* (Nov).

Film:

Annie Hall (director, Woody Allen).
Close Encounters of the Third Kind (director, Steven Spielberg).
The Getting of Wisdom (director, Bruce Beresford).
The Last Waltz (starring Bob Dylan and The Band).
Padre Padrone (directors, Paolo and Vittorio Taviani).
Providence (director, Alain Resnais).
Saturday Night Fever (starring John Travolta).
Star Wars (director, George Lucas).
That Obscure Object of Desire (director, Luis Buñuel).

Radio:

In Britain, last edition of BBC Radio's *The Navy Lark* (running since 1959).

Television:

Broadcast in Japan of *A Wandering Life*.
Broadcast in USA of *Roots*, based on the book by Alex Haley (1976).
New programmes in Britain include: *Abigail's Party* (BBC), by Mike Leigh; *Professional Foul* by Tom Stoppard.
Scum, by Roy Minton, made by the BBC and set in a borstal (secure home for young offenders), is banned from transmission until 1983.

Birth of first 'test-tube baby' ... Cambridge sinks in English university boat race ... Advent of Dallas ...

o Politics, Government, Law, and Economy

Chapman Pincher, *Inside Story*.

In China, the late Mao Zedong's collection of thoughts, known as the 'Little Red Book', is denounced (29 Oct).

In USA, foundation of the Manhattan Institute for Policy Research.

In USA, the Government Ethics Law (signed 26 Oct) provides an absolute protection for civil servants bringing evidence of corruption or mismanagement to the attention of Congress or the people.

Radio broadcasts of the British Parliament begin (3 April).

The European Court affirms the superiority of Community law over the national law of member states.

In USA, Cleveland, Ohio, is the first US city to default on debts since the Depression (16 Dec).

cent of electorate in consultative referenda for devolution to take effect.

30 in Britain, Conservative leader Margaret Thatcher, in an interview, refers to the legitimate fears of white Britons concerning 'swamping' by immigrants.

B **February**

1 Start of 'Information scandal' or 'Muldergate' in South Africa when the auditor general reports to Parliament that the Department of Information had made unauthorized expenditure in attempt to counter the country's negative image abroad; Justice Anton Mostert is appointed to undertake inquiry.

3 EC and China conclude their first trade agreement.

4 Junius Jayawardene becomes president of Sri Lanka.

14 President Carter of USA proposes the sale of 50 jet fighters to Egypt.

16 British House of Commons passes Bill establishing direct elections to European Assembly.

C **March**

3 In Rhodesia Ian Smith and three black leaders sign agreement for a power-sharing government and eventual majority rule, but Mugabe and Nkomo's Patriotic Front is excluded.

5 new Chinese constitution affirms the rule of law.

11 in Italy, in the 'Historic Compromise', a new government led by Giulio Andreotti is installed with the support of the Communist Party.

12 (and 19) National Assembly elections in France return the Right to power with diminished majority.

14 Israel invades southern Lebanon.

16 *Amoco Cadiz* oil tanker runs aground off Brittany, France.

16 Red Brigade terrorists kidnap former Italian Prime Minister Aldo Moro.

18 death sentence passed on former Pakistani Prime Minister Zulfikar Ali Bhutto.

22 first United Nations 'UNIFIL' ('UN Interim Force in Lebanon') troops arrive in Lebanon.

25 US coal-miners' strike ends.

D **April**

6 US mandatory retirement age raised from 65 to 70.

7 German Chancellor Schmidt proposes European currency stabilization plan; later enacted as the European Monetary System (EMS).

18 Panama Canal Treaty ratified by the US Senate.

25 European Court of Human Rights condemns judicial birching in Isle of Man as degrading.

27 Communist and Islamic forces take power in Afghanistan.

E **May**

1 Britain's first May Day public holiday.

8 in Britain, opposition amendment to Budget passed in Commons, reducing income tax by 1p (10, amendment is carried against the government to raise the threshold for higher tax rates from £7,000 to £8,000).

8 in South Africa, Prime Minister Vorster accepts responsibility for unauthorized expenditure of Information Department.

9 Aldo Moro found dead in Rome after Italian government refuses to make concessions to his captors.

10 nine people die in Islamic fundamentalist riots in Qom, Iran.

16 Rhodesian forces kill 94 at a black political meeting.

18 Yuri Orlov, Soviet human-rights campaigner, is sentenced to seven years in a labour camp.

25 David Steel announces end of the Lib–Lab Pact.

F **June**

6 in California, USA, 'Proposition 13' to cut local property taxes is passed in a referendum by large majority.

13 Romanian President Nicolae Ceauşescu visits Britain, staying with the Queen at Buckingham Palace.

13 Israelis pull out of south Lebanon but fighting erupts in the north.

15 President Leone of Italy resigns after financial scandal (8 July, Alessandro Pertini sworn in).

15 President Vorster abolishes South Africa's Information Department. Information Secretary Eschel Rhoodie resigns.

24 South Yemeni parcel bomb kills president of North Yemen.

26 the president of South Yemen is assassinated, by the faction who murdered the president of North Yemen.

G **July**

5 Coup in Ghana replaces General Acheampong with his deputy, Fred Akuffo.

7 Solomon Islands gain independence.

14 Soviet dissident Anatoly Shcharansky sentenced to 13 years in jail.

21 British Chancellor Denis Healey announces a 5-per cent guideline for wage increases in the next year.

24 in Britain, George Davis, released from prison after a campaign in 1975–76, is sentenced to 15 years for armed robbery

Ford Motors fined $125 million in California, USA, for fitting faulty fuel tanks (7 Feb).

First meeting held, in Bonn, West Germany, of the 'Group of Seven' largest capitalist economic powers (USA, Canada, Japan, West Germany, France, Italy, Britain).

Deregulation of the airline industry in the USA.

P Society, Education, and Religion

In USA, in Regents of the University of California v. Bakke, the Supreme Court rules (28 June) in favour of 'positive discrimination' for the admission of disadvantaged applicants to colleges (African-Americans and Hispanics), but that the University of California Medical School was wrong to reject the white applicant Allan Bakke.

At University of Chicago, USA, Hannah Gray is inaugurated as the first woman president of a US university (6 Oct).

In USA, a man is found not guilty of raping his wife (27 Dec), in what was seen as a test case on relations between the sexes.

The mandatory retiring age for most people in the USA is raised from 65 to 70 (bill signed 6 April).

In China, after the fall of the 'Gang of Four', a new constitution declares that education should be developed to raise the cultural and scientific level of the whole nation; a new standardized curriculum and textbooks are produced, marking a return to a more academic curriculum.

In Pakistan, President Zia ul-Haq orders that education should place greater emphasis upon loyalty to Islam.

New core curriculum at Harvard University, USA, is designed to ensure 'literacy in the major forms of intellectual discourse' (approved 2 May).

In Britain, publication of the Warnock Report on children with special educational needs.

The Waddell Committee recommends a new examination in England and Wales to replace the 'O' level and the Certificate of Secondary Education (CSE).

Deaths of Pope Paul VI (6 Aug) and his successor John Paul I (26 Sept); John Paul's successor, John Paul II (Karol Wojtyla, Archbishop of Kraków), is the first non-Italian Pope since 1522.

General Synod of the Church of England rejects the ordination of women to the priesthood and episcopate (8 Nov).

Jürgen Moltmann, *The Church in the Power of the Spirit*.

Q Science, Technology, and Discovery

Konica introduces the first camera with automatic focus.

USA bans use of chlorofluorocarbons (CFCs) as spray propellants in order to reduce damage to the ozone layer.

Launch of US satellite *Seasat 1* to measure temperature of sea surfaces, wind and wave movements, ocean currents, and icebergs.

Two Soviet cosmonauts spend a record 139 days and 14 hours in space (15 June–2 Nov).

Launch of US space probes *Pioneer 1* (20 May) and *2* (8 Aug); they go into orbit around Venus on 4 and 9 Dec.

Soviet spacecraft *Venera 11* and *12* soft-land on Venus.

Discovery of Charon, a moon orbiting Pluto.

W Paul measures the life of a neutron — about 15 minutes.

In USA, W Gibson and associates at Harvard make bacteria manufacture insulin in response to instructions from synthetic DNA.

In Britain, birth of the first 'test tube' baby (created by in vitro fertilization), Louise Brown (25 July).

Cyclosporin A introduced as immunosuppressant drug in organ transplant surgery.

R Humanities

Footprints of a hominid, made 3.6 million years ago, found near Laetoli, Tanzania.

Excavation of tomb of Philip of Macedon (died 336 BC) at Vergina in northern Greece.

Discovery of the foundations of the Aztec great temple under the centre of Mexico City.

Geoffrey Barraclough (ed.), *The Times Atlas of World History*.

Richard Bradley, *The Prehistoric Settlement of Britain*.

Alan Macfarlane, *The Origins of English Individualism*.

Mark Girouard, *Life in the English Country House*.

J M Roberts, *The French Revolution*.

Encyclopedia of American Foreign Policy.

Paul Thompson, *The Voice of the Past: Oral History*.

Arthur Schlesinger, Jr, *Robert Kennedy and his Times*.

Daniel Dennett, *Brainstorms*.

Nelson Goodman, *Ways of Worldmaking*.

S Art, Sculpture, Fine Arts, and Architecture

'Paris-Berlin', exhibition at the Pompidou Centre, Paris.

'The State of British Art', Institute of Contemporary Art, London.

Painting, etc:

Sandro Chia, *Perpetual Motion*.

after being caught in the act and pleading guilty.

26 in Britain, the TUC resolves not to support Chancellor Healey's 5-per-cent pay policy.

31 Queen Elizabeth gives Royal Assent to Devolution bill for Scotland and Wales.

H August

3 De Lorean Motor Company announces intention to build a factory in Belfast, Northern Ireland, for production of sports cars.

4 former Liberal Party Leader Jeremy Thorpe and three others are charged with conspiracy to murder Norman Scott between 1968 and 1977. Thorpe is also charged with incitement to murder.

6 death of Pope Paul VI.

8 Rhodesian government announces intention to scrap racial discrimination in public places.

12 Japan and China sign Treaty of Peace and Friendship.

22 (–24) in Nicaragua, Sandinista guerrillas seize the parliament building in Managua.

22 death of President Kenyatta of Kenya (10 Oct, succeeded by Daniel arap Moi).

25 Spain abolishes the death penalty in peacetime.

26 Albino Luciani, Patriarch of Venice, is elected Pope; he takes the name John Paul I.

27 new Iranian government of Sharif-Emami lifts ban on political parties.

J September

5 (–17) in USA, summit between Carter, Sadat, and Begin at Camp David, Maryland; concludes with a 'framework' peace treaty ending 30 years of hostility between Israel and Egypt.

7 British Prime Minister James Callaghan makes surprise announcement that there will be no general election in 1978.

8 in Iran, demonstrations in Tehran lead to 95 deaths.

11 exiled Bulgarian author Georgi Markov dies in London (2 Jan 1979, inquest finds that he was unlawfully killed by the injection of a poison pellet through an umbrella).

15 Spanish parliament recognizes Basque demand for autonomy.

16 earthquake in Iran kills 21,000.

16 Rhodesian executive council starts conscripting blacks to fight the Patriotic Front.

19 Bingham Report reveals that BP and Shell had broken oil sanctions against Rhodesia (now Zimbabwe) and that British ministers concealed knowledge of this.

20 B J Vorster resigns as prime minister of South Africa, on grounds of ill health (29, P W Botha replaces him. 10 Oct, Vorster becomes president).

21 in Nigeria the outgoing military regime promulgates a new constitution based on that of the USA.

28 sudden death of Pope John Paul I.

28 Camp David accord approved by the Israeli parliament, the Knesset.

30 Tuvalu, formerly the Ellice Islands, gains independence.

K October

2 British Labour Party conference votes against the Labour government's pay policy.

4 renewed battles in Beirut kill 500.

5 Swedish centre-right government collapses over nuclear power (13, replaced by a minority Liberal government under Ola Ullsten).

10 British unions and government fail to resolve their differences on pay during talks at 10 Downing Street.

12 border clashes between Uganda and Tanzania caused by President Amin's expansionist claims on Tanzanian territory.

16 Karol Wojtyla, Archbishop of Cracow, is elected Pope; he takes the name John Paul II.

24 US airline industry deregulated.

26 World Health Organization announces that smallpox has been eradicated except for laboratory stocks.

29 in South Africa a newspaper reveals that the former Information Department funded the *Citizen*, a pro-government English-language newspaper.

31 Iranian oil workers commence strike action.

L November

1 US dollar rises sharply after President Carter announces a major support plan, including higher interest rates.

2 in South Africa Justice Mostert, against request from Prime Minister Botha for confidentiality, releases information from his inquiry into the former Information Department (7, former Information Minister C P 'Connie' Mulder resigns from cabinet; Botha dismisses Mostert and appoints Justice Rudolf Erasmus to conduct new inquiry).

3 Dominica gains independence.

5 referendum in Austria stops Zwentersdorf nuclear power station from being switched on.

6 military government appointed in Iran.

Anselm Keifer, *Untitled.*

Sculpture:
Christo, *Wrapped Walkways.*
Barry Flanagan, *As Night.*

Architecture:
Norman Foster, Sainsbury Centre, University of East Anglia, England.
I M Pei, extension to the National Gallery, Washington, DC, USA.

T Music
György Ligeti, *Le Grand Macabre* (opera).
Andrzej Panufnik, *Metasinfonia.*
Krzysztof Penderecki, *Paradise Lost* (opera).
Aribert Reimann: *Lear* (opera).
Evita (musical), text by Tim Rice, music by Andrew Lloyd Webber (first performed at the Prince Edward Theatre, London, 21 June).
Abba, *The Album.*
Blondie, *Parallel Lines.*
Kate Bush, 'Wuthering Heights', *The Kick Inside.*
Chic, 'Le Freak'.
Donna Summer, 'McArthur Park'.
Talking Heads, *More Songs About Buildings and Food.*
Disco music popular: the Bee Gees' *Saturday Night Fever* becomes the biggest-selling soundtrack album yet.
The film of *Grease* (starring John Travolta and Olivia Newton-John) produces the best-selling singles 'You're The One That I Want' and 'Summer Nights'.

U Literature and Drama
J G Farrell, *The Singapore Grip.*
Graham Greene, *The Human Factor.*
John Irving, *The World According to Garp.*
Armıstead Maupin, *Tales of the City.*
Iris Murdoch, *The Sea The Sea.*
Yuri Trifonov, *Starik.*

Drama:
Brian Clark, *Whose Life is it Anyway.*
David Hare, *Plenty.*
Harold Pinter, *Betrayal.*

V Births and Deaths
Jan 13 Hubert Humphrey dies (66).
Jan 14 Kurt Gödel dies (71).
Feb 11 James B Conant dies (84).
April 14 F R Leavis dies (82).
May 15 Robert Menzies dies (83).
Aug 6 Pope Paul VI dies (80).
Aug 22 Jomo Kenyatta dies (89).
Sept 17 Willy Messerschmitt dies (80).
Nov 15 Margaret Mead dies (76).
Nov 18 Giorgio de Chirico dies (90).
Dec 8 Golda Meir dies (80).
Dec 14 Salvador de Madariaga dies (92).

W Everyday Life
Disco culture at its height.
Sneakers (training shoes) account for 50 per cent of shoe sales in the USA.
In Britain, divorce of Princess Margaret from the Earl of Snowdon (24 May).

X Sport and Recreation
In cricket, New Zealand beats England in a Test match for the first time, after 48 years of matches (15 Feb).
Leon Spinks beats Muhammad Ali on points to win the World Heavyweight boxing title (15 Feb); seven months later, Ali regains the World Boxing Association version of the title, beating Spinks on points in New Orleans (17 Sept); meanwhile Larry Holmes beats Ken Norton on points in Las Vegas (10 June) and wins the World Boxing Council crown.
The Cambridge boat sinks in the English University Boat Race (25 March).
Naomi James completes her solo round-the-world voyage (8 June), taking two days fewer than Sir Francis Chichester in 1967.
Host nation Argentina wins the soccer World Cup, beating the Netherlands in the Final 3–1 (25 June).
European golfers are allowed to compete alongside British and Irish players in Ryder Cup matches against the USA, in an attempt to produce a more even contest.

Y Media
150th anniversary of British weekly the *Spectator.*
In USA, re-launch of *Life* magazine (Oct).
Launch of the *Daily Star* (2 Nov), a new British tabloid newspaper.
In Britain, suspension of *The Times*, *The Sunday Times*, and *Times* supplements as a result of an industrial dispute (30 Nov).

Film:
The Deer Hunter (director, Michael Cimino; starring Robert de Niro).
The Marriage of Maria Braun (director, Rainer Werner Fassbinder).
Martin (director, George Romero).
Midnight Express (director, Alan Parker).
Superman (director, Richard Donner; starring Christopher Reeve).

Television:
Broadcast in USA of *Dallas.*
New programmes in Britain include: *All Creatures Great and Small* (BBC); *The BBC Television Shakespeare* (–1985); *Lillie* (LWT), starring Francesca Annis as Lillie Langtry; *The Mayor of Casterbridge*

7 US mid-term elections produce small Democratic losses in Congress.
7 (–17 Dec) bakery workers' strike in Britain.
8 Uganda drops territorial claim on Tanzania.
8 in India, Indira Gandhi returns to the Lok Sabha in a by-election.
19 in Guyana 911 die in mass suicide at the People's Temple in the Jim Jones cult centre.
20 (–13 Dec) in Britain, committal hearings in Minehead concerning charges against Jeremy Thorpe and others produce lurid publicity.
22 Ford workers in Britain accept 17-per-cent pay offer, a flagrant breach of the 5-per-cent pay policy.
25 Robert Muldoon returns to power in New Zealand with much reduced majority for the National Party.
27 Japanese Prime Minister Takeo Fukuda resigns (7 Dec, succeeded by Masayoshi Ohira).
27 Tanzanian troops move into Ugandan border areas.
30 in Britain, Times Newspapers suspend publication of their papers indefinitely because of industrial dispute.

M **December**
5 In South Africa the Erasmus Commission issues report on the Information scandal, but ignores allegations that President Vorster knew about the unauthorized expenditure.
6 James Callaghan announces that Britain will not join the new European Monetary System.
13 government commercial sanctions against Ford for breaching the pay policy voted down in British Parliament.
15 USA and China agree to normalize diplomatic relations (effective from 1 Jan 1979).
17 OPEC decides to raise oil prices by 14.5 per cent by the end of 1979.
19 (–26) in India, Indira Gandhi is expelled from the Lok Sabha for contempt and imprisoned.
25 Vietnam begins full-scale invasion of Cambodia.
30 committee of US House of Representatives concludes that a second gunman was involved in the assassination of President John F Kennedy in 1963.
31 government of Iran admits that nearly all production and export of oil has been halted.

Revolution in Iran ... 'Winter of discontent' in Britain ...
USSR invades Afghanistan ...

A **January**
1 USA and China open diplomatic relations.
3 (–7 Feb) lorry drivers go on strike in Britain, causing widespread interruption of supplies.
4 the shah of Iran appoints Dr Shakpur Bakhtiar prime minister as concession to popular discontent.
7 Vietnamese troops and Cambodian rebels capture Phnom Penh and oust the Khmer Rouge regime.
10 in Britain most petrol tanker drivers return to work.
11 (–14) state of emergency in Northern Ireland because of tanker strike.
16 the shah of Iran and his family flee Iran for Egypt.
20 Tanzanian troops invade Uganda after border clashes.
22 in Britain one-day strike of public sector workers closes schools and hospitals (–6 Mar, continuing industrial action by local authority workers such as dustmen and grave-diggers; –20 Mar, health service workers take industrial action; the *Sun* labels the surge of strikes 'the winter of discontent', an allusion to Shakespeare's 'Now is the winter of our discontent...').
26 (–29) Islamic revolutionary violence in Tehran, Iran.
31 in Italy the Andreotti government resigns, ending the 'Historic Compromise' between Christian Democrats and Communists.

B **February**
1 Ayatollah Khomeini returns to Iran from exile in Paris (since 1964).
8 USA cuts off aid to Somoza regime in Nicaragua for human-rights violations.
12 Dr Bakhtiar flees Iran; a Revolutionary Council loyal to Ayatollah Khomeini is created, with Mehdi Bazargan as designate prime minister.
14 the US Embassy in Tehran, Iran, is briefly seized by protesters.

(BBC), adapted by Dennis Potter and starring Alan Bates; *Pennies from Heaven* (BBC), by Dennis Potter; *The South Bank Show* (LWT), an arts programme presented by Melvyn Bragg.

In Britain, the BBC broadcasts the 667th and final episode of *Z Cars*, and the final edition of *The Black and White Minstrel Show*.

Accident at Three Mile Island nuclear plant ... Possible discovery of 'black hole' ... M T Clanchy's Memory to Written Record ...

o **Politics, Government, Law, and Economy**

Andrew Boyle, *The Climate of Treason.*

British House of Commons establishes new structure of 14 Select Committees to examine the expenditure, administration and policies of principal government departments.

France imposes a prohibitive tariff on British lamb exports in defiance of the European Court.

P Atiyah, *The Rise and Fall of Freedom of Contract.*

Oil prices double under the impact of the Iranian revolution.

European Monetary System (EMS) and its Exchange Rate Mechanism (ERM) are established to regulate European currency fluctuations.

Successful completion (12 April) of the Tokyo Round of negotiations of the General Agreement on Tariffs and Trade (GATT).

In USA, the federal government saves the

Chrysler motor company from bankruptcy with a loan guarantee for $1.5 billion.

P **Society, Education, and Religion**

In USA, in United Steelworkers of America v. Weber, the US Supreme Court rules that companies can give preference in training for better jobs to African-Americans provided that white workers are not debarred and only until the racial imbalance of a workforce has been corrected (27 June).

In Britain, the Williams Report on obscenity (published 28 Nov) recommends liberalization of controls on content but increased restriction on displays in shops.

Abortion is legalized in France.

Christopher Lasch, *The Culture of Narcissism.*

In USA, creation of a Department of Education, administered by a secretary with cabinet rank.

In England and Wales, the Education Act repeals the comprehensive school legislation of 1976, freeing local authorities

14 British government and TUC sign a Concordat to end the 'winter of discontent' strikes.

17 (–5 Mar) China makes punitive incursions into Vietnam.

19 President Zia ur-Rahman's Bangladesh Nationalist Party wins elections in Bangladesh.

20 in Northern Ireland, 11 members of a loyalist gang known as the 'Shankill butchers' are sentenced for 19 sectarian murders in Belfast following a sensational trial.

22 St Lucia becomes independent.

23 (–16 Mar) war between North and South Yemen.

23 Rhodesian planes attack rebel camps in Zambia.

c March

1 Referendums on devolution in Scotland and Wales; devolution is approved in Scotland by 51.6 per cent of voters but those approving fall short of the required 40 per cent of the electorate (32.9 per cent of electorate voted Yes, 30.8 per cent No, 36.3 per cent did not vote). 79.8 per cent of voters in Wales reject devolution (11.9 per cent voted Yes, 46.9 per cent No, 41.2 per cent did not vote).

7 in Britain, the Callaghan government establishes the Clegg Commission on Comparability to examine the grievances of public sector workers.

10 general strike begins in Nicaragua.

12 New Jewel movement under Maurice Bishop seizes power in Grenada.

13 European Monetary System (EMS) becomes operational.

15 civilian government committed to democratization takes office in Brazil.

15 CENTO defence pact collapses.

22 IRA assassinates British ambassador to the Netherlands in The Hague.

26 Egypt and Israel sign peace treaty in Washington, DC, USA.

27 Hafizullah Amin becomes prime minister of Afghanistan.

28 British Labour government loses a motion of no confidence by 310–311 in the House of Commons. Prime Minister Callaghan calls a general election.

30 in Britain, bomb planted by the Irish National Liberation Army kills Airey Neave, Conservative spokesman on Northern Ireland, in the House of Commons car park.

31 Malta cuts military links with Britain.

d April

1 Following a referendum Iran is declared an Islamic Republic by Ayatollah Khomeini.

2 publication of interim Erasmus report on the Information scandal in South Africa which clears serving politicians.

4 Zulfikar Ali Bhutto is executed in Pakistan for conspiracy to murder.

7 former Prime Minister Hovaida becomes a victim of a purge of the Shah's former officials in Iran.

10 (–20) multi-racial elections held in Rhodesia.

11 Kampala falls to Tanzanian and rebel forces. Idi Amin flees (13, Yusufu Lule is inaugurated as president of Uganda).

16 in South Africa Connie Mulder is expelled from the National Party following the information scandal.

18 100 children killed in demonstration against school uniforms in Bangui, Central African Empire.

23 violence at National Front election meeting in Southall, London, leaves dead a teacher, Blair Peach.

e May

2 Riots in Longwy, France, over proposed closure of steel plants.

3 Conservatives win British general election with 339 seats. Labour wins 269, Liberals, 11, Unionists, 12, Scottish Nationalists, 2, Plaid Cymru 2 (Conservatives win 43.9 per cent of votes cast, Labour, 36.9 per cent, Liberals, 13.8 per cent).

4 Margaret Thatcher becomes Britain's first woman prime minister.

5 rebel guerrillas in El Salvador capture the French, Venezuelan, and Costa Rican embassies (last embassy recaptured 1 June).

8 (–22 June) trial of former Liberal leader Jeremy Thorpe and three others for alleged plot to murder Norman Scott; all are acquitted, but Thorpe never resumes his political career.

10 in USA, President Carter's plan for petrol rationing is rejected by Congress.

15 British government abolishes Prices Commission and price controls.

22 in Canada, Pierre Trudeau's Liberal government loses the general election. Joe Clark is appointed prime minister of Progressive Conservative minority government.

25 crash of DC-10 aircraft at Chicago kills 273 and causes the grounding of DC-10s in USA 29 May–13 July.

28 Greece signs Treaty of Accession to EC, for entry in 1981.

from compulsion to introduce comprehensive education.

The Inner London Education Authority votes (18 Sept) to ban corporal punishment from its 1,000 schools by Feb 1981.

Overseas students at British universities are required to pay the full cost of their courses.

Foundation of Green College, Oxford, England.

Michael Rutter and others, *Fifteen Thousand Hours*.

Mother Teresa awarded the Nobel Peace Prize.

Pope John Paul II makes the first ever papal visit to Ireland (29 Sept–1 Oct).

Robert Runcie appointed to replace Donald Coggan as Archbishop of Canterbury (appointment announced 7 Sept; Runcie enthroned 25 March 1980).

General Synod of the Church of England refuses to allow women priests ordained abroad to celebrate holy communion.

Publication of the New International Version of the Bible.

Q Science, Technology, and Discovery

Major accident at the Three Mile Island nuclear power station in Pennsylvania, USA (29 March).

The Philips Company launches the LaserVision video disc system.

First spreadsheet programme for personal computers — expands business use of PCs.

Matsushita in Japan develops a pocket-size flat-screen TV set.

The human-powered aircraft *Gossamer Albatross* crosses the English Channel.

First successful launch of the European Space Agency's *Ariane* rocket (4 Dec).

The US space station *Skylab 1* falls back to Earth after travelling 140 million km (87 million mi) in orbit since 1973.

US space probes *Voyager 1* and *2* explore the moons of Jupiter; *Voyager 1* discovers a ring around Jupiter and two moons (the 15th and 16th).

US space probe *Pioneer 11* travels through the rings of Saturn, which are found to be made of ice-covered rocks.

Soviet cosmonauts Vladimir A Lyakhov and Valery V Ryumin set new record for time spent in space of 175 days, 36 mins; (25 Feb–19 Aug).

The satellite *HEAO2* (*High Energy Astronomy Observatory* — later renamed the Einstein Observatory) discovers a possible 'black hole' in the constellation Cygnus X-1.

US astronomers John A Eddy and Aram A Boornazian announce that the Sun is shrinking at a rate of 1.5 m/5 ft per hour.

Physicists in Hamburg at DESY (Deutsches Elektron Synchroton) observe gluons — particles that carry the strong nuclear force which holds quarks together.

Inauguration of European Molecular Biology Laboratory at Heidelberg, West Germany.

The US Surgeon-general publishes a 1,200-page report confirming that cigarette smoking causes cancer and is linked with numerous other diseases.

R Humanities

M T Clanchy, *From Memory to Written Record: England 1066–1307*.

Charles Phythian-Adams, *Desolation of a City: Coventry and the Urban Crisis of the Late Middle Ages*.

Robert Dallek, *Franklin D Roosevelt and American Foreign Policy, 1932–1945*.

F H Hinsley et al., *British Intelligence in the Second World War* (–1990).

E H Gombrich, *The Sense of Order: A Study in the Psychology of Decorative Art*.

Jean-François Lyotard, *The Post-modern Condition*.

Thomas Nagel, *Mortal Questions*.

S Art, Sculpture, Fine Arts, and Architecture

French government accepts large gift of works from the Picasso estate (museum to be established in Paris).

'Paris–Moscou', exhibition at Pompidou Centre, Paris.

Velázquez, portrait of *Juan de Pareja* sold at Christie's for $5.5 million, the most expensive painting bought at auction.

Jennifer Durrant is first woman artist in residence at Oxford University, England.

Rome art critic Achille Bonito Olivia coins term 'Transavanguardia' to denote painters who had gone beyond modernism and had established a broader attitude to art.

Painting, etc:
Philip Guston, *The Rug*.

Sculpture:
Joseph Beuys retrospective at Guggenheim Museum, New York, installed by the artist.

Judy Chicago, *The Dinner Party*.

Architecture:
B E P Akitek (with I M Pei as consultant), Overseas Chinese Banking Corporation Headquarters, Singapore.

Aldo Rossi, Teatro del Mondo, Venice.

T Music

Alban Berg, *Lulu* (opera), first complete performance (with the score of Act 3 orchestrated by Friedrich Cerha).

John Cage, *Roaratorio*.

Jacob Druckman, *Aureole*.

F **June**

1 Bishop Abel Muzorewa, a black leader, is appointed prime minister of the renamed Zimbabwe Rhodesia.

3 (–4) Italian general election, in which the Communist Party loses ground.

4 President Vorster of South Africa resigns after the final Erasmus Report shows that he knew about illegal activities at Information Department.

4 Flight-Lieutenant Jerry Rawlings leads military coup that deposes President F Akuffo of Ghana.

7 (and 10) first direct elections for the European Parliament; low turnout and results influenced by popularity of national governments; in Britain the Conservatives win 60 seats, Labour, 17, Liberals, 0 (Conservatives win 48.4 per cent of votes cast, Labour, 31.6 per cent, and Liberals, 12.6 per cent); the Scottish Nationalists win 1 seat, the Ulster Unionists, 3.

12 British Chancellor Geoffrey Howe's first budget reduces income tax and increases VAT.

14 (–26) in Nicaragua, Sandinista rebels close in on the capital Managua.

15 (–18) President Carter of USA and Leonid Brezhnev of USSR hold summit in Vienna, Austria, ending with signing of the SALT II treaty limiting nuclear weapons.

G **July**

11 In India, the Janata Party loses overall control of the Lok Sabha through defections.

15 Morarji Desai resigns as Indian prime minister (28, replaced by Charan Singh).

16 Saddam Hussein becomes president of Iraq.

16 in USA, President Carter proposes radical measures to deal with the energy crisis and speaks of 'a crisis ... of our national will'.

17 Anastasio Somoza, dictator of Nicaragua, flees to the USA.

19 in Nicaragua, Sandinista rebels take Managua and set up a new government.

29 Argentina and Britain re-establish diplomatic relations at ambassadorial level.

H **August**

1 British government accepts Clegg Commission's recommendation of large pay rises for some public sector workers.

1 (–8) Commonwealth Conference in Lusaka proposes a conference to settle the Zimbabwe Rhodesia problem.

3 in Iran supporters of Ayatollah Khomeini dominate the new constituent assembly.

3 a military coup in Equatorial Guinea deposes President Macias Nguema.

5 Mauritania renounces claims to Western Sahara and makes peace with the Polisario guerrillas of Western Sahara.

14 17 die when a hurricane hits boats participating in the Fastnet yacht race.

15 Andrew Young, US ambassador to the UN, resigns when it is revealed that he had unauthorized contact with the PLO.

27 Earl Mountbatten and three others killed by an IRA bomb while boating in County Sligo in the Republic of Ireland.

27 18 soldiers and a civilian are killed in an IRA attack at Warrenpoint in Northern Ireland.

J **September**

6 30,000 'boat people' who have fled from Vietnam are allowed to settle in the USA.

7 death toll from Hurricane David in the Dominican Republic reaches 1,100.

10 (–21 Dec) Lancaster House conference held in London to seek settlement of the Rhodesia problem.

11 death of President Agostinho Neto of Angola (20, replaced by Jose Eduardo dos Santos).

12 telephone division of the British Post Office is established as separate company, British Telecommunications.

16 in Swedish general election, non-Socialist parties retain power with majority of one seat.

16 overthrow of President Nur Mohammad Taraki of Afghanistan, replaced by Hafizullah Amin.

20 in the Central African Empire, former President David Dacko overthrows his uncle Emperor Bokassa; the Empire reverts to Republic status.

24 (–29) trial of Macias Nguema, former President of Equatorial Guinea, who is found guilty of genocide and executed.

29 (–1 Oct) Pope John Paul II makes first papal visit to Ireland.

K **October**

A civilian government takes power in Nigeria after 13 years of military rule.

2 the conference of the British Labour Party votes for mandatory reselection of sitting MPs.

7 Liberal Democrat Party wins a narrow victory in Japan's general election.

8 Eschel Rhoodie of South Africa's Information Department is sentenced to six years' imprisonment for fraud.

14 Israeli Foreign Minister General Moshe Dayan resigns in protest against Israel's stand on Palestinian autonomy.

16 President Zia of Pakistan cancels elections and bans political activity.

Maurice Ohana, *Livres de Prodiges*.

Wolfgang Rihm, *Jacob Lenz* (opera).

Michael Tippett, String Quartet No. 4.

Sweeney Todd (musical), lyrics and music by Stephen Sondheim (first performed at the Uris Theatre, New York, 1 March).

Abba, 'Voulez Vous'.

Boomtown Rats, 'I Don't Like Mondays'.

The Clash, *London Calling*.

Elvis Costello, 'Oliver's Army'.

Gloria Gaynor, 'I Will Survive'.

Pink Floyd, 'Another Brick In The Wall'.

The Police, 'Message in a Bottle', *Regatta de Blanc*, 'Walking on the Moon'.

Sugar Hill Gang, 'Rapper's Delight', an early 'rap' hit.

Donna Summer, *Bad Girls*.

Supertramp, *Breakfast in America*.

Village People, 'YMCA' (released in 1978).

Neil Young, *Rust Never Sleeps*.

At a pop concert in Cincinnati, Ohio, USA, given by the British group The Who, 11 people are crushed to death and 28 injured (3 Dec).

First digital recording in Britain.

u Literature and Drama

J G Ballard, *The Unlimited Dream Company*.

Italo Calvino, *If on a Winter's Night a Traveller*.

Joan Didion, *The White Album*.

Odysseus Elytis, *Maria Nefeldi*.

Nadine Gordimer, *Burger's Daughter*.

Milan Kundera, *The Book of Laughter and Forgetting*.

Norman Mailer, *The Executioner's Song*.

Bernard Malamud, *Dubin's Lives*.

Peter Matthiessen, *The Snow Leopard*.

V S Naipaul, *A Bend in the River*.

Craig Raine, *A Martian Sends a Postcard Home* (poems).

Alain Robbe-Grillet, *Le Rendez-vous*.

Philip Roth, *The Ghost Writer*.

William Styron, *Sophie's Choice*.

Louis Zukofsky, *A* (poems).

Drama:

Caryl Churchill, *Cloud Nine*.

Dorothy Hewett, *The Man from Mukinupin*.

Bernard Pomerance, *The Elephant Man*.

Peter Shaffer, *Amadeus*.

Martin Sherman, *Bent*.

David Williamson, *Travelling North*.

v Births and Deaths

Jan 5 Max Born dies (96).

Jan 5 Charlie Mingus dies (56).

Jan 26 Nelson Rockefeller dies (70).

Feb 9 Dennis Gabor dies (78).

Feb 12 Jean Renoir dies (84).

March 16 Jean Monnet dies (90).

May 6 Bernard Leach dies (92).

May 8 Talcott Parsons dies (76).

May 14 Jean Rhys dies (88).

May 29 Mary Pickford dies (86).

June 11 John Wayne dies (72).

July 29 Herbert Marcuse dies (81).

Aug 16 John Diefenbaker dies (83).

Aug 27 Louis (Earl) Mountbatten dies (79).

Sept 22 Otto Frisch dies (74).

Sept 27 Gracie Fields dies (81).

Oct 30 Barnes Wallis dies (92).

Dec 30 Richard Rodgers dies (77).

w Everyday Life

Brighton, in S England, is the first British seaside resort to provide an area designated for nudists (9 Aug).

x Sport and Recreation

Trevor Francis moves from Birmingham City to Nottingham Forest in the first £1 million transfer deal in English football (14 Feb); the record is broken again when Steve Daley of Wolverhampton Wanderers moves to Manchester United for £1.45 million and Andy Gray from Aston Villa to Wolverhampton for £1.47 million.

Wales wins the rugby Triple Crown for the fourth successive year (17 March) and the Five Nations championship for the second year running.

West Indies retain the cricket World Cup, beating England by 92 runs in the Final at Lord's (23 June).

British athlete Sebastian Coe is the first man to hold three indoor world records simultaneously, for the 800 m, the mile and the 1,500 m (15 Aug).

The 'Packer dispute' is settled when the Australian Cricket Board grants Channel Nine exclusive rights to televise Test cricket in Australia.

African-American boxer John Tate wins the World Boxing Association Heavy-weight title in Pretoria, South Africa, defeating the white South African Gerrie Coetzee on points over 15 rounds before 80,000 spectators, the largest-ever live audience for a heavyweight title fight (20 Oct).

International Olympic Committee decides (by 62 votes to 17) to admit athletes from the People's Republic of China to the next Olympic Games (26 Nov).

Stewards agree to stage women's races at the Henley Royal Regatta, England, from 1981 (12 Dec).

Scottish and English Football Associations decide that tickets for future England v. Scotland matches at Wembley, London, will not be sold north of the border, to prevent drunken Scottish fans from causing

16 British government announces plans to sell 5 per cent of its holding in British Petroleum, in order to raise £290 million, leaving the government with just over 25 per cent of BP.

23 in a surprise move (after Chancellor Howe has had a sleepless night) the British government abolishes exchange controls.

23 the former shah of Iran is flown to the USA for medical treatment.

23 Václav Havel and five other Czech dissidents are convicted of subversion.

25 referendums in Spain approve devolution of power to Catalonia and Euzkadi (the Basque provinces).

26 president of South Korea, Park Chung-Hee, is assassinated by his secret service.

27 St Vincent and Grenadines gains independence.

30 Robert Boulin, French minister of labour, accused of a scandal over property purchases, commits suicide.

L November

1 British government announces spending cuts for 1980–81 financial year of £3.5 billion.

4 Iranian students seize the US embassy in Tehran, taking 63 US citizens and 40 others hostage; they demand the return of the shah for trial.

6 Ayatollah Khomeini's Islamic Revolutionary Council takes power in Iran from the provisional government.

7 Senator Edward Kennedy announces challenge to President Carter for the Democratic nomination for the 1980 presidential election (8, Governor Jerry Brown of California announces candidacy for Democratic nomination.

13 Ronald Reagan, former governor of California, declares candidacy for Republican nomination.

12 in response to the seizure of US hostages in Iran, President Carter of USA imposes an embargo on Iranian oil (14, Iranian assets in the USA are frozen).

13 publication of *The Times* is resumed after a stoppage of almost a year.

15 following the publication of Andrew Boyle's *The Climate of Treason*, alleging that a senior figure had been a USSR agent, Margaret Thatcher announces that the agent was Professor Sir Anthony Blunt, Surveyor of the Queen's Pictures and her art adviser; Blunt is stripped of his knighthood.

15 Minimum Lending Rate reaches a record 17 per cent.

19 (–28) strikes at some British Leyland car plants following the dismissal of 'Red Robbo', alias Derek Robinson, a union shop steward.

19 US House of Representatives votes $1.56 billion aid to the Chrysler Car Corporation.

20 about 200 armed militants seize the Grand Mosque in Mecca, apparently in protest at corruption of Saudi regime (23, siege ended by Saudi Arabian troops).

22 former British Labour Party Chancellor Roy Jenkins floats the idea of a realignment of centre-left politics in his Dimbleby Lecture on BBC television.

28 Syrian Ambassador to the UN, Hammoud El-Choufi, resigns from his post, accusing the government of President Hafez al Assad of corruption, repression, and opportunism.

29 (–30) EC summit in Dublin, Ireland, at which Margaret Thatcher demands a rebate against British contributions to the Community.

30 British Steel announces loss of 50,000 jobs.

M December

2 mob burns US embassy in Tripoli.

5 Jack Lynch resigns as Prime Minister of Eire (7, replaced by Charles Haughey).

10 the rebel parliament in Zimbabwe Rhodesia winds itself up, ending UDI.

12 Lord Soames arrives in Zimbabwe Rhodesia to oversee formal end of British rule.

13 the Canadian government of Prime Minister Joseph Clark is defeated in a confidence debate. Clark calls an election.

18 Canadian Liberal Pierre Trudeau reverses decision to retire from party leadership.

21 Lancaster House agreement signed in London, providing for an end to Rhodesian civil war and introduction of majority rule (28, ceasefire in Rhodesia).

25 USSR invasion of Afghanistan, in bid to halt civil war and protect USSR interests.

27 President Amin of Afghanistan killed and replaced by Babrak Karmal.

31 at year end oil prices are 88 per cent higher than at the start of 1979.

31 publication of British New Year's Honours List in which Prime Minister Thatcher bestows political honours for the first time since 1974.

disorder in London (20 Dec); the same day the Pools Promoters Association announces annual donations of £3.5 million to a trust investigating crowd behaviour and other social problems associated with soccer.

y Media

Financier James Goldsmith launches *Now!* magazine in Britain (Sept).

One of Canada's most important newspapers, the 111-year-old *Montreal Star*, ceases publication eight months after a lengthy strike over the introduction of new technology and manning practices (25 Sept).

Offices of *The Times of Malta* are fire-bombed by demonstrators celebrating 30 years of Dom Mintoff as leader of the Labour Party and prime minister; a Church daily, *Il Hajja*, also has its offices destroyed (15 Oct).

In Britain, resumption of publication of *The Times*, *The Sunday Times*, and supplements (13 Nov).

Film:

Alien (director, Ridley Scott).

Kramer vs. Kramer (director, Robert Benton).

Mad Max (director, George Miller; starring Mel Gibson).

Manhattan (director and star, Woody Allen).

Man of Marble (director, Andrzej Wajda).

Monty Python's Life of Brian (director, Terry Jones; starring the Monty Python team).

Nosferatu (director, Werner Herzog).

Tess (director, Roman Polanski).

Television:

There are now 150 million television sets in the USA.

In Canada, start of broadcasts via satellite.

New programmes in Britain include: *Life on Earth* (BBC), presented by David Attenborough; *Tales of the Unexpected*, based on stories by Roald Dahl; *Testament of Youth*, based on the autobiography of Vera Brittain; *Tinker, Tailor, Soldier, Spy* (BBC), based on the novel by John le Carré and starring Alec Guinness; *Year Zero — The Silent Death of Cambodia*, a report by John Pilger.

Independence of Zimbabwe ... Start of Iran–Iraq War ...
Emergence of 'Solidarity' in Poland ...

A **January**

1 UN Secretary General Kurt Waldheim visits Tehran to seek release of US hostages.
2 (–2 Apr) British national steel strike.
3 Congress (I) Party wins sweeping victory in Indian general election.
6 total death-toll in Northern Ireland since 1969 exceeds 2,000.
8 US President Carter describes Soviet invasion of Afghanistan as greatest threat to peace since World War II (23, warns USSR against interference in Persian Gulf).
22 USSR sends dissident physicist Andrei Sakharov into internal exile at Gorky.
23 Israel completes withdrawal from 18,000 sq km/7,000 sq mi of Sinai peninsula.
25 Abolhassan Bani-Sadr becomes president of Iran.
29 Canada announces escape of four US diplomats from Iran on Canadian passports.
30 British Department of Employment reports more working days lost through strikes in 1979 than in any year since 1926.

B **February**

12 International Olympic Committee rejects US demand for cancellation or relocation of Moscow Olympics.
14 polling begins in Rhodesia for 20 white seats in new parliament (27, polling for 80 black seats begins).
18 Liberals defeat Progressive Conservatives in Canadian general election. Pierre Trudeau becomes prime minister.
19 in Britain, publication of Employment Bill outlawing secondary picketing and requiring unions to hold secret ballots before strikes.
22 proclamation of martial law in Kabul, Afghanistan, as resistance to Soviet invaders continues.
24 (–11 Mar) UN Commission visits Iran but fails to see US hostages.
26 Israel and Egypt exchange ambassadors for first time.

C **March**

4 in Rhodesia (now Zimbabwe) ZANU wins Rhodesian general election (11, Robert Mugabe forms coalition government with Joshua Nkomo as minister of home affairs).
11 President Zia crushes attempted military coup in Pakistan.
16 proclamation of martial law in Aleppo as political violence sweeps Syria.
17 free House of Commons vote approves government appeal for British boycott of

Moscow Olympics (25, British Olympic Association decides to send team).
18 USA bans sale of high-technology equipment to USSR.
19 British government declares that private consortium may construct Channel Tunnel, but no public money will be forthcoming.
20 in Britain, Lord Underhill, the former national agent of the Labour Party, publishes documents detailing methods by which the Party had been infiltrated by the Trotskyite Revolutionary League under the name of 'Militant Tendency'.
24 Archbishop Oscar Romero shot dead while celebrating mass in San Salvador (30, violence at his funeral kills 40).
26 British Budget increases spending on defence, police and pensions, and raises duties and prescription charges.
27 147 British and Norwegian workers die when Alexander Kielland oil-platform collapses in North Sea.
31 in Spain, Basque regional parliament opens in Guernica.

D **April**

2 In Britain, young blacks riot in St Paul's district of Bristol after police raid on a club used by the black community.
6 10,000 Cubans seek political asylum in Peruvian embassy in Havana.
7 USA bans trade with Iran, breaks off relations, and expels Iranian diplomats.
7 Iraqi artillery bombards Iranian border town of Oweisa.
9 major Israeli raid on Palestinian positions in southern Lebanon.
10 Spain agrees to re-open border with Gibraltar (closed 1969).
14 Israel and Egypt decide to hold negotiations on Palestinian autonomy.
18 Rhodesia gains legal independence as Zimbabwe under President Canaan Banana.
23 Saudi Arabia expels British Ambassador in protest at a British television programme about execution of a Saudi princess and her lover for adultery.
25 US commando mission to rescue hostages in Iran fails with loss of eight lives (29, Cyrus Vance resigns as US secretary of state; succeeded by Edmund Muskie).
28 EC summit in Luxembourg fails to reach agreement on Britain's demand for rebate payment against contributions.
30 Queen Juliana of the Netherlands abdicates in favour of Crown Princess Beatrix.
30 terrorists seize Iranian embassy in London, demanding release of political prisoners in

*Brandt Report on North–South relations ... Launch of the Sony
'Walkman' ... The New Grove Dictionary of Music ... MCC
members attack umpires ...*

o Politics, Government, Law, and Economy

In South Africa, constitutional changes are made following publication of the report of the Schlebusch Commission (8 May): the Senate is abolished (21–22 May); the president is given power to nominate 20 members of the House of Assembly; and an advisory President's Council is formed, comprising 60 members (no Africans) appointed by the president (takes office in Oct).

In USA, the 'Abscam' ('Arab Scam') investigation, in which FBI agents posing as Arab oilmen find several members of Congress willing to take bribes, and one who confesses on camera: 'I have larceny in my blood' (eight members of Congress are found guilty, with the last being sentenced on 1 May 1981).

In Britain, publication of government White Paper *The Interception of Communications in Great Britain* (1 April); Home Secretary William Whitelaw tells the House of Commons that police and secret services will continue to employ telephone-tapping and interception of mail in the fight against espionage, subversion, and terrorism; a senior judge will check and monitor operations.

The case Regina v. Scuig establishes that entrapment is not a defence in English common law.

The 'Isoglucose' case in England establishes the right to consultation of the European Parliament.

Companies Act in Britain makes 'insider dealing' in shares a criminal offence.

The Brandt Report, *North–South: A Programme for Survival* advocates fundamental change in relations between the industrial Northern hemisphere and the poor Southern hemisphere (published 12 Feb).

In USA, passage of Comprehensive Environmental Responses, Compensation, and Liability Act (commonly called 'Superfund').

General Motors in USA makes its first loss since 1921.

In USA, the trucking industry is deregulated.

Britain becomes a net exporter of oil (June).

British government privatizes Ferranti electronics, Fairey, and British Aerospace.

p Society, Education, and Religion

Half of married British women go out to work, the largest proportion anywhere in the European Community (reported 3 Jan).

Housing Act gives council tenants in Britain the right to buy their homes at cheap rates.

Janet Radcliffe Richards, *The Sceptical Feminist: A Philosophical Enquiry*.

In France, government regulations reduce university autonomy, placing restrictions on the numbers and types of courses.

In Japan, introduction of a new curriculum for elementary schools.

The Education Act in Britain introduces the 'Assisted Places Scheme', subsidising independent school places for able children from disadvantaged backgrounds.

Following the USSR's invasion of Afghanistan (25 Dec 1979), the Conference of Islamic Foreign Ministers calls on Muslims to boycott the Moscow Olympics.

The British television film *Death of a Princess*, about the enforcement of Islamic law in Saudi Arabia, causes widespread controversy in the Islamic world.

The South African government withdraws Bishop Desmond Tutu's passport.

The *Alternative Service Book 1980* is published as the first authorized prayer book of the Church of England since 1662.

q Science, Technology, and Discovery

Japanese Company Sony launches the 'Walkman', a small portable, personal tape recorder/player.

Launch of 10-year World Climate Research Program to study prediction of climate changes and human influence on climate change.

Intelsat 5 communication satellite launched, capable of relaying 12,000 telephone calls and two colour television channels.

Intelpost, the first public international electronic facsimile service.

People's Republic of China launches its first inter-continental ballistic missile.

Soviet cosmonauts Valery V Ryumin and Leonid I Popov set another record for time spent in space, 185 days.

Very Large Array (VLA) satellite at Socorro, New Mexico, USA, enters service; its 27 dishes are equivalent to one dish 27 km/17 mi in diameter.

US space probe *Voyager 1* flies past Saturn; it discovers the planet's 13th, 14th, and 15th moons and transmits information about the planet and its moons and rings.

Astronomers Uwe Fink and associates report

Iran (Special Air Service storms embassy, 5 May).

E **May**

1 USSR's traditional May Day parade is boycotted by ambassadors of 15 countries because of invasion of Afghanistan.

1 Sweden is practically at a standstill as pay negotiations crumble amidst strikes and lock-outs.

4 death of President Tito of Yugoslavia; replaced by eight-man collective presidency.

10 Franco-African agreement to form 30-nation French-speaking commonwealth.

14 President Sadat of Egypt discontinues talks with Israel on Palestinian autonomy.

14 in Britain, TUC 'day of action' against government policies evokes little response.

18 EC imposes trade sanctions against Iran.

20 referendum in Quebec on possible separation from Canada produces a 59.9 per cent vote against.

26 George Bush abandons bid for Republican nomination for US presidency.

28 first Islamic parliament (Majlis) opens in Iran.

30 New Hebrides appeals for British and French help to suppress rebellion on Espiritu Santo (24 July, Anglo-French force occupies the island).

30 EC foreign ministers agree on a rebate to Britain of £710 million.

F **June**

3 US nuclear alert when computer error indicates missile attack by USSR.

9 in speech in London, Roy Jenkins floats idea of creating new radical centre party in British politics.

11 Colonel Khadaffi halts 'liquidation' of Libyan exiles, except those collaborating with US, Israel, or Egypt.

12 death of Masayoshi Ohira, prime minister of Japan (Zenko Suzuki succeeds, 17 July).

17 British Ministry of Defence announces plan to deploy US Cruise missiles at Greenham Common and Molesworth military bases.

17 (–21) in South Africa, over 30 die in clashes with police in black townships around Cape Town.

22 1,000 die in ethnic violence in Tripura, India.

25 Basque terrorists explode bombs on Costa Blanca to disrupt Spanish tourist trade.

26 French President Giscard d'Estaing discloses France's capability to produce neutron bomb.

G **July**

1 Increase in meat prices prompts industrial unrest in Poland (24, Polish government approves wage rises).

1 John Anderson announces independent candidature for US presidency.

2 South Africa withdraws from Angola after three-week raid on guerrilla bases.

3 Bank of England reduces minimum lending rate from 17 to 16 per cent.

10 British Labour Party issues radical proposals for nationalization and price controls.

15 British government decides to replace Polaris with US *Trident-1* nuclear missile system in mid-1980s.

17 Republican Party convention in Detroit nominates Ronald Reagan as presidential candidate; he chooses George Bush as running-mate for vice-president.

18 British annual inflation rate stands at 21 per cent after first fall in two years.

19 Olympic Games open in Moscow, boycotted by 45 nations.

27 inauguration of President Fernando Belaunde Terry ends 12 years of military rule in Peru.

29 British Steel announces record losses of £545 million.

30 New Hebrides becomes independent as Vanuatu.

30 the Israeli Knesset proclaims unified Jerusalem the capital of Israel.

H **August**

2 Right-wing Italian terrorists kill 82 with bomb at Bologna railway station.

4 abolition of Clegg Commission on pay comparability in British public sector.

5 Belgian parliament passes Bill dividing country into three autonomous linguistic regions.

12 Senator Edward Kennedy withdraws from contest for Democratic presidential nomination after Jimmy Carter wins vote in the rules committee by 545 votes.

13 (–28) French fishermen blockade Channel ports in campaign for government aid.

14 Polish strikers occupy Lenin shipyard in Gdansk.

14 Democratic Party convention in New York nominates President Carter and Vice-President Mondale for second term.

20 USSR jams Western radio broadcasts for first time in seven years to prevent news of widespread strikes in Poland.

26 leadership changes in China consolidate power of pragmatic reformers led by Deng Xiaoping.

27 British unemployment total exceeds 2 million.

the discovery of a thin atmosphere on Pluto.

A new vaccine for prevention of hepatitis B is tested in the USA; it has a success rate of 92 per cent.

The Swiss firm Biogen produces human interferon in bacteria for the treatment of diseases.

Munich firm develops the lithotripter, a machine that uses sound waves to break up kidney stones.

A team at the Washington University School of Medicine (St Louis, Missouri, USA) transplants insulin-producing pancreatic islets from a rat to a mouse, opening up the possibility of making similar transplants from animals to humans.

A gene is transferred from one mouse to another.

In Diamond v. Chakrabarty, the US Supreme Court rules that a microbe created by genetic engineering can be patented (16 June).

M Ikeya and T Liki of Yamaguchi University, Japan, announce a new method of dating fossils: electron spin resonance spectroscopy, which measures the amount of natural radiation received by such remains.

R **Humanities**

John Baines and Jaromír Málek, *Atlas of Ancient Egypt.*

Jessica Rawson, *Ancient China: Art and Archaeology.*

Encyclopedia of American Economic History.

Stephan Thernstrom (ed.), *Harvard Encyclopedia of American Ethnic Groups.*

W A McCutcheon, *The Industrial Archaeology of Northern Ireland.*

Michael Baxandall, *The Limewood Sculptors of Renaissance Germany.*

Norbert Lynton, *The Story of Modern Art.*

Jerome J McGann (ed.), *Lord Byron: The Complete Poetical Works* (–1993).

Bernard Crick, *George Orwell: A Life.*

Stanley Sadie (ed.), *The New Grove Dictionary of Music and Musicians.*

Donald Davidson, *Essays on Action and Events.*

Richard Rorty, *Philosophy and the Mirror of Nature.*

Dr Anthony Kenny, Master of Balliol College, Oxford, is expelled from Czechoslovakia following a police raid on the flat of the Czech dissident philosopher Dr Julius Tomin (12 April); Dr Kathleen Wilkes, Tutor in Philosophy at St Hilda's College, Oxford, is arrested and expelled for the same reason on 20 May.

S **Art, Sculpture, Fine Arts, and Architecture**

Interest in figurative painting revives.

Picasso exhibition at the Museum of Modern Art, New York.

'The Avant-Garde in Russia', exhibition Los Angeles County Museum, Los Angeles, USA.

Painting, etc:

Sandro Chia, *Excited Pastoral.*

Cindy Sherman, *Untitled no 66.*

Sculpture:

Georg Baselitz, *Model For a Sculpture.*

Tony Cragg, *Plastic Palette I.*

Richard Deacon, *If the Shoe Fits.*

Architecture:

Francisco Saénz de Oíza, Banco de Bilbao, Centro Azca, Madrid, Spain.

T **Music**

Elliott Carter, *Night Fantasies.*

Peter Maxwell Davies, *The Lighthouse* (opera).

Philip Glass, *Satyagraha* (opera).

Oliver Knussen, *Where the Wild Things Are* (opera).

Krzysztof Penderecki, Symphony No. 2.

Barnum (musical), lyrics by Michael Stewart, music by Cy Coleman (first performance at the St James Theatre, New York, 30 April).

Les Misérables (musical), lyrics by Herbert Kretzmer, music by Claude-Michel Schönberg (first performed at the Palais de Sports, Paris, 17 Sept).

Blondie, 'Atomic', 'Call Me'.

David Bowie, 'Ashes to Ashes', *Scary Monsters.*

Elvis Costello, 'I Can't Stand Up for Falling Down'.

Jam, 'Going Underground'.

Joy Division, *Closer*, 'Love Will Tear Us Apart'.

Pink Floyd, *The Wall.*

Bruce Springsteen, *The River.*

UB40, *Signing Off.*

Ska revival by British bands, e.g. Madness and The Specials.

U **Literature and Drama**

Joseph Brodsky, *A Part of Speech.*

Anthony Burgess, *Earthly Powers.*

Truman Capote, *Music for Chameleons.*

Umberto Eco, *The Name of the Rose.*

Russell Hoban, *Riddley Walker.*

Zhang Jie, *Leaden Wings.*

John Le Carré, *Smiley's People.*

Shiva Naipaul, *Black and White.*

V S Naipaul, *A Bend in the River.*

John Kennedy Toole, *A Confederacy of Dunces* (posthumous).

31 Lech Walesa, leader of Gdansk strikers, signs agreement with Polish government allowing formation of independent trade unions and granting release of political prisoners.

J September

1 Conference of British TUC at Brighton deplores Employment Act and calls for campaign of non-co-operation with government.

5 Stanislaw Kania succeeds Edward Gierek as first secretary of Polish Communist Party.

9 closure of British Embassy in Tehran.

10 Libya and Syria proclaim union.

11 referendum in Chile approves eight-year extension of Pinochet's military government.

12 General Kenan Evren heads military take-over in Turkey.

12 Ayatollah Khomeini sets out conditions for release of US hostages in Iran.

22 Iraq invades Iran in attempt to gain control of Shatt al-Arab waterway.

22 Indian government assumes emergency powers to combat violence in southern India.

28 President Zia of Pakistan visits Tehran and Baghdad in attempt to mediate in Iran–Iraq War.

K October

1 British Labour Party conference in Blackpool votes for unilateral nuclear disarmament, withdrawal from EC and mandatory re-selection of MPs.

5 West Germany re-elects Chancellor Helmut Schmidt's coalition with increased majority.

6 British prison officers begin work-to-rule, refusing to admit new prisoners.

6 in Britain, Transport Act ends monopoly on long-distance coach travel.

10 in Britain, Margaret Thatcher tells Conservative Party conference of her determination to persist with monetarist policies: 'U-turn if you want to; the Lady's not for turning'.

10 earthquake in Algeria kills 20,000.

15 James Callaghan resigns as leader of the British Labour Party.

17 Queen Elizabeth II pays first State visit to Vatican by British monarch (22, the Pope annuls 1633 condemnation of Galileo).

21 sterling exchange rate reaches $2.45 for first time since 1973.

23 Nikolai Tikhonov succeeds Alexei Kosygin as Soviet prime minister.

24 Polish authorities register a new independent trade union, named 'Solidarity'.

26 London protest march by Campaign for Nuclear Disarmament attracts 50,000.

27 (–18 Dec) in Northern Ireland, seven IRA prisoners in the Maze prison on hunger strike, demanding 'political status'.

L November

4 In US presidential election, Republican Ronald Reagan wins a sweeping victory over President Carter. Reagan wins 489 electoral votes, Carter, 49. Popular vote: Reagan, 43,899,248; Carter, 35,481,435; John Anderson (Independent), 5,719,437. Republicans win control of the Senate and gain 33 seats in the House of Representatives.

10 in Britain, Michael Foot defeats Denis Healey to become leader of Labour Party, winning 139 votes to Healey's 129 in the second ballot.

10 (–11 Dec) British firemen work to rule in pay dispute.

20 treason trial of former Chinese leaders, the 'Gang of Four', opens in Beijing.

24 British Chancellor Sir Geoffrey Howe announces £1.06 billion reduction in public spending and £3 billion increase in taxation.

27 four Welsh nationalist extremists jailed for arson attacks on holiday homes.

27 British government announces aim of cutting 100,000 jobs from civil service.

30 Syria masses troops on Jordanian border; Jordan calls up reserves.

M December

2 EC warns USSR against military intervention in Poland.

3 start of major Soviet offensive against Afghan resistance fighters.

4 Francisco Sá Carneiro, prime minister of Portugal, dies in air crash (21, Francisco Pinto Balsemão succeeds).

8 Margaret Thatcher and Charles Haughey, meeting in Dublin, agree to establish commission to examine Anglo–Irish links respecting Northern Ireland.

8 former Beatle John Lennon is murdered in New York.

10 President Brezhnev of USSR calls on West and China to make Persian Gulf and Indian Ocean 'a zone of peace'.

15 Milton Obote becomes president of Uganda after first elections in 18 years.

16 OPEC increases crude oil prices by 10 per cent.

16 unveiling of memorial in Gdansk, Poland, to workers killed in riots of Dec 1970.

21 Iran demands 'deposit' of $24,000 million for release of US hostages; (29, US refuses to pay).

27 violent anti-USSR demonstrations in Tehran on anniversary of invasion of Afghanistan.

Sean O'Faolain, *Midsummer Night Madness and Other Stories*.
Patrick White, *The Twyborn Affair*.
Heathcote Williams, *Whale Nation*.
Tom Wolfe, *The Right Stuff*.

Drama:
David Edgar (adaptor), *Nicholas Nickleby*.
Brian Friel, *Translations*.
Ronald Harwood, *The Dresser*.
Greg McGee, *Foreskin's Lament*.
Mark Medoff, *Children of a Lesser God*.
Sam Shepard, *True West*.
Howard Brenton, *The Romans in Britain*, at the National Theatre, London, causes controversy on account of scenes involving nudity and sexual violence; prosecution for obscenity is threatened (all tickets are sold).
Peter Brook's Centre International de Créations Théâtrales is given the New York Drama Critics' Circle Award.

v Births and Deaths
Jan 18 Cecil Beaton dies (76).
Feb 17 Graham Sutherland dies (76).
March 18 Erich Fromm dies (79).
March 26 Roland Barthes dies (64).
March 31 Jesse Owens dies (66).
April 15 Jean-Paul Sartre dies (74).
April 29 Alfred Hitchcock dies (80).
May 4 Tito dies (87).
June 7 Henry Miller dies (88).
July 1 C P Snow dies (74).
July 24 Peter Sellers dies (54).
July 27 Muhammad Reza Shah Pahlavi dies (60).
Aug 6 Marino Marini dies (79).
Sept 8 W F Libby dies (71).
Sept 17 Jean Piaget dies (84).
Oct 26 Marcello Caetano dies (74).
Nov 22 Mae West dies (88).
Dec 3 Oswald Mosley dies (84).
Dec 8 John Lennon dies (40).
Dec 16 Harland 'Colonel' Sanders dies (90).
Dec 18 Alexei Nikolaievich Kosygin dies (76).
Dec 22 Karl Doenitz dies (89).
Dec 31 Marshall McLuhan dies (69).

w Everyday Life
Eruption of the Mt St Helens volcano in Washington state, USA (18 May).

x Sport and Recreation
Nigel Short, age 14, from Bolton in Britain, becomes youngest International Master in the history of chess (11 Jan).
Alan Minter is the first British fighter to win a world title in the USA since Ted 'Kid' Lewis in 1917 when he wins the World Middleweight title, beating Vito Antuofermo in Las Vegas (16 March).

Liverpool Football Club win the English League Championship for the second year running, the fourth time in five years, and the 12th time in all — a record (3 May).
Cliff Thorburn of Canada is first non-British player to win the world snooker championship (5 May).
A C Milan, one of Italy's top football teams, is relegated to the second division by a Disciplinary Commission of the Italian League; the Commission found the club president and several key players guilty of fraud, bribe-taking, and fixing games (18 May).
The European Football Association (EUFA) fines the English Football Association £8,000 because of the 'violent and dangerous conduct of English supporters' who rioted during England's opening match against Belgium in Turin (12 June); police had used tear gas to break up the rioting and the match was stopped for five minutes when players became affected by gas.
At the Wimbledon tennis tournament in London, Bjorn Borg of Sweden wins his fifth consecutive Men's Singles title (5 July); during the championships electronic fault-finding equipment is introduced for use by line judges.
The centenary Test match between England and Australia is held at Lord's (28 Aug–2 Sept); the match is drawn after 10 hours are lost to rain — on the Saturday MCC members assault the umpires.
The 22nd Olympic Games are held in Moscow, USSR (19 July–3 Aug). Following the Soviet invasion of Afghanistan, the Games are boycotted by 65 countries, most notably the USA, West Germany, Japan, and Kenya. The USSR wins 80 gold medals; East Germany, 47; Bulgaria, Cuba, and Italy, 8 each; Hungary, 7; Romania and France, 6 each; Great Britain, 5; Poland, Sweden, and Finland, 3 each.

y Media
Japan's leading newspaper, *Asahi Shimbun*, is produced by use of new technology — 'untouched by human hands' (24 Sept).
London's *Evening News* is merged into the *Evening Standard* (31 Oct).

Film:
Elephant Man (director, David Lynch).
The Empire Strikes Back (director, Irvin Kershner).
Heaven's Gate (director, Michael Cimino; having cost $40 million, the film was withdrawn after being lambasted by critics).

*Riots in Britain ... Socialist government in France ... Martial law
in Poland ...*

A January

1 Greece becomes 10th member of EC.

5 in Britain, Margaret Thatcher sacks Norman St John-Stevas as Leader of the Commons.

6 Gaston Thorn succeeds Roy Jenkins as president of European Commission.

13 Namibian peace conference breaks up without agreement in Geneva.

15 the Pope receives official 'Solidarity' delegation led by Lech Walesa.

20 inauguration of Ronald Reagan as 39th president of USA.

20 Iran releases all 52 US hostages (held since 4 Nov 1979) after agreement is signed in Algiers releasing Iranian assets in USA.

25 former British Labour ministers Roy Jenkins, Dr David Owen, William Rodgers and Shirley Williams issue the 'Limehouse Declaration', advocating a new central political position to pursue radical change, and form the 'Council for Social Democracy'.

25 show trial in Beijing, China, convicts 'Gang of Four' of treason. Chiang Ch'ing, widow of Chairman Mao, receives suspended death sentence.

29 Adolfo Suárez resigns as Spanish prime minister (10 Feb, succeeded by Leopoldo Calvo Sotelo).

B February

3 Gro Harlem Brundtland becomes first woman prime minister of Norway.

6 Revd Ian Paisley stages midnight parade of 500 Protestants with fire-arm certificates on his 'Carson trail' in Northern Ireland.

9 General Wojciech Jaruzelski replaces Josef Pintowski as prime minister of Poland.

12 fighting breaks out between rival ex-guerrilla forces in Zimbabwe (16, Joshua Nkomo persuades his supporters to lay down their arms).

18 British National Coal Board withdraws pit closure plan to avert strike by miners.

18 US President Reagan proposes spending cuts of $49,000 million and 30 per cent reduction in taxation over three years.

20 USA accuses USSR and Cuba of attempting to subvert El Salvador.

23 200 civil guards storm Spanish parliament and hold MPs at gun-point in coup attempt (24, guards surrender after denunciation by King Juan Carlos).

C March

2 12 British MPs and nine Peers resign Labour whip to sit as Social Democrats (16, one Conservative MP joins them).

10 austere British Budget raises duties and freezes income-tax allowances.

22 USSR extends Warsaw Pact manoeuvres in Poland until 7 Apr.

26 in Britain, official launch of Social Democratic Party (SDP), with programme of incomes policy, proportional representation, and support for EC and NATO.

27 USSR brands Polish trade union 'Solidarity' counter-revolutionary.

30 US President Reagan wounded in assassination attempt in Washington, DC.

30 academic economists sign memorial calling on British government to abandon hardline monetarism.

Kagemusha (Akira Kurosawa).

Melvin and Howard (director, Jonathan Demme).

My Brilliant Career (director, Gillian Armstrong).

Ordinary People (director, Robert Redford; starring Mary Tyler Moore).

Raging Bull (director, Martin Scorsese).

The Shining (director, Stanley Kubrick; starring Jack Nicholson).

Television:

In USA, there are now 35 television stations broadcasting mainly religious programmes.

New programmes in USA include *Hill Street Blues* (NBC).

The British programme *Death of a Princess* (ATV), about the execution of a Saudi princess for adultery (broadcast 9 April), causes a rift between Saudi Arabia and Britain (broadcast in USA on 12 May, attracting record audience).

New programmes in Britain include: *Bergerac* (BBC; –1991); *The Flipside of Dominic Hide*, starring Peter Firth; *Staying On* (Granada), starring Trevor Howard and Celia Johnson; *Yes Minister* (BBC), a comic drama series caricaturing British government (–1982).

Introduction of the French high-speed train ... Abolition of death penalty in France ... First London Marathon ...

o Politics, Government, Law, and Economy

J L Sundquist, *The Decline and Resurgence of Congress*.

States in the Persian Gulf (Abu Dhabi, Bahrain, Kuwait, Oman, Qatar, and Saudi Arabia) establish the Gulf Cooperation Council (May).

'P2' scandal reveals corruption and conspiracy in the Italian political class and establishment.

French National Assembly abolishes the death penalty and thereby use of the guillotine (30 Sept).

Contempt of Court Act brings the British practice on this matter into line with the European Convention on Human Rights.

Royal Commission on Criminal Procedure recommends extension of police powers of arrest and search (8 Jan).

In Britain, Peter Sutcliffe, the 'Yorkshire Ripper', is found guilty of the murder of 13 women (22 May) and sentenced to life imprisonment.

International Meeting on Cooperation and Development held by representatives of 22 countries at Cancún, Mexico (22–23 Oct), to discuss economic problems facing developing countries.

In USA, President Reagan gets a large tax-cut package through Congress.

Milton Friedman, *Monetary Trends in the United States and the United Kingdom*.

British government sells National Freight Corporation to management-led consortium (19 Oct; 30, sells 50 per cent of shares in Cable and Wireless Ltd).

p Society, Education, and Religion

In referendum, Italian voters decide in favour of a right to abortion (17 May).

Sandra Day O'Connor is appointed the first woman justice of the US Supreme Court (25 Sept).

Susan Brown is the first woman cox in the English Oxford and Cambridge boat race, steering the Oxford crew to victory (4 April).

Andrea Dworkin, *Pornography*.

Betty Friedan, *The Second Stage*.

British Nationality Act replaces universal British subjecthood with three status categories (British citizenship with right of abode, citizenship of dependent territory, overseas citizenship).

European Court rules that dismissal for refusing to join union 'closed shop' is a violation of human rights.

In USA, the Education Consolidation and Improvement Act reduces federal spending on education.

First bachelors' university degrees are awarded in China.

Japan introduces a new curriculum for lower secondary schools.

Legislation in Japan permits the establishment of a 'University of the Air'.

Education Act in Britain places new duties upon local education authorities to integrate children with special educational needs into mainstream schools, along the lines suggested by the Warnock Report of 1978.

British government reduces grant to universities by 3 per cent (13 March).

The Unification Church ('Moonies') in Britain loses a libel action against the *Daily Mail*

D **April**

1 Introduction of food rationing in Poland.

1 heavy fighting in Beirut, Lebanon, between Arab peace-keeping force and Christian militias.

7 referendum in Philippines grants sweeping powers to President Marcos.

9 in Northern Ireland, Bobby Sands, imprisoned IRA hunger-striker, wins by-election in Fermanagh and South Tyrone (dies 5 May).

10 (–12) severe riots in inner London area of Brixton.

17 Polish farmers win right to form independent trade union.

28 Foreign Office advises British nationals to leave Lebanon as conflict intensifies between clients of Syria and Israel.

30 Central Committee of Polish Communist Party approves programme of moderate reforms.

E **May**

6 USA expels all Libyan diplomats because of Libyan support for terrorism.

8 (–27) US peace envoy, Philip Habib, tours Middle East.

10 François Mitterrand becomes first Socialist president of France with 51.7 per cent of vote to Valéry Giscard d'Estaing's 48.3 per cent.

13 gunman seriously wounds Pope John Paul II in assassination attempt in St Peter's Square (22 July, Mehmet Ali Agca jailed for life in Italy).

21 President Mitterrand appoints Pierre Mauroy as French prime minister.

26 Italian government falls after revelations of infiltration by Masonic Lodge 'Propaganda 2' (24 July, Italy bans secret societies).

30 assassination of President Zia ur-Rahman of Bangladesh (succeeded by vice-president Abdus Sattar).

F **June**

8 Israeli air force bombs Osirak nuclear reactor under construction near Baghdad (19, UN Security Council condemns attack after Iraq denies military use).

11 Fianna Faíl loses general election in Republic of Ireland (30, Garret FitzGerald becomes prime minister at head of Fine Gael–Labour coalition).

12 General Jaruzelski reconstructs Polish government to tackle economic crisis.

16 in Britain, Liberals and SDP issue joint statement, *A Fresh Start for Britain*.

21 Socialists win landslide victory in second round of elections to French National Assembly (23, new government includes three Communists).

22 in Iran, Ayatollah Khomeini denounces President Bani-Sadr (who flees to France, 29).

28 bomb attack on offices of Islamic Republican Party kills 74 in Tehran, Iran, including Chief Justice Ayatollah Beheshti.

30 British government announces that the armed survey ship HMS *Endurance*, on patrol in the South Atlantic, will be withdrawn and not replaced.

G **July**

4 (–6) arson and riots in Toxteth district of Liverpool, England; disturbances follow in Manchester, Brixton, Reading, Hull, and elsewhere.

17 Israeli jets attack Palestinian areas of Beirut (29, Israel and PLO agree cease-fire after two weeks of fighting in southern Lebanon).

23 Polish government announces plans to cut rations and quadruple food prices.

24 Muhammad Ali Rajai elected president of Iran.

24 flood in Sichuan province of China makes up to 1.5 million people homeless.

29 the Prince of Wales and Lady Diana Spencer marry in St Paul's Cathedral, London.

H **August**

3 (–5) in Poland, 'Solidarity' blockades Warsaw city centre in protest at food shortages.

3 strike by US air traffic controllers; 6, they are dismissed for not complying with presidential order to return to work.

9 in USA, President Reagan announces decision to proceed with manufacture of neutron bomb.

13 East Germany officially celebrates 20th anniversary of Berlin Wall.

16 USSR postpones Polish debt repayments and increases supplies of raw materials and consumer goods to Poland.

19 US air force shoots down two Libyan fighters during naval exercises off the coast of Libya in the Gulf of Sirte.

20 Bank of England abolishes the Minimum Lending Rate.

26 P W Botha confirms that South African troops are fighting guerrillas in Angola.

30 bomb in Tehran kills President Rajai and Prime Minister Bahonar of Iran.

J **September**

4 Warsaw Pact begins largest military exercises in Baltic since World War II.

4 assassination of French ambassador to Lebanon in Beirut.

5 (–10) first national congress of 'Solidarity' union in Gdansk, Poland.

concerning an article about its treatment of members and the wealth of founder Sun Myung Moon.

The General Synod of the Church of England votes overwhelmingly to recognize the sacraments of the Free Churches and their women ministers and to allow women to be ordained to the Anglican diaconate (12 Nov).

The Salvation Army withdraws from the World Council of Churches because of its financial support for African guerrilla movements.

Q Science, Technology, and Discovery

French railways introduce their high-speed train, the Train à Grande Vitesse (TGV).

In Britain, opening of suspension bridge over the River Humber in NE England — the world's longest suspension bridge (opened by Queen Elizabeth II on 17 July).

The IBM company launches its personal computer, using the Microsoft disc-operating system (MS-DOS) which becomes a standard programme throughout the computer industry.

Launch of two-dimensional fluorescent lamp.

First pocket-size television produced, by British inventor Sir Clive Sinclair.

The *Solar Challenger* aircraft, powered by solar cells, crosses the English Channel.

First flight of the American reusable space shuttle (12–14 April), using the orbiter *Columbia* (second shuttle flight 12–14 Nov).

US space probe *Voyager 2* photographs the rings and moons of Saturn and transmits scientific data (Aug).

Astronomers at the University of Wisconsin, USA, discover the most massive star yet known, R136a, which is 100 times brighter than the Sun and 2,500 times larger.

US Center for Disease Control recognizes AIDS (Acquired Immune Deficiency Syndrome), thought to be caused by the HIV virus.

The US Food and Drug Administration grants permission to Eli Lilley and Co to market insulin produced by bacteria, the first genetic engineering product to go on sale.

Scientists at Ohio University, USA, transfer a gene into a mouse — the first transfer of a gene from one animal species to another.

Chinese scientists make the first clone of a fish (a golden carp).

Chemists devise a way of giving polymers some properties of metals; this enables scientists at the University of Pennsylvania, USA, to construct the first 'plastic battery'.

R Humanities

UNESCO, *General History of Africa*.

Peter Salway, *Roman Britain* (in 'Oxford History of England' series).

David Hill, *An Atlas of Anglo-Saxon England*.

Anthony Fletcher, *The Outbreak of the English Civil War*.

E A Wrigley and R S Schofield, *The Population History of England, 1541–1871: A Reconstruction*.

Mark Girouard, *The Return to Camelot: Chivalry and the English Gentleman*.

Paul Langford (ed.), *The Writings and Speeches of Edmund Burke* (–).

Stephen Koss, *The Rise and Fall of the Political Press*, Volume 1 (Volume 2, 1984).

G E Mingay (ed.), *The Victorian Countryside*.

Thomas C Cochran, *Frontiers of Change: Early Industrialization of America*.

James M McPherson, *Ordeal by Fire: The Civil War and Reconstruction*.

P J Waller, *Democracy and Sectarianism: A Political and Social History of Liverpool, 1868–1939*.

Kenneth O Morgan, *Rebirth of a Nation: Wales 1880–1980*.

Avner Offer, *Property and Politics 1870–1914*.

Martin J Wiener, *English Culture and the Decline of the Industrial Spirit, 1850–1980*.

John Carey, *John Donne*.

Jürgen Habermas, *The Theory of Communicative Action*.

R M Hare, *Moral Thinking*.

Alisdair MacIntyre, *After Virtue*.

S Art, Sculpture, Fine Arts, and Architecture

Following the restoration of democracy in Spain, Picasso's *Guernica* is taken from the Museum of Modern Art, New York, to the Prado in Madrid, Spain.

'20th-century British Sculpture' exhibition at the Whitechapel Gallery, London.

'A New Spirit in Painting', exhibition at the Royal Academy, London.

Figuration Libre movement, France, based on comic strips and graffiti.

Painting, etc:

Francesco Clemente, *Toothache*.

Richard Long, *Terracotta Circle*.

David Salle, *An Illustrator Was There*.

Sculpture:

Carl André, *Niner*.

Tony Cragg, *Britain Seen From the North*.

Architecture:

Denys Lasdun, Redhouse and Softly, European Investment Bank, Luxembourg.

Tom Wolfe, *From Bauhaus to Our House*.

T Music

Ghiya Kancheli, Symphony No. 6.

György Kurtág, *Messages of the Late Miss R V Troussova*.

9 French government announces national-ization of 36 banks and 11 industrial groups.

16 British Liberal Party conference in Llan-dudno votes for electoral alliance with SDP.

20 Belize becomes independent within the Commonwealth.

27 Denis Healey narrowly defeats Tony Benn in vote for deputy leadership of British Labour Party (Healey wins 50.426 per cent of votes, Benn 49.574 per cent).

κ **October**

2 Hojatoleslam Ali Khameini elected presi-dent of Iran (29, Hosein Musavi becomes prime minister).

3 in Northern Ireland, IRA hunger-strike at Maze prison ends after 10 deaths.

6 assassination of President Sadat of Egypt (14, succeeded by Hosni Mubarak).

18 Panhellenic Socialist Movement wins Greek general election (21, Andreas Papandreou forms first Socialist govern-ment in Greek history).

18 General Jaruzelski, prime minister of Poland, succeeds Stanislaw Kania as first secretary of Polish Communist Party.

23 Presbyterian Church of South Africa con-ducts mixed race marriages in defiance of apartheid laws.

L **November**

1 Antigua and Barbuda become independent within the Commonwealth.

1 Tunisian government wins all seats in first multi-party elections since 1959.

4 crisis talks in Poland between General Jaruzelski, Lech Walesa, and Polish pri-mate Cardinal Glemp.

6 Margaret Thatcher and Garret FitzGerald, meeting in London, agree to establish Anglo–Irish inter-governmental Council (23, protest strikes in Northern Ireland).

14 Gambia and Senegal form confederation of Senegambia.

18 President Reagan of USA offers to cancel deployment of Cruise and Pershing miss-iles in Europe if USSR dismantles medium-range missiles targeted on Western Europe.

20 USSR contracts to supply Siberian natural gas to West Germany.

25 Arab summit conference in Fez quickly reaches deadlock over Saudi Arabian peace plan for Middle East.

28 National Party wins very narrow victory in New Zealand general election.

M **December**

1 US–Soviet talks on arms limitation open in Geneva.

9 USSR allows Lisa Alekseeva to emigrate after 17-day hunger-strike by her stepfather Andrei Sakharov.

13 imposition of martial law in Poland: mass detention and curbs on civil liberties and trade unions.

14 Israel formally annexes the Golan Heights, occupied in 1967.

18 reported suicide of Mehmet Shehu, prime minister of Albania (later denounced as US–Soviet–Yugoslav spy).

22 General Leopoldo Galtieri becomes presi-dent of Argentina.

29 President Reagan of USA introduces econ-omic sanctions against USSR for compel-ling Poland to adopt martial law.

31 Lieutenant Jerry Rawlings stages his second military coup in Ghana.

Arvo Pärt, *Passio domini nostri Jesu Christi secundum Joannem*.

Alfred Schnittke, Symphony No. 3.

Karlheinz Stockhausen, *Donnerstag aus Licht* (opera).

Cats (musical), by Andrew Lloyd Webber, based on poems by T S Eliot (first performed at the New London Theatre, 11 May).

Adam and the Ants, *King of the Wild Frontier*, 'Prince Charming', 'Stand and Deliver'.

Phil Collins, 'In The Air Tonight'.

Brian Eno, *My Life in the Bush of Ghosts*.

Grandmaster Flash and the Furious Five, *The Message* (a seminal hip-pop album).

The Human League, *Dare*, 'Don't You Want Me?'

Police, 'Every Little Thing She Does Is Magic', *Ghost In The Machine*.

Diana Ross and Lionel Richie, 'Endless Love'.

Soft Cell, 'Tainted Love'.

The Specials, 'Ghost Town'.

Suicide, *Half Alive*.

Ultravox, *Vienna*.

u Literature and Drama

Raymond Carver, *What We Talk About When We Talk About Love*.

William Golding, *Rights of Passage*.

Alasdair Gray, *Lanark*.

Minoru Oda, *Hiroshima*.

Salman Rushdie, *Midnight's Children*.

Martin Cruz Smith, *Gorky Park*.

Paul Theroux, *The Mosquito Coast*.

D M Thomas, *The White Hotel*.

Mario Vargas Llosa, *The War of the End of the World*.

Publication of Terence Kilmartin's reworking of Scott Moncrieff's translation of Proust's *Remembrance of Things Past*.

Drama:

Edward Bond, *Restoration*.

Nell Dunn, *Steaming*.

Harvey Fierstein, *Torch Song Trilogy*.

Charles Fuller, *A Soldier's Play*.

Tom Kempinski, *Duet for One*.

Mike Leigh, *Goose Pimples*.

Ariane Mnouchkine, *Mephisto*.

Sharon Pollock, *Blood Relations*.

Arnold Wesker, *Caritas*.

v Births and Deaths

Jan 5 Harold Clayton Urey dies (87).

Jan 23 Samuel Barber dies (70).

April 8 Omar Bradley dies (88).

April 12 Joe Louis dies (66).

May 30 Zia ur-Rahman dies (45).

July 1 Marcel Lajos Breuer dies (79).

Sept 12 Eugenio Montale dies (84).

Oct 6 Anwar Sadat dies (62).

Oct 16 Moshe Dayan dies (66).

Nov 10 Abel Gance dies (92).

Nov 22 Hans Krebs dies (81).

w Everyday Life

x Sport and Recreation

First London Marathon held, with 7,055 competitors (29 March).

In Britain, Shergar, ridden by Walter Swinburn, wins the Derby by 10 lengths, the longest winning distance yet in the 20th century (3 June).

In cricket, in the Third Test at Headingley, Leeds, home team England beat Australia by 18 runs after being forced to follow on (21 July), only the second time this has happened in 104 years of Test cricket.

In nine days (Aug), British athletes Steve Ovett and Sebastian Coe establish three world records for the mile; the record is cut by over 1 second to 3 minutes 47.53 seconds.

First English soccer League match is played on artificial turf (at Loftus Road ground of Queen's Park Rangers, London).

y Media

Rupert Murdoch buys *The Times* and other *Times* newspapers in Britain.

Now! magazine in Britain is closed after 18 months (March).

Roland 'Tiny' Rowland's Lonrho company purchases the *Observer* in Britain (effective from July).

In USA, the *Washington Star* ceases publication (Aug).

Film:

Atlantic City (director, Louis Malle; starring Burt Lancaster).

Chariots of Fire (director, Hugh Hudson).

Diva (director, Jean-Jacques Beneix).

Excalibur (director, John Boorman).

The French Lieutenant's Woman (director, Karel Reisz; starring Meryl Streep and Jeremy Irons).

Man of Iron (director, Andrzej Wajda).

My Dinner with André (director, Louis Malle).

On Golden Pond (director, Mark Rydell; starring Katharine Hepburn and Henry Fonda — his last film).

Ordinary People (director, Robert Redford).

Reds (director, Warren Beatty).

Yol (director, Yilmaz Guney).

Television:

There are now regular television transmissions in 137 countries.

The government of Indonesia bans television commercials.

New programmes in USA include *Dynasty*.

New programmes in Britain include: *Brideshead Revisited* (BBC), based on the novel by Evelyn Waugh; *Cagney and Lacey*; *Country* (BBC), by Trevor Griffiths; *Only Fools and Horses*; *Postman Pat* (BBC).

Falklands War ... Israel invades Lebanon ... 'Solidarity' banned in Poland ...

A January

8 Spain agrees to end blockade of Gibraltar (Dec, frontier opened).

19 Polish authorities announce increases in food prices of between 200 per cent and 400 per cent from 1 Feb.

21 members of Britain's National Union of Mineworkers (NUM) vote to accept a wage increase of 9.3 per cent.

24 Egypt's President Mubarak announces policy of non-alignment and seeks assistance from USSR on industrial projects.

26 according to government statistics, unemployment in Britain passes 3 million.

29 US government agrees to cover Poland's debt payments.

31 Israel agrees to UN peace-keeping force in Sinai.

31 curfew imposed in Gdansk, Poland, following riots over price increases.

B February

9 EC and USA announce end to East–West talks in Madrid until martial law in Poland is lifted.

9 British Prime Minister Thatcher, in House of Commons, defends plan to scrap the South Atlantic survey ship HMS *Endurance.*

17 Joshua Nkomo dismissed from Zimbabwe government.

19 court martial opens in Spain of 32 officers charged with involvement in 1981 attempted coup (3 June, sentenced to 30 years' imprisonment).

19 receivers appointed to failed government-supported De Lorean Car Company in Northern Ireland.

23 members of Ugandan Freedom Movement attack capital Kampala.

C March

1 General Jaruzelski visits Moscow, USSR, for talks on situation in Poland.

10 USA imposes embargo on Libyan oil imports and on exports of high-technology goods to Libya.

11 British government announces intention to purchase Trident II submarine-launched missile system to replace Polaris.

15 President Daniel Ortega suspends Nicaraguan constitution and declares one-month state of siege.

19 Argentine scrap-metal dealer lands on island of South Georgia and raises Argentine flag.

23 military coup in Guatemala.

24 military coup in Bangladesh.

25 in Scotland, Roy Jenkins of SDP wins Glasgow Hillhead in by-election from Conservatives.

D April

2 Argentine troops invade Falkland Islands. Britain breaks diplomatic relations with Argentina.

3 UN Security Council Resolution 502 demands withdrawal of Argentine forces from Falklands.

4 Lord Carrington resigns as British foreign secretary; succeeded by Francis Pym.

4 first ships of British Royal Navy Task Force sail for Falklands.

7 US Secretary of State Alexander Haig offers to mediate in Falklands dispute.

11 EC imposes sanctions on Argentina.

12 Britain declares 320-km/200-mi maritime exclusion zone round Falkland Islands.

15 five Muslim fundamentalists executed in Cairo, Egypt, for involvement in assassination of President Sadat.

17 Queen Elizabeth proclaims new Canadian constitution, severing Canada's last colonial links with Britain.

19 British government rejects Haig plan to resolve Falklands conflict (29, Argentine government follows suit).

25 British forces recapture South Georgia.

30 in USA, Reagan administration imposes economic sanctions on Argentina and offers to supply war materials to Britain.

E May

1 50,000 Solidarity supporters demonstrate against martial law (4, military controls tightened).

1 British Royal Air Force bombs Port Stanley airport on Falkland Islands.

2 British submarine HMS *Conqueror* sinks Argentine cruiser *General Belgrano*, killing 368.

3 Israeli Prime Minister Begin announces that Israel will assert sovereignty over occupied West Bank.

4 Argentine missiles sink British destroyer HMS *Sheffield*; 20 killed.

6 Conservatives make large gains in British local elections.

21 British troops land on East Falkland Island and establish bridgehead at Port San Carlos.

22 Pope celebrates Mass for Peace in Rome with English and Argentine cardinals.

28 British troops recapture Port Darwin and Goose Green in East Falkland, taking 1,400 Argentines prisoner.

Canada repatriates constitution ... Rat gene transferred to mouse
... Attenborough's Gandhi *... Spielberg's* ET *...*

o Politics, Government, Law, and Economy

In People's Republic of China, new constitutions of the Communist Party and the State transfer power back to the bureaucracy and the leadership, serving the interests of leader Deng Xiaoping.

United Nations Law of Sea Conference agrees international convention governing use and exploitation of sea and seabed (30 April).

Repatriation of the Canadian constitution (its removal from British law to place it entirely under Canadian control) removes Canada's last legal link with Britain.

The British government proposes new political institutions in Northern Ireland in the White Paper *A framework for Devolution* (published 4 April); it envisages a new elected Northern Ireland Assembly.

Local Government Finance Act increases British central government's control over local authority spending.

British Criminal Justice Act creates new system of custodial offences for young offenders, but removes imprisonment and Borstal detention as punishments.

International commodity prices reach their lowest point since World War II.

Mexico defaults on a loan payment, leading to general concern about the ability of Third World countries to meet their international debts and about consequences of defaults for lending nations; the International Monetary Fund intervenes with debt rescheduling and imposes austerity measures on debtor countries.

In USA, deregulation of Savings and Loan financial institutions leads to an upsurge in bad loans and fraud.

Braniff International is the first US airline ever to file for bankruptcy (13 May).

British company Laker Airways, providing cheap trans-Atlantic flights, collapses with debts of £270 million (4 Feb).

The US Congress passes a tax-raising package to fight the growing budget deficit (a 5-per cent tax on petrol is called a 'user fee').

p Society, Education, and Religion

In the second half of 1982, unemployment in USA reaches its highest level since the recession of the 1930s, with 12 million out of work, representing a rate of 10.4 per cent.

In USA, the Equal Rights Amendment (passed by Congress in 1972), prohibiting discrimination on the basis of sex, fails to secure ratification of a sufficient number of states to ensure inclusion in the Constitution (30 June); opponents to the Amendment include Phyllis Schlafly, an anti-feminist who mounted the 'Stop ERA' campaign.

In USA, President Reagan announces 'New Federalism', by which the responsibility for funding several welfare measures is left to the states.

US Supreme Court, in NAACP v. Clairborne Hardware Co, overturns judgement making National Association for the Advancement of Colored People liable for damages arising from business boycott (2 July).

Canadian Charter of Rights and Freedoms.

Joel Garreau, *The Nine Nations of North America*.

UNESCO sets 2000 as target year for the eradication of illiteracy in Africa.

Japan introduces new upper secondary school curriculum and standardized textbooks.

Ruling by European Court of Human Rights allows British parents to refuse use of corporal punishment on children at school (25 Feb).

The European Court of Human Rights condemns the use of the tawse in Scottish schools.

In USA, a federal court in Little Rock, Arkansas, declares it unconstitutional to teach creationism on a par with evolutionary theory.

Assemblies of the Presbyterian Church and the United Presbyterian Church in the USA agree to merge (with votes on, respectively, 15 and 29 June), ending a split dating from the American Civil War.

The Israeli invasion of Lebanon (5 June) produces mixed reactions in both Israel and in the world Jewish community.

Publication of *The Final Report* of the Anglican–Roman Catholic International Commission (ARCIC).

Church of England working party produces the report *The Church and the Bomb*, supporting unilateral nuclear disarmament.

General Synod of the Church of England fails to gain necessary majority for a proposed covenant of unity with the Methodists, the United Reformed Church, and the Moravians.

Britain and the Vatican resume full diplomatic relations after break of over 400 years (16 Jan).

q Science, Technology, and Discovery

Compact disc (CD) players go on sale.

The first 'clone' of an IBM personal computer

28 (–2 June) first-ever Papal visit to Britain.

F **June**

3 Israel's ambassador to Britain, Shlomo Argov, is shot and wounded in London street.

4 Israeli jets bomb guerrilla targets in Lebanon in retaliation for Argov shooting.

5 Israeli armed forces invade Lebanon (6, Israeli and Syrian forces clash in southern Lebanon; UN Security Council calls for halt to fighting).

7 rebel forces in Chad capture capital, Ndjamene, overthrowing regime of President Goukouni Oueddi.

8 in the Falklands, British landing ships *Sir Tristram* and *Sir Galahad* are attacked in Bluff Cove, 40 killed.

11 Israeli forces defeat Syrian armour around Lake Karoun.

13 French government announces freeze of prices and incomes following devaluation of franc (to last until 31 Oct).

14 Argentine forces surrender at Port Stanley, ending Falklands War. 255 Britons and 652 Argentines died in Falklands conflict.

14 Israeli forces surround 6,000 PLO guerrillas in West Beirut.

17 President Galtieri resigns; replaced by General Alfredo Saint Jean.

22 leaders of three Kampuchean factions meet in Kuala Lumpur to form opposition government-in-exile.

22 US government extends prohibition on supplying materials for Euro–Siberian gas pipeline to overseas companies manufacturing under licence.

23 Argentine air-force and navy commanders resign from military junta on appointment of General Reynaldo Bignone as president.

25 US secretary of state, Alexander Haig resigns; succeeded by George Shultz.

27 Israel demands surrender of PLO guerrillas in West Beirut (29, offers to allow them to leave Beirut with arms).

G **July**

2 In Britain, Roy Jenkins elected leader of SDP.

6 in Britain, Lord Franks appointed to chair committee of Privy Councillors to investigate background to Falklands invasion.

11 Argentina recognizes de facto cessation of hostilities with Britain (12, British government declares end to hostilities in South Atlantic).

13 Iranian troops enter Iraq, aiming to take Basra; offensive is repulsed.

17 Israeli Prime Minister Begin gives PLO guerrillas in West Beirut 30 days to leave.

20 PLO offers acceptance of UN Security Council Resolution 242 (recognizing Israel's right to exist) in return for US recognition of PLO (25, Palestinian leader Arafat signs document accepting Resolution 242; 26, USA refuses to recognize PLO).

23 International Whaling Commission votes for complete ban on commercial whaling by 1985.

26 Falklands Thanksgiving Service at St Paul's Cathedral, London, after which Archbishop Runcie is criticized for his even-handed sermon.

29 Arab League announces PLO's intention to leave West Beirut, Lebanon.

H **August**

6 Italian authorities order liquidation of country's largest privately owned bank, the Banco Ambrosiano of Milan.

12 EC protests against President Reagan's embargo on use of US technology in construction of West European–Soviet gas pipeline.

17 China and USA agree gradual reduction in US arms sales to Taiwan.

19 Israeli Cabinet accepts US plan to evacuate PLO guerrillas and Syrian troops from Beirut (21, first convoys of guerrillas leave for Cyprus; 30, Yassir Arafat leaves for Tunisia).

23 Lebanese Chamber of Deputies elects leader of Christian Phalangists, Bashir Gemayel, president.

26 Argentine government lifts ban on political parties.

J **September**

1 (12) 12th Congress of Chinese Communist Party in Beijing. Hua Guofeng, who had succeeded Chairman Mao, is removed from Politburo.

13 report by Lord Shackleton on scope for economic development of the Falkland Islands recommends investment of £100 million.

14 President-elect Bashir Gemayel of Lebanon killed in Beirut bomb explosion (23, brother Amin sworn in as president).

17 West German government collapses following withdrawal of Free Democrat ministers (1 Oct, Christian Democrat–Free Democrat coalition government formed under Helmut Kohl).

18 over 800 Palestinians killed after Christian Phalangist militiamen enter West Beirut refugee camps (25, protests in Israel over Beirut massacre; 28; Prime Minister Begin agrees to independent three-man board of inquiry into massacre).

is produced, using the same operating system as the IBM personal computer.

First flight by Boeing 757 airliner (19 Feb).

Soft landings on Venus by Soviet space probes *Venera 13* (1 March) and *14* (4 Nov).

Orbiter *Columbia* makes the first deployment of a satellite from the US space shuttle (11 Nov).

Astronomers at Villanova University in Pennsylvania, USA, announce the discovery of rings around Neptune.

A gene controlling growth is transferred from a rat to a mouse; the mouse grows to double size.

In USA, a new kind of artificial heart keeps a patient alive at the University of Utah Medical Center for 112 days (implanted 2 Dec).

US Congress passes Endangered Species Act Amendments.

Scientists at Darmstadt, West Germany, announce the production of element 109 (29 Aug).

R Humanities

The Cambridge Ancient History, Volume 3, 2nd edition (–).

James Campbell (ed.), *The Anglo-Saxons*.

Keith Wrightson, *English Society, 1580–1680*.

Roy Porter, *English Society in the Eighteenth Century*.

R C O Matthews, C H Feinstein, and J C Odling-Smee, *British Economic Growth 1856–1973*.

The Cambridge History of Classical Literature, Volume 2 (Volume 1, 1985).

Michael Millgate, *Thomas Hardy: A Biography*.

A J Ayer, *Philosophy in the Twentieth Century*.

Richard Rorty, *The Consequences of Pragmatism*.

S Art, Sculpture, Fine Arts, and Architecture

Young British sculptors gain notoriety — Tony Cragg, Richard Deacon, Bill Woodrow, Barry Flanagan.

'Zeitgeist', exhibition at the Martin Gropius Bau, Berlin, West Germany.

Switzerland and Britain collaborate on largest retrospective exhibition of the works of Jean Tinguely.

Painting:

Georg Baselitz, *Last Supper in Dresden*.

Anish Kapoor, *White Sand, Red Millet, Many Flowers*.

Julian Schnabel, *Humanity Asleep*.

Sculpture:

Daniel Buren, *Installation*, for the Kassel Documenta.

Jenny Holzer, *Times Square* (sculpture).

Architecture:

Kisho Kurokawa, Saitama Prefectural Museum of Art, Japan.

Richard Rogers, Inmos Microprocessor Factory, Gwent, Wales.

T Music

Luciano Berio, *La vera storia* (opera).

Edison Denisov, *Death is a Long Sleep*.

Mauricio Kagel, *Rrrrrrr...*

William Mathias, *Lux Aeterna*.

Boris Tishchenko, Second Violin Concerto.

Abba, *The Visitors*.

ABC, *Lexicon of Love*.

Laurie Anderson, *Big Science*.

Clash, *Combat Rock*.

Culture Club, 'Do You Really Want To Hurt Me?'

Dexy's Midnight Runners, 'Come On Eileen'.

Dire Straits, *Love Over Gold*.

J Geils Band, 'Centrefold'.

Michael Jackson, *Thriller*.

Kraftwerk, 'The Model'.

Madness, 'House of Fun'.

Paul McCartney and Stevie Wonder, 'Ebony and Ivory'.

Prince, *1999*.

Richard and Linda Thompson, *Shoot Out the Lights*.

U2, 'New Year's Day'.

Simon and Garfunkel's reunion concert in Central Park.

U Literature and Drama

Isabel Allende, *The House of the Spirits*.

Saul Bellow, *The Dean's December*.

André Brink, *A Chain of Voices*.

Charles Bukowski, *Ham on Rye*.

Carlos Fuentes, *Distant Relations*.

Thomas Keneally, *Schindler's Ark*.

Primo Levi, *If Not Now, When?*

Harry Mulisch, *The Assault*.

V S Pritchett, *Collected Stories*.

John Updike, *Rabbit is Rich*.

Edmund White, *A Boy's Own Story*.

Drama:

John Byrne, *The Slab Boys*.

Tadeusz Cantor, *The Dead Class*.

Caryl Churchill, *Top Girls*.

Harvey Fierstein, *Torch Song Trilogy*.

Michael Frayn, *Noises Off*.

Simon Gray, *Quatermaine's Terms*.

David Mamet, *Edmond*.

Julian Mitchell, *Another Country*.

19 Social Democrats win Swedish general election.

26 Israeli troops withdraw from West Beirut; replaced by peace-keeping force of French, Italian and US troops.

K October

7 Record day's trading on New York Stock Exchange; 147,070,000 shares change hands.

8 new law in Poland bans Solidarity and forbids setting up of new trade unions.

10 USA imposes trade sanctions on Poland.

11 Sikhs besiege Indian Parliament in New Delhi following murders of Sikhs in Punjab state.

12 PLO leader Yassir Arafat holds talks with King Hussein of Jordan over proposed establishment of Palestinian state confederated with Jordan.

13 strikes in Polish shipyards end when military law enforced.

19 Northern Ireland Office announces closure of De Lorean car plant. John De Lorean arrested in Los Angeles, USA, on drugs charges.

20 Sinn Féin wins five seats in elections to Northern Ireland Assembly.

28 Socialists win Spanish general election.

30 new Portuguese constitution comes into force, military influence in government ended.

L November

2 Democrats make large gains in US midterm elections. Republicans retain control of Senate.

2 NUM votes 61 per cent against strike action over pay and pit closures.

7 military coup in Upper Volta.

10 in USSR, President Brezhnev dies (12, Yuri Andropov elected First Secretary of Soviet Communist Party).

11 bomb destroys Israeli military HQ in Tyre, Lebanon; 100 killed.

11 SDLP and Sinn Féin boycott opening of new Northern Ireland Assembly.

12 in Poland, Solidarity leader Lech Walesa released from detention.

16 Sino-Soviet talks open in Moscow, first since 1969.

22 Ramiz Alia becomes new Albanian head of state, replacing Haxhi Lleshi.

M December

5 Greater London Council invites Danny Morrison and Gerry Adams of Sinn Féin to London (8, government bans them from entering the British mainland).

6 in Northern Ireland, 17 killed in bomb explosion at public house in Ballykelly, County Londonderry.

7 US House of Representatives rejects President Reagan's request for $988 million to build and deploy first five of 100 MX missiles.

12 in Britain, 20,000 women encircle Greenham Common air base in protest against proposed siting of US Cruise missiles there.

14 in Ireland, Dr Garret Fitzgerald is elected prime minister at head of Fine Gael–Labour coalition government.

15 IMF agrees credits of $4.5 billion to Brazil to enable it to service its foreign debts.

19 Poland's Council of State announces suspension of martial law (from 31).

Neil Simon, *Brighton Beach Memoirs*.
Bode Sowande, *Flamingo*.
Tom Stoppard, *The Real Thing*.
Britain's Royal Shakespeare Company moves into its new London home, the Barbican Theatre.

v Births and Deaths
Feb 6 Ben Nicholson dies (87).
Feb 17 Thelonius Monk dies (61).
March 8 R A Butler dies (79).
May 12 Humphrey Searle dies (66).
July 29 Vladimir Zworykin dies (92).
June 10 Rainer Werner Fassbinder dies (36).
June 12 Dame Marie Rambert dies (94).
June 21 Prince William of Britain born (–).
Aug 5 John Charnley dies (70).
Aug 29 Ingrid Bergman dies (67).
Sept 1 Wladyslaw Gomulka dies (77).
Sept 14 Grace Kelly dies (53).
Oct 18 Pierre Mendès-France dies (75).
Nov 5 Jacques Tati dies (74).
Nov 10 Leonid Brezhnev dies (75).
Dec 20 Artur Rubinstein dies (95).

w Everyday Life
In Britain, Michael Fagan, a burglar, breaks into Buckingham Palace in London, steals a bottle of wine from a cellar, and enters the Queen's bedroom; the Queen awakes to find him drinking and only manages to obtain help when Fagan asks for a cigarette (7 July).
Time magazine's 'Man of the Year' is 'Pac-Man', a character from a computer game that sweeps the USA in 1982.
Inland Telegram service in UK ends (2 Oct).

x Sport and Recreation
15 England cricketers are banned from Test cricket for three years for participation in a cricket tour of South Africa, breaking an international ban on sporting links with that country.
The Australia rugby league team wins all 22 matches on its tour of Britain and France.
The soccer World Cup is held in Spain; Italy beats West Germany 3–1 in the Final.

Daley Thompson of Britain wins the European decathlon title in Athens, setting a new world record of 8,743 points; he simultaneously holds the Olympic, Commonwealth, and European decathlon titles.
In USA, the professional football season is interrupted by a players' strike, lasting 57 days (20 Sept–22 Nov). The dispute is settled by a Collective Bargaining Agreement which establishes a minimum salary for players and introduces severance pay to help those moving to other careers.

y Media
In USA, publication of *USA Today*, an all-colour national newspaper (15 Sept).
In Britain, launch of the *Mail on Sunday* (Oct).

Film:
Bladerunner (director, Ridley Scott; starring Harrison Ford).
Diner (director, Barry Levinson).
ET (director, Steven Spielberg).
Fanny and Alexander (director, Ingmar Bergman).
Fitzcarraldo (director, Werner Herzog).
Gandhi (director, Richard Attenborough; sets world record for the number of extras).
An Officer and a Gentleman (director, Taylor Hackford; starring Richard Gere).
Passion (director, Jean-Luc Goddard).
The Return of Martin Guerre (director, Daniel Vigne).
Tootsie (starring Dustin Hoffman).

Television:
In USA, television commercials are deregulated, removing restrictions on content and length (23 Nov).
New programmes in USA include *Cheers* (NBC; –1993).
Start of broadcasts by Britain's Channel 4 television station; also of S4C, a station transmitting some programmes in Welsh.
New programmes in Britain include: *Boys from the Blackstuff*, a play by Alan Bleasdale; *The Flight of the Condor* (BBC); *A Kind of Loving* (Granada); *Smiley's People*, starring Alec Guinness; *Wogan*, chat show with Terry Wogan.

Cruise missiles deployed in Britain ... USSR shoots down Korean
passenger jet ... USA invades Grenada ...

A January

6 In reshuffle of British cabinet Michael Heseltine becomes defence secretary.

13 Saudi Arabia re-establishes diplomatic links with Libya.

17 Nigeria orders expulsion of 2 million illegal immigrants.

18 in Britain, Franks Report published; it exonerates Margaret Thatcher's government of blame for Argentine junta's decision to invade Falkland Islands on 2 April 1982.

18 Group of Ten leading countries agree increase in funds of 'General Arrangements to Borrow' unit of IMF from $7.1 billion to $19 billion.

19 South Africa re-imposes direct rule on South-West Africa (Namibia).

24 32 Italian Red Brigade terrorists jailed for kidnap and murder of Aldo Moro in 1978.

27 US–Soviet talks resume in Geneva with USSR proposing nuclear-free zone for central Europe.

B February

8 Kahane Commission on Beirut massacre (18 Sept 1982) condemns Israeli government and recommends dismissal of Defence Minister Sharon (11, Sharon resigns).

15 Christian Phalangist militia withdraws from Beirut, giving Lebanese government control over the city.

19 Joshua Nkomo held by Zimbabwean police.

24 in India, 1,500 reported dead in violence during local elections in Assam.

24 in Britain, Liberals win Bermondsey by-election from Labour.

24 western banks underwrite $5 billion loan to Mexico; also short-term loan of $433 million.

28 in Britain, Yorkshire and South Wales miners called out on strike to protest against planned pit closures.

C March

3 British National Union of Mineworkers executive calls ballot for national strike.

5 Labour Party wins Australian general election.

6 Christian Democrats win general election in West Germany. Green Party wins 24 seats in Bundestag.

9 Joshua Nkomo flees Zimbabwe (15 Aug, returns).

14 OPEC agrees to cut oil prices for first time since formation in 1961; price of Saudi light crude reduced from $34 a barrel to $29.

17 Chad seeks assistance of UN in border dispute with Libya.

23 President Reagan proposes 'Star Wars' defence system for USA, using satellites to detect enemy missiles and effect destruction.

28 chairman of British Steel, Ian MacGregor, appointed chairman of National Coal Board.

31 President Reagan of USA halts sale of F-16 fighter aircraft to Israel until its troops are fully withdrawn from Lebanon.

D April

10 US Middle East peace plan collapses when Jordan withdraws from talks.

12 Vietnam claims victory over Kampuchean rebels.

22 leader of Polish Solidarity trade union Lech Walesa returns to work at Lenin Shipyard, Gdansk.

24 Socialist Party loses majority in Austrian elections (11 May, coalition government formed under Dr Fred Sinowitz).

24 Turkey's military government permits formation of political parties; ban remains on 150 leading politicians.

E May

4 Iran outlaws Tudeh, Iranian Communist Party, and expels 18 Soviet diplomats.

4 President Reagan of USA declares support for aim of Nicaraguan Contras to overthrow Sandinista government.

17 Israel and Lebanon sign agreement providing for withdrawal of Israeli troops from Lebanon within three months.

25 USA agrees to export high-technology items to China.

F June

1 Civilian members of Palestinian Al Fatah faction declare opposition to Arafat's leadership of PLO.

9 Conservatives win overall majority of 144 seats in British general election, taking 397 seats, against Labour, 209, Liberal–SDP Alliance, 23, others 21 (Conservatives win 42.4 per cent of votes cast, Labour, 27.6 per cent, Liberal–SDP Alliance, 25.4 per cent).

First US woman in space ... Publication of the 'Hitler Diaries' ...
Australia wins America's Cup ...

o Politics, Government, Law, and Economy

In South Africa, formation of the United Democratic Front (UDF) (Aug), an anti-apartheid organization which attracts two million members in affiliated clubs, societies, and churches (the president is Dr Allan Boesak).

The government of South Africa holds referendum of white voters on Constitution Act, providing for parliament to be reconstituted as three chambers (one each for whites, coloureds, and Indians) and for parliament to elect the president; two-thirds of voters support the plan (2 Nov).

British government White Paper proposes abolition of Greater London Council and metropolitan counties (7 Oct).

The number of Members of Parliament in Britain is increased to 650; the pay of MPs is linked to civil service rates.

In USA, in Immigration and Naturalization Service v. Chadha, the Supreme Court's ruling invalidates the legislative veto of delegated powers (23 June).

NHS hospitals in Britain are obliged to allow private contractors to tender for cleaning, catering, and laundry services (from 8 Sept).

Hitachi Ltd pleads guilty in US federal court to charges of conspiracy to obtain classified information on IBM computers (8 Feb).

USSR announces reforms allowing factory managers greater autonomy over wages, bonuses, and technical innovations (26 July).

P Society, Education, and Religion

US Congress votes to make birthday of Martin Luther King (15 Jan) a federal holiday from 1986 (legislation signed 2 Nov).

In USA, Harold Washington is elected the first African-American mayor of Chicago (13 April).

Guion Bluford is the first African-American to go into space, in the US space shuttle (launched 30 Sept).

In Akron v. Akron Center for Reproductive Health, the US Supreme Court limits power of state and local governments to restrict access to legal abortions (15 June).

Wearing of seat belts by front-seat car passengers made compulsory in Britain.

Ernest Gellner, *Nations and Nationalism*.

In USA, the National Commission on Excellence in Education's report, *A Nation at Risk* (published 26 April), is sharply critical of declining standards.

In Belgium, school-leaving age extended to 18.

Technical and Vocational Education Initiative launched in Britain.

Schools Council abolished in Britain.

In Iran, Ayatollah Khomeini declares that Islam is a 'religion of the sword' and sends armed pilgrims to Mecca.

A referendum in the Republic of Ireland results in a two to one majority for enshrining the existing legal ban on abortion in the national constitution.

General Synod of the Church of England rejects support for unilateral nuclear disarmament.

United Reformed Church becomes the first church in Britain officially to support unilateral nuclear disarmament.

Q Science, Technology, and Discovery

IBM in the USA produces the first personal computer with a built-in hard disc.

Apple Computers in USA devise a computer programme featuring 'pull-down' menus with instructions given by means of a 'mouse' control box.

Japan launches the 'fifth generation' computer project, aiming to produce a machine capable of 1 billion computations per second.

Launch of Infrared Astronomical Satellite, designed to detect infrared radiation from objects in space (25 Jan).

US space probe *Pioneer 10* is first human-made object to leave solar system (13 June).

A mission by space shuttle *Challenger* (18–24 June) includes the first US woman to go into space, Sally Ride.

Soviet probes *Venera 15* and *16* (launched on 5 and 7 June) enter orbit around Venus (10 and 14 Oct).

Observation of 'W' and 'Z' sub-atomic particles in experiments at CERN, Switzerland; the existence of these particles had been predicted as carriers of the weak nuclear force (June).

First experiments with Joint European Torus equipment at Culham, England, attempting to generate electricity by means of nuclear fusion.

In USA, a research team at the University of California at Los Angeles performs the first successful transfer of a human embryo.

Researchers isolate the hormone (produced by the heart) that regulates blood pressure (June; synthesized in Aug).

Andrew W Murray and Jack W Szostak create the first artificial chromosome.

9 new centre-left coalition government under Mario Soares takes office in Portugal.

11 British Cabinet reshuffle: Nigel Lawson becomes chancellor of the exchequer; Sir Geoffrey Howe, foreign secretary; Leon Brittan, home secretary; Cecil Parkinson, trade and industry secretary.

12 Michael Foot announces intention to resign as leader of British Labour Party.

14 in Britain, Roy Jenkins resigns leadership of SDP (21, Dr David Owen named as successor).

16 Pope begins eight-day visit to Poland and has talks with General Jaruzelski and Lech Walesa (19, Polish government warns Church to stay out of politics).

17 British annual rate of inflation falls to 3.7 per cent, lowest in 15 years.

24 Yassir Arafat is ordered out of Syria; Syrian tanks besiege PLO guerrilla bases in Lebanon.

27 British defence secretary announces plan to build £215 million airport for Falkland Islands.

G **July**

6 British Defence White Paper *Statement on the Defence Estimates* re-states government's plan to deploy Cruise missiles at Greenham Common and Molesworth.

12 in Britain, secretary of state for employment announces further reforms in Trade Union law, including compulsory strike ballots.

16 nine-nation committee of Organization of African Unity calls on foreign countries to end involvement in civil war in Chad.

20 Israeli Cabinet agrees on partial withdrawal of troops from Lebanon, redeployed south of Chouf Mountains.

21 Polish government announces end to martial law and amnesty for political prisoners.

25 Sri Lankan government imposes curfew following attacks on Tamil community (28, ban imposed on political parties advocating partition).

28 US House of Representatives votes to end covert aid to Nicaraguan contras by 30 Sept.

H **August**

2 Libyan planes bomb Faya-Largeau in Chad (7, France sends paratroops to supplement 500 'military instructors' in Chad).

8 military coup in Guatemala.

11 Faya-Largeau in Chad falls to Libyan troops (19, further 3,500 French troops sent to assist President Habre).

12 President Zia of Pakistan announces elections for March 1985 and end of martial law.

14 French police seize large consignment of arms bound for IRA.

19 40,000 Argentines protest at proposed amnesty for military personnel involved in human-rights violations during 1970s.

20 President Reagan of USA lifts ban on export of pipe-laying equipment to USSR.

21 Philippines opposition leader Benigno Aquino assassinated at Manila airport.

28 Israeli Prime Minister Menachim Begin announces intention to resign (15 Sept, succeeded by Yitzhak Shamir).

J **September**

1 269 killed when South Korean Boeing 747 airliner is shot down by Soviet fighter after straying into Soviet air space near Sakhalin Island (5, West European nations impose 14-day ban on Aeroflot flights).

4 civil war breaks out in Lebanon's Chouf mountains following withdrawal of Israeli troops.

6 final document of European Conference on Security and Co-operation adopted in Madrid, pledging governments to continue 'Helsinki process' of peaceful settlement of disputes and increased respect for human rights.

6 USSR admits military chiefs ordered fighters to stop flight of stray Korean airliner (8, US Secretary of State Shultz describes Soviet response to South Korean airliner disaster as inadequate).

11 violent protests in Chile on 10th anniversary of military coup.

16 in USA, CIA denies South Korean airliner was engaged in spying.

19 Caribbean islands of St Kitts-Nevis achieve independence from Britain.

21 demonstrators in Philippines demand resignation of President Marcos (29, Marcos orders closure of any newspaper alleging army officers involved in murder of Aquino).

26 ceasefire agreed in Lebanon; government agrees to conference of national reconciliation.

K **October**

2 Neil Kinnock elected leader of British Labour Party.

5 Nobel Peace Prize awarded to Polish Solidarity leader Lech Walesa.

6 Indian government takes over direct control of Punjab state in response to growing violence.

10 in Philippines, commission investigating Aquino murder resigns (22, Marcos appoints new commission).

Fernand Daffos extracts the blood from a foetus and diagnoses disease in the foetus.

Researchers at the US National Cancer Institute and at the Pasteur Institute in Paris, France, isolate the virus thought to cause AIDS; it becomes known as the HIV virus.

R Humanities

Paul Ratchnevsky, *Genghis Khan: His Life and Legacy*.

Peter Clark, *The English Alehouse: A Social History 1200–1830*.

Daniel J Boorstin, *The Discoverers*.

Maldwyn A Jones, *The Limits of Liberty: American History 1607–1980*.

Final (48th) volume of W S Lewis (ed.), *Horace Walpole's Correspondence*.

C A Bayly, *Rulers, Townsmen and Bazaars: North Indian Society in the Age of British Expansion, 1770–1870*.

P J Waller, *Town, City, and Nation: England 1850–1914*.

John Campbell, *F E Smith*.

Alan Bullock, *Ernest Bevin: Foreign Secretary*.

Clifford Geertz, *Local Knowledge: Further Essays in Interpretive Anthropology*.

Karl Popper, *Realism and the Aim of Science*.

S Art, Sculpture, Fine Arts, and Architecture

London auctioneers Sotheby's bought by Alfred Taubman of USA.

'The Temporary Contemporary', exhibition Los Angeles Museum of Contemporary Art, Los Angeles, USA.

'The Essential Cubism', exhibition at the Tate Gallery, London.

Painting:

Cindy Sherman, *Untitled* No. 131.

Sculpture:

Joseph Beuys, *Untitled Vitrine*.

Richard Deacon, *For Those Who Have Ears*.

Jenny Holzer, *New York City*.

Niki de Saint Phalle, Jean Tinguely, Fountain, Pompidou Centre, Paris.

Architecture:

Tadao Ando, Rokko Housing, Hyogo, Japan.

Sir Leslie Martin, Gulbenkian Foundation for Modern Art, Lisbon, Portugal.

T Music

Leonard Bernstein, *A Quiet Place* (opera).

Harrison Birtwistle, *The Mask of Orpheus* (opera).

Pierre Boulez, *Répons*.

Witold Lutoslawski, Symphony No. 3.

Olivier Messiaen, *Saint François d'Assise* (opera).

Alfred Schnittke, String Quartet No. 3.

La Cage aux Folles (musical), by Jerry Herman and Harvey Fierstein (first performed at the Palace Theatre, New York, 21 Aug).

David Bowie, 'Let's Dance' (single and album).

Phil Collins, 'You Can't Hurry Love'.

Duran Duran, 'Is There Something I Should Know?'

The Fall, *Perverted by Language*.

Marvin Gaye, 'Sexual Healing'.

Michael Jackson, 'Beat It', 'Billy Jean'.

Michael Jackson and Paul McCartney, 'Say, Say, Say'.

Madonna, *Madonna*.

Men At Work, *Business As Usual*.

Police, 'Every Breath You Take', *Synchronicity*.

REM, *Murmur*.

Z Z Top, *Eliminator*.

U Literature and Drama

Isaac Asimov, *Foundation's Edge*.

Malcolm Bradbury, *Rates of Exchange*.

Anita Brookner, *Look At Me*.

Hugo Claus, *Sorrow of Belgium*.

Ariel Dorfman, *Widows*.

Gabriel García Márquez, *Chronicle of a Death Foretold*.

Andrew Harvey, *A Journey in Ladakh*.

Elizabeth Jolly, *Miss Peabody's Inheritance*.

William Least-heat Moon, *Blue Highways*.

Norman Mailer, *Ancient Evenings*.

R K Narayan, *A Tiger for Malgudi*.

Salman Rushdie, *Shame*.

Alice Walker, *The Color Purple*.

Drama:

Howard Barker, *Victory*.

Howard Brenton, *The Genius*.

Harvey Fierstein, *La Cage aux Folles*.

David Hare, *A Map of the World*.

David Mamet, *Glengarry Glen Ross*.

Marsha Norman, *'Night Mother*.

Sam Shepard, *Fool for Love*.

V Births and Deaths

Feb 23 Adrian Boult dies (93).

Feb 25 Tennessee Williams dies (71).

March 3 Arthur Koestler dies (77).

March 6 Donald Maclean dies (69).

March 8 William Walton dies (80).

March 15 Rebecca West dies (90).

April 30 George Melitonovich Balanchine dies (79).

May 21 Kenneth Clark dies (82).

May 31 Jack Dempsey dies (87).

July 1 R Buckminster Fuller dies (87).

July 24 Georges Auric dies (84).

July 29 Luis Buñuel dies (83).

Aug 5 Joan Robinson dies (79).

12 Chinese Communist Party commences biggest purge of membership since Cultural Revolution; qualifications of 40 million party members to be reviewed.

14 British Trade and Industry Secretary Cecil Parkinson resigns following revelations of adultery with his secretary, Sarah Keays (16, succeeded by Norman Tebbit).

19 left-wing military coup in Grenada, in which Prime Minister Maurice Bishop is killed.

22 anti-nuclear protests held across Europe against deployment of US Pershing II and Cruise missiles.

23 attacks by suicide bombers kill 242 US and 62 French troops in peace-keeping force in military compound, Beirut, Lebanon.

25 US Marines invade Grenada to depose military government (28, USA vetoes UN resolution deploring invasion).

30 Radical Party, led by Raoúl Alfonsín, gains absolute majority in Argentine elections.

31 Governor-General of Grenada, Sir Paul Scoon, confirms that he requested assistance from East Caribbean forces and indirectly from USA.

L **November**

4 Governor of Grenada declares state of emergency.

9 China's Foreign Ministry announces intention to declare unilateral policy on Hong Kong in Sept 1984 if no agreement has been reached with Britain.

14 Defence Secretary Heseltine announces arrival of first Cruise missiles at Greenham Common (15, 141 people arrested at demonstration outside Greenham Common airbase).

14 Turkish Cypriot Legislative Council issues unilateral proclamation of independence of Turkish part of island (18, UN Security Council Resolution 541 declares action illegal).

21 Official Unionist Party withdraws from Northern Ireland Assembly.

22 West German Bundestag votes for deployment of Pershing II missiles in country.

23 USSR walks out of arms limitation talks in Geneva following deployment of US missiles in Europe (24, President Andropov announces USSR to increase number of submarine missiles targeted at USA).

M **December**

6 Turkey's National Security Council dissolved, ending three years of military rule.

9 former British Foreign Secretary Lord Carrington named as successor to Dr Joseph Luns as secretary general of NATO from 1984.

10 Raoúl Alfonsín installed as President of Argentina, ending eight years of military rule.

17 IRA car bomb explodes outside Harrods department store in London, killing six.

20 Yassir Arafat and 4,000 supporters evacuated from Lebanon.

25 Egypt and Jordan sign accord restoring economic relations.

29 USA announces intention of withdrawing from UNESCO at end of 1984, alleging that the organization 'exhibited hostility towards the basic installations of a free society'.

31 coup led by Major-General Mohammed Buhari ousts government of President Shagari of Nigeria.

Miners' strike in Britain ... IRA bombs British government ...
Indira Gandhi assassinated ...

A **January**

1 Brunei becomes independent after 95 years as British Protectorate.

1 19-member Supreme Military Council assumes power in Nigeria.

10 'amity talks' convened in Sri Lanka between Tamil and Sinhalese representatives.

17 35-nation conference on disarmament in Europe opens in Stockholm.

18 President of American University in Beirut, Malcolm Kerr, is shot dead by pro-Iranian group.

19 Islamic Conference Organization votes to invite Egypt back to membership (suspended since Camp David accord).

19 USA partly lifts trade sanctions on Poland.

25 British government announces that staff at Government Communications Headquarters (GCHQ) in Cheltenham to be deprived of right to belong to trades unions (21 Feb, government announces that most GCHQ workers have accepted offer of £1,000 to surrender union rights).

Aug 18 Nikolaus Pevsner dies (81).
Nov 25 Anton Dolin dies (79).
Dec 20 Bill Brandt dies (78).
Dec 25 Joan Miró dies (90).

w Everyday Life

In USA, start of craze for Cabbage Patch dolls.

x Sport and Recreation

In cricket, Australia defeats England and regains the Ashes (7 Jan).

In Britain, Lester Piggott, riding Teenoso, wins a record ninth Derby (1 June).

The first five horses home in the Cheltenham Gold Cup in Britain are all trained by Michael Dickinson.

The first World Athletics Championships are held in Helsinki, free of boycotts, with 157 nations competing; the USA leads the gold medal table with 8.

In yacht-racing, the USA fails to win the America's Cup for the first since the race series began in 1870; the victor is the Australian yacht *Australia II*.

y Media

Stern magazine in Germany publishes extracts from 'The Hitler Diaries' (May), which are considered authentic by historian Hugh Trevor-Roper but later exposed as a fake produced by a dealer in Nazi memorabilia.

In Britain, Eddie Shah launches the Messenger group of free newspapers in Warrington, produced by non-union workers; 29 Nov, police used to break union picket.

Film:

The Ballad of Narayama (director, Shohei Imamura).

The Big Chill (director, Lawrence Kasdan).

Danton (director, Andrzej Wajda).

The King of Comedy (director, Martin Scorsese; starring Robert de Niro).

Local Hero (director, Bill Forsyth).

El Norte (director, Gregory Nava).

Pauline on the Beach (director, Eric Rohmer).

The Right Stuff (director, Philip Kaufman).

Rue Cases Nègres (director, Euzhan Palcy).

Rumblefish (director, Francis Ford Coppola).

Zelig (director and star, Woody Allen).

Television:

East German television buys US films starring Robert Redford to schedule against competition from West German television.

Launch in Britain of 'TV AM', breakfast-time television station.

New programmes in Britain include: *An Englishman Abroad* (BBC), by Alan Bennett; *Blackadder* (BBC; –1989), starring Rowan Atkinson; *Birth of a Nation* (Central), the first of four dramas by David Leland; *The Winds of War*.

Humans thought to be closely related to chimpanzees ... Dr Alec Jeffreys invents 'genetic fingerprinting' ...

o Politics, Government, Law, and Economy

Rates Act gives the British government the power to override decisions of local councils on their property tax (rate) levels.

British Police and Criminal Evidence Act ('PACE') reforms police powers of entry, search, and arrest, and revises rules on treatment and interrogation of suspects.

The Data Protection Act regulates the use of computer data in Britain and establishes the office of the Data Protection Registrar to oversee the requirements of the Act; the Act gives people the right of access to computerized information about themselves.

In USA, American Telephone and Telegraphy Co (AT&T) is broken up into regional telephone systems, a research company, and a residual corporation dealing with long-distance connections (1 Jan).

British government sells shares in British

B February

1 Nissan announces plan to build pilot car-assembly plant in England.

6 in Lebanon, President Gemayel orders 24-hour curfew as Shi'ite Muslim and Druze militias over-run West Beirut.

7 President Reagan orders US marines to withdraw from Beirut (26, last US marines leave).

9 President Andropov of USSR dies (13, Konstantin Chernenko named first secretary of Soviet Communist Party).

11 Iraq commences bombing of non-military targets in Iran.

27 Iraq announces blockade of main Iranian oil terminal at Kharg Island and threatens to attack oil tankers loading there.

C March

1 Joint South African-Angolan monitoring commission begins supervision of South African troop withdrawal from southern Angola.

1 in Britain, Tony Benn, out of Parliament since 1983 election, wins Chesterfield by-election for Labour.

4 Speaker of Iranian Parliament claims 400 Iranian soldiers killed by Iraqi chemical weapons.

7 Polish students stage sit-in at Stanislaw Staszic College in Mietne to demand restoration of crucifixes in classrooms.

8 leaders of British NUM support planned strikes in Yorkshire and Scotland over proposed pit closures.

12 (−20) new Lebanon reconciliation conference in Lausanne.

12 in Britain, miners' strike spreads to 100 pits (15, only 21 pits working, most of these in Nottinghamshire).

13 British Budget raises income tax allowances, abolishes employers' National Insurance surcharge, begins reduction of Corporation Tax to 35 per cent over three years, and plans Borrowing Requirement of £7,250 million (2.5 per cent of GDP).

23 in Britain, Sarah Tisdall, junior Foreign Office clerk, jailed for leaking secret documents on arrival of Cruise missiles in Britain to the *Guardian* newspaper.

31 Indian government agrees to amend Punjabi constitution to acknowledge Sikhism as religion distinct from Hinduism.

D April

3 Indian state of Punjab is declared 'dangerously disturbed area' (5, government imposes detention without trial).

4 in Britain, bailiffs clear women's peace camp at Greenham Common.

5 in Britain, Nottinghamshire miners reject NUM Executive Committee's recommendation not to cross picket lines.

6 Polish government and Catholic Church agree compromise on display of crucifixes in state schools and other public places.

12 British NUM President Arthur Scargill vetoes proposed national ballot on continuation of pit strike.

17 in London, WPC Yvonne Fletcher killed and 11 others injured when gunmen inside Libyan People's Bureau fire on demonstrators (22, Britain breaks diplomatic relations with Libya; 27, siege of building ends).

20 demonstrations in West Germany against deployment of US missiles in Europe.

E May

2 Publication of report of New Ireland Forum, formed by three main parties in Ireland and the SDLP in Northern Ireland. It advocates creation of united Ireland by federation of Ireland and Northern Ireland or by government of Northern Ireland under joint authority of Britain and Ireland.

2 dissident Soviet physicist Andrei Sakharov begins hunger strike when authorities refuse to allow wife, Yelena Bonner, to travel abroad for medical treatment (6 Aug, ends).

3 opposition parties gain seats in British local elections.

10 International Court of Justice at The Hague rules that USA should cease blockade of Nicaraguan ports.

10 Danish Parliament votes to halt payments to NATO for deployment of Pershing II and Cruise missiles in Europe.

14 opposition makes gains in Philippine elections.

23 in British miners' strike, talks between Arthur Scargill and Ian MacGregor on pit closures break down.

24 five former El Salvador National Guardsmen found guilty of murder of three US nuns and female lay assistant in 1980.

24 US House of Representatives votes to continue military aid to El Salvador, but against further aid to Nicaraguan Contras.

24 Iranian war planes attack oil tankers off coast of Saudi Arabia (27, USA sends Stinger anti-aircraft missiles to Saudi Arabia in case of Iranian attack).

29 in Britain, 64 injured and 84 arrested in confrontation between pickets and police at

Telecom, for the first time using techniques of mass marketing with the intention of creating a nation of small shareholders.

Texaco Inc acquires the Getty Oil Co in the largest business merger in US history.

P Society, Education, and Religion

United Nations holds its second Conference on World Population, in Mexico (6–13 Aug); representatives of 149 countries adopt 88 recommendations.

In USA, Christine Craft, a newsreader who was demoted to reporter because she was considered 'Too old, unattractive, and not deferential enough to men', is awarded damages of $325,000.

In Britain, Brenda Dean is the first woman to lead major British union; elected leader of print union SOGAT '82 (March).

In Britain, report of Committee of Inquiry into Human Fertilization and Embryology, chaired by Dame Mary Warnock, recommends control of research into 'test-tube' babies and ban on surrogate motherhood agencies (published 18 July).

Bath houses closed in San Francisco, USA, to slow the spread of AIDS.

British House of Commons passes new divorce law, allowing spouses to end marriage after one year (14 June).

USA withdraws from UNESCO, alleging that it is too critical of American policy.

In USA, the 'Perkins' Vocational Education Act provides financial incentives for state developments to encourage vocational education and links between school and industry.

In USSR, school reforms include lengthening compulsory schooling to 11 years (to 12 years in the Baltic republics of Estonia, Latvia, and Lithuania).

Council for the Accreditation of Teacher Education established in Britain.

British Parliament approves the new GCSE (General Certificate of Secondary Education) examination, to replace 'O' level and CSE from 1988.

In India troops lay siege to the Golden Temple in Amritsar where Sikh militants had barricaded themselves in an attempt to secure special status for Amritsar and constitutional recognition for Sikhism.

The Roman Catholic church in Chile officially backs demonstrations against violations of human rights for the first time under the regime of General Augusto Pinochet.

The Roman Catholic Sacred Congregation for the Doctrine of the Faith publishes *An Instruction on Certain Aspects of the Theology of Liberation*, warning against acceptance of Marxist ideology (3 Sept).

Leading proponent of liberation theology, Father Leonardo Boff of Brazil, appears before the Doctrinal Office of the Vatican, accompanied by two Brazilian cardinals.

The Concordat of 1929 between the Vatican City State and Italy is revised, with Roman Catholicism losing its status as official state religion of Italy.

In USA, the Supreme Court, in Lynch v. Donnelly, rules that the public financing of Nativity scenes does not violate the principle of separation of Church and State (5 Mar).

US evangelists Billy Graham and Luis Palau hold missions in Britain.

The appointment of Rev Professor David Jenkins as Bishop of Durham in England arouses controversy because of the Bishop-elect's views on Christian doctrine; after the Bishop's consecration in York Minster (6 July) lightning strikes the Minster (9 July), prompting discussion about a possible act of God.

G A Lindbeck, *The Nature of Doctrine.*

Q Science, Technology, and Discovery

Two US shuttle astronauts make untethered space walks, using jet-propelled back packs to move in space (7 Feb).

An Indian astronomer discovers two more rings around Saturn.

US astronomers working in Chile photograph a partial ring system around Neptune.

US astronomers photograph a planet system around the star Beta Pictoris.

An Australian woman gives birth to a child created by in vitro fertilization of her husband's sperm with another woman's egg (Jan).

An Australian woman gives birth to a child developed from a previously frozen fertilized embryo.

William H Clewall of the University of Colorado, USA, performs the first successful operation on an unborn foetus.

Surgeons at Loma Linda University Medical Center in California, USA, transplant the heart of a baboon into a two-week-old girl; the patient survives for 20 days (dies 15 Nov).

In USA, the Texas Board of Education repeals rule requiring evolution to be taught as one of several theories, rather than as fact (14 April).

From studies of DNA, Charles G Sibley and Jon E Ahlquist argue that humans are more closely related to chimpanzees than to other great apes and that humans and apes diverged approximately 5–6 million years ago.

In Britain, Dr Alec Jeffreys of the University of Leicester discovers that a core sequence

Orgreave coke works (30, Arthur Scargill arrested and charged with obstruction).

F June

1 US Secretary of State Shultz calls on Nicaraguan government to stop support for rebels in El Salvador.
2 South African Prime Minister Botha meets Margaret Thatcher at Chequers; the first visit by a South African prime minister to Britain in 23 years.
6 250 Sikh extremists killed when Indian troops storm Golden Temple at Amritsar (11, Sikh soldiers mutiny at eight army bases in protest at attack).
10 Iraq seeks UN supervision of agreement with Iran to stop attacks on civilian areas.
14 Dutch parliament approves cabinet decision to delay final decision on deployment of Cruise missiles.
14 in British by-election, SDP wins Portsmouth South from Conservatives.
25 (–26) summit conference of EC heads of government at Fontainebleau, France, reaches agreement on British budget contribution.
27 British unions hold 'day of action' in support of striking miners.
29 Indian Prime Minister Indira Gandhi dismisses governor and police chief of Punjab.

G July

4 Lebanese Army units take over positions in Beirut from militias.
5 former Nigerian Transport Minister Umaru Dikko, exiled in Britain, found inside crate at Stansted airport (12, Britain expels two Nigerian diplomats).
10 (–20) national dock strike in Britain over use of non-registered labour.
14 Labour Party defeats ruling National Party in New Zealand general election.
16 British High Court rules ban on union membership at GCHQ illegal (6 Aug, Court of Appeal overturns ruling; 22 Nov, House of Lords upholds ban).
18 in USA, Democratic Party Convention in San Francisco selects Walter Mondale and Geraldine Ferraro (first woman to be nominated) as Party candidates for president and vice-president.
19 Jacques Delors named president of European Commission from Jan 1985.
21 James F Fixx, author of *The Complete Guide to Running*, the 'joggers' Bible', dies of a heart attack while jogging.

H August

1 Legal moves begun to seize assets of South Wales miners after they fail to meet deadline for payment of fine.
3 Upper Volta renamed Burkina Faso ('land of upright men').
4 violent clashes between Tamils and Sinhalese in Sri Lanka.
8 Robert Mugabe announces plan for one-party state in Zimbabwe.
13 federation established between Libya and Morocco.
16 John De Lorean acquitted in USA of eight charges of drug-trafficking.
22 in USA, Republican Party Convention in Dallas nominates President Reagan and Vice-President Bush as party's nominees for November election.
23 in USSR, Yelena Bonner, wife of dissident physicist Sakharov, sentenced to five years' internal exile.
24 (–18 Sept) national dock strike in Britain, sparked by Hunterston dockers attempting to block coal supplies to Ravenscraig steel works in support of miners.
31 Yitzhak Shamir and Shimon Peres agree to form government of national unity in Israel and to alternate in post of prime minister.

J September

3 14 die in rioting in Sharpeville and other black townships around Johannesburg.
4 Progressive Conservatives defeat ruling Liberals in Canada's general election.
9 British Coal Board Chairman Ian MacGregor arrives for talks with Arthur Scargill in Edinburgh with carrier bag over his head.
12 in Britain, High Court grants eviction order against Greenham Common peace camp.
14 South African Prime Minister Botha sworn in as country's first executive president (17, first 19-member multi-racial Cabinet sworn in).
17 France reaches agreement with Libya for withdrawal of both countries' forces from Chad by mid-November.
20 in Lebanon, bomb explodes at US embassy in Beirut, killing 23.
22 new Bishop of Durham, Dr David Jenkins, describes British Coal Board Chairman Ian MacGregor as an 'imported, elderly American' (27, Archbishop of Canterbury expresses regret at remarks).
25 Jordan restores full diplomatic relations with Egypt.
26 draft agreement for return of Hong Kong to China in 1997 signed by British and

of DNA is unique to each person; this examination of DNA, known as 'genetic fingerprinting', can be used to establish family relationships and in criminal investigations.

Allan Wilson and Russell Higuchi of the University of California at Berkeley, USA, clone genes from an extinct animal, the zebra-like quagga.

Element 108 synthesized.

R Humanities

Kenneth O Morgan (ed.), *The Oxford Illustrated History of Britain*.

J Catto, *The Early Oxford Schools*, the first volume in The History of the University of Oxford (–).

J H Elliott, *Richelieu and Olivares*.

Leslie Bethell (ed.), *The Cambridge History of Latin America* (–1991).

Encyclopedia of American History.

David Hempton, *Methodism and Politics in British Society, 1750–1850*.

Kenneth O Morgan, *Labour in Power, 1945–1951*.

Donald Davidson, *Inquiries into Truth and Interpretation*.

Nelson Goodman, *Of Mind and Other Matters*.

S Art, Sculpture, Fine Arts, and Architecture

In Britain, first Turner Prize for Painting is awarded to Malcolm Morley.

Frank Stella is first visual artist to hold post of Charles Eliot Norton Professor of Poetry at Harvard University, USA.

'Primitivism in the Twentieth Century', exhibition at Museum of Modern Art, New York.

Neo-Geo movement in the USA.

Painting, etc:

Hans Haacke, *Taking Stock*.

Sculpture:

Tony Cragg, *St. George and the Dragon* (sculpture).

Architecture:

High Tech, Classicism — two extremes in architectural design.

Philip Johnson, John Burgee, AT&T Building, New York.

James Stirling, Neue Staatsgalerie, Stuttgart, West Germany.

The Prince of Wales, in an address to the Royal Institute of British Architects at Hampton Court, London (30 May), attacks Modern Architecture (describing the proposed extension to the National Gallery as 'a carbuncle on the face of an old friend').

T Music

Robert Ashley, *Perfect Lives* (video opera).

Luciano Berio, *Un re in ascolta* (opera).

Philip Glass, *Akhnaten* (opera).

Krzysztof Penderecki, *Polish Requiem*.

Michael Tippett, *The Mask of Time*.

Sunday in the Park with George (musical), lyrics and music by Stephen Sondheim (first performed at the Booth Theatre, New York, 2 May).

Band Aid, 'Do They Know It's Christmas?'

Phil Collins, 'Against All Odds, Take A Look At Me'.

Einsturtzende Neubauten, 'Strategien gegen Architekturen'.

Frankie Goes to Hollywood, 'Relax', 'Two Tribes', 'Welcome To The Pleasure Dome'.

Madonna, *Like a Virgin*.

Prince, *Purple Rain*.

Special Aka, 'Free Nelson Mandela'.

The Smiths, *The Smiths*.

Bruce Springsteen, *Born in the USA*.

U2, *The Unforgettable Fire*.

The Band Aid single 'Do They Know It's Christmas?' raises £8 million for famine relief in Africa.

U Literature and Drama

Martin Amis, *Money*.

J G Ballard, *The Empire of the Sun*.

S S Bhoosnurmath, *The Grand Man/Bhavya Manava*.

Aldo Busi, *Seminar on Youth*.

J M Coetzee, *The Life and Times of Michael K*.

Jan Drzezdzon, *God's Face/Twarz Boga*.

William Goyen, *Arcadio*.

Stefan Heym, *The Wandering Jew*.

F Sionil Jose, *Po-on* (5th and final volume of *The Pretenders*).

Milan Kundera, *The Unbearable Lightness of Being*.

Graham Swift, *Waterland*.

Ibrahim Tahir, *The Last Imam*.

William Trevor, *Fools of Fortune*.

New edition of James Joyce's *Ulysses*, correcting 5,000 errors.

Start of public lending right (PLR) in Britain: payments to authors on library loans.

Drama:

Grupa Chwilowa, *A Miraculous Story*.

Terry Johnson, *Cries from the Mammal House*.

Sharman Macdonald, *When I was a Girl I used to Scream and Shout*.

Stephen Poliakoff, *Breaking the Silence*.

Neil Simon, *Biloxi Blues*.

August Wilson, *Ma Rainey's Black Bottom*.

Chinese representatives at ceremony in Beijing.

K October

10 In Britain, NUM fined £200,000 for contempt of court for attempting to discipline non-striking members.

12 in Britain, IRA bomb explodes at Grand Hotel, Brighton, during Conservative Party Conference, killing 4, injuring 32, and nearly killing Margaret Thatcher (13 Nov, fifth person dies).

16 pit deputies' union NACODS votes for strike (24, called off).

20 Central Committee of Chinese Communist Party agrees programme of economic reforms, giving factory managers greater autonomy.

23 in Philippines, official report into Aquino murder (21 Aug 1983) claims 26 people, including top military officials, involved.

27 Polish authorities admit that missing pro-Solidarity priest, Father Jerzy Popieluszko, was murdered by members of security police (30, priest's body found in reservoir; 31, three officers to be charged).

31 Indian Prime Minister Indira Gandhi assassinated by Sikh bodyguards; her son Rajiv sworn in as prime minister. Communal violence follows.

L November

2 Angola offers to reduce number of Cuban troops in country if South Africa agrees to relinquish control of Namibia.

4 Sandinista Front wins Nicaraguan elections. Daniel Ortega elected president with 63 per cent of popular vote.

4 British RAF begins airlift of food supplies to famine-stricken Tigre province of Ethiopia.

6 in US presidential election Republican President Ronald Reagan, with 525 electoral college votes, wins landslide victory over Democrat Walter Mondale, with 13 college votes. Reagan wins all states bar Minnesota and District of Columbia. Republicans retain majority in the Senate and increase representation in House of Representatives. Popular vote: Reagan,

54,455,075 (58.8 per cent); Mondale, 37,577,185 (40.6 per cent).

12 (–15) Organization of African Unity summit in Addis Ababa calls for massive international aid for Africa.

16 President Mitterrand of France acknowledges Libyan troops still in Chad in defiance of agreement.

20 shares in British Telecom offered to public; issue is four-times over-subscribed (3 Dec, trading opens with premium of 45p above offer price of £1.30p).

20 North Wales branch of NUM votes to end strike.

26 US restores full diplomatic relations with Iraq (severed in 1967).

30 two striking miners charged with murder of cab driver in South Wales, by dropping block on car from bridge (May 1985, convicted of murder; Oct, reduced to manslaughter).

M December

1 King Hussein of Jordan holds talks with Egypt's President Mubarak in Cairo on peace initiatives for West Bank.

3 leak of toxic gas from Union Carbide pesticide plant near Bhopal, India, kills 2,500 and injures 200,000.

7 front page article in China's *People's Daily* argues that Marxist theory is not solution to all of the country's economic problems (10, 'correction' criticizes article for failure to emphasize continued importance of Marxist principles).

7 Tamil terrorists attack Sri Lankan army convoy, killing 100.

15 Soviet Politburo member Mikhail Gorbachev visits London and states that USSR is willing to negotiate large reductions in nuclear weapons. Margaret Thatcher declares 'I like Mr Gorbachev. We can do business together'.

18 British government announces plan to privatize the Trustee Savings Bank.

22 Dom Mintoff resigns as prime minister of Malta; succeeded by Dr Carmello Mifsud Bonnici.

24 Congress (I) Party of Rajiv Gandhi wins large majority in Indian general election.

28 sterling falls to $1.1627, down 27 cents on year.

Teatr Nowy, *The End of Europe* wins 'Grand Prix' at Theatre of Nations, Nancy.

v Births and Deaths

Jan 14 Ray Kroc dies (81).
Jan 20 Johnny Weissmuller dies (79).
Feb 20 Mikhail Sholokov dies (78).
March 5 Tito Gobbi dies (68).
March 6 Martin Niemöller dies (92).
March 30 Karl Rahner dies (80).
April 5 Arthur Harris dies (91).
April 8 Pyotr Kapitza dies (89).
April 16 Count Basie dies (79).
May 19 John Betjeman dies (76).
June 22 Joseph Losey dies (75).
June 25 Michel Foucault dies (57).
June 30 Lillian Hellman dies (77).
July 26 G H Gallup dies (82).
Aug 5 Richard Burton dies (58).
Aug 14 J B Priestley dies (89).
Oct 14 Martin Ryle dies (66).
Oct 21 François Truffaut dies (52).
Oct 31 Indira Gandhi dies (66).
Dec 28 Sam Peckinpah dies (59).

w Everyday Life

Publication of *The Yuppie Handbook* draws attention to the 'young upwardly mobile professional', one of the defining icons of the mid 1980s.

Celebration at Walt Disney World, Orlando, Florida, USA, of 50th anniversary of Donald Duck (June).

In USA, home video-taping is ruled legal by the Supreme Court in Sony v. Universal City Studios (17 Jan).

x Sport and Recreation

Before the English University Boat Race, the Cambridge boat collides with a stationary barge (17 March)

Sweden wins Lawn Tennis's Davis Cup for the first time, beating the USA 4–1 in the Final.

In three competitions (European Championships, Winter Olympics, World Championships), the British ice dancers Jayne Torvill and Christopher Dean are awarded 59 'perfect' scores of 6.

The 23rd Olympic Games are held in Los Angeles, USA (28 July–12 Aug), and are boycotted by the Soviet bloc, with the exception of Romania, and by Iran and Libya, in retaliation for the USA boycott of the Moscow Olympics in 1980. The USA wins 83 gold medals; Romania, 20; West Germany, 17; China, 15; Italy, 14; Canada and Japan, 10 each; New Zealand, 8; Yugoslavia, 7; South Korea, 6; Britain, France, and the Netherlands, 5 each. In the athletics, Carl Lewis of the USA wins four gold medals.

y Media

Stock-market flotation of the Reuters news agency.

In Britain, Robert Maxwell buys the *Mirror* group of newspapers (13 July).

In Britain, the *News of the World* is relaunched as a tabloid paper.

Film:

Man of Flowers (director, Paul Cox).

A Nightmare on Elm Street (director, Wes Craven).

Nostalgia (director, Andrei Tarkovsky).

Once Upon a Time in America (director, Sergio Leone).

Paris, Texas (director, Wim Wenders).

A Passage to India (director, David Lean).

A Sunday in the Country (director, Bertrand Tavernier).

Terminator (director, James Cameron; starring Arnold Schwarzenegger).

End of capital allowances on films in Britain — producers announce they will leave the country.

Television:

In USA, 75 million people watch *The Day After*, about the effects of nuclear attack.

New programmes in USA include *Miami Vice*.

New programmes in Britain include: *The Jewel in the Crown*; *The Living Planet*; *Rainy Day Women* (BBC), by David Pirie; *Spitting Image* (Central), satire of contemporary politics using puppets; *Threads*, which dramatizes the presumed effects of a nuclear explosion over the city of Sheffield in N England.

In Britain, Edgar Reitz's *Heimat*, an epic lasting almost 16 hours, is shown on BBC television.

Sinking of the Rainbow Warrior ... *TWA and* Achille Lauro
hijacks ... Anglo–Irish Agreement *...*

A **January**

7 (–8) US Secretary of State Shultz and USSR Foreign Minister Gromyko hold talks in Geneva over resumption of arms control negotiations.

14 Israeli Cabinet agrees three-stage withdrawal from occupied Lebanon, commencing Feb.

14 Hun Sen elected prime minister of Kampuchea in succession to late Chan Sy.

17 (–20) summit conference at UN between President Kyprianu of Cyprus and Turkish Cypriot leader Rauf Denktaş fails to resolve differences.

18 in Britain, FT 100 Share Index exceeds 1,000 points for first time.

18 panel of prosecutors in Philippines announces sufficient evidence to charge 26 with involvement in murder of Benigno Aquino (1 Feb, trial opens).

25 President Botha opens South Africa's new three-chamber Parliament for whites, Indians, and coloureds.

B **February**

4 in USA, President Reagan's defence budget calls for tripling of expenditure on 'Star Wars' research programme.

5 Gibraltar's frontier gates with Spain reopened after 16 years.

7 four Polish secret police officers found guilty of murder of Father Jerzy Popieluszko, sentenced to between 14 and 25 years in jail.

10 imprisoned ANC leader Nelson Mandela refuses South African government's offer of freedom, conditional on his renouncing violence.

11 former British Ministry of Defence official Clive Ponting acquitted of charges of leaking documents relating to the sinking of Argentine cruiser *General Belgrano* during Falklands War.

19 Irish Dáil passes emergency law enabling government to seize up to IR £10 million from Provisional IRA bank accounts.

27 NCB announces that over 50 per cent of Britain's miners are back at work.

C **March**

1 Julio Sanguinetti takes office as Uruguay's first elected president in 12 years.

3 in Britain, NUM delegates conference votes to return to work without settlement of strike.

10 President Chernenko of USSR dies.

11 Mikhail Gorbachev is named first secretary of Soviet Communist Party; he calls

for more *glasnost* ('openness') in Soviet life and later pursues policy of *perestroika* ('reconstruction').

12 (–23) further round of US–USSR arms talks in Geneva.

15 military rule ends in Brazil.

20 Belgian parliament approves deployment of Cruise missiles.

21 South African police fire on crowds at Uitenhage on 25th anniversary of Sharpeville massacre, killing 18 (22, judicial commission of inquiry announced).

29 (–30) summit of EC heads of government in Brussels agrees terms for admission of Spain and Portugal on 1 Jan 1986.

D **April**

2 Israeli Army removes 1,100 Lebanese prisoners from detention camps in southern Lebanon to Israel.

6 coup in Sudan led by General Swar al-Dahab.

7 Soviet leader Gorbachev announces moratorium on missile deployments in Europe until Nov and offers to hold summit talks with President Reagan.

11 Enver Hoxha, first secretary of Albanian Communist Party and national leader for more than 40 years, dies. Ramiz Alia named new first secretary.

15 South Africa accepts recommendations of Parliamentary committee to abolish laws forbidding inter-racial marriage and sexual intercourse.

15 President Botha announces that South African forces in Angola will leave by 18.

22 trial opens in Argentina of nine former military leaders, including Galtieri.

26 Warsaw Pact leaders agree to renew military alliance for further 30 years.

E **May**

1 USA imposes financial and trade sanctions on Nicaragua.

1 in Poland, 10,000 Solidarity supporters clash with police during May Day demonstrations in Gdansk.

10 (–13) Sikh extremists bomb three Indian cities, 84 reported dead.

14 146 die in Tamil attack on Sri Lankan city of Anuradhapura.

19 Shi'ite Muslim militia attempts to drive Palestinians from refugee camps of Sabra, Shatila, and Bourj-el-Barajneh in Beirut, Lebanon.

20 Israel releases 1,150 prisoners under supervision of International Red Cross in

Famine in Ethiopia ... Hole discovered in ozone layer ...
Unseeded man wins Wimbledon title ...

o Politics, Government, Law, and Economy

A Heath, R Jowell, and J Curtice, *How Britain Votes*.

P Whitehead, *The Writing on the Wall*.

In South Africa, an act of parliament provides for the introduction of Regional Services Councils, with indirectly elected representatives of white, coloured, and African councils (from 1987).

British Ecology Party changes its name to the Green Party.

Gramm–Rudman Act passed in USA, requiring automatic spending cuts if the federal budget deficit persists.

US Congress passes the Superfund Improvement Act, tightening environmental protection law.

Anti-discrimination section of Canada's federal constitution (Charter of Rights and Freedoms) incorporated into law (17 Apr).

Proceedings in British House of Lords televised for first time (23 Jan).

In USA, in Garcia v. San Antonio MTA, the Supreme Court severely qualifies state immunity from federal regulation under the 10th Amendment (19 Feb).

In USA, the Supreme Court, in Federal Election Commission v. National Conservative Political Action Committee, strikes down restrictions on spending by Political Action Committees (18 March).

Crown Prosecution Service established in England and Wales, taking over responsibility for criminal prosecutions from the police.

British election law amended, raising the deposit for candidates from £150 to £500.

World Bank sets up fund for Africa.

In USA, R J Reynolds and Nabisco merge in a deal that pioneers the use of 'junk bonds'.

Pound–dollar rate touches $1.03, the lowest ever.

Meeting of the 'Group of Five' (or 'G5' — USA, Japan, West Germany, Britain, France), in New York, reaches the Plaza Accord: the countries will cooperate to maintain stability of exchange rates (21–22 Sept).

Agriculture legislation in USA provides for crop insurance and low-cost, long-term loans to farmers.

Nissan of Japan negotiates single-union deal with Amalgamated Union of Engineering Workers for employees at new car construction plant at Washington, NE England.

International Whaling Commission bans commercial whaling, in order to prevent extinction of whales.

p Society, Education, and Religion

Major famine in Ethiopia.

Citizens of western countries are spurred to action against famine in Africa by such events as the Live Aid concerts (13 July).

International Women's Development Agency founded; United Nations holds Decade of Women conference in Nairobi.

Japanese Diet approves bill to remove restrictions on women's work (17 May).

12-day conference opens in Nairobi to mark end of UN Decade for Women.

In Republic of Ireland, the Dáil legalizes shop sales of contraceptives (20 Feb).

The House of Lords in Britain, in the Gillick case, permits doctors to prescribe oral contraceptives to girls aged under 16 without parental consent (17 Oct).

Bernie Grant elected leader of Haringey Council, Britain's first black council leader; Venerable Wilfred Wood consecrated Bishop of Croydon, Britain's first black bishop (both 30 Apr).

US film star Rock Hudson is the first celebrity to die of AIDS (2 Oct); on 16 Dec it is reported that 8,000 Americans have died from the disease.

European Court of Human Rights finds Britain guilty of sex discrimination in immigration policy (28 May).

US Congress passes Safe Drinking Water Act Amendments.

Ruth Lawrence achieves the best first-class mathematics degree at the University of Oxford, England, at age 13 (4 July).

Dons at Oxford University, England, vote to refuse Margaret Thatcher (an Oxford graduate) an honorary doctorate (29 Jan).

Britain withdraws from UNESCO, complaining about the organization's anti-Western bias (5 Dec).

Doctrinal Office of the Vatican imposes one year's silence on Father Leonardo Boff of Brazil, a leading exponent of 'liberation theology'.

Dr Allan Boesak, President of the World Alliance of Reformed Churches, is arrested during a demonstration in Cape Town, South Africa.

General Synod of the Church of England approves ordination of women to the diaconate by large majority.

Synod held in Rome to assess impact of reforms of Second Vatican Council (24 Nov).

exchange for last three soldiers held by Palestinians.

25 10,000 die as cyclone hits southern Bangladesh.

F **June**

2 President Jayawardene of Sri Lanka discusses violence in his country with Indian Prime Minister Rajiv Gandhi.

6 skeleton thought to be remains of Auschwitz doctor Josef Mengele exhumed in Brazil (21, identity confirmed by team of forensic experts).

10 Israel completes withdrawal from all bar 'security zone' in southern Lebanon.

12 Spain and Portugal sign treaty of accession to EC.

14 two Shi'ite Muslim gunmen hijack TWA jet with 145 passengers and crew of eight, demanding release of 700 prisoners held by Israel. One passenger, a US Navy diver, is shot dead (17, hostages removed from jet, in Beirut, Lebanon, and held in south Beirut).

15 South Africa names multi-racial administration for Namibia but retains control of foreign policy and defence.

23 Air India Boeing 747 crashes into Atlantic off Irish coast killing all 329 on board. Terrorist bomb suspected.

30 39 US hostages from TWA jet taken to Damascus, released following Syrian intervention.

G **July**

2 Andrei Gromyko named president of USSR; Edvard Shevardnadze becomes foreign minister.

11 explosion sinks Greenpeace ship *Rainbow Warrior* in Auckland harbour, New Zealand, killing one man — ship was in South Pacific to disrupt French nuclear tests (two people later charged with explosion and discovered to be French agents).

18 (–20) Organization of African Unity Conference in Addis Ababa declares that most African countries on verge of economic collapse.

20 South African government declares state of emergency in 36 districts in response to increased violence.

24 Indian Prime Minister Rajiv Gandhi announces agreement with Sant Harchand Singh Longowal, leader of Sikh community in Punjab, aimed at reducing tension in state.

27 coup in Uganda, led by Brigadier Tito Okello, ousts President Milton Obote.

H **August**

4 Black miners in South Africa's gold and coal mines go on indefinite strike, demanding end to state of emergency.

15 President Botha of South Africa re-states commitment to apartheid and rules out parliamentary representation for blacks.

22 in Britain, 54 die in fire on board jet at Manchester airport.

23 West German counter-espionage official Hans Joachim Tiedge seeks asylum in East Germany (28, head of West German Secret Service sacked).

26 report exonerates French government of involvement in sinking of *Rainbow Warrior*; findings rejected by New Zealand government (27, French Prime Minister Laurent Fabius orders further investigations).

27 South African civil rights activist Rev Allan Boesak arrested on eve of leading march to prison where Nelson Mandela held (28, violence when police seek to prevent march).

27 military coup in Nigeria, led by Major-General Ibrahim Babangida.

J **September**

2 Cabinet reshuffle in Britain: Douglas Hurd becomes home secretary; Leon Brittan, trade secretary.

2 Pol Pot resigns as commander in chief of Khmer Rouge Army; replaced by Sol Senn.

9 USA announces selective economic sanctions against South Africa.

10 EC foreign ministers approve sanctions against South Africa (Britain delays decision until 25).

13 Britain expels 25 Soviet diplomats and officials for alleged espionage activities (14, USSR expels 25 Britons; another round of expulsions follows).

16 10 Politburo members and 64 members of Central Committee of Chinese Communist Party resign, to make way for younger men.

17 in West Germany, secretary in Chancellor Kohl's office defects to East Germany.

19 over 7,000 die in earthquake in Mexico City.

20 French Defence Minister Charles Hernu resigns and Admiral Pierre Lacoste, head of foreign service, is dismissed over *Rainbow Warrior* affair.

22 French Prime Minister Fabius admits that *Rainbow Warrior* was sunk by French secret service agents.

26 elections held for Hong Kong's Legislative Council; first in 100 years of colonial rule.

28 (–29) riots in Brixton, London, following police wounding of black woman, Cherry Groce.

K **October**

1 Israel attacks PLO headquarters in Tunis killing 60; revenge attack for murder of three Israelis in Cyprus.

In Britain, the Methodist Conference votes against its members becoming Freemasons, and bans Masonic meetings on its premises.

David Brown, *The Divine Trinity*.

Q Science, Technology, and Discovery

The British Antarctic Survey detects a hole in the ozone layer over Antarctica.

US space shuttle *Discovery* (launched 27 Aug) deploys three satellites; the crew also retrieve, repair, and redeploy an orbiting satellite.

Crew of the shuttle *Atlantis* undertake construction exercises to develop skills for building a large orbiting space station.

Launch of European, Japanese, and Soviet probes to rendezvous with Halley's comet in 1986.

Astronomers at Cornell University, USA, report the discovery of eight infrared galaxies located by the Infrared Astronomical Satellite.

Two groups of researchers discover rings around Neptune.

A woman in the USA treated for infertility gives birth to septuplets; three survive, but with medical problems (May).

In USA, lasers are used in surgery, to clean out clogged arteries.

Researchers locate gene markers on chromosomes for cystic fibrosis and polycystic kidney disease.

Evidence found for the existence of fullerenes (buckyballs), a new elemental form of carbon.

R Humanities

J J Scarisbrick, *The Reformation and the English People*.

Paul Slack, *The Impact of Plague in Tudor and Stuart England*.

Alan Everitt, *Landscape and Community in England*.

J C D Clark, *English Society, 1688–1832*.

Cyril Ehrlich, *The Music Profession in Britain since the Eighteenth Century: A Social History*.

J M Winter, *The Great War and the British People*.

Judith M Brown, *Modern India: The Origins of an Asian Democracy*.

Margaret Drabble (ed.), *The Oxford Companion to English Literature*, 5th edition.

Jürgen Habermas, *The Philosophical Discourse of Modernity*.

P F Strawson, *Scepticism and Naturalism: Some Varieties*.

Bernard Williams, *Ethics and the Limits of Philosophy*.

S Art, Sculpture, Fine Arts, and Architecture

Picasso Museum opens in Paris, France.

Saatchi Collection opens in London.

Turner Prize in Britain awarded to Howard Hodgkin.

Exhibition 'German Art in the Twentieth Century 1905–1985', Royal Academy, London.

Painting, etc:

Cindy Sherman, *Untitled* No. 140.

Sculpture:

Arman, public sculpture: a heap of suitcases outside the Gare St Lazare, Paris, France.

Christo wraps Pont Neuf, Paris.

Anselm Kiefer, *The High Priestess*.

Architecture:

Richard Meier, Museum für Kunsthandwerk, Frankfurt-am-Main, West Germany.

Norman Foster, Hong Kong and Shanghai Bank Headquarters, Hong Kong.

Richard Rogers, Lloyds Building, City of London.

T Music

Benjamin Lees, *Memorial Candles*.

Andrew Lloyd Webber, *Requiem*.

Witold Lutoslawski, *Chaine*.

André Previn, Piano Concerto.

Alfred Schnittke, *(K)ein Sommernachtstraum*.

Toru Takemitsu, *Riverrun*.

Phil Collins, *No Jacket Required*.

Dire Straits, *Brothers in Arms*.

Paul Hardcastle, '19'.

Whitney Houston, 'Saving All My Love For You'.

The Jesus and Mary Chain, *Psychocandy*.

Madonna, 'Into The Grove', 'Material Girl'.

The Pogues, *Rum, Sodomy and the Lash*.

The Smiths, *Meat is Murder*.

Sonic Youth, *Bad Moon Rising*.

Tears for Fears, *Songs From The Big Chair*.

Wham!, 'I'm Your Man'.

Live-Aid — televised concerts in USA and Britain to raise funds for famine relief; USA for Africa produces the single 'We Are The World'.

U Literature and Drama

Aas Foss Abrahamren, *The Bird and the White Tablecloth*.

Brian Aldiss, *The Helliconia Trilogy*.

Julian Barnes, *Flaubert's Parrot*.

Angela Carter, *Nights at the Circus*.

Alexander Kaletski, *Metro, A Novel of the Moscow Underground*.

Ivan Klima, *My First Loves*.

R M Lamming, *In the Dark*.

Doris Lessing, *The Good Terrorist*.

Lars Lundkvist, *Korn*.

Grace Paley, *Later the Same Day*.

6 riots in Tottenham, London, during which PC Keith Blakelock is murdered.

7 four Palestinian guerrillas hijack Italian cruise liner *Achille Lauro* with 450 people on board in Mediterranean (9, hijackers surrender to Egyptian authorities after killing one US passenger, Leon Klinghoffer, a crippled elderly Jew).

10 US jets intercept plane carrying hijackers from Egypt to Tunis and force it to land in Sicily. President Mubarak accuses USA of 'piracy'.

12 USA protests when Italian authorities release Mohammed Abbas, terrorist alleged to have been behind *Achille Lauro* hijack.

18 British miners in Nottinghamshire and South Derbyshire vote to disaffiliate from the NUM and form the Union of Democratic Mineworkers (UDM).

27 Julius Nyerere retires as president of Tanzania after 24 years; succeeded by Ali Hassan Mwinyi.

L **November**

2 South African government imposes emergency restrictions on reporting of unrest.

4 two French secret service agents plead guilty to manslaughter and sabotage in sinking of *Rainbow Warrior* (21, sentenced to 10 years in prison).

6 General Jaruzelski resigns as prime minister of Poland to become chairman of council of state. Professor Zbigniew Messner named new prime minister.

13 estimated 25,000 killed when Nevado del Ruiz volcano in Colombia erupts.

15 Anglo-Irish Agreement signed at Hillsborough Castle, giving the Republic of Ireland a consultative role in the affairs of Northern Ireland; British Treasury Minister Ian Gow resigns in protest.

24 Egyptian commandos storm hijacked Egyptian airliner at Malta airport; 60 killed.

29 black union leaders in South Africa form new union covering 500,000 workers: Congress of South African Trade Unions (COSATU).

M **December**

2 Court in Philippines acquits 26 accused of complicity in Aquino murder. Aquino's widow, Corazon, announces she will run for presidency against Marcos.

3 Church of England publishes report *Faith in the City*, critical of government policies on inner cities; government spokesmen denounce it as 'Marxist'.

9 five former members of Argentina's military junta found guilty of human-rights violations.

11 police and Loyalist demonstrators clash as first conference under Anglo-Irish Agreement held in Belfast, Northern Ireland.

17 Ulster Unionist MPs all resign from House of Commons over Anglo-Irish Agreement.

17 in Uganda, General Tito Okello and Yoweri Museveni of National Resistance Army sign peace accord.

21 South African police forcibly remove Winnie Mandela from her home in Soweto.

21 Haitians demonstrate against government of Jean-Claude Duvalier.

25 fighting breaks out on border between Mali and Burkina Faso.

30 General Zia ends martial law in Pakistan.

31 King Hussein of Jordan meets President Assad of Syria—first meeting for six years.

Patrick Suskind, *Perfume*.
Anne Tyler, *The Accidental Tourist*.
Kurt Vonnegut, *Galapagos*.
Ted Hughes is appointed Britain's Poet Laureate.

Drama:
Howard Brenton and David Hare, *Pravda*.
Jean-Claude Carrière and Peter Brook, *The Mahabharata*.
Christopher Hampton, *Les Liaisons dangereuses*.
Louis Nowra, *The Golden Age*.

v **Births and Deaths**
Jan 22 Arthur Bryant dies (85).
March 11 J M G M Adams dies (53).
March 28 Marc Chagall dies (97).
April 13 Oscar Nemon dies (79).
June 2 George Brown dies (70).
July 17 Susanne Langer dies (89).
Sept 17 Laura Ashley dies (60).
Oct 10 Orson Welles dies (70).
Nov 3 J M Wallace-Hadrill dies (69).
Nov 28 Fernand Braudel dies (83).
Dec 7 Robert Graves dies (90).

w **Everyday Life**
In USA, the Coca-Cola company introduces a sweeter formula for its drink, but has to reinstate the old formula under the Classic name following protests.

x **Sport and Recreation**
In snooker, Dennis Taylor of Northern Ireland beats Steve Davis of England on the last ball of the 35th and final frame to win the Embassy World Professional Championship in Sheffield, England (28 April); 18.5 million people watch the final stages on television.
In England, 55 die when fire destroys the main stand at Bradford City's Valley Parade ground (11 May).
In Belgium, 39 people are killed at the Heysel Stadium in Brussels following a riot by Liverpool fans before the European Cup Final between Liverpool and Juventus of Italy (29 May); as a consequence, English football clubs are banned from all European competitions.
In tennis, Boris Becker, at 17 years and 227 days, wins the Men's Singles title in the Wimbledon tournament, London (7 July): he becomes the youngest winner, the first West German winner, and the first unseeded player to win the title.

In cricket, England regains the Ashes (2 Sept), beating Australia 3–1 in the six-Test series.
Europe's golfers, captained by Tony Jacklin, win the Ryder Cup at the Belfry, England (15 Sept), the first European team to defeat the US team since 1957.

Y **Media**
Express newspapers are bought by United Newspapers.
Canadian Conrad Black takes control of *Telegraph* newspapers (Dec).

Film:
Australian businessman Rupert Murdoch buys 50 per cent of the Twentieth-Century Fox film company in the USA (8 April).
1985 sees cinema audiences in Britain rise by 33 per cent to 70 million.
Back to the Future (director, Robert Zemeckis).
Brazil (director, Terry Gilliam).
Colonel Redl (director, Istvan Szabo).
Kiss of the Spider Woman (director, Hector Babenco; starring William Hurt).
Out of Africa (director, Sydney Pollack; starring Meryl Streep and Robert Redford).
Ran (director, Akira Kurosawa).
Trouble in Mind (director, Alan Rudolph).

Television:
In USA, Capital Cities Communications buys (17 March) the American Broadcasting Company (ABC), and Australian businessman Rupert Murdoch purchases most of Metromedia's television stations (6 May), forming Fox Television Inc. (4 Sept, Murdoch becomes a US citizen in order to comply with US law prohibiting aliens from owning television stations in the USA).
New programmes in USA include *The Golden Girls* (NBC).
In Britain, the BBC bans *At the Edge of the Union* on account of its interviews of IRA members — TV journalists strike.
The War Game, about the possible effects of a nuclear attack on Britain, is broadcast by the BBC after 20 years' suppression.
New programmes in Britain include: *EastEnders* (BBC), a 'soap opera' set in the East End of London; *Edge of Darkness* by Troy Kennedy Martin; *Taggart*; *The Triumph of the West* (BBC), an interpretation of world history presented by J M Roberts;

USA bombs Tripoli ... Explosion at Chernobyl nuclear power station ... State of Emergency in South Africa ...

A January

1 Spain and Portugal become 11th and 12th members of EC.

7 USA imposes sanctions on Libya for involvement in international terrorism.

9 Michael Heseltine resigns as British defence secretary following Cabinet disagreement over future of ailing Westland helicopter company (known as 'Westland affair'); succeeded by George Younger (24, Trade Secretary Leon Brittan also resigns, over leak of letter; 25, replaced by Paul Channon).

25 USSR leader Gorbachev proposes 15-year timetable for elimination of all nuclear weapons.

22 in India, three Sikhs sentenced to death for murder of Indira Gandhi.

23 polling in 15 Northern Ireland constituencies following resignations of Ulster Unionists; all former MPs are re-elected except for Enoch Powell.

26 National Resistance Army takes over Ugandan capital (29, Yuweri Museveni sworn in as Uganda's president).

28 US space shuttle *Challenger* explodes shortly after take-off, killing crew of seven.

B February

7 Presidential election in Philippines (9, computer operators from Commission on Elections protest, claiming vote rigging).

7 President Jean-Claude Duvalier of Haiti flees to France following anti-government demonstrations. General Henri Namphy forms new government.

11 USSR releases Jewish dissident Anatoly Shcharansky and three others in exchange for five East Europeans.

15 opposition members walk out of Philippines parliament when President Marcos declares himself victor in election.

19 Iran takes Iraqi oil port of Faw, giving it control of mouth of Shatt al-Arab waterway.

22 Defence Minister Juan Ponce Enrile and Deputy Chief of Staff Fidel Ramos take over headquarters of Philippines Defence Ministry and declare opposition to President Marcos and support for Corazon Aquino.

24 President Marcos flees Philippines. Corazon Aquino sworn in as president.

28 Sweden's Prime Minister Olof Palme assassinated in Stockholm street.

C March

2 Queen Elizabeth signs Australia Bill in Canberra, severing remaining legal ties with Britain.

6 USSR Communist Party Congress agrees sweeping changes in membership of Central Committee and Politburo.

7 South African government lifts state of emergency imposed in July 1985.

12 Spain votes in referendum to remain in NATO, but not in command structure.

16 opposition parties win narrow majority in French general election, ending five years of Socialist rule (20, Jacques Chirac, Gaullist leader, appointed prime minister).

D April

1 Price of North Sea oil falls below $10 a barrel for first time.

4 (–7) Contadora group, meeting in Panama, fails to reach agreement on ending fighting in Central America.

5 bomb attack on 'La Belle' discotheque in West Berlin, frequented by US servicemen, kills two and injures 200; Libyan involvement suspected.

11 Brian Keenan, lecturer at American University of Beirut, Lebanon, is taken hostage.

14 House of Commons rejects bill to deregulate Sunday trading in England and Wales.

15 bombers from US warships and bases in Britain attack targets in Libya; 100 killed, 1 plane shot down.

17 bodies of two kidnapped Britons and one American found near Beirut, Lebanon; they had been murdered after the US raid on Libya.

17 John McCarthy, acting bureau chief for Worldwide Television in Beirut, is taken hostage.

18 President Botha of South Africa announces end to country's pass laws, restricting movement within the country.

18 bomb discovered in El Al passenger's luggage at Heathrow airport, London. Jordanian Nezar Hindawi is arrested for attempted bombing.

26 major accident at Chernobyl nuclear power station near Kiev, USSR, announced after abnormally high levels of radiation reported in Sweden, Denmark, and Finland.

30 2,000 police and paramilitary commandos enter Sikh Golden Temple at Amritsar, India, to expel militants.

*British government plans 'poll tax' ... Return of Halley's Comet
... David Morgan's* The Mongols ... *Major changes in British
newspaper industry ...*

o Politics, Government, Law, and Economy

David Stockman, *The Triumph of Politics: How the Reagan Revolution Failed.*

In Britain, abolition of the Greater London Council and six other metropolitan local authorities (31 March).

In Britain, representatives of the *Independent* and *Guardian* newspapers withdraw from daily briefings by government press officers to accredited 'lobby' journalists.

British Government Green Paper proposes introduction of the Community Charge (popularly known as the 'poll tax') in place of domestic rates.

British defence secretary announces scrapping of British GEC Nimrod early-warning aircraft programme and plan to order six US-built Boeing 'AWACS' planes.

In USA, William Rehnquist is appointed Chief Justice of the Supreme Court.

The Public Order Act increases police powers over gatherings and processions in Britain.

US national debt reaches $2 trillion.

Oil oversupply leads to a slump in prices, to $6 a barrel compared to over $30 in the early 1980s; this leads to an increase in prosperity in industrial countries and states not dependent on oil revenues.

'Big Bang' deregulation of the London stock exchange abolishes distinctions between various types of trader (27 Oct).

In USA, Tax Reform Act passed to simplify the federal tax system.

Comprehensive Anti-Apartheid Act in USA imposes strict sanctions on South Africa and causes many multinational firms to disinvest (General Motors ceases operations in South Africa on 22 Oct).

British government privatizes British Gas and British Airports Authority.

Nissan of Japan opens car assembly plant in Sunderland, NE England (8 Sept).

p Society, Education, and Religion

After 37 years, the US Senate ratifies the United Nations Convention on the Prevention and Punishment of the Crime of Genocide (19 Feb).

Referendum in the Republic of Ireland rejects proposal to allow divorce (27 June).

Liechtenstein allows women to vote for first time in elections to National Diet.

In USA, the Supreme Court, in Local 93 International Association of Firefighters v. City of Cleveland, supports use of preferential quotas in the hiring of employees (2 July).

The Simpson–Mazzoli immigration law in the USA gives legal status to many illegal immigrants.

US Senate votes for change in immigration laws, making employers who knowingly hire illegal aliens subject to civil fines (signed 7 Nov).

US Supreme Court rules, in Bowers v. Hardwick, that Georgia's law prohibiting oral and anal intercourse is not unconstitutional (30 June).

British junior Health Minister Edwina Currie blames poor health of northern Britons on ignorance (23 Sept).

In South Africa, repeal of the Urban Areas Act (including removal of the pass laws).

In Britain, the National Society for the Prevention of Cruelty to Children (NSPCC) reports doubling in number of reported cases of child sex abuse during year.

Education Act in Britain defines the duties and responsibilities of school governors.

The British government announces a new type of secondary school, the City Technology College, to be jointly financed by industry and the state.

National Council for Vocational Qualifications established in Britain to coordinate standards.

House of Commons votes to abolish corporal punishment in state schools (22 July).

A major Vatican document, *Instruction on Christian Freedom and Liberation*, recommends passive resistance against injustice and countenances armed struggle as 'a last resort to put an end to obvious and prolonged tyranny.'

The Vatican declares Father Charles Curran of the USA unfit to teach Catholic theology because of his writings on divorce, contraception, abortion, and homosexuality.

The Dutch Reformed Church in South Africa declares that racism is a sin.

Anglicans and Methodists in Britain are urged to support 'effective economic sanctions' against South Africa.

q Science, Technology, and Discovery

In France, foundation of the Museum of Science and Industry at La Villette, Paris.

Jeana Yeager and Dick Rutan of USA fly round the world in their *Voyager* aircraft without refuelling (Dec).

The first 'lap top' computer introduced in the USA.

US space probe *Voyager 2* passes close to

E **May**

3 175 police and 150 demonstrators injured in violent protests outside News International's plant at Wapping, London.

4 Babrak Karmal resigns as general secretary of People's Democratic (Communist) Party of Afghanistan; replaced by Najibullah, former head of Afghan secret police.

10 Britain expels three Syrian diplomats for alleged involvement in terrorism (11, Syria expels three British diplomats).

18 Sri Lankan forces seek to establish control over Jaffna peninsula in north, held by Tamil insurgents.

24 (–26) Presidents of Nicaragua, Guatemala, El Salvador, Honduras and Costa Rica sign Declaration of Esquipulas at summit in Guatemala, endorsing Contadora peace treaty and calling for end to US military intervention in area.

25 30,000 blacks expelled from homes in Crossroads squatter camp near Cape Town, South Africa.

F **June**

2 1,000 Sikhs arrested in Punjab during protests on second anniversary of army attack on Golden Temple.

8 former UN Secretary General Kurt Waldheim elected president of Austria.

10 in Britain, Patrick Magee convicted of murder of five people through bombing of Grand Hotel in Brighton (23, jailed for life).

12 President Botha announces state of emergency throughout South Africa in response to deteriorating security situation.

12 report of Commonwealth Eminent Persons Group published, calls for economic sanctions against South Africa.

12 in Britain, Northern Ireland secretary announces dissolution of Northern Ireland Assembly set up in 1982.

20 conference of 120 nations in Paris organized by UN Special Committee against Apartheid, OAU, and Non-Aligned Movement, calls for sanctions against South Africa.

26 (–27) EC summit conference at The Hague, the Netherlands, appoints Sir Geoffrey Howe to lead peace mission to South Africa.

G **July**

5 Leader of Turkish Cypriots, Rauf Denktaş, refuses UN request for talks on re-opening of border dividing island.

7 French agents jailed for sinking of *Rainbow Warrior* released into French custody.

11 inflation in Britain falls to 2.5 per cent, lowest since Dec 1967.

11 British newspapers banned from printing extracts from *Spycatcher*, the memoirs of former MI5 officer, Peter Wright.

17 US senate approves treaty allowing extradition of suspected IRA terrorists to Britain.

24 British government appoints advisory council to administer Turks and Caicos islands following resignation of chief minister and two others over alleged constitutional malpractice.

29 Howe mission to South Africa fails to secure release of Nelson Mandela or lifting of ban on ANC.

H **August**

3 (–5) special conference in London of seven Commonwealth leaders to consider policies on South Africa. Britain is only country to oppose sanctions programme.

11 154 Tamil refugees from Sri Lanka rescued from lifeboats off Newfoundland coast.

12 USA suspends defence obligations to New Zealand following Labour government's espousal of anti-nuclear policy and denial of access to New Zealand facilities for US warships and military aircraft.

18 Israel and USSR hold talks in Helsinki, Finland, on plight of Jews in USSR, first such talks for 19 years.

22 1,700 die in Cameroon when toxic gas erupts from volcanic Lake Nyas.

23 Gennady F Zakharov, USSR diplomat accredited to UN, arrested by FBI and charged with spying (30, US newspaper correspondent Nicholas Daniloff arrested in Moscow and charged with spying).

J **September**

6 President Pinochet of Chile survives assassination attempt; state of siege declared.

7 Rt Rev Desmond Tutu enthroned as first black Archbishop of Cape Town, South Africa.

11 share prices on Wall Street, New York, register biggest fall since 1929 due to renewed fears of inflation.

16 EC foreign ministers agree to prohibit new investment in South Africa.

17 US State Department orders 25 members of USSR mission to UN out of the country by Oct.

30 Neil Kinnock pledges a future Labour government will close all US nuclear bases in Britain.

K **October**

2 US Senate votes to impose economic sanctions on South Africa, overturning presidential veto.

Uranus (Jan); photographs taken by the probe reveal 10 unknown satellites.

Explosion of US space shuttle *Challenger* (28 Jan) leads to suspension of shuttle flights.

Launch of Soviet *Mir 1* space station (19 Feb), intended to be permanently occupied.

Return of Halley's Comet; it is photographed by five space probes, including the European probe *Giotto*, which flies into the comet's tail (14 March).

British surgeons perform the first heart, lung, and liver transplant.

Surgeons develop an operation for removing tissue from the cornea by laser.

The US government announces a structure for the supervision of research and applications in genetic engineering (June).

Scientists at the Massachusetts Institute of Technology, USA, announce discovery of the first gene that inhibits growth; it inhibits the cancer retinoblastoma.

Announcement of the approximate location of a gene causing Duchenne muscular dystrophy; this makes possible screening to find carriers of the gene.

US Department of Agriculture permits the Biological Corporation of Omaha to market a virus produced by genetic engineering.

US Food and Drug Administration approves use of the monoclonal antibody OKT3 in organ transplant surgery.

German physicist Johannes Bednorz and Swiss physicist K A Müller, at IBM in Switzerland, announce discovery of a new superconducting material, in which superconductivity occurs at a higher temperature ($30°K$) than hitherto known; the potential for use of superconductivity is increased.

R **Humanities**

Marjorie Chibnall, *Anglo-Norman England, 1066–1166.*

David Morgan, *The Mongols.*

Oliver Rackham, *The History of the Countryside.*

G R Elton, *The Parliament of England, 1559–81.*

D E Underdown, *Revel, Riot and Rebellion: Popular Politics and Culture in England, 1603–60.*

Bernard Bailyn, *The Peopling of British North America.*

Final (4th) volume of *The Collected Works of Walter Bagehot*, edited by Norman St John-Stevas.

Jack Simmons, *The Railway in Country and Town, 1830–1914.*

Adrian Hastings, *A History of English Christianity, 1920–1985.*

Robert Rhodes James, *Anthony Eden.*

Arthur M Schlesinger, Jr, *The Cycles of American History.*

Stanley Wells and Gary Taylor (eds.), *William Shakespeare: The Complete Works.*

Final (4th) volume of the *Supplement to the Oxford English Dictionary.*

D K Lewis, *On the Plurality of Worlds.*

Thomas Nagel, *The View from Nowhere.*

S **Art, Sculpture, Fine Arts, and Architecture**

Opening of Palazzo Grassi, Venice, Italy; first exhibition: 'Futurism and Futurisms'.

Painting:

Frank Auerbach, *Head of Catherine Lampert.*

Lucien Freud, *Painter and Model.*

Sculpture:

Turner Prize in Britain awarded to Gilbert and George.

Louise Bourgeois, *Articulated Lair.*

Jeff Koons, *Rabbit.*

Architecture:

First show of British Architecture at Royal Academy, London, devoted to Richard Rogers, Norman Foster, and James Stirling.

Gae Aulenti and international team of architects, Musée d'Orsay, Paris, France.

Arata Isozaki, Museum of Contemporary Art, Los Angeles, USA.

T **Music**

Harrison Birtwistle, *Yan Tan Tethera* (opera).

Elliott Carter, String Quartet No. 4.

Sofia Gubaidulina, *Stimmen... Verstummen.*

Michael Nyman, *The Man who Mistook his Wife for a Hat* (opera).

Krzysztof Penderecki, *Die schwarze Maske* (opera).

Kevin Volans, *White Man Sleeps.*

Udo Zimmermann, *The White Rose* (opera, second version).

Chess (musical), lyrics by Tim Rice, music by Bjorn Ulvaeus and Benny Anderson (first performed at Prince Edward Theatre, London, 14 May).

Phantom of the Opera (musical), lyrics by Charles Hart, music by Andrew Lloyd Webber (first performed at Her Majesty's Theatre, London, 9 Oct).

Husker Du, *Candy Apple Grey.*

Peter Gabriel, *So.*

Genesis, *Invisible Touch.*

Madonna, *True Blue.*

Petshop Boys, *Please*, 'West End Girls'.

Prince, 'Kiss'.

Run DMC, 'Walk This Way'.

Paul Simon, *Graceland.*

Simply Red, 'Holding Back The Years'.

5 USSR human-rights campaigner Dr Yuri Orlov released from Siberian exile and flown to USA.

11 (–12) US–USSR mini-summit in Reykjavik, Iceland, fails to reach agreement on arms control, after President Reagan refuses to abandon Strategic Defense Initiative ('Star Wars').

12 Queen Elizabeth II begins week-long visit to China, first by reigning British monarch.

19 President Machel of Mozambique and 28 government officials killed in air crash in South Africa.

20 Yitzhak Shamir succeeds Shimon Peres as Israeli prime minister under terms of 1984 rotation agreement.

20 Israeli nuclear technician Mordechai Vanunu kidnapped in London after revealing details of Israel's nuclear resources (9 Dec, Israelis admit to holding Mordechai Vanunu).

24 Britain breaks off diplomatic relations with Syria for alleged involvement in plot to bomb El Al jet (Apr).

L **November**

2 US hostage David Jacobsen freed in Beirut, Lebanon, following intervention of British envoy Terry Waite.

3 Joaquim Chissano elected president of Mozambique.

3 details of US arms deal with Iran to secure release of Beirut hostages appears in Lebanon magazine.

4 Democrats gain control of Senate in US mid-term elections.

10 President Ershad announces end to martial law in Bangladesh.

13 US President Reagan admits to secret arms deal with Iran, but denies involvement in hostage deal.

14 US securities dealer Ivan F Boesky fined $100 million for illegal insider dealing.

25 President Reagan's National Security Adviser, Vice-Admiral John Poindexter, resigns and aide, Lieutenant-Colonel Oliver North, is dismissed from National Security Council after revelation that money from arms sales was channelled to Contra rebels in Central America (26, Reagan appoints former Senator John Tower to head inquiry into role of National Security Council in 'Iran-Contra scandal').

27 French high school and university students protest at government education reforms (8 Dec, reform bill withdrawn).

M **December**

8 (–11) food riots force Zambian government to reverse decision to double price of maize flour.

19 USSR authorities announce Andrei Sakharov and Yelena Bonner to return to Moscow after seven years' internal exile.

19 in USA Lawrence E Walsh appointed special prosecutor to investigate Iran-Contra scandal.

30 Esso announces withdrawal from South Africa.

The Smiths, *The Queen is Dead.*
Bruce Springsteen, *Live, 1975–1985.*

u Literature and Drama
Peter Ackroyd, *Hawksmoor.*
Fleur Adcock, *The Incident Book.*
Yuz Aleshkovsky, *Kangaroo.*
Louise Erdrich, *The Beet Queen.*
William Gaddis, *Carpenter's Gothic.*
Günter Grass, *The Rat.*
David Grossman, *Smile of the Lamb.*
Andrew Harvey, *Burning Houses.*
Garrison Keillor, *Lake Wobegon Days.*
Vikram Seth, *The Golden Gate.*
Endu Shusaku, *Scandal.*
In USA, the librarian of Congress, Daniel Boorstin, names Robert P Warren as first official poet laureate (26 Feb).

Drama:
Larry Kramer, *The Normal Heart.*
Richard Nelson, *Principia Scriptoriae.*
August Wilson, *Fences.*

v Births and Deaths
Jan 4 Christopher Isherwood dies (81).
Jan 23 Joseph Beuys dies (64).
Feb 16 Edmund Rubbra dies (84).
March 6 Georgia O'Keefe dies (98).
March 30 James Cagney dies (86).
April 14 Simone de Beauvoir dies (78).
June 13 Benny Goodman dies (77).
June 14 Jorge Luis Borges dies (86).
July 26 Averell Harriman dies (94).
Aug 31 Henry Moore dies (88).
Nov 8 Vyacheslav Molotov dies (96).
Dec 16 Serge Lifar dies (81).
Dec 29 Harold Macmillan dies (92).

w Everyday Life
In New York, the Statue of Liberty is reopened, by President Reagan in the presence of President François Mitterrand of France, following refurbishment (4 July).
The Singer company in the USA announces its withdrawal from the manufacture of sewing machines, in order to concentrate on aerospace products.
In Britain, the Prince of Wales admits he talks to plants (21 Sept).

x Sport and Recreation
After 10 successive defeats, Cambridge wins the English University Boat Race.
An estimated 30 million people take part in Sportaid's 'Race Against Time', a series of fun runs held around the world to raise money for the starving of Africa (25 May).
In the soccer World Cup, held in Mexico, Argentina beats West Germany 3–2 in the final (29 June).
The women golfers of Britain and the Republic of Ireland win the Curtis Cup at Prairie Dunes, Kansas, their first victory in the USA and their first in the series since 1956.
Mike Tyson of the USA beats Trevor Berbick of Canada in two rounds to win the WBC World Heavyweight title in Las Vegas, USA (22 Nov); at 20 years, he is the youngest-ever champion.

y Media
In Britain, production of *The Times, Sunday Times*, the *Sun*, and the *News of the World* is moved overnight from premises in central London to a new plant in Wapping, E London (24–25 Jan).
Eddie Shah launches *Today*, Britain's first full-colour, low-cost tabloid newspaper (4 March); sales fail to achieve target levels and the paper is sold to 'Tiny' Rowland's Lonrho company.
In Britain, Andreas Whittam-Smith and associates launch the *Independent* (7 Oct).

Film:
Betty Blue (director, Jean-Jacques Beneix).
Blue Velvet (director, David Lynch).
Caravaggio (director, Derek Jarman).
Dona Herlinda and her Son (director, Jaime Humberto Hermosillo).
Hannah and her Sisters (director, Woody Allen).
Jean de Florette (director, Claude Berri).
My Beautiful Laundrette (director, Stephen Frears).
Platoon (director, Oliver Stone).
Sacrifice (director, Andrei Tarkovsky).
She's Gotta Have It (director and star, Spike Lee).
Something Wild (director, Jonathan Demme).
Stand By Me (director, Rob Reiner).
Top Gun (director, Tony Scott; starring Tom Cruise).

Television:
New programmes in Britain include: *Bread* (BBC), a comedy based in Liverpool, by Carla Lane; *Casualty*, a hospital drama; *Inspector Morse* (Central), based on the novels of Colin Dexter; *The Singing Detective* (BBC), a television play by Dennis Potter.

Iran–Contra hearings in USA ... Single European Act in force ...
US–Soviet agreement on intermediate nuclear forces ...

A January

6 Portuguese Council of State agrees to restore Macao to China before 2000 (13 Apr, Portugal signs agreement to return Macao in 1999).

9 South African government bans all reporting of activities of ANC.

15 US–USSR arms control talks resume in Geneva.

20 Archbishop of Canterbury's envoy Terry Waite disappears in Beirut, Lebanon (2 Feb, reported to be 'under arrest' in Beirut).

21 new coalition government takes office in Austria under Dr Franz Vranitzky.

24 162 police and 33 demonstrators injured in clashes outside Rupert Murdoch's News International plant at Wapping, London.

27 USSR leader Gorbachev proposes reforms, including secret ballots for election of party officials.

B February

5 SOGAT ends picket of Wapping plant.

5 Iran launches missile attack on Baghdad, Iraq (19, truce agreed in 'war of cities').

9 Sino–USSR talks on border held in Moscow, first since 1979.

10 USSR government announces release of 140 political dissidents.

10 Robert McFarlane, former US national security adviser, attempts suicide after implicated in Iran-Contra scandal.

17 in Republic of Ireland, Fianna Fáil is returned as largest party in general election.

22 4,000 Syrian troops enter West Beirut in effort to end fighting between Shi'ite Muslim and Druze forces.

26 in USA, report of Tower Commission, which investigated White House management during the period of the 'Iran–Contra affair', is critical of White House Chief of Staff Donald Regan (27, Regan replaced by former Senator Howard Baker).

28 USSR leader Gorbachev proposes separate agreement abolishing intermediate-range nuclear weapons in Europe and drops insistence on curtailment of US 'Star Wars' programme.

C March

2 (–4) US–USSR proposals on medium-range missiles tabled at Geneva.

4 in USA, President Reagan accepts full responsibility for Iran–Contra scandal.

6 Townsend Thoresen cross-channel ferry *Herald of Free Enterprise* capsizes off Zeebrugge, Belgium, killing 187.

10 Charles Haughey elected prime minister of Republic of Ireland.

17 British Budget reduces basic rate of income tax to 27 per cent, introduces new personal pension scheme, announces borrowing requirement of £7 billion.

19 Czechoslovak leader Gustáv Husák announces political and economic reforms.

25 6th National People's Congress opens in Beijing; Prime Minister Zhao Ziyang confirms new liberal economic policies.

D April

7 (–8) Syrian forces relieve Palestinian refugee camps of Shatila and Bourj-el-Barajneh in Lebanon after five-month siege by Shi'ite Amal militia.

8 state of siege allowed to lapse in Paraguay, in force since 1947.

10 Gorbachev announces that USSR is prepared to negotiate on short- as well as intermediate-range missiles.

12 general election in Fiji won by Indian-dominated coalition.

17 (–19) in Argentina, army officers mount rebellion.

17 Tamil terrorists ambush buses near Trincomale, Sri Lanka, killing 129.

20 (–26) Palestinian National Council meets in Algiers; re-elects Arafat leader, but reduces his authority.

25 in Britain, IRA car bomb kills Lord Justice Maurice Gibson and Lady Gibson.

27 US Justice Department bars President Waldheim of Austria from entering the USA because of his alleged involvement in Nazi atrocities.

E May

6 Ruling National Party wins sweeping victory in South African general election. Conservatives become second-largest party.

7 Conservatives make gains in British local elections.

8 in Northern Ireland, nine IRA men killed in battle with police and troops after attempted bomb attack on police station in Loughall, Co Armagh.

10 Nationalist Party defeats ruling Labour Party in Malta's general election.

11 Indian government imposes direct rule on Punjab.

14 coup in Fiji led by Colonel Sitiveni Rabuka.

14 Egypt breaks off diplomatic relations with Iran over financing of Islamic fundamentalism.

Single European Act ... Allan Bloom's Closing of the American
Mind *... Death of Fred Astaire ...*

o **Politics, Government, Law, and Economy**

Paul Kennedy, *The Rise and Fall of the Great Powers*.

Peter Wright, *Spycatcher: The Making of an Intelligence Officer* (published first in the USA, then in Australia and Ireland).

In USA, in McCleskey v. Kemp (22 Apr), the Supreme Court rules that statistical demonstration of racism in the application of the death penalty is not sufficient to make it a cruel and unusual punishment (and therefore unconstitutional).

In USA, Senate Committee rejects Robert Bork, nominated by President Reagan, as a justice of the Supreme Court because of his conservative political and legal views (23 Oct).

In Britain, the Access to Personal Files Act puts right to consult manual files on the same level as that for computer files under the Data Protection Act.

Finance ministers of six Western countries make the Louvre Accord, agreeing measures to stabilize the dollar (Feb).

Members of the European Community complete ratification of the Single European Act; it comes into force on 1 July, starting the creation of a single market in Europe by 1993.

Japan privatizes its national railways, by transfer of system to seven private companies (1 Apr).

British Airways acquires British Caledonian for £237 million (16 July).

P **Society, Education, and Religion**

Formal announcement that world population has reached 5,000,000,000, double the level of 1950 (11 July).

Global Fund for Women founded.

In USA, the Supreme Court, in California Federal Savings and Loan Association v. Guerra, upholds California law obliging employers to grant pregnant women up to four months' unpaid leave (13 Jan).

Family clinics in USA that counsel people about abortion are denied federal aid.

Vatican document, *Instruction on Respect for Human Life in its Origin and on the Dignity of Procreation: Replies to Certain Questions of the Day*, condemns artificial methods of fertilization and calls for ban on experiments on living embryos (10 March).

Superior Court Judge in 'Baby M' case in USA denies parental rights to surrogate mother (31 March).

Court of Appeal in Britain rejects appeal by man to prevent a woman carrying his child from having an abortion (30 Apr).

House of Lords in Britain approves sterilization of 17-year-old subnormal girl.

Allan Bloom, *The Closing of the American Mind*.

Randy Shilts, *And the Band Played On: Politics, People and the AIDS Epidemic*.

Teachers' Pay and Conditions Act in Britain abolishes union–employer negotiating machinery.

British government announces (11 Sept) intention to abolish the Inner London Education Authority.

The Vatican announces plans to renew contact with dissident French Archbishop Marcel Lefèbvre.

Patriarch Demetrios I of Constantinople joins in blessing crowds in St Peter's Square, Rome.

In USA, the Supreme Court, in Edwards v. Aguillard (19 June), strikes down state laws requiring schools to give equal time to 'creationist science', as violating the Constitution's separation of Church and State.

In England (2 Dec), the anonymous preface to the new edition of the *Crockford's Clerical Directory* is critical of the Archbishops of Canterbury and York, and of the general leadership of the Church of England; its author, Dr Gareth Bennett of New College, Oxford, commits suicide (7 Dec).

General Synod of the Church of England debates homosexuality; published report states that sexual intercourse belongs properly within marriage, and that homosexuals should be met with compassion and a call to repentance.

Doctrine Commission of the Church of England publishes the report *We Believe in God*.

Q **Science, Technology, and Discovery**

An advanced supercomputer enters service, the Numerical Aerodynamic Simulation Facility, able to do 1,720,000,000 computations a second.

First suspect is convicted in Britain of two murders by evidence derived from genetic fingerprinting.

First glass-fibre optic cable laid across the Atlantic Ocean.

Digital audio tape cassettes, producing high-quality sound, go on sale.

International protocol to limit use of damaging CFCs.

17 Iraqi Exocet missile hits USS *Stark* in Persian Gulf, killing 37.

29 19-year-old West German, Mathias Rust, lands small plane in Moscow's Red Square (30, commander-in-chief of USSR Air Defences dismissed).

F **June**

1 Lebanese Prime Minister Rashid Karami killed by bomb explosion on helicopter.

3 in Canada, Prime Minister Mulroney and prime ministers of the 10 provinces make the Meech Lake Accord whereby Quebec would be recognized as a 'distinct society'; the Accord requires ratification by the provinces.

4 West German Bundestag endorses US–USSR plan to eliminate medium-range missiles from Europe.

11 Conservatives win British general election with overall majority of 101, winning 375 seats, against Labour, 229, Liberal–SDP Alliance, 22 (Conservatives win 42.3 per cent of votes cast, Labour, 30.8 per cent, Liberal–SDP Alliance, 22.6 per cent).

14 large gains for Socialists in Italian general election.

18 unemployment in Britain falls below 3 million.

21 multi-candidate lists introduced in 5 per cent of constituencies in USSR local elections.

25 Károly Grósz, a reactionary, becomes Hungary's prime minister and later introduces an austerity programme to deal with economic problems.

G **July**

1 Single European Act in force, improving EC procedures and introducing qualified majority voting in Council of Ministers.

7 in USA, in evidence before Iran–Contra hearings, Colonel Oliver North claims his actions were sanctioned by superiors.

14 opposition parties become legal in Taiwan.

17 in USA, Vice-Admiral John Poindexter states that he authorized diversion of funds to Contra rebels.

20 UN Security Council adopts Resolution 598 calling on Iran and Iraq to implement cease-fire.

21 US offers naval protection to Kuwaiti tankers in Persian Gulf.

22 USSR leader Gorbachev offers to dismantle all short- and medium-range missiles in USSR.

29 President Jayawardene of Sri Lanka and Prime Minister Gandhi of India sign agreement aimed at ending communal violence in Sri Lanka.

H **August**

4 Tamil rebels in Sri Lanka agree to surrender arms to Indian peacekeeping force.

6 in Britain, Dr David Owen resigns leadership of SDP, following vote in favour of merger negotiations with Liberals (28, succeeded by Robert Maclennan).

7 Arias Plan for peace in Central America signed by presidents of Guatemala, El Salvador, Honduras, Nicaragua, and Costa Rica.

12 in USA, President Reagan insists he was not told of diversion of funds from arms sales to Nicaraguan Contras.

19 gunman Michael Ryan kills 16 in English town of Hungerford, before shooting himself (22 Sept, government bans automatic weapons of kind used by Ryan).

19 Zimbabwe's House of Assembly agrees change to constitution, abolishing 20 seats reserved for whites.

19 USA announces restoration of full diplomatic relations with Syria.

30 in Britain, Dr David Owen announces formation of breakaway 'continuing' SDP.

J **September**

3 Coup in Burundi; Military Committee for National Redemption formed.

6 Radical Civic Union Party loses majority in Argentina's Chamber of Deputies.

7 East German leader Honecker begins five-day official visit to West Germany; first by East German leader.

11 UN Secretary General Javier Pérez de Cuéllar begins peace mission to end Iran–Iraq War.

15 diplomatic relations established between Albania and West Germany.

15 (–17) US Secretary of State Shultz and USSR Foreign Minister Shevardnadze reach agreement on elimination of intermediate-range nuclear weapons.

17 in Britain, Liberal Party Assembly votes for merger talks with SDP.

17 constitutional affairs committee of President's Council in South Africa recommends repeal of 1953 Separate Amenities Act and relaxation of 1950 Group Areas Act.

25 second coup in year in Fiji led by Colonel Sitiveni Rabuka.

K **October**

1 Violent demonstrations against Chinese rule in Tibetan capital, Lhasa.

3 Canada and USA agree moves to reduce tariffs and economic barriers.

6 Colonel Rabuka declares Fiji a republic.

8 in Britain, inquest jury returns verdict of unlawful killing on 187 victims of Zeebrugge ferry disaster.

Start of construction of Channel Tunnel between England and France (Nov).

Launch of the USSR's *Energia* superbooster, the world's most powerful space launcher with thrust of 3 million kg/6.6 million lb.

Soviet cosmonaut Yuri V Romanenko spends a record 326 days in the *Mir* space station (6 Feb–29 Dec).

Observation of radio waves from 3C326, believed to be a galaxy in the process of formation.

Discovery of the first supernova (explosion of a star) to be observed since 1604 (24 Feb).

Harvey Butcher of Groningen, Netherlands, estimates that the Universe is younger than 10 billion years.

First successful five-organ transplant, in which a three-year-old girl in the USA receives a new liver, pancreas, small intestine, and parts of the stomach and colon.

Surgeons at the University of Pennsylvania Hospital, USA, transplant an entire human knee.

Canadian surgeons use a laser to clear a blocked coronary artery.

A South African woman gives birth to triplets formed from her daughter's transplanted embryos.

The US Patent and Trademark Office announces its intention to allow the patenting of animals produced by genetic engineering (April).

British scientist Sir Walter Bodmer and associates announce the discovery of a marker for a gene that causes cancer of the colon.

David C Page and associates announce the discovery of a gene that initiates the development of male features in mammals.

Chinese scientists insert genes controlling human growth hormones into goldfish and loach, they grow to four times the normal size.

Discovery of ceramics with superconducting properties.

R Humanities

R R Davies, *Conquest, Co-existence and Change: Wales 1063–1415.*

Maurice Howard, *The Early Tudor Country House: Architecture and Politics, 1490–1550.*

David Cressy, *Coming Over: Migration and Communication between England and New England in the Seventeenth Century.*

Simon Schama, *The Embarrassment of Riches.*

Robert Gildea, *Barricades and Borders: Europe 1800–1914.*

Charles Phythian-Adams, *Re-thinking English Local History.*

Richard Ellman, *Oscar Wilde.*

Jacques Derrida, *Of Spirit: Heidegger and the Question.*

Hilary Putnam, *The Many Faces of Realism.*

S Art, Sculpture, Fine Arts, and Architecture

Christie's sells Vincent van Gogh's *Irises* for £30 million, a world record sale price for art of any kind.

Turner Prize in Britain awarded to Richard Deacon.

'British Art of the Twentieth Century', exhibition at the Royal Academy, London.

Painting, etc:

Barbara Kruger, *I Shop Therefore I Am.*

Andres Serrano, *Piss Christ.*

Jeff Stultiens, *His Eminence, Cardinal Basil Hume, OSB, Archbishop of Westminster.*

Sculpture:

Richard Deacon, *The Back of my Hand* (sculpture).

Architecture:

Le Corbusier retrospective exhibitions held at the Hayward Gallery, London, and Pompidou Centre, Paris, France.

Architecture:

Renzo Piano, de Menil Museum, Houston, Texas, USA.

James Stirling and Michael Willford, Clore Gallery, Tate Gallery, London.

Olympia and York property company takes over development of Canary Wharf, London Docklands; architects: Cesar Pelli, Adamson Associates, Frederick Gibberd and Partners.

T Music

John Adams, *Nixon in China* (opera).

Elena Firsova, *Earthly Life.*

John Harbison, *The Flight into Egypt.*

Nigel Osborne, *The Electrification of the Soviet Union* (opera).

Joan Towers, *Silver Ladders.*

The Beastie Boys, 'Fight For Your Life To Party', *Licensed To Kill.*

Ferry Aid, 'Let It Be'.

Whitney Houston 'I Wanna Dance With Somebody', *Whitney Houston* (the first record album by a woman singer to go straight to number one in the album charts).

Michael Jackson, 'Bad'.

Los Lobos, 'La Bamba'.

Marrs, 'Pump Up The Volume'.

George Michael, 'Faith'.

Prince, 'Sign Of The Times'.

Starship, 'Nothing's Gonna Stop Us Now'.

U2, *The Joshua Tree.*

13 (–17) Commonwealth Conference in Vancouver. Britain dissents from declaration on South Africa.

15 military coup in Burkina Faso.

15 Queen Elizabeth accepts resignation of Ratu Sir Penaia Ganilau as governor general of Fiji, ending 113-year colonial link.

16 'Great Storm' sweeps across SE England, felling 15 million trees; reckoned to be worst storm in Britain for 300 years.

19 in New York, Dow Jones Average falls 508.32 points (23 per cent), precipitating large falls in share values across world.

19 US destroyers and commandos attack Iranian oil installations in Persian Gulf.

25 (–1 Nov) 13th Communist Party Congress in Beijing. Deng Xiaoping retires as general secretary and Politburo member.

L November

1 French authorities uncover arms haul on trawler *Eksund*, thought to be bound for IRA.

2 USSR leader Gorbachev, in speech to mark 70th anniversary of Russian Revolution, criticizes Stalin for political errors.

8 in Northern Ireland, IRA bombs explode at Remembrance Day service in Enniskillen, Co Fermanagh, killing 11 (15, Catholic Bishops in Northern Ireland and Republic denounce IRA violence).

8 (–11) Arab summit meeting in Jordan. Syria's President Assad agrees to end political and military support of Iran.

11 in USSR, Boris Yeltsin dismissed as chief of Moscow Communist Party after he criticizes the slow pace of reforms.

18 in USA, report of joint Senate/House of Representatives Iran–Contra Committee blames President Reagan for abuse of law; eight Republicans refuse to sign report.

18 Ethiopian government announces that 5 million people are facing starvation in northern provinces.

18 30 die in fire at King's Cross Underground Station, London.

23 (–24) Secretary of State Shultz and USSR Foreign Minister Shevardnadze agree treaty to eliminate all intermediate-range nuclear (INF) weapons.

24 Li Peng succeeds Zhao Ziyang as China's prime minister.

24 government of Ireland agrees new extradition arrangements with Britain, removing right to claim exemption for politically motivated crime.

M December

7 (–10) US–USSR Summit in Washington, DC, USA. Reagan and Gorbachev agree to eliminate intermediate nuclear forces.

17 Gustáv Husák resigns as general secretary of Czechoslovak Communist Party; succeeded by Milos Jakeš.

21 2,000 killed in ferry disaster in Philippines.

22 Prime Minister Mugabe and Joshua Nkomo agree to unite ZANU (PF) and ZAPU parties.

22 UN Security Council criticizes Israeli action against Palestinians protesting on West Bank and Gaza Strip.

28 Tunisia and Libya restore diplomatic relations.

31 US dollar reaches all-time low against major currencies.

The Sugarcubes, 'Birthday'.

u Literature and Drama

Chinua Achebe, *Anthills of the Savannah.*
Margaret Atwood, *The Handmaid's Tale.*
Bruce Chatwin, *Songlines.*
Robertson Davies, *What's Bred in the Bone.*
Nadine Gordimer, *A Sport of Nature.*
George Higgins, *Outlaws.*
Kazuo Ishiguro, *An Artist of the Floating World.*
Penelope Lively, *Moon Tiger.*
Haruki Marukami, *Norwegian Wood.*
Toni Morrison, *Beloved.*
Howard Norman, *The Northern Lights.*
Michael Ondaatje, *In the Skin of a Lion.*
Christopher Ricks (ed.), *The New Oxford Book of Victorian Verse.*
Michele Roberts, *The Book of Mrs Noah.*
Colin Thubron, *Behind the Wall.*
Tom Wolfe, *Bonfire of the Vanities.*

Drama:

Caryl Churchill, *Serious Money.*
Alma de Groen, *The Rivers of China.*
Iain Heggie, *A Wholly Healthy Glasgow.*
Lanford Wilson, *Burn This.*

v Births and Deaths

Feb 4 Liberace dies (67).
March 3 Danny Kaye dies (74).
March 19 Duc Louis de Broglie dies (94).
April 11 Primo Levi dies (67).
June 2 Andrés Segovia dies (93).
June 22 Fred Astaire dies (88).
Aug 17 Rudolf Hess dies (93).
Oct 3 Jean Anouilh dies (77).
Oct 19 Jacqueline du Pré dies (42).
Oct 29 Woody Herman dies (74).
Nov 30 James Baldwin dies (63).

w Everyday Life

In USA, a toy manufacturer suffers severe losses by mass-producing dolls of Oliver North, an aide involved in the Iran–Contra scandal.

In Britain, it is announced that Enid Blyton's 'Noddy' books will be altered to replace the golliwogs with gnomes.

x Sport and Recreation

In cricket, Sunil Gavaskar of India, playing in his 124th Test match, becomes the first batsman to score 10,000 Test runs (7 March).

In cycling, Stephen Roche is the first Irishman and the second rider from beyond continental Europe to win the Tour de France (26 July).

Laura Davies is the first British golfer to win the US Women's Open Championship (28 July).

Europe's golfers win the Ryder Cup in the USA for the first time (27 Sept).

British champion jockey Lester Piggott is jailed for three years for tax evasion (23 Oct).

y Media

Robert Maxwell launches the *London Daily News* (Feb), a new London evening newspaper; it is foiled by a temporary relaunch of the *Evening News* and closes in July.

In Britain, attempt made to establish the *News on Sunday*, a new left-wing Sunday newspaper (April–Nov).

Lonrho sells the British tabloid *Today* to Rupert Murdoch (July).

Film:

Fatal Attraction (director, Adrian Lyne; starring Michael Douglas and Glenn Close).
The Last Emperor (director, Bernardo Bertolucci).
Pelle the Conqueror (director, Bille August).
Robocop (director, Paul Verhoeven).
The Untouchables (director, Brian de Palma; starring Kevin Costner).
Wall Street (director, Oliver Stone).
Whooping Cough (director, Peter Gardos).
Wings of Desire (director, Wim Wenders).
Italy lifts ban on *Last Tango in Paris.*

Television:

Federal Communications Commission abandons requirement that broadcasters must present all sides of controversial issues (4 Aug).

*USSR withdraws from Afghanistan ... Death of President Zia
ul-Haq ... George bush elected US president ...*

A **January**

2 Canada and USA sign free-trade agreement.

3 Margaret Thatcher becomes longest-serving British prime minister in 20th century.

8 New York stock market registers third largest one-day fall in history, with Dow Jones average closing 140.58 points down on the day.

17 presidential elections held in Haiti amidst allegations of voting irregularities.

22 USA submits draft space defence treaty at US–USSR disarmament talks in Geneva.

25 Ramsewak Shankar is inaugurated as president of Surinam, bringing end to eight years of military rule.

26 celebrations in Sydney mark bicentenary of arrival of European settlers in Australia.

29 talks in Luganda achieve agreement for Cuban military withdrawal from Angola.

B **February**

2 2,000 nurses and other health workers in London hospitals hold a one-day strike over pay.

7 Leslie Manigat inaugurated as president in Haiti, ending two years of military rule.

8 Mikhail Gorbachev announces that USSR troops will begin withdrawal from Afghanistan on 15 May.

8 International Commission finds that Kurt Waldheim, president of Austria, knew about wartime atrocities in the Balkans, but clears him of war crimes.

10 over 100 people die in violence during local elections in Bangladesh.

20 Regional Soviet in Nagorno-Karabakh votes for region to be transferred from Azerbaijan to Armenia.

23 torrential rain in Brazil leaves 275 reported dead and 25,000 homeless.

23 US Secretary of State George Shultz arrives in Israel at start of Middle East peace mission.

26 in USSR, Gorbachev makes unprecedented television appeal for calm after week of nationalist demonstrations in Armenia.

29 in South Africa, Archbishop Desmond Tutu and 100 clergy detained in Cape Town while protesting at curbs imposed (on 24 Feb) on anti-apartheid organizations.

C **March**

1 USSR troops enforce curfew in Sumgait in Azerbaijan following deaths in ethnic violence.

6 three suspected IRA terrorists are shot dead by British SAS team in Gibraltar.

14 three days of clashes begin between China and Vietnam over the disputed Spratly Islands.

15 in Britain, in the Budget, Chancellor Nigel Lawson reduces standard rate of income tax in Britain to 25 per cent and replaces all higher rate taxes with single rate of 40 per cent.

20 elections to National Assembly in El Salvador won by right-wing Nationalist Republican Alliance.

23 Contra commanders and government officials sign 60-day cease-fire agreement in Nicaragua.

29 British Secretary for Trade and Industry Lord Young announces sale of Rover car group to British Aerospace.

D **April**

2 Indian forces seal border with Pakistan against infiltration of Sikh extremists after 120 deaths in week of violence in the Punjab.

3 peace agreement between Ethiopia and Somalia ends 11 years of border conflict.

5 Shi'ite Muslim extremists hijack a Kuwait Airways 747 airliner, forcing it to fly to Iran and to Cyprus, where two hostages are shot dead (20, hijack ends in Algiers).

10 hundreds of deaths in explosion at army ammunition dump near Islamabad in Pakistan, for which Afghan agents are believed responsible.

16 assassination of military commander of PLO, Abu Jihad, in Tunis.

18 US planes and warships destroy two Iranian oil platforms and attack ships in the Persian Gulf in retaliation for damage to a US frigate.

22 France flies in military reinforcements when three gendarmes are killed and others captured by Kanak separatists in New Caledonia.

25 in Israel, John Demjanjuk ('Ivan the Terrible') is sentenced to death for war crimes in the gas chambers in the Treblinka concentration camp.

E **May**

2 Thousands of shipyard workers go on strike in Poland and seven Solidarity leaders are detained.

3 Islamic Jihad free three French hostages in Lebanon amidst allegations that France had done a deal with Iran.

6 Pope John Paul II begins a 13-day tour of Uruguay, Bolivia, Peru, and Paraguay.

First woman bishop in US Episcopal Church ... Harvard patents genetically engineered mouse ... Steffi Graf wins tennis 'grand slam' ...

o Politics, Government, Law, and Economy

Legalization of political opposition in Hungary.

In USSR, Supreme Court approves posthumous judicial rehabilitation of Nikolai Bukharin and nine other Soviet leaders executed or imprisoned after 1938 'show trial' (4 Feb).

British House of Commons votes to allow its proceedings to be televised (9 Feb).

In Britain, the Liberal Party (23 Jan) and the Social Democratic Party (31 Jan) vote to form a new party (from 3 March), the Social and Liberal Democrats (known as the Liberal Democrats from 16 Oct 1989); Dr David Owen and supporters refuse to accept the merger and remain the 'continuing' SDP.

In Britain, the White Paper *The Next Steps* recommends hiving off parts of the British civil service into autonomous agencies.

Local Government Act in Britain requires local authorities to put more services out to competitive tendering.

In Brogan v. UK the extended detention provisions of the Prevention of Terrorism Act (1974) are found to be in conflict with the European Convention on Human Rights.

The right to silence of accused people is abolished in Northern Ireland.

USA and Canada sign a free-trade agreement.

Financial Corporation of America becomes the largest bankruptcy in American history, with losses of $33.9 billion.

Britain's chancellor, Nigel Lawson, prepares for British entry into the Exchange Rate Mechanism (ERM) by making the pound 'shadow' the Deutschmark.

In Britain, persistent disagreement between Prime Minister Thatcher and Chancellor Lawson on exchange rate policy unsettles money markets.

In bid to reduce over-production of foodstuffs, the European Community agrees the 'Set-aside' agriculture policy, whereby farmers are subsidized for taking land out of production.

p Society, Education, and Religion

In USA, installation of Eugene Antonio Marino as the first African-American Roman Catholic archbishop (5 May).

Following the introduction of youth training, social security benefits in Britain are withdrawn from people aged 16–18.

Charges for eye tests and dental checks are introduced in Britain.

The 'Baker' Education Reform Act in Britain introduces a ten-subject national curriculum, testing at four 'key stages', envisages further City Technology Colleges and permits schools to 'opt out' of local education authority control.

In England and Wales, General Certificate of Secondary Education examinations replace GCE Ordinary levels and the CSE.

The Higginson Report, recommending broader courses of study to replace GCE Advanced levels in England and Wales, is shelved by the government.

The Holy Shroud of Turin, claimed by some to be Christ's mortuary cloth, is shown by carbon dating to date from the 14th century.

Dissident French Archbishop Marcel Lefèbvre consecrates four bishops in his traditionalist movement and is automatically excommunicated by the Catholic Church.

In the Apostolic Letter *Mulieris Dignitatem* Pope John Paul II reiterates his opposition to women priests.

In USA, Barbara Harris, a divorcee, is elected as first woman bishop in the Anglican communion (25 Sept), to serve as suffragan Bishop of Massachusetts (consecrated 11 Feb 1989).

The headquarters of the South African Council of Churches is bombed.

The Lambeth Conference of Anglican Bishops is held in Canterbury, SE England (17 July–7 Aug).

The film *The Last Temptation of Christ*, directed by US director Martin Scorsese, is widely regarded as blasphemous.

q Science, Technology, and Discovery

The *Daedalus 88* sets new record for human-powered flight, covering 119 km/74 mi in 3 hr 54 min.

US 'Stealth bomber', invisible to radar and heat-seeking missiles, goes on public display (Nov).

Serious damage is done to computer systems world-wide by 'viruses' implanted by 'hackers' breaking into computer networks.

Launch of two Soviet *Phobos* space probes (7 and 12 July), to study Phobos, one of the moons of Mars; *Phobos 1* is accidentally sent a 'suicide' instruction.

Israel launches a satellite (19 Sept), for geophysical studies.

8 President Mitterrand (Socialist) defeats Jacques Chirac (Gaullist) in French Presidential elections, with over 54 per cent of poll.

10 Chirac resigns as French prime minister and is replaced by Michel Rocard (Socialist).

15 USSR troops begin withdrawal from Afghanistan after eight and a half years.

19 Sikh rebels surrender after occupying Golden Temple in Amritsar, N India.

23 in Britain, the second largest turn-out of peers in the 20th century secures majority of 134 for the Government's Poll Tax Bill in the House of Lords.

F June

1 Reagan and Gorbachev sign Intermediate-range Nuclear Forces (INF) treaty at Moscow Summit (29 May–2 June).

2 in Australia, Canberra High Court dismisses British Government's appeal against sale of Peter Wright's book *Spycatcher*, after 18 months of legal proceedings.

5 in Moscow, leading world churchmen celebrate 1,000 years of Christianity in Russia.

19 Leslie Manigat, civilian president of Haiti, is deposed by a military coup and replaced by General Henri Namphy.

23 USSR troops move into parts of Armenia, Azerbaijan, and the disputed region of Nagorno-Karabakh, as ethnic violence enters its fifth month.

28 (–1 July) at 19th Communist Party conference at Moscow, President Gorbachev outlines plans for changes in the administrative structure of the USSR, intended to make the Party more democratic and businesses more autonomous.

G July

3 US warship *Vincennes* shoots down Iranian civilian airliner in the Persian Gulf, with loss of 290 lives.

6 explosion on North Sea Piper Alpha oil platform kills 167.

6 presidential elections in Mexico won by Carlos Salinas de Gortari, of the ruling Institutional Revolutionary Party.

11 Nicaragua expels US ambassador and seven colleagues, on charge of inciting violent anti-government incidents.

18 70th birthday of ANC leader Nelson Mandela marked by worldwide protests calling for his release from prison in South Africa.

28 Israeli representative makes first official visit to USSR since breaking of diplomatic relations in 1967.

31 King Hussein of Jordan announces plans to cut legal and administrative ties with the occupied West Bank.

H August

7 Over 1 million people in Sudan are homeless after widespread flooding in Khartoum and surrounding provinces.

8 Iraq and Iran announce ceasefire.

17 President Zia ul-Haq and the US ambassador to Pakistan are killed when plane carrying them explodes in mid-air; state of emergency is declared.

25 centre of Lisbon, Portugal, gutted by fire.

31 Lech Walesa holds first talks with Polish authorities since the banning of Solidarity in 1981.

31 widespread flooding in Bangladesh leaves 25 million homeless.

J September

4 Demonstrations by Serbs and Montenegrins in Yugoslavia calling for martial law in Kosovo and protection from Albanian separatists.

18 in Haiti General Namphy is deposed in military coup.

20 in speech to Council of Europe at Bruges, Margaret Thatcher warns against the folly of moves towards political and economic union of Europe.

21 state of emergency declared in Nagorno-Karabakh, USSR.

22 Brazil concludes agreement with creditor banks, rescheduling debts of US$62,100 million.

29 Nobel Peace Prize awarded to UN peace-keeping forces.

30 major changes are made in USSR Politburo, including retirement of President Andrei Gromyko and dismissal of leading figures.

K October

1 Mikhail Gorbachev is elected president of USSR by Supreme Soviet.

2 founding of Estonian Popular Front.

3 Chad and Libya end war and establish diplomatic relations.

6 Algerian government introduces emergency measures, following rioting against rising prices and unemployment.

11 Ladislav Adamec replaces Lubomir Štrougal as prime minister of Czechoslovakia as part of major changes in government and Communist Party.

19 British home secretary announces ban on broadcasting of interviews with 11 terrorist organizations, including Sinn Féin.

First mission of the US shuttle for almost three years (29 Sept–3 Oct).

Soviet uncrewed space shuttle *Buran* ('blizzard') makes its inaugural flight, under radio control (15 Nov).

Simon J Lilly of the University of Hawaii, USA, reports the location of a galaxy about 12 billion light years from Earth, adding to evidence about the date of galaxy formation.

Stephen Hawking, *A Brief History of Time*.

A French company markets the abortion-inducing drug RV486; anti-abortion groups protest.

US scientists announce a project to compile a complete 'map' of human genes; establishment of the Human Genome Organization (HUGO) in Washington, DC, USA.

US Patent and Trademark Office grants Harvard University a patent for a mouse developed by genetic engineering (Apr).

R Jaenisch and associates implant a human gene, connected with a hereditary disorder, into a mouse.

The first dairy cattle are produced by cloning embryos.

R **Humanities**

A rich tomb of *c.* AD 300 is found near Sipan in Peru.

John Cannon et al. (eds.), *The Blackwell Dictionary of Historians*.

Christopher Brooke, Roger Highfield, and Wim Swaan, *Oxford and Cambridge*.

E A Wrigley, *Continuity, Chance, and Change: The Character of the Industrial Revolution in England*.

James McPherson, *Battle Cry of Freedom*.

Eric Foner, *Reconstruction: America's Unfinished Revolution*.

Colin Holmes, *John Bull's Island: Immigration and British Society, 1871– 1971*.

J M Winter, *The Experience of World War I*.

Eighth and final volume of the official biography of Winston Churchill by Martin Gilbert.

Sir Henry Phelps Brown, *Egalitarianism and the Generation of Inequality*.

Neil Sheehan, *A Bright Shining Lie: John Paul Vann and America in Vietnam*.

John Sutherland, *Longman Companion to Victorian Fiction*.

Ted Honderich, *The Consequences of Determinism*.

Alisdair MacIntyre, *Whose Justice? Which Rationality?*

S **Art, Sculpture, Fine Arts, and Architecture**

Jasper Johns's *False Start* sold for $17,050,000, a world record for contemporary art and for a work by a living artist.

Turner Prize in Britain awarded to Tony Cragg.

Painting:

Francesco Clemente, *Paradigm*.

Peter Halley, *Red Cell*.

Sculpture:

Tony Cragg, *Generations*.

Anish Kapoor, *Mother as Void*.

Rachel Whiteread, *Closet*.

Architecture:

'Deconstructivist Architecture' exhibition at the Museum of Modern Art, New York.

T **Music**

Kalevi Aho, Symphony No. 7.

György Ligeti, Concerto for Piano and Orchestra.

Marcel Landowski, Symphony No. 4.

Witold Lutoslawski, Piano Concerto.

Meredith Monk, *Book of Days*.

Conlon Nancarrow, String Quartet.

Karlheinz Stockhausen, *Montag aus Licht* (opera).

Rich Astley, 'Never Gonna Give You Up'.

Bros, 'I Owe You Nothing'.

Tracy Chapman, *Tracy Chapman*.

Guns 'n' Roses, *Appetite For Destruction*.

k d lang, *Shadowland*.

Def Leppard, *Hysteria*.

Kylie Minogue, 'I Should Be So Lucky'.

My Bloody Valentine, *Isn't Anything*.

The Pixies, *Surfer Rosa*.

Public Enemy, *It Takes A Nation Of Millions To Hold Us Back*.

Sonic Youth, *Daydream Nation*.

U2, *Rattle and Hum*.

Rock stars make world-wide tour to give concerts in aid of Amnesty International.

Concert held at Wembley Stadium, London, to celebrate the 70th birthday of Nelson Mandela.

U **Literature and Drama**

Kobo Abe, *The Ark Sakura*.

Saul Bellow, *More Die of Heartbreak*.

Peter Carey, *Oscar and Lucinda*.

Anita Desai, *Baumgartner's Bombay*.

Stephen Dobyns, *The Two Deaths of Señora Puccini*.

Janet Frame, *The Carpathians*.

Gabriel García Márquez, *Love in the Time of Cholera*.

Thomas Harris, *The Silence of the Lambs*.

David Lodge, *Nice Work*.

Eduardo Mendoza, *The City of Marvels*.

Brian Moore, *The Colour of Blood*.

Milorad Pavic, *Dictionary of the Khazars*.

Salman Rushdie, *The Satanic Verses*.

26 simultaneous elections to white, black, coloured, and Indian local councils held for first time in South Africa.

31 Polish government announces closure of Gdansk shipyard.

L **November**

1 Israeli elections produce no clear winner.

2 Margaret Thatcher begins three-day visit to Poland, in which she holds talks with the prime minister and meets Lech Walesa at Gdansk shipyard.

8 in US presidential elections Republican George Bush, with 426 electoral college votes, defeats Democrat Michael Dukakis, with 112 votes, but the Democratic Party increases its majority in the Senate and House of Representatives. Popular vote: Bush, 48,886,097; Dukakis, 41,809,074.

15 PLO parliament in exile declares an independent state of Palestine.

16 parliament in Estonia votes to give itself rights to veto laws from Moscow.

16 Benazir Bhutto's Pakistan People's Party win 94 seats in general election (2 Dec, she is sworn in as prime minister of Pakistan).

21 general election in Canada won by Progressive Conservative Party led by Prime Minister Brian Mulroney.

22 in Britain, Queen's Speech at state opening of Parliament announces bills for Privatization of water and electricity services.

23 two regions of Azerbaijan placed under state of emergency following ethnic clashes.

24 Egypt and Algeria restore diplomatic relations.

M **December**

7 In New York, President Gorbachev announces plans to reduce USSR armed forces and conventional weapons.

12 34 die in rail crash at Clapham Junction in South London, the worst rail accident in Britain for 20 years.

4 Spain has 24-hour general strike, the first such for 50 years.

15 USA resumes contacts with PLO after 13-year boycott.

16 Edwina Currie, under secretary of state for health, resigns after allegation of widespread salmonella infection in British egg production leads to collapse in egg sales.

21 terrorist bomb explodes on Pan Am Boeing 747 airliner flying over Lockerbie in Scotland, killing all on board and 11 on the ground.

22 agreement reached at UN for Namibian independence, with phased withdrawal of Cuban forces.

30 Government of Yugoslavia, led by Branko Mikulic, resigns as parliament blocks economic reform package.

Anatoli Rybakov, *Children of the Arbat* (published after a 20-year ban in the USSR).

Wole Soyinka, *Ake*.

Adam Zameenzad, *My Friend Matt and Hena the Whore*.

Drama:

David Henry Hwang, *M Butterfly*.

David Mamet, *Speed-the-Plow*.

Gieve Patel, *Mister Behram*.

Sam Shepard, *A Lie of the Mind*.

Timberlake Wertenbaker, *Our Country's Good*.

Richard Eyre replaces Peter Hall as Director of Britain's National Theatre.

v Births and Deaths

Feb 2 Solomon dies (85).

Feb 5 Ove Arup dies (92).

Feb 15 Richard Feynman dies (69).

April 12 Alan Paton dies (85).

April 23 Michael Ramsey dies (83).

Aug 14 Enzo Ferrari dies (90).

Oct 2 Alec Issigonis dies (81).

Oct 28 Pietro Annigoni dies (78).

Dec 30 Isamu Noguchi dies (84).

w Everyday Life

In USA, the 'kiss-'n-tell' memoir of Donald Regan, former White House chief of staff, reveals that President Reagan set dates for important meetings and decisions according to information from his wife's astrologer (3 May).

x Sport and Recreation

'Sandy' Lyle is first British golfer to win the US Masters, held at Augusta, Georgia (10 April).

Tottenham Hotspur Football Club, London, pays record £2 million transfer fee to Newcastle United for Paul Gascoigne (July 7).

The 24th Olympic Games are held in Seoul, South Korea (17 Sept–2 Oct), and are free of boycotts. The USSR wins 55 gold medals; East Germany, 37; USA, 36; South Korea, 12; West Germany and Hungary, 11 each; Bulgaria, 10; Romania, 7; France and Italy, 6 each; China, Great Britain, and Kenya, 5 each. In the Athletics, Ben Johnson of Canada wins the 100 m in a world record time of 9.79 seconds; he is then stripped of the title when drug tests reveal traces of an anabolic steroid, stanozol.

Steffi Graf of West Germany becomes only the third woman to win the Grand Slam of all four major tennis tournaments; she also wins an Olympic gold, following the restoration of tennis to the Olympic Games at Seoul.

India refuses entry to cricket players who had sporting contacts with South Africa, forcing England to call off its winter tour (9 Sept).

y Media

British weekly *New Society* is merged into *New Statesman* (Feb).

In Britain, the *Sun* pays £1 million to Elton John to settle the pop singer's libel claim out of court.

Eddie Shah launches a new British daily paper, the *Post*, but it folds after 33 issues (Nov–Dec).

Film:

Au Revoir les Enfants (director, Louis Malle).

Dead Ringers (director, David Cronenberg).

Die Hard (director, John McTiernan; starring Bruce Willis).

A Fish Called Wanda (director, Charles Crichton, starring John Cleese).

The Last Temptation of Christ (director, Martin Scorsese).

Rain Man (director, Barry Levinson; starring Dustin Hoffman and Tom Cruise).

Salaam Bombay (director, Mira Nair).

Torch Song Trilogy (starring Harvey Fierstein).

Women on the Verge of a Nervous Breakdown (director, Pedro Almodovar).

Television:

New programmes in Britain include: *Red Dwarf* (BBC); *A Very British Coup* (Channel 4).

*Massacre in Tiananmen Square ... Collapse of communism in
Eastern Europe ...*

A January

2 Ranasinghe Premadasa sworn in as president of Sri Lanka.

6 USSR announces mass rehabilitation of thousands of citizens who were victims of Stalin's purges 1930–50.

7 Emperor Hirohito of Japan dies after a 62-year reign; his son, Crown Prince Akihito, succeeds him.

10 Cuban troops begin withdrawal from Angola.

11 149 countries agree declaration outlawing use of poison gas, toxic, and bacteriological weapons.

11 Hungarian parliament passes law allowing formation of political parties.

15 riot police in Prague break up demonstration marking 25th anniversary of Jan Palach's suicide in protest at Soviet invasion of Czechoslovakia.

19 Ante Marković is named prime minister of Yugoslavia.

20 George Bush inaugurated as 41st president of USA.

23 274 die in earthquake in Tajikistan, USSR.

31 trial begins of Colonel Oliver North, US marines officer at centre of Iran–Contra affair.

B February

2 President Botha resigns as leader of ruling National Party in South Africa, following a stroke; F W de Klerk succeeds him.

2 Carlos Andrés Pérez sworn in as president of Venezuela.

3 35-year-old regime of President Alfredo Stroesner in Paraguay is overthrown by military coup led by General Andrés Rodríguez, who replaces him as president (1 May, Rodríguez gains landslide victory in elections).

9 in Jamaican general election, Michael Manley's People's National Party wins landslide victory over ruling Jamaica Labour Party.

14 in Iran, Ayatollah Khomeini issues fatwa against Salman Rushdie, calling for his death for blasphemy in his book *The Satanic Verses*; Rushdie goes into hiding.

18 President Najibullah imposes state of emergency in Afghanistan to bolster authority.

21 Václav Havel, dissident Czech playwright, is imprisoned for inciting public disorder in Prague in Jan.

C March

5 Cabinet resigns in Sudan. Prime Minister Sadiq al-Mahdi agrees to form coalition government and introduce a peace plan to end civil war.

7 Iran breaks off diplomatic relations with Britain over the Rushdie affair.

7 China imposes martial law in Lhasa, Tibet.

15 demonstration in Budapest calling for democracy and national independence.

19 Alfredo Cristiani (Arena party) gains outright victory over Dr Fidel Chavez Mena (Christian Democrats) in El Salvador presidential election.

24 *Exxon Valdez* oil tanker runs aground in Prince William Sound, Alaska, spilling estimated 64 million litres/11 million gallons of oil (27, USA declares state of emergency).

26 voters have a choice of candidates for first time in elections for Congress of People's Deputies in USSR. Boris Yeltsin, dismissed from the Politburo 17 months before, gains 89 per cent of vote in his Moscow constituency, while many senior Party officials fail to get elected.

28 Solomon Mamaloni, new prime minister of the Solomon Islands, announces intention of turning the Islands into a republic, ending 100-year link with British Crown.

D April

5 Lech Walesa and Polish government sign agreement for political and economic reforms.

6 (–13) in trial of Oliver North in USA, North says that he acted on orders in arranging arms deals with Iran and diverting the profits to Nicaraguan Contras (4 May, found guilty).

17 Solidarity is legalized in Poland.

17 students march on Beijing's Tiananmen Square to call for democracy.

20 first multi-party elections in Czechoslovakia since 1946.

25 Japanese Prime Minister Noboru Takeshita resigns over bribery scandal; replaced by Sosuke Uno.

26 anti-Senegalese violence in Mauritius leaves 400 dead (28, revenge killings in Senegal).

E May

2 Hungarian troops start to dismantle 350 km/ 218 mi-long security fence along border with Austria.

3 centre-right coalition under Ruud Lubbers in the Netherlands becomes first European

Hugo Young's One of Us ... *I M Pei's Louvre Pyramid ... John Tavener's* Protecting Veil ... *President Bush spurns broccoli ...*

o Politics, Government, Law, and Economy

Denis Healey, *The Time of My Life*.

Peter Hennessy, *Whitehall*.

Proceedings of the British House of Commons are televised for first time (21 Nov).

In Britain, the Security Services Act places MI5 and MI6 under a degree of judicial supervision; reform of Official Secrets Act creates clear categories of secret information, disclosure of which would be a criminal offence.

In USA, the Supreme Court, in Texas v. Johnson, rules (21 June) that the Constitution's guarantee of free speech includes the act of trampling or burning the national flag (President Bush and the House of Representatives express dismay at the ruling); the ruling is confirmed in 1990 in US v. Eichmann (11 June).

The Court of First Instance is established to take the pressure off the European Court of Justice.

Following complaints from Muslims living in Britain about Salman Rushdie's novel *The Satanic Verses*, the British Home Office announces that Blasphemy Law will not be extended to cover Islam (on 14 Jan, Muslims in Bradford, N England, publicly burn Rushdie's novel).

The British Court of Appeal is given power to review sentences that are considered lenient.

In England and Wales, the defendant's right of peremptory challenge of jurors is abolished.

In Britain, the 'Guildford Four' are cleared on appeal of bombing convictions (passed in Oct 1975) after serving 14 years of their life sentences (17 Oct).

The 'Factortame' case rules that the British Merchant Shipping Act is in conflict with European law and therefore invalid.

Members of the Association of South-East Asian Nations (ASEAN) join Canada, Australia, New Zealand, Japan, and South Korea in forming the Council for Asia–Pacific Economic Co-operation.

Leaders of Morocco, Libya, Algeria, Tunisia and Mauritania form new economic bloc called Arab Maghreb Union (17 Feb).

In USA, bailout package for troubled Savings and Loan institutions goes into operation.

p Society, Education, and Religion

South African law commission publishes working paper calling for the abolition of apartheid and introduction of universal franchise (11 March).

In USA, in Webster v. Reproductive Health Services, the Supreme Court upholds a state law in Missouri that prohibits public hospitals and clinics from performing abortions except where the mother's life is in danger (3 July).

In Wards Cove Packing v. Antonio, the US Supreme Court overturns a decision of 1971 and transfers the responsibility for deciding whether women and minorities should receive special treatment in employment from employers to employees (5 June).

In Martin v. Wilks, the US Supreme Court rules that disappointed white workers can challenge affirmative action employment arrangements (12 June).

Summit of European Community at Strasbourg, France, adopts European Social Charter on workers' rights, with Britain dissenting (8–9 Dec).

Celebrations held to mark 200th anniversary of start of French Revolution (14 July).

Forcible repatriation begins of Vietnamese boat people from Hong Kong (11 Dec).

Children Act in Britain compels parents in divorce cases to consider the interests of their offspring in divorce settlements and gives children the statutory right to be consulted.

J Masson, *Against Therapy*.

Australian Research Council established.

In Canada, School Achievement Indicators Program begins.

In Britain, several National Curriculum subject working-party reports and final orders are published.

Six Jesuit priests, their housekeeper, and her 15-year-old daughter are tortured and murdered at the University of Central America, San Salvador, El Salvador (16 Nov).

Mikhail Gorbachev is the first leader of the USSR to visit the Vatican; he and John Paul II agree to reestablish diplomatic relations between the USSR and the Vatican (1 Dec).

Václav Havel attends a thanksgiving mass in St Vitus' Cathedral, Prague, after his inauguration as president of Czechoslovakia (29 Dec).

Pastor Lázlo Tökes of Timişoara plays a prominent part in the Romanian Revolution.

q Science, Technology, and Discovery

US space shuttle launches the probe *Magellan*

government to resign over an environmental issue, when Liberal Democrats refuse support for proposals for financing of anti-pollution measures.

6 elections held in Panama, subsequently annulled by General Noriega.

14 Carlos Menem (Peronist) defeats Eduardo Angeloz (ruling Radical party) in Argentinian presidential elections (8 July, Menem takes over as president on resignation of Alfonsín).

17 in Poland, Roman Catholic Church is given status unparalleled in Eastern Europe, with restoration of property confiscated in the 1950s and the right to run schools.

19 Ciriaco de Mita announces resignation of centre-left government in Italy (23 July, Giulio Andreotti becomes prime minister of similar coalition).

F **June**

3 In China, People's Army tanks move into Tiananmen Square in Beijing, killing 2,000 pro-democracy protesters.

3 Ayatollah Khomeini, spiritual and political leader of Iran, dies.

4 Solidarity achieves landslide victory in elections to Polish parliament.

12 President Gorbachev of USSR and Chancellor Kohl of West Germany sign Bonn Document affirming right of European states to determine their own political systems.

18 Andreas Papandreou's Pasok Government loses overall majority in general election in Greece (2 July, interim government of New Democracy and Communists, led by Tzannis Tzannetakis, is sworn in).

23 President Jose Eduardo dos Santos of Angola and Dr Jonas Savimbi, leader of UNITA rebels, sign declaration ending 14-year civil war in Angola.

28 Tamil Tigers in Sri Lanka agree to ceasefire, which lasts until 5 Nov.

29 government of Sadiq al-Mahdi in Sudan is overthrown in coup.

G **July**

2 IRA car bomb explodes in Hanover, the first of a series of attacks on British army personnel stationed in West Germany.

3 Britain states that there will be no automatic right of abode in Britain for Hong Kong residents worried about the colony's future under Chinese rule.

19 Polish parliament elects General Jaruzelski (the only candidate) to new post of President, by just one vote.

23 elections for the Upper House in Japan end 34-year-old Liberal Democrat majority.

28 Hojatoleslam Ali Rafsanjani is elected first executive president of Iran.

H **August**

1 State price controls are abolished in Poland, and food prices rise by up to 500 per cent.

7 David Lange resigns as prime minister of New Zealand and is succeeded by Geoffrey Palmer.

8 resignation of Japanese Prime Minister Soske Uno as result of sex scandal; succeeded by Toshiki Kaifu (9, sworn in).

19 Communists agree to join a Solidarity-led coalition in Poland.

24 Solidarity candidate Tadeusz Mazowiecki is elected prime minister of Poland.

23 over 2 million people in Baltic republics of USSR form human chain in nationalist demonstration marking 50th anniversary of USSR–German non-aggression pact.

J **September**

1 USA breaks off diplomatic relations with Panama.

6 in whites-only election in South Africa, National Party is returned with reduced majority and F W de Klerk is elected president.

6 in Dutch general election Christian Democrats led by Ruud Lubbers remain largest party (7, form coalition with Labour).

10 Hungary allows East Germans to cross freely to the West.

11 Norwegian elections take place under new system, which favours small parties (16 Oct, Conservative-led coalition takes office).

11 creation of New Forum opposition group in East Germany.

12 Solidarity-dominated government takes office in Poland, the first government in Eastern Europe since 1940s not under Communist control.

14 Sam Najoma, president of SWAPO, returns to Namibia after nearly 30 years of exile.

17 north-east Caribbean is hit by Hurricane Hugo.

24 Arab League ceasefire enables civilians to return to homes in Beirut after six months of fighting.

26 Vietnamese troops withdraw from Kampuchea.

27 national parliament of Slovenia approves constitutional amendments giving right to secede from Federation of Yugoslavia.

28 Ferdinand Marcos, former ruler of Philippines, dies in exile in Hawaii.

K **October**

4 Mass demonstration in Leipzig demands political reform in East Germany.

7 Hungarian Socialist Workers' Party votes for its own dissolution.

(4 May) to map the surface of Venus using radar.

US space probe *Voyager 2* reaches Neptune (25 Aug) and transmits pictures; it discovers a great dark spot on the planet.

US shuttle launches the probe *Galileo* (18 Oct) to explore Jupiter.

Launch of the US COBE (Cosmic Background Explorer) satellite to study microwave background radiation, thought to be a vestige of the 'big bang'.

Inauguration of LEP (Large Electron Positron Collider) at the CERN research centre in Switzerland (14 July); the new accelerator has a circumference of 27 km/16.8 mi.

Stanley Pons and Martin Fleischmann announce (March) that they have achieved nuclear fusion at room temperature; other scientists fail to replicate their experiment.

M Harrison and colleagues remove a foetus from its mother's womb, operate on its lungs, and return it to the womb.

Researchers in Toronto, Canada, identify a gene responsible for cystic fibrosis.

Scientists in Britain introduce genetically engineered white blood cells into cancer patients, to attack tumours.

Convention on International Trade in Endangered Species agrees total ban on trading in ivory (16 Oct).

R Humanities

Peter Brown, *The Body and Society*.
The Cambridge History of Japan (–).
Remains of the Rose and Globe Theatres uncovered in London, where Shakespeare's plays were originally performed.
Colin Morris, *The Papal Monarchy*.
Christopher Dyer, *Standards of Living in the Later Middle Ages: Social Change in England, c. 1200–1520*.
Christopher Brooke, *The Medieval Idea of Marriage*.
Gervase Rosser, *Medieval Westminster, 1200–1540*.
Lyndal Roper, *The Holy Household: Women and Morals in Reformation Augsburg*.
David H Fisher, *Albion's Seed: Four British Folkways in America*.
Paul Langford, *A Polite and Commercial People: England 1727–1783* (in 'New Oxford History of England' series).
Simon Schama, *Citizens*.
Drew R McCoy, *The Last of the Founding Fathers: James Madison and the Republic Legacy*.
Nathan O Hatch, *The Democratization of American Christianity*.
Richard Holt, *Sport and the British*.
Avner Offer, *The First World War: An Agrarian Interpretation*.

Paul Fussell, *Wartime*.
Hugo Young, *One of Us*.
The Victoria History of the Counties of England celebrates 200 volumes with exhibition 'Particular Places' at the British Library, London, and accompanying book (same title) by Christopher Lewis.
J A Simpson and E S C Weiner (eds.), *The Oxford English Dictionary*, 2nd edition.
David Armstrong, *A Combinatorial Theory of Possibility*.
Gilbert Harman, *Skepticism and the Definition of Knowledge*.
Willard V Quine, *Pursuit of Truth*.

S Art, Sculpture, Fine Arts, and Architecture

'Italian Art in the Twentieth Century' exhibition at the Royal Academy, London.

Painting, etc:
Therese Oulton, *Passage*.

Sculpture:
Turner Prize in Britain awarded to Richard Long.
Richard Deacon, *Kiss and Tell*.
Architecture: I M Pei, Pyramid, Musée du Louvre, Paris, France.
Johann Otto von Spreckelsen and Paul Andreu, La Grande Arche, La Défense, Paris, France.
HRH The Prince of Wales, *A Vision of Britain: A Personal View of Architecture*.

T Music

John Cage, *Europera III/IV*.
Magnus Lindberg, *Kinetics*.
Colin Matthews, *Hidden Variables*.
Nicholas Maw, *Odyssey*.
John Tavener, *The Protecting Veil*.
Michael Tippett, *New Year* (opera).
Opening of Bastille Opera in Paris, France.
Aspects of Love (musical), lyrics by Don Black and Charles Hart, music by Andrew Lloyd Webber (first performed at the Prince of Wales Theatre, London, April).
Black Box, 'Ride On Time'.
Jive Bunny, *Swing The Mood*.
Fine Young Cannibals, *The Raw And The Cooked*.
Guns 'n' Roses, *G 'N' R Lies*.
Madonna, 'Like A Prayer'.
The Neville Brothers, *Yellow Moon*.
Prince, 'Batman' (single and album).
Lou Reed, *New York*.
Simple Minds, *Street Fighting Years*.

U Literature and Drama

Breyten Breytenbach, *Memory of Snow and Dust*.

8 Latvian Popular Front announces intention to seek independence from USSR.

9 Rezso Nyers is elected president of newly formed Hungarian Socialist Party.

11 Poland opens borders with East Germany and declares it will accept refugees.

17 earthquake in San Francisco, USA, kills at least 273.

18 Erich Honecker resigns from leadership of Party and State in East Germany; Egon Krenz succeeds him.

23 new Hungarian Republic is declared, with a constitution allowing multi-party democracy.

24 US television evangelist Jim Bakker sentenced to 45 years imprisonment for fraud.

26 Nigel Lawson resigns as chancellor of the exchequer in Britain. John Major replaces him.

31 Turgut Özal is elected president of Turkey in succession to General Kenan Evren.

L November

1 President Ortega's Sandinista regime in Nicaragua ends 19-month ceasefire with Contra rebels.

5 Greece holds second election of year (23, new government sworn in, led by Prof Xenophon Zolatas).

7 East German government led by Willi Stoph resigns amid continuing pro-reform demonstrations.

7 Namibia begins five days of polling to elect first independent government of Africa's last colony.

8 Jordan holds first parliamentary election since 1967.

9 East Germany announces opening of its border with West Germany. The authorities begin demolishing sections of the Berlin Wall the following day.

9 China's senior statesman, Deng Xiaoping, resigns as chairman of Central Military Commission.

10 Petar Mladenov replaces Todor Zhivkov as general secretary of Communist Party in Bulgaria, ending Zhivkov's 35-year dictatorship.

13 Hans Modrow elected prime minister in East Germany.

16 F W de Klerk announces end of Separate Amenities Act in South Africa.

17 fighting in San Salvador as rebel guerrillas win over parts of the city.

17 police break up peaceful demonstration in Prague.

22 in India's general election, Congress Party led by Rajiv Gandhi loses parliamentary majority (2 Dec, new multi-party government is sworn in under V P Singh).

22 President René Muawad of Lebanon (5, elected) dies in bomb explosion (24, succeeded by Elias Hrawi).

27 general strike in Czechoslovakia calls for end to Communist rule.

28 Czechoslovak Prime Minister Ladislav Adamec formally renounces Communist monopoly on power.

M December

2 Presidents Bush of USA and Gorbachev of USSR declare end of Cold War.

3 Politburo and Communist Party Central Committee resign in East Germany after revelations of widespread corruption (8, former leader Erich Honecker charged with abuse of office).

10 new government takes power in Czechoslovakia, led by Marian Calfa, with non-Communist majority.

14 Patricio Aylwin (Christian Democrat) wins overwhelming victory in presidential elections in Chile.

17 army fires on demonstration in Timişoara, Romania, killing about 100 people, but rumours report far higher figure (20, President Ceauşescu declares state of emergency as protests spread).

17 Fernando Collor de Mello (Conservative) narrowly wins presidential election in Brazil (15 Mar 1990, takes office).

19 US troops invade Panama to overthrow regime of General Noriega.

22 army joins forces with anti-government demonstrators in Romania and overthrows President Ceauşescu (25, Nicolae and Elena Ceauşescu are captured, given summary trial and executed by the army).

22 ceremonial opening of the Brandenburg Gate.

26 in Romania, interim government is formed by National Salvation Front; it announces constitutional changes, guarantees rights of national minorities, allows for freedom of worship and a free market economy, and promises free elections.

27 Egypt and Syria resume full diplomatic relations.

29 Václav Havel is elected Czechoslovakia's first non-Communist president for 41 years.

Annie Dillard, *The Writing Life*.
David Grossman, *See Under: Love*.
Shusha Guppy, *The Blindfold Horse*.
Rodney Hall, *Kisses of the Enemy*.
James Hamilton-Paterson, *Gerontius*.
John Irving, *A Prayer for Owen Meany*.
Kazuo Ishiguro, *Remains of the Day*.
David Leavitt, *Equal Affections*.
Bharati Mukherjee, *Jasmine*.
Cheng Naishen, *The Piano Tuner*.
Amy Tan, *The Joy Luck Club*.

Drama:

Matsuyo Akimoto, *Suicide for Love*.
David Mamet, *A Life in the Theatre*.
Joshua Sobol, *Ghetto*.

v Births and Deaths

Jan 7 Hirohito dies (87).
April 12 Sugar Ray Robinson dies (67).
April 30 Sergio Leone dies (60).
June 3 Ruhollah Khomeini dies (87).
June 27 A J Ayer dies (78).
July 11 Laurence Olivier dies (82).
Sept 22 Irving Berlin dies (101).
Sept 30 Virgil Thomson dies (92).
Dec 22 Samuel Beckett dies (83).
Dec 25 Nicolae Ceauşcu dies (71).
Dec 26 Lennox Berkeley dies (86).

w Everyday Life

In USA, President Bush expresses his distaste for broccoli, and his power as leader of the free world never to have to eat the vegetable again; broccoli-growers protest and deliver a consignment to the White House.
In Britain, acid-house rave parties attract tens of thousands of young people, despite a clampdown by police.

x Sport and Recreation

Cycling's first World Cup is won by Sean Kelly of the Republic of Ireland.
In England, 96 Liverpool fans die in a crush during the Football Association Cup semi-final against Nottingham Forest at Hillsborough, Sheffield (15 Apr).
In cricket, Australia regains the Ashes (1 Aug), beating England 4–0 in the six-Test series.
Britain and Ireland's amateur golfers win the Walker Cup against the USA for the first time since 1971; their victory is their first in the United States (17 Aug).
During the 1988–89 English horse-racing season, Peter Scudamore becomes the first National Hunt jockey to saddle 200 winners in one season; on 18 Nov he sets a new record of 1,139 wins over jumps.
Martine le Moignan is the first British player to win the women's squash World title.

y Media

Launch of the *Sunday Correspondent* in Britain (17 Sept); closed in Nov 1990.

Film:

Batman (director Tim Burton).
Crimes and Misdemeanours (director, Woody Allen).
Do the Right Thing (director, Spike Lee).
Driving Miss Daisy (director, Bruce Beresford).
My Left Foot (director, Jim Sheridan).
Sex, Lies and Videotape (director, Steven Soderbergh).
When Harry Met Sally (director, Rob Reiner).

Television:

At start of broadcasting of British House of Commons, members are deluged with advice about how to improve their appearance.
Launch of satellite station Sky TV in Britain (5 Feb).
New programmes in Britain include: *Birds of a Feather*; *Death on the Rock*, a controversial account of the killing (in March 1988) of IRA bombers in Gibraltar by members of the SAS; *Round the World in Eighty Days*, featuring Michael Palin; *Tumbledown*, about the Falklands War; *Twin Peaks* by David Lynch.

Re-unification of Germany ... Iraq invades Kuwait ... Resignation
of Margaret Thatcher as British prime minister ...

A January
3 In Panama, General Noriega surrenders to US authorities and is taken to Florida to face charges of drug-smuggling.

15 Soviet troops are sent into Nagorno-Karabakh to quell continuing ethnic violence.

15 Bulgarian National Assembly votes to end Communist monopoly on power.

18 Azerbaijan declares war on Armenia.

19 Soviet troops fire on demonstrators in Baku, Azerbaijan.

22 Yugoslavia's Communist Party votes to abolish Party's monopoly on power.

26 Indian troops bring Kashmir under direct rule and enforce curfew, following deaths in separatist violence and the resignation of the state government.

B February
1 Bulgarian government resigns (8, new all-Communist government is formed).

1 Yugoslav government sends troops to Kosovo province in attempt to end clashes between ethnic Albanians and Serbian authorities.

2 President de Klerk ends 30-year ban on the African National Congress (ANC).

7 Central Committee of Communist Party in USSR votes to end Party's monopoly on political power.

11 Nelson Mandela is released after 27 years in prison in South Africa.

15 Social-Democrat government in Sweden resigns (26, leader Ingvar Carlsson is reappointed as prime minister of new Social Democrat government).

16 SWAPO leader, Sam Nujoma, is elected first president of independent Namibia (21, Republic of Namibia becomes an independent sovereign state).

21 authorities in Kenya ban demonstrations after protests calling for President Moi's resignation and demanding an inquiry into the murder of the foreign minister.

24 nationalists defeat Communist candidates in Lithuanian elections.

25 in elections in Nicaragua, US-backed coalition under Violeta Chamorro defeats Ortega's Sandinista government.

26 USSR agrees to withdraw troops from Czechoslovakia by July 1991.

C March
6 In Afghanistan, government of President Najibullah puts down attempted coup.

10 General Avril resigns as president of Haiti (12, Ertha Pascal-Triuillot succeeds him).

11 Lithuania declares independence from USSR.

12 Dr Vitautis Landsbergis is elected Lithuanian president.

13 Israel's national unity coalition government collapses after Prime Minister Yitzhak Shamir dismisses Deputy Prime Minister Shimon Peres.

15 Gorbachev sworn in as first executive president of USSR.

18 in East Germany's first free elections since 1933, 'Alliance for Germany' wins 48 per cent of vote.

24 ruling Labor Party is returned for fourth term in Australian general election.

25 Soviet authorities send tanks to Vilnius, capital of Lithuania, to discourage proponents of secession.

30 Estonia suspends Soviet constitution on its territory.

31 huge anti-poll tax demonstration in Trafalgar Square, London, ends in rioting and looting.

D April
1 In Britain, 1,000 inmates riot in Strangeways Prison, Manchester, and take over large parts of the prison (25, last prisoners surrender after storming of the prison by specially trained officers).

1 Robert Mugabe gains decisive victory in presidential elections in Zimbabwe, and ruling ZANU–PF wins 117 of the 120 seats.

3 King Baudouin of Belgium steps down from throne temporarily to allow passing of new law legalizing abortion, which he refused to sign on principle.

4 Chinese People's Congress approves the Basic Law, a mini constitution for Hong Kong after the 1997 take-over by China.

8 New Democracy Party gains narrow majority in Greek general election; 11, Constantine Mitsotakis takes office as prime minister.

8 centre-right Democratic Forum and allies win landslide victory in Hungarian general election.

11 parts for a 'supergun' destined for Iraq detained by Customs officers on Teesside, Britain.

11 three hostages released in Lebanon after a French arms deal with Libya in contravention of the EC embargo.

12 Lothar de Maizière sworn in as prime minister of coalition in East Germany.

18 USSR cuts off oil supplies to Lithuania.

Guinness trial in Britain ... Japan puts satellite in orbit around Moon ... Deaths of Lewis Mumford and A J P Taylor ...

o Politics, Government, Law, and Economy

K Phillips, *The Politics of Rich and Poor*.

J Rosenau, *Turbulence in World Politics*.

The British government bans the broadcasting of speakers from unconstitutional parties in Northern Ireland (the ban principally affects Sinn Féin).

In Britain, Dr David Owen's 'continuing' Social Democratic Party is wound up.

National Health Service and Community Care Act introduces self-managing trust hospitals and fund-holding general practitioners into British National Health Service, creating the so-called 'internal market'.

European Court of Justice is reported to be taking one and a half years to deal with references from national courts and two and a half to process direct actions.

EC Summit opens in Rome (27 Oct); with exception of Britain, members vote to begin second stage of economic and monetary union by 1994 and to achieve single currency by 2000.

In England and Wales, the Courts and Legal Services Act extends rights of audience in courts (permitting solicitors to appear in some courts) and permits 'no win, no fee' method of charging legal costs.

The 'Guinness trial' in Britain (12 Feb–27 Aug), in which four senior businessmen are convicted of theft, false accounting, and creating a false market in shares during the Guinness company's takeover of Distillers Group (April 1986); the trial is the most expensive in British history.

Poland introduces the harshest transitional austerity programme in Eastern Europe.

Clean Air Act in USA raises standards for emissions made by industrial concerns.

Zimbabwean Parliament legislates for nationalization of white-owned farms at fixed compensation (12 Dec).

In USA, junk bond brokers Drexel Burnham Lambert file for bankruptcy following indictment (in 1989) of leading bond-dealer Michael Milken.

AT&T telephone service in USA interrupted several times because of faulty software.

p Society, Education, and Religion

Americans with Disabilities Act gives rights of access to public facilities and employment equality to disabled people.

Britain introduces separate taxation for married women.

World Summit for Children is held in New York (29 Sept).

David Dinkins becomes first African-American mayor of New York (1 Jan).

Drug possession criminalized in Italy (law repealed by referendum in 1993).

Mike Davis, *City of Quartz: Excavating the Future in Los Angeles*.

Naomi Wolf, *The Beauty Myth: How Images of Beauty are Used Against Women*.

Publication of research suggesting link between exposure to radiation at Sellafield nuclear reprocessing plant in NW England and cases of leukaemia in employees' children (15 Feb).

Home-produced beef is banned in British schools and hospitals (15 May) as result of concern over 'mad-cow disease' (bovine spongiform encephalopathy, or BSE).

In Britain, a call for a Royal Commission on Education from Sir Claus Moser, president of the British Association for the Advancement of Science, is rejected by the government.

Further National Curriculum subject working-party reports and final orders are published in Britain.

British education secretary John MacGregor states that new national curriculum for history should place greater emphasis on dates and facts (26 July).

Chief inspector of schools in Britain reports that one in three children is 'getting a raw deal' from the state education system (5 Feb).

Inauguration (11 May) of collegiate status of Rewley House in the University of Oxford, England (renamed Kellogg College 1 Oct 1994).

Levels of British student grants are frozen and supplemented by 'top-up' loans (Sept).

The world's largest cathedral is consecrated by Pope John Paul II in Yamoussoukro, Ivory Coast.

George Carey, Bishop of Bath and Wells, is named as successor to Robert Runcie as Archbishop of Canterbury (25 July).

In Saudi Arabia approximately 1,400 Muslim pilgrims are crushed to death in stampede in overcrowded tunnel leading from Mecca to hill outside (2 July).

Law forbidding religious propaganda in Albania is repealed.

A new Council of Churches for Britain and Ireland replaces the British Council of Churches; Roman Catholics and Black-led churches participate for the first time.

John MacQuarrie, *Jesus Christ in Modern Thought*.

E May

1 Opposition demonstrations disrupt May Day parade in Red Square, Moscow, USSR.

4 Latvia declares itself an independent sovereign state.

4 Constantine Karamanlis is re-elected president of Greece.

8 Estonia declares independence from USSR.

20 Romania holds first free elections since 1937; National Salvation Front wins two-thirds of seats and Ion Iliescu wins landslide victory in presidential elections.

22 North and South Yemen merge to form Yemen Republic.

24 Princess Anne, the Princess Royal, visits USSR in first official British royal visit since 1917 Revolution.

27 National League for Democracy wins multi-party elections in Burma (now Myanmar), though army later refuses to hand over power.

27 Cesar Gaviria Trujillo of ruling Liberals is chosen as president-elect in elections in Colombia.

29 Boris Yeltsin elected president of Russian Federation, defeating Gorbachev's candidate.

F June

5 Communist hardliner, Vladimir Ivashko, elected president of Ukraine.

7 President de Klerk lifts four-year state of emergency from all parts of South Africa except Natal province.

8 Civic Forum triumphs in first free elections in Czechoslovakia since 1946.

8 Russian parliament votes that its laws should take precedence over those of USSR (12, Russian Federation formally declares itself a sovereign state).

11 Alberto Fujimori defeats author Mario Vargas Llosa in presidential elections in Peru.

12 Yitshak Shamir forms new right-wing coalition government in Israel.

12 in Algerian local elections, fundamentalist Islamic Salvation Front wins control of most municipal and provincial assemblies

14 mobs of miners patrol the streets of Bucharest, Romania, attacking anti-government demonstrators.

20 Uzbekistan declares independent sovereignty.

21 major earthquake in NW Iran.

22 Manitoba and Newfoundland refuse to ratify Meech Lake Accord recognizing Quebec as a 'distinct society'.

29 Lithuania suspends declaration of sovereignty during negotiations with Soviet government.

G July

1 East Germany cedes sovereignty over economic, monetary, and social policy to West German government and Bundesbank; Deutschmark becomes official currency.

2 Imelda Marcos is acquitted of plotting to steal funds from the Philippines for private use.

6 Petar Mladenov resigns as president of Bulgaria.

8 Indian army takes direct control of Kashmir after separatist violence.

12 Boris Yeltsin and other reformers resign from Communist Party in USSR.

16 Ukrainian parliament votes for sovereignty and to become a neutral state.

19 Iraqi troops start massing on the border with Kuwait, following threats over disputed territory.

20 IRA bomb explodes at Stock Exchange in London.

29 free elections held in Mongolia.

29 troops loyal to President Doe in Liberia massacre at least 600 refugees sheltering in a church in the capital Monrovia (5 Aug, USA sends marines to evacuate US citizens from Monrovia).

30 in Britain, Ian Gow, Conservative MP for Eastbourne, is murdered by IRA car bomb.

H August

2 Iraqi forces invade Kuwait; deposed emir flees to Saudi Arabia.

3 Arpád Göncz sworn in as president of new Democratic Republic of Hungary.

4 Iraqi troops mass on border with Saudi Arabia.

6 UN Security Council imposes sanctions against Iraq, including oil embargo.

6 president of Pakistan dismisses government of Benazir Bhutto on charges of corruption and ineptitude.

7 President Bush sends US forces to Saudi Arabia to prevent Iraqi invasion.

8 West African states send multi-national force to end civil war in Liberia.

9 Iraq announces annexation of Kuwait.

14 in USSR, President Gorbachev issues decrees rehabilitating those repressed by Stalin and restoring citizenship to exiled dissidents including Alexander Solzhenitsyn.

15 Iraq makes peace with Iran, accepting all Iranian terms.

19 coalition government in East Germany collapses.

19 Iraq rounds up Western nationals in Kuwait and deports them to Iraq to serve as 'human shields' at military installations.

Q Science, Technology, and Discovery

Japan launches the first probe to be sent to the Moon since 1976 (24 Jan); it places a small satellite in lunar orbit (March).

The space shuttle *Discovery* places the Hubble Space Telescope in Earth orbit (24 April); the main mirror proves to be defective.

Launch of the German-built X-ray *Röntgensatellite* (1 June).

The US *Magellan* radar mapper arrives in orbit around Venus (10 Aug); it transmits the most detailed pictures of the planet's surface yet produced.

US astronomer Mark R Showalter discovers an 18th moon of Saturn when researching pictures transmitted by *Voyager 2*.

Surgeons at Guy's Hospital in London perform the first surgery on a baby in its mother's womb (30 Jan).

Pierre Chambon and associates announce the discovery of gene that may be important in the development of breast cancer.

Bowel and liver grafts are transplanted at the University of Western Ontario, Canada, enabling the patient to resume a normal diet for the first time ever.

First human gene experiment: defective white blood cells are taken from a four-year-old girl, given a gene that controls an enzyme in the immune system, and reinserted.

Six institutions are selected to participate in the project for mapping the genes of selected human chromosomes.

Chemists at the Louis Pasteur University, Strasbourg, France, announce the creation of nucleohelicates, compounds that mimic the double helix structure of DNA.

Canadian scientists discover fossils of the oldest known multi-cellular animals, dating from 600 million years ago.

R Humanities

Maurice Keen, *English Society in the Later Middle Ages, 1348–1500*.

Conrad Russell, *The Causes of the English Civil War*.

F M L Thompson (ed.), *The Cambridge Social History of Britain 1750– 1950*.

Peter Ackroyd, *Dickens*.

David Cannadine, *The Decline and Fall of the British Aristocracy*.

Ross McKibbin, *The Ideologies of Class: Social Relations in England 1880– 1950*.

Kenneth O Morgan, *The People's Peace: British History 1945–1990*.

Donald Davidson, *Structure and Content of Truth*.

Karl Popper, *A World of Propensities*.

S Art, Sculpture, Fine Arts, and Architecture

Jenny Holzer is the first woman to represent the USA at the Venice Biennale, Italy.

''Monet in the '90s' exhibition at the Royal Academy, London.

Painting, etc:
John Greenwood, *That's My Bus*.
Andres Serrano, *Red Pope I, II, III*.

Sculpture:
Damian Hirst, *My Way*.
Jeff Koons, *Jeff and Ilona (Made in Heaven)*.
Rachel Whiteread, *Valley*.

Architecture:
Terry Farrell, practical completion of Charing Cross redevelopment, London.

T Music

Brian Ferneyhough, String Quartet No. 4.

Hans Werner Henze, *Das verratene Meer* (opera).

Robin Holloway, *Clarissa* (opera).

György Ligeti, Concerto for Violin and Orchestra.

David Matthews, *Romanza*.

Judith Weir, *The Vanishing Bridegroom* (opera).

Babes in Toyland, *Spanking Machine*.

Happy Mondays, *Pills 'n' Thrills and Bellyaches*.

Ice Cube, *Amerikkka's Most Wanted*.

Jane's Addiction, *Ritual De Lo Habitual*.

Sinead O'Connor, 'Nothing Compares To You'.

Pink Floyd perform *The Wall* in Berlin, Germany.

Concert held at Wembley Stadium, London, to celebrate the release of Nelson Mandela.

U Literature and Drama

Martin Amis, *London Fields*.
Nicholson Baker, *Room Temperature*.
A S Byatt, *Possession*.
Penelope Fitzgerald, *The Gate of Angels*.
Firdaus Kanga, *Trying to Grow*.
Ian McEwan, *The Innocent*.
David Malouf, *The Great World*.
Paul Muldoon, *Madoc*.
V S Naipaul, *India*.
Thomas Pynchon, *Vineland*.
Piers Paul Read, *On the Third Day*.
Mordechai Richler, *Solomon Gursky Was Here*.
Adam Zameenzad, *Cyrus Cyrus*.
Alexander Solzhenitsyn is awarded the Russia State Literature Prize for *The Gulag Archipelago*.

21 400 die in clashes between ANC and Zulu Inkatha movement in Transvaal townships in South Africa.

24 British hostage Brian Keenan, held in Lebanon since 1986, is released.

31 East and West Germany sign reunification treaty.

J September

3 In Yugoslavia, Albanians in Kosovo stage 24-hour strike, following imprisonment of trade union leader Hajrullah Gorani.

4 Geoffrey Palmer resigns as Labour prime minister of New Zealand. Michael Moore replaces him.

10 President Samuel Doe of Liberia dies after being captured by rebel faction; Prince Johnson takes over government.

10 Cambodian factions agree on peace formula to end civil war.

27 Britain and Iran resume diplomatic relations broken over the Rushdie affair.

28 in Yugoslavia, Serbian parliament adopts new constitution stripping province of Kosovo of its autonomy.

K October

2 German Democratic Republic ceases to exist at midnight; 3, East and West Germany are reunited.

5 on final day of Labour Party Conference, British Conservative government announces entry of sterling into the European Exchange Rate Mechanism (on 8).

5 US House of Representatives rejects federal budget; non-essential federal services begin to close down after Bush refuses to grant emergency funding; 9, emergency bill is signed; 27 and 28, budget is passed by both Houses.

8 Israeli police fire on demonstrators at Temple Mount, Jerusalem. Israel later refuses to co-operate with UN attempts to carry out inquiry into the incident.

15 Nobel Peace Prize is awarded to Mikhail Gorbachev of USSR.

19 ruling South African National Party formally opens its membership to all races.

24 Benazir Bhutto's Pakistan People's Party suffers overwhelming defeat to Islamic Democratic Alliance in Pakistan general election (6 Nov, Nawaz Sharif is sworn in as prime minister).

27 National Party led by James Bolger defeats ruling Labour Party in New Zealand elections.

28 non-Communist parties triumph in elections in Georgia, USSR, with calls for independence and a market economy.

29 coalition government in Norway resigns (30, Gro Harlem Brundtland forms minority Labour government).

L November

1 In Britain, Geoffrey Howe, leader of the House of Commons, resigns from government over differences with Margaret Thatcher on approach to EC.

7 Mary Robinson wins election to become first woman president of Republic of Ireland.

7 government of V P Singh resigns in India.

12 enthronement of Emperor Akihito of Japan.

18 Socialist Party of Labour, a recreated Communist Party, is founded in Romania.

20 election held for leadership of the British Conservative Party, with Michael Heseltine as challenger to Margaret Thatcher; Thatcher fails to secure the margin needed for reelection, with 204 MPs' votes against Heseltine's 152 (22, Thatcher stands down from second ballot).

23 Soviet parliament grants President Gorbachev emergency powers to maintain order in USSR.

25 Christian militias withdraw from East Beirut in agreement to create reunified city.

26 Lee Kuan Yew resigns as Singapore's prime minister after 31 years in office.

27 John Major wins second ballot for leadership of British Conservative Party with 185 votes to 131 for Michael Heseltine and 56 for Douglas Hurd; Heseltine and Hurd withdraw from third ballot; John Major becomes Conservative leader.

28 Margaret Thatcher resigns as British prime minister; succeeded by John Major.

M December

2 Helmut Kohl is returned as chancellor in election in united Germany.

6 Saddam Hussein announces freeing of all Western hostages in Kuwait and Iraq.

9 Lech Walesa achieves landslide victory in Polish presidential election.

9 Slobodan Milosovic (Serbian Socialist Party) is elected president in Serbia's first free elections for 50 years.

14 Polish government of Tadeusz Mazowiecki resigns (29, Lech Walesa nominates Jan Krzystof Bielicki as prime minister).

16 Fr Jean-Bertrand Aristide wins first-ever presidential election in Haiti.

17 Lothar de Maizière resigns from German government after allegations that he worked for the Stasi (secret police).

20 Eduard Shevardnadze resigns as USSR foreign minister declaring that the USSR is heading for dictatorship.

23 in Yugoslavia, Slovenia votes for independence in plebiscite.

Drama:
Robert Lepage, *Tectonic Plates*.
Yuri Trifonov, *Exchange*.
Derek Walcott, *Remembrance*.
Temporary closure of the Royal Shakespeare Company's London theatres due to lack of funds.

v **Births and Deaths**
Jan 26 Lewis Mumford dies (94).
March 12 Rosamund Lehmann dies (89).
April 15 Greta Garbo dies (84).
June 20 Steen Rasmussen dies (92).
Sept 7 A J P Taylor dies (84).
Sept 26 Alberto Moravia dies (82).
Sept 30 Patrick White dies (78).
Oct 14 Leonard Bernstein dies (72).
Dec 2 Aaron Copland dies (90).

w **Everyday Life**
Pop band Milli Vanilli are exposed as actors who mime the words.

x **Sport and Recreation**
In cricket, Richard Hadlee of New Zealand becomes the first bowler to take 400 Test wickets (4 Feb).
US boxer James Buster Douglas wins the world Heavyweight title, knocking out Mike Tyson of the USA in the 10th round of their fight in Tokyo, Japan (11 Feb); Douglas later loses the title to Evander Holyfield of the USA (25 Oct).
Jockey Lester Piggott returns to the saddle five years after retiring and two years after completing a jail sentence for tax avoidance; he becomes the oldest ever flat-race jockey in Britain.
Martina Navratilova of the USA wins her ninth Women's Singles title in the Wimbledon tennis tournament, London (7 July), beat-

ing the record of Helen Wills Moody, set between 1927 and 1938.
In the soccer World Cup, held in Italy, West Germany beats Argentina 1–0 in the Final (8 July).
Yorkshire Cricket Club in England lifts its ban on players born outside the county (27 Nov).

y **Media**
Launch in Britain of the *Independent on Sunday* (Jan).
Robert Maxwell publishes the *European*, a weekly English-language newspaper for circulation throughout Europe (May).
To improve voluntary regulation of the British press, the Press Council is abolished, to be replaced on 1 Jan 1991 by the Press Complaints Commission.

Film:
Cinema Paradiso (director, Giuseppe Tornatore).
City of Sorrows (director, Hou Xiaoxian).
Cyrano de Bergerac (director, Jean-Paul Rappeneau).
Dances With Wolves (director and star, Kevin Costner).
Delicatessen (directors, Jean-Pierre Jeunet and Marc Caro).
Distant Voices (director, Terence Davies).
Dreams (director, Akira Kurosawa).
Jesus of Montreal (director, Denys Arcand).
Silence of the Lambs (director, Jonathan Demme; starring Jodie Foster and Anthony Hopkins).

Television:
New programmes in Britain include: *One Foot in the Grave* (BBC); *The Trials of Life* (BBC), presented by David Attenborough; *Your Cheatin' Heart* (BBC), by John Byrne.

*Disintegration of Yugoslavia ... Coup against President
Gorbachev ... Demise of the USSR ...*

A January

6 In Guatemala, Jorge Serrano Elias is elected successor to President Vinicio Cerezo.

7 5,000 ethnic Greek Albanians flee to Greece amid chaos in Albania.

8 government of Kazimiera Prunskiene in Lithuania resigns over price increases.

13 Soviet troops storm television station in Vilnius, Lithuania.

13 Mario Soares elected president of Portugal for second term.

15 Iraq fails to meet UN deadline for withdrawal from Kuwait.

16 US-led coalition commences air offensive 'Operation Desert Storm' to liberate Kuwait from Iraqi occupation.

17 King Olav of Norway dies, aged 87; his son succeeds as Harald V.

18 Iraq launches Scud missiles against Israel.

25 Iraq pumps oil into the Gulf causing largest-ever slick.

26 rebels in Somalia overrun Mogadishu. President Barre flees to Kenya and United Somali Congress appoints Ali Mahdi Mohammed as prime minister.

3 Latvia and Estonia vote for independence in referenda.

6 Chandra Shekhar resigns as prime minister of India.

7 Albanian refugees land at Italian ports in defiance of the authorities.

11 trial begins of former Greek Prime Minister Andreas Papandreou on bribery charges.

17 referendum in USSR gives slim majority for Gorbachev's proposal for renewed federation of socialist sovereign republics.

17 Serbia suspends the provincial Kosovo constitution and use of Albanian for official purposes is declared illegal.

24 Nicephore Soglo defeats President Kerekou in Benin's first democratic elections for 20 years.

26 Iraqi government forces bomb Kirkuk, held by Kurdish rebels; by 30, Iraqi government has recovered most of the country.

31 ruling Communist Party of Labour wins majority in free elections in Albania.

31 military structure of Warsaw Pact is dissolved.

B February

1 President F W de Klerk announces plans for repeal of laws underpinning apartheid in South Africa.

7 IRA mortar bombs cause damage at 10 Downing Street in London, where a Cabinet meeting was in progress.

9 Lithuanian referendum approves proposal for independence.

14 Peruvian cabinet resigns in split over economic crisis.

22 hundreds of Kuwait oil wells are set alight by Iraqi soldiers as they face defeat (3 Nov, last fire extinguished).

23 martial law declared in Thailand, following the overthrow of the government of Chatichai Choonhavan.

24 US-led coalition in Gulf launches ground offensive against Iraqi forces.

27 coalition forces enter Kuwait City and declare Kuwait liberated.

28 President Bush announces suspension of hostilities in Kuwait and Iraq.

C March

1 In Iraq popular revolt against government begins in Basra and spreads to other Shi'ite cities; separate Kurdish revolt starts in the north.

D April

9 Parliament of Georgia votes to assert independence from USSR.

11 Iraqi forces attack Kurdish refugees within US exclusion zone.

17 British, French, and US troops start to enter northern Iraq to establish and guard camps for Kurdish rebels.

13 Giulio Andreotti forms a new government in Italy.

22 agreement is reached on a 50-year moratorium on mineral exploration in Antarctica.

23 British government announces proposals for a new 'council tax' to replace the community charge ('poll tax') in 1993.

30 Kurdish refugees begin to move into Western-protected havens.

30 Major-General Justin Lekhanya, military leader in Lesotho, is overthrown by Colonel Elias Ramaema.

E May

9 Yugoslavia's Collective State Presidency grants special powers to Yugoslav National Army for operations in Croatia, freeing it from effective government control.

12 multi-party elections in Nepal won by Congress Party.

Repeal of South Africa's apartheid legislation ... Birtwistle's Sir
Gawain ... The Oxford Dictionary of Byzantium ...

o Politics, Government, Law, and Economy

Noam Chomsky, *Deterring Democracy.*

E J Dionne, *Why Americans Hate Politics.*

British Prime Minister, John Major, launches the 'Citizen's Charter' (22 July), a scheme for setting standards of public services and providing for compensation when standards are not met.

Remains of Frederick the Great of Prussia re-interred in Potsdam (18 Aug).

German government votes to move government from Bonn to Berlin (20 June).

President Bush makes controversial nomination of conservative African-American Judge Clarence Thomas to the US Supreme Court; during the televised Senate confirmation hearing, Prof Anita Hill accuses Judge Thomas of sexual harassment; the Senate approves the nomination 52–48 (15 Oct), the narrowest margin in the Court's history.

Kermit L Hall et al. (eds.), *The Oxford Companion to the Supreme Court of the United States.*

In Britain the 'Birmingham Six' are released after Appeal Court finds their conviction in 1974 for IRA pub bombings in Birmingham 'unsafe and unsatisfactory' (14 Mar).

Criminal Justice Act in Britain introduces income-related fines and prevents judges from taking previous convictions into account when passing sentence.

In Regina v. Gibson (the 'foetal earrings case') in England, the Court of Appeal upholds a conviction of outraging public decency, a revived common law offence.

Collapse of the Bank of Credit and Commerce International in western countries (July), after discovery of massive fraud and involvement in organized crime, arms dealing, and the drug trade.

Indian government abandons centralized planning and introduces reforms to liberalize the economy (24 July).

European Bank of Reconstruction and Development, to assist economic development in East European and the former USSR, is opened in London (5 April); its splendid offices feature specially purchased marble.

Pan Am airline (founded 1927), burdened with massive debts, is closed down (4 Dec).

British output falls by 2.5 per cent, the steepest decline since the 1930s.

p Society, Education, and Religion

Legal framework for apartheid in South Africa is destroyed with repeal of Land Acts, Group Areas Act (4 June), and 1950 Population Registration Act (17 June).

Belgian parliament changes constitution to allow women to accede to the throne (13 June).

British government announces appointment of Stella Rimington as first woman head of MI5 (16 Dec).

Edith Cresson becomes first woman prime minister of France (15 May).

US armed forces in the Gulf War include 30,000 women.

In Britain, the House of Lords rules that a husband can be guilty of marital rape (23 Oct).

James Lincoln Collier, *The Rise of Selfishness in America.*

Paul Fussell, *BAD or, The Dumbing of America.*

Joel Garreau, *Edge City: Life on the New Frontier.*

Julia Neuberger, *Whatever's Happening to Women? Promises, Practices and Payoffs.*

In USA, National Literacy Act.

In Australia, strategic review of educational research makes wide-ranging recommendations.

Russian ministry of education launches Programme for the Stabilization and Development of Education.

First compulsory tests for seven year-olds are held in Britain, but few head teachers agree to declare the results, fearing the implications of 'league tables'.

Dinesh d'Souza, *Illiberal Education: The Politics of Race and Sex on Campus.*

Royal representation at the multi-faith Commonwealth Day service in Westminster Abbey, London (8 Mar).

Dr George Carey succeeds Dr Robert Runcie as Archbishop of Canterbury; his enthronement service (19 April) includes modern informal music, reflecting the new archbishop's more evangelical vision of the Church of England.

Rabbi Dr Jonathan Sacks is installed as British chief rabbi (1 Sept).

Pope John Paul II awards the title 'Venerable' to 19th-century British Cardinal John Henry Newman.

Jürgen Moltmann, *History and the Triune God.*

q Science, Technology, and Discovery

Richard Branson and Per Lindstrand complete first hot-air balloon crossing of Pacific Ocean (17 Jan).

World Ocean Experiment (WOCE) pro-

14 in South Africa, Winnie Mandela, wife of ANC leader Nelson Mandela, sentenced to six years imprisonment for kidnap and accessory to assault.

15 Edith Cresson appointed prime minister of France, after resignation of Michel Rocard.

15 cease-fire begins in Angola.

16 Karl Otto Pöhl, president of the Bundesbank, resigns over differences with the German government over monetary policy.

17 Somali National Movement declares northern Somalia independent.

21 Rajiv Gandhi, former Indian prime minister, is assassinated by a Tamil suicide bomber during India's general elections campaign.

12 President Mengistu of Ethiopia flees to Zimbabwe as rebel forces close in on Addis Ababa.

28 Ethiopian People's Revolutionary Democratic Front capture Addis Ababa and end 17 years of Marxist rule.

26 Zviad Gamsakhurdia elected president of Georgia.

31 President Dos Santos and Jonas Savimbi, leader of UNITA, sign peace agreement in Lisbon to end civil war in Angola.

F June

4 Albanian government resigns after three-week strike.

4 Mouloud Hamrouche, prime minister of Algeria, resigns after security forces fire on Islamic Salvation Front rioters in Algiers.

7 Islamic Salvation Front ends protests in exchange for promise of elections.

12 Blaise Compaoré, military leader of Burkina Faso, dissolves revolutionary government and calls for new constitution.

12 Boris Yeltsin becomes first ever directly elected leader of the Russian Federation.

17 Population Registration Act repealed in South Africa, bringing end apartheid system.

20 P V Narasimha Rao is appointed Indian prime minister at head of minority government.

25 republics of Croatia and Slovenia declare independence from Yugoslavia.

G July

1 Protocol signed in Prague marks formal end to Warsaw Pact.

1 EC ministers order total arms embargo on Yugoslavia and agree to send monitoring mission.

18 floods in China submerge over 20 million hectares/50 million acres of farmland.

31 Presidents Bush of USA and Gorbachev of USSR sign Strategic Arms Reduction Treaty (START) to reduce arsenals of long-range nuclear weapons by a third.

H August

6 Bangladesh abandons presidential system of government and returns to parliamentary rule.

8 John McCarthy, British journalist held hostage in Lebanon, is released after 1,943 days in captivity.

15 UN Security Council condemns Iraq for hindering work of UN inspectors by denying access to nuclear facilities.

19 Communist hardliners, led by Gennady Yanayev, stage coup in USSR against President Gorbachev, who is placed under house arrest in the Crimea; radio and television stations are shut down and military rule imposed in many cities.

20 Estonia declares independence.

21 coup in USSR collapses following widespread popular resistance led by Boris Yeltsin (22, Gorbachev returns to Moscow).

21 Latvia declares independence.

24 Mikhail Gorbachev resigns as first secretary of USSR Communist Party (29, Russian parliament suspends Communist Party and seizes its assets).

27 Croatian town of Vukovar falls to Serb-dominated army after 86-day siege.

28 Soviet government is dismissed and KGB collegium disbanded.

30 Azerbaijan declares independence.

J September

2 Central government in USSR is suspended pending formulation of new constitution.

6 Soviet authorities make formal grant of independence to Latvia, Lithuania and Estonia.

7 EC-sponsored peace conference on Yugoslavia opens in The Hague, chaired by Lord Carrington.

11 withdrawal of Soviet troops from Cuba is announced.

15 ruling Social Democrats lose general election in Sweden and Swedish Prime Minister Ingvar Carlsson resigns (4 Oct, Carl Bildt forms right-wing coalition).

18 Yugoslav state of Macedonia declares independence (but international recognition is withheld).

22 Armenia declares independence.

25 UN imposes mandatory arms embargo on Yugoslavia.

25 peace accord is signed in El Salvador to end 11-year civil war.

26 troops are deployed in Romania after two days of riots by miners demanding higher

gramme set up to monitor ocean temperatures, circulation, and other parameters.

The US space shuttle deploys the 17-tonne Arthur Holly Gamma Ray Observatory in Earth orbit (7 April).

A mission by the US shuttle *Columbia* carries the Space Life Sciences-1 laboratory, in which astronauts conduct experiments on themselves, rats, and jellyfish polyps.

Chemist Helen Sharman is the first Briton to go into space, as a participant in a Soviet space mission (18–26 May).

The US space probe *Galileo* takes the first high-quality picture of an asteroid, called Gaspra (Oct).

The Jodrell Bank radio astronomy centre near Manchester reports the possible discovery of a planet orbiting pulsar star PSR 1829–10.

Astronomers at Mt Palomar, California, USA, announce the discovery of the most distant object yet seen, a quasar.

Launch of the European Space Agency's first Remote-sensing satellite (*ERS-1*) into polar orbit to monitor Earth's temperature from space.

In Britain, first production of a significant amount of power by atomic fusion by JET (Joint European Torus) at Culham near Oxford.

Heart surgeons develop a way of repairing damaged hearts using muscles from the patient's body.

Researchers announce the discovery of a gene responsible for mental handicap.

Chemists isolate fullerenes — a new form of elemental carbon.

R Humanities

Discovery in the Italian Alps of the preserved body of a man from *c.* 3,300 BC, with clothes, bow, arrows, axe, and other implements.

Alexander P Kazhdan et al. (eds.), *The Oxford Dictionary of Byzantium.*

Albert Hourani, *A History of the Arab Peoples.*

Henry Mayr-Harting, *Ottonian Book Illumination: An Historical Study.*

Michael Lynch, *Scotland: A New History.*

Felipe Fernández-Armesto, *Columbus.*

Euan Cameron, *The European Reformation.*

Conrad Russell, *The Fall of the British Monarchies, 1637–1642.*

Jack P Greene, J R Pole (eds.), *The Blackwell Encyclopedia of the American Revolution.*

Frank A J L James (ed.), *The Correspondence of Michael Faraday* (–).

Jack Simmons, *The Victorian Railway.*

John Harriss (ed.), *The Family: A Social History of the Twentieth Century.*

Robert Dallek, *Lone Star Rising: Lyndon Johnson and His Times, 1908–60.*

Twentieth Century British History issued (–).

Michael Dummett, *The Logical Basis of Metaphysics.*

Thomas Nagel, *Equality and Partiality.*

S Art, Sculpture, Fine Arts, and Architecture

Thyssen Collection of paintings opened in Madrid, Spain.

Turner Prize in Britain awarded to Anish Kapoor.

'High and Low' exhibition at the Museum of Modern Art, New York.

'Metropolis' exhibition, Martin Gropius Bau, Berlin, West Germany.

'Pop Art' exhibition at the Royal Academy, London.

Architecture:

Sir Norman Foster, Sackler Galleries, Royal Academy, London; Stansted Airport, Essex, SE England.

Robert Venturi and Denise Scott Brown, Sainsbury Wing, National Gallery, London.

T Music

Frangis Ali-Zade, String Quartet.

Malcolm Arnold, Symphony No. 9.

Harrison Birtwistle, *Sir Gawain and the Green Knight* (opera).

Friedrich Cerha, *Langegge Nachtmusik.*

John Corigliano, *The Ghosts of Versailles* (opera).

Bryan Adams, 'Everything I Do, I Do For You'.

Guns 'n' Roses, *Use Your Illusion II.*

Nirvana, *Nevermind*–emergence of grunge music from Seattle, USA.

Primal Scream, *Screamadelica.*

Public Enemy, 'Apocalypse '91: The Empire Strikes Back'.

REM, *Out Of Time.*

Rock star Freddie Mercury dies of AIDS (24 Oct).

U Literature and Drama

William Boyd, *Brazzaville Beach.*

James Broughton, *The Androgyne Journal* (poems).

Angela Carter, *Wise Children.*

Richard Condon, *The Final Addition.*

Bret Easton Ellis, *American Psycho.*

Ben Okri, *The Famished Road.*

Jean Rouaud, *Les Champs d'Honneur.*

John Updike, *Rabbit at Rest* (concluding volume of *Rabbit* quartet).

Derek Walcott, *Omeros* (poems).

wages; government led by Petre Roman resigns and Teodor Stolojan is named prime minister on 1 Oct.

30 President Aristide is overthrown in coup in Haiti (8 Oct, military install Judge Joseph Norette as provisional president).

K October

1 In USSR, Leningrad reverts to name St Petersburg.

1 Yugoslav federal army begins siege of Dubrovnik (7, federal jets attack Croatian capital, Zagreb).

6 ruling Social Democratic Party in Portugal gains outright majority in general elections.

8 Abdur Rahman Biswas is elected president of Bangladesh.

13 Bulgarian Socialist Party suffers overwhelming defeat in elections (8 Nov, Filip Dimitrov becomes first non-communist prime minister since 1944).

15 parliament in Bosnia-Herzegovina votes to declare independence.

20 peace agreement is signed in Rome to end civil war in Mozambique.

20 Suleyman Demirel's True Path Party tops the poll in general election in Turkey.

21 President Mobutu of Zaire sacks Prime Minister Etienne Tshisekedi, provoking violent rioting (31, opposition movement forms rival government).

23 four factions in Cambodia sign peace accord in Paris to end civil war.

27 Poland holds first free parliamentary elections since World War II, but result is inconclusive, with no party polling more than 12 per cent.

31 President Kaunda suffers defeat in Zambian elections.

L November

5 Robert Maxwell, British publishing tycoon, dies after falling overboard from his yacht off the Canary Islands.

6 Philippines hit by floods and landslides.

8 EC foreign ministers decide to impose immediate economic and trade sanctions against Yugoslavia and suspend the peace conference (2 Dec, sanctions are dropped against all republics except Serbia and Montenegro).

13 hundreds of civilians evacuated from Dubrovnik, Croatia, under UN ceasefire.

14 Prince Sihanouk returns to Cambodia after 13 years' exile.

18 Terry Waite, envoy to the Archbishop of Canterbury and the last British hostage in Lebanon, is freed after 1,763 days in captivity.

24 general election in Belgium produces gains to Flemish extremists and Green Party.

M December

2 Joseph Cicipio, US hostage in Lebanon is released, followed by Alan Steen (3) and Terry Anderson (4).

3 general assembly of Kenya votes to end one-party state.

5 Robert Maxwell's business empire collapses with huge debts and revelations about misappropriation of money in pension funds.

8 leaders of Russia, Belarus, and Ukraine agree to formation of Commonwealth of Independent States (CIS) (21, eight of the nine other USSR republics sign the agreement).

9 (–10) summit of EC heads of government at Maastricht in Holland agree treaty on closer economic and political union.

13 UN ends ban on sporting, scientific, and academic links with South Africa.

19 Paul Keating replaces Bob Hawke as prime minister and leader of Australian Labor Party.

20 Ante Marković resigns as federal prime minister of Yugoslavia.

25 Mikhail Gorbachev resigns as president of USSR; the USSR officially ceases to exist.

26 Islamic Salvation Front defeats ruling National Liberation Front in first round of Algerian elections.

Drama:
Alan Bennett, *The Madness of George III*.
Steven Berkoff, *Kvetch*.
Ariel Dorfman, *Death and the Maiden*.
Kuniu Shimuzu (adapted by Peter Barnes), *Tango at the End of Winter*.
James Stock, *Blue Night in the Heart of the West*.

v Births and Deaths
Feb 21 Margot Fonteyn dies (71).
April 3 Graham Greene dies (86).
May 31 Angus Wilson dies (77).
Nov 5 Robert Maxwell dies (68).
Nov 18 Gustáv Husák dies (78).

w Everyday Life
In USA, the 'coffee culture' emerges from the foggy streets of Seattle, Washington State.
Sonic the Hedgehog leads Sega's computer-game war against Nintendo.

x Sport and Recreation
In cricket, England beats the West Indies in a Test match in England for the first time in 22 years (10 June).
South Africa is re-admitted to the International Olympic Committee (9 July) and to the International Cricket Conference (10 July).
In the third World Athletics Championships in Tokyo, Mike Powell of the USA sets a new world record for the Long Jump of 8.95 m (29 ft 4.5 in), beating the record set by Bob Beamon in 1968 — the oldest in track and field athletics (30 Aug).
Twenty-two soccer clubs break away from the English Football League, under the auspices of the Football Association, to form a 'premier league'; it commences in Aug 1992.
The English club Liverpool returns to European football (18 Sept) after expiry of the six-year ban imposed after Heysel stadium disaster (1985).

y Media
Closure of the *Listener* magazine in Britain (first published 1929).
A consortium led by Canadian businessman Conrad Black takes over the Fairfax Group of newspapers in Australia.
Robert Maxwell purchases the *New York Daily News* (13 March).
Circulation figures of British daily newspapers: *Daily Express*, 1,518,764; *Daily Mail*, 1,683,768; *Daily Mirror*, 3,641,269; the *Sun*, 3,665,006; *Today*, 459,621; *Daily Telegraph*, 1,058,082; the *Independent*, 372,240; *Financial Times*, 287,120; the *Guardian*, 409,660; *The Times*, 387,386.
Following the death of British businessman Robert Maxwell (5 Nov), the *Mirror* group is taken over and run by receivers; the *European* ceases publication (revived in 1992).

Film:
Barton Fink (directors, Joel and Ethan Coen).
Beauty and the Beast (director, Walt Disney).
Le Belle Noiseuse (director, Jacques Rivette).
The Double Life of Véronique (director, Krzysztof Kieślowski).
Europa Europa (director, Agnieszka Holland).
JFK (director, Oliver Stone).
Ju Dou (director, Zhang Yimou).
Terminator 2: Judgement Day (director, James Cameron; starring Arnold Schwarzenegger).
Thelma and Louise (director, Ridley Scott).
The Vanishing (director, George Sluizer).

Television:
New programmes in Britain include: *GBH*, by Alan Bleasdale; *Noel's House Party* (BBC); *Prime Suspect*, starring Linda La Plante.

British Conservatives elected for fourth term ... Riots in Los
Angeles ... Bill Clinton elected president of USA ...

A January

1 Boutros Boutros-Ghali becomes UN secretary general on retirement of Javier Pérez de Cuéllar.

1 Serbia and Croatia agree UN plan for deployment of peacekeeping forces.

2 opposition Democratic Party forms in Kenya under Mwai Kibaki.

6 President Zviad Gamsakhurdia of Georgia flees to Armenia at end of two-week siege of government buildings in Tbilisi by rebel forces (16, Gamsakhurdia declares war on rebels).

8 Laurent Fabius replaces Pierre Mauroy as Socialist Party leader in France.

11 President Chadli Benjedid of Algeria resigns as armed forces take control to thwart electoral victory by Islamic Salvation Front (12, High Security Council cancels second round of poll).

15 EC recognizes Croatia and Slovenia as independent republics.

19 Zhelyu Zhelev elected president of Bulgaria.

23 UN imposes arms embargo on Somalia in attempt to end civil war.

23 resignation of government in Estonia over inability to deal with fuel and food shortages.

26 EC lifts economic sanctions on South Africa.

30 Charles Haughey, prime minister of Ireland, resigns after allegations are made of telephone-tapping (6 Feb, Albert Reynolds succeeds as prime minister).

B February

1 UN-negotiated truce comes into effect in El Salvador.

2 Serbs accept UN peace plan.

9 Algerian government declares state of emergency after two days of clashes between fundamentalists and security forces.

9 first democratic local elections in Romania for 45 years bring end to one-party rule.

18 Sikh militants murder 17 people in Indian Punjab in attempt to enforce boycott of state elections.

22 ruling Nationalist Party wins general election in Malta.

23 ceasefire agreed in Somalia.

C March

1 Referendum in Bosnia-Herzegovina, boycotted by Bosnian Serbs, decides in favour of becoming an independent sovereign state.

2 violent clashes take place in Sarajevo between militant Serbs, Croats, and Muslims.

3 former USSR troops begin withdrawal from Lithuania.

5 Christian Democrat Jean-Luc Dehaene agrees to form coalition government in Belgium after three-month political crisis.

12 Mauritius becomes a republic within the Commonwealth.

18 white electorate in South Africa votes for constitutional and political reform.

22 Socialist Party in France suffers crushing defeat in regional elections.

22 opposition Democrat Party in Albania wins absolute majority in general election, ending 45 years of Communist rule.

D April

2 Edith Cresson resigns as Prime Minister of France and is replaced by Pierre Bérégovoy.

5 President Alberto Fujimori of Peru suspends the constitution and dissolves Congress with military backing (22, after international criticism Fujimori promises to return Peru to democracy within 12 months).

6 in Italy's general election, established parties suffer losses to the Lombard League, the Greens, and the anti-Mafia La Rete Party.

7 EC formally recognizes independence of Bosnia-Herzegovina; fighting escalates as federal air force aids Serb forces.

8 Serb and federal army forces begin bombardment of Sarajevo in Bosnia-Herzegovina.

9 British general election confounds predictions of opinion pollsters by returning the Conservatives for a fourth term, though with a reduced majority of 21. Conservatives win 336 seats, Labour, 271, Liberal Democrats, 20 (Conservatives receive 41.9 per cent of votes cast, Labour, 34.4 per cent, and Liberal Democrats, 17.8 per cent).

13 Neil Kinnock and Roy Hattersley resign as leader and deputy leader of British Labour Party.

13 in South Africa, Nelson Mandela announces separation from his wife Winnie, whose apparent involvement in criminal activity was damaging the ANC's reputation.

16 President Najibullah of Afghanistan is overthrown. Mujaheddin rebels close in on Kabul.

*First woman speaker of British House of Commons ... J K
Galbraith's* Culture of Contentment *... Methodist Church
condemns patriarchy ...*

o Politics, Government, Law, and Economy

Donald Barlett and James B Steele, *America: What Went Wrong?*.

Francis Fukuyama, *The End of History and the Last Man*.

Steven M Gillon, *The Democrats' Dilemma: Walter F Mondale and the Liberal Legacy*.

Ian Gilmour, *Dancing with Dogma*.

David Osborne and Ted Gaebler, *Reinventing Government*.

Muslim faction in Britain inaugurates self-styled 'Parliament' in London.

Referendum among Inuit people in northern Canada endorses creation of Nunavut, a semi-autonomous Inuit territory (12 Nov).

Russia and Ukraine agree to divide Black Sea fleet (12 Jan).

Ratification, after 200 years, of 27th Amendment to the US Constitution, concerning Congressional pay.

Carl Bildt announces end of Sweden's policy of neutrality (13 Feb).

Cabinet committee membership lists are published for the first time in Britain.

King Fahd of Saudi Arabia grants 'Basic Law' giving constitutional rights (1 Mar).

UN votes (31 Mar) to impose sanctions on Libya after refusal to hand over two men suspected of involvement in Lockerbie bombing (15 Apr, sanctions come into effect).

Manuel Noriega, former ruler in Panama, is convicted (9 Apr) in Miami, USA, of drug trafficking and racketeering.

John Gotti, head of largest Mafia family in New York, is convicted of murder and racketeering (2 Apr).

In Britain, the House of Lords, in Regina v. Brown (the 'Spanner case'), holds that consensual acts of sado-masochism are criminal assaults where the harm done is more than 'trifling'.

Peter Clowes, former head of the Barlow Clowes investment group in Britain, the Channel Islands, and Gibraltar, is convicted of fraud and theft involving over £113 million (10 Feb).

Establishment of Council of Baltic Sea States (5 March), to aid economic development and strengthen links with the European Community.

Price controls are lifted in Russia, Ukraine and many other CIS republics (2 Jan).

In USA, General Motors announces loss for 1991 of $7.2 billion, a world record (24 Feb).

The Lloyds insurance market in London reveal losses of £2 billion, the first in a series of severe losses.

Dealers use the trading floor of the London stock exchange for the last time (31 Jan).

Al Gore, *Earth in the Balance*.

p Society, Education, and Religion

In USA, voters in California elect Diane Feinstein and Barbara Boxer as their senators.

In Britain, Betty Boothroyd is elected the first woman speaker of the House of Commons (27 Apr).

Barbara Mills, QC, is appointed first woman director of public prosecutions in England and Wales (6 Feb).

In USA, in Planned Parenthood v. Casey, the Supreme Court upholds a state law in Pennsylvania requiring women seeking abortions to hear representations against such action; teenagers must have the consent of one parent or a judge (29 June).

J K Galbraith, *The Culture of Contentment*.

Theda Skocpol, *Protecting Soldiers and Mothers: The Political Origins of Social Policy in the United States*.

Demonstrations held in many Latin American countries against celebrations of 500th anniversary of arrival of Columbus in the Americas (12 Oct).

Germany's asylum law is tightened to give powers to refuse entry to economic migrants (6 Dec).

Education Law in Russia provides for the development of testing procedures and the raising of educational standards.

Education systems in the five former East German states are reorganized in line with those in the rest of Germany.

In Britain, the Department of Education and Science is renamed the Department for Education (DfE).

The Education Act in Britain establishes the Office for Standards in Education ('Ofsted'), responsible for overseeing four-yearly inspections of schools by independent teams of inspectors.

'Three Wise Men' criticize state of primary education in Britain.

Polytechnics and several colleges of higher education in Britain are granted university status.

Roman Catholic Church introduces new

23 (–7 May) disruptive public service strike in Germany; unions seek higher pay to compensate for economic conditions arising from reunification (dispute ends with agreement on 5.4 per cent increase).

29 in USA, four white policemen in Los Angeles are acquitted of beating an African-American motorist, despite video-tape evidence; 30–3 May, 58 people die in riots and looting which break out in protest at the acquittals.

E May

6 Lebanese government resigns over worsening economic situation.

8 demonstrators clash with riot police in Bangkok, Thailand, as they call for resignation of unelected Prime Minister General Kraprayaon (20, king of Thailand promises constitutional amendments in return for an end to the demonstrations).

20 Papua New Guinea reaches peace agreement with secessionists on Bougainville Island.

25 Oscar Scalfaro is elected president of Italy.

30 UN imposes ban on trade, air, and sporting links and an oil embargo on new Yugoslav state because of continuing Serbian aggression in Bosnia-Herzegovina.

F June

2 Danish referendum votes against ratification of the Maastricht Treaty.

5 Polish government is voted out of office by parliament; Waldemar Pawlak replaces Jan Olszewski as prime minister.

6 elections in Czechoslovakia result in victory for pro-independence parties in Slovakia and for pro-federal parties in the Czech lands.

16 Fidel Ramos wins Philippines presidential election.

18 referendum in Republic of Ireland endorses ratification of Maastricht Treaty.

18 39 people are killed in 'Boipatong massacre' in South Africa, allegedly by Inkatha supporters (20, police fire on black residents in Boipatong).

23 ANC withdraws from constitutional discussions in protest at the violence.

23 Labour Party wins convincing victory over ruling Likud Party in Israeli general election.

29 President Mohammed Boudiaf of Algeria assassinated by Islamic fundamentalists (2 July, Ali Kafi becomes new president).

G July

5 UN military observers arrive in Somali capital, Mogadishu, to help distribute food aid.

7 Abdul Sabbur Fareed becomes new prime minister of Afghanistan.

9 Chris Patten sworn in as 28th governor of Hong Kong, replacing Lord Wilson of Tillyorn.

15 in Algeria, president and vice-president of Islamic Salvation Front sentenced to 12 years' imprisonment for conspiracy against the state.

17 President Hável of Czechoslovakia resigns after Slovak deputies vote to declare their republic a sovereign state.

18 in Britain, John Smith is elected leader of the Labour Party and Margaret Beckett deputy leader.

28 Italian government forces through emergency legislation to cut federal budget and prevent bankruptcy.

29 Erich Honecker, former East German leader, is forced to leave Chilean embassy in Moscow, to face trial in Germany on manslaughter charges for the killing of people who tried to escape over the Berlin Wall.

H August

3 ANC begins 'mass action' protest campaign in South Africa.

7 agreement reached in Rome to end civil war in Mozambique.

13 UN condemns the Serbs' 'ethnic cleansing' (forced removal) programme as a war crime.

19 Sir Lyndon Pindling loses general election and resigns as president of Bahamas after 25 years.

22 (–26) five nights of serious rioting at a reception centre for asylum seekers in Rostock marks resurgence of anti-foreigner violence in eastern Germany.

24 Hurricane Andrew hits Bahamas and coast of Florida; insurance claims make this the most expensive natural disaster in US history.

27 Lord Owen replaces Lord Carrington as EC's chief mediator on Yugoslav crisis.

27 USA, Britain and France impose air exclusion zone in southern Iraq to protect Shi'ite Muslims from air attacks.

29 ceasefire begins in Afghanistan after three weeks of heavy fighting between pro-government forces and the Mujaheddin faction.

J September

7 President Rakhmon Nabiyev is forced to resign in Tajikistan.

12 Ramiz Alia, former president of Albania, is arrested on charge of misuse of state funds and abuse of power.

catechism, replacing the catechism of 1566 (16 Nov).

Vatican formally rehabilitates Galileo Galilei, forced by the Inquisition in 1633 to recant his assertion that the Earth orbits the Sun (31 Oct).

Unconfirmed children are allowed to receive communion in the Church of Scotland.

Ten women are ordained to the Anglican priesthood in Australia, despite a ruling against by the New South Wales Court of Appeal.

Senior Church of England bishops devise a two-tier system of episcopal oversight to enable opponents of women priests to stay within the Church in the event of the General Synod voting in favour of women's ordination.

The Church of England General Synod votes to allow women to be ordained to the priesthood (11 Nov).

In Britain, a Methodist Church report supports inclusive language in publications and condemns patriarchy as deep sin.

N T Wright, *The New Testament and the People of God*.

Q Science, Technology, and Discovery

President Bush announces (11 Feb) that the USA will phase out CFCs by 1995, five years earlier than planned; Michael Heseltine makes a similar announcement for Britain (14).

The United Nations holds a Conference on Environment and Development in Rio de Janeiro, Brazil, attended by delegates from 178 countries (3–14 June); most countries sign binding conventions on prevention of climate change and preservation of biodiversity.

Launch of *Endeavour*, a new-type US space shuttle orbiter (May).

Astronauts on the US space shuttle fit a new motor to a satellite (*Intelsat-6*) and fire it into a new orbit (14 May).

The US space probe *Ulysses* flies over the north and south poles of Jupiter, to enter a trajectory for reaching the south pole of the Sun (8 Feb); it transmits data about Jupiter's magnetosphere.

The *COBE* (*Cosmic Background Explorer*) satellite detects ripples thought to originate in the formation of galaxies.

Sperm cells are discovered to have odour receptors and may therefore reach eggs by detecting scent.

The first transplant of a baboon liver into a human.

R Humanities

Eamon Duffy, *The Stripping of the Altars: Traditional Religion in England, 1400–1580*.

Andrew Pettegree, *Emden and the Dutch Revolt: Exile and the Development of Reformed Protestantism*.

Bruce Redford (ed.), *The Letters of Samuel Johnson* (–1994).

Melvyn P Leffler, *A Preponderance of Power*.

John Carey, *Intellectuals and the Masses: Prejudice Among the Literary Intelligentsia, 1800–1939*.

Robert P Newman, *Owen Lattimore and the 'Loss' of China*.

John L Gaddis, *The United States and the End of the Cold War*.

William Bright (ed.), *International Encyclopedia of Linguistics*.

The Cambridge History of the English Language.

Tom McArthur (ed.), *The Oxford Companion to the English Language*.

Anthony Huxley et al. (eds.), *The New Royal Horticultural Society Dictionary of Gardening*.

S Art, Sculpture, Fine Arts, and Architecture

Turner Prize in Britain awarded to Grenville Davey.

'Matisse' exhibition at the Museum of Modern Art, New York.

'The Russian Utopia' exhibition at the Guggenheim Museum, New York.

Sculpture:

Damian Hirst, *The Physical Impossibility of Death in the Mind of Someone Living*.

T Music

York Georg Höller, *Aura*.

Robert Moran, *From the Towers of the Moon* (opera).

Andrzej Panufnik, Cello Concerto.

Aulis Sallinen, *Kullervo* (opera).

Alfred Schnittke, *Life with an Idiot* (opera).

Michael Tippett, String Quartet No. 5.

Genesis, 'We Can't Dance'.

P J Harvey, *Dry*.

Whitney Houston, 'I Will Always Love You'.

Morrisey, *Your Arsenal*.

The Orb, *U F Orb*–ambient house music.

REM, *Automatic for the People*.

Shamen, *Ebeneezer Goode*.

Simply Red, *Stars*.

Snap, 'Rhythm Is A Dancer'.

AIDS awareness benefit concert held at Wembley, London, in memory of Queen's Freddie Mercury.

U Literature and Drama

Harold Brodkey, *The Runaway Soul*.

Jung Chang, *Wild Swans*.

Jim Crace, *Arcadia*.

Robertson Davies, *Murther and Walking Spirits*.

16 sterling crisis: British Chancellor of Exchequer Norman Lamont increases base rate from 10 per cent to 12 per cent, then to 15 per cent in attempt to defend the pound against speculative selling; sterling is withdrawn from the ERM and allowed to 'float'; base rate returns to 12 per cent (22, cut to 9 per cent).

20 French referendum produces vote narrowly in favour of Maastricht Treaty.

20 right-wing parties win strong position in parliament in Estonia's first post-independence elections.

23 (–24) over 80 are killed in flash floods in France.

24 thousands of citizens flee NW Liberia as battles rage following breakdown of peacekeeping.

24 David Mellor, first British national heritage secretary, resigns after tabloid press reveals affair with an actress and acceptance of gifts from daughter of a senior PLO official.

25 ceasefire between Azerbaijan and Armenia over disputed region of Nagorno-Karabakh, but each side accuses the other of breaking it before the end of Sept.

29 (–30) first multi-party elections held in Angola. 17 Oct, results give victory for ruling Popular Movement for Liberation of Angola Workers' Party.

K October

5 General election in Guyana results in narrow victory for People's Progressive Party, ending 28-year rule of People's National Congress.

11 President Paul Biya wins slim majority in Cameroon's first multi-party elections.

13 in Britain, announcements are made that coal production will cease at 31 of the country's 50 pits (19, government postpones some of the closures after huge outcry and public support for the miners).

26 Canadian referendum rejects Charlottetown reform agreement which would grant concessions to French-speaking Quebec.

L November

3 Democrat William Jefferson ('Bill') Clinton, governor of Arkansas, wins the US presidential election with 370 electoral college votes. President Bush (Republican) gains 168 electoral votes and H Ross Perot (Independent) fails to win any, although he took 19 per cent of the popular vote. In the Congressional elections, Democrats retain control of both chambers. Popular vote: Clinton, 43,728,375; Bush, 38,167,416; Perot, 19,237,247.

16 Goldstone Commission in South Africa exposes evidence of state 'dirty tricks' campaign against the ANC.

18 in Pakistan Benazir Bhutto is tear-gassed by government forces as she leads march to Islamabad calling for fresh elections.

20 in Britain, fire ravages Windsor Castle, the monarch's second main residence.

22 in legislative elections in Peru, parties supporting President Fujimori achieve absolute majority in the new Democratic Constituent Congress, though only 38 per cent of the electorate vote; elections are boycotted by main opposition parties.

27 Dos Santos and Savimbi issue Namibia Declaration committing themselves to acceptance of Bicesse Peace Accord and continuing UN presence in Angola.

30 (–4 Dec) SWAPO win landslide victory in elections in Namibia.

M December

2 Prime Minister of Greece Constantine Mitsotakis dismisses entire cabinet after facing dissent over austerity measures and his moderate position over Macedonia (3, new cabinet is appointed).

6 Hindu extremists demolish 16th-century mosque at Ayodhya, provoking sectarian violence throughout India which claims over 1,200 lives.

9 US troops arrive in Mogadishu, Somalia, to oversee delivery of international food aid, in operation 'Restore Hope'.

9 in Britain, separation is announced of Prince and Princess of Wales (married 1981).

11 (–12) Edinburgh summit of EC heads of state meets Danish objections to Maastricht Treaty.

16 Israeli cabinet approves order to deport 415 Palestinians to Lebanon. Lebanon refuses to accept the deportees, who are forced to set up camp in 'no man's land' in security zone in south Lebanon.

16 Czech National Council adopts Constitution for the new, separate, Czech Republic to come into being on 1 Jan 1993.

20 Slobodan Milosevic is re-elected to Serbian presidency and his Socialist Party of Serbia wins gains in legislative elections.

21 High Court rules that British government's decision to close 31 pits was illegal and had ignored right of mineworkers and trade unions to be consulted.

29 Fernando Collor de Mello resigns as president of Brazil as impeachment proceedings begin against him in the Senate (30, found guilty of corruption and official misconduct, and banned from public office for eight years).

Martin Goodman, *On Bended Knees*.
Ian McEwan, *Black Dogs*.
Toni Morrison, *Jazz*.
Michael Ondaatje, *The English Patient*.
Adam Thorpe, *Ulverton*.
Jeff Torrington, *Swing Hammer Swing!*
Foundation of the British Literature Prize as Britain's premiere literary award.

Drama:
Jim Cartwright, *The Rise and Fall of Little Voice*.
John Guare, *Six Degrees of Separation*.
Tony Kushner, *Angels in America*.
David Mamet, *Oleanna*.
Théâtre de Complicité, *Street of Crocodiles*.

v Births and Deaths
Jan 11 W G Hoskins dies (83).
March 9 Menachem Begin dies (78).
May 8 F A von Hayek dies (92).
April 6 Isaac Asimov dies (72).
April 23 Satyajit Ray dies (70).
April 27 Olivier Messiaen dies (83).
April 28 Francis Bacon dies (82).
May 6 Marlene Dietrich dies (90).
June 28 John Piper dies (88).
July 4 Willem Visser't Hooft dies (91).
Aug 12 John Cage dies (79).
Oct 8 Willy Brandt dies (78).
Nov 7 Alexander Dubček dies (70).

w Everyday Life
In USA, a talking Barbie doll that says, 'Math class is tough' is withdrawn after protests against the example it sets to girls.
Buckingham Palace announces (19 Mar) the separation of Duke and Duchess of York (married 1986).
The *Daily Mirror* (20 Aug) publishes compromising photographs of the Duchess of York on holiday in France with a so-called 'financial adviser' (24, newspapers carry transcript of a telephone conversation allegedly between Princess of Wales and an intimate male friend).
In Britain, Princess Royal is granted divorce from Captain Mark Phillips (23 April).

x Sport and Recreation
Cricketer David Gower breaks Geoffrey Boycott's record of runs scored for England, reaching a total of 8,154 while playing in Test against Pakistan (6 July).
The 25th Olympic Games are held in Barcelona, Spain (25 July–9 Aug). The Unified Team (comprising the 11 nations of the Commonwealth of Independent States and Georgia) wins 45 gold medals; USA, 37; Germany, 33; China, 16; Cuba, 14; Spain, 13; South Korea, 12; Hungary, 11; France, 8; Australia, 7; Italy and Canada, 6 each.
Nigel Mansell of Britain, driving a Williams–Renault, wins the Formula One Drivers' World Championship (16 Aug), setting a new record of nine Grand Prix victories in one season.
The Toronto Blue Jays become the first team from outside the USA to win baseball's World Series (24 Oct).
US boxer Riddick Bowe wins the World Heavyweight title, out-pointing Evander Holyfield of USA in Las Vegas, USA (13 Nov).
Lennox Lewis becomes the first British-born World Heavyweight boxing champion in the 20th century, when Riddick Bowe vacates the WBC version of the title (14 Dec).

y Media
David and Frederick Barclay purchase the title of the *European* and relaunch the paper.
Closure (8 April) of *Punch* in Britain (first published 1841).

Film:
The Best Intentions (director, Bille August).
Howard's End (directors, James Ivory; starring Anthony Hopkins and Emma Thompson).
Malcolm X (director, Spike Lee).
Orlando (director, Sally Potter).
The Player (director, Robert Altman).
Strictly Ballroom (director, Baz Luhrmann).
Tous les Matins du Monde (director, Alain Corneau).

Radio:
Launch in Britain of Classic FM, a national station specializing in popular classical music (7 Sept); programmes include *Classic America* presented by Mel Cooper.

Television:
In USA, 60 per cent of households receive cable television.
In Australia, the Donaher family of Sydney appears in a fly-on-the-wall documentary series made by Sylvania Waters.
New programmes in Britain include: *Absolutely Fabulous* (BBC) by Jennifer Saunders; *Between the Lines* (BBC); *Eldorado* (BBC), a 'soap opera' about British expatriates in Spain, which proves an expensive flop; *Pole to Pole* with Michael Palin.

Peace agreement between Israel and PLO ... Yeltsin clashes with Russian parliament ... Initial problems for Clinton's administration ...

A January

1 European Community's single market comes into force.

1 Czech and Slovak republics become separate sovereign countries.

3 Presidents Bush and Yeltsin sign START II (second Strategic Arms Reduction Treaty) committing USA and Russia to dismantle two-thirds of nuclear warheads.

6 President Alberto Fujimori re-establishes constitutional government in Peru.

9 government troops in Angola capture headquarters of UNITA leader Jonas Savimbi in Huambo.

13 allied forces carry out air strikes against targets in southern Iraq.

13 former leader of East Germany Erich Honecker is released from prison in Berlin and allowed to join wife in Chile (8 Feb, returns for final session of trial).

14 in USA, President Clinton's choice for post of attorney general, Zoë Baird, is revealed to be under investigation for non-payment of tax (withdraws on 22 after revelation that she employed an illegal immigrant; 5 Feb, second choice Kimba Wood withdraws on the same grounds).

18 elections in Haiti boycotted by most electors.

19 legislation permitting contact between Israeli citizens and the PLO passes final reading in Israeli parliament; 21, PLO leader Yassir Arafat is interviewed on Israeli television.

20 inauguration of William Jefferson Clinton as 42nd president of USA.

21 Clinton appoints his wife, Hillary, to head task force on health reforms (plan unveiled, 22 Sept).

21 to honour campaign pledge, President Clinton orders defense secretary to draft order removing ban on homosexuals in the US armed services; opposed by Colin Powell, chairman of the joint chiefs of staff, and Sam Nunn, chairman of Senate Armed Services Committee (28, Clinton delays lifting of ban, but prohibits questions about recruits' sexual orientation).

B February

10 In Italy, first of a series of ministerial resignations as corruption scandal shakes government.

22 UN Security Council decides to create war crimes tribunal relating to former Yugoslavia — the first such tribunal since Nuremberg (1945–46).

24 Brian Mulroney resigns as Canadian prime minister.

26 bomb explosion damages World Trade Center in New York.

C March

1 US forces carry out air-drop of relief supplies to areas in eastern Bosnia-Herzegovina cut off from UN operations.

7 56-day siege of Huambo ends as Angolan armed forces withdraw before UNITA bombardment.

10 fighting breaks out in Italian senate as Prime Minister Giuliano Amato is heckled over corruption allegations.

10 in USA, gynaecologist Dr David Gunn is shot dead by an anti-abortion activist in Pensacola, Florida, in wave of violent attacks on abortion clinics by 'Rescue America'.

12 emergency session of Russian Congress votes to restrict powers of president and defeats Yeltsin's constitutional amendments (20, Yeltsin announces 'special rule' and sets date for referendum on constitution; 28, attempt to dismiss Yeltsin is defeated in Congress).

12 North Korea withdraws from Treaty on Non-Proliferation of Nuclear Weapons.

12 Labor Party under new Leader Paul Keating wins fifth consecutive victory in general election in Australia, with slight increase in share of vote.

16 in Britain, Chancellor Norman Lamont announces imposition of Value Added Tax on domestic fuel.

20 in Bosnia-Herzegovina, UN supervises evacuation of civilians from Srebrenica, besieged for almost a year (siege ends 18 April).

20 IRA bombs explode in centre of Warrington, NW England, killing two children.

24 Ezer Weizman is elected president of Israel (sworn in 13 May); Binyamin Netanyahu replaces Yitzhak Shamir as leader of Likud Party.

27 Jiang Zemin becomes state president of China.

29 Edouard Balladur becomes prime minister of France after victory for right-wing RPR–UDF alliance in elections; ruling Socialist Party retain only 54 of their 252 seats.

Gun control in USA ... Pope issues Veritatis Splendor *... Opening of Buckingham Palace to the public ... Disaster at the Grand National ...*

o Politics, Government, Law, and Economy

Timothy Garton Ash, *In Europe's Name.*

Alan Clark, *Diaries.*

Paul Kennedy, *Preparing for the 21st Century.*

Sidney M Milkis, *The President and the Parties: The Transformation of the American Party System since The New Deal.*

Margaret Thatcher, *The Downing Street Years.*

In Italy, end of the 'First Republic' as referendum supports change to the electoral system, replacing proportional representation by one-member constituencies.

In Australia, Prime Minister Paul Keating announces that the country will become a republic by 2001 (19 Sept).

First direct elections to national assembly held in Cuba (25 Feb), with official turn-out of 99.6 per cent.

British Labour Party Conference narrowly supports Labour leadership's plan to replace use of bloc votes in selection of parliamentary candidates by 'one member, one vote', known as 'OMOV' (29 Sept).

Following the implementation of the Maastricht Treaty (1 Nov), the EC Council of Ministers is renamed the EU Council and the Commission of the EC becomes the European Commission.

Queen Elizabeth II of Britain and the Prince of Wales both volunteer to pay income tax and capital gains tax on their private income; the Queen also takes over civil list payments to junior members of the royal family (announced 11 Feb).

In USA, the Brady Act (named after former White House press secretary James Brady, who was wounded during attempted assassination of President Reagan in 1981) introduces some controls on acquisition of firearms (signed 30 Nov).

Bernard Schwartz, *A History of the Supreme Court.*

Morton Horowitz, *The Transformation of American Law: 1860–1960.*

Criminal Justice Act in Britain abolishes income-related fines (introduced 1991).

In Britain, in M v. Home Office, the House of Lords rules that the then home secretary, Kenneth Baker, was in contempt of court to deport a Zaïrean refugee against the instructions of a court order.

The Court of Appeal in Britain provides the basis for a new tort of harassment in Khorsandjan v. Bush.

In Britain, nurse Beverley Allitt is convicted of murdering four babies under her care at the Grantham and Kesteven hospital (17 May).

In Britain, two 11-year-old boys, Robert Thompson and Jon Venables, are convicted of the murder of two-year-old James Bulger in Liverpool, NW England, in Feb.

GATT arbitration rules that EC import restrictions on bananas unfairly limit Latin American imports (26 May).

Jacques Attali of France resigns as president of the European Bank of Reconstruction (16 July), after it is revealed that in its first period of operation it spent twice as much on refurbishment of its London headquarters as on loans to Eastern Europe.

The international community lifts sanctions against South Africa (8 Oct).

Oil is discovered off the Falkland Islands (1 Dec).

Conclusion in Geneva, Switzerland, of the 'Uruguay Round' of negotiations for a revised General Agreement on Tariffs and Trade (started Sept 1986); 117 nations agree the GATT Final Act (15 Dec).

p Society, Education, and Religion

In USA, President Clinton signs (5 Feb) the Family Leave Act; employers with more than 50 employees have to provide time off work for parents after the birth of a child.

Janet Reno becomes the first woman attorney general of the USA (confirmed 12 March).

Judge Ruth Ginsburg becomes the second woman member of the US Supreme Court (takes seat 1 Oct).

In USA, in speech to the National Governors' Association (2 Feb), President Clinton announces promise to 'end welfare as we know it', so that it ceases to be 'a way of life'.

Community Care Act in Britain changes the way in which health and social services deal with the elderly, disabled, and mentally ill (in theory providing for care at a more local level rather than in institutions).

Abolition of Wages Councils removes controls on low pay in Britain enacted since 1909.

In Britain, the House of Commons votes for partial deregulation of Sunday trading in England and Wales (8 Dec); small stores are completely deregulated, large stores can open for six hours.

The Republic of Ireland decriminalizes homosexuality and equalizes age of consent for heterosexuals and homosexuals at 17 (24 June).

D **April**

10 In South Africa, Chris Hani, a leading figure in the African National Congress (ANC), is assassinated by a member of Afrikaner Resistance Movement.

11 in Israel, occupied territories are 'closed' in attempt to stem violence.

25 Russian referendum produces vote of confidence in Yeltsin.

29 Brazil's Supreme Court rules that former president Fernando Collor de Mello be indicted for passive corruption and criminal association.

E **May**

1 Ranasinghe Premadasa, president of Sri Lanka, is assassinated during parade in Colombo.

4 UN takes over military and humanitarian effort in Somalia from US-led task force.

4 businessman Asil Nadir, awaiting trial in Britain for theft and false accounting after collapse of Polly Peck, jumps bail and flees to Northern Cyprus.

4 opening of Scott inquiry into British Government's involvement in export of arms to Iraq.

6 UN Security Council declares 'safe areas' in Sarajevo, Tuzla, Zepa, Goradze, Bihac, and Srebrenica in Bosnia-Herzegovina (30, Bosnian Serbs attack Goradze and Srebrenica).

7 in South Africa, multi-party talks in Johannesburg reach agreement for holding of non-racial elections by April 1994.

13 USA formally abandons Strategic Defence Initiative.

18 in second referendum, Denmark approves the Maastricht Treaty by a narrow majority.

19 USA recognizes government in Angola.

24 Eritrea becomes independent from Ethiopia.

24 demonstrations are held in Lhasa, Tibet, after arrest of dissidents; Western observers investigating human-rights abuses cut short their visit.

27 US House of Representatives narrowly votes to approve President Clinton's programme of tax increases and spending cuts.

29 five Turkish women are killed in a neo-Nazi arson attack in Solingen, Germany (Turkish demonstrations and rioting throughout Germany over following days).

F **June**

3 In USA, President Clinton withdraws nomination of Lani Guinier for head of Justice Department's Civil Rights Division after reading her work on quotas and empowerment of minorities.

4 rebellion amongst army in Azerbaijan; (18, President Abulfaz Elchibey is forced to leave Baku).

5 Somali National Forces attack Pakistani troops serving with the UN.

6 guerrillas attack refugee camp near Harbel in Liberia and massacre over 450 people.

11 Ali Akbar Rafsanjani, president of Iran, is re-elected for second term.

13 Kim Campbell, Progressive Conservative, becomes first woman prime minister of Canada.

15 last Russian troops leave Cuba.

23 international sanctions are imposed on Haiti.

23 presidential elections in Nigeria are annulled (unrest persists into July).

25 armed supporters of Afrikaner Volksfront storm Johannesburg World Trade Centre, scene of talks on constitutional future of South Africa.

26 USA makes missile attack on Iraqi intelligence headquarters in Baghdad, in retaliation for alleged plot to kill George Bush, former president of the USA.

G **July**

3 Peace agreement signed between exiled president of Haiti, Jean-Bertrand Aristide and General Raoul Cédras, leader of 1991 coup.

10 water supply is cut off in Sarajevo, Bosnia-Herzegovina, when fuel supplies fail to get through besieging Serb forces.

18 after governing Japan since 1955, the Liberal Democrats lose their overall majority in general election (6 Aug, replaced by seven-party coalition).

18 in Pakistan, under pressure from army chief of staff, President Ghulam Ishaq and Prime Minister Sharif both resign after power struggle.

19 in USA, President Clinton and the defense department reach compromise on service by homosexuals in the US armed forces: homosexuals are allowed to serve provided that they neither declare homosexuality nor engage in homosexual activity (effective from 1 Oct).

22 in Britain, government fails to win vote on the Maastricht Treaty in House of Commons; 23, government policy is confirmed by vote of confidence, proposed by Prime Minister John Major with threat of dissolution if the government loses.

29 in Israel, John Demjanjuk, sentenced to death in 1988 for war crimes committed as death-camp guard 'Ivan the Terrible', is cleared by the Supreme Court after the identification is doubted.

Members of Yanomami tribe in Brazil are massacred by gold and tin miners (15 Aug).

Robert Hughes, *The Culture of Complaint: The Fraying of America.*

The Education Act makes it easier for schools in England and Wales to 'opt out' of local authority control; permits the establishment of specialist Technology Colleges; and provides for the establishment of a Funding Agency for Schools and for 'Educational Associations' to run schools judged to be 'failing'.

Learning to Succeed, the report of the Paul Hamlyn National Commission on Education in Britain, calls for greater public and private investment in education, universal nursery schooling, a General Teachers' Council, and reform of educational administration at the central and local levels.

The British government agrees to reduce the content of the National Curriculum and to modify testing arrangements in the light of prolonged teachers' industrial action and the findings of an enquiry chaired by Sir Ron Dearing, Chairman of the Schools Curriculum and Assessment Authority.

The Universities' Funding Council and Polytechnics' Central Funding Council in Britain are dissolved and replaced by the Higher Education Funding Council (HEFC).

Three colleges in Oxford are the first former men's colleges in England's 'ancient universities' of Oxford and Cambridge to announce the appointment of women heads of house (Prof Marilyn Butler as rector of Exeter College, Prof Averil Cameron as warden of Keble College, and Dr Jessica Rawson as warden of Merton College).

In USA, FBI siege of headquarters of Branch Davidian cult in Waco, Texas, ends after 51 days, with the compound consumed by fire; cult leader David Koresh is amongst the dead (19 April).

Chief Rabbi of Israel visits Pope John Paul II at Castel Gandolfo, Italy (22 Sept), first such meeting (30 Dec, Vatican and Israel sign 'fundamental agreement' whereby the Vatican recognizes Israel).

Catholic bishops in Cuba issue pastoral letter pleading for social and political reforms (Sept).

Methodist Conference in Britain affirms teaching of 'chastity for all outside marriage and fidelity within it' (June).

Papal encyclical Veritatis splendor (*The Splendour of Truth*) is published (5 Oct); it condemns relative moral judgements and affirms Catholic moral teaching.

Ordination of women in Church of England approved by House of Commons (29 Oct)

and House of Lords (2 Nov).

E P Sandars, *The Historical Figure of Jesus.*

B Metzger and Michael D Coogan, *The Oxford Companion to the Bible.*

Q Science, Technology, and Discovery

Sir Ranulph Fiennes and Dr Michael Stroud of Britain complete the first unsupported crossing of Antarctica on foot, having covered 2,160 km/1,350 mi in 95 days (11 Feb).

Publication in USA (15 Sept) of The National Information Infrastructure: Agenda for Action, proposing framework for the creation of a national 'information highway'.

The Hubble Space Telescope (placed in Earth orbit, 1990) is repaired, at a cost of $360 million, by five US astronauts operating from the US space shuttle (7 Dec).

US loses contact with its *Mars Observer* space probe (cost, $980 million).

Jane Luu and David Jewitt, working in Hawaii, USA, announce discovery of four large ice objects beyond Pluto in the solar system.

In Princeton, USA, the most successful nuclear fusion experiment yet, when hydrogen isotopes are heated to 300 million degrees, creating 3 million watts of power.

In USA, US Congress cancels the proposed Superconducting Super Collider particle accelerator.

Publication of spectacular pictures of individual atoms, obtained by use of a scanning tunnelling microscope.

British mathematician Andrew Wiles solves 'Fermat's Last Theorem', a mathematical problem posed by the French mathematician Pierre de Fermat, 1601– 65.

An ice core drilled in Greenland, providing evidence of climate change over 250,000 years, suggests that sudden fluctuations have been common and that the recent stable climate is unusual.

Dean Hammer and colleagues at the US National Cancer Institute publish the approximate location of a gene that could predispose male humans to homosexuality.

R Humanities

R H Britnell, *The Commercialisation of English Society, 1000–1500.*

Peter Coss, *The Knight in Medieval England, 1000–1400.*

Barbara Harvey, *Living and Dying in England 1100–1540: The Monastic Experience.*

Simon Thurley, *The Royal Palaces of Tudor England: Architecture and Court Life, 1460–1547.*

Hugh Thomas, *The Conquest of Mexico.*

J M Neeson, *Commoners: Common Right,*

31 King Baudouin of Belgium dies suddenly of heart attack, aged 62 (Aug 9, his brother Albert of Liège is sworn in as king).

H **August**

2 Following speculative pressure on currencies in the European Exchange Rate Mechanism, the Mechanism comes close to collapse and currencies are allowed to fluctuate within broad band of 15 per cent on either side of central rates.

4 President Juvénal Habyarimana and Rwandan Patriotic Front sign peace accord.

10 in USA, President Clinton signs budget and deficit reduction plan.

21 UN relief convoy arrives in Mostar, Bosnia-Herzegovina.

27 General Ibrahim Babangida steps down as president of Nigeria, handing power to non-elected interim government.

J **September**

7 Body of Ferdinand Marcos is returned to Philippines for burial; 24, his widow Imelda is sentenced to imprisonment for corruption.

13 in Washington, DC, USA, peace agreement (the 'Declaration of Principles') is signed between Israel and the Palestine Liberation Organization, providing for Israeli withdrawal from Gaza Strip and Jericho; Yassir Arafat and Yitzhak Rabin shake hands.

17 the remains of General Wladyslaw Sikorski, leader of Polish government in exile during World War II, are reinterred in his home country.

19 Polish general election gives victory for former communists.

21 Yeltsin suspends Russian parliament and calls elections; Supreme Soviet defies this action and swears in Alexandr Rutskoi as president.

27 White House in Moscow, seat of Russian parliament, is sealed off by troops (telephone links, water and electricity supplies had been cut off in preceding days).

K **October**

4 Rebels holding out in Moscow parliament building surrender after fire breaks out following shelling from army tanks loyal to President Yeltsin; state of emergency in force until 18 Oct.

6 in Pakistan, general election produces hung parliament; 19, Benazir Bhutto is sworn in as prime minister.

9 General Aydid, leader of warring faction in Somalia, announces unilateral ceasefire.

15 Nobel Peace Prize is awarded jointly to F W de Klerk and Nelson Mandela of South Africa.

20 emergency measures imposed in Kenya after renewed ethnic violence in Rift Valley.

21 President Melchior Ndadaye and six senior ministers are killed during attempted army coup in Burundi.

25 Liberal Party wins decisive victory in Canadian general election; Progressive Conservative Party, in office since 1984, retains only two seats, while Bloc Québecois becomes second-largest party (4 Nov, Liberal leader Jean Chrétien is sworn in as prime minister).

28 in USA, bush fires break out in southern California; conflagration reaches suburbs of Los Angeles, leaving many homeless and causing damage of over $1,000 million.

31 referendum held in Peru on President Fujimori's draft constitution, allowing president to stand for further term of office and re-introducing death penalty for terrorism.

L **November**

1 Maastricht Treaty (the Treaty on European Union) comes into force; the European Community becomes the European Union (EU).

6 in New Zealand, Jim Bolger's National Party retains office following general election.

14 Farooq Ahmed Leghari becomes president of Pakistan.

17 military coup ends brief period of civilian rule in Nigeria; defence minister General Sanni Abacha takes over as head of state.

17 US House of Representatives approves North American Free Trade Agreement negotiated with Canada and Mexico.

M **December**

2 In Colombia, Pablo Escobar Gaviria, head of Medellín drug-trafficking cartel, is shot dead by police.

7 multi-racial Transitional Executive Council takes over government in South Africa to prepare for elections.

11 Eduardo Frei Ruíz-Tagle of Coalition for Democracy, is elected president of Chile.

12 in legislative elections in Russia, largest share of vote (22.8 per cent) goes to nationalist Liberal Democratic Party of Russia, led by Vladimir Zhirinovsky; voters approve Yeltsin's draft constitution in simultaneous referendum.

14 Downing Street declaration sets out principles for peace talks on Northern Ireland.

Enclosure and Social Change in England 1700–1820.

Stanley Elkins and Eric McKitrick, *The Age of Federalism.*

Margaret Conrad and Alvin Finkel, *History of the Canadian Peoples, Volume 1, Beginnings to 1867* (–).

Dorian Gerhold, *Road Transport before the Railways: Russell's London Flying Waggons.*

David Montgomery, *Citizens and Workers.*

Denis Mack Smith, *Mazzini.*

David Levering Lewis, *W E B Du Bois: Biography of a Race.*

Jordan Schwarz, *The New Dealers: Power Politics in the Age of Roosevelt.*

Peter Preston, *Franco.*

Philip Ziegler, *Harold Wilson.*

John Campbell, *Edward Heath: A Biography.*

Andrew Motion, *Philip Larkin: A Writer's Life.*

Mary Jane Phillips-Matz, *Verdi.*

Michael Dummett, *Origins of Analytical Philosophy.*

Thomas Hurka, *Perfectionism.*

Larry S Temkin, *Inequality.*

s Art, Sculpture, Fine Arts, and Architecture

Bomb attack in Florence damages part of Uffizi gallery (27 May).

It is revealed that Russia possesses the 'Schliemann Gold' — objects found by Heinrich Schliemann at Troy in 1873 which disappeared from Berlin in 1945.

Exhibition 'From Cézanne to Matisse — the Barnes Collection' is held at the Musée d'Orsay, Paris, France (–1994); this is the first time that items from the Collection have left Pennsylvania, USA.

Sculpture:

Hans Haacke, *Installation*, at the German pavilion, Venice Biennale, Italy.

Rebecca Horn, *Binoculars in Conversation.*

Orlan, conceptual/performance work, SoHo, New York, is beamed worldwide by closed circuit television; consists of one operation in a series to give the artist the mouth of François Boucher's *Europa*, the nose of a Diana from the School of Fontainebleau, and forehead of Leonardo da Vinci's *Mona Lisa*, the chin of Sandro Botticelli's *Venus*, and the eyes of Gérome's *Psyche.*

Vong Phaophanit, *Neon Rice Field.*

In Britain, Rachel Whiteread is awarded the Turner Prize for *House*, the plaster cast of the inside of a house in the East End of London (also receives prize for the 'worst artist of the year').

T Music

Michael Berkeley, *Baa-Baa Black Sheep* (opera).

Jonathan Harvey, *Inquest of Love* (opera).

George Lloyd, *Symphonic Mass.*

Deborah Mollison, *Ocean Witness.*

Dmitri Smirnov, *Song of Liberty.*

Iannis Xenakis, *The Bacchae.*

Ace of Base, 'All She Wants', 'The Sign'.

Bjork, *Debut.*

Phil Collins, *Both Sides.*

Meat Loaf, 'I'd Do Anything for Love (But I Won't Do That)', *Bat Out of Hell II.*

Mr Blobby, 'Mr Blobby'.

Morrisey, *Vauxhall and I.*

Rise of Ragga.

Suede, *Suede.*

Take That, *Everything Changes*, 'Pray', *Take That And Party.*

U2, *Zooropa.*

U Literature and Drama

Isabel Allende, *The Infinite Plain.*

Ana Castillo, *So Far From God.*

Amy Clampitt, *A Silence Opens* (poems).

Roddy Doyle, *Paddy Clarke Ha Ha Ha.*

Gita Mehta, *A River Sutra.*

Caryl Phillips, *Crossing the River.*

Vikram Seth, *A Suitable Boy.*

Carol Shields, *The Stone Diaries.*

Drama:

David Beard, *Oneonta.*

Jonathan Harvey, *Beautiful Thing.*

Edna Mazya, *Games in the Backyard.*

Harold Pinter, *Moonlight.*

Tom Stoppard, *Arcadia.*

V Births and Deaths

Jan 6 Dizzy Gillespie dies (75).

Jan 24 Thurgood Marshall dies (84).

Feb 6 Arthur Ashe dies (49).

April 8 Marian Anderson dies (96).

Oct 31 Federico Fellini dies (73).

W Everyday Life

In USA, the runways at Los Angeles airport are closed for about 40 minutes while Christophe, a fashionable Beverly Hills hairdresser, cuts President Bill Clinton's hair on board his official plane, Air Force One; in addition to the cost of disrupting air traffic, the cut costs $200 and the incident becomes known as 'Hairgate' (22 May).

Crown Prince Naruhito of Japan marries Masako Owada (9 June).

Buckingham Palace, London, is opened to the general public (from 6 Aug); money from entrance fees to be put towards the restoration of Windsor Castle.

Genetic materials from the Duke of Edinburgh

*Democracy in South Africa ... Rwandan civil war ... Cease-fire in
Northern Ireland ...*

A January

1 Zapatista National Liberation Army leads rebellion of Indian groups in state of Chiapas, Mexico.

13 national assembly in Burundi elects Cyprien Ntaryamira as president.

16 radical Yegor Gaidar resigns from Russian cabinet in protest at conservatism of government policy; 26, Boris Fedorov also resigns.

17 major earthquake hits southern California, USA; 57 are killed and 25,000 made homeless.

19 proposed reforms against political corrup-tion in Japan are defeated in upper house; 29, compromise is reached removing weighting given to rural votes and limiting, rather than prohibiting, corporate dona-tions to politicians.

31 Gerry Adams, president of Irish republican party Sinn Féin, is granted a visa to visit the USA.

B February

5 Mortar attack on market place in Sarajevo, Bosnia-Herzegovina, kills at least 68 civilians.

16 Greece imposes trade ban on Macedonia.

and other relatives of the Romanov royal family in Russia are compared, using techniques of 'genetic fingerprinting', with the supposed remains of Nicholas II and his family, proving that the remains are genuine.

x **Sport and Recreation**

Nigel Mansell of Britain wins an Indycar Grand Prix at his first attempt, in Queensland, Australia (21 March).

In horse racing, the Grand National (held at the Aintree course in NW England) is declared void after two false starts. Over half the runners fail to respond to the second red (cancellation) flag and complete the course. The void race is won by Esha Ness, ridden by John White (3 April).

In soccer, in England, Arsenal is the first team to win the Football Association Cup and League Cup in the same season, beating Sheffield Wednesday in both finals (18 April, 20 May).

In the World Athletics Championships in Stuttgart, Germany, Sally Gunnell of Britain establishes a new world record in winning the Women's 400 m hurdles (27 Aug).

Evander Holyfield of the USA defeats Riddick Bowe to win the World Boxing Association and International Boxing Federation versions of the World Heavyweight boxing title (6 Nov).

Y **Media**

Films:

The Age of Innocence (director, Martin Scorsese).

Groundhog Day (starring Bill Murray).

In the Name of the Father (director, Jim Sheridan; starring Daniel Day Lewis).

Jamon Jamon (director, Bigas Luna).

Jurassic Park (director, Steven Spielberg).

Les Nuits Fauves (director and star, Cyril Collard).

Olivier Olivier (director, Agnieszka Holland).

Philadelphia (director, Jonathan Demme; starring Tom Hanks).

The Remains of the Day (director, James Ivory).

The Scent of Green Papaya (director, Tran Anh Hung).

Schindler's List (director, Steven Spielberg).

Shadowlands (director, Richard Attenborough; starring Anthony Hopkins).

Strawberry and Chocolate (directors, Tomas Guttierez Alea and Juan Carlos Tabio).

Radio:

In Britain, launch of the national pop station Virgin Radio (April).

Following a campaign against the BBC's plan to stop broadcasting Radio 4 on long wave, the proposal is withdrawn, enabling listeners in Europe to continue to hear *The Archers* and other popular programmes.

Television:

US businessman Rupert Murdoch purchases Star TV, a five-channel satellite station based in Hong Kong and broadcasting to an estimate 40 million viewers in Asia.

In Britain, following competition for franchises, four commercial stations lose their licences and are replaced by new companies.

German armed forces permitted outside NATO area ...
Inauguration of Channel Tunnel ...

o **Politics, Government, Law, and Economy**

Henry Kissinger, *Diplomacy.*

Paul Whiteley, *True Blues: The Politics of Conservative Party Membership.*

Bob Woodward, *The Agenda: Inside the Clinton White House.*

NATO summit in Brussels, Belgium (10–11 Jan), launches 'partnership for peace' programme to encourage co-operation with former members of Warsaw Pact.

Libya and United Arab Emirates extend application of Islamic law, the sharia (respectively 17 and 20 Feb).

Legislation in Latvia imposes language test for citizenship and excludes former military personnel (21 June).

Government of the People's Republic of China announces (9 July) that Hong Kong's legislative council will be terminated on China's resumption of sovereignty in 1997; it rejects the reform package approved in the colony on 30 June.

Federal Constitutional Court in Germany approves principle that Germany's armed forces can be deployed outside the NATO area in collective operations (12 July).

21 former head of CIA Soviet counter-intelligence, Aldrich Hazen Ames, is arrested with his wife on charges of having spied for the USSR.

23 in Bosnia-Herzegovina, ceasefire between Bosnian and Croat forces.

25 over 50 Palestinians are massacred in gun attack by an Israeli settler on a mosque in Hebron; 26, Israeli government seals off the West Bank and Gaza Strip.

26 amnesty is announced in Russia for political prisoners, including leaders of the attempted coup in 1991.

c **March**

1 Negotiations are concluded on enlargement of European Union to include Sweden, Finland, and Austria; on 16, Norway is also included.

1 International Atomic Energy Agency inspection team enters North Korea, but is not given access to certain sites.

18 Bosnia-Herzegovina and Croatia sign accord on creation of a federation of Bosnian Muslims and Croats.

20 in Tunisia, first elections are held under new legislation ensuring presence of opposition in the legislature.

22 South Korea places forces on full alert after breakdown of talks with North Korea.

24 allegations are made in the US Congress that President and Mrs Clinton may have used their investment in the Whitewater Development Corporation in Arkansas for improper purposes, especially in connection with the failed Madison Guaranty Savings bank (the affair becomes known as 'Whitewatergate').

24 factions in Somalia sign peace agreement (25, US troops withdraw).

26 (–27) in Italy, Freedom Alliance led by businessman Silvio Berlusconi wins parliamentary elections.

31 in South Africa, President F W de Klerk imposes state of emergency in KwaZulu–Natal after anti-election demonstration is organized by the Inkatha Freedom Party.

31 in Bosnia-Herzegovina, Serbs bombard safe areas in Goradze and Srebrenica.

D **April**

6 The presidents of Rwanda and Burundi, respectively Juvénal Habyarimana and Cyprien Ntaryamira, are killed in an air crash; violence erupts on huge scale, with hundreds killed in Rwanda's capital Kigali.

8 Morihiro Hosokawa resigns as prime minister of Japan after weakening of coalition and accusations of financial misconduct.

10 NATO authorizes air strikes on Serbian posts near Goradze; 22, Goradze falls to Serb forces.

14 Greece deprives former king, Constantine II, of his Greek citizenship.

10 in South Africa, the Inkatha Freedom Party agrees to take part in all-race general election.

20 the government of Angola and UNITA reach agreement over principles for new elections.

23 (–27) in South Africa, terrorist attacks by white right-wing groups attempting to disrupt elections.

26 (–29) first non-racial general election in South Africa, which results in an overwhelming victory for the African National Congress.

E **May**

8 (and 29) Elections in Hungary result in clear majority for former communist Socialist Party.

9 ceasefire established in Nagorno-Karabakh (Armenian-populated enclave in Azerbaijan), with support of international peacekeeping force.

10 in South Africa, Nelson Mandela is sworn in as president; on 11, new cabinet includes representatives from all four racial groups into which the population had been divided under apartheid.

12 in Britain, sudden death of John Smith, leader of the Labour Party (21 July, Tony Blair is elected leader).

13 Israel withdraws military forces from the Jericho area of the occupied West Bank to make way for self-rule by Palestinian National Authority; on 18, withdraws from Gaza Strip.

14 government of Georgia and rebels in the breakaway region of Abkhazia agree cease-fire.

26 President Clinton of USA renews 'most favoured nation' status for China, despite previous insistence that trading relations be linked to improvement of China's record on human rights.

F **June**

1 South Africa rejoins the Commonwealth.

8 in Bosnia-Herzegovina, ceasefire signed by leaders of the Bosnian Serbs and the Bosnian Federation; soon broken by violations.

12 in USA, President and Mrs Clinton testify under oath about involvement in the Whitewater financial scandal (26 July, Congressional committee begins hearings into the affair).

In USA, in J E B v. Alabama Ex Rel T B, the Supreme Court rules (19 April) that sexual discrimination in the selection of juries is a violation of the equal protection guarantee in the 14th Amendment to the Constitution.

The Criminal Justice Act in Britain criminalizes trespass and squatting, restricts the right to silence, and introduces a new police caution.

In Virginia, USA, Lorena Bobbitt is cleared (21 Jan) of maliciously wounding her husband after she cut off his penis (June 1993); it was accepted that she had become temporarily insane.

In USA, Paula Jones files case against President Clinton alleging sexual harassment when he was governor of Arkansas (6 May); a federal judge rules (21 July) that the case can be held pending until it has been determined whether an incumbent president is immune from civil law suits that predate his presidential term.

North American Free Trade Agreement (NAFTA), between Mexico, the USA, and Canada goes into operation (1 Jan).

Second stage of economic and monetary union in Europe comes into force with establishment of European Economic Area (1 Jan).

At the 'Summit of the Americas', held in Miami, Florida, USA (9–11 Dec), leaders of 34 countries agree to create the Free Trade Area of the Americas by 2005.

In Ouro Preto, Brazil, the presidents of Argentina, Brazil, Paraguay, and Uruguay sign pact (17 Dec) creating the Southern Common Market (Mercosur), the world's second-largest customs union (in force from 1 Jan 1995).

Private banks established in Iran for the first time since the nationalization of banking in 1979 (14 June).

In Britain, British Coal is privatized with the sale of 22 deep mines and 32 opencast pits (29 Dec).

New currency, the real, is introduced in Brazil (1 July).

P **Society, Education, and Religion**

United Nations Fund for Population Activities holds the third International Conference on Population and Development in Cairo, Egypt (5–13 Sept); delegates give special attention to the education of women and endorse a Programme of Action to stabilize population growth; but the Vatican and other states criticize the Programme's implicit acceptance of abortion and extramarital sexual intercourse, and some Arab and Muslim countries boycott the Conference.

In USA, 'Take Your Daughter to Work Day' involves 3 million women and their children.

In USA, Freedom of Access Act declares that the obstruction of abortion clinics and places of worship is a federal offence (signed 26 May).

Voters in California, USA, approve Proposition 187, which would stop illegal immigrants from receiving non-emergency health care, welfare, and education (8 Nov); restraining orders prevent immediate implementation, pending judgement on the Proposition's constitutionality.

In Oregon, USA, voters support Measure 16, permitting euthanasia in regulated circumstances for the terminally ill (8 Nov).

Labour law approved in China, establishing a minimum wage, and eight-hour working day, and prohibiting child labour (5 July).

As part of agreement with the World Bank and the International Monetary Fund, Burkina Faso agrees to end the practice of female circumcision.

Homosexual age of consent lowered to 18 in Britain.

In Baltimore, Maryland, USA, leading African-Americans hold the National African-American Leadership Summit to explore and reconcile differences among African-Americans (12–14 June).

In USA, Benjamin Chavis, director of the National Association for the Advancement of Colored People, is dismissed on account of the Association's debt, his lavish expense-account life-style, and because he committed the NAACP to meet an out-of-court settlement for sexual harassment (20 Aug).

Members of Council of Europe approve Convention on the Protection of National Minorities (10 Nov).

French parliament passes law requiring use of 3,500 terms and technical expressions in preference to foreign equivalents in public notices, contracts and public culture (5 May).

Human Development Report 1994 (published 1 June) ranks countries according to the Human Development Index (based on life expectancy, education, and purchasing power); Canada ranks first.

Richard Bernstein, *Dictatorship of Virtue: Multiculturalism and the Battle for America's Future.*

Stanley Fish, *There's No Such Thing as Free Speech And It's A Good Thing, Too.*

Education Act in England and Wales establishes the Teacher Training Agency, permitting schools to train teachers alone or in

14 United Nations completes programme to destroy Iraq's chemical weapons, in accordance with peace terms agreed after Gulf War.

15 Jimmy Carter, former president of the USA, visits North Korea and helps defuse crisis over nuclear inspections.

23 France sends troops into Rwanda to protect refugees and support humanitarian effort.

23 in Ecuador, Land Development Law is suspended after widespread protests by indigenous population, who claim that it removed their grazing and watering rights.

24 (–25) summit of EU heads of government at which, on 25, Prime Minister John Major of Britain vetoes nomination of Jean-Luc Dehaene, prime minister of Belgium, as president of the European Commission (15 July, Jacques Santer, prime minister of Luxembourg, is chosen as president).

29 in Japan, following collapse of previous coalition, Tomiichi Murayama of the Social Democratic Party, becomes prime minister.

G **July**

1 Yassir Arafat, chairman of the Palestine Liberation Organization, enters Gaza, setting foot on Palestinian territory for the first time for 25 years; on 5, visits Jericho.

8 leader of North Korea, Kim Il Sung, dies at age of 82.

16 (–22) fragments of the comet Shoemaker-Levy 9 collide with Jupiter.

18 Rwandan Patriotic Front claims victory in Rwandan civil war; Pasteur Bizimungu assumes presidency; 24, over 2 million Rwandans are reported to have left the country; international relief effort airlifts supplies to vast refugee camps on the borders as cholera spreads and many refugees remain afraid to return home (1 Aug, UN establishes commission to investigate human rights violations in Rwanda).

23 military coup in the Gambia deposes President Jawara; on 26, 29-year-old coup leader, Yahya Jammeh, names himself president and promises elections.

25 King Hussein of Jordan and Yitzhak Rabin, prime minister of Israel, sign joint declaration in Washington, DC, USA, formally ending their conflict (26 Oct, peace treaty is signed in a desert ceremony on border between Jordan and Israel).

29 in USA, a doctor and his escort are shot dead by a prominent anti-abortionist in Pensacola, Florida.

31 UN Security Council authorizes 'all necessary means' to remove military regime in Haiti.

H **August**

3 General strike in Nigeria in support of Chief Moshood Abiola, the presumed victor in the annulled presidential election of 1993, who is charged with treason by the military regime (4 Sept, end of strike by oil workers).

11 President Fidel Castro of Cuba lifts restrictions on those wishing to leave Cuba, provoking a major exodus from the island; by end August, 20,000 have left; on 19, President Clinton of USA removes automatic refugee status for Cubans fleeing to USA (9 Sept, restrictions on departures are reintroduced after agreement is reached between Cuba and USA).

14 'Carlos the Jackal' (José Angel García Talavera), wanted for numerous terrorist attacks, is arrested in Khartoum, Sudan.

16 Sri Lankan ruling party, the United National Party, is defeated in legislative elections, and replaced by 'People's Alliance', a left-wing coalition led by Chandrika Kumaratunga.

21 in Bosnia-Herzegovina, government forces take rebel Muslim enclave of Bihac.

22 Ernesto Zedillo becomes president of Mexico after election victory for centre-right Institutional Revolutionary Party.

29 Russian troops withdraw from Estonia and, on 30, from Latvia.

31 in Northern Ireland, Irish Republican Army announces complete cessation of violence (16 Sept, British government lifts broadcasting ban on representatives of Sinn Féin).

J **September**

6 Landslide victory for Labour Party in Barbados, led by Owen Arthur, who becomes prime minister.

8 last Russian troops leave Polish soil; foreign troops make formal departure from Berlin, Germany.

12 Parti Québecois wins overall majority in provincial legislature in Quebec, Canada.

19 US troops invade Haiti, encountering no resistance; on 26, USA lifts sanctions.

26 in USA, President Clinton's attempts to introduce health-care reforms collapse in face of opposition from legislature.

28 car ferry *Estonia* sinks in the Baltic off Finland, with estimated loss of 900 lives.

29 Willy Claes is appointed secretary general to NATO.

K **October**

13 Raoul Cédras, leader of deposed junta in Haiti, takes exile in Panama.

15 President Aristide returns to Haiti after three years in exile; on 17, Aristide agrees

partnership with a higher education institution.

In USA, President Clinton launches the Americorps national service programme (12 Sept), providing government assistance with college costs for students undertaking community service.

In USA, the Hartford Board of Education is the first Board to privatize its schools, in a bid to raise standards (3 Oct); Education Alternatives Inc takes over the management of the Board's schools (providing education for 24,000 pupils) and curriculum development, and can keep half of budget savings as profit.

In England, first women priests in Church of England are ordained in a service at Bristol Cathedral (12 March).

In USA, death of Rabbi Menachem Schneerson, leader of the Jewish Lubavitcher sect and regarded by followers as the Messiah (12 June).

Series of murders and suicides in Switzerland and Canada are linked to the religious sect the Order of the Solar Temple (Sept).

Q Science, Technology, and Discovery

Inauguration of Channel Tunnel between Britain and France, with ceremony attended by Queen Elizabeth II and President Mitterrand (6 May).

Swedish government approves 'Öresund link' project to connect Sweden with Denmark by bridge and tunnel (16 June).

In Oslo, Norway, representatives of 25 European countries and Canada sign United Nations protocol on reducing sulphur emissions, a cause of acid rain (14 June).

The Russian space mission *Soyuz-TM 18* to the *Mir* space station (launched 8 Jan) includes Dr Valeri Polyakov, who plans to spend 14 months at the space station to study the effect on the human body of being in space for the time required to travel to Mars.

Publication of first discoveries from the Keck telescope on Mauna Kea, Hawaii, USA; the telescope's mirror is made of 36 hexagonal segments.

Asteroid detected (13 March), by the Spacewatch telescope at Kitt Peak, Arizona, USA, as likely to pass nearer to Earth than the Moon (attempts to observe its passage were unsuccessful).

The Hubble Space Telescope takes clear pictures of galaxies in their infancy (published 6 Dec).

Electrical flashes in Earth's upper atmosphere first examined by plane (8 July), by team from the University of Alaska Statewide System, Fairbanks, Alaska, USA.

R Humanities

Susan Reynolds, *Fiefs and Vassals: The Medieval Evidence Reinterpreted.*

John Blair, *Anglo-Saxon Oxfordshire.*

Christopher Dyer, *Everyday Life in Medieval England.*

J R Maddicott, *Simon de Montfort.*

Pierre Chaplais, *Piers Gaveston: Edward II's Adoptive Brother.*

Wallace T MacCaffrey, *Elizabeth I.*

C P R Currie and C P Lewis (eds.), *English County Histories.*

Robert Gildea, *The Past in French History.*

Clyde A Smith et al. (eds.), *The Oxford History of the American West.*

Eric Hobsbawm, *Age of Extremes: The Short Twentieth Century, 1914–1991.*

Anthony Seldon and Stuart Ball (eds.), *Conservative Century: The Conservative Party since 1900.*

A J Nicholls, *Freedom with Responsibility: The Social Market Economy in Germany, 1918–1963.*

Gerhard L Weinberg, *A World at Arms: A Global History of World War II.*

Douglas Brinkley and David Facey-Crowther, *The Atlantic Charter.*

Michael R Beschloss and Strobe Talbot, *At the Highest Levels: The Inside Story of the End of the Cold War.*

Francis Haskell, *History and its Images: Art and the Interpretation of the Past.*

Humphrey Burton, *Leonard Bernstein.*

Jancis Robinson (ed.), *The Oxford Companion to Wine.*

William Child, *Causality, Interpretation, and the Mind.*

S Art, Sculpture, Fine Arts, and Architecture

The Tate Gallery, London, selects Bankside Power Station as the future home for London's first Museum of Modern Art.

Painting, etc:

Some Went Mad: Some Ran Away exhibition at the Serpentine Gallery, London.

Completion of the controversial cleaning of Michelangelo's paintings in the Sistine Chapel in the Vatican.

Miquel Barcelo, *Untitled* series on paper.

Sculpture:

Mona Hatoum, *Corps Etranger* (video).

Damian Hirst, *Away from the Flock.*

Architecture:

Giorgio Grassi wins competition to rebuild the Neues Museum, Berlin, Germany.

I M Pei, design for the Basil and Elise Goulandris Foundation Museum of Modern Art, Athens, Greece.

to leave the Roman Catholic priesthood in attempt to mend relationship with the Vatican, which opposed his liberation theology and had been the only sovereign state to recognize Cédras's military regime.

15 the Nobel Peace Prize is awarded to Palestinian leader Yassir Arafat, and to Shimon Peres and Yitzhak Rabin of Israel.

16 ruling centre-right coalition led by Helmut Kohl retains office after German general election, but with reduced majority.

20 Israel closes borders with West Bank and Gaza after Hamas attacks, including suicide bombing of a bus in Tel Aviv.

21 USA and North Korea reach agreement over nuclear programme, in which North Korea agrees to submit to nuclear inspections and USA agrees to finance changeover to light-water reactors and to give diplomatic recognition to North Korea.

27 Mozambique holds multi-party elections (19 Nov, results give victory for President Joaquim Chissano).

31 Lusaka Protocol is signed in latest attempt to end Angolan civil war.

L November

2 Rising in northern Pakistan in protest calling for introduction of Islamic law.

7 South Korea lifts ban on direct trade with North Korea.

7 South African government dismisses 2,000 army trainees who had gone absent without leave in protest at camp conditions and the failure to integrate ANC's military wing into new National Defence Force.

8 UN Security Council sets up International Criminal Tribunal for Rwanda to prosecute those responsible for genocide.

8 Democrats suffer dramatic defeat in US mid-term elections; Republicans gain a majority in the Senate and win control of the House of Representatives for first time in 40 years.

9 in Sri Lanka, Prime Minister Chandrika Kumaratunga becomes first woman president; her mother takes over as prime minister.

10 Iraq recognizes independent sovereignty of Kuwait.

10 in Angola, Huambo, the main stronghold of UNITA, falls to government forces.

11 USA ends arms embargo against former Yugoslavia.

12 (–13) riots and demonstrations in East Timor draw attention to oppression by Indonesian authorities.

17 Albert Reynolds resigns as prime minister of Republic of Ireland after collapse of his coalition government following the appointment of controversial attorney general Harry Whelehan as president of the High Court by Reynolds and Fianna Fáil ministers in absence of Labour Party colleagues (11 Nov).

18 violent clashes in Gaza Strip between Palestinian police force and supporters of Hamas and Islamic Jihad.

21 (–25) NATO airstrikes on Serb positions in Bosnia-Herzegovina in response to bombing of Bihac.

22 Italian Prime Minister Silvio Berlusconi is revealed to be under investigation for bribery.

25 (–26) in breakaway Russian republic of Chechenya, opposition forces with Russian backing launch unsuccessful attack on the capital Grozny; on 29, Yeltsin issues an ultimatum, requiring both sides in Chechenya to lay down their arms.

27 (–28) Norwegian referendum rejects EU membership.

M December

11 Russian forces invade the breakaway republic of Chechenya.

14 President Yeltsin of Russia issues ultimatum to leader of Chechen rebels, Dzhokhar Dudayev: lay down arms or face invasion of Chechen capital Grozny.

15 in Republic of Ireland, following the resignation of Albert Reynolds as prime minister, John Bruton of Fine Gael forms a new coalition and becomes prime minister.

20 Jimmy Carter, former president of the USA, negotiates cease-fire in Bosnia-Herzegovina, beginning on 23 Dec and lasting for four months.

21 warring factions of Liberia sign peace agreement in Ghana, ending civil war.

22 Silvio Berlusconi, the new prime minister of Italy, resigns to avoid probable defeat in no-confidence vote in parliament.

31 Russian forces launch offensive against Grozny, the capital of the breakaway republic of Chechenya.

31 warring parties in Bosnia-Herzegovina sign further accord calling for 'complete cessation of hostilities'.

Enzo Piano Building Workshop, Kansai Airport Terminal Building, Japan.

T Music
George Benjamin, *Sudden Time*.
Harrison Birtwistle, *The Second Mrs Kong* (opera).
Peter Maxwell Davies, Symphony No. 5.
John Tavener, *The Apocalypse*.
Xaver Paul Thomas, *Draussen vor der Tür* (opera).
Judith Weir, *Blond Eckbert* (opera).
All-4-One, 'I Swear'.
The Beastie Boys, *Ill Communication*.
Blur, *Parklife*.
Mariah Carey, *Music Box*.
Elvis Costello, *Brutal Youth*.
D-Ream, 'Things Can Only Get Better'.
M People, *Elegant Slumming*.
Oasis, *Definitely Maybe*.
Pink Floyd, *The Division Bell*.
Prince, *Come*.
REM, *Monster*.
Rolling Stones, *Voodoo Lounge*.
Snoop Doggy Dogg, *Doggy Style*.
Wet Wet Wet, 'Love Is All Around'.
Kurt Cobain of Nirvana commits suicide (8 April).
Rise of 'Jungle Music' in Britain.
In Rome, Italy, a judge rules (30 Dec) that US pop star Michael Jackson plagiarized a song by Italian singer Al Bano and bans the sale of Jackson's album *Dangerous* on which the song ('Will You Be There?') appears.

U Literature and Drama
John Barth, *Once Upon a Time*.
Harold Brodkey, *Profane Friendship*.
James Broughton, *Little Sermons on the Big Joy* (poems).
Peter Carey, *The Unusual Life of Tristan Smith*.
Jonathan Coe, *What a Carve Up*.
E L Doctorow, *The Waterworks*.
Paul Durcan, *Give Me Your Hand* (poems).
Shusaku Endo, *Deep River*.
James Fenton, *Out of Danger* (poems).
William Gaddis, *A Frolic of His Own*.
Joseph Heller, *Closing Time*.
Alan Hollinghurst, *The Floating Star*.
John Irving, *A Son of the Circus*.
Amin Maalouf, *The Rock of Tanios*.
Hilary Mantel, *A Cold Climate*.
Candia McWilliam, *Debatable Land*.
V S Naipaul, *A Way in the World*.
Susan Powers, *The Grass Dancer*.
Barbara Trapido, *Juggling*.
Russian writer Alexander Solzhenitsyn returns to Russia after 20 years in exile (27 May).

Drama:
Edward Albee, *Three Tall Women*.
Terry Johnson, *Dead Funny*.
David Mamet, *The Cryptogram*.
Arthur Miller, *Broken Glass*.
Robert le Page, *The Seven Streams of the River Ota*.

V Births and Deaths
Feb 19 Derek Jarman dies (52).
April 22 Richard Nixon dies (81).
July 29 Dorothy Hodgkin dies (84).
Sept 17 Karl Popper dies (92).
Dec 4 G R Elton dies (73).
Dec 13 Antoine Pinay dies (102).
Dec 20 Dean Rusk dies (85).
Dec 24 John Osborne dies (65).

W Everyday Life
President Clinton of USA, who studied at Oxford University, England, from 1968 to 1970 but left without taking a degree, returns to Oxford for award of an honorary doctorate of civil law by diploma (8 June).
In USA, Frank Corder, a truck-driver from Maryland, commits suicide by crashing a two-seater Cessna aircraft on to the south lawn of the White House (12 Sept).
Russian presidential plane lands at Shannon airport in Republic of Ireland, but President Yeltsin remains on board, failing to meet the prime minister of Ireland who was waiting for him on the runway (30 Sept).

X Sport and Recreation
In chess, Peter Leko becomes the world's youngest-ever grand master (Jan 30).
In cricket, Indian bowler Kapil Dev takes his 432nd Test wicket when playing against Sri Lanka at Ahmedabad, India, setting a new world record (8 Feb).
The West Indies cricket team dismisses England for 46 (30 March), the lowest total reached by an English side since 1887.
West Indian cricketer Brian Lara sets four records: he makes highest individual Test scores of 375 runs (18 April, playing against England in Antigua) and 501 runs (6 June, playing in England for Warwickshire at Edgbaston); during the June match he also achieves a record seven centuries in eight innings and scores a record 390 runs in one day (3 and 6 June respectively).
Andrés Escobar, the Colombian soccer player who scored an own goal in the match that eliminated Colombia from the World Cup, is murdered on his return to Medellín (2 July).
Brazil wins the soccer World Cup final, held at Pasadena, California, USA, defeating Italy on penalties after extra time (17 July).

Financial crisis in Mexico ... Bomb attack in Oklahoma City ...
Assassination of Itzhak Rabin ... Peace treaty for Bosnia-Herzegovina ...

A **January**

1 Cease-fire begins in Bosnia-Herzegovina (agreed 31 Dec 1994).

1 Austria, Finland, and Sweden join the European Union (1 Jan), increasing the Union's population from 345 million to 368 million.

2 in Chechenya, Russia, Chechen fighters repel the Russian offensive against the capital Grozny (started 31 Dec 1994); Russian army resumes offensive the following day.

3 financial crisis in Mexico as value of the peso (floated Dec 1994) falls; President Ernesto Zedillo announces spending cuts, agreements with unions on wages, and international credit facilities.

4 in USA, inauguration of the 104th Congress; Newt Gingrich is elected speaker of the House of Representatives, the first Republican speaker since 1955. The Republican-dominated House immediately abolishes three minor committees and many subcommittees, and sets a six-year term limit for chairmen and maximum tenure of eight years for the speaker.

5 Speaker Newt Gingrich embarks on the 'Contract with America', the programme of legislation proposed by the Republicans in the Nov 1994 elections which they intend to implement in the first 100 days of Congress.

5 former president of Malawi Hastings Banda is arrested on murder charges (trial starts 10 July; acquitted 23 Dec).

10 Japan and USA finalize financial services agreement, permitting greater access to Japan's corporate bond markets for foreign firms.

13 following the resignation of Silvio Berlusconi as prime minister of Italy (22 Dec 1994), President Oscar Scalfaro invites Lamberto Dini, an independent, to form a

Two stages of the Tour de France cycle race are held in S England (6–7 July).

English athlete Sally Gunnell wins the 400 m hurdles at the European Athletics Championships (12 Aug) and thereby becomes the first woman to hold world, Olympic, European, and Commonwealth titles, and the world record at the same time.

In USA, proposed capping of baseball players' salaries results in strike (12 Aug–2 April 1995) and first-ever cancellation of the World Series.

British golfer Nick Faldo wins the 'Million Dollar Challenge' held at Sun City, South Africa; his prize of $1 million is the largest prize ever in golf.

ᵧ Media

In Britain, control of the *Independent* and the *Independent on Sunday* is acquired by a consortium led by the Mirror Group Newspapers (18 March).

Newspaper price war in Britain: the *Telegraph* cuts its sale price (22 June) in response to price cut by *The Times* in 1993; the *Independent* follows (31 July).

Films:

The Adventures of Priscilla, Queen of the Desert (director, Stephen Elliot).

L'Enfer (director, Claude Chabrol).
Faraway, So Close (director, Wim Wenders).
Forrest Gump (director, David Zemeckis; starring Tom Hanks).
Four Weddings and a Funeral (director, Mike Newell).
Geronimo (director, Walter Hill).
Leon (director, Luc Bresson).
Natural Born Killers (director, Oliver Stone).
Pulp Fiction (director and writer, Quentin Tarantino).
Quiz Show (director, Robert Redford).
Speed (director, Jan de Bont; starring Keanu Reeves).
Three Colours Red (director, Krzystof Kieslowski).

Radio:

In Britain, the BBC launches Radio Five Live, a channel dedicated to news and sport (28 March).

Television:

New programmes in Britain include: *Beyond the Clouds* (Channel 4), about life in a Chinese town; *Charles — The Private Man, The Public Role* (ITV); *Middlemarch* (BBC), based on the Novel by George Eliot; *Thatcher: The Downing Street Years*.

Trial of O J Simpson ... Collapse and rescue of Barings bank ...
Pope apologizes to women ... Radio presenter deceives Queen ...

○ Politics, Government, Law, and Economy

Vernon Bogdanor, *The Monarchy and the Constitution.*

Ivor Crewe and Anthony King, *SDP: The Birth, Life, and Death of the Social Democratic Party.*

George M Fredrickson, *Black Liberation: A Comparative History of Black Ideologies in the United States and South Africa.*

Francis Fukuyama, *Trust: The Social Virtues and the Creation of Prosperity.*

Newt Gingrich, *To Renew America.*

Will Hutton, *The State We're In.*

Max Kaas, Kenneth Newton, Elinor Scarbrough (eds.), *Beliefs in Government* (5 volumes).

Christopher Lasch, *The Revolt of the Elites and the Betrayal of Democracy.*

The imam of the main Paris mosque, Dalil Boubakeur, presents a 'Muslim Charter' and announces the foundation of a Representative Council of Muslims (10 Jan).

The British Labour Party replaces 'clause IV' of its 1918 constitution (advocating public ownership) with a statement of aims and values (adopted by executive committee 13 March; confirmed by special party conference 29 April).

The Nolan Report on standards in British public life (commissioned in 1994 after the revelation that two MPs had accepted payment for asking questions in the House of Commons; published 11 May) recommends: appointment of a Parliamentary Commissioner for Standards; disclosure of MPs' parliament-related consultancy work and remuneration; that ministers who wish to accept business appointments within two years of leaving office should obtain permission from an advisory committee; appointment of an independent commissioner to scrutinize appointments to government (new government sworn in 17 Jan).

13 as financial crisis in Mexico worsens, President Clinton of the USA authorizes loan guarantees of US$40 billion to stabilize the peso and prevent Mexico from defaulting on short-term debts (31, guarantees increased to $50.76 billion).

17 earthquake in the Kansai region of Japan, which devastates the city of Kobe, kills over 5,000, and leaves 310,000 homeless.

19 in Grozny, Chechenya, Russian troops capture the presidential palace, main centre of Chechen resistance.

26 in USA, the House of Representatives approves constitutional amendment requiring a balanced budget by 2002, as proposed in the Republicans' 'Contract with America' (2 March, the amendment fails to secure the necessary two-thirds support in the Senate by one vote).

28 USA and Vietnam agree to open liaison offices in each other's capital and exchange diplomats.

30 following heavy rain in north-west Europe, 250,000 people in the Netherlands leave their homes in the country's largest peacetime evacuation when major rivers threaten to burst their banks (–1 Feb).

B February

8 In Russia, the pro-separatist president of Chechenya, Dzhokhar Dudayev, announces that he and his military units are leaving the capital Grozny, conceding its loss; fighting continues to the south and east of Grozny.

8 500,000 miners from 200 of Russia's 228 coal mines hold a day-long 'warning strike', demanding payment of wage arrears.

21 in South Africa, the Inkatha Freedom Party led by Chief Gatsha Buthelezi walks out of parliament (5 March, agrees to return).

22 at press conference in Belfast, Northern Ireland, the prime ministers of Ireland and Britain, John Bruton and John Major, present a 37-page framework document for all-party peace negotiations over the future of Northern Ireland.

28 President Lee Teng-hui of Taiwan unveils plaque commemorating native Taiwanese massacred by Nationalist troops from the Chinese mainland on 28 Feb 1947 (23 March, Taiwan's parliament approves payment of compensation to victims' relatives).

C March

2 Giulio Andreotti, former prime minister of Italy, is sent for trial charged with member-

ship of the mafia (26 Sept, trial opens in Palermo, Sicily).

3 UN troops complete withdrawal from Somalia in Operation United Shield.

5 in Estonia, general election is won by the Coalition Party of former communists and the Rural People's Union, ousting the reformist Fatherland Party.

5 all members of Hong Kong's regional and urban councils are elected for the first time; 'pro-democracy' parties do well.

6 Russian army claims complete control of Grozny, capital of rebel Chechenya.

9 President Ernesto Zedillo of Mexico announces further austerity measures in attempt to stem his country's financial crisis and the fall in value of the peso.

9 Canadian patrol boats seize a Spanish trawler just outside Canada's territorial waters (crew released 15 March).

10 in USA, President Clinton's nominee for director of the CIA, General Michael Carns, withdraws after it is revealed that he violated immigration and labour laws in his employment of a Filipino man.

11 in Burundi, murder of Ernest Kabushemeye, minister of mines and energy and Hutu leader of the Rally of the Burundian People, sparking off ethnic clashes, the flight of refugees, and fears of genocide similar to the 1994 massacres in Rwanda.

16 President Clinton meets Gerry Adams, leader of the Irish party Sinn Féin, at the White House, Washington, DC, and permits him to raise funds in the USA.

20 on the underground railway in Tokyo, Japan, a release of nerve gas kills 12, injures about 5,000 and paralyzes the system; on 22, police raid the offices of the Aum Shinrikyo religious sect (founded 1987) in Kamikuishiki, S Honshu; 16 May, the sect's leader, Shoko Asahara, is arrested.

20 truce in Bosnia-Herzegovina broken, when the Bosnian army attacks Serb positions; Serbs respond with attacks on government forces and Muslim towns (–30).

26 seven members of the European Union (Belgium, France, Germany, Luxembourg, Netherlands, Portugal, Spain) remove internal border controls and tighten controls on external borders.

27 President Nelson Mandela dismisses his wife Winnie from her cabinet position for insubordination (reinstated 11 April because Mandela had failed to undertake required consultations with political leaders; dismissed again 14 April).

27 Jim Bolger, prime minister of New Zealand, meets President Clinton during the first visit to the USA of a New Zealand

'quangos'. On 6 Nov MPs vote for compulsory declaration of members' earnings from parliament-related consultancy work, against government recommendation.

In USA, legislation passed under the Republicans' 'Contract with America' includes the Unfunded Mandates Bill (signed 22 March), which prohibits federal government from imposing unfunded tasks on states, and the Shareholder Lawsuits Bill (vetoed by President Clinton 19 Dec, veto overridden 22 Dec). Three bills to impose term limits on Congress members are defeated; a fourth bill is passed, but by an insufficient majority required for a constitutional amendment (29 March).

The US Supreme Court rules, in US Term Limits, Inc. v. Thornton, that state legislation to limit the number of terms served by representatives in the federal Congress is unconstitutional (22 May).

In Miller v. Johnson, the US Supreme Court rules that it is unconstitutional for race to be used as a 'predominant factor' in drawing boundaries for electoral districts (29 June).

China makes agreement with USA (26 Feb) for protection of intellectual property rights in China (the USA was concerned to limit Chinese pirating of US material).

In South Africa, the Constitutional Court rules that the death penalty is incompatible with the Bill of Rights included in the interim constitution (June).

In USA, African-American former football star O J Simpson is tried for murder of his former wife Nicole Brown Simpson and her friend Ronald Goldman (on 12 June 1994); trial (popularly dubbed the 'trial of the century') opens 24 Jan, Simpson is acquitted on 3 Oct in a verdict widely ascribed to racial motives.

In Britain, Rosemary West is given 10 life sentences (22 Nov) for murder of 10 young women and girls, most of whom had been buried at her home in Gloucester. Her husband, Fred, who had been charged with 9 of the murders and the murder of his first wife, had committed suicide by hanging in prison on 1 Jan.

Inauguration (1 Jan) of the World Trade Organization, successor organization to the General Agreement on Tariffs and Trade, to regulate commercial relations between the signatories of the GATT international trade agreement.

Inauguration (1 Jan) of the Southern Common Market or Mercosur, the world's fourth largest free-trade grouping, comprising Argentina, Brazil, Paraguay, and Uruguay.

Britain's oldest merchant bank, Barings, collapses (in administration 26 Jan) after

Nicholas Leeson, a futures trader based in Singapore, accumulates losses of £625 million. Barings' main operating sections and liabilities for Far East losses are sold to the Netherlands-based Internationale Nederlanden Groep NV for £1 (6 March). Leeson is arrested at Frankfurt airport (2 March) and eventually agrees to return to Singapore (29 Oct) where he pleads guilty to two charges of deception and cheating (sentenced to 6½ years in prison, 2 Dec).

In Japan, bond trader Toshihide Iguchi of Daiwa Bank is charged (26 Sept) with incurring losses of US$1.1 billion through unauthorized dealing, the largest ever loss made by a Japanese bank. The bank's president, chairman, and two senior executives later resign.

The European Union and Turkey agree to form a trade alliance (6 March).

The US dollar reaches its lowest ever exchange rates against the German mark and Japanese yen (7 March).

In Britain, Glaxo takes over Wellcome (offer accepted 8 March), forming the world's largest pharmaceuticals company.

P **Society, Education, and Religion**

World Employment 1995, published by the International Labour Organisation (22 Feb), reports that 33 per cent (820 million people) of the global workforce are either unemployed or under-employed.

United Nations holds World Summit on Social Development in Copenhagen, Denmark (6–13 March); delegates endorse plan aimed at eradicating world poverty and combating social injustice.

Pope John Paul II publishes letter to women, acknowledging that the Roman Catholic Church had marginalized and discriminated against women, but maintains ban on women priests and reiterates that abortion is a grave sin (10 July).

The fourth United Nations World Conference on Women is held in Beijing, China (4–15 Sept), concluding with the adoption of a Platform of Action. Non-Governmental Organisations hold a parallel Forum on Women at Huairou, N of Beijing (31 Aug–8 Sept), which is marred by accusations that the Chinese authorities had harassed delegates.

In Republic of Ireland, the Dáil legalizes the provision of information about foreign abortion services (8 March; approved by Senate 14 March; declared constitutional by Supreme Court and promulgated 12 May).

In USA, it is reported that Norma McCorvey has joined the anti-abortion group Oper-

prime minister since 1984 (in Dec 1994, the US government had recognized New Zealand's ban on ships carrying nuclear weapons).

D **April**

6 US House of Representatives passes the 10th and final item in the Republicans' 'Contract with America' programme, having failed to pass only one item. By this date, however, the Senate has approved only the House procedural reforms and the Line-Item Veto Bill which would permit the president to veto items in appropriations bills without rejecting an entire bill.

9 reelection of Alberto Fujimori as president of Peru, the first person to be elected for a second consecutive term (sworn in 28 July).

16 Canada and the European Union make agreement ending their long-running dispute over fishing in NW Atlantic and providing for the conservation of fish stocks.

19 in USA, bomb explodes in car park underneath federal office block in Oklahoma City, Oklahoma, killing 166 (including 19 children) and injuring over 400, the worst terrorist attack in US history. Later in the day, Timothy McVeigh is stopped for speeding and subsequently recognized as a suspect bomber; on 21, suspect Terry Nicholas is arrested.

19 in Japan, poisonous phosgene gas is released in a crowded train at the main railway station in Yokohama; about 370 people are treated in hospital (21, gas is released in a department store in Yokohama).

22 in USA, special prosecutor Kenneth Starr separately interviews President and Hillary Clinton about their involvement in the Whitewater Development Corporation and related matters.

23 socialist Lionel Jospin is surprise victor in first round of French presidential elections with 23.3 per cent of the vote; Jacques Chirac (Gaullist) is second with 20.8 per cent.

30 cease-fire in Bosnia-Herzegovina expires; during May violence escalates.

E **May**

4 Local government elections in England and Wales produce the worst results for the Conservative Party since World War II.

7 Jacques Chirac (Gaullist) wins second round of French presidential elections with 52.6 per cent of the vote; Lionel Jospin (socialist) achieves 47.4 per cent (17, President Mitterrand transfers power to Chirac

who appoints Alain Juppé as prime minister).

7 in Kenya, conservationist and palaeontologist Richard Leakey announces plan to found new political party and accuses President Daniel arap Moi of mismanagement and corruption. (New party's name, Safina, meaning 'Noah's ark', announced on 13 June.)

10 British government minister Michael Ancram meets representatives of Sinn Féin, led by Martin McGuiness, in Belfast, Northern Ireland, the first meeting of a government minister and Sinn Féin since 1973. (24, Sir Patrick Mayhew, secretary of state for Northern Ireland, meets Gerry Adams, president of Sinn Féin, in Washington, DC, USA.)

12 Review and Extension Conference of Parties to the 1968 Treaty on Non-Proliferation of Nuclear Weapons, in New York, ends with agreement to extend the Treaty indefinitely.

14 Carlos Menem (Peronist) reelected as president of Argentina with 49.8 per cent of the vote (sworn in 8 July).

16 Polish currency, the zloty, is floated on international currency markets.

26 Bosnian Serbs begin seizure of UN troops as hostages, in response to proposed NATO air strikes; by June over 377 troops have been taken (released 2–18 June).

28 in local elections in Spain, the conservative Popular Party wins largest share of vote (43 per cent against 29 per cent for socialists), taking control of most cities.

31 Lord Owen resigns as EU mediator in former Yugoslavia; succeeded on 12 June by Carl Bildt, former prime minister of Sweden.

F **June**

3 NATO defence ministers agree creation of a Mobile Theatre Reserve (known as the 'rapid reaction force') for use in Bosnia-Herzegovina, to be operational by mid-July.

7 in televised address to parliament, the prime minister of Australia, Paul Keating, announces a timetable for turning Australia into a republic by 2001. He also indicates his preference for the country's president to be nominated by the prime minister, to inherit many of the powers of the governor-general, and for politicians to be barred from the presidency unless they have been out of office for five years.

9 the Japanese Diet adopts a resolution expressing regret at the country's acts during World War II, but is criticized abroad for failure to apologize.

ation Rescue (11 Aug). Under the legal pseudonym Jane Roe, McCorvey had once sought a legal abortion, leading to the 1973 Supreme Court decision in Roe v. Wade which legalized abortion.

Referendum in Ireland votes to lift constitutional ban on divorce, by majority of 9,114 votes (25 Nov).

After its population had reached 1.2 billion five years earlier than expected, China announces stricter enforcement of its population control policy of 'one child per family' (14 Feb).

In the Netherlands, a district court finds Dr Henk Prins guilty of murder for killing a three-day-old severely handicapped baby (in March 1993), but withholds punishment on the ground that the killing was 'justifiable' (26 April).

Australia's Northern Territory passes the world's first voluntary euthanasia law, legalizing the killing of terminally ill patients (25 May).

The World Health Authority (WHO) reports that AIDS cases worldwide now exceed 1 million (3 Jan).

Citizenship law in Estonia extends the residence qualification for citizenship from two to five years (approved by parliament 19 Jan).

Lithuanian is established by law as the country's official language (approved by parliament 31 Jan).

The Netherlands government announces (9 Feb) the end of military conscription (from 1 March).

The Netherlands parliament makes denial of the Jewish Holocaust a criminal offence (3 Feb).

Mary Fulbrook, *Anatomy of a Dictatorship: Inside the GDR 1949–1989*.

Romanian parliament prescribes Romanian as the language of tuition and examination in universities and colleges (law promulgated 24 July; minority groups protest in July and Aug).

Federal Constitutional Court in Germany rules that the practice of hanging crucifixes in the classrooms of state schools in Bavaria is contrary to the Basic Law (10 Aug). Chancellor Helmut Kohl describes the ruling as 'incomprehensible' and 30,000 people protest in Munich against the ruling (23 Sept). The Bavarian parliament passes a law permitting crucifixes unless parents object (13 Dec).

The Synod of the Evangelical–Lutheran Church in Sweden accepts (28 Aug) a government proposal to separate Church and State by 2000, ending the establishment created in 1527.

Q Science, Technology, and Discovery

At the international climate conference held in Melbourne, Australia, it is reported that periodic disruptions of surface currents (which may cause climate changes) have been discovered in the Atlantic and Indian Oceans.

Russian cosmonaut Valeri Poliakov, on board the *Mir* space station, breaks record for the longest stay in space with his 366th day (9 Jan; returns to Earth 22 March after 439 days in space).

Russian cosmonaut Yelena Kondakova, also on the *Mir* space station, sets new record for time spent in space by a woman, returning to Earth (22 March) after 170 days.

US space shuttle *Atlantis* docks with the Russian *Mir* space station (29 June–4 July) in the first superpower link-up in space since 1975.

US craft *Galileo* launches a probe into Jupiter's atmosphere (5 Dec) and then goes into orbit around the plant (6 Dec) to conduct studies.

An outbreak of the deadly Ebola virus occurs in Zaire (confirmed by World Health Organization on 11 May).

Scientists announce the discovery of a new form of matter, called a Bose-Einstein condensate (because its existence had been predicted by Albert Einstein), created by cooling rubidium atoms to just above absolute zero.

Surgeons at Duke University, North Carolina, USA, report (April) the successful transplant of genetically altered hearts of pigs into baboons, a notable advance in trans-species operations.

Stephen Westaby of the John Radcliffe Hospital, Oxford, England, makes first implant of a battery-operated heart (23 Oct).

John Carey (ed.), *The Faber Book of Science*.

R Humanities

Felipe Fernández-Armesto, *Millennium*.

Rosamund McKitterick (ed.), *The New Cambridge Medieval History: 700–900*.

R W Southern, *Scholastic Humanism and the Unification of Europe (–)*.

R R Davies, *The Revolt of Owain Glyn Dŵr*.

Jonathan Israel, *The Dutch Republic: Its Rise, Greatness and Fall, 1477–1806*.

J M Winter, *Sites of Memory, Sites of Mourning: Studies in the Social and Cultural History of Modern Warfare*.

I C B Dear (ed.), *The Oxford Companion to the Second World War*.

Michael Kazin, *The Populist Persuasion: An American History*.

Robert H Wiebe, *Self-Rule: A Cultural History of American Democracy*.

9 the presidents of Ukraine and Russia, Leonid Kuchma and Boris Yeltsin, meeting at Sochi in Russia, reach agreement to end dispute over the former Soviet Black Sea fleet: fleet to be divided equally, with Russia then purchasing part of the Ukrainian fleet.

10 the Shell oil company begins towing its disused North Sea oil platform Brent Spar to a dumping site in the Atlantic; 16, Greenpeace activists occupy the platform; 20, following boycott of Shell petrol stations in Germany and the Netherlands, company cancels the dumping.

13 Jacques Chirac, president of France, announces series of eight nuclear tests at Mururoa atoll in the Pacific (breaking France's self-imposed halt in testing of April 1992).

14 Bosnian government forces launch major offensive against Bosnian Serb forces; in response, Bosnian Serbs renew bombardment of Sarajevo.

14 rebel Chechen unit seizes hostages in the Russian town of Budennovsk and holds them in the town hospital; 19, most hostages are freed and Chechens allowed to return to Chechenya.

22 John Major, prime minister of Britain, announces sudden resignation as leader of the Conservative Party in bid to restore his authority; 26, John Redwood, secretary of state for Wales, resigns from government and announces candidature for leadership.

23 department store collapses in Seoul, South Korea, killing 521.

23 Chechen and Russian officials make preliminary peace agreement: Chechen fighters to disarm; all but 8,000 Russian troops to leave Chechenya; elections to be held in Chechenya in Sept.

G **July**

4 John Major reelected leader of the British Conservative Party with 218 votes against 82 votes for John Redwood with 22 MPs abstaining or spoiling their ballot papers. Major's victory is followed by a cabinet reshuffle (5 July) in which Michael Heseltine is appointed deputy prime minister.

10 in Burma (now Myanmar), opposition leader Aung San Suu Kyi is unexpectedly released from house arrest (arrested July 1989); 10 Oct, is reinstated as general secretary of the National League for Democracy.

11 Serbs capture the UN-designated safe area of Srebrenica in eastern Bosnia-Herzegovina; Muslim women and children are moved to Tuzla while men are held back and allegedly massacred.

11 President Clinton announces intention of USA to establish full diplomatic relations with Vietnam.

11 President Yeltsin of Russia is rushed to hospital; on 18, in interview from hospital, admits to having had heart attack; returns to work on 7 Aug.

14 Serbs attack safe haven of Zepa in eastern Bosnia-Herzegovina, which falls on 25.

18 in USA, Senate panel begins hearings into Whitewater affair.

20 Serbs and allies attack the safe haven of Bihać in NW Bosnia-Herzegovina; on 27, Croat troops enter Bosnia to relieve pressure on Bihać.

21 (–26) China tests missiles in vicinity of Taiwan.

22 in USA, the special prosecutor investigating the Whitewater affair, Kenneth Starr, again interviews President and Mrs Clinton under oath.

25 bomb explodes on train at St Michel underground station, Paris, killing 7 and injuring 84.

26 US Senate passes bill enabling the USA unilaterally to lift the embargo on supply of arms to forces in Bosnia-Herzegovina; passed by House on 1 Aug but vetoed by President Clinton on 11 Aug.

28 Vietnam is first communist state to be admitted to the Association of South-East Asian Nations (ASEAN).

28 name of Bombay, India, is changed to Mumbai (Bambai in Hindi) following decision taken by the Maharashtra state government.

30 Chechen and Russian representatives sign peace agreement in Grozny.

H **August**

4 (–9) Croat armed forces invade and occupy the Serb-inhabited Krajina in Croatia; Serb refugees pour into Serb areas of Bosnia-Herzegovina and Serbia.

9 US government announces new initiative to seek peace between factions in Bosnia.

15 on 50th anniversary of end of World War II, the prime minister of Japan, Tomiichi Murayama, expresses a 'feeling of deep remorse' and offers 'heartfelt apology' about Japan's actions in the war.

19 six main factions in Liberian civil war sign peace accord in Abuja, Nigeria.

28 stock exchange opens in capital of Mongolia, Ulan Bator.

J **September**

1 Six-member Council of State is inaugurated in Liberia; on 3, the Council announces formation of new transitional government.

Alonzo L L Hamby, *Man of the People: A Life of Harry S Truman*.
Jonathan Keates, *Purcell: A Biography*.
Stanley Fish, *Political Correctness: Literary Studies and Political Change*.

s Art, Sculpture, Fine Art, and Architecture

Paintings and engravings from 18,000 to 15,000 BC are discovered in a network of caves near Vallon-Pont-d'Arc in southern France (18 Jan).

Centenary of the Venice Biennale, curated by Gerard Regnier (alias Jean Clair), the first non-Italian director of the visual arts for the Biennale.

First modern art museum in the Russian Federation, the Museum of Modern Russian Art, opens at Vladivostok; it includes 100 paintings donated by the collector Alexander Glezer.

Painting, etc:
Kathy Prendergast, *Two Hundred Words for Lonely* (Prendergast also wins the prize for the best young artist, the Premio Duemila, at the Venice Biennale).
Bill Viola, *Buried Secrets* (video).

Sculpture:
Christo, *Wrapped Reichstag* (Berlin).
Nam June Paik, *Cybertown* – a global community connected through the Internet.

Architecture:
Jacques Herzog and Pierre de Meuron win competition for design of the Tate Gallery of Modern Art at Bankside, London.

T Music

Alexander Goehr, *Arianne* (opera).
Benedict Mason, Clarinet Concerto.
Steve Reich, *Proverbs*.
Poul Ruders, Concerto for Viola and Orchestra.
Kaija Saariaho, *Graal Théâtre*.
Mikis Theodorakis, *Elektra* (opera).
Michael Tippett, *The Rose Lake*.
The Beatles, *Anthology 1*, 'Free As A Bird' – first new Beatles single for 25 years.
Blur, *The Great Escape*.
Bon Jovi, *These Days*.
Coolio, *Gangsta's Paradise*.
Michael Jackson, *HIStory*.
Alanis Morrisette, *Jagged Little Pill*.
Oasis, *(What's the Story) Morning Glory*.
Pink Floyd, *Pulse*.
Pulp, *Different Class*.
The Rolling Stones, *Stripped*.
Queen, *Made In Heaven*.
Simply Red, *Life*.
Bruce Springsteen, *The Ghost of Tom Joad*.
Neil Young (and Pearl Jam), *Mirrorball*.

In Britain, 'Britpop' comes to the fore: white, guitar-based bands (such as Blur, Oasis, and Pulp) playing song-based pop-rock, often influenced by the Beatles and 1960s British pop.

U Literature and Drama

Martin Amis, *The Information*.
Kate Atkinson, *Behind the Scenes at the Museum*.
Pat Barker, *The Ghost Road*.
James Elroy, *American Tabloid*.
Robert Harris, *Enigma*.
Sean O'Brien, *The Ghost Train* (poems).
Philip Roth, *Sabbath's Theater*.
Salman Rushdie, *The Moor's Last Sigh*.
Barry Unsworth, *Morality Play*.
In Britain, collapse of the Net Book Agreement (established 1 Jan 1900, whereby publishers set retail prices of books), when Penguin, HarperCollins, and Random House announce their withdrawal from the Agreement (26 Sept).

Drama:
Sebastian Barry, *The Steward of Christendom*.
Jez Butterworth, *Mojo*.
David Edgar, *Pentecost*.
David Hare, *Skylight*.
Patrick Marber, *Dealer's Choice*.
Timberlake Wertenbaker, *Break of Day*.

V Births and Deaths

May 24 Harold Wilson dies (79).
June 23 Jonas Edward Salk dies (80).
Oct 9 Alec Douglas-Home (Lord Home) dies (92).
Oct 22 Kingsley Amis dies (73).
Nov 23 Louis Malle dies (63).

W Everyday Life

Customs officers in Sweden catch a woman entering the country with 65 baby snakes hidden in her bra (Jan); she claimed that she planned to start a reptile farm.
In Canada, radio presenter Pierre Brassard, imitating prime minister Jean Chrétien, phones Queen Elizabeth II in London and broadcasts their discussion (28 Oct).

X Sport and Recreation

Rugby Football League in Britain votes for the formation of a 14-team Super League, involving British and French clubs, with play to be held during summer months (8 April); the proposal is backed by Rupert Murdoch's News International Corporation. A proposed amalgamation of several clubs is dropped after vigorous protests.
The Rugby World Cup is held in South Africa. In the final, in Johannesburg, the host nation defeats New Zealand 15–12 after extra time (24 June).

4 three US servicemen allegedly rape a 12-year-old girl in Okinawa, Japan, causing protests against US military forces in Japan.

5 first French nuclear test explosion at Mururoa atoll in the S Pacific, followed by large-scale riots on Tahiti and protests elsewhere in the Pacific region.

8 in Geneva, Switzerland, representatives of the 'Contact Group' (Britain, France, Germany, Russia, USA) and the foreign ministers of Bosnia-Herzegovina, Croatia, and Yugoslavia agree basic principles for a peace accord between the warring parties in Bosnia (foreign ministers reach further agreement in New York on 26).

11 Bosnian government forces launch offensive in western and central Bosnia-Herzegovina, which reduces Serb-controlled territory from 70 to 50 per cent.

11 Mexican government and Zapatista National Liberation Army sign accord establishing procedures for dealing with the grievances of Zapatista rebels.

11 Vladimir Meciar, prime minister of Slovakia, announces convertibility of the Slovak crown from 1 Oct; on 26, Czech republic makes koruna widely convertible from 1 Oct.

12 in France, General Jean-Louis Mourut, head of the army historical service, admits that the Dreyfus affair of 1894 was a 'military conspiracy ... partly founded on false documents'.

15 the president of Kazakhstan decrees transfer of the country's capital from Alma Ata in the south to Akmola in the north, the latter being better placed for controlling the country's largest concentration of Russians.

17 in final elections to the Legislative Council ('Legco') in Hong Kong before the restoration of Hong Kong to China, the Democratic Party wins 19 of 60 seats.

19 in USA, the *Washington Post* includes a 35,000-word manifesto insert written by the terrorist bomber known as the 'Unabomber' who had been active for 17 years.

27 Britain and Argentina make agreement for oil and gas exploration in South Atlantic SW of the Falkland Islands with a joint commission overseeing the exploration.

κ October

1 Nigeria's head of state, General Sanni Abacha, announces that military government will continue until 1 Oct 1998.

5 President Clinton of USA announces agreement of 60-day cease-fire in Bosnia-Herzegovina from 10 Oct (comes into effect on 12).

7 British MP Alan Howarth announces intention to resign from the Conservative Party and join Labour (29 Dec, MP Emma Nicholson announces resignation from Conservative Party to join Liberal Democrats).

15 Silvio Berlusconi, former prime minister of Italy, and his brother Paolo are committed for trial on corruption charges.

16 'Million Man March' held in Washington, DC, USA, organized by Louis Farrakhan, leader of the Nation of Islam. Farrakhan urges an estimated 837,000 African-American males to moral and spiritual renewal and denounces white racism.

17 armed forces in Sri Lanka launch the 'Rivirasa' ('Sunshine') offensive against Tamil rebels' stronghold of Jaffna.

20 Willi Claes, secretary general of NATO, resigns after the Belgian parliament votes to lift his immunity from prosecution so that he can be tried for alleged corruption.

26 President Yeltsin of Russia is again rushed to hospital; 27 Nov, moves to sanatorium (–26 Dec).

28 fire in underground railway system in Baku, Azerbaijan, kills over 300 people.

30 referendum held in Quebec; voters narrowly defeat the proposal that the province should leave the Canadian federation (50.56 per cent against, 49.44 in favour).

L November

1 Opening of peace talks between parties in conflict in Bosnia-Herzegovina, held at the Wright-Paterson airforce base near Dayton, Ohio, USA. Delegations are headed by Alija Izetbegovic, president of Bosnia; Franjo Tudjman, president of Croatia; and Slobodan Milosevic, president of Yugoslavia acting also for Bosnian Serbs.

3 Queen Elizabeth II gives royal assent in Wellington, New Zealand, to legislation returning land and granting compensation to the Tainui Maori tribe and apologizing for consequences of British aggression in late 1860s.

4 Itzhak Rabin, prime minister of Israel, is assassinated at peace rally in Tel Aviv by Jewish law student Yigal Amir, who was protesting against cession of land to Palestinians.

5 Javier Solana Madariaga, foreign secretary of Spain who had a history of opposition to NATO, is appointed secretary general of NATO.

10 Nigerian authorities hang writer Ken Saro-Wiwa and eight others who had cam-

At World Athletics Championship in Gothenberg, Sweden, Jonathan Edwards of Britain is the first person to jump over 18 m in the triple jump (7 Aug). He sets two new world records of 18.16 m (59.58 ft) and 18.29 m (60 ft).

The governing body of Rugby Union, the International Rugby Football Board, votes to end the game's 'amateur only' status (27 Aug), after Australian media magnate Kerry Packer threatened to create a breakaway professional organization.

In USA, Cal Ripken Jr of the Baltimore Orioles baseball team breaks Lou Gehrig's record of playing 2,130 consecutive games (6 Sept).

The amateur golfers of Britain and Ireland defeat the USA in the Walker Cup, held at Porthcawl, Wales (10 Sept). The final score of 14–10 is the largest margin of victory over the USA ever achieved in the competition. Shortly afterwards (24 Sept) European golfers narrowly defeat the USA in the Ryder Cup (14½–13½), held at Oak Hill Country Club, New York.

Cyclist Miguel Induráin of Spain is the first person to win the Tour de France in five successive years (23 July).

Y **Media**

In Britain, closure of *Today* (last issue 17 Nov).

David and Frederick Barclay purchase the *Scotsman* group of newspapers (3 Nov).

Film:

In USA, Steven Spielberg, Jeffrey Katzenberg, and David Geffen found Dreamworks SKG, the first major Hollywood studio to be founded since 1935.

The American President (director, Rob Reiner; starring Michael Douglas).

Apollo 13 (director, Ron Howard; starring Tom Hanks).

Babe (director, Chris Noonan).

Braveheart (director and star, Mel Gibson).

Bridges of Madison County (director, Clint Eastwood; starring Meryl Streep and Clint Eastwood).

Carrington (director, Christopher Hampton; starring Emma Thompson and Jonathan Pryce).

Casino (director, Martin Scorsese; starring Robert de Niro and Sharon Stone).

Circle of Friends (director, Pat O'Connor; starring Minnie Driver, Geraldine O'Rawe, and Saffron Burrows).

Goldeneye (director, Martin Campbell; starring Pierce Brosnan as James Bond and Judi Dench as 'M').

Heat (director, Michael Man; starring Robert de Niro and Al Pacino).

In the Heat of the Sun (director, Jiang Wen).

Land and Freedom (director, Ken Loach).

The Madness of King George (director, Nicholas Hytner; starring Nigel Hawthorne; script by Alan Bennett).

Nixon (director, Oliver Stone; starring Anthony Hopkins).

Pocahontas (directors, Mike Gabriel and Eric Goldberg).

Il Postino (director, Michael Radford; starring Massimo Troisi, who died 12 hours after the end of filming).

The Shawshank Redemption (director, Frank Darabont; starring Morgan Freeman).

Ulysses' Gaze (director, Theo Angelopoulos; starring Harvey Keitel).

Vanya on 42nd Street (director, Louis Malle).

Waterworld (director, Kevin Reynolds; starring Kevin Costner; the first film costing US$200 million).

While You Were Sleeping (director, John Turteltaub; starring Sandra Bullock).

Radio:

Launch in UK (14 Feb) of Talk Radio UK (or TRUK), a national commercial station based on the format of US shows presented by outspoken and often offensive 'shock jocks'.

Launch in the London area of Britain of Premier Radio, the country's first Christian station (10 June), and Viva, an all-women's station (3 July).

New programmes in Britain include *20/20 : A View of the Century*, written and presented by John Tusa (BBC). BBC Radio 3 broadcasts *Fairest Isle*, a festival of programmes celebrating British music, with some programmes commemorating the tercentenary of Henry Purcell's death.

Television:

Iranian parliament passes law banning import, distribution, and private use of satellite reception dishes (15 Feb).

Launch of BBC Prime and BBC Gold, British satellite channels available in Europe.

In Britain, the Princess of Wales is interviewed on the BBC's current affairs programme *Panorama* (20 Nov), attracting a record audience of 21.1 million.

New programmes in Britain include: *People's Century* (BBC), *Pride and Prejudice* (BBC).

paigned against environmental damage in the Ogoni region; 11, Nigeria is suspended from the Commonwealth.

12 Croatian government and Serb leaders sign agreement for reintegration of Eastern Slavonia, the last Serb-held part of Croatia.

13 Commonwealth admits Mozambique, a former Portuguese colony.

13 in dispute with Republicans in Congress over 1996 US budget, President Clinton blocks two temporary funding measures, resulting in closure of non-essential government functions from 14; 19, resolution provides funding to 15 Dec.

15 Alain Juppé, prime minister of France, announces reforms to social security system to reduce expenditure; followed by protest strikes and indefinite railway strike from 23 Nov after cuts in railway system are announced.

19 former communist Aleksander Kwasniewski defeats President Lech Walesa in presidential elections, winning 51.7 per cent of votes against Walesa's 48.3 per cent (Kwasniewski sworn in on 23 Dec).

20 in Sri Lanka, government forces enter Jaffna; 24, seal off the town.

20 Andreas Papandreou, 76-year-old prime minister of Greece, is rushed into hospital, suffering from pneumonia.

21 parties in Bosnia peace talks initial comprehensive plan.

27 opening of International Criminal Tribunal in Arusha, Tanzania, to handle charges arising from the conflict in Rwanda.

28 in London, on eve of President Clinton's visit to the British Isles, the prime ministers of Britain and Ireland, John Major and John Bruton, announce establishment of three-man commission to examine decommissioning of terrorist arms and the aim of holding all-party talks on Northern Ireland by end of Feb 1996.

30 President Clinton visits Northern Ireland; 1 Dec, visits Dublin, Ireland.

M December

14 Formal signing of peace plan for Bosnia-Herzegovina at the Elysée Palace, Paris; creates two entities within Bosnia, a Muslim–Croat federation with 51 per cent of territory and a Serb republic with 49 per cent. UN peacekeeping force will be replaced by NATO implementation force.

16 many US government functions are again closed as temporary finance provision expires and budget dispute between President Clinton and Republicans in Congress continues.

23 bodies of 16 members of the Solar Temple religious sect are found in a clearing near Grenoble, France; 14 were probably shot by two who then committed suicide.

Index

The entries in this index refer to a year and a letter. For example, for '1943 D' the reader should turn to the year '1943', then look for the letter 'D' in the margin. Letters A to M are on the left-hand pages, O to Y on the right-hand pages.

Air France, 1933 O, 1945 O, 1976 F
Air India, 1985 F
Aisne, River, 1914 J, 1917 D
Aisne, First Battle of the, 1914 J
Aisne, Second Battle of the, 1917 D
Aitape, 1944 D
Aitken, Max, 1977 Y
Ajman, 1971 M
Al-Akhbar, 1944 Y
Akhmatova, Anna, 1921 U
Akihito, Emperor of Japan, 1933 V, 1989
    A, 1990 L
Akimoto, Matsuyo, 1989 U
Akitek, B E P, 1979 S
Akmola, 1995 J
Akrotiri, 1967 R
Akuffo, Fred, 1978 G, 1979 F
Alabama, 1963 P
Alain-Fournier, 1913 U
El Alamein, 1942 F, 1942 K
Alaska, 1903 K, 1906 E, 1959 A, 1968 O,
    1977 O, 1989 C,
Alaska, University of, 1994 Q
Alaska Highway, 1942 O
Albania, 1921 L, 1945 L, 1987 J
    allied with China, 1966 L
    atheist state, 1968 P
    Balkan Wars, 1912 M
    becomes kingdom, 1928 J
    becomes republic, 1924 M
    Corfu Channel dispute, 1949 O
    defensive alliance with Italy, 1927 L
    diplomatic relations with Greece
        restored, 1971 E
    elections, 1991 C, 1992 C
    frontier treaty, 1926 G
    heads of state, 1982 L
    Hoxha dies, 1985 D
    independence, 1917 F
    Italy invades, 1939 D
    Khrushchev visits, 1959 E
    and Kosovo, 1990 B
    leaves Warsaw Pact, 1968 J
    Mehmet Shehu commits suicide, 1981
        M
    Muslim rising, 1937 E
    People's Republic, 1946 A
    poor relations with Yugoslavia, 1927
        F
    principality created, 1913 E, G
    refugees from, 1991 A, C
    religion in, 1990 P
    revolt, 1910 D
    Serbs invade, 1913 K
    strikes, 1991 F
    Treaty of Tirana, 1926 L
    USSR breaks off relations with, 1961
        M
    Warsaw Pact, 1955 E
    World War I, 1918 E
    and Yugoslavia, 1988 J
Albanian Orthodox Church, 1937 P
Albee, Edward, 1928 V, 1959 U, 1960 U,
    1961 U, 1962 U, 1966 U, 1994 U
Albeniz, Isaac, 1909 T
Albers, Josef, 1949 S
Albert I, King of the Belgians, 1909 M,
    1926 G, 1934 B
Albert, Eugen d', 1903 T
Albert, Lake, 1910 E
Albert of Liège, King of the Belgians,
    1993 G
Alberta, 1905 J
Albertini, Luigi, 1952 R
Albertville, 1964 F
Alcalá Zamora, Niceto, 1931 D, M
Alcatraz Island, 1934 W, 1963 O

Alcock, J W, 1919 Q
Alcoholics Anonymous, 1935 P
Aldeburgh Festival, 1948 T
Aldermaston Marches, 1958 O, 1963 D
Aldershot, 1972 A
Aldiss, Brian, 1985 U
Aldrich, Robert, 1967 Y
Aldwych Theatre, London, 1905 U
Alea, Tomas Guttierez, 1993 Y
Alekseva, Lisa, 1981 M
Alemán, Miguel, 1946 G
Aleppo, 1980 C
Aleshkovsky, Yuz, 1986 U
Alessandri, Arturo, 1932 M
Aleutian Islands, 1942 F, 1943 E
Alexander, King of Greece, 1917 F, 1920
    G, M
Alexander I, King of Serbia, 1901 B,
    1903 F, 1918 M, 1929 A, 1934 K
Alexander, A V, 1940 E
Alexander, General, 1945 D
Alexander, Samuel, 1920 R
Alexander Kielland oil platform, 1980 C
Alexandra, Queen of England, 1902 H
Alexandra, Tsarina, 1916 M
Alexandria, 1921 E, 1951 X
Alexandropol, Treaty of, 1920 M
Alfonsín, Raoül, 1983 K, L, 1989 E
Alfonso XIII, King of Spain, 1902 E,
    1923 J, 1931 D
Alford, Kenneth J, 1913 T
Alfvén, Hugo, 1919 T
Algeciras, Act of, 1906 D
Algeciras Conference, 1906 A
Algeria, 1992 G
    admitted to Arab league, 1962 H
    Algerian War, 1955 H, J, 1958 E, K,
        1960 A, F
    civilian government restored, 1958 M
    constitution, 1963 J
    coup, 1961 D
    earthquakes, 1980 K
    and Egypt, 1988 L
    Evian agreements, 1962 C
    Ferhat Abbas proclaims Provisional
        Government, 1958 J
    France sends troops to, 1954 M
    French political crisis, 1958 E
    general elections, 1991 M, 1992 A
    independence, 1962 G
    insurrection, 1954 K
    joins Arab Magreb Union, 1989 O
    local elections, 1990 F
    presidents, 1992 F
    prime ministers, 1961 H, 1962 J
    referendums, 1958 J, 1959 J, 1961 A
    riots, 1988 K, 1991 F
    state of emergency, 1992 B
    World War II, 1942 L
Algiers, 1943 H, 1960 A, 1991 F
Ali, Mohammed, Shah of Persia, 1908 F
Ali, Muhammad (boxer), 1942 V, 1974
    X, 1975 X, 1978 X
Ali, Muhammad (prime minister of
    Pakistan), 1953 D
Ali, Rashid, 1941 D, E
Ali ibn-Hussein, King of the Hejaz, 1924
    K
Ali-Zade, Frangis, 1991 T
Alia, Ramiz, 1982 L, 1985 D, 1992 J
Alka-Seltzer, 1931 W
All-4-One, 1994 T
All-African People's Conference, Accra,
    1958 M
All-America Football Conference, 1946
    X
'All Blacks' (New Zealand Rugby
    Union), 1905 X, 1925 X

All England Lawn Tennis and Croquet
    Club, 1922 X
All-India Congress Committee, 1945 J
All-India Congress Party, 1937 C, D
All India Muslim League, 1906 O
All-India Village Industries Association,
    1934 K
Allegheny river, 1937 P
Allen, P S, 1906 R
Allen, Steve, 1954 Y
Allen, Woody, 1935 V, 1969 U, 1972 Y,
    1977 Y, 1979 Y, 1983
    Y, 1986 Y, 1989 Y
Allenby, Edmund, 1917 F, M, 1919 C
Allende, Isabel, 1982 U, 1993 U
Allende, Salvador, 1970 J, 1972 D, 1973 J
Allgemeiner Deutscher
    Nachrichtendienst, 1946 Y
Allied Control Commission, 1945 F, L,
    1946 C, 1947 C, 1948 C
Allied Supreme Council (World War I),
    1919 L, 1921 E, H
Alliluyeva, Svetlana, 1967 C
Allitt, Beverley, 1993 O
Alma Ata, 1995 J
Alma-Tadema, Lawrence, 1909 S
The Almanac Singers, 1940 T
Almodovar, Pedro, 1988 Y
Alpert, Herb, 1962 T
Alsace-Lorraine, 1911 E, 1913 L
Alther, Lisa, 1976 U
Althusser, Louis, 1965 R, 1976 R
Altizer, T J, 1966 P
Altman, Robert, 1925 V, 1970 Y, 1973 Y,
    1975 Y, 1992 Y
Alvarez, 1959 Q
Alvin Theatre, New York, 1927 U, 1930
    T
Alwyn, William, 1977 T
Amalgamated Society of Railway
    Servants, 1901 O
Amalgamated Union of Engineering
    Workers, 1943 P, 1972 L
Amanullah, Emir, 1929 E
Amasia Protocol, 1919 F
Amato, Giuliano, 1993 C
Ambassador Theatre, New York, 1921 U
Amdahl, Gene, 1967 Q
American Air Force Band, 1942 T
American Automobile Association
    (AAA), 1902 P
American Bar Association, 1908 O
American Broadcasting Co (ABC), 1943
    Y
American City Planning Institute, 1916 P
American Civil Liberties Union, 1920 P
American Enterprise Association, 1943 O
American Expeditionary Force, 1919 P
American Express, 1958 W
American Federation of Arts, 1909 S
American Federation of Labor (AFL),
    1900 P, 1935 P, 1936 P, 1937 P,
    1955 P
American Federation of Musicians, 1901
    T, 1935 T
American Football Conference (AFC),
    1969 W
American Football League, 1960 X, 1966
    X
American Jewish Committee, 1906 P
American League of Professional
    Baseball Clubs, 1900 X
American Legion, 1919 P
American Medical Association, 1937 P
American Newspaper Guild, 1933 Y
American Professional Football
    Association, 1919 X

Ardizzone, Edward, 1940 S
Arendt, Hannah, 1951 O, 1958 R, 1961 O, 1963 O
Argenteo, Dominick, 1976 T
Argentina, 1914 E, 1987 J
  ban on political parties, 1982 H
  basketball, 1950 X
  commercial agreement with Spain, 1946 K
  constitution, 1956 E
  coup, 1976 C
  disputed ownership of Falkland Islands, 1955 E
  divorce legalized, 1954 P
  Eva Perón dies, 1952 G
  Falklands conflict, 1976 A, 1982 C-G, 1983 A
  Falklands conflict trial, 1985 D
  general elections, 1973 C, 1983 K
  human rights, 1983 H, 1985 M
  Irigoyen resigns, 1930 J
  lands in South Georgia, 1982 C
  military rule, 1983 M
  Perón goes into exile, 1955 J
  presidents, 1946 B, 1951 L, 1973 J, 1974 G, 1981 M, 1982 F, 1989 E, 1995 E
  re-establish relations, 1979 G
  revokes oil concessions, 1928 J
  riots, 1973 F
  Southern Common Market, 1995 O
  Wheat Agreement, 1933 H
Argov, Shlomo, 1982 F
Ariane rockets, 1979 Q
Arias Plan, 1987 H
Arica, 1922 G
Arica-Tacna dispute, 1929 F
Ariès, Philippe, 1960 R, 1977 R
Arif, Abdul Rahman, 1966 D
Arif, Abdul Salam, 1963 B
Aristide, Jean-Bertrand, 1990 M, 1991 J, 1993 G, 1994 K
Arizona, 1912 B, P, 1974 P
Ark Royal, 1941 L
Arkansas, 1994 C
Arkle (racehorse), 1966 X
Arlen, Harold, 1954 U
Armagh, 1968 L
Arman, 1960 S
Armenia, 1915 D, E, 1919 E, 1920 M, 1988 B, C, F, 1990 A, 1991 J, 1992 A, H
Armenian Church, 1902 D
Armitage, Kenneth, 1951 S, 1954 S
Armory Show, New York, 1913 S
Armstrong, David, 1989 R
Armstrong, E, 1933 Q
Armstrong, Gillian, 1980 Y
Armstrong, Henry 'Homicide Hank', 1938 X
Armstrong, Louis, 1901 V, 1925 T, 1932 T, 1964 T, 1971 V
Armstrong, Neil, 1969 G
Army Appropriations Bill (US), 1901 C
Army Bill (Germany), 1911 B
Army Comrades Association (Irish Free State), 1932 B
Arnaz, Desi, 1951 Y
Arness, James, 1956 Y
Arnhem, 1944 J
Arnim, General Hans-Jürgen von, 1943 D
Arnold, Malcolm, 1973 T, 1976 T, 1991 T
Arnold, T, 1937 O
Arnstein, M, 1968 Q
Aron, Raymond, 1938 R
Arp, Jean, 1916 S, 1932 S, 1933 S

Arrabel, Fernando, 1958 U
Arras, 1917 C
Arras, Battle of, 1917 D
Arsenal Football Club, 1928 X, 1935 X, 1993 X
Art Institute of Chicago, 1925 U
Artaud, Antonin, 1938 U
Arthur, Owen, 1994 J
Artois, Battle of, 1915 E, J
Arts Council of Britain, 1945 T
Arup, Ove, 1988 V
Asaff, George, 1915 T
Asahara, Shoko, 1995 C
Asahi Shimbun, 1980 Y
Ascari, Alberto, 1952 X
Ash, Timothy Garton, 1993 O
Ashanti, 1957 B
Ashanti Kingdom, 1901 J
Ashanti rising, 1900 L
Ashberry, John, 1975 U
Ashe, Arthur, 1943 V, 1975 X, 1993 V
Ashfield, 1977 D
Ashley, Laura, 1925 V, 1967 W, 1985 V
Ashley, Robert, 1984 T
Ashton, T S, 1948 R
Asiago offensive, 1916 E
Asian Games, New Delhi, 1951 X
Asian Legal Consultative Committee, 1957 D
Asian Socialist Conference, Rangoon, 1953 A
Asimov, Isaac, 1920 V, 1951 U, 1983 U, 1992 V
Asociación Interamericana de Radiodifusión (AIR), 1946 Y
Asquith, Anthony, 1948 Y
Asquith, H H, 1925 A
Asquith, H H, 1905 M, 1911 G
  becomes prime minister, 1908 D
  coal strike, 1912 C
  death, 1928 V
  dissolves parliament, 1909 M
  general elections, 1910 L, 1922 L
  Imperial Conference, 1911 E
  World War I, 1914 C, 1915 E, 1916 M
Assad, Hafez al, 1979 L, 1987 L
Assali, Sabri el, 1954 B
Assam, 1944 C, 1983 B
Associated Press, 1900 Y, 1952 Y, 1958 Y
Association for the Advancement of Creative Musicians, 1965 T
Association Football Players' Union, 1907 X
Association of South-East Asian Nations (ASEAN), 1967 O, 1989 O, 1995 G
Astaire, Fred, 1935 Y, 1987 V
Astier Laws, 1919 P
Astley, Rich, 1988 T
Aston, University of, 1966 P
Aston, F W, 1919 Q
Aston Villa football club, 1979 X
Astor, Colonel J J (Lord Astor), 1923 Y
Astor, Mary, 1921 Y
Astor, Lady Nancy, 1919 P
Asturias, Miguel, 1946 U
Aswan Dam, 1902 M
Aswan High Dam, 1956 G, 1958 K, 1959 L, 1960 R, 1971 B
AT&T *see* American Telephone and Telegraph Co
Atatürk, Kemal (Mustafa Kemal):
  Amasia Protocol, 1919 F
  death, 1938 L, V
  elections, 1923 K, 1927 J
  Erzurum Congress, 1919 G
  name, 1934 P

The New Turkey, 1927 O
  new Turkish assembly opens, 1920 D
  war with Greece, 1921 H
Athenia, 1939 J
Athens:
  bomb attack on Israeli aircraft, 1968 M
  military coup, 1967 D
  riots, 1901 P, 1954 M
  terrorist attacks, 1973 H
  World War I, 1916 K
  World War II, 1944 K, L, M
Athens Polytechnic, 1975 M
Athos, Mount, 1913 P, 1924 P
Atiyah, P, 1931 V, 1979 O
Atkin, Lord, 1932 O
Atkinson, Kate, 1995 U
Atkinson, R, 1929 Q
Atkinson, Rowan, 1983 Y
Atlanta World, 1928 Y
Atlantic Charter, 1941 H
Atlantic Congress, 1959 F
Atlantic Ocean:
  aircraft crossings, 1941 Q
  Alcock and Brown cross, 1919 Q
  cross-Atlantic radio signals, 1901 Q
  currents, 1995 Q
  transatlantic telephone services, 1927 W
Atlantis space shuttle, 1985 Q, 1995 Q
Atlas, Charles, 1926 W
Atlas computer, 1961 Q
Atlas satellites, 1958 Q
Atletico Madrid, 1963 X
Atomic Energy Commission, 1946 M, 1949 G, 1950 A, Q
Atomic Research Centre, 1945 Q
Attali, Jacques, 1993 O
Attenborough, David, 1954 Y, 1967 X, 1979 Y, 1990 Y
Attenborough, Richard, 1923 V, 1969 Y, 1982 Y, 1993 Y
Atterberg, Kurt, 1933 T
Attica Prison, New York, 1971 J
Attlee, Clement, 1936 F
  becomes leader of Labour Party, 1935 K, L
  death, 1967 V
  general elections, 1945 G, 1950 B
  Lynskey tribunal, 1948 L
  party political broadcasts, 1947 Y
  retirement, 1955 M
  and Spanish Civil War, 1937 M
  World War II, 1940 E, 1942 B, 1945 G
Attu, 1942 F, 1943 E
Atwood, Margaret, 1987 U
Aubers Ridge, Battle of, 1915 E
Auden, W H, 1907 V, 1930 U, 1932 U, 1935 U, 1936 U, 1937 U, 1938 U, 1945 U, 1948 U, 1950 U, 1956 U, 1973 V
Audubon Society, 1905 P
Auerbach, Frank, 1986 S
August, Bille, 1987 Y, 1992 Y
Aulen, G, 1931 P
Aulenti, Gae, 1986 S
Auletta, 1943 J
Aum Shinrikyo sect, 1995 C
Aung San Suu Kyi, 1995 G
Auric, Georges, 1920 T, 1983 V
Auriol, Vincent, 1947 A
Aurobindo, Sri, 1950 U
Auschwitz, 1942 P, 1945 A, 1957 S
Austin, J L, 1962 R
Austin, Mary, 1903 U
Austin Motor Company, 1952 O
Austin Seven, 1922 O

Colton, California, 1907 C
Coltrane, John, 1964 T
Columbia Broadcasting System (CBS), 1927 Y, 1938 Y, 1940 Y, 1941 Y, 1948 Y, 1951 Y
Columbia Pictures, 1924 Y
Columbia Record Company, 1948 T
Columbia space shuttle, 1981 Q, 1982 Q, 1991 Q
Columbia University, New York, 1912 Y, 1924 Y, 1968 D
Columbus, Christopher, 1992 P
Columbus, New Mexico, 1916 C
Colvin, Howard, 1954 R
Combes, Émile, 1902 F, 1904 P
Comden, Betty, 1944 T, 1953 T
Comfort, Alex, 1944 U
Comecon *see* Council for Mutual Economic Assistance
Cominform, 1947 K, 1948 F, G, 1956 D
Comintern *see* Third International
Commager, Henry Steele, 1930 R, 1960 R, 1966 O, 1968 R
Commerce and Labor, Department of (US), 1903 O
Commission on Civil Rights (US), 1947 P
Commission for Relief and Reconstruction of Europe, 1919 A
Committee for Economic Development (US), 1942 O
Committee on Equal Employment Opportuniy (US), 1962 P
Committee of Imperial Defence, 1902 M
Committee for Industrial Organization (US), 1935 P, 1937 P
Committee of National Defence (Spain), 1936 G
Committee on National Expenditure (GB), 1922 O
Committee of National Liberation (France), 1943 F, H, 1944 F
Committee for National Liberation (Poland), 1944 O
Committee on the Neglect of Science, 1916 P
Common, Alf, 1902 X, 1905 X
Common Agricultural Policy, establishment, 1962 O
Common Market *see* European Economic Community; European Community; European Union
Commonwealth:
British Citizenship Act, 1948 P
Colombo Conference, 1950 O
Elizabeth II claims, 1953 L
finance ministers meeting, 1954 A
founded, 1921 O
Mozambique joins, 1995 L
name, 1949 O
prime ministers' meetings, 1961 C
South Africa leaves, 1961 C
suspends Nigeria, 1995 L
see also individual countries
Commonwealth Conferences, 1952 L, 1953 F
Commonwealth Eminent Persons Report, 1986 F
Commonwealth Immigrants Act (GB) 1962 O
Commonwealth of Independent States (CIS), 1991 N
Commonwealth Law Conference, London, 1955 O
Commonwealth Party (Great Britain), 1943 B, D, 1944 A
Commonwealth Prime Minister's Conference, 1965 F

Commonwealth Reconstruction Training Scheme, 1945 P
Commonwealth Relations Office (GB), 1947 O
Commonwealth Trade and Economic Conference, Montreal, 1958 J
Commonwealth Transantarctic Expedition, 1958 Q
Communist Labor Party (US), 1919 J
Communist Party (GB), 1922 F, 1932 X
Communist Party (US), 1919 J
Communist Youth Congress, Warsaw, 1955 H
Community Care Act (GB), 1993 P
Como, Perry, 1945 T, 1958 T
Comoro Islands, 1975 G
Companies Act (GB), 1980 O
Compass, Operation, 1940 M
Compiègne, 1918 F, L
Comprehensive Environmental Responses, Compensation, and Liability Act (US), 1980 O
Compton-Burnett, Ivy, 1911 U, 1925 U, 1929 U, 1935 U, 1941 U, 1944 U, 1955 U
Compton, Denis, 1947 X
Compton, Sir Edward, 1967 D
Compton Report, 1971 L
Conant, James B, 1956 P, 1978 V
Concorde, 1962 L, 1969 Q, 1976 A, Q
Condon, Richard, 1991 U
Coney Island, New York, 1907 G
Confederation of Autonomous Right Wing Groups (CEDA, Spain), 1933 L
Confederation of British Industry (CBI), 1965 O, 1972 H, 1974 B
Confederazione Generale de Lavoro, 1906 P
Conference on the Law of the Sea, 1958 O
Confessional Church (Germany), 1933 P
Congo Republic:
Belgian aid suspended, 1967 H
cease fire, 1962 K
foreign hostages killed, 1965 F
forms confederation, 1961 C
Hammarskjöld killed, 1961 J
independence, 1960 F, G
Kasavubu overthrown, 1965 L
Lumumba killed, 1961 A
mercenaries in, 1964 H
name change, 1971 K
People's Republic declared, 1964 H
prime ministers, 1960 J, 1961 B, G, 1964 G, 1965 K
rebels take Albertville, 1964 F
Stanleyville captured, 1964 L
UN in, 1960 H, 1961 M, 1962 J, M, 1963 A, 1964 F
see also Belgian Congo; Zaire; French Congo; Katanga
Congregational Christian Churches (US), 1961 P
Congrès Internationaux d'Architecture Moderne, 1928 S
Congress for Cultural Freedom, 1950 P
Congress of Industrial Organization, 1955 P
Congress of Industrial Reorganization, 1937 P
Congress of Racial Equality (CORE), 1943 P
Congress of Soviet Writers, 1934 U
Congresses of the Chinese Communist Party, 1982 J
Coniston Water, 1967 Q

Conkin, Paul, 1967 R
Connecticut, 1974 P
Connell, Evan, 1958 U
Connelly, Marc, 1930 U
Connery, Sean, 1962 Y, 1963 Y, 1964 Y
Connie's Inn, Harlem, 1929 T
Connolly, Cyril, 1935 U, 1938 U, 1944 U
Connolly, Maureen 'Little Mo', 1953 X, 1970 X
Conqueror, HMS, 1982 E
Conrad, Joseph, 1900 U, 1902 U, 1904 U, 1907 U, 1911 U, 1914 U, 1915 U, 1924 V
Conrad, Margaret, 1993 R
Conservative Nationalists (Germany), 1924 M
Conservative Party (Canada), 1911 K
Conservative and Unionist Party (GB): leaders, 1911 L, 1990 L
unite with Liberal Unionists, 1914 E
see also Britain, by-elections; Britain, general elections; local elections
Consolidated Talking Machine Co. (US), 1900 T
Constant, 1949 S
Constantine I, King of Greece, 1915 C, 1917 F, 1920 M, 1922 J
Constantine II, King of Greece, 1964 C, 1965 G, 1967 M, 1994 D
Constantine, Learie, 1901 V, 1971 V
Constantinople, 1914 H, 1918 L
see also Istanbul
Consumer Credit Protection Act (GB), 1968 O
Consumer Products Safety Act (GB), 1972 O
Consumers' Association, 1957 O
Contadora, 1986 D, E
Contempt of Court Act, 1981 O
Convalescent Home, Purkersdorf, 1903 S
Convention on Trade in Endangered Species, 1989 Q
Conway, Russ, 1959 T
Coogan, Michael D, 1993 P
Cook, E T, 1903 R
Cook, Michael, 1975 U
Cook, Peter, 1960 U, 1962 Y, 1965 Y
Cook, Thomas, 1972 O
Cooke, Alistair, 1946 Y, 1972 Y
Cooke, Deryck, 1959 R, 1964 T
Coolidge, Calvin, 1920 F, 1923 H, 1924 F, L, 1925 C, 1933 V
Coolio, 1995 T
Cooper, Alfred Duff, 1938 K
Cooper, Alice, 1972 T
Cooper, Gary, 1929 Y, 1932 Y, 1934 Y, 1943 Y, 1952 Y
Cooper, Gladys, 1971 V
Cooper, Gordon, 1963 Q
Cooper, Mel, 1992 Y
Cooper, Merian C, 1933 Y
Cooperative League (US), 1911 O
Coover, Robert, 1969 U
Copeland, Thomas W, 1958 R
Copenhagen, 1969 W
Copland, Aaron, 1900 V, 1925 T, 1938 T, 1942 T, 1943 T, 1944 T, 1946 T, 1953 R, 1973 T, 1990 V
Copperfield Affair, 1914 W
Coppola, Francis Ford, 1939 V, 1971 Y, 1974 Y, 1983 Y
Coptic Church, 1945 P
Copts, 1910 D
Copyright, International Convention on, 1908 O
Copyright Act (GB), 1911 O
Copyright Act (US), 1909 O, 1912 O

Coral Sea, Battle of, 1942 E
Corbett, Harry, 1953 Y
Corbett, Ronnie, 1971 Y
Le Corbusier, 1914 S, 1918 S, 1922 S,
     1925 S, 1926 S, 1929 S, 1930 S,
     1947 S, 1950 S, 1951 S, 1955 S,
     1957 S
Corder, Frank, 1994 W
Cordle, John, 1977 G
Córdoba, 1955 J
Corfu, 1916 A, 1923 H, 1923 J
Corfu Channel, 1949 O
Corfu Declaration, 1917 G
Corigliano, John, 1938 V, 1991 T
Cork, 1920 M
Corneau, Alain, 1992 Y
Cornelius, Henry, 1954 Y
Cornell, Joseph, 1940 S
Cornell University, 1985 Q
Coronel, Battle of, 1914 L
Corregidor, 1942 E
Corsica, 1938 L, 1943 J
Cortines, Adolfo Ruíz, 1952 G
Corvo, Baron, 1905 U
Corwin, Edward S, 1914 O, 1919 R
Cosgrave, Liam, 1973 C
Cosgrave, William T, 1922 J, 1927 J,
     1933 J, 1965 V
Cosmas, Desmond, 1970 P
Costa, Lucio, 1956 S
Costa Blanca, 1980 F
Costa e Silva, President, 1968 M, 1969 H
Costa-Gavras, Constantin, 1969 Y
Costa Rica, 1920 L, 1921 C, 1987 H
Costello, Elvis, 1954 V, 1977 T, 1979 T,
     1980 T, 1994 T
Costello, John, 1951 F, 1954 F, 1976 V
Costner, Kevin, 1987 Y, 1990 Y, 1995 Y
Cotentin Peninsula, 1944 F
Cotton Club, Harlem, 1923 T
Coty, René, 1953 M
Coughlin, Father Charles E, 1926 P, 1934
     P
Coulton, G G, 1930 R
Council for the Accreditation of Teacher
     Education, 1984 P
Council of Action for Peace and
     Reconstruction, 1935 G
Council for Asia-Pacific Co-operation,
     1989 O
Council of Baltic Sea States, 1992 O
Council for Churches in Britain and
     Ireland, 1990 P
Council of Europe:
     calls for European army, 1950 H
     creation of, 1949 E
     Cyprus joins, 1961 E
     Eden Plan, 1952 J
     European Convention on Human
          Rights, 1950 O
     European Political Community, 1953
          A
     Greece leaves, 1969 M
Council for Mutual Economic Assistance
     (Comecon), 1949 A, O
Council for National Academic Awards,
     1964 P
Council for the Preservation of Rural
     England, 1926 P
Country Music Hall of Fame, 1961 T
Courageous, HMS, 1939 J
Courland, Latvia, 1915 D
Courrières mine, 1906 C
Court, Margaret, 1970 X
Court of Appeal (GB), 1932 O, 1966 O
Court of Appeals (US), 1924 P
Court of Cassation (Italy), 1900 B

Court of Criminal Appeal (GB), 1966 O
Court of First Instance, 1989 O
Courtauld Institute, 1931 P
Courtney, Tom, 1964 Y
Courts and Legal Services Act (GB),
     1990 O
Cousins, Frank, 1966 G
Couve de Murville, 1968 G
Coventry, 1907 W, 1940 L, 1941 D
Coventry Cathedral, 1962 S
Coward, Noël, 1924 U, 1925 U, 1929 T,
     1930 U, 1931 T, U, 1934 T, 1941 T,
     U, 1945 Y, 1973 V
Cowell, Henry, 1912 T, 1923 T, 1935 T,
     1941 T
Cowling, Maurice, 1967 R
Cox, C B, 1969 P
Cox, H E, 1965 P
Cox, James M, 1920 G, 1920 L
Cox, Paul, 1984 Y
Crabb, Lionel, 1956 D
Crabbe, Buster, 1936 Y
Crace, Jim, 1992 U
Craft, Christine, 1984 P
Cragg, Tony, 1980 S, 1981 S, 1982 S,
     1984 S, 1988 S
Craig, Christopher, 1952 O
Craig, E G, 1905 R
Craig, Sir James (Viscount Craigavon),
     1921 B, F
Crane, Hart, 1926 U, 1930 U
Crankshaw, Edward, 1963 R
Craven, Avery, 1942 R
Craven, Wes, 1984 Y
Crawford, Broderick, 1949 Y, 1956 Y
Crawford, Joan, 1945 Y
Crawford, O G S, 1921 R, 1927 R, 1928 R
'Crazy Horse Saloon', Paris, 1951 W
Cream, 1966 T, 1969 T
Credit-Anstalt, 1931 E
Creedence Clearwater Revival, 1970 T
Creighton, D G, 1964 R
Creole Jazz Band, 1922 T
Cresson, Edith, 1991 E, 1991 P
Cressy, David, 1987 R
Creston, Paul, 1945 T
Crete:
     Greece annexes, 1913 L, M
     revolt against Turkish rule, 1905 C
     union with Greece, 1908 K
     World War II, 1940 L, 1941 E
Crewe, Ivor, 1995 O
'Crichel Down' affair, 1954 O
Crichton, Charles, 1954 Y, 1988 Y
Crichton, Michael, 1969 U
Crick, Bernard, 1980 R
Crick, Francis, 1916 V, 1953 Q, 1961 Q
Crimea, 1919 D, 1921 K, 1944 D
Criminal Justice Act (GB), 1963 O, 1967
     O, 1991 O, 1982 O, 1993 O, 1994 O
Criminal Law Act (GB), 1977 O
Criminal Law Revision Committee, 1958
     O
Cripps, Sir Stafford, 1940 E, 1942 B, L,
     1950 K, 1952 V
Crisis, 1910 P
Cristiani, Alfredo, 1989 C
Criterion (GB), 1922 U
La Critica, 1904 R
Croatia and Croats:
     boycott Yugoslav Parliament, 1935 F
     and the breakup of Yugoslavian, 1991
          E, H, 1992 A, 1994 C
     declares independence, 1991 F
     and Eastern Slavonia, 1995 L
     invasion of Krajina, 1995 H
     separatism, 1928 H, 1929 A

World War II, 1941 D
     in Yugoslavia, 1946 A
Croce, Benedetto, 1902 R, 1904 R, 1909
     R, 1917 R, 1952 V
Croft, Michael, 1956 U
Croly, H D, 1909 P, 1914 Y
Cromer, Earl of, 1908 R
Cronberg, 1906 H
Cronenberg, David, 1988 Y
Cronin, A J, 1937 U
Cronje, Piet, 1900 B
Cronkite, Walter, 1968 Y
Crookes, William, 1900 Q
Crosby, Bing, 1903 V, 1937 T, 1940 Y,
     1942 T, Y, 1954 Y, 1977 V
Crosland, Anthony, 1956 O, 1975 E, 1976
     C, 1977 B
Cross, F H, 1957 R
Cross, Jasper, 1970 K
Cross, Peter, 1993 R
Crosse, Gordon, 1974 T
Crossman, Richard, 1907 V, 1950 O,
     1974 V, 1975 J, O
Crowley, Mart, 1969 U
Crown Lands ordinance, 1902 J
Crown Proceedings Act (GB), 1947 O
Crowther Report, 1959 P
Croydon, 1950 W
Crudup, Arthur 'Big Boy', 1954 T
Cruise, Tom, 1986 Y
Crum, George, 1970 T
Crump, Diane, 1970 X
Crusader, Operation, 1941 L
Cruz Report, 1955 L
Cruze, James, 1925 Y
Crystal Palace, Sydenham, 1936 W
Ctesiphon, Battle of, 1915 L
Cuba:
     Batistà flees, 1959 A
     Batistà overthrows government, 1933
          H, 1952 C
     Batistà regime tried, 1959 O
     Bay of Pigs invasion, 1961 D
     Castro imprisoned, 1953 G
     Castro lands in, 1956 M
     complains of US aggression, 1060M
     constitution, 1900 L, 1901 C, F, 1957
          K
     Cubans invade Panama, 1959 D
     demands for reform, 1993 P
     and El Salvador, 1981 B
     elections, 1993 O
     emigration, 1994 O
     expropriates US property, 1959 F
     land expropriation, 1960 O
     land reform, 1959 O
     Liberals revolt, 1906 G
     missile crisis, 1962 K, L
     Organization of African States and,
          1975 G
     presidential election, 1901 M
     presidents, 1906 J, 1955 B, 1959 A, G
     press restrictions, 1959 Y
     recognizes China, 1960 J
     refugees, 1980 D
     trade with Europe, 1964 A
     troops in Angola, 1984 L, 1988 A,
          1989 A
     US aid, 1960 E, J
     US influence in, 1901 O
     US marines land in, 1917 C
     US military rule ends, 1901 E
     US diplomatic relations, 1961 A, 1977
          E
     US trade and shipping embargos,
          1960 K, 1963 B
     and USSR, 1962 A, J, 1963 B, D, 1991
          J, 1993 F

Dassin, Jules, 1948 Y, 1955 Y, 1962 Y
Data Protection Act (GB), 1984 O, 1987 O
Data Protection Register, 1984 O
Daughters of the American Revolution, 1939 T
Davey, Grenville, 1992 S
Davidson, Donald, 1980 R, 1984 R, 1990 R
Davidson, Randall, Archbishop of Canterbury, 1903 P, 1928 P
Davidson, Roger H, 1969 O, 1977 O
Davie, Michael, 1976 U
Davies, Harold, 1965 G
Davies, Laura, 1987 X
Davies, R R, 1987 R, 1995 R
Davies, R W, 1950 R
Davies, Robertson, 1987 U, 1992 U
Davies, W H, 1908 U
Dávila, Carlos, 1932 F
Davis, Bette, 1950 Y
Davis, Dwight Filley, 1900 X
Davis, George, 1975 H, 1976 E, 1978 G
Davis, H W C, 1905 R
Davis, J W, 1924 L
Davis, Joe, 1927 X
Davis, Luther, 1953 T
Davis, Mike, 1990 P
Davis, Norman, 1971 R
Davis, R H C, 1957 R, 1967 R
Davis, Steve, 1985 X
Davis, Stuart, 1924 S
Davis, W J, 1924 F
Davis Cup (tennis), 1900 X, 1966 X, 1973 X, 1984 X
Davison, Emily Wilding, 1913 P
Dawes, Charles, 1923 L, 1924 D, F, 1951 V
Dawes Plan, 1924 G, H
Dawson, Geoffrey, 1912 Y, 1923 Y, 1941 Y, 1944 V
Dawson Scott, Mrs, 1922 U
Dawson's Field, 1970 J
Day, Doris, 1954 T, 1956 T
Day Lewis, Cecil, 1935 U, 1938 U, 1953 U, 1972 V
Day Lewis, Daniel, 1993 Y
Dayan, Moshe, 1915 V, 1979 K, 1981 V
Dazai, Osamu, 1947 U
De Andrea, John, 1970 S, 1975 S
de Beauvoir, Simone, 1986 V
de Beer, E S, 1955 R, 1976 R
De Beers, 1959 O
de Bont, Jan, 1994 Y
de Broglie, Duc Louis, 1987 V
de Filippo, Eduardo, 1946 U
De Forest, Lee, 1908 Y, 1910 V, 1961 V
De Forest Radio Telephone Co., 1907 Y
de Gasperi, Alcide, 1946 F, 1947 B, E, 1950 A, 1953 G, 1954 V
de Gaulle, Charles:
  Adenauer visits, 1958 J
  Algerian referendum, 1959 J, 1961 A
  Algerian War, 1958 E, K, 1961 D
  asks Pompidou to remain in office, 1962 K
  becomes president, 1958 M, 1959 A
  and Britain's EEC entry, 1963 A, 1967 E
  and Canada, 1967 G
  death, 1970 V
  declares state of emergency, 1961 D
  devaluation, 1968 L
  and EC, 1969 B
  forms government, 1958 F
  Franco-German treaty, 1963 A
  general elections, 1948 L

and NATO, 1966 B
offers Algeria independence, 1960 A
presidential elections, 1965 M
Provisional Government, 1944 K, 1945 L, 1946 A
Rassemblement du Peuple Français, 1947 D, K
resigns, 1969 D
student riots, 1968 E
summit meetings, 1960 E
Vietnam War, 1966 K
visits Britain, 1961 L
visits USSR, 1959 C, 1966 F
World War II, 1940 F, H, 1943 F, 1944 H
de Gortari, Carlos Salinas, 1988 F
de Groen, Alma, 1987 U
de Havilland, Olivia, 1949 Y
de Klerk, F W:
  becomes president, 1989 J
  birth, 1936 V
  declares state of emergency, 1994 C
  end of apartheid, 1991 B
  ends ban on ANC, 1990 B
  ends separate amenities, 1989 L
  lifts state of emergency, 1990 F
  Nobel Peace Prize, 1993 K
  succeeds Botha, 1989 B
de Klerk, Michael, 1921 S
de Kooning, Willem, 1940 S, 1944 S, 1945 S, 1948 S, 1949 S, 1952 S, 1955 S
de la Huerta, Adolfo, 1923 M
de la Mare, Walter, 1921 U, 1935 U
De Lorean, John, 1982 K, 1984 K
De Lorean Car Company, 1978 H, 1982 B, K
de Maizière, Lothar, 1990 D, M
De Maria, Walter, 1977 S
de Mello, Fernando Collor, 1989 M, 1992 M, 1993 D
de Mille, Cecil B, 1915 Y, 1934 Y, 1952 Y, 1959 V
de Mita, Ciriaco, 1989 E
de Nicola, Enrico, 1946 F
de Niro, Robert, 1974 Y, 1978 Y, 1983 Y, 1995 Y
de Palma, Brian, 1987 Y
De Priest, Oscar, 1928 P
de Quay, J E, 1959 E
de Saint Phalle, Niki, 1969 S
de Salvo, Albert, 1967 O
de Santi, Giuseppe, 1948 Y
de Sica, Vittorio, 1946 Y, 1948 Y, 1951 Y, 1971 Y
de Valera, Éamon:
  becomes president, 1932 C, 1966 F
  becomes president of Sinn Féin Dáil, 1919 D
  becomes prime minister again, 1957 B
  British-Irish Treaty, 1921 M, 1922 A
  constitutional reform, 1937 F
  death, 1975 V
  elections, 1932 B, 1933 A, 1937 G, 1954 F
  founds Fianna Fáil, 1926 E
  government accepts his terms, 1923 D
  heads coalition, 1951 F
  imprisoned, 1923 H
  Irish Civil War, 1921 G
  Irish Republic proclaimed, 1919 A
  organizes Republican Society, 1922 C
  resigns, 1922 A, 1926 C, 1959 F, 1973 E
  takes seat in Dáil, 1927 H
  vote of confidence, 1953 G
de Vries, Hugo, 1900 Q

De Vries, Peter, 1954 U
de Wet, Christian, 1914 K
Deacon, Richard, 1980 S, 1982 S, 1983 S, 1989 S
Dead Sea, 1968 L
Dead Sea Scrolls, 1947 R
Deakin, F W, 1962 R
Dean, Basil, 1926 U
Dean, Brenda, 1984 P
Dean, Christopher, 1984 X
Dean, James, 1954 Y, 1955 Y, 1956 Y
Dean, John, 1973 F
Dean Witter, 1924 O
Deane, Phyllis, 1962 R
Dear, I C B, 1995 R
Dearing, Sir Ron, 1993 P
Dearmer, Percy, 1906 P, 1925 P
Deauville, 1913 W
Debierne, A, 1910 Q
Debré, Michel, 1962 D
Debrecen, 1944 M
Debs, Eugene V, 1918 J, 1920 L
Debussy, Claude, 1902 T, 1905 T, 1908 T, 1913 T, 1918 V
Debye, P J W, 1930 Q
Déchelette, Joseph, 1908 R
Dee, Kiki, 1976 T
Def Leppard, 1988 T
Defence of the Realm Act (GB), 1914 O, 1916 L
Defense, Department of (US), 1949 O
Degania Aleph, 1909 P
Degas, Edgar, 1917 V, 1919 S
Dehaene, Jean-Luc, 1992 C, 1994 F
Del Tredici, David, 1976 T
Delafield, E M, 1930 U
Delaney, Shelagh, 1959 U
'Delaney clause', 1958 O
Delaunay, Robert, 1910 S, 1912 S
Delcassé, Théophile, 1903 G, 1904 D, 1905 F, 1915 K
Delhi:
  Asian Games, 1951 X
  demonstrations, 1951 F
  riots, 1924 G, 1966 C, L
  television introduced, 1959 Y
Delhi Durbar, 1903 A, 1911 M
Delhi Pact, 1931 C, 1950 D
Delius, Frederick, 1904 T, 1907 T, 1912 T, 1934 V, 1953 T
Dell, Ethel M, 1912 U, 1939 V
Dello Joio, Norman, 1951 T
Delluc, Louis, 1922 Y
Deloria, Vine, 1969 P
Delors, Jacques, 1984 G
Delvaux, Paul, 1938 S
Demerdjis, Prime Minister, 1936 D
Demetrios I, Patriarch, 1987 P
Demirel, Suleyman, 1991 K
Demjanjuk, John, 1988 D, 1993 G
Demme, Jonathan, 1980 Y, 1986 Y, 1990 Y, 1993 Y
Democratic Party (US) see United States of America, Congressional elections; United States of America, presidential elections
Demonstration Cities and Metropolitan Redevelopment Act (US) 1966 P
Dempsey, Jack, 1919 X, 1926 X, 1983 V
Demuth, Charles, 1928 S
Denby, Edwin, 1924 B
Dench, Judi, 1995 Y
Deng Xiaoping, 1904 V, 1966 L, 1977 G, 1980 H, 1982 O, 1987 K, 1989 L
Denikin, Anton, 1919 B, J, K, M, 1920 C
Denisov, Edison, 1968 T, 1982 T
Denktas, Rauf, 1985 A, 1986 G

Handy, W C, 1912 T, 1914 T
Hangzhou, 1937 M
Hanham, H J, 1959 R
Hani, Chris, 1993 D
Hankey, Lord, 1961 R
Hankou, 1926 J, 1927 B, 1938 K
Hanks, Tom, 1993 Y, 1994 Y, 1995 Y
Hanley, James, 1931 U
Hanoi, 1940 J, 1945 H, 1946 M, 1954 K,
    1966 M
Hanover, 1945 D
Hanson, Howard, 1938 T
Hansson, Per, 1946 K
Happy Mondays, 1990 T
Hapsburg monarchy, 1937 B
Hara, Takashi, 1921 L
Harald V, King of Norway, 1991 A
Harappa, 1915 R, 1943 R
Harbach, Otto, 1924 T, 1926 T
Harbel, 1993 F
Harbin, 1909 K
Harbison, John, 1987 T
Harburg, E Y, 1947 T
Hardcastle, Paul, 1985 T
Harden, Arthur, 1906 Q
Hardie, Keir, 1915 V
Hardin, Ty, 1958 Y
Harding, Sir John, 1955 J, L, 1956 H,
    1957 L
Harding, Warren G, 1920 F, L, 1921 C, D,
    O, 1922 C, 1923 H, V
Hardy, Oliver, 1957 V
Hardy, Thomas, 1901 U, 1904 U, 1919 U,
    1928 V
Hare, David, 1978 U, 1983 U, 1985 U,
    1995 U
Hare, R M, 1948 R, 1963 R, 1981 R
Harijan (India), 1933 Y
Harland and Wolff, 1974 G
Harlem, 1964 G
Harlem Globetrotters, 1927 X
Harley, William, 1903 W
Harley-Davidson motorcycles, 1903 W
Harlow, Jean, 1933 Y
Harman, Alec, 1957 R
Harman, Gilbert, 1989 R
Harmsworth, Alfred *see* Northcliffe, Lord
Harmsworth, Harold (Lord Rothermere),
    1940 V
Harnack, A von, 1901 P
Harnick, Sheldon, 1964 T
Harold II, King of England, 1956 W
HarperCollins, 1995 U
Harriman, Averell, 1941 J, 1942 H, 1944
    K, 1951 G, 1986 V
Harrington, M, 1961 P
Harris, Arthur, 1984 V
Harris, Barbara, 1988 P
Harris, Frank, 1900 U
Harris, Joel Chandler ('Uncle Remus'),
    1908 V
Harris, José, 1972 R, 1977 R
Harris, Joseph P, 1963 O
Harris, Ralph, 1957 O
Harris, Robert, 1995 U
Harris, Roy, 1933 T, 1939 T, 1944 T
Harris, Thomas, 1988 U
Harris, Wilson, 1963 U
Harrison, Brian, 1971 R
Harrison, C Ross, 1907 Q
Harrison, George, 1960 T, 1970 T
    see also Beatles
Harrison, M, 1989 Q
Harrison, Wallace K, 1947 S
Harrison Narcotic Act (US), 1914 O
Harriss, John, 1991 R
Harrods, 1983 M

Harroun, Ray, 1911 X
Hart, Charles, 1986 T
Hart, H L A, 1961 O
Hart, Lorenz, 1936 T
Hart, Moss, 1930 U, 1948 U
Hart, Robert, 1906 E
Hart, William S, 1913 Y
Hartford Board of Education, 1994 O
Hartley, L P, 1947 U, 1953 U
Hartmann, Karl, 1963 T
Hartnell, William, 1963 Y
Hartshorne, Charles, 1937 R
Hartung, Hans, 1956 S
Hartz, Louis, 1955 O
Harvard College Laboratory, 1976 P
Harvard University, 1978 P, 1988 Q
    Graduate School of Business
    Administration, 1908 P
Harvey, Andrew, 1983 U, 1986 U
Harvey, Barbara, 1993 R
Harvey, John, 1947 R, 1954 R
Harvey, Jonathan (author), 1993 U
Harvey, Jonathan (composer), 1993 T
Harvey, Lawrence, 1958 Y
Harvey, P J, 1992 T
Harvey, Paul, 1932 R
Harwell, 1945 Q, 1947 Q, 1956 Q, 1961
    Q
Harwich, 1918 L
Harwood, John, 1922 Q
Harwood, Ronald, 1980 U
Hary, Armin, 1960 X
Hašek, Jaroslav, 1922 U
Hashem, Ibrahim, 1957 D
Haskell, Dr Coburn, 1902 X
Haskell, Francis, 1994 R
Hassan, King of Morocco, 1972 H
Hastie, William H, 1937 P
Hastings, Adrian, 1986 R
Hatch, Nathan O, 1989 R
Hatch Act (US), 1939 O
Hatoum, Mona, 1994 S
Hattersley, Roy, 1992 D
Haughey, Charles, 1925 V, 1970 E, 1979
    M, 1980 M, 1987 C, 1992 A
Hauptmann, Bruno, 1932 W
Hauptmann, Gerhart, 1912 U, 1946 V
Hausmann, Raoul, 1918 S, 1919 S, 1921
    S
Havana, 1900 L, 1960 B, 1980 D
Havas news agency, 1944 Y
Havel, Václav:
    becomes president, 1989 M, P
    birth, 1936 V
    convicted of subversion, 1979 K
    imprisoned, 1989 B
    resigns, 1992 G
Havilland, Geoffrey de, 1965 V
'Haw Haw, Lord', 1939 Y
Hawaii, 1989 J
    becomes 50th state, 1959 H
    Keck telescope, 1994 Q
    territory of USA, 1900 D
    World War II, 1941 M, 1942 P
Hawke, Robert (Bob), 1929 V, 1991 M
Hawking, Stephen, 1942 V, 1988 Q
Hawkins, Jack, 1953 Y
Hawks, Howard, 1930 Y, 1932 Y, 1944
    Y, 1946 Y, 1948 Y, 1953 Y, 1959 Y
Hawthorne, Nigel, 1995 Y
Hay, Donald, 1946 Q
Hay, John, 1900 F, 1905 V
Hay-Herrán pact, 1903 A
Hay-Pauncefote Convention, 1901 L,
    1912 H
Hayakawa, Sessue, 1914 Y
Hayashi, Tadasu, 1901 K

Hayek, Friedrich von, 1944 P, 1960 R,
    1992 V
Hayes, Lee, 1940 T
Hayes, Patricia, 1971 Y
Haynes, Johnny, 1961 X
Haynsworth, Clement, 1969 O
Hays, Samuel P, 1957 R
Hazza el-Majali, 1960 H
Head Start programme, 1965 P
Headingly, 1975 H
Healey, Denis, 1917 V, 1974 E, 1975 D,
    1976 J, 1978 G, 1980 L, 1981 J,
    1989 O
Healy, Tim, 1922 M
Heape, 1923 Y
Hearst, Patricia, 1975 J, 1976 C
Hearst, William Randolph, 1904 Y, 1907
    Y, 1924 Y, 1930 Y, 1951 V
Heath, A, 1985 O
Heath, Donald, 1950 B
Heath, Edward:
    becomes leader, 1965 G
    becomes prime minister, 1970 F
    birth, 1916 V
    calls election, 1974 B
    entry to EEC, 1961 L, 1971 E
    and the miners, 1974 A
    and Northern Ireland, 1971 J, 1972 C
    pay policies, 1973 A
    resigns, 1974 E, 1975 B
    three-day week, 1973 M
    visits China, 1974 E
    visits Eire, 1973 J
Heath, Ted (musician), 1944 T
Heathrow Airport, 1946 O, 1977 M, 1986
    D
Heaviside, Oliver, 1902 Q
Hebrew University, Jerusalem, 1925 P
Hebron, 1994 B
Hecht, Ben, 1928 U
Heckel, Erich, 1910 S
Hedtoft, Hans, 1950 K, 1953 J
Hefner, Hugh, 1953 Y, 1962 P
Hegedüs, Andras, 1955 D
Heggie, Iain, 1987 U
Heidegger, Martin, 1927 R, 1929 R, 1976
    V
Heifetz, Jascha, 1917 T
Heimwehr (Austria), 1936 K
Heinlein, Robert, 1961 U
Heisenberg, Werner, 1926 Q, 1927 Q,
    1952 R, 1958 R
Heitler, W, 1927 Q
Heizer, Michael, 1969 S
Hejaz, 1916 F, 1917 A, 1924 K, 1926 A,
    1927 E, 1929 H
    see also Saudi Arabia
Hejaz railway, 1900 J, 1908 J
Helensburgh, 1902 S
Heligoland, Battle of, 1914 H
Helion, Jean, 1947 S
Helios spacecraft, 1975 Q
Heller, Joseph, 1961 U, 1994 U
Helles, Cape, 1915 D, 1916 A
Hellman, Lillian, 1905 V, 1907 V, 1934
    U, 1939 U, 1941 U, 1984 V
Hellman, Monte, 1971 Y
Helsingfors, 1918 D
    see also Helsinki
Helsinki, 1918 A, 1952 X, 1986 H
Helsinki Conference on Security and
    Co-operation in Europe, 1975 H
Helsinki Convention on Nordic Co-
    operation, 1962 C
Hemingway, Ernest, 1926 U, 1927 U,
    1929 U, 1932 U, 1937 U, 1940 U,
    1950 U, 1952 U, 1961 V, 1964 U

Ishaq Yusof Bin, 1965 H
Isherwood, Christopher, 1904 V, 1928 U, 1935 U, 1937 U, 1938 U, 1964 U, 1986 V
Ishiguro, Kazuo, 1987 U, 1989 U
Iskander Mirza, 1956 B, 1958 K
Islamabad, 1966 S, 1988 D, 1992 L
Islamic Conference Organization, 1984 A
Isle of Man, 1978 D
Isle of Wight, 1925 X
Isonzo, First Battle of the, 1915 F
Isonzo, Second Battle of the, 1915 G
Isonzo, Third Battle of, 1915 K
Isonzo, Fourth Battle of the, 1915 L
Isonzo, Fifth Battle of the, 1916 B
Isonzo, Sixth Battle of the, 1916 H
Isonzo, Seventh Battle of the, 1916 J
Isonzo, Eighth Battle of the, 1916 K
Isonzo, Ninth Battle of the, 1916 K
Isonzo, Tenth Battle of the, 1917 E
Isonzo, Eleventh Battle of the, 1917 H
Isonzo, River, 1915 F
Isozaki, Arata, 1974 S, 1976 S, 1986 S
Israel:
    agreement with Lebanon, 1983 E
    aircraft bombed at Athens, 1968 M
    attacks factories in Cairo, 1970 B
    attacks Iraq, 1981 F
    attacks Jordan, 1968 L, M
    attacks terrorist positions, 1974 E
    bombs Egypt, 1970 D
    bombs Palestinians in Jordan, 1968 H
    ceasefire with PLO, 1981 G
    coalition government, 1951 K, 1954 A, 1990 C
    creation of, 1948 E
    definition of Jews, 1970 C
    demonstrations, 1990 K
    deports Palestinians to Lebanon, 1992 M
    Egypt closes Gulf of Aqaba, 1967 E
    Eichmann arrested, 1960 E
    exchanges ambassadors with Egypt, 1980 B
    fighting with Egypt, 1969 G, J, L, M
    fighting with Syria, 1970 A, 1972 L, 1973 J, 1974 D
    fighting in West Beirut, 1982 G, H
    general elections, 1976 M, 1977 E, 1988 L
    and Golan Heights, 1981 M
    government of national unity, 1984 H
    Gulf War, 1991 A
    Hamas attacks, 1994 K
    invades Egypt, 1973 K
    and Iraq, 1969 A
    Jews in USSR, 1986 H
    and Jordan, 1966 L, 1968 A, 1969 D, 1994 G
    Knesset established, 1949 O
    Lebanese conflicts, 1972 A, 1978 C, F, 1980 D, 1981 G, 1982 F, J, L, P, 1983 G, 1985 A, D, F
    makes Jerusalem capital, 1949 M
    Munich Olympics murders, 1972 J
    nuclear weapons, 1974 M, 1986 K
    occupied territories, 1969 M, 1971 B, 1993 D
    Palestinan autonomy, 1979 K, 1980 D, E
    Palestinians massacred, 1994 B
    peace with Egypt, 1971 A, B, 1977 L, 1978 A, J
    and the PLO, 1993 A, J
    presidents, 1952 M, 1993 C
    prime ministers, 1953 M, 1955 L, 1974 F, 1977 D, E, 1983 H, 1986 K

    raids PLO in Tunis, 1985 K
    releases prisoners, 1985 D
    satellites, 1988 Q
    shells Egyptian oil refineries, 1967 K
    ships sunk, 1970 B
    and Sinai Peninsula, 1957 A, 1967 F, 1975 J, 1980 A
    Six-Day War, 1967 F
    storms hijacked plane at Entebbe, 1976 F
    Suez War, 1956 J-L
    and Syria, 1966 G, H, 1967 D
    terrorist attacks, 1969 D, 1970 E
    truce with Jordan and Egypt, 1970 H
    and UN, 1982 A, 1987 M, 1990 K
    unifies Jerusalem, 1967 G, 1980 G
    US arms supplies, 1970 C, 1983 C
    and USSR, 1953 B, G, 1988 F
    and the Vatican, 1993 P
    war-crime trials, 1961 O, 1988 D, 1993 H
    War of Independence, 1948 E, G, 1949 B, 1956 D
    West Bank, 1982 E
    withdraws from Jericho, 1994 E
    withdraws from UN Mixed Armistice Commission, 1954 C
    Yitzhak Rabin assassinated, 1995 L
    Yom Kippur War, 1973 K, L, 1974 A
    see also Palestine
Israel, Jonathan, 1995 R
Israeli-Jordan Mixed Armistice Commission, 1956 K
Issigonis, Alec, 1906 V, 1948 W, 1959 W, 1988 V
Istanbul, 1909 D, 1920 B, C, 1922 G, K, 1923 K, 1955 J, 1960 D
    see also Constantinople
Isthmian Canal Act (US), 1902 F
Istria, 1920 L
Italian Communist Party, 1921 A, B
Italian Socialist Party, 1921 A
Italian Somaliland, 1925 K, 1934 M, 1935 F, 1941 B
Italy:
    abortion, 1981 R
    adopts gold standard, 1928 O
    annexes Fiume, 1919 J, 1924 C
    Anti-Comintern Pact, 1937 L
    antisemitism, 1938 K
    'Aventine Secession', 1924 F
    Ballila, 1926 P
    Belgrade Pact, 1937 C
    blockades Venezuela, 1902 M, 1903 B
    bombards Corfu, 1923 H, J
    coalition government, 1916 F
    commercial treaties, 1922 E
    constitution, 1947 M
    corruption scandals, 1993 B, C
    criminal code, 1927 O
    currency devalued, 1949 O
    customs union with France, 1949 C
    defensive alliance with Albania, 1927 L
    devalues lira, 1936 K
    divorce, 1970 P, 1974 P
    drugs, 1990 P
    earthquake, 1908 M
    education, 1968 P, 1977 P
    elections, 1900 F, 1904 K, 1923 L, 1924 D, 1929 C, 1948 D, 1953 F, 1958 E, 1976 D, 1979 F, 1987 E, 1992 D, 1994 C
    electoral reform, 1928 E, 1953 A
    EEC formed, 1957 C
    Fascist Congress, 1922 K

    Fascist militia, 1923 A
    Fascists march on Rome, 1922 K
    financial policies, 1992 G
    financial scandals, 1978 F
    floods, 1966 L, S
    Franco-Italian Entente, 1902 L
    friendship treaty with Austria, 1930 B
    friendship treaty with Ethiopia, 1928 H
    friendship treaty with Greece, 1928 J
    friendship treaty with Hungary, 1927 D
    friendship treaty with Romania, 1926 J
    general strike, 1904 J, 1922 G
    general strike prevented, 1902 B
    government overthrown, 1901 B
    'Historic Compromise', 1978 C, 1979 A
    Hoare-Laval Pact, 1935 M
    industrial reorganization, 1926 O
    invades Albania, 1939 D
    invades Ethiopia, 1935 K, 1936 E
    Italian-Turkish War, 1911 J, 1912 C
    labour charter, 1927 D
    Lateran Treaties, 1929 P
    League of Nations sanctions, 1936 G
    leaves League of Nations, 1937 M
    and Libya, 1937 C, 1938 K
    loses Dodecanese Islands, 1920 H
    Moro kidnapped, 1978 C, E
    Mussolini becomes dictator, 1925 A
    Mussolini founds Fasci d'Italiani di Combattimento, 1919 C
    naval rearmament, 1930 D
    'No Force Declaration', 1932 M
    nuclear force, 1963 A
    'occupation of the factories', 1920 J
    occupies Somaliland, 1925 K
    P2 scandal, 1981 E, O
    parliamentary conflict, 1900 B
    parliamentary reorganization, 1928 O
    peace treaty, 1947 B
    political parties dissolved, 1926 L
    political reform, 1925 O
    presidents, 1946 F, 1948 E, 1955 D, 1962 E, 1964 M, 1992 E
    prime ministers, 1906 E, 1909 M, 1917 K, 1919 F, 1947 B, E, 1950 A, 1953 G, 1954 A, B, 1955 F, 1957 E, 1958 F, 1959 A, 1960 B, 1976 B, 1989 E, 1991 D, 1994 M, 1995 A
    Racconigi agreement, 1909 K
    Rapallo Treaty, 1924 J
    and Red Sea, 1926 J
    republic, 1946 F
    riots between Fascists and Communists, 1921 B
    Rome-Berlin axis, 1936 L
    Rome Pact, 1933 F, 1936 C
    and Spanish Civil War, 1937 F
    strikes, 1969 O
    and Tangier, 1928 G
    terrorism, 1980 H, 1983 A
    Treaty of Nettuno, 1925 G
    Treaty of Rapallo, 1920 L
    Treaty of Tirana, 1926 L
    and Trieste, 1953 E, 1954 K
    Triple Alliance, 1902 F, 1907 G
    and the Vatican, 1984 P
    war debts, 1925 L
    Western European Union, 1955 C
    women enfranchised, 1946 P
    World War I, 1914 H, 1915 D-F, H, K, L, 1916 B, E, H-K, 1917 E-F, H, K, M, 1918 F, 1918 K

K

Kabalevsky, Dmitri, 1948 T
Kabul, 1980 B, 1992 D
Kabushemeye, Ernest, 1995 C
Kádár, János, 1956 K, L, 1957 F
Kaempfert, Bert, 1961 T
Kafi, Ali, 1992 F
Kafka, Franz, 1916 U, 1920 U, 1924 V,
    1925 U, 1926 U, 1927 U
Kagel, Mauricio, 1971 T, 1982 T
Kahanamoku, Duke, 1920 X
Kahane Commission, 1983 B
Kahn, Louis, 1901 V, 1951 S, 1958 S,
    1959 S, 1962 S, 1963 S, 1972 S,
    1977 S, 1974 V
Kaifeng, 1938 F
Kaifu, Toshiki, 1989 H
Kalatozov, Mikhail, 1957 Y
Kaletski, Alexander, 1985 U
Kálmán, Emmerich, 1915 T, 1924 T
Kaluga, 1941 M
Kamenev, Lev, 1935 A
Kamerlingh-Onnes, Heike, 1908 Q, 1911
    Q
Kamil, Mustafa, 1907 M
Kamishari, 1936 Q
Kampala, 1979 D
Kampuchea, 1985 A, 1989 J
Kancheli, Ghiya, 1981 T
Kandel, I L, 1933 P
Kander, John, 1966 T
Kandinsky, Wassily, 1908 S, 1909 S,
    1910 S, 1911 S, 1912 S, 1913 S,
    1914 S 1933 S, 1936 S, 1940 S, 1944
    V
Kanga, Firdaus, 1990 U
'Kangaroo' clause (GB), 1911 D
Kania, Stanislaw, 1980 J, 1981 K
Kansas, 1912 P, 1947 W
Kantorowicz, Ernst H, 1927 R
Kapitza, Pyotr, 1938 Q, 1984 V
Kapoor, Anish, 1982 S, 1988 S
Kapp, Wolfgang, 1920 C
Kapp Putsch, 1920 C, 1925 H
Kaprow, Allan, 1966 S
Karachi, 1953 A
Karajan, Herbert von, 1954 T
Karamanlis, Constantine, 1961 K, 1963
    F, 1974 G, 1990 E
Karami, Rashid, 1987 E
Karelia, 1941 F
Karelian Autonomous Republic, 1956 G
Karelian Isthmus, 1940 B, C
Kariba Dam, 1960 O
Karloff, Boris, 1931 Y, 1934 Y, 1935 Y,
    1969 Y
Karmal, Babrak, 1979 M, 1986 E
Károlyi, Count, 1932 J
Karoun, Lake, 1982 F
Karpov, Anatoly, 1975 X
Karrer, O Paul, 1931 Q, 1938 Q
Kars, 1918 C
Kars, Treaty of, 1921 K
Karume, Abdul Amari, 1964 B
Kasavubu, Joseph, 1960 F, J, 1961 B, D,
    1965 K, L
Kasdan, Lawrence, 1983 Y
Kashmir, 1947 K, M, 1951 G, 1952 G,
    1962 M, 1963 E, 1965 J, 1990 A, G
    see also Jammu and Kashmir
Kassem, Brigadier Abdul Karim, 1958 G,
    1961 F, 1963 B
Kästner, Erich, 1974 V
Katanga, 1960 G, H, 1961 J, M, 1962 J,
    M, 1963 A, F
Katsura, Prince, 1912 M
Katyn massacre, 1943 D
Katzenberg, Jeffrey, 1995 Y

Kaufman, George S, 1927 T
Kaufman, Philip, 1983 Y
Kaufmann, George, 1930 U
Kaunda, Kenneth:
    birth, 1924 V
    electoral defeat, 1991 K
    nationalizes copper mines, 1969 H
    as prime minister of Northern
        Rhodesia, 1962 M, 1964 A
    as president, 1964 K
    released from prison, 1960 A
Kautsky, Karl, 1919 R
Kavanagh, P J, 1966 U
Kavanagh, Patrick, 1942 U
Kawabata, Yasunari, 1937 U, 1951 U,
    1968 U, 1972 V
Kawara, On, 1970 S
Kawawa, Rashidj, 1962 A
Kaye, Danny, 1913 V, 1954 Y, 1987 V
Kazakhstan, 1995 J
Kazan, Elia, 1947 U, 1951 Y, 1954 Y,
    1956 Y
Kazantzakis, Nikos, 1946 U
Kazhdan, Alexander P, 1991 R
Kazin, Michael, 1995 R
Kazvin, 1911 L, 1945 L
KDKA radio station, 1920 Y
Keasey, Ken, 1962 U
Keates, Jonathan, 1995 R
Keating, Paul, 1944 V, 1991 M, 1993 O,
    1995 F
Keating-Owen Act (US), 1916 P
Keaton, Buster, 1917 W, 1924 Y, 1966 V
Keays, Sarah, 1983 K
Keel, Howard, 1954 Y
Keele University, 1949 P, 1962 P
Keeler, Christine, 1963 C, F
Keen, Maurice, 1990 R
Keenan, Brian, 1986 D, 1990 H
Kefauver Committee, 1950 P
Keifer, Anselm, 1978 S
Keiller, Alexander, 1928 R
Keillor, Garrison, 1974 Y, 1986 U
Keir, Gillian, 1975 R
Keitel, Harvey, 1995 Y
Keitel, Wilhelm von, 1938 B, 1945 E
Keith, A B, 1912 O, 1936 R
Keith, Arthur, 1948 Q
Keller, Helen, 1903 P, 1968 V
Kellogg, Frank Billings, 1925 A, 1927 M,
    1928 D, 1937 V
Kellogg, W K, 1906 W, 1951 V
Kellogg-Briand pact, 1928 F, H, J, 1929
    A, B, G, 1933 F
Kellogg College, Oxford, 1990 P
Kelly, Ellsworth, 1953 S, 1961 S
Kelly, Gene, 1951 Y, 1952 Y
Kelly, Grace (Princess Grace of Monaco),
    1928 V, 1952 Y, 1954 Y, 1956 W,
    1982 V
Kelly, Sean, 1989 X
Kemal, Mustafa see Atatürk, Kemal
Kemal, Yasar, 1958 U
Kemal Pasha, 1922 L
Kempinski, Tom, 1981 U
Kendall, E C, 1915 Q, 1935 Q, 1972 V
Kendrew, J C, 1960 P
Keneally, Thomas, 1982 U
Kennan, George, 1952 K
Kennedy, Edward, 1969 G, 1970 D, 1979
    L, 1980 H
Kennedy, Jacqueline, 1953 W
Kennedy, John F:
    assassination, 1963 L, V, 1964 O,
        1968 V, 1978 M
    becomes president, 1960 L, Y, 1961 A
    and Berlin, 1961 F, H, 1963 F

    birth, 1917 V
    civil rights, 1963 F
    Cuba missiles crisis, 1962 K, L
    establishes Peace Corps, 1961 P
    and Laos, 1961 C
    marriage, 1953 W
    meets Macmillan, 1961 M
    Nassau conference, 1962 M
    tariffs, 1962 O
Kennedy, Margaret, 1926 U
Kennedy, Paul, 1987 O, 1993 O
Kennedy, Robert, 1925 V, 1968 B, F
Kenny, Anthony, 1980 R
Kent, University of, 1965 P
Kent State University, 1970 D
Kenton, Stan, 1940 T
Kentucky Derby, 1970 X
Kenya:
    abandons one-party state, 1991 M,
        1992 A
    Asian emigration, 1968 B
    bans demonstrations, 1990 B
    becomes republic, 1964 M
    Britain annexes, 1920 G
    conflict with Somalia, 1967 K
    constitutional conference, 1960 A,
        1961 L, 1962 B
    education, 1974 P
    elections, 1961 D
    elephant hunting ban, 1973 H
    emergency ends, 1959 L, 1960 A
    ethnic violence, 1993 K
    'Hola incident', 1959 C
    independence, 1963 M
    Kenyatta's conviction quashed, 1953
        G
    Mau Mau emergency, 1952 K, 1953
        D, H, 1955 A
    Safina party formed, 1995 E
    as a single-party state, 1964 L
    state of emergency, 1960 A
    white settlers denounce government
        policy, 1935 J
    World War II, 1941 A, B
Kenya African Union, 1952 K, 1953 F
Kenyatta, Jomo:
    becomes president, 1964 M
    death, 1978 H, V
    imprisoned, 1953 D, G
    released, 1961 D
Kenyon, Kathleen, 1952 R, 1957 R
Ker, W P, 1923 R
Kerekou, President, 1991 C
Keren, 1941 C
Kerensky, Alexander, 1917 E-J, L, P,
    1970 V
Kern, Jerome, 1917 T, 1927 T
Kerner Report, 1968 P
Kerouac, Jack, 1922 V, 1957 U, 1958 U,
    1969 V
Kerr, Deborah, 1956 Y
Kerr, Sir John, 1975 L, 1977 G
Kerr, Malcolm, 1984 A
Kerr-McGee, 1974 O
Kerry football club, 1915 X
Kerschner, Irvin, 1980 Y
Kesselring, Albert, 1960 V
Ketèlbey, Albert, 1915 T, 1920 T
Kettering, C F, 1911 Q
Keuffel und Esser, 1976 Q
Key, V O, 1949 O, 1961 O
Keynes, John Maynard, 1919 O, 1930 O,
    1933 O, 1936 O, 1946 V
Keystone films, 1911 Y
Keystone Kops, 1913 Y
Khabarovsk Protocol, 1929 M
Khachaturian, Aram, 1940 T, 1942 T,
    1954 T

World War II, 1945 H
see also North Korea; South Korea
Korean War, 1950 F-G, J-M, O, 1951 A,
    C-H, K-M, 1952 F, M, P, 1953 D, E,
    G
Koresch, David, 1993 P
Kornberg, Arthur, 1957 Q
Korngold, Erich, 1920 T
Kornilov, General Lavr, 1917 J
Korsch, Karl, 1923 R
Košice, 1945 D
Košice Programme, 1945 D, O, P
Kosinski, Jerzy, 1965 U, 1971 U
Kosovo, 1988 J, 1990 B, J, 1991 C
Kosruth, Joseph, 1966 S
Koss, Stephen, 1981 R
Kossel, 1916 Q
Kostov, Traicho, 1950 B
Kosygin, Alexei Nikolaievich:
    becomes prime minister, 1964 K
    birth, 1904 V
    death, 1980 V
    suceeded as prime minister, 1980 K
    visits Beijing, 1969 J
    visits Britain, 1967 B
    visits Prague, 1968 E
Kotalawala, Sir John, 1953 K, 1956 D
Kotex, 1921 W
Koundouriotis, George, 1926 H
Koundouriotis, Admiral Pavlos, 1924 C
Koussevitsky, Serge, 1924 T
Kowal, Charles T, 1974 Q, 1975 Q
Kozintsev, Grigori, 1964 Y
Kraemer, H, 1938 P
Kraftwerk, 1974 T
Krajina, 1995 H
Kraków, 1914 M, 1918 L, 1945 A
Kramer, Larry, 1986 U
Kraprayaon, General, 1992 E
Krasnoyarsk, 1920 A
Krassin, Leonid, 1920 E
Kray, Reginald, 1969 C
Kray, Ronald, 1969 C
Krebs, Hans, 1900 V, 1932 Q, 1981 V
Kreisler, Fritz, 1919 T
Kremlin, hot line, 1963 F, O
Křenek, Ernst, 1927 T
Krenz, Egon, 1989 K
Kreps, Juanita, 1972 P
Kretzmer, Herbert, 1980 T
Kreuger, Ivar, 1932 O
Kriegsrohstoffabteilung (KRA), 1915 O
Kripke, Saul, 1973 R
Kristallnacht, 1938 L
Kroc, Ray, 1902 V, 1954 O, 1984 V
Kroetz, Franz, 1972 U
Kroger, Helen, 1969 G
Kroger, Peter, 1969 G
Kronstadt naval base, 1921 C
Kruger, Barbara, 1987 S
Kruger, Paul, 1900 C, J, K, 1904 V
Krupp, 1903 O
Ku Klux Klan, 1915 P, 1965 C, K
Kuala Lumpur, 1942 A, 1969 E, 1982 F
Kubrick, Stanley, 1928 V, 1957 Y, 1960
    Y, 1962 Y, 1964 Y, 1968 Y, 1971 Y,
    1980 Y
Kuchma, Leonid, 1995 F
Küchü, Fazil, 1960 H
Kühlmann, Richard von, 1917 H
Kuhmo, Lake, 1940 B
Kuhn, R, 1933 Q
Kuhn, Thomas S, 1962 R, 1970 R, 1977 R
Kuleshov, Lev, 1924 Y, 1925 Y
Kumoratunga, Chandrika, 1994 H, L
Kun, Béla, 1919 H
Kundera, Milan, 1979 U, 1984 U

Küng, Hans, 1928 V, 1971 P
Kurds, 1924 L, 1930 G, 1970 C, 1974 E,
    1991 C, D
Kurile Islands, 1945 H
Kurokawa, Kisho, 1970 S, 1972 S, 1982 S
Kurosawa, Akira, 1910 V, 1948 Y, 1950
    Y, 1951 Y, 1952 Y, 1954 Y, 1957 Y,
    1958 Y, 1961 Y, 1980 Y, 1985 Y,
    1990 Y
Kursk, 1941 L, 1943 B
Kursk Salient, 1943 G
Kurtág, György, 1981 T
Kushner, Tony, 1992 U
Kut-al-Imara, 1915 J, L, M, 1916 D, 1917
    B
Kutno, 1914 L
Kuwait:
    admitted to Arab League, 1961 G
    Britain and, 1961 F
    Gulf War, 1990 G, H, M, 1991 A, B
    Iraq claims, 1961 F
    Iraq recognizes, 1994 L
    OPEC, 1960 O
    US and, 1987 G
Kuwait Airways, 1988 D
Kuwait Oil Company, 1946 O
Kuybyshev, 1941 K
Kuyper, Dr Abraham, 1901 G
Kwajalein, 1944 B
Kwasniewski, Aleksander, 1995 L
KwaZulu, 1971 O
KwaZulu-Natal, 1994 C
Kyprianu, President, 1985 A

L

La Follette, Robert, 1911 A, 1915 P, 1924
    L
La Plante, Linda, 1991 Y
La Scala Opera, Milan, 1950 T
Labis, 1964 J
Labor Party (US), 1923 B
Labour, Ministry of (GB), 1917 O
Labour Exchanges (GB), 1910 P
Labour Party GB:
    first Labour government, 1924 A
    see also Britain, general elections;
        Britain, local elections
Labour Representation Committee (GB),
    1900 B
Labrador, HMCS, 1957 Q
Lacan, Jacques, 1966 R
Lack, David, 1966 Q
Lacombe, Georges, 1939 Y
Lacoste, Pierre, 1985 J
Ladd, Alan, 1953 Y
Ladisla, J, 1938 W
Ladoga, Lake, 1939 L, 1940 B, C
Ladurie, E Le Roy, 1966 R
Ladysmith, 1900 B
Laetoli, 1978 R
Lagerlöf, Selma, 1901 U
Lagos, 1954 O
Lagos Charter, 1962 A
Lahore, 1965 J
Laika, 1957 Q
Laing, R D, 1960 P
Lakatos, Imre, 1976 R
Lake Havasu City, 1971 W
Lakehurst Naval Station, New Jersey,
    1937 E
Laker, Freddie, 1966 O, 1977 J
Laker, Jim, 1956 X
Laker Airways, 1966 O, 1982 O
Lakonia, 1963 M
Lamarr, Hedy, 1933 Y

Lamb, Henry, 1940 S
Lambert, Constant, 1929 T
Lambeth Bridge, London, 1932 W
Lambton, Anthony, 1973 E
Lamming, R M, 1985 U
Lamont, Norman, 1992 H, 1993 C
Lamour, Dorothy, 1940 Y
Lampedusa, Giuseppe di, 1958 U
Lampell, Millard, 1940 T
Lamprecht, Gerhard, 1931 Y
Lancaster, Burt, 1946 Y, 1953 Y, 1957 Y
Lancaster University, 1964 P
Lance, Bert, 1977 J
Land Charges Act (GB), 1925 O
Land Registration Act (GB), 1925 O
Lander, Susanne, 1985 V
Landes, David, 1958 R, 1969 R
Landlord and Tenant Act (GB), 1954 O
Landon, Alfred M, 1936 L
Landowski, Marcel, 1988 T
Landrum-Griffin Act (US), 1959 O
Landsat satellites, 1972 Q
Landsbergis, Vitautis, 1990 C
Landsteiner, Karl, 1900 Q
Lane, Allen, 1936 U
Lane, Burton, 1947 T
Lane, Carla, 1986 Y
Lane, Elizabeth, 1965 P
Lane, Hugh, 1915 S
lang, k d, 1988 T
Lang, Andrew, 1905 R
Lang, Cosmo, Archbishop of Canterbury,
    1928 P, 1930 P
Lang, Fritz, 1918 Y, 1919 Y, 1921 Y,
    1922 Y, 1924 Y, 1926 Y, 1931 Y,
    1933 Y, 1953 Y, 1976 V
Lang, Paul Henry, 1942 R
Lang Vei, 1967 C
Lange, David, 1989 H
Lange, Dorothea, 1939 P
Langemark, 1915 D
Langer, Susanne, 1942 R
Langford, Paul, 1981 R, 1989 R
Langmuir, Irving, 1912 Q
Laniel, Joseph, 1953 F, 1953 M
Lankester, Ray, 1916 P
Lansbury, George, 1912 F, L, 1935 A, K,
    1940 V
Lansdowne, Lord, 1900 K, 1903 E, 1911
    E, 1917 L
Lansing, Robert, 1915 F
Lantz, Herman, 1958 P
Lanyon, Peter, 1951 S
Laon, 1918 K
Laos:
    ceasefire, 1961 E
    and China, 1962 J
    civil war, 1969 C, E
    communists take over, 1975 M
    coup, 1960 H
    emergency, 1959 J
    Geneva conferences on, 1961 E, 1962
        A, G
    indepence, 1954 G
    Kennedy and, 1961 C
    martial law, 1960 J
    North Vietnam offensive, 1969 G, J,
        1970 B
    provisional government formed, 1962
        E
    rebellion, 1960 M
    renewed fighting, 1962 D
    S Vietnam invades, 1971 B
    signs ceasefire, 1973 B
    UN to be sole arbiter of disputes, 1959
        B
    US bombs, 1973 E, H

Chinese Civil War, 1945 K
creates People's Republic of China, 1949 K
death, 1976 J, V
denounced, 1978 O
dogmatism condemned, 1960 H
Khrushchev visits, 1958 G
'Long March', 1934 K
plot to kill, 1972 H
succeeded, 1976 K
swims down Yangzi River, 1966 G
and USSR, 1970 A
Maoris, 1995 L
Maphylaxis, 1902 Q
Marber, Patrick, 1995 U
Marc, Franz, 1911 S
Marcel, Gabriel, 1921 U, 1927 R
March, Fredric, 1954 Y
Marchand, L A, 1973 R
Marciano, Rocky, 1923 V, 1952 X, 1956 X, 1969 V
Marco Polo Bridge, 1937 G
Marconi, Guglielmo, 1901 Q, 1937 V
Marconi Company, 1913 F, 1919 Y, 1920 Y, 1922 Y
Marconi Report, 1913 F
Marconiphone Company, 1933 Q
Marcos, Ferdinand, 1968 J, 1969 K, 1972 Y, 1973 A, 1981 D, 1983 J, K, 1986 B, 1989 J, 1993 G
Marcos, Imelda, 1990 G, 1993 F
Marcus, Frank, 1965 U
Marcus Island, 1942 B
Marcuse, Herbert, 1941 R, 1955 R, 1964 R, 1969 R, 1979 V
Marder, A J, 1940 R, 1961 R
'Mareth Line', 1943 C
Margaret, Princess, 1955 W, 1960 W, 1978 W
Marianas Islands, 1944 F
Marie-Claire, 1954 Y
Marienbad, 1907 J
Marin, Dvoboj, 1936 X
Marine Insurance Act (GB), 1906 O
Mariner spacecraft, 1964 Q, 1965 Q, 1971 Q, 1974 Q
Marinetti, Filippo Tommaso, 1909 S
Marini, Marino, 1901 V, 1947 S, 1980 V
Marino, Eugene Antonio, 1988 P
Maris, Roger, 1961 X
Maritain, Jacques, 1920 P, 1932 R, 1943 P, 1973 V
Market Garden, Operation, 1944 J
Markov, Georgi, 1978 J
Marković, Ante, 1989 A, 1991 M
Marmon Wasp, 1911 X
Marne, First Battle of the, 1914 J
Marne, Second Battle of the, 1918 G
Marne, River, 1914 J, 1918 G
Marquand, David, 1977 R
Márquez, Gabriel García, 1967 U, 1983 U, 1988 U
Marrakesh, 1908 H
Marrs, 1987 T
Mars, Frank, 1923 W
Mars Observer spacecraft, 1993 Q
Mars spacecraft, 1971 Q
Marseilles, Agreement of, 1935 A
Marsh, Fredric, 1935 Y
Marshall, Alfred, 1923 O, 1924 V
Marshall, General George, 1942 D, 1946 B, 1947 A, F, 1949 A, 1950 J, 1951 E, 1959 V
Marshall, Thurgood, 1908 V, 1967 O, 1993 V
Marshall Aid (Marshall Plan), 1947 F, G, 1948 C, S, 1949 M, 1950 F, M, 1951 M

Marshall Islands, 1942 B, 1954 C
Martin, F X, 1976 R
Martin, Frank, 1940 T
Martin, Kingsley, 1969 V
Martin, Sir Leslie, 1983 S
Martin, Troy Kennedy, 1985 X
Martin Committee (Australia), 1964 P
Martini, Arturo, 1930 S
Martino, Donald, 1970 T
Martinu, Bohuslav, 1945 T, 1955 T, 1961 T
Marukami, Haruki, 1987 U
Marvin, Lee, 1967 Y
Marx, Louis, 1929 W
Marx, Wilhelm, 1923 L, M, 1924 E, 1925 A, D, 1926 E, 1927 A, 1928 F
Marx Brothers, 1933 Y, 1935 Y, 1941 Y
Mary, Queen, consort of George V, 1953 V, 1967 F
Maryland, University of, 1920 P
Marylebone Cricket Club (MCC), 1903 X, 1968 X
Masaryk, Jan, 1945 D, 1948 B, C
Masaryk, Tomáš, 1918 L, 1927 E, 1935 M, 1937 V
Mascagni, Pietro, 1921 T
Mascall, Eric, 1949 P
Masefield, John, 1902 U, 1911 U, 1923 U, 1930 U, 1941 U, 1967 V
Masina, Giulietta, 1954 Y
Mason, Benedict, 1995 T
Mason, James, 1954 Y, 1964 Y, 1966 Y
Mason, Philip, 1953 R
Maspero, H, 1927 R
Massachusetts, 1912 P, 1927 O, 1931 O
Massachusetts Institute of Technology, 1955 Q, 1986 Q
Massawa, 1941 D
Massenet, Jules, 1902 T
Massey, Raymond, 1954 Y
Massey, Vincent, 1926 L, 1952 A, 1967 V
Massey, W F, 1912 G, 1919 H, 1925 E
Massie, Bob, 1972 X
Masson, André, 1925 S
Masson, J, 1989 P
Massu, Jacques, 1960 A
Massy, Arnaud, 1907 X
Masterman, C F G, 1902 O, 1909 P
Masters, John, 1954 U
Masters, W, 1966 P
Mastroianni, Marcello, 1962 Y
Masuria, Winter Battle of, 1915 B
Masurian Lakes, Battle of, 1914 J
Mata Hari, 1917 K
Mateos, López, 1964 G
Matheson, M C, 1906 R
Mathis, Johnny, 1960 T
Matisse, Henri, 1900 S, 1904 S, 1905 S, 1906 S, 1907 S, 1908 S, 1910 S, 1911 S, 1913 S, 1916 S, 1921 S, 1925 S, 1928 S, 1931 S, 1932 S, 1949 S, 1951 S, 1952 S, 1953 S, 1954 S, V, 1992 S
Matrimonial Causes Act (GB), 1923 O
Matsukata, 1912 M
Matsusshita, 1979 Q
Matteotti, Giacomo, 1924 F
Matterhorn, 1965 X
Matthau, Walter, 1960 Y
Matthew, H C G, 1968 R
Matthew, Robert, 1951 S
Matthews (neurologist), 1929 Q
Matthews, Colin, 1989 T
Matthews, Donald, 1990 T
Matthews, Donald R, 1960 O
Matthews, John, 1975 R

Matthews, R C O, 1982 R
Matthews, Stanley, 1953 X, 1965 X
Matthews, W, 1970 R
Matthiessen, Peter, 1965 U, 1979 U
Mattingly, Garrett, 1959 R
Mau Mau, 1952 K, 1953 D, H, 1955 A, 1959 C
Maud, Queen of Norway, 1905 L
Maude, Angus, 1949 P
Maudling, Reginald, 1961 L, 1962 G, 1965 G, 1970 F, 1972 G
Maugham, Somerset, 1915 U, 1919 U, 1921 U, 1922 U, 1926 U, 1927 U, 1928 U, 1930 U, 1938 U, 1944 U
Mauna Kea, 1994 Q
Maupin, Armistead, 1978 U
Mauriac, François, 1923 U, 1932 U, 1964 O, 1970 V
Maurice, Major-General Sir Frederick, 1918 E
Mauritania, 1907 W
Mauritania, 1958 M, 1960 L, 1961 K, 1975 L, 1976 D, 1979 H, 1989 O
Mauritius, 1965 J, 1989 D, 1992 C
Mauroy, Pierre, 1981 E, 1992 A
Maurras, Charles, 1905 R
Mauss, Marcel, 1925 R
Maw, Nicholas, 1989 T
Mawer, A, 1924 R
Max, Prince of Baden, 1918 K, L
Maxim, Hudson, 1927 V
Maxwell, H, 1903 R
Maxwell, Robert, 1923 V, 1955 Q, 1968 Y, 1975 Y, 1984 Y, 1987 Y, 1990 Y, 1991 L, M, V, Y
Maxwell Davies, Peter, 1969 T, 1972 T, 1980 T
May, Ernest, 1976 R
May Committee, 1931 B, G
May Day holiday, 1978 E
Maya civilization, 1949 R
Mayaguez, 1975 E
Mayakovsky, Vladimir, 1928 U, 1930 U
Mayer, René, 1953 A, E
Mayfair, London, 1958 W
Mayhew, Christopher, 1966 B
Mayhew, D, 1974 O
Mayhew, Sir Patrick, 1995 E
Mayr-Harting, Henry, 1972 R, 1991 R
Maze prison, Belfast, 1981 K
Mazowiecki, Tadeusz, 1989 H, 1990 M
Mazya, Edna, 1993 U
Mboya, Tom, 1930 V, 1964 M, 1969 V
The MC5, 1969 T
Mead, G H, 1932 R
Mead, Lake, 1936 O
Mead, Margaret, 1901 V, 1928 P, 1930 R, 1949 P, 1953 R, 1978 V
Mears, G C, 1932 O
Meat Inspection Act (US), 1906 O
Meat Loaf, 1993 T
Mecca, 1916 F, 1926 A, 1979 L, 1990 P
Meciar, Vladimir, 1995 J
Medal of Congress (US), 1922 F
Medal of Freedom (US), 1945 P
Medical Research Council, 1957 Q
Medina, 1908 J
Mediterranean, 1914 H, 1941 C
Mediterranean Games, Alexandria, 1951 X
Medoff, Mark, 1980 U
Mee, Arthur, 1919 Y
Meech Lake Accord, 1987 E, 1990 F
Mehta, Gita, 1993 U
Meier, Richard, 1985 S
Meighen, Arthur, 1920 G, 1921 M, 1926 F

Nagy, Imre, 1953 G, 1955 D, 1956 K, L, 1958 F, V

Nahas Pasha, Mustafa, 1927 H, 1928 C, 1930 A, 1936 E, 1944 K, 1950 A, 1952 A

Naipaul, Shiva, 1980 U

Naipaul, V S, 1932 V, 1957 U, 1961 U, 1964 U, 1972 U, 1979 U, 1980 U, 1990 U, 1994 U

Nair, Mira, 1988 Y

Nairobi, 1948 D

Naishen, Cheng, 1989 U

Najibullah, President, 1986 E, 1989 B, 1990 C, 1992 D

Najoma, Sam, 1989 J

Namibia, 1961 D, 1966 O, 1981 A, 1985 F, 1988 M, 1989 J, L, 1990 B, 1992 L

Namier, Lewis, 1929 R, 1948 R, 1960 V

Namphy, General Henri, 1986 B, 1988 F, J

Namsos, 1940 D

Namur, 1944 M

Namur, Battle of, 1914 H

Nancarrow, Colon, 1988 T

Nanga Parbat, 1953 Q

Nanjing, 1911 L, M, 1913 J, 1927 C, 1928 F, 1931 J, 1937 M, 1938 C, 1949 A, D

Nanning, 1939 L

Nanshan, Battle of, 1904 E

Naples, 1943 K

Narayan, R K, 1961 U, 1983 U

Narizzano, Silvio, 1966 Y

Narlikar, J V, 1964 Q

Naruhito, Crown Prince, 1993 W

Narva, 1918 C, 1918 L

Narvik, Battles of, 1940 D, E

Nash, John, 1940 S

Nash, Johnny, 1972 T

Nash, Malcolm, 1968 X

Nash, Ogden, 1961 U

Nash, Paul, 1918 S, 1940 S, 1943 S

Nash, Walter, 1957 L

Nashville, Tennessee, 1944 T, 1961 T

Nasser, Gamal Abdel:
    becomes deputy prime minister, 1953 F
    becomes president, 1956 F
    birth, 1918 V
    British-Egyptian agreement, 1954 K
    closes Suez Canal, 1967 F
    confiscates property, 1961 P
    death, 1970 J, V
    and Israel, 1967 E
    meets Tito, 1956 A
    rise to power, 1954 B, D, L
    Suez canal tolls, 1957 C
    Suez War, 1956 G, J
    United Arab Republic, 1958 B

Nation, Carry, 1900 P, 1911 V

Nation of Islam, 1995 K

National Academy of Recording Arts and Sciences (US), 1958 T

National Advisory Committee on Civil Disorders (US), 1968 P

National Aeronautics and Space Administration (NASA), 1958 Q

National African-American Leadership Summit, 1994 O

National American Women's Suffrage Association, 1913 P, 1915 P

National Art Collections Fund (GB), 1903 S

National Association for the Advancement of Colored People (NAACP), 1909 P, 1910 P, 1920 P, 1935 P, 1994 O

National Black Political Assembly (US), 1972 P

National Brass Championship (GB), 1900 T

National Broadcasting Company (NBC), 1926 Y

National Cancer Institute (US), 1954 Q, 1983 Q, 1993 Q

National Child Labor Committee, 1904 P

National Coal Board, 1972 M, 1981 B

National Council of Churches of Christ, 1950 P

National Council of Labour (GB), 1937 J

National Council for Vocational Education, 1986 P

National Defense Education Act (US), 1958 P

National Economic Development Council (UK), 1960 O

National Endowment of the Humanities (US), 1966 R

National Enterprise Board, 1975 A, O

National Federation of Anglers, 1903 X

National Food Kitchens (GB), 1918 P

National Football Conference (NFC), 1969 X

National Football League (US), 1922 X, 1929 W, 1935 X, 1940 X, 1966 X, 1960 X

National Forests Commission (US), 1906 O

National Free Church Council (GB), 1940 P

National Freight Corporation (GB), 1981 O

National Front (GB), 1977 H, L, 1979 D

National Gallery, London, 1939 T, 1947 S

National Gallery of Art, Washington, DC, 1937 S, 1941 S

National Health and Community Care Act (GB), 1990 O

National Environment Policy Act (US), 1969 O

National Health Insurance Act (GB), 1911 E, 1912 P

National Health Service (GB), 1946 P, 1948 P, 1956 P, 1974 O

National Incomes Committee (GB), 1963 D

National Industrial Recovery Act (US), 1933 O, 1935 O

National Insurance Act (GB), 1946 P

National Labor Relations Board (US), 1937 O

National Labor Service Act (US), 1942 K

National League of Handicrafts Societies (US), 1907 S

National League on Urban Conditions Among Negroes (US), 1911 P

National Library of Canada, 1967 R

National Library of Scotland, 1923 R

National Maritime Museum, Greenwich, 1937 R

National Negro Finance Corporation, 1924 P

National Organization of Women (NOW), 1966 P

National Park Service (US), 1916 O

National Party of Work (Hungary), 1912 E

National People's Army (East Germany), 1956 O

National People's Congress, China, 1987 C

National Petroleum Corporation (Mexico), 1937 C

National Physical Laboratory (GB), 1914 Q, 1950 Q

National Playing Fields Association (GB), 1933 X

National Progressive Republican League (US), 1911 A

National Reclamation Act (US), 1902 O

National Recovery Administration (US), 1933 O

National Registration Act (GB), 1915 P

National Republican Convention (US), 1900 F

National Resistance Council (France), 1943 E

National Review (US), 1955 O

National Savings (GB), 1916 W

National Security Council (US), 1947 O, 1986 L

National Service, Ministry of (GB), 1916 O

National Socialist Party (Germany) *see* Nazis

National Socialist Party (Hungary), 1937 K

National Society for the Prevention of Cruelty to Children (NSPCC), 1986 P

National Theatre, London, 1963 U, 1975 U, 1988 U

National Union of the Left (France), 1928 D

National Union of Mineworkers (NUM, GB), 1973 L, 1982 A, L, 1983 C, 1984 C, D, K, L, 1985 C, K

National Union Party (Portugal), 1930 G

National Union for Social Justice (US), 1934 P

National Viewers' and Listeners' Association (GB), 1965 Y

National Wage Labor Board (US), 1942 P

National Wildlife Federation (US), 1936 Q

National Youth Administration (US), 1936 P

National Youth Theatre (GB), 1956 U

Nationalist Party (South Africa), 1915 K, 1924 F, 1934 F

Native Americans, 1924 P, 1946 P

Native Representative Council (South Africa), 1951 P

NATO (North Atlantic Treaty Organization), 1949 K, 1962 K
    air defence, 1960 J
    Atlantic Congress, 1959 F
    and Cyprus crisis, 1957 C
    de Gaulle and, 1966 B
    Eire and, 1949 B
    and European Defence Community, 1952 B
    foundation of, 1949 D
    France and, 1963 F, 1966 C, G
    Greece withdraws from, 1964 H, 1974 H
    headquarters, 1967 C
    integrated defence force, 1950 M
    and Malta, 1972 C
    missile deployment, 1984 E
    Mobile Theatre Reserve, 1995 F
    nuclear force, 1962 M, 1963 K
    'partnership for peace', 1994 O
    Poland asks NATO to acknowledge Oder-Neisse line, 1960 G
    Polaris, 1963 B
    proposed missile bases in Greece, 1958 A
    secretary generals, 1983 M, 1994 J
    and Serbia, 1994 D

Porter, Cole, 1929 T, 1932 T, 1934 T, 1948 T, 1964 V
Porter, Katherine Anne, 1962 U
Porter, Quincey, 1950 T
Porter, Roy, 1982 R
Portland Spies, 1961 O
Portman, John, 1973 S
Portsmouth, 1955 K, 1956 D
Portsmouth, Treaty of, 1905 J
Portsmouth football club, 1956 X
Portsmouth South, 1984 F
Portugal:
    and Angola, 1961 F, 1970 M, 1975 A
    autonomy for Mozambique, 1970 M
    concordat with Vatican, 1940 P
    and Congo, 1927 G
    constitution, 1911 H, 1933 C, 1976 D, 1982 K
    coups, 1926 E, G, 1974 D, 1975 L
    dictatorship, 1945 K
    EC entry, 1985 C, F, 1986 A
    elections, 1934 E, M, 1945 L, 1953 L, 1969 K, 1975 D, 1991 K
    European Free Trade Association, 1959 L
    financial crisis, 1902 E
    Indian enclaves, 1957 L
    insurrection, 1915 E
    king assassinated, 1908 B
    left-wing government, 1974 G
    and Macao, 1987 A
    Mozambique atrocities, 1973 G
    political parties, 1930 G
    political prisoners released, 1974 E
    presidents, 1915 H, 1918 M, 1928 C, 1974 J, 1991 A
    prime ministers, 1932 G, 1968 J, 1980 M, 1983 F
    republic proclaimed, 1910 K
    revolt against Carmona dictatorship, 1927 B
    revolution in Lisbon, 1921 K
    and Rhodesian oil ban, 1966 C
    riots, 1919 D
    royalist rising, 1913 K
    Salazar's rise to power, 1928 D
    separation of Church and State, 1911 P
    and South Africa, 1928 J
    terrorism, 1973 A
    World War I, 1916 C
    World War II, 1943 K
Portuguese South-East Africa, 1900 J
Posen, 1918 M
Post, 1988 Y
Post, Wiley, 1933 Q
Post Office (GB), 1912 O, 1922 Y, 1957 W, 1959 W, 1968 O, 1979 J
Post Office Savings Bank, Vienna, 1904 S
Post Office Tower, London, 1965 W
Postgate, R, 1946 R
Potemkin (Russian battleship), 1905 F
Potemkin, Vsevolod, 1928 Y
Potenza, 1943 J
Potomac Charter, 1954 F
Potsdam, 1010 L, 1991 O
Potsdam Conference, 1945 G, 1952 C
Potter, David M, 1954 R, 1968 R, 1973 R
Potter, Dennis, 1978 Y, 1986 Y
Potter, Sally, 1992 Y
Pottle, F A, 1950 R
Poujade, Pierre, 1956 A
Poujadists, 1956 A
Poulantzas, N, 1973 P
Poulenc, Francis, 1920 T, 1924 T, 1957 T, 1959 T, 1963 V
Poulsen, V, 1902 Q

Poulson, John, 1972 G, 1974 B, 1977 G
Pound, Ezra, 1911 U, 1915 U, 1919 U, 1928 U, 1948 U, 1950 U, 1972 V
Pound, Roscoe, 1921 O, 1944 O, 1964 V
Pousseur, Henri, 1969 T
Powell, Adam Clayton Jr, 1944 P
Powell, Anthony, 1905 V, 1931 U, 1951 U
Powell, C F, 1947 Q
Powell, Colin, 1993 A
Powell, Enoch, 1958 A, 1963 K, 1965 G, 1968 D, 1969 F, 1974 B, 1986 A
Powell, Felix, 1915 T
Powell, Michael, 1937 Y, 1941 Y, 1943 Y, 1946 Y, 1947 Y, 1959 Y
Powell, Mike, 1991 X
Powell and Moya, 1950 S
Power, Eileen, 1924 R, 1941 R
Powers, Gary, 1960 E
Powers, Susan, 1994 U
Powicke, F M, 1947 R, 1953 R
Powys, John Cowper, 1929 U, 1933 U
Powys, Theodore Francis, 1928 U
Poznán, 1956 F
Prague, 1939 C, 1972 G, 1989 A, L, 1991 G
Prasad, Rajendra, 1950 A
Pratt, David, 1960 D
Pravda, 1912 Y, 1917 W
Premadasa, Ranasinghe, 1989 A, 1993 E
Premier Radio, 1995 Y
Preminger, Otto, 1954 Y, 1957 Y, 1959 Y, 1960 Y, 1962 Y, 1963 Y
Prendergast, Kathy, 1995 S
Prentice, Reg, 1974 P, 1975 G, 1976 M, 1977 K
Presbyterian Church, 1900 P, 1982 P
Presidential Succession Act (US), 1947 O
Presley, Elvis, 1935 V, 1954 T, 1956 T, Y, 1957 T, 1958 W, 1961 T, 1962 T, 1977 H, T, V
Press Association, 1920 Y, 1925 Y, 1951 Y
Press Complaints Commission, 1990 Y
Press Council, 1953 Y, 1990 Y
Pressburger, Emeric, 1941 Y, 1943 Y, 1946 Y, 1947 Y
Prestes, Dr Júlio, 1930 K
Preston, Peter, 1993 R
Preto, Ouro, 1994 O
Pretoria, 1900 F
Prevention of Terrorism (Temporary Provisions) Act (GB), 1974 O
Prévert, Jacques, 1946 U, 1977 V
Previn, André, 1985 T
Price Administration, Office of (US), 1941 O, 1942 O
Price Stabilization, Office of (US), 1953 O
Prices Commission (GB), 1973 A
Prices and Incomes Board (GB), 1965 C, E
Priestley, J B, 1929 U, 1932 U, 1934 U, 1937 U, 1958 O, 1984 V
Primal Scream, 1991 T
Primo de Rivera, Miguel, 1923 J, 1930 A, V
Prince, 1982 T, 1984 T, 1986 T, 1987 T, 1989 T, 1994 T
Prince of Wales, 1941 M
Prince William Sound, 1989 C
Princess Juliana canal, 1935 O
Princeton, 1993 Q
Princeton, University of, 1930 P
Princip, Gavrilo, 1914 F
Prins, Dr Henk, 1995 P
Prinz Eugen, 1941 E

Prior, James, 1972 L
Pripet Marshes, 1916 F
Pritchett, V S, 1956 U, 1982 U
Private Eye, 1962 Y
Privy Council, 1933 E, 1946 O
Prix Goncourt, 1945 U
Prix Louis Delluc, 1937 Y
Pro-Treaty Party (Ireland), 1922 C
Proctor and Gamble, 1967 O
Procul Harum, 1967 T
Production, Ministry of (GB), 1942 O
Professional Golfers' Association, 1901 X, 1916 X
Profumo, John, 1963 C, F, G, J, P
Progressive ('Bull Moose') Party (US), 1912 O
Progressive Education Association (USA), 1918 P, 1955 P
Progressive Republican Party (US), 1912 F, H
Prohibition:
    New Zealand rejects, 1919 P
    Norway introduces, 1919 P
    in USA, 1900 P, 1911 J, 1919 K, 1920 A, 1922 O, 1923 F, 1924 A, 1931 O, 1933 M, P
Prokofiev, Sergei, 1917 T, 1921 T, 1925 T, 1935 T, 1936 T, 1938 T, 1940 T, 1942 T, 1944 T, 1946 T, 1953 V, 1954 T
Promenade Concerts, London, 1944 T, 1948 T
Promotion of Bantu Self-Government Act (S Africa) 1960 A
Prothero, R E, 1912 R
Proust, Marcel, 1913 U, 1922 V, 1927 U, 1981 U
Prouvé, Jean, 1958 S
Prunskiene, Kazimiera, 1991 A
Prussia, 1910 E, F, 1914 H, J, 1917 D, 1932 D, G, 1944 G
    see also Germany
Pryce, Jonathan, 1995 Y
Przemysl, 1915 C, F
Ptashne, Mark, 1968 Q
Pu Yi, Emperor of China, 1932 B
Public Enemy, 1988 T, 1991 T
Public Order Act (GB), 1936 O, 1937 A, 1986 O
Public Records Act (GB), 1958 O
Public Safety Act (Ireland), 1927 G
Public Works Administration (US), 1933 P
Publication of Man, 1901 R
Publications Control Board (S Africa), 1963 P
Puccini, Giacomo, 1900 T, 1904 T, 1910 T, 1917 T, 1918 T, 1924 V, 1926 T
Puddefoot, Syd, 1922 X
Pudovkin, Vsevolod, 1926 Y, 1927 Y
Puerto Rico:
    association with USA, 1952 O
    becomes US territory, 1901 O, 1917 O
    Foraker Act, 1900 E
    nationalism, 1950 K
Pulitzer, Mrs Joseph, 1912 Y
Pulitzer Prizes, 1917 U
Pullman Company, 1936 P
Pulp, 1995 T
Punch, 1992 Y
Punjab, 1947 P, 1982 K, 1983 K, 1984 C, D, 1987 E, 1988 D, 1992 B
Purcell, E W, 1946 Q
Purcell, Henry, 1995 Y
Purdy, James, 1959 U
Pure Food and Drugs Act (US), 1906 O
Pusan, 1950 G

Rimington, Stella, 1991 P
Rimsky-Korsakov, Nikolai, 1909 T
Rio de Janeiro, 1992 Q
Rio de Janeiro Non-aggression Pact, 1933 J
Rio Grande, 1911 A
Ripken, Cal Jr, 1995 X
Rise of Ragga, 1993 T
Rivera, Diego, 1947 S
Rivers, Larry, 1953 S, 1961 S
Rivet, A L F, 1958 R
Rivette, Jacques, 1974 Y, 1991 Y
Rivonia Trial (S Africa), 1963 K, 1964 F, L
Riyadh, 1976 K
RNA, 1970 Q
Road Traffic Act (GB), 1934 O
Robards, Jason, 1959 Y
Robbe-Grillet, Alain, 1960 U, 1979 U
Robbins, Jerome, 1961 Y
Robbins, Marty, 1953 T
Robbins Committee, 1965 B
Robbins Report, 1963 P
Robens, Lord, 1971 A
Roberts, Frederick, Earl, 1914 V
Roberts, J M, 1976 R, 1978 R, 1985 X
Robertson, Anna M see Moses, Grandma
Robertson, John, 1976 A
Robertson, William, 1915 M
Robeson, Paul, 1925 T, 1928 T, 1976 V
Robin, Leo, 1949 T
Robinson, Derek, 1979 L
Robinson, Edward, 1910 U
Robinson, Edward G, 1965 Y
Robinson, G N, 1960 P
Robinson, Heath, 1944 V
Robinson, Jackie, 1941 X, 1947 X
Robinson, James Harvey, 1912 R
Robinson, Janice, 1994 R
Robinson, Joan, 1983 V
Robinson, John, 1963 P
Robinson, Mary, 1990 L
Robinson, Sugar Ray, 1921 V, 1946 X, 1951 X, 1964 X, 1989 V
Robinson College, Cambridge, 1977 P
Robson, Arthur, 1923 Y
Rocard, Michel, 1988 E, 1991 E
Rochberg, George, 1972 T
Roche, Kevin, 1975 S
Roche, Stephen, 1987 X
Roche and Dinkeloo, 1976 S
Rock Sand (racehorse), 1935 X
Rockall, 1971 L
Rockefeller, John D, 1911 O, 1937 V
Rockefeller, Nelson, 1908 V, 1968 D, 1979 V
Rockefeller Commission (US), 1975 F
Rockefeller Foundation (US), 1913 P
Rodchenko, Alexander, 1918 S
Rodgers, Jimmie, 1928 T
Rodgers, Richard, 1902 V, 1936 T, 1943 T, 1945 T, 1949 T, 1951 T, 1956 Y, 1958 Y, 1959 T, 1979 V
Rodgers, William, 1981 A
Rodin, Auguste, 1900 S, 1902 S
Rodrigo, Joaquin, 1940 T
Rodríguez, Andrés, 1989 B
Roeg, Nicholas, 1970 Y, 1973 Y, 1976 Y
Roehm, Ernst, 1934 F
Roethke, Theodore, 1953 U, 1958 U
Rogers, Ginger, 1935 Y, 1937 Y
Rogers, Richard, 1933 V, 1977 S, 1982 S, 1985 S, 1986 S
Rohmer, Eric, 1983 Y
Rokeby Venus, 1914 C
Rolfe, Frederick see Baron Corvo
Rolland, Romain, 1900 U, 1904 U, 1943 U

Rolling Stone, 1967 T
The Rolling Stones, 1961 T, 1964 T, 1965 T, 1968 T, 1971 T, 1972 T, 1973 T, 1976 T, 1994 T, 1995 T
Rolls, Charles, 1904 O
Rolls-Royce, 1904 O, 1970 L, 1971 B
Romains, Jules, 1922 U, 1932 U
Roman, Petre, 1991 J
Roman Catholic Church see Catholic Church
Romanenko, Yuri V, 1987 Q
Romanes Lectures, 1958 S
Romania:
    alliance with Czechoslovakia, 1921 D
    alliance with Poland, 1926 C
    alliances with Yugoslavia, 1921 F, 1947 M, 1949 K
    Balkan Entente, 1934 B, 1938 G
    Balkan Wars, 1913 F
    barter arrangement, 1955 H
    Ceausescu overthrown, 1989 M
    collectivization of agriculture, 1949 O
    condemns Czech invasion, 1968 H
    constitution, 1948 D, 1952 O
    coup, 1944 H
    earthquake, 1977 C
    elections, 1946 L
    floods, 1970 E, 1990 E
    friendship treaty with Italy, 1926 J
    frontier treaty, 1920 H
    head of state, 1967 M
    invades Hungary, 1919 H, L
    Iron Guard, 1938 D, L, 1939 J
    language, 1995 P
    'Little Entente', 1920 H, 1933 B, 1934 C
    Litvinov Protocol, 1929 B
    local election, 1992 B
    miners unrest, 1990 F, 1991 J
    Moldavian revolt, 1907 C
    National Peasant Party dissolved, 1947 G
    nationalization, 1948 O
    New States treaty, 1920 H
    Nixon visits, 1969 G
    peace treaty, 1947 B
    prime ministers, 1933 M, 1937 M, 1945 C
    religious influence, 1989 P
    Socialist Party of Labour founded, 1990L
    union with Transylvania, 1918 M
    and USSR, 1934 F, 1969 B
    Warsaw Pact, 1955 E
    World War I, 1916 H, J, K, M, 1917 M, 1918 E
    World War II, 1940 F, G, J-L, O, 1941 G, M, 1944 D, J
Romanov dynasty, 1917 C, 1993 W
Romberg, Sigmund, 1924 T, 1926 T
Rome:
    international conference on immigration, 1924 E
    Olympic Games, 1960 X
    terrorist attack on airport, 1973 M
    World War II, 1943 G, J, 1944 F
Rome, Treaty of, 1957 C, O
Rome Pact, 1933 F, 1936 C
Romero, George, 1968 Y, 1978 Y
Romero, Oscar, 1980 C
Rommel, Field Marshal Erwin, 1941 B-D, 1942 A, F, K, 1943 D, 1944 K
Roncalli, Cardinal Angelo see John XXIII, Pope
Röntgen, Wilhelm, 1901 Q
Room, Abram, 1927 Y
Roosevelt, Eleanor, 1962 V

Roosevelt, F D, 1933 P, 1935 A, 1939 Q, T, Y
    assassination attempt, 1933 B
    and Basic English, 1943 P
    becomes president, 1932 L, 1933 C
    death, 1945 D, V
    defence expenditure, 1939 A
    education policy, 1938 P
    employment reforms, 1941 P
    'fireside chats', 1933 C
    'Hundred Days', 1933 C
    leaves gold standard, 1933 D
    'New Deal', 1932 G, 1933 O, 1935 P
    nominated for vice-presidency, 1920 G
    and outbreak of war, 1939 D
    presidential elections, 1936 L, 1936 O, 1940 L, 1944 L
    and Spanish Civil War, 1937 A
    and Supreme Court, 1937 O
    tariff reforms, 1934 F
    World War II, 1939 L, 1940 O, 1941 A, H, M, 1942 F, P, 1943 A, E, G, H, L, 1944 J, 1945 B
Roosevelt, Theodore:
    and American Football, 1905 X
    becomes president, 1901 J
    death, 1919 V
    ends coal strike, 1902 K, O
    entertains Booker T Washington, 1901 P
    Hague peace conference, 1907 F
    History as Literature 1914 R
    inaugurates Pacific communications cable, 1903 Q
    Mount Rushmore Memorial, 1941 W
    nature conservation conference, 1908 O
    'The New Nationalism', 1910 H
    nominated as vice-president, 1900 F
    presidential elections, 1904 L, 1912 H, L
    and Progressive Republican Party, 1912 F, O, 1916 F
    reformed spelling, 1906 P
    and Russo-Japanese War, 1905 J
    and teddy bears, 1902 W
    wildlife refuges, 1903 O
    wounded by fanatic, 1912 K
Root, E, 1917 F
Roper, Lyndal, 1989 R
Roque, Jacqueline, 1961 W
Rorty, Richard, 1931 V, 1980 R, 1982 R
Rose, L Arthur, 1937 T
Rose, Reginald, 1954 Y, 1957 Y
Rose Ball, American football, 1902 X
Rosebery, Lord, 1905 L, 1929 V
Rosen, Charles, 1971 R
Rosenau, J, 1990 O
Rosenberg, Albert, 1930 O
Rosenberg, Isaac, 1915 U
Rosenberg, Julius and Ethel, 1950 O, 1951 O, 1953 O
Rosenthal, Jack, 1976 Y
Ross, Diana, 1981 T
Ross, Harold, 1925 Y
Ross, Jerry, 1954 T, 1955 T
Ross, Mrs, 1925 P
Rossellini, Roberto, 1945 Y, 1946 Y
Rossen, Robert, 1949 Y
Rosser, Gervase, 1989 R
Rossi, Aldo, 1979 S
Rossiter, Clinton, 1956 O
Rosso, Medardo, 1906 S
Rostand, Edmond, 1900 U, 1918 V
Rostok, 1992 H
Rostov, 1941 L, 1942 G, 1943 B

U